German-Americana in Europe

Two Guides to Materials Relating to American History in the German, Austrian, and Swiss Archives

Don Heinrich Tolzmann

HERITAGE BOOKS
2015

HERITAGE BOOKS
AN IMPRINT OF HERITAGE BOOKS, INC.

Books, CDs, and more—Worldwide

For our listing of thousands of titles see our website
at
www.HeritageBooks.com

Published 2015 by
HERITAGE BOOKS, INC.
Publishing Division
5810 Ruatan Street
Berwyn Heights, Md. 20740

Copyright © 1997 Don Heinrich Tolzmann

All rights reserved. No part of this book may be reproduced or transmitted in any form or by any means, electronic or mechanical, including photocopying, recording or by any information storage and retrieval system without written permission from the author, except for the inclusion of brief quotations in a review.

International Standard Book Numbers
Paperbound: 978-0-7884-0674-4
Clothbound: 978-0-7884-6172-9

Contents

Since this book combines two works, the page numbers are not sequential throughout. At the beginning of each volume, there is a more thorough table of contents for the pages in that range.

Editor's Introduction   v-x

Volume 1:
Guide to the Manuscript Materials Relating to American History in the German State Archives

Preliminary pages and table of contents   i-viii

Main text   1-324

Index   325-352

Volume 2:
Guide to the Materials for American History in Swiss and Austrian Archives

Preliminary pages and table of contents   i-x

Main text   1-268

Index   269-299

Editor's Introduction

The importance of German-language source material for American history cannot be underestimated. Altogether, approximately eight million German-speaking immigrants have come to America since the 17th century, when the first Germans arrived at Jamestown, Virginia in 1608.

Today, more than sixty million descendants comprise the nation's largest ethnic element, the German-Americans. Moreover, Germany and the various German-speaking countries and states have throughout history played a role in various aspects of the social, cultural, political, economic, and political relations with America.

Harold Jantz commented on the significance of German sources for an understanding of American history, stating "how important it is, indeed essential to extend one's research beyond the normally accessible British and American sources."[1] Elsewhere, the editor has also emphasized this point, observing that "important primary and secondary sources have been ignored and overlooked. The kind of history thus presented is, hence, only a fragment of the story, but is often presented, as if it were the whole story."[2]

Hence, for the aforementioned reasons, German source materials in the German-speaking countries of Europe provide much that is elemental to an understanding of the history of the U.S. The keys for accessing these sources will be found in this work, which consists of two major guides to the archives of Germany, Austria, and Switzerland.

Although completed before the First World War, these guides have never really been replaced. They remain invaluable guides for establishing the availability of archival materials on a particular topic.[3] The particular value of these guides is their focus on German-Americana, as they were compiled by two well-known German-American historians, Marion Dexter Learned (1857-1917) and Albert Bernhardt Faust (1870-1951). Since the publication of these guides, other works have appeared, which survey the holdings of the archives of the German-speaking countries, but their focus is not on German-Americana, but on Americana in general.

For example, the German Society for American Studies published *Amerikana in deutschen Sammlungen. Ein Verzeichnis von Materialien zur Geschichte der Vereinigten Staaten von Amerika in Archiven der Bundesrepublik Deutschland.* (München: Omnia, 1967), a five volume work. This does not replace the earlier guides for two reasons: First, the particular focus is not on German-Americana, as it aims to cover the entirety of American history. Second, it does not include coverage, of course, of Austria and Switzerland.

These volumes will be especially useful for guiding the user to the appropriate archive and in identifying the kinds of materials available on a wide range of topics dealing with the relations between the German-speaking countries and America. Indeed, they particularly illuminate the many sources dealing with German immigration and settlement in the U.S., and are essential for anyone engaged in research in the area.[4]

In the first volume dealing with archives in Germany, the material is organized in an arrangement descending from state to municipal archives. In each section the items are arranged in alphabetical sequence, and the majority of the records are in German, English, and French. Records include the following: papers, passenger lists, personal diaries, letters, etc., and mainly date from the eighteenth and nineteenth centuries.

Access to this material is provided by a quite detailed index. Of course, libraries and archives in the eastern German provinces, which were lost as a result of the Second World War, suffered a harsh fate, including theft and destruction. Nevertheless, this guide will be of value in seeking what was once to be found, and which might in some cases again be locatable. [5]

In the second volume, forty-six archives and libraries in Austria and Switzerland are surveyed. The arrangement is in the descending order from cantonal to municipal institutions. Most of the entries are in German with a summary regarding their content in English. This volume also contains a very detailed index. Together with the first volume, it provides a basic guide to sources, which will be of great use to the field of German-American Studies.

Notes

1. Cited in Don Heinrich Tolzmann, ed., *German Allied Troops in the American Revolution: J.R. Rosengarten's Survey of German Arhives and Sources.* (Bowie, MD: Heritage Books, Inc., 1993), p. xxii-xxiii. See esp. "American History From German Archives," pp. 5-9; "American History From German Sources," pp. 43-49; and "Bibliographical Guides," p. 94.

2. See Don Heinrich Tolzmann, ed., *The Sioux Uprising in Minnesota, 1862: Jacob Nix's Eyewitness History.* (Indianapolis: Max Kade German-American Center, Indiana University-Purdue University & the Indiana German Heritage Society, 1994), p. xi-xii.

3. For a directory with addresses of archives in the German-speaking countries, see Ernest Thode, *Address Book for Germanic Genealogy.* Fourth Edition. (Baltimore: Genealogical Publishing Co., Inc., 1991), pp. 76-159.

4. For bibliographical guides to German-American history, see Don Heinrich Tolzmann, *German-Americana: A Bibliography.* (Bowie, MD: Heritage Books, Inc., 1995) and by the same author, *Catalog of the German-Americana Collection, University of Cincinnati.* (München: K.G. Saur, 1990), and Margrit B. Krewson, *German-American Relations: A Selective Bibliography.* (Washington, D.C.: Library of Congress, 1995).

5. For further information regarding the impact of the war on libraries and archives, see Pierce Butler, *Books and Libraries in Wartime*. (Chicago: University of Chicago Pr., 1945); Hilda Uren Stubbings, *Blitzkrieg and Books: British and European Libraries As Casualties of World War II*. (Bloomington, IN: Rubena Pr., 1993); and Klaus-Dieter Lehmann and Ingo Kolasa, *Die Trophäenkommissionen der Roten Armee: Eine Dokumentensammlung zur Verschleppung von Büchern aus deutschen Bibliotheken*. (Frankfurt am Main: Klostermann, 1996).

1.

Guide to the Manuscript Materials

Relating to American History

in the German State Archives

By Marion Dexter Learned

PREFACE.

The task of examining the German Archives was different from that of my predecessors in other archives, in that the number of depositories was large and the character of the collections varied, and relatively little was known in detail in America about the actual contents of most of these archives. Accordingly, I was allowed great freedom in the plan of procedure and method of examining the archives. Since, however, but seven months could be devoted to the research—February to September, 1909—the Director of the Department of Historical Research gave specific instructions that the scope of the task should be so restricted that the collecting of materials in Germany might be finished within that period. The most practicable plan was to limit the research, in the first instance, to the State Archives, for the following reasons:

(1) They contain the state papers and other official matter corresponding to the materials which the Carnegie Institution has had examined in the archives of other countries;

(2) They are the best organized and administered archives in the German Empire;

(3) The municipal archives are so numerous, and in some cases so incompletely organized, that much time would be expended in finding relatively little valuable material;

(4) The ecclesiastical collections seemed less important because they contain as a rule papers bearing specifically on none but religious affairs in America;

(5) A systematic examination of parish archives and private collections could be made most advantageously with the co-operation of a larger force and of the officials and owners of the collections.

The search began with the State Archives of Prussia and Bavaria, which contain the greater part of the official material relating to America. In addition to the thirty or more state archives personally examined, reports were received from the remaining state archives, giving lists of such materials as relate to America.

Besides the fifty or more state archives, some municipal archives were examined, particularly those known to have important materials bearing on the subject in hand.

In the arrangement of materials Prussia and Bavaria have been given the first place, in consideration of the great amount of matter which they contain. The provincial archives are then arranged in their respective groups in their order. Then follow in one alphabetical order the remaining territorial states, together with the Hanseatic or city states, and the imperial domain of Alsace-Lorraine, and lastly the municipal archives, so far as examined. The arrangement of materials in the respective archives follows the serial or numerical order, because it seemed simpler and less confusing than the chronological order, which would have necessitated frequent repetitions of the "signatures".

In cases where ministerial papers or series of volumes break off abruptly in the archives, the continuation will usually be found in the respective ministries themselves, and can be consulted, usually, by presenting an exact statement of the matter required to the Minister of State.

The enumeration of specific documents in the various archives has usually not extended beyond a systematic attempt to list the salient pieces, or those most important for American history. It has been made exhaustive only in the case of volumes I. and II. of " General Controlle, Königl. Geheimes Ministerial Archiv, Tit. LVIII., Nr. 7 ", and in that of the group of material called " Repositur XI. 21 a " (both at Berlin).

In copying the titles I have followed the orthography of the documents. In the few cases, where the copy was furnished by the copyist in the archives, the orthography is sometimes modernized.

The construction of a guide to fifty archives in the seven months allotted me was only possible because of the ready and efficient co-operation accorded me in the course of my labors. It gives me great pleasure to acknowledge my indebtedness to the General Director of the State Archives of Prussia, Wirkl. Geh. Ober-Regierungsrat Dr. Reinhold Koser, to Geh. Archivrat Dr. Paul Bailleu, and his colleagues in the Royal Privy State Archives of Prussia, to Geh. Archivrat Dr. Gustav Könnecke and his colleagues of the State Archives in Marburg, and to the directors of the other provincial state archives of Prussia and their colleagues. Also to His Excellency Karl Theodor Ritter von Heigel, President of the Bavarian Academy, to Kämmerer und Ministerialrat Freiherr von Hirschberg, Director of the Royal Bavarian Privy State Archives, to Dr. Franz Ludwig Ritter von Baumann, Director of the Royal Bavarian General National Archives, to Geh. Archivrat Dr. Georg M. Jochner and his colleagues, and to Kgl. Reichsarchivsrat Franz Löher and Assessors Dr. Franz Deybeck and Dr. Alfred Altmann, and to the directors of the other circuit archives of Bavaria. The nature of my work put me under obligations also to the directors of the archives of other states, particularly to Geh. Archivrat Dr. P. Zimmermann, Director of the Ducal Archives in Wolfenbüttel, and to Senatssekretär Dr. Anton Hagedorn and his colleagues of the Staatsarchiv in Hamburg, to Syndicus Dr. W. von Bippen of the State Archives in Bremen, to Director Professor Dr. Jos. Hansen of the Historical Archives in Cologne, to Director Dr. G. Freiherr Schenk zu Schweinsberg and Dr. J. R. Dieterich of the Grand-Ducal House and State Archives in Darmstadt, to Director Geh. Regierungsrat Dr. Otto Posse and his colleagues of the Royal Saxon Central State Archives in Dresden, to Director Professor Dr. R. Jung and his colleagues of the City Archives at Frankfort, and to Dr. J. Th. Müller, Archivist of the Moravian Archives at Herrnhut.

M. D. LEARNED.

PHILADELPHIA, January 3, 1911.

TABLE OF CONTENTS.

	PAGE
PREFACE	iii
GERMAN STATE PAPERS RELATING TO AMERICA	1
Early Emigration	1
Auxiliary German Troops and the Revolution	5
Diplomatic and Commercial Relations and Later Emigration	6
GERMAN ARCHIVES	11
Classes of Archives	11
Organization, Administration, and Equipment of the State Archives	14
PRUSSIA	17
Aurich	17
Berlin	17
Royal Privy State Archives of Prussia	17
General Controlle	18
Aüswärtiges Amt	39
Ministerium des Innern	71
Archives of the Ministry of War	76
Breslau	78
Royal State Archives	78
City Archives	82
Coblenz: Royal State Archives	84
Danzig: Royal State Archives	87
Düsseldorf: Royal State Archives	92
Hannover: Royal State Archives	97
Königsberg: Royal State Archives	107
Magdeburg: Royal State Archives	109
Marburg: Royal State Archives of the District of Cassel	112
Ministerium des Auswärtigen	131
Repertorium über die Regierungs Hoheit Repositur	135
Archiv der Kurhessischen Gesandtschaften	137
Kurhessisches Ministerium des Innern	138
Additional Collections (Accessionen)	138
Documents on the III. English-Waldeck Regiment	144
Documents on the Wildunger Brunnen	149
Münster: Royal State Archives of the Province of Westphalia	150
Osnabrück: Royal State Archives	154
Posen: Royal State Archives	157
Schleswig: Royal State Archives	160
Sigmaringen: Royal State Archives	163
Stettin: Royal State Archives of the Province of Pomerania	164
Wetzlar: Royal State Archives	168
Wiesbaden: Royal State Archives	169
BAVARIA	173
Munich	173
Royal Bavarian Privy State Archives	173
Royal Bavarian General National Archives	191
The Royal Bavarian Circuit Archives	191
Royal Bavarian Circuit Archives of Lower Bavaria in Munich	192

Table of Contents

	PAGE
BAVARIA—Continued	
Amberg: Circuit Archives	201
Bamberg: Circuit Archives	204
Landshut: Circuit Archives	207
Neuburg: Circuit Archives	209
Nuremberg: Circuit Archives	211
Speyer: Circuit Archives of the Palatinate	214
Würzburg: Circuit Archives of Lower Franconia and Aschaffenburg	216
ALSACE-LORRAINE	223
Colmar: District Archives of Upper Alsace	223
Metz: District Archives of Lorraine	223
Strassburg: District Archives of Lower Alsace	224
ANHALT (Zerbst): Ducal House and State Archives	228
BADEN (Karlsruhe): Grand-Ducal General National Archives	229
BREMEN: State Archives	238
BRUNSWICK (Wolfenbüttel): Ducal Brunswick-Lüneburg National Central Archives	248
Riedesel Papers	248
Other Papers	263
HAMBURG: State Archives	266
Hauptmeldeamt der Polizei in Hamburg	273
HESSE (Darmstadt): Grand-Ducal Hessian House and State Archives	275
LIPPE (Detmold): House and National Archives of the Principality	278
LÜBECK: State Archives	279
Vereinigte Staaten von Nord Amerika (auch Texas)	279
Mittelamerikanische Staaten	281
Südamerikanische Staaten	283
Acta Hanseatica	288
Urkunden (Trese)	289
MECKLENBURG-SCHWERIN (Schwerin): Grand-Ducal Privy and Central Archives	291
MECKLENBURG-STRELITZ (Neustrelitz): Grand-Ducal Central Archives	291
OLDENBURG: Grand-Ducal House and Central Archives	292
REUSS, ELDER LINE (Greitz): State Archives of the Principality	293
REUSS, YOUNGER LINE (Gera): General Archives	293
SAXE-ALTENBURG (Altenburg): Ducal Government Archives	293
SAXE-COBURG-GOTHA (Coburg and Gotha): Ducal Saxon House and State Archives	293
SAXE-MEININGEN (Meiningen): Privy State Archives	294
SAXE-WEIMAR-EISENACH (Weimar): Grand-Ducal and Ducal Saxon State Archives	295
SAXONY (Dresden): Royal Saxon Central State Archives	296

Table of Contents

	PAGE
SCHAUMBURG-LIPPE (Bückeburg): Ministerial Archives	302
SCHWARZBURG-RUDOLSTADT (Rudolstadt): Archives of the Principality	302
SCHWARZBURG-SONDERSHAUSEN (Sondershausen): National Archives of the Principality	302
WALDECK (Arolsen): Archives of the Principality	302
WÜRTTEMBERG (Stuttgart and Ludwigsburg): Royal Privy House and State Archives	303
Staatsarchiv Filiale in Ludwigsburg	303
Ministerium des Innern in Ludwigsburg	305
MUNICIPAL AND OTHER LOCAL ARCHIVES	308
Cologne: Historical Archives	308
Frankfort-on-the-Main: City Archives	310
Herrnhut: Moravian Archives	314
Karlsruhe: City Archives	318
Mannheim: City Archives	319
Neuwied: Archives of the Principality of Wied-Neuwied	322

CARNEGIE INSTITUTION OF WASHINGTON
PUBLICATION NO. 150

PAPERS OF THE DEPARTMENT OF HISTORICAL RESEARCH
J. FRANKLIN JAMESON, Editor

The Lord Baltimore Press
BALTIMORE, MD., U. S. A.

GERMAN STATE PAPERS RELATING TO AMERICA.

1. EARLY EMIGRATION.

It is one of the anomalies of history that the German states, which next to the British Isles furnished the largest and most important ethnical element in the population of the United States, should have founded no politically distinct colonies in this vast territory of the Western world. This fact, so strikingly in contrast with the colonizing policies of other European states, particularly of Spain, Portugal, France, England, Holland, and Sweden, finds its explanation in the political, economic, and social conditions prevailing in the old German Empire during the period of colonization in America. In the epoch of discovery in the Western world individual Germans had their interest and share. This was notably the case in the great commercial cities of South Germany, which were dominated by rich merchant princes. The same is true to some extent of the merchant adventurers of North Germany, as for example Peter Minuit of Wesel, who was successively governor of the Dutch settlement of Manhattan Island (1626), and founder of New Sweden (1638) on the Delaware.

As a matter of fact it was the two great merchant families of Augsburg, the Welsers and the Fuggers, with their affiliated houses in Nuremberg and Ulm, that were most prominent in the Spanish colonization of South America in the second quarter of the sixteenth century, 1529 and 1533 respectively. These colonizing projects of the Germant merchant princes, however, during the reign of the Hapsburg Emperor Charles V., appear as episodes in the history of Spanish colonization and not as specifically German efforts in settling the New World. Accordingly, the documents relating to these early German colonial enterprises are preserved in the Welser and Fugger archives and in some cases in the Spanish and English records; nevertheless a few fragments of the Fugger papers dating from the years 1533-1534 are found in the Royal Bavarian General National Archives in Munich.[1]

It is not till the period of "territorial absolutism" that the state papers relating to America begin to appear as a part of the governmental business of the German principalities. Most of these earlier papers deal with the two great questions of the time—confessional liberty and emigration. The Peace of Westphalia was the beginning of a new epoch in the religious and political history of Europe in general, and of the German states in particular. The great religious conflict which had brought on the Thirty Years' War was subordinated in the final issue to political interests. The treaties of Westphalia reduced the political supremacy of the Emperor to the minimum, and vested correspondingly greater authority in the German princes, thus giving to the rulers of principalities or individual states a distinct autonomy, which enabled the ruler to reign absolutely over his subjects. Thus each petty prince began to say what was attributed particularly to Louis XIV. of France, " L'état c'est moi"! In like manner the Peace of Westphalia in 1648 dealt a severe blow at the confessional supremacy of the Roman Catholic Church, in spite of the fierce protestations of the Pope, and supported with certain

---

[1] There is curious reference to an Indian chief in a letter of Landgraf Philipp zu Hessen directed to the Elector Augustus of Saxony 1561 (see *infra*, p. 299).

limitations the general principle of confessional freedom secured in France by the Edict of Nantes, inasmuch as it recognized religious liberty for the three established confessions, Catholic, Lutheran, and Calvinist or Reformed. Thus the Peace of Westphalia, instead of eliminating the causes of political and religious conflict, introduced new complications, which led to endless strife in Church and State.

In the wake of the Thirty Years' War followed a far-reaching wave of religious sectarianism. Even before the war a number of sects had arisen to disturb and alarm the orthodoxy of both Catholic and Lutheran. The followers of Johann Huss and of Caspar Schwenkfeld had been the subjects of persecution, and the Mennonites as successors of the Waldenses had awakened suspicion both in Holland and in Germany. In 1670 the strongholds of Lutheranism were threatened by the appearance of the Pietists under the leadership of Jacob Spener in Frankfort-on-the-Main. The peril threatened by these sects was the more grave because they inculcated certain fundamental doctrines based on primitive Christianity, particularly the refusal to bear arms and to take the civil oath, as promulgated by the General Conference of the Mennonites held at Dordrecht in 1632, and the doctrine of spiritual regeneration, the most essential principle of all these sects. These cardinal principles of primitive Christianity were in direct conflict with the military and political temper of the time. It was natural that the state authorities should keep a watchful eye on the confessional irregularities of Separatists. In 1659 the Swiss Reformers inaugurated their fiercest persecution of the Mennonites. From this time on there are many state papers found in the German archives relating to that sect.

The General-Landesarchiv in Karlsruhe is particularly rich in records relating to the religious affairs of this period and even earlier. Under the rubric " Generalia: Religion: Die Wiedertäufer in Kurpfalz ", are mandates and other papers from the years 1566, 1571, 1603, 1610, 1664, 1698, and later, and under " Pfalz, Generalia: Religion: Nachrichten über Religionssecten der Wiedertäufer und Quaker in der Pfalz insbesondere die Concession der Wiedertäufer 1651-1679 " are many papers relating to the Mennonites of Steinfurt, Alzei, and other places, and to the " exercitium religionis ".

The papers relating to emigration begin to appear systematically during this period of religious disturbance and territorial absolutism. As early as 1660 we find reference to the efforts of Louis XIV. to extend French influence in America, in the edict of Louis King of France and Navarre authorizing Nicolas de Gargot to establish French colonies in Newfoundland, to carry on trade with the savages and bring them into the fold of the Catholic Church. In the state archives of Strassburg are a number of documents dating from 1669 and later, relating to the efforts of Louis XIV. to check or control French emigration.[1]

As a sequel to the visits of William Penn and other Quakers among the Mennonites along the Rhine, and Penn's invitation to the Germans to settle in his new province of Pennsylvania, we find a fresh interest awakening among the German sects, and a desire to emigrate to America. In the Royal Bavarian Privy Archives in Munich is a newly discovered German translation of William Penn's *Letter to the Committee of the Free Society of Traders of London*. This manuscript is the more interesting as it shows that Penn's

---

[1] Compare also the papers relating to the colonization of Cayenne (Würzburg, Hist. Saal. VII., Fach 49).

letter undoubtedly passed into German translation about the same time the Dutch translation was published.[1]

A new impulse was given to the religious unrest by the Revocation of the Edict of Nantes in 1685. Thousands of Protestants were forced out of France, and sought refuge in the German lands beyond the Rhine, in Holland, and later in America. These Huguenot refugees were an important factor in preparing the way for the great Palatine exodus of 1709. In addition to this calamity of the Revocation of the Edict of Nantes, came the struggle of the Reformed Church for recognition in the Rhine countries, particularly in the Rhenish Palatinate, a struggle which resulted in religious liberty for the Reformed in 1705. In the midst of these religious turmoils the Rhenish Palatinate became the scene of the ravages of two wars, the war of the Palatine Succession, 1688 to 1697, in which Louis XIV. reduced most of the thriving villages of the Palatinate to ashes; and the war of the Spanish Succession, which in 1707 laid its heavy hand likewise upon the Palatinate. Thus a bare subsistence for the Palatines at home became an impossibility, and they finally, under the protection of Queen Anne of England, followed in the steps of the Huguenots to New York, and of the Mennonites to Pennsylvania. The exodus of so many subjects threatened the Rhine countries with depopulation, and the ruling princes were forced to take the severest measures to retain their subjects at home.

The striking paucity of the records of this Palatine emigration in the Palatinate itself has led to the supposition that the papers were destroyed during the wars. But it seems quite likely that few local records were kept in the Palatinate itself of the fugitive subjects, as they fled before invading armies and in most cases never returned to identify themselves. While the records in the Palatinate proper are thus scanty, there still exist many papers relating to the Palatines in the Bavarian archives at Munich and those of Baden in Karlsruhe and Hesse-Nassau in Wiesbaden. These papers consist of numerous edicts issued by the Elector Count Palatine, by the Emperor, and the Count of Hesse-Nassau. Taken together they furnish a fairly complete history of the conditions prevailing in the Rhineland, the causes and extent of the migration and the vigorous efforts made by the respective governments to prevent wholesale emigration. In these records the genesis of the several state policies toward the question of emigration can be traced step by step from the simple form of the cameral order and the princely edict to the more complicated diplomatic agreements with neighboring states, and finally with the United States of America, when the colonies had gained their independence.

The steps in this early state legislation concerning emigration are many but relatively simple. We find edicts forbidding subjects to emigrate without the permission of the government; orders issued to the judiciary districts, or local courts, to examine the reasons in the applications of subjects wishing to emigrate, to make inventories of their property and unpaid debts, and to see that the prospective emigrant paid his debts and the emigrant tax (or tithe) before leaving the country. The countries lying along the route of the Rhine were forced to formulate measures regulating the passage of emigrants through their territory, thus bringing about diplomatic correspondence between the several states. In 1709 the number of wandering strangers became

---

[1] The document has now been printed in *German American Annals* for March-April, 1910, and by Emil Heuser in *Pennsylvanien im 17. Jahrhundert und die ausgewanderten Pfälzer in England* (Neustadt a. H., 1910).

so great that the closest inspection was instituted, and rigorous ordinances passed regulating their stay in the respective states. A further source of trouble to the state authorities was found in the emigration agents, the so-called "Emissarii", or later in the eighteenth century, "Neuländer", who kept up an incessant agitation among the German peasants and small tradesmen year after year. Edicts were issued imposing severe penalties upon the emissaries. The expulsion of these agents was the more difficult because of the great inducements held out by the owners and masters of ships carrying on the emigrant traffic with America and also by the further fact that the English government and the provincial proprietaries were aiding and abetting the shippers.

As the lists on later pages will show, the Royal Bavarian Privy State Archives and the Royal Bavarian Provincial Archives, the Grand Ducal General National Archives in Karlsruhe, the Ducal Archives in Darmstadt, the State Archives in Wiesbaden, Coblenz, and other provinces contain vast numbers of state papers relating to the several phases of the emigration problem from 1709 onward. The records are particularly full in reference to the emigration tax (*Nachsteuer, Abzugsgeld,* etc.) and the system of passports (*Freizügigkeit, Passwesen,* etc.), and furnish many lists of names and particulars of emigrants to America and other countries.

In addition to the state papers relating to the emigration in general there are also many valuable records relating to individual German settlements in America and to colonizing societies formed in Germany. While in some instances records of these colonizing enterprises have been preserved in America, these papers in the German archives are for the most part new and unpublished sources.

As early as 1706, two years before Kocherthal prepared the way for the exodus of the Palatines, the "High German Society of Langensalza" ("Hochteutche Compagnie von Langensalza") was organized and making plans for a Thuringian settlement on the "Island of Carolina" ("Insul Carolina"). In the Royal State Archives at Dresden there is a most valuable collection of papers relating to this enterprise. It seems quite likely that this High German Society bears some historical relation to the High German Society of Frankfort-on-the-Main, of which Pastorius was the agent in the settlement of Germantown in 1683. There is also the further coincidence that the enterprise was to be under the guidance of a great Quaker.[1]

In like manner the emigration of the Salzburg Lutherans to Georgia in 1732 has left its traces in the state archives of Munich and Bamberg. The Moravians who first accompanied the Salzburgers to Georgia and later settled in Pennsylvania and elsewhere, have also left many records behind them, the most of which are found in Herrnhut. Nevertheless there are also papers relating to the Moravians in the Grand Ducal Archives at Weimar. In the State Archives in Breslau are important papers relating to the Schwenkfelders who emigrated to America in 1734. The attempt of the Waldo's to effect a large German settlement in New England attracted great attention in Germany, and gave rise to many state papers relating to the enterprise, particularly to the settlement in Massachusetts (Maine), concerning which there is much manuscript material in the State Archives at Ludwigsburg (Württemberg), and in the State Archives in Wiesbaden. These papers extend over a period of more than twenty years, some of them dating as late as 1771.

---

[1] It is interesting that the idea of an "island" colony was quite general in the minds of these early emigrants. The records refer to the "Insul Pensilvania," the "Insul Carolina," and in 1720 even to the "Insul Mississippi".

2. AUXILIARY GERMAN TROOPS AND THE REVOLUTION.

The military operations of the American Revolution introduced a new element into the relations of Germany and America, and called forth extensive diplomatic correspondence, as well as a great mass of other materials relating to the war, thus opening a new epoch in the history of German emigration and diplomacy. The state papers arising out of the events of the war consist of several distinct classes of documents:

1. Contracts between George III. of England and the German princes, the Landgrave of Hesse, the Duke of Brunswick-Lüneburg, the Duke of Hesse-Hanau, the Duke of Anhalt-Zerbst, and the Margrave of Anspach-Bayreuth, for auxiliary troops to serve with the English forces in America, together with the official and private correspondence relating thereto.
2. Regulations and instructions for the recruiting and organizing of troops for English service.
3. Papers relating to the passage of the auxiliary troops through the several principalities en route for England, and the return of the surviving troops to their home-quarters after the close of the war.
4. The monthly and other official reports of the condition of the troops in America, the final balance-sheets for the payment of these subsidies, and the settlements of these balances through the bankers.
5. Correspondence of officers and men relating to the movements of the troops and the events of the war in America.
6. Parole and order books used by the officers of the auxiliary troops.
7. Diaries and journals kept by the officers and men of the auxiliary troops in America.
8. Maps and plans of battles illustrating the topography of the scenes of the war in America.

These papers are widely distributed among the German state archives. The largest collections are found in the following archives:

1. The State Archives at Marburg, which contain the most extensive collection of papers relating to the Revolution, including a fairly complete set of monthly reports, a large number of diaries and journals, considerable official and private correspondence, the papers of the final settlement of subsidies, a number of order books and a large collection of maps of various parts of America.
2. The Ducal Archives in Wolfenbüttel, which contain the original parchment contracts with George III., in a fine state of preservation, papers relating to the recruiting and organization of the Brunswick troops, diaries relating to the Revolution, keys to the cipher codes, paroles, countersigns, and scouting marks, reports of Riedesel and other officers, maps relating to America, and most important of all, the very extensive correspondence of Riedesel, including his official letters before, during, and after the Revolution, and letters written to him by the officers and men, amounting in all to several hundred letters,

treating of almost every conceivable phase of the war in America.
3. The Royal Bavarian Circuit Archives in Bamberg, containing papers relating to subsidy contract between George III. and the Margrave of Brandenburg-Bayreuth and other matter, including poems concerning the departure of the Brandenburg-Bayreuth troops for America.
4. The Royal Bavarian Circuit Archives in Würzburg, containing a large collection of papers relating to the passage of the Ansbach-Bayreuth troops through the episcopal domains of Würzburg en route for England.
5. The State Archives in Hannover, containing similar papers relating to the passage of the auxiliary troops through Hanoverian territory on their way to England.

These last two collections contain matter hitherto unknown to most historians of the American Revolution, and shed much light upon the diplomatic machinery brought to bear, as well as upon the details of transporting and provisioning the troops in their overland march to the sea. In addition to these above mentioned collections there are papers in the Ducal Palace and State Archives in Zerbst relating to the Anhalt-Zerbst troops, and in the State Archives in Marburg relating to the Waldeck regiment in English service in America.

The state papers relating to German troops in English service furnish a new point of view of the relations of England to the German states, and show that the system of employing auxiliary forces in Germany for English military service began long before the American Revolution, and was in full force during the French and Indian War.

3. DIPLOMATIC AND COMMERCIAL RELATIONS AND LATER EMIGRATION.

It is easy to trace in the German state papers, more particularly those of Prussia, the beginnings of American diplomatic relations with Germany during the American Revolution. Two factors are important in these early official transactions between the United American Colonies and the King of Prussia, the desire of Frederick the Great to extend Prussian trade in America, and the efforts of the American colonies to secure recognition by foreign powers. Out of these two motives acting one upon the other, sprang the interesting acts of our first diplomacy with Prussia. One of the early policies of Frederick the Great had been that of effecting commercial treaties with those countries which had extensive colonies in America. As early as 1747 and 1753 he entered into such commercial relations with France, in 1756 with England, and in 1771 with Spain, with the purpose of extending the Prussian linen trade in America in exchange for tobacco and other commodities from the American colonies. The outbreak of the American Revolution naturally interrupted this growing commerce with America. The King of Prussia and the American agents abroad, as well as the leaders of the Revolution at home, were fully alive to the situation. The Declaration of Independence had scarcely dried upon the parchment before the American agents abroad began to seek negotiations with a view to establishing trade relations with the King of Prussia in the hope of thereby securing some form of recognition, at least of the diplomatic independence of the colonies. There is no more interesting chapter in the history of our diplomatic relations with Europe than that of the diplomatic correspondence between our American agents abroad, notably Arthur Lee in Paris, and Schulenburg, Frederick the Great's Minister of State in Berlin, and the highly significant marginal comments affixed by Frederick in his own hand to Schulenburg's official dispatches. In these documents can be traced the shrewd diplomacy of the great king in his efforts to take the first advantage for the interest of Prussian trade without violating his relations with neighboring powers.

As early as July 29, 1776, Montessuy, Prussian Minister in Paris, sent an interesting communication to Schulenburg in Berlin concerning the tobacco trade with America. All eyes were naturally intent upon the acts of the American Congress at Philadelphia. In October we find the king commanding Schulenburg to receive Carmichael only as a " simple négociant ", and to avoid giving any official sign of recognition of the colonies. Likewise in the following year the king remained firm in his opposition to the admission of American privateers to Prussian ports, commanding Schulenburg to reject Arthur Lee's proposals with the following significant words, " mit complimenten abweissen. Fred." (Oct. 16, 1777). When Arthur Lee made new commercial proposals in January, 1778, the king wrote Schulenburg more favorably, but still declared that an open alliance would be premature. As the negotiations proceeded, interesting private adventurers come into play. A certain Jew of Philadelphia, Jacob by name, proposed a plan for regulating commercial relations between Prussia and America. At length, Sept. 10, 1783, after the United Colonies had gained their independence, the king opened public, cordial negotiations with the new Republic of the West.

In the very beginning of the new republic other German states took up the question of entering into diplomatic and trade relations with the United States. As early as May, 1783, we find documents relating thereto in the Royal State Archives in Dresden. The business relations of Germany and America became more complicated. Even before the close of the Revolution the question of settling estates of Germans in America and of German Americans in Germany had given rise to extensive transactions, such, for example, as the estate of Maria Dildey and the property of Georg Christoph White in the parish of Raleigh in Virginia, 1780; the inheritance of the Ravenhorst heirs in Ebenezer, Georgia, 1784; and many others in various parts of the two countries. As early as 1784 we find Thieriot, Saxon commissioner of trade in Philadelphia, busy with the organization of a trade society to carry on commerce between Saxony and America. In 1791 Paleske was appointed Prussian consul-general for North America, and in 1798 J. E. C. Schultze, a merchant in Baltimore, was appointed consul for Baltimore. In 1799 the treaty of friendly and commercial intercourse between the United States and Prussia was renewed with additional articles abolishing the alien inheritance tax and making other provisions touching other conditions that concerned the commercial relations of the two countries. In 1801-1802 the settlement of commercial claims against American merchants assumes new proportions, notably the claims of Engmann, Mottern, and Boehm against Consul Schultze in Baltimore (1801) and the claim of Engel of Züllichau against Jacob Mark and Company in New York. In 1803 H. von Seckendorf forms the project of maintaining a Saxon chargé d'affaires in America.

The restoration of the rights of the princes which followed the Vienna Congress of 1815, and was advanced by the reactionary policy of the régime of Metternich, gave rise to a new epoch of political unrest throughout the German states and led ultimately to renewed emigration of discontented and persecuted Germans to America. The twenty years of German emigration which followed the closing of the Turner Halls in Germany in 1819, contributed an enormous mass of state papers to the records of the German archives. In almost every German state the most stringent measures were taken to suppress the excesses of German students in the universities, and the republican sentiments of the Turner organizations, thus forcing hosts of well-educated German subjects to emigrate. The strongest current of emigration was turned toward the United States. So great became the interest in the New World, that it seemed impossible to check the emigration. The next question was how to regulate the emigration of German subjects, and to protect them against ill treatment and fraud on the part of colonizing and shipping agents. In one notable instance we find a German prince, Bernhard, duke of Saxe-Weimar-Eisenach, visiting the New World to see it with his own eyes, in the years 1825-1826. Two years before, in 1823, we find documents relating to the organization of the " American Company of the Elbe " (" Elb-Amerikanische Compagnie "). The following year, 1824, the treaty between the United States of America and Russia regarding the trade in the South Sea attracted considerable attention in Germany. In the same years a new and significant territory for German colonization was opened in Brazil, thus diverting the stream of emigrants for a time to South America, especially emigrants from Austria and South Germany. The records relating to this emigration are very full, particularly in the Royal Privy State Archives of Bavaria in Munich. The beginning of this emigration to Brazil was made by Georg Anton Schäfer, a German physician in Brazil, who returned to Europe in 1822, claiming to have a secret mission from the Emperor of Brazil to the Emperor of Austria, relating to the new scheme of founding a German colony in Brazil. In 1827 we find papers relating to the recognition of the Empire of Brazil. Since that time the interest of the Germans in Brazil has been a constant quantity in the state papers.

It was during this period that the lands of Missouri and neighboring states were discovered as a new and inviting country for German colonists. The echoes of Gottfried Duden's travels in Missouri and the western states of North America in the years 1824-1827 are clearly reflected by the state papers in the Prussian, Bavarian, Saxon, and other state archives. In 1828 the treaty of commerce and navigation was consummated between Prussia and North America, and in 1832 the " Thuringian Emigration Society " was organized.

Meanwhile other important questions, particularly that of the American tariff, had been agitating the minds of the Germans. In 1833 the German Tariff Union (Deutscher Zollverein) came into the foreground of the state papers, and the financial crisis in America between 1830 and 1840 awakened the gravest apprehensions in German commercial circles. As the relations of the German and American states became more complicated, it was found necessary to make provisions against irresponsible adventurers and other dangerous persons; accordingly, treaties between Bavaria and Prussia, and the United States, were effected in 1852-1854 for the purpose of extraditing fugitive criminals.

In the early forties of the nineteenth century the records call attention again to the German emigration to Texas. Even before this period there are state papers relating to Texas as a part of Mexico, for there had been an emigration to " Colorado ", Texas, as early as 1823. Now, however, 1844, the more systematic plan of colonization in Texas, stimulated by Castro's accounts in European papers, was inaugurated by the society of German princes and nobles called the " Verein zum Schutze der deutschen Auswanderer in Texas ", which was formed at Mainz. In 1844-1845 we find papers relating to the importation of articles from the Hanse towns and the Baltic ports of Prussia under discussion, and in 1845 papers and reports of Gerolt, minister resident in Washington. Meanwhile the emigration grows apace and gives rise to the formation of societies for the direction of emigration and the founding of colonies, particularly the " Verein zur Centralisation deutscher Auswanderung und Colonisation " in Berlin and the " Deutsche Colonisations-Gesellschaft für Central-Amerika ". These and similar societies now enter into co-operation with the older German societies in America, especially with the " Deutsche Gesellschaft von Pennsylvania ", " Deutsche Gesellschaft von Maryland ", " Deutsche Gesellschaft von New York ", and " Deutsche Gesellschaft von New Orleans ", whose reports were forwarded frequently to the central bureau in Berlin. Hamburg and Bremen now became prominent ports for the shipping of German emigrants, and the senates of these two Hanse towns turned their attention to the protection of German emigrants, and aided in the formation of bureaus of information for emigrants. In 1855 the first annual report of the " Nachweisungs-Bureau der Auswanderer-Behörde in Hamburg " was published.

About the middle of the nineteenth century the great current of German emigration passed out by way of Hamburg and Bremen, giving a new impulse to the shipping between these ports and the great seaboard cities of the United States. The governments having developed a system of police inspection, now gave minute attention to all the details of emigration. The emigration societies already mentioned co-operated with the several emigrant bureaus in Berlin, Hamburg, Bremen, and other places, and a full account was kept, so far as it was obtainable, of the individual emigrants. It not infrequently happens that as many as twenty or thirty papers grow out of the case of a single emigrant before he embarks for the New World. An interesting list of such papers concerning an emigrant from Neustadt-on-the-Wald-Naab in Bavaria in 1851-1852 is here given as an example of such emigrant literature:

Acten-Renner des K. Landgerichts Neustadt W/N.

Auswanderung des Leonhard Bettmann von Flossenburg und der Müllerstochter Anna Maria Maierhoefer von Gailertsreuth betff.

Datum			Vortrag	Num. Curr.
Tag	Monat	Jahr		
14	Dezbr.	1851	Bericht der Gemeindeverwaltung Flossenburg..	1
3	Januar	1852	Protokoll	2
"	"	"	Signatur an die Gemeindeverwaltung Gailertsreuth	3
"	"	"	Schreiben zum K. protest. Pfarramt Floss....	4
"	"	"	Schreiben an das protest. Vikariat Flossenburg	5
"	"	"	Bekanntmachung	6
8	"	"	Protokoll	7
15	"	"	Protokoll	8
17	"	"	Protokoll	9
18	"	"	Vollzugsnachweis	10
17	"	"	Protokolls-Fortsetzung	11
28	"	"	Schiffahrts-Contract	12

2

Datum			Vortrag	Num. Curr.
Tag	Monat	Jahr		
31	Januar	1852	Bekanntmachung im Intelligenzblatte für die Oberpfalz und von Regensburg............	13
2	Feb.	"	Bericht der Gemeindeverwaltung Flossenburg..	14
6	"	"	Schuldenforderung	15
10	"	"	Schreiben des K. protest. Vikariats Flossenburg	16
8	"	"	Bericht der Gemeindeverwaltung Gailertsreuth	17
16	"	"	Protokoll	18
21	"	"	Protokoll	19
19	"	"	Protokoll	20
24	"	"	Protokoll	21
23	"	"	Circular	22
27	"	"	Protokoll	23
4	März	"	Protokoll	24
"	"	"	Ausgabsmandat	25
"	"	"	Vollzugsausweis	26
8	"	"	Protokoll	27
"	"	"	Auswanderungsbewilligung	28
7	"	"	Schreiben an das K. Rentamt Weid[e]n......	29
9	"	"	Taufzeugniss	30

Neustadt W/N am 8ten März 1852.

In the cities of Hamburg and Bremen records were made of the emigrants shipping from these ports. In Hamburg, for example, in the central police station, a complete record of emigrants passing through the city from 1834 to 1867 is found in the " Protocoll der Aufenthalts-Karten ". This early list has been continued as " Das Melde-Register ", giving lists of emigrants down to the present time. This is one of the most valuable emigrant records in the German Empire. A similar list or record of emigrants seems to have been kept also in Bremen, but has been destroyed, unfortunately, down to within ten years of the present time. The German Lloyd has, of course, a full list of cabin passengers sailing on Lloyd ships. The best continuous account of the German emigration during the second half of the nineteenth century is preserved in the records in the Privy State Archives in Berlin, among the papers of the Foreign Office under the rubric " Auswanderungen, Generalia " and " Auswanderungen ausser Europa ". These records contain not only the ministerial acts relating to emigration but an almost complete printed literature in the way of pamphlets, shipping circulars, and the like, bearing upon the various phases of emigration.

In this brief survey it has been possible to show how the incidental events of early colonization in America have led, in the course of the centuries, from the simple edict prohibiting emigration, to the far-reaching and highly complicated commercial, diplomatic, and cultural relations which have brought every town and village, nay, every citizen of Germany and America into sympathetic touch in the present epoch.

GERMAN ARCHIVES.

The results of historical research in Germany are apparent in the organization and administration of archives of various kinds. Active inquiry in all the fields of German history has called into requisition the sources of state and municipal as well as private collections, and the greatest liberality has been shown in opening these collections to investigators. Thus the various depositories with their own several distinctive features in the way of materials and method of administration have come to the aid of historical science.

CLASSES OF ARCHIVES.

In the course of the centuries the sources of German history have grown up under the varying forms of government and complex agencies of culture, and a great variety of collections has naturally developed, each having its own individuality and historic value. The following classes of German archives come under contribution for materials relating to American history.

State Archives (Staatsarchive). The most important and extensive collections of German historical documents are the state papers which make up to a large extent the State Archives. These archives vary in number from one or two depositories in the smaller states to ten in Bavaria and eighteen in Prussia. The state archives are an essential part of the several ministries, especially the ministries of foreign affairs and of internal affairs, corresponding to our departments of State and of the Interior. The earlier state papers of the ministries are transferred in great part from the ministerial depositories to the state archives, although there is no uniform method of transference even in the same state. The kind of papers to be transferred and the period from which the papers are to be taken are determined by considerations of space, need of documents for scientific purposes, character of the documents, and the frequency with which they are required in the work of the respective ministries. In some cases the documents have been transferred down to a very late date; in others, certain groups of state papers are still deposited *in toto* with the ministry.

In the capitals of the larger states, like Prussia and Bavaria, there are two kinds of state archives, constituting in some of the states separate and distinct depositories: the Privy State Archives (*Geheimes Staatsarchiv*) and the Provincial State Archives, called in Bavaria Circuit Archives (*Kreisarchive*). The privy archives and the provincial state papers are deposited together in many of the smaller states. The privy archives contain the documents of the archives of the respective ruling houses (*Hausarchiv*), as they relate to the government and to the economies and personal affairs of the court. The Royal Privy Archives of Prussia and Bavaria are depositories of rare value, both as regards domestic and foreign affairs, and are particularly rich in matter relating to American history. In these privy state papers are found the confidential transactions of the government, much of the matter in cipher.

The German state archives are distributed as follows:

Prussia: The Royal Privy State Archives in Berlin and the Royal Prussian State Archives located in Aurich, Breslau, Coblenz, Danzig, Düsseldorf, Hannover, Königsberg, Magdeburg, Marburg, Münster, Osnabrück, Posen, Schleswig, Sigmaringen, Stettin, Wetzlar, and Wiesbaden.

Bavaria: The Royal Privy State Archives in Munich, the Royal Bavarian General National Archives in Munich, and the Royal Bavarian Provincial or Circuit Archives located in Amberg, Bamberg, Landshut, Munich, Neuburg-on-the-Danube, Nuremberg, Speyer, and Würzburg.

Alsace-Lorraine: District Archives of Upper Alsace, in Colmar; District Archives of Lorraine, in Metz; District Archives of Lower Alsace, in Strassburg.

Anhalt: Ducal House and State Archives, in Zerbst.

Baden: Grand-Ducal General National Archives, in Karlsruhe.

Bremen: State Archives.

Brunswick: Ducal Brunswick-Lüneburg National Central Archives, in Wolfenbüttel.

Hamburg: State Archives.

Hesse: Grand-Ducal Hessian House and State Archives, in Darmstadt.

Lippe: House and National Archives of the Principality, in Detmold.

Lübeck: State Archives.

Mecklenburg-Schwerin: Grand-Ducal Privy and Central Archives, in Schwerin.

Mecklenburg-Strelitz: Grand-Ducal Central Archives, in Neustrelitz.

Oldenburg: Grand-Ducal House and Central Archives, in Oldenburg.

Reuss, Elder Line: State Archives of the Principality, in Greiz.

Reuss, Younger Line: General Archives, in Gera.

Saxe-Altenburg: Ducal Government Archives, in Altenburg.

Saxe-Coburg-Gotha: Ducal Saxon House and State Archives, in Coburg and in Gotha.

Saxe-Meiningen: Privy State Archives, in Meiningen.

Saxe-Weimar-Eisenach: Grand-Ducal and Ducal Saxon State Archives, in Weimar.

Saxony: Royal Saxon Central State Archives, in Dresden.

Schaumburg-Lippe: Ministerial Archives, in Bückeburg.

Schwarzburg-Rudolstadt: Archives of the Principality, in Rudolstadt.

Schwarzburg-Sonderhausen: National Archives of the Principality, in Sondershausen.

Waldeck: The (relevant) Archives of the Principality are not found in Arolsen, the capital, but are deposited in the State Archives at Marburg.

Württemberg: Royal Privy House and State Archives in Stuttgart, and the Filiale, including the Department of the Interior, in Ludwigsburg.

Municipal Archives (Stadtarchive). In most of the important cities archives are to be found containing matter relating to the legislative and administrative functions of the municipality. In the Hanse towns the municipal archives are often deposited with the state archives, which relate to the general functions of the city in its capacity as a state. In these city states, Hamburg, Lübeck, and Bremen, the archives combine the collections of state papers with collections of local records. In some cases cities which were formerly free cities of the Empire, but later descended to the rank of ordinary municipalities, have retained their state papers; as for example, the city of Frankfort-on-the-Main. In other cities the municipal archives and the state archives are still distinct depositories, as in the case of Nuremberg, with its municipal archives (*Stadtarchiv*) and its provincial or circuit state archives (*Kreisarchiv*). When municipal archives are mentioned in this work, they are understood to be archives of cities which have no state functions, or, in the case of the Hanse towns, archives of the city as a municipality, in distinction to the city as a state. The number of municipal archives is very large and the collections vary greatly in character and value. In some cases the history of municipal affairs is kept in the form of a city chronicle. This was formerly a common form of city record, and many of the older city chronicles have been committed to print and are invaluable historical documents. (*Cf. Die Chroniken der deutschen Städte.*)

Village and Parish Records. As the cities have kept record of the municipalities, so the village communities have in many cases preserved valuable records, except where they have been destroyed by fire or war, as is unfortunately the case with many villages in the Rhenish Palatinate and other districts in the track of pillaging armies. The village, or community, or parish archives contain a variety of documents, such as the church records of marriages, births, baptisms, and deaths, and matter relating to the local government of the community or parish. These records contain important information concerning the German emigration to America, and are invaluable for the genealogist.

Ecclesiastical Archives. There are many large collections of ecclesiastical documents in Germany, under the general control of the respective confessions, Catholic, Lutheran, Reformed, Moravian, and the like. Notable among these collections are those in Zweibrücken, Kiel, Cologne, and Herrnhut. All these collections have important bearing on the history of these religious bodies in America, and some of them have already been consulted by American investigators. An inventory or guide to these depositories would be of great service to historians both in Europe and America.

In some cases the ecclesiastical collections are deposited, in part at least, in the state archives, as for example, in Hamburg and Marburg. Most of the state archives contain, as a matter of course, state papers relating to church affairs.

Private Archives. Among the many private or family archives of Germany, two are especially interesting to students of American history, *viz.*, those of the Welser and the Fugger families. Much has already been written of the history of these two families, and it is expected that the Welser and Fugger collections will soon be thoroughly exploited and their contents made accessible in printed form. The work of Dr. Jansen of Munich on the Welser manuscripts is already well in hand. There are many important and valuable old family archives throughout the German Empire, which would no doubt amply repay an examination for sources of American history. Another important class of private collections is family correspondence and other personal papers relating to transactions of individuals and business firms with America. Private correspondence is a particularly valuable source of information concerning economic, domestic, and political conditions in America. In some parts of Germany, for example Baden and the Rhenish Palatinate, a plan of systematically collecting private family papers has already been proposed. In many provinces these papers have found their way into more central depositories.

Historical Societies and their Collections. An important adjunct to the official state and municipal agencies for preserving historical materials is found in the provincial and other historical societies of Germany. In most provinces such societies have been formed and are devoting themselves to the collection and preservation of local records and objects illustrating the history of the people. The collections of objects forming local museums, especially in the provinces of Hesse and of the Rhineland, have a peculiar value in the study of the domestic life of the Germans in America. These local historical societies could render American historical research a lasting service by systematically collecting private family papers and making them accessible to American investigators.

ORGANIZATION, ADMINISTRATION, AND EQUIPMENT OF THE STATE ARCHIVES.

The state papers naturally claim our first attention, inasmuch as they are the official expression of the relations of Germany and America.

Organization. As has been already intimated, the state archives in the larger states are thoroughly organized as a part of the governmental records. The various collections of documents are classified, repertorized, and arranged in cases, shelves, or partitions (*Fächer*). The repertories are general catalogues containing the titles and numbers not of separate documents or papers, but of fascicles or bundles of papers. Large bundles are called *Convolute*. Each convolute contains a large number of fascicles or smaller packages of documents. A fascicle or parcel or volume often contains as many as two or three hundred papers, and a convolute may contain as many as a thousand papers, about as many as one can conveniently carry. The repertories, or catalogues, are usually in the form of bound books. In Würzburg and Karlsruhe a kind of slip or card system is in use, but the card system of catalogue, giving the title of separate documents, is not in general use in the archives, although it is being introduced into the university libraries, and in the circulating libraries, notably in the Lesehalle of Hamburg, where a particularly interesting and ingenious form of card catalogue is employed.

It will be seen thus that the repertories of the state archives are little more than guides to bundles or fascicles of papers. The work of calendaring, or even cataloguing, the single papers of an archive collection would be enormous. The papers are usually arranged more or less chronologically in the respective fascicles, much in the same order in which they were made; hence it is important to know not only the general title of the fascicle but also the period covered by the papers in the fascicle. In exceptional cases in the materials relating to America the folios are numbered, thus greatly facilitating reference. As a matter of course, each paper or official document has a number referring to the transaction in the records of the ministry, but it was not found practicable to give these numbers in the case of separate documents referred to in this guide, because the chronological reference seemed more serviceable.

Administration. The state archives of the larger states particularly are well administered, and even in the smaller states where the archival materials are less extensive, there is always an efficient archivist who is especially qualified for his work. Those states having a complex system of archives have a correspondingly elaborate system of archival administration.

In Prussia the Royal Privy State Archives of Berlin and the seventeen Provincial State Archives are under the general supervision of the General Director, while each of the individual archives has its own special Director. In Bavaria the Royal Bavarian Privy State Archives, the Royal Bavarian General National Archives, and the eight Provincial or Circuit Bavarian State Archives are under the supervision of a General Directorate, and the Provincial Bavarian State Archives (*Kreisarchive*) are under the immediate supervision of the Director of the Royal Bavarian General National Archives. In other states the state archives are likewise administered by state authorities.

This centralized administration of the state archives under the rigorous system of civil service prevailing throughout the German states makes it possible, and indeed imperative, to maintain a thoroughly trained staff of archivists and to administer the archival affairs with special reference to the needs of scientific research. The archivists are not only well trained and well educated men but specialists and investigators in their own chosen fields; they fully appreciate the difficulties which confront the historian in the several fields and at the same time understand the importance of accuracy in technical details. Thus the investigator finds in the German archivist not a mere custodian or antiquarian, whose business it is to guard the archives and prate about notable local events and personages, but rather an efficient and helpful colleague eager to aid in advancing research. Indeed, it may be said that the entire system of state archives is devoted largely to the service of research.

The conditions and rules for the use of the archival materials are most generous, and are themselves a high testimonial to the generosity and intelligence of the administration. Materials may be consulted in the archives where they are deposited during the working hours, or by a liberal system of transfer or loan documents may be sent to other archives or libraries, under certain conditions, to be consulted by the investigator. This liberality in loaning materials is observed both by the archives and by the libraries in Germany. The investigator may select some particular depository as the centre for work, and have sources sent to him from other archives with the consent of the depository in which he is working. The procedure is this: The investigator asks the depository or archives, in which he is working, to request the archives containing the desired materials to have them sent for his use. The investigator pays express and other charges both ways and the depository in which he is working vouches for the proper return of the materials loaned. In the case of very rare or valuable documents it is better and more courteous to go and consult them in the depository in which they are found, and thus avoid unnecessary concern or risk in transportation.

In the matter of formalities it is very important that the foreign investigator should observe the customs of the land. While the archivists from the director down are always most courteous, it is well to observe the formality of applying to the official head or director for the privilege of consulting the archives, and it is very fitting that the investigator at the close of his researches in a depository should thank the director and his colleagues for courtesies extended. In case the investigator is commissioned by an institution to make researches, he should bear credentials from the institution and when possible have his request sent directly from the institution to the General Director of the archive which he wishes to consult. If this is done long enough in advance the officials of the respective archives will make a preliminary search and summary of the materials desired and thus facilitate the work of the investigator.

The rules of the archives regulating the use of the materials are usually printed, and shown to the investigator before he begins his work. The regulations vary often according to the classes of investigators, and the formalities differ according as the applicant is a native or a foreigner. In some archives, and in the case of certain kinds of documents, the investigator may be asked to subscribe to more specific conditions; as for example in the case of genealogical researches, where the material desired may affect the private history of families still living. Some archives require also the presentation of a printed copy of the result of the investigation when published.

As a rule investigators are not admitted to the stack and may consult the repertories only when it is necessary. Even then permission must be granted by the director. The investigator will not find it necessary to enter the stack except when he needs to inform himself of the method of arranging materials. He can always obtain the materials more expeditiously by asking the archivist for them.

Equipment. The state archives differ greatly in the manner of equipment. In the earlier period, when the archives were reorganized, there was a tendency to appropriate older buildings, such as castles, judicial, or other government buildings, for archival purposes, as for example, the castles at Königsberg, Posen, Osnabrück, Marburg, Landshut, Würzburg, Ludwigsburg, and Darmstadt, and the older public buildings of Berlin, Hannover, Wolfenbüttel, Coblenz, Schleswig, the State Archives in Munich, and the Royal Saxon Archives in Dresden. In recent years much attention has been given to the erection of new buildings for state archives. These modern structures are built on the most approved plan, and equipped with modern appliances, in the way of fire-proof vaults for valuable manuscripts, iron or steel cases, cement floors, and the like. In the older buildings some interesting devices were found for safe-guarding the records. In Strassburg, for example, the most valuable documents are stored near the front end of the building, so that they can be easily removed in case of fire. In Neuwied there is a peculiar precaution against the destruction of archives by flood from the Rhine. Here the documents are placed on shelves in portable boxes which can be closed by means of doors and hastily transported to another place by means of wagons. Among the newer structures are the archive buildings in Breslau, Bamberg, Magdeburg, Münster, Düsseldorf, Karlsruhe, and Bremen. Some of these are models of architectural beauty and practical utility.

PRUSSIA.

BERLIN.[1]

ROYAL PRIVY STATE ARCHIVES OF PRUSSIA.

(KÖNIGLICH GEHEIMES STAATSARCHIV.)

Located Berlin, C. 2, Klosterstrasse 76, these include the Privy State Archives of the Mark of Brandenburg, the Privy Ministerial Archives, and the Archives of the former Kingdom of Westphalia. The archives are now located in the old castle of the electors of Brandenburg hard by the Gray Cloister. The administrative offices are in a newer building adjoining.

The papers of the Royal Privy Prussian State Archives are grouped according to the departments (*Behörden*) in which they originated and are arranged for the most part chronologically in the order in which they were made. This accounts for the fact that the materials relating to America are found under different rubrics. In the early colonial and revolutionary period, particularly during the reign of Frederick the Great, the machinery of the Prussian government was comparatively simple, consisting of the several departments and the king's cabinet as a central regulative called *General Controlle*. Business might originate in the several departments or even outside of them by official or private initiative and then be communicated through the Minister of War and State, who was in effect the prime minister to the king. The king considered the matter and dictated his order to the secretary, who jotted it down usually in pencil on the document itself, or the king wrote the order in his own hand on the margin of the document. The order was then sent to the Minister of War and State, who in turn communicated it to the respective department or person concerned. In case of important matters the Minister of War and State set up a brief, usually in French, for the king, summing up the points of the question and adding any suggestions he might have to make, and forwarded the same to the king. It sometimes happened that private persons tried to reach the king directly, as in the case of William Lee, the American representative, who addressed a letter to the king. But the king even in such cases forwarded the communication to his minister to be answered as the latter saw fit. The papers thus passing between the king and the Minister of War and State constitute the collection designated as *General Controlle* or later as *Cabinets-Sachen*. Naturally these materials are very miscellaneous in character.

The other materials relating to America are found in the departments or ministerial divisions. It not unfrequently happens that papers relating to the same matter are found both in the Cabinets-Sachen and in the ministerial division. This applies particularly to the communications of the foreign legations. The despatches from London, Paris, etc., often in cipher with transliterated copies, are found among the Cabinets-Sachen. Thus it happens that the despatches from the Prussian minister in London during the American Revolution are found under the rubric " Geh. Kabinets-Registratur, 1688-1786 ". In like manner the corresponding legations in Madrid, the Hague, etc., may contain incidental matter relating to America.

[1] In alphabetical order the Prussian State Archives at Aurich would come before Berlin; but nothing relating to America in those archives survived a conflagration which took place there some years ago.

The correspondence of the American representatives, Carmichael, Arthur and William Lee, and others, was directed for the most part to Schulenburg, the Minister of War and State. In the case of the purchase of arms for the American forces in the Revolution, Franckenstein, the Minister of Finance, was called into requisition. The extensive correspondence relating to the trade treaty (*Commercien Tractat*) between Prussia and the United States, which continues through the entire period of the Revolution till 1785, when the final treaty was signed, is found under the General Controlle (Cabinets-Sachen) for these years.

In the later periods after Prussia and the United States began to treat as independent nations, and the question of emigration, the rights of emigrants, the settlement of estates, the extradition of criminals, the regulation of tariffs, and the like, took on larger proportions, the documents relating to these subjects are found in the respective section of the Department of Foreign Affairs (Amt der Auswärtigen Angelegenheiten or Auswärtiges Amt = A. A.). Into this department of foreign affairs came not only the usual business of the Foreign Office with the consulates, legations, ministers, and ambassadors of different places and periods in America, but also reports and other papers from the various emigration societies, shipping agents, and the like, so that one can say that the material in detail for a history of emigration to America is preserved in the records of the Foreign Office.

Hours: Week days except Saturdays from 9 to 3. Saturdays from 9 to 2.

GENERAL CONTROLLE. KÖNIGL. GEHEIMES MINISTERIAL ARCHIV. TIT. LVIII., NO. 7.[1]

Vol. 1. Acta betreffend den Americanischen Handel und Krieg. 1776, 1777.

Extractus. The king to Schulenburg. Potsdam, Aug. 9, 1776. Referring to Montessuy's proposal that the king open trade negotiations with the American colonies. The king thinks it too hazardous but wishes Schulenburg to consult with Finanz Rath Magusch about prices of Virginia tobacco and then to decide. (German.)

Montessuy's letter to the king with the proposals, dated Paris, July 29, 1776. (French.)

Pro Memoria, giving prices of tobacco in London in 1773. Signed Magusch. Berlin, Aug. 16, 1776. (Copy. German.)

Schulenburg to Montessuy, " Agent de S. M. le Roi de Prusse à Paris ". Berlin, Sept. 12, 1776. (Copy. French.)

Montessuy, stating that the proposal in regard to arms can not be entertained but that he shall try in some other way to secure Virginia tobacco. (French.)

Montessuy (to Schulenburg), stating that he forwards the articles of (the king's) communication in question to the colonies. Paris, Oct. 5, 1776. (French.)

Schulenburg's reply, urging upon Montessuy the greatest caution to do nothing in the negotiation of a " commerce d'échange " with the colonies, that might compromise the king. Berlin, Oct. 16, 1776.

---

[1] Photographic reproductions of the three volumes calendared below are to be found in the collections of the Emperor William Institution of German American Research at the University of Pennsylvania. Information concerning the photographs may be obtained from M. D. Learned, Director of the Institution.

Montessuy to Schulenburg, relating to tobacco, Carmichael, the purchase of a frigate arriving in Bordeaux with list of tobaccos, etc. Paris, Oct. 11, 1776. (French.)
Schulenburg communicates the king's order of Aug. 9, 1776, and other questions for Montessuy to inquire into. (French.)
Schulenburg to the king, with the king's marginal note: "bené mais cela ne durera pas parce que Les Anglais ont battû les Collonies Federic", enclosing the *mémoire*, which was a draft to be copied. Berlin, Oct. 21, 1776. (French.)
Schulenburg to von Görne relating to the French ship of 5 pieces, 450 tons, which the French expect in Bordeaux and wish to sell. Berlin, Oct. 21, 1776.
Von Görne to Schulenburg, ordering Montessuy to withdraw his participation in the sale of the French ship. Berlin, Oct. 22, 1776. (German.)
Schulenburg to Montessuy, sharply calling him to account for precipitancy, and telling him to let the "Compagnie maritime" conduct its own affairs with reference to the ship. Berlin, Oct. 23, 1776. (French.)
Montessuy (to Schulenburg) apologizing for his haste in the matter. Paris, Nov. 8, 1776. (French.)
Schulenburg to Magusch on interview with Carmichael in Berlin, with the marginal note: " P. S. Da H. Carmichael nichts als Englisch spricht, so werden Sie wohl thun, sich nach einem zuverlässigen und verschwiegenen Dolmetscher umzusehen ".
Report of the interview with Carmichael and the directions given him for shipping tobacco, etc., giving Emden as preferred harbor, or in case of greater security a French port. (Exceedingly valuable matter reflecting the conditions of trade and shipping in America and Europe.) Nov. 28, 1776. (German.)
Abschrift des Herrn Carmichael Antwort auf das was an Ihn unterm 27. Nov. c. ergangen ist. Berlin, Nov. 29, 1776. (German.)
Magusch to Schulenburg communicating the interview with Carmichael. Berlin, Nov. 20, 1776. (German.)
Schulenburg reports the matter to the king. Berlin, Nov. 30, 1776. (French.)
The king's reply that a treaty of commercial exchange such as Carmichael proposes is fraught with "mille difficultés". Signed "Federic". The king is willing to consent to having tobacco come through French ports and has ordered Goltz in Paris to do so. Potsdam, Dec. 2, 1776. (French.)
Magusch to Schulenburg, stating that he has notified Carmichael. Berlin, Dec. 3, 1776. (German.)
Copie: "Mein Herr", etc., being a report of the negotiation for tobacco from Virginia through France. Dec. 3, 1776. (German.)
Letters of Montessuy recommending Carmichael (to Schulenburg). Paris, Oct. 10, 1776. (French.)
"Mémoire" with an English postscript in Carmichael's hand.
Carmichael to Schulenburg. Havre, Jan. 19, 1776. (French.)
German translation of the same.
Magusch to Schulenburg, on Carmichael. Berlin, Feb. 4, 1776. (German.)
"Extract eines Schreibens von New York vom 5 Jan. 1777", giving interesting account of the attack at Trent[on], etc.

"Uebersetzung eines Schreibens an den H. Geheimen Rath Magusch", Paris, Mar. 7, 1777, with original notes: "Leurs propositions de Commerce n'étant pas acceptables". Frederick's official reply to Schulenburg. The king says he does not wish to choke off the colonies by refusing their proposals outright, etc. Potsdam, Mar. 12, 1777. (French.)
Lettre de Mrs. [Messrs.] Franklin et Deane. Paris, Feb. 14, 1777.
Lettre de Mr. Carmichael. Paris, Feb. 18, 1777.
Schulenburg to Franklin and Deane. Berlin, Mar. 14, 1777. (French.)
Schulenburg to Carmichael. Berlin, Mar. 15, 1777. (French.)
Carmichael to Schulenburg, on shipping of tobacco. Paris, Mar. 30, 1777. (French trans.)
Letter of B. Franklin, Silas Deane, and Arthur Lee, ministers plenipotentiary from the Congress of the United States of America, on shipping and commerce. Paris, Apr. 19, 1777.
French translation of the same.
Schulenburg to the king, telling of the arrival and mission of Franklin, Deane, and Lee in France. Berlin, May 5, 1777. (French.)
Frederick (signed "Federic") to Schulenburg. Potsdam, May 6, 1777. (French.)
Schulenburg to Coeper in Potsdam, relating to Franklin, etc. Berlin, May 7, 1777.
Coeper to Schulenburg. Potsdam, May 8, 1777. (German.)
Schulenburg to the king; concept copied in. Berlin, May 9, 1777. (French.)
Schulenburg to the king, same date with the king's original note. (French.)
Schulenburg to Messrs. Franklin, Deane, and Lee in Paris. Berlin, May 11, 1777.
Schulenburg to "M. le Baron de Goltze Colonel et Chambellan du Roi et son envoyer extraordinaire" in Paris. Same date. (French.)
Arthur Lee to Schulenburg. Paris, May 8, 1777. (English.)
French translation of the same.
Goltz to Schulenburg. Paris, May 9, 1777. (German.)
Schulenburg to Arthur Lee in Paris. Berlin, May 29, 1777. (French.)
Schulenburg to Goltz in Paris. Same date. (French.)
Arthur Lee to Schulenburg, enclosing lists of articles of export. Berlin, Sunday, June 8, 1777. (English.)
French translation of the same.
Schulenburg to Arthur Lee (in Berlin). Berlin, June 9, 1777. (French.)
Arthur Lee to Schulenburg, relating to the establishing of "companies of Insurance" at Rouen and Nantes, and commerce with America, and enclosing note, begging the minister to accept a corrected copy of the "Articles of Confederation" and of the "Constitution of Pennsylvania". Berlin, June 10, 1777. (English.)
French translation of the same.
Letter of Frederick ("Federic") instructing Schulenburg. Mokrau, June 10, 1777. (French.)
Schulenburg to the king. Berlin, June 15, 1777. (Copied in clear draft.)
Schulenburg to Lee, expressing interest in Lee's proposals of a commercial treaty and enclosing the list of vessels, captains, pilots, and sailors in Prussia. Berlin, June 18, 1777. (French.)

Arthur Lee to Schulenburg. Berlin, June 29, 1777. (English.)
French translation of the same.
Schulenburg to the king, relating to Lee's request for the freedom of German ports for American vessels, such as France and Spain have granted. Berlin, June 21, 1777. (French.)
Frederick's reply to Schulenburg, that he continue to treat with Lee but in such wise that Lee himself will see the futility of the king's entrance into compacts which would disturb his relations with England. (French.)
Schulenburg to Lee. Berlin, June 26, 1777. (French.)
Schulenburg to Finkenstein. Same date.
Finkenstein to Schulenburg. Potsdam, June 28, 1777. (French.)
Schulenburg to Goltz in Paris. Berlin, June 30, 1777. (French.)
Director Neudi in Hamburg to Schulenburg, calling attention to the effort of the Americans, Lee and Steffens, in Berlin to purchase cloth, etc., in Germany, especially in Prussia, and suggesting the forming of a commercial treaty with America. N.'s informant was John Parish, an English merchant and commissioner of the Americans, who had received a commission 3 months before from Congress to make a purchase in the sum of 100,000 rts. Hamburg, June 26, 1777.
Schulenburg to Neudi. Berlin, July 3, 1777. (German.)
The king to Schulenburg, referring Lee (who has made a communication direct to his Majesty!) to Schulenburg, who will guard his (Lee's) secret. Potsdam, July 3, 1777. (French.)
Schulenburg to the king, reporting the interview with Lee, enclosing a clean copy for the king with His Majesty's marginal notes. Berlin, July 3, 1777. (French.)
Schulenburg to the king, relating to the same. Same date. Also clean copy. (French.)
The king's instruction to Schulenburg. Potsdam, July 4, 1777. (French.)
Letter of Schulenburg, notifying the king of the communication of the king's orders to Lee and of Lee's intended departure after seeing the futility of his mission in Berlin. Berlin, July 6, 1777. The same calligraphed for the king with marginal note of the king. (French.)
Letter of Stephen Sayre requesting Schulenburg " to return to Berlin for a few days " to hear his new proposals, different from those of Lee and approved by the Earl of Chatham. Hotel Corsica, Berlin, July 11, 1777. (English.)
Letter of Sayre, asking whether he may communicate his proposals through Mr. Bourke and save His Excellency the trouble of coming back to the city. Berlin, July 14, 1777. (English.)
French translation of Sayre's letter of July 11.
French translation of Sayre's letter of July 14.
Desegner to Schulenburg, enclosing translation of Sayre's letter. July 16, 1777. (French.)
Letter of Desegner [de Segner], giving an account of Sayre and Lee's pending contract with Schmitz for cloth, etc. Berlin, July 23, 1777. (French.)
P. S. note signed by Dörnberg, giving a report of the interview with Sayre and Sayre's adverse account of Lee, and the ten proposals

made by Sayre. Berlin, July 26, 1777. Also a supplement, dated Berlin, July 27, 1777. (French.)
Schulenburg's acknowledgment of the above.
Desegner to Schulenburg, reporting the king's order relating to Sayre's proposals with special reference to agriculture and mechanical trades. Berlin, July 30, 1777. (French.)
Desegner to Schulenburg, communicating a most important letter of the king to Sayre, relating to Elbing, to the shipping with England, to confidential letters of Chatham, etc. Berlin, Aug. 3, 1777. (French.)
Letter of Desegner to Schulenburg (?), quoting the passage in Sayre's letter asking permission to speak directly with the king. The department is in dismay over the presumption! Berlin, Aug. 5, 1777. (French.)
Baron de Goltz's cipher despatch to Schulenburg (?) relating to the proposals of Sayre.
Arthur Lee to Schulenburg (?), relating to the establishment of insurance companies in Germany. Paris, Aug. 15, 1777. (English.)
French translation of the same.
Schulenburg's communication to the king ("Au Roi"). Berlin, Sept. 6, 1777. (French.) Draft and calligraphed copy with the king's comment: "Das gehet nicht an er will in unsere Havens ein laufen das ist ihm schon abgeschlagen Fr."
Seconde lettre de M. Sayre au Roi.
Pensées sur l'agriculture.
Considérations sur la manière de perfectionner les voitures et les grands chemins de ce pais.
Troisième lettre de M. Sayre au Roi, relating to Elbing, etc.
Idées sur la manière de former un établissement dans l'isle Dominique, dans le cas que la propriété peut s'en aquerir de la grande Bretagne pour la Prusse (enclosing table of probable incomes from the island).
Arthur Lee to Schulenburg relating to entrance of armed vessels into Prussian ports, etc., dated Paris, Sept. 21, 1777 (English), enclosing " Mémoire " of 10 pp. concerning borrowing money.
French translation of Lee's letter and " Mémoire ".
Schulenburg to the king, draft and calligraphed copy with the king's remark: " Mit Complimenten abweisen Fred." Berlin, Oct. 6, 1777. (French.)
Copy of Arthur Lee's letter of Sept. 21, 1777. (French.)
Schulenburg's reply to Lee, relating to the loan. Berlin, Aug. 8, 1777. (French.)
The king to Schulenburg, referring Sayre to S. to " arrange " his affair. Potsdam, Oct. 17, 1777. (German.)
Sayre to the king. Berlin, Oct. 15, 1777. (French.)
Schulenburg to the king. Draft and copy with the king's marginal reply.
Schulenburg to Sayre postponed to the following year. Berlin, Oct. 22, 1777. (French.)
Schulenburg to Görne relating to the same subject. Same date. (German.)
Schulenburg to Görne, giving Sayre's address in Paris (Banquier Panchaud).

Arthur Lee to Schulenburg, regretting his failure to find favorable consideration of his plan on the part of the king. Paris, Oct. 23, 1777. (English.)
French translation of the same.
Schulenburg to the king, relating to Lee's request for information whether England is to secure troops from Germany, Russia, and Denmark, with the king's note in reply at the bottom: " rien de Russie, rien de Danemarc, mais quelques centaines d'hommes d'Anspach et du Pr. de Hesse Fr." Berlin, Nov. 4, 1777. (French.)
Copy of Arthur Lee's letter calligraphed for the king. Paris, Oct. 23, 1777. (French.)
Görne to Schulenburg, referring to the king's order relating to Sayre's whaling project. Berlin, Oct. 18, 1777. (German.)
Schulenburg to Arthur Lee, apprising him frankly of the recruiting of German troops in Brunswick, Hesse, and Anspach. Berlin, Nov. 6, 1777. (French.)
Carmichael to Schulenburg, relating the tacit permission to American cruisers to enter Prussian ports, etc., under the guise of a trade compact. Hotel de Vauban, Rue de Richelieu, Paris, Nov. 2, 1777. (English.)
French translation of the same.
Schulenburg to Magusch relating to the same. Berlin, Nov. 21, 1777. (German.)
Arthur Lee to Schulenburg, announcing the appointment of " William Lee Esqr Commissioner of Congress at the Court of Berlin with full powers to conclude a treaty of amity and commerce with the King of Prussia ". Paris, Nov. 13, 1777. (English.)
French translation of the same.
Schulenburg to the king, notifying the latter of content of Lee's letter, and the king's marginal note: " Festina Lente Fr." Draft and calligraphed copy. Berlin, Nov. 25, 1777. (French.)
Calligraphed copy (for the king) of Lee's letter.
Schulenburg to Arthur Lee, replying that William Lee is at liberty to come as a private person, but will not be received as an official envoy. Berlin, Nov. 28, 1777. (French.)
Arthur Lee to Schulenburg, thanking him for his letter. (English.)
French translation of Arthur Lee's letter.
Magusch to Schulenburg, on tobacco from Virginia, etc. Berlin, Nov. 28, 1777. (German.)
Schulenburg to Carmichael. Berlin, Dec. 1, 1777. (French.)
Schulenburg to Görne, on the scheme. Berlin, Dec. 3, 1777. (German.)
Arthur Lee to Schulenburg, giving account of Ticonderoga. Paris, Nov. 30, 1777. (English.)
Schulenburg to the king, enclosing French translation of Lee's letter (draft and calligraphed copy). Berlin, Dec. 11, 1777, with the king's comment: " Grand Merci Fr."
Schulenburg to Lee, asking for positive facts to settle conflicting reports and assuring Lee of the interest the king has in the success of the American colonies.
Arthur Lee to Schulenburg, on the departure of Washington and the capital at Philadelphia. Paris, Dec. 4, 1777. (English.)

Schulenburg to the king, communicating Lee's letters. Draft and calligraphed copy with the king's note: " Ceci est fort beau, mais il faut Luy dire que j'attens a reconnaitre L'Independence des Americains Lors que la France en aura fait autant Federic ". Berlin, Dec. 15, 1777.
Schulenburg to Arthur Lee in Paris. Berlin, Dec. 18, 1777. (French.)
Carmichael to Schulenburg, on the capitulation of Burgoyne, etc. Paris, Dec. 6, 1777. (English.)
French translation of the same.
Schulenburg's reply to Carmichael. Berlin, Dec. 20, 1777. (French.)
Notes relating to the opening of Sayre's letter to Görne. Berlin, Dec. 19, 1777. (German.)
Schulenburg to Sayre at Altona. Berlin, Dec. 20, 1777. (French.)
Arthur Lee to Schulenburg. " We have heard reports of his Majesty's gracious interposition relative to the march of troops hird against us, which I hope are well founded." Paris, Dec. 11, 1777.
Transcript of the capitulation of Burgoyne from official reports.
French translation of Lee's letter of Dec. 11, 1777.
Schulenburg to Arthur Lee in Paris, confirming the report that the king had refused permission to the allied troops to pass through his dominions. Berlin, Dec. 23, 1777. (French.)

Vol. 2. Acta den Americanischen Handel und Krieg betreffend von 1778 bis 17. Juni 1783.

The king to Schulenburg, asking for his opinion of a " Seehandlungs Entreprise " submitted by " Girardot Haller und Compagnie zu Paris ". Berlin, Jan. 3, 1778. (German.)
Schulenburg's report and reply to the king, strongly condemning the scheme so far as Prussia is concerned.
The king's order to Schulenburg to reply that he can not entertain such proposals, because he has no fleet. Berlin, Jan. 4, 1778. (German.)
Arthur Lee to Schulenburg, giving account of the war and asking at the close whether arms can be purchased at the king's manufactory. Paris, Dec. 28, 1778.
Schulenburg to the king, enclosing a French translation of Lee's letter.
The king's hearty reply giving order that whatever the Americans order in the way of arms be at once furnished them. Berlin, Jan. 13, 1778. (German.)
Merchant Splittgerber sends Schulenburg pieces of arms. Berlin, Jan. 14, 1778. (German.)
Schulenburg's reply to Lee, saying that France must first recognize American independence, because it is most directly interested, and that the king would have no difficulty in admitting American vessels to Prussian ports, if he had a fleet to avenge attacks, and that the king allows free purchase of arms at his manufactory, enclosing a list of prices. Berlin, Jan. 16, 1778. (French.)
William Lee to Schulenburg, wishing to count the King of Prussia among the first to acknowledge American independence, and to prevent England from getting more German troops. Paris, Jan. 16, 1778.

Schulenburg to the king, enclosing French translation of W. Lee's letter. Jan. 31, 1778.
The king to Schulenburg, declaring his inability to enter into any commercial relations with the Americans at present. Potsdam, Feb. 1, 1778. (French.)
Schulenburg to W. Lee, reminding him of the "bonnes dispositions du Roi pour Vos commettants" as expressed in a letter to A. Lee, and assuring him that England will get no considerable reinforcements of German troops. Berlin, Feb. 3, 1778.
Arthur Lee to Schulenburg, thanking Schulenburg for assurances of the king's good will. Paris, Feb. 2, 1778.
French translation of the same.
Arthur Lee to Schulenburg, giving a report of Washington's shutting Howe in at Philadelphia. Nantes, Feb. 12, 1778.
French translation of the same.
W. Lee to Schulenburg, reports from letters from London which say: "we have detached the King of Prussia from the American Interest by paying his demands". Paris, Mar. 6, 1778.
French translation of Lee's letter.
Schulenburg to William Lee, thanking for news, etc. Berlin, Mar. 21, 1778.
W. Lee to Schulenburg, announcing that the King of France has openly acknowledged American Independence and American "Commissioners in that capacity were publickly introduced this day at Versailles: the French Ambassador having before avowed to the King of Great Britain the Treaty which his Majesty of France had concluded with the United States; in consequence of which t'is believed, that War is by this time declared in London against France". Paris, Mar. 20, 1778.
French translation of the same.
Schulenburg to the king, announcing Lee's letter, and enclosing copy of it in French translation. Berlin, Mar. 30, 1778. (French.) The king's reply on the margin: "il faut luy repondre que Nous etions si ocupez de L'allemagne dans ce moment que Nous ne pourrions point pensser a L'amerique que Nous les reconoitrions vollontier independence mais que dans ce moment ci cela ne Leur pouroit procurer aucun avantage, et nous estre fort prejudiciable Federic".
Schulenburg to W. Lee, enclosing the king's reply. Berlin, Apr. 4, 1778. (French.)
Order for passage of the guns to be shipped by Splittgerber to the Americans. Signed "Fred." Berlin, Mar. 23, 1778.
Letter of Schulenburg, sending the king's order. Berlin, Apr. 24, 1778. (German.)
W. Lee to Schulenburg, containing severe reproof. Frankfort-on-the-Main, Apr. 9, 1778. (English.)
French translation of the same.
French translation of Lee's letter dated "Frankfort sur le Main, Apr. 18, 1778" (*cf.* the next).
W. Lee to Schulenburg, announcing his appointment to manage American affairs at the courts of Vienna and Berlin, and bringing up again the question of commercial relations with the United States. Frankfort, Apr. 18, 1778.

Schulenburg to the king, communicating the matter. Aug. 24, 1778. (French.)
The king to Schulenburg, bidding him reply that such an alliance would be of no utility to the colonies, because he could not support the treaty with force, and that the maritime powers alone can take part in such affairs. Schoenwalde, Apr. 27, 1778. (French.)
W. Lee to Schulenburg, announcing the arrival of Adams as commissioner at Versailles. Frankfort, Apr. 24, 1778. (English.)
French translation of the same.
Schulenburg to the king, sending Lee's letter. Berlin, Aug. 30, 1778. (French.)
Schulenburg to W. Lee, communicating the king's reply. Same date.
The king to Schulenburg, on Lee's letter of Aug. 14, 1778, saying: " Il faut avouer que cela est beau. . . . . Mais les affaires que j'ai ici M'occupent infinement plus, que celles la ".
Letter of Schulenburg issuing pass for American purchase of arms (" Zollfrei "). Berlin, Apr. 24, 1779. (German.)
W. Lee to Schulenburg, on the Bavarian succession, commercial agreement, etc. Frankfort, July 17, 1778.
French translation of the same.
Schulenburg to the king, enclosing this letter. Berlin, July 25, 1778. (French.)
Schulenburg to W. Lee, enclosing the king's reply. Berlin, Aug. 7, 1778. (French.)
The king's reply (*cf.* the last), ordering Schulenburg to reply " was Jch 10 mall gesagt, nemlich Jch haette keine Flotte ", etc. Jaromirs, July 30, 1778.
W. Lee to Schulenburg. Frankfort-on-the-Main, Aug. 28, 1778.
Ditto, Oct. 31, 1778, giving account of the progress of the war in America.
French translation of the same.
Schulenburg to W. Lee. Berlin, Nov. 10, 1778.
Arthur Lee to Schulenburg, on the arms ordered of Splittgerber, and enclosing Splittgerber's bill. Chaillot, near Paris, Oct. 21, 1778. (English.)
French translation of the same.
Schulenburg to Splittgerber, on the arms. Berlin, Nov. 27, 1778. (German.)
Splittgerber's heirs to Schulenburg, with copy of prices of arms. Berlin, Nov. 28, 1778.
French translation of the same.
Schulenburg to Arthur Lee, attempting to clear up the misunderstanding about the guns ordered.
W. Lee to Schulenburg, still feeling his way to the commercial treaty. Frankfort-on-the-Main, Dec. 1, 1778. (English.)
French translation of the same.
Schulenburg to Finkenstein, enclosing W. Lee's letter, dated Berlin, Dec. 8. 1778, relating to armed vessels entering Prussian ports. (French.)
Finkenstein's reply to the same.
Schulenburg to the king, on the same. Berlin, Dec. 16, 1778. (French.)
Order of the king regarding the same. Breslau, Dec. 29, 1778. (French.)
Letter of Schulenburg, enclosing the king's reply to W. Lee. Berlin, Jan. 2, 1779. (French.)

Arthur Lee to Schulenburg, sharply condemning the specimen of musket as "one of the worst I ever beheld". Paris, Dec. 16, 1778. (English.)
French translation of the same, enclosing extracts from the minutes of Congress on European barbarities.
Manifesto and French translation, signed by Laurens. Oct. 30, 1778.
W. Lee to Schulenburg, in reply to the information that Prussian ports are open to all nations, and saying that, before American vessels could enter Prussian ports with confidence, some kind of convention with the United States should be made. Frankfort-on-the-Main, Jan. 30, 1779.
Schulenburg to "Comte de Finkenstein, Ministre d'État et du Cabinet du Roi à Breslau", on Lee's letter of Jan. 30, 1779, and enclosing a French translation. Berlin, Feb. 9, 1779.
Schulenburg to W. Lee, giving the king's answer that American vessels may enter as others the Prussian ports, but that he thinks a convention superfluous. Berlin, Feb. 17, 1779.
Finkenstein to Schulenburg, giving plainly the effect of a convention: "La demande d'une déclaration qui comprendroit les états unis de l'Amérique au nombre des nations, équivaudroit la reconnoissance de leur indépendance, et les mettroient dans le cas d'en faire parade et de nous compromettre avec la Cour de Londres". Breslau, Feb. 14, 1779.
W. Lee to Schulenburg, saying that he did not understand foreign tongues very well (!) and that he was glad to learn that American vessels might have the same privileges as others in Prussian ports, and referring also to the final settlement of the Austrian succession. Frankfort, Feb. 27, 1779. (English.)
French translation of W. Lee's letter.
Schulenburg to Finkenstein, reporting his reply to Lee. Berlin, Mar. 16, 1779. (French.)
Schulenburg to Finkenstein, respecting Arendt. Berlin, July 22, 1779. (French.)
Arendt's pedigree by himself. Berlin, July 21, 1779. (French.)
Schulenburg to Arendt, advising him to address himself directly to the merchants. Berlin, July 25, 1779. (French.)
W. Lee to Schulenburg, reporting events in America and expressing the hope that the king may soon renew his good will toward the Americans in an active way. Frankfort, Aug. 28, 1779. (English.)
French translation of the same.
Schulenburg's reply to Lee. Berlin, Sept. 20, 1779. (French.)
W. Lee to Schulenburg, expressing hope that the Prussians may effect peace between England and the United States, and assurance that the English people wish peace, etc. Frankfort, Oct. 1, 1779. (English.)
French translation of the same.
A. Gillon to Schulenburg, as to re-entering Prussia. Frankfort-on-the-Main, Oct. 2, 1779. (French.)
A. Gillon to "Pierre Hasenclever Negt à Berlin", same subject. Frankfort, Nov. 30, 1779. (French.)
Schulenburg to Gillon at Amsterdam. Berlin, Dec. 13, 1779. (French.)

William Carmichael to Schulenburg, opening the question of friendship and flattering the King of Prussia a bit. Madrid, Mar. 9, 1780. (English.)
French translation of the same.
Schulenburg to Carmichael, excusing himself from discussing a convention as Prussia has no " homme de confiance " at Madrid, etc. Berlin, Aug. 7, 1780. (French.)
Krieges-Rath Cranz (Crantz) to Schulenburg, relating to Geh'rath van der Hay and the " Handlungs Etablissement " at Emden (same as Lee's proposals in the main). Berlin, Apr. 16, 1780. (German.)
Letter of Schulenburg declining to have the matter go through his hands and referring the petition to the king direct.
Crantz to Schulenburg, on Van der Hay's proposals. Berlin, Apr. 27, 1780. (German.)
Schulenburg to Crantz, same subject. Berlin, Apr. 23, 1780. (German.)
W. Lee to Schulenburg, giving reports from America and enclosing extract from a private letter of Clinton. Brussels, May 25, 1780. (English.)
French translation of the same.
Letter of Schulenburg, reporting his letter to the king. Berlin, June 1, 1780. (French.)
William Carmichael to Schulenburg, giving reports of America. Aranjuez, June 8, 1780. (English.)
French translation of the same.
William Carmichael to Schulenburg, only general reference to recognition. Madrid, Nov. 19, 1780. (English.)
French translation of the same.
W. Lee to Schulenburg, inquiring what manufactures can be had at Emden by American merchants, what duties are levied, etc. Lee speaks only for himself, not for the Congress. Brussels, Dec. 28, 1780. (English.)
French translation of the same, with the last paragraph crossed out in red ink.
Schulenburg to the king, enclosing Lee's letter, except the last paragraph, which might bring up the question of a treaty again.
King's reply, declaring that perfect neutrality must be kept with the Americans as with all states. Berlin, Jan. 9, 1781. (German.)
Arendt to Schulenburg. Berlin, Dec. 12, 1782.
Schulenburg to Arendt, thanking him for the " plans " and " échantillons d'argent ", sent him by Arendt, but discouraging him of all hope of being engaged for service on the canal. Berlin, Dec. 13, 1782. (French.)
Baron Director Stilke in Magdeburg to Schulenburg, recommending the " berühmter Künstler " Jacob, a Jew of Philadelphia.
Jacob's memorial to the king, offering a plan of Prussian " commercie in America ". Euthen, May 27, 1783. (German.)
Schulenburg's reply to Stilke, stating that the plan is not feasible. Berlin, June 17, 1783. (German.)[1]

[1] For English translations of some of the foregoing letters to and from the American agents, see Jared Sparks, *Diplomatic Correspondence of the American Revolution*; and Francis Wharton, *The Revolutionary Diplomatic Correspondence of the United States*. A few of the German letters were printed, mostly in extract, by Friedrich Kapp in his *Friedrich der Grosse und die Vereinigten Staaten von America*.

Rep. XI. 21 a. Conv. 1. Amerika. Verein. Staaten, 1778-1801 (1817).

Amerika 1. 1 a. Abschrift eines Briefes des Baron von Schulenburg an Arthur Lee in Paris. Jan. 16, 1778. (Original in the Library of Harvard University.) Then follows a note relating to the lost (?) journal of Count Donop.

Amerika 1. 2. Acta die Erbschaftsforderungen des Ackerbürgers Kühn in Amerika betrf. Contains documents relating to the estate of Maria Dildey and to her mother's brother George Christoph White's property in the parish of Raleigh in Virginia and dated as follows: Feb. 12, 1780; Sept. 17, 1782; Feb. 18, 1785; June 27, 1793; Jan. 31, 1794; July 31, 1796; June 21, 1798; July 6, 1816; Jan. 10, 1817.

Amerika 1. 3. Acta Vereinigte Provinzen von Amerika betr. This fascicle contains valuable papers relating to General von Steuben and the early relations of Prussia and America, among which the following may be noted:

Fol. 1. Traduction d'une Résolution du Congrès. En Congrès le 5 8br 1780.

Foll. 2-3. Letter of Madeweiss addressed: " Hochwohlgebohrener Freyherr, Hochgebietender Herr wirklicher Geheimer Etats Kriegs und Kabinets Minister, gnädiger Herr ", dated Stuttgardt, Oct. 24, 1781, relating to General von Steuben and his connection with Prussian military service and his troubles with General von Anhalt. The answer to the letter is given by Graf Hertzberg as coming from King Frederick the Great, as is indicated at the top of the letter under date of Nov. 6 of the same year.

Fol. 4. Extrait d'une Lettre du Général et Inspecteur général de toutes les armées Américaines, Baron de Steuben, à un de ses amis à Stouccard, du Camp près de Richmond le 26 Mai 1781. Very interesting documents relating to Steuben's position in Europe and America.

Fol. 5. Letter (in French) of United States chargé d'affaires Dumas to Baron Hertzberg, Prussian Minister of State, Feb. 26, 1783, relating to American military service. The letter is in reply to an inquiry of Lincoln, Secretary of War, in which he had asked for a detailed account of the pay, rations, subsistence, etc., of the Prussian army. Hertzberg replies, that the detailed answer would require much correspondence and could be more easily obtained through Steuben.

Amerika 1. 5. Presented in full detail, as follows:

Repositur XI. 21 a. Conv. 1. 5.

Extrait de la dépêche du B. de Goltz. Dec. 2, 1783.

Duplicat E. S. ad Relationem No. 15. The Hague, Feb. 20, 1784. (Beginning " Je me suis appliqué à remplir les ordres immédiats ", etc. Cipher transliteration between the lines.)

Letter of Struensee. Berlin, Feb. 28, 1784. (German.)

Letter of Finkenstein. Mar. 8, 1784.

Schulenburg to the " Department der Auswärtigen Angelegenheiten ", asking for return of " Originalien " relating to the treaty. Berlin, Mar. 8, 1784.

Letter of Finkenstein to Schulenburg. Berlin, Mar. 8, 1784, with a copy of letter of Frederick to Schulenburg, dated Potsdam, Mar. 7, 1784. (Both German.)
Traité d'amitié et de commerce conclu entre S. M. le Roi de Suède et les États Unis de l'Amérique Septentrionale (10 pages) fait à Paris le 3 Avril 1783. Signed: Gustave Philippe Comte de Creutz.
Extrait de la dépêche du Sr. de Thulemeier. Mar. 9, 1784.
Extrait de la dépêche du Sr. de Thulemeier. Mar. 12, 1784.
Finkenstein to Schulenburg. Berlin, Mar. 20, 1784.
Finkenstein to Schulenburg. Berlin, Apr. 3, 1784.
Schulenburg to " Dep. d. Ausw. Angelegenheiten ". Berlin, Apr. 3, 1784.
Extrait de la dépêche du Sr. de Thulemeier. Mar. 30, 1784.
Reponse. Berlin, Apr. 6, 1784.
Thulemeier " au Department des Affaires Étrangères ". The Hague, Mar. 30, 1784.
Copie d'une lettre adressée [by Thulemeier] au Sieur Adams, Ministre Plénipotentiaire des États Unis de l'Amérique à la Haye. The Hague, Mar. 25, 1784.
Finkenstein to Schulenburg, sending copy of Thulemeier's postscript and asking for copy of the form of treaty approved by the king with the United States.
Schulenburg to Department of Foreign Affairs, declaring that rough cloth and woolen wares should come second not last on the list. Berlin, Apr. 8, 1784.
Traité d'Amitié et de Commerce conclu entre S. M. le Roy de Prusse et les États Unis le l'Amérique Septemtrionale (27 articles, 14 pages), with an " article séparé " relating to renewal after fifteen years.
Letter of Finkenstein announcing the intention to send the treaty to Congress by the first ship to Philadelphia or Boston, " dahero diese Unterhandlung nunmehro wohl eine Zeitlang ruhen wird ". Aug. 20, 1784.
Thulemeier to the king (" Duplicat "), enclosing " Observations faites par Sieur Adams, sur le projet d'un Traité ", etc. The Hague, May 18, 1784. (Important, 2 pages.)
Finkenstein to Schulenburg, relating to Adams's " Anmerkungen ". Berlin, May 25, 1784. (German.)
Schulenburg to Department of Foreign Affairs, asking whether Thulemeier shall be instructed to proceed with the negotiation. Berlin, May 30, 1784.
Frederick to Schulenburg, relating to religious liberty and harboring vessels of reprisal, etc. (Important, 2 pages.)
Duplicat E. S. ad Relationem No. 100, enclosing the draft (projet), English and French in opposite columns, of the treaty. (27 articles, 22 pp.)
" Plein Pouvoir " given to Adams, Franklin, and Jefferson to effect the treaty, signed by Thomas Mifflin and Chas. Thomson, Sec. May 12, 1784.
Finkenstein to Schulenburg, relating to changes made by the United States in the text of the treaty. Berlin. Dec. 17, 1784. (German.)

Schulenburg to the Department, relating to the "Contre-Projet" and particularly to articles 13 and 23.
Schulenburg to the Department of Foreign Affairs, sending a concept of the report.
Finkenstein to Schulenburg, relating to the "Contre-Projet", especially article 13, contraband, etc. Berlin, Dec. 25, 1784.
Schulenburg to Department of Foreign Affairs, Berlin, Dec. 30, 1784, enclosing report, dated Berlin, Dec. 24, 1784, and addressed "au Roi". (13 pp.)
Thulemeier to the king, relating to declaring the port of Emden or Stettin free, with a copy of the communication of Adams, Franklin, and Jefferson, requesting free ports, dated Passy, Jan., 1785 (2 pp.), addressed to Thulemeier at the Hague. The Hague, Feb. 11, 1785.
Thulemeier to the king relating to "nouvelles Ouvertures" of the American plenipotentiaries, with a copy of the "Ouvertures" in English and French, dated Passy, Mar. 14, 1785. The Hague, Apr. 15, 1785.
Schulenburg to the Department, etc., on points in the Contre-Projet.
Finkenstein to Schulenburg, on the Contre-Projet, Article 19, etc. Berlin. Apr. 15, 1783.
Schulenburg to the Department of Foreign Affairs, relating to Article 19 and containing copy of the king's order to Thulemeier to yield the point, etc. Berlin, Apr. 21, 1785. (German.)
Peter Hasenclever to Hertzberg, commenting on the treaty. Landeshutt. Apr. 16, 1785. (German.)
Thulemeier to the king, stating that the only point in the treaty to be settled is the term of years (the Americans having suggested ten years), and enclosing copy of the treaty as agreed upon. The Hague, June 17, 1785. (French.)
Order of Frederick to the Ministre d'État et de Cabinet le Comte de Finkenstein. Potsdam, July 8, 1785. (French.)
Letter of Finkenstein (and Hertzberg) authorizing Thulemeier to sign for ten years. Berlin, July 9, 1785. (German.)
Letter of Finkenstein and Hertzberg, informing the king of the act. July 9, 1785.
Finkenstein and Hertzberg to Thulemeier, with subscript to Schulenburg relating to correction of some errors in the text. July 9, 1785.
Schulenburg to the Department of Foreign Affairs, relating to errors in translation and copy of the "observation". July 9, 1785. (German.)
Thulemeier to the king, giving notice of the exchange, etc. The Hague, July 22, 1785. (French.)
Thulemeier to the king, on Adams's request for explanations touching tobacco, indigo, oil, etc. The Hague, Aug. 5, 1785. (French.)
Finkenstein (and Hertzberg) to Schulenburg, touching the reply to Adams. Berlin, Aug. 12, 1785.
Schulenburg to the Department, on same subject. Kehnert, Aug. 21, 1785. (German.)
Finkenstein (and Hertzberg) to Thulemeier, on same subject. Berlin, Aug. 30, 1785. (French.)

Thulemeier to the king, on Franklin's signing the treaty and on ratification by Congress, enclosing a copy of the English translation of the " Plein Pouvoir ", etc.

Finkenstein and Hertzberg recommending that the king receive the copy presented by Mr. Schort, although it contains unessential errors of the scribe. Berlin, Aug. 30, 1785. (French.)

Ratification of the treaty (in rough copy or draft) by the king, dated Berlin, Sept. 24, 1785, with signatures of Finkenstein and Hertzberg (the treaty was signed Sept. 10 by the Americans.) (French.)

Finkenstein and Hertzberg to Thulemeier, communicating the king's order (to finish the exchange). Berlin, Sept. 28, 1785. (French.)

Finkenstein and Hertzberg to Schulenburg, same subject. Same date.

Schulenburg to the Department, same subject. Berlin, Oct. 3, 1785. (German.)

Thulemeier to the king, notifying him of the assurance of the American ratification, etc. The Hague, Oct. 11, 1785. (French.)

Thulemeier to the king, advising him of Adams's arrival to exchange the ratification papers. The Hague, Aug. 8, 1786. (French.)

Struensee to the Cabinet Minister, on the treaty. Berlin, Aug. 13, 1786. (German.)

Palleske to Struensee, giving account of trade conditions in America, etc. Philadelphia, June 28, 1786. (German.)

Henry Edmund v. Lutterloh to the king, relating to treaty. Wilmington, " à l'America ", Sept. 16, 1786. (French.)

Lutterloh to " Excellence " (Schulenburg), same subject. Wilmington, Sept. 14, 1786.

Lutterloh's proposal for a " Handels Compagnie ". Wilmington, North Carolina, Feb. 25, 1786. (German.)

Note relating to ratification. Aug. 24, 1790. (German.)

Finkenstein (and Hertzberg) to Schulenburg, stating that Wrede of Baltimore and Ludlow of New York have asked to be appointed Prussian consuls and asking the opinion of the Minister on the subject. Berlin, Oct. 28, 1785. (German.)

Thulemeier to the king, notifying him that at the request of Daniel Crommelin and Son in Amsterdam he presents the following request. The Hague, Oct. 30, 1786. (French.)

Request of Crommelin and Son, relating to trade with America. Amsterdam, Oct. 18, 1786. (French.)

Reply of Schulenburg, stating that there is as yet no prospect of direct trade with America, and that the request will be scrutinized, etc. Berlin, Oct. 30, 1786. (German.)

Wrede's application. Berlin, Oct. 25, 1786. (German.)

Testimonial for Wrede. Berlin, Oct. 11, 1786. (German.)

Letters of Finkenstein and Hertzberg, communicating the decision that Wrede is not well enough known to be made consul and will have to become qualified (German), and that Ludlow can not be appointed for the same reason (French). Both dated Berlin, Nov. 1, 1786.

Finkenstein and Hertzberg to the merchant Heinrich Willmanns of Bremen ("der auch zum Konsul ernannt werden will") stating that His Majesty the King "aber nunjetzo keinen Gebrauch davon machen könnten, da Ihro Unterthanen noch keinen Handel nach Amerika treiben und derselbe nach den Westindischen Inseln nicht offen noch frei ist folglich ein Preussischer Konsul dort von keinem Nutzen seyn kann". Berlin, Dec. 21, 1786. (German.)

Application of Willmanns. Bremen, Dec. 12, 1786. (German.)

Three papers relating to Lutterloh's application for the position of consul general in America. Wilmington, N. C., Aug. 31, 1788. (French.)

Rep. XI. 21 a. Conv. 1 (continued).

Amerika 1. 6. Acta das Gesuch der Ravenhorstschen Erben wegen der Erbschaft von ihrem zu Ebenezar [Georgien] verstorbenen Bruder betrf. 1784.

America 1. 7. Contains papers relating to inheritances, *a-h*, except *b* and a part of *e*. 1785-1790.

Amerika 1. 8. Die Bestellung des Paleske zum General-Consul in den Nord-Amerikanischen Staaten betr. und wegen Erweiterung des Handels der Preussischen Unterthanen in Nord-America, inl. Paleske, wegen seiner Wieder-Ansetzung, und wegen Remuneration. 1791-1801.

Rep. XI. 21 a. Conv. 2. Amerika. Verein. Staaten. 1795-1804.

2. 2 a-m (excepting d).

Prod.¹ a. Betr. Die Fieselmannsche Erbgelder (33 Rthl. 30 gr.) nach Providence [Rhode Island] in Nord-America. 1792. Seven papers and a note referring to the location of the "Laws of the United States", etc.

Prod. b. Acta de 1793-1799, d. 3. Febr. wegen des in Nordamerica herrschenden gelben Fiebers u. der zu Marocco ausgebrochenen Pest. (3 papers.)

Prod. c. An die Dorothea Sophia Riedeln geb. Boerstlingen allhier. Ihre Erbschafts-Forderung in America btr. 1794. (3 papers.)

Prod. e. Three papers relating to the efforts of Colonel Peers to enlist officers on the lower Elbe and in Prussia for American service. 1797.

Prod. f. A letter of John Quincy Adams (in French) addressed to Comte de Haugwitz, Prussian Minister of State, explaining the power of Congress and of the President of the United States. Berlin, Feb. 24, 1798.

Prod. g. Das Gesuch des Nordamerikanischen Gesandten Adams um Erlaubnis zum Ankauf von 10,000 Gewehren. Nov. 30, 1798. (3 papers.) Request declined because the 300,000 already granted to the Americans have not been replaced and the supply can not be further reduced. Dec. 31, 1798.

---

¹ Produkt.

Prod. h. Correspondence between Baron Alvensleben and Adams in regard to forwarding letters to Dr. Thomas Parker in Philadelphia. Incidental reference to the Pennsylvania "Gutsbesitzer Humphry und Moses Marschal Esqurs", as having sent seeds of trees and useful plants to Germany (Prussia). 1798. (3 letters.)

Prod. i. Papers relating to the plan of James Swan of Boston, member of the legislature of Massachusetts, to establish commercial relations between the Prussian states and North America and to introduce the sugar maple into Germany. Jan. and Feb., 1800. (2 papers with Baron Alvensleben's remarks on the scheme.)

Prod. k. Extrait de la Dépêche du Baron Jaccobi Klaest [Kleist?] à Londres en date du 1 d'Août 1800. Relates to the appointment of Merry as minister to the United States in place of Liston. Reference also to Jefferson and the presidency of the United States.

Prod. l. Ex actis v. 31 Jan: 1800 btr. die von England nachgesuchte Getreide Ausfuhr aus den Preuss. Staaten. A paper with note relating to the exportation of 4 million piasters from America to the Prussian states.

2. 3. Acta des Jonas Hirschel Bluch Erbschafts-Angelegenheiten in Nord America betr. A thick fascicle of papers giving much interesting detail. 1797-1804.

2. 4. Acta den Austritt des Cantonisten [Johann Christoph] Wieting [aus Stendal, now living in Conagoherry (Canajoharie?) in New York] ausser Landes und dessen Citation in America. 1797. (9 papers.)

2. 5. Acta betrf. die Accreditirung des Adams als Ministre Plénipotentiaire der Staaten von America und dessen Rappel. 1801. Hearty approval of the appointment of Mr. Adams. There are 22 papers in all, including copy of Adams's commission in English.

2. 6. Acta wegen Bestellung des Kaufmann [J. E. C.] Schulze [Schultze] zum Consul zu Baltimore. 1798-1801. (17 papers.)

2. 7. Acta des Königl. Geheimen Staats-Archivs betreffend den am 11. Juli 1799 mit den Staaten von America erneuerten Freundschafts- und Handlungs-Tractat. A thick fascicle of papers with the remark that the original of the "Tractat" is to be found in the Geheimes Archiv-Cabinet sub. Nr. 338 B. The paper opening the subject is by John Q. Adams and written in French. 1798-1801.

2. 8. Acta betr. das Gesuch des Brauers Gehrcke zu Stargard wegen seines nach Amerika gereisten Sohnes. 1799-1800. (10 papers.)

Rep. XI. 21 a. Conv. 3. u. Reste von Conv. 4. et seq. Amerika. Verein. Staaten. 1801-1817 (1828).

3. 1. Acta die Forderung der Handlungshäuser Engmann und Mottern und Boehm an den ehemaligen Consul Schulz in Baltimore betr. 1801-1802. (7 papers.)

3. 2. Acta die Forderung des Kreis-Steuer-Einnehmers Engel zu Züllichau an das fallirte Handelshaus Jacob Mark u. Comp. in Neuyork. 1802-1805. (Small fascicle of papers.)

3. 3. Acta betr. das Verwendungsgesuch des [Martin Ernst Gottfried] Scheffler in Sachen gegen Kaufmann Taakes u. Cons. in Hamburg.
Intus: wegen verschiedener aus Hamburg nach Nord Amerika verschleppter Königl. Unterthanen.
Namensliste der nach Amerika gebrachten Unterthanen, und Formular zur eventuellen Anzeige in den öffentlichen Blättern. 20 Juli 1802. Czolbe, Wilke, Fluege, und Halle aus Danzig, Nov. 10, 1802; Hohmann und Kriek aus dem Halberstadschen, Sept. 15, Nov. 6, 1802; Pohl und Memel, Nov. 9, 1802; Walter und Krahl aus Ostpr., Dec. 12, 1802; Wilke, Mueller und Weber aus Pommern, Dec. 16, 1802; Wiesener (Pommer), Jan. 16; Hecht, Schmidt, Schaefer, und Holzmann aus Magdeburg, Dec. 16, 1802; Knorr, Mueller, und Seidel aus Schlesien, Jan. 7, 1803; Wilking und Weber aus dem Mindenschen, Dec. 12, 1802–Mar. 12, 1803.
Wegen Verschickung verschiedener Königl. Unterthanen zum Englischen Kriegsdienst. 1802-1805. A thick fascicle of papers containing much valuable information, among them an indenture given by Scheffler to Jonathan Bradfield, dated Philadelphia, Sept. 16, 1800, and a list of the fellow-passengers of Scheffler: Namens Verzeichnis der Mitgereisten unter denen die so grosse Menge Preussen am mehrsten zu brauern [?]. (102 names in all.)
Verzeichnis der im J. 1801 von Hamburg mit dem Schiff *Anna* Cap. Jürgens nach Philadelphia geschickten 31 Königl. Unterthanen nebst den für erbetenen Loskaufgeldern.
"Hansel a Jew Boy", etc. A very interesting story of a Jew boy seeking passage for America. May 16, 1804. (English.)

3. 4. John M. Forbes wird zum Nord-Americanischen Consul in Hamburg und dem Niedersächs. Kreise ernannt. Cf. R. 16 n. 112. A.

3. 5. Acta das Gesuch des Handlungs-Commis Pöhlmann wegen des Nachlasses seines Bruders in New York betr. 1803-1804.

3. 6. Acta die Ansprüche des Weigel et Cons. zu Ansbach und die Verlassenschaft des zu Philadelphia verstorbenen Zuckerbäcker George Utz betr. 1803-1817.

3. 7. Acta betr. die Abschoss-Freiheit mit den Americanischen Freistaaten. Mar. 31, 1804. (Abschoss = alien inheritance tax.)
Acta wegen der Abschoss-Verhältnisse mit den Nord-Americanischen Freistaaten. Nov. 29, 1803.
Acta wegen des Abschosses von dem väterlichen Erbtheil des Juden Hendel Hertz zu Philadelphia. The copy of article X. of the convention between Prussia and the United States, July 11, 1799, abolishing the Abschoss, is now found R. 9 BBB. I.

3. 8. Acta das Engagement deutscher Eingeborenen für die Vereinigten Staaten von Nord-America betr. Apr. 19, 1805.
Interesting account of the efforts of the merchants Wills and Co. in Amsterdam to engage Germans between 16 and 45 years of age for service in the United States, and the protest made against these efforts by von Seibert in Frankfort.
List of sailings of the transports. Feb. 28, 1805.

3. 9. Acta betr. den Antrag des Kaufmanns John Speyer, den Ankauf Schlesischer Leinwand mit Landesprodukten aus New-York acquittiren zu dürfen. Dec. 12, 1810.
3. 10. Acta betr. das Gesuch des Steven John Bramson um Ertheilung des Consulats in Amerika. July 12, 1810.
3. 11. Verordnung wegen Abbrechung des Handels-Verkehrs mit den Vereinigten Staaten von Nord-Amerika. Berlin, July 19, 1810. (Printed. 2 copies with reference to R. 7 and 201.)
4. 1. Acta betr. die Ansprüche des Gottlieb Friedr. Reichert an die Erbschaft der zu Philadelphia verstorbenen Anne Gottliebe Schneider. 1815-1816.
4. 2. Acta des Ministeriums der auswärtigen Angelegenheiten betr. die angebliche zur Bewaffnung der Amerikanischen Insurgenten von den diesseitigen Landen nach Triest hin stattfindenden Gewehrhandel. Sept. and Nov., 1817.
7. 1 a. Print of commercial treaty between Prussia and America. May 1, 1828. (French and German.)
17. Acta betr. die Forderung des Dernisch und Geissler an das Haus John Jac. Sommer in Philadelphia. Mar. 4, 1816. (*Cf.* Intercessionen, D. 1.)

Rep. 92. Hardenberg B. 8.

Acta Koenigl. Geheimen Staats-Archivs betr. Vorschlag des g. Graf, die Inseln Rotunda und Sombrera in Besitz zu nehmen. 1795. On the inside is the following: " 1795, Sept. 2. Acta betr. den Vorschlag des M. C. Graf in Augsburg. Zwecke der Etablirung des deutsch Westindischen Handels die Inseln Rotunda und Sombrera in Besitz zu nehmen und im demnächstigen Frieden förmlich abtreten zu lassen ".
" Pro memoria " of Jacob, a Jew, in Philadelphia, addressed to the Kgl. General Directorium in Berlin, proposing a plan of commercial exchange and offering to conduct such an exchange of Prussian wares in America in consideration of a yearly pension for life and travelling expenses to Berlin. The document of Jacob is important as showing possible articles of export and import and proposing thus early a " Handlungs-Compagnie ". Euthen, May 27, 1783. The German text of this " Pro memoria " is printed in the *Publications of the American Jewish Historical Society*, no. 16 (1907), pp. 85 *et seq.*

Rep. 96.

28. A. *Frankreich* 1775, Januar-Juni. Des preuss. Gesandten Br.'s v. Goltz Depeschen.
Vol. VII. Dispatches from the Paris office (in French in part transliterated from cipher) and the royal dispatches in reply, also transliterated in part from cipher.
28. B. *Frankreich* 1775, Juli-Decbr. Immediat-Depeschen. These papers furnish a good example of the pro-American sentiment in France, notably the dispatch of Goltz, Fontainebleau, Nov. 5, 1775, and the reply, Potsdam, Nov. 9, 1775. King Frederick directs Goltz to send him any news on the war in America which he may receive in France.

35. B. *Gross Britannien* 1775. Des preuss. Gesandten Gf. v. Maltzan Depeschen.

Vol. X. Dispatches of Maltzan in London and the replies from Potsdam and Berlin, transliterated in part from cipher. The answers of the king contain the same personal touches which characterize his other dispatches, as for example, the dispatch to Maltzan, Potsdam, Mar. 29, 1775, which gives an interesting glimpse of the king's economy in the matter of postage: " Enfin selon vos comptes de 1771 et 72 Le port le letres en Angl. va bien haut, et il me semble, que pour la menager, vous pourries bien vous borner à une seule depeche dans quinze jours ", etc. In the dispatch, dated Oct. 30, 1775, to Maltzan we read, evidently from the king: " Un corps de 20 a 30 m hs n'est pas une trouppe si aisé à rassembler. Je ne comprens pas même, qui pourroit ou voudroit la fournier a l'Angleterre."

Much is said in the dispatches of the possible assistance from Russia. A dispatch of Frederick dated Potsdam, Nov. 6, 1775, shows him to be fully and rightly convinced, that Prussia would not furnish England with auxiliary troops to fight against America. The king of Prussia is very positive in his determination not to furnish troops: " il me semble que Le souvenir de la conduite de l'Angl. dans la derne. guerre devroit bien lui faire perdre toute esperance, de pouvoir M'engager jamais a lui en [des troupes] fournir. Aussi serez vous bien prudent [?] de ne vous avancer en rien à ce sujet, afin que Je ne sois pas obligé, à vous donner un dementi formel et sur ".

35. H-K (really H-I).

H. *Grossbritannien* 1781. Des Gesandten Grafen Maltzan Depeschen, etc. Dispatches, to a considerable extent in cipher, between Maltzan in London and the ministry in Berlin, among them one dated London, Feb. 27, 1781, showing that a proposal of peace for England and the colonies would be more welcome from St. Petersburg than from Madrid, and disclosing interesting intrigues in European diplomacy.

73. C. *Politica* 1776, 1777. Des prss. Gen. Maj. W. v. Anhalt Geheime Aufträge für den Kumpel [Kümpel] u. den Herzer. Dazu Oberst Arendt 1781 (containing the following):

Letter of General von Anhalt recommending Captain Fatiasch, a comrade of Kümpel, for a special commission. Potsdam, Nov. 9, 1776.

Reply to the same. Nov. 10, 1776.

Letter of General von Anhalt relating to Goldmeier.

Letter of Herzer requesting an annual compensation.

Letter of General von Anhalt to Herzer, relating to the report of Herzer, etc. Mar. 8, 1777.

Letter of General von Anhalt relating to the same.

Letter of Arendt. Philadelphia, Dec. 2, 1780. (French.)

Account of the battle, surrender, and forces at York [Town]. (French. Important.)

224. A. Acta des Kabinets Friedrich Wilhelms II. Handels- und Zoll Sachen, 1786-1797. Fascicle of 28 documents containing among other things:

Instruction für die zur Aufhebung der Monopolien allerhöchst verordnete Immediat-Commission. Berlin, 1786.

"Pro Memoria" relating to commerce between Prussia and the Austrian states. (Copy.)

Paper of Schulenburg, relating to the "Pro Memoria" of Obrist Lutterloh touching European trade with America. Reasons why such commercial agreements can not yet be made are given, among them the inability of Americans to pay. Berlin, Aug. 27, 1786.

Letter of Finanz-Rath von Wöllner relating to wool and indigo. Berlin, Nov. 11, 1786.

Matter relating to the export of money, etc. Jan. 21, 1787.

Paper signed by Werder, relating to a proposal made by the merchant Hasenclever of Landshut for the formation of a "Handlungs Gesellschaft von Stettin nach Nord America". The document is referred for further investigation to the "Combinirten General Departement".

Letter from E. Sinde, relating to a "Handlungs-Institut". Berlin, Feb. 11, 1791.

Papers of Struensee relating to finance and trade.

224. C. Acta des Kabinets Friedrich Wilhelm's II. Consulats und Schiffahrts-Sachen. 1787-1795.

Papers relating to the appointment of a consul for Virginia and Maryland, signed by Schulenburg. Mar. 29, 1787.

Papers relating to other countries, such as Friesland, the Netherlands, and the Baltic ports, Danzig and Königsberg.

424. K (aus Kabinetssachen R XI. 1784).

Anno 1784 im July entworfene Uebersicht des Nord-Americanischen Handels. A large table of statistical matter relating to the thirteen colonies or states arranged under the following heads: Grafschaften, deutsche quadrat-Meilen, Einwohner (weisse, Neger, Wilde), Handlungsstädte und Seehäfen, Einfuhr, Producten und Ausfuhr, Flüsse, Seen, Küsten und Bayen, Specialien, Generalien, Fabriquen und Manufacturen. An important document containing an astonishing amount of information concerning the colonies.

Other references to America may be found in the correspondence between the Foreign Office in Berlin and the legations in England and France. They are listed as follows in the repertorium:

Grossbritannien.

1765-1781. Grf. v. Maltzan, preuss. Kammerherr u. Gesandter, etc.

Vol.	I.	1765 u. 1766.	Fach 34, Lit. A.
Vol.	II.	1767.	" " " B.
Vol.	III.	1768.	" " " C.
Vol.	IV.	1769.	" " " D.
Vol.	V.	1770.	" " " E.
Vol.	VI.	1771.	" " " F.
Vol.	VII.	1772.	" " " G.
Vol.	VIII.	1773.	" " " H.

Vol. IX. 1774. Fach 35, Lit. A.
Vol. X. 1775.   "   "   " B.
Vol. XI. 1776. "   "   " C.
Vol. XII. 1777. "   "   " D.
Vol. XIII. 1778. "   "   " E.
Vol. XIV. 1779. "   "   " F.
Vol. XV. 1780. "   "   " G.
Vol. XVI. 1781. "   "   " H.

1781-1786. Grf. v. Lusi, preuss. Gesandter, und seine Depeschen aus London.

Vol. I. 1781. Mar.-Dec. Fach 36, Lit. A.
Vol. II. 1782.   "   "   " B.
Vol. III. 1783. "   "   " C.
Vol. IV. 1784.   "   "   " D.
Vol. V. 1785.   "   "   " E.
Vol. VI. 1786.   "   "   " F.
Vol. VII. 1787. "   "   " G.

Frankreich.
1772-1786. Br. v. Goltz, preuss. Oberst, Kammerherr und Gesandter, seine Depeschen aus Paris, etc.

Vol.   I., II. u. III. de 1769. Fach 26, Lit. H, I, K.
Vol. IV.   1772.   " 27, "   E.
Vol. V.   1773.   "   "   "   F.
Vol. VI.   1774.   "   "   "   G.
Vol. VII. u. VIII. 1775.   " 28, "   A, B.
Vol. IX.   1776.   "   "   "   C.
Vol. X.   1777.   "   "   "   D.
Vol. XI.   1778.   "   "   "   E.
Vol. XII. u. XIII. 1779.   "   "   "   F, G.
Vol. XIV. u. XV.   1780.   "   "   "   H.
Vol. XVI. u. XVII. 1781.   " 29, "   A, B.
Vol. XVIII. u. XIX. 1782. "   "   "   C, D.
Vol. XX. u. XXI.   1783.   "   "   "   E, F.
Vol. XXII.   1784.   "   "   "   G.
Vol. XXIII.   1785.   "   "   "   H.
Vol. XXIV.   1786.   "   "   "   I (Jan.-Aug.).

AUSWÄRTIGES AMT.

Abteilung I. Rep. 1. Amerika.

No. 1. Acta betr. die Mission bei den Nord-Americanischen Freistaaten. July 2, 1817–May 7, 1824.

Creditiv für den Legations-Rath Greuhm als Minister-Resident. July 2, 1817.

Bestellung als General Consul. Instruction als solcher, vid. in actis der II Section.

Ausstellung des G. Sasse als Legations Secretair. July 17, 1817.

Dessen Vereidung. July 26, 1817.

Autorisation, dass Sasse nach Europa zurückgesendet werden kann. Jan. 12, 1819.

Ls. R. Greuhm wird überlassen, mit Urlaub nach Berlin zurückzukehren. Feb. 22, 1819.

Sasse ist Ende Juny in Berlin eingetroffen. 1819.
Ls. R. Greuhm ist den 24 Juny abends in Berlin angekommen. 1820.
Herrn Ls. R. Greuhms abermalige Sendung nach Nordamerica.
Genehmigt von Sr. Majestät durch Cab. Order d. d. Teplitz, Aug. 25, 1822.
Reiset von Berlin ab nach Bremen. den 6 Juny 1823.
Hat sich von Bremen nach Hamburg begeben und dort am 8 July nach America eingeschifft, wo er den 31 Aug. landet.
Stirbt den 1 Dec. 1823 in Washington.

No. 2. Washington. Correspondance avec la mission du Roi. Oct. 31, 1817-Feb., 1819.
Copies of letter of John Quincy Adams. Oct. 31, 1817.
Liste des Agents diplomatiques Résidans près les États Unis d'Amérique. 1817.
Letters of Greuhm in French and German, enclosing clippings, reports, etc., relating to America. Such for example as the following:
" Sur les relations commerciales entre les États Unis et la Grande Bretagne." 1818.
Letter of Ancillon to Greuhm containing important reflections and remarks relating to America, particularly that dated Berlin, Mar. 21, 1818, showing that the political situation of the United States is becoming more and more involved with European diplomacy.

No. 3. Acta betr., etc. (as no. 1). Apr. 21–Dec. 31, 1819. Letters mostly in German from Greuhm relating to American affairs.

No. 4. Acta betr., etc. Mar. 31–June 14, 1820. Letters and clippings from Greuhm.

No. 7. Acta betr., etc. June 11, 1825–Dec. 14, 1826. For the most part letters and clippings from Niederstetter in Philadelphia relating to both North and South American affairs, with special reference to commerce and trade, and enclosing important clippings and other printed matter.
" Empfehlungsbrief " for Prince de Hardenberg. Jan. 9, 1826.

No. 8. Acta betr., etc. Jan. 25, 1827–Nov. 4, 1830. Continuation of Niederstetter's letters and clippings relating thereto.

No. 9. Acta betr., etc. June 19, 1834–Dec. 13, 1835. Letters, clippings, and other printed matter sent by Rönne to the Ministry of Foreign Affairs in Berlin. Important official correspondence.

No. 11. Acta betr., etc. Jan. 2, 1836–Dec. 12, 1837. Letters and clippings from Rönne continued.

No. 13. Acta betr., etc. Jan. 5–Dec. 14, 1838. Letters, etc., of Rönne continued.

No. 14. Acta betr., etc. Jan. 13, 1839–Dec. 8, 1841. Letters and clippings from Rönne continued.

ABTEILUNG I. C.

6. Washington. Polit. Schriftwechsel mit der Königl. Mission. Jan. 4, 1842–Jan. 18, 1844.
Letters from Rönne in Washington giving detailed accounts of matters before Congress, including even such as a petition of some citizens of Massachusetts brought before Congress by J. Q.

Adams, Jan., 1842, concerning the dissolution of the Union. In most cases clippings and other printed matter accompany the letters.

10. Washington. Politischer Briefwechsel, etc. Dec. 6, 1844–Apr. 11, 1849.
Letters from Schmidt in New-York and Gerolt in Washington, with numerous clippings, giving much attention to the Mexican War.
Important letter of Gerolt dated Washington, Jan. 28, 1847, relating to the settlement of the dispute with England about the Oregon Territory and the new tariff.

15. Washington. Politischer Briefwechsel, etc. July 22–Dec. 24, 1850. Continuation of papers of a similar character.

16. Washington. Politischer Briefwechsel, etc. May 25–Dec. 3, 1850. Contains similar matter.

17. Washington. Politischer Briefwechsel, etc. Jan. 4, 1851–Dec. 23, 1854.
Papers dealing with the finance, gold production, public lands, etc., in the United States.
Papers calling attention to the need of a German steamship line to the United States and direct railroad communication between the Atlantic coast and California.
Papers relating to the attitude of political parties in the United States, the influence of the Knownothings and the position of the Mormons.

26. Washington. Politischer Briefwechsel, etc. Jan. 13, 1855–Dec. 29, 1856.
Similar papers relating to politics, shipping, and the like.

28. Washington. Politischer Briefwechsel, etc. Mar. 9, 1857–Jan. 12, 1859.
The same kind of matter continued.

31. Washington. Politischer Briefwechsel, etc. Feb. 9–Dec. 31, 1859. The same matter continued.

32. Washington. Politischer Briefwechsel, etc. Jan. 16–Dec. 31, 1860.
Papers relating to the failure of Congress to prevent a dissolution of the Union, opposition to Lincoln in the slave states, South Carolina's Declaration of Independence and other details relating to the matter.

Abteilung II. Rep. 6. Handel, Nord-Amerika.

1. Vol. 1. Acta des Ministeriums der auswärtigen Angelegenheiten betr. die Handelsverhältnisse mit den Nordamerikanischen Freistaaten. Jan. 21, 1818–Dec. 31, 1819. A thick volume of papers containing among other documents the following:
Correspondence between Consul General Greuhm in Washington and the Foreign Office in Berlin.
Correspondence between J. W. Schmidt and Legationsrat Jordan.
Correspondence between von Bülow in Berlin and Freiherr von Humboldt in London.
Correspondence of Graf von Bernstorff, Prussian Minister of State in Berlin, with Greuhm in Washington.
Statistical reports, newspaper clippings, and other printed matter relating to America.
Letter of John Quincy Adams to Consul General Greuhm, referring to a " perfect reciprocity in respect to the payment of duties upon the vessels of the United States and their Cargos in the

Prussian ports, on condition that the same principles should be applied to Prussian vessels and their Cargos in the ports of the United States ". Washington, May 7, 1819. (English.)

A number of letters relating to the above matter together with a report bearing the title: " Number of Vessels and Amount of Tonnage, belonging to Great Britain and the United States, and all other Powers respectively, which entered in the United States of America from each Nation and its Several Dependencies during the year ending 31st December 1818 ".

Exports von Producten aus Charleston in Süd-Carolina. Oct. 1, 1818–Sept. 30, 1819.

1. Vol. 2. Acta des Ministeriums, etc. . . . . Jan. 15, 1820–Oct., 1824. Contains among other papers the following:

Letter of Graf von Bülow acknowledging the report of the exports to South Carolina and Georgia for the preceding year.

Correspondence relating to the reports of Consul General Greuhm in Washington and to questions of American imports from Germany, American finance, the exclusion of American ships from the British West Indies, and the renewal of friendly trade relations with England.

Correspondence between Consul General Greuhm and Graf von Bernstorff, relating to American commerce, revenue, taxes, etc., and their bearing on German trade.

Printed reports and other matter relating to American finance.

Circular to Collectors, Naval Officers and Surveyors. Treasury Department, Comptroller's Office, Nov. 18, 1819, etc.

Decisions of the Supreme Court of the United States, etc.

Greuhm to von Bernstorff, on the ruling of the United States, touching the cruising of an American citizen under a foreign flag against American vessels. The letter refers to this procedure as " eine Lehre, die dem allgemeinen Völkerrechte, den besonderen Verträgen der Vereinigten Staaten mit fremden Mächten und den eigenen Congress Acten schnurstracks entgegen läuft". Mar. 3, 1820.

A report of vessels of the United States entering various ports, etc.

Greuhm to von Bernstorff, giving an interesting account of the question of slavery, incidental to the admission of the territory of Missouri. Jan. 31, 1820.

Von Bülow to von Bernstorff, relating to the exportation of Prussian linen to North America. Sept. 29, 1820.

Communication of C. M. Grünter of Aachen, setting forth the importance of Prussia's making friendly trade treaties with North America as with Spanish and Portuguese colonies, etc. The letter contains an epitome of Prussia's foreign trade relations. Sept. 19, 1816.

Communications from Bremen, Hamburg, etc., relating to American tariff and showing that the Prussian ministers were in the closest touch with American commercial affairs.

1. Vol. 3. Acta des Ministeriums, etc., ... April, 1825–Nov. 30, 1828. Contents similar to the matter in the foregoing volumes. The following may be specially noted:

Papers relating to the tariff of the United States, including among others "Liste des objets, dont l'importation exempte de droits et permise aux Mexique, etc." 1825.

Important communications from Regierungsrat Niederstetter, chargé d'affaires in Washington, giving an account of his experience and mission in Washington in the interests of Prussian trade in America and incidentally shedding much light upon Prussian "Handelspolitik". The most important letters bear the following dates: Jan. 16, 1826; Dec. 12, 1826; May 9, 1827; May 2, 1828; June 20, 1828. Enclosed with the above are newspaper clippings, and a printed copy of the "Treaty of Commerce and Navigation between the United States of America and His Majesty the King of Prussia. May 9, 1828".

1. Vol. 4. Acta des Ministeriums, etc. ..... Jan., 1829–Oct., 1833. Contains important matter relating to the practical application of the commercial treaty in detail and to other matters touching the commercial relations of Prussia and America.

1. Vol. 5. Acta des Ministeriums, etc. ..... Jan., 1834–June, 1836. Continuation of the same general matter, of which the following is worthy of note:

Communications of Diergardt to the Foreign Office, Jan. 19, 1834, and later.

Letter from Rönne, Dec. 18, 1840, and another from Wheaton to Werther, Jan. 21, 1841.

Correspondence of Alvensleben, Rönne, H. H. Meier (addressed to Daniel Jenifer of Maryland, etc., enclosing clippings, etc.).

1. Vol. 6. Acta des Ministeriums, etc. ..... July, 1836–Dec., 1837.

Correspondence between Baron von Rönne in America and the Foreign Office in Berlin.

Confidential correspondence between Baron von Rönne and Abbott Lawrence, M. C., touching the question of linen tapes, etc. Note particularly the letters dated Jan. 12 and Feb. 15, 1836.

Printed bills and reports of the Secretary of the Treasury of the United States.

Correspondence between Baron von Rönne and John Forsyth, Secretary of State.

Letter of Alvensleben to the ministry, showing how the matter of the treaty progressed but slowly. Berlin, July 30, 1836.

Letters from German shippers relating to trade.

Correspondence of Wheaton addressed to Eichhorn and continued on into the next volume.

Much printed matter and important tabular statements of imports for the year ending Sept. 30, 1835.

1. Vol. 7. Acta des Ministeriums, etc. ..... Jan.-Dec., 1838. Continuation of correspondence and discussion of the conditions of American trade and commerce, among others a letter of Baron von Rönne, Northampton, Oct. 30, 1837, referring to the speeches of Webster, Clay, Calhoun, King, Rives, Sargent, and others.

A copy of the *Staats und Gelehrte Zeitung des Hamburgischen unparteiischen Correspondenten* of Feb. 10, 1838.

Letter of Henry Wheaton announcing his appointment as plenipotentiary to effect a treaty of navigation and commerce between the United States and Prussia. Mar. 24, 1838.
Letter of President Van Buren appointing Wheaton.
Much official correspondence relating to this treaty with the text and the translations of the important documents enclosed.

1. Vol. 8. Acta des Ministeriums, etc. . . . . . Jan., 1839–Dec., 1840. Continuation of matter contained in vol. 7, and among other papers:
   Letter of Joshua Dodge to Wheaton.
   Certified translation of Wheaton's communication of Feb. 23, 1839, to Baron Werther.
   Communications of Jordan and Alvensleben.
   Papers of Controleur J. N. Barker of Mar. 4, 1839, in French copies.
   Original and French translation of Wheaton's communication to Werther of July 11, 1839.
   Report on tobacco made by Joshua Dodge to Wheaton. Aug. 31, 1839.
   Correspondence on the subject of tobacco.

1. Vol. 9. Acta des Ministeriums, etc. . . . . . Jan.-Dec., 1841. Continuation of correspondence in vol. 8.
   Correspondence relating to the tariff in German silk. The letter of Alvensleben is of special importance, as giving the progress of the negotiations.

1. Vol. 10. Acta des Ministeriums, etc. . . . . . Jan., 1842–Feb. 28, 1844.
   Reports from Rönne relating to American trade.
   Correspondence on tariff, etc., enclosing: *Neues Tarif-Gesetz der Ver. Staaten von Nordamerica.* Jan. 23, 1843. (Print of German translation.)
   Correspondence between Wheaton, Rönne, and the ministry relating to the tariff.
   Reappointment of Wheaton as plenipotentiary to the court of Prussia by President Tyler. Dec. 7, 1843.
   Interesting clipping from supplement no. 20 of the *Weser-Zeitung* for Jan. 23, 1844, relating to German trade with America.
   Letter of Diergardt in Viersen to Gen. Direktor Kühne in Berlin. Jan. 13, 1844.
   Handelsvertrag zwischen Preussen und den übrigen Staaten des Deutschen Zoll- und Handels-Vereins einerseits und den Vereinigten Staaten von Amerika andererseits. MS. German and English in opposite columns.

1. Vol. 11. Acta des Ministeriums, etc. Feb.-July, 1844. Contains among other papers:
   Printed copy of *Commissions-Bericht über das der hohen II. Kammer zur Zustimmung vorgelegte provisorische Gesetz vom 13. October 1842 den Vereinszolltarif für die Jahre 1843, 1844, und 1845 betreffend. Erstattet von dem Abgeordneten Bassermann (Protokoll der 35. öffentl. Sitz. vom 4. März 1844).*
   Original projet of 9 articles in English.
   Correspondence relating to the *Bericht* and modifications, etc.
   Confidential original notes with signatures, copies, and translations of the various forms of the treaty, etc.
   A list of particular articles included in the treaty.

1. Vol. 12. Acta des Ministeriums, etc. . . . . . July, 1844–Dec., 1845. Continuation of papers relating to tariff.
    Letters from the Prussian Consul Schmidt in New York containing important matter.
    Printed reports, clippings from newspapers such as the *Weser-Zeitung* of Aug. 6, 1844, the *Madisonian* of Washington of July 26 and Aug. 3, 1844, and the *Cölnische Zeitung* of June 26, 1844.
    Address of the Democratic Association, Apr. 29, 1844, relating to " the treaty in favor of American Tobacco, Cotton, Rice, and Lard rejected by the old Whigs ". (Printed pamphlet.)
    Reports of Gerolt, minister resident in Washington, of Mar. 26, 1845, giving important details of the new cabinet.
    Clipping from *Niles's Register* and from German newspapers.
1. Vol. 13. Acta des Ministeriums, etc. . . . . . Jan.-Dec., 1846. Continuation of correspondence in the foregoing volume.
    Papers relating to the details of American affairs, often in most out-of-the-way places.
    Papers relating to a single wire telegraph. Jan. 14, 1846.
    Table of articles and proposals of new duties on such articles. Mar. 10, 1846.
1. Vol. 14. Acta, etc., betr. die Handels- und Schiffahrt-Verhältnisse mit den Vereinigten Staaten von Amerika. Jan.-Dec., 1847.
    Letters of J. Buchanan, Gerolt, and the minister.
    Papers relating to the extension of the Prussian treaty with the United States, dated May 1, 1828, to other states of the Zollverein.
    Confidential copies of the " Protocoll of the Conference ". Washington, Feb. 23, 1847.
    " Comparative Statement " of the articles to be taxed and table of articles for the German States.
    Long document of A. J. Donelson to Baron de Canitz, minister of state. Berlin, July 8, 1847.
1. Vol. 15. Acta, etc., Jan., 1848–Dec., 1851.
    Further papers dealing with the tariff.
    Rupture of the negotiations, the attitude of Haiti, etc. Mar. 18, 1848.
    " Statements of the principal articles imported directly from Hanse towns and the Prussian ports on the Baltic Sea compared with the same articles imported by Holland, Belgium, and France in the years 1844, 1845, 1846 " (taken from the Report of the Secretary of the Treasury).
    Elaborate statistical tables. 1850.
1. Vol. 16. Acta, etc. Jan., 1852–Mar., 1857.
    Tables sent from Washington giving imports into New York for 1851 and following years.
    Correspondence of Gerolt with the minister, enclosing extracts, clippings, bills before Congress, etc.
1. Vol. 17. Acta, etc. Apr., 1857–Aug., 1862.
    Important papers relating to political events in America.
    Report of the decisions of the Commission of Claims under the convention of Feb. 8, 1852, between the United States and Great Britain.
    Gerolt to Manteuffel, referring to the claims. Apr. 8, 1857.
    Letters of Gerolt reflecting the danger of discussion at this time.

Correspondence following every significant step of the secession movement and showing great concern for the interests of German trade.

Much printed matter enclosed, such as printed pamphlets, clippings, reports, and the like, especially: *Disunion and Its Results to the South,* and *Letter from a Resident of Washington to a Friend in South Carolina* (Washington, 1861). Pamphlet. "Amtlicher Bericht über den jetzigen Zoll-Tarif", etc., by Friedr. Kühne of the firm Knauth, Nachod, and Kühne. New-York, Aug., 1861.

Important papers relating to the cotton trade in New Orleans, etc.

Ten papers relating to American affairs forwarded by Gerolt. July 29, 1862.

1. Vol. 18. Acta, etc. Sept., 1862–Dec., 1869.

Papers relating to American tariff, which was agitating the German mind, because of the increase (for war revenue). New Orleans, Baltimore, and New York are the chief centres of German commercial interest. The papers are for the most part colorless so far as the political issues are concerned, but there are numerous printed pamphlets, reports, etc., which reflect the state of things.

Bericht über die Lage und den Handel der Vereinigten Staaten von Nord-Amerika, von Friedrich Kühne, Consul, Mitglied des Bankhauses Knauth, Nachod, and Kühne. (New York, Juli 1865.) Print.

Communication of Delbrück, addressed to the "Handelskammer" of Gladbach, Elberfeld, Düsseldorf, Krefeld, Aachen, Eupen, Duisburg, Lennep, Solingen, Stolberg, Hagen, Lüdenscheid, Iserlohn, Breslau, and "die Herren Aeltesten der Kaufmannschaft", declaring "von einer diplomatischen Einwirkung auf die Regierung in Washington entsprechende Erfolge mit Wahrscheinlichkeit nicht in Aussicht zu nehmen". Berlin, Oct. 19, 1866.

1. Vol. 19. Acta, etc. Jan., 1870–June, 1873. More papers relating to the tariff with important printed reports enclosed.

2. Acta des Ministeriums der auswärtigen Angelegenheiten betr.:

No. 2. Die Beschuldigungen gegen den Capitain Schultz vom Schiffe *Ceres* wegen übler Behandlung der Ausgewanderten nach America. 1817-1824. Intus: Nordamerikanischerseits genommene Massregeln wegen Ueberfüllung der Schiffe d. 26. Feb. [18]20; Diesseitige Bestimmungen d. 17. Juny [18]20. See also Schiffsachen Gen. N. 52.

No. 3. Die errichtete Societät-Handlung unter der Firma "Factorei für den Debit Preussischer und Deutscher Fabrikate und Produkte". 1824.

No. 4. Die Verordnung bei den Nordamerikanischen Freistaaten, wegen des ungehinderten Durchgangs der Gegenstände, welche von dem Grafen von Sack und anderen Reisenden Botanikern an die diesseitigen Institute und Gärten gespendet werden. 1826, 1827.

No. 5 Die Zusammenstellung der Steuer-Abgaben und Handelsgesetzen in den Vereinigten Staaten von Amerika. 1828-1867.

No. 6. Die Beschwerde des Bevollmächtigten der Preussischen See-Assecuranz-Compagnie Wiszmann zu Stettin gegen den g. Gasziot wegen angeblicher Assecuranzbetrügerei bei dem nach Amerika gesegelten Schiffe *Leonidas.* 1836-1838.

No. 7. Acta betr. die Verhältnisse der in Süd-Carolina gegründeten " Amerikanisch-Deutsche Handels- und Versicherungs-Gesellschaft ". 1836-1839. Intus: Antrag des Delius wegen eines Consulats.

No. 8. Die Beschwerde des Nordamerikanischen Consuls Dr. Rivinus zu Dresden über Beschädigung seiner Effecten bei deren Revision zu Halberstadt.

No. 9. Die See- und Nachsteuer an den Küsten der Vereinigten Staaten von Amerika. 1845-1869.

No. 10. Die Verschiedenen Beschwerden und Reclamationen gegen die Zollbehörden in den Vereinigten Staaten von Amerika. Vol. I. 1846-1874.

5. Vol. I. Acta, etc., betr. wegen Anstellung einiger Preussischen Consuls in Nord-America. 1802-1817. Intus:
Charlestowner Consulat erhält Steinmetz 12 Febr: 2 [1802].
Bramson Bewerbung um das Consulat zu Baltimore, Philadelphia und New York 4 Aug. 2. Pass für ihn 18 Aug. 2 [1802].
Krumbhaar [zu Philadelphia].
Mathias [als Consul in Baltimore und Philadelphia].
Ralph Bennet Forbes bittet um das Consulat zu New Hampshire, Massachusetts, Rhode Island, Connecticut d. 14 Feb. [18]15.
Wegen der Zoll-Abgaben in den Nord Americanischen Staaten vom den Fremden Schiffen d. 26 Oct. [18]15.
Seckendorff.
F. W. Am Ende bittet um Anstellung zu New Orleans d. 19 März.
Correspondenz mit dem Finanz-Ministerium wegen Besetzung der Consulat-Stellen überhaupt d. 17 Juny [18]16.
Eduard Waldeck d. 18 Juny 1816.
George Delius d. 7 Septbr. [18]16, n. 5788.
J. W. Schmidt wird Consul zu New York d. 30 Nov. d. 19 Dec. [18]16.
C. M. Grünter d. 14 Jan. [18]17.
Valuable information concerning all the places in question, shedding much light upon the history of the Germans in these cities.

5. Vol. II. Acta, etc., betr. den königl. Preussisch. Gesandschaftsträger und General Consul bei den Vereinigten Staaten von Nord Amerika, vom Juli 1817 bis September 1840. Contains matter similar to that in the preceding volume.

5. Vol. III. Acta, etc. Mar., 1841–Nov., 1852. Continuation of the same kind of matter.

15. Handels- und Schiffs-Sachen. Acta betr. die Pressung des Lehrers Julius Lembke zu Matrosendiensten auf dem Amerikanischen Schiffe *Bengal* durch dessen Captain Burgess u. Beschwerde des Lembke dieserhalb. Dec., 1870.

19. Vol. I. Acta, etc., betr. die angetragene Errichtung eines Preussisch. Consulats in St. Louis, Staat Missouri, am Mississippi in den Vereinigten Staaten von Nordamerika. June, 1840–Oct., 1861.

The first paper is a letter from George Engelmann, M. D., addressed to Eichhorn, giving a most interesting account of the growth of the city of St. Louis and the outlying region. Berlin, May 28, 1840.

Letter from C. Ritter touching the same matter. Berlin, May 27, 1840.

Correspondence between the Foreign Office in Berlin and Rönne, Prussian minister, relating to the same question.

Letter of Schumacher in Baltimore and C. Ulrici and Compagnie in St. Louis to Rönne.

Matter relating to the appointment of Angelrodt as consul in St. Louis and to the decoration of Angelrodt with the Order of the Red Eagle of the fourth class.

31. Vol. I. Acta des Ministeriums der auswärtigen Angelegenheiten betr. die Errichtung eines Consulats zu Newbedford, in den V. St. v. Amerika, Staat Massachusetts. Mar., 1846–Feb., 1858.
42. Vol. I. Acta, etc., betr. das Königlich Preussische Consulat zu Milwaukee, Staat Wisconsin. May, 1850–Nov., 1862.
55. Acta, etc., betr. das Preussische Consulat zu Detroit im Staat Michigan. Sept., 1855–May, 1858.
68. Acta, etc., betr. das Königliche Consulat zu La Porte, Staat Indiana. Dec., 1858–Jan., 1859.
73. Acta, etc., betr. das Königliche Consulat zu New Albany, Staat Indiana. June-Sept., 1860.

ABTEILUNG III. REP. I.

2. Vol. 1. Now to be found under R. 73, no. 68, 2. Acta generalia, betr. die Auswanderungen aus den Niederrheinischen Provinzen nach Polen, America, etc. Intus:

Die Auswanderung Baierscher Unterthanen in diesseitige Provinzen. Mar. 22, 1816.

Die erschwerte Auswanderung des Scheuffelhuth. Einwanderungen und Auswanderungen im Coblenzer Regierungs-Bezirk.

Wehrpflichtige in Sachsen. Emigration.

Dansard, Auswanderung nach America. Jan. 11, 1816–Nov. 25, 1816. The matter relating to Poland is important and interesting when compared with that relating to America. The motive of the emigrants and their keen insight into the advantages offered in Russian Poland are significant. Many names are found in these papers which have later bearing on America. An important paper is a communication of Otterstedt, Aug. 19, 1816, setting forth the attitude toward the Jews.

Communications of Baron von Zwackh to Baron von Otterstedt, notably, one dated Speyer, Aug. 8, 1816, with enclosed clipping.

Papers referring to the "Pariser Tractat" and its consequences.

"Die Auswanderung nach den Holländischen Kolonien und besonders nach Nord-Amerika betreffend", enclosing a printed pamphlet of 101 pages entitled: *Erinnerungen an meine teutschen Landsleute, welche versucht seyn sollten aus Europa zu wandern,* von Dr. Wilhelm Butte (Cologne, 1816), a somewhat discouraging account of America.

Papers relating to the emigration from Cologne, Trier, etc.

Matter relating to the " Russischen Colonisten-Werber ", who are busy in Frankfort-on-the-Main.
Important letter of Ingersleben to Hardenberg, showing the change of sentiment toward emigration. Coblenz, Nov. 4, 1816.
Papers relating to the emigration of the book-binder Nikolaus Dansard to America. 1816.

2. Vol. 2. Acta betr. die Auswanderungen aus den Niederrheinischen Provinzen nach Polen, America, etc.
Das Einwandern Baierscher Unterthanen nach dem Posenischen d. 15ten April [18]17. Jacob Breininger d. 15, April [18]17.
Papers relating to emigration in general and to the privilege of emigration within six years (the " sexennium " provided by the Peace of Paris) from all the provinces ceded by France, particularly Schuckmann's letter to the Ministry of Foreign Affairs, Dec. 10, 1816, and the reply.
Correspondence relating to emigration from particular places or districts.
Papers relating to the permission for certain Germans to emigrate to America: Friedrich Jung, laborer of Oberraden, and Jacob Mertgen, carpenter of Niederhonefeld. 1817.
Correspondence relating to the great emigration during the " Sexennium ", some 3000 wishing to go from Trier alone. Number of emigrants to America mentioned by name, together with the place of residence, trade, and number of children, etc.
Communication of Schultheis and Dr. Ebermaier to the Oberpräsident Gr. v. Solms, stating that emigration from Württemberg, Switzerland, and bordering French departments to Holland has so increased in the last six weeks that several thousand have passed down the Rhine and some 80,000 intend to go to America. Laubach, May 9, 1817.
More correspondence relating to this emigration, such as letters of June 6 and 22, 1817; and other papers relating to the inspection of passes, from which we learn incidentally that the emigrants from South Germany and Switzerland shipped almost exclusively down the Rhine.
Matter relating to the new kind of passes, addressed by Scholtz to the Minister of Foreign Affairs. Jan. 24, 1817.
An important " Verzeichniss " of names of emigrants. July 5, 1817.
Clippings from the *Stuttgarter Zeitung* of June 17, 1817.
Auszug eines Publikandums gegeben Warschau in der Staatsverwaltungssitzung. May 3, 1817.
More lists of emigrants. June and July, 1817.
Much correspondence with other German states, notably with Bavaria toward the close of the volume.

2. Vol. 3. Acta des Ministeriums der auswärtigen Angelegenheiten betr. die Auswanderungen aus Deutschland und der Schweiz nach Polen, America, etc. Apr. 1, 1819-Dec. 31, 1824.
Papers relating to emigration in general.
Correspondence of Graf von Bernstorff in Berlin and Zastrow, Prussian minister in Munich.
Letter addressed to the ministry relating to Bahia in Brazil. Apr. 29, 1819.

Copy of an important communication from Frankfort-on-the-Main, Apr. 18, 1819, enclosed with the above letter and other papers bearing upon the subject.
Papers relating to emigrants to Russian Poland.
Letter on the refusal to allow German and Swiss emigrants to enter the Netherlands unless they have sufficient cash to complete the journey to America. May 17, 1819.
Much correspondence relating to this subject.
Clippings from the *Bremer Zeitung*, no. 139, 1819, relating to Captain Steiger and his company of emigrants from Switzerland, and also from the *Privilegierte wöchentliche gemeinnützige Nachrichten von und für Hamburg*, May 26, 1819.
Papers relating to the efforts to settle the lands of Colonel James Swan, of Boston, which he sold in Virginia and Kentucky to Morcadier and which the latter sold to a French and a German stock company. The French company is headed by Le Mercier, the physicist, Jerome, and Graf von Redern; the German company by Graf von Waldeck, Fürst von Fürstenberg, and the family von Gültlingen in Württemberg.
Küster to von Bernstorff, enclosing the statutes of the above-mentioned society as well as other papers directed to Bernstorff. Stuttgart, May, 1819.
Letter of Greuhm, giving an interesting account of the course of emigration to the Western states and of the captain of the ship *Ceres* of Danzig, which has now redeemed its record. Washington, Sept. 9, 1819.
Extract of a document of Secretary John Quincy Adams beginning thus: " The Government of the United States has never adopted any measures to encourage or invite immigration from any part of Europe," etc. Washington, June 14, 1819.
Papers relating to the ship *Johanna*, of Stettin, now in Philadelphia. Oct. 6, 1819.
" Bordereau über das Gepäck " and other matters relating to shipping to America.
Clippings, etc., from newspapers, especially from the *Altonaischer Mercurius*, Dec. 14, 1824.
Further papers relating to emigration to Brazil.
Correspondence of Gottfried Werner and others. 1824.

2. Vol. 4. Acta des Ministeriums der auswärtigen Angelegenheiten betr. Polen: Die Auswanderungen aus Deutschland und der Schweiz nach Holland, Polen, America, etc. Jan., 1825–Aug. 31, 1826.
Papers relating to Prussians, subject to military duty, on the ship *Caroline*, bound for Brazil, including: *Staats- und Gelehrte Zeitung des Hamburgischen unparteiischen Correspondenten* of June 11, 1825.
Papers relating to Major Schäffer and others, and to the ships *Wilhelmine* and *Germania*, in connection with German colonists going to Brazil.

2. Vol. 5. Acta, etc. June, 1827–Dec., 1828.
Papers relating to the emigration, continued, and showing the connection of the movement in Germany with the Austrian emigration

to Brazil, enclosing the following: *Amtsblatt der Regierung zu Trier* for Jan. 9, Mar. 8, Mar. 27, Apr. 3, and Apr. 26, 1828, relating to the emigration to Brazil.

Letter of Nagler to Bernstorff, relating to the ship, *Olympe,* bound for Buenos Ayres, from Havre. Frankfort-on-the-Main, Feb. 5, 1828.

Auszug aus dem Berichte der königlichen Regierung Vice-Praesidenten H. Fritsche. Coblenz, Mar. 25, 1828, giving the following data: Auswanderungen, 121 Männer, 133 Frauen, 194 Kinder, überhaupt 448 Individuen ausgewandert, und zwar 313 nach Brasilien.

Einige Nachrichten über Brazilien zur Belehrung für die Auswanderungslüstigen, besonders in der Eifel. (Printed by Hetzrodt und Sohn in Trier. No. 59.)

2. Vol. 6. Acta, etc. Mar., 1829–Nov., 1833.

More papers relating to the emigration to Brazil.

Letter of Ober-Präsident von Vincke of Münster, to the ministry in Berlin, relating to the formulation of an " Uebersiedlungsplan ", for which he has asked the assistance of Bergamtdirektor Schmidt, who is at present in Mexico, collecting information concerning German trade there. 1829, 1830.

Papers relating to Pernambuco.

Correspondence relating to shipping from French ports to America. 1831.

Amerikanische Colonisations-Gesellschaft, Freiburg in Breisgau den 1. Maii, 1832. At the end the name of Heinrich Benedikt von Hermann, Engelgasse, no. 15. At the beginning appear the following names of agents:

Frankreich: Herren Solms and Comp. in Strassburg; Herr Slade in Havre; Herren Guillot and Comp. daselbst.

Deutschland: Herr H. B. von Hermann, zu Freiburg im Breisgau.

Nord-Amerika: Herr J. M. Lafitte in Baltimore; Herr Solms in Philadelphia.

Papers relating to Mexico. June, 1832.

Papers relating to shipping from Havre and the Low Countries.

Papers relating to Portuguese, French, and Germans and to the various countries, Brazil, French ports, Low Countries, etc.

Printed pamphlet of 14 pages entitled *Wohlgemeinter Rath der Vorsteher der Deutschen Gesellschaft in New York, an Deutsche, die nach den Vereinigten Staaten von N. Amerika auszuwandern beabsichtigen* (New-York, 1833), and a number of letters relating to the same.

Requests of individual Germans of Saarbrücken and other places for permission to emigrate to North America. 1833.

Printed pamphlet of 60 pages, entitled *Rechts-Verhältnisse der Württembergischen Auswanderer: Ein Handbuch für Obrigkeiten,* etc. (Heilbronn, 1833.)

Partial list of emigrants by way of Havre. August, 1833. Nos. 1 to 1725 wanting in the list.

2. Vol. 7. Acta, etc. Apr., 1834–Dec. 31, 1836.

Gesuche um Erlaubniss zum Auswandern nach Amerika.

Das Auswandern Militairpflichtiger betr.

Obrigkeitliche Verordnung (of the Senate of Bremen, June 13 and 19, 1832).
More correspondence relating to Prussian emigrants shipping by way of France, enclosing the following printed pamphlets: *Wohlgemeinter Rath der Deutschen Gesellschaft von Maryland an Deutsche die irgend ein Interesse an der Auswanderung nach den Vereinigten Staaten von Nord-Amerika fühlen* (Baltimore, gedruckt bey J. H. Dreyer u. Sohn, 1834) and also *Proceedings of the State Convention of Mechanics, Held in Utica, Aug. 21-22, 1834*, etc.
Correspondence relating to both pamphlets.
Communication of Sydow, enclosing a partial list of emigrants. Apr. 26, 1836.
Important communication by " Friedrich Stohlman, vormaliger Lehrer an der Schule, wie auch Organist und Kantor an der Kirche in Klein-Bremen ", beginning as follows: " Vereinigte Staaten Nord-Amerikas, Staat Pennsylvanien an den Grenzen Ohios und Kanadas; Stadt Erie (am See gleichen Namens) den 27ten März, 1836 ". (No. 3818, May 7, 1836, middle of the volume.)
First report of the director of the South Australian Company. 1836.
Frankfürter Repertorium für Handel- und Finanz-Wesen, etc. 1836.

2. Vol. 8. Acta, etc. Feb., 1837–Sept., 1840. Contains among other papers:
Beilage zum Frankfürter Journal, Feb. 2, 1837, with a notice of Blum, Spediteur, of Forbach.
Verordnung in Betreff der Verschiffung der über Hamburg nach andern Welttheilen Auswandernden; Auf Befehl eines Hochedlen Raths der freien und Hansestadt Hamburg, etc. Feb. 27, 1837.
Papers relating to the Chevalier de Bloem, Officier Supérieur du Génie et Directeur Général des Mines et Hautes Fourneaux du Brésil, enclosing his visiting card with " Hotel du Roi de Portugal " written on it, and the following paper: " Koningrijk der Nederlanden. Besluit van den 28. December, 1837 (Staatsblad, no. 81), houdende nadere bepalingen omtrent den doortogt van landverhuizende Personen ", etc. (Dutch and German on opposite columns.)
Papers relating to Guiana, Apr. 29, 1838, enclosing the following printed matter:
Bedingungen für Arbeiter in Demerara, signed by Dr. Strecker. Mainz, Oct. 10, 1838.
Indenture of Johannes Kehr to Bernhard Ries, merchant in London, also relating to Guiana.
Extract from the *London Times* of Dec. 13, 1838, relating to the Guiana Colony and the Germans.
Polizey-Bekanntmachung, das Auswanderungswesen hierselbst betreffend. Hamburg, July 31, 1839.
Copy of the Report of the Meeting of the 3d of March, 1840, at the house of Mr. Waitz, on invitation of Waitz and Dunker.
Reise-Beförderung nach den Vereinigten Staaten von America durch den unterzeichneten autorisirten und beeidigten Schiffs-Makler, William Gibson zu Hamburg (1840).

Notwendige Anzeige für Auswanderer sowie Entlarvung und Abfertigung der Bremer Schiffsmakler, Lüdering, Traub, und Duntze (Hamburg, 1839, pp. 32).

Obrigkeitliche Verordnungen of the Senate of Bremen. Apr. 8, 1840.

2. Vol. 9. Acta, etc. Jan., 1841–Dec., 1842.

Correspondence relating to the shipping of emigrants from French harbors to America, including lists of ships and number of passengers.

Von Rochow to von Werther, relating to emigration to South Australia and enclosing interesting printed matter relating to Australia. Feb. 28, 1841.

Correspondence with Eichhorn enclosing the following print: *Die Vorsteher der Deutschen Gesellschaft in New York an ihre Landsleute, welche nach den Vereinigten Staaten von Nord-Amerika auszuwandern beabsichtigen* (1841).

Matter relating to the Lutheran Confession, enclosing a printed circular in German and English on opposite columns treating of the emigration to Jamaica (1835) and also the following: *The New British Colony, Province of Victoria, in Central America*, June, 1840 (*J. Cunningham, Printer, Crown-court, Fleet Street, London*); *Ist eine Vereinigung zwischen Lutheranen und den verschiedenen Glaubens Partheien der sogenannten Reformirten möglich?* (Altona, 1841).

Auswanderungen aus dem Grossherzogthum Kurhessen während des Jahres 1841 (accompanied by the following prints): *Antrag des Abgeordneten v. Werner, die Bildung eines Emigrations- und Colonisations-Vereins betreffend* (Nov. 6, 1844); *Prospectus über einen Verein für Deutsche Auswanderer; Entwurf zum Statut d. Ver. f. d. A.* (Düsseldorf, June 20, 1843).

Obriglichkeitliche Verordnung (of the Senate of Bremen, June 6, 1842).

2. Vol. 10. Acta, etc. Apr., 1843–Dec., 1844.

Papers relating to expedition to St. Thomas. 1843.

Map of " The Territory of Verapas " in Central America.

Papers relating to Guatemala.

Rapport Officiel de M. De Puydt, Colonel du Génie, Chef de la Commission d'Exploration dans l'Amérique Centrale (Bruxelles, Lesigne Frères, Imprimeurs de la Compagnie Belge de Colonisation, 1842).

Compagnie Belge de Colonisation fondée sous le Patronage du Roi: Statuts, Contrats et Chartes (Brussels).

Communauté de l'Union, fondée par la Compagnie Belge de Colonisation, et approuvée par Arrêté Royal en date du 26 Novembre, 1842 (Brussels).

Clippings relating to the same subject from the *Moniteur Belge*, etc.

Darstellung der neuen Colonie Süd-Australien, etc.

2. Vol. 11. Acta, etc. Jan.-May, 1845. Matter relating to the " Auswanderungs- und Colonisations-Verein", enclosing copies of statutes, etc., and the following print:

Revidirte Verordnung in Betreff der Verschiffung der über Hamburg direkt nach andern Welttheilen Auswandernden. Mar. 26, 1845.

5 b. Vol. 1. Auswärtiges Amt, III b., Akten betr. die Staatsangehörigkeit der in den Vereinigten Staaten von Amerika lebenden Deutschen und umgekehrt. Einzelfälle. Aug., 1830–Sept., 1863. A collection of miscellaneous papers relating to Germans in many parts of America, including requests for permission to emigrate to America, and to the transference of property belonging to Germans in America through the German legation, with passes and other related papers.

5 b. Vol. 2. Auswärtiges Amt, etc., und die Ertheilung von Entlassungsurkunden an dort lebende Deutsche. Jan., 1864–Apr., 1876. Contains matter similar to that of Vol. I.

5 b. Vol. 3. Auswärtiges Amt, etc. July, 1876–Dec., 1883.

11. Vol. 1. Auswanderungen ausser Europa. Acta des Ministeriums der auswärtigen Angelegenheiten betr. die Ueberwachung und Leitung der Auswanderungen aus Deutschland nach den Nord- und Südamericanischen Staaten und Australien und die Fürsorge für die Deutschen Ansiedler in Bezug auf das Kirchen und Schulwesen, Erhaltung der Sprache und Nationalität, etc. July, 1844–May, 1846. *Cf.*: (1) Acta Auswand. nach America. Ausw. Gen. 2. (2) Auswand. nach Texas. Ausw. ausser Europa 2. (3) Consulat in Adelaide in Australien. No. 27.

Matter relating to the reports of Consul Harrassowitz in La Guayra and the emigration from Baden to Venezuela. July-Sept., 1844.

Correspondence of Arnim and Bülow.

Letter of Eichhorn to Bülow, Feb. 17, 1845, emigration to Texas, enclosing the following manuscript: "Pro Memoria Eichhorns über die Stellung Preussens zu den Deutschen Auswanderern, namentlich in Nordamerika." (10 pages, folio.) An interesting passage runs thus: "Ein Zehntel der Deutschgermanischen Stämme bewohnt die Staaten und Territorien der Union und diese deutsche Bevölkerung beträgt mehr als ein Viertel der Gesammt-Bevölkerung, fast ein Drittel der freien Bevölkerung der Vereinigten Staaten".

Correspondence with v. Rochow, the Prussian Minister in Stuttgart. Mar., 1845.

Clippings from the *Beilage zur Allgemeinen Zeitung,* Mar. 6, 1845, relating to the German settlement in Texas.

Letters of Eichhorn to Bülow and Consul Schmidt.

Correspondence between the Foreign Offices of Darmstadt and Berlin.

Beraldingen in Stuttgart to Bülow, on emigration to America. Apr. 24, 1845.

The Prussian consul at Antwerp to Bülow, enclosing extracts, reports to the "Commission de la Navigation Transatlantique" and much other correspondence relating to the passage of Prussian subjects. June 4, 1845. (French.)

Important matter relating to shipping in connection with the emigration question, especially that of Consul Carp of Rotterdam. 1845.

Correspondence between Gerolt in Washington and the Foreign Office in Berlin, enclosing clippings from no. 638 and no. 639 of the *Weser-Zeitung* relating to the emigration to Texas.

Letters relating to emigration to New York and to Brazil, and particularly a document from the consul general in Rio de Janeiro, Dec. 15, 1845, directed to the Foreign Office in Berlin, enclosing an "Auszug" and a print of the *Auswanderungs-Contrakt für Brasilien* (1837).
Clippings from *Extrabeilage zu No. 85 und No. 88 der Frankfurter Oberpostamt-Zeitung* of Mar. 26, 1846, relating to the emigration to Brazil.
Wheaton to Baron de Canitz, on the law relating to emigrants. Berlin, Apr. 14, 1846. (French.)

11. Vol. 2. Acta, etc. June-Dec., 1846.
Correspondence relating to the report of Dr. Ludwig Colmann, practising physician in London, in reference to Germans on the emigrant ship *Patell* from Bremen.
Matter from Schmidt in New York, relating to Carp in Rotterdam. Apr. 5, 1846.
Clippings from the *Frankfurter Journal*, May 2, 1846, relating to Wamberzie and Crooswick, American shipping agents.
Correspondence between the ministries in Berlin and Carlsruhe, etc., relating to emigration.
Correspondence of June, 1846, relating to Brazil, enclosing a print entitled *Homoeopathy, the Healing Art*, by Dr. Colmann (London, 1843).
Letter of Consul General Schmidt, in New York, and matter relating to the legislature in Pennsylvania, and the act of Mar. 5, 1828.
French papers relating to Brazil, signed by Le Vicomte d'Abrantez. Swinemünde, July 20, 1846.
Letter of Werner, Prussian consul in Havre. July 23, 1846.
Extracts of *Gazette de Cologne*. Aug., 1846.
Report of Consul Theremin, in Rio de Janeiro. June 30, 1846.
Map, relating to Brazil.
Matter relating to Texas and Brazil, Aug. 25, 1846, and enclosing *Allgemeines Organ für Handel und Gewerbe* of Nov. 17, 1846.
Matter relating to " Friedensunterhandlungen am La Plata ". Nov. 30, 1856.

11. Vol. 3. Acta, etc. Jan.-June, 1847. Continuation of subjects in volume 2.
Much statistical matter relating to emigration by way of Antwerp, of which the following is interesting: In 1845, 5221 emigrants; 1846, 13,178. American ships [bearing American flags], 48; English, 15; Austrian, 7; Sardinian, 6; Bremen, 3; Swedish, 2; Holland, 2; Hanoverian, 2; Prussian, 1; Russian, 1; Mecklenburg, 1; Danish, 1.
Statistics giving destination of emigrants and number landing in each harbor, as follows: New York, 7581; Galveston, 2276; Rio, 1661; New Orleans, 1204.
Many papers relating to the emigration to Brazil and shipping by way of Antwerp. 1846 and 1847.
Matter, dated Jan. 30, 1847, relating to Texas, and Carl Detrue et Comp. in Dunkirk, etc., enclosing clipping from the London *Morning Post*, Jan. 27, 1847, dealing with the emigration to Mosquitia.

Papers relating to the passage of Swiss by way of Germany, Apr. 22, 1847, and to the passenger bill of Washington, Mar., 1847, enclosing a copy of the *Weser-Zeitung* of May 5, 1847, treating the bill, also a clipping from the *Beilage zur Grossherzoglich Hessischen Zeitung* of 1847, p. 828.
Obrigkeitliche Verordnung über die Beförderung von Schiffs-passagieren of the Senate of Bremen. May, 1847. (Print.)
Regierungs-Blatt für das Königreich Württemberg, no. 2. Jan. 14, 1847. (Print.)
Report of Consul General Schmidt. New York, Feb., 1847.
Clipping from *Berlinische Nachrichten*. June 13, 1847.

11. Vol. 4. Acta, etc. July-Dec., 1847.
Decree of the kingdom of the Netherlands. Dec. 28, 1837. (Dutch and German.)
Matter relating to Bluefields and the porcelain factory. July 1, 1847.
More papers relating to Brazil, enclosing a printed decree of the Herzoglich Nassauische Landesregierung, dated Wiesbaden, May 8, 1847.
" Deutsche Auswanderung nach Chili, etc. A. Reid, M. D." Valparaiso, July, 1847. (Important manuscript.)

11. Vol. 5. Acta, etc. Jan.-Dec., 1848.
Statistics according to " Precurseur " covering the years 1833 to 1847. Letters of Carp, in Rotterdam.
Papers relating to the shipping of grits and rice. Dec., 1847.
Letter of John Suscombe, Persian vice consul, on the case of the emigrant Schröder, etc. Plymouth, Jan. 18, 1848.
Matter relating to Dr. Otto Blumenau, of Braunschweig, and the emigration to Brazil. Nov., 1847.
Papers relating to the Germans in the Orkneys. 1847.
German report, or memorial, summing up the proceedings of the session of the " Germanisten-Versammlung " of Sept. 26, 1846, containing resolution to appoint a commission to find ways and means for preserving German nationality and speech outside of German lands. Accompanying this motion is Professor Franz Lieber's " Schreiben über die Nationalität der Deutschen in den Vereinigten Staaten von Nord-Amerika ".
A bill to make further provision for the carriage of passengers by sea to North America. Feb. 11, 1848. (Print, English.)
Jahresbericht des Direktoriums des Deutschen Volks-Vereins in der Stadt New-York: von Februar, 1847, bis dahin 1848.
Important manuscript copies of ship accounts, etc. Feb., 1848.
An English letter of Francis Fox, etc.

11. Vol. 6. Acta, etc. Jan., 1849-June, 1850.
Prospektus des Central-Vereins für Auswanderung in Köln und Düsseldorf, genehmigt von der hohen Stadts-Regierung unter Zusicherung angemessener Unterstützung der diesseitigen Consuls, so wie des Minister Residenten bei den Vereinigten Staaten von Nord-America (Cologne and Düsseldorf, Sept. 16, 1848).
Die Hoffnung, Concessionierte deutsche Bureaux für Auswanderung nach Amerika von I. M. Bielefeld, in Mannheim, together with ship circular and the *Moniteur Belge* of June 4, 1849.

Manuscript report of the conference of the commission in Berlin, giving the names of those present: Frantz, Schöner, Hellwig, and Puttkammer (chairman). Sept. 4, 1849.
Matter communicated from London relating to Quebec, Canada. Jan. 3, 1850. (English and German.)
Important matter relating to the " Spediteurs ".
Manuscript entitled " Bedingungen, bei Zulassung von Agenten für Ausländer, welche den Transport von Auswanderern mitnehmen ".
Matter relating to the shipping society and enclosing the print entitled *Revidierte Verordnung in Betreff der Verschiffung der über Hamburg direkt nach andern Welttheilen Auswandernden.* June 3, 1850.

11. Vol. 7. Acta, etc. July, 1850–June, 1851.
Matter relating to shipping in Bremen as represented by Consul Delius and the consulate in Havre.
Correspondence of the " Central Verein für Auswanderung ".
Matter relating to the emigration to Costa Rica. July, 1850.
Prospect. Zeitschrift für Auswanderung und Colonisation, Handel und Schiffahrt, herausgegeben vom Berliner Verein zur Colonisation, redigirt von C. P. Schneitler, etc.
Manuscript containing 22 questions relating to Central America.
Matter relating to Chili, enclosing reports of the Deutsche Gesellschaft von New Orleans.
List of ship agents with important letter relating to shipping. Oct. 12, 1850.
Papers relating to the formation of the " Colonisations-Gesellschaft für Central-Amerika ". Dec. 10, 1850.
Bedingungen der Anwerbung, a printed circular with original proof and the revise.
" Nachweisungsbureau für Auswanderer in Bremen." (Manuscript dated 1851.)
Papers relating to Swiss emigration by way of Havre. Apr., 1851.
Abgedrungene Erwiederung auf die in den Beilagen der [Augsburger] *Allgemeinen Zeitung No. 96, 97, u. 98 erschienenen Reiseskizzen aus Havre zur Geschichte der Auswandererleiden.* (Important print.)
" Hamburger Verordnungen " of 1850-1851.

11. Vol. 8. Acta, etc. July, 1851–June, 1852.
Papers relating to emigration by way of Havre.
Instructions to the legations in Brazil, Mexico, New Granada, and the Central American states.
Extracts and questions of Hr. Wr. and answers by Drs. R. and L.
Matter relating to Peru. London, Sept. 17, 1851.
Matter relating to Costa Rica. San José, Feb., 1849.
Erster Bericht des Nachweisungs Burcau in Bremen (1851).
Communications from Gerolt in Washington relating to emigration societies.
Important communication from Dr. Th. A. Tellkampf in New York. Nov. 24, 1851.
" Beantwortung der Fragen über Colonisation in Central-America in 1851 ". (Important manuscript.)

Correspondence of the " Berliner Verein " relating to Brazil. Jan., 1852.
Matter relating to the emigration to Texas.
Bericht der Deutschen Gesellschaft in Maryland (1852).
Auswanderung nach Peru. Circular dated Bremen, Sept., 1851, signed
    by Bödeker.
*Staats-Contract vollzogen von dem General-Commandanten der Marine,
    Don Francisco Forcelledo,* etc. (Print.)
" Bedingungen der Ueberfahrt von Bremen nach Peru, etc."
" An deutsche Auswanderer " [nach Peru].
Copies of the newspaper *Hansa* of Mar. 3, 6, 9, 13, 1852, relating to Peru.
Collection of laws and resolutions of the province of San Pedro do Rio
    Grande do Sul. Oct. 20, 1851. (Portuguese.)

11. Vol. 9. Acta, etc. July, 1852–Dec., 1853.
Reports of Consuls Hebeler in London and Vogel in New Orleans, relat-
    ing to the payment of indemnity " gegen Aushändigung der
    Englischen Pickets ". July 12, 1852, etc.
Matter relating to the emigration to Texas and shipping via Liverpool
    and New Orleans to Galveston and Indianola. Feb., 1852.
Communication of D. H. Klaener, of Galveston. July 17, 1852, and later.
Printed reports of the German Society of Maryland and the German
    Society of New Orleans.
" An Act relating to the Importation of Passengers ", passed by the Gen-
    eral Assembly of Maryland, Dec., 1849.
" Gesetz-Entwurf betreffend die Beförderung von Auswanderern." Jan.,
    1853.
Matter relating to La Guayra, Dec. 8, 1852, with a subscription list headed
    by Harrassowitz.
" Zweiter Bericht des Nachweisungsbureau für Auswanderung in
    Bremen." 1853.
Clippings relating to the " revidierte Verordung in Betreff der Beförde-
    rung von Auswanderung, etc." Apr. 2, 1853.
" Verordnung das heimliche Auswandern von Soldaten und Militär-
    dienstpflichtigen betreffend." Darmstadt, May 23, 1853.

11. Vol. 10. Acta, etc., die Ueberweisung und Leitung der Auswanderungen
    aus Deutschland nach überseeischen Ländern und die Für-
    sorge für die deutschen Ansiedler in Bezug auf Kirchen- und
    Schulwesen, Erhaltung der Nationalität und Sprache, etc.
    Jan.-Oct., 1854.
Letter of Consul Burchardt in Liverpool. May 9, 1854.
" Auswanderung. Dritte Rechnungschaftsbericht des Hamburger Ver-
    eins zum Schutze von Auswanderern, etc." Mar., 1854.
Report of Delius in Bremen.
Letters from many parts of Germany relating to emigration.
Letters from New Braunfels, Texas. May 3, 1853, etc.
Obrigkeitliche Verordnungen of the Senate of Bremen. June 7, 14,
    1854.
Printed notice of the formation of the " Deutsche Katholische Einwan-
    derungs-Gesellschaft ", signed by Clemens Richard, Sec.
    Cincinnati, Feb. 1, 1854.
Papers signed by Pommer Esche.
Copy of *Staats- und Gelehrte Zeitung des Hamburgischen Unparteiischen
    Correspondenten.* June 29, 1854.

Bittburger Intelligenzblatt, No. 68, 1857, containing article entitled "Hauptexpedition für Auswanderer nach America von Carl Maibücher in Köln".
"Auszug aus dem *Wittlicher Intelligenz Blatt*, No. 27, Mar. 29, 1857."

11. Vol. 14. Acta, etc. Mar., 1859–Dec., 1864.
An Act to amend the Law relating to Emigrants. (Print, 1858.)
Papers relating to the Germans in "Hatszel Grune", in Wisconsin. 1857 and 1859.
Catalogue of the shippers authorized by Edward Ichon (manuscript), and printed circular, dated July 15, 1861.
Papers relating to forwarding of emigrants, including a "Beförderungs Schein", dated Jan. 1, 1861.
Gesetz und Verordnung über die Durchreise und weiter Beförderung von Auswandernden. Gratis. Loo, Aug. 1, 1861. (Dutch and German.)
Manuscript list of ships and number of passengers arriving in New York, 1862, enclosing important letter, dated Apr. 17, 1863, relating to emigration.
Matter relating to the emigration to Canada during the progress of the Civil War in the United States and enclosing important papers, such as "Embarcation Form", etc.
Letter addressed to Bismarck Schönhausen, reporting that a shipload of 700 foreigners had arrived in Boston and had been enlisted by the governor of Massachusetts for the Union army, with a number of papers relating thereto. Washington, Aug. 10, 1864.
Matter relating to P. J. Steffen's efforts to secure workmen in Elberfeld for Pennsylvania coal mines, enclosing a printed copy of the *Laws to Encourage Immigration and to regulate the Carrying of Passengers,* Mar. 24, 1860.
Aufruf und Warnung an Auswanderungs-Lustige in Deutschland, issued by the "Komité der deutschen Vereine". Aug. 26, 1864.
Letter of Guido de Grabow to Seward, Secretary of State, Sept. 11, 1864, and Seward's reply, Sept. 16, 1864.

11. Vol. 15. Acta, etc. Jan., 1865–June, 1866.
Weighty correspondence of Eulenburg, Minister of the Interior, Bismarck, Minister of State, and the Ministry of Foreign Affairs, with Gerolt in Washington, relating to the "frivolen Menschenhandel", which is decoying Germans into the American army. These papers and those following give a vivid impression of the situation in America as seen from the German point of view. The following print is enclosed: *Answers of the Governor of Massachusetts to Inquiries Respecting Certain Emigrants who have arrived in this Country from Europe, and who are alleged to be illegally enlisted in the Army of the United States, and other Papers on the same Subject* (Washington, 1864).
Papers relating to the cases of Martin H. Dreier and Jacob Rübel in the matter of their complaint of ill-treatment in the Central Guardhouse of Washington, notably the letter of T. W. Büddecke to Baron Gerolt in Washington. Feb. 21, 1865.

Der von der Königlichen Regierung concessionirte von Hamburger und Bremer Rhedern und Schiffseignern bevollmächtigte Hauptagent H. C. Platzmann expedirt vermittels seines Auswanderer- und ueberseeischen Geschäfts-Comtoirs zu Berlin, etc. (Printed circular. 1854.)

11. Vol. 11. Acta, etc. Nov., 1854–Apr., 1855.
Papers relating to Texas and New Orleans.
" Procès verbal d'expertise ", a French list of provisions from Antwerp to New York.
" Emigrant Eisenbahn-Passage-Billet No. 63, Berlin, 28 September, 1854." (Messrs. Rischmueller and Loescher in New York.)
Matter relating to shipping offices in New York, New Orleans, Baltimore, Philadelphia, St. Louis, and Quebec.
Matter relating to the emigration from Hamburg, Bremen, Oldenburg, etc.
" Entwurf eines Staatsvertrages zur Regelung des Auswanderungswesens ", enclosing reports.
" Uebereinkunft zwischen dem Grossherzogthum Hessen, den Königreichen Preussen, Bayern u. Württemberg, dem Grossherzogthum Baden, dem Kurfürstenthum Hessen, dem Grossherzogthum Oldenburg, dem Herzogthum Nassau, dem Landgrafenthum Hessen-Homburg und der freien Stadt Frankfurt, Massregeln zur Verhütung heimlicher Auswanderung betreffend."

11. Vol. 12. Acta, etc. May, 1855–Feb., 1856.
Report of ships sailing to America in 1854 and other important matter connected therewith.
Letter of Bloomfield to Baron Manteuffel with confidential memorandum. Berlin, Apr. 30, 1855.
" Verordnungen in Betreff des Auswandererwesens." (Hamburger Rath, Versammlung of Apr. 30, 1855.)
A printed copy of *Königlich Preussischer Reise-Pass für das Ausland*, with names filled in.
Paper issued by the consul general in New York.
" Ueberfahrts-Vertrag der Haupt-Agentur von Heinr. Jos. Maasen und Co. in Cöln, 25 April, 1855."
Copy of *Allgem. Auswanderungs-Zeitung Rudolstadt* of Aug. 20, 24, 1855, containing the following article : " Einwanderung, die Quelle nationaler Grösse ".
Communication of Gessler in Stuttgart, containing an important résumé. Aug. 13, 1855.
" Auszug aus dem politischen Bericht No. 1, vom 13ten Jan. 1856 ", relating to Panama, etc.

11. Vol. 13. Acta, etc. Mar., 1856-Feb., 1859. Continuation of matter in preceding volume.
" Schiffs-Accord " of Joseph Stöck in Kreuznach, etc., referring to the " Reglement " of Sept. 6, 1853.
Erster Jahresbericht über die Wirksamkeit des Nachweisungs-Bureau der Auswanderer Behörde in Hamburg während des Zeitraums vom 1. Mai bis 31 December 1855.

Papers relating to the ship, *Wm. Nelson,* 1865.
Papers relating to the contract of M. D. Ross, of Boston, Mass., and Julian Allen, of New York, in the matter of filling the quota of 300,000 volunteers.

11. Vol. 16. Acta, etc. July, 1866–Mar., 1868.

Correspondence between Gerolt and Bismarck relating to the aims and tendencies of the newly founded society, "Die Deutsche National-Gesellschaft zum Schutze der Einwanderer, Egg Harbor City, New Jersey", enclosing letter from the president of the society, and the following printed circular relating to emigrants traversing Great Britain: *Avis aux Émigrants Français traversant la Grande Bretagne* (in four languages).

Papers relating to labor conditions in New York, notably one treating of the Tischler Verein, dated Mar. 5, 1867.

Clippings from the *Auswanderer Zeitung* of Bremen, Mar. 25, 1867, and the *New Yorker Handels Zeitung,* Aug. 1, 1867, containing an article entitled " Unmenschliche Behandlung deutscher Einwanderer ".

Matter relating to the treatment of German immigrants by the Grand Trunk Railroad in Canada. July 15, 1867.

Warning to the German Society of New York. Mar. 4, 1866. (Print.)

List of rations for voyagers dated Brussels, Apr. 26, 1855, and other matter relating to the shipping of passengers, dated 1867.

Matter relating to Strauss, agent in Antwerp, and to the ship *Giuseppe Baccarcici* and the case of Caspar Graff, with report of the Board of Commissioners of Emigration.

" Preussen in Bezug auf die Auswanderung nach Brasilien, etc."

Matter relating to the treatment of passengers on board the ship *Wilberforce,* enclosing a letter from the government Immigration Office in Quebec, Nov. 9, 1867.

Report of Messrs. Kapp and Bissinger to the Board of Commissioners of Emigration referring to the ship *Leibnitz.* New York, 1868.

" Mittheilung des Senats an die Bürgerschaft." Hamburg, Mar. 9, 1868.

11. Vol. 17. Acta, etc. Apr., 1868–Dec., 1869.

" Bericht des Ausschusses zur Prüfung des dringlichen Antrages des Senats (No. 22) wegen eines Nachtrages zu den Verordnungen in Betreff des Auswandererwesens 1868 ", enclosing among other things a manuscript relating to the " Schauerliche Behandlung deutscher Einwanderer über Quebec ", Aug. 25, 1867.

Matter relating to the ship *Leibnitz,* enclosing a clipping relating to " Die ungeschützten Deutschen ". Dec. 12, 1868.

Reference to the steamer *Cella.* Also a number of clippings.

11. Vol. 18. Acta, etc. Jan., 1870–Oct., 1872.

Matter relating to the shipping of Germans by water and by rail.

Letter of Civil Engineer Heinrich Carl Schmidt of Independence, Washington County, Texas, to Bismarck, asking for a place as commissioner and trade agent to regulate the emigration to America. Interesting clippings enclosed.

Circular relating to Panama.

11. **Vol. 19.** Acta, etc. Nov., 1872–Dec., 1873.
Matter relating to the ship *Wangerland* with important clippings, passenger contracts and the like.
Petition or protest of passengers, dated "Atlandischer Ocean, Apr. 23, 1873", with many signatures relating to bad treatment on the *Columbia*. (Interesting for signatures.)
Correspondence of the North German Lloyd with list of officers and agents. 1873.

11. **Vol. 20.** Acta, etc. Jan., 1874–Dec., 1875.
Much matter relating to emigration via Bremen. Statistics, reports, clippings, and the like.
Correspondence with London office relating to the shipping act and to the case of Johann Ristau and August Julius Becker and their bill of exchange on Kummer and Becker in Baltimore.

18. Acta betr. die Ueberwachung der Auswanderung aus Deutschland nach der Westküste von America. Oct., 1852–Aug., 1863. (Intus: Chile, Peru; cf. Ausw. auss. Europa, 17, 45, and 46.)
Letter of Julie Hasskarl in the commission of her husband. Düsseldorf, Aug. 3, 1853.
Important document containing regulations of Peru to facilitate the settlement of the Amazonas region, signed by José Rufino Echenique and José Manuel Firado. Apr. 15, 1853.
Papers relating to the ship *Norton* sailing from Antwerp with 300 German emigrants for Callao. Apr. 14, 1857.
Papers relating to the German settlement in Valdivia. Jan. 22, 1862.
Letter of Theodor Müller to Bismarck, Lima, May 27, 1863, enclosing copies of documents relating to the perils of shipping to the Canacas [Islands], including a document from Christopher Robinson, special envoy of the United States, and clippings from Lima newspapers.

19. **Vol. 1.** Acta betr. Ueberwachung der Auswanderung aus Deutschland nach den V. St. von America. Nov., 1852–Dec., 1866.
Papers relating to the laws and regulations of the United States concerning immigrants and including reports from consuls describing the conditions of emigrants in America, particularly in Texas, and clippings from the *Galveston-Zeitung* of Feb. 6, 1852, from the *National Intelligencer* of Washington, Sept. 9, 1852, and an ordinance for the improvement of the harbor opposite the southern part of the city of St. Louis, Apr. 29, 1850.
Verfassung und Neben-Gesetze des Deutsch-Texanischen Freundschaftsbundes in Galveston, Texas (1848, gedruckt in Ch. Büchners Galveston Zeitung Office).
Jahresbericht der Deutschen Gesellschaft (St. Louis) vom 1. März 1851.
Annual Meeting of the German Society (St. Louis). 1852 and 1855.
Reports of the German Society of New Orleans and of the German Society of New-York.
Correspondence between von Grabow and Fernando Wood, mayor of New-York, relating to the entrance of immigrants.
Memorial of the "Emigrations-Commision" of New-York. Nov., 1855. (German print.)

Papers relating to the arrival of immigrants in the United States including circular from the Department of State at Washington.
"Die Gefahren des Contrahierens in Europa für Inland-Reisen in Amerika", signed by 6 foreign consuls. New York, Feb. 2, 1852.
Circular Nr. 1, new series, in Relation to the Purchase of Public Lands, etc. (Washington, 1855).
Clippings from the *New-Yorker Staatszeitung* of 1866 and letter from New Orleans dated Jan. 18, 1866.

19. Vol. 2. Acta betr., etc. Jan., 1867–Aug., 1870.
Clipping from the *Georgia Weekly Telegraph*, Sept., 1866; article by Germanicus (Col. Frankschaller).
Important letters from Gerolt in Washington. 1867.
Letters from H. F. Wellinghoff to A. Schumacher, Präsident der D. Gesellschaft von Maryland, on the settlement of German immigrants. Baltimore, Feb. 2, 1867. (German.)
Broadside placard of the regulations in Castle Garden. (German.)
Papers relating to individual immigrants, requests for information concerning the commission of emigration, etc.

19. Vol. 3. Acta, etc. Apr., 1871–May, 1875.
Papers relating to complaints of Christian Rust against the Pennsylvania Central Rail Road. June, 1869.
Papers relating to the admission of immigrants and to individual Germans brought to the notice of the consuls.
Unfavorable report of H. Clausenius in Chicago on the climatic conditions of the settlement Saxonia in Schoolcraft Co., Michigan. 1873.
Papers relating to "Nativismus", with clippings from the *New Yorker Staatszeitung* of Apr. 7, 1874, containing an article entitled: "Die gestrige Massen-Versammlung der Deutschen; Eine grossartige Demonstration gegen den Nativismus".
C. Tholen of Leavenworth, Kansas, to Bismarck, complaining of the ungrateful attitude of the liberated negroes toward the Germans. Sept. 26, 1874.
Fred. Hess to Friedrich Kapp in Berlin, inquiring into the report published in a Chicago German paper, that the princes Putbus and Lichnowski, the dukes of Ratibor and Sagan, Count Radziwill and others had formed a society with the special purpose of encouraging a systematic return of German Americans to their Vaterland. Fort Dodge, Iowa, Mar. 4, 1875.
Hess to Bismarck with clipping. Mar. 5, 1875.
Papers relating to the importation of aliens. 1875.

19. Vol. 4. Acta, etc., vom June, 1875–Aug., 1877.
Papers relating to the immigration laws and test cases.
Report of shipping with Hamburg, etc., enclosing many miscellaneous communications from the consuls, such as statistics of German immigrants, etc.

19. Vol. 5. Acta, etc. Oct., 1877–Oct., 1879.
"Bericht über die Thätigkeit des Reichskommissars zur Ueberwachung des Auswandererwesens während des Jahres 1877."
Matter relating to Gottlob Friedrich Spahrmann. 1879.

ABTEILUNG III. REP. 8. INTERCESSIONEN.

1. Vol. I. Acta des Ministeriums der auswärtigen Angelegenheiten betr. die Beschaffung von Geburts und Todtenscheinen und von Civil-Personen aus den Amerikanischen Staaten für Preussische Unterthanen. Mar., 1829–Nov., 1847. Very miscellaneous aggregations of papers relating to Germans in many parts of America both North and South, to efforts to obtain property, family data, and the like—a rich source for German genealogy.
1. Vol. II. Acta, etc. Jan., 1848–Dec., 1851. Matter similar to that of the preceding volume.
Papers relating to Heinrich Lütkens (alias Hermann Ross), who died on board ship near Philadelphia.
Death of Friedrich Wilhelm Gerfen, tailor in Columbia, Lancaster Co., Penn., and of the weaver Ludwig Meyer, who was drowned near Albany, N. Y.
Many other official documents directed by the consuls or consul general or the Department of the Interior to the Minister of Foreign Affairs, with the official replies.
1. Vol. III. Acta, etc. Jan., 1852–Dec., 1853. Continuation of vol. II. Correspondence between Gerolt in Washington and the Foreign Office and others, representing official affairs in America. Among the papers are many relating to individuals.
1. Vol. IV. Acta, etc. Jan., 1854–Mar., 1855. Continuation of the same kind of papers.
1. Vol. V. Acta, etc. Apr.-Dec., 1855. Continuation of similar papers, including an interesting document entitled " Den Todtenschein des Paul von Eckartsberg betr."
1. Vol. VI. Acta, etc. Jan.-Sept., 1856. Continuation of similar material, including an interesting case: " Den Todtenschein des Georg Karp betreffend ".
1. Vol. VII. Acta, etc. Oct., 1856–Sept., 1857. Similar to the foregoing volumes.
1. Vol. VIII. Acta, etc. Oct., 1857–Aug., 1858. The same kind of matter as in the foregoing.
This series continues to volume LXIX., coming down to the year 1883. The contents are indicated by the brief analysis of the first eight volumes given above. The series contains much material valuable to the genealogist.
5. Vol. I. Acta des Ministeriums der Auswärtigen Angelegenheiten betr. die Nachlassregulirungen verschiedener im Kriege der V. St. v. America gegen Mexico verstorbener Personen aus Preussen und anderen deutschen Staaten. Dec., 1854–Dec., 1857. Contains a list of 50 names as an index in the beginning of the volume and also a list of 22 names furnished by the Prussian consul general Schmidt of New York, Nov. 3, 1854. The letter of the consul general mentions the settlement and payment of estates as a chief occasion for such papers.
5. Vol. II. Acta, etc., betr. die Nachlassregulirungen verschiedener im Kriegsdienst der V. St. v. America verstorbener Personen aus Preussen und anderen deutschen Staaten; desgleichen, die Pensionszahlung an deren Witwen und Waisen. Jan., 1858–

Dec., 1859. In the beginning of the volume is an index of 41 names. A good specimen of these papers relating to a similar case is the group referring to Johanne Wilhelmine Elisabeth Peters, numbered III 4762 pr. Mar. 22, 1859. 17 pages of text in all.

5. Vol. III. Acta, betr., etc. [the title is in the main the same as in vol. I.] Jan., 1860–Dec., 1861. Index list of 31 names.
5. Vol. IV. Acta, etc. Jan., 1862–Apr., 1863. Index list of 40 names, repeated in part from the preceding.
5. Vol. V. Acta, etc. May-Nov., 1863. Index list of 52 names, of which the following is the first example: Betrifft das Gesuch des Johann Oster zu Nauenheim im Kreise Mayen, um Auszahlung seiner Nordamerikanischen Militair-Pension durch die Preussischen Behörden ohne Vermittelung des Nordamerikanischen Consuls zu Frankfurt a./M., and inclosing rescript no. 16336 of Nov. 29, 1862.
5. Vol. VI. Acta, etc. Dec., 1863–Apr., 1864. Index list of 52 names. Similarly, the ensuing volumes have index lists of from 25 to 100 names.
5. Vol. VII. Acta, etc. May, 1863–Sept., 1864.
5. Vol. VIII. Acta, etc. Oct., 1864–Feb., 1865.
5. Vol. IX. Acta, etc. Mar.-June, 1865.
5. Vol. X. Acta, etc. July-Sept., 1865.
5. Vol. XI. Acta, etc. Oct.-Nov., 1865.
5. Vol. XII. Acta, etc. Dec., 1865–Jan., 1866.
5. Vol. XIII. Acta, etc. Feb.-Mar., 1866.
5. Vol. XIV. Acta, etc. Apr.-May, 1866.
5. Vol. XV. Acta, etc. June-Aug., 1866.
5. Vol. XVI. Acta, etc. Sept.–Nov. 8, 1866.
5. Vol. XVII. Acta, etc. Nov.-Dec., 1866.
5. Vol. XVIII. Acta, etc. Jan.–Feb. 14, 1867.
5. Vol. XIX. Acta, etc. Feb. 15–Apr., 1867.
5. Vol. XX. Acta, etc. May-June, 1867.
5. Vol. XXI. Acta, etc. July-Aug., 1867.
5. Vol. XXII. Acta, etc. Sept.–Nov. 14, 1867.
5. Vol. XXIII. Acta, etc. Nov. 15, 1867–Jan., 1868.
5. Vol. XXIV. Acta, etc. Feb.–Mar. 8, 1868.
5. Vol. XXV. Acta, etc. Mar. 9–Apr. 3, 1868.
5. Vol. XXVI. Acta, etc. Apr. 4–May 15, 1868.
5. Vol. XXVII. Acta, etc. May 10–July 9, 1868.
5. Vol. XXVIII. Acta, etc. July 10–Sept. 19, 1868.
5. Vol. XXIX. Acta, etc. Sept. 20–Oct., 1868.
5. Vol. XXX. Acta, etc. Nov. 1-30, 1868.
5. Vol. XXXI. Acta, etc. Dec., 1868–Jan., 1869.
5. Vol. XXXII. Acta, etc. Feb.–Mar. 15, 1869.
5. Vol. XXXIII. Acta, etc. Mar. 16–Apr. 14, 1869.
5. Vol. XXXIV. Acta, etc. Apr. 15–May 22, 1869.
5. Vol. XXXV. Acta, etc. May 23–June 30, 1869.
5. Vol. XXXVI. Acta, etc. July 6–Aug., 1869.
5. Vol. XXXVII. Acta, etc. Sept.-Oct., 1869.
5. Vol. XXXVIII. Acta, etc. Nov.–Dec. 15, 1869.
5. Vol. XXXIX. Acta, etc. Dec. 16, 1869–Feb. 10, 1870.

5. Vol. XL. Acta, etc. Feb. 11–Mar., 1870.
5. Vol. XLI. Acta, etc. Apr.–May 14, 1870.
5. Vol. XLII. Acta, etc. May 15–June, 1870.
5. Vol. XLIII. Acta, etc. July–Aug., 1870.
5. Vol. XLIV. Acta, etc. Sept.–Oct., 1870.
5. Vol. XLV. Acta, etc. Nov.–Dec., 1870.
5. Vol. XLVI. Acta, etc. Jan.–Mar., 1871.
5. Vol. XLVII. Acta, etc. Mar. 9–May 14, 1871.
5. Vol. XLVIII. Acta, etc. May 15–July 15, 1871.
5. Vol. XLIX. Acta, etc. July 16–Sept., 1871.
5. Vol. L. Acta, etc. Oct.–Nov., 1871.
5. Vol. LI. Acta, etc. Dec., 1871–Jan. 19, 1872.
5. Vol. LII. Acta, etc. Jan. 20–Mar. 23, 1872.
5. Vol. LIII. Acta, etc. Mar. 24–May 11, 1872.
5. Vol. LIV. Acta, etc. May 12–July 12, 1872.
5. Vol. LV. Acta, etc. July 13–Sept., 1872.
5. Vol. LVI. Acta, etc. Oct.–Dec. 11, 1872.
5. Vol. LVII. Acta, etc. Dec. 12, 1872–Feb. 12, 1873.
5. Vol. LVIII. Acta, etc. Feb. 13–Apr., 1873.
5. Vol. LIX. Acta, etc. (After "Verstorbener" follows: "Deutscher Unterthanen".) May–July, 1873. Two papers relating to Wilhelm von Steuben (correspondence between the German minister in Brazil and the Foreign Office in Berlin.)
5. Vol. LX. Acta, etc. Aug.–Oct., 1873.
5. Vol. LXI. Acta, etc. Nov., 1873–Jan., 1874.
5. Vol. LXII. Acta, etc. Feb.–Apr., 1874.
5. Vol. LXIII. Acta, etc. May–July 14, 1874.
5. Vol. LXIV. Acta, etc. July 15–Oct. 18, 1874.
5. Vol. LXV. Acta, etc. Oct. 19, 1874–Jan. 12, 1875.
5. Vol. LXVI. Acta, etc. Jan. 13–May 15, 1875.
5. Vol. LXVII. Acta, etc. May 16–Aug., 1875.
5. Vol. LXVIII. Acta, etc. Sept.–Dec. 12, 1875.
5. Vol. LXIX. Acta, etc. Dec. 14, 1875–Mar., 1876.
5. Vol. LXX. Acta, etc. Apr.–June 1876.
5. Vol. LXXI. Acta, etc. July–Oct., 1876.
5. Vol. LXXII. Acta, etc. Nov., 1876–Jan., 1877.
5. Vol. LXXIII. Acta, etc. Feb.–Apr., 1877.
5. Vol. LXXIV. Acta, etc. May–June, 1877.
5. Vol. LXXV. Acta, etc. July–Aug., 1877.
5. Vol. LXXVI. Acta, etc. Sept.–Nov., 1877.
5. Vol. LXXVII. Acta, etc. Dec., 1877–Feb. 25, 1878.
5. Vol. LXXVIII. Acta, etc. Feb. 26–Apr., 1878.
5. Vol. LXXIX. Acta, etc. May–July 15, 1878.
5. Vol. LXXX. Acta, etc. July 16–Oct., 1878.
5. Vol. LXXXI. Acta, etc. Nov., 1878–Jan., 1879.
5. Vol. LXXXII. Acta, etc. Feb.–Apr. 12, 1879.
5. Vol. LXXXIII. Acta, etc. Apr. 16–July, 1879.
5. Vol. LXXXIV. Acta, etc. Aug.–Oct. 30, 1879.
5. Vol. LXXXV. Acta, etc. Nov., 1879–Mar., 1880.
5. Vol. LXXXVI. Acta, etc. Apr.–Aug., 1880.
5. Vol. LXXXVII. Acta, etc. Sept., 1880–Jan., 1881.
5. Vol. LXXXVIII. Acta, etc. Feb.–July, 1881.
5. Vol. LXXXIX. Acta, etc. Aug.–Dec., 1881.

ABTEILUNG III. REP. 10. JUSTIZ, VEREINIGTE STAATEN.

1. Acta des Ministeriums der auswärtigen Angelegenheiten betr. die von dem Nordamerikanischen General Consul Saabye zu Copenhagen nachgesuchte Auslieferung des zu Danzig eingezogenen Matrosen Stromski. (Beginning with a letter dated Copenhagen, Feb. 22, 1817.)
3. Vol. I. Acta des Ministeriums der auswärtigen Angelegenheiten betr. die Verhältnisse mit den Nordamerikanischen Freistaaten wegen gegenseitiger Auslieferung der Verbrecher. Mar., 1835–Dec., 1844.

The first case is that of Emil Römer, a clerk of the brothers Heucken in Aachen, for theft of 10,000 fl. The first document is dated from the post office in Aachen, Feb. 27, 1835.

An interesting caricature in colors entitled "Executive Mercy and the Bambers" (New York, H. R. Robinson; with German explanation of the cut).

The remaining and larger part of the volume is given up to the Römer case.

4. Vol. I. Acta des Ministeriums der auswärtigen Angelegenheiten betr. die Verhältnisse mit den Nordamerikanischen Freistaaten (in some volumes, "mit den Vereinigten Staaten von Nord-America") in Justizangelegenheiten, Eidesabnahme, etc. Nov., 1835–Nov., 1847. Among the papers are a large number relating to Salomon Wittgenstein's oath and his law suit with the Ebeling heirs in Paderborn (1838).
4. Vol. II. Acta, etc. Jan., 1848–Dec., 1850. Miscellaneous matter relating to law suits, etc.
4. Vol. III. Acta, etc. Jan., 1851–Dec., 1853.
4. Vol. IV. Acta, etc. Jan., 1853–June, 1854.
4. Vol. V. Acta, etc. July, 1854–June, 1855.
4. Vol. VI. Acta, etc. July, 1855–June, 1856.
4. Vol. VII. Acta, etc. July, 1856–June, 1857.
4. Vol. VIII. Acta, etc. July, 1857–June, 1858.
4. Vol. IX. Acta, etc. July, 1858–Mar., 1859.
4. Vol. X. Acta, etc. Apr.-Dec., 1859.
4. Vol. XI. Acta, etc. Jan.-Sept., 1860.
4. Vol. XII. Acta, etc. Oct., 1860–May, 1861.
4. Vol. XIII. Acta, etc. June, 1861–Feb., 1862.
4. Vol. XIV. Acta, etc. Mar.-Dec., 1862.
4. Vol. XV. Acta, etc. Jan.-Dec., 1863.
4. Vol. XVI. Acta, etc. Jan.-Dec., 1864.
4. Vol. XVII. Acta, etc. Jan.-Dec., 1865.
4. Vol. XVIII. Acta, etc. Jan.-Sept., 1866.
4. Vol. XIX. Acta, etc. Oct., 1866–July, 1867.
4. Vol. XX. Acta, etc. Aug., 1867–May, 1868.
4. Vol. XXI. Acta, etc. June-Nov., 1868.
4. Vol. XXII. Acta, etc. Dec., 1868–June, 1869.
4. Vol. XXIII. Acta, etc. July, 1869–Mar., 1870.
4. Vol. XXIV. Acta, etc. Apr.-Sept., 1870.
4. Vol. XXV. Acta, etc. Oct., 1870–Mar., 1871.
4. Vol. XXVI. Acta, etc. Apr.-Aug., 1871.
4. Vol. XXVII. Acta, etc. Sept., 1871–Feb., 1872.

4. Vol. XXVIII. Acta, etc. Mar.-Sept., 1872.
4. Vol. XXIX. Acta, etc. Oct., 1872-Feb., 1873.
4. Vol. XXX. Acta, etc. Mar.-Sept., 1873.
4. Vol. XXXI. Acta, etc. Oct., 1873-Feb., 1874.
4. Vol. XXXII. Acta, etc. Mar.-June 9, 1874.
4. Vol. XXXIII. Acta, etc. June 10-Sept., 1874.
4. Vol. XXXIV. Acta, etc. Oct.-Dec., 1874.
4. Vol. XXXV. Acta, etc. Jan.-Apr. 15, 1875.
4. Vol. XXXVI. Acta, etc. Apr. 16-July 15, 1875.
4. Vol. XXXVII. Acta, etc. July 19-Oct., 1875.
4. Vol. XXXVIII. Acta, etc. Nov., 1875-Jan., 1876.
4. Vol. XXXIX. Acta, etc. Feb.-May, 1876.
4. Vol. XL. Acta, etc. June-Aug., 1876.
4. Vol. XLI. Acta, etc. Sept.-Nov., 1876.
4. Vol. XLII. Acta, etc. Dec., 1876-Feb., 1877.
4. Vol. XLIII. Acta, etc. Mar.-Apr., 1877.
4. Vol. XLIV. Acta, etc. May-June, 1877.
4. Vol. XLV. Acta, etc. July-Aug., 1877.
4. Vol. XLVI. Acta, etc. Sept.-Oct. 15, 1877.
4. Vol. XLVII. Acta, etc. Oct. 16-Dec. 13, 1877.
4. Vol. XLVIII. Acta, etc. Dec. 14, 1877-Jan. 31, 1878.
4. Vol. XLIX. Acta, etc. Feb.-Mar. 20, 1878.
4. Vol. L. Acta, etc. Mar. 22-May 9, 1878.
4. Vol. LI. Acta, etc. May 10-June 30, 1878.
4. Vol. LII. Acta, etc. July 1-Aug. 22, 1878.
4. Vol. LIII. Acta, etc. Aug. 23-Oct. 7, 1878.
4. Vol. LIV. Acta, etc. Oct. 10-Nov., 1878.
4. Vol. LV. Acta, etc. Dec., 1878-Jan. 25, 1879.
4. Vol. LVI. Acta, etc. Jan. 26-Mar., 1879.
4. Vol. LVII. Acta, etc. Apr.-May 23, 1879.
4. Vol. LVIII. Acta, etc. May 24-July 21, 1879.
4. Vol. LIX. Acta, etc. July 22-Sept. 30, 1879.
4. Vol. LX. Acta, etc. Oct.-Nov., 1879.
4. Vol. LXI. Acta, etc. Dec. 1, 1879-Jan. 31, 1880.
4. Vol. LXII. Acta, etc. Feb.-Mar., 1880.
4. Vol. LXIII. Acta, etc. Apr.-May, 1880.
4. Vol. LXIV. Acta, etc. June-Aug., 1880.
4. Vol. LXV. Acta, etc. Sept.-Oct., 1880.
4. Vol. LXVI. Acta, etc. Nov.-Dec., 1880.
4. Vol. LXVII. Acta, etc. Jan.-Mar., 1881.
4. Vol. LXVIII. Acta, etc. Apr.-May, 1881.
4. Vol. LXIX. Acta, etc. June-Aug. 12, 1881.
4. Vol. LXX. Acta, etc. Aug. 13-Oct. 27, 1881.
4. Vol. LXXI. Acta, etc. Oct. 29, 1881-Jan., 1882.
4. Vol. LXXII. Acta, etc. Feb.-Apr. 24, 1882.
4. Vol. LXXIII. Acta, etc. Apr. 25-June, 1882.
4. Vol. LXXIV. Acta, etc. July-Sept. 12, 1882.
4. Vol. LXXV. Acta, etc. Sept. 13-Nov., 1882.
4. Vol. LXXVI. Acta, etc. Dec., 1882-Feb., 1883.
4. Vol. LXXVII. Acta, etc. Feb. 8-Mar., 1883.
4. Vol. LXXVIII. Acta, etc. Apr.-May, 1883.
4. Vol. LXXIX. Acta, etc. June-July, 1883.

Vol. LXXX. Acta, etc. Aug.–Sept. 10, 1883.
Vol. LXXXI. Acta, etc. Sept. 11–Nov., 1883.
Vol. LXXXII. Acta, etc. Dec., 1883–Jan. 17, 1884.
Vol. LXXXIII. Acta, etc. Jan. 18–Feb., 1884.
Vol. LXXXIV. Acta, etc. Mar.–Apr. 19, 1884.
Vol. LXXXV. Acta, etc. Apr. 23–May, 1884.
Vol. LXXXVI. Acta, etc. June–July, 1884.
Vol. LXXXVII. Acta, etc. Aug.–Oct. 15, 1884.
Vol. LXXXVIII. Acta, etc. Oct. 16–Dec., 1884.
Vol. LXXXIX. Acta, etc. Jan.–Feb., 1885.
Vol. XC. Acta, etc. Mar.–Apr., 1885.
Vol. XCI. Acta, etc. May–June 20, 1885.
Vol. XCII. Acta, etc. June 22–Aug. 31, 1885.
Vol. XCIII. Acta, etc. Sept.–Oct., 1885.
Vol. XCIV. Acta, etc. Nov.–Dec., 1885.

ABTEILUNG III. REP. 14. NACHRICHTEN AUSSER EUROPA.

1. Vol. I. Acta des Ministeriums der auswärtigen Angelegenheiten betr. die verschiedenen Berichte und Nachrichten des Preussischen Gesandtschaftsträgers und General Consuls bei den Nordamerikanischen Freistaaten zu Philadelphia über Gewerbe, Handels- und andere Gegenstände. Oct., 1825–Dec., 1827.

Official letters of von Schuckmann of the Ministry of the Interior to von Bernsdorff of the Prussian cabinet.

Letters of von Bülow to Niederstetter in Philadelphia treating of the condition of manufacture in the United States, with special reference to New England, the manufacture of flour in America, the Erie Canal which was just finished, etc.

Letters of Niederstetter reporting practically everything of interest to the Germans in the progress of American arts and invention, such as Brewster's vertical spinning frame, Oliver Evans's work on construction of mills, transactions of the Franklin Institute, Aug. Day's stove which analyzes water, etc.

Clippings from American newspapers.

Notice of treaties such as " Of- und Defensiv Allianz-Vertrag zwischen Columbien und Mexico ".

Letters relating to the military conditions of America with reference to Harrison's general position, showing our importance at that time for the evolution of military affairs in Germany.

Letters of Gilbert Brewster proposing to set up machines in Prussia, leaving it to the Prussian government to fix the compensation.

Letter of Niederstetter, May 15, 1826, relating to Cuba.

Other letters, illustrating the influence of American inventions and discoveries upon German arts and science.

1. Vol. II. Acta, etc. Jan., 1828–Dec., 1834.

A great variety of papers relating to the ever growing export of German manufactures to America and the persistent study of American conditions on the part of the Germans.

Papers relating to American finance, with much correspondence and numerous reports.

Matter relating to exploration of the South Seas. Mar., 1828.
Decision of the King of the Netherlands in the boundary dispute between New Brunswick and the United States. July 26, 1832 [Jan. 10, 1831].
Discussion of the situation in Mexico. 1834.
Other papers, relating to the coinage of money, shipping, etc., 1834.
1. Vol. III. Acta, etc. Jan., 1835–Dec., 1838.
Correspondence between von Rönne and the Foreign Office in Berlin and other papers relating to shipping.
Papers relating to the American revenue surplus, " a thing unknown in Europe ".
" Demetz et Blouet sur les penetantiers [pénitenciers] américains " and correspondence of the Minister of the Interior in Paris with the Prussian Minister of Foreign Affairs. Paris, Sept. 29, 1837.
Important correspondence of Gustav Gossler in Boston, and of von Rönne relating to shipping.
1. Vol. IV. Acta, etc., die verschiedenen Berichte und Nachrichten des Preussischen Residenten und der Consuln in den Vereinigten Staaten von America über Handel, Gewerbe, etc. Jan., 1839–July, 1843.
Correspondence of von Rönne relating to American trade conditions.
Matter relating to the outbreak of the Mexican War.
Matter relating to the United States Treasury Bill of 1840.
Matter relating to the Oregon Territory, its occupation and exploration. 1842.
1. Vol. V. Acta, etc. Feb., 1844–Dec., 1846.
Consular reports from Baltimore, Philadelphia, Boston, Charleston, and New Orleans, with matter relating thereto.
Report of F. L. Braun of Baltimore, giving an important summary of the shipping to foreign ports. Jan., 1845.
Reports of Gerolt, Jan., 1845, of Nagel from New Orleans, of Schmidt from New York, the general character of which can be described in Gerolt's words: " Uebersendung von verschiedenen Dokumenten in Bezug auf die Politik, Verwaltung, Finanzen, Handel, Industrie, Agrikultur, Geographie, Statistik, neue Erfindungen, etc., der Vereinigten Staaten, nebst einer Sammlung von verschiedenen Saamen ".
1. Vol. VI. Acta, etc. (the title is slightly changed in this volume). Feb., 1847–Sept., 1849.
Matter relating to shipping and trade, enclosing reports and lists of imports and shipping in general to New York harbor. 1846.
Much printed matter accompanying these reports.
1. Vol. VII. Acta, etc. Feb., 1850–Dec., 1852.
Consists largely of reports, printed matter, and correspondence relating to questions affecting Germany, such as land titles in California and the like.
Mention of Professor A. D. Bache's correction of hydrographic errors near the harbor of San Francisco (1851); Dr. Page's experiments in electro-magnetic locomotives.
Important statistics of exports and imports.

A large envelope of papers, reports, and clippings relating to Prussian ships landing in New York harbor. 1851.
Important account of California sent to Gerolt from San Francisco. Feb., 1852.
1. Vol. VIII. Acta, etc. Jan., 1853–Oct., 1854.
Much matter relating to steam shipping, with reference to the caloric engine of Ericsson, etc. 1853.
List of documents sent to the Foreign Office in Berlin, relating to the Peale and other patents. Feb., 1853.
Interesting papers and letters relating to the Central West, the tobacco market of Cincinnati, the trade with New Orleans, etc.
A Review of the Trade and Commerce of Cincinnati, by Richard Smith (1852).
Matter relating to the commerce of St. Louis.
1. Vol. IX. Acta, etc. Nov., 1854–Aug., 1858. Continuation of similar matter.
1. Vol. X. Acta, etc. Feb., 1859–Dec., 1862. (There is a gap in the papers from Sept., 1858, to Jan., 1859.)
1. Vol. XI. Acta, etc. Jan., 1863–June, 1866.
1. Vol. XII. Acta, etc. Aug., 1866–Dec., 1868. (The papers seem not to tally exactly with the labels on the volumes.)
1. Vol. XIII. Acta, etc. June, 1874–Jan., 1880. (In red ink: " Die Akten sind geschlossen. Forts. in den Akten Volkswirtschaft V. St. v. N. America ".)
5. Vol. —. Nachrichten ausser Europa vom Novbr., 1833.
One small separate fascicle containing a report of Schmidt in New York. 1833.

Ministerium des Innern.

Archiv I. B. des Ministerii des Innern.
Acta betr. die Thüringische Auswanderungsgesellschaft. July 7, 1832.
Contains among other things:
Copy of the *Intelligenz-Blatt für den Bezirk des Königlichen Oberlandesgerichts von Sachsen*. May 16, 1832.
Letter to Tzschoppe and Tzschoppe's reply.
Correspondence between the police and the Oberpräsidium in Magdeburg.
Communication of the Ober Regierungsrath and the Ministerium des Innern.

Rep. 77. Tit. CCXXVI.
68. Vol. 1. Acta die von den Regierungen eingereichten Uebersichten von den stattgehabten Auswanderungen betr., sowie die Nachrichten des statistischen Büreaus über die stattgehabten Ein- und Auswanderungen. (*Conf.* Acta no. 108, vol. 10.) Oct. 25, 1817–Dec. 6, 1855. Official papers relating to emigration including valuable lists of names, such as the following:
Nachweisung der in der Königlichen Regierungs Bezirk von Coblenz während dem 3ten Quartal des Jahres 1817 ertheilten Auswanderungs-Erlaubnisse.
Statistical tables giving numbers of emigrants from the various districts.

Occasional lists of names, as for example, for the year 1852, with the formula used in other states: Name | Stand | Letzter Wohnort | Zahl d. Angehörigen | Vermögen | Gegend.
108. Vol. 10. Acta betr. die Bildung von Vereinen zur Leitung der Auswanderungen und Begründung von Colonien, sowie die Sucht zur Auswanderung im Allgemeinen. Jan. 22, 1849–June 13, 1852.

Important official correspondence relating to the letter of Dr. Falk, dated Dec. 29, 1849, and addressed to the Ministry of State in Berlin and dealing with the question of the "Commission zur Prüfung" and to the question of protecting emigrants, etc., with Falk's "Gutachtung" of June 4, 1849, enclosed. Both sides of the emigration question are discussed and attention is drawn to the fact that those remaining in Germany have a better chance for development after the population has been thinned by emigration.

Papers relating to German colonization in Chili, signed by Puttkammer. 1850.

Papers relating to admission to the Medical Invalid and General Life Assurance Society of London. Apr., 1850.

Antrag um die Erlaubniss zur Errichtung von Agenturen für Auswanderer. Apr. 17, 1850.

Letter of Charles de Forster to the ministry calling attention to the concessions of rich lands for emigrants in Costa Rica. Feb. 22, 1850.

Papers relating to similar questions in Central America.

Jahresbericht der deutschen Gesellschaft der Stadt New York. Feb., 1849-1850.

Papers relating to the emigration to Texas, particularly western Texas, and containing particulars of Dr. von Herff of Darmstadt, for some years resident in Texas. Apr., 1850.

Papers of July 11, 1850, and later, relating to the "Berliner Verein zur Centralisation deutscher Auswanderung und Colonisation".

Document of "Bernhard Doctor" of Frankfort-on-the-Main, July 29, 1850, to the Ministry of the Interior, relating to emigration to North America, enclosing copy of a circular entitled "the Universal Emigration and Colonization Company, Embracing the Principles of Freehold Assurance" and the "Union Deutsch-Englisch-Amerikanischer Bureaux zur Beförderung der Auswanderungen nach Amerika". 1850.

Papers relating to emigration to New Granada, etc. 1850.

Clippings of the *Frankfurter Oberpostamts-Zeitung* of Dec. 5, 1850, and of the *Hamburger Nachrichten*.

Matter relating to the notice given by the English government touching emigration to Australia, enclosing a shipping circular dated June, 1851.

Bericht des Vereins zum Schutze deutscher Einwanderer in Texas (Wiesbaden), referring also to a pamphlet of Doctor von Herff entitled: *Geregelte Auswanderung.*

Instruction für Auswanderer nach Texas. Print, containing the names of the committee and answers to thirty important questions. Wiesbaden, May 10, 1851.

Denkschrift, signed by Hermann, Fürst zu Wied, Präsident des Vereins zum Schutze deutscher Auswanderer in Texas. Wiesbaden, May 12, 1851.

An Auswanderer! Rath, Auskunft und Belehrung ertheilt unentgeldlich das Bureau des Vereins zur Centralisation deutscher Auswanderung und Colonisation in Berlin, Unter den Linden, No. 54 und 55. (Print.)

Letter of Bibra containing a list of the names of members of the Verein. Neuwied, July 4, 1851.

Manuscript entitled "Finanz-Plan für den Texas Verein", signed by Bibra. Feb. 11, 1851.

Papers relating to the "Deutscher Colonisations Gesellschaft für Central-Amerika". Dec. 9, 1851, and later.

Organ zur Beförderung der Kolonisation und des Gewerbfleisses in Deutschland (Prospekt und Descriptions-Einladung). (Print. Dresden, Aug., 1857.)

Börsen-Halle. Hamburgische Abend Zeitung für Handel, Schiffahrt und Politik (Jan. 13, 1852).

Letter of Gerolt, "die Einwanderung in Philadelphia und New Orleans betreffend." Washington, Nov. 13, 1851.

Oeffentliche Warnung! vor der Auswanderung nach den Besitzungen der " Fünf der angesehensten Landgut-Besitzer des Kaiserreichs Brasilien" in der Provinz Rio de Janeiro. (Print, issued by the Berlin "Verein zur Colonisation Deutscher Auswanderer, etc.", under date of Jan. 17, 1852.)

Amtsblatt der Königlichen Regierung zu Potsdam und der Stadt Berlin. Printed, together with the "Statuten der deutschen Colonisations-Gesellschaft für Central-Amerika", Feb. 20, 1852.

Deutsche Gesellschaft von New Orleans, Sitzung der Direktion am 7ten Januar, 1852 (print).

An Alle welche Auswandern wollen! (Mar. 15, 1852; issued by the same society).

Bremen als Einschiffungsplatz für deutsche Auswanderer: Wahrheit gegen Unwahrheit. (Print. Cf. *Bremer Handelsblatt No. 30*, of May, 1852.)

Hansa, Centralorgan für deutsche Auswanderung (Hamburg, May 3, 1852).

Auswanderung: Erster Rechenschaftsbericht des Hamburger Vereins zum Schutze von Auswanderern erstattet in der General-Versammlung des Vereins am 25 Februar, 1852, Hamburg. (Print.)

Erster Bericht über die Wirksamkeit des Nachweisungs-Bureau für Auswanderer in Bremen. (Druck von C. Schuenemann; Mar.-Oct., 1852.)

Vol. 11. Acta betr. die Bildung von Vereinen, etc. July 5, 1852–Dec. 7, 1854. Continuation of matter relating to emigration as in preceding volume:

Correspondence with Gerolt in Washington relating to emigration and giving a number of important names, such as, F. L. Brauns, in Baltimore, Dr. Juris H. Ludewig Löscher, Richard or Bernhard Bresslauer aus Reichenbach in Schlesien, Pastor

Brandt, Castro in Texas, J. W. Jockusch in Galveston, Kaufmann Heinrichsen in San Francisco. References also made to Central America, Mexico, the American and Pacific Ship Canal Company (printed copy of whose charter is enclosed), to California and to the constitution of the German Society of New York.
Bericht der Deutschen Gesellschaft von New York (June-July, 1849).
Annual Report of the Commissioners of Emigration of the State of New York (Feb., 1852). The following prints are enclosed:
Altonaer Zeitung. Sept. 10, 1852.
Beilage zur Königlichen Preussischen Staats-Anzeiger. Apr. 1, 1853.
Zweiter Bericht des Nachweisungs-Bureau für Auswanderer in Bremen, 1853 and 1854.
Obrigkeitliche Verordnung, die Beförderung von Schiffspassagieren betreffend, issued by the Senate of Bremen, June 14, 1854.
Verordnung vom 26ten October, 1854, forbidding the sale of tickets to emigrants from Hesse.
Sammlung von Gesetzen, etc., für Kurhessen, Jahr 1854, no. 19, Oct.

Vol. 12. Acta betr. die Bildung von Vereinen, etc. Jan. 13, 1855-Nov. 30, 1858.
" Betreffend den Abschluss von Auswanderungs-Verträgen durch den Agenten A. W. Berger ausserhalb des Bezirks für welchen die Concession ertheilt ist." Nov. 5, 1854.
Le Moniteur Universel, Journal Officiel de l'Empire Français. Jan. 17, 1855.
Erster Jahresbericht and circulars of information issued by the " Nachweisungs-Bureau der Auswanderer-Behörde in Hamburg ". 1855.
Papers relating to the conditions in Castle Garden, etc. Aug. 14, 1856, Feb. 26, 1857, etc.
Neuester Bericht über die Empfangs- und Weiterbeförderungs-Verhältnisse der Auswanderer in New York, von Eduard Pelz.
Einzel-Abdruck aus den Mittheilungen von Nordamerika (Frankfurt-am-Main, Druck von C. Adelmann, 1856).
Bericht des Nachweisungs-bureau in Bremen.
Important matter relating to the " Beförderung der Verbrecher ", showing that the question of criminals had become very serious at this time.
" Den Auswanderungs-Unternehmer Strauss zu Antwerpen betreffend ", Oct. 1857, etc. (Very interesting series of papers inclosing: *Die Deutsche Platz- und Schutzagentur für Auswanderer,* etc. G. A. Wundermann und Söhne in Antwerpen. Printed circular.)

Rep. 81.
149. Acta der Gesandschaft zu Hamburg betr. die Reichsgesetzwidrige Anwerbung Reichsständiger Unterthanen zur Bevölkerung

des Genesee Districts in Amerika. 1792. On the inside original cover is written: "Die Amerikanische Werbung von Berczy betreffend d. 27 April, 1792, nebst Beilagen". (39 papers in all.)

Papers relating to the efforts of "William Berczy bevollmachtigter der Genesee Association" to secure settlers for the Genesee lands in New York. The following important prints are enclosed:

Bericht über den Genesee-District in dem Staate von New York der vereinigten Staaten von Nord-Amerika nach der im Jahr 1791 Englischen herausgegebenen Ausgabe übersetzt (Gedruckt im Dezember 1791).

Auszug der Anmerkungen zum Unterricht derjenigen Europäer, die sich in Amerika niederzulassen gesonnen sind, von dem letztlich verstorbenen berühmten Dr. Franklin. (8 pages in German.)

Mandat wider die Kolonisten-Werbungen .... Actum und Decretum in Senatu Hamb. Publikatumque d. 7. Maii, 1792.

168. Acta der Königl. Preuss. Gesandschaft am Niedersächsischen Kreise, betreffend die von dem aus Danzig gebürtigen Kaufmannsdiener Ernst Gottfried Scheffler gegen den hiesigen Kaufmann Taackes et Consorten angebrachte Denunciation pcto. getriebenen Menschen-Handels nach America incl. der Schefflerischen Privatsatisfaction. Angefangen den 29ten December 1801, beendigt den 7ten October 1802-1803. (64 papers in all.)

Rep. 84. I.

41. Acta Specialia des Ministerii zur Revision der Gesetzgebung und Justiz-Organisation in den neuen Provinzen.

Die Ueberhand nehmenden Auswanderungen und die Emanirung eines Strafgesetzes gegen die Verführung zum Auswandern. Jan., 1819. A thin fascicle of papers relating to the enactment of the law and reciting the events leading up to it, and enclosing printed matter relating thereto.

Rep. 84. XII.

2. Acta des Justiz-Ministeriums betreffend die Beschuldigungen gegen den Schiffs-Capitain Schulz vom Preuss. Schiffe die *Ceres*, wegen seiner Beschuldigung der Ausgewanderten nach Amerika. Mar. 1, 1818–Dec. 20, 1823.

Rep. 84. XIV. II.

1. Acta generalia des Justiz-Ministeriums zur Revision der Gesetzgebung, etc., betreffend das Auswandern diesseitiger Unterthanen nach fremden Staaten. 1832-1846. A thin fascicle containing:

"Vorlagen, etc.", to the law regulating emigration to Greece in the expectation of a "Subsistenz" declaration, of manufacturers, the establishment of new industries, and the emigration of working men.

Papers of Sept., 1839, relating to the emigration of Johann Heinrich Feldwisch or Feldwich (of Ladbergen) to America.

Request of widow von Münchhausen for permission to emigrate, enclosing a printed pamphlet entitled: *Die Auswanderungen in Ihrer Beziehung zum Staate, als manuscript gedruckt* (Köln im August 1846, 14 pp.).

ARCHIVES OF THE MINISTRY OF WAR.

(ARCHIV DES KRIEGSMINISTERII.)

The archives of the Royal Prussian Ministry of War are not a part of the Royal State Archives, but are separate archives, housed in the building of the War Ministry, on the corner of Wilhelmstrasse and Leipzigerstrasse. The ministry has kindly supplied the following extracts, having a bearing on American history, from its manuscript catalogue of materials which originally formed a part of the archives of the War Ministry of Hesse Cassel, but which, unless the contrary is stated below, are now preserved in Berlin, at the Kriegsministerium. The Roman numerals indicate sections in the repertory. The Arabic numerals are those of the fascicles in the respective sections. The fascicles having been renumbered from the old lists of the original repertory, it is desirable to retain both old and new numbers.

AUSZUG AUS DEM REPERTORIUM DES KURHESSISCHEN KRIEGSMINISTERIUMS.

X. *Garnison Cassel. Militär- Witwen- und Waisenkasse in Cassel.*

New nos.

253. Verzehrung der Militär-Witwen-Kassen-Pensionen im Auslande. 1831-1864. (Preserved in the Intendantur of the XI. Army Corps at Cassel.)

Zu XII. Invalidenhaus Carlshafen.

Old nos.
(150.) 53. Die bei der Kriegs- und Carlshafener Lazarettkasse im Rückstande gebliebenen Kapitalzinsen, Rückzahlungen, und sonstigen Einnahmeposten. 1814-1835. 1 vol.

XXII. Bergfestung und Garnison Spangenberg.

(41¹.) 1. Besetzung der Kommandantenstellen und Emolumente. 1759-1866.

XXV. Festung und Garnison Ziegenhain.

(33.) 1. Bestellung, Besoldung, und Emolumente eines Kommandanten. 1760-1804.

XXVII. Rapporte und Grundlisten.[1]

(536, 537.) 1. Rapporte vom Hessen-Hanauischen Jäger-Korps. 1777. Tom. I. u. II.
(538, 540.) 2. Grundliste desgleichen. 1783. Tom. I., II., u. III.
(541.) 3. Desgleichen desgleichen Husaren und Jägerkorps von 1783 und 1784.
(542.) 4. Desgleichen über angeworbene Jäger von 1780.

[1] All the troops designated under XXVII. served as auxiliaries to the British army in the war in America, 1776-1783. Their *Rangirlisten* were transferred in 1867 to the Royal State Archives in Marburg.

des Genesee Districts in Amerika. 1792. On the inside original cover is written: "Die Amerikanische Werbung von Berczy betreffend d. 27 April, 1792, nebst Beilagen". (39 papers in all.)
Papers relating to the efforts of "William Berczy bevollmachtigter der Genesee Association" to secure settlers for the Genesee lands in New York. The following important prints are enclosed:
Bericht über den Genesee-District in dem Staate von New York der vereinigten Staaten von Nord-Amerika nach der im Jahr 1791 Englischen herausgegebenen Ausgabe übersetzt (Gedruckt im Dezember 1791).
Auszug der Anmerkungen zum Unterricht derjenigen Europäer, die sich in Amerika niederzulassen gesonnen sind, von dem letztlich verstorbenen berühmten Dr. Franklin. (8 pages in German.)
Mandat wider die Kolonisten-Werbungen .... Actum und Decretum in Senatu Hamb. Publikatumque d. 7. Maii, 1792.

168. Acta der Königl. Preuss. Gesandschaft am Niedersächsischen Kreise, betreffend die von dem aus Danzig gebürtigen Kaufmannsdiener Ernst Gottfried Scheffler gegen den hiesigen Kaufmann Taackes et Consorten angebrachte Denunciation pcto. getriebenen Menschen-Handels nach America incl. der Schefflerischen Privatsatisfaction. Angefangen den 29ten December 1801, beendigt den 7ten October 1802-1803. (64 papers in all.)

Rep. 84. I.

41. Acta Specialia des Ministerii zur Revision der Gesetzgebung und Justiz-Organisation in den neuen Provinzen.
Die Ueberhand nehmenden Auswanderungen und die Emanirung eines Strafgesetzes gegen die Verführung zum Auswandern. Jan., 1819. A thin fascicle of papers relating to the enactment of the law and reciting the events leading up to it, and enclosing printed matter relating thereto.

Rep. 84. XII.

2. Acta des Justiz-Ministeriums betreffend die Beschuldigungen gegen den Schiffs-Capitain Schulz vom Preuss. Schiffe die *Ceres*, wegen seiner Beschuldigung der Ausgewanderten nach Amerika. Mar. 1, 1818–Dec. 20, 1823.

Rep. 84. XIV. II.

1. Acta generalia des Justiz-Ministeriums zur Revision der Gesetzgebung, etc., betreffend das Auswandern diesseitiger Unterthanen nach fremden Staaten. 1832-1846. A thin fascicle containing:
"Vorlagen, etc.", to the law regulating emigration to Greece in the expectation of a "Subsistenz" declaration, of manufacturers, the establishment of new industries, and the emigration of working men.
Papers of Sept., 1839, relating to the emigration of Johann Heinrich Feldwisch or Feldwich (of Ladbergen) to America.

Request of widow von Münchhausen for permission to emigrate, enclosing a printed pamphlet entitled: *Die Auswanderungen in Ihrer Beziehung zum Staate, als manuscript gedruckt* (Köln im August 1846, 14 pp.).

ARCHIVES OF THE MINISTRY OF WAR.
(ARCHIV DES KRIEGSMINISTERII.)

The archives of the Royal Prussian Ministry of War are not a part of the Royal State Archives, but are separate archives, housed in the building of the War Ministry, on the corner of Wilhelmstrasse and Leipzigerstrasse. The ministry has kindly supplied the following extracts, having a bearing on American history, from its manuscript catalogue of materials which originally formed a part of the archives of the War Ministry of Hesse Cassel, but which, unless the contrary is stated below, are now preserved in Berlin, at the Kriegsministerium. The Roman numerals indicate sections in the repertory. The Arabic numerals are those of the fascicles in the respective sections. The fascicles having been renumbered from the old lists of the original repertory, it is desirable to retain both old and new numbers.

AUSZUG AUS DEM REPERTORIUM DES KURHESSISCHEN KRIEGSMINISTERIUMS.

X. Garnison Cassel. Militär- Witwen- und Waisenkasse in Cassel.

New nos.

253. Verzehrung der Militär-Witwen-Kassen-Pensionen im Auslande. 1831-1864. (Preserved in the Intendantur of the XI. Army Corps at Cassel.)

Zu XII. Invalidenhaus Carlshafen.

Old nos.
(150.)   53. Die bei der Kriegs- und Carlshafener Lazarettkasse im Rückstande gebliebenen Kapitalzinsen, Rückzahlungen, und sonstigen Einnahmeposten. 1814-1835. 1 vol.

XXII. Bergfestung und Garnison Spangenberg.

(41¹.)   1. Besetzung der Kommandantenstellen und Emolumente. 1759-1866.

XXV. Festung und Garnison Ziegenhain.

(33.)   1. Bestellung, Besoldung, und Emolumente eines Kommandanten. 1760-1804.

XXVII. Rapporte und Grundlisten.[1]

(536, 537.)   1. Rapporte vom Hessen-Hanauischen Jäger-Korps. 1777. Tom. I. u. II.
(538, 540.)   2. Grundliste desgleichen. 1783. Tom. I., II., u. III.
(541.)   3. Desgleichen desgleichen Husaren und Jägerkorps von 1783 und 1784.
(542.)   4. Desgleichen über angeworbene Jäger von 1780.

---

[1] All the troops designated under XXVII. served as auxiliaries to the British army in the war in America, 1776-1783. Their *Rangirlisten* were transferred in 1867 to the Royal State Archives in Marburg.

Berlin

(543-545.)   5. Desgleichen vom Hessen-Hanauischen Freikorps von 1781. Tom. I., II., u. III.
(546-549.)   6. Desgleichen desgleichen von 1782. Tom. I., II., III., u. IV.
(550.)   7. Desgleichen von Offizieren und Mannschaften des Hessen-Hanauischen Corps (Jahre nicht angegeben).
(551.)   8. Desgleichen vom Hessen-Hanauischen Garde-Grenadier-Regiment 1769.
(552.)   9. Grundliste vom Hessen-Hanauischen Regiment Erbprinz (Jahre nicht angegeben).
(553.)   10. Desgleichen desgleichen (1. Bataillon). Tom. I.
(554.)   11. Desgleichen desgleichen (1. Bataillon). Tom. II., vom Ausmarsch aus Hanau im Jahre 1776 bis zur Rückkunft aus Amerika im Jahre 1783 in 6 Kompagnien.
(555.)   12. Grundliste vom Hessen-Hanauischen Regiment Erbprinz (1. Bataillon). Tom. III., über präsente Mannschaften in Canada.
(556.)   13. Desgleichen vom Hessen-Hanauischen Grenadier-Bataillon (Jahre nicht angegeben).
(557.)   14. Desgleichen von der Hessen-Hanauischen Artillerie-Kompagnie, vom Ausmarsch aus Hanau in 1776 bis zur Rückkehr aus Amerika in 1783.

XXXI. Pensionen, Unterstützungen, Gnadengehalte, Wartegelder, p.p.

(135, 136.)   2. Bezahlung der verwilligten Pensionen in das Ausland. 1786-1867 (2 volumina).
(249.)   5. Pensionsbewilligungen für Unteroffiziere und Soldaten des amerikanischen Kriegs, bezw. deren Witwen. 1831-1835.
(245.)   6. Pensionsgesuche amerikanischer Krieger p.p., welche in den abgetretenen Gebietsteilen wohnen. 1831-1840.
(141.)   7. Etats über den Zu- und Abgang der amerikanischen Pensionen. 1831-1833.
(145.)   8. Abhörung der Rechnungen über amerikanische Pensionen. 1831-1838.
(248.)   9. Anfang des Bezuges der bewilligten amerikanischen Pensionen. 1833-1837.
   10. Unrechtmässig von den Witwen Dessel und Heinemann bezogene amerikanische Pensionen. 1841-1844. (Now preserved in the Intendantur of the XI. Army Corps at Cassel.)
(147, 246, 535.)   11. Pensionslisten der amerikanischen Krieger. 1831-1847. 3 vol.
(247.)   12. Pensionslisten der Witwen von amerikanischen Kriegern. 1831-1835.

XXXIII. Ordres und Dienstlitteralien.

   2. Hof- und Staatshandbücher von 1771-1777, 1781 und 1782, 1784, 1785 und 1786, 1788 und 1789, 1790, 1791 und 1792, 1794-1796, 1798, 1799, 1800-1805, 1814, 1815, 1816-1820, 1823-1831, 1833-1846, 1851-1863, inclusive.

BRESLAU.

ROYAL STATE ARCHIVES.

(KÖNIGLICHES STAATSARCHIV.)

These, the collective archives for the province of Silesia, are located in a splendid new building, with modern equipment, in Thiergartenstrasse 13. The collections are very rich, containing some 85,000 documents besides a collection of seals and a reference library.

Hours: March till October from 8 to 1; November till February from 8.30 to 1.30; afternoons, Mondays, Wednesdays and Thursdays, from 4 to 7.

Rep[ositur] 14. (P[reussisches] A[rchiv]) 28 m. Copy of an edict " wegen Unterbringung ", etc. Seelowitz, Mar. 8, 1742.
I. 42 k. Acta Generalia vom Abzug und Austreten der Unterthanen.
  (1) Acten der Kgl. Regierung zu Reichenbach. 1816-1819 (1764 and 1789).
  (2) Acten der Kgl. Regierung zu Breslau. 1855 and 1873.
    Paper dated Breslau, Aug. 1, 1764, referring to the " Arbeitshaus-Edikte " of Mar. 24, 1747, and relating to deserters in the war with Russia and the funds for disabled soldiers.
    Papers relating to individual emigrants, requests and permissions to emigrate and the like.
VIII. 53 b. Acta wegen der Emigranten und deren Etablissement betrf. 1742, 1748 (also 1769-1804). Contains papers relating to the " Böhmischen und anderen Emigranten " such as the following:
  Official papers containing orders and regulations concerning the settlement and assistance of these emigrants dated Zirlau, June 9, 1742, also another dated May 30, 1742.
  Matter relating to the Bohemians settling in Münsterberg, Frankenstein, and Reichenbach.
  Edict wegen Unterbringung und Placirung der so genannten Schwenckfelder in Sr. Königl. Majestät Schlesischen und uebrigen Landen. De dato Seelowitz den 8 Martii 1742 (Breslau zu haben in J. J. Korns Buchladen). The second part of the volume contains rescripts and edicts relating to the " Professionisten " and " Fabrikanten ", such as:
  Königlich Preussisches Patent, betreffend die geneigte Aufnahme der Auswärtigen vom Adligen Stande, etc. De dato Berlin d. 5 Januar 1770. (Printed by Schweickhardt in Glogau.)
  Edict of Frederick, Berlin. Jan. 5, 1770, and accompanying it the following:
  Declaration des Edicts de dato Berlin den 5ten Januarii 1770 (dated Potsdam, Apr., 1770).
  Erneuertes Edict relating to the same. Mar. 8, 1775.
  Publicandum betreffend die den Ausländern bei ihrem Anzuge in Schlesien zu bewältigende Vortheile (Potsdam, Sept. 19, 1784. Printed by Korn in Breslau).

Breslau 79

VIII. **185 a.** Acta der Königlichen Regierung zu Reichenbach bzw. zu Breslau betreffend den Handel mit den Nord-Amerikanischen Frey-Staaten. 1816-1853 (1816-1818, 1853).

Papers relating to trade with North America, with Spanish America, and to the linen industry in Scotland and Ireland, as reported by the Prussian consul, Boetger. St. Thomas, Feb. 20, 1816.

Correspondence relating to the trade conditions in Germany, Holland, etc., and America.

VIII. **185 aa.** [Registratur der Königl. Regierung zu Oppeln, etc.] Acta betr. den Handel mit Amerika. 1828-1830; 1851-1853.

Matter dated May 14, 1828, relating to discrimination duties of tonnage, etc.

Other papers relating thereto.

VIII. **185 b.** Vol. I. Acta [der Kriegs- und Domänenkammer] bezw. der Regierung zu Breslau vom Commercio mit Amerika, Anstellung eines General Consuls zu Philadelphia. 1791-1798; 1818-1841.

Begins with papers relating to the appointment of Carl Gottfried Paleske, " negotiant ", in Philadelphia as consul in North America, Sept. 19, 1791.

Reports relating to commerce and trade with America in general, with the West Indies, etc.

Papers relating to the question of neutral harbors in the war of 1798 with many documents in copy relating thereto and setting forth incidentally the importance of the Prussian commercial treaty for the separate provinces such as Silesia.

Papers relating to the tariff in the republic of Haiti, dated May 28, 1827.

IX. **25 l.** Acten der Königlichen Regierung, Abteilung des Innern, Gewerbe-Polizei-Verwaltung zu Oppeln, betreffend die in London stattfindende allgemeine Ausstellung von Industrie-Erzeugnissen aller Völker. Desgleichen in New York. May 5, 1850-June 27, 1853.

With the papers is enclosed a print entitled: *Bekanntmachung,* etc., signed by von der Heydt, Minister of Trade, giving the plan and particulars of the exposition. Erfurt, Apr. 10, 1850.

X. **28 g.** Vol. I.-II. Acta betr. die Anträge der Separatisten zum Auswandern in andere Weltheile.

Vol. I. Mar., 1836–Dec. 31, 1838.

Papers relating to the request of Carl Gottlob Helling and Consort for money to emigrate to America. Breslau, Mar., 1836.

Papers relating to individuals, requests for permission to emigrate, passes, etc.

Much important matter for the genealogist.

Vol. II. Jan., 1839–July 31, 1845.

Papers relating to the Separatists emigrating to America. Australia, etc. Important lists of names such as:

" Liste der aus dem Kreise Oels ausgewanderten Separatisten-Familien." Gives the following detailed information: Aufenthaltsort | Name | Stand und Gewerbe | Datum des Emigrations-Consensus | Tag der Auswanderung.

M[inisterial] R[egistratur], Pars VI.
  No. 14. Vol. I.-II. Acta vom Mutuellen-Commercio zwischen Schlesien und America.
   Vol. I. 1779–Dec., 1801. Contains among other papers the following:
   Extract aus der Königl. Cabinets-Ordre de dato Breslau den 11 Januar 1779. Relates to the American Colonel Arend and the linen trade with America, how it can be restored to its former status, etc. The document is signed: " Friedrich ".
   Letter in French of Colonel Arendt asking for an audience.
   Letters to and from Arendt, some 30 in all, bringing out in full the history, character and schemes of Arendt. The letters are as follows:
   Letter of Arendt. Breslau, Jan. 23, 1779.
   Letter of Arendt. Feb. 6, 1779.
   Letter (in German) addressed to von Zedlitz. Breslau, Feb. 13, 1779.
   Autograph letter of von Zedlitz.
   Autograph letter of von Zedlitz. Feb. 23, 1779.
   Letter to Arendt. Breslau, Feb. 24, 1779.
   Letter to Arendt. Feb. 26, 1779.
   Letter of Arendt asking for the Order of the Cross of our Lady in Halberstadt instead of that of Peter and Paul, as first proposed. Feb. 25, 1779.
   Letter of Arendt to von Zedlitz. Feb. 27, 1779.
   Paper relating to Arendt's matriculation.
   Letter to von Zedlitz. Feb. 28, 1779.
   Letters of Arendt to von Zedlitz. Mar. 8, 16, 1779.
   Note of von Zedlitz.
   Letters of Arendt to von Zedlitz. Mar. 22, 23, 1779.
   Official letter to von Zedlitz. Apr. 3, 1779.
   Letter of Arendt to von Zedlitz. Apr. 26, 1779.
   Important report of the " Kaufmanns Aeltesten " of Breslau, directed against the shipping of linen to America. Jan. 20, 1779.
   Arendt's memorial sent to von Zedlitz. Jan. 29, 1779.
   Letter of von Zedlitz to Arendt. Apr. 3, 1779.
   Letter of Arendt requesting an interview. Mar. 31, 1779.
   Arendt's request to be elevated to the nobility, addressed to von Hoym, Minister of State.
   Official reply to Arendt in reference to the linen trade with America. Apr. 10, 1779.
   Letter of Arendt to the Minister of State, asking for the king's decision. Apr. 11, 1779.
   Letter of Arendt to von Hoym.
   Letter of Arendt to von Görne, Minister of State. Apr. 13, 1779.
   Letter of Arendt. Breslau, Apr. 14, 1779.
   Royal order to pay Arendt 200 Reichsthaler for his expenses in the interest of Prussian trade, signed by von Hoym. Apr. 16, 1779.

French letter of Arendt, reporting an interview with Mr. Lee in Frankfort-on-the-Main in reference to the question of commerce between Prussia and America.
Der Gebürgs Handel-Stand berichtet unterthänigst wegen den zu einer Reise nach Nordamerica vorzuschlagenden Subjectis. Other reports relating thereto.
Papers directed by the king to von Hoym.
Extract of a letter of Frederick the Great, stating that he has written to Minister Franklin in Paris in regard to commerce with the United States.
Autograph letter of the king (in French), directed to von Hoym.
A number of papers relating to trade with America and containing important matter leading up to the first commercial treaty between Prussia and the United States.
Reports giving statistics in regard to tariff and the like. 1783.
Matter relating to the export of linen from Hirschberg, Schmiedeberg, and Greiffenberg to England and America. Mar., 1783.
Papers relating to Prussian export to America via England. 1784.
Reports of Frederick the Great's efforts to establish the Prussian linen trade in North America in accordance with a rescript of Nov. 25, 1783.
Papers relating to the further extension of trade relations with America.
Letter of Peter Hasenclever, relating to export and import trade with America. Apr. 30, 1790.
Papers relating to the performance of the treaty between Prussia and the United States. 1790 and 1791.
Copy of the patent of consul-general issued to Paleske in Philadelphia and signed by King Frederick William II. Berlin, Aug. 14, 1791. (French.)
Other papers relating to Paleske in Philadelphia, which was then the consular centre of Prussian relations to America.

Vol. II. Jan., 1802–1804. Papers relating to the insolvency of the Prussian consul Schultze in Baltimore and the appointment of another consul.

Rep. 28. F[ürstentum] Liegnitz. X. F. u. I. u. II. Acta betr. die Schwenckfelder in den Fürstenthümern Liegnitz und Jauer und ihre Bedrückung durch Kath. Missionare. (1734-1738), 1732-1737.
Suppliken von Harpersdorfer, Armenruher, Lang-Neudorfer, und Lauterseiffer Unterthanen, die in der Schwenckfelder Religion geboren aber zur Augsburgischen Konfession übergetreten sind, auch ihrer Grundherrschaften an den Kaiser; Kaiserliche Reskripten an das Oberant.

Rep. 199. (M. R.) **XVIII.** No. **1.** Vol. **1.** Acta vom erlaubten Aufenthalt der (. . . .) Schwenck-Felder und Herrnhuter in denen königl. Preuss. Schlesischen Landen (Mar., 1742–Nov., 1754).
Official papers relating to the Schwenkfelders and Moravians, such as edicts, rescripts and the like, shedding much light upon the attitude and efforts of the government in the interests of these sects.

"Mehr als in 100 Familien bestehen die Anzahl, darunter allerhand Fabricanten und nutzbahre Handwercker sich befinden." These intend to leave their old seats and move their "Seminarium Theologicum samt dem aufgerichteten Paedagogio" to Silesia (Oct. 7, 1743).
Rep. 199. C-O. (Journal über eingegangene Cabinets Ordres.)
No. 4. 1778-1783.
Fol. 366 refers to Franklin in Paris and commercial relations between Prussia and America.
Fol. 557 relates to American merchants.
No. 5. 1784-1789.
Fol. 25. Matter relating to American trade.
Fol. 327. Matter relating to "immediaten Handel", particularly the linen trade with America. Mar. 17, 1784.
Fol. 571. Report for Feb., 1784.

CITY ARCHIVES.

(STADTARCHIV.)

Located Rossmarkt 7-9; contains some 30,000 original documents and letters, about 10,000 book manuscripts and account books, and over 5000 fascicles of official papers.[1]
Repert. No. 2. Litt. K.
433. Acta der Breslauischen Kaufmanns-Aeltesten betreffend die Handels Verhältnisse mit den amerikanischen Ländern. Jan. 26, Feb. 9, 1798; Nov. 18, 1797–May 15, 1848.
Papers relating to the permission to sail neutral ships from neutral ports to Spanish America, particularly to carry on trade with the West Indies.
Matter relating to the appointment of Johann Ernst Christian Schultze as consul in Baltimore. Sept. 12, 1798.
Fol. 24. Important *Circulair,* containing among other things reference to the "Patriotische Vorschläge" made by von Humboldt and dated Berlin, Mar. 23, 1798.
Fol. 25. Refers to the part played by Mr. Henry, consul general in Madrid.
Fol. 26. Copy of Humboldt's "Patriotische Vorschläge". Mar. 23, 1806.
Fol. 28 b *et seq.* Trade statistics for 1802 and 1803.
Fol. 43. Copy of an important letter from Philadelphia. July 12, 1822.
Fol. 45 *et seq.* Papers relating to the tariff in Mexico, with lists of names of the people concerned. 1825.
Fol. 77 *et seq.* "Liste der in der Republik Mexico ansässigen deutschen Handels-Häuser", with the following rubrics: Wohnort | Staat | Firma | Interessenten der Firma | Vaterland oder Geburtsort | Geschäft. *Circa* 1830.
Fol. 87-88. List of merchants and manufacturers interested in Breslau. 1832.

---

[1] Students of ecclesiastical history will find rich collections in the newly founded (1896) Diözesanarchiv.

Many other papers reflecting the intimate relations between Breslau and Mexico and other parts of America, with copies of documents enclosed.

Fol. 166. Report of the Prussian consul general in Rio de Janeiro. 1845.

Verzeichniss des Breslauer Börsen Archivs (Breslauer Kaufmannschaft) beendet 1772 Mai 24. A manuscript volume containing 3 parts as follows: A. Geschriebene gebundene Bücher Nr. 1-162; B. Acten Nr. 163-968; C. Gedruckte Bücher (18 numbers in all).

A later hand has added: " Systematische Index zum Repertorium des Börsenarchivs ", Sections I.-V.: I. Handel; II. Bank- und Börsenwesen; III. Zoll-Accise-Steuerwesen; IV. Die Kaufmannschaft als Corporation; V. Stellung der Kaufmannschaft zur Stadt, zur Provinz und zum Staate. Breslau, July 3, 1879.

The " Protokolle oder Copierbücher der Breslauer Kaufmannschaft " date back to 1623. The " Acta Publica " begin 1705, but the " Juden Amts Protokoll " goes back to Apr. 27, 1702, and continues to Apr. 30, 1704, and then, after a gap, from Dec. 18, 1729, to Mar. 12, 1734. From 1770 on proposals were made by the " Kaufmannschaft " with a view to improving Breslau's commercial relations with the outside world (*cf.* Verzeichniss Nr. 297-299, etc.).

The following numbers are of interest here:
- **388.** Frauenverein zur Verpflegung verwundeter und kranker Krieger im Lazaret zu St. Barbara. 1813-1814.
- **455.** Paper relating to the trade with Spain. 1771-1793.
- **456.** *Id.* 1797-1821.
- **476.** Handlungsdiener Institut. Vol. I., 1774-1813. Vol. II., 1815-1853.
- **504.** Indigo den Handel damit betr. 1800.
- **521.** Jus importandi. 1754-1878. (*Cf.* Kretschmersche Armen Posteritäts Casse, Nr. 536-540, vols. I.-III., 1712-1840.)
- **586** *et seq.* Leinwand. 1771—.
- **592-854.** Leinwand. 1767—.
- **846** *et seq.* Tabak. 1767-1793.

Rep. **199. VI. 17 b.** Handel nach Spanien. Vols. I.-IV. 1740-1806.
17 c. Handels Compagnie in Cadiz. 1771.
17 d. Extra Gesandten nach Spanien. 1780.

COBLENZ.

ROYAL STATE ARCHIVES.

(KÖNIGLICHES STAATS-ARCHIV.)

Located in the old Deutsch-Ordenshaus, entrance Castorhof 35. Contains some 80,000 documents from the seventh century on. Well repertorized.
Hours: Week days from 8 to 1.
Bibliography: 1. *Uebersicht über den Inhalt der kleineren Archive der Provinz* [Publicationen der Gesellschaft für Rheinische Geschichtskunde]. Bd. I., II., and to be continued. Zweiter Band bearbeitet von Dr. Armin Tille and Dr. Johannes Krudewig. (Bonn, Hermann Behrendt, 1904.) 2. *Uebersicht über die Bestände des K. Staatsarchivs zu Coblenz*, von Dr. Eduard Ansfeld, Archivdirektor zu Magdeburg [Mittheilungen der K. Preussischen Archivverwaltung, 6]. (Leipzig, Hirzel, 1903.) Excellent index to the volumes.

GRAFSCHAFT SAYN ALTENKIRCHEN.

Abth. **A**. Tit. I. Abzugssachen.

No. 6. Acta Generalia betr. die Erhebung des zehnten Pfennigs oder der Nachsteuer in der Grafschaft Sayn-Altenkirchen. 1742-1802.

No. 23. Jahr 1709. (No. 34, a new provisional numbering.) Acta den von verschiedenen Unterthanen der Grafschafft Sayn vorhabenden Abzug nach der in America gelegenen Königl. Engelländ. Insul Pennsylvania, und Fürstl. Sachsen-Eisenach Seits hierwieder ergangene Verordnung betr.

Contains 2 papers: first, a letter to Johann Wilhelm Herzog zu Sachsen, Jülich, Cleve, und Berg, dated Altenkirchen, June 6, 1709, giving an account of the craze which has seized the Germans to emigrate to the "Island of Pennsylvania", and stating that they have passage given them in Rotterdam free of cost, and promises of land as well, and that the Evangelical and Lutherans particularly are tempted by these inducements. The second paper is a "Verordnung" dated June 13, 1709, and ordering that the property of those subjects who emigrate without permission shall be confiscated.

No. 39. Die Auswanderung armer Einwohner der Dörfer Daaden und Biersdorf nach Amerika und die ihnen ertheilte Erlaubniss zum Verkauf ihrer Häuser. 1753.

No. 44. Verordnung betr. die Auswanderung junger Burschen ohne Erlaubniss der Herrschaft. 1784.

No. 45. Verordnung betr. die Auswanderung ohne Herrschaftliche Genehmigung (Kgl. Altenk.). 1698.

GRAFSCHAFT SPONHEIM BADEN SOHREN.

1926. Auswanderer nach Pensilvanien. Contains 2 papers.

A request of Peter Velten and Johannes Meinhardus, giving an account of Velten's escape to Pennsylvania and asking for forgiveness, etc. Sohren, Sept. 11, 1717.

The second paper contains an interesting recital of the case and a reply to the request.

Papers relating to the inheritance of Johann Peter Martini of Traben-on-the-Mosel residing in Upper Milford, Northampton Co., Pa. 1770-1772.

Oberamt Kirchberg.

1990. Untersuchungssache in specie Böslicher Austritt. Die ohne erhaltene Manumission nach Neu Engelland ausgewanderte Gebrüder Alberthal von Sohren, und die Confiscation derselben zurückgelassenen Vermögens betr. 1771.

Amt. Martinstein.

2374. Untersuchungs Sache, etc. Verschiedene böslich ausgetrettene Unterthanen des Amts Martinstein bet. 1776, 1777, 1785.

12 folios of papers relating to the disappearance of Christoph and Johannes Kuhn (Kühn ?), Schulze zu Martinstein.

Also papers relating to Maria Magdalena Scherhammerin of Martinstein and her emigration to America.

A third bundle of papers relating to Philipp Wagner's son as an emigrant to Poland.

2627. Betrifft die Neuländer. 1764. One manuscript folio containing the " Verordnung " prescribing that those who have received manumission to emigrate " in das neue Land " (America) must leave within 3 weeks, while those going to the Banat of Temesvár in Hungary are more favored by the state.

2640. A " Verordnung", regulating the form of application for emigrants going to Hungary, to New England, Pomerania, etc. Kirchberg, Dec. 14, 1770.

8446. Vermögungsausfolgung von Verschollenen. 1777-1782. Two fascicles of papers containing names of Germans who had emigrated to America. The papers give many hints as to letters written to and from America. Valuable for the genealogist.

Oberamt Saarbrücken.

II. No. 5. Verbot der Auswanderung und Massregeln dagegen. 1764-1785.

II. No. 6. Das Schuldwessen der nach Amerika ausgewanderten Einwohner von Carlsbrunn (Eberhard u. Kramer). 1779-1781.

Repert. 35 a. II. Deutsche in Amerika. Aus Acten der Waisen Schreiberei Saarbrücken. (Unter dem unterstrich. Namen zu finden.)

Anna Maria geb. Kramer verhei. Kohler nach Pennsylvanien (aus Carlsbrunn) ; Joh. Martin (Joh. Georg u. Martin u. Ludwig) Kramer zogen etwa 1773 nach Pennsylvanien aus Carlsbrunn.

Hans Georg Repperts Witwe aus Carlsbrunn 1691 nach A[merika], etc.

Letter of Joh. Paul Sturmfelz to his brother Joh. Peter Sturmfeltz in Gmünden. Sturmfelz gives his address as follows: To Mr. Paul Sturmfeltz, to the care of Mr. William Wister or Henry Thiell in Philadelphia. July 10, 1785.

IV. No. 1. Erhebung des Abzugsgeldes. 1729-1736.
"Verordungen" arranged chronologically under the several districts in alphabetical order, as for example:
Kurtrier. Innere Landesverw[altung] i. Allg.
[Bd.] No. 47. Kurfürstl. Gnädigstes Prümer-Amts Befelcheren-Buch ab Anno 1674 bis 1740.
No. 48. *Id.*, 1741-1757.
No. 49. *Id.*, 1758-1763.
No. 50. *Id.*, 1764-1769.
No. 51. *Id.*, 1770-1779.

DANZIG.
ROYAL STATE ARCHIVES.
(KÖNIGLICHES STAATSARCHIV.)

Located Hansaplatz 5, in a new building. Contains not only the records of Danzig but also those of Marienwerder, which have recently been deposited here. The importance of Danzig now as the great corn mart of the Vistula and the capital of the province of West Prussia and as a strategic military and trade centre since the days of the Teutonic Order and the Wars of the Roses, and of the strong Hanseatic trade of the Baltic in the fourteenth and fifteenth centuries, makes its records specially valuable for the history of shipping on the Baltic.

Hours: Monday to Friday, 8 to 1; Saturday, 8 to 12.

Königl. Ober-Präsidium von Preussen.
Abt. 161.
    12. Auswanderungen im Jahr 1827 betreffend. 1827-1828.
    23. Consense zu Auswanderungen aus dem königlich Preuss. Staaten betreffend. (Vol. I. of the older signature). Nov. 18, 1817–Mar. 2, 1819.
    24. Die Auswanderungen Consense betr. 1819-1826. (Vol. II. of the older signature.)

Abt. 180.
    1936. Auswanderungen aus dem Kreise Berent. 1824-1858.
    1937. *Id.*, dem Kreise Berent. 1858-1873.
    1938. *Id.*, dem Kreise Karthaus. 1862-1867.
    1939. *Id.*, dem Kreise Karthaus. 1867-1881.
    1940. *Id.*, der Stadt Danzig. 1840-1843.
    1941. *Id.*, der Stadt Danzig. 1843-1850.
    1942. *Id.*, der Stadt Danzig. 1861-1866.
    1943. *Id.*, dem Landkreis Danzig. 1830-1843.
    1944. *Id.*, dem Landkreis Danzig. 1843-1861.
    1945. *Id.*, dem Landkreis Danzig. 1862-1877.
    1946. *Id.*, der Stadt Elbing. 1852-1873.
    1947. *Id.*, dem Landkreis Elbing. 1851-1874.
    1948. *Id.*, dem Kreise Marienburg. 1841-1845.
    1949. *Id.*, dem Kreise Marienburg. 1845-1857.
    1950. *Id.*, dem Kreise Marienburg. 1857-1864.
    1951. *Id.*, dem Kreise Marienburg. 1864-1869.
    1952. *Id.*, dem Kreise Marienburg. 1869-1876.
    1953. *Id.*, dem Kreise Neustadt. 1818-1849.
    1954. *Id.*, dem Kreise Neustadt. 1849-1865.
    1955. *Id.*, dem Kreise Neustadt. 1865-1866.
    1956. *Id.*, dem Kreise Neustadt. 1866-1873.
    1957. *Id.*, der Pr. Stargard. 1826-1851.
    1958. Auswanderung des Bauern Michael Prill aus Jungfernberg. 1847-1849.
    1970. Errichtung von Auswanderungs-Agenturen. 1868-1869.
    1971. *Id.* 1869-1870.

1972. *Id.* 1870-1872.
1972 a. *Id.* 1873-1874.
1974. Nachweisung der vorgekommenen Auswanderungen und hierauf Bezug habende Bestimmungen. 1855-1863.
1975. Die Bestrafung unerlaubter Auswanderungen. 1837-1843.
2881. Die Reisen hoher Personen durch die Preussischen Staaten (Militär-Registratur). 1852-1886.
316. Acta der Königlichen Preuss. Regierung Marienwerder betr. die Jahresberichte der Auswanderungs-Agenten. 1868-1872.

Abt. 181.
2281. Statistiches Bureau enthaltend die Nachweisungen von den in Preussen vorgekommenen Ein- und Auswanderungen. Tabellen über Ein- und Auswanderungen. Vol. I. Jan. 14, 1863–Jan. 14, 1865.
2282. *Id.* Vol. II. Jan. 18, 1866–Jan., 1873.
2283. *Id.* Vol. III. Jan. 2, 1873–Mar. 11, 1874.
2284. Korrespondenz in Ein- und Auswanderungs-Angelegenheiten. Vol. I. Mar. 11, 1863–May 13, 1878.
2285. *Id.* Vol. II. Nov. 1, 1878–Mar. 13, 1882.

Abt. 184. Landratsamt Berent. Auswanderungen. Passwesen.
75. Auswanderungen. 1859-1867.
76. *Id.* 1867-1872.
82. *Id.* 1873-1879.
77. *Id.* 1880-1882.
78. *Id.* 1883-1899.
79. Auswanderungsagenten. 1861-1892.
80. Einwanderungen und Ertheilung der Naturalisationsurkunden für Ausländer. 1832-1874.
73. Correspondenzen in Passangelegenheiten. 1879-1885.
74. *Id.* 1885-1891.

Abt. 189. Landratsamt Karthaus.
1. Auswanderungen und Uebersiedlungen auswärtiger und preussischer Unterthanen in das diesseitige Staatsgebiet. 1832-1857.
2. *Id.* 1857-1860.
3. *Id.* 1860-1861.
4. *Id.* 1861-1863.
5. *Id.* 1863-1865.
6. *Id.* 1865-1866.
7. *Id.* 1866-1868.
8. *Id.* 1868.
9. *Id.* 1868-1873.

Abt. 191. Landratsamt Neustadt.
78. Auswanderungen. Bd. 6. 1881-1883.
114. *Id.* Bd. 2. 1865-1870.
145. *Id.* Bd. 1. 1854-1865.

Abt. 194. Landratsamt Briesen.
13. Auswanderungen. 1897-1902.

Abt. 195. Landratsamt Deutsch-Krone. Aus- und Einwanderungen. Passwesen.

Danzig

53. Betreffend die nachgesuchten Auswanderungskonsense für preussische Unterthanen nach Nord America. 1862.
54. Auswanderungskonsense für preussische Untertanen nach Nord Amerika. 1867.
55. *Id.* 1868.
56. Auswanderungen aus dem preussischen Staate. 1872.
57. *Id.* 1874-1881.
58. Einwanderungen resp. Naturalisationen. 1853-1879.
59. Auswanderung aus dem preussischen Staate und Niederlassungen von Ausländern in demselben, desgleichen Heimatsscheine. 1826-1863.
60. *Id.* 1862-1880.
61. Erhebungen über Auswanderungen. 1881-1882.
62. *Id.* 1882.
63. *Id.* 1883.
64. *Id.* 1884.
65. *Id.* 1885.
68. *Id.* 1886-1888.
69. *Id.* 1888-1891.
70. *Id.* 1891-1895.
71. Fremden Polizeiliche Kontrolle der Herbergen. 1883-1890.
72. Massregeln zur Beseitigung des Landstreichens und Bettelei. 1878-1890.
74. Mittheilungen über Auswanderungen. 1881-1888.
75. *Id.* 1889-1892.
76. *Id.* 1892-1894.
77. *Id.* 1894-1897.

Abt. 196. Landratsamt Flatow.
84. Auswanderungen. 1844.
85. *Id.* 1853-1854.
86. *Id.* 1854.
87. *Id.* 1855.
88. *Id.* 1856.
89. *Id.* 1857.
90. *Id.* 1859-1870.
91. *Id.* 1844-1847.
92. Uebersichten über Ein- und Auswanderungen. 1868-1870.
93. Ertheilung von Heimatsscheinen und Aufnahme in den Preussischen Unterthanen-Verband. 1839-1853.
95. Uebersichten über Ein- und Auswanderungen. 1871-1882.
96. Die am 1. November j. J. einzureichende Uebersicht der vorgekommenen Ein- und Auswanderungen. 1845-1869.
97. Aufnahme in den Preussischen Unterthanen-Verband. 1853-1871.
297. Auswanderungsangelegenheiten spec. 1870-1874.
304. Ertheilung der Auswanderungskonsense spec. 1847-1853.
308. Uebersichten über Ein- und Auswanderungen. 1882-1898.

Abt. 198. Landratsamt Konitz. Aus- und Einwanderungen.
56. Die Einwanderung von Ausländern. 1826-1858.
67. Auswanderungen nach Polen, Amerika, etc. 1847-1862.
68. Auswanderungen, etc. 1860-1883.
69. Ausweisung ausländischer Unterthanen. 1852-1884.

71. Die vorgekommenen Auswanderungen. 1883-1885.
70. Kontrolle der russisch-polnischen Ueberläufer. 1883-1892. (Cf. Abt. 201, Nr. 106-108.)
72. Das Auswanderungswesen. 1886-1891.
73. Id. 1881-1892.

Abt. 201. Landratsamt Marienwerder. Auswanderungen. Wanderungen. Passwesen.
106-108. Auswanderungen im Allgemeinen. 1881-1896.

Abt. 203. Landratsamt Schlochau. Auswanderungen. Wanderungen. Passwesen.
27. Auswanderungen. 1871-1888.
28. Id. 1888-1891.

Abt. 204. Landratsamt Schwetz. Aus- und Einwanderungen. Landesverweisungen. Naturalisationen.
135. Ertheilung der Entlassungsurkunden und Naturalisationen. Bd. 5. 1861-1868.
136. Id. Bd. 4. 1854-1864.
137. Ertheilung der Auswanderungskonsense und Auslieferung der Ueberläufer. Bd. 2. 1827-1850.
143. Verheirathung der inländischen Frauenzimmer mit vormaligen Polnischen Soldaten oder Ausländern und Ertheilung der Fraukonsense. 1838-1865.
336. Landesverweisungen und Auswanderungen. Bd. 1. 1853-1879.
337. Id. Bd. 2. 1879-1892.
338. Ertheilung der Entlassungs- und Naturalisations-urkunden. 1869-1877.
324. Ertheilung der Heimatscheine. 1842-1888.
325. Ertheilung der Reisepässe. Bd. 2. 1880-1883.
375. Id. Bd. 4. 1885-1890.
376. Id. Bd. 5. 1890-1896.
417. Id. Bd. 3. 1883-1885.

Abt. 205. Landratsamt und Kreisausschuss Strasburg. Aus- und Einwanderungen. Passwesen, Naturalisation. 1864-1866.
2. Naturalisationen. 1864-1866.
10. Bestimmungen über Ein- und Auswanderungen. 1845-1889.
13. Naturalisationen. 1860-1862.
16. Id. 1870-1871.
17. Id. 1871-1872.

Abt. 206. Landratsamt Stuhm. Auswanderungen. Einwanderungen. Passwesen.
27. Passsachen. 1860-1862.
59. Passertheilungen. Vol. 1. 1877-1878.
60. Passertheilungen. Vol. 2. 1879-1884.
105. Passertheilungen und Visirungen. 1858-1860.
134. Auswanderungsangelegenheiten. 1869-1882.
142. Die Ertheilung von Aus- und Inlandspässen. 1874-1877.
155. Passangelegenheiten und sonstige Atteste. 1817-1856.

Abt. 207. Landratsamt Thorn. Aus- und Einwanderungen. Passwesen.
8. Auswanderungen nach Polen und Amerika. 1860-1872.
9. Auswanderungen. Gen. 1818-1881.

> 10. Ein- und Auswanderungen. 1880-1881.
> 11. Id.
> 12. Uebersiedlung von Ausländern nach Preussen. Gen. 1839-1840.
> 232. Passwesen. 1849-1855.
> 233. Pass- und Fremdenwesen im Allgemeinen. 1844-1875.
> 40. Ausweisungen. 1870-1877.
> 41. Id. 1875-1882.
> 47. Naturalisationen.
> 48. Id.
> 49. Id.
> 50. Id.
> 51. Id. } 9 vols. 1845-1875.
> 52. Id.
> 53. Id.
> 54. Id.
> 55. Id.

Gewerbe (Handel, Industrie, Fabriken).
> 167. Handel und Industrie. Gen. 1844-1868.
> 167 a. Handel und Industrie im Allgemeinen. 1876-1884.
> (Cf. also Nos. **170** and **173**.)

Serie I. A. No. 7. Acta die Auswanderungen betr. 1737-1864.
     C. Nos. **40, 41, 42, 35, 95, 106, 146, 147, 152, 155, 157, 163**.

DÜSSELDORF.
ROYAL STATE ARCHIVES.
(KÖNIGLICHES STAATSARCHIV.)

Located in a fine new building, Prinz Georgstrasse 78, and contains some 100,000 documents with numerous state papers from 648 A. D. down to the present time. The collections are particularly interesting because of the many historical vicissitudes of the Lower Rhine, many of which, notably the French régime (Fremdherrschaft), have left a deep impress upon the records.
Hours: 8 to 1.

Grossherzogthum Berg. Ministerium des Innern. Statistik.
    2. Acta das Niederlassen der Ausländer im Grossherzogth. und das Auswandern hiesiger Unterthanen ins Ausland resp. die Erlangung des Bürgerrechtes betr. in specie im Siegdept. 1810-1812.

Grossherzogtum Berg. Praef[ectur] des Rhein-Dep[artements]. Statistik.
    60. Bevölkerungs-Aufnahme im Rhein-Depart. und Veränderungen. 1810-1813.
    70. Grossherzogthum Berg: Acten der Praefectur des Rhein Departements, Division des Innern, Bureau der Statistik; betreffend die Aus- und Einwanderungen und Vermögens Ex- und Importationen. 1809-1811.
    A thin parcel of papers, the earliest of which bear date of 1809 but refer in some instances to 1808. The " Formular " is in both French and German, but the text is, for the most part, German.

Regierung Düsseldorf. Landrathsamt **Cleve** (2).
    [Conv.] **1.** Vol. I.-III. Acta Spec. betreffend Ein- und Auswanderungen. 1847-1849; 1849; 1849-1850.
    [Conv.] Vol. IV.-V. Acta Spec., etc. 1851; 1852-1853.
    [Conv.] Vol. VI.-VII. Acta Spec., etc. 1853-1854; 1854-1857.
    [Conv.] Vol. VIII.-X. Acta Spec., etc. 1857-1861; 1862-1866; vol. X., Ueberschriften der jährlichen Ein- und Auswanderungen. 1863-1883.

Landrathsamt Düsseldorf.
    No. I. Acta betreffend Passwesen. Vol. I. 1847-1862.

B. XI. Landrathsamt **Elberfeld.**
    No. I. Acta betr. Uebersichtung der Zustände der Ein- und Auswanderungen. 1845-1868.

Regierungs Bezirk Aachen. Landrathsamt **Erkelenz** (11).
B. XI.
    No. **1.** Acta betreffend Auswanderungsconsense. 1817-1838.
    No. **2.** Acta betr. die Anfertigung der Statistischen Tabellen. Vol. 1, 1825-1839; vol. 2, 1839-1854; vol. 3, 1854-1864.

Düsseldorf

Regierungs Bezirk Aachen. Landrathsamt Erkelenz (13).
B. XI.
    No. 6. Acta Spec. und Gen. betr. die jährlichen Tabellen der Geburten, Trauungen und Sterbefälle, etc.
    No. 7. Acta Spec. betr. Volksaufnahme. 1871-1875.
    No. 8. Acta Spec. 1875-1877.
B. XI. Landrathsamt Essen.
    No. 1. Acta betreffend Uebersichten der Ein- und Auswanderungen. 1869-1882.
B. XI. Landrathsamt Geldern.
    No. I. Vol. I. Acta betreffend Ein- und Auswanderungen. Specialia. Aufenthalt der Ausländer im Inlande. Ausweisung. 1850-1854.
B. XI. Landrathsamt Gladbach.
    No. 1. Acta betr. die Auswanderungen in fremde Staaten. 1828 (1820)-1852.
    No. 2. Acta betr. die Einwanderungen in den hiesigen Staat. 1833-1851.
B. XI. Landrathsamt Gravenbroich.
    No. 1. Acta Specialia Einwanderungen. Aufnahme von Ausländern betr. 1833-1852.
    No. 2. Acta Specialia, etc. 1857-1868.
B. XI. Landrathsamt Gummersbach.
    No. 1. Generalia betr. Auswanderungen. 1816-1850. Papers (for the most part in German) relating to emigration in general, especially to Russia and Poland (1816), emigration and military service (1818). Those bearing more particularly on America are:
Ertheilung von Auswanderungsconsensen, etc.
List of "Paquebots reguliers à voile entre Anvers et New York". 1844.
    No. 2. Generalia betr. die Einwanderungen im Kreise Grummersbach. 1829-1843.
B. XI. Landrathsamt Jülich (6).
    No. 1. Acta. betr. Auswanderungen Königl. Preussischer Unterthanen ins Ausland. 1816-1848.
Verordnungen, Nachweise. Register (Listen) der Ausgewanderten, etc.
Registratur d. Jülich-Berg. Landes Archivs.
    391. Geh. Rat. Verhandlungen betreffend das Auswandern Jülich-Bergischer Unterthanen. 1764-1803. The inside title-page bears the following heading: "Verhandlungen betreffend das Auswandern Jülich-Bergischer Einsassen in fremde Staaten und das Einwandern fremdherrlicher Unterthanen und die deshalb erlassenen Landesherrlichen Verordnungen". 1764-1803. A number of these "Verordnungen" will be found printed in Scotti's *Sammlung der Jülich-Bergischen Verordnungen.* A most valuable collection of papers, including among others the following:
Documents relating to subjects who emigrate "um sich in den neuen französischen Etablissemens in America niederzu-

schlagen ". There seems to have been doubt in the minds of the authorities as to the disadvantage of letting these emigrants go: " ob die leute besonders so der Gemeinheit mehr schad als nuetzlich seyend, fortziehen lassen, und auf anmelden, nach vorgängiger liquidation und zahlung der schulden, erlaubnus ertheilen solle ". (*Verordnung* dated, Ollendorf, Mar. 15, 1764, and signed by Kurfürst Otto.)

Papers relating to the efforts of " Frantz Caspar Hasenclever aus dem Hasenclev Kirspels ", who has been established for three years in Rotterdam and is secretly inducing " eyssen- und stahlfabricanten, auch zimmerleuthe, welche die zugehörige werckstätte, in specie Hämmer zu bawen verstehen, heimlich ['Nach New Jorrck'] anzuwerben ". (Document dated Mar. 20, 1764.)

Papers relating to the Emissarii in the Palatinate, particularly the *Verordnungen* of Pfalzgraf Carl Theodor, of the year 1764 and following.

Papers relating to the emigration of Germans to Spain together with important printed matter in 1767. (Compare similar documents in the General Landesarchiv in Carlsruhe.)

Verordnung of Joseph II., Vienna, June 7, 1768, and other material relating to Thierriegel's scheme of a German colony in Spain.

Printed *Verordnungen* of 1801-1803 relating to " Vermögens Exportationen ", etc.

B. XI. Landrathsamt **Mettmann** [Kreis Elberfeld].

No. 1. Acta Generalia betr. die Einwanderungen von Ausländern respective Polen. Gesetz über die Erwerbung und den Verlust der Eigenschaft als Preussische Unterthanen, sowie über den Eintritt in fremde Staatsdienste, von 31 Dezember 1842. 1843-1864.

No. 3. Acta Generalia, betr. die Ein- und Auswanderungen. 1852-1860.

B. XII. Landrathsamt **Mettmann.**

No. 1. Acta betr. den Handelverkehr mit den östlichen und westlichen Provinzen der Preuss. Monarchie, so wie mit sonstigen Ländern. 1819-1861.

B. XI. Landratsamt **Montjoie.**

No. 1. Acta betr. die Auswanderungsgesuche und Auswanderungen im Kreise Montjoie. Vol. 1 u. 2. 1817-1850.

Gen. Gouvernement des **Nieder-** und **Mittel-Rheins.**

Sec. 3. Capt. 19. No. 20. Acta betr. die im Jahre 1813 durch die französische Duanen geschehene Wegnahme von Colonial-Waaren nach dem Decret von Nossen 8. May 1813 und desfalsige Reclamationen um Wiedererstattung. 1814-1815.

B. XI. Landratsamt **Rheinbach.**

Acc. 3/1898.

No. 1. Ein- und Auswanderungs-Nachweisen. 1845-1880. Contains statistical lists and matter relating to emigrants in detail.

Düsseldorf

Roerdepartement: Praefectur III. Division 2. Bureau 6. Handel.
   No. 29. Anschluss des Grossherzogthums Berg an Frankreich. Handelsbeziehungen Crefelds zu Amerika. Behandlung (Verbrennung) englischer Waren. Anweisung für die Fabrikation (Färberei). 1809-1811.
   Papers largely in French. Those relating to Crefeld and America depict the state of things after the interruption of commerce with America in 1809, particularly the effect of this interruption on the manufacturers. The following papers are worthy of note:
   Communications to the prefect of the department of Aix-la-Chapelle. Aug. 5, 1809.
   Exportation en Amérique de velours de Creveld.
   A communication of the Minister of Interior, referring to the wretched conditions of the workmen " en raison de la facilité inattendue qu'ont eu les fabricieux de faire passer de velours en Amérique par le Dannemark"). Aug. 29, 1809.

Roerdepartement. Kantonal-Archiv Moers.
   II. E. 9. Papers relating to emigrants, 1810-1812, and furnishing the following particulars in tabular form as rubricated below: Noms | Prenoms | Qualité Profession Fonctions | Naissance | Domicile à l'Étranger | Age | Emploi | Epoque d'absence | Consistance | Permission, etc. | Renseignement.
   II. B. No. 4. Korrespondenz in Polizeisachen. An interesting bundle of papers relating to the police methods of the period of the French domination. 1812-1813.
   Nr. 5. Actes concernants les Passeports an 9 (de la République). 2 papers.
   Nr. 6. Passwesen. Sicherungsatteste. 1812-1813.

Roerdepartement. Gouvernements-Commissariat.
   IV. 61. 2. Acta Generalia, betr. das Pass-Wesen. 1814-1816.
   IV. 62. 2. Acta betr. das Pass-Wesen. Bezirk Aachen. 1814-1816.

B. XI. Landratsamt **Solingen**.
   Nr. 1. Acta betr. die Auswanderungen, sowie statistischen Nachweisen über die Ein- und Auswanderungen. 1863-1873.

B. XI. Landratsamt **Waldbroel**. Registratur des landratlichen Officii zu Waldbroel.
   No. 2. Acta Specialia betr. die ausländischen Einwanderungen. 1840-1843.

Stadt **Wesel**.
   Capsula 204.
   No. 4. Police Passeport. 1808-1812. Papers for the most part in French and quite important.
   No. 5. Registre d'ordre pour la délivrance des passeports à l'Intérieur. 1810, 1811. 3 fascicles.
   Registre des passeports. 1813.
   Einschreibungs-Register der Aufenthalts-Karten für die Stadt und das Amt Wesel pro 1815. 1 fascicle.
   No. 6. Acte wegen Ertheilung der Reise-Pässe. 1813-1826.
      Deponirte ausgelaufene Pässe und Atteste, auch Certificate worauf Aufenthalts- oder Sicherheits-Konsense ertheilt worden sind.

Capsule 209.
  No. 13. Acta betr. Auswanderungen und Heimathsscheine. Specialia. 1842-1854. Important matter relating to emigration to various countries.
  No. 19. Acta betr. Auswanderungen. 1853-1862 (marked vol. II., and continuation of no. 13).
  No. 20. Acta Specialia betr. Einwanderungen aus dem Auslande. Naturalisations-Urkunden. 1818-1862.
  No. 40. Acta betr. die Auswanderungen, sowie die Gesuche um Erlaubniss zur Auswanderung. 1818-1839.

HANNOVER.
ROYAL STATE ARCHIVES.
(KÖNIGLICHES STAATSARCHIV.)

Located: Am. Archive 1. Embrace the archives of the former electorate and kingdom of Hanover. Permission to consult the collections must be obtained, in the case of Germans, from the " Oberpräsident der Provinz ". Foreigners address their requests to the " Präsident des Staatsministeriums ", or through the " Generaldirektor der Staatsarchive " in Berlin.[1]

Hours: 8 to 1.

Bibliography: Max Bär, *Geschichte des Königlichen Staatsarchivs zu Hannover* [Mittheilungen der K. Preussischen Archivverwaltung, 2] (Leipzig, Hirzel, 1900); Max Bär, *Uebersicht über die Bestände des K. Staatsarchivs zu Hannover* [ditto, 3] (Leipzig, Hirzel, 1900).

Des[ignation] 9. A. America. Staaten von Süd u. Nordamerica.
  No. 1. Betr. einen Antrag des Nordamericanischen Residenten Wheaton zu Berlin, wegen Abschliessung eines Handels- u. Schiffahrtsvertrages zwischen dem Königreiche Hannover und den vereinigten Staaten von Nordamerica. 1835. *Vid.* Acta sub Rubro: Seeschiffahrt, in sp. Vereinigte Staaten von Nordamerica.
  No. 2. Betr. den von dem Consul der Nordamericanischen Freystaaten, John Cuthbert zu Hamburg, in Beziehung auf die in Ostfriesland gefänglich eingezogene Mannschaft eines gestrandeten americanischen Schiffes, welche des Mordes des Capitains und Steuermanns desselben höchst verdächtig gemacht, gerichteten Antrag auf die Auslieferung derselben zur Transportirung nach Amerika. 1838.
  No. 3. Betr. die von dem am Pabstlichen Hofe ancreditirten Geschäftsträger der Republik Neu-Granada durch die diesseitige K. Gesandtschaft in Rom geschehene Mittheilung der Probe einer Baumrinde, welche die Heilkraft einer Chinarinde besitzen soll. 1838.
  No. 4. Betr. eine Beschwerde des Nordamericanischen Consuls zu Hamburg, über das Verfahren des Amts Zeren gegen den Nordamericanischen Geistlichen Henry Hiesland, hinsichtlich dessen Reiselegitimation, 1839, 1840. *Vid.* Acta, Passwesen, Fasc. 17.
  No. 5. Betr. die Erleichterung officieller Communicationen nach den Nordamericanischen Freystaaten in Privatangelegenheiten, und die dabey in Frage gekommene Vermehrung der diesseitigen Consuln in den Nordamericanischen Freystaaten. 1840. *Vid.* Acta, Königliche Consulate, Generalia, no. 6.

---

[1] The collections of city documents down to 1815, and index to 1848, and the like, are found in the Stadtarchiv (in the City or " Kestner " Museum), open 11 to 1.

No. 7. Betr. die Beförderung der Correspondenz zwischen dem Königl. Ministerio und den Königl. Consulaten in Nordamerika. 1841. *Vid.* Acta, Königl. Consulate, Generalia, Fasc. 7.

No. 9. Betr. die etwaige Auslieferung des anjetzt in der Strafanstalt zu Stade befindlichen H. H. Norden aus Sottrum an die Behörden des Nordamericanischen Freystaates Maryland, und die dabei in Frage gekommene gegenwärtige Staatsangehörigkeit des Norden. 1842.

No. 10. Betr. den Antrag des Americanischen Consuls F. J. Grund zu Bremen, wegen Auslieferung Americanischer Gefangenen von dem Americanischen Schiffe *Maryland,* welche durch das Amt Lehe verhaftet sind. 1842.

No. 11. Betr. die Adresse des Königl. Notifications-Schreiben an die Nordamerikanischen Regierungen. 1843. *Vid.* Acta sub Rubro: Notificationes. Generalia, Fasc. 2.

No. 12. Betr. die diesseitigen Handelsverhältnisse mit den Nordamerikanischen Freystaaten, in sp. den von Letzteren auf ausländisches Leinen gelegten Zoll. 1844. *Vid.* Acta sub Rubro: Seeschiffahrt, Amerika.

No. 13. Betr. des Carl Schäfer, dermalen zu Hamburg, Colonisations-Project in der Republic Guatemala. Dessen zu Guatemala erfolgtes Ableben u. Nachlass. 1844, 1860.

No. 14. Betr. die von der K. K. Gesandtschaft hieselbst geschehene Mittheilung des Extracts eines zu Baltimore von einer Commission behuf Ermittelung Verletzungen der Nordamerikanischen Naturalisationsgesetze aufgenommenen und dem Senate der Vereinigten Staaten vorgelegten Protocolls, insbesondere die Einwanderungen von Verbrechern in die Nordamerikanischen Freistaaten. 1845, 1851.

Desgleichen eine Anfrage des allhier als Agenten der Vereinigten Staaten von Nord Amerika beglaubigten Agenten Dudley Mann, über die im hiesigen Königreiche etwa vorkommenden Auswanderungen verurteilter Verbrecher oder entlassener Sträflinge nach den Vereinigten Staaten. 1847, 1848, 1855.

No. 15. Botschaft des Präsidenten der Vereinigten Staaten von Nordamerika, James K. Polck. Washington, Dec. 2, 1845.

No. 16. Betr. eine von dem Königl. Consulate in Bremen eingesandte Druckschift unter dem Titel: *Das Oregon Gebiet.* 1846.

Die Rede des General Cass gehalten in dem Senate der Nordamerikanischen Freistaaten, betreffend den Streit mit Grossbritannien über das Oregon Gebiet. 1846.

No. 18. Betr. das angeblich unter der deutschen Bevölkerung in den Vereinigten Staaten von Nord-Amerika stattfindende politische Treiben in Beziehung auf Deutschland. 1847. *Vid.* Acta sub Rubro: Policey-Sachen, Fasc. 73.

No. 19. Betr. die durch den Nord-Amerikanischen Agenten Mann beantragte Erlassung oder Ermässigung der Eingangsabgabe von ungeschältem Reis. 1847. *Vid.* Sub Rubro: Seeschiffahrt, Vereinigte Staaten von Nord-Amerika, Fasc. 8.

No. 20. Betr. die von dem Consul Delius in Bremen angeregte Betheiligung an der Colonisation von Mittel-Amerika. 1850.

No. 21. Betr. das für die Angehörigen der Republik Venezuela über die Bewilligung von Moratorien erlassene Gesetz. 1850, 1857.
No. 22. Betr. eine von dem Consulate in Newjork eingesandte *Shipping and Commercial List.* 1851.
No. 23. Betr. die Anherosendung der für die Königl. Universitätsbibliothek in Göttingen bestimmten Public Documents mehrerer der Vereinigten Nordamerikanischen Staaten. 1851.
No. 24. Betr. die Verhaftung mehrerer Matrosen der Nordamerikanischen Bark *Arethusa* durch das Amt Lehe. 1852.
Desgl. des Nordamerikanischen Schiffes *Hellespont* in Bremerhaven. 1859. (Seeschiffahrt, Hannover, no. 59.)
No. 25. Betr. die für New-York beabsichtete grosse Kunst und Gewerbe Ausstellung. 1852.
Die von dem Gewehrfabrikanten Crause in Herzberg zur Ausstellung in New-York gesandten Gegenstände. 1855.
Die von dem Leinenfabrikanten G. H. Heller in Göttingen. 1858.
No. 26. Betr. den zwischen Preussen und den Vereinigten Staaten wegen Auslieferung flüchtiger Verbrecher abgeschlossenen Vertrag. 1853, 1855. Desgl. den zwischen Hannover u. den Vereinigten Staaten abgeschlossenen dessfalsigen Vertrag.
No. 27. Betr. das von dem Gesandten Grafen Kielmansegge in London für die Königl. Universitätsbibliothek in Göttingen bestimmte Werk, *Annual Report of the Superintendent of the United States Coast Survey.* 1853, 1854. Ferner die Einsendung verschiedener anderer Werke.
No. 28. Den zwischen Russland und den Vereinigten Staaten abgeschlossenen Seerechtsvertrag. 1854. *Vid.* Handels- u. Schiff-Sachen, Seeschiffahrt, Vereinigte Staaten von Nordamerika, no. 10.
No. 29. Die Einleitung einer Verhandlung mit der Regierung der Vereinigten Staaten über die diesseitige Gesetzgebung hinsichtlich der Auswanderungs-freiheit und Militairpflichterfüllung. 1853 *seqq. Cf.* Militairsachen, no. 653.
No. 30. Betr. die Verhältnisse des Kaiserreichs Brasilien. 1856. *Cf.* Brasilien.
No. 31. Betr. die Verrichtung processualischer Handlungen als Eidesabnahme, Zeugenvernehmung in den Vereinigten Staaten von Nord-Amerika durch öffentliche Notare. 1859.
No. 32. Betr. das dem Kongress in Lima vorgelegte Gesetz über die Verhältnisse der in Peru lebenden Fremden. 1860. *Cf.* Peru.
No. 33. Betr. die Lossagung des Staates Süd-Carolina von dem Vereine der nordamerikanischen Freistaaten. 1861.
No. 34. Betr. die Beschwerde des J. B. Mott aus Boston über die hiesige Königl. Polizei-Direktion, wegen Verletzung seines Reisepasses. 1861.
No. 35. Betr. die gesetzlichen Bestimmungen über das Bürgerrecht in den Vereinigten Staaten von Amerika, insbesondere hinsichtlich der Erwerbung desselben von Seiten der einwandernden Fremden. 1861.

No. 36. Betr. die Staatsangelegenheitsverhältnisse der nach Amerika ausgewanderten Hannoveraner. 1862, 1863, 1865.
No. 37. Betr. den Regierungsantritt des Präsidenten der Republik Paraguay Don Francisco Solano Lopez. 1863. Cf. Paraguay.
No. 38. Betr. den Regierungsantritt des Präsidenten der Republik Peru Don Miguel San Roman. 1863. Cf. Peru.
No. 39. Betr. das neue Münzwesen der Republik Peru und den dagegen erhobenen Protest. 1863.
No. 40. Betr. die Erhebung des Herrn Jesus Jimenes in San José zum Präsidenten der Republik Costa-Rica. 1863.
No. 41. Betr. die einstweilige Wahrnehmung der Geschäfte eines Ministers der auswärtigen Angelegenheiten von Seiten des Juan José Ulloa. 1863. Cf. Costa Rica.
No. 42. Betr. die Frage, mit welchem Lebensjahre die Rechte der Volljährigkeit in den Vereinigten Staaten von Nordamerika eintreten. 1864.
No. 43. Betr. die Ernennung des Bankiers und Senators Fortlage in Osnabrück zum Commissioner of Deeds für den Staat Missouri. 1864-1865.
No. 44. Betr. das Notificationsschreiben des Präsidenten der Republik Uruguay. 1864.
No. 45. Betr. die Angelegenheiten der Republik Peru. 1864. Offensiv- und Defensiv-Allianz zwischen Chile und Peru gegen Spanien. 1866. Cf. Acta, Spanien, no. 37.
No. 46. Betr. die Gesetzgebung des Staates New York über die Verjährung von Klagen und Forderungen. 1865.
No. 47. Betr. die im Staate New-York incorporirte, in der Stadt New-York domicilirte Lebensversicherungsgesellschaft Germania. 1865.
No. 48. Betr. die Einsendung eines Exemplars der von einer Regierungs-Kommission ausgearbeiteten Generalkarte von Columbien nebst einem vollständigen Atlas aller die Union bildenden Staaten. 1866.
No. 49. Betr. die Aufnahme des William Wolf aus Pittsburgh in die Irrenanstalt zu Göttingen. 1866.

Des[ignation] 9. E. Emigration.
No. 2. Die nähere Ermittelung der zur Anzeige gekommenen Betrügereyen, denen fremde das hiesige Land durchziehende Auswanderer durch angebliche Agenten im hiesigen Königreiche ausgesetzt seyn sollen. 1841.
No. 3. Betr. das Erbieten des K. Consuls Schulze zu New-Orleans, wegen der den Hannoverschen Auswanderern nach jenem Theile von Nord-Amerika zu verschaffenden Erleichterung und Abwendung der denselben bisher auf den Dampfschiffen betroffenen Unglücksfälle. 1841. Vid. Acta K. Consulats in sp. Consulat zu New-Orleans.
No. 4. Betr. die mit dem Senat der freyen Stadt Hamburg eigeleitete Communication über die zu treffenden Anordnungen wegen Sicherstellung des hiesigen Königreiches gegen das Eindringen mitteloser fremder Auswanderer, die beabsichti-

gen, sich behuf ihrer Einschiffung nach Hamburg zu begeben. 1841.
No. 5. Betr. die von der K. Niederländischen Gesandschaft hierselbst beantragte Bekanntmachung einer Verfügung des K. Niederländischen Gouvernements, hinsichtlich der Beförderung deutscher Auswanderer. 1844. Ferner die Behandlung deutscher Auswanderer in den Niederländischen Seehäfen. *Vid.* Acta sub Rubro: Niederlande, Fasc. 129. 1846.
No. 6. Betr. die von der K. Landdrostei hieselbst beantragte Einziehung von Nachrichten über die in anderen deutschen Staaten bestehenden Vorschriften bey Auswanderungen nach Amerika, etc. 1846.
No. 7. Betr. eine Anzeige abseiten der König. Gesandtschaft zu London n. Hamburg von der Uebervortheilung Hannoverscher Auswanderer durch einige hierländische Agenten; ferner die Regelung des Auswanderungswesens. 1847, 1851 *seq. Cf.* Holstein 98.
No. 8. Betr. die vom K. Ministerium des Jnneren beantragte Einziehung von Erkundigungen über die Bestimmungen, welche in anderen deutschen Bundesstaaten wegen Aufnahme-Zusicherungen bey Einwanderungen bestehen. 1846, 1847.
No. 9. Betr. die Uebersiedlung diesseitiger Unterthanen nach Australien durch Beihülfe der South-Austral-Company in London zu den Uebersiedlungskosten. 1848.
No. 10. Betr. eine Anfrage Baierns über die hiesigen Ansichten hinsichtlich der Auswanderungsfrage. 1849. *Vid.* Acta, Bundest. Verh. Lit. A., Fasc. 33.
No. 11. Betr. die von dem Senate zu Bremen in Anregung gebrachte übereinstimmende Gesetzgebung für die Hannoverschen, Oldenbergschen, und Bremenschen Weserhäfen hinsichtlich des bei der Untersuchung und Verproviantirung der Auswandererschiffe zu beobachtenden Verfahrens. 1850. *Vid.* Seeschiffahrt, Gen. u. Var., Fasc. 11.
No. 12. Betr. die gesetzlichen Vorschriften über die Auswanderung in das Hamburgische Gebiet. 1851.
No. 13. Betr. die von dem Königlich-Preussischen General-Consul Hebeler in London verfasste Darstellung des jetzigen Auswanderungswesens. 1852.
No. 14. Betr. die Auswanderung hiesiger Unterthanen. 1852. *Cf.* Acta, no. 493, den Vertrag wegen der Uebernahme der Auszuweisenden.
No. 15. Betr. die von dem Senate zu Bremen mitgetheilten Entwürfe zu einem Staatsvertrage hinsichtlich der Regelung des Auswanderungswesens. 1852.
No. 17. Betr. Massregeln zur Verhinderung der heimlichen Auswanderung böswilliger Schuldner nach Amerika. 1853.
No. 18. Betr. die Eheschliessungen von Auswanderern. 1853.
No. 19. Betr. die Verordnung des Senats der freien Stadt Bremen vom 15-17. Mai 1854 über das Verbot des Verkaufs von Billets zur Weiterbeförderung von Auswanderern von dem überseeischen Landungsplatze nach dem Bestimmungsort im Jnnern. 1854.

No. 20. Betr. die Staatsangehörigkeit der im Auslande lebenden Hannoveraner. 1859.
Verzeichnis der Acten der Geheimen Canzlei in London, England.
    No. 1-159. Relations of Hanover with England in general.
        Matter relating to 10,000 troops furnished England by Hanover in 1701 and later.
        Matter relating to similar service on the part of Braunschweig-Lüneburg in 1702 and later.
        Matter relating to treaties between Hanover and England and Sweden and Holland.
    Nos. 128-141. Berichte und Zeitungen aus London. 1717.
    No. 150. Matter relating to furnishing England with troops, by Count Solms.
    No. 159. Zusammenstellung über die von England unterhaltenen deutschen Truppen.
Des[ignation] 92. 1714-1837.
    D. Aussereuropäische Staaten.
        XLI, 134. Die von den Abgeordneten der Spanisch-Südamerikanischen Provinzen (Republik Columbia) nachgesuchte Anerkennung der Independenz. 1822-1824.
        Die Gelangung des Vicente Guerrero zur Präsidentur in Mexico. 1829.
        XLI, 135. Kaiserthum Brasilien.
            a. Die Werbungen Deutscher durch Major Schäffer für Brasilien und dessen Austreten als Brasilianischer Agent. 1824-1825.
            b. Die Anerkennung des Kaiserthums Brasilien. 1826.
            c. Den als Brasilianischen diplomatischen Agenten aufgenommenen Oberstleutenant Schäffer. 1826.
            d. Brasiliens Krieg mit den Vereinigten Staaten von Rio de la Plata. 1826.
            e. Abdikation des Kaisers Don Pedro I. zu Gunsten Don Pedro II. 1831.
        XLI, 137. Die Volksunruhen im Jahre 1831.
        XLI, 138. Condition, etc.
            1. Brasilien. Geschäftsträger Cheval. Meneze Vasconcellos de Drummond u. Consuln Kaltmann in Hannover, Taaks zu Emden. 1829-1831.
            2. Mexico. Geschäftsträger von Gorostiza u. die Ernennung des v. Uslor zum Hannov. Handelsagenten in Mexico. 1826-1827.
It would be well for the investigator interested in minor South American or West Indian or British American countries to examine the diplomatic records relating to these countries.
Des[ignation] 41. E. Acten Verzeichniss des Churfürstl. Hannoverschen General Commandos. Durchmärsche der fremdländischen Truppen durch hannoversches Gebiet. 1776-1800.
    I. Braunschweiger.
        No. 1. Durchmarsch der 1 Divis. Herzoglich Braunschw. Truppen durch das Hannoversche Land, behuf ihrer Einschiffung zu Stade. Bestand: 1 Grenad. Bataillone; 1 [Infant.] Regt. v.

Riedesel; 1 Regt. Prinz Friedrich. Deren Marschrouten und Verpflegung. Convention zwischen Preussen und Braunschweig wegen gegenseitiger Durchmärsche de 1697. (Subsidien Tractat de 1768.) Feb.-Mar., 1776.

No. 2. Durchmarsch der 2 Division Herzogl. Braunschw. Truppen, bestehend aus den Regtn. v. Rhetz, v. Specht, und den leichten Batt. v. Barner. Marschrouten für dieselben. Instruction f. d. Regiments- Commandeurs-Gage und Verpflegung der Truppen während ihres Transports zu Schiffe. Eidesformular für dieselben als Engl. Subsidien Truppen. Jan.-Mar., 1776.

No. 3. Rapporte des Majors v. Malorte über die Führung und Einschiffung der Braunschweigischen Truppen. Jan.-Mar., 1776.

No. 4. Berichte des Majors Malortie an den Feldmarschall v. Spörken, über die Führung und Einschiffung der Braunschweigischen Truppen. (Important account of expenses and list of officers.) Jan.-May, 1776.

II. Churhessen A. 1. Division.

No. 5. Verhandlung der Regierung zu Hannover mit dem Feldmarschall v. Freytag wegen des Durchmarsches der Hessischen Truppen im Allgemeinen. Correspondenz mit dem die Engl. Werbungen leitenden Obersten Faucitt. Jan., 1776.

No. 6. Correspondenz zwischen dem Ministerio und dem Feldmarschall v. Freytag wegen Durchmarsch der Hess. Truppen. Ernennung der betr. Marsch-Commissäre und Massregeln zur Verhütung der Desertionen von Hessischen Truppen. Feb., 1776.

No. 7. Instruction für den Obersten und Gen. Quartiermstr. v. Estorf, den Amtmann Dreppenstedt, und andere als Marsch-Commissaire bestellte Offiziere betr. Feb., 1776.

No. 8. Rapporte des Hauptmann Niemeyer über die Durchführung der in Colonne Hessischer Truppen, bestehend aus dem Grenad. Batt. von Block, Regimente v. Mirbach, v. Donop, Erbprinz. Mar., 1776.

No. 9. Rapporte des Capit. Lieutenants v. Langen über den Durchmarsch folgender Hessischer Truppen, als: Grenad. Bataillon v. Minnigerode, Regiment v. Losberg, Regiment v. Rall und v. Kniphausen. Mar., 1776.

No. 10. Correspondenz des Genl. Qrtmstr. v. Estorf mit dem Hess. Genl. Lt. v. Gohr u. v. Heister nebst einem Gesammt Etat der Hessischen an England überlassenen Truppen. Jan.-Mar., 1776.

No. 11. Correspondenz des Oberst u. Gen. Qrtmstr. v. Estorf mit dem Landgrafen Friedrich v. Hessen, dem Hess. Gen. Lt. v. Schlieffen, dem Engl. Obersten Faucitt und dem Hess. Obersten v. Junken. Mar., Apr., 1776.

No. 12. Verhandlungen mit den versch. Aemtern und Gerichten über den Durchmarsch und die Verpflegung der fragl. (Hessischen) Truppen. Feb., Mar., 1776.

No. 13. Correspondenz des Gen. Qrtmstr. v. Estorf mit dem Amtmann Hintze zu Lilienthal über die Bequartirung der Truppen im Bremenschen. Feb., Mar., 1776.
No. 14. Correspondenz des Gen. Qrtmstr. v. Estorf mit den Braunschweigischen und Fürstlich Hildesheimischen Marsch Commissairen. Feb., 1776.
No. 15. Correspondenz des Gen. Quartmstr. v. Estorf mit der freien Reichstadt Bremen. Feb., Mar., 1776.
No. 16. Das Embarquement der Hessischen Truppen zu Bremerlehe betr. Verzeichniss der Transportschiffe und der Vertheilung der Truppen auf denselben. Mar., Apr., 1776.
No. 17. Berichte des General Qrtmstr. v. Estorf an das Ministerium über den beschafften Durchmarsch und die Einschiffung der Truppen, desgl. über die Oldenburgsche Zollfreiheit und gelegentliche Desertionen Hannov. Soldaten. Mar. 11–Apr. 19, 1776.
No. 18. Berichte des General Qrtrmstr. v. Estorf an den Feldmarschall v. Spörcken über den fraglichen Durchmarsch. Mar. 17–Apr. 19, 1776.
No. 19. Berichte der Marsch-Commissaire an den Feldmarschall v. Spörcken über den fragl. Durchmarsch. (Very important for the lists of regiments, etc.) Feb., Mar., 1776.
No. 20. Eides-formular für die Hessischen Subsidial Truppen und einige Verzeichnisse von Hessischen Offizieren. (Contains list of " Commandeurs der Grenadier Bataillone ".)
No. 21. Marschrouten der Hessischen Truppen durch das Churfürstenthum Hannover, wobei auch solche welche bereits 1756 für das Bremensche entworfen sind.
No. 22. Varia, den Hessischen Durchmarsch betreffend. Jan.-Apr., 1776. (Contains " Specificationen ", " Berechnungen ", lists of supplies, of regiments, etc.)

II. Churhessen A. 2. Division.
No. 23. Correspondenz des Gen. Qrtrmstr. v. Estorf mit dem Gen. Lieut. v. Gohr wegen des Marsches der 3. Division unter Commando des GLt. v. Knyphausen von Cassel bis Ritzebüttel. (Contains important lists of regiments, etc.) May, 1776.
No. 24. Ein Project über den Wasser-Transport der fraglichen Truppen von Münden bis Bremerlehe.
No. 25. Verhandlungen zwischen dem Ministerio und dem Gen. Qrtrmstr. v. Estorf über den Durchmarsch und die Verpflegung der Hess. Truppen, bestehend aus 1. Comp. Feldjäger, drei Regtrn. v. Wuttginau, v. Wissenbach, v. Bünau, v. Hayn und dem Grenad. Batt. v. Köhler. Apr., May, 1776.
No. [26]. Rapporte von der als Marsch-Commissaire bestellten Hauptleutn. Niemeyer und v. Wangenheim über die Führung der Truppen bis zu ihrer Einschiffung zu Ritzebüttel. May, June, 1776.
No. 27. Generelle Verhandlungen der Hannov. Regierung mit dem Feldmarsch. v. Spörcken und von Hardenberg über den Durchmarsch Braunschweigischer, Hessischer, und Wal-

Hannover

deckscher Truppen. Die darüber erstatteten Berichte an den König von England. (Contains among other things important decrees in printed copies and some lists of companies, etc.) Jan.-Dec., 1776.

No. 28. Verhandlung der Hannoversch. Regierung mit dem Feldmarschall v. Spörcken und v. Hardenberg über den Durchzug Braunschw., Hessischer, und Waldeckscher Truppen in den Jahren 1777-1781.

No. 29. Varia und Brieffe den 2ten Marsch der Hessischen Truppen betreffend. Mar.-May, 1776.

III. Anhalt-Zerbster.

No. 30. Verhandlungen der Hannov. Regierung mit dem Feldmarschall v. Hardenberg, dem Engl. Gen. Major Faucitt und der Anhaltischen Regierung über den zu gestattenden Durchmarsch eines an England überlassenen Grenadier Bataillons. Jan.-Mar., 1778.

IV. Anspacher, Hanausche, und Waldecksche Recruten Transporte.

No. 31. Correspondenz der diesseit. Regierung mit dem Feldmarschall v. Hardenberg über die Escortierung dieser Recruten Transporte. Feb., Mar., 1778.

No. 32. Escortirung verschiedener nach Amerika bestimmter Recruten Transporte. Mar.-May, 1782.

V. Rückmarsch der versch. von Amerika zurückkehrenden fremden Corps betr.

No. 33. Rapporte und Berichte wegen der Rückmärsche der fremden Truppen, welche aus Amerika bei Stade und Bremerlehe ausgeschifft werden und weiter nach ihren resp. Ländern die Marsch-Anweisungen erhalten haben. 1783-1784. The first paper is a " Berechnung des Verlustes deutscher Truppen in Amerika ", a most important paper, giving 8662 men as the " Total Verlust ".

X. Fremde Werber u. Recrut. Transporte.

No. 41. Werbungen des Oberstlt. v. Scheither u. anderer Personen für die Krone v. England. Gestattung von Werbeplätzen im hiesigen Lande und Transport der Recruten betr. 1775-1776. A list of eight papers containing earlier negotiations of Faucitt in enlisting recruits in Hanover. The first paper announces an " Accord " that Col. Faucitt with Lieut.-Col. Scheither shall recruit 4000 men and deliver them at Stade. This paper is dated: " Hanover den 7ten Nov. 1775 ". The " Rescript " signed by George III. is dated: " St. James den 7ten Nov. 1775 ", and addressed: " An den Feldmarschall v. Spörcken ". According to this agreement it is assumed that no Hanoverian troops be engaged: " Wie Wir nun voraussetzen, dass derselbe sich in Unsern dortigen Landen aller Werbung enthalte und keinen Einheimischen engagiere ", etc.

No. 42 a. Aufnahme Englischer Werbe-Commandos im Lande. (Taken from the Repertorium.) 1776-1796.

No. 44. Ueberlassung diesseitiger Off. und Mannschaften an das nach Amerika bestimmte Hanauische Jäger-Corps betr. 1777.

The following rubrics may be consulted for scattered references to
    America:
Armatur und Pferde-Equipagen betreffend, etc. Cavallerie, nos. 43, 46,
    47, 65, 66, 67, 69, 70, 71, 72, 73, 114 a.
Infanterie, nos. 5, 6, 8, 9, 10, 11, 12, 13.
Artillerie-Regiment und Ingenieur-Corps:
    No. 4. Correspondenz mit Georg III. während der Zeit 1774-1802.
    No. 10. Munition.
    No. 13. Correspondenz der Kriegs-Kanzlei, etc.
Avancement, etc.
    No. 22. Verzeichnisse von den in den Jahren 1776-1790 stattgehabten Avancements.

KÖNIGSBERG.
ROYAL STATE ARCHIVES.
(KÖNIGLICHES STAATSARCHIV.)

Located in the old castle (Schloss) in the corner beyond and over the "Court of Blood" (Blutgericht), which is now a wine cellar and restaurant. This castle was formerly the seat of the Teutonic Order and later the residence of Frederick William III. of Prussia after the troublous times of 1807. It was here that the great plans which led to the rehabilitation of Prussia and the Empire were formed. Incorporated with the State Archives is a valuable collection of papers relating to the Bourse (Kaufmannschaft) of Königsberg. The Handels-Kammer, however, still has many records not yet handed over to the State Archives. For these the investigator must consult the Syndicus of the Handels-Kammer.

Hours: 8 to 1.

Vasallen-Tabellen (Fernere Vasallen-Tabellen in der Registratur des Etatsministeriums 110 g).

109 g. Generalia wegen verbothener Peregrinationen ausser Landes. Item Vasallen-Tabellen.

Contains edicts relating to emigration. The earliest patent relating to emigration is dated Nov. 20, 1643: "Patent vom 20ten Nov. 1643 wegen examinerung der frembden Passagiers".
"Patent vom 30ten Jan. 1686. Von der Peregrination, dass selbige nicht ohne Consens unternommen werden soll." (A printed copy of the edict issued by Frederick William from Potsdam.)

Edict of the Elector of Brandenburg regulating emigration and migration. Königsberg, Oct. 11, 1700.

Edicts of 1739 and following years relating to sending children abroad, and to emigration in general.

127 a. Acta des Ostpreussischen Etats-Ministeriums, betr. des Kaufmannes Carl Gottfried Paleske zu Philadelphia.

Wegen einer Bestellung zum General Consul in den Vereinigten Nord-Americanischen Staaten zur Beförderung und Ausbreitung des Handels und der Schiffarth nach Nord-America. 1791.

Litt. A. No. 7. Acta des Vorsteher-Amts der Kaufmannschaft zu Königsberg betreffend die Auswanderungen. 1737-1864.

Edict of Frederick William I., ordering passes for all subjects leaving the country. Königsberg, May 7, 1737.

Papers from 1848 on relating to shipping by way of Bremen and to trade in general.

Printed matter relating to emigration, of which the following is an interesting specimen: *Reisegelegenheit für Passagiere nach California*, signed by A. Schreiber, and giving the terms on which passage can be made. Stettin, Jan., 1849.

Matter relating to the *Deutsche Auswanderer-Zeitung.* Nov., 1851, and Jan. 2, 1852.

Matter relating to Das Auswanderer-Haus zu Bremerhafen (no. 1736, Apr., 1852. Cut and description.)
Bremen als Einschiffungsplatz für deutsche Auswanderer, Wahrheit gegen Unwahrheit (May, 1852).
Berichte of the Nachweisungsbüreau in Bremen.

Litt. C. No. 24. Acta, etc., betreffend die Nordamerikanische Consuls in Preussen. 1830-1872.
Notice of the appointment of the merchant Friedrich Schellow as American consul at Stettin, Königsberg, May 5, 1830, the appointment of Stadtrath Berent Lorck as consular agent of the United States in Königsberg, June 20, 1832, and similar later acts.

Litt. C. No. 34. Acta, etc., betreffend die Preuss. Consuls in den Hansastädten. 1812-1865.
Small fascicle of papers beginning with the notice of appointment of legation and consular secretary Kolster at Hamburg, Königsberg, Jan. 6, 1812.
Papers relating to shipping at Cuxhaven. 1846.

Lit. C. No. 40. Acta, etc., betreffend die Preuss. Consuls in Nordamerika. 1791-1870.
Papers relating to the appointment of Carl Gottfried Paleske, merchant, as consul general at Philadelphia. Oct. 14, 1791.
Similar papers relating to consular appointments at later times.

Litt. C. No. 95. Acta, etc., betreffend die Preuss. Consuls in Süd-Amerika. 1842-1873.

Litt. C. No. 101. Acta, etc., betreffend die Anlegung preussischer Colonien in Nord-America.

Litt. C. No. 106. Acta, etc., betreffend Preuss. Consuls in Mexico. 1848-1866.

The following numbers are presumably still in the Handels-Kammer:

Litt. C. No. 2. Acta, etc., die Colonisten betr. 1721-1752.
No. 41. *Id.*, Preussische Consuls in Brazilien betr.
No. 146. *Id.*, die Preuss. Consuls in Central-Amerika betr. 1863-1869.
No. 147. *Id.*, die Preuss. Consuls in Chili betr. 1844-1869.
No. 152. *Id.*, die Preuss. Consuls in Westindien.
No. 155. *Id.*, betr. die deutschen Konsulate in fremden Landen überhaupt.
No. 157. *Id.*, die Fremden Konsulate in Deutschland.
No. 163. *Id.*, Correspondenz mit London.
No. 35. *Id.*, Preussische Consuls in England betr. 1800-1870.

Litt. D. No. 14. Acta, Prozess des Kaufmanns G. A. Dieckmann in Bremerhafen wider die Allgem. Vers. Ges. für See- Fluss- und Land-Transport in Dresden, Hauptagent hier Kfm. Otto Schröder.

Litt. H. No. 8. Acta Ober-Praesidialia. Handels und Schiffahrts Angelegenheiten. Vol. I. Dec. 29, 1818–June, 1826.

Litt. S. No. 34. Acta die Ueberladung der Schiffe mit Passagieren betr. 1826-1827.

MAGDEBURG.

ROYAL STATE ARCHIVES.
(KÖNIGLICHES STAATSARCHIV.)

Located: Augustastrasse 25, in a fine new fire-proof building with excellent appointments.[1]

Hours: 8 to 1 and (except Saturdays) 3 to 5.

GRAFSCHAFT MANSFELD.

Rep. **XXI**. Nr. 11. Acta die Englischen und Russischen Colonisten betr. ergangen 1753, 1766. Conspectus Actorum:
  Nr. 1. Des Kgl. Cammer Präsidentur v. Platen Hochwürd. und Hochwohlgeb. Schreiben. Fol. 1.
  Nr. 2. Umlauff an Sämtl. Gerichtsobrigkeiten. Fol. 3.
  Nr. 3. Den Policey Reutern einhalts des vorstehenden Schneibens Ordre ertheilet. Fol. 4.
  Nr. 4. Bericht an des Kgl. Cammer Präsident von Platen Hochw. Fol. 4.
  Nr. 5. Umlauff wie er präsentirt. Fol. 6.

Contains 9 papers in all, the first 3 dating from the year 1753 and relating to the emissaries who are inducing the Mansfelders to emigrate. The first document is dated June 1, 1753, and prescribes strict vigilance on the part of the police to keep out the emissaries who stealthily slip into the land, "um Teutsche zu denen Englischen Colonien in America anzunehmen und zu debauchiren". The authorities are ordered to watch, "dass dergleichen Emissaires sich nicht in hiesige Landen weder öffentl. einfinden, noch heimlich einschleichen, um Unterthanen oder andere Leuthe, zu gedachten Englischen Colonien in Afrika oder sonsten, zu engagiren oder zu debauchiren". Severe regulations are made ordering the close inspection of the "Gasthöfe, Schenke und Krüge", and affixing a penalty for the slightest negligence in the examination of passengers. Lists of the court districts and the dates of presentation are entered on the document.

The papers dated 1766 are 8 in number and deal with the "intendirte Verleitung der Unterthanen zur Emigration nach Russland" and are accompanied with a copy of the "Rescript die intendirte Verleitung zur Emigration nach Russland betr." The rest of the papers in this group deal particularly with the emigration to Russia.

KÖNIGL. PROVINCIALARCHIV ZU MAGDEBURG.

Rep. **A. 8.** Magdeb. Cammer I. 921. Acta die von Hamburg aus nach Nord-America geschickte Königl. Preussische Unterthanen und die desfals veranlasste Untersuchung, item nach England de ao. 1802 [-1804].

---

[1] Attention is called also to the collections of the Stadtarchiv, located Hauptwache 4

Contains 26 papers including tabular lists, etc., relating to the shipping of 32 Prussian subjects of Magdeburg on a ship sailing from Hamburg to Philadelphia in Mar., 1801, who, unable to pay the 20 guineas passage money, bound themselves to serve out the amount: "dass sie sich gegen die Eigentümer des Schifs verbindlich gemacht haben, sich zur Abverdienung obiger Se. nach ihrer Ueberkunft, von einer dazu verordneten Societät nach ihrem Gewerbe und Kenntnissen unterbringen zu lassen. Da sich aber eine solche Societät zu Philadelphia gar nicht gefunden, vielmehr die bemerkten Subjecte sich haben endlich überliefern müssen", etc. Among the names mentioned are the following from Magdeburg (Province): Carl Hecht aus Halle; Schäfer, Bäcker aus Magdeburg; Andreas Schmidt, aus Halle; Holtzmann, Tischler aus Magdeburg. The document directs the "Cammer" of Magdeburg to search for the relatives of these redemptioners and to co-operate with the government in Berlin in relieving them of their misery. Signed: "Berlin den 20. Juli 1802, auf seiner Königl. Majestät allergnädigsten Spezial-Befehl. Alvensleben". An exceedingly interesting fascicle of papers showing the thoroughness with which the Prussian authorities, even at that time, investigated questions relating to emigration. In this connection the following might be consulted for similar matter: Rep. der Acta der Grafschaft Mansfeld (Rep. XXI. Nr. 1-10), particularly the papers relating to "Neuanbauende Ausländer".

MAGDEB. KGL. REG. I ABTEILUNG. POLIZEI-REGISTRATUR (II).

Rep. C. 28. Abt. I. Anbau und Desmembrationssachen. Generalia.
Nr. 67. Auswanderungsgesuche aus dem Kreise Aschersleben. 6 Bde. 1852-1880.
Nr. 68. *Id.*, Calbe. 8 Bde. 1852-1878.
Nr. 69. *Id.*, Gardelegen. 9 Bde. 1852-1876.
Nr. 70. *Id.*, Halberstadt. 6 Bde. 1852-1876.
Nr. 71. *Id.*, Jerichow I. 6 Bde. 1852-1878.
Nr. 72. *Id.*, Jerichow II. 5 Bde. 1852-1876.
Nr. 73. *Id.*, Magdeburg. 15 Bde. 1852-1877.
Nr. 74. *Id.*, Neuhaldensleben. 3 Bde. 1852-1876.
Nr. 75. *Id.*, Oschersleben. 3 Bde. 1852-1876.
Nr. 76. *Id.*, Osterburg. 5 Bde. 1852-1876.
Nr. 77. *Id.*, Salzwedel. 5 Bde. 1852-1876.
Nr. 78. *Id.*, Stendal. 4 Bde. 1852-1876.
Nr. 79. *Id.*, Wanzleben. 3 Bde. 1852-1876.
Nr. 80. *Id.*, Wolmirstedt. 3 Bde. 1852-1890.
Nr. 81. *Id.*, Wernigerode. 3 Bde. 1852-1876.
Nr. 83. Das Auswanderungs- und Heimathschein-Gesuch des G. C. Weinschenk hier 1848-1852 (verkauft).
Nr. 87. Das Auswanderungsgesuch des Heinrich Könnecke 1857 (verkauft).
Nr. 84-89. Papers relating to other individuals.

Magdeburg 111

Armensachen, Specialia.
    Nr. 109, relating to a German returned from America, 1845-1847 (verkauft).
Pass Sachen, Specialia.
    Nr. 1-14, scattered references.
    Nr. 134. Die Uebernahme von Agenturen der ausländischen Renten-, Aussteuer-, Witwen-, und Lebensversicherungsgesellschaften. 1837-1857.
    Nr. 231-253. Die hier unter polizeilicher Aufsicht stehenden Personen. A-Z. 1846-1879.
    Nr. 290. Transport Russisch-Polnischer Unterthanen aus dem Oesterreichischen Staate nach Frankreich und Belgien.
    Nr. 291. Conzessionierung von Agenturen zur Annahme und Beförderung von Ausländern.
    Nr. 1-322. Papers relating to insurance societies, etc.
    Nr. 365. Das Geschäft der Beförderung von Auswanderern seitens der Inhaber der Firma Carl Pokrantz et Co. in Bremen. 1853-1862.
    Nr. 366. *Id.*, F. Y. Wichelhausen et Comp. zu Bremen. 1853-1859.
    Nr. 367. *Id.*, Luedering et Comp. zu Bremen. 1853-1882.
    Nr. 369. *Id.*, Valentine Lorenz Meyer zu Hamburg. 1853-1857.
    Nr. 390. *Id.*, F. B. Boedeker Jun. H. et Heinecken Nachfolger in Bremen. 1854-1869.
    Nr. 409. *Id.*, Eduard Thon zu Bremen. 1856-1898.
Unterstützungs Sachen, Specialia.
    Nr. 103-117 (verkauft).
Versicherungs Sachen, Spezialia.
    Lit. L. Nr. 10. Lebensversicherungs-Gesellschaft Germania in New York. 1868-1894.
    Nr. 14. Lebensversicherungs-Gesellschaft Manhattan in New York. 1871-1874.
    Nr. 22. Equitable Lebensversicherungs-Gesellschaft in New York. 1877-1894.
    Nr. 25. New York Lebensversicherungs-Gesellschaft. 1882-1899.
    Nr. 27. Mutual Life Assurance Company. New York. 1886-1895.
Oberpräsidium, Sectio II., Generalia.
    F. Nr. 11. Aus- und Einwanderungsangelegenheiten. Abschuss. Only this number has been handed over to the archives; the others are still among the government papers.
Oberpräsidium, Sectio II., Specialia.
    Nr. 1, relating to the same subject in the year 1817. The remaining papers are in the Oberpräsidium.

MARBURG.
ROYAL STATE ARCHIVES OF THE DISTRICT OF CASSEL.
(KÖNIGLICHES STAATSARCHIV FÜR DEN REGIERUNGS BEZIRK CASSEL.)

Located in the castle, which was formerly the residence of the landgraves of Hesse, and in which in 1529, at the call of Philip the Magnanimous, the famous dispute between Luther, Melanchthon, Zwingli, Oecolampadius, and others concerning transsubstantiation took place. The collections of parchment documents and other rare papers number about 100,000 and are made up from three other archives: (1) the archives of the suppressed electorate of Hesse-Cassel, containing the papers relative to the American Revolution, and in part formerly preserved in the Wilhelmshöhe Schlossbibliothek near Cassel; (2) the archives of Fulda, containing rare and precious parchments, documents from the reign of Pippin on; (3) the archives of Hanau.

Hours: 8 to 1.

In addition to the Königlich Preussische und Grossherzoglich Hessische Samtarchiv, the castle contains a rare collection of objects illustrating Hessian life and customs.

O. W. S. Fach 1247. Kriegssachen 1776-1782. Untersuchungs-Akten betrffd Affaire von Trenton. Thick fascicle of papers containing among other things the following:
Die Action bey Trentown in Nord-America den 26. Debris 1776. Signed: " L. C. von Heister Hauptmann im Hessen Cassellisch Leib Dragoner Regiment". 28 pp. Hamburg, Sept. 16, 1787.
Acta, die Ueberrumpelung der Hessischen Brigade Rall bei Trenton betreffend, namentlich Berichte des Generaleutnants v. Knyphausen an den Landgrafen Friedrich II. zu Hessen mit Protocollen, etc. 1778-1782.
Extracts of a letter of the Landgraf to Lieutenant Generals Heister and Knyphausen, copies of order from James Grant, communications from Rall, Joseph Reed, Donop, Stirling, A. Leslie, Wrede, Thos. Gamble, John Cadwalader, also correspondence between Grant, Leslie, and Donop (in copy).
" Species Facti " of the battle of Trenton, signed by Scheffer. Philadelphia, May 25, 1778.
" Species Facti " signed by Matthaeus, and copy of the " Relation "of Baum, captain in Knyphausen's regiment, dated Philadelphia, May 20, 1778.
Plans of the battle of Trenton (in colors).
Kriegsprotocoll, with seals of the F. Hess: Oberauditoriat.
Special Protocoll II. Die Untersuchung der Surprise zu Trenton, Verhöre des Regiment von Lossberg betr. Two thick fascicles containing important lists.
Special Protocoll, Verhör des Regiments von Knyphausen.
Protocoll, Verhör des Grenadier Regiments Rall modo vacant von Wölwarth betr.
" Gutachten " of Wangermann. Cassel, Dec. 22, 1778.

Marburg 113

Extracts from papers relating to the surprise with the votum signed by Wotheisen.
The Landgraf to Knyphausen. Weissenstein, Apr. 22, 1779.
Kasseler Kriegskollegium to the Landgraf. Cassel, Apr. 15, 1782.
Letters of Knyphausen to the Landgraf.
Correspondence between Grant, Leslie, and Donop.
Communications to and from Knyphausen.

O. W. S. Fach 1248. Journal vom Hessisch. Corps in Amerika unter dem Gen. v. Heister, 1776–June, 1777 ("aus der Wilhelmshöher Schlossbibliothek durch seine Majestät König Wilhelm I. überwiesen"). Volume of papers bound in vellum numbered CXVIII., belonging to series of volumes bound uniformly, to which the following volumes also belong. Bl. 1-252. Contains copies of the Journal of General Heister's corps, beginning with Feb. 3, 1776. Most valuable matter for the history of the Revolution, as the journals were kept from day to day in the headquarters of the General Staff, and give an account of the movements of the German auxiliaries.

O. W. S. 1248. Relationes vom Nord-Amerikanischen Kriege unter dem Commandier. Gener. v. Heister ("aus der Wilhelmshöher Schlossbibliothek"). 1776, 1777. Vols. I., II., III., IV., V., with a series number CXIX., CXX., CXXI., CXXII., CXXIII., and bound uniformly with the preceding volume CXVIII.

Vol. I. Contains original communications sent by Heister and Knyphausen to the Landgraf of Hesse. The first is dated Cassel Jan. 23, 1776, and is a letter signed by Heister, accepting the appointment of the Landgraf and stating the compensation as follows: 741 1/2 Rth per month while on German soil and £180 while on English soil.
Letters of Faucitt to Heister.
Letters of Francis Carr Clerke to Knyphausen.
Rapport von denen zu der 1ten Brigade der 1ten Division gehörigen Regimentern, Grenadier-Battaillons und Jäger Comp. vom 3ten Martii 1776, and similar ones of Mar. 7, 13, 19, 21, 1776, and later dates.
Monatliche Tabelle von sämtlichen zu der 1ten Division gehörigen Regimentern, etc., pro Martio 1776.
Official papers relating to the mustering of troops, lists of officers and numbers of men.
Communications of Mirbach and an autograph letter of the Landgraf dated Cassel, May 13, 1776.
Letter of Sir George Osborn, announcing his appointment by Faucitt.
Original seal accounts of forces from Heister.
Répartition Des Trouppes Hessoises sur les Vaisseaux suivantes après leur Élargissement à la Rade de Spithead ce 28me Avril 1776, and others of a similar character.
Communications, reports, etc., of Schmidt to the Landgraf and replies thereto.

Communications from Lieutenant von Linckersdorff to the Landgraf.

Im Congress, den 14ten August 1776, a printed paper making overtures to the Germans to leave the British lines and settle in the United States, endorsed: " Auf Verordnung des Congresses, John Hancock, President, Bezeugts Charles Thompson, Secretär ". One printed page accompanied by the emblem with the legend: " Hearts of Oak ".

Pencil sketch of " Flatbusch " or " Flack-busch ".

List of officers and of the musquetiers of the forces.

Valuable historical matter, dated New York, Feb. 27, 1777.

Vol. II. Relationes vom Nord-Amerikanischen Kriege unter dem Commandier. Gen. v. Knyphausen. 1777, 1778. II. (From the Wilhelmshöhe Schlossbibliothek.) Matter relating to Knyphausen's forces quite similar to that of vol. I. relating to Heister's forces, including:

Reports of Lossberg and other officers concerning the movement of the German forces in America.

German translation of a letter of General Howe dated: " Dalworth nahe bey Chad's Ford den 12ten Septbr 1777 ".

Copy of an interesting letter of Howe to Donop, thanking Captain Stamford for his bravery at the Waters Edge and stating that he has sent 20 guineas to be distributed among the Hessian Grenadiers who followed Captain Moncrief on the 11th inst. and drove the enemy from the boats. Germantown, Oct. 13, 1777.

Tabelle von denen Hochfürstl. Hessischen Troupen in America. Sept., 1777.

Communication of J. Matthäus. Relation um die feindliche Armée unter General Washington, welche 14 Engl. Meilen von Philadelphia, auf den Gebirgen von Whitmarsh der Gegend Norrington stehet, ihren linken Flügel an den Wisahiccon und den Rechten gegen den Deleware 6 Meilen en front extendiret, etc. Winchester, Sept. 29, 1777.

Anlagen zu den von Donop. Journal von Lit. A. bis hh. inclusive. (Copies of important notes and reports.)

Vol. III. Same title as vol. II. 1779, 1780. (From the Wilhelmshöhe Schlossbibliothek.) Continuation of similar papers, among them the following:

Copies of Letters and " Articles of Capitulation " of April 10–May 11, 1780 (South Carolina: printed by Robertson, Macdonald, and Cameron), with many papers relating thereto.

Proceedings of the Board to examine John André. Sept. 29, 1780.

Vol. IV. Same title as preceding. 1781, 1782. (From the Wilhelmshöhe Schlossbibliothek.) Contains among other papers the following:

Reports and letters from Knyphausen and from other officers to him, particularly from Lieut. Müller, Motz, J. W. Endemann, Auditeur Steuber, v. Seitz, Capt. Reiffurth, Graf,

Arnold Larbusch, Linsing, Ewald, v. Münchhausen and v. Löwenstein.

Liste von Gebliebenen und Verwundeten Officiers in der Affaire bey Guildford Court-House am 15ten Mart. 1781.

Liste derer Trouppen unter Ordre des General Lieutenant Milord Cornwallis, so würklich in der Action den 15ten März a. c. bey Guilford Court House unter dem Gewehr gewesen und in der Action Todt geschossen, Blessiert und Vermisst worden.

Reports of Du Buy from Cape Fear River, N. C., Apr. 24, 1781, of v. Fuchs from Portsmouth, Va., May 13, 1781, of v. Bose from Charlestown, May 4, 1781, of Lieut.-Col. v. Wurmb, July 4, 1781. (Copies.)

Letter of H. Clinton commending v. Wurmb, July 7, 1781. (Copy.)

Sundry other reports accompanying the orders of the War Department of the Landgraf of Hesse, enclosing much printed matter relating to the war such as *A Declaration,* signed by H. Clinton and Mt. [Marriot] Arbuthnot and dated Dec. 29, 1780, offering clemency to the colonies. It is accompanied by copies of the *Royal Gazette* of 1781 and 1782.

Vol. V. Relationes vom Nord-Amerikanischen Kriege unter dem Commandir. Gen. v. Lossberg. 2. (From the Wilhelmshöhe Schlossbibliothek.) 1782, 1783, 1784. 274 *et seq.*

Contains papers similar to those in the preceding volumes, including the following:

Reports of Lossberg to the Landgraf and replies thereto, together with originals and copies.

" Rapport B.", giving list of dead and wounded under v. Bose at York Town, Oct. 19, 1781. (Fol. 133.)

" Rapport C.", giving account of the troops at Bedford, Long Island, in May, 1783. (Fol. 135.)

Letter of Guy Carleton to the Landgraf commending General Lossberg upon his embarcation for Europe, dated New York, Nov. 15, 1783, and the reply of the Landgraf in French. (Fol. 206-209.)

Gef. 1249. Kriegssachen 1783-1789 [1792]. A thick unbound volume of papers containing among others the following papers: " List of troops of Hesse Cassel " (a recent typewritten copy, evidently new. On the second and last page at the left and right are these signatures: " N. York. 1783. Copied by Fredk. Mackenzie, Major R. W. F.—Wm. Wiederhold Lt. Regt. du Corps ").

Hessen-Cassel'scher Kriegsstaat (Americanischer Krieg). Die nach der Rückkehr des im Amerikanischen Krieg für den Dienst der Krone England angenommenen Hessen-Cassel'schen Auxiliar-Corps von demselben abgehenden Bediensteten, deren Wiederanstellung, Pensionirung, etc., betr. A very important list of officers and subalterns. About 1783.

Den Marsch der aus America zurückkommenden Fürstl. Hessischen und anderen Trouppen, und die den ersteren zum Theil angewiesene Stand Quartiere btr. 1783, 1784.

Die von den Städten Rinteln und Oldendorff gebetene Vergübung der im Herbst 1783 aus America zurückgekommenen Trouppen gelieferten Mundportionen betr. 1786, 1788, 1789. A thick bundle of papers bound in paper relating to the return of the Hessians from America and containing among others:

 Letter of Karl Alexander, margrave of Anspach-Bayreuth, asking for the passage of his troops through the domains of his "Vetter" in the same manner as they had been allowed to go to embark for America, together with papers relating thereto, giving the "Marschroute" for each detachment. [*Cf.* Würzburg.] Anspach, Aug. 19, 1783.

Aufnahms und Fahr Patent für einen Transport Hanauischer Trouppen, containing lists of troops, etc. Cassel, Aug. 21, 1783.

Papers from the Geheimen Kriegs-Canzley, with orders signed by Gen.-Lt. v. Jungkenn.

Designation des an nachbenahmte Land-Räthe und Commisarios locorum, für die von denen Untherthanen behuf des Marsches des an die Crone England überlassenen HLöbln. Corps gestellte Fuhren, auch Zug- und Reitpferde zur weiteren Distribution zu vergütenden Geldbetrags und zwar: "Summa 2030.8 Schreibe Zweitausend und Dreissig Rthlr. 8 alb. Cassel den 30n Dec. 1776". Also amounts aggregating 4422 Rthlr. 8 for the years 1776-1784.

Hessen-Cassel'sche Militairsache. Ponton. Der gewesene Vorrathsfischer Wilhelm Gärtner (Gärdner) in Cassel findet in der Fulda auf dem Sandwerre ein kupfernes Schiff, welches zum Zeughause abgeliefert wird. 1789.

The last item and the papers which follow relate to events after the return of the troops from America.

Gef. 1268. Journal von der Campagne in America. Tom. I., II., III., IV., V., VI., VII., VII., IX., X., XI. (From the Wilhelmshöhe Schlossbibliothek durch seine Majestät König Wilhelm I. überwiesen.) This series is bound in thin folio volumes, in brown leather. The volumes have also the old serial numbers, CXXVI., etc.

Tom. I. Contains the following important matter: "Diarium" kept by P. W. Schäffer, "Regiments Auditeur". May 15, 1776–1777.

Journal von der Reise des Detachements der Hochfürstl. Hessischen, Hessen Hanauischen, und Herzoglich Braunschweigischen Trouppen von New-York nach Canada unter dem Commando des Obristen Lentz, Schiff *John*. 1782.

Journal der Reise derer Teutschen Trouppen von Quebec nach Deutschland, verfertiget am Bord des Transport Schiffs *Hero* vom 1ten August, 1783.

Journal von der Reise des Hochfürstl. Hessen Hanauischen Hochlöbl. 1ten Bataillon des Regiment Erbprintz, Artillerie und Jäger Corps von Bremerleh nach Hanoverisch Minden auf der Weser vom 25ten Sept., 1783.

Das von dem, bey dem Hochlöbl. Hessen Hanauischen Infanterie Regiment Erbprintz stehenden Lieutenant und Regiment Quartier Meister Sartorius geführte Journal der Reise nach Amerika, nebst der Fortsetzung desselben von den daselbst gehaltenen Feldzügen. (Mar.-July, 1777. Evidently a copy and incomplete.)

General Quartier Trois Rivières den 31ten May 1777. Marsch Disposition der teutschen Trouppen bis zum General Rendez vous Comberland Head von der ganzen Armée.

Castell Town de 21ten July 1777. Ordre. Also a number of similar orders for the same year.

Tom. II. Contains among other papers the following:

Kurze Reise Beschreibung derer Landgräflich Hessischen Truppen, unter Commando des Herrn General Lieutenant von Heister Excellenz von Bremerleh nach America. (Continued down to Nov. 28, 1777. The order of battle for the British is enclosed.)

Tom. III. Relationes des Hochfürstl. Hessischen Corps in America von 1776-1782. Geführt durch den Obristen Bauermeister. The Relationes are made up of separate sections kept evidently on loose sheets and later put together as a whole. The sheets vary in size from folio to quarto. The whole is an important account of the campaigns, giving much detail of the movements of the forces.

Tom. IV. Contains letters (originals, copies, and extracts) of German officers in America. 1776-1780. Among the interesting things are the following:

Letter dated Hallifax in New Scottland on board the ship *Mallaga*, July 2, 1776. (German.)

Copy of a letter of Kriegs Rath Lorenz, written on the transport *Eagle* near New York, Aug. 14, 1776.

Col. v. Hering to General v. Losberg. Long Island, Sept. 1, 1776.

Copy of a letter of Wagner written to a friend. Long Island, Sept. 5, 1776.

Copies of two unsigned letters written from Long Island. Sept. 3 and 24, 1776.

Sumarischer Extract aus denen Monatlichen Listen von dem in der Crone England Dienst und Sold stehenden Fürstl. Hessischen Corps in America pro Sept. et Octobri 1776.

Liste der von dem Corps des General Lieut. v. Knyphausen bey der Attaque vom 16 9bris 1776 Todgeschossen[en], Blessirten und Vermissten.

Copy of a German letter written by a Hessian officer from the camp at King's Bridge. Nov. 19, 1776.

Von dem Secretario des Herrn Generals von Heister im Lager bei Kingsbridge den 25. Nov., 1776. (Important.)

Extract Schreibens aus America. Trenton, Dec. 18, 1776.

Extract Schreibens d. Lieut. Henkelmann vom Steins Regiment an den Secretarius Strieder in Cassel. " Im Lager bey Fort Knyphausen ", Jan. 1, 1777. Together with other similar letters.

Copy of a letter of a Hessian captain in Howe's Regiment to his brother in H. auf Biback bey Hentolphelp (?). Aug. 30, 1777.

Lists of killed, wounded, and missing officers, etc.

Long French communication of Donop, giving a report of affairs in America, 1776-1777, including the battle of Trenton.

Letter of Chaplain Theobald to his father, the pastor in Döringen, describing the hardships of the preceding summer. New-Port, R. I., Mar. 26, 1778. Another from the same. Apr. 3, 1778.

Copy of a letter of an officer of the Grenadier Battalion of Minnegerode. Middletown, Sandy Hook, July 3, 1778.

Letter of Freiherr v. Diemar enclosing a list of those who had gone over to his Hussars. Kingsbridge, Nov. 9, 1779.

Plan of Savannah and environs, together with a "Relation". 1779.

More letters of Diemar with a copy of a printed invitation to the Germans to join his corps of Hussars. The print begins: "An alle brave Deutsche", etc., and is dated "Lager zu Kings-Bridge den 12ten August 1779".

Manuscript list of men in the Hussar squadron.

Journal der Expedition auf Charlestown in Süd Carolina unter Commando Sr. Excell. General en Cheff Sir Henry Clinton. Dec. 18, 1779.

Plan der Belagerung von Charlestown.

Liste Générale du Corps des Troupes Allemandes commandé par le Major Général de Riedesel, conformé à l'État recu de Charlotteville en Virginie de ce date. New York, Aug. 1, 1780.

Printed *Proceedings of a Board of General Officers Respecting John André.*

"Auszug" of a letter printed in the *Pennsylvanische Zeitung,* Oct. 4 (1780 ?), relating to André.

Proposed Winter Quarters. 1780.

State of the Regiment of Brunswick Dragoons .... Re-establishment on the 5th of January to the 20th of July 1781.

Unterthänigste Relation von der Belagerung zu York Town in Virginien.

Plan von St. Augustin und dem Fort St. Moris in Ost Florida, in Süd America.

Tom. V. 1776-1780. Contains among other things:

Liste von dem Hochfürstl. Hessen Hanauischen Hochlöblichen Infanterie Regiment Erbprinz, wie selbiges den 25ten Merz 1776 zu Wilhelmstadt auf die Englische Schiffe embarquiret worden.

C. de Creuzbuorg to His Serene Highness. Wilmstadt, Mar. 24, 1776. (French.)

Sir Joseph Yorke to His Serene Highness. The Hague, Mar. 29, 1776.

Same to same. Apr. 2, 1777.

Letters of Col. Rainsford to His Serene Highness, dated The Hague, Mar. 29, 1776; London, May 14, 1776, etc. (French.)

Extract of a letter of Charles Douglas, dated from his ship *Isis* before Quebec, thanking his Excellency Sir Joseph Yorke for "fresh acknowledgments". The letter sheds interesting light on the "Rebels". May 14, 1776.

Extract of a German letter of Fändrich Heerwagen. Prairie St. Magdelaine, Aug. 24, 1776.

Another. Masquinonge, Nov. 16, 1776.

Letter of Guy Carleton relating to the Hessian troops. Quarters General at Quebec, Dec. 16, 1776. (French.)

Carleton to Brig.-Gen. Gall. Same place, Jan. 23, 1777.

Kurzer Auszug aus einem Journal vom 16 Juni 1776 als den Tag unseres debarquements bis den 8ten Mertz 1777 in dem Winterquartier. Signed by J. F. Heerwagen, "Fändrich".

Fortsetzung des Diarij von Prairie aus. Sept. 5, 1776–June 19, 1777.

Liste des Verlustes derer deutschen Trouppen, etc., at Bennington, Aug. 16, 1777.

General Disposition der Armée (at Bennington).

Puncten der Capitulation den 16ten bey Stillwather. Signed by John Burgoyne and Horatio Gates. Oct. 16, 1777.

Hauptmann von Geismar to his father, Ober-Jäger-Meister von Geismar. Albany, Oct. 20, 1777. (Copy.)

Liste denominative des différents Corps composant L'Armée de Son Excellence Lieutenant-Général Bourgogne, l'année 1777, dans l'Expédition de Canada contre les Rebelles.

Quartiers d'Hiver pour les Troupes Allem: en Canada, 1776-1777. (A fine pen sketch.)

Quartier d'Hiver pour les Troupes de Bronswic de la Première Division en Canada, 1776-1777.

Liste Générale de la Perte totale dans l'Armée de la Majesté Brittannique sous le Commendement de Msr. le Général Bourgogne dans la Campagne de 1777.

Copia Schreibens des Lieutenant Heerwagen an seine Eltern zu Hanau. Winter Hill near Boston, Jan. 8, 1778. (Interesting.)

Liste Générale du Corps des Troupes Allemandes, commandées par le Major Général de Riedesel fait à Cambridge ce 1er Juin 1778. (Three different lists.)

Unterthänigstes Pro Memoria. Signed by O. A. Wegener, and containing an important list of companies. Hanau, Sept. 8, 1779.

Statif of the British and German Troops. Charlotte Ville Barracks, Oct. 20, 1779.

Parade Rapport vom Teutschen Corps vom 4ten Junij 1780 auf des Königs Geburts Tage. Signed by Gall.

Vom Englischen Corps auf Sr. Majestät Geburts Tag den 4ten Junij 1780. Signed by Gall. Barracks, Albemarle in Virginia.

Tom. VI. Briefe von sämtlichen Generals aus America. 1778-1783. A thick volume of correspondence beginning with: "Extract eines Schreibens aus New York vom 20ten Sept 1778", and closing with: "Extrait de la lettre du Ministre plénipot:

Bron. de Kutzleben, à son Altesse Sérénissime Monseigneur le Landgrave régnant de Hesse, etc., Londres ce 30 Décembre 1783", enclosing a paper entitled " Embarquement zu New York ". A most important collection of original letters from Gall, Knyphausen, v. Heckenberg, v. Fuchs, Lossberg, Benning, v. Cochenhausen, v. Riedesel, W. P. Philips (who gives a glowing testimonial to the spirit of the Hessian artillery in a letter, dated New York, May 18, 1780), and Guy Carleton.

Tom. VII. Briefe des Major Pausch aus America. An important collection of original letters directed to the Landgraf of Hesse. May, 1776–Nov. 6, 1783.

Tom. VIII. Schreiben von commandirten Officiers des 1ten Bataillons in America. Begins with a letter of von Germann dated Mar. 23, 1776, and closes with a letter from Johannes Mörschell, Feuerwerker, dated Oct. 1, 1780. Among them are letters from Geismar, Gall, Ludwig von Passern [?], von Schöll, von Eschwege, von Lindau, von Buttlar, von Schachten, Dufais, Lieut. Zincke, Heerwagen, Ludw. Kempfer. The collection contains also a petition in behalf of Fähnrich Burckhard, signed by 14 officers and accompanied by a letter of Burckhard, dated Lancaster, July 7, 1781, and other letters by him and by Capt. Kirchhoff, Andreas Koch, Lieut. Carl Dittmar Spangenberg, Joh. Mich. Bach, Capt. Franck, Lieut. Bünau, and Sartorius.

Tom. IX. Correspondenz mit dem Obersten Lentz von der Zeit seines geführten Commandos über das 1te Bataillon Hessen Hanauisc[hen] Grenadier Regiments von 1781-1783. There is a second part of the volume entitled: Ordre-Buch Berthier den 21ten Decembre 1776, including orders and extending over 129 folio pages, and continuing to Oct. 6, 1787.

Tom. X. Correspondenz mit dem Oberst Lieutenant v. Jan[ecke] Chef des Frey Corps von 1781 bis 1783. The volume contains valuable letters and closes with the following: Conduiten-Liste von denen Officiers des Löblich-Hessen-Hanauischen Frey Corps vom 1ten Januar 1783.

Vol. XI. Englische Zeitungen. Contains English " Requisitions " and " Observations " of Carleton, Burgoyne, and others. The first part of the volume contains official proclamations in print, and clippings from English newspapers, chiefly from the London *Gazette* relating to the American Revolution.

O. W. S. **1268.** Journal vom Hochlöbl. Regiment Prinz Carl von Anfang bis zu Ende des Americanischen Krieges, Jan. 14, 1776–Nov., 1784. It contains 22 folios with 40 written pages and gives a list of companies and officers and an account of events in which the regiment took part. It closes with the following: " Hersfeld den 10ten Nov. 1784 J. H. Pfaff, Regts Qtiermeister ".

Journal des Regiments von Ditfurth von der Amerikanischen Campagne. Entries usually very brief. The journal is signed: " C. Wende, R. Qtier Meister ". Feb. 11, 1776–Nov. 14, 1783.

Marburg

CXXXVII. Ordre Buch des Regiments. (From the Wilhelmshöhe Schlossbibliothek.) The title-page runs: " Ordre Buch vor das Hochfürstlich Hessen Hanauische Hochlöbliche 1te Battaillon Erb-Prinz. Angefangen den 10ten October, zu Point Levis im Lager 1782 ". Imperfect. 60 closely written pages large folio. Bound in brown leather. Oct. 10, 1782–Nov. 1, 1783.

Ordrebuch von der Campagne in Amerika vom 13 Apr. 1777 bis 15 Dec. 1781. (From the Wilhelmshöhe Schlossbibliothek.) 206 pp.

General Ordrebuch. (From the Wilhelmshöhe Schlossbibliothek.) 157 pp. Begins at Cambridge, Apr. 4, 1778, and closes with the minutes of a court-martial, New York, Jan. 1, 17, 1783.

Musterliste sämtlicher Hessen-Hanauischen Truppen in Amerika. (From the Wilhelmshöhe Schlossbibliothek.) 143 pp. Mar., 1776–July, 1783.

Militär-Berichte und Relationen, die Operationen des hessischen Corps im amerikanischen Kriege betreffend. (From the Wilhelmshöhe Schlossbibliothek.) 231 pp. 1776-1782.

O. W. S. 1386. Tagebuch eines Grenadiers vom Fürstlich Hessen Hanauischen Infanterie Regiment Erbprinz, Compagnie des Obristlieutenants Lenz, Burschen beim Stabs Capitän späteren Brigade Major Friedrich Wilhelm von Geismar. On a separate wrapper the explanation: " Enthält die Blätter mit Seitennummern von 1-192 von denen das Blatt mit den Seiten 7-8 fehlt, über die Erlebnisse während des Nordamerikanischen Unabhängigkeits-Kriegs vom Tage des Ausmarsches von Hanau 15ten März 1776 bis zum 14ten December 1778 ". The manuscript is made up of loose sheets and breaks off abruptly. An interesting diary containing much detail, a good specimen of which is the account of Canada, pp. 59 *et seq.*

W. S. 1386.

I. B. a. 2. Journal des Hochlöbl. Fuselier Regiments v. Alt Lossberg. Geführt durch den Regiments Quartier Meister Heusser, vom Aus Marsch aus der Garnison Rinteln an, bis zur Zurück Kunft des gedachten hochlöblichen Regimentes aus America. (From the Wilhelmshöhe Schlossbibliothek.) Evidently a clean copy of an earlier draft, a very interesting diary containing official lists of companies, an account of the movements of the army and considerable other detail. Pp. 307. Mar. 10, 1776–Oct. 5, 1783.

I. B. a. 3. Journal des Hochfürstl. Hessischen Grenadier-Regiments von Bischhausen. (From the Wilhelmshöhe Schlossbibliothek. Copied for Lowell 1882, and for Lidgerwood in 1909.) Thin quarto, 84 written pages, signed I. W. Endemann. A straightforward, well constructed, and interesting account of the movements of the regiment and the progress of the war. Contains many citations from speeches. Mar. 4, 1776–Nov., 1, 1782.

I. B. a. 4. Journal vom Hochlöbl. Leib Infanterie Regiment. " Die von dem Jahr 1779 bis incl: den 22ten May 1784 sowohl in

America als Engeland durch den Regiments-Quartier-Meister Berkewitz für das Hochlöbliche Leib-Infanterie Regiment gesammelten Vorfälle und Nachrichten." (From the Wilhelmshöhe Schlossbibliothek.) 94 written pp. Signed " von Kospoth ; Bockewitz, Regiments-Quartier Mstr." Contains interesting detail concerning America, such as the account of horse races, etc.

I. B. a. 5. Journal von dem Hochlöbl. Regiment von Donop modo v. Knyphausen. Vom 29ten Febr. 1776 als dem Tag des Marsches aus Hessen, bis zum 17ten May 1784, als zum Tage des Ein Marsches in die Garnison zu Cassel. Geführt durch den Auditeur und Regiments Quartiermeister Zinn. (From the Wilhelmshöhe Schlossbibliothek.) 69 written pages. Bound in brown leather. On the last page is written: " Carl Philipp Heymell ". Brief but important for data relating to the regiment.

I. B. a. 6. Das Regiment von Knyphausen, etc. (no separate title). Begins with the formation of the regiment as the Hansteinisches Regiment, Anno 1684, and continues till October 16, 1783, when the regiment returned to the garrison in Ziegenhain. Closes with the following in a different hand: " Geführt und aufgestellt von Lieutenant Ritter ". 157 written pp. The detail, though brief, is accurate. A good example is the account of the battle of Trenton and of the movements in the battle of Brandywine.

I. B. a. 7. Journal von dem Hochfürstlich Hessischen des General Lieutenant von Bose Hochlöbl. Infanterie Regiment seines in ao. 1776 aus Hessen nach America geschehenen Aus Marsches, bis zum Jahr 1783 wiederum gethanen Ein Marsches zur Garnison Hoffgeismar. (From the Wilhelmshöhe Schlossbibliothek.) 296 pp. Bound in half leather. A sober military account with but meagre general detail, signed: Carl Bose.

I. B. a. 9. Ordre Buch vom Hochlöblichen Regiment von Mirbach vom 10ten März 1777 bis den 24ten Juny 1780. (From the Wilhelmshöhe Schlossbibliothek.) 420 written pp. Begins with an account of the troops and the order of battle.

I. B. a. 10. Journal vom H. Löbl. Leib Infanterie Regiment modo Erbprinz angefangen im Februario 1776 da solches nach America marschirte geendigt Ende Maji 1784, da das Regiment nach der Retour von America in Marburg seinem neuen Stand Quartier einrückte. The title-page adds, " Nach der retour von America in die bestimmte Garnison zu Marburg in Oberhessen einrückte geführt vom Stabs-Auditeur und Regiments-Quartiermeister Lotheisen". 134 written pp. The journal opens with the historical account of the " Subsidien Tractat " between Great Britain and the Landgraf of Hesse Cassel, Jan. 15, 1776, and contains a plain account of the campaigns.

I. B. a. 11. Journal von Sr. Hochfürstl. Durchlaucht Prinz Friedrichs Hochlöblichen Infanterie Regiment von 1776 bis Ende 1783. The title-page adds: " Vom Aus Marsch nach America vom 2ten Martii 1776 bis zu dessen Zurückkunft am 19ten Novembris 1783 ; Worin alle die Vorfälle und Begebenheiten, so dieses Hochlöbl. Regiment in denen Campagnen in America beigewohnet und betroffen aufgezeichnet sind vom Regiments Quartier Meister Ludewig ". 135 written pp. Bound in red. Contains a plain but accurate account of the movements of the forces, lists of the companies and the general make-up of the regiments, together with some good sidelights on the battle of Yorktown.

I. B. a. 12. [LXIII.] Journal von dem Hochfürstl. Hessischen des Generalmajors von Knoblauch Löblichen Garnisons Regiment seith dem Americanischen Krieg, von ao. 1776 bis Ende 1783. (From the Wilhelmshöhe Schlossbibliothek.) An important and full account of the regiment, especially good for details concerning the equipment of the forces, food stuffs and the like. Two plans are inclosed: " Wie das Corps in einem Treffen campiren soll "; and " Wie das Corps in 2 Treffen campiren soll ". The journal contains also a list of the regiments at the embarcation from New York, Nov. 6, 1778, and is signed: " H. von Knoblauch ". 625 pp.

I. B. a. 13. Journal vom Löbl. Regiment v. Benning de 1776-1783. The title-page runs: Journal vom Löblichen Garnisons-Regiment von Huyn nachhero von Benning de ao. 1776 bis medio Nov. 1783 geführt durch mich Regiments Qtermstr. Kleinschmidt. 150 written pp. An important account with much valuable detail. It begins by relating how Col. Faucitt came to Cassel, Dec., 1775, and made overtures to Landgraf Friedrich looking toward the " Subsidien-Tractat " for troops to serve six years. The text of important documents and of addresses, delivered to the troops upon taking oath of service in April, 1776, are incorporated. The journal contains also a list of the English ships and commanding officers, together with a " Zee Journal " of the voyage to America with the log in 1776. Among the other interesting papers to be noted are the following:

Pp. 50-52. Address (in English) made to Lord Percy and his reply on his departure for England. May 5, 1777.

P. 65 *et seq.* Copy of the Declaration of Independence.

Pp. 72-75. Important data relating to the scarcity and price of foods.

Pp. 79-80. Letter to Mr. Southwick from the " Female supporters of Liberty ".

Speech of the " Yioux " chief to General Carleton. (German translation.)

Pp. 109 *et seq.* Speeches (in English) on the departure of Maj. Gen. de Huyn, with the signatures of those concerned. Oct. 15, 1779.

" The following is said to be a Copy of an Avertisement stuck up at publick Places in Philadelphia on the late arrival there of General Horatio Gates.

" Millions! Millions! Millions! Reward. Strayed, deserted, or stolen from the subscriber on the 16th of August last near

Cambden, in the State of South-Carolina, a whole Army, consisting of Horse, Foot and Draggons, to the Amount of near 10000, as has been said, with all their Bagage, Artillerie, Woggons and Camp Equipage. The subscriber has very strong suspicions from Information received from his Aid de Camp, that a Certain Charles Earl Cornwallis was principally concerned in carrying of the said Army with their Bagage, etc. Any Person or Persons civil or military, who will give information either to the Subscriber or to Charles Thompson, Esqr., Secretary to the Continental Congress, where the said Army is, so that they may be recovered and reallied again, shall be entitled to demand from the Treasurer of the united states the sum of Tree Millions of Paper Dollars as soon as the can be spared from the public funds and another Million for apprehending the Person principally concerned in taken the said Army of. Proper Passes will be granted by the President of the Congress to such Persons as incline to go in search of the said Army, and as a further Encourragement, no Deduction will be made from the above Reward on account of any of the Militia who compose Part of the said Army, not being to be found or heard of, as no Dependence can be placed on their Services, and nothing but the most speedy flight can ever save their Commander.

"Horatio Gates M. Gen. and late Commander in Chief of the Southern Army.

"Philadelphia the 30th of Augt. 1780."

I. B. a. 14. Journal des Grenad. Bataillons Block nachher von Lengerke. Journal des untergehabten Grenad. Bataillons derer in America geschehenen Feld-Züge von 1776-1784. (From the Wilhelmshöhe Schlossbibliothek.) 44 written pp., bound in leather and gilt. Signed: "Extrahirt Rinteln den 17ten Septembr. 1784. G. E. v. Lengerke".

I.B. a. 15. Journal vom dem Hochlöbl. Hessischen Grenadier Bataillon olim von Minnigerode modo von Löwenstein vom 20ten januarii 1776 bis den 17ten Maij 1784. (From the Wilhelmshöhe Schlossbibliothek.) 380 written pp. Gives a good account of the standing of the troops Oct. 19, 1781, as well as much other valuable detail. The journal is signed: "S. A. Ungar gewesener Regiments Quartier Meister und Auditeur bey dem Hochlöbl. Grenadier Bataillon von Löwenstein".

I. B. a. 16. Journal vom Grenadier Bataillon Platte von 1776-1784. (From the Wilhelmshöhe Schlossbibliothek.) The title-page has, after Platte: "vom 16ten Februar. 1776 bis den 24ten Maij, 1784. Geführt durch den Regiments-Quartier Meister Carl Bauer". 442 written pp. The account really begins Feb. 14, 1776, and contains much valuable detail concerning the equipment of the forces, e. g., that the battalions, having been equipped with new arms, first fired with cartridges on Mar. 19 and 20, 1776. The journal contains an account of the route of march and of places in America, e. g., detailed description of Savannah and its environs with its vegetation, alligators, and the like (pp. 229 *et seq.,* Feb., 1780).

I. B. a. 17. Journal von H. F. H. Hochlöblichen F. J. Corps in America. (From the Wilhelmshöhe Schlossbibliothek.) The title-page has: Journal Geführt Bey dem Hochlöblich Hessischen Feld-Jäger Corps während denen Campagnen der Königl. Brittanischen Armée in North-America. Angefangen den 23ten July 1777 von dem Tage wo der Oberstlieutnant Ludwig Johann Adolph von Wurmb das Commando über dieses Corps übernahm und geendigt den 20ten April 1784 bey der erfolgten Retour derer sämtlichen Hochfürstlich-Hessischen Trouppen aus America". 238 written pp. Begins with a brief sketch of the corps and gives occasional details of local interest, *e. g.,* an account of a negro guide, who showed the Germans the road at Turkey Point, Aug. 28, 1777, the Germans evidently having no map of the region. The operations in Pennsylvania and around Philadelphia are described with interesting details, and excerpts from the *Philadelphische Zeitung* show that they read this paper carefully.

I. B. a. 18. Ordres, vom 7ten May 1777 biss den 30 Apr. 1783. (From the Wilhelmshöhe Schlossbibliothek.) 135 written pp. Bound in dark linen cloth. Contains not only the orders but minute instructions in detail, anticipating contingencies of bad weather and other unfavorable conditions; a most instructive presentation of the tactics employed in the movements of the forces. Clippings from the *Neue Europäische Zeitung,* Hanau, Jan. 13, 1781, are inclosed.

I. B. a. 18½. Tagebuch meines Vaters des damaligen Capitains, späterhin Oberstlieutnants und ritterschaftlichen Ober Einnehmers des adeligen Stiftes Kaufungen Friedrich von der Malsburg aus dem Hause Escheling. 160 closely written pages in large folio. Bound in brown leather. Copy of an earlier original. The diary begins Feb. 11, 1776, and continues with minute detail to Dec. 31, 1776, closing with an account of the winter quarters at Newport. The march to the sea, the passage through England and across the Atlantic, as well as things in America, are described in much detail. Some 50 pages are devoted to observations concerning the Atlantic Ocean.

I. B. b. 19. Relationes aus Amerika vom Hess. Hanauisch Infanter. Regiment. (From the Wilhelmshöhe Schlossbibliothek.) 126 leaves. Bound in leather. Consists of letters and reports from various persons such as v. Gall and others. The last letter of v. Gall is dated London, Mar. 6, 1781.

I. B. b. 20. Relationes aus Amerika vom Hessen-Hanauisch. Jäger-Corps. (From the Wilhelmshöhe Schlossbibliothek.) Thick quarto volume bound in half leather and containing autograph letters from de Creuzbourg and much interesting matter relating to the conduct of the soldiers and to desertions from the army, enclosing among other things the following: Beyläufiger Plan des Forts Carillon oder Ticonderoga.

Conduitten Liste von denen Officiers des Löbl. Hessen Hanauischen Jäger Corps vom 1ten Januarii 1778 und zwar von den 4 Sec: Lieutenants. Same of the captains and first lieutenants.

The correspondence is very private in character, relating chiefly to official matter communicated by Creuzbourg to the Erbprinz in autograph letters.

I. B. b. 21. Journal vom Jäger Corps [Hanauisches Jäger Corps]. (From the Wilhelmshöhe Schlossbibliothek.) Made up of separate sections written evidently in the camp on different sizes of paper and later bound in leather. Contains among other things the following:

Plan der Situation auf Mount Independence bey Carillon vor der Retraite.

Plan der Cantonnements der Trouppen in Canada bey einem befürchteten Einfall in die Provintz.

Pen picture of a Blockhouse or Fort.

Colored ink sketches of the following: Carriole, Travail, Raquette, Casse-tete, Peau de Buffle.

I. B. b. 22. Ordre Buch von Hessen Hanauisch. Regiment von 1. Januari 1777 bis 9: April 1777. (From the Wilhelmshöhe Schlossbibliothek.) Thick quarto volume of orders bound in paper boards, containing matter of the greatest variety from the various officers, and valuable as a source for the tactical history of the campaigns. The book is made up of different sections, one of which has a special title-page dated Jan. 1, 1777, and consisting of 24 pp., while another, of 24 pp., contains paroles, etc.

O. W. S. 1433. Rep. D. Kriegsministerium.

A. 2 a. Engl. Subsidien Gelder 1776-1784. Contains the following fascicles in large folio bound in paper:

1. Geld- und Natural-Berechnungen über die von Fürstl. Montierungs Commission, von 1777 an bis 1784 behuf des Hlöbl Corps nach America gesandten Armatur-Stücke, Lederwerck. Reit-Equipage, Feld Requisiten, auch Officiers-Uniforms und kleine Montierungs Stücke für Unter Officiers und Gemeine.

2. Vorläufigs unvollkommene Entwürfe zum Feld Kriegs Zahlungs Etat des der Crone England zum Dienst in Nord America in Sold überlassenen Hfürstl. Hessen Cassell. Corps der 12/m Mann und zwar

Für 4 Grenadier Bataillons

15 Infanterie Regimenter

Das Artillerie Corps à 3. Compagnien mit Staab und Train. 1776.

Das Feld Jäger Corps à 1 berrittene und 5 unberittene Compagnien samt dem Staab. 1777.

3. Rang-Reglement de dato Braunschweig den 13 Martii 1762.

4. Noten derer bey denen Banquiers van Notten in London und Amsterdam, zur Disposition Fürstl-General Kriegs Commissariats, nach und nach auf denen verschiedenen Rechnungen der Tractatsmässig Engl. Gelder vorräthig ge-

Marburg

wesenen Beträge. Na. geht nur bis Ende April 1783. 1780-1783.
5. Summarischer Abschluss derer
  1. Bey der Englischen Tresorerie bis Ende 1781 rückständigen und
  2 und 3. Bey denen Banquiers van Notten and Comp. in London und Amsterdam mit Ende Martii 1782 baar vorrätigen Gelder.
6. Status derer bey der Engln. Tresorerie seit 1776 rückständigen auch bey den Banquiers van Notten and Compe. in London und Amsterdam vorräthigen Tractatsmässigen Gelder, de a'is 1778, 1779, 1780, 1781, 1782.
7. Zur Final Soldeyen-Liquidation mit der Königl. Tresorerie in London. General Abstracte und Abschlüsse, auch Erläuterungen und sonstige Literalien und Nachrichten über den Geld und Land- auch Schiffs Provisions Empfang behuf des Hochlöbl. Corps in America und Canada, item beym Rücktrajet bis Bremer-Lehe de a'is 1776–May 1784.
8. Original Berechnungen des Geheimen Raths Alt in London über die Tractatsmässige Zahlungen de a'is 1755 bis inclus. 1763. Nebst denen daraus gezogenen General Aufrechnungen dieser Gelder de a'is 1756 bis incl. 1763. Ferner, Des Geheimen Legations Raths Alt in London Privat- oder Particulier Rechnungen de a'is 1756 bis 1763. These papers are important as preliminary to the engaging of the auxiliary troops for the English crown. In them we see that the business of engaging auxiliaries began long before the Revolution.
9. Englische Subsidien-Gelder. Berechnungen von dem Jahr 1779.
10. Subsidien Rechnung nebst Urkunden vom Jahr 1784.

O. W. S. 1513.
8810. IV. B. 6. 7. Regiment Wuttginau später Landgraf. Monatliche Listen, etc., vom Jan. 1767-1783. Contains the following fascicles:
  6. Leib Infant. Regmt 2tes Bataillon. Monatliche Listen vom Infanterie Regimt v. Wuttginau, de annis 1767, 1768, 1769, 1770.
  7. Monatliche Listen, etc., hernach seit Mart. 1777 Landgraf de annis 1771, 1772, 1773 Jan.–Jun., 1776, Sept.–Dec. 1777, nebst Ranglisten.
Monatliche Listen, etc., vom Infanterie Regiment Landgraf und seit May 1783 Leib Regiment Infanterie de annis 1778, 1779, 1780, 1781, 1782, 1783 Jan.-Apr.
8814. Fuss Rgt Erbprinz (Wilhelm) VIII. 6. Rapports 1775 bis 1780. Contains " Monatliche Tabellen und Listen ".
8815. Inf. Rgt. Erbprinz dann Pr. Wilhelm. Mon. Rapp. u. Mon. Listen 1781-85 VII. 7, 8, 9. Includes one fascicle marked thus:
Regiment Erbprinz 1tes Bataill. Monatliche Listen von des Erbprinz Infanterie Regiment, und seit 1784 Prinz Wilhelm [Infanterie Regiment] de annis 1781 Jan.–Oct., Nov., Dec.,

1782 Jan., Feb., Mart., Aug.–Nov., 1783 Jan., Feb., May, Jun., 1784 Jul.–Dec., 1785 Jan.–Sept.
O. W. S. 1514.
8819. (VI. B. 2, 3). Regt Mirbach von Jung Lossberg. Monatliche Listen 1770-1784. Rang-Listen 1770-1776. Contains the following:
Regiment Erbprinz 2tes Bataill. Monatliche Listen von dem Infanterie Regiment Vacant Pr. v. Anhalt und seit Apr. 1770 v. Mirbach de annis 1770, 1771, 1772, 1773 Jan.–Jul., 1776 Apr.–Dec., 1777, 1778.
Monatliche Listen, etc., von Mirbach und seit Feb. 1781 Jung v. Losberg de annis 1779, 1780, 1781, 1782, 1783, 1784 Jan.–Mai.
8824. VI. A a 3. Regt. Prinz Carl. Mon. Rapports 1770-1784. Anc[iennitäts] Ranglisten 1770-1776. The fascicle contains the following:
I. G. No. 13. Monatliche Listen vom Infanterie Regiment Prinz Carl de annis 1770, 1771, 1772, 1773 Jan.–Jun.
I. G. No. 14. Monatliche Listen, etc., de annis 1776 Sept.–Dec., 1777, 1778, 1779, 1780, 1781, 1782 Jan.–Mai, Juli–Dec., 1783, 1784 Jan.–Apr.
Anciennitäts [Rang] Listen 1770 Apr. u. Aug., 1771 Apr., 1772 Apr., 1773 Apr., 1774 Sept., 1775 Feb., 1776 Feb.
8826. Rgt v. Gräffendorf. VI. A. b. 6.
Ranglisten, 1763-1767.
Mon. Listen, 1763-1767.
Rgt Prinz Sachsen Gotha. 7.
Ranglisten, 1767-1775.
Mon. Listen, 1767-1773.
Rgt v. Trümbach. 8.
Rangl[isten], 1776.
Mon. Listen, 1776-1778.
Rgt. v. Bose. 9.
Mon. Listen, 1779-1783.
Contains the following bundles of papers corresponding to numbers 6-9 above:
Regiment Prinz Carl 2tes Bataill.
I. G. Nr. 26. Monatliche Listen vom Regiment Infanterie von Gräffendorf de annis 1763, 1764, 1765, 1766.
I. G. No. 27. Monatliche Listen, etc.; und seit Sept., 1767, Prinz von Sachsen Gotha; de annis 1767, 1768, 1769, 1770, 1771, 1772, 1773, Jan.–Jun.
I. G. No. 28. Monatliche Listen, etc., und seit Jan., 1779, von Bose, de annis 1776 Apr.–Dec., 1776, 1777, 1778, 1779, 1780, 1781, 1782 Jan., Feb., Apr., 1783 incl.
Anciennitäts [Rang] Listen, Mai 1763–Feb. 1776.
O. W. S. 1515.
8836. IItes Grenadier Bat. (später F. v. Eschwege) Block, v. Lengerke. Rapporte von April 1776 bis Januar 1784. (IV., VI., VIII., No. 678). Contains 4 fascicles as follows:
1. (VI. B. 2). Ranglisten Rgt. von Mirbach. 1745-1776.

Marburg

2. Grenadier Bat. Block. Rapports vom April 1776 bis incl. Februar 1777.
3. Monatliche Listen vom Grenadier Bataillon Block, hernach seit Mart. 1777 v. Lengerke; zuletzt eingegang. 1tes Grenadier Bataillon de annis 1776 Apr.–Dec., 1777, 1778, 1779–Dec.
4. Monatliche Listen, etc., de annis 1780, 1781, 1782, 1783 Jan.–Sept., Nov.–Dec., 1784 Jan.

8837. I. Grenad. Bat. v. Linsingen. April 1776-84 März. III., IV., VI. Contains 2 bundles of papers with this title.
1. Monatliche Listen vom Grenadier Bataillon v. Linsing[en], zuletzt eingegang. 2tes Grenadier Bataillon, de annis 1776 Apr.–Dec., 1777, 1778, 1779.
2. Monatliche Listen, etc., de annis 1780, 1781, 1782, 1783 Jan.–Jul., Sept.–Dec., 1784 Jan.–Feb., Mart.

O. W. S. 1516.

8848. XXXII A. 13. Fuss-Regt. von Ditfurth, Rapporte u. Ranglisten 1766–1783 Juli. The full title of the papers is: Monatliche Tabellen vom Fusilier [Regiment] v. Ditfurth, zuletzt eingegang. Vacante Bataillon de annis 1763, etc., 1773, 1776-1783. The " Rang Listen " run from 1 to 17 and extend from May, 1765, to Feb., 1776, with interruptions.

8850. Leichtes Infant. Bataillon v. Bülow 1779 bis 1788. Contains the reports of Bülow to the Landgraf and the replies from the war office.

8851. Leichtes Infant. Bataillon Lentz 1788-89.

8853. Feld Jäger Corps 1776-1784. The cover contains the following list of contents:
Monatliche Listen vom Feld-Jäger-Corps de annis 1776 Apr.–Dec., 1777, 1778, 1779, 1780, 1781 Jan.–Aug., 1783 Jan.–Jun., Aug.–Dec., 1784 Jan.–Feb.
Monatliche Liste vom Hochlöblich-Hessischen Feld-Jäger-Corps, vom Monat September 1778.
These are the official returns from the commanding officers of the auxiliary German troops in America and furnish the basis upon which the English subsidies were to be paid. The remarks at the foot of each list give important particulars concerning the death of officers and the loss of men.

O. W. S. 1517.

8862. Garnisons-Reg. v. Wilcke 1764-1789. A thick unbound volume of original papers from E. H. v. Wilcke to the Landgraf with the replies thereto. Important official matter relating to the officers and men under Gen. Lieut. v. Wilcke's command. Among the papers are lists of deserters and the like. The second part of the volume is made of original papers labelled: Acta des Regiments v. Hanstein 2te Bataill. von 1664-1789.

8865. Has no title, but contains the following fascicles:
Monatliche Listen vom Garnisons Regiment v. Seitz zuletzt v. Porbeck de anno 1776, Apr.–Dec.
Monatliche Listen vom Garnisons Regiment v. Seitz zuletzt v. Porbeck de annis 1777, 1779, 1780, 1781, 1782, 1783 Jan.–Jul.

O. W. S. 1518.
8873. Garnisons Reg. von Bünau 1776-1787. Contains the following fascicles:
1. 1776 Eingeg. Colson, etc., Monatliche Listen vom Garnisons-rgt v. Bünau, de 1776, Sept.-Dec.
2. Monatl. Listen des Garnis.-reg. v. Bünau; zuletzt v. Colson. 1777.
3. *Id.*, 1778.
4. *Id.*, 1779.
5. *Id.*, 1780.
6. *Id.*, 1781.
7. *Id.*, 1782.
8. *Id.*, 1783 Jan.–Febr., Apr., Mai, Jun., Aug.–Nov. Fehlen Mart., Jul., Dec.
9. Garnisons-Reg. von Bünau. 1785-87.
10. *Id.*, 1784-87. Acten.

O. W. S. 91. L. Friedrich II. Correspondenz cum variis 1743-1779. A thick fascicle of papers with the following written in blue ink on the cover: Hess. Kass. Personalien. Landgraf Friedrich II zu Hessen-Cassel (Correspondenz desselben mit den innen verzeichneten Personen, grössten Teils in Privatangelegenheiten). Contains the following:
1. Acten des Erbprinzen Friedrich (später F. II). Includes interesting military pay rolls of December 1752.
2. L. Friedrich II. (Corresp. c. variis).
3. Bundle of original personal autograph and other letters of the Landgraf. 1773.
4. Landgraf Friedrich II. zu Hessen Cassel (Corresp.). 1771-1779.
5. Letter of H. Wagner in Marburg, May 11, 1776, enclosing a note to the Landgraf written in praise of the Hessian troops in America: " Des Regierenden Herrn Landgrafen von Hessen Cassel Hochfürstlichen Durchlaucht bey der Musterung Höchst Dero Trouppen in tiefster Ehrfurcht überreicht von Johann Konrad v. Einem ".
6. 2 German poems of 5 pages beginning:
" Was seh ich? Sind dies nicht die Enkel jener Katten," etc., and
" Nach der am Hochfürstl. Hessen-Casselischen Löwen-Ordens-Tage den 19 Nov. 1771 angeführten Italienischen Oper *Andromeda*."
L. Friedrich II. (Correspondenz 1780-83 cum Variis.)
L. Friedrich II. Correspondenz. Varia. Paper cover has the following:
1. Landgraf Friedrich II. zu Hess. Cassel. Correspondenz zwischen dem Obristen v. Pirch bey dem Königl. Preussischen Infanterie Regiment .... dessen Inhaber der Landgraf Friedrich II. zu Hessen war, bezw. dem Regiments u. Quartiermeister Trendelenburg daselbst, und dem Hof-Intendanten Ordensrat Döring zu Cassel, die Berechnung der Gelder der Leib-Compagnie, Uebersendung der Ueberschüsse der Montierungsstücke, die schlechte Dienstführung des v.

Trendelenburg, Cautionsleistung von Seiten desselben, etc.,
betreffend. 1779, 1780, 1781, 1782, 1783, 1785, 1786.
2. Ministerial Relationes vom Monath April 1759.
3. Relationes ad Ser'mum nos'i Ministerii de 21 Jul. 1770.
4. Papers of 1770.
5. Papers of 1776.
6. Papers of 1784.
7. Papers of 1780, 1781.
8. Ministerial Correspondence. 1784.
9. Correspondence. 1762-1775.
10. Correspondence. 1782.
11. Correspondence. 1760.
12. Correspondence with various persons.

MINISTERIUM DES AUSWÄRTIGEN (OR, DES AEUSSEREN UND
DES HAUSES).

O. W. S. 1039.
Nr. 136. Akten betreffend die Accreditirung des Kaiserlich-Brasilianischen Geschäftsträgers am D. Bunde, Dr. Jean Alves Loureiro in gleicher Eigenschaft am Kurfürstlichen Hofe. 1857–Aug., 1863.
Nr. 137. Akta betreffend die Accreditirung des Chevalier Vianna de Lima als Kaiserlich-Brasilianischen Geschäftsträgers am Kurfürstlichen Hofe. Aug., 1863.
Nr. 304. Akta betr. die Bestellung des Kaufmanns Faber in New-York zum Kurhessischen Consul in den Vereinigten Staaten von Nord-America. 1831.
Nr. 315. Akten betr. die Allerhöchste Ernennung des Kaufmanns August Fritze zu New-York zum Kurhessischen Consul daselbst. 1856. Resignation accepted Jan. 1, 1859.
Nr. 316. Akten betr. die Allerhöchste Ernennung des Kaufmanns Th. Wagner, zu Galveston, Staat Texas, zum Kurhessischen Consul daselbst. 1856.
Nr. 317. Akten betr.
I. Die Allerhöchste Ernennung des Kaufmanns E. Angelbrodt zu St. Louis, in den Vereinigten Staaten von Nord-America, zum Kurhessischen Consul daselbst. Mar. 20, 1857. Allerhöchste Entlassungs Rescript vom 24/2 1865.
II. Sowie des Kaufmanns Robert Barth zu St. Louis, zum Kurhessischen Vice-Consul daselbst. Mar. 10, 1860. Barth made consul by rescript of Feb. 24, 1865.
Nr. 318. Akten betr. die allerhöchste Ernennung des Kaufmanns C. F. Adä, in Cincinnati, Staat Ohio, zum Kurhessischen Consul daselbst. 1857.
Nr. 319. *Id.* Richard Thiele, New-Orleans. 1855.
Nr. 321. *Id.* Friedrich Kühne, New-York. 1856-1859.
Nr. 323. *Id.* Werner Dresel, Baltimore. 1860.
Nr. 326. *Id.* Clamor Friedrich Hagedorn, Philadelphia. 1853-1866 (Verabschiedet am 11 Oct., 1865).
Nr. 327. *Id.* Christian Friedrich Mebius, San Francisco. 1863-1865.

Nr. 328. Akten betr. Handels- und Verkehrs-Berichte der Kurhessischen Consuln in den Vereinigten Staaten von Nord-America. Vol. I. and II. 1858 et seq.

Nr. 329. Akten betr. Patent des Carl Graebe, in Cassel, als Consul der Vereinigten Staaten von America, für das Kurfürstenthum Hessen und dessen Anerkennung als solche. 1835.

Nr. 330. Die Bestellung des Samuel Rücker aus Louisiana zum Consul der Vereinigten Staaten von Nord-America, für das Kurfürstenthum Hessen. 1854.

Nr. 332. Akten betr. die Bestellung des Kaufmanns Friedrich Möller dahier, zum Consul des südamerikanischen Freistaats Uruguay für Kurhessen. 1858.

Nr. 334. *Id.* Friedrich Möller zum Consul der Argentinischen Confoederation (Süd-America), für Kurhessen. 1860.

Nr. 335. *Id.* Louis Peixoto de Lacerda Werneck zum Kaiserlich Brasilianischen General-Consul für Kurhessen. 1863.

Nr. 336. *Id.* William W. Murphy zum Consul der Vereinigten Staaten von Nord-America für das Kurfürstenthum Hessen. 1861.

Nr. 337. Akten betr. die Versagung des Exequatur an Consuln und Agenten auswärtiger Staaten. 1847.

Nr. 373. Akten betr. die Mission des Kaiserlich Mexicanischen Gesandten am Deutschen Bunde, Don Thomas Murphy, an Se. Königl. Hoheit den Kurfürsten, zur Ueberreichung des Notificationsschreibens Sr. Majestät des Kaisers Maximilian von Mexico über allerhöchst dessen Thronbesteigung. 1864.

Nr. 588. Akten betr. den Bundesbeschluss wegen Organisation der Auswanderung Angehöriger der deutschen Bundesstaaten. 1856.

Nr. 589. Akten betr. die Unterdrückung des Sclavenhandels. 1843. Refers to the " Traité conclue entre les cinq Puissances ayant pour objet la suppression de la Traite des Noirs, et signé à Londre le 20 Decembre 1841 ". The fascicle contains also a printed copy of the document enclosed in a letter of W. Fox Strangways, dated Frankfort-on-the-Main, Apr. 20, 1842, and other papers relating thereto.

Nr. 773. Akten betr. die Auswanderung Kurhessischer Unterthanen nach Amerika. 1832, 1833.

Nr. 774. *Id.* die Entlassung von Militairpersonen aus dem Kurhessischen Unterthanen-Verband. Vol. I.-III. 1832 et seq.

Nr. 775. *Id.* die Verhandlungen wegen der von Baiern vorgeschlagenen Uebereinkunft hinsichtlich gleichförmiger Grundsätze über Militairpflichtigkeit in Beziehung auf Auswanderungsfreiheit. 1817, 1818.

Nr. 777. *Id.* die vom Brasilianischen Gouvernement den Auswanderern aller Länder dargebotenen Vortheile. 1833.

Nr. 779. *Id.* das K. K. Oestereichische Auswanderungs-Patent vom 24. März 1832.

Nr. 780. *Id.* die Auswanderungs-Angelegenheiten im Allgemeinen, sowie deshalbige Verordnungen, Bestimmungen, und Nachweisungen. Vol. I., 1851 et seq. Vol. II., 1857.

Marburg

Nr. 782. *Id.* Uebereinkunft mit andern deutschen Bundesstaaten bezüglich der Massregeln zur Verhütung heimlicher Auswanderung. 1855.
Nr. 783. *Id.* die Auswanderung Kurhessischer Unterthanen nach Russland und die desshalbigen Bestimmungen. 1833.
Nr. 784-794. *Id.* Heimatsverhältnisse. Conventionen wegen Uebernahme Ausgewiesener. 1820-1850.
Nr. 795. *Id.* die Heimatsverhältnisse einzelner Personen.
Nr. 815-819. *Id.* besondere Verhältnisse der Juden 1829-42.
Nr. 944-963. *Id.* öffentliche Ruhestörungen und Unordnungen insbesondere auch revolutionäre Umtriebe. 1820-1849.
Nr. 967-977. *Id.* Aufenthalt Kurhessischer Unterthanen im Auslande. 1821-1846.
Nr. 978-990. Passangelegenheiten. 1817-1862.
Nr. 992-1004. Verbreitung verbotener und politisch schädlicher Zeit- und anderer Schriften. 1820-1852.
Nr. 1229. Acta betr. Abschliessung eines Handels- und Schiff-Fahrts-Vertrages zwischen dem grossen deutschen Zollverein und den Vereinigten Staaten von Nordamerika. 1838.
Nr. 1235. *Id.* den Höchstgenehmigten Abschluss eines Handels- und Schiffahrts-Vertrages zwischen Preussen, namens der sämtlichen Zollvereinsregierungen, und der Republik Venezuela. 1845.
Nr. 1239. *Id.* den Freundschafts-, Handels- und Schiff-Fahrts-Vertrag mit Mexico. 1854.
Nr. 1240. *Id.* Salvador. 1854.
Nr. 1241. *Id.* den Handels- und Schiffahrts-Vertrag mit Uruguay. 1855.
Nr. 1242. *Id.* Dominica. 1856.
Nr. 1244. *Id.* den Freundschafts-, Handels- und Schiff-Fahrts Vertrag mit der Argentinischen Conföderation. 1857.
Nr. 1245. *Id.* den Handels- und Schiff-Fahrts-Vertrag mit Paraguay. 1859.
Nr. 1247. *Id.* Chili. 1860.
Nr. 1248. *Id.* Peru. 1861.
Nr. 1253. *Id.* Columbia. 1865.
Nr. 1256. *Id.* Vereinbarungen mit den Vereinigten Staaten von Nordamerika:
1. wegen der Verhältnisse der Unterthanen des einen Theils, welche in dem Gebiete des anderen verweilen;
2. über Verhältnisse der Consuln;
3. über Aufhebung des Heimfallrechtes und der Nachsteuer;
4. über Handels-Erleichterungen (nicht abgeschlossene Verhandlungen). 1835 *et seq.*
Nr. 1261. *Id.* Handels- und Schiff-Fahrts-Vertrag zwischen den Hansastädten, Lübeck, Bremen und Hamburg, und der Republik Venezuela, zu Caracas am 27. Mai 1837 abgeschlossen. 1837.
Nr. 1263. *Id.* Kurhessische Zustimmung zu den Handelsverträgen der Königreiche Baiern und Württemberg mit der Republik Mexico von 1832. 1835.

Nr. 1266. *Id.* den diesseitigen Beitritt zu dem zwischen den Königlichen Regierungen von Preussen und den Niederlanden abgeschlossenen Vertrage über die Zulassung von Handels-Consuln in den überseeischen Niederländischen Colonien. 1856.

Nr. 1294. *Id.* Handelsbeziehungen zwischen den Staaten des deutschen Zollvereins und dem Kaiserthum Brasilien. 1845.

Nr. 1295. *Id.* die von einer amerikanischen Gesellschaft unternommene, und von Preussen bei den übrigen Zollvereins-Regierungen befürwortete Dampfschiff-Fahrts-Verbindung zwischen Bremen und New-York. 1846.

Nr. 1319. *Id.* die diesseits gewünschte Aufhebung oder Herabsetzung der in Amerika angeordneten hohen Einfuhrzölle auf deutsches, in specie hessisches Leinen und deshalbige Verwendung durch den Kurhessischen Consul Faber in New-York. 1832, 1833.

Nr. 1345. *Id.* die Bestimmungen bezüglich der Zulassung ausländischer Handels- und Gewerbe-Gesellschaften und deren Erwerbung von Grundeigenthum. 1858.

Nr. 1403. *Id.* die Auslieferung der von dem Geheimen Legationsrathe v. Langsdorff aufbewahrten, auf das Schüttlersche Gut Cambervell in Jamaika sich beziehenden Papiere an das Grossherzogl. Badische Ministerium der auswärtigen Angelegenheiten. 1833 *et seq.*

Nr. 1470-1471. *Id.* Erlangung und Verabfolgung von Tauf- und Trauscheinen. Vol. I.-IV. 1840.

Nr. 1472-1476. *Id.* Erlangung und Verabfolgung von Todesscheinen. Some 18 volumes. 1817-1840.

Nr. 1481. *Id.* die in Anspruch genommene Militairpflichtigkeit der nach Amerika ausgewanderten bezwse. entlassenen Unterthanen. 1836.

Nr. 1496. *Id.* die Grossherzogl. S. Weimarischer seits gewünschte Theilnahme der in gedachtem Herzogthum befindlichen, ehemals Kurhessischen Unterthanen, welche dem amerikanischen Kriege als solche beigewohnt haben, an der durch die Landstände den Kurhessischen amerikanischen Kriegern zugesicherten Unterstützung.

Nr. 1517. *Id.* die Abschliessung eines Freizügigkeits-Vertrages mit Nordamerika. 1844.

Nr. 1537. *Id.* die Ermächtigung der Kurhess. Consuln in Nordamerica zur Vornahme von Handlungen der freiwilligen Gerichtsbarkeit, als Aufnahme von Vollmachten, Verzichts-Erklärungen, etc., so wie zur Abnahme von Schiedseiden. 1857.

Nr. 1584. *Id.* Verhandlungen in Berlin zum Abschluss eines Vertrages über gegenseitige Auslieferung flüchtig gewordener Verbrecher zwischen Preussen und den übrigen Staaten des Zollvereins einerseits und den Vereinigten Staaten von Nordamerika andererseits. 1843.

Nr. 1589½. *Id.* Vertrag zwischen den Vereinigten Staaten v. Nordamerika u. Preussen u. dem deutschen Bund betr. die Auslieferung von Verbrechern. 1852.

Nr. 2281-2294. *Id.* Diplomatische Briefe und Berichte (first half of the nineteenth century).

Marburg

REP. ÜBER DIE REGIERUNGS HOHEITS REPOSITUR.

Gef. 4. Fasc. 8. Acta, die wegen der geheimen Umtriebe und gefährlichen Verbindungen von Sr. Königl. Hoheit dem Kurfürsten erlassenen Verkündigung betreffend. 1819.

Gef. 41. Fasc. 5. Papers relating to the Herrnhuter in the Hessian states.

Gef. 42. Fasc. 44. Mennonites in the Hessian states.

Gef. 89. Fasc. 8. Acta die Erwerbung des Bürgerrechtes im Auslande mit Beibehaltung des diesseitigen Unterthanen Rechtes betr. Vol. I., 1824-1846; vol. II., 1849-1865.

Fasc. 9. Acta die Ertheilung von Heimatsscheinen betr. Vol. II., 1839-1846.

Fasc. 10. *Id.* Vol. III. 1847—.

Fasc. 11. Acta die jährlichen Uebersichten über die Aufnahmen in den Unterthanen Verband betr. 1861-1867.

Gef. 98. Fasc. 12. Acta die Auswanderung mehrerer Unterthanen ins Ausland betr. 1817-1835.

Fasc. 13. Acta die mit der freien Hansastadt Bremen verabredete wechselseitige Freizügigkeit betr. Vol. I., 1817-1847; vol. II., 1848—.

Fasc. 15. Acta die Auswanderung hessischer Unterthanen nach Brasilien betr. 1820-1848.

Fasc. 16. Acta die zu ergreifenden Maasregeln, dass die Kurhessischen Unterthanen nicht durch den in Hamburg erlassenen Aufruf an deutsche Jünglinge zum Kampfe gegen die Türken, zum Auswandern verführt werden, betr. 1821.

Fasc. 17. Acta die Auswanderung Kurhessischer Unterthanen nach Amerika betr. Vol. II. 1824 (vernichtet).

Fasc. 18. Acta Generalia die Auswanderung Kurhessischer Unterthanen in das Ausland betr. Vol. I. 1825-1841.

Fasc. 18 a. Acta Generalia, die Entlassung weiblicher Unterthanen behufs Verheirathung im Ausland betr. 1851.

Fasc. 19. Acta die Auswanderung Kurhessischer Unterthanen nach America betr. Vol. III. 1832-1833 (vernichtet).

Fasc. 21. *Id.* Vol. IV. 1833—(vernichtet).
Fasc. 22. *Id.* Vol. V. 1834-1836 (vernichtet).
Fasc. 23. *Id.* Vol. VI. 1836 (vernichtet).
Fasc. 24. *Id.* Vol. VII. 1836 (vernichtet).
Fasc. 25. *Id.* Vol. VIII. 1837 (vernichtet).
Fasc. 26. *Id.* Vol. IX. 1838-1839 (vernichtet).
Fasc. 27. *Id.* Vol. X. 1839-1840 (vernichtet).
Fasc. 28. *Id.* Vol. XI. 1840-1841 (vernichtet).

Cf. 2826/57 R[egierungs] Pr[esidial Abt.] I. (in Cassel).

Fasc. 29. Acta die Auswanderung Kurhessischer Unterthanen in das Ausland betr. Vol. II. 1842-1848.

Fasc. 30. Acta, die Entlassung aus dem Unterthanenverbande zur Auswanderung nach Amerika betr. Vol. XII. 1842-1843.

Fasc. 32. Acta, die tabellarischen Uebersichten über die Gesuche um Entlassung aus dem Unterthanen Verbande btr. Vol. I. 1840-1844.

Fasc. 33. Acta die Auswanderung nach Amerika betr. Vol. XIII. 1843-1844.

Fasc. 35. *Id.* Vol. XIV. 1844-1845.
Fasc. 37. *Id.* Vol. XV. 1845-1846.
Fasc. 38. *Id.* Vol. XVI. 1846.
Fasc. 39. *Id.* Vol. XVII. 1846-1847.
Fasc. 40. *Id.* Vol. XVIII. 1847.
Fasc. 41. *Id.* Vol. XIX. 1847-1848.
  Id. Vol. XX. 1848.
Fasc. 42. *Id.* Vol. XXI. 1848-1849.
Fasc. 36. Acta, die tabell. Uebersichten über die Gesuche um Entlassung aus dem Unterthanen Verbande betr.
  Vol. II. 1845-1847.
  Vol. III. 1848.
  Vol. IV. 1850-1854.
  Vol. V. 1855-1856.
  Vol. VI. 1857.
  Vol. VII. 1860[?].
Fasc. 43. Acta die Regelung des Gewerbes zur Beförderung der Auswandernden betr. 1852.
Fasc. 44. Acta die Agenturen zur Vermittelung des Transports von Auswanderern betr.
  Vols. I-XI. 1853-1863.
  Vol. XII. 1864.
  Vol. XIII. 1865, 1867.
Fasc. 45. Acta die Auswanderung Kurhessischer Unterthanen in das Ausland betr.
  Vol. I. 1851-1853.
  Vol. II. 1854-1857.
  Vol. III. 1858-1863.
  Vol. IV. 1864-1867.
Fasc. 46. Acta betr. die Aushändigung der Zinsabschnitte von den seitens der Auswanderungs-Agenten als Caution hinterlegten Staatsschuld-Verschreibungen.
  Vol. I. 1862-1864.
  Vol. II. 1865.
Fasc. 47. Acta Generalia betr. die Uebersichten über die Auswanderung aus Hessen. 1853.
Gef. 101. Fasc. 1. Acta, die Auswanderung hessischer Unterthanen nach London, Verabfolgung ihres Vermögens dahin und davon zu entrichtendes Abzugsgeld betr.
  Vol. I. 1778-1822.
  Vol. II. 1823-1848.
Fasc. 5. *Id.*, nach Lübeck. 1832-1847.
Gef. 102. Fasc. 1. *Id.*, nach Oesterreich.
  Vol. I. 1760-1837.
  Vol. II. 1838-1848.
Fasc. 2. *Id.*, nach Portugal. 1795.
Fasc. 6. Acta, die Freizügigkeit zwischen dem Königreich der Niederlanden und Kurhessen betr. 1821-1856.
Gef. 103. Fasc. 2. Acta die Auswanderung, etc., nach Schweden betr. 1752-1845.
Fasc. 3. *Id.*, Schweiz. 1765-1843.
Fasc. 4. *Id.*, Schleswig. 1768-1819.
Fasc. 6. *Id.*, Russland. 1794-1845, 1849-1860.

Gef. 104. Fasc. 2. *Id.*, Ungarn. 1777-1836.
Gef. 125. Fasc. 4. Acta, die vom K. Preussischen Staats- und Policey-Ministerio zu Berlin wegen der durch Steckbriefe verfolgten Personen erlassenen Verordnungen betr. 1815.
Gef. 127. Fasc. 1. Acta, die Verhältnisse mit dem Staate Missouri betr. 1859.

ARCHIV DER KURHESSISCHEN GESANDTSCHAFTEN.

Gesandtschaft zu Berlin.

No. 46. Diplomatische Tagesberichte der Gesandten. Feb. 8, 1820-1866.
No. 60 a. Bestellung des Carl Graebe zum Nordamerikanischen Consul für Kurhessen, resp. das in seinem Ernennungs-patente vorgekommene Form-Versehen. 1835.
No. 61. Correspondenz mit dem Kurfürstlichen Ministerium des Aeusseren betr. die zwischen dem Preussischen Minister der auswärtigen Angelegenheiten von Werther und dem Nordamerikanischen Gesandten Wheaton in Berlin wegen der dem letzteren von dem Eigenthümer seiner früheren Wohnung zurückerhaltenen Effecten und darüber in Beziehung auf die Rechte der Exterritorialität der Diplomaten sich erhobenen Streitigkeit gewechselten Noten; letztere in Abschrift. 1839.
No. 73 a. Betr. die Kurhessische Verfassungsangelegenheit und die politischen Zustände im Kurstaate. 1851-1862.
No. 150. Betr. Unterhandlungen mit den Vereinigten Staaten von Nord-Amerika in Bezug auf die Regelung der gegenseitigen Handels- und Unterthanen-Verhältnisse. 1835-1838.
No. 150 a. Betr. die Vertretung Kurhessens durch die Königl. Preuss. Regierung bei Abschluss eines Auslieferungsvertrages mit den Nordamerikanischen Freistaaten. Auswechselung der Ratificationsurkunden, 1844-1846. Auslieferung des wegen Unterschlagung in Untersuchung gezogenen Rentmeisters Jeremias Hoffmann. 1853-1856.
No. 151. Betr. Abschliessung eines Handelsvertrages zwischen dem Zollverein und den Nordamerikanischen Freistaaten. 1844.
No. 151 a. Betr. die Abschliessung eines Freizügigkeits-Vertrages zwischen Kurhessen und den Nordamerikanischen Freistaaten, 1844-1847; sowie Kurhessische Ratificationsurkunde über den zwischen Kurhessen und den Nordamerikanischen Freistaaten abgeschlossenen Freizügigkeitsvertrag vom 2. Mai 1846. Two copies. (*Cf. Verz. der Hess. Staatsverträge,* no. 44, where are stated the reasons for failure to exchange ratifications.)
No. 161. Betr. Abschluss eines Handels-Vertrages des Zollvereins mit Venezuela; Bedenken der Kurf. Regierung gegen die Fassung des § 12, die Culturfreiheit betr. 1846.
No. 163. Betr. die Abschliessung eines Handels- und Schiffahrts-Vertrages des Zollvereins mit Belgien, überhaupt die diplomatischen Handels-Verhältnisse betr. 1844-1847. Schreiben des Kurfürst. Ministers des Auswärtigen in Betreff eines Actien-Unternehmens, etc.

KURHESS. MINISTERIUM DES INNERN.

II. *Hoheits-Repositur.*
Cl. 14. No. 1. Die Aufnahme zum Unterthan und verwandte Gegenstände im Allgemeinen. 1822.
No. 3. Gesuche von Candidaten der Theologie um Ertheilung, bezw. um Erhaltung der Kurhessischen Unterthanen-Rechte. 1825. Vols. I., II.
No. 4. Die Auswanderungen, Entlassungen aus dem Unterthanen-Verbande überhaupt. Vols. I., II., III., IV., V. 1821, 1823-1840, 1841-1848, 1849-1854, 1855.
No. 5. Das Auswandern Kurhessischer Unterthanen nach Brasilien. 1824.
No. 7. Die Annahme eines ausländischen Staatsbürgerrechts neben Beibehaltung des Kurhessischen. 1821.
No. 8. Den Erwerb und den Verlust der Staatsangehörigkeit. 1834.
No. 9. Die Verabfolgung des Vermögens gewesener Kurhessischer Unterthanen pp. in das Ausland und den Bezug von Vermögen aus dem Auslande von Seiten Kurhessischer Unterthanen. 1816.
No. 10. Die in Folge des Art. 18 des Bundes-Kartels ertheilten Auswanderungs-Consense, Entlassungen aus dem Kurhessischen Unterthanen-Verbande, Wiederaufnahme zum Unterthan. Vols. I., II. 1832-1837, 1838.
No. 11. Trauungen von Ausländern, etc. 1825, 1836.
No. 13. Die Auswanderung Kurhessischer Unterthanen nach Russisch-Polen. 1837.
No. 16. Das über Auswanderungen zu erlassende Gesetz. 1841.
Nos. 17, 18. Unterthanenrechte für Ausländer.
No. 21. Die Niederlassung deutscher Colonisten im südlichen Theile der Republik Chili. 1849.
No. 23. Die periodischen Uebersichten über die stattgehabten Auswanderungen. Vols. I., II., III., IV., V. 1850-1853, 1854-1858, 1859-1862, 1863.
No. 24. Die behufs Auswanderung aus der Staatscasse nachgesuchte Unterstützung. 1852. (Reg. Archiv Cassel.)
No. 25. Die Regelung des Gewerbes der Beförderung von Auswanderern und die deshalb erlassene Verordnungen vom 23ten Februar 1853 sowie vom 26ten December 1844.
No. 26. Die Gestattung von Uebernahme von Agenturen, behufs Vermittlung des Transportes von Auswanderern. Vols. I., II. 1853-1859, 1860—. (Reg. Archiv Cassel.)
No. 27. Gesuch um Ansiedlung in Kurhessen. 1855.
No. 28. Trauungen im Auslande. 1856.
No. 29. Ausbürgerrecht. 1840.

ADDITIONAL COLLECTIONS (ACCESSIONEN).
Acc. 1896/7.

VII. Nr. 7. Intercessionalia seit dem Jahre 1860 oder bis 1860 reichend, in Erbschafts- und Vermögens-Angelegenheiten überhaupt (alphabetisch geordnet). 22 Convolute.

Nr. 26. Akten betr. die Ermittelung der Erben der in Mexico gefallenen, aus Kurhessen gebürtigen, Soldaten der Vereinigten Staaten Nordamerikas. 1848—.

Nr. 27. Das Guthaben bezws. den Nachlass der in Kriegsdiensten der Vereinigten Staaten Nordamericas gestandenen und aus Kurhessen gebürtigen Soldaten betr. Vol. I., 1862-1864; vol. II., 1865—; vol. III., 1867—.

VIII. B. Nr. 197. (In Handbibliothek des Staatsarchivs.) Extra-Beilage zu Nr. 13. des *Oberhessischen Provinzial Wochenblattes*. A print containing:

" Bekanntmachung der Kurfürstlichen Regierung der Provinz Oberhessen." Marburg, Mar. 25, 1833.

" Wohlgemeinter Rath der Vorsteher der Deutschen Gesellschaft in New-York an Deutsche, die nach den Vereinigten Staaten von Nord-Amerika auszuwandern beabsichtigen." New York, Jan. 1, 1833. (Reprint.)

Acc. 1903/9, Verzeichniss XII. der Acten Kurfürstlicher Reg. Cassel (Provinz Niederhessen), das Polizeiwesen betreffend.

Auswanderung betreffend.

No. 1. Instruktion für deutsche Auswanderer nach Texas nebst der neuesten Karte dieses Staates nach dessen Grenzbestimmungen durch Congressbeschluss vom September 1850. Sodann einer Spezialkarte über den vermessenen Theil des Grantgebietes des Texas-Vereins und einzelnen Plänen der von denselben gegründeten Städte Neu Braunfels, Friedrichsburg, und Indianola. Herausgegeben von dem Verein zum Schutze deutscher Einwanderer in Texas. 1851.

No. 2. Die Auswanderung Kurhessischer Unterthanen nach Amerika betreffend. 1849-1850.

No. 3. Die Auswanderung Kurhessischer Unterthanen nach Preussen, Holland, und Sachsen.

No. 4. Die Auswanderung Kurhessischer Unterthanen nach Hamburg, Lübeck, Bremen und Frankfurt a/M.

No. 9. Auswanderung in das Ausland im Allgemeinen betreffend. Vol. IV., 1853-1857; vol. V., 1858-1864; vol. VI., 1865-1867.

No. 10. Die Tabellarischen Uebersichten über die Gesuche um Entlassung aus dem Unterthanen-Verbande betreffend. Vol. I., 1840-1844; vol. II., 1845-1847.

No. 11. Die Tabellarischen Uebersichten über die Gesuche um Entlassung aus dem Unterthanen-Verbande betreffend. Vol. IV., 1853-1854; vol. V., 1855-1856; vol. VII., 1860-1867.

No. 12. Die Agenturen zur Vermittelung des Transportes von Auswanderern betreffend. Vol. I., 1853; vol. II., 1853; vol. III., 1854; vol. VI., 1856-1857; vol. VIII., 1859-1860; vol. IX., 1860-1861; vol. XI., 1862-1863; vol. XII., 1864; vol. XIV., 1867.

No. 13. Generalia, die Auswanderung Kurhessischer Unterthanen in das Ausland betreffend. Vol. I., 1851-1853; vol. II., 1854-1857; vol. III., 1858-1863; vol. IV., 1864-1867.

No. 64. Generalia, das Passwesen überhaupt betreffend. Vol. II. 1862-1867.

No. 138 a. Zusammenstellung der Ergebnisse aus den in Deutschland geführten Untersuchungen bezüglich des politischen Treibens in der Schweiz, insbesondere der Verbindung " Das junge Deutschland" nach den der Bundes Central-Behörde bis 14 Januar 1836 zugekommenen Akten. 1836.

No. 160. Register über die von Kurhessischer Regierung der Provinz Niederhessen ertheilten Gestattung zur Uebernahme von Agenturen behufs Vermittelung des Transports von Auswanderern betreffend. 1833.

Acc. 1903/9, Verzeichniss XIII. der Acten der Kurfürstlichen Regierung zu Cassel, Handels- und Gewerbe-Angelegenheiten betreffend.

No. 8. Die Verordnung vom 23 März 1835, das Wandern, die Versammlungen, und Verbindungen der deutschen Handwerksgesellen betreffend. 1835-1858. (*Cf.* No. 29.)

No. 21. Die Agenturen zur Vermittelung des Transports von Auswanderern betreffend. Bd. IV., 1855; V., 1856; VII., 1857-1858; X., 1861-1862; XIII., 1865-1866.

No. 38. Die Uebersichten über den Geschäftsbetrieb der in der Provinz Niederhessen zugelassenen Feuerversicherungsgesellschaften betreffend. 1865-1867.

No. 97. Die Zunftordnung vom Jahre 1816. III., 1835-1847; IV., 1848-1854; V., 1855-1859; VI., 1860-1867.

No. 119. Die Bildung eines Handwerkervereins betreffend. 1845.

No. 120. Die Kommission für Gewerbe- und Handels-Angelegenheiten und die Abgabe der nunmehr zu deren Geschäftskreise gehörigen Akten u. s. w. betreffend. 1854-1859.

No. 122. Die Aufstellung einer Gewerbestatistik des Zollvereins betreffend. 1861-1864.

No. 203. Generalia. Das Konzessionenwesen betreffend. II. 1830-1836.

No. 204. Generalia. Das Konzessionenwesen betreffend. III. 1836-1845; IV., 1846-1852; V., 1853-1858; VI., 1859-1867.

Acc. 1903/9, Verzeichniss XIX. der Acten der Kurfürstlichen Regierung zu Marburg, Polizeiwesen betreffend.

No. 20. Die landwirtschaftliche Statistik. 1866.

No. 21. Ausarbeitung von Kreisstatistiken in Kurhessen. 1866-1867.

No. 78, 79, 80, 81, 82, 83, 84. Die Aufnahme von Ausländern. 1821-1865.

No. 92, 94. (Different stages of the subject.)

No. 99. Die Entlassung aus dem Unterthanen-Verbande und darauf bezügliche Gegenstände. Bd. IV. 1853-1857.

Acc. 1903/9, Verzeichniss XX. der Acten der Kurfürstlichen Regierung zu Marburg, Handels- und Gewerbe-Angelegenheiten betreffend.

No. 5. Generalia. *a.* Die Zulassung ausländischer Feuer- u. Lebensversicherungs- und Renten-Anstalten.

b. Das Projekt zur Gründung eines Kredit-Institutes pp. vom Finanzkandidat Fenner von Fenneberg betreffend. 1844-1854.

No. 6. Generalia, relating to same as no. 5 a above. 1865-1867.
No. 27. Generalia, die Fabrikation des irdenen Geschirres in der Provinz, auch die Ausfuhr des Thones, und die desfallsigen Verfügungen, desgleichen die Hebung der Thongewerbe betreffend. 1822-1867. Cf. no. 34.
No. 28. Generalia. Runkelrüben und Zuckerfabriken. 1837.
No. 29. Generalia, die gebetene Minderung der auf dem ausländischen Leder ruhenden Eingangssteuer betreffend. 1825-1827.

Acc. 1903/9. Verzeichniss XXI. der Acten der Kurfürstlichen Regierung zu Marburg, Polizeiwesen betreffend.

R.? S. S. 3564. No. 1. Generalia: (1) Die Auswanderungen; (2) Die Agenten zur Vermittelung des Transports der Auswanderer betreffend. 1864-1867. Vol. VII.
No. 19. Generalia, Reisepass-Wesen und alle darauf Bezug habenden Gegenstände, insbesondere auch die Beglaubigung von Legitimationspapieren betreffend. 1858-1867.
No. 27. Die Gestattung eines temporären Aufenthalts von Fremden im Kreise Marburg und Beschwerden wegen Verweigerung desselben betreffend. 1850-1864.
No. 28. Die Gestattung eines temporären Aufenthalts von Fremden in der Stadt Marburg und Beschwerden wegen Verweigerung desselben betreffend. 1850-1867.
No. 35. Cf. similar act for Kirchhain. 1852-1867.

Acc. 1903/9. Verzeichniss XXVI.

No. 28. Die über den Aufenthalt von Fremden in der hiesigen Provinz erlassene allgemeine Verfügungen betreffend, etc. 1825-1866.

Acc. 1903/9. Verzeichniss XLV.

No. 59. Generalia, die Jahresberichte der Distrikts-Vereine über den Zustand des Handels und des Gewerbes betreffend. 1840-1847.

Akten Repertorium der Kurfürstlichen Kommission für statistische Angelegenheiten, acc. 1909, 29.

5 i. Ein- und Auswanderungen.
  91. Akten betreffend die Einwanderungen in Kurhessen.
    Fasc. I. 1855-1864.
    Fasc. II. 1865—.
  92. Akten betreffend die Auswanderungen aus Kurhessen.
    Fasc. I. 1852-1863.
    Fasc. II. 1864.
  92. Akten betreffend die von der kurfürstlichen Regierung zu Cassel abgegebenen, von den unteren Verwaltungsbehörden aufgestellten Verzeichnisse über Auswanderungen in den Jahren 1857-1863.
  92. Register über die Auswanderungen. 1852-1862.
    Band A. Provinz Niederhessen.
    Band B. Provinz Oberhessen und Fulda.
    Band C. Provinz Hanau, sowie Schmalkalden und Rinteln.

92. Register über die Aus- und Einwanderungen von 1863. One volume, another containing the " Aemter-, Kreis-, und Provinzabschösse ".

Repertorium über die Wilhelmshöher Kriegskarten.

The Repertorium contains a list of 44 volumes of maps, with an alphabetical list of geographical names at the end and another of the orders of battle. The maps are listed here as they come in the order of volumes. The two volumes devoted particularly to the American wars are 28 and 29 with this title:
" Plans vom Nord-Americanischen Kriege von 1775-1782." I Theil, 1775-1777 (=28) ; II Theil, 1777-1782 (=29).
Outside of volumes 28 and 29 none relating to America were noticed. Those with reference to Winchester, 1756, etc., all bear on England and the position of the Hessian troops, but not on America. (*Cf.* Bd. 24, nos. 7 and 8.)

Tabellen der hessischen Regimenter, zusammengestellt durch Major a. D. von Gironcourt im Jahre 1879.

A tabulation of Hessian troops, giving names of troops and chief, formation and numerical strength, garrison, campaigns, withdrawals, and accessions. From these tables I give the following outline:

Leibgarde Regiment.
    A. 1 [tes] Bataillon 1776-1784 in Amerika.
    B. 2 [tes] Bataillon 1776-1783 in Amerika.
        Hessen Hanauisches Regiment. Chef, Erbprinz Wilhelm von Hessen. In Canada.
        Fusilier Regiment. General von Lossberg (Oberst v. Minnigerode und Löwenstein).
        Grenadier Regiment. Oberst Rall.
Erstes Inf. Regiment (Kurfürst).
    A. 1 [tes] Bataillon. Stamm[1] Leib Fusilier Regiment. Exped. nach England 1756. Erbprinz Friedrich von Hessen.
        Leib Infanterie Regiment 1776-1783 in Amerika. Com. Oberst von Linsingen.
    B. 2tes Bataillon. Stamm Reg. Landgraf Wilhelm VIII. Exped. nach England 1756.
        Regiment Landgraf. Landgraf Friedrich II. Die Grenadierkompagnie wurde 1. des zweiten Gren. Bataillons. 1776 Block, 1777 Lengerke, in Amerika 1776-1784.
Zweites Inf. Regiment (Landgraf Wilhelm von Hessen).
    A. 1 [tes] Bataillon Gen. Major Prinz J. C. Isenburg-Birstein. Exped. in England 1756. v. Isenburg-Birstein. Gen. Lt. Donop Comp. wurde 2 [te] des 2. Gren. Bat. Com. Oberst von Block in Amerika 1776—. Oberst Lengerke.
    B. 2 [tes] Bataillon von Fürstenberg. 1 [ein] Bat. Exped. nach England 1756. Gen. Lt. von Knyphausen in Amerika 1776-1783.

---

[1] *I. e.*, the base of the regiment, its first organized form.

Marburg

Drittes Inf. Reg. (Prinz Friedr. Wilhelm von Hessen).
A. 1 Bataillon. Stamm Füsil. Reg. Landgraf Carl.
    a. 1. Bat. Exped. nach England 1756. Die Gren. Comp. wurde 2 [te] des zweiten Gren. Bat. (Oberst Block) in Amerika 1776-1783.
    b. 2. Bataillon. Füsil. Reg. Landgraf Carl in Schottland 1742, 1746. Regiment von Trümbach in Amerika 1776-1783. Regiment Bose at Guilford 1780.
B. 2 [tes] Bataillon. Stamm 2 [tes] Bat. Reg. Pr. von Solms. Die Gren. Comp. wurde 4 [tes] Gren. Bat. Linsingen in Amerika 1776—. Reg. (von Lossberg) in Amerika 1780-1781.
Jäger Bataillon. 4 [tes] Jäger Corps (Hanauisches Jägercorps) in Amerika 1776—.
Schützen Bataillon. Stamm: 1 [tes] Bat. Reg. Pr. von Solms.
    Fusilier Regiment Erbprinz Wilhelm von Hessen. Die Grenadierkompagnie wurde des 3. Gren. Bat. (Minnigerode) in Amerika 1776-1783.
Vacantes Bataillon. A. 1 [tes] Bataillon.
    Regiment F. M. v. Canitz. Ein Bat. Exped. nach England 1756. Fusilier Reg. (Ditfurth, Minnigerode) in Amerika 1776-1783.
Garnisons Reg. von Porbeck. (Gen. Lt. Stein, Oberst Köhler) in Amerika 1776-1783.
Garnisons Reg. Köhler. (Gen. Maj. v. Wisserbach, Oberst J. C. Köhler) in Amerika 1776-1783.
Garnisons Reg. v. Knoblauch (Oberst v. Huyn) in Amerika 1776-1783.
Garnisons Reg. v. Colson (Oberst v. Bünau) in Amerika 1776—. (*Cf.* Platte und Graf.)
Artillerie Reg. 6te Comp. Feld Artillerie.
    1 Comp. Garnisons Artillerie.
    1 Husaren Comp. (*Cf.* 1600 Schützen Baurn.)

Marburg. Cross or supplementary reference. (See the Uebersicht Rep. or " Uebersicht der Abteilungen ".)

Correspondence with the governments of (Denmark) England, Holland, Sweden, France, Spain, Portugal, also correspondence with the Hessian legations in the same countries, especially *circa* 1704, which is preceded by the Geheimraths-Correspondence, 1677-1727. (39 vols.) Especially to be examined:

    Correspondenz des Gesandten von Görtz in England und Holland.
    Correspondenz des Obermarschalls Fr. von Kettner 1723 (one vol., England).
    Correspondenz der Agenten Abr. und Fae Maudry zu Genf, 1722-1755. 1 vol.
    Correspondenz des Gesandten Gen. v. Rotberg in Basel, 1720-1722 und 1724-1730. 1 vol.
    Correspondenz des Holländischen Gesandten Runkel in der Schweiz, 1705-1707. 1 vol.
    Correspondenz des Mr. Sande im Haag, 1701-1703. 1 vol.
    Correspondenz des Holländischen Gesandten Volkeniers in der Schweiz, 1704. 1 vol.
    Correspondenz des Raths Vultejus im Haag, 1721-1730, 1730-1743. 2 vols.

Correspondenz des Gesandten v. Alt in London, 1735-1739, 1740-1741, 1744-1746, 1747-1751. 5 vols.
Correspondenz des Gesandten v. Diemar in London, 1730-1732 (2 vols.), 1733-1735 (1 vol.).
Correspondenz des Gesandten im Haag, 1739-1742, 1742-1743, 1743, 1744, 1745, 1747, 1748-1750. 7 vols.
Correspondenz des Gesandten v. Alt in London, 1733-1759 (24 vols.) and 1766-1768 (5 vols.).
Correspondenz des Gesandten v. Diemar in London, 1730-1731, 1733-1734. 1 vol.
Correspondenz des Gesandten v. Diemar in London, 1735, und Bonn, 1736. 1 vol.
Correspondenz des Gesandten v. Diemar in Stockholm, Hannover und London, 1734-1741. 1 vol.
Correspondenz des Agenten A. G. v. Fabrice. 1746-1751 ?
Correspondenz des Agenten v. Fagel im Haag, 1715-1730, und 1735-1744. 1 vol.
Correspondenz des Agenten Ant. Mann im Haag, 1735, und 1739-1741, 1742-1760 (12 or 18 ? vols.), 1760-1761 (12 vols.).
Correspondenz des Gesandten Fr. Carl v. Moser zu Wien und im Haag, 1763-1766. 1 vol.
Correspondenz des Agenten Warmholtz im Haag, 1740. 1 vol.
Correspondenz des (Agenten) v. Welderen im Haag, 1731-1754. 1 vol.
Correspondenz des Legationsraths Neuhard im Haag, 1762 (1 vol.), 1768-1771 (5 vols.).
Correspondenz des Gesandten Oynhausen im Haag, 1765-1769. 1 vol.

DOCUMENTS ON THE III. ENGLISH-WALDECK REGIMENT.

As explained under Waldeck, *infra,* the historical archives of that principality have for the most part been transferred from Arolsen to Marburg. This transfer included the following documents respecting the auxiliary troops which the Prince of Waldeck furnished to the King of Great Britain during the war for American independence:

944a. Generalia, das III. Englisch-Waldeckische Regiment in America betr. 1776-1784.
950. Repertorium das in anno 1776 in Königlich Grossbrittanischem Sold errichtete III. Waldeckische Regiment betr.
949. Die wegen des III. Englisch-Waldeckischen Regiments geführte Korrespondenz zwischen dem Fürstlichen Kabinett und König Georg III. von England, dem Unterhändler Generalmajor William Faucitt und andern Angehörigen des englischen Hofes. 1775-1784.
964. Verhandlungen des Präsidenten von Zerbst mit dem englischen Hofe, namentlich mit Faucitt, wegen des englisch-waldeckischen Soldregiments. 1776-1783.
943. Die von dem Geheimen Secretär Frensdorff zur Erhebung von Werbegeldern für das III. englisch-waldeckische Regiment nach London unternommene Reise nebst Einnahme- und Ausgabe-Rechnung. 1778.
962. Berichte des Geheimen Secretärs Frensdorff aus London über seine dortigen Unterhandlungen wegen des III. englisch-waldeck-

ischen Soldregiments. Mit Rechnung über Einkäufe für den Fürsten. 1780-(1781).
980. Betr. das III. englisch-waldeckische Soldregiment, in specie enthaltend die Korrespondenz zwischen dem Geheimen Secretär Frensdorff und dem Agenten Hesse in London. Tom. I. 1776-1780.
982. *Id.* Tom. II. 1781-1786.
996. Betr. das III. englisch-waldeckische Soldregiment in specie enthaltend die Rechnungen des Militäragenten Hesse in London. 1776-1785.
042. Betr. sämtliche Forderungen Waldecks an die englische Tresorie wegen des III. Regiments. 1784.
967. Abrechnungen mit der englischen Regierung wegen des III. englisch-waldeckischen Regiments. Generalia. 1776-1787.
963. Betr. das III. englisch-waldeckische Soldregiment in specie enthaltend Instruction für den Regimentskommandeur, Kriegsartikel, Exerzierreglement. 1776.
942. Musterrollen des dritten englisch-waldeckischen Soldregiments. 1776-1783.
1008. Das III. englisch-waldeckische Soldregiment. Werbungssachen. Allgemeines. 1776-1785.
1012. Verhandlungen des Arolser Kabinetts mit dem Major H. E. Lutterloh betr. Werbungen für das dritte englisch-waldeckische Soldregiment. 1775-1776.
1013. Das III. englisch-waldeckische Soldregiment. Verhandlungen mit verschiedenen kleinen Reichsständen zum Zwecke der Soldatenwerbung in deren Gebiet. 1776.
1014. *Id.* Soldatenwerbungen in Hessen-Homburg und Solms 1777-1778, in Wittgenstein, 1780-1781, 1785.
1009. Betr. auswärtige Werbungen für das III. englisch-waldeckische Soldregiment, 1776-1777:
A. in Mühlhausen, Nordhausen, und auf dem Eichsfeld;
B. in Hildesheim;
C. in Hamburg und Bremen;
D. in Frankfurt, Wetzlar, Wittgenstein;
E. in Pyrmont;
F. in Stade.
1010. Werbungen in Hamburg. 1776, 1781.
1031. Werbungen des Fähnrichs, Lieutenants Le Suire. 1776-1782.
1016. Werbungen des Sergeanten Göbel in Friedberg, Wetzlar, Worms, and Speyer. 1777-1783.
1015. Soldatenwerbungen in Wetzlar, auf dem Eichsfelde, in Waldeck, und in Friedberg. 1777-1783.
1011. Betr. die von dem Waldeckischen Agenten Zanders im Haag vorgeschossenen Gelder zur Bestreitung der Werbekosten für das dritte englisch-waldeckische Regiment. 1780-(1784).
1017. Betr. Anwerbungen von Soldaten für das dritte englisch-waldeckische Regiment in America durch den Lieutenant Heus in Pyrmont. 1780-1782.
1018. Werbungen des Sergeanten Gerle. 1776-1783.
1019. Werbungen des Hauptmanns v. d. Osten-Sacken in Friedberg und Wetzlar. 1781-1782.

1020. Werbungen des Hauptmanns v. Romrodt im Solmsischen. 1776-1778.
1021. Werbungen des Lieutenants Noezel in Franken. 1777-1778 (1781).
1022. Werbung des Lieutenants Becker in Wetzlar (und Friedberg). 1776-1777.
1023. Werbung des Lieutenants Becker in Wittgenstein und Erbach. 1777.
971. Betr. die Versuche bei der Bildung des dritten englisch-waldeckischen Soldregiments freiwillige waldeckische Landeskinder anzuwerben. 1776.
973. Dienstentlassungen von Soldaten des I. und II. holländisch-waldeckischen Regiments zwecks Uebertritts in das dritte englisch-waldeckische Soldregiment. 1776, 1777.
977. Enthaltend Pässe und Leumundszeugnisse für Soldaten des nachmaligen dritten englisch-waldeckischen Soldregiments. 1775.
997. Löhnungs- und Ausgabebuch des zum dritten englisch-waldeckischen Soldregiment in America bestimmten Rekrutentransports *Hameln.* Mar. 2, 1781.
998. Summarische Uebersicht über Unkosten und Löhnung für die zum dritten englisch-waldeckischen Regiment in America bestimmten Rekruten. Pyrmont, Jan.-Apr., 1782.
999. Beläge zu dem Löhnungs- und Ausgabebuche des zum dritten englisch-waldeckischen Soldregiment in America bestimmten Rekrutentransports *Hameln.* Mar. 1, 1781.
1000. Einnahme- und Ausgabeberechnung des Majors v. Seebisch über einen Rekrutentransport für das dritte englisch-waldeckische Soldregiment in America. Mit den Belägen, Aufgestellt. Apr. 4, 1782.
1001. Ausgabeberechnung bei dem Rekrutentransport für das dritte englisch-waldeckische Regiment auf dem Marsche und in Hameln. Mit den Belägen. Nov. 28, 1777–Mar. 7, 1778.
1002. Equipage- und Rekrutentransporte zum dritten englisch-waldeckischen Regiment in America. 1782-1783.
1003. Rekrutentransporte zum dritten englisch-waldeckischen Soldregimente nach America. 1776-1778.
1004. Equipage- und Rekrutentransporte zum dritten englisch-waldeckischen Soldregimente nach America. 1779-1781.
1005. Ausgaberechnung des Hauptmanns v. Seebisch über den Rekrutentransport zum dritten englisch-waldeckischen Regiment nach Staten-Island. 1778.
1006. Berechnung aller Schulden des 1777 in Staten-Island angekommenen Rekrutentransports zum dritten englisch-waldeckischen Soldregiment. 1777.
1007. Rechnung des Hauptmanns v. Seebisch über die Kosten des Rekrutentransports. Mar. 6, 1778–Feb. 27, 1779.
945. Löhnungs- und Rechnungsbuch derer zum III. Hochfürstlich Waldeckischen Regiment bestimmten Rekruten des Jahres 1782.
946. Beläge zu: Grundliste, Löhnungs- und Rechnungsbuch derer zum III. hochfürstlich Waldeckischen Regiment bestimmten Recrouten des Jahres 1782.
966. Jährliche Etats des dritten englisch-waldeckischen Soldregiments. 1776-1782.
970. Grundlisten des dritten englisch-waldeckischen Soldregiments in America. 1776-1777, 1783.

Marburg

- **968.** Die Stärke des dritten englisch-waldeckischen Regiments betr. 1776-1783.
- **960.** Betr. Deserteurs und solche, die sich der Wehrpflicht entzogen haben. 1776-1787.
- **969.** Betr. Desertion zweier Soldaten vom dritten englisch-waldeckischen Regiment. 1782.
- **978.** Verzeichnis des Abgangs an Toten, Verabschiedeten, und Deserteurs (Offiziere und Mannschaften). 1776-1783.
- **983.** Personalia der Offiziere und Mannschaften. 1776-1785.
- **984.** Betr. das kriegsgerichtliche Verfahren gegen den Hauptmann Alberti sen. wegen seines Benehmens vor, während und nach seiner spanischen Gefangenschaft. 1779-1780 (1782).
- **985.** Militairgerichtliches Verfahren gegen den Major v. Seebisch wegen Vergehens im Dienst. 1782.
- **986.** Militairgerichtliches Verfahren gegen den Vicekorporal Reichert wegen Verleitung zur Desertion. 1782.
- **987.** Betr. Fürstliche Gnadengeschenke an die zurückgelassenen Angehörigen von Soldaten des III. englisch-waldeckischen Soldregiments. 1776-1783.
- **944.** Montirungssachen. 1776-1784.
- **1047.** Montirungsverzeichnisse. 1777-1784.
- **979.** Equipagelieferungen durch den Hoffactor Jacob Marc bezw. die Gebrüder Marc (und den Hofagenten Stieglitz). 1776-1784.
- **952.** Tuchlieferungen von G. F. Besseling in Rotterdam. 1779-1780.
- **953.** Gewehrlieferungen aus Holland für das dritte englisch-waldeckische Regiment. 1777-1780.
- **954.** Monturlieferungen des Goldschmieds Berges. 1779-1782.
- **955.** Gewehrlieferungen des Büchsenmachers Thomas Wilhelm Pistor in Schmalkalden. 1776-1782.
- **956.** Waffenlieferungen der Schwertfeger Georg Conrad Schömckell und Johann Conrad Sch. seel. Wittib in Cassel. 1776-1782.
- **957.** Gewehrlieferungen von G. A. Ampfurt in Hameln. 1777-1778.
- **958.** Zeltlieferungen des Tapezierers Diederich in Cassel. 1777-1778.
- **959.** Lieferungen der Cülter Tuchfabrik. 1777-1783.
- **948.** Bilancen über Einnahme und Ausgabe. 1776-1783.
- **1038.** Beläge 1-195 zu Seite 3-41 des Journals des Regierungsrates Frensdorff über Einnahme und Ausgabe für das dritte englisch-waldeckische Soldregiment. Mar. 10, 1770–Mar., 1785.
- **1033.** Regimentsrechnung des Regierungsrates Frensdorff über Einnahme und Ausgabe. Mar. 8, 1776-Sept. 22, 1777.
- **1035.** Belege 1-89 zu Seite 3-25 der Regimentsrechnung des Regierungsrates Frensdorff über Einnahme und Ausgabe. Mar. 8, 1776–Sept. 22, 1777.
- **1036.** Beläge 1-68 zu Seite 31-47 der Regimentsrechnung des Regierungsrates Frensdorff über Einnahme und Ausgabe. Mar. 8, 1776–Sept. 22, 1777.
- **1044.** Belege 1-33 zu einer nicht vorhandenen Rechnung des Geheimen Sekretärs Frensdorff das III. englisch-waldeckische Regiment betr. 1776-1783.
- **1046.** Belege A-F zu einer nicht vorhandenen Rechnung, das dritte englisch-waldeckische Regiment betr. 1777-1778.

1032. Regimentsrechnung des Regierungsrats Frensdorff über Einnahme und Ausgabe. 1777-1781.
1034. Belege 1-176 zu Seite 5-59 der Regimentsrechnung des Regierungsrates Frensdorff über Einnahme und Ausgabe. 1777-1781.
1039. Belege 1-156 zu Seite 62-117 der Regimentsrechnung des Regierungsrates Frensdorff über Einnahme und Ausgabe. 1777-1781 (incomplete).
1048. Journal des Regierungsrates Frensdorff über Einnahme und Ausgabe. Mar. 10, 1777–Mar., 1785. Hierzu 6 Pakete Beläge.
1049. Belege 1-119 zu Seite 43-71 des Journals, etc.
1050. Belege 1-24 zu Seite 75-85 des[selben].
1051. Beläge 1-175 zu Seite 87-115.
1052. Beläge 1-43 zu Seite 119-141.
1053. Beläge 1-68 zu Seite 145-169 und 1-4 zu Seite 171.
1041. Belege A 1-186 zu einer Rechnung Frensdorffs. Sept., 1781–Aug., 1782.
1045. Beläge a-v zu einer nicht vorhandenen Rechnung des Geheimen Secretärs Frensdorff gehörend. 1781-1782.
1043. Belege 1-79 zu einer nichtvorhandenen Rechnung des Geheimen Sekretärs Frensdorff. 1782-1783.
1024. Ausgaberechnung des Regimentsquartiermeisters Wiegand vom III. englisch-waldeckischen Regiment. Mit den Belegen. Mar. 18–May 20, 1776.
1025. Ausgaberechnung des Regimentsquartiermeisters Wiegand. Mit den Belegen. May 20–July 26, 1776.
1026. Ausgaberechnung desselben. Mit den Belegen. July 27, 1776–June 24, 1777.
1027. Ausgaberechnungen desselben. Mit den Belegen. June 25, 1777–Dec. 24, 1778.
1028. Ausgaberechnungen desselben. Mit den Belägen. Dec. 25, 1780–Dec. 24, 1782.
1029. Ausgaberechnungen desselben. Mit den Belegen. Dec. 25, 1778–Dec. 24, 1780.
1040. Einnahme und Ausgaberechnung des Regimentsquartiermeisters Wiegand für den in spanischer Gefangenschaft gewesenen Teil des dritten englisch-waldeckischen Regiments von 1780 Juni 25–1782 Juni 24, sowie für den in New-Towtown gewesenen Teil von 1781 Dec. 25–1782 Juni 24. Mit den Belegen.
1030. Ausgaberechnungen des Regimentsquartiermeisters Wiegand. Mit den Belägen. Dec. 25, 1782–Oct. 24, 1783.
993. Bestallung des Juden Philipp Marc als Kommissar für das dritte englisch-waldeckische Soldregiment. 1776.
981. Briefwechsel zwischen dem waldeckischen Regimentscommissar Jacob Marc in London und dem Geheimen Sekretär Frensdorff in Arolsen. 1781-1782.
994. Berechnung mit den Gebrüdern Marc wegen Lieferungen an das dritte englisch-waldeckische Regiment in America. 1778-1782 incl.
995. Schreiben des Kommissars für das dritte englisch-waldeckische Soldregiment Philipp Marc. 1777–1782.
988. Verpflegungszettel. 1776-1783. Tom. I. (Ausgestellt vom Lieutenant und Regimentsquartiermeister Wiegand.)

Marburg

989. *Id.*, Tom. II. (Ausgestellt vom waldeckischen Kommissar Phil. Marc.)
990. *Id.*, Tom. III.
992. *Id.*, Tom. IV.
991. Zusammenfassende Verpflegungszettel des dritten englisch-waldeckischen Regiments. 1776-1783.
947. Rechnungen über Verpflegung von Mannschaften des dritten englisch-waldeckischen Regiments in Hospitälern in America. 1776-1783.
965. Schriftwechsel mit dem englisch-hannöverschen Residenten Bütemeister und dem Chevalier Yorke im Haag betr. die Postverbindung zwischen Waldeck und dem III. Soldregiment in America. 1776-1778.
972. Berichte vom dritten englisch-waldeckischen Regiment an den Fürsten und Frensdorff. 1776-1785.
974. Berichte des Kommandeurs des dritten englisch-waldeckischen Soldregiments in America, Oberstleutnants (dann Obersten) von Hansleden an den Fürsten und an Frensdorff. 1776-1780.
975. Korrespondenz des Fürsten und Frensdorffs mit dem Oberstleutnant von Horn vom III. englisch-waldeckischen Soldregiment in America. 1776-1784.
976. Schreiben des Geheimen Secretairs Frensdorff an den Kommandeur des dritten englisch-waldeckischen Soldregiments in America, Obersten von Hansleden. 1776-1781.
951. General-Contobuch über Soll und Haben der Offiziere und Mannschaften. 1776 *et seq.*
1037. Kontobuch des Regierungsrates Frensdorff über Soll und Haben von Offizieren und Mannschaften des dritten englisch-waldeckischen Soldregiments in America. 1776-1781.
961. Die Rückkehr des dritten englisch-waldeckischen Soldregiments aus America in die Heimat. 1783-1784.

DOCUMENTS ON THE WILDUNGER BRUNNEN.

3187. Geschäftlicher Verkehr zwischen dem Geheimen Secretär Frensdorff und der Firma Joh. Caspar Brust in Bremen betreffend die Ausfuhr des Wildunger Wassers (auch den Verkehr mit dem waldeckischen Regiment in America). Tom. I. 1774-1782.
3167. *Id.*, Tom. II. 1783-1807.

MÜNSTER.
ROYAL STATE ARCHIVES OF THE PROVINCE OF WESTPHALIA.
(Königliches Staatsarchiv der Provinz Westfalen.)

Located in a new building, quite in contrast with the older structures in the centre of the city, particularly the Rathaus with its reminiscences of the Peace of Westphalia. For the records of the kingdom of Westphalia consult the Royal Privy Prussian Archives in Berlin.[1]
Hours: 8 to 1.

Acta der Königlichen Regierung Arnsberg.

Ober-Präsidial-Registratur (Fach 1, no. 4) 77. Acta betreffend die jährlichen Nachweisungen der Königl. Regierungen über die vorgekommenen Auswanderungen. 1855-1863.

Ober Präsidium B. Handlungs Sachen. Fach 68, no. 21 (185). Acta betr. die Rheinisch-Westindische Handels-Gesellschaft; und den Deutsch-Amerikanischen Bergwerks-Verein. 1821. Contains valuable printed matter such as circulars, pamphlets, and the like, relating to both organizations, 1831-1835, also important correspondence between Staatsminister von Bülow, Graf von Bernstorff and Wittgenstein in Berlin, and between Ober-Präsident von Vincke, in Münster, and Becher, in Elberfeld, and others. A number of important reports of the enterprise is enclosed, such as: " Resultat des Mexicanischen Geschäfts der vorliegenden Rechnungs Periode von 1 Feb. 1830 bis 31 Dec. 1831, Zeitraum von 23 Monaten," and " Uebersichten der durch die Rheinisch-Westindische Kompagnie bis zum 31 Dezember 1831 seewärts ausgeführten Waaren".

Fach 68, no. 22 a, 240, I. Acta betr. den diesseitigen Handel mit Nord und Süd Amerika, und die Anordnung der Konsulate. 1821-1866. Valuable volume containing papers, applications, and the like, relating to the establishment of new consulates and reflecting the commercial conditions of the respective countries and the reasons for establishing consulates. Much important printed matter is enclosed.

Id., 242, II. Acta betr. den diesseitigen Handel mit Nord- und Süd- Amerika, und die Anordnung der Consulate. 1866-1874.

B. 45. Betreffend das Auswandern der Fabrik-Arbeiter. 1815.

B. 70, Polizei Registratur. Betreffend die Nachweisungen der vorgekommenen Aus- und Einwanderungen. Vol. V. 1874-1878.

V. 18, Kreis Registratur Soest. Acta Auswanderungs Consense betreffend. Vol. I. 1817-1846. Desgleichen wegen der von auswärtigen Staaten geforderten werdenden Heimathscheinen.

VII. 6, Kreisreg. Dortmund. Acta spec. betreffend die Ein- und Auswanderungen. 1856-1866.

VIII. 7, Amt Bochum. Acta betreffend die statistischen Tabellen über die Aus- und Einwanderungen. 1864-1884 incl.

---

[1] The investigator's attention is called also to the collections of the Handelskammer. and the Archiv des Vereins für Geschichte und Altertumskunde Westfalens.

Access. 16, 1908 (Amt Boele).
IX., no. 155. Acta Ansiedlung und Auswanderung betr. 1821-1851.
No. 156. Acta specialia betr. die Ansiedlungen, Ein- und Auswanderungen. 1851-1856.
Kreis Registratur Hagen.
IX. 42. Acta Gener. betr. die Auswanderungen diesseitiger Unterthanen. 1831-1869.
43. Acta Specialia betr., etc. 1852-1866.
45. Acta Specialia, etc. 1819-1852.
154. Acta Spec. betr. den Unterstützungs-Verein der kleinen Fabrikanten und Handwerksmeister der Gemeinde Eckesey. 1875-1882.
Kreis Iserlohn.
C. 287. X. 100. Acta betreffend die Auswanderungen und den Abschoss. 1817-1852. Requests for permission to emigrate and matter relating thereto.
A. N. Z., Kreis Reg. Wittgenstein.
XIV. 15. Acta Emigration diesseitiger und Reception fremder Unterthanen betr.
Vol. I. 1844-1847.
Vol. II. 1847-1850.
Vol. III. 1850-1854.
Vol. IV. 1854-1857.
16-16 a. Acta Emigration, etc.
Vol. I. 1832-1835.
Vol. II. 1833.
Vol. III. 1835-1836.
Vol. IV. 1837-1844.
Vol. V. 1858-1868.
Amts Registratur Arfeld.
XIV. 113. Acta betreffend Emigration von Jnländern und Reception von Ausländern in dem Jahren 1845 bis 1855 incl.
114. Acta Specialia Emigration von Inländern und Reception von Ausländern vom Jahre 1856 incl. und weiter bis 1866 incl.

Regierung Minden.

Access. 18, 1904. 14 I. Acta spec. betr. die Einreichung der Nachweisungen über die Ein- und Auswanderungen pro 1856 bis 1865 incl. Statistical tables like those given for the other departments, but disappointing, except that the agents are mentioned by name.
14 II. Acta spec., etc. 1860–Sept., 1864.
14 III. Acta spec., etc. 1866-1871.
14 IV. Acta spec., etc. 1871-1873.

Regierung Münster.

Kreis Ahaus.
33. Acta Gener. betr. die Auswanderungen. 1817-1857.
Kreis Borken.
Access. 27, 1908, 77. Acta betr. die jährliche Nachweisungen der Ein- und Ausgewanderten. 1862-1889.

IV. 39. Acta Generalia betreffend die Auswanderungen. 1817-1866.
Contains important matter relating to the emigration of subjects from the " Fabrik-Gegenden ", such as the following and documents relating thereto:
Verfügung des Hohen-Finanz Ministerium vom 4. d. M. [1817, March].
Edikt vom 2 Juli 1812.
Printed notice of the Ober Präsident Vincke, dated Münster, Mar. 12, 1817, and directed to the various provincial administrations to take all possible measures to stem the tide of emigration.
Important printed circulars and other matter used as bait ("Lockspeise") to induce emigration to America.

Kreis [Registratur] Ludinghausen.
IV. 47. Acta Specialia betreffend die Auswanderungen. 1857-1861.
IV. 48. Acta Specialia, etc. 1819-1843.
IV. 49. Acta Specialia, etc. 1847-1850.
IV. 50. Acta Specialia, etc. 1846.
IV. 51. Acta Specialia, etc. 1862-1871.

A. N. Z., 181. Acta betreffend die Auswanderungen nach Amerika:
Vol. 1. May 6, 1828–Aug. 13, 1833.
Vol. 2. Aug. 24, 1833–May 30, 1836.
Vol. 3. June 4, 1836–Apr. 3, 1837.
The general character of these papers is much the same for the volumes of the several periods. The first volume may be taken as a characteristic example. It contains, among other things, the following:
Papers relating to 18 persons from Bavarian families who have left home to ship from Bremen to Brazil.
A printed pamphlet with the following title: *Einige Nachrichten über Brasilien, zur Belehrung für die Auswanderungslustigen, besonders in der Eifel,* closing with the words: " Bleibet im Lande, und nähret euch redlich. Geschrieben in der Eifel, im März, 1828. G. B."
Militäratteste. Auswanderungsgesuche und Consense. (All important for names and other personal data.)
Vol. 4. Apr. 7–Oct. 10, 1837.
Vol. 5. July, 1837–Mar., 1838.
Vol. 6. Mar. 24, 1838–May 23, 1839.
Vol. 7. June 2, 1839–Aug. 23, 1840.
Vol. 8. Aug. 24, 1840–July 8, 1841.
Vol. 9. July 2, 1841–Apr. 27, 1842.
Vol. 10. May 3, 1842–May 5, 1843.
Vol. 11. May 9–Nov. 10, 1843.
Vol. 12. Jan. 14–Mar. 31, 1844.
Vol. 13. Apr. 1–May 30, 1844.
Vol. 14. June 3–Aug. 7, 1844.
Vol. 15. Aug. 8, 1844–Feb. 24, 1845.
Vol. 16. Mar. 4–June 30, 1845.
Vol. 17. July 4–Aug. 23, 1845.
Vol. 19. Sept. 5, 1845–Jan. 27, 1846.
Vol. 20. Feb. 6–Mar. 9, 1846.

Vol. 21. Mar. 9–May 5, 1846.
Vol. 22. May 7–July 10, 1846.
Vol. 23. July 15–30, 1846.
Vol. 24. Aug. 1–11, 1846.
Vol. 25. Aug. 12–19, 1846.
Vol. 26. Aug. 21–31, 1846.
Vol. 27. Sept. 1–30, 1846.
Vol. 28. Oct. 3, 1846–Feb. 26, 1847.
Vol. 29. Mar. 1–30, 1847.
Vol. 30. Apr. 1–June 14, 1847.
Vol. 31. June 17–Aug. 23, 1847.
Vol. 32. Aug. 20–Sept. 20, 1847.
Vol. 33. Sept. 22, 1847–Mar. 11, 1848.
Vol. 34. Mar. 13–Aug. 11, 1848.
Vol. 35. Aug. 15, 1848–Feb. 5, 1849.
Vol. 36. Feb. 5–26, 1849.
Vol. 37. Feb. 27–Mar. 31, 1849.
Vol. 38. Apr. 2–June 30, 1849.
Vol. 39. July 5, 1849–Mar. 2, 1850.
Vol. 40. Mar. 4–Aug. 26, 1850.
Vol. 41. Aug. 28, 1850–Feb. 28, 1851.
182. Acta betreffend die Uebersichten der Ein- und Auswanderungen.
Vol. 1. June, 1845–Apr., 1856.
Vol. 2. 1856-1860.
Vol. 3. 1861-1864.
Vol. 4. 1865-1869.
Vol. 5. Missing.
Vol. 6. 1872-1876.
Vol. 7. 1877-1878.
Vol. 8. 1879-1880.
Vol. 9. 1881-1882.
Contain important statistical matter, such as reports, with lists of names of emigrants and personal facts relating to them.
Access. 1, 1907. 455. Nachweise der Ein- und Auswanderungen. Numerical reports arranged according to districts and places and containing important matter relating to individuals.
456. Acta betr. die mit den Bevölkerungs Listen eingekommenen Nachweisen der Ein- und Ausgewanderten. 1832.
457. Acta betr. die Nachweisen der Ausgewanderten. 1834. Contains most valuable matter among which is the following: Namentliches Verzeichniss derjenigen Individuen aus dem Kreise Tecklenburg, welche sich der heimlichen Auswanderungen nach Nord Amerika schuldig gemacht haben.

OSNABRÜCK.
ROYAL STATE ARCHIVES.
(KÖNIGLICHES STAATSARCHIV.)

Located in the royal castle and contains some 18,000 documents dating from the tenth century down, and also the manuscript collections of the Historischer Verein.

Rep. 122. VII. a.
F. Colonien.
- g. VII. 243. Acta in Betr. der beabsichtigten Erleichterungen des Handelsverkehrs mit Holland. 1832.
- gg. VII. 525. Ertheilung von Pässen. Vol. I., II.
- 527. Corresp. mit d. Sicherheits Polizei-Commision zu Hannover.
- 538. Einnahme und Ausgabe an Passformularen vom 1ten März 1818 an.
- 548. Austeilung von Attesten behufs Auswanderungen hiesiger oder Aufnahme fremder Unterthanen.
- 554. Verm. d. Pass- u. Fremden-Polizei nach der Kgl. Verord. v. 9. Mai u. der ministeriellen Instruction vom 30. Mai 1836. (Missing.)
- 558. Acta in Betr. polizeilicher Massregeln gegen unstatthafte Durchzüge deutscher Auswanderer nach den Niederlanden behufs dortiger Einschiffung nach Amerika. The character of the contents may be inferred from the following: "Denjenigen Auswanderern, denen Pässe auf das Königreich der Niederlande lauten oder welche auf Befragen angeben, ihren Weg dahin nehmen zu wollen, ohne daneben eine solche schriftliche Autorisation einer Königlich Niederländischen Behörde des Auslandes aufweisen zu können, den Eintritt in das Königreich zu verweigern, oder solche sofort zurückzuweisen". (Osnabrück, Mar. 20, 1828.)
- 559. Acta in Betr. eines Polizei-Reglements für die Stadt Meppen. 1829.
- 560. Acta in Betr. verbotener Bücher u. Druckschriften. 1831.
- 564. Acta das Auswanderungsgesuch des Ferdinand Wendel .... nach Amerika betr. 1836.
- 565. Acta das Passwesen betreffend.
- 566. Acta untersuchte Polizei Vergehen betr. 1841.

VII. b. No. 1. Acta betr. nach Amerika ausgewanderte Eingesessene. 1842-1849. (Some 30 papers.)

ARCHIV DES AMTES WITTLAGE.
II. 1823-1852. (Cf. Regiminalia, Fach 19.)
Fach 24. Aeltere Landes Verordnungen.
Fach 25. No. 43-49. Sieben Bände Spangenbergs Sammlung der Verordnungen.
No. 50-53. Vierzehn Bände Osnabrücker Anzeigen. 1826-1838.

Fach 26. No. 1-27. Osnabrücker Anzeigen, 1826-1851; Fünf Bände Polizei Blatt, 1847-1851.
Fach 47. No. 1. Acta betr. Sammlung alter Pässe und Wanderbücher. 1814-1826.
No. 2. Acta betr. Sammlung, etc. 1822-1840.
No. 3. Acta betr. Pass- und Pass-Visa-Register. 1814-1845.
No. 4. Acta betr. Anschaffung der Pass-, etc., Formulare. 1826-1852.
No. 5. Acta betr. Nachrichten wegen verdächtiger Subjecte in Rücksicht auf Pass-Ertheilungen. 1826-1843.
No. 6. Acta betr. Sammlung alter Pässe und Wanderbücher. 1840-1844.
No. 7. *Id.*, 1844, 1845.
No. 8. *Id.*, 1846–Aug. 1, 1847.
Fach 49. Aufnahme von Heurlingen, nos. 1-41.
50. Ertheilung von Taufscheinen.
92. No. 16. Acta betr. das Erscheinen eines aufwieglerischen Gedichts, Auswanderung nach Amerika betr. 1833. (Missing.)
No. 21. Acta betr. Auswanderungen nach Amerika. 1834-1838.
No. 31. Acta betr. Uebersiedlung der Wagabunden Familien Boehme und Tewitz zu Hunteburg nach Amerika. 1839.
No. 80. Acta betr. die Anstellung von Agenten zur Beförderung von Schiffs-Passagieren nach überseeischen Häfen. 1852.
No. 86. Acta betr. Verfügungen zur Verhütung der Auswanderungen nach Nordamerika. 1843-1852.

Amt Wittlage-Hunteburg.

B. Regiminalia.
Fach 46. Wagabunde und Reisende.
No. 18. Die Ueberlassung Sträfling Jobst Heinrich Wellmann aus Bohmte nach Nordamerika betr. 1842.
19. Die Uebersiedelung der Gebrüder Fritz und Johann Heinrich Mosel aus der Bauerschaft Hitz- und Jüstinghausen mit ihren Familien nach Nordamerika betr. 1843.

Rep. des Amts Iburg, VIII. Polizei-Sachen.

H. Sitten- und Ordnungs-Polizei. 7. Auswanderungswesen.
Fach 304. Akt No. 2. Archiv Fach 385. Acta betr. die Uebersiedelung, etc.
311. No. 1. Archiv Fach 390. Acta betr. die höheren Orts vorgeschriebenen polizeilichen Massregeln in Ansehung der aus Süddeutschland als Kolonisten nach Brasilien durch das Königreich Hannover reisenden Auswanderer. 1826.
No. 2. Acta betr. vorgekommene Einsprüche und Bedenklichkeiten über beabsichtigte Auswanderungen. 1829.
No. 3. Acta betr. landespolizeiliche Fürsorge für Auswanderer durch zeitgemässe Warnungen gegen vorgekommene Auswanderungs-Verleitungen. 1832.

No. 4. Acta betr. höheren Orts vorgelegten Uebersichten der stattgefundenen Auswanderungen nach Amerika. 1832-1847.
No. 5. 391. Acta betr. Konzessionierung von Schiffsmaklern und Agenten und deren Ueberwachung. 1834.
No. 6. Acta betr. die durch Vermittelung der Hannoverschen Konsuln in Nord-Amerika in geeigneten Fällen eingezogenen Nachrichten über Ausgewanderte. 1840.
No. 7. Acta betr. die Auswanderung der Familie Sprengelmeyer aus Hagen nach Nord-Amerika durch Vermittelung des Hannoverschen Konsulats in Bremen. 1845.
No. 8. Acta betr. die Beförderung der Auswanderer von Harburg nach den Vereinigten Staaten von Nord-Amerika. 1851.

III. MILITÄR SACHEN.

F. Entlassungen aus dem Untertanen-Verbande.
  Fach 61. Akt No. 1. Archiv Fach 82. Akta betr. Chelsea Out Pensioners. 1815-1859.
  Fach 62. Akt. No. 1. Archiv Fach 83. Akta betr. Auswanderungs-Konsense. 1819-1828.
    2. Archiv Fach 83. Acta betr. Allgemeines und Verschiedenes. 1823-1829. 2 vols.
    14. Archiv Fach 85. Acta betr. Allgemeines, etc. 1866.
    18. Archiv Fach 86. Acta Gener. Verordnungen, Ausschreiben und sonstige allgemeine Verfügungen. 1866 *et seq*.

NIEDERGRAFSCHAFT UND AMT LINGEN.

[Rep. 122. VI. b.] The part in brackets=older Rep. number=Lokat, etc. Other numbers still in force when they are not in square brackets.
Lokat I. 135, 8. [No. 630.] Acta betr. die Auswanderungen nach Amerika. 1852-1879. (About 4 papers.)
  6. [631.] *Id.*, 1834-1838. (About 40 papers.)
    [632.] Acta betr. die Ertheilte Auswanderungs-Consense an militärpflichtige Eingesessene. 1851.
    633. *Id.*, Ertheilte Consense zu Auswanderungen. 1840.
  1. [634.] Acta, etc., Aus- und Einwanderungen. 1800-1813.
    636. Acta, etc., Auswanderungs-Konsense. 1824.
  3. [637.] *Id.*, 1826.
For church records in general see Oberconsistorium in Hannover; though some are in the Osnabrück Staatsarchiv.

POSEN.
ROYAL STATE ARCHIVES.
(KÖNIGLICHES STAATSARCHIV.)

Located in the old castle, Schlossberg. The papers relating to emigration to America, etc., are still deposited in the Ministerial Building, close under the roof, but fairly well classified and arranged in compartments (Fächer). Through the efforts of one of the archivists and the courtesy of the Ober-Präsident access was given for the purpose of making a hasty inventory.

Hours: Week days, 9 to 3.

I. Acta generalia der Königlichen Regierung zu Posen betr. die Auswanderungen der Einwohner aus den Königl. Staaten.
   Fach 13.
   1. Gesuche um Emigrations Consense.
   2. Acta des Königl. Oberpräsidii, betr. die Auswanderung der Unterth. d. Gr. Herz. Posen.
   3. Nachweisung sämtl. ausgewanderten Personen und Sujets, mixte.
II. Landes Sachen. Sect. 1. In Bezug auf fremde Staaten. c. Auswanderungen.
   Vol. I. Angefangen October 1815, geschlossen April 1821. Begins with an edict of July 9, 1812, signed by Hardenberg, and enclosing circulars and statistical lists according to the *Bezirke.*
   Vol. II. May, 1821–July, 1833.
   Vol. III. Aug., 1833–July, 1840.
   Vol. IV. July, 1842–Mar. 10, 1855.

In addition to the 3 rubrics above follow:
   4. Uebersichtliche Nachrichten über Aus- und Einwanderung.
   5. Geschäftsführung und Caution der Auswand. Agenten.
      Vol. V. Mar., 1855–Aug., 1868.
   Fach 14.
      Vol. VI. Sept., 1868–Feb., 1882.
      Vol. VII. Feb., 1882–1890.
      Vol. VIII. 1890–Sept., 1891; and continuing on to the present.
   Acta, etc., betreffend Verleitung zur Auswanderung.
   Vol. I. Apr., 1884–Nov., 1887. Königliche Regierung zu Posen Präsidial Abtheilung Registratur I.
      Acta Sammelberichte zur Rund-Verfügung vom 30. Juli 1891 Nr. 6097/91CA betreffend Auswanderungen nach Brasilien.
      Acta, etc., betr. die Auswanderungen. 1866-1887.
      Acta, etc., betr. die Untersuchung des Herrn v. Zakrzewski und z Kalisch wegen Ermunterung hiesiger Einwohner zur Auswanderung. Nov., 1824.

Polizei-Registratur Tit. II. Sect. P. No. 64.
Acta betr. Uebersichten der Ausgewanderten Personen bezw. Verleitung zum Auswandern. 1881.
Acta, etc., betr. die von Ausländern nachgesuchten Concessionen zum Besitz von Gütern im hiesigen Regierungs Bezirke. Mar., 1838–June, 1839.

Fach 15. Acta der Königl. Regierung zu Posen Präsidial Abteilung Registratur I A 2. Acta betr. die Anträge von Ausländern um Gestattung der Einwanderung aus dem Kreis Adelnau. Ein- und Auswanderungen. 1828-1867.
Fach 16. *Id.*, 1867-1901.
Fach 17. *Id.*, Kreis Birnbaum. 1829-1855.
Fach 18. *Id.*, Kr. Bomster. 1829-1865.
Fach 19. *Id.*, Buk. 1821-1864.
Fach 20. *Id.*, Fransladt. 1828-1862.
Fach 21. *Id.*, Kosten.
Fach 22. *Id.*, Kröben. 1828-1887.
Fach 23, 24. *Id.*, Kotoschin. 1828-1864, 1864-1891.
Fach 25. *Id.*, Meseritz. 1829-1858.
Fach 26. *Id.*, Obornik. 1827-1859.
Fach 27. *Id.*, Pleschen. 1827-1865.
Fach 28. *Id.*, Posen. 1826-1860.
Fach 29. *Id.*, Samter. 1826-1862.
Fach 30. *Id.*, Schildberg. 1829-1861.
Fach 31. *Id.*, Schrimm. 1829-1855.
Fach 32. *Id.*, Schroda. 1829-1859.
Fach 33. *Id.*, Wreschen. 1829-1898.
Fach 34, 35. *Id.*, Posen Stadt. 1829-1853, 1853-1863.
Fach 36. *Id.*, Einwanderungen. 1819-1821.

Acta der Königlichen Regierung I zu Posen betreffend die Anträge von Ausländern in die hiesige Provinz, etc.

Fach 1. Einwanderungen. 1829-1842.
Fach 2. *Id.*, 1842-1848.
Fach 3. *Id.*, 1846-1851.
Fach 4. *Id.*, 1851-1853.
Fach 5. *Id.*, 1853-1856.
Fach 6. *Id.*, 1857-1862.
Fach 7. *Id.*, 1862-1864.
Fach 8. *Id.*, 1871-1877.
Fach 9. *Id.*, 1877-1884.
Fach 10. *Id.*, 1884-1899.
Fach 11. *Id.*, Ostrowo. 1888-1889.
Fach 12. Nachrichten über Aus- und Einwanderungen. 1868-1888.
Fach 62. Auswanderungsagenten, A-F.
Fach 63. *Id.*, G-M.
Fach 64. *Id.*, N-Z.
Fach 65. Auswanderungs-Angelegenheiten.
Fach 2. No. 2. Acta, etc., betreffend die *Deutsche Auswanderer-Zeitung* (1865).
No. 4. Acta, etc., betreffend Requisitionen in Versicherungs-Auswanderungs-Angelegenheiten. Angef. 1864, geschl. [1873]. Contains important printed matter, such as shipping circu-

lars, etc., relating to the ships *Leibnitz* and *Liebig,* and also a sample copy of the *Mittheilungen des Vereins zum Schutze deutscher Auswanderer in Berlin,* no. 1, 1868; *Correspondenz für Deutschland* (no. 19), per Dampfer *Oneida,* Rio de Janeiro den 8 Juni 1868. Interesting matter relating to a concert by the Liedertafel for the benefit of a fund to build a German school in Rio. Clippings from the *Deutsche Auswandrer-Zeitung in Bremen,* 19. Jahrgang, no. 9, Feb. 28.

Fach 3. No. 3. Acta betreffend Verleitung zum Auswandern nach Brasilien. Angef. 1895, geschl. ———.

No. 5. Acta betreffend die Quartal Nachweisungen über erfolgte Auswanderung. Angef. 1893, geschl. [1895].

Fach I., etc. Acta betreffend die Auswander. Agenten. Some 60 numbers, each relating to an emigration agent or agency from the sixties to about 1900. Valuable list.

SCHLESWIG.
ROYAL STATE ARCHIVES.
(Königliches Staatsarchiv.)

Located in an old building formerly the residence of the curate, then a gymnasium, and very primitive, in keeping with the older part of the town of Schleswig itself. The archives comprise the state papers of the three duchies, Schleswig, Holstein, and Lauenburg. The ecclesiastical collections however are deposited in Kiel. It is evident that many papers relating to America are still kept in the ministerial archives and at Copenhagen.

Bibliography: Georg Hille, *Uebersicht über die Bestände des K. Staatsarchivs zu Schleswig* [*Mitteilungen der K. Preussischen Archivverwaltung*, 4]. (Leipzig, Hirzel, 1900.)

Hours: 9 to 2.

A. XVIII. Nr. 390. Betr. das Gesuch mehrerer der Theologie Beflissenen in Kiel um Reservation der Candidatenrechte für den Fall der Uebernahme eines geistl. Amts in Nordamerika. July 5, 1845. A thin parcel of papers relating to candidates of theology, who are going to preach in America, and containing among others:

Verzeichnis der unbeförderten Candidaten der Theologie in den Herzogthümern Schleswig und Holstein. Michaelis, 1844.
   I. Solche, die vor Errichtung des für beide Herzogthümer gemeinschaftlichen Examinations-Collegii geprüft sind und zwar: A. auf Gottorf (1-39); B. in Glückstadt (40-70).
   II. Von dem gemeinschaftlichen Examinations-collegio geprüfte Candidati (71-210). The papers give a historical perspective back to 1777.

Forordninger for Hertugdommet Slesvig. 1856.
Verordnungen für das Herzogtum Schleswig. 1856.
No. 62. Extract eines Schreibens, dass es behufs der Auswanderung nach Nordamerika einer ausdrücklichen Entlassung aus den dänischen Unterthanenverbande nicht bedürfe. Apr. 21, 1856. (Print.)

Schleswig-Holsteinische Blätter für 1839, herausgegeben von Dr. C. Weiberg, Advocaten in Schleswig. Band 7, Kap. XXIII: "Ein Blick auf Nordamerika". (An article by the editor dealing with constitutional liberty as realized in America.)

Nr. 4860. Externa, Nordamerika. A fascicle, about 5 inches thick, of miscellaneous papers relating to America, of which the following are the most important:

Two papers dealing with the "heimliche Werbung für die Genesse Colonie in Nordamerika" in Hamburg and adjacent places. The papers are dated June 20 and June 30, 1792.

Papers relating to the ratification of the appointment of John M. Forbes as vice-consul in Tönning, Husum, and Friedrichstadt. Copenhagen, July 12, 1806.

Paper relating to the arrest of an American. Sept. 24, 1807.

Papers relating to the unloading of the American ships *Perseverance* and *Missouri*. Rendsburg, Nov. 2, 1807.
Papers relating to the arrest of Reuben Smith. Rendsburg, Nov., 1807.
"Pro Memoria" concerning the arrival of American ships and their admission to the harbor. Copenhagen, Feb., Mar., and May, 1809.
"Forordning" (Danish), signed by King Frederick VI. Copenhagen, May 15, 1809. 8 papers relating to the landing of American ships with the following prescription: "Dass diejenigen amerikanischen Schiffe, welche directe von Amerika nach dänischen Häfen abzusegeln gedenken, sich bey ihm [dem Generalconsul in Nordamerika] oder seinen Vice-Consuln am Orte der ausgehenden Expedition melden und von ihm einen Attest über die Beschaffenheit der Ladung, deren Bestimmung und Eigenthum, nebst hizugefügtem Namen des Schiffes und Schiff-Capitains erwerben."
Matter relating to suspicious English wares found on American ships. Copenhagen, Jan. 16, 1810.
Anzeige für das Handlungshaus Fabritius et Wever zu Kopenhagen. Jan. 27, 1810.
Bundle of Danish and German papers relating to wares brought to Tönning by American ships from Jan. to Dec., 1809, enclosing a printed list of ships and some newspaper clippings.
Papers relating to the American ship *Congress* from Baltimore. Copenhagen, May 19, 1810.
Papers relating to the American ship *Charles King* from Philadelphia. Copenhagen, June 12, 1810.
Papers relating to the American ship *William*. Copenhagen, May 12, 1810.
Papers relating to the American brig *Luna* from New York.
Papers relating to suspicious wares on American ships. July, 1810.
Papers relating to the inspection of wares on American ships entering the harbors of Schleswig-Holstein. July, 1810.
Papers regulating the entrance of American ships and requiring that no ships with the American flag shall enter Tönning. July 28, 1810.
Papers relating to the inspection and duty of American ships in the Alster.
Thick parcel of papers relating to the American ship *President Adams* from Boston. July, 1810.
Papers relating to the American ships *Edward, President Adams, Neutrality*, and *Plato*. 1810.
Papers relating to the exclusion of North American ships from all the harbors of the duchy of Holstein. Aug., 1810.
Papers relating to the exclusion of American ships from Tönning and Husum. Aug., 1810.
Lists of American ships whose "Duplicat Atteste" have been sent in. July, 1810.
Papers relating to the ship *Thomas Wilson* from Philadelphia. Aug., 1810.
Papers relating to the ships *John Drew, Pilgrim*, and *Golden Fleece*. Sept., 1810.

List of ships with " Duplicat Atteste ". Sept. 11, 1810.
Papers relating to the American ship *Adriane*. Oct. 23, 1810.
Id., to the American ship of Andreas Schaabye. Nov. 6, 1810.
Id., to the American ship *Dolby*. Nov. 10, 1810.
Id., to American ships with " Duplicat Atteste ". Dec. 4, 1810.
Id., to the American ship *The Oriental*. Feb. 9, 1811.
Id., *Washington*. Mar. and May, 1811.
Id., *Charlotte A. Plimpton*. Mar. 27, 1811.
Id., to American ships under English convoy. May 18, 1811.
Id., to the American ship *Friendship*. June 8, 1811.
Id., to American ships and their certificates. June, 1811.
Id., to the American ship *Minerva Smith*. June 22, 1811.
Id., to the American ship *Ganges*. Aug. 17, 1811.
Id., to John Michael Forbes, as American consul in Kiel, etc. Sept. 17, 1811.
Id., to the surrender of the papers of condemned American ships. Nov. 9, 1811.
Id., to the American firm Brown and Ives concerning the ship *Asia*. Nov. 12, 1811.
Id., to the American ship *Stranger* in Kiel. Dec., 1811.
Id., to the appointment of John M. Forbes as consul general. Aug. 23, 1817.
Id., to American shipping. Sept. 27, 1817.
Id., to the American emigrants Heinrich and Ida Andreä. Mar. 16, 1840.

SIGMARINGEN.

ROYAL STATE ARCHIVES OF SIGMARINGEN.

(KÖNIGLICHES REGIERUNGS-ARCHIV FÜR DIE HOHENZOLLERNSCHEN LANDE.[1])

Located in the Hohenzollern Castle, now restored, the seat of the Hohenzollern at Sigmaringen, an island of Prussian domain far away in South Germany shut in by Bavaria and Württemberg. In addition to the archives are the valuable records of the Fürstlich Hohenzollernsches Haus- und Domänen-Archiv, located in the new building.

I. Repert. C. I. 2. d. No. 7. Auswanderung Fürstl. Hohenzoll.-Sigmar. Unterthanen in die benachbarten Staaten und bezieh. nach Amerika and die Erhebung des Vermögens Abzugs betr. 1785-1834. 420 leaves. Leaves 1-349 relate to emigrants to neighboring European countries, 350 to 420 concern emigrants to America. Among the papers the following are noteworthy:

Papers relating to Martin Saile (Sailr ?). 1833.

Mehrere Familien von Glatt und Jettensee, who wish to go to America. *Cf.* paper dated Jan. 25, 1833, giving a brief résumé of the conditions of emigration at this time and showing that the desire to emigrate is increasing and that subjects wishing to leave sell their property with the purpose of paying their passage money, some giving the flimsy excuse of wishing to marry. The document continues: " Allein nicht nach Amerika wohin die Reisse mit so vielen Gefahren und Resico verknüpft ist, und die Auswanderer als Bettler allem Elende preiss gegeben sind, sondern nach Griechenland. In diesem günstigen Clima [von Griechenland], bei der verwunderten dortigen Einwohnerzahl dürfte eine Colonisation mit ungleich günstigeren Aussichten vorgenommen, und vom Staate aus selbst geleitet werden können, als nach America ".

Names of emigrants are given in the papers from which one can see the obverse of this unfavorable picture of American conditions as the following passage will show: " Der so vielen guten in unserem deutschen Vaterlande eingegangenen Berichten aus Nord Amerika zufolge, wurde bei zweien meiner Sohnen (!) der Wunsch rege, dass auch sie ihr Glück in jenem Erdtheile unfehlbar machen können und werden ". This document is dated Jan. 24, 1833. The remaining papers give the names of emigrants and data concerning them.

---

[1] Or, as it is now called, Königliches Staatsarchiv.

STETTIN.
ROYAL PRUSSIAN STATE ARCHIVES OF THE PROVINCE OF POMERANIA.
(KÖNIGLICH PREUSSISCHES STAATSARCHIV FÜR DIE PROVINZ POMMERN.)

Located in a new building, Kaskutschstrasse 13, entrance from the Turnerstrasse. Stettin is the capital of Pomerania. The history of that land under the dukes of Pomerania till 1637, under Swedish domination from 1648 till 1720, and under Prussian rule in part from 1720 and completely from 1815, gives the records in the State Archives a peculiar interest. The records of the Estates and of the Chamber of Commerce as well as those of most of the cities of the province are deposited in the State Archives.

Hours: Week-days, 8 to 2.

ABTEILUNG I. TITEL II a. SECT. 3. NO. 10.
ACTA DER KÖNIGLICHEN REGIERUNG ZU STETTIN.

Packet (Fasc.) 27.

Vol. 8. Acta der Königlichen Regierung zu Stettin betreffend die Auswanderungen nach Amerika. June, 1852–May, 1853. Papers relating to individual emigrants, Auswanderungskonsense, Entlassungsurkunden. The papers are important for names of emigrants, not only to North America, but to America and the West Indies in general.

Papers relating to the ship *Norma* with names of passengers, and to shipping.

Paper relating to emigrants to Texas, and funds taken along by Carl Johann Albrecht of Graatz. Aug. 6, 1852.

Lists of intended emigrants to America from the year 1853.

Vol. 9. Acta der Königlichen Regierung, etc. May, 1853–Feb., 1854. Similar papers, list of emigrants from the several " Aemter " or " Kreise ".

With a paper, dated Anclam, Feb. 24, 1854, is enclosed an interesting printed circular or prospectus relating to the colony of Icaria, with the title: *Einladungsschrift an die Auswanderer nach den Vereinigten Staaten von Nordamerika: Ikarische Colonie, eine Gütergemeinschaft—ihre Grundsätze Brüderlichkeit—incorporirt im Staate Illinois (Nauvoo), und im Staate Iowa; die Gründung des Sozialphilosophen und Bürger Cabet, ehemals Generalprocurator und Deputirter in Franckreich.* A broadside signed Nauvoo, 1853, by Cabet, President der Ikarischen Gemeinschaft, with a cut of Cabet, etc.

Packet 28.

Vol. 10. Acta der Königlichen Regierung, etc. (Feb.) Apr., 1853–Mar., 1854.

Vol. 11. *Id.,* (Feb.) Apr., 1854–Mar., 1855.

Packet 29.
   Vol. 12. *Id.*, (Feb.), 1855–July, 1855. Contains special extract from nos. 102 and 104 of the *Norddeutsche Zeitung*, relating to Pastor Meinel.
   Vol. 13. *Id.*, July, 1855–Mar., 1856.
Packet 30.
   Vol. 14. *Id.*, (Mar.) Apr.–July, 1856.
   Vol. 15. *Id.*, July, 1856–Mar., 1857. Interesting "Urlaubspass" of the Grenadier Gottfried Gorges. Berlin, Sept. 25, 1856.
Packet 31.
   Vol. 16. *Id.*, Mar.-May, 1857.
   Vol. 17. *Id.*, May, 1857–Jan., 1858.
Packet 32.
   Vol. 18. *Id.*, Jan.-Dec., 1858.
   Vol. 19. *Id.*, Jan., 1859–Apr., 1860. Includes "Acta personalia des Magistrats der betreffenden Orte, wie Naugardt", relating to individuals, etc. With "Reise-Route No. 65", or pass dated Stargard, Mar. 15, 1800, *cf.* paper of July 25, 1859.
Packet 33.
   Vol. 20. *Id.*, May, 1860–Aug., 1861.

TIT. 12. SECT. 1. COMMERCIEN SACHEN.

Nr. 59. Acta wegen des Commercii mit Franckreich. Jan., 1747.
Nr. 104. Acta wegen einer mit Franckreich geschlossenen Convention. 1753. *Cf.* same relations with Spain, 1771, and England.
Acten des Königlichen Kommerz-Kollegiums.
   I. Generalia.
      2. Wegen der Errichtung des Justizwesens bey der Handlung und bey dem etablirten Neuen Commercien Collegio. 1755-1764.
   II. Specialia. C.
      1. Wegen Contrabandes auf der See bey itzt im Kriege verwickelten Mächten Engelland und Franckreich. 1756.
      2. Von dem Zustande des Commercii pro 1756, item: Verbesserung desselben. 1757, 1760.
No. 171. (Krieges Archiv.) Acta Camerae.
Dass wegen des abgebrochenen Commercii zwischen Engelland und America ratione des Krieges zubefürchtenden starcken Banquerouts in Engelland, Holland, und Hamburg, und dass die Pommersche Kaufleute dabei alle Vorsicht gebrauchen möchten. An edict of Frederick the Great, dated Berlin, Aug. 13, 1777, and signed by Schulenburg. Directed "An die Pommersche Krieges und Domänen Cammer Generale".
A paper relating thereto. Stettin, Aug. 19, 1777.
No. 188. Acta Camerae.
Wegen Bestimmung des Gewinns welchen die Preussischen See Schiffer durch Fracht-Fahrten fremder Kaufleute verdienen. Imgleichen
Wegen des See Commercii der Königl. Preuss. Unterthanen nach Beendigung des gegenwärtigen See-Krieges zwischen England und America.

Paper sent by Schulenburg to the Finanz Rath and Cammer Präsident von Schöning in Stettin, June 17, 1782, and followed by a "Rechnung des National-Gewinns eines Schiffes von 100 Hollandischen Lasten im vorigen Jahre", and other important and interesting papers.

Paper relating to "Gewisse Handlungs-Angelegenheiten", signed by E. Bauer. Stettin, Aug. 28, 1776.

Papers relating to German trade with the Levant. In this connection *cf.* Bauer's report of Aug. 12, 1782 (Stettin).

The later papers of the volume consist of reports, letters, and other official papers relating to the progress of (German) Pomeranian trade and shipping till 1791.

No. 216. Wegen einer nach Hofe einzusendenden Nachweisung von dem Werthe aller der Waaren, welche aus Franckreich und dessen Colonien in West- und Ost-Indien im Jahre 1788/89 in der Provinz Pommern Seewärts eingebracht sind. 1790.

No. 887. Acta betr. das Edict wegen künftiger Errichtung des Mennonisten Wesens. Sept., 1789.

TITEL 19. SECT. 1. GENERALIA COMMERCIEN-SACHEN ("POLIZEI REGISTRATUR").

No. 19. Acta Wegen der gänzlichen Handels Sperre gegen Engelland und verbotener Einfuhr aller aus Europäischen Häfen kommenden Ost- oder Westindischen Colonialwaren. Imgleichen wegen Bestellung der Handlungs-Commissarien. Dec., 1808-May, 1813.

Correspondence of "Königl. Preuss. Accise and Zoll-Departement" with the "Pommersche Kriegs- und Domänen-Kammer zu Stettin", with printed circulars and "Formel". The "Formel" begins: "Zur Unterdrückung des Verkehrs mit England und Schweden hat das Königl. General Accise-Departement die Veranstaltung getroffen, dass Seitens der Accise-Aemter über die aus diesseitigen Staaten auswärts zu versendenden Waaren Ursprungs-Atteste ertheilt werden", etc. Stettin, Dec. 7, 1808.

Also the "Reglement" in German and French. Königsberg, June 17, 1808. (Several copies.)

Also Verordnungen, etc., relating to the same. These papers and those which follow have special reference to the British West Indies of course, but concern indirectly the trade with America.

No. 26. Vol. 1. Acta der Königl. Regierung von Pommern, die Handels Verhältnisse zwischen den Preussischen und Nordamericanischen Staaten betreffend. Nov., 1815–July, 1846.

Contains papers relating to the shipping regulations of the U. S. (Zoll, Steuern, etc.); official correspondence between Pomeranian towns and merchants and the Polizei-Deputation; important shipping invoices, especially of May, 1816.

Also statistics of ships in the harbor of Swinemünde, 1814, 1815, and Sonder-Zoll-Sätze.

Important report of the Pomeranian government on the trade of Baltic ports with American states (U. S.). Stettin, June 19, 1816.
Correspondence between Bülow and Oberpräsident Sack, in reference to reports of Greuhm in Washington touching the regulations of shipping. Mar. 17, 1819.
Reports of exports to, and imports from the United States for various years.
Import of American flour to West Indies and South America. Report of Rönne. Baltimore, July 20, 1836.
Statistics of imports to America. 1836.
Report of imports from U. S. to Swinemünde for 1842 (copy), 1844, etc.
No. 90. Acta der Königl. Regierung zu Stettin, betreffend die Errichtung einer Rheinländisch Westindischen Handelsgesellschaft zu Elberfelde im Regierungs Departement Düsseldorf, Dec., 1821. Three papers. The plan of the society is not included.

WETZLAR.
ROYAL PRUSSIAN STATE ARCHIVES.
(KÖNIGLICH PREUSSISCHES STAATSARCHIV.)

In a letter of Feb. 25, 1910, the chief archivist of this archive informs the compiler of this volume that the Königliches Staatsarchiv at Wetzlar contains only the documents in legal cases tried before the Reichskammergericht which formerly sat in that town, with the addition of a part of the papers in cases tried before the Prussian court now held there; that the latter, naturally, contain no material for American history, and that it is extremely improbable that anything of the sort would be found among the former. " It is true," he adds, " that an American might have sued a German of the Empire in the Reichskammergericht for non-delivery of goods, or some matter respecting payment, or the like. I have never come upon such a document, but it is of course within the realm of possibility that a few such documents may be here. To establish their presence would, however, be extremely laborious, for the documents are arranged according to the names of the plaintiffs, in alphabetical order. Accordingly in order to prove that such documents are or are not here it would be necessary to go through all the indexes—about fifty great folios—page by page and number by number. That would cost much time and money, and at the best would yield only a few notes almost without value.

"Besides the papers named, there are deposited in the Staatsarchiv here:
1. The Allmenröder collection of documents, and
2. The so-called Old Archive of the town of Wetzlar. Neither of these contains any material for American history."

The Staatsarchiv is situated on the ground floor of the Court House in this place.

Hours: 8 to 1.

WIESBADEN.
ROYAL STATE ARCHIVES.
(Königliches Staatsarchiv.)

Located Mainzerstrasse 80, in a relatively new building, well adapted to the purpose, and standing on the edge of the city, less exposed to danger from fire. The archives contain the records of Hesse-Nassau, some 60,000 documents in all, dating from 910 on.

Hours: Daily from 8 to 1.

V. Fürstlich Nassau Using.

Gen. XIV. c. N. 18. Auswanderung nach Amerika aus dem Amt Hochheim (only one paper). 1805.

VI. Nassau Weilburg.

Gen. XIV. c. N. 17. Verordnungen in specie die Emigration derer Unterthanen betreffend. (1690) 1699-1792. These decrees are important as giving a brief survey of the progress of legislation regulating emigration.

The rescripts of 1709 and 1740 contain matter bearing on the emigration to America. Occasionally inventories of emigrants are inclosed, as in the case of Daniel Wörner, dated Mar. 30, 1781.

Other interesting papers mention the names and confession of manumitted emigrants, Mennonites, Catholics, etc.

Other important printed matter relating to the Commissarii is inclosed.

VII. Altes Dillenburger Archiv.

P. 493. Abzug einiger Unterthanen in Pennsylvaniam betr. anno 1709. This is a most valuable collection of original papers dating from the period of the great exodus of the Palatines. The package contains original requests ("Gesuche") of those wishing to emigrate, some 60 papers in all. The last sheet contains a valuable list of names with the following title: Verzeichnus deren Underthanen, so umb den Abzug angehalten und darzu die Bewilligung erhalten, als die Aemter Herborn, Offenbach, Bicken, Medenbach, Gontersdorf u. Merckenbach, Ambdorff, Statt Wiedorff, Goffenhayn, Mademühlen, Rabenschiedt. Summa 35 Mann, 37 Weiber, 107 Kind, noch 2 ledige von Mademühlen.

VII. Regierung Dillenburg.

R. 206. Reg. A. [Regierungs Acta] über die Emigrationen nach fremden Colonien. Vol. I.-X. in 4 Einzelaktenstücken.

Vol. I. Reg. Acta über die Emigrationen nach fremden Colonien. 1750-1766. Contains a minute account of the Waldo colony in Maine. A large number of manuscripts and official refer-

ences to the scheme as well as rare and important printed matter are found in the volume, such as the following:
Continuation der gesammelten Nachrichten und Verordnungen die neu angebaute Massachusetts und in specie Broad-Bay und Neu-Germantown in Neu-Engelland betr.
Extracts in German from the *Kaiserl. Reichs-Post Ztg.*, no. 47, Mar. 23, 1753.
Extract des See-Contracts von 1751.
Extract aus der *Lancastrischen Zeitung* in Pennsylvanien 6tes Stück. Mar. 25, 1753.
Order issued by Thomas Holles from Whitehall. Mar. 2, 1753.
A printed Verordnung relating to the emissary George Lübke and to the emigration to South Carolina. Cassel, Feb. 27, 1753.
Important lists of emigrants, particularly one from Amt Beilstein, dated Sept. 7, 1753.

Vol. II. Reg. Acta Emigrations Verordnungen. 1776-1783. Relating to emigration and forwarding of estates to America and Prussia, etc.

Vol. III. R. A. Emigrationes der Unterthanen and deshalb erlassenen Verordnungen. 1784-1785.

Vol. IV. R. A. über die Emigrationen. 1785, 1786.

Vol. V. R. A. über die Emigrationen nach auswärtigen Kolonien.

Vol. VI. R. A. über die Emigrationen nach fremden Colonien. 1788.

Vol. VII. R. A. wegen der Emigrationen nach fremden Colonien. 1789.

Vol. VIII. R. A. wegen der Emigrationen nach fremden Colonien. 1789.

Vol. IX. R. A. über Auswanderungen und hinterlassenes Vermögen der Emigrirten betr. Erbschaftsangelegenheiten von Ausländern in hiesigen Landen, etc. 1803.

Vol. X. R. A. Auswanderungen ausserhalb Deutschlands. 1804-1806.

R. A. des Fabrikanten Carl Bartholomäus Ehefrau zu Philadelphia gebohrne Metzlerinn aus Herborn und deren Mutter, jetzt des Moritz Dobels Ehfrau in Tulpehoken in Pensylvanien, um Verabfolgung ihrer älterlichen und grossälterlichen Verlassenschaft. 1791.

R. A. Johannes Müller und Joh. Jost Müllers Wittib zu Rüdershausen so dann Daniel Brachthäuser daselbst wegen Confiscation des Vermögens ihrer nach America gewanderten Schwäger, Joh. Jost Schmidts und Joh. Jost Hofheinz, von Rüdershausen betr. 1789-1790.

R. A. das Gesuch der Anna Elisabeth, Conrad, und Johann Jacob Drewitz zu Ukersdorf, um Erlaubniss nach America ziehen zu dörfen, desgleichen deren hinterlassenes Vermögen und dessen Benutzung betr. 1773-1796.

R. A. Die Wiederaufnahme der ausgewanderten Joh. Friedr. Jüngsten Ehfrau von Herborn, in hiesiges Land, Unterstützung, und Erziehung ihrer Kinder betr. 1790-1793.

R. A. Verbot gegen Colonisten Anwerbung. 1804.

VIII. Staats Verträge.

Artikel 99 a. Nass. Ratification des zwischen den Vereinigten Staaten v. Nordamerika u. dem Zollverein geschlossenen Handelsvertrages vom 25/3, 1844.

116. Nordamerikan. Ratification des zwischen den Vereinigeten Staaten u. Nassau abgeschlossenen Freizügigkeitsvertrages d. d. Berlin 27/5, 1846.

VIII. Herzogthum Nassau.

Gen. XVII a. St. M. Die Ernennung eines Consuls für Californien (v. Witzleben, Finkler).

XXV. Gemeinschaften 1 a. Amt Nassau Dreiserisch.

Gen. VIII e. Nr. 11.
- *a.* Das Abkehren einiger Unterthanen nach Pensylvanien, Hungarn, betreffende Schriften. 1709.
- *b.* Die aus dem Ambt Nassau in Hungarn gezogene Unterthanen und deren Leibeigenschaftserlassung betr. 1724.

In fascicle *a* are two important papers: One paper dated May 23, 1709, being a request of Heybach for instructions forbidding the emigration of Leonardt Hinnigoffen and Wilhelm Duffing a former schoolmaster and such others as may wish to emigrate; the second is a reply to the former dated June 12, 1709, prohibiting them " in die Insel pensylvanien zu ziehen". The two papers occupy 5 pages folio. The second bundle, *b*, contains papers relating to the emigration from Nassau-Saarbrücken to Hungary which was then beginning to break the way for the larger exodus later in the century.

VIII. Hesse Homburg.

Gen. XIV c. Nr. 33. Schreiben des H. Consuls für die Vereinigten Staaten v. Nordamerika betr. Passwesen in den Vereinigten Staaten, dergl. Postverbindungen mit New Orleans. 1862-1865.

XII. Nassau Katzenellenbogen.

Gen. XIV c. N. 2. Emigrationes nach Pensylvanien, Ungarn, und Littauen, etc. 1709-1787 (1709, 1723, 1724, 1726, 1786). Contains a bundle of papers relating to emigration in the years given in parenthesis.

Order of Ernst Ludwig, landgrave of Hesse-Darmstadt, requiring more accurate information concerning emigration, with the following prescription: " Indessen niemand ausser Landes zu ziehen gestattet er habe dann bey uns dessfalz nachgesucht". The paper states: " Dass Viele Unterthanen aus dem Land giengen und vorschützten dass die Lasten So sie zu tragen all zu gross auch neben der schweren Contribution der licent gleichwie in der Pfaltz in unsere Landen introduciret werden solte ". Darmstadt, May 1, 1709.

Paper reciting: "Dass alle diejenigen so von unsern Unterthanen ferner ausserhalb Landes ziehen wollen, zuförderst umb Unsere Gnädigste Erlaubnuss gebührende Nachsuchung thun". Those who do not comply with this condition are punishable both in property and person. Apr. 29, 1709.

"Verordnung" of Ernst Ludwig requiring of emigrants "Abzug-Scheine". Oct. 11, 1723.

List of names of emigrants to Hungary. Mar. 26, 1724.

"Verordnung" dated Darmstadt, Oct. 30, 1766, relating to the famine of that year and the consequent "Emigrations-Sucht".

VIII. Herz. Nassau.

Gener. XIV c. Acta regim.

Die Auswanderungen nach Nordamerika. 1847-1848 (ungeordnetes).

Die Auswanderungen in den Freistaat Texas. 1843-1844.

VIII. St. M. (Berliner Abgabe).

Conv. 40. Auswanderungs-Sachen. Auswanderungs Agenten. 1855, 1864.

XVIII. Herz. Homburg.

Gen. XIV c. N. 16. Auswanderungen (darunter Jahresberichte aus New Orleans). 1834-1863.

XXIII. Wied-Neuwied.

Gen. VIII b. 2. Güter zu Alsbach betr. (property of Joh. Thiel Böckling). 1722-1805.

Gen. VIII. 6. Acta die Verpachtung des Herrschaftlichen Hoffs zu Alsbach betr. ingl. dessen Versteurung und Verkauff an Neu Wied brtr. Bendorff. 1744, 1749, 1761, 1771. The fascicle contains some 40 papers, one of which recites that Böckling has not only failed to renew his fief at Alsbach "sondern nuhnmehro auch Sein Vaterland verlassen und in die Engelländische sogenante Carolinam verrayssen will". Feb. 22, 1740.

Ungeordn. Ausw. Sachen.

Statistische und polit. Berichte des nass. Consuls Carl Adae für den Staat Ohio (Cincinnati). 1854-1866.

Zwei Berichte des Consuls Freudenthal an den nass. Staatsminister Prinzen Wittgenstein über Vorgänge in New-Orleans. (Orig.) 1862.

BAVARIA.

The Royal Bavarian State Archives are distributed in ten different depositories in various parts of the kingdom, including the Royal Bavarian State Archives (Staatsarchiv), the Royal Bavarian General National Archives (Reichsarchiv), both located in Munich, and the eight Royal Bavarian Circuit Archives located in Amberg, Bamberg, Landshut, Munich, Nuremberg, Neuburg a. D., Speyer, and Würzburg.

MUNICH.
ROYAL BAVARIAN PRIVY STATE ARCHIVES.
(Königlich Bayerisches Geheimes Staatsarchiv.)

Located at Neuhauserstrasse 51, entrance Maxburgstrasse, Parterre. This archive contains the records of the central government in its relations with the several ministries or departments, including royal edicts and other official orders relating to emigration and papers dealing with foreign affairs and the like. The papers are arranged in cases of different colors and designated by the color of the case and the number in the case. Permission to use the materials must be obtained through the Director (Vorstand) of the Royal Bavarian Archives Commission. The rules stated below, approved by the Ministry of the Interior, regulate the use of the archive material.

Hours: Week-days, 8 to 2.

Bestimmungen für die Benützer des Kgl. Bayer. Geheimen Staats-Archives.
(Genehmigt mit höchster Entschliessung des k. b. Staatsministeriums des Kgl. Hauses und des Aeussern vom 10. März 1900, Nr. 3503^I.)

1. Gesuche um Benützung des k. Geheimen Staatsarchives sind in der Regel schriftlich einzureichen.

In dem Gesuche sind die gewünschten Archivalien genau zu bezeichnen oder, wenn dies nicht möglich ist, das historische Faktum oder das Rechtsverhältnis anzugeben, zu dessen Aufhellung das Gesuch gestellt wird.

Die Gesuche dürfen nicht allgemein gestellt werden, sondern müssen einen bestimmten und deutlich erkennbaren Zweck, sowie den Umfang der beabsichtigten Forschung ersehen lassen.

Demgemäss darf sich ein Gesuch nicht allgemein auf Benützung einer ganzen Abteilung des Archives noch auf eine grössere Zeitepoche erstrecken, sondern es hat sich auf eine bestimmte Frage und einen nicht zu weit bemessenen Zeitraum zu beschränken.

2. Wünscht ein Archivbenützer später seine Forschungen weiter auszudehnen, als er anfangs beabsichtigte, so hat er seine diesbezüglichen Wünsche in einem neuen Gesuche darzulegen.

3. Jedem Gesuche ist die Angabe der über eine Materie bereits vorhandenen Litteratur und, soweit thunlich, eine kurze Darlegung des Sachverhaltes auf Grund derselben beizufügen.

4. Bei Gesuchen um Benützung des Archives für privatrechtliche Zwecke ist ein persönliches oder rechtliches Interesse nachzuweisen.

5. Gesuche, welche den unter § 1—4 aufgeführten Anforderungen nicht entsprechen, werden behufs Ergänzung zurückgegeben.

6. Gesuchsteller, welche auf dem Archive bis dahin unbekannt sind, haben sich auf Verlangen entsprechend zu legitimieren.

7. Archivbenützern, welche ihr Gesuch mündlich vorbringen und die erforderlichen Darlegungen mündlich geben, werden entsprechende Gebrauchsformulare zum sofortigen Ausfüllen zur Verfügung gestellt.

9. Die Verbescheidung der Benützungsgesuche erfolgt schriftlich oder mündlich.

10. Im Falle der Genehmigung wird den Gesuchstellern bei ihrem Erscheinen im Archive das Ergebnis der gepflogenen Recherche bekannt gegeben.

11. Anfragen von auswärts werden durch kurze Mitteilungen über das Vorhandensein, den Umfang und die allgemeine Beschaffenheit der einschlägigen Archivalien beantwortet.

Eine förmliche Bearbeitung der einschlägigen Materie auf Grund der vorhandenen Archivalien kann von Privaten nicht beansprucht werden.

12. Die Benützung der Archivalien hat im k. Geheimen Staatsarchive in Gegenwart eines Archivbeamten oder Praktikanten zu geschehen.

13. Den Benützern kann unter keinen Umständen gestattet werden, Archivalien aus dem Amtsgebäude zu entfernen.

14. Versendungen von Archivalien finden nicht statt.

15. Dagegen kann gestattet werden, dass von einem anderen Archive Archivalien zur Benützung hier anwesender Forscher an das k. Geheime Staatsarchiv gesendet werden.

Für die Benützung dieser Archivalien gelten vorliegende Bestimmungen. Die Transportkosten hat der betreffende Forscher zu tragen.

16. Die Einsichtnahme in den alphabetischen Zettelkatalog, die Urkundenrepertorien und das alphabetische Repertorium kann bis zur Fertigstellung eines chronologischen Benützerrepertoriums nur ausnahmsweise in Gegenwart des mit der Recherche betrauten Referenten gestattet werden.

Auszüge und Notizen aus den Katalogen und Repertorien dürfen ohne Genehmigung nicht gemacht werden.

17. Die Archivalien werden immer nur in angemessenen Partien, wobei jedoch die Wünsche der Benützer thunlichste Berücksichtigung finden, ausgefolgt.

18. Die Archivalien sind mit thunlichster Sorgfalt zu behandeln.

Auf die unversehrte Erhaltung der Siegel ist besonderes Augenmerk zu richten.

Jede Art der Beschädigung und Beschmutzung, das Anbringen von Berichtigungen, Zeichen oder Zusätzen, die Behandlung mit Reagentien, die Schädigung durch Ausschneiden oder Rasuren ist strengstens verboten.

Archivalien dürfen auch nicht als Unterlage verwendet werden.

Ein absichtliches Verfehlen gegen diese Bestimmungen hebt die erteilte Erlaubnis zur Benützung des Archives auf.

19. Jedem Benützer wird zur Aufbewahrung seiner Archivalien ein eigenes Fach angewiesen.

20. Jeder Benützer ist verpflichtet, so oft er das Archiv verlässt, die Archivalien in der gleichen Ordnung, in welcher er sie erhalten hat, dem beaufsichtigenden Beamten zurückzustellen.

21. Einem etwaigen Wunsche eines Archivbenützers, schon benützte Archivalien behufs späteren Nachschlagens oder Vergleichens zurückzubehalten, wird, soweit thunlich, willfahrt werden.

22. Im Benützungszimmer soll Ruhe herrschen. Das Rauchen ist ausnahmslos untersagt, ebenso ist das Mitbringen von Hunden verboten.

23. Archivalien dürfen von einem Benützer nicht ohne ausdrückliche Genehmigung dritten Personen gezeigt, bezw. zur Benützung weiter gegeben werden.

24. Die Archivbenützer sind verpflichtet, die von ihnen gemachten Abschriften und Excerpte aus den Archivalien des k. Geheimen Staatsarchives auf Verlangen zur Einsicht vorzulegen.

25. Den Archivbenützern ist es gestattet, sich unter eigener Verantwortung vertrauenswürdiger Personen als Kopisten zu bedienen. Dieselben sind jedoch vorher dem Vorstande namhaft zu machen.

26. Auch den Angestellten des k. Geheimen Staatsarchives bleibt es unbenommen, ausser den Dienststunden für Archivbenützer Abschriften und Excerpte gegen entsprechende Honorierung anzufertigen.

27. Die Anfertigung von Kopien und Excerpten durch das k. Geheime Staatsarchiv für Privatbenützer kann nur ausnahmsweise stattfinden.

Die amtliche Beglaubigung von Abschriften durch das k. Geheime Staatsarchiv unterliegt den gesetzlichen Gebühren.

28. Zum Gebrauche innerhalb des Archives steht den Benützern eine Nachschlagebibliothek zur Verfügung.

Auf Ansuchen werden den Archivbenützern Bücher und andere Hilfsmittel aus der Amtsbibliothek gegen Legschein zur Benützung in den Archivräumen zur Verfügung gestellt.

Den Archivbenützern ist es nicht gestattet, von Archivalien, Handschriften, Büchern, Landkarten der Amtsbibliothek und von anderen Hilfsmitteln der Archivverwaltung eigenmächtig Kenntnis zu nehmen.

29. Bleibt ein Archivbenützer ohne vorherige Anzeige länger als 6 Wochen aus, so werden die für ihn bereit liegenden Archivalien eingestellt. Deren Wiedervorlage kann nur auf schriftliches Ansuchen erfolgen.

30. Jeder Archivbenützer verpflichtet sich, der Bibliothek des k. Geheimen Staatsarchives ein Exemplar der im Druck erschienenen Arbeiten zu übermitteln, welche er auf Grund bezw. unter Benützung von Archivalien des k. Geheimen Staatsarchives herausgibt.

31. Vor Beginn der Arbeiten hat jeder Archivbenützer einen Revers folgenden Inhalts zu unterzeichnen:

"Ich bestätige hiemit, dass mir die Bestimmungen für die Benützer des k. Geheimen Staats-Archives vom 1. April 1900 bekannt gegeben worden sind und verspreche genaue Befolgung derselben."

München, den 1. April 1900.

Kasten schwarz.

154/11. Fol. 1-42 incl. Acta die Königlich gros brittanischen- u. Churhanoverische Gesandtschaft an dem Churpfaltz Bayerischen Hof betr. 1756, 1757, 1776, 1777, 1779, 1780, 1783, 1784, 1797, 1798. Letters in Latin accrediting Morton Eden, John Trevor, Thomas Walpole, Arthur Paget, etc.

209/13. Act die in denen Churbayer. Landen nicht [zu] gestattende fremde Werbungen und die sich desswegen ergebene verschiedene Differenzen betr. 1763-1769. Sheds only sidelights upon America.

321/1-5, 7. Haslang, Avis d'Angleterre. Consists of six folio volumes of papers, including correspondence between the legation in London and the ministry in Munich, copies of state papers, the king's messages to Parliament and printed treaties. The correspondence of Count Haslang, minister plenipotentiary in London, with his brother in Munich is one of the most valuable diplomatic correspondences on record, so far as America is concerned, as it reflects the diplomatic relations of England with the states of Europe during the periods of the French and Indian War and the Revolution. An analysis follows.

321/1. Correspondance du Comte d'Haslang. 1751-1753.
321/2. Correspondance du Comte d'Haslang. 1754-1757. This volume contains papers relating to the bill naturalizing the Jews in England and the following relating to the Old French War:

Letter of Haslang in London to his brother in Munich. Aug. 23, 1754.

Traduction de la Harrangue du Roi de la Grande Bretagne, prononcée aux deux Chambres du Parlement, le jeudi 14. Novembre 1754.

Letter of Haslang dated May 9, 1755, dealing with the four articles proposed by the English:

    1. que les françois se retirent a 20 lieuës sur la côte meridionale du fleuve de St. Laurent;

    2. à 20 lieuës de la Baye françoise;

    3. à 20 lieuës du territoire, qui est entre l'Ohio et le Wabash;

    4. à 20 lieuës des Lacs de Ontario et de Erie, qui se jettent dans la rivière de St. Laurent. Les quels la France ne sauroit jamais accepter, etc.

Letter of Haslang, containing the important news of the capture of Beauséjour by the English, by which they expect to become masters of the isthmus or Bay of Fundy; that a part of the fleet of Boscawen has blockaded Louisburg; that General Braddock is on the Ohio to attack Crownpoint; that the French are forming a camp between Dunkirk and Graveline; and that it is also feared that Europe is soon to be involved; that of the 8000 men which Hesse is to furnish, 1600 are cavalrymen. Hannover, Aug. 7, 1755.

Letter of Haslang: " Notre grande attention est sur l'aboutissement du different entre les 2 puissance la France et l'Angleterre et tout le monde souhaiteroit fort que l'affaire puisse être accommodée ou du moins q'une affaire dans la partie du monde Americal, n'allume point la guerre en Europe", etc. Aug. 19, 1755.

Letter of Haslang, referring to Mr. Fox and Parliament and the importance of this session of Parliament. London, Oct. 17, 1755.

Letter of Haslang, expressing the fear of an invasion of England by the French and stating that a declaration of war must soon be made. London, Oct. 31, 1755.

Extrait d'une lettre du Major General Johnson du camp à Lake George en Amérique de 9. Septembre 1755.

Letter of Haslang, referring to the treaty with Russia, to the 5000 sailors now prisoners in the various parts of the realm, and to the 6000 reinforcements received by Major General Johnson. London, Nov. 4, 1755.

Traduction de la Harrangue de Sa Majesté, etc., le 13. Novembre 1755. Reference to the troubles between England and France and to the treaties with Russia and the Landgrave of Hesse-Cassel.

Letter of Haslang, stating that prizes are continually taken and amount to more than a million pounds sterling, although war has not been formally declared between England and France; reference to the return of the squadrons of De la Motte and of Admiral Boscawen, Holburne and Mostyn; complaints of Baron Munchhausen against Mr. de Schneid in Ratisbon. London, Nov. 18, 1755.

Addresse de la Chambre des Seigneurs au Roi le vendredi 14 Novembre 1755.

Addresse de la Chambre des Communes, samedi le 15. Novbre. 1755.

Letter of Haslang, referring to the transfer of the chancellorship of the exchequer from Mr. Legge to George Lyttelton, to the passage of a bill in the Commons subsidizing 50,000 sailors for the following year, to the earthquake of Lisbon, to the sale of prizes, etc. London, Nov. 25, 1755.

Letter of Haslang, enclosing printed copies of treaties with Russia and Hesse-Cassel. London, Nov. 5, 1755.

Letter of Haslang, referring to the agreement of the King of Prussia to resist by force of arms any entrance of foreign troops, and mention of the payment of £30,000 by England in consequence. [Nov. ?] 20, 1755.

Letters of Feb. and Mar., 1756, relating to the imminent declaration of war and to the advance of the French on the island Minorca.

Letter of Haslang, giving two reasons brought forward by the Crown: first to condemn the prizes taken from the French, and second to prevent other nations such as the Swedes, Danes, Hollanders, etc., from giving commercial assistance to France. London, May 18, 1756.

Correspondence relating to the king's message to Parliament, May 27, 1756, and to the effect of the struggle between England and France on European politics, showing that England had been careful in making treaties with the German and other European states, in anticipation of the conflict with France.

Other letters referring to operations in Minorca. June and Aug., 1756.

Letter of Haslang, referring to the return of a part of the garrison of Oswego, sent by Vaudreuil, commander in chief of the French forces in America. London, Nov. 12, 1756.

Letter of Haslang, referring to the departure of 16 vessels of the line for Cork to embark 6000 men for America, and to be followed by 2000 Scottish mountaineers and nine more warships, altogether 8000 men and 25 ships: " C'est le plus fort embarquement qui ait été fait de memoire d'hommes, et qui coute un million cent mille Lvstrg [Livres sterling]. Depuis on a encore resolu de faire lever 3m h's de troupes de plus pour la Marine ". London, Mar. 4, 1757.

Letter of Haslang, referring to the imminent rupture between Russia and Prussia. London, Mar. 18, 1757.

Letter of Haslang, referring to the militia bill for raising 30,000 men from the several provinces of England. Apr. 29, 1757.

321/3. Correspondance du Comte d'Haslang, etc. 1758-1759. The correspondence of this year deals largely with the military disturbances in Europe. The following have direct bearing on America:

Letter of Haslang, referring to the siege of Louisburg. Aug. 19, 1758.

Papers of Jan. and Feb., 1759, with many references to the pending treaty between England and France, revealing the complicated motives prevalent in the European states, especially the German states.

Draft of a treaty between England and Bavaria and papers relating thereto.

Extrait des Articles de la Capitulation faite le 1er mai dernier entre leurs Excellences le Major General Barrington, chef d'Escadron Moore et Mr. Nadan Dutreil, and letters referring thereto. June, 1759.

Letter of Haslang, giving news of the French quitting "Ticonderogo" and going to Crownpoint, and of General Wolfe's debarkation with 4000 men before Quebec. Sept. 7, 1759.

Letter of Haslang, referring to the Six Nations and calling Niagara " la clef à tout ce continant, qui ou ouvre, ou ferme la communication de tous les Natifs de la dite Amerique; des Six Nations, des Ohioes, Shawanoes, Miamis ", etc., and enclosing a list of French vessels commanded by De la Clue. Sept. 11, 1759.

Letters of Haslang, giving an account of the siege of Quebec. London, Oct. 16, 19, 1759.

Papers relating to the capitulation before Quebec on Sept. 18, 1759.

Pasquinade faite à Londres sur le Roi de France. Sept. 27, 1759.

Copy of a letter of Lord Holderness to Count Haslang, giving the strength of the English navy.

321/4. Correspondance du Comte d'Haslang, etc. 1760-1764. Contains among other things the following:

Two important balance-sheets: Per contra pour argent Payé entre le 11 Janvier 1759 et le 11 Janvier 1760. On the back are these rubrics: Savoir | Echiquier | Compagnie des Indes | Banque d'Angleterre | Compagnie du Sud.

Letter of Haslang, reporting a letter received from Capt. Allen regarding military affairs in America. London, Sept. 2, 1760.

Letter of Haslang, giving a report of the capture of Montreal, with extracts of the articles of capitulation. London, Oct. 7, 1760.

Letter of Haslang, referring to the proclamation of George III. made on the previous Sunday, with the following remark: " et il paroit au moins exterieurement, que le Defunct est déjà oublié. Sic transit gloria mundi ". Oct. 28, 1760.

Letter of Haslang, stating that Lord Egremont and General Yorke have been appointed to attend the Congress for arranging the terms of peace. The same letter refers to Haslang as being " en liaison avec la famille de Fugger " (in Augsburg). Apr. 17, 1761.

Papers relating to the places proposed for the Congress. Mar., 1761.

Letter of Haslang and other papers relating to the Congress.

Letter intimating the cession of all Canada. June 26, 1761.

Letter of Haslang, full of important historical detail. July 14, 1761.

Letter giving a report of Major Gates concerning the progress of the war in Martinique. Mar. 23, 1762.

Letters relating to the war in the West Indies.

Letter of Haslang, referring to new efforts to arrange peace between France and England conjointly with Spain. May 21, 1762.

Letter of Haslang, giving an account of the operations in Newfoundland and showing incidentally that the American colonies were the diplomatic barometer of Europe. July 7, 1762.

Memoir pour Mr. le Comte d'Haslang, enclosed with a letter of the latter dated Aug. 31, 1762, relating to the political situation.

Letter of Haslang, reporting the bombardment of Havana, etc. Sept. 10, 1762.

Traduction d'une lettre qui a été distribuée avanthier à la bourse Royale: " L'Amerique Septentrionale, ce puissant Empire, que nous avons depuis peu consideré comme la base et l'elevation de notre Commerce, est à present meprisée ". (Important document of 4 pages folio.)

Copie des Articles Préliminaires signés à Fontainebleau le 3 Novembre 1762.

Letter of Haslang, enclosing an important note in French referring to Frederick the Great's designs with Bavaria and Suabia. Oct. 17, 1762.

Copie du Traité Définitif de Paix, signé à Paris le 10 Fevrier 1763. (Print.)

321/5. Correspondance du Comte d'Haslang, etc. 1765-1768.

Letters of Haslang, giving an account of the financial settlement between England and France regarding prisoners of war. Apr. 29.

Termes et Conditions suivant lesquels l'affaire des Billets et lettres de change du Canada doit être accommodée. Important account of the financial condition of the time.

Project de l'addresse des Pairs. Referring to the dissatisfaction and disruption in America.

321/7. Les Relations d'Angleterre 1770. (Haslang). Contains among other papers the following bearing upon America:

Messages of King George to the Elector Maximilian Joseph and replies thereto.

Letter of Haslang, referring to the revocation of the " examen de la requête des Negociants de Londres qui trafiquent dans l'Amerique Septentrionale ". Feb. 13, 1770.

Letter of Haslang, relating to the resolution of the colonies in America not to admit certain English goods. Mar. 2, 1770.

Letter of Haslang, including the following significant passage: " Les Americains ne paroissent point encore satisfaits des Droits qu'on a supprimés sur le papier, le verre, et les couleurs à l'exception de celui sur le Thé ". Also other important details concerning New York, Newport, and Boston. July 20, 1770.

344/27. Beschreibung über Pennsylvania et Philadelphia. 1683. (Ex archivo Solisburcensi Recepi 1790 Roth.) Contains fol. 1-30 in manuscript with the following title:

Ein Brief von William Penn Eigenthumbs-Herrn und Befehlshabern in Pennsylvania in America zu denen Verordneten Der freyen gesellschaft in der Handlung derselben Landschafft, wohnende in Londen; so da in sich hält Eine allgemeine Beschreibung derselben Landschafft, Ihres grundes, der Lufft, dess Wassers, der Jahreszeiten, und was sie hervorbringt, so wohl von Natur als durch Kunst Wie auch von Ihren eingebohrnen, oder Ursprünglichen einwohnern, derselben sprachen gebräuchen und Weisen, Kost, Häussern oder wigwams, Freygebigkeit, leichten art zu leben, arzney, begräbnissen, opferung und gesängen, Feyer und Festtagen, Regierung und ihrer ordnung in Ratshalten bey Verhandlung Landes und Ihrem Gericht gegen missethätern, Ingleichen von denen ersten anbauern, denen Niederteutschen, etc., und von dem gegenwärtigen Zustand und aufrichtung auch herrlichen Zu- und aufnehmen der besagten Provinz und dem gerichts Rath, Welchem beygefüget ist eine Nachricht Von der Statt Philadelphia so jüngstens angeleget worden; Dessen anlage zwischen zweyen schiffbaren Strömen Delanware und Skulkil, nebenst einem Ab- und grund-riss derselben (Worinnen der Verkauffer ihre Los durch einsezte gewisse Zahlen unterschieden seyn) Wie auch die glückliche und vortheilhaffte anstalt der erwehnten gesellschafft in derselben Statt und Landschafft. Londen 1683.

This document has been printed by M. D. Learned in *German American Annals,* Mar.-Apr., 1910, and by Heuser, *Pennsylvanien im Siebzehnten Jahrhundert* (1910).

444/14. Les Affaires d'Angleterre (Comte de Haslang). 1778-1786. Graf Haslang mit Graf Seinsheim. Among the letters (which are not chronologically arranged) are:

Letter of Haslang to Seinsheim, referring to Clinton's orders, to the evacuation of Philadelphia, and to the operations of Washington and Lafayette. London, Aug. 24, 1778.

Letter of Haslang to Seinsheim, giving an account of Cornwallis's winter quarters, the passage of the Schuylkill, etc. London, 1778.

Letter of Haslang to Seinsheim, referring to the bills proposed for the reconciliation of America. Mar. 12, 1778.
Letters of Haslang designated: Correspondance de S. E. M. le Comte de Haslang à Londres de ao. 1778 et 79.
Briefe vom H. Grafen v. Haslang in London 1779.
Id., 1780.
Id., 1781.
Id., 1782.
Id., 1785.
Id., 1786.

457/20. Bairische Kreis-Sachen. 1768. Contains four parcels of papers, the third of which has the following matter of special interest: Manuscript letter with an edict of Emperor Joseph on parchment of the year 1768, with a signature of the emperor, and other papers relating to the edict and treating of the question of preventing emigration from Regensburg, Cologne, Nuremberg, Lübeck, Ulm, Frankfort, Bremen, and Hamburg.
Letter to the Archbishop of Salzburg, relating to emigration. Aug. 6, 1768.
Letter to the Bavarian estates.
Letter of Maximilian Joseph.
Letter of the consul of Nuremberg to the Prince Elector. Aug. 29, 1768.
Letter to Archbishop Sigismund of Salzburg.
Letter of the consul of Nuremberg addressed to the "Durchlauchtigster Fürst". Nov. 3, 1768.
Conclusum ad Proponendum XImum. Oct. 13, 1768.
Letter to the Archbishop of Salzburg. Munich, Nov. 15, 1768.
An die Abgesandte des gegenwärtig versamelten Erbl. Fränckischen Kreises zu Nürnberg im Namen des Erbl. Bayer. Kreises. Nov. 15, 1768.
Letter from Sigismund in Salzburg to the "Fürst". Dec. 5, 1768.

476/22. Das Auswanderungsgesetz betr. 1799.

476/81. Gesandschafts Diarium vom 13. Mai 1790 bis 31. Dezember 1799.

476/82. Die Französischen Emigranten und deren Niederlassung im Fränk. Kreis betr. 1792.

502/1-6. Haslang, 1777-1782. Contains the same kind of material as the other correspondence:

502/1. Letters referring to the military operations in America.
Letters referring to communications from General Howe, dated Philadelphia, Oct. 29, 1777, describing the occupation of the city.
Letters dated London, Dec., 1777, and later, giving an important account of the German troops.

502/2. Haslang, 1778.
Letter giving an account of the French forces in America. London, Dec. 18, 1778.
Letter containing a protest against the action of England. Dec. 8, 1777.

Letter giving an account of the expedition in New Jersey. Dec. 4, 1777. These letters are contemporaneous history of the details of the Revolution and show clearly that the war in America with its strong French support was a continuation, in the minds of Europeans, of the war between England and France.

Papers relating to the recall of Baron Münchhausen, Hessian captain and aide-de-camp of General Howe, and his appointment by the Landgrave as aide-de-camp. July, 1778.

Courrier Politique et Littéraire or *French Morning Post* of May 6 and 9, 1778, enclosed in a letter of May 12, 1778.

Letters relating to Cornwallis. 1778.

502/3. Haslang, 1779. Continuation of the correspondence giving news in detail of the progress of the war in America, the troubles between England and France, and the course of political events in England and Ireland:

Letter of Haslang, addressed to S. E. M. le Cte de Haslang, relating to Paul Jones: "Si l'escadron de Paul Jones n'est pas bien considérable, on tachera sans doute de le déloger bientôt de ces parages, ou il fait en attendant, à ce que je vois, des torts assez considérable[s]". Mannheim, Oct. 9, 1779.

Letter of Haslang, giving full news from America of the Isle of St. John, Savannah, Stono Ferry, order of General Lincoln, New London, New Haven, New York, etc., and of the depredations of Paul Jones off the coast of Yorkshire, stating on the strength of a letter from Hull, that Paul Jones took 16 vessels laden with merchandise in the river and offered a naval spectacle which struck consternation into the people of Hull. London, Sept. 28, 1779.

Other letters (a number of them addressed to His Excellency Baron de Vieregg) containing similar references to Paul Jones and giving information concerning the movements of the English fleet.

Copie du Manifeste remis par l'Ambassadeur d'Espagne au Lord Weymouth. London, June 16, 1779.

Letter of Haslang to Vieregg, giving an interesting account of the operations of Clinton, Vaughan, Johnson, and Sullivan, and of Charleston and the "Volontaires de la Caroline". London, July 13, 1779.

Letter of Haslang to Vieregg, giving a detailed account of the operations in Georgia. Apr. 23, 1779.

502/4. Haslang, 1779, 1780.

Letters of G. Fantina in Berlin to Vieregg in Munich, referring to the military operations in Europe.

Les Articles de la Capitulation signé[s] a Charles-Town le 12 May dernier [1780]. (Enclosed in a letter of June 20, 1780, addressed by Haslang to Vieregg.)

Letter of Haslang, relating to the capitulation at Charles-Town. June 16, 1780.

Letter of Haslang to Vieregg dated Dec., 1779, enclosing copies of the *London Gazette* of Dec. 21-25, 1779.

Letter to Haslang, referring to Major André and General Arnold. Munich, Nov. 26, 1780.
Letter of Haslang to Vieregg, referring to the discussion between Mr. Fox and Lord George Germain concerning the recognition of American independence. London, Nov. 10, 1780.
Letter of Haslang to Vieregg, giving an account of operations at Pensacola and along the Mississippi. Apr. 4, 1780.

502/5. Haslang, 1781. Letters of Haslang in London to Vieregg containing important reference to America:
Letter giving an account of the terrible earthquake and hurricane in Jamaica. Feb. 5, 1781.
Letter giving an account of the operations in Canada and of a sally of 200 Indians under Lieut. Woughton toward the Connecticut River. Feb. 9, 1781.
Letter giving an account of the mutiny of 1300 Pennsylvania troops at Morristown, on account of lack of food, clothing, and pay. Feb. 23, 1781.
Letter dated Apr. 3, 1781, containing a communication from Cornwallis at Turkey-Creek.
Letter reporting the defeat of Cornwallis. Nov. 30, 1781.

502/6. Haslang, 1782. Correspondence of Haslang and Vieregg continued:
Letter of Haslang, quoting Lord Cavendish concerning the American Revolution: " Que la grande Bretagne étoit à present engagée dans une Guerre dispendieuse avec la France, l'Espagne, et la Hollande sans un seul Allié ". London, Mar. 12, 1782.
Letter of Haslang, referring to the technicality of the phrase " à l'Amérique " in the bill before the House of Commons. July 5, 1782.
Letter of Haslang, referring to the *New York Gazette*, the *Pennsylvania Gazette*, and the letter of Guy Carleton to General Washington, which Washington forwarded to Congress, and also to the resolutions made at Philadelphia. London, July 15, 1782.

502/7. Haslang et Lerchenfeld, Londres 1783. Contains a number of prints, such as the following:
Provisional Articles of Peace, signed at Paris, the 30th of November, 1782, by the Commissioners of His Britannick Majesty, and the Commissioners of the United States of America.
Preliminary Articles of Peace, between His Britannick Majesty, and the Most Christian King. Signed at Versailles, the 20th Jan. 1783.
Articles Préliminaires de Paix, entre sa Majesté Britannique et les Etats Généraux des Provinces Unies des Pais-Bas. Signés a Paris, le 2 Sept. 1783.
Traité Définitif entre la Grande Bretagne et les États Unis d'Amérique au Nom de la Très Sainte et Indivisible Trinité (signed at Versailles, 1783).
Letters of Lerchenfeld and Vieregg relating to these treaties.

Declaration de ses Droits faite par les Corps Volontaires de la Province d'Ulster en Irlande dans l'Assemblée de leur Délégués tenue à Duncannon le 8 Septembre 1783. (Copy.)

Letter of C. W. Kellerhoff in London to Vieregg, referring to the disturbances caused by the refugees in Baltimore, who had not yet been able to return to their countries and did not wish to become American citizens, and to the resolutions of that city regarding these refugees. Sept. 26, 1783.

Copy of Ayre's *Sunday London Gazette and Weekly Monitor*, Aug. 10-17, 1782, enclosing a communication from George Washington with the following heading: " There is something so truly interesting and important in the following Circular Letter from his Excellency George Washington, Commander in Chief of the army of the United States of America, that we cannot think its extreme length will be an objection to our readers ". The communication [his circular to the governors] is dated at the headquarters in Newburgh, June 18, 1783.

Letter of Kellerhoff to Vieregg, referring to the United States and to Washington's letter of resignation. London, Aug. 19, 1783.

Letter of Kellerhoff to Vieregg, referring to the American army. Aug. 15, 1783.

Letter of Lerchenfeld, referring to Washington as a second Cromwell. London, Aug. 8, 1783.

Letter of Kellerhoff to Vieregg, containing information concerning the refugees and loyalists in America, and stating that the governor of Florida had invited them to his province. Reference is also made to Franklin's return from Paris to America. Aug. 1, 1783.

Letters of Haslang to Vieregg at the close of the volume, containing references to the treaty with the United States of America, etc.

502/8-11. Correspondance du Comte de Haslang, 1785-1788.

502/12. Correspondance Ministérielle avec le Comte de Hasslang et le Sr. Dufossey à Londres. 1790.

502/13-19. Correspondance avec le Comte de Haslang à Londres. 1791-1798.

535/1-5. Mémoires sur la Guerre. Tom. I.-V. 1756-1760.

535/6. Mémoires concernans la Guerre pour la Succession d'Autriche. Tom. I.

535/7. Lettres particulières de l'Électeur Charles Théodore aux princes et princesses de la Maison.

535/8. No. 2. Mémoires sur la Guerre.

535/9. No. 3. Différentes Dépêches à Mr. le Comte de Wickenburg et Goldstein et Vieregg. 1799.

535/10. No. 4. Marquis Curtis à Naples. 1784.

535/11. No. 6. Le Baron de Hinckel, Ministre de Hollande. 1797.

535/12. No. 7. Ministre de Saxe, Comte de Görtz. 1796.

535/13. No. 8. Le Ministre d'Angleterre, Chevalier Walpole. 1784.

535/14. No. 10. John Trewor [Trevor] Engl. Gesandter mit H. Vieregg. 1780-1783.

535/15. Lettres de S. A. S. E. Bavaro-Palatine Charles Théodore à son Ministre le Comte d'Oberndorf. 1778-1795.

564/70. Die Auswanderungen und Vermögens-Exportationen aus der Rheinpfalz in fremde Staaten überhaupt betr. 1801.

564/72. Die Einwanderungen und Vermögens-Importationen aus fremden Staaten in das Herzogthum Berg. 1801.

564/73. Die Auswanderungen und Vermögens-Exportationen aus dem Herzogthum Berg in fremde Staaten betr. 1801.

593/15. Grossherzogtum Berg. Grundsätze bey Aus- und Einwanderungen. 1806, 1809, 1810, 1813.

598/1. Handelsverhältnisse zwischen sämtlichen Zollvereins-Staaten, mit Hannover, Oldenburg u. Braunschweig.

598/2. Die Aufnahme anderer Staaten in den deutschen Zollverein nach den Zoll- u. Handelsverträgen v. J. 1833, 1835 u. 36 u. nach den H. Conf. Verhandl. H. Prot. v. 12ten Septbr. 1836 § 35, hier die Unterhandlungen der Zollvereins-Staaten resp. Preussen u. Churhessen mit Hannover, Braunschweig, Oldenburg, über Handels- u. Zollverhältnisse u. über ein Zoll-Cartell; die Handels-, Zoll- u. Schiffahrts-Verhältnisse, Mass-Gewicht-Münzänderung in Braunschweig; Handels-Consulate; Eisenbahnen u. Handelsverhältnisse mit Bremen; Zoll- u. Handelsvertrag zwischen Hannover, Braunschweig; Freundschafts-, Handels- u. Schiffahrtsvertrag zwischen Lübeck, Bremen u. Hamburg u. den Vereinigten Staaten von Nordamerika; Handels- u. Schiffahrts-Vertrag zwischen Frankreich u. Mecklenburg; Münzgesetze in Hannover; Handelsverhältnisse mit Lippe-Detmold, Amer. u. Deutschland. 1835-1837. A thick fascicle or volume of papers enclosing also copies of newspapers relating to trade conditions and:
Valuable papers relating to American trade with Germany.
A document addressed to the King of Hannover, and signed by Hormayer, giving a graphic description of the condition of American banks and finance in 1837, as the following passage will show: " Die Nachrichten aus Amerika lauten noch immerfort höchst ungünstig und entmuthigen jeden direckt oder indireckt Betheiligten. Die Fallimente der bedeutendsten Häuser sind jetzt in New-York auf 200 Millionen, in New-Orleans auf 120 Millionen Dollars gestiegen; selbst die Banken stellen ihre Baarzahlungen ein. Unter solchen Umständen sind unruhige Auftritte wohl zu fürchten. Bereits meldet man von schlimmen Bewegungen aus New-Orleans und Washington, wo die Metropolitan-Bank soeben ihre Zahlungen suspendirt hat". Hannover, June 25, 1837.
Liste der Ao. 1836 in Bremen eingeführten Waaren, nach dem Durchschnittspreise berechnet.
Woll-Einfuhr in England 1834 bis 1837.

598/4-6. Allgemeine Maassregeln zur Aufrechthaltung der gesetzlichen Ordnung und Ruhe in den deutschen Bundesstaaten. Revolutionäre Umtriebe an den Universitäten. 1819-1829.

598/7-11. Allgemeine Maassregeln, etc. 1820-1849.

598/12-23. Die Central-Untersuchungs-Commission zu Mainz.
598/24. Die von Seite der Central-Untersuchungs-Com. zu Mainz eingeleitete Untersuchung über die seit 1819 auf den deutschen Universitäten noch andauernden Burschenschaftlichen Verbindungen u. Umtriebe, sowie die von Seite des K. Bayer. Gouvernements ergriffenen Massregeln gegen diese gesetzwidrigen Verhandlungen u. Zusammenkünfte der Studierenden. 1821, 1822.
598/25-26. *Id.* 1822, 1823.
599/1-12. Allgemeine Maassregeln zur Aufrechthaltung der Ordnung und Ruhe in den deutschen Bundesstaaten in Ansehung der bei den deutschen Universitäten entdeckten revolutionären Umtriebe. 1824-1830. Numbers 11 and 12 deal particularly with " Passwesen ", both for " Inländer " and " Ausländer ".
600/1. *Id.* Continued.
600/2-182. Pass- und Fremden Polizei. Den Eintritt, Aufenthalt und die Behandlung fremder Militärpersonen in Bayern. 1806-1842.
606/3-8. *Id.* Continued.
606/3. Notizen über den allgemeinen Welthandel von dem K. Gesandten von Hormayer, eigentlich Handels- u. Zoll- dann Schiffahrts-Verhältnisse mit Süd u. Norddeutschland, und den überseeischen Staaten. Deutsche Auswanderungen; Leinen u. Garnhandel; Absatz Bayerischer Produkte; Eisenbahnen; Notizen über Industrie u. Gewerbe, Hanseatische Welthandel, und Handels-Verträge, etc., vom Monat Febr. 1838 bis zum Monat Dezbr. 1839. Conv. I. Nos. 1-92. Large bundle of papers in pasteboard cover, containing invaluable statistics and other details concerning the trade relations of Germany and America.
606/4. *Id.* Jan.-Dec., 1840. Conv. II. Nos. 93-169.
606/5. *Id.* Jan., 1841–Jan., 1842. Conv. III. Nos. 1-45.
606/6. *Id.* Jan.-Dec., 1845. Conv. IV. Nos. 1-73.
606/7. *Id.* Jan.-Apr., 1846. Conv. V. Nos. 1-70.
606/8. *Id.* May, 1846–Aug., 1847. Conv. VI. Nos. 1-75.
614/24. Auswanderungen und Passanten. 1820-1824. A bundle of 31 papers with a brief calendar in the front.
An den Kgl. Residenten Frhn. von Hertling in Frankfurt geh. Werbungen zur Emigration nach Brasilien betr. Ministerial Erlass. Munich, Feb. 20, 1824. Among the names mentioned in this paper are (1) Georg Ant. Schäfer, native of Münnerstadt in the Lower Rheinkreis, sometime physician in Brazil, who returned 1822 to Germany claiming to have a secret mission from the Emperor and Empress of Brazil to the Emperor of Austria; (2) Dr. Med. Kretzschmer of Frankfort-on-the-Main, who had some connection with Schäfer.
614/25. A paper relating to Kretzschmer and the emigration to Brazil.
614/26. Ministerial order. Frankfort a. M., Mar. 20, 1824, relating to Schäfer and Kretzschmer. Apr. 26, 1824.
614/27. Paper relating to the permission to emigrate.
614/28. Paper referring to an article in the *Mannheimer Zeitung*, relating to the treatment of the Germans in Brazil.

614/29. Letter dated Frankfort a. M., May 16, 1824, signed by Inig, giving more details on the same subject and enclosing copies of the *Zeitung der Freien Stadt Frankfurt* of Feb. 16 and May 4, 1824, with articles relating to Brazil.
614/30-31. Werbungen zur Auswanderung nach Brasilien betr. (Enclosing clippings from newspapers of 1824.)
616/102. Bestimmungen der Militärpflichtigkeit in Beziehung auf Auswanderungen, dann die der Landwehrpflicht bei Auswanderungen. 1819-1821.
618/247. Note an das K. Württemberg. Staats-Ministerium, Werbungen zur Auswanderung nach Amerika (no. 6276; original in Stuttgart ?). Oct. 29, 1817.
618/248. Süddeutsche Auswanderer u. deren Durchzug nach Oesterreich. 1818. Copy of the " Massregeln " is enclosed.
618/250. Auswanderungen nach Russland, insbesondere die Umtriebe der Würtemb. Unterthanen Werner, Feigel, etc., u. Auswanderungen aus dem Rheinkreis. 1819, 1821. Contains copy of the *Kgl. Privilegirte Stuttgarter Zeitung* of May 21, 1821, and a French communication from Comte de Rechberg to Comte de Lagarde, minister of France, dated Munich, Sept. 13, 1819.
618/251. Auswanderungen durch mystische Umtriebe. 1820. Relates to Handelsmann Wörner and to Feigel in Giengen and to Brugget of Heidenheim.
618/259. Auswanderungen K. Unterthanen nach Amerika. 1831. Official note addressed by the ministry in Munich to the Bavarian ministry in Stuttgart. Relates to the regulations for issuing papers in the case of families accredited by the American consul Louis Mark in Bamberg. July 18, 1831.
620/311. Bestimmungen der Militärpflichtigkeit rücksichtlich der Auswanderungen. 1817, 1818.
622/1-21. Acten-Produkte der bayer. Gesandtschaft in Wien. IV. Gesandtschaftliche Gegenstände. B. Ein- und Auswanderungen und Vermögensexportationen. Oesterreichische Verordnungen wegen Auswanderungen. 1767, 1768.
622/1-25. Acten der Königlichen Bayerischen Gesandtschaft in Wien. Oesterreichische Verordnungen wegen Auswanderungen. 1767, 1768.
647/314-718. Landesabwesende Untertanen.
648/1-134. *Id.*
648/135-144. Ein- und Auswanderungen Stadt Augsburg (1809-1817). Tabellarische Uebersichten. 1811, 1812, 1813, 1814, 1815, 1816.
648/151. Ein- und Auswanderungen 1809-1817. (Relates chiefly to Austria, Bohemia, Silesia, Switzerland, and France).
648/152-159. Aus- u. Einwanderungen. 1818-1820.
648/160-164. Ausw. u. Vermögensexportationen. 1812.
648/165-171. *Id.* 1810-1811.
648/172-175. *Id.* 1811.
648/176-182. *Id.* 1811.
648/183-188. *Id.* 1811.
648/189-194. *Id.* 1810.
648/195-201. *Id.* 1810.

648/201. Ein- und Auswanderungen resp. Aus- und Einwanderungen. 1809-1810.
649/1-38. Auswanderungen u. Vermögens-Exportationen in Tabellen nach den Kreisen. 1810-1821. These tables give detailed information of the emigrant and his property. The list of names does not mention the destination in all cases but only the place whence the emigrant comes. The fuller detail must be obtained from the original papers, relating to permission to emigrate, etc.
649/39-273. Einwanderungen u. Vermögensimportationen: Specialia. 1800-1825.
650/1-86. Nachtrag: Einwanderungen u. Vermögensimportationen. Specialia. 1825-1847. Interesting cases of Joseph Haidt aus Amerika, 1840, and of the Postmaster "Huber aus Warior Bridge", 1840-1847.
650/87-982. Auswanderungen u. Vermögensexportationen. Specialia. 1800-1836.
651/1-935. Auswanderungen, etc. 1781-1843.
652/1-928. Auswanderungen, etc. 1799.

Kasten Grau.
102. Gesandtschaft zu Paris.
Act. No. 101. Den Krieg zwischen den Vereinigten Staaten von Nordamerika und Grossbritannien betreffend. 1812. Contains among other things a letter in French addressed to the Minister of the United States, dated Paris, Aug. 21, 1812, enclosing a printed copy of *War Declared against Great Britain by the United States of America, with an Exposition of its Motives,* signed by Madison, President, and Monroe, Secretary of State.
103. Gesandtschaft zu Paris.
Fasc. 17 b. Die Auswanderung nach Amerika betr. 1847. Refers to the regulations regarding the transportation of emigrants.
104. Gesandtschaft zu Paris.
Act. No. 445. Die Auswanderung nach Nordamerika im Allgemeinen betreffend. 1832-1838. Stringent regulations of France requiring that the emigrant shall have 800 francs for himself or 1700 francs for his family. Important correspondence between Munich and Paris, relating to the matter, enclosing a list of provisions needed for the transit to New York and a list of the Bavarian commissariats for 1836-1837, together with the number of emigrants.
105. Gesandtschaft zu Paris.
Fasc. 26. Act. No. 446. Literarische Correspondenz mit Nordamerika betreffend. 1829. Relates to the transmission of Adolf Amman's packages through the Paris or London legation.
109. Act. No. 86. Der Vollzug des Art. 20 des Handels-Vertrages vom 29. Februar 1851, in spec. der gegenseitig zu gewährende Consular-Schutz in Nord-Amerika.
110. Gesandtschaft zu Karlsruhe.
Act. No. 231. Betreff: den Auslieferungsvertrag zwischen Preussen und Nordamerika; Bayerns Nichtbetheiligung an demselben. 1852.

Act. No. 361. Betreff: Heimliche Auswanderung nach Amerika. 1836-1855. Contains 11 papers dealing with the following: Complications due to the rigid passes, etc., of the French government.
Adventures of Braditsch "Miliz-General in dem Nordamerikanischen Staate Maine".
The emigration of 1849.
Secret emigration to lands beyond the sea, especially to the United States of America, with mention of special points to be guarded against.

118. Gesandtschaft zu London.
Act. No. 774. Betreff: Ernennung Bayrischer Handels-Agenten in Amerika. 1825-1827. Contains 13 papers in all relating to the appointment of the following agents:
Joh. Herrmann Christen Brink [ten Brink] zu Rio de Janeiro.
Peter Peyke in Bahia.
Hermann Nolte in Mexico.
G. P. Sprotto in La Guayra.
Johann Eschenburg in Buenos Ayres.
Act. No. 547. Betreff: Auslieferungs-Vertrag zwischen Bayern und Preussen mit den Vereinigten Staaten von Nordamerika wegen flüchtiger Verbrecher. 1843-1844. Some 60 papers in all.

120. Gesandtschaft zu London.
Act. No. 950. Betreff: Das Bayrische Auswanderungsgesetz von 1799. A letter to Haslang enclosing a printed copy of the rescript of July 5, 1799.
Act. No. 954. Betreff: Die Auswanderung nach dem Reiche des Mosquito-Königs in Amerika, 1842. Contains the following papers:
Letter of George Upton to A. Y. Schäzler. 68 Old Broad St., Mar. 30, 1842.
Two unsigned letters to George Upton. London, Mar. 31, 1842.
Unsigned letter in French addressed to Lord Aberdeen. London, Apr. 4, 1842.
Letter of Aberdeen to Cetto. Foreign Office, May 7, 1842.
Act. No. 955. Betreff: Die Auswanderung nach Buenos Ayres. 1855.
Paper relating to the operations of Franz Dessauer in Aschaffenburg in soliciting emigrants.
Copy of an important document addressed by Private Secretary Mayer to the legation in Paris.
Act. No. 956. Betreff: Die Auswanderung nach Canada. 1857.
A letter from the ministry in Munich to the legation in London.
Correspondence between the Foreign Office and the legation in London. It is noteworthy that this letter speaks of the German emigration to Canada as having increased of late and of the advantages of Canada over the United States as a desirable country for settlers.
Act. No. 964. Betreff: Auswanderungs- und Vermögens-Exportations-Gesuch des Johann Baptist Kohler aus Dingisweiler. 1836-1837.

Act. No. 968. Betreff: Gesuch des Generalagenten G. H. Paulsen zu Mainz um die Bewilligung zur Vermittlung von Ueberfahrtsverträgen und zur Aufstellung von Auswanderungs-Agenten nach Amerika. 1847-1848.

Act. No. 1108. Betreff: Geldbeiträge für die deutschen Verwundeten. 1866. Correspondence between the ministry in Munich and the legation in London.

Act. No. 1158. Betreff: Literarische Correspondenz mit Nordamerika. 1829. Relating to the permission to transmit free of cost packages of historical writings to Adolf Amman in North America and of correspondence of the Salzburg colonies to Munich. Mar. 9, 1829. *Cf.* Kasten Grau 105, fasc. 26, Act. no. 446.

Kasten Roth.

102/412. *Freundschaft-, Handels- und Schiffahrts-Vertrag zwischen Preussen und den übrigen Staaten des Zollvereins einerseits und der Argentinischen Konföderation andererseits.* Nov. 19, 1857. (Printed in German and Spanish.)

102/413. Tratado de Amistad Comercio y Navigacion entre la Confederacion Argentina por una parte y la Prussia y los otros Estados del Zollverein Aleman por la otra parte. Manuscript in Spanish and German, evidently the original, as it bears the signature and seal of Argentina. June 3, 1859.

102/414. Certified copy accompanying the 4 copies of the Tratado.

Gesandtschaft Wien.

No. 5. Amerika.
  Fol. 1. An die Gesandtschaft in Wien. Die Freystaaten in dem nördlichen und südlichen Amerika betreffend. Jan. 10-16, 1843. Inquiry how these states are formed and which states have been recognized by the Austrian government.
  Fol. 2-12. Papers relating to the interests of Bavarian manufacturers in Valparaiso, that were injured by the Spanish bombardment of the city in 1866. Indemnity asked for. Replies enclosed.
  Fol. 13-17. Den Nordamerikanischen Pass-Beamten Georg Plitt betreffend. 1839-1840.
  Fol. 18-19. Die Marine Sternwarte in Washington betr. Apr. 22 and 25, 1873.

No. 5. Brasilien.
  Fol. 1-3. Urkunden-Beglaubigung betreffend (by Notary Carl Börsch in Edenkoben, etc.). 1863.
  Fol. 4. Ausschreibung der Kais. Brasilianischen Gesandtschaft in Wien wegen Aufführung seines Monumentes für weil. S. Maj. den Kaiser Dom Pedro I. betreffend. 1856.

No. 6. Sardinien.
  Bericht den zwischen Sardinien u. Ver. Staaten von Nordamerika abgeschlossenen Handels- u. Schiffahrts-vertrag betr. Dated Vienna, Apr. 12, 1839; date of treaty Nov. 26, 1838.

No. 131. Konsulatswesen. 1813-1879.
  Vorrechte, Vollmachten u. Uniform der Konsuln.

Revision des bayr. Konsulatswesens, öster. Konsulargebühren. 1831-1856.
Personalien, Correspondenzen bei den einzelnen K. Konsulaten: in Brasilien (Rio de Janeiro), Californien, Brody, Fiume, Gibraltar, Hamburg, Lissabon, Livorno u. den annexierten italienischen Staaten (1864), Messina, New Orleans, Nord-Amerika, Odessa, Pesth, Philadelphia, Triest, Türkei, Venedig, Wien. 1813-1872.
Fremde Konsulate in Bayern (Oesterreich, Spanien, Schweden, Portugal). 1857.
Organisation der deutschen Reichs-Konsulate. 1871-1879.

Fol. 6. Brasilien; Das Kgl. Consulat in Rio de Janeiro betreffend. Oct. 31, 1853.
Fol. 7. Die Errichtung eines Konsulats in Californien betr. June 8, 1861.
Fol. 17. Die Errichtung eines Konsulats in New Orleans betreffend. Nov. 23, 1854.
Fol. 21. Den Vollzug des Art. 20 des Handels Vertrages vom 19ten Februar 1853, resp. den gegenseitig zu gewährenden Consular-Schutz in Nord-Amerika betreffend. June 4, 1855, etc.
Fol. 25. Complaint sent by Seward, Sec. of State, to J. Lothrop Motley, minister at Vienna, against Consul Hagedorn of Philadelphia; Motley's letter in French, investigation of the affair. 1865.

ROYAL BAVARIAN GENERAL NATIONAL ARCHIVES.

(KÖNIGLICH BAYERISCHES ALLGEMEINES REICHSARCHIV.)

Ludwigstrasse, 23. In the same building with the Royal Court and State Library. These archives are the administrative centre for the eight provincial or circuit archives of Bavaria. The rules and regulations for the use of this and the other state archives are formulated in the *Ministerial-Bekanntmachung, Gesetz- und Verordnungsblatt für das Königreich Bayern,* no. 9, Munich, Mar. 2, 1899, and printed in the *Archivalische Zeitschrift,* neue Folge, XI. 230 *et seq.,* Jahrgang 1904.

Hours: March to October, 8 to 2. November to February, 8.30 to 2.

From this archive the compiler derived but one document for American history:

Raimundus Fuggers zu Augsburg Schreiben an Herzog Ott Heinrich mit Nachrichten über ds neu gefundene land Peru. 1534. Fragment, 9 leaves folio.

THE ROYAL BAVARIAN CIRCUIT ARCHIVES.

These provincial depositories, distributed according to circuits (Kreise) and perpetuating to some extent the traditions of the circuits of the Empire made by Emperor Maximilian, contain the provincial state papers. Accordingly, papers of a provincial or local character may be found in the circuit archives corresponding to those of a more general nature found in the Royal Privy State Archives in Munich, and dealing with the same subject. The circuit archives are here arranged in alphabetical order, except that those of Munich come first, following immediately upon the other archives of the kingdom.

ROYAL BAVARIAN CIRCUIT ARCHIVES OF LOWER BAVARIA IN MUNICH.
(KÖNIGLICH BAYERISCHES KREISARCHIV.)

The archive is at Himbelstrasse 1 a. The papers are classified according to subjects, grouped in separate divisions under General Registratur (G. R.), and the Department of the Interior and the like, and arranged in bundles (Fascikel). The materials relating to America were not all repertoried at the time this search was made. Indeed, many parcels included in the following list had to be marked as the search was going on.

The rules for the use of archival materials in general have been referred to above. In case of certain investigations relating to family history a special form must sometimes be subscribed to, in order to guard against reckless publication of private matters.

G. R. Fasc. 405/1. 2. 4. 5. 6.

405/1. General Acta. A large bundle of papers including printed decrees, of which the following are worthy of mention:

Printed edict against emigration, containing 10 paragraphs. Paragraph X. refers to the mandate of 1598 requiring the people to attend service on holidays, to put aside heretical books, etc., to hold themselves aloof from sectarian services, and not to marry their children in sectarian places. Munich, Dec. 20, 1644.

A similar edict of Maximilian Emanuel, prescribing that the emigrant shall be at least 16 years of age and well instructed in " gewohnlicher Gleubens Profession ". The edict contains 11 commands, the tenth of which refers particularly to women wishing to emigrate. Munich, Dec. 5, 1681.

A large broadside edict of Karl Albrecht, containing 12 injunctions, prescribing, among other things, that children in foreign countries must not attend non-Catholic schools. Munich, Sept. 22, 1738.

A manuscript document of Louis XIV., authorizing " Nicolas Gargot Sr. de la Rochette, Chevallier de notre ordre de St. Michael, Marechal de Bataille ", to extend French dominion in America. St. Jean de Luz, May, 1660.

Edict of Karl Albrecht confirming former edicts relating to emigration. Munich, Apr. 30, 1732.

Edict of Friedrich Wilhelm I., king of Prussia, with the title: *Erneuertes Patent Dass die Aus fremden Landen nach Berlin ziehende Manufacturiers, Fabricanten und Handwercker Die hierin benannte Beneficia und Freyheiten geniessen sollen. De Dato Berlin, den 3ten August, 1734.* (Regenspurg, Gedruckt bey Johann Caspar Memmel.)

Patent . . . . von Ihro zu Ungarn und Böhmen Königl. Maj., etc., directed against the " Werber " (emissarii). Jan. 5, 1744.

On the top of the bundle were the following:

Edict of Maximilian Joseph directed against " aussländische Emissarii in Unseren Landen ". Munich, Feb. 28, 1764.

Edict of Maximilian Joseph, following up the preceding. Jan. 3, 1766. A number of printed copies.

Verruf repeating the order of the " Rescriptum dehortatorium " of July 7, 1768. Munich, Aug. 5, 1768.

A number of edicts of 1768 relating to emigration.
Papers relating to the emigration to Hungary, 1772. Several hundred Bavarians seem to have gone to Hungary in this year.
Höchst Landesherrliche Verordnungen, showing that the emigration to Hungary and Austria is still going on, an emigration which turned the tide of population from America to southeastern Europe. Munich, July 5, 1799.
405/2. General Emigrations Acten. Papers relating to the migration to Bohemia, Poland, and Hungary. 1615-1773.
405/3. General Emigrations Acta. 1802-1804. Regulating the removal of children from Bavaria and neighboring lands to Austria, and of young apprentices still bound to learn a trade.
405/4. General Emigrations Acta. Papers relating to military service of emigrants. 1792-1808.
405/5. General Emigrations Acta. Papers relating to property of emigrants, etc. 1780-1808.
405/6-409/13. Papers dealing with German emigration to Austria, France, Hungary, Italy, Sardinia, etc. Those relating to France at least have some bearing upon America.
409/14. Emigrations-Acta. 1768, 1771, 1772, 1773, and 1777-1797.
A document dated Abbach, Feb. 26, 1771, states that the number of emigrants from the Breisgau, Schwarzwald, Switzerland, and Lorraine to Hungary in the year 1770 was 19,556 persons not including children. This shows that the trend of emigration had turned toward the east even before the American Revolution.
Important document appealing to the Elector to ameliorate the intolerable condition of his subjects. Burghausen, Jan. 19, 1772.
410-417. Emigrations-Acta, on emigration to Hungary, etc. 1799-1808.
418/33. Die Einwanderung der Fremden ins Land, dann Vermögens Importationen, im Gegensatze derley Exportationen u. Emigrationen. 1796-1804.
418/34. Similar papers relating to emigration of individuals from neighboring lands, differences concerning tax, property, etc. 1781-1811.
418/35. Papers relating to property of emigrants. 1807-1808.
418/36. Papers relating to the immigration from France to Bavaria. 1794-1804.
418/37. Papers forbidding the French to purchase property in Bavaria. 1799.
418/38. Verwendung des in das Ausland gehenden Vermögens. 1817-1820.
418/39. Akt von 1801-1804.
419/41. Conv. I. Die Auswanderung der Familie Häusler nach Amerika betr. Nos. 1-28. 1810-1814.
The case of Häusler is quite a typical one. He was born in Munich, June 17, 1784. His father went to France and then to America, 1786, having a pass signed by General Moreau. Young Häusler (Klemens Joseph) was a saddler by trade and a Catholic. His father, formerly in the Bavarian postal service, now (1811) has a farm ("Plantage") at Baltimore ("Baldemor"). No. 13 of the papers in this bundle con-

tains Häusler's autobiography. No. 24 contains copies of the *Augsburger Ordinari Postzeitung* of Feb. 20 and Apr. 9, and of other German and French newspapers of 1812. No. 28 contains the decision of the court as regards Häusler's estate.

Conv. II. Auswanderungen nach Amerika. An otherwise unnumbered fascicle containing references to:
(1) Wilhelm Friedrich Freiherr von Karwinsky ("Karrwiensky"), who emigrated to Brazil in 1821. (2) Coppersmith Anton Schmied of Landshut, who emigrated with wife and 3 children to live with his brother Johann, silversmith, in Havana, Cuba. 1819. (9 papers.) (3) Franz Xavier Fessel ("Fesl") of Munich and his emigration to America. 1811. (9 papers.)

420. Auswanderung u. Vermögensexportationen nach den Niederlanden, Päbstl. Staaten, Polen, Preussen, Regensburg, Russland, Sachsen, Ungarn, Württemberg, Würzburg.
421. Auswanderungen, etc., nach Italien, etc.
422. Auswanderungen, etc., nach fremden Staaten. 1804-1816.
423. Auswanderungen, etc. 1817.
424. Auswanderungen, etc. 1818.
425/46-48. Emigrations-Wesen.
46. Act der Regierung des Isarkreises. Auswanderungen und Vermögens-Exportationen von Baierischen Unterthanen in fremde Staaten. 1819-1821.
47. Auswanderungsgesuche. 1822.
48. Auswanderungen. 1823.
428/53. Emigrations-Wesen.
Vermögens Confiscationen Baierischer Unterthanen wegen unerlaubten Auswanderungen. 1809-1814.
Die im Ausland sich aufhaltenden Bair. Unterthanen betr. 1812-1813.
Die sich in ausländischen Diensten aufhaltenden Baiern betr. 1812-1813.
429. Emigrations Wesen. Einwanderungen auswärtiger Unterthanen in das Königreich Baiern. (Arranged alphabetically, A-K.)
430. Emigrations Wesen, L-Z.
431/59. Emigrations-Wesen vom Salzburgischen Gebieth oder ehemaligen Salzachkreise betr. 1808-1817. Papers dealing with the following subjects:
Emigration from Salzburg to Bavaria. 1808.
Estates going to Austria by inheritance. 1809.
Salzburgers attending schools and universities elsewhere.
Emigration of French subjects. 1810.
Emigration of subjects liable for military duty. 1810.
Die in Deposito befindlichen Nachsteuer Gelder wegen Auswanderung in die neu acquirirten Gebieths Theile u. in die Oesterreich. Staaten, 1811.
Ausw. d. Doblingerschen Familie nach Oesterreich. 1811.
Ausw. und Vermögens Exportation überhaupt. 1811-1815.

Verordnungen der Kurfürstlichen Landesdirection von Baiern. 1804.

Allgemeine Verordnung das Wandern der Handwerker betreffend. 1807. This rescript prescribes definite conditions under which artisans and trades people shall be allowed to leave the country. Section 3 requires that a list or "Wanderbuch" shall be kept containing the names of all such emigrants and giving at the same time the birthplace, the judicial district, the trade of the parents, the age, profession, and the beginning and end of the "Wanderzeit", etc.

Auszug aus dem Edicte vom 24. September 1799 über die Organisation des Schulwesens.

Nachsteuer u. Freizügigkeits Verhältnisse mit Baaden, Berg, Sachsenweimar, Franckfurt, Preussen, Sachsen, der Schweiz.

Nachsteuer, etc., mit Frankreich u. Illyrien.

Freizügigkeit mit Würtemberg.

431/60. Emigrations Wesen vom Unterdonaukreise namentlich von Passau betr. 1764-1806.

432/61-64. Emigrations Wesen.
- **61.** Acta die ausgewanderten Französischen Geistlichen und deren Aufenthalt betr. 1791-1793.
- **62.** Acta die ausgewanderte Französische geistliche und weltliche Personen, dann deren Aufenthalt dahier. Conv. VI. Jan.-July incl., 1795.
- **63.** Die Trappisten Emigranten.
- **64.** Certificata oder Reiss Pass für jene Personen, so in Bayern nicht ansässig somit für Ausländer oder Emigranten sind. 1799-1806.

433/65. Emigrations Wesen. Lit. A-G. Alphabetical list of French émigrés. Französische Emigranten. 1799.

Id. 1790-1799.
Id. 1775, 1798-1799.
Id. 1799-1802.
Id. 1796, 1837.
Id. 1797-1802.

434/*ad* **65.** Emigrations Wesen. Lit. G-Z. 1796-1806.

435/66. Die fremden Emigranten nach Baiern in genere, dann aus Frankreich. 1784-1793.

435/67. Die fremden Emigranten, etc. 1794-1796.

436/68. Emigrations Wesen. General Acta, die Französischen Emigranten in genere. 1797.

436/69. *Id.* General Acta, die Französischen Emigranten in genere. 1798. Valuable matter relating to the French emigrants such as the following:

Alphabetisches Verzeichniss derjenigen Ausgewanderten resp. Fremden, welche seit dem 10ten October 1798 wiederholt neuerdings die gnädigste Erlaubnis erhalten, in dem Lande Baiern auf unbestimmte Zeit sich aufhalten zu dürfen. (About 1000 names.)

Verzeichniss Jener Personen, welche nach verschiedenen Landen mit hoher Oberlandes Regierungs Genehmigung Pässe erhalten, von 21. May 1798 anfangend [bis 1800].

437/70. Emigrations Wesen. General Acta. Die Französischen Emigranten in genere. 1799. Matter similar to that of the preceding, containing among other things the following:
Verzeichniss. 1796. (Containing a list of the French priests in Bavaria and also a list of French émigrés in Landshut, in Munich, and other places. Valuable material for genealogical purposes.)

437/71. *Id.* Die Französischen Emigranten in genere. 1800-1804.

438/72. *Id.* Französische Emigranten Anzeigen von Seite der Landgerichte. 1800-1803.

439/73. *Id.* Französische Emigranten Anzeigen von Seiten der Landgerichte. 1804-1806.

440/74. Emigrations-Wesen. Anzeigen über die in den Regierungsbezirken, München, Landshut, Straubing, und Burghausen sich aufhaltenden französischen Emigranten. 1797.

441/75. Emigrations-Wesen.
Gerichtliche Anzeigen der sich im Regierungsbezirk Burghausen befindlichen Emigranten, so auf ausgefertigten Befehl de [20] May 1801 haben verfasst werden müssen. Nos. 1-19 incl.
Anzeigen der sich im Regierungsbezirk Landshut befindlichen Emigranten, etc. Nos. 1-19 incl.
Gerichtliche Anzeigen, etc. Regierungsbezirk Straubing, etc. Nos. 1-26 incl.

A[emter] R[egistratur] II.
Fasc. 164/848⅓. Die Rechtsverhältnisse in Amerika betr. Refers to a communication of Consul Angelrodt in St. Louis enclosing a printed sheet with the title: *Die Erbberechtigung der Ausländer (Fremden oder Aliens) in einzelnen Staaten von Nord-Amerika betreffend* (St. Louis, Missouri, 1859).

A[emter] R[egistratur] I.
167/4. Verzeichnisse über stattgehabte Aus- und Einwanderungen. Beim K. Bayer. Landgerichte Ebersberg. 1818-1851. Contains a valuable list of names of emigrants, also a number of printed rescripts.[1]

391/5. Pfleggericht Rauschenberg. Acta Ein- und Auswanderungen. 1731-1805. Contains papers relating to the following:
The emigration of 400 Protestants from Salzburg. 1731.
Papers directed "ad Deputationem Secretam". Important for names and condition of Salzburgers, giving minute details of the Salzburg troubles.
Papers relating to the Salzburgers for the years 1789 to 1805. Important for names of individuals.

391/6. Pfleggericht Rauschenberg. Acta Verordnungen über die Freizügigkeit. 1768, 1802.

452/67. [No. 544.] Akten des Königlichen Landgerichts Laufen über staatsrechtliche Gegenstände betreff. Verordnungen und Akten über unbefugte Auswanderungen und Vermögens exportationen, dann Rückkehr. Die Ausgewanderten im Allgemeinen. 1812-1853.

---

[1] These were examined only as far as the letter M, as they were not repertorized further.

453/22. Generalien. Ein- und Auswanderungen im Allgemeinen. 1810-1856. Contains, among other things, Auswanderungs-Tabelle, Einwanderungs-Tabelle, for 1805.
453/23. Generalien. Auswanderungs-Agenten. 1841-1855. Important papers addressed to the police relating to agents who are forwarding emigrants to America. The following are noteworthy:

Paper relating to a certain Johann Hjelm, a Swede in Havre, who is about to establish agencies in Bavaria and has employed a certain Friedrich Carl Mayer in Bergzabern as his agent. Munich, Apr. 22, 1841.

Matter relating to a Frenchman Metro, in company with Wenz, supposed to be from Zweibrücken, operating under the firm name " Metro, Wenz, and Co.", who are making contracts for the transportation of emigrants.

Printed circulars issued by " Das Nachweisungsbureau für Auswanderer in Bremen ". 1857.

Letter of W. L. Marcy from the State Department at Washington, dated Jan. 31, 1857, relating to traffic, and 2 letters of G. C. Verplanck to Marcy touching the same subject.

453/25. Generalien. Auswanderungen insbesondere, nach Algier, Australien, Belgien, Brasilien, Canada, La Plata-Staaten, Frankreich, Griechenland, Oesterreich, Polen, Preussen, Reuss-Plauen, Russland, Ungarn, Wallachei, Württemberg. 1819-1861. Contains papers of official character relating to the emigration to these lands, only indirectly bearing on America.
453/26. Generalien. Auswanderungen nach Amerika u. Reisen dorthin. 1843-1861.
453/27. Generalien. Vermögensexportationen, Nachsteuer und Freizügigkeitsverhältnisse. 1811-1836.
453/28. Acta des Königlichen Landgerichts Tittmoning. Generalien. Die Bayrische Auswanderung mit Tabell. Uebersicht, etc. 1853-1858.

R[egierungs] A[cten].
1154/60. Presidial-Acten der Königl. Regierung von Oberbayern. H. Polizei-Gegenstände. C. Sicherheits-Polizei.

Die Münchener Auswanderungs-Gesellschaft. 1850. Relates that the society's aim is not only to encourage emigration but to diffuse democratic principles, with the purpose of overthrowing the present order. The document gives also a brief sketch of the society and the names of the officers and place of meeting. One of the papers states that " der grösste Theil unserer dermaligen Mitglieder gesonnen ist, sich nach Dalton, einer im Norden des Staates Georgia am Fusse der Allegahny-Gebirge gelegenen neu gegründeten Stadt zu begeben, und da der Weg dahin von Charleston aus in 1½ Tagen auf der Eisenbahn zurückgelegt werden kann, so ist unsere Gesellschaft bei der kürzlichen Anwesenheit des Generalagenten Washingt. Finlay dahier, mit demselben in Unterhandlung getreten ", etc. Feb. 27, 1850.

1157/130. Presidial Acten, etc. H. Polizei-Gegenstände. C. V. Personalia.
Braditsch N. Nordamerikanischer General. Refers to the adventures of the so-called Militia General Braditsch of the state of Maine, who attracted much attention in Bremen, Münster, and other places, and had certain escapades in Hungary. Braditsch passed himself off as a "Fiumaner" [man of Fiume], which the document says is corroborated by his dialect.
1245/94. Auswanderung aus Giesing nach Nord-Amerika. 1846. The names mentioned are Herzog, Niederreiter, and Wagener. A copy of the *Münchener Tageblatt* of Apr. 8, 1846, enclosed.
1245/95. Auswanderungen nach Nord-Amerika im Jahre 1846 betreffend, mit einer Tabelle. Under the same signature are seven other fascicles devoted to the years 1847, 1848, 1849, 1850, 1851, 1852, 1853. Reports giving the numbers of emigrants, place of birth, amount of property they possessed, etc. In the same bundle are some 42 small papers relating to the emigrants of this year.
1245/105. Das Gesuch des Xaver Ammer Sattlergütlers von Unterschleissheim um Bewilligung zur Auswanderung nach Nordamerika (Marienstadt in Pennsylvanien). 1845.
1245/107. Michael Albrecht Gütlerssohn von Perlach. 1847.
1245/108. Maria Eigner Bauerstochter von Gusshübl.
1245/127. Nikolaus Bröder (or Bräder) Gesuch um Erlaubniss zur Auswanderung nach Amerika. 1837.
1245/135. Joseph Blum Sattlergeselle aus Pförring Gesuch, etc., nach Amerika. 1840.
1245-143. Andreas Birki Gutsbesitzers Sohn von Gern Gesuch, etc., nach Illinois. 1845.
1245/147. Gesuch des Peter Beuschl von Körsching, der Witwe Maria Anna Beer von da, und der Korbinian Reinwald von Oberdalling . . . . nach Nordamerika. 1845.
1245/148. Max Baum aus Neuhausen nach Pennsylvanien. 1845.
1246/150-309.
1247/310-472.
1248/473-681.
1249/682-834. } Contain references to about 120 emigrants.
1250/835-950.
1251/951-984.

The "Gerichts-Literalien" or "Literalien der altbayerischen Land- und Pfleggerichte", were not fully repertoried and could not be examined.

1794/6. Acten der Königl. Reg. von Oberbayern. Kammer des Innern. Die Bayerische Auswanderung. 1855, de anno 1852. The introductory paragraph gives a general idea of the contents: "Den K. Regierungen, K. d. J., wurde durch die Ministerial-Entschliessung vom 3 Januar 1843, No. 24, 455, der Auftrag ertheilt, am Schlusse eines jeden Jahres eine möglichst genaue Uebersicht der stattfindenden Auswanderungen unter Angabe des Standes und Vermögens der Ausgewanderten, des muthmasslichen Grundes ihrer Auswanderung, des vorläufig bezeichneten Reisezieles und des eingeschlagenen We-ges in Vorlage zu bringen". The volume contains valuable statistical tables giving a number of emigrants from several police districts and much information concerning the individual emigrants. The same volume contains papers dated as late as 1868.

1794/11. Rotulus Actorum. Betreff: Auswanderungen nach Amerika. Minist. Rescripte, Auswanderungen nach Brasilien. Jan. 7, 1825, no. 642; May 22, no. 9817; Aug. 23, no. 15,731; Sept. 13, no. 17,038; Apr. 27, 1826, no. 8198; May 19, no. 9534. Minist. Rescr. Auswanderungen nach Amerika ist bei den Inn. Acten, Auswanderungen nach Nordamerica, 2 Juli, 6309. Contains misgivings that the Germans have been decoyed to Brazil. Some of the documents relate to individual emigrants and regulations concerning emigration. About 40 papers in all.

1794/12. Aus- und Einwanderungen, dann Vermögens Ex. u. Importationen nach u. aus Canada. Generalia. 1855. (3 papers.)

1794/13. Aus- u. Einwanderungen, dann Vermögens Ex. u. Importationen nach u. aus Demerara. Generalia. 1839.

1795/37. Rückwanderungen aus Nordamerika. 1856. The first page contains the following:

"Königreich Bayern. Staatsministerium des Innern.

"Nach öffentlichen Blättern soll im verflossenen Jahre eine nicht unbeträchtliche Anzahl von Deutschen, welche nach Nordamerika ausgewandert waren, in die vormalige Heimath zurückgekehrt sein.

"Da die Nachrichten, welche hierüber sowohl von den amerikanischen Einschiffungs- als auch von den europäischen Landungsplätzen veröffentlicht wurden, nicht entnehmen lassen, ob und in welchem Umfange diese Rückwanderung auch nach Bayern stattgefunden hat, das unterfertigte Staatsministerium aber wünschen muss, in dieser Beziehung verlässigen Aufschluss zu erhalten: so wird die K. Regierung, K. d. J. beauftragt, Erhebungen darüber anzuordnen, wie viele aus dem Regierung-Bezirk ausgewanderte Familien und ledige Manns- und Frauenspersonen im Kalenderjahre 1855 aus Amerika zurückgekehrt sind?

"Hiebei ist zugleich zu ermitteln, wielange die zurückgekehrten in Amerika waren, in welchem Staate sie sich zuletzt aufhielten, welche Gründe sie zur Rückkehr bewogen, in welchen Vermögens- und Erwerbs-Verhältnissen sie anlangten, welche Reiselegitimation sie besassen, in welchem amerikanischen Hafen sie sich einschifften und in welchem europäischen Hafen die Landung erfolgte?"

The fascicle contains documents relating to the years 1855-1863, including important tabulated matter for 1858-1859 and 1859-1860.

M[inisterial] A[kten des Innern].

1064/1. Ch. geheimer Raths Act. Generalia. Auswanderungs Verbot de Ao. 1796 usq. 1804. This like most of the "Verbote" deals with emigration in general. Many papers relate to the confiscation of the property of emigrants, who left without the consent of the government. The papers are important for names of emigrants, as the question of the destination of the emigrant was of importance to the government.

1064/2. Acta das Verboth der Auswanderung nach Oesterreich während gegenwärtigen Kriegs betr. A large volume of papers bound in paper. 1796-1799.

1064/33. Geheime Raths-Acten K. Staats-Ministerium des Innern vom J. 1830. Betreff: Das Gesuch des Andreas Pirkl von Perlach um Bewilligung zur Auswanderung nach York in Oberkanada. 1830.

1064/131. Geheime Raths-Acten, etc., vom J. 1835. Exportation des Vermögens des Joseph Völker von Stetten, gegenwärtig zu Barrington in Nordamerika betreffd. Völker, born in Stetten 1774, emigrated 1789. His authorized agent, Melchior Zink of Stetten, gained a decision in his favor.

M. A. N. E.

561. Bureaux Akten des K. Staatsministeriums des Innern. München. Auswanderungsgesellschaft. Bundle of 15 papers, including a printed notice of the Münchener Auswanderungs-Gesellschaft (Jan. 1850). Important matter relating to this society. Feb. 27–Nov. 27, 1850.

1918. Tabellarische Uebersicht der Auswanderungen nach überseeischen Ländern in Kalenderjahre 1857.

1919. *Id.*, der Auswanderungen nach europäischen Ländern im Kalenderjahre 1857.

1920. *Id.*, der Rückwanderungen aus Nordamerica im Kalenderjahre 1857.

1921. *Id.*, der Einwanderungen im Kalenderjahre 1857.

1922. *Id.*, der Auswanderungen aus dem Königreiche Bayern im Kalenderjahre 1857.

AMBERG.
ROYAL BAVARIAN PROVINCIAL (CIRCUIT) ARCHIVES.
(KÖNIGLICHES KREISARCHIV.)

A very old and valuable collection dating back to 1437, and containing sixteen rooms filled with records, about 16,000 fascicles.

Hours: 8 to 12 and 2 to 4.30.

Zugang 86; Fasc. No. 1; Akt. No. 7. Acta des Königlichen Landgerichts Riedenburg. Uebersicht über die Auswanderungen nach Nordamerika, Oesterreich, Württemberg, etc. 1843-1861. Contains the following matter of importance:

Papers relating to statistical lists (Uebersichten) which are to be taken because of the increased importance of emigration to North America, and are to begin with the year 1842. The fascicle contains important lists of this character giving the names of emigrants from 1845 to 1846 and for the year 1854.

Zugang 51; Fasc. No. 2; Akt. No. 10. Akten über die jährlichen Verzeichnisse hinsichtlich der nach Nordamerika auswandernden Individuen. Ks. Landght. Wilseck. 1838-1848 (1860). Contains important lists of names of emigrants and data relating thereto, particularly the following:

Verzeichniss über die Ein- und Auswanderungen, welche sich seit der Errichtung des diesseitigen Landgerichtes ergeben haben. Königliches Landgericht Wilseck. Contains from 300 to 400 names.

Verzeichniss über die nach Nordamerika ausgewanderten Individuen pro 1841-42 bis 1845-46. Königliches Landgericht Wilseck. Contains 25 names.

Uebersicht der jährlichen Auswanderungen nach Nordamerika 1845-46 bis 1859-60. Contains 164 names.

Zugang 127; Fasc. 26; Akt. No. 312. Act. der K. B. Regierung der Oberpfalz und von Regensburg. Kammern des Innern. Die alljährliche Uebersicht über deutsche Auswanderung nach Nordamerika betrf. 1843-1852. Contains lists of emigrants such as the following:

Verzeichniss der aus dem Regierungs-Bezirke der Oberpfalz u. von Regensburg nach Nordamerika im Jahre 1842 ausgewanderten Individuen. This and the succeeding lists give the following information: " Vor- und Zuname | Stand | Heimathsort | Datum der erhaltenen Ausw. Bewilligung | Muthm. Grund der Auswanderung | Vorläufiges bez. Reiseziel | Eingeschlagener Weg | Besondere Bemerkungen ". In these lists the emigrant alone is counted and not the children who went with him. (20 names of emigrants in all.)

Uebersicht der aus dem Regierungs-Bezirk der Oberpfalz u. von Regensburg im Lauf des Jahres 1843 nach Nordamerika ausgewanderten Individuen. (46 names in all.)

Verzeichniss der aus dem Regierungs-Bezirke der Oberpfalz, etc., in Jahre 1844 ausgewanderten Individuen. (134 names.)

Verzeichniss, etc. 1844-1845. (330 names.)
Two short lists for the year 1845-1846.
Verzeichniss, etc. 1845-1846. (471 names.)
Id. 1846-1847. (365 names.)
Id. 1847-1848. (197 names.)
Id. 1848-1849. (145 names.)
Id. 1849-1850. (75 names.)
Id. 1850-1851. (146 names.)
Id. 1851-1852. (681 names.)
Akt. No. 313. Die jährlich zu erstattende Uebersicht über die bayerische Auswanderung. 1853 bis 1860/61. Contains statistical tables for the years 1853-1860, but is chiefly valuable as giving the numbers of the emigrants, not the names, while the papers accompanying these reports are often valuable for the individuals. One of the summaries will give an idea of the contents: Emigrants to European lands, 130; amount of property, 10,566 Fl.; emigrants to North America, 762; amount of property, 225,486¼ Fl.
Zugang 161; Akt. No. 1444. Akt. des Königlichen Landgerichts Neustadt a. W. Fascikl., Einzelne Gesuche und Verhandlungen um Reisepässe zum Wandern nach Amerika betr.
Akt. No. 1448. Generalia. Acta des Kgl. Landgerichts Weiden. Betreff: Uebersicht der Auswanderungen nach Nordamerika; dann Einwanderungen in das Königr. Bayern; hier den Rechenschaftsbericht. 1843-1861. Contains written reports and the following " Uebersichten ":
Uebersicht der Auswanderer im Jahre 1843-44. Königliches Landgericht Weiden. The report includes the following rubrics: Name and former residence | calling | property | presumable reason for emigrating | land to which the emigrant is going.
Uebersicht der Auswanderer im Jahre 1844-45. (34 names.)
Uebersicht der beim Königl. Landgerichte zu Weiden im Etatsjahre 1845-46 vorgekommenen Auswanderungen nach Nordamerica. (11 names.)
Id. 1846-1847. (4 names.)
Id. 1847-1848. (8 names.)
Id. 1848-1849. (10 names.)
Tabellarische Uebersichten for the later years give only the figures without the names of the emigrants.
Akt. No. 1467. Auswanderung nach Nordamerika der Johann Georg Sauerschen Eheleute von Irchenreuth betrf. 1845. A very interesting and characteristic bundle of 17 papers, illustrating the complications often encountered by the emigrant in quitting his native land.
Akt. No. 1468. Acta des Königlichen Landgerichts Weiden. Auswanderung nach Nordamerika der Rösch, Andreas, Oekonomiebürgers, Eheleute von Kaltenbrunn und der Trötsch, Katharine, ledig, von dort. 1845-1847.
Akt. No. 1469. Auswanderung nach Nordamerika des Dobner, Wolfgang, Schneidermeister von Kaltenbrunn. 1845-1853. (A bundle of 25 to 30 papers.)

Amberg

Akt. No. 1472. Das Auswanderungsgesuch des Johann Adam Schwabenländer von Mantl und dessen Eheweib Anna Sabeia und deren 3 minderjährigen Kinder nach Nordamerika betrd. 1848-1854.
Akt. No. 1474. Act des Königl. Bayer. Landgerichts Neustadt a. d. W. Auswanderung des Bernhard Wittmann von Flossenburg und der Müllerstochter Anna Maria Maierhöfer von Gailertsreuth.
Zugang 165; Akt. No. 46, 57, 76, 77, 78, 79, 80, 81, 82, 83, 84, 85, 86, 87, 88, 89, 90, 91, 92, 93, 94, 95, 96, 97, 98, 99, 100, 101, 102, 103, 104, 105, 106, 107, 107, 108, 109, 110, 111, 112, 116, 117, 118, 119, 120, 121, 122, 123, 124, 125, 126, 127, 128, 129, 130, 131, 132, 133, 134, 135, 137, 138, 139, 140, 142, 145, 145, 146, 147, 148, 149, 150, 151, 152, 153, 154, 155, 156, 157, 158, 159, 160, 161, 162, 164, 165, 166, 167, 168, 169.

BAMBERG.
ROYAL BAVARIAN PROVINCIAL (CIRCUIT) ARCHIVES.
(KÖNIGLICH BAYERISCHES KREISARCHIV.)

Located Hain-Soden-Strasse, in a fine new but low building in one end of which the director resides. The collection embraces the old archives of the prince-bishops of Bamberg and of the princes of Anspach-Bayreuth, as well as the modern Bavarian papers. It contains 70,000-80,000 documents from the year 1097 on, several hundred codices, departmental and fief books, state papers, and other manuscripts from 1154 on to the present.

Hours: 8 to 4.

L. 595. Fasc. 1. N. Schränke.
A. 2. Subsidien-Tractat mit Gross Brittanien d. a. 1777.
Copia vidimata des Tractats über die den 1. Februarii 1777 in Königl. Gross-Brittanischen Sold zum Dienst in America überlassene 2 Regimenter Infanterie nebst einer Compagnie Jäger. Anspach, Aug. 13, 1778. This contract between the King of Great Britain and the Margrave of Brandenburg-Anspach and Bayreuth contains 14 articles in French. The copy is certified and has the grand seal of the privy council of the margrave.

Copia de Copia vidimata des Tractats über die den 1. Februarii 1777 in Königl. Gross Brittanischen Sold zum Dienst in America überlassene 2 Regimenter Infanterie nebst einer Compagnie Jäger. Anspach, Aug. 13, 1778. (French.) This document like the preceding has this date: " Faite à Anspach ce 1. Fevrier 1777 ", and is signed by William Faucitt and Charles de Gemmingen. Then follows this note in German: " Vorstehende Abschrift ist von dem im Plassenburgischen geheimen Archiv verwahrten Onolsbachischen Original-Vidimus getreulich genommen und mit solchem aufmerksamst collationirt worden. Bayreuth den 26 May 1777. In fidem Philipp Ernst Spiess ".

A. 3. Acta die in Königl. Grossbrittan. Sold nach America überlassene Hochfürstl. Brandenburg. Kriegs-Völker betr. d. a. 1777. folg. 16 Produkte. Contains the following papers:

Foll. 1-5. Klagelied eines deutschen Biedermannes im Jahre 1776. Two pages of introduction and then a German poem, in eight seven-line strophes, entitled, " Abschiedsgedanken von einem Grenadier zu Bayreuth den 28. Februar 1777 ", and another poem in German in eight six-line strophes entitled, " Abschieds-Lied von einem Jäger, 1777 ".

Fol. 6. List of troops reviewed Mar. 25, 1777.

Fol. 8. Extract aus dem 54 Stück der *Hamburger Zeitung* de anno 1777.

Fol. 10. Interesting German letter written by Hoffman to a Regierungs Rath. 6 pp. Philadelphia, Jan. 19, 1778.

Fol. 13. Notes and extracts concerning soldiers taken captive. Oct. 21, 1781.

Fol. 14. Report from a Holland paper of Dec., 1781, stating that two days after the capitulation the Anspach troops, officers and men, offered their services to Lauzun, but that the duke replied that they belonged to the Americans and he could not give them over to French service without the consent of his master the king and of Congress.

Fol. 15. A curious printed decree dated Onolsbach [=Anspach], Dec. 21, 1781, prohibiting with penalty the passing of unwarranted censure on the capture of the " Hochfürstl. Regimenter in America ".

Fol. 17. Printed order from the Chamber in Bayreuth, containing orders of the margrave issued to all the districts touching the following points: Fornication, entering foreign military service, settling and marrying in the native land. 1783.

Fol. 19-24. Geschichte aus dem Bayreuthischen neuen Zeitungs-Calander de ao. 1778 die in Englischen Sold nach America abgegangene 2 Hochfürstl. Brandenburg. Regimenter, nebst dem dazu gehörigen Jäger Corps betr. A very important official account of the motives for sending mercenaries to aid the English—the Protestant cause protected by George II., the relations of Germany to the ruling house in England, etc.

Foll. 73-75 give a very interesting description of Washington.

Fol. 79-110 contains extracts from various German newspapers in the years 1777-1783.

Fol. 79. *Erlanger Real-Zeitung*, Num. 20, Mar. 11, 1777.

Fol. 80 et seq. *Bayreuther Zeitungen*, Num. 50, Mar. 1, 1777; Num. 53, Apr. 22, 1777; Num. 60, May 20, 1777, containing lists of the troops who embark.

Fol. 90. A pen sketch of two American soldiers labelled " Americaner Soldat ".

Fol. 109-110. Auf die Zurückkunft der Anspacher Truppen aus Amerika den 18. Nov. 1783. (A German poem of 10 eight-line strophes.)

Fol. 112. Extrait d'une Gazette Angloise.

Fol. 113. A German poem of 5 four-line strophes by Regierungs-Rath Petermann of Bayreuth.

Fol. 114. Morgen-Gesang eines Anspachischen Offiziers in Amerika vor einer Schlacht. (6 four-lined strophes.) Gesang nach der Schlacht. (9 four-lined strophes; *cf. Bayreuther Zeitung*, no. 143, Nov. 30, 1780.)

Rep. 168. Vrz. 16. No. 1-5. Statistische Tabellen von Gemeinden des K. Bezirksamtes Bayreuth über Ein- und Auswanderungen. 1890-1893.

Rep. 27. No. 95. 246/15. Die Handelsverhältnisse mit der Republik Buenos Ayres betr. 1856.

Verzeichniss derjenigen Artikel, welche nach Angabe des General-Consuls der Republik Buenos Ayres für Bayern F. Dessauer zu Aschaffenburg in Buenos Ayres sehr gangbar und coulant zu verwerthen sind.

Fach No. 19. Acta des Königl. Bezirksamts Stadtsteinach.
  Akt. No. 119, 121, 122, 123, 124, 126, 127, 128, 130, 131, 132, 133, 134, 137, 138, 140, 143, 144, 147, 148, 150, 151, 152, 153, 154, 155, 156, 157, 158, 159, 163, 167, 169, 170, 171, 172, 173, 174, 175, 176, 177, 178, 180, 181, 182, 183, 184, 185, 186, 188, 189, 190, 191, 193, 194, 195, 197, 198, 201, 202, 203, each number relating to an emigrant between the years 1865 and 1869.

LANDSHUT.
ROYAL BAVARIAN PROVINCIAL (CIRCUIT) ARCHIVES.
(KÖNIGLICH BAYERISCHES KREISARCHIV.)

Located in the royal castle Trausnitz, which, like the city of Landshut itself, is a well-preserved monument of the great German past. Contains over 3000 documents, 400 codices, and 23 rooms full of state papers.
Hours: Mar. 1–Nov. 1, 8 to 12, 3 to 5; Nov. 1–Mar. 1, 8.30 to 12, 2 to 4. Saturdays during the morning hours only.

Rep. **XXVII d.** Fasc. **107.** Ein- und Auswanderungen nebst Vermögens In- und Exportation. 1833. A statistical report giving the numbers of emigrants to various countries. 4982 went with permission, 1342 without. 4883 went to America. Of these 4000 were from the Rheinkreis.
    Ein- und Auswanderungen, etc. 1834.
    Ein- und Auswanderungen, etc. 1835.

Rep. **XCVII a.** Verz. III.
- Fasc. **1.** No. **45.** Landgericht Abensberg. 1814-1846. Contains requests of subjects for permission to emigrate to America and other lands. The papers relating to America are scattered through the bundle.
- Fasc. **2.** No. **46.** Landgericht Bogen. 1841-1846.
  - No. **47.** Landgericht Deggendorf. 1815-1846.
  - No. **48.** Landgericht Dingolfing. 1845-1846.
  - No. **49.** Landgericht Eggenfelden. 1811-1846.
- Fasc. **3.** No. **50.** Landgericht Grafenau. 1815-1846.
  - No. **51.** Landgericht Griesbach. 1819-1846.
  - No. **52.** Landgericht Hengersburg. 1839-1846.
  - No. **53.** Landgericht Kehlheim. 1811-1846.
- Fasc. **4.** No. **54.** Landgericht Kötzting. 1818-1846.
  - No. **55.** Landgericht Landau. 1813-1846.
  - No. **56.** Landgericht Landshut. 1820-1846.
  - No. **57.** Magistrat Landshut. 1817-1846.
  - No. **58.** Landgericht Mallersdorf. 1817-1846.
- Fasc. **5.** No. **59.** Landgericht Mitterfels. 1808-1846.
  - No. **60.** Landgericht Osterhofen. 1840-1846.
  - No. **61.** Landgericht Passau II. 1840-1845.
  - No. **62.** Landgericht Passau I. 1842-1846.
  - No. **63.** Landgericht Passau. 1814-1837.
- Fasc. **6.** No. **64.** Stadtmagistrat Passau. 1817-1844.
  - No. **65.** Landgericht Pfarrkirchen. 1817-1846.
- Fasc. **7.** No. **66.** Landgericht Regen. 1814-1845.
  - No. **67.** Landgericht Rottenburg. 1842-1846.
  - No. **68.** Landgericht Rotthalmünster. 1840-1846.
  - No. **69.** Landgericht Simbach. 1818-1846.
  - No. **70.** Landgericht Straubing. 1811-1846.

Fasc. 8. No. 71. Stadtmagistrat Straubing. 1808-1846.
No. 72. Landgericht Viechtach. 1817-1846.
No. 73. Landgericht Vilsbiburg. 1824-1846.
No. 74. Landgericht Vilshofen. 1819-1846.
Fasc. 9. No. 75. Landgericht Wegscheid. 1815-1845.
No. 76. Landgericht Wegscheid. 1821-1838.
Fasc. 10. No. 77. Landgericht Wolfstein. 1815-1846.
No. 78. Herrschaftsgericht Zeitskofen. 1815-1833.

NEUBURG.
ROYAL BAVARIAN PROVINCIAL (CIRCUIT) ARCHIVES.
(KÖNIGLICH BAYERISCHES KREISARCHIV.)

These archives, housed in the west wing of the castle, comprise, besides modern Bavarian documents, the old archives of the principality of Pfalz-Neuburg, of the diocese of Augsburg, and of many Swabian free cities and other jurisdictions.

A. B. Fasc. 29/09. Die Bayerischen Auswanderungen betfd.; dann Einwanderung, Auswanderung nach Amerika. 1853-1861. Fascicle of papers of various character, containing among other things:

A ministerial rescript prescribing that at the end of each calendar year beginning with 1853 reports shall be made, in accordance with the enclosed blanks, of those who have emigrated in that year. Augsburg, Nov. 21, 1853.

Tabellarische Uebersicht der Auswanderungen nach überseeischen Ländern aus dem K. Landgerichts Bezirke Burgau im Kalender-Jahre 1853.

Papers relating to the immigration and emigration down to the year 1860.

A paper dated Nov. 7, 1856, relates to statistical tables of the Israelites, explaining that although the immigration of Jews was prohibited by the edict of June 10, 1813, in the West Rhenish provinces yet the conferring of citizenship by royal decree upon foreigners is not excluded. The document states that, "die Zahl der aus Nordamerika zurückgekehrten vormals bayerischen Unterthanen nicht unbeträchtlich ist, und angenommen werden darf, dass diese Rückwanderungen vorerst in erheblichem Maase noch fortdauern werden; von jenen Zurückgekehrten aber, welche die Naturalisation in Amerika erworben haben, ohne Zweifel eine nicht geringe Zahl das bayerische Indigenat durch Ansässigmachung wieder erwerben wird".

Another paper gives these particulars as required of those who returned from America: "Wielange und in welchem Staate er in Nordamerika sich aufgehalten hat, welche Gründe ihn zur Rückkehr bewogen, welche Reiselegitimation er besass, in welchem amerikanischen Hafen die Einschiffung und in welchem europäischen Hafen die Landung erfolgte, endlich in welcher Weise die Staatsangehörigkeits- und Heimathsfrage geregelt werde".

Zusammenstellung der erlassenen Verordnungen bezüglich der Auswanderung nach Nordamerika. Augsburg, Aug. 25, 1856. The 14 points in question are:

1. Data to be taken with respect to sex.
2. The emigrant is to be instructed and warned in regard to the danger, in accordance with the rescript of June 17, 1846, Nr. 28,063.

3. Age, state of family, birth, etc.
4. Statement of the amount of property.
5. Military certificate.
6. Publication of the case, in accordance with the edict, in the official record of the district or in the local papers.
7. Name of the agent with whom sailing is taken.
8. Special method of hastening departure.
9. Military and other credentials in particular.
10. Regulation of marriage in the foreign land, according to the rescript of July 12, 1808.
11. Passes.
12. Special particulars relating to passes.
13. Stamp tax.
14. Request for passes to North America are to be made in accordance with the regulation of June 27, 1850, Nr. 12,853.

Tabellarische Uebersicht der Auswanderungen nach überseeischen Ländern aus dem K. Landsgerichts Bezirke Burgau im Kalender Jahr 1856. Contains among other papers:
A model pass form.
Paper relating to emigration to Brazil. Burgau, July 24, 1858.
Papers relating to Johann Bader of Wettenhausen and his permission to emigrate.
Tabellarische Uebersicht d. Ausw. nach Europ. Ländern aus d. K. Landgerichts-Bezirke Burgau im Kal. Jahr 1857.
Tabellarische Uebersicht der Einwanderungen in den Reg-Bez. von Schwaben u. Neuburg im K.-J. 1857.
Rückwand. aus N. Amerika. 1858.
Verzeichniss der Ein- u. Ausw. während dem Laufe des Jahres 1844-1845. Contains a list of some 80 emigrants to America with very full particulars of each individual, giving even the amount of money each possessed.

NUREMBERG.
ROYAL BAVARIAN PROVINCIAL (CIRCUIT) ARCHIVES.
(KÖNIGLICH BAYERISCHES KREISARCHIV.)

Located in Archivstrasse. Entrance at the rear of the building from the court. The archives are those of the old imperial free city of Nuremberg, together with those of many lesser jurisdictions.[1]

193/19. (Ansbach, Bezirksamt), Acta, Verordnungen über die Judenaufnahme, Judenschutzbriefe und Schutzgelder enthaltend. 1582-1738.

193/38. Acta des Landesgerichts Ansbach, die jüdischen Glaubensgenossen (Judenschutz, Beschäftigung, Aufsicht, Matrikel, etc.) betreffend. 1807-1873. (Sundry papers are found in Fasc. 197 for Dinkelsbühl and other places.)

193/57. Acta des Kameralamts Colmberg, die Verfassung der Judengemeinden, Name, Beruf der Vorsteher derselben betreffend. 1804-1805.

193/87. Ordnung und Formalien, welche bei Abschwörung des Judeneides in der Synagoge zu beobachten. 1747.

195 a. Cadolzburg Amtsgericht. Fürstlich Brandenburg allgemeine Ausschreiben und Verordnungen, nach alphabetischer Ordnung. (*Cf.* 191. J. 12-200. Z. 21. 1685-1755.)

197/656. Topographische Beschreibungen des Königl. Landgerichts Dinkelsbühl. 1809-1827. (Enthält die bezüglichen Aufzeichnungen nach den einzelnen Gemeinden nach dem Stand von 1809 bis 1827.)

197/661. Statistische Erhebungen über die Bevölkerung. 1852. (Enthält die Tabellen der Geburten, Trauungen, Sterbefälle, Ein- und Auswanderungen pro 1844-5 bis 1850-1.)

197/663. *Id.*, 1857, for the years 1851-2–1855-6.

197/664. *Id.*, 1858, for the years 1856-7–1857-8.

197/665. *Id.*, 1859, for the year 1858-9.

197/666. *Id.*, 1860-1, for the years 1859-60 and 1860-1.

197/667. Erstattung der Jahresberichte pro 1808-9 bis 1831-2. 3 Akten 1809-1832. (Enthält diese Jahresberichte mit Tabellen über Bewegung der Bevölkerung, etc.)

197/668-671. Same 1833-44 for years 1830-1844.

197/973. Zunftbuch der Metzger in Weiltingen. 1712.

197/974. Zunftbuch der Schneider. 1730.

197/975. Zunftbuch der Leinweber. 1750.

197/976. Zunftbuch der Schuhmacher. 1668.

197 c. Dinkelsbühl Königl. Bezirksamt. Fach No. 58. Ein- und Auswanderungen.

2606. Ein- und Auswanderungen. 1824. (Veraltete Entschliessungen im bezeichneten Betreffe.)

2607. *Id.*

---

[1] Valuable collections bearing upon Nuremberg history are also to be found in the city archives (Stadtarchiv); hours, 9-12, 3-5.

2608. Auswanderungsgesuche nach Nordamerika pro 1853. This is a most important fascicle of papers relating to emigrants to America. It includes:
1. Verzeichniss der im Jahre 1853/54 nach Amerika Ausgewanderten oder mittels Reisepass Abgereisten: Vor- und Zuname, Stand, Alter, Wohnort, also the amount of money. 126 names in all.
2. The official " Gesuche " and papers relating thereto.
201. Feuchtwangen Königl. Bezirksamt. Fach 82.
1641. Akt. 1114. Auswanderungsgesuch des Nathan Holzinger nach Amerika (the following numbers give separate names as here indicated). 1867.
1642. Akt. 1115. Nach Amerika. 1867.
1646. Akt. 1119. Id.
1652. Akt. 1125. Id.
1663. Akt. 1136. Nach Amerika. 1868.
1673. Akt. 1146. Id.
1674. Akt. 1147. Nach Amerika. 1868-73.
202/100. Acta Generalia des Königl. Landgerichts Kadolzburg, mit Tabellen über Ein- und Auswanderungen und Vermögens Importationen. 1808-1819.
202/101. Ein Band dergleichen Acta über Ein- und Auswanderungen, die Verordnungen gegen unerlaubte Auswanderungen, Untauglichkeitsnachweise Militärpflichtiger, Freizügigkeit mit Baden, Oesterreich, etc., Nachsteuer- und Abgangs-freiheit zwischen den deutschen Bruderstaaten, gesetzwidrige Werbungen zur Auswanderung, etc., betreffend. 1810-1849.
202/105. Acta Generalia des Königl. Landgerichts Cadolsburg. Aus- und Einwanderungen und deshalb zu erstattende Berichte betreffend. Mit Tabellen. 1819-1833.
202/333. Auswanderungssachen betreffend. 1836.
209. Hipoltstein II. Königl. Bezirksamt.
162. Akta die französische Immigration betreffend. 1794-1804. There were also nos. 23-30 entitled: Verschiedene Generalien 1793-1803, and no. 33: Zusammenstellung der Verordnungen von 1799 an bis 1832.
215. Neustadt a. A. Königl. Bezirksamt.
164. Acta des Königl. Landgerichts Markt Erlbach. Auswanderung nach Brasilien, Algier, etc. 1826. Verordnung dated Ansbach, May 10, 1826, issued from the Kammer des Innern, repudiating the authenticity of Major Schäffer's representations of the advantages in Brazil, and summarizing in a most enlightening manner the conditions under which settlers had to take up land and the disadvantages accompanying the emigrant thither, as the following passage shows: "Dass Familien auf freie Ueberfahrt sich keine Rechnung machen können, unverheirathete Mannspersonen unter 32 Jahren dieselben aber nur dann erhalten, wenn sie sich *unbedingt* dem Dienste des Kaisers ergeben wollen ".
737-758. Ein- und Auswanderungsgesuche. 1853-1857. The number of papers in each fascicle is given in the manuscript cata-

logue. These papers are more specifically listed in the Repertorium, which gives for example under 737:

"A^{II} d. B.
No. 102 bis 108} Ein- und Auswanderungsgesuche. 1857-1860."

An occasional document under other rubrics as nos. 779, 783, 787, 789, and others under "Religiöse Sekten", 1828-1848, relating to the revolutionary disturbances, also reflects light on the emigration, especially nos. 825-830 on the censorship and the press. (*Cf.* also Polizei.)

220. Rothenburg o. T. Königl. Bezirksamt. Staatsrechtliche Gegenstände.
  992-1035. Each of these numbers is a thin separate Heft in pasteboard, and each refers to an emigrant.
222. Schwabach Königl. Bezirksamt.
  863-946.

The following also have occasional references to emigrants to America:
198. Eichstädt Bezirksamt.
200. Erlangen Bezirksamt.
195. Cadolsburg Königl. Rentamt.
192 a. Altdorf Königl. Rentamt.
206, 206 a, 222. Heilsbronn Königl. Bezirksamt.

SPEYER.
ROYAL BAVARIAN PROVINCIAL (CIRCUIT) ARCHIVES OF THE PALATINATE.
(KÖNIGLICH BAYERISCHES KREISARCHIV DER PFALZ.)

Archive material of the Electoral Palatinate, of Pfalz-Zweibrücken, the bishoprics of Speyer and Worms, etc.[1]

Bestand Kurpfalz. Rep. 1. No. 35[1]. Lagerort 1/1. Acta Generalia betr. Ein- und Auswanderungen, auch Bürger-Annahmen. 1685-1779.

Edict of the Elector Palatine Charles II., giving freedom to the inhabitants of "Altzey, Odernheim, Pfeddersheim, Freinsheim; in den Flecken, Dalsheim, Osthofen, Westhofen, Altheim am Alt Rhein, Pfiffligheim, Rheintürkheim, Armsheim, Altzheim bey Gronau, Edingkoven, Edigkeim, Epstein, Friedelsheim, Lobloch, Ormsheim und Schauernheim", from "Wildfang und Leibeigenschaft". (Print. Heidelberg, Feb. 16, 1685.)

Edict of the Elector Palatine Charles III. Philip, prescribing "dass keine frembde, welche nicht anvorderist ihres untadelhaften Wandels und Aufführens gehörig und genugsame Zeugnuss und Legitimation vorbringen, mithin dass selbige wenigstens einhundert Rthlr. baaren Gelds in eigenem Vermögen haben, eydlich darthun können", etc. Mannheim, Apr. 8, 1727. (Print.)

Regulations concerning taxes. Mannheim, Dec. 19, 1738. (Print.)

Edict of the Elector Palatine's government, Mannheim, June 21, 1752. An important document having special reference to America, as the first part will show: "Man hat eine geraume Zeit hero mit besonderem Missvergnügen wahrnehmen müssen, wie dass viele hiesigen Chur-Pfältzischen Unterthanen aus hiesigen Chur-Pfältzischen Landen nacher Pennsylvanien und sonstigen Americanischen Provintzen, wie auch nacher anderen weit entlegenen frembden Landen, von sicheren abgeschickten oder aus solchen Landen zurückkommenden Personen unterm Vorwand der zu besorgen habenden Geschäfften und Besuchung ihrer Anverwandten uder sonsten ausgekünstelten Vorspiegelungen durch verkehrtes Anbringen zu deren augenscheinlichen Schaden auch gemeiniglich darauf erfolgenden eigenen grössten Leidwesen ohnerlaubterweis verführet werden", etc.

Order relating to the right of citizenship in the duchies Neuburg and Sulzbach. Dec., 1753. (Print.)

Order placing a threefold penalty upon those who sell their property before obtaining "Manumissionsscheine, oder venia emigrandi". Mannheim, Mar. 4, 1760.

Rescript enforcing the observance of the rescript of Mar. 3 "und wie übrigens in dem Kayserlichen *Reichs-Post-Zeitungs Blatt* Nro. 147, unter dem Articul London vom 4ten Septembris lauffenden Jahres eine rührende Beschreibung des Erbarmnus würdigen Zustands einer Anzahl von 600 armer unglück-

---
[1] Local material of value is deposited in the archives of the city of Speyer.

licher Personen, Männer, Weiber und Kinder, eingeflossen ist, die ein sicherer Officier unter allehand blendenden Vorspiegelungen, sonderheitlich, dass Sie auf seine Kosten nach America in die daselbst von ihme anzulegende Pflanzung überbringen wolte, aus ihrem teutschen Vaterland gezogen, nachgehends in der Gegend von London, in einem Land dessen Sprache sie nicht kundig, ohne alle Hülfe verlassen, so dass deren viele, bey damahls eingefallenen starcken Regen-Wetter hungerig, bloss ohne Dach und Fach im Feld herumgeirret, andere unter gehäufften Krankheiten, und in dem Jammer vollesten Zustand geschmachtet, bey 200 aber, wegen nicht bezahlter Fracht, auf denen Schiffen, mit welchen sie angekommen, dem Hunger, Ungezieffer, und Unflath, mithin gewissen Verderb ausgesetzet verbleiben müssen". Mannheim, Nov. 27, 1764. (Printed.)

Rescript stating that so many of the serving class have emigrated that there is great lack of servants. Mannheim, Mar. 3, 1764. (Printed.)

Rescript dated Mannheim, Sept. 18, 1765, removing the expense and inconvenience encountered by those who wanted to become "Bürger und Beysassen" and showing incidentally how difficult it was to obtain reliable certificates of baptism, and that the certificates of citizenship were sometimes obtained by foreign and unknown ship agents. The rescript is printed and refers to previous rescripts of the following dates: Feb. 5, 1753; Nov. 3, 1759; Nov. 7, 1760; Jan. 23, 1762; Aug. 26, 1763; Feb. 1, 1764; Jan. 30 and Feb. 13, 1765.

Rescript specifying the conditions of citizenship for various classes of subjects, native and foreign born. Mannheim, Aug. 13, 1771. (Printed.)

Similar rescripts of Dec. 22, 1772, and Aug. 30, 1775.

Copies of letters addressed to the Elector Palatine by Oberdorff. Mannheim, Jan. 7 and Aug. 7, 1778.

Paper addressed to the elector, relating to duties imposed upon those who have emigrated to Hungary. Mannheim, Apr. 21, 1746.

Paper relating to emigrants who have returned from the "Neues Land" and have become a burden to the village communities, and prescribing that they shall be put into military service. Schwetzingen, May 29, 1764.

The remaining papers of the fascicle relate to emigration in general, or to emigrants to Galicia, etc.

WÜRZBURG.
CIRCUIT ARCHIVES OF LOWER FRANCONIA AND ASCHAFFENBURG.
(Kreisarchiv für Unterfranken und Aschaffenburg.)
Located in the left wing of the Royal Castle. Contains, among other things, the old archives of the prince-bishops of Würzburg and the electors of Mainz.

Hours: Daily from 8 to 4.

His. Saal **VII**. Fasc. 11. **N.** 171, und Misc. 4391. (Formerly D 74 a.) Acten der Würzburger geh. Kanzlei betr. den Subsidienvertrag mit Hannover. Darunter, Erlasse des Königs Georg von England, 1755, 1756.

N. 172, 174. Politische Zeitungen, etc., and other matter relating to the Würzburg troops. Possibly some reference to the French and Indian War, but not very likely.

Fach **49**, nun **59**, **N. 32**. Akt des Kgl. Kreisarchives Würzburg. Guinea bezw. Guiana (called Cayenne in the Acta), Colonisationsproject der Katholischen Fürsten, namentlich der Kurfürsten von Mainz und Bayern. 1660-1670. The following " Acta sub lege remissa " relating to the colony are noted as being deposited in the Reichsarchiv in Munich:

1. Schreiben des französischen Ministers Colbert an den Kurfürsten von Mainz. Paris, Oct. 21, 1665. (German translation ?).
2. Vertragsprojekt über Kolonisation mit den Gegenbemerkungen Frankreichs, bezw. der westindischen Compagnie. (French.)
3. Schreiben des Joh. Daniel Crafft (vermutlich Kurmainzischen Gesandten in Paris und an einen Beyerischen Beamten gerichtet) über das Projekt. Mainz, Dec. 7, 1665.

These three acta are noted as belonging (1882) to a group of unordered papers and have the nos. 6, 7, 8, respectively. It is possible that other papers exist, relating to the same subject.

Another plan of colonization connected with this was the project of Count Friedrich Kasimir of Hanau. The Reichsarchiv in Munich contains also " sub lege remissionis " among the " Fürstensachen " an act with the following title: " Ihre Hochgrävl. Gnaden Herrn Friedrichs Casemirn Gravens zu Hanau Vorhaben undt Reysse nacher Westindien betr." 1669. This document contains the draft of a number of letters to the count concerning the plan from the year 1669 and 1670, written doubtless by his brother-in-law, the last count Palatine of Veldenz, Lauterecken, and Lützelstein—Leopold Ludwig (died 1694). Contains 6 sheets in all and a " Denkschrift " entitled:

"Gründlicher Bericht von Beschaffenheit.... dess in America.... in der Landschaft Guiana gelegenen Strich Landes, welchen die Edle priviligirte West-Indische Compagnie der vereinigten Niederlanden.... an den.... Herrn Friedrich Casimir, Grafen zu Hanauw.... cedirt und über lassen hat.... 54 pp. Frankfurt, 1669.

Militärsachen No. 95. (Formerly Fasc. 5 of No. 33.) A fascicle of 64 papers relating to the passage of the Anspach troops on their way to Great Britain in 1777. Among the papers are the following:

Letter of notification sent by Friedrich Carl Alexander, margrave of Brandenburg, etc., to Adam Friedrich, bishop of Bamberg and Würzburg, with the following: "Wir haben Ihro Gros Britanische Majestät, zu Höchst Jhro Dienst, ein Corps Unserer Trouppes von 1200 Mann, mit Innbegrif einer Compagnie Jäger, in Sold überlassen, welches zu Anfang des nechst kommenden Monaths März auf dem Mayn eingeschifft, und zu Wasser an den Ort seiner Bestimmung gebracht werden solle". Then follows the request that the troops with their equipments be allowed to pass " Zoll Mauth auch sonstiger Abgaben frei " and be granted the privilege to purchase " Naturalien " for the journey. Onolsbach [=Anspach], Feb. 3, 1777.

The protocol and the resolution of the Camera. Feb. 13, 1777.

Letter addressed to the " Hofkriegs Rath ".

Die Bewirthung deren durch das Fürstl. Würtzburg nacher America passirenden Fürstl. Anspach. General Staabs und Capitains betr.

Letter of Franz von Gebsattel to the Reichs Fürst, asking for more information as to the time when the troops will be embarked at Ochsenfurth. Würzburg, Feb. 27, 1777.

Actum in consilio bellico. Würzburg, Feb. 27, 1777.

Letter from von Hygle to the bishop, giving an account of the situation at Uffenheim. Uffenheim, Mar. 8, 1777.

Similar reports relating to the passage of the troops at other points.

Letter of Baron von Stetten, stating that the margrave has sent a " Douceur " of 100 Gulden to the hussars, who escorted the troops to Würzburg. Mar. 11, 1777.

Letter of recognition sent by the margrave to the bishop, thanking the latter for the attention and friendly escort, " jene gantz ausserordentliche Gewogenheit und Attentionen ", given the troops.

Special distinction accorded to certain officers by the margrave.

French letter of M. De Cressener ministre plénipot[re] de sa M. B. aux Électeurs de Mayence, Treves, Cologne, et au Cercle de Westphalie, etc., thanking the Bishop of Würzburg for his assistance. Bonn, Apr. 15, 1777.

French reply to this communication stating that it was the bishop's friendship for the margrave which prompted the friendly service.

Group of similar papers relating to the passage of supplementary troops through the Würzburg territory. Dec., 1778.
Papers relating to the passage of further troops, 40 Jäger and 180 infantry. Jan., 1781.
Request of the margrave for the passage of 260 Jäger recruits. Feb., 1782.

No. 96. (Formerly Fasc. 5 of No. 33.) Anspach Troupen. Derselben Durchmarsch durch die Würzburg. Lande (to the Netherlands, Mar., Apr., May, 1778, Jan., 1779). Contains 14 papers that have apparently only indirect bearing upon America.

No. 97. (Formerly Fasc. 5 of No. 33.) Geistliche Regierung, den zum Fürstl. Anspachischen nacher Engelland abgegangenen Troupen Transport für die darunter befindliche Catholiquen abgegebenen Exjesuiten Priester Piret (Pirett in the German documents) betr. 1777. Contains 11 papers relating to the appointment of the ex-Jesuit priest, Franz Piret, as " Feld Caplan der unter Meinen in Grossbrittanischen Sold überlassenen Trouppes befindlichen Mannschafft, Catholischer Religion ". The papers consist of the following:

Copy of a letter of the margrave addressed to Gebsattel, announcing Piret's appointment and ordering him to be ready to sail on the transport-ship on the 9th inst. Onolsbach, Mar. 2, 1777.
Letters from the Archbishop of Cologne in Latin.
Letter of Alexander to the Bishop of Bamberg, acknowledging his consent to the appointment of Piret. (Affords a good example of the baroque official German style of the time.)

No. 98. (Formerly Fasc. 5 of No. 34.) Bericht des Generals von Stetten verschiedene kriegerische Nachrichten von Amerika betr. 1777, 1778. Contains 3 papers in all:

Letter addressed to the Reichsfürst reporting that the Imperial Minister von Erthal has passed out the Sanderthor, etc., and that " schriftliche Americanische Nachrichten seind mir von meinem gewesenen Herrn Land Commendeur Grafen von Isenburg mit heutiger Post zugeschickt worden ". Würzburg, Oct. 1, 1777.
Paper requesting more particular information from the general respecting events in America. Bamberg, Oct. 5, 1777.
Letter of Ysenbourg to the Reichsfürst. Jan. 1, 1778.

G(eneralia) 149. Act des Rentamts Römershag. Nachsteuer u. Abzugsfreiheit (Freizügigkeit). 1804-1838.

G. 1081. Bezirksamt Karlstadt V. Thuengen. Aus- und Einwanderung. 1808-1815.

G. 1410. (Des Fürstlich Leiningschen Herrschaftsgerichts Amorbach Administrativ-Akten.) Betr. Aus- und Einwanderungen, Vermögens Aus- und Einführungen, Nachsteuer, Generalia. 1786-1855. A very thick volume with the following contents:
A. Kur-Mainzer Verordnungen. 1786-1802.
B. Fürstl. Leiningische Verordnungen. 1803-1810.
C. Grossherzogl. Hessische Verordnungen. 1807-1815.
E. Königl. Bayrische Verordnungen. 1816-1855.

Important material for the history of the action of the government on the question of emigration. Among the *acta* of special importance for the emigration to America are the following:

Rescripts referring to the emigration of 1709 and dealing with the question of " Freizügigkeit ".

Auswanderungen nach Brasilien betr. Würzburg, Feb. 5, 1824.

Geheime Werbungen für Brasilien betr. Würzburg, May 30, 1824.

Das Auswandern nach Brasilien betr. Würzburg, June 16, 1825.

Das Auswandern nach Brasilien betr. Apr. 20, 1826.

Auswanderung nach Brasilien betr. Würzburg, May 4, 1826.

Die Auswanderungen und Vermögensexport nach d. nordam. Staaten betr. May 12, 1832.

Auswanderungen nach Frankreich betr. Apr. 26, 1832, *et seq.*

Die Auswanderungen u. Vermögensexp. nach d. Nordam. Staaten betr. May 12, 1832.

Auswanderung mehrerer Familien nach Amerika. Würzburg, Dec. 26, 1832, *et seq.*

Auswanderungen nach Nordamerika betr. Dec. 18, 1839.

Verordnung. Nov. 11, 1840.

Verordnung relating to Fichtel and Brandes. Dec. 10, 1841.

Verordnung relating to Rodolf (Rudolf) and Texas. Mar. 11, 1842.

Verordnung relating to the agent Finlay at Mainz. Apr. 29, 1847.

Verordnung relating to the emigration of Germans subject to military duty. Nov. 12, 1847.

Verordnung relating to G. Link. Nov. 30, 1849.

Verordnung relating to secret emigration. May 14, 1852.

Letter relating to the emigration to America, directed to Landrichter Hastig in Amorbach by Franz Dessauer, who has as his letter-head " General-Agentur für Auswanderungen nach Nord- und Südamerika ". July 21, 1852.

Verordnung relating to emigration to Brazil. July 30, 1852.

Verordnung relating to the appointment of agencies. Nov. 19, 1852.

Verordnung relating to appointment of agents, especially in Württemberg and Switzerland, and mentioning a certain merchant, Glück, of St. Gall, as emissary of the house of Steinmann and Drevet in Brazil. May 15, 1853.

V. 2. Amorbach. 1/2. Ausw. erlaub. für Anna Maria Spies von Preunschen. 1817.

V. 7. Amorbach. 1/7. Gesuch d. Franz Schiedig von Kirchzell. 1810.

V. 19. Amorbach. 1/19. Ausw. erlaub. für Johann Michael Balles aus Weckbach. 1817.

V. 138. Amorbach. 3/140. Gesuch d. F. J. Breunig von Weilbach. 1808.

V. 195. Amorbach. 4/199. Gesuch d. B. Zeller von Hambrunn. 1808.

V. 207. Amorbach. 5/211. Gesuch d. E. Brohm von Amorbach. 1809.

V. 208. Amorbach. 5/212. Gesuch d. Kuhr von Amorbach. 1810.
V. 209. Amorbach. 5/213. Gesuch d. Emich u. K. Schiel von Amorbach. 1810.
V. 215. Amorbach. 5/219. Gesuch d. G. T. Link von Neudorf. 1816.
V. 352. Amorbach. Akt, Generalien, Verordnungen, etc., gegen die (heimlichen) Auswanderungen von Unterthanen aus dem Churfürstenthum Mainz und bezw. Fürstenthum Aschaffenburg. 1754-1805.
V. 353. Amorbach. Bitte des Georg Steigerwald. 1803.
V. 882. Aschaffenburg. 6/127. Gesuch des M. Kollmann u. S. Schwab zu A. 1814.
V. 1488. Alzenau Ldg. 14/296. Ausw. Erlaubnis für Peter Schneider aus Michelbach. 1809.
V. 1573. Alzenau Ldg. Berichte der Amtskellerei Alzenau über Vermögensconfiscationen heimlich ausgewanderter Unterthanen unter Anlage summarischer Vermögens- und Schulden-Verzeichnisse der Ausgewanderten. 1789, 1791.
V. 1718. Alzenau Ldg. Akt, Steinheimer Oberamtsgericht, die heimliche Auswanderung von Unterthanen aus den Orten Horstein und Wasserlos betr. 1786.
V. 1723. Alzenau Ldg. 17/A 429. Gesuch des aus Kahl heimlich entwichenen Gerhard Zahn, etc. 1790.
V. 2099. Ldg. Alzenau. 24/718. Gesuch des Seb. Siegler zu Gross-Ostheim. 1815.
V. 2112. Ldg. Alzenau. 24/730. Ausw. d. H. Heilmann zu Geiselbach. 1804.
V. 2116. Ldg. Alzenau. 24/735. Ausw. d. Ehefrau des J. Ritter zu Hörstein. 1805.
V. 2464. Ausw. d. Schäfer zu Lohr. 1788.
V. 2507. Confisc. d. Verm. d. Joh. Fleckenstein von Rechtenbach. 1789-1790.
V. 2640. Entlassung d. J. Ritter zu Aschaffenburg. 1808.
V. 2724. Entlassung des Georg Scheibler aus Hösbach aus der Nachbarschaft. 1807.
V. 15663. Adm. 694/13217. Auswanderungsgesuche und deren Verbescheidung. 1814-1816.
V. 17313. Adm. 744/14359. Aus- und Einwanderungen in den Landgerichtsbezirken des Landcommisariates Würzburg; im I Quartal 1806; Berichte und Tabellen hierüber. 1806.
V. 17314. Adm. 745 u. 746/14360-61. Ein- und Auswanderungen, Vermögensexportationen, Nachsteuerentrichtungen, Confiscation des Vermögens von Deserteuren verbotwidrige Ansässigmachung und Copulationen, etc. 1806-1814.
V. 17315. Adm. 746/A 14361. Statistische Tabellen und Verzeichnisse über Aus- und Einwanderungen, Vermögens-Ex- und Importationen im Grossherzogthum Würzburg in den Jahren 1809-1814. W. Staatsratsakt.
V. 17316. Adm. 746/A 14361. Alphabetisches Register über Auswanderungsgesuche von den Jahren 1809-1814. Aktenstück des Staatsrathes zu Würzburg. Important list giving the place from which and to which the emigrant went, in all some 500 names, but few references to America.

V. 17317. Adm. 746/A 14361. Abänderung der Strafe für verbotswidrige Auswanderungen weiblicher Personen. 1809.
V. 17319. Adm. 746/A 14361. Auswanderungen und Vermögensexportationen, Nachsteuerverhältnisse, Confiscationen, Erbschaftsaushändigungen, etc. 1814-1817.
V. 17323. Adm. 747/A 14362. Verbot der Vermögensverabfolgung an Angehörige des Unterwalden in der Schweiz. 1815.
V. 17332. Adm. 747/14360. Auswanderungen und Vermögensexportationen, Nachsteuerverhältnisse und Freizügigkeitsverträge mit anderen Staaten, etc. 1814-17. Sammelakten der K. Hofcommission Aschaffenburg.
V. 17336. Adm. 747/A 14360. Verbot der Vermögensverabfolgung an Angehörige des Cantons Unterwalden in der Schweiz, etc. 1815.
V. 17340. Adm. 747/A 14360. Ein- und Auswanderungen, Vermögens-Im- und Exportationen im Bezirke der Landgerichte des Landcommissariates Schweinfurt. Berichte und Tabellen hierüber. 1804-1807.
V. 17343. Adm. 747/A 14360. Ein- und Auswanderungen, Vermögens-Im- und Exportationen im Bezirke der Landgerichte des Landcommissariates Würzburg. Berichte und Tabellen hierüber. 1804-1805.
Ger[icht] Gerolzhofen. 50 (III). Auswanderungen aus dem Amte Prichsenstadt, Gesuche hierwegen, Erhebung der Nachsteuer. 1804-1805.
Ger. Hofheim. 337 (XIX). Klage der Gemeinde Lendershausen gegen die dortigen Ganerben (Stein zum Altenstein, Truchsess v. Wetzhausen u. das sächs. Amt. Königsberg) wegen der Einrichtung des Abzugsgeldes oder der Nachsteuer. 1734-1743, 1755. Act der Regierung zu Würzburg.
Ger. Karlstadt. 121 (III). Berichte und Anzeigen über Ein- und Auswanderungen im Bezirke des Landcommissariates Karlstadt. 1804-1805. Akt des Landcommissärs des Districtes Karlstadt.
Ger. Klingenbach. (*Cf.* IX, Nr. 150.) Gesuch des Barth. Schmitt von Neuenbuch. 1814.
Ger. R. Miltenberg. (*Cf.* VIII, Nr. 440.) Gesuch des Frz. Ant. Scheuermann von Hambrunn. 1814.
441. Gesuch des Bonifaz Friedel z. Kirchzell. 1814.
443. Gesuch des A. M. Hummel von Weckbach. 1814.
455. Gesuch des N. Repp von Watterbach. 1814.
456. Gesuch des Ant. Klein von M. 1814.
466, 469. Gesuch des Franz Ludw. Jäger von M. 1814.
506. Gesuch des Franz Mathes Lindner von Wiesenthal. 1814.
Ger. Rothenfels. 299 (X). Tabellen über Ein- und Auswanderungen im Gerichtsbezirke Rothenfels. 1825-1852.
Ger. Schweinfurt. 47 (III). Auswanderungsgesuche der B. Gademann, des Chr. Herold, E. H. Cramer, J. A. Gottschalk, der A. M. Glückert, des J. P. Herold, der W. W. Casius, der Marg. Heunisch, der A. B. Cramer, und der A. R. Silbermann von Schweinfurt. (13 papers.) 1807-1809.
G. 1410. Gericht Amorsbach. (*Cf.* G. 1411 also, Gericht Kleinheubach, 1817-1849.) Aus- u. Einwanderungen, Vermögens Aus- u. Einführungen, Nachsteuer. 1786-1855.

G. 3209. Erhebung der Nachsteuer von mehreren aus dem Amte Lohr weggegangenen Unterthanen, u. (2) Erlasse über Freizügigkeit. 1580-1788.
G. 12937. Nachsteuerherabsetzung zwischen der Kurpfalz und Würzburg, etc. 1742-1793.
G. 15704. Befolgung des Vertrages mit Kurmainz wegen der Nachsteuer. 1722.
Miscell. 1090. Aktenstücke betr. die Abzugs- und Nachsteuer u. die desshalb getroffenen Vereinbarungen mit Schwarzenberg, Zobel, Bechtolsheim, Hannover, Corvey, etc. 1602-1775, 1800.
Miscell. 1168. Die Aufhebung der Nachsteuer zwischen Würzburg und Hessen-Hanau. 1773.

ALSACE-LORRAINE.
COLMAR.
DISTRICT ARCHIVES OF UPPER ALSACE.
(Bezirks-Archiv des Ober-Elsass.)

Hours: 8.00 to 12.30 and 4 to 6.

1. Passeports à l'étranger—Instruction. An 12–1868.
2. Passeports à l'étranger—Correspond. An 12–1870.
3. Émigration—Instruction. An 9–1864.
4. Émigration—statistique et affaires diverses. 1852-1870.
5. Réfugiés étrangers. 1833-1870.

METZ.
DISTRICT ARCHIVES OF LORRAINE.
(Bezirks-Archiv von Lothringen.)

Founded in 1790 by resolution of the French National Assembly. The building stands on the Regierungsplatz (Place de la Préfecture), adjoining the Bezirkspräsidium. The archives contain, from the French period, the following series: A, Actes du pouvoir souverain; B, Justice (Parlement of Metz, Chambre des Comptes, etc.); C, Administrations provinciales; D, Instruction publique; E, Féodalité, communes, bourgeoisie, et familles; G, Clergé séculier; H, Clergé régulier; L and Q, Administration du département de la Moselle, etc., 1790-1798; M-Z, documents of the French administration from 1798 to 1870, and of the German since 1870. See *Inventaire Sommaire des Archives Départementales de la Moselle (Lorraine)*, t. I., series A-E; t. II., series G; t. III., series H; and *Inventaire des Aveux et Dénombrements, 1534-1745.*

Hours: 9 to 12 and 3 to 6.

The inventories show only the following American items:

Série A. 1. Édit autorisant la vente du tabac de France, d'Amérique et mâtiné du Brésil, etc., à 20 sous la livre pour les deux premiers et à 40 sous celui du Brésil. 1648-1691.

Série C. 21. Lettre du duc de Choiseul refusant à M. de Murray, neveu du général de ce nom, l'autorisation de s'instruire dans les écoles françaises, parce que " les ministres anglais n'accorderaient jamais leur permission à un Français d'aller s'établir à Chatam ou dans tout autre port, et que d'ailleurs la France n'a pas eu à se louer d'eux dans le Canada ". 1768.

Série C. 839. Lettres de Calonne et mémoires des fermiers généraux relativement à la fraude qui se fait sur les cafés des îles et colonies françaises de l'Amérique destinés pour la consommation du royaume. 1784.

The following modern portions might, it is reported, be taken into consideration.

Série L. VIII. 22. Étrangers. Police des étrangers, expulsions et secours.
Série L. XIII. 9. Familles étrangères. Rapatriement.
Série L. XVI. 9. Industrie et commerce. Importations et exportations.
Série M X. 10, 1. Émigration. Instructions et correspondance générale.
Série M. X. 10, 2. Agents d'émigrations.
Série M. X. 10, 4. Émigrations vers les divers pays.
Série M. X. 13-16. Étrangers. Extradition, surveillance, expulsion, rapatriement, statistiques.
Série M. X. 30. Passeports à l'étranger.
Série M. XV. 7. État civil. Étrangers à la France. Résidences.
Série M. XV. 8. Français à l'étranger. Résidences.
Série M. XVIII. 17-18. Exportations. Blé, avoine et divers.
Série M. XVIII. 46. Traités de commerce. Transit de commerce.

STRASSBURG.

DISTRICT ARCHIVES OF LOWER ALSACE.

(BEZIRKS-ARCHIV DES UNTERELSASS.)

Located in Fischartstrasse. Contains some 40,000 parchments from 815 A. D. to 1870. The repertoria are in French, and contain in many cases an "analyse des pièces" (titles of the *acta* with brief account of contents). See *Inventaire Sommaire des Archives Départementales du Bas-Rhin*, four vols. (1863-1872). Permission to consult the papers is given by the Bezirks-Präsident.[1]

Hours: Daily from 9 to 12 and 3 to 6.

Série C. Article 263. Intendance. Emigration en les pays étrangers; et passages des familles étrangers dans les colonies et autres parties de la France. 1669-1774. The volume contains 6 groups of papers entered in the repertorium as follows:

1. Avis de Mr. de Vanolles et lettres diverses à lui écrites ou par lui écrites, concernant la nommée Reimberg, soupçonnée d'avoir débauché des ouvriers de Lyon pour les faire passer à l'étranger. 5 pièces. Mar. 20-31, 1748.
2. Lettres et pièces concernant les émigrans de 1749 et les Embaucheurs et Émigration dans la nouvelle Angleterre dont une du Sr. Boediger, les autres non signées de 1751. This analytical title gives in general the content of the parcel. The repertorium then continues:

Ordonnance du subdélégué de l'intendance Gayot concernant les émigrations (1749) et les embaucheurs.
Déclaration du Roi de 1669 concernant les émigrations.
Lettres de Mr. Aigrefeuille à l'intendant d'Alsace concernant les émigrants. 1753.

---

[1] Other valuable collections are found in the Stadtarchiv, located Spitalplatz 8, containing some 12,000 official documents and numerous state papers. With it are connected the Archiv des Stifts "Unser lieben Frauen Werk" of Münster and the Archiv des Hospitalstifts St. Wilhelm of Münster. Permission to consult these collections is given by the Burgomaster. Hours: Daily from 9 to 12 and 3 to 6; Saturdays from 8 to 1.

The contents in particular are the following:
- Fol. 1. Lettre de Mr. Boettiger facteur de la fonderie de Lettres de Lucher. Oct. 15, 1751. Relates to the shipping of emigrants to New England and advises that emigrants wait until April of the following year because of the lateness of the season. Interesting information about shipping from London and Holland, enclosing the following:
- Fol. 2-3. Extrait des avertissemens et Reglemens concernant la Baye de Massachusett dans la Nouvelle Angleterre.
- Fol. 4-6. Extrait d'une Lettre de Boston dans la Nouvelle Angleterre du 15 Juin vieuxstyle de l'an 1751.
- Fol. 7-8. Letter of Gayot. Strassburg, June 20, 1749.
- Fol. 9-10. Letter of Billandes. Oberbronn, June 15, 1749.
- Fol. 11-14. Déclaration du Roi, forbidding emigration and commanding emigrants to return. Aug. 13, 1669.
- Fol. 15-20. Letters of D'Aigrefeuille. May, 1753.

3. This parcel contains 18 papers, touching the general question of emigration, rights of emigrants, and the relation of French subjects to England, etc., enclosing:
  Extrait des Registres du Conseil Souverain d'Alsace, etc. 1669-1753.
  Mémoires, correspondances, édits des Rois Louis XIV. et Louis XV., déclaration, ordonnances concernant les émigrations.
  Réclamation du Sr. Bardet, ingénieur au service du Roi des deux Siciles et par les sieurs André et Jean Barth, établi à Frankfort sur le Main, qui réclament leur biens à eux échus par succession. 18 papers. 1669-1753.

4. Lettres et pièces concernant les Lettres de Change tirés sur la Cayenne et les porteurs de papiers du Canada. 1762-1763.
  Correspondance entre le baron de Lucé intendant d'Alsace et le duc de Choiseul. 4 papers.

5. États des familles étrangères qui sont parties de Strasbourg pour se rendre à Cayenne en 1764. 1763-1764.
  Avances faites par les receveurs des finances et des deniers royaux pour fournir à la subsistance des dites familles.
  Lettres et pièces qui y ont rapport. 21 papers. This is the most important matter I have yet found relating to Cayenne.
  The following papers deserve special mention:
  Matter giving the routes of the emigrants. Feb. 8, 1764.
  Papers containing a list of emigrants. Nov. 14, 1763.
  Extensive lists of emigrants written on printed forms giving the following information: Nombre de familles, Noms des Particuliers, Age, Profession, Religion, Lieux de Naissance, Jurisdictions. These lists have the following dates: Strassburg, July 3, 1763, Jan. 24, June 20, 23, Aug. 18, 23, 24, Sept. 3, 7, Oct. 8, 1764; Landau, Nov. 20, 1763. Then follow:
  Avances faites par M. Chastel pour le service des colonies pendant l'année 1763. (Important matter.)

6. Familles allemandes envoyées dans différentes seigneuries et abbayes de la France. 2 papers. 1763-1764.

M. Administration Générale: Police Générale.
> An XI à 1812. Émigration en Amérique et Russie et autres pays. 1791 à 1812. The papers furnish names and other particulars of those emigrants who came under the eye of the police. Some of the papers give accounts of money expended in aiding emigrants. Important printed matter, such as circulars of information, is enclosed.
> 1816 à 1818. Émigration en Crimée. 1816.
> Émigrés rentrés. Correspondance. 1817.
> Émigration. Correspondance. 1818.
> 1828 à 1837. Émigrations. États Nominatifs des émigrés partis pour l'Amérique. 1828-1837. Contains much statistical matter and the following papers:
>> État numérique, giving a list of emigrants between 1828 and 1837 for all the cantons and communes of the Department of the Lower Rhine.
>> État des habitants of the several communes, giving data under the following heads, in French and German: Numéro d'ordre, Noms et Prénoms, Profession, Nombre des individus, Sommes emportées en numéraire, Observations.
>> Letter addressed to the prefect of the Lower Rhine enclosing an important communication from Weisskopf on Paris, and giving information concerning land for sale in America, and referring to Mr. Keating, who furnished the writer with money to go to " Karthaus bei Clearfield " (Pennsylvania). 1830.
>> Another paper with the following notice: *Felder zu verkaufen im Auslande, insgesamt oder in kleinen Portionen.* The land is described as lying on the Susquehanna, which is compared with the Seine at Paris. The tract comprises about 28,000 acres. References are given to the following agents: 1. Weisskopf in Paris; 2. Naigeon, a lawyer in Paris; 3. Bartolomée Mahler in Strassburg; 4. John Keating in Philadelphia; 5. Price in Havre de Grace.
> Parcel of letters addressed to the prefect of the Lower Rhine, and referring to the cholera epidemic in Strassburg and the emigration to America. 1832.
> Correspondence with the Minister of the Interior at Carlsruhe relating to emigrants.
> Correspondence of the Bureau de Police relating to emigration to America. June, 1833.
> Émigrés d'Amérique, notes, etc. 1842.
> Émigrants allemands pour l'Amérique en 1849. Enclosing declarations, giving names of emigrants, etc.
> Émigration pour l'Amérique. Correspondance. Important bundle of letters containing minute information concerning emigrants.

Amerika. Ausland. 1819-1844. Auswanderung. Contains the following, each consisting of official papers relating to individual emigrants, giving names, trades, etc.

1. Émigration. Correspondance. Renseignement. 1819.
2. Émigration pour l'Amérique. 1819.
3. Émigration pour l'Amérique. 1824.
4. *Id.* 1823.
5. *Id.* 1823.
6. *Id.* 1822.
7. *Id.* 1822.
8. *Id.* 1823.
9. *Id.* 1823.
10. *Id.* 1823.
11. *Id.* 1823.
12. *Id.* 1821.
13. *Id.* 1822.
14. *Id.* 1824.
15. *Id.* 1824.
16. *Id.* 1827.
17. *Id.* 1823.
18. *Id.* 1826.
19. *Id.* 1823.
20. *Id.* 1820.
21. *Id.* 1822.
21. *Id.* 1822.
22. *Id.* 1821.
22. *Id.* 1822.

Also other papers relating to the years 1829, 1831, 1838, 1839, 1846, 1847.

M. Adm. Gen. Police Générale.
Recherches dans l'intérêt des familles.
Personnes A-K and L-Z. (2 volumes not dated.)
Personnes A-G, H-M, N-Z. (3 volumes dated.)
Successions de Français décédés à l'Étranger et d'étrangers décédés en France. Correspondance, Renseignement.
Familles A à Z et pièces collectives. (1 volume.)
Familles A-W. 1849-1869. (1 volume.)
Under these rubrics and perhaps elsewhere are many loose papers not yet arranged, such for example as the following:
Émigrations, Instructions sur l'Émigration à Buenos Ayres. 1859.
Rapport à son Excell. Le Ministre de l'Intérieur sur l'Émigration. 1857-1862.

ANHALT (ZERBST).
DUCAL HOUSE AND STATE ARCHIVES.
(HERZOGLICHES HAUS- UND STAATSARCHIV.)

Located in the Ducal Castle, these archives contain the following collections: the general archives of Anhalt, 941-1603; the Senioratsarchiv, 1603-1863; the archives of the former separate principalities of Dessau, from 1603; Cöthen, 1603-1847; Bernburg, 1603-1863; Zerbst, 1603-1793; and those of the related lines of Harzgerode, 1635-1709; and Hoym, 1718-1812.

Hours: 9 to 2.

C. 16 (formerly F. 134 Nr. 4-25, 135 Nr. 1). Kriegskanzleiakten. 1777-1785.

BADEN (KARLSRUHE).
GRAND-DUCAL GENERAL NATIONAL ARCHIVES OF BADEN.
(GROSSHERZOGLICH BADISCHES GENERAL-LANDESARCHIV.)

These archives include the Archives of the Grand Ducal Family, the Grand Ducal Palace and State Archives, and the National Archives (Landesarchiv). The archives are deposited in a fine new fire-proof building, Nördliche Hildapromenade 2, equipped with modern appliances such as photographic apparatus, exhibition hall and the like. The fascicles are numbered in this collection seriatim, thus simplifying the signatures. Three volumes have thus far appeared (1901, 1907, 1908) of the official *Inventare des Grossherzoglich Badischen General-Landesarchivs, herausgegeben von der Grossherzoglichen Archivdirektion*. Undoubtedly there are in this archive many papers relating to individual emigrants, but they are very scattered and would require much time for search. Reference may here be made to Dan. Häberle, *Auswanderung und Koloniegründungen der Pfälzer im 18. Jahrhundert* (Kaiserslautern, 1908).

Hours: 9 to 12 and 3 to 6.

In addition to the General-Landesarchiv in Karlsruhe there are also several provincial archives in the grand-duchy of Baden. As these were of a more local or municipal character they were not examined for the present Guide. They doubtless contain, like most other local archives, much valuable matter relating to emigrants to America.

5. Abzugsrecht. Die Einführung der Nachsteuer in Kurpfalz, derselben Modifikationen, Gutachten über Nachsteuer von freien Gütern u. Bedienten. 1550-1779.
84. Baden-Durlach: Ordnungs- und Policey-Sache. Die wegen des Emigrirens der Underthanen in Pennsylvanien ergangene und publicirte Verordnung betr. 1737, 1745.
216. Amt Durlach, Wegzug. Die Auswanderung mehrerer Schutz verwandten Bürger und Hintersassen in dem Oberamt Durlach. 1771. (Relates largely to Cleves.)
217. Durlach, Blankenloch, Büchig, Grozingen, Wegzug. Jakob Seelands, Andreas Waldenmeyers, und Jakob Landmessers von Blankenloch und Büchig Manumissions Gesuch um nach Pennsylvanien zu emigriren, imgleichen zerschiedene Grözinger und Durlacher Innwohner gebetenen Wegzug ins Preussische betr. 1770, 1771.
477. Durlach, Pennsylvanien, Erbschafts Sache. Die Abfolgung des dem in der Englischen Provinz Pensulvanien wohnhaften Johannes Knabschneider zu Durlach zuständigen Vermögen betrf. 1769.
505. Amt Pforzheim, Wegzug. Die Auswanderung mehrerer schutzverwandten Bürger und Hintersassen in dem Oberamt Pforzheim. 1769, 1771, 1787. Relates to Pennsylvania, in particular to Michel Wessenbacher with his six children, 1769, and others.

Zugang 1891. No. 24. V. Gen. Den Abzug mit den Amerikanischen Staaten betr. 1817, 1818, 1819, 1821, 1830, 1832, 1833, 1840, 1841, 1844, 1854, 1855, 1858, 1864.
Zugang 1899. No. 53. II. Gen. 47. Die Vorladung der in das Ausland insbesondere nach Amerika Ausgewanderten bey Verlassenschafts- und sonstigen Theilungen betr. 1834, 1835, 1836, 1850.
Zugang 1901. No. 24. V. Gen. Ministerium des Innern. Generalia.
639. Die Auswanderungen nach den verschiedenen Theilen von America. 1818-1821, 1824-1828, 1830, 1831. Pars IIda.
640. Die Auswanderungen, etc. 1832-1836. Pars IIItia.
641. Die Auswanderungen, etc. 1837-1847. Pars IVta.
643. Die Auswanderungen, etc. 1842, 1847-1850. Die im Ausland in einer hülflosen Lage sich befindenden Auswanderer und deren Unterstützung und Armensache (Curen). Die Cur- und Verpflegkosten armer Kranken, etc. I Teil.
644. Die Leitung des Auswanderungswesens betr. 1851-1852. Die im Ausland, etc. II Teil.
645. *Id.* 1853-1855. III Teil.
646. *Id.* 1855-1857. IV Teil.
648. Die Auswanderung nach Amerika insbesondere den Verein zum Schutz deutscher Einwanderer nach Texas betr. 1847, 1848, 1850, 1851, 1855.
649. Die Auswanderung nach Amerika hier Die Agenten für Vermittelung des Transports von Auswanderern nach Amerika im Grossherzogthum betr. 1847-1849. I Thiel.
652. Die Auswanderung, etc. 1853-1857, 1864. IV Theil.
656. Die Gesuche mehrerer zur Conscription für 1850 flüchtigen aus dem Mittelrheinkreis um Erlaubniss zur Auswanderung nach Amerika betr.
658. Die Gesuche von Einwohnern aus verschiedenen Gemeinden des Mittelrheinkreises um Unterstützung zur Auswanderung nach Amerika (und Gewährung von Steuerbeiträgen). 1851-1854. T. I.
659. Die Staatsbeiträge zur Auswanderung verschiedener Personen aus dem Mittelrhein Kreis betr. 1855-1859. T. II.
660. Die Bewilligung von Staatsbeiträgen zur Auswanderung verschiedener Personen aus dem Mittelrheinkreis. 1860-1864. Pars [T.] III.
661. Die Unterstützung mehrerer Einwohner aus verschiedenen Gemeinden des Oberrhein Kreises zur Auswanderung (und Gewährung von Steuerbeiträgen) betr. 1851, 1852. Fasc. I. These cases of assistance by the state shed new light on the history of the German emigration of this period and deserve a special treatment.
662. Die Unterstützung, etc. 1853-1857. Pars (Fasc.) II.
663. Staatsbeitrag zur Verbringung verschiedener Individuen aus dem Oberrheinkreis nach Amerika betr. 1858-1864. Pars III.
664. Gesuche von Einwohnern aus verschiedenen Gemeinden des Seekreises um Unterstützung zur Auswanderung nach Amerika (und Gewährung von Steuerbeiträgen). 1851-1853. Vol. I.

665. Die Unterstützung verschiedener Bewohner des Seekreises zur Auswanderung nach Amerika, etc., betr. 1854-1864. Vol. II.
666. Die Auswanderung nach Surinam betr. 1852.
667. Die Leitung des Auswanderungswesens insbesondere den Untergang des Auswanderungsschiffes *Powhatan* und die dabei verunglückten Badischen Auswanderer betr. 1854.
668. Die Auswanderungen nach Brasilien betr. 1854, 1856-1861. Pars I. A thick fascicle of papers containing:
A volume of papers, resolutions, and the like, of the ministry relating to the emigration to Brazil, and enclosing important printed matter in German and French.
A bundle of papers enclosed in pasteboard entitled: Beilagen No. 1-12, Die Auswanderung nach Brasilien betreffend.
Gehorsamster Bericht des Unternehmens für Beförderung von Auswanderern, Kaufmann Emil Giehne in Karlsruhe, die Auswanderung nach Brasilien betreffend. Dated Karlsruhe, July 28, 1858, and enclosing 9 printed pamphlets relating thereto; also a manuscript Pro Memoria by T. C. Strauch and a communication of F. Keller, of the year 1857.
670. Bericht des Gross. Consuls in Havre vom 22ten d. Mts. den Untergang des Auswandererschiffs *Luna* betr.
929. Badische Markgrafschaft, Wegzug IV. 2. Die wegen des Auswanderns der Unterthanen erlassenen Verordnungen betr. 1785, 1787, 1790, 1800, 1803, 1804, 1805, 1808.
930. Die wegen des Auswanderns, etc. 1809, 1810. Pars II.
933. IV. 1. Die an verschiedene Grossherzogliche Unterthanen ertheilte Emigrations-Erlaubniss in den Jahren 1809, 1810, 1811, 1816, 1817, 1818, 1819, 1821, 1824, 1826 betr.
934. Die tabellarische Uebersicht der Auswandernden betr. 1817. Contains important lists of emigrants with the usual particulars of the district, the name, condition, number of children, number in the family, destination.
935. Die Auswanderungen nach den verschiedenen Theilen von America betr. 1816, 1817, 1832. Pars I. A volume of valuable papers containing decrees, rescripts, and the like, relating to the general question of emigration and to emigrants; also passports, original letters, relating to shipping from Amsterdam and Basel, printed broadsides and a report entitled: "Das Auswandern nach Amerika betr.", dated Amsterdam, May 12, 1817.
1029. Die Auswanderungen nach Russland und anderen Staaten betr. 1824-1827.
1053. Dreisam Kreis, Stadt Freiburg. Wegzug, Auswanderungsgesuch bei der Stadt Freyburg dann Abzugs u. Auswanderungsgebühren betr. 1790, 1807.
1170. Nachlass Mone. Aufsätze für Zeitungen:
(b) über die Auswanderung nach Texas, f. 21-27.
A manuscript article prepared for print with the original title: "Der Deutsche Adelsverein für Auswanderer und der Staat Texas". This original title is stricken out and the following is written above it: "Ueber die Auswanderung nach Texas. Von einem Deutschen in Texas".

1687. Amt Karlsruhe. Carlsruhe-Augspurg. Wegzug. Des Wegzugs Erlaubniss.
1729. Amt Durlach. Wegzug. Bitte verschiedener Personen um Wegzug bet. 1794-1810. Contains an original " Abschiedspass " of Grenadier Gottfried Geyger of Durlach.
1954. Grossherzog. Bad. Directorium des Dreisam Kreises, Stadt Freyburg. Generalia. Wegzug. Betrff. verschiedene Auswanderungs Gesuche in der Stadt Freyburg. 1800-1807.
2164. Baden. Generalia. Erbschaften. Die Vorsichtsmassregeln bey Vermögens Ausfolgungen nach Amerika betr. 1786.
2651. Pfortzheim. Wegzug. Die dem Handelsmann Schlosser zu Pfortzheim gnädigst ertheilte Erlaubniss zu seinem vor habenden Wegzug von da nach America betrf. 1751.
4174. Papers relating to the Mennonites.
4211. Schutzgeld der Mennoniten.
4212. *Id.*
4213. *Id.*
4229. Gemischte Sachen, Taufe, etc. Erziehung der Kinder, Eheliche Verbindungen a. 1766.
4230. Verzeichnisse der Mennoniten, Aufstellung, etc.
4231. Wasser-Waidgenuss der Mennoniten.
4237. Schutzgeld der Mennoniten.
4238. *Id.*
4239. *Id.*
4286. Kirchen Theilung unter die Katholischen und Reformirten 1706-1707. An original manuscript with the title: Tabell der Kirchen Theilung under die Catholische und Reformirte in denen Chur Pfältzischen Stätten und Dörfern diess- und Jenseit Rheins. In Anno 1706 vorgenommen. (*Cf.* 4350, a. 1697.)
4331, 4332. Verbot der Pietisten u. Separatisten Sekten.
4333. Pfalz, Generalia, Religion. Die Wiedertäuffer in Kurpfalz. 1566, 1571, 1603, 1610, 1664, 1698, 1744. (12 papers in all.)
4334. Gnädigste Verordnung, wie Es mit Einlössung der von den Wiedertäuffern erkaufften Güthern gehalten werden solle. Volumen I. 1662-1763.
4335. Papers relating to the burial-places of the Mennonites.
4336. Pfalz, Generalia, Religion. Nachrichten über die Religionssekten der Wiedertäufer und Quäker in der Pfalz, insbesondere die Concessionen der Wiedertäufer. 1651-1679. Contains petitions of Mennonites for equal privileges with other sects and many other interesting matters connected with the Mennonite assemblies.
4337. Pfalz, Generalia, etc. 1680-1743. Two thick bundles of papers important for the history of the Mennonites and Quakers in the Palatinate. Band I. contains among other interesting papers the following:
Paper mentioning Jacob Groff, Hans Mendt, and Hans Mayer as Mennonites of Steinfurt. Oct. 5, 1656.
Various papers relating to the " exercitium religionis " among the Mennonites.

Paper directed to the " Burggraff und Lantschreiber zu Alzei " dated Kriegsheim (" Chrysheim ") 15. 7 Mo. 1660, and signed: " By ons die de Spotters Quakers nennen ".

Verzeichnus Der Jenigen Wiedertäufferischen Persohnen, so zu Steinfirth bey der Versamblung befunden worden den 2. Martij Ao 1661. (Important list of 53 names.)

Another paper giving names and property of Anabaptists. Apr. 24, 1661.

Extracts of a protocol, showing that, while Mennonite meetings were not prohibited, an exact account of those present was kept. Oct. 23, 1661.

A paper in English signed Jno. P. Hilley (Hiller ?), addressed " To the Prince Elector at Hidelberg ", exhorting the elector to his Christian duty, and written in a very Quakerish tone. June 15, 1664.

Verzeichnus derer in dem Oberambt Altzey befindlichen Menisten was selbige, etc. (Includes Kriegsheim and 20 other places.)

A printed sheet entitled, *Eine Warnung an alle Menschen,* signed by James Parnel, printed in Amsterdam by Christoff Cunrad, 1670, with six signatures written on the back.

Papers relating to the Mennonites of Osthofen. 1670 et seq.

Bd. II. Continues the same kind of matter as vol. I., among which the following are noteworthy:

Schrift von Jahns Reinhard Herman, Pfarrer zu Nider Florsheim, replying to Peter Hendrichsen von Amsterdam. 1680. (Copy.)

Document mentioning the Quakers and referring to " Roger Longworth und Roger Haydocke von Doeten aus Engelland 150 Englische Meilen hinder Londen ". Alzei, Aug. 15, 1681.

Document relating to the Quakers and containing this interesting passage : " Nachdem die Quäcker zü Kriegsheim vormahlen Menisten gewesen, und nach von dieser auf Jene närrische Sekte gefallen ", showing that Mennonites became Quakers. Aug. 11, 1684.

Another paper referring to the Quakers: " Wegen einiger Quäckern, so aus Kriegsheim hinweg zu ziehen Vorhabens ", and the condition under which they are allowed to go. Alzei, May 23, 1685.

Specification der Jungen Menonisten so sich in Churpfaltz Landen befunden, etc. Oct. 28, 1685.

Unthgst. Gehorsamste Die teutsche Wormbsser judenschafft. (Directed to the elector.)

List of Mennonite children and others. 1685.

Tabelle Deren in Chur Pfaltz befindlicher Menonisten, welche das schuldige Schutzgeld, und welche solches nicht entrichten, und zahlt die Familie Jährlichs sechs, die wittiben nur halb so viel, etc.

4328. Papers relating to the Mennonites. Lists, etc.
4355. *Id.*
4359. *Id.*
5090. Ertheilung von Pässen. 1704-1802.
5105. Verordnung wegen der fremden Bettler. 1710-1721.

5651. Vertrag zwischen dem Schiffmann Horst in Heidelberg u. einer Anzahl Auswanderer wegen ihrer Beförderung nach Rotterdam. Heidelberg, Feb. 7, 1754.
The package of papers marked: Polizei, siehe auch: Medizinalanstalten, contains some important numbers.

6487. Verordnung, directed against the efforts of emissaries to induce the Palatines to emigrate to foreign colonies, and against enlisting emigrants for the service of foreign rulers. 1766-1809.

6529. Acta Unterthanen, welche ohne Obrigkeitliche Erlaubniss emigriren, deren sämtliches Vermögen soll confiscirt werden. 1739. *Cf.* still earlier papers of the year 1658, relating to the same matter; and **6538, 6539, 6540, 6541** (1762-1808) relating to "Wegzug".

6733. Kurpf. Verordnungen, directed against the emigration of subjects. 1753-1766. *Cf.* also **6727.**

6735. Acta die aus der Pfaltz nach Pennsylvanien gehende Unterthanen betref. Heidelberg, May 22, 1709. A thin parcel of papers containing the following:

Matter relating to the scarcity of grain and bread and a contract with a certain Jew for 10,000 Centners for the troops, with the remark, that the emigration "in die sogenannte Landschaft Pensylvaniam" has contributed much to this state of things.

An order dated Düsseldorf, May 12, 1709, to regulate or prevent emigration to Pennsylvania, and a similar paper dated June 9 relating to the same subject.

Order relating to emigrants and the excitement "wegen der nach der Insel Pennsylvanien", etc. June 12, 1709.

Paper relating to the distribution of the 10,000 Centners of flour bought for the troops. June 13, 1709.

Order relating to the restitution of the flour mentioned above. June 13, 1709.

Order relating to 127 families from the Upper Rhine (but none from the Palatinate) arrived at Düsseldorf. Düsseldorf, June 25, 1709.

Order assigning lands to 241 persons who wish to settle in the Palatinate. Düsseldorf, June 27, 1709.

Order relating to six families, that had actually settled, and to the settlement of Martinus Storck in Alzei, where he claims to have two brothers. June 27, 1709.

Order relating to the Reformed in the Palatinate, and addressed to the "Präsidenten zu Londen Steingens". July 5, 1709.

Paper addressed to Regierungsrat-Präsidenten Freiherrn von Hillesheim, and relating to those who had settled in Alzei instead of going to Pennsylvania. Heidelberg, July 30, 1709.

Order releasing these settlers from taxes for the current year. Aug. 8, 1709.

Paper of the same date addressed to the President at Amsterdam, asking for the publication, in the Palatinate and in the Netherlandish gazettes, in the French language, of a notice of those who have made trouble. Düsseldorf, Aug. 13, 1709.

6736. Pfalz, Wegzug, Einschrankung desselben. Measures to limit the emigration of Palatines from the Palatinate. 1741. (2 papers.)
6737. Pfalz, Leibeigenschaft u. Wegzug. Ohne die diesfallsige Erlaubniss sollen keine Güter Versteigungen vorgenommen werden. 1741, 1750, 1760. The article of 1750 refers to emigrants who have sold their personal property and turned it into cash. *Cf.* also 6539, 6540, 6541.
6557. Das verbotswidrige Auswandern von Personen weiblichen Geschlechts u. die Nachricht von der Vermögens-Confiscation in besonderen Fällen. 1792-1796.
6740. Acta das von Johann Caspar Thürriegel vorhabende Unternehmen zur Entführung deren Unterthanen nacher Spanien betr. 1767, 1768. Enclosing a very interesting printed circular entitled: *Glucks-Hafen oder Reicher Schatz-Kasten, welchen der Spanische Monarch, als einer derer reichesten Königen, zum Trost und Nutzen aller Teutschen und Niederländischen Bauersleuten, Taglöhnern, Handwerksmännern, Burschen oder Gesellen, Jungen und Alten, Ledig- und Verheurateten, Manns- und Weibs-Personen und kleinen Kindern aufgeschlossen hat,* etc. 1667. 12 quarto pages, 10 of which are printed, with the written signature, "Johann Caspar von Thürriegel", on the last printed page. A powerful bait held out to the starving Germans.
6741. Documents warning the German Palatines not to be misled by Thürriegel's inducements. 1767-1770.
6743. Generalia. Acta die auss diesseitigen in die Insel Cajenne und Preussische Landen ziehende Unterthanen betrf. Hierunter seynd alle frembde Landen begriffen. 1763-1764. Vol. I. Contains requests and directions sent to 20 districts, relating to the emigration to Prussia and other lands, among them " das sogenannte Franzoe Newe Land " or " das sogen. newe Land " (Cayenne), with mention of 86 souls in one instance in the year 1764. Mention is also made of Pennsylvania.

Verordnungen und Verbote betr. die Emissarii, etc. A print is enclosed with the title, *Wider das Mord- Raub- und Diebs-Volk auch anderes Herrenlose Gesindel und wie gegen solches, nach der äussersten Strenge, zu verfahren,* issued by " Derer Fürsten und Ständen des Löbl. Ober-Rheinischen Creyses allhier versammlete Räthe, Botschafftere und Gesandte ". Frankfort, Mar. 9, 1763.

Extracts from the protocolls relating to the emigrants.

Interesting inventories of property sent to Prussia.

6744. Pfalz, Generalia, Wegzug. Den Wegzug der Kurf. Unterthanen in andere Länder, insbesondere auch nach der Insel Cajenne. 1764-1804. Contains matter quite similar to that in vol. I., referring to the tedious procedure in the matter of property of emigrants, to manumissions, double emigrant tax, etc. Also papers relating to the emigration to Russia, particularly to the southern provinces of Russia in 1804.
8241. Papers relating to the burial-places of the Mennonites.

8242. Papers relating to the Mennonites.
8561. Pfalz, Generalia, Religion. Die mit der Königl. schwedischen Gesandtschaft gepflogene Correspondenz in Religions Angelegenheiten. 1699-1700. A very heated correspondence with the elector in reference to the religious agreement of the Peace of Westphalia.
9847. Baden-Durlach, America. Bürgerrechts Veränderung und Translationes domicilii. Aus Anlass der bey denen Underthanen in Teutschland und der Schweitz eingerissene Sucht in Carolina, Pensylvania auch andere Englische Provincen dasiger Gegend zu ziehen, gesammelte Nachrichten von dem Zustand solcher Landen auch dem Vortheil oder Schaden, den die Transmigranten daselbst zu erwarten [haben]. 1727-1737. Contains:

Extracts from the protocol of the council of Carlsruhe. Dec. 9, 1737.

Extract Schreibens von H. Güldin aus Pensylvania vom 8ten 9bris 1727. A most glowing account of the health conditions in Philadelphia—3 burials in one day!

Verordnung of the burgomaster and council of Basel against emigration to Carolina, dated Apr. 20, 1735, and referring to similar ordinances of Dec. 11, 1734, and Mar. 9, 1735.

Abschrift eines Brieffs von Hans Martin an seine zwo Töchtern zu Basel. Pennsylvania. Nov. 6, 1735. (Reference is made also to Carolina.)

Extract Schreibens von Hans Martin aus Pensilvania vom 6ten 9bris 1735 an H. Candidat. (Relates to Pennsylvania and Carolina.)

Extractus Eines Auss Pensilvania vom 6ten 9bris 1735, an H. Fattet geschriebenen Brieffs. (Relating also to Carolina.)

Copy of another letter of Hans Martin, of same date, relating to Pennsylvania and Carolina.

Extract Schreibens von Londen den 7ten Martii 1736, so von Herrn Wettstein Hoff-Prediger des Printzen von Wallis überschrieben und im Aprili 1736 von allen Cantzlen auff der Landschafft zu dem Canto Basel verlesen worden. (Relating to " Neu Georgien das besser Theil von Carolina ".)

Extract Schreibens auss Pensilvania den 16ten Octobris 1736, von Andres Bonj, addressed: " Geliebter Vetter Martin ". A valuable letter warning in a postscript against " Menschen Diebe " in Rotterdam.

Extract auss Durs Thommens Brieff, dene Er an Meister Johannes Fischer geschrieben auss Philadelphia den 19ten Weinmonath 1736. (Relates to Carolina.)

Ausszug auss Catharina Thommens, obigen Tochter Brieff an Ebengemeldten.

Letter of Durss Thommen to Candidate Annoni. Philadelphia, Oct. 20, 1736.

Extract Schreibens von Balthasar Rupanus auss Termidorg [?] 6 Meil von Philadelphia in Pennsylvania. (Gives a favorable account of Pennsylvania.)

Copia Schreibens von Maria Martin an Ihre Schwester Barbara Rudi Suters dess Würths Frau zu Brattelen.

Copia von Maria Martins Schreiben an Ihren Sohn Johannes Schwob in Brattelen den 10ten Wintermonath 1736.

Copy of a letter of Joggi Thommen with the following endorsement: " Geschrieben den 11ten 9bris 1736, von mir Joggi Thommen ".

Einige Fragen So Herr Chevalier Schaub auff Begehren Herrn Deputat Raillards an Jemend von der Regierung von Neu Georgia gestellt, unndt dero Beantwortung. An important document bringing out many particulars concerning the conditions in New Georgia.

Wegzug, Repositur II. 1. Die Organisation der deutschen Auswanderung betr. 1848.

[Vol. 420.] Die Auswanderung nach Texas betr. 1848-1855.

BREMEN.
BREMEN STATE ARCHIVES.
(BREMISCHES STAATSARCHIV.)

Each of the three imperial free cities or old Hanse towns, Bremen, Hamburg, and Lübeck, has its state archives, containing the official records of the city both as state and as municipality. Those of Bremen are located in a fine new brick building on the Tiefer with entrance from Klosterstrasse. They contain documents of the city of Bremen as far back as 1159. The collections are well repertorized and arranged. Permission to consult the collections is given by the Inspector of the Archives through the Archivist.

Hours: 9 to 2, and 3 to 7.

B. Hanseatica.
B. 9. b. a. 18. Manzarillo.
B. 9. c. 7. Bilbao.
B. 13. Verhältnisse der Hansastädte mit den Vereinigten Staaten von Nordamerica.
B. 13. a. Im Allgemeinen und Diversa. A thick parcel of miscellaneous papers containing among others the following:
    Letter from Henry Heyman to the Burgomaster of Bremen, giving notice of the fact that the English have obtained satisfaction for a ship captured by the Spanish at Nootka Sound (which the Spanish claim) and released by the Viceroy of Mexico. London, May 7, 1790.
    Papers relating to Moritz Castens of Richmond County, Georgia, and his claim to an inheritance. 1822.
    Treaty between Denmark and the United States. Washington, Apr. 26, 1826.
    Treasury Circular and Navigation Act (1817).
    Notice of the Agricultural Society of South Carolina and the Profits of the New Trade of Rough Rice (1827). Addressed with a letter of Nov., 1827, to the Senate of Bremen.
    Shipping and Commercial List (New York, May, 1828).
    Communications of Richard Ward to the Senate of Bremen, relating to piracy on the high seas. New York. June 15 and Sept. 13, 1828.
    Statement of the Number of Hogsheads of Maryland Tobacco shipped from Baltimore in the years 1821-1833.
    Uebersicht des Geschäfts von Nord-Americanischen Tobacen im Jahre 1834.
    Statistische Notizen über den Handel der Vereinigten Staaten von Nordamerica und der Republik Venezuela, mit besonderer Beziehung auf Deutschland. Sept. 30, 1835. (Print.)
    Letter from Caspar Meier and Co., relating to finance and trade. New York, May 16, 1837.
    Obrigkeitliche Verordnung of the Senate of Bremen, regulating the shipping of emigrants to the United States. Jan. 15, 1838.

Evangelischer Verein für deutsche Protestanten in Nord-Amerika. Bremen, Nov., 1839. (Printed circular.)
Papers relating to countervailing duties, etc.
Papers relating to the crew of the ship *Clementine*. July, 1842.
Herrn Sen. Adamis Aufmachung der von 1830 bis 1842 (auch von 1819-1821) in Bremen ein- u. ausgelaufenen Americanischen Schiffe. May 2, 1842.
List of state documents sent to the Senate of Bremen.
Letter from the United States Consul Dudley Mann to the Senate, taking exception to an article in the *Bremen Gazette* of Feb. 18, 1845.
Extracts from the Protocoll of the Senate of Bremen.
Letter from Minister Wheaton in Berlin commending Dr. Scherer.
Statistische Notizen zu dem Zwecke gesammelt um die Bedeutung des Hanseatischen Handelsverkehrs mit den Vereinigten Staaten verglichen mit denjenigen anderer Länder ins Licht zu stellen, aus der Zeit wo das seit 1827 bestehende Reciprocitätsverhältniss durch die Whig-Partei in Amerika bedroht erschien. 1843-1845.
Verordnung of May 11, 1846, supplementing those of Apr. 8, 1840, June 6, 1842, and May 30, 1845, " die Beförderung der Auswanderer durch Bremer Schiffe betreffend ". (Printed.)
Empfehlung für Auswanderer nach New York. Bremen, Oct. 14, 1846.
Die Inspection für das Auswanderungswesen. (Printed.)
Bericht der Deputation wegen Revision der Accise und Schiffahrts-Abgaben. June 4, 1847. (Printed.)
Auszug aus dem Senatsprotokoll den 5. Januar 1848. (Relating to Gevekoht's Pro Memoria concerning shipping and trade with the United States.)
Extract from the Protocoll of the Senate of Bremen, relating to the frigate *St. Lawrence*. Oct. 3, 1848.
Extract of the Protocoll of the Senate of Bremen, relating to a letter from the citizens of Lafayette in Louisiana and the sending of a German flag. Feb. 9, 1849.
Letter from Fr. Rodewald, relating to "Organisations Tendenzen" in the United States and enclosing clippings. New York, Oct. 22, 1851.
Matter relating to the Exhibitions of New York and Dublin and the international postage.
Correspondence between the Department of State in Washington and the Austrian chargé d'affaires, relating to Martin Koszta. New York, 1853. (Printed.)
A number of reports and prints relating to the Exposition in New York, 1853, treaties between the United States and Argentina, 1853-1855, and the convention between the United States and France, 1853.
Letter of Hermann Heye, relating to dutiable wares. Nov. 11, 1853.

Auszug aus dem Beschluss der Bürgerschaft vom 19 Nov. 1851. (Relating to the Washington Monument.)

Acta betreffend die Uebersendung einer Sammlung Bremischer Münzen an die Amerikanische Münzsammlung zu Philadelphia und darauf erfolgtes Gegengeschenk einer Sammlung amerikanischer Münzen. Oct. 14, 1853–Sept., 1854.

Verhandlungen betreffend die Entschädigung von der Amerikanischen Regierung für die bei dem Bombardement von Graytown (18. Juli 1854) zu Schaden gekommenen Hanseatischen Staatsangehörigen. Sept. 8, 1854–Nov. 4, 1856.

Acta betreffend die Gleichstellung Bremens mit anderen bisher bevorzugten Europäischen Export-Häfen hinsichtlich der Berechnung der bei der Verzollung von Waaren in den Häfen der Verein. Staaten zu erhebenden Commission. Oct. 24–Nov. 30, 1859.

Acta betreffend die von der Handelskammer in Anlass eines vorgekommenen Falles nachgesuchte Intervention der Gesandschaft in Washington, auf eine Abänderung der in der Amerikanischen Zollgesetzgebung bestimmten Haftbarkeit des Schiffes wegen Zolldefraudationen, auch wenn sie von einzelnen Passagieren begangen sind, hinzuwirken, u. dieserhalb mit der Gesandschaft stattgehabte Correspondenz. Oct. 16–Dec. 7, 1863.

Wasserschout. Abstract logs für Lieutenant Maury.

Acta betreffend die diesseitigen Beileidsbezeugungen in Anlass der Ermordung des Präsidenten der Vereinigten Staaten von America, Abraham Lincoln. Apr. 28, June 9, 1865.

Letter of Charles C. Leigh relating to the National Freedmen's Relief Association, enclosing a pamphlet: *Die Befreiten Sclaven in Amerika* (Bremen, 1865).

Paper relating to the list of those fallen and buried in the war, sent by the consul at Philadelphia. Jan., 1867.

Matter relating to the "Tributes of the Nations to Abraham Lincoln". Sept. 15-24, 1868.

Extract of the Protocoll of the Senate of Bremen relating to Wells's pamphlet on the tariff. Jan. 31–Apr. 1, 1870.

Extract of the Protocoll of the Senate of Bremen, relating to the invitation of the Prison Association of New York. Aug. 13, 1869–Feb., 1872.

Extract of the Protocoll of the Senate of Bremen, relating to health regulations.

Extract of the Protocoll of the Senate of Bremen, relating to the invitation of the Northern Pacific Railroad. May 19–Oct. 23, 1883.

Acta betreffend die Beileidsbezeugungen des Senats in Anlass der Ermordung des Präsidenten der Vereinigten Staaten von America, McKinley. Sept. 24, 1901.

B. 13. b. Hanseatische diplomatische Agenten, Consuls, u. s. w., bei ihnen und Correspondenz mit denselben.

0. Im Allgemeinen. 1816-1869. Contains among other papers the following:
Protocoll Extracts relating to the appointment of a Hanseatic minister to the United States, 1816; of a common agent to the United States, 1818; the appointment of a diplomatic agent to the United States and the recommendation of Fürstenwerther; the establishment of a Bremen consulate in America, 1826-1832; the request of Consul Meier, New York.
Vollmacht für Gevekoht. Nov. 28. 1845.
Matter relating to the appointment of H. H. Papendiek as consul for Bremen in Milwaukee. Apr., 1850.
Papers relating to the conclusion of a treaty between the Hanseatic towns and the United States concerning the mutual extension of the judicial right to the consuls. Apr. 17, 1850–Apr. 15, 1853.
Papers relating to the appointment of Rudolph Schleiden as minister of Bremen. May, 1853.
Application of James Wenz for the vice-consulate of Bremen in Minnesota. Oct., 1855.
Application of Dr. Hermann Brandis in Hoboken for the consulate of Bremen in New Jersey. Dec. 4, 1856.
Application of the Hanoverian consul A. G. Wilmanns of Milwaukee for the Bremen consulate of Wisconsin, Illinois, Iowa, Indiana, Michigan, and Minnesota. Oct. 3, 1857.
Application of Frederick Hertel of Chicago for the consulate of Bremen in Chicago. Mar. 10, 1862.
Application of Gottfrey Snydacker for the Bremen consulate in Chicago.
Papers relating to the settlement of disputes between shipmasters and crews on board of ships, and instructions regarding the same.

1. In Washington.
   a. Rudolph Schleiden Ministerresident. 1853. Generalia und Diversa. 1853-1901. Among the papers are the following:
   Duplicate, Concepte u. vermischte Papiere, die Sendung des R. Schleiden nach Washington betreffend. 1853.
   Instructionen, etc., for Schleiden. Apr., 1853.
   Instructions to Schleiden regarding the Ocean Steam Navigation Co. Mar. 13, 1854.
   Acta betreffend die Attaschierung des Dr. Juris Carl Julius Schellbass bei der Bremischen Gesandtschaft zu Washington. Dec., 1856.
   Papers relating to the claims of Rücker, Riensch and Co. against the United States. Nov. 3, 1858–May 6, 1859.
   Papers relating to the appointment of Dr. Johannes Rösing as secretary to the legation. Nov. and Dec., 1862.
   Acta betreffend die Errichtung einer gemeinsamen Hanseatischen Ministerresidentur zu Washington und Uebertragung desselben auf den bisherigen Bremischen Ministerresidenten daselbst Dr. Rudolph Schleiden. June 18, 1862–Jan. 12, 1863.

b. Dr. Johannes Rösing Geschäftsträger. 1865. Generalia et diversa. Papers relating to the appointment of Rösing as minister resident for the Hanseatic towns and to the inner affairs of the legation.
2. In Baltimore. 1797-1842.
3. In New York. 1815-1866.
4. In New Orleans. 1817-1866.
5. In Philadelphia. 1827-1868.
6. In Charleston. 1828-1867.
7. In Boston. 1828-1867.
8. In Alexandria. 1828-1852.
9. In Savannah. 1830-1865.
10. In Richmond, Norfolk, and Petersburg. 1844-1866.
11. In St. Louis. 1846-1862.
12. In Galveston. 1846-1867. For the papers of the period before annexation see below, C. 26.
13. In San Francisco. 1850-1868.
14. In Indianola. 1853-1868.
15. In Mobile. 1842-1866.
16. In Cincinnati. 1853-1864.
17. In Key-West (Florida). 1860-1867.

B. 13. c. Verträge und Tractaten.
  1. Hauptacte.
    a. Von der ersten Anknüpfung mit denselben bis zum Abschluss des Vertrags v. 20. Dec. 1827 und dessen Additionalartikels v. 4. Jan. 1828. (1782-1829.)
    b. Von 1829—. Anmerkungen: Die Akten wegen der Dampfschiffahrt zwischen Bremen und New York s[iehe] R. 11. 0. 2. a; Wegen der Auslieferung von Verbrechern s. D. 19. e. 5. f; Die Verhandlungen über den Hanseatisch-Amerikanischen Vertrag vom 30. April 1852 wegen der richterlichen Befugnisse der Consuls. s. in B. 13. b. 1.

P. 7. C. 2. P. 3. San Juan de Puerto Rico.
    S. 4. Santiago de Cuba.
    T. 5. Trinidad.

P. 8. A. 12. Aufrufung desselben [Bürgerrechts] und Ertheilung von Emigrationsscheinen, u. s. w., mit oder ohne Reservation des Bürgerrechts.
    a. Generalia et diversa. Anmerkung: Wegen Emigration von Nichtbürgern, die hierselbst ansässig gewesen sind vergl. P. 8. B. 10, aus dem Gebiet vgl. o. 1. qq. 7, sowie die Akten Gemeindebürgerrecht bei den einzelnen Ortschaften.
    b. Einzelne Fälle: 1. A-L; 2. M-Z: 3. Auswanderungsfreiheit v. 25. Juni 1849.
    d. Gesuche um Ertheilung von Auswanderungsconsensen nach Erlass der Verordnung vom 25. Juni 1867 wegen Einführung der allgemeinen Wehrpflicht ohne Stellenvertretung, etc.
    e. Ertheilung von Auswanderungsconsensen an solche junge Leute, welche ihre Militärpflicht durch den Dienst als einjährige Freiwillige genügt haben.

P. 8. B. 8.
    a. vor 1840. Anmerkung: Auswanderungen aus dem Reiche, s. H. 4. q.; nach Brasilien, s. C. 12. e.; Wegen der Schiffs- und Proviantbesichtiger siehe P. 8. B. 8. c. 4. b.
    b. von 1840-1850.
    c. von 1851.
        1. Generalia et diversa: (a) bis 1860 incl.; (b) von 1861-1870; (c) von 1871—.
        2. Gesetzliche Bestimmungen, Verordnungen, Regulative, etc., das Auswandererwesen betreffend: (a) bis 1862 incl.; (b) von 1863—. (Anm.: Die Acten, betr. das Reichsgesetz über das Auswanderungswesen, s. M. 6. e. 7.)
        3. Deutsche Auswanderer-Zeitung: (a) Im Allgemeinen; (b) die Zeitung selbst, 1-12, 1852-1875.
        4. Behörde für das Auswandererwesen.
            a. Im Allgemeinen und diversa. Hierbei liegen Protocolle der Behörde für das Auswanderungswesen v. 21/1 57 bis—, in Abschrift.
            b. Schiffs- und Proviantbesichtiger und deshalb erlassene Verordnungen (1860 Juli mit den Buden u. Ladungsbesichtigern vereinigt, daher von da an in Ss. 2. a. 7. m.)
        5. Nachweisungsbureau für Auswanderer.
        6. Passagier- und Schiffsexpedienten und Agenten.

P. 8. B. 9. Aufenthalt von in Vegesack recipierten Personen in Bremen, s. P. 13. b. 29. b.

B. 13. e. Internationale Ausstellungen daselbst [*scil.* in den Vereinigten Staaten] 1876-1903. Papers relating to the exposition in Philadelphia, 1876, and in Chicago, 1903.

C. 4. b. 6. d. 1. New Providence.
        2. Montreal; Quebec.
        3. Halifax.
        4. Jamaica; Kingston.
        5. St. John, N. B.
        6. Bermudas.

C. 4. b. 14. New Castle.

C. 7. i. 4. St. Thomas.

(*Cf.* 1. C. 24 b for Dominican Republic.)

C. 12. Verhältnisse der Hansastädte mit Brasilien.

C. 12. a. Im Allgemeinen und Diversa.

C. 12. b. Hanseatische Consuln, u. s. w., in Brasilien, auch Verhandlungen mit denselben.
  1. Im Allgemeinen.
  2. Zu Rio Janeiro.
    a. Im Allgemeinen, namentlich nicht realisierte Anmeldungen zu dieser Stelle.
    b. General-Consul G. E. Stuhlmann. 1818-1820.
    c. Vice Consul Joh. Friedr. Bothe. 1820-1822.
    d. General-Consul I. H. Chr. Ten-Brink. 1823-1837.
    e. General-Consul Christian Stockmeyer, 1837-1854. Supplementary to this *cf.* Fasc: "Ad C. 12. b. 2. e.", containing printed matter relating to the Stockmeyer papers.
    f. General-Consul Alexander Georg Mosle. 1854-1858.
    g. General-Consul Christian Stockmeyer. 1857—.

3. Zu Bahia.
4. Zu Pernambuco.
5. Zu Montevideo, s. C. 20 Uruguay.
6. Zu Rio Grande do Sul.
7. Zu Santos.
8. Zu Porto Alegre.
9. Zu Pará.
10. Zu Ceará und Rio Grande do Norte.

C. 12. c. Von Seiten Brasilien bei den Hansestädten angestellte diplomatische Agenten, Consuls, u. s. w.
1. Im Allgemeinen.
2. Vor der gänzlichen Trennung von Portugal.
3. Nach der gänzlichen Trennung von Portugal.
   a. Im Allgemeinen.
   b. Bei den Hansestädten gemeinschaftlich.
      1. Commandeure Georg Anton von Schäffer, diplomatischer Agent. 1825.
      2. Anton Joseph Rademaker, Consul. 1826-1829.
      3. Antonio da Silva Caldeira, General-Consul. 1829 u. 1830.
      4. Antonio de Menezes Vasconcellos de Drummond, Geschäftsträger, General-Consul. 1831.
      5. Marcos Antonio de Aurojo, Geschäftsträger und General-Consul, 1834, sod. Ministerresident, 1851, u. ausserordentl. Gesandter und bevollm. Minister, 1857.
      6. Jose Lucio Correia, General-Consul. 1852.
      7. Francisco Moniz Bareto d'Aragão, General-Consul. 1863.
      8. Le Chevalier Vianna de Lima, sodann Baron de Jauru, ausserordentl. Gesandter u. bevollm. Minister. June, 1868–Jan., 1890.
      9. Ygnacio José Alves de Souza, jr., Generalkonsul. Feb., 1890.
   c. Bei Bremen allein.
      1. Ludw. Friedr. Kalkmann, Vice Cons., 1827-1847, Consul, 1847.
      2. Hermann Wätjen, Vice Cons. 1848-1849.
      3. Franz Friedr. Droste, Vice Cons. 1849.
      4. Heinr. Wilh. Witte, Consul. 1867-1880.
         Aug. Franz Friedr. von Heymann, Vice K. 1881-1884.
         Albert Bartram, Vice Konsul. 1885-1895.
         de Alzevedo Barroso Bastos, Consul. 1891-1892.
         Carl Fränkel, Consul. 1892-1896.
         F. C. A. Runken, Vice Konsul. 1895-1896.
      5. Dr. José Marcelino de Moraes Barros, Vice Konsul, 1896-1898; sodann 1899—.
         Carl Weltmann, Handelsagent sod. Vicekonsul. 1896-1899.
         Chr. Ad. Tohlmann, Handelsagent. 1898.

C. 12. d. Handels- und Schiffahrts Vertrag. 1827.
1. Hauptakte.
2. Vorrath des gedruckten Vertrages.

C. 12. e. Auswanderungen nach Brasilien. (1826-1874.) Most important parcel of papers relating to the Germans in Brazil. The earlier documents are particularly valuable for the history of the beginnings of German emigration to that country. Among them the following are worthy of note: Correspondence between the Senate of Bremen and the Duchy of Darmstadt, 1826 and 1827, showing that there was a strong current of emigration from South Germany to Brazil and that emigrants were tempted by the promise of free passage to America by way of Bremen. Rigid measures were taken but, as the papers state, with little avail: " indem durch sie [die Massregeln] zwar wohl die Wirkungen des Uebels verhindert, nicht aber dessen Ursachen gehoben werden können ". (Letter addressed by the minister of Bremen to the Ministry of Foreign Affairs in Darmstadt, May 11, 1826.)

Acta betreffend die Auswanderer nach Brasilien namentlich Verhandlungen über diesen Gegenstand mit dem Cabinetsministerium zu Hannover, dem Ministerium der auswärtigen Angelegenheiten zu Stuttgart, dem Staatsministerium zu Cassel, und dem Staatsministerium zu Darmstadt. Apr. 14–Dec. 22, 1826.

Papiere betr. die Polizeiliche Beaufsichtigung sowie die Unterstützung der in den Jahren 1827-1828 für Brasilien engagirten am Buntenthorsteinweg einquartirten Auswanderer.

Verhandlungen des Senats mit den Regierungen des Grossherzogtums Hessen, des Königreichs Württemberg, des Grossherzogthums Baden und mit dem Senate der Stadt Frankfurt a. M. betreffend Wahrnehmung des Interesses derselben in Rücksicht auf die Auswanderungen nach Brasilien, u. s. w., durch Herrn Senator Dr. Gildermeister bei dessen Sendung nach Rio Janeiro. Dec. 14, 1826–Apr. 26, 1828.

Important extracts from the Protokoll of the Senate, relating to emigration.

Copies of Portuguese papers from the government of Brazil and other sources.

Printed pamphlets and circulars in German and Portuguese relating to Brazil.

Extracts from the Protokoll of the Senate of 1874, relating to emigrants returning from Brazil.

C. 13. Verhältnisse der Hansestädte mit Mexico.
C. 13. a. Generalia et diversa. (Supplementary to this *cf.* **C. 13. a.** Add., consisting of printed matter.)
C. 13. b. Erste Anknüpfung der Verhältnisse, auch Abschliessung eines Handels-Tractats.
  1. Hauptacte.
  2. Vacat.
  3. Kündigung des Vertrages von 1832, Abschluss des Vertrages von 1855, und weitere Acta.
C. 13. c. Gegenseitige Handels- u. Diplom. Agenten, etc.
  1. Hanseatische in Mexico.
      a. Im Allgemeinen (Generalia).
      b. Zu Mexico.
      c. Zu Vera Cruz.

d. Zu Tampico.
e. Zu Mazatlan.
f. Zu Campeche.
g. Zu Colima und Manzanillo.
h. Zu Tepic und San Blas.
2. Mexicanische bei den Hansestädten.
C. 14-15. Verhältnisse der Hansastädte mit Haiti.
C. 14. a. Mit Haiti insbesondere.
1. Generalia et diversa.
2. Consulat:
a. In Port au Prince (Port Républicain).
b. In Cap Haitien.
3. Haitisches Consulat hieselbst.
C. 14. b. Mit der Dominikanischen Republik.
1. Generalia et diversa.
2. Consulat in Porto Plata.
3. Dominikanisches Consulat hieselbst.
C. 15. Verhältnisse der Hanseatischen Städte zu Peru.
C. 15. a. Im Allgemeinen und diversa.
C. 15. b. Gegenseitige Handelsagenten, Consuls, etc.
1. Hanseatische in Peru:
a. Im Allgemeinen.
b. Consulat in Lima und Callao.
2. Peruanische bei den Hansestädten.
a. Im Allgemeinen (ohne Acten).
b. Peruanisches Consulat hieselbst.
C. 16. Verhältnisse der Hansestädte zu Columbien.
C. 16. I. Vor der Theilung Columbiens in mehrere Staaten.
a. Im Allgemeinen und diversa.
b. Anknüpfung der Verhältnisse.
c. Gegenseitige diplomatische Agenten, Consuls, u. s. w., bis 1828 incl.
C. 16. II. Nach der Teilung Columbiens.
1. Venezuela.
a. Generalia et diversa.
b. Verträge mit Venezuela auch Acta den Verkehr mit Venezuela überhaupt betreffend.
c. Gegenseitige diplomatische Consuln, u. s. w.
1. Generalia.
2. Hanseatische in Venezuela:
a. Im Allgemeinen.
b. Zu Laguaira.
c. Zu Puerto Cabello.
d. Zu Bolivar (Angostura).
3. Venezuelische bei den Hansestädten.
2. Ecuador.
3. Neugranada (Columbien).
a. Generalia et diversa.
b. Hanseatische Consuln in Neugranada.
c. Neugranadische (Columbische) Consuln in den Hansestädten.
C. 17. Verhältnisse der Hansestädte zu den Barbaresken. This Convolut is labelled R. 11. ee. 3 von Barbaresken.

C. 17. a. Varia.
C. 17. b. Acta des durch Marocanische Corsaren 1790 aufgebrachten Bremischen Schiffs *Elisabeth*, Capitain Vögels. 1798 *et seq.*
C. 17. c. Die in Algier aufgebrachte Ladung des mit Linnen von Bremen nach Sevilla befrachteten Schwedischen Schiff's *Anna Elisabeth*. Capitain C S. Wieksten. 1814.
C. 17. d. Die im Englischen Canal von den Barbaresken genommenen Hansischen Schiffe, namentlich die *Leda* von Bremen. 1817.
C. 18. Verhältnisse der Hansestädte zu Buenos-Aires.
C. 18. a. Im Allgemeinen und diversa.
C. 18. b. Gegenseitige Handelsagenten. Consuls, etc.
  1. Hanseatische in Buenos-Aires (Argentinien):
    a. Im Allgemeinen.
    b. Consulat in Buenos-Aires.
  2. Argentinische bei den Hansestädten:
    a. Im Allgemeinen.
    b. Generalconsulat hieselbst.
C. 19. Verhältnisse der Hansestädte zu Chile.
C. 19. a. Generalia et diversa.
C. 19. b. Gegenseitige Handelsagenten, Consuls, etc.
  1. Hanseatische in Chile:
    a. Im Allgemeinen.
    b. Consulat zu Valparaiso.
    c. Consulat zu Valdivia und Curral.
    d. Consulat zu Tolcahuano und Concepcion.
  2. Chileanische bei den Hansestädten.
C. 20. Verhältnisse der Hansestädte zu Uruguay (Montevideo).
C. 20. a. Generalia et diversa.
C. 20. b. Gegenseitige Handelsagenten, Consuls, etc.
  1. Hanseatische in Uruguay:
    a. Im Allgemeinen.
    b. Consulat in Montevideo.
  2. Uruguayische bei den Hansestädten:
    a. Im Allgemeinen.
    b. Consulat später Gen. Consulat in Hamburg.
    c. Viceconsulat hieselbst.
C. 23. Verhältnisse zu Central America.
C. 23. a. Generalia.
C. 23. b. Allgem. Verhältnisse zu den einzelnen Staaten.
  1. Zu Guatemala.
  2. Zu Nicaragua.
  3. Zu Costarica.
C. 23. c. Consulate in Centralamerica.
  1. Generalia.
  2. Generalconsulat in Guatemala.
  3. Consulat in Greytown u. für Mosquitia.
  4. Consulat zu Isabel u. Santo Tomas.
  5. Consulat zu San José u. Punto Arenas.
C. 26. Verhältnisse der Hansestädte zu Texas.
C. 27. *Id.*, zu Paraguay.
C. 30. *Id.*, zu Bolivia. (6 papers in all.)
C. 37. *Id.*, zu Cuba. (1 paper. 1903.)

BRUNSWICK (WOLFENBÜTTEL).
DUCAL BRUNSWICK-LUNEBURG NATIONAL CENTRAL ARCHIVES.
(HERZOGLICH BRAUNSCHWEIG-LÜNEBURGISCHES LANDESHAUPTARCHIV.)
Located in the old Gerichtsgebäude. Contains much valuable material relating to America. Records are well in hand and may be consulted by permission of the Minister of State obtained through the Director.
Hours: 9 to 1 and 3 to 5.

The most valuable materials relating to America are original contracts made by King George of England for Brunswick-Lüneburg auxiliary troops to serve in America to put down the Revolution, and the extensive Riedesel Correspondence, preserved by General von Riedesel and containing many hundred letters and communications, which passed between him and his prince, officers, and others during the period of the Revolution. The correspondence has not been catalogued nor fully indexed, but after it was handed over to the Archives it was carefully arranged and furnished with an alphabetical list of the correspondents by the directors of the Archives.

RIEDESEL PAPERS.
Gewölbe III. Repert. 20 a. Briefschaften und Akten des Generallieutenants Friedrich Adolf von Riedesel, Freiherr zu Eisenbach.
  I. Aus der Zeit vor dem Nordamerikanischen Kriege. Seite 1-9.
  II. Aus der Zeit des Nordamerikanischen Krieges. Seite 10-24.
  III. Aus der Zeit nach dem Nordamerikanischen Kriege. Seite 25-33.
This is the title as given in the special Repertorium of the collection. It is Part II. which particularly concerns America, as the following numbers will show.
v. Riedesel. II. 1. 57 Schreiben des Herzogs Karl I. zu Br. u. Lün. z. T. mit Anlagen. 1776-1777 (14 of 1776, 24 of 1777, 19 undated). Contains letters of Duke Karl I. to Riedesel relating chiefly to the condition and movements of the army, replies to reports and other more personal matter. Communications are enclosed also from other officers. The letters of the duke to Riedesel are written in a familiar and friendly tone. In II. 1 are found:
  " Specifique Berechnung derer, den ausmarschirten Regimentern und Corps auf Verlangen überschickten Armatur-Stücken und Feld-Requisiten, und was ihnen desfalls zu decourtiren. Summa 1425 Rthlr., 20 Gyl., 2 d."
  Letter to Westernsee, commissary of war, containing an order for supplies to be sent to Hamburg for the English. Braunschweig, July 25, 1777.
  The duke to Riedesel, relating to the decline of English " Wechsel-Cours " in Braunschweig to 5 Rthlr. and 18 Gyl., and ordering that for the troops already sent into the English service the rate of exchange shall be 5 Rthlr. and 20 Gyl., " aus besondern Gnaden ". July 26, 1777.

v. Riedesel. II. 2. 9 Schreiben des Erbprinzen bez. Herzogs Karl Wilhelm Ferdinand aus Halberstadt u. Braunschweig. Dabei Aufzeichnungen über die Stellung u. Tätigkeit v. Riedesels, den Character Karl Wilhelm Ferdinands u. a. 1776-1782 (4 of 1776, 2 of 1780, 2 of 1781, 1 of 1782). Contains letters relating to the troops in America and to the disposition of the troops after the close of the war in America:
A letter of Duke Karl Wilhelm, discussing Riedesel's plan of leaving a portion of the troops in the English service after the close of the war, and another proposal to send troops into Prussian service, which latter plan the duke does not approve, because the King of Prussia has not changed his budget and does not need extra troops. Braunschweig, Aug. 1, 1780.

v. Riedesel. II. 3. 92 Entwürfe von Berichten, etc., v. Riedesels an die Herzöge Karl und Karl Wilhelm Ferdinand. 1776-1783 (one of 1776, 2 of 1777, 6 of 1778, 4 of 1779, 10 of 1780, 21 of 1781, 19 of 1782, 28 of 1783, 1 n. y.). Reports partly in German and partly in French, in many cases more than drafts, being original official documents relating to the most various subjects concerning the movements, provisioning, and payment of the troops. This is important matter bearing upon the fiscal side of the war, as will be seen from a passage in a letter dated Sept. 5, 1780, referring to " die Art, wie die Hessen mit der Tresorie handeln, und ich bin von guter Hand versichert worden, dass der durchl. Land Graff, ohnerachtet der Geschichte von Trenton, und der Folgen nach in Gefangenschaft seyenden Hessen, so über 400 Mann ausmachen England dem Landgraffen zu Hessen nicht einen Heller schuldig ist ".

v. Riedesel. II. 4. 33 Schreiben Herzog Ferdinands z. Br. u. Lün. d. d. Braunschweig, Magdeburg, Vechelde, etc., und 28 Entwürfe von Schreiben Riedesels an den Herzog mit Anlagen. 1776-1783 (10 and 10 of 1776, 4 and 8 of 1777, 2 and 2 of 1778, 1 and 1 of 1779, 6 and 5 of 1780, 4 of 1783). Contains among other things a very interesting letter of Duke Ferdinand to Riedesel dated Mar. 25, 1776, and Riedesel's reply.

v. Riedesel. II. 5. 19 Originalschreiben v. Riedesels an Herzog Ferdinand z. T. mit Randbemerkungen von der Hand des Herzogs. 1776-1782 (5 of 1776, 3 of 1777, 2 of 1778, 1 of 1779, 4 of 1780, 1 of 1781, 2 of 1782).

v. Riedesel. II. 6. a. Schreiben des Herzogs Friedrich August zu Br. Lün.-Oels d. d. Berlin und Sanssouci und 1 Schreiben Riedesels an den Herzog. 1776, 1777. The letter of Friedrich August dated Berlin, Oct. 4, 1777, relates to the taking of Boston, etc. b. Ein Schreiben v. Riedesels an den Herzog Ludwig Ernst zu Br. u. Lün. 1780.

v. Riedesel. II. 7. 6 Schreiben des Erbprinzen Wilhelm v. Hessen, Grafen v. Hanau, und 10 Schreiben von Riedesels an ihn. Letters relating to the troops of Hesse Hanau and containing the order that troops shall in no case return to Europe without special orders to that effect. There are also other letters relating to the Hesse Hanau troops. 1780-1783.

v. Riedesel. II. 8. Contains letters from:
  Abbott, Edward, Capitän der Art. 1782. (2 letters, English.)
  Affleck, Edmund, Schiffskapitän. 1781. (2, English.)
  Albus, G., Leut. im v. Diemarschen Hus. Corps. New Utrecht, 1780-1781. (2, German.)
  Van Alstine, Peter, Capit. bez. Major Refugés. Port Smith Town. 1781. (3, English.)
  Amherst, Lord, General, 1777, 1779. (3, French.)
  Arbuthnot, Vice-Admiral. 1781. (1, English.)
  Archdale, R., Cap. 17. Reg. Dragon. 1781-1782. (12, English.)
  Arnold, B., General. Portsmouth, 1781. (1, English.)
  Axtell, W., Oberst. Flatt Bush, 1781. (2, English.)
v. Riedesel. II. 9. 99 Schreiben an bez. von Riedesel. Verzeichniss inliegend 1776-1783. The correspondence includes the following names:
  v. Bärtling, August, Kapitän. Westmunster, 1778-1780. (19, from and to B.)
  v. Barner, W., Major. St. François, 1777. (2.)
  Barnes, John, Kapitän d. Artillerie. Sorel, 1782-1783. (8, from and to B.)
  Battersby, Ja., Kapitän im 29. Regt. Brooklyn, 1781. (2.)
  Baum, Oberstleut. 1777. (1, to B.)
  Becker, A. L. n. y. (1.)
  Becker, Kathol. Geistlicher. Rivier onel, 1783. (1.)
  Beckwith, Ferd. A., Major. Isle aux Noix, 1782. (2, 1 to B.)
  Beckwith, Geo., Kapitän. New York, 1782. (2.)
  Belair, Louis, Maître de poste. Trois Rivieres, n. y. (1.)
  Bell, W., Serj.-Major. 1782. (1.)
  Bese, Louise, Frl. Wolfenbüttel, 1776. (1.)
  Best, Konrad, Fänrich. 1783. (1.)
  Bibby, T., Dep. Adj. Gen. New York, 1781. (3.)
  Bickell, Leutnant. Portsmouth, 1781. (1.)
  Blackley, James. St. John's, 1782. (1.)
  Blake, Mary. n. y. (1.)
  Bland, Theo., Oberst. Charlottesville, 1779. (7, from and to B.)
  v. Bodingen, Hauptmann. Brooklyn, n. y. (1, to B.)
  Boilan, Capitain de Milice. Chambly, 1782. (2, to B.)
  Bornemann, Leutnant. 1780. (1.)
  Borthwick, Wm., Hauptmann der Art. Sorel, 1782. (1.)
  v. Bose, Carl, Hess. Gener. Major. Newport, 1778-1781. (5, from and to B.)
  Boyd, William, Hauptmann. n. y. (3.)
  Brehm, D., Hauptmann, Barrack-Master General. 1781-1783. (8.)
  Breva, A. W., Leutnant. Albany, etc., 1777-1779. (4.)
  Brown, Oberst, 1780. (1.)
  Bruen, Henry, Major. New York, 1781. (2.)
  Bryan, Eduard. 1781. (1.)
  Buisson, Jean Baptiste. Aux Trois Rivières, 1783. (2, 1 to B.)
  Burgoyne, John, Generalleut. Quebec, etc., 1776, 1777. (20, from and to B.)
  v. Buttlar, Hauptmann. Stäntawn, 1779. (1.)

v. Riedesel **II. 10.** Contains letters from or to:
    de Cabanal. 3 Rivières, 1782. (1.)
    Caldwell, Henry, Oberst. Belmont, Quebeck, New York, St. John's, etc., 1782. (2.)
    Campbell, Alex., Hauptmann bez. Major. 1781-1783. (28.)
    Campbell, Brig.-General. 1782. (2.)
    Carleton, Christ., Hauptmann bez. Major. Isle-aux-Noix, St. Charles, 1776-1782. (6, from and to C.)
    Carleton, Guy, Generalleutnant. Chambly, etc., 1776-1777. (38, 21 to C.)
    Carleton, Thomas, General. Montreal, Trois Rivières, Quebeck, 1776-1777, 1781, 1782. (14, from and to C.)
    Carter, T., Major. Rutland, 1778. (2.)
    Chambers, W., Commodore. St. John's, Sorel, 1782, 1783. (14, from and to C.)
    Chandler, K. Quebec, 1782. (5.)
    Chandler, Thomas. St. John's, 1782. (1.)
    Clarke, Jon., Commis. New York, London, 1781-1782. (3.)
    Clarke, Tho., General. Quebec, 1782, 1783. (12, from and to C.)
v. Riedesel. **II. 11.** 107 Briefe des Leutnants Friedrich Cleve vom Stabe v. Riedesels. Dabei auch Briefe dieses an C. 1778-1783. These letters are for the most part in German. A number of the earlier ones of Cleve are in French. The correspondence is most valuable for the technical history of the war.
v. Riedesel. **II. 12.** Berichte des Hauptmanns H. Urban Cleve (z. T. Duplikate u. Triplikate) nebst zahlreichen Anlagen, Abschriften von Berichten Cleves an den Herzog, Briefen Verschiedener, auch v. Riedesels an Cleve, Listen, Quittungen, etc., etc., in Orig. u. Abschrift. 1777, 1781-1783, and n. y. A rich source of minute information, containing valuable documents, both in manuscript and in print, relating to the war. Among the documents is a printed "Pardon Card", signed by Riedesel and dated: "Sorel in Canada, Jan., 1782", promising pardon to all deserters from the English army, if they will return to service. The card is English on one side and has the confirmation of the promise and the signature in German on the other side. Another interesting paper is the "Specification" of documents contained in the chests of Cleve, and also of the baggage for the troops, etc.
v. Riedesel. **II. 13.** Letters from or to:
    Clinton, Sir Henry, General. Brooklyn, etc., 1778-1781. (27, 25 to C.)
    Clover, Brig.-General. n. y. (1, to C.)
    Clerke, Francis Carr, Adjutant Burgoynes. Fort Ann, etc., 1777. (9.)
    v. Cochenhausen. Bei Fort Knyphausen, 1778. (1.)
    Cochrane, John, Zahlmeister. Quebec, 1783. (1.)
    Collier, W. New York, 1780-1781. (2.)
    Conway, H. S., General. London, 1779, 1780. (2, 1 to C.)
    Cornwallis, Lord, Generalleutnant. New York, Wynnesborough, 1780, 1781. (7, 3 to C.)
    Corry, James. St. John, 1782. (1.)

Couwenhoven (?), Capitain. 1781. (1.)
Cramahé, H. T., Leutnant Gouverneur. Quebek, 1776-1777. (10, from and to C.)
v. Creuzberg, C., Hessen-Hanauischer Oberst. Lager bei Pointe aux Fer, etc., 1781-1784. (52, 3 to C.)
Crosbie, Oberst. New York, 1780. (1.)
Croxal, M. Lon[g] Island, 1780. (1.)
Cruse, P. S., Leutnant. Baraquen bei Charlottenville, 1780. (2, 1 to C.)
Cuff, W., Major. Brooklyn, 1781. (1.)
Cusseau, Major. Denysés, 1780. (1.)

v. Riedesel. II. 14. Letters from or to:
Dalrymple, Oberst. Brooklin, 1781. (1.)
Davis, Abel, American Prisoner. Sorel, 1782. (1.)
Day, Nath., Generalkommissar. Quebeck, 1781-1783. (12.)
Dechambault. Montreal, 1783. (1.)
Dehnhard, Stabsfeldwebel (Hessen-Hanau). Berthier, 1777. (1.)
Delancey, Oliver, Major, Adjut. General. New York, etc., 1780-1781. (21, from and to D.)
Depaky, Rice, Hauptmann, Quartiermeister General. n. y. (1, to D.)
Descheneaux, Crevier, Hauptmann der Miliz. St. François, 1782. (1.)
Deville. (1.)
Dickson, H., Hauptmann. St. John's, 1783. (1.)
Diehl, John Justus, Hauptmann. Montreal, 1782. (1.)
v. Diemar, Friedr. Frh., Hauptmann. New York, etc. 1779-1781. (18, from and to D.)
v. Ditfurth, Kammergerichtsassessor. Wetzlar, 1781-1783. (2.) Dabei Abschrift von Briefen v. D's u. des Landgrafen von Hessen, 1776-1779.
Dominque, Hauptmann. Pointe Olivier, 1781. (1.)
Dommes, Aug. Friedr., Hauptmann. Westminster, 1778. (1.)
Dougall, Alex. M. [McDougall], General (Amerika). Fishkill, 1778. (1.)
Du Buy, Oberstleutnant. Nord Carolina, 1781. (1, copy.)
Dumford, Ingénieur. Landing Place East Bay, 1777. (2.)
Dunlop, Hauptmann. (3.)
Dunn, Joseph, Fähnrich. Hallet's Cove, 1781. (1.)
Duport, R., Assistant Quarter Master General. Sorel, 1777. (2.)
Dupré, George, Oberst d. Miliz. Quebeck, 1777, 1782. (6, from and to D.)

v. Riedesel. II. 15. Letters from or to:
Edmondstone, Archibald. London, 1778-1781. (11, from and to E.)
Edmondstone, A., Jun., Hauptmann. Orange Courthouse, etc., London, 1778, 1780. (18, from and to E.)
Effingham, Countess of. Stoke, [1776-1777]. (2, 1 to her.)
v. Ehrenkrook, Karl Friedrich, Major. Winchester, 1781. (2, 1 to E.)
Elphinstone, G. B., Hauptmann. Warwick. (1.)

Ernst, Friedr. Brooklyn. (2.)
Ewald, Hauptmann. Chesapeak (Virginia), 1781. (3, to E.)
v. Riedesel. II. 16. Letters from or to:
  Fawcett, W., Generalmajor. London, etc., 1780-1787. (7, 3 to F.)
  Ferguson, Leutnant. St. John's, 1782. (1.)
  Feronee, v. Rotencreuz, Geheimerrat. Braunschweig, 1781. (1.)
  Fitzgerald, Elisabeth. Quebeck, 1782. (1.)
  v. Filzhofer, Leutnant. Point Olivier, 1782. (7.)
  Finley, Hugh. Quebeck, 1776, 1781. (3.)
  Förster, G., Major. Cambridge, etc., 1778, 1779. (4.)
  Fontain, Oberst. 1779. (1, to F.)
  Forbes, D., Hauptmann. St. John's, 1781, 1782. (10, from and to F.)
  Fox, Oberst. New York and Bedford, 1781. (2.)
  Foy, Ed., Hauptmann. Trois Rivières, 1776, 1777. (18.)
  v. Francken, Major. La Prairie, 1782. (1.)
  Fraser, Al., Brigadiergeneral. Montreal, 1777. (1.)
  Fraser, Tho., Leutnant, bez. Hauptmann. Yamaska Lower Blockhouse, etc., 1782, 1783. (30.)
  Fraser, W., Hauptmann. Yamaska Upper Blockhouse, etc., 1781-1783. (66, from and to F.)
  Fraser, Sekretär to Foy. Department. (1, to F.)
v. Riedesel. II. 17. Letters from or to:
  Freeman, Quin John, Aide de Camp. New York, adjutant Burgoyne's, 1780, 1783, 1787. (116, from and to F.)
  Fricke, H., Hauptmann. Westminster, Rutland, 1778-1780. (20.)
v. Riedesel. II. 18. Letters from or to:
  Gall, W. R., Brigadiergeneral. Berthier, Stendown, 1776-1782. (67, from and to G.)
  Gamble, Tho., Major, Generalquartiermeister. Quebec, St. John's etc. (53.)
  Gamble, Mos., Leutnant. (1.)
v. Riedesel. II. 19. Letters from or to:
  Gates, Horatio, General. Camp on Behmus's Heights, 1777. (2.)
  Gauguette, Joseph. (1.)
  Gebhard, Theodor, Leutnant. Rutland, 1781-1783. (7, from and to G.)
  v. Geismar, Hauptmann, bez. Major. Stantown, Charlotte Ville, Hanau, etc., 1779, 1780, 1784, 1786. (15.)
  Gerlach, J. D., Hauptmann. Trois Rivières, Quebec, etc., 1776-1783. (131, from and to G., with enclosures.)
v. Riedesel. II. 20. Letters from or to:
  Germain, Lord George. London, 1776, 1778-1781. (39, from and to G.)
  Gill, John. Montreal, 1782. (1.)
  v. Gleissenberg, Hauptmann. Albani, 1777, 1778. (5, from and to G.)
  Glover, John, General. Cambridge, 1778. (4, 1 to G.)
  Gödecke, H., Oberfeldkassier. Montreal, etc., 1776-1778. (16, 3 to G.)
  Gore, Jean u. Co. London, 1776. (4.)
  Gräfe, Aug., Cornet. Bennington, 1777, 1778. (7, 1 to G.)

Grant, J., Fähnrich. New York, 1781. (1.)
Grau, C. W. F., Leutnant. Elisabethtowns Point, 1780. (1.)
Green, Charles, Aide de Camp. Ticonderoga, 1777. (1, to Maj.-Gen. Phillips.)
Greene, Nath. Westpoint Garrison, 1779. (1.)
Grigsby, Mary. (1.)
Gugy [?], C. 1777. (1.)
Gunn, Major. (2, to G.)

v. Riedesel. II. 21. Letters from or to:
v. Hagen, J. W., Leutnant (Hessen-Hanau). Herrichs, 1781. (1.)
Hairre, Oberst. 1779. (1, to H.)
Haldimand, Fred., General. Quebec, Montreal, etc., 1778-1783. (311, from and to H.; 46 of 1781, 183 of 1782, 78 of 1783.) The letters are in English and French and constitute an exceedingly interesting and varied correspondence.

v. Riedesel. II. 22. 110 Schreiben an bez. von Riedesel. Verzeichnis inliegend 1776-1785. Contains letters to or from the following:
Hamilton, James, Brig.-General. Ticonderoga, 1777, 1779, 1781. (11.)
Handfield, W. Halifax, 1782. (1.)
Harbord, Hauptmann. Winchester u. Lancaster, 1781. (3, 1 to H.)
Harvie, Jon., Oberst (Amer.). 1779. (6, from and to H.)
v. Harstall, Leutnant. New York u. Braunschweig, 1781, 1782. (4, from and to H.)
Hassard, Thomas, Hauptmann (u. John Brangon Amer.). (1.)
Hauss, Jobst Heinrichs Witwe. Braunschweig, 1780. (1.)
Haynes, T., Hauptmann. 1776. (1.)
Henderson, Hauptmann. (1, to H.)
Heath, Generalmajor (Amer.). Boston, 1778. (17, from and to H.)
Heerwagen, J. F., Fähnrich (Hessen-Hanau). St. Dennys, 1776. (1.)
Henny, Mark, [McHenry?], Oberst, Sekretär d. Gen. Washington. 1779. (1.)
Henry, James W., General. Middlebrook, 1779. (4, 3 to H.)
v. Hesler, Curt, Leutnant. 1777. (1.)
Hewlett, Rich., Oberstleutnant. Loyds Neck, 1781. (6.)
Hill, J., Oberstleutnant. Charlotte Ville, 1779. (4, from and to H.)
Hinnitz [?]. Denyh's [?].
Hinüber, Charles (Geheimer Legationsrat). London, New York, 1780. (1.)
Hocking, R., Leutnant u. Ingenieur. St. John u. Isle aux Noix, 1781, 1782. (11, from and to H.)
Hogel, Francis. Verchere, 1782. (1.)
Holland, Sam. Bei Quebeck, etc., 1782, 1783. (3.)
Hooke, G. P., Hauptmann. Denyees, 1781. (1.)
Hope, Henryk, Oberst, Quart. M. Gen. Quebeck, 1782, 1783, 1785. (11.)
Hooper, Oberst. Bethlehem, 1779. (1.)

Houghton, Rich., Leutnant (Indians of Cachnawaga). Cachnawage, 1782, 1783. (9.)
How, William, General. 1778. (1, to H.)
Hoyer, Wilhelm. Lancaster, 1781. (1.)
Hoyes [Noyes ?], Robert. St. John's. 1782. (1.)
Hubert, Oberst. (1.)
Huff, Paul, Major. Fort Slougan, 1781. (1.)
Hughes, David, D. C. of Prisoners. Hagerstown, 1779. (1.)
Hughes, James, Agent. Fort George, 1777. (1.)
Hunter, James u. Adam. Fredericksburg, 1779. (1.)

v. Riedesel. II. 23. Letters from or to:
Irving, Amelius, Major. Skenesborough, etc. 1777-1780. (17, from and to I.)
Jaritz, Erasmus, Oberleutnant. Brooklyn, 1781. (1, with 3 inclosures.)
Jefferson, Gouverneur v. Virginien. (1, to J.)
Jenison, Jean, Seigneur de Saint Charles. 1776. (1.)
Jessup, Eben. Verchere, 1782, 1787. (2.)
Jessup, Edward, Major, Oberst. Verchere, etc., 1782, 1783. (24, from and to J.)
Jones, David, Leutnant. Yamaska, 1782. (1.)
Jones, John, Capitain, Dragonen. Sorel, 1781, 1783. (4.)
Johnson, John, Oberleutnant. Montreal, 1782, 1783. (4.)
Jordan, Jacob, Zahlmeister. Montreal, 1776, 1777. (4.)

v. Riedesel. II. 24. Letters from or to:
Kay, William. Montreal, 1782. (2.)
Kelsick, Richard. Isle of Bee, 1781. (1.)
Kingston, Rob., Adjutant Burgoynes. Cambridge, etc., 1777, 1778. (11, in part orders.)
v. Kniphausen, Generalleutnant. Philadelphia, York Island, etc., 1778-1784. (32, from and to K.)
v. Kospoth, Generalmajor. New York, 1780-1781. (3, 2 to K.)
Krause, John Christoph, sen. Braunschweig, 1780. (1.)
v. Kuntzsch, T. F., Leutnant (Hess.). (1.)

v. Riedesel. II. 25. Letters from or to:
Labonne. Aux Trois Rivières, 1782. (1.)
La Fayette, Marquis. 1777. (1, to L.)
Lampman, Jno. 1777. (2, 1 to L.)
Langemeyer, Sekretär. 1778. (2, 1 to L.)
Lawe, Geo. Montreal, 1782. (1.)
Leaver [?], Deal. Bremerleh, 1783. (2.)
Lee, Will. R., Oberst. Cambridge, 1777. (4, from and to L.)
Leger, Barry St., Oberst. Chamblee, Montreal, etc., 1776. (79, from and to St. L.)
Leland, Brig.-General. 1780. (1.)
Le Maische, Fran., Generaladjutant. Quebeck, 1781. (11, from and to L.)
v. Lentz, Oberstleutnant. [Hess. bez. Anhalt. Bei St. Jean, Lancaster, etc.], 1776, 1780, 1783. (11, from and to L.)
Lernoult, R. B., Generaladjutant. Montreal, Quebeck, 1782, 1783. (15.)

v. Riedesel. II. 26. Letters from or to:
>Lind, Oberstleutnant. 1779. (3, 1 to L.)
Lindsay, Wm. (1.)
v. Loos, Oberst. Point Levy, Quebeck, etc., 1780-1784. (37, from and to L.)
Lorentz, J. G., Kriegsrat u. Generalkommissar. New York, Broklin, 1779-1781. (9, from and to L.)
Lorentz, Rich., Feld Kriegs-Kassier (Hess.). New York, Kassel, 1781-1784. (4.)
v. Lossberg, Generalmajor. Newport, Morrishause, etc. 1778, 1780. (27, from and to L.)
Lott, Jeromus, Oberstleutnant. (1.)
Ludlow, Dan. 1781. (1.)
Ludlow, Geo. D. (1.)
Ludlow, G. G. Loyds Neck, 1780, 1781. (14.)
Lutwidge, Hauptmann. Ticonderoga, 1777. (1.)

v. Riedesel. II. 27. Letters from or to:
>Macbean, Forbes, Oberstlt. d. Art. Quebec, Sorel, 1781-1783. (11, 1 to M.)
Macdonald, John, Major. Newtown, 1781. (1.)
Macdukel, General. Newpurry, Harsbroek, 1775. (4, from Riedesel.)
Mackay, Jannet, Mrs. Berthier, 1782. (2.)
Mackenzie, Fred., Capitain. Hauptquartier, 1781. (4.)
Marsh, J., Oberst. New York, 1781. (1.)
Marsh, William. St. John, 1782, 1783. (3.)
Marshall, Capitain. Brooklyn, 1781. (1.)
Mathews, R., Capitain. Quebec, 1782-1783. (8.)
Maurer, J., Capitain, Montreal. 1782-1783. (8.)
de Meibom, Herz. Braunschw. Major. Westminster, 1777, 1778 (6 of 1777, 1 to M.; 14 of 1778, 2 to M.). Lankaster, 1779-1781 (11 of 1779, 9 to M.; 17 of 1780, 6 to M.; 16 of 1781, 6 to M.).
Melzheimer, Feld Prediger. Brimfield, 1778. (1.)
Melvin u. Wills. Quebec, 1782. (1.)
Mendonsa, Peter. Madeira, 1781. (3, 1 to M.)

v. Riedesel. II. 28. Letters from or to:
>v. Mengen, Otto Carl Anton, Herzl. Br. Oberstlt. Virginien, 1780-1782. (8 of 1780, 5 to M.; 15 of 1781, 6 to M.; 4 of 1782, 3 to M.).
Mercer, Alex., Capitain. New York, 1781. (1.)
Mersereau, Joshua. Elisabeth Town, 1782. (1.)
Metzner, P., Brigademajor. New York, 1781. (2.)
Monsell, William, Major. St. John's, 1783. (7.)
Montgolfier. Upper Montreal, 1782, 1783. (2.)
Morin, Jean, Capitain. St. Roche, 1782. (1.)
Murray, Michael. Barrack Office, Quebec, 1776-1783 (2 of 1776, 8 of 1777, 1 of 1780, 23 of 1782, 2 to M.; 12 of 1783, 2 to M.).
Murray, Tho., Aid de Camp. New York, 1780, 1781. (2.)

v. Riedesel. II. 29. Letters from or to:
>Nairne, John, Major vom 53. Reg. Isle aux Noix, 1781-1783. (40, 2 to N.)

Neveusevertre [?], Colonel. 1782. (2.)
Noiseux. 1782. (1.)
Norton, Wm., Hauptmann. St. Charles, 1782. (5.)
Olivier, Louis. Berthier, 1776. (2, 1 to O.)
Ouvrier, Lud. Benj., Prof. d. Theol. in Giessen. Giessen, 1781. (1.)
Paine, W., Doctor. London, 1781. (1.)
Paterson, Brig.-General. Staten Iland, 1781. (1.)
Pattison, Jac., Art. Capitain, dann Major. London, 1781. (1.)
Pausch, G. Cambridge, 1778-1783. (14, 3 to P.)
Pflüger, geb. Baum, Witwe des Leut. in Wolfenbüttel. Quebec, 1783. (1, to P.)
v. Riedesel. II. 30. Letters from or to:
    Phillips, W., Generalmajor. Chambly, Montreal, etc., 1776. (10.) Montreal, etc., 1777. (11.) Cambridge, etc., 1778. (34, 8 to P.) Colonel Carters House, 1779. (53, 5 to P.) New York, etc., 1780. (43, 9 to P.) New York, 1781. (12, 1 to P.) n. p., n. y. (22.)
    Pinuchne [?]. Chatham, 1781. (1.)
    Piper, John, Capitain, Quart. Mstr. Gen. Rhode Island, Newport, 1778. (3.)
    v. Pöllnitz, Hauptmann. Trois Rivières, New York, Sorel, 1777-1783. (37, 3 to P.)
    Powl, Brig.-Gen. St. Johns, 1776. (1.)
    Prant, James. Quebec, 1782. (1.)
    Pringle, T. 1781. (1.)
    Pritchard, Azar. Sorel, St. Johns, 1781, 1782. (2.)
    v. Prüschenck, Oberstlt. Jericho, Westburry, 1780. (3, 1 to P.)
v. Riedesel. II. 31. 85 Schreiben an bezw. von Riedesel und Companie-Listen. Verzeichnis inliegend 1776-1791 und o. J.
Quincy, Oberst. Braintree, 1778. (9, 2 to Q.)
Quintal, Michael, Capitain. Verchere, 1782. (1.)
Ramsay, Geo. Will. n. p., n. y. (1.)
v. Rauschenplat, Geo., Major, dann Oberstlt. St. Antoine, etc. (7, 2 to R.) Gives the names of the men in his company.
Reinking, F. C., Leutnant. Winchester, 1781. (2, 1 to R.)
v. Rhetz, Aug. Wilh., Gen. Leut. Wolfenbüttel, Braunschweig, 1776, 1780. (2.)
Rice, Capitain. Aus Colle near Charlotteville, 1779. (1.)
Richardson, John. Montreal, 1776. (1.)
v. Riedesel, Schwägerin d. Generals, D. R. née H. H. June 6, 1781. (1.)
v. Riedesel, Charles [Fr.], Bruder d. Generals. Lauterbach, July 9, 1782. (1.)
v. Riedesel, Joh. Conrad, Oberst u. Kammerherr. Braunschweig, 1776-1782. (32, French.)
Rogers, Jac., Major. Fort St. John's. 1782-1783. (4.)
v. Romrod, Carl, Hessischer Oberst. Cantonnement bei Fort Knyphausen, 1782. (2, 1 to R.)
Roohr, D. J. G. P. Forces. New York, 1780. (1.)
Ross, Colonel. n. d. (1.)
Ro .... [?] Anton Florens. Rittberg, 1783. (1.)

Roussel, J. B. Longueil, 1781. (1.)
Ruff, Joh. Conrad, Capitain. Carlston u. Flatbush, 1781. (2.)
R .... [?] K. Leutnant. St. John, 1783. (1.)
v. Riedesel. II. 32. Letters from or to:
  Sandwich, Earl. Admiralty, 1776. (4.)
  Sartorius, Lieutenant u. Reg. Quartermstr. In den Barraquen, 1776. (2, 1 to S.)
  Saucier, Louis, aide de post. La Rivière du Loup. (1.)
  Saunders, A. Isle au[x] Noix, 1782, 1783. (22.)
  Saur, C. H. Wolfenbüttel, 1777, 1780, 1781. (4.)
  Schachten (aus Hessen?). Auf den Barraquen, 1779. (1.)
  Schank, John. Quebec, 1782, 1783. (7.)
  Schlagenteufel, Capitain d. Braunschweig. Regt. v. Specht. 1780. (1.)
  Schmidt, Capitain bei der Blankenburgischen Land. Comp. Blankenburg, 1781. (2, 1 to S.)
  Schmidt, Fr., Hofmeister. Cassel, 1781. (1, to Lt. Col. v. Riedesel.)
  v. Schöle, Offizier d. Hess-Hanauischen Truppen. Rivière Quelle, 1782. (1.)
  Schuyler, Ph., Major Gen. Saratoga, 1783. (5, 1 to S.)
  Scott, Sco 1779. (1.)
  Scott, T. C. W. Sorel, 1781. (2.)
  Scott, Edward. Jamaica, 1781. (1.)
v. Riedesel. 11. 33. 78 Schreiben an bezw. von Riedesel nebst Anlagen Verzeichnis inliegend 1776-1785.
  Seddon, George, Cabinet Maker. London, 1783. (1.)
  Shelburne, Earl. Sorel, Isle aux Noix, etc., 1776, 1782. (10.)
  Sherwood, J., Capitain. Loyal Block-House, 1782, 1783. (19.)
  Skeenes, Benj., Colonel. Clarendon, 1777. (1.)
  Smith, George, Dr. St. John, 1782-1783. (10.)
  Sotheron, Capitain. (1.)
  Specht, Anton, Officier. Rutland, 1781. (1.)
  Specht, A. C. (Ant. Christoph), Dechant des Math. Stifts z. Braunschw. Braunschweig, 1781. (2.)
  Specht, J. H., Oberst. Braunschweig, 1782. (5, 3 to S.)
  v. Speth. Ernst Lud. Wilh. Friedr., Gen. Major. Chatham, New York, Wolfenbüttel, 1778, 1781. (6, 2 to S., with enclosure.)
  Stapleton, D. A. G. New York Head Quarters, 1781. (1.)
  Stedenson [Stevenson?], Cha. London, 1785. (1.)
  v. Stein, Hessischer Major. Fleusching, Deneycis, Newtown, etc., 1781. (7.)
  St. Germain. St. Sulpice, 1777. (1.)
  St. Onges, General. 1780-1782. (5.)
  Stutzer, J. B., Cornet. Brimfield, Lancaster, 1778, 1780. (3.)
  Suffolk, Lord. St. James, 1776. (2.)
  Sutherland [Sullivan?], Colonel. Brooklyn, 1781. (2, 1 to S.)
v. Riedesel. II. 34. Letters from or to:
  Tanswell, Jacob. Quebec, 1782. (1.)
  Theobald, Officier in Hessisch-Hanauischen Diensten. Herford, 1778. (1.)
  Theodore, F., Curé. Becancourt, 1776. (4.)

Thomae, A. J., Hauptm. Führer d. 1. Rekruttransport. Quebec, Trois Rivières, Spithead, 1777, 1779. (6, 1 to T., with 16 appendices.) Important because it contains lists of the men of the several companies, etc.
Tonnacourt, Geo. Trois Rivières, 1776-1782. (14, 1 to T.)
Torriano, Cha., Lieutenant. 1779. (2, 1 to T.)
Trottig, Jean, Capitain. Batiseau, 1777. (1.)
v. Riedesel. II. 35. Letters from or to:
  v. Tunderfeld, Carl, Hauptmann, aide de Camp. Quebec, etc., 1776-1783 (52 of 1776, 45 of 1777, 1 of 1779, 2 of 1780, 23 of 1781, 59 of 1782, 4 to T.; 33 of 1783, 3 to T.; 5, n. y., 1 to T.).
v. Riedesel. II. 36. Letters from or to:
  Tuttle, Stephen. (1.)
  Twiss, W., Hauptmann. Camp at Point au Fer, 1776. (1.) Ingénieur-Département. Quebec, etc., 1781, 1782. (57, 3 to T.)
  Tyler, W., Leutnant. St. John's, 1782. (2.)
v. Riedesel. II. 37. Letters from or to:
  v. Unger, Leutnant. Quebec, 1783. (1.)
  Vallancy, Capitain, Gen. Quart. Mstr. Cambridge, Charlotte Ville, etc., 1778, 1779. (15, 3 to V.)
  Verreau, Joseph, Prêtre. St. Roch, 1782. (4.)
  Vogel, C. H. Hannover, 1776. (1.)
  Voigt, Geh. Registrator. Braunschweig, 1776. (1.)
  Voigt, Joh. Andr. Philadelphia, 1780. (1.)
v. Riedesel. II. 38. 63 Schreiben an bezw. von Riedesel nebst 1 Liste. Verzeichnis inliegend.
  Waddington, B. New York, 1781. (1.)
  Wail. 1777. (1.)
  Walch, Mathew, Master. Sorel, 1783. (1.)
  Wallace, Hugh Alex. New York, 1782. (1.)
  Wallach, Moses Abraham. Winterhill, 1778. (1.)
  Wallop, B. H., Brigade Major. Jamaica, 1781. (4.)
  Watson, Josiah. Alexandria, 1779. (1.)
  Walter, [J. ?]. (1.)
  Warner, Levi. St. John's, 1782. (1.)
  Washington, G., General. Head Quarters Valley Forge, etc., 1778-1781. (11, 9 to W.)
  Wasmus, Jno. Friedr., Escadron Chirurgus. Brimfield u. Rutland, 1778-1781. (5.)
  Watson, Brook. Montreal, Quebec, u. London, 1776, 1779-1783. (26, 1 to W.)
  [Watson and Rashleigh. London, 1782.]
  Weise, Capitain. Charles Town, 1781. (3, and 1 list of arms.)
  Wende, C., Reg. Quartiermeister v. Ditfurthschen Reg. New York, 1778. (1.)
  Westensee, P. F. H. Braunschweig, 1777. (1.)
  v. Westphalen, Georg Philip, Frh. Landgraf Drost früher Geh. Sect. S. Herz. Ferd. 1776. (1.)
  Wicke, Wilhelm, Soldat. Philadelphia, 1780. (1.)

Wied, Dan. 1781. (1.)
v. Wietersheim, Hauptmann. St. Antoine, 1782. (1.)
v. Riedesel. II. 39. Letters of:
  Willoe, Sam. Quebec, London, Sorel, etc., 1776-1787. (74.)
v. Riedesel. II. 40. Letters from or to:
  v. Wilmowsky, Major. Brooklyn, 1781. (1, to W.)
  Winkelmann. Abbensen, 1781. (2.)
  Winslow, Joshua. Quebec, 1783. (3, 1 to W.)
  v. Winzingerode, Oberst. Cassel, 1776-1781. (4.) Ziegenhayn u. Mastricht, 1783-1791. (7.)
  Wood, Capitän. St. John's, 1782. (1.)
  Right Worshipfull Sir. (1.)
  v. Wurmb, Hess. Officier, Oberstlt. Rohd Island, 1777. (1.) Kingsbridge, 1778. (1.) Long Island, 1779. (1.) Westburry, 1780. (24.) Westburry, etc., 1781. (49, 2 to W.) Deneysis, 1782. (1.) Huntington, Johnshouse, etc., 1783. (4.) Chatham, New York, Cassel, 1784. (14.)
v. Riedesel. II. 41. Briefe und Eingaben von verschiedenen Einwohnern Amerikas mancherlei Angelegenheiten betr. grossenteils undatiert. 1776-1782. A most curious, interesting, and in certain particulars valuable bundle of papers, odds, and ends relating to the American Revolution, personal matter concerning the family v. Riedesel and other information. One particularly interesting document is the proclamation of Riedesel dated on the back " Trois Rivières ce 23me Nov. 1776 " and signed by Riedesel.
v. Riedesel. II. 42. Briefe mit unlesbaren Unterschriften, Bruchstücke von Briefen, Entwürfe von Briefen Riedesels ohne Adressen, dabei ein Gedicht auf R.'s Geburtstag. 1778, etc. A curious miscellany containing matter with French transcription interlined and a great variety of papers valuable for the historian.
v. Riedesel. II. 43. Acta die Einrichtung eines neuen Corps zum englischen Dienst betr. 3 vols. Vol. I., Dec. 2-22, 1775; vol. III., Jan. 6-16, 1776; vol. IV., Jan. 16–Feb. 22, 1776. [Vol. II. wanting.]
  Vol. I. Dec. 2-22, 1775. This volume is bound in paper. It contained originally, according to the table of contents, 96 numbers or papers and 2 additional documents marked a and b at the beginning of the list. The following numbers are of particular interest:
  a. Schreiben Ser^{mi}, directed to Riedesel. Braunschweig, Dec. 2, 1775.
  b. Schreiben des Erbprinzens Durchl. Two important early documents relating to the German mercenaries for English service in America.
  No. 1. Project d'un Traitté a conclure pour un Corps, etc.
  2, 3 u. 4. 3 Stück Brouillons zum neuen Corps.
  5. Aufsatz zur Instruction für die Werber.
  6. Desgleichen für 1 Officier auf Werbung.
  7. Aufsatz, wie ad Nr. 5.
  8. Benennung der Werbe Posten.
  9. Benennung einiger Unterofficiers, zur Werbung.

10. Plan von diesem neuen Corps.
11. Brouillon von den erforderl. Officiers, von hiesigen Regimentern.
12. Brouillon vom Grenad. Mousq. u. einem Frey Battaillon.
13. Erklärungen der Officiers, ob sie mitmarschieren wollen.
14. Unterthänige Anfragen über einige Punkte zur Werbe Instruction.
15. Untert. Pro Mem. ad Ser^{mum} nebst beygesetzter höchsten Antwort, die zu veranstaltende Werbung betr.

These first 15 papers will give an idea of the contents of the volume and indicate the value of the documents for the historian. Judging from the applications of officers for acceptance in the corps, one can hardly say that the officers of the German mercenaries were " verkauft wie Vieh ". To be sure the recruiting officers were instructed to employ their persuasive art in making the situation " recht angenehm " for the recruits. With number 93 are enclosed two colored plates of soldiers in uniform worn in the service.

Riedesel II. 44. Acta betr. den mit England, 1776 abgeschlossenen Subsidienvertrag, die Instruction von Riedesels zur Führung der Braunschweig[ischen] Truppen, etc. 1776. Contains the following documents of importance:

Copies of the " Subsidien Tractate " printed in Frankfort and Leipzig. 1776.

Projet d'un Traitté à conclure pour un Corps de 4000. Hommes d'Infanterie et de 300. Hommes de Cavallerie des Trouppes de Bronsvic [Dec. 1775, 17 articles].

Treaties of the Duke of Brunswick with the Landgrave of Hesse Cassel and the Count of Hanau, in three columns side by side. (English MS.)

Eydes Foronel [German].

Decree of the Duke of Brunswick and Lüneburg to carry out the terms of the treaty. Brunswick, Jan. 16, 1776. (French.)

Instruction für Unsern von Gottes Gnaden Carl Herzog zu Braunschweig und Lüneburg, etc., Obristen und lieben Getreuen Friedrich Adolph von Riedesel, das demselben über die in Königln. Grossbrittannischen Sold marchirende Trouppen anvertraute Ober-Commando betreffend. Jan. 10, 1776. (14 pp.)

v. Riedesel. II. 45. Ciffern schlüssel, Paroles, Countersigns, Scouting Marks, etc. The two sheets of scouting marks are exceedingly interesting and cover in all 5 pages. There are 3 pages of paroles.

v. Riedesel. II. 46. Tagebuch der Braunschweigischen Truppen in Nordamerika unter dem Befehle des Generalmajors v. Riedesel. Zwei im wesentlichen gleiche Niederschriften: I. Feb. 22, 1776–June 1, 1777; II. Feb. 22, 1776–Jan. 15, 1779. The exact title of the first diary runs thus: " Journal der Hochfürstl Braunschweigischen Trouppen nach Nord America unter dem Befehl der Herrn General-Major v. Riedesel ". It contains 108 written folio pages, averaging about 600 words, and also a few simple plans but no maps. The second diary contains 320 written folio pages with some 500 words to the page, thus containing nearly twice the number of words in I.

v. Riedesel. II. 47. Auszüge aus verschiedenen Journalen, sowie sonstige Aufzeichnungen über Kriegsereignisse und militärische Angelegenheiten verschiedener Art. (Das Scheibenschiessen 1776; Winterquartiere 1779; Das Embarquement der für Canada von New York bestimmten Truppen 1781, etc., sowie Ausführungen gegen ein zu Boston gedrucktes Blatt 1777-1783.) Contains a large amount of valuable detail, such as the list of men, papers relating to the embarcation, together with "A Journal of the proceedings of the Fleet and Army after leaving New York, Saturday 25th December 1779", and many other original notes and papers used doubtless in making up the "Journal".

v. Riedesel. II. 48. Acta betr. die Capitulation von Saratoga am 16. October 1777 und die Auswechselung der in Kriegsgefangenschaft geratenen Offiziere. Desgl. die von diesen zu fordernden Couragegelder und die zu York-Town verlorene Bagage. 1777, 1782. Contains among other valuable matter:

1. Papers relating to the convention of October 13, 1777, a large bundle containing among others the document entitled: "Pièce Justificatoire du Général Major Riedesel, sur les évènements de la Campagne de 1777 en Amérique", 15 written pages in French.
2. An extensive collection of original papers relating to the exchange of prisoners, containing among other things lists of names and official papers relating thereto.

v. Riedesel. II. 49. Generalordres, Vorschriften, etc., des Generalmajors v. Riedesel; Ordres, etc., des Englischen Oberbefehlshabers; Rescripte des Herzogs; Befehle des Königs, etc. 2 vols.

Vol. I. Feb. 16, 1776-1780.
Vol. II. 1781–Oct., 1783.

v. Riedesel. II. 50. Zwei Ordrebücher des Braunschw. Truppencorps in Nordamerika.

Vol. I. June 5, 1776–Dec. 11, 1782.
Vol. II. Jan. 19–July 6, 1783.

v. Riedesel. II. 51. Acta betr. die den Truppen im englischen Solde gewährten Gagen, ihren Abmarsch, u. ihre Einschiffung nach Amerika. 1776. Pay-rolls, details of the march, numerical lists, details relating to the blacksmiths, etc.

v. Riedesel. II. 52. General-Kassenextrakte, Abrechnungen des Truppencorps und einzelner Truppenteile über Sold, Subsistenz-Quartier-Gelder, Bekleidung, Fouragegelder, etc., etc. Listen über Vorräte, etc. Allerlei Rechnungen, etc., etc. 3 vols.

Vol. I. 1776-1779.
Vol. II. 1780-1782.
Vol. III. 1783-1784 u. o. J.

These papers are important for the lists of the men in the several companies and the pay received by each, as well as other details relating to the expenses of the army.

v. Riedesel. II. 53. Acta betr. die Fürstl Feld-Kriegskasse, die Rechnungführung im Allgemeinen und die Abrechnung mit den Regimentern vor dem Abmarsche aus Amerika. 1783. Balance sheets of accounts and general summaries of the expenses of the war.

v. Riedesel. II. 54. Listen, etc., über die Stärke der Braunschweigischen Truppen insgesammt, sowie ihre einzelnen Theile. Desgl. Namenrollen u. Namenslisten der Letzteren. 1776-1783. Important lists of names and reports of marches in the several campaigns.

v. Riedesel. II. 55. Listen über Zugang und Abgang bei den Braunschw. Truppen, über Gefangene, Todte, und Verwundete. 1777-1783.

v. Riedesel. II. 56. Listen über Hessische und andere Truppen 1776-1782. Contains names of Hessian (Hanau) soldiers, also of Yamasca 2d Company.

v. Riedesel. II. 57. Acta betr. die Stellung von Riedesels in der Freimaurerloge zu Quebeck und freimaurerischen Angelegenheiten sonst.

v. Riedesel. II. 58. Landkarte, auf Leinwand aufgeklebt: *New England*, by Thomas Jefferys. Nov., 1774.

v. Riedesel. II. 59. Landkarte, auf Leinwand aufgeklebt: *Province of New York with Part of Pennsylvania and New England*, by Captain Montresor. 1775.

v. Riedesel. II. 60. Landkarte auf Leinwand aufgeklebt: *Nord Amerika*, by John Rocque. 1761.

v. Riedesel. II. 61. Plan von London. n. p., n. d.

OTHER (THAN RIEDESEL) PAPERS.

Acta Militaria. I. 83. Den Amerikanischen Feldzug der Herzoglich Braunschweigischen Truppen betreffende Instructionen für die Regiments Chefs, die Generalstabs- und Regiments-Auditeurs und die Compagnie-Chirurgen. 1776.

Acta Militaria. I. 84. Amerikanische Briefe an des Herrn Erbprinzens Hochfürstl. Durchl. Contains letters of:

1. Riedesel. 1776, 1777.
2. v. Specht. 1776, 1777.
3. Christian Julius Prätorius. 1776, 1777. Encloses a manuscript entitled " Journal vom 2ten Juni bis den 17 Juli 1777", with flags on colored sheets. (4 pp.)
4. v. Mengen. 1776, 1777.
5. Christian Senf. 1776.
6. Gerlach. 1776. Contains the following relating to winter quarters: Quartiers d'Hiver Pour les troupes Allemandes en Canada. 1776-1777. One large sheet with the title: " Quartiers d'iver Pour les troupes Angloises en Canada ".

Bündnisse, Verträge, etc. Nr. 506. König Georgs III. Vollmacht für seinen Gesandten, den Obersten Wilh. Faucitt, mit dem Herzoge Carl zu Braunschweig u. Lüneb. einen Subsidientractat abzuschliessen. " Dabantur in Palatio nostro Divi Jacobi 21. Die Mensis Decembris Anno Domini 1775 Regnique Nostri 16." Original, with the king's signature and the seal in a silver case. A splendid parchment document in Latin, well preserved, and endorsed: " Colonel Faucitt. Full Power".

Bündnisse, Verträge, etc. Nr. 507. Subsidientractat des Herzogs Carl zu B. u. L. mit dem Könige Georg III. von England wegen Ueberlassung eines zu dem Kriege in Amerika bestimmten Truppencorps von 3964 Mann Infanterie und 336 Mann leichter Cavallerie. Von den beiderseitigen Ministern abgeschlossen. d. d. Mart. The document is in French and contains 15 articles together with " État des Trouppes qui passeront à la Solde de Sa Majesté Brittannique ".

Bündnisse, Verträge, etc. Nr. 508. Separat Artikel, welcher bestimmt, dass der König von England die im Vertrage festgesetzten Hülfsgelder für die Braunschweigischen Truppen im Amerikanischen Kriege fortzahlen soll, wenn der Herzog von Braunschweig durch Kaiserl. Aufgebot zur Verteidigung des Reichs verhindert ist, die jährlichen Rekruten zu stellen, und dass diese Verminderung des Truppencorps nur Einfluss auf den Sold haben soll. " Fait à Brunswic ce 9me Janvier 1776." Original parchment, with the signatures of the two plenipotentiaries, and a " Notte sur l'État de Solde de deux Mois énoncée dans l'Article XIII du Traitté ", also a statement of the payments for 60 and 61 days ; each has the two signatures. Notte concernant l'Argent de Livree.

Bündnisse, Verträge, etc. Nr. 509. Subsidientractat des Herzogs Carl zu Braunschweig u. Lüneb. mit dem Könige Georg III. von England wegen Ueberlassung eines zu dem Kriege in Amerika bestimmten Truppencorps von 3964 Mann Infanterie und 336 Mann leichter Cavallerie. Vom Könige Georg III. ratificirt. " Quae dabantur in Palatio Nostro Divi Jacobi 19. Die Mensis Januarii, anno Domini 1776, Regnique Nostri 16." Original, with the king's signature, and the seal in a silver case. The treaty is on heavy sheepskin and in French. It contains in all 15 articles.

Gewölbe II. Repert. 22. Consulat zu St. Louis, etc. Contains the following entries : Herzogl. Braunschw. Consulat in St. Louis (geführt 1855-1856 von A. E. Koels, 1857-1859 von E. C. Angelrodt) :

1. Registrande :
   a. Ueber Legalisation von Documenten. 1855-1863.
   b. Ueber Erledigung der Geschäfte. 1855-1863.
2. Verschiedene Schreiben aus dem Jahr 1856, u. A. den Tod des Sohnes Hans des Hofjägermeisters v. Veltheim betr.
3. Kopierbuch, die abgegangenen Schreiben von 1857-1869 enthaltend.
4. Registrande über Legalisation von Documenten. 1863-1868.
5. Registrande über Erledigung der Geschäfte. 1863-1868. (Sodann eingegangene Briefe für Bayern, Baden, Württemberg, u. Hessen, 1869-1870.)
6. Abschrift einer Instruction für den Braunschw. Consul der Vereinigten Staaten von Nord-Amerika (Consul Samson für die südlichen Staaten der Union) vom 25 März 1854. Eingetauscht Okt. 1900 vom Seminaroberlehrer Fr. Jeep.

410. Fragment eines Tagebuchs über die Braunschweigischen Truppen im Amerikanischen Feldzuge. July 2–Oct. 26, 1777. 136 pages octavo.
761. II. Reise Beschreibung erster Division der Fürstl. Braunschweigischen Trouppen nach America. Gesammelt von Julius Friedrich Wasmus, 1776. 264 quarto pages of text, 40 pages of index.

Acta der Geheimen Kanzlei des Herzoglichen Staatsministeriums. E. Varia.

Nr. 9. Acta betr. Todesscheine. 1832-1867. 4 vols.
Nr. 12. Acta Ertheilung von Heimathsscheinen betr. 1820, 1837-1849.
Nr. 13. Acta Pässe betr. 1813-1861. 3 vols., 1813-1837, 1838-1850, 1851-1861.
Nr. 13 a. Reisepässe betr.
Nr. 14. Acta das Wandern der Handwerksgesellen in der Schweiz betr. 1852-1863.
Nr. 14 a. Acta die Wiederaufnahme der Ausgewiesenen betr. 1836-1853.
Nr. 16. Emigrations-Consense betr. 1851-1871. 17 vols.

HAMBURG.
STATE ARCHIVES.
(Staatsarchiv.)

Located in the lower and upper stories of the new City Hall (Rathaus). In the lower part a special fire-proof vault contains the rare documents and oldest records, such as parish books, charters, and the like. The collections, which are those of an old imperial free city and state, are accessible to 1848. Permission to consult the materials is given by the Senate through the Director of the Archives, Senatssecretär Dr. Anton Hagedorn, who has kindly furnished the 81 numbered items given below as a list of the chief American contents of the archives. The orthography has been modernized by the copyist.

Hours: 9 to 5.

Bibliography: 1. Ernst Baasch, *Beiträge zur Geschichte der Handelsbeziehungen zwischen Hamburg und Amerika.* (Separate reprint from *Festschrift der Hamburgischen Amerika-Fair, 1892.*) 2. *Inhaltsverzeichnis zu den Protokollen der Bürgerschaft in den Jahren 1859 bis 1900* (Hamburg, 1902). (Leaving only the gap 1848-1858 inaccessible to the investigator.)

1. Cl. I. Lit. Nc. Nr. 41. Akten, betreffend den Vorschlag der hiesigen Amsterdamer Boten wegen Annahme und Beförderung der nach den 13 vereinigten amerikanischen Staaten abzusendenden Briefschaften. 1788, 1793.
2. ————. Nr. 47. Vorschläge des Amsterdamer Boten Andr. von Beseler wegen Einrichtung einer amerikanischen Postexpedition und Gesuch um Verfügung in Ritzebüttel, dass die mit den Schiffern von Amerika kommenden Briefe, wenn die Schiffe in Cuxhaven aufgehalten würden, durch ausserordentliche Gelegenheit heraufbefördert werden möchten. 1794.
3. ————. Nr. 51. Ansuchen der Privatunternehmer der amerikanischen Briefbeförderung, sie zur ausschliesslichen Beförderung der von Amerika hier ankommenden Briefe in den Stand zu setzen, und Verhandlungen darüber mit den Kommerzdeputierten. 1796-1797.
4. ————. Nr. 52. Akten, betreffend die nach dem Tode von A. v. Beseler erfolgte Uebertragung der amerikanischen Post expedition an die Interessenten der hiesigen Bremer fahrenden Post. 1798-1800.
5. ————. Nr. 58 C. Beschwerde des Charles H. Vogel über die Direktion der amerikanischen Briefbeförderungsanstalt. 1805.
6. ————. Nr. 63. Ansuchen der amerikanischen Postinteressenten um Erlassung der Rekognition an die Kammer während der Stockung der Seefahrt von hier. 1809.
7. ————. Nr. 81. Beschwerde der Interessenten der amerikanischen Post über Eingriffe der Schiffsmakler. 1817, 1820.
8. Cl. VI. Nr. 16 p. Vol. I., Fasc. 1. Akten, betreffend die Handelsverhältnisse mit den Vereinigten Staaten. Konsulats-Zertifikation. Zollbefreiungen. Rückzahlung des Fremdenzolls (discriminating duties), etc. 1815, 1823-1827.

9. ———. Fasc. 1 a. Ratsprotokollextrakte und Aktenstücke, betreffend Glückwunschschreiben des Senats an den Kongress der nordamerikanischen Staaten zur erworbenen Unabhängigkeit mit Empfehlung zur Begünstigung wechselseitiger Handelsbeziehungen. (Nos. 1-7.) 1783-1891.
No. 1. Contains congratulations of the Hamburg Bourse, dated Mar. 26, 1783, and sent by the senate of Hamburg.
No. 2. Contains " Extractus Protocolli senatus Hamburgensis" containing the following interesting passage: " Die in voriger Session verlesenen Schreiben an die Nord-Americanischen Staaten und an Herrn Francklin mitzuteilen ". Mar. 28, 1783.
No. 3. Resolution of the senate as to the form of the congratulation and the manner of sending it, the same date.
No. 4. The original English letter or resolution of Congress returning thanks to the city of Hamburg for its good wishes. The resolution is signed by Charles Thomson as secretary. The German translation is inclosed. Oct. 29, 1783.
No. 5. Letter of acknowledgment from Elias Boudinot, president of Congress, dated Princeton, Nov. 1, 1783. A German translation is enclosed and the paper now has the following endorsement: " Im Jahre 1902 aus dem Nachlass von Hauptmann C. F. Gaedechens ans Archiv gesandt ".
No. 6. Auszug aus einem Schreiben des Herrn Dr. Baasch vom 11. October 1891 an Herrn Senatssekretair Dr. Hagedorn betr. Benutzung der Archivalien.
No. 7. Copy of Boudinot's letter noted above.

10. ———. Fasc. 3. Kongressakte vom 6 Januar 1829, durch welche der einjährige Termin für zollfreie Wiederausfuhr aus den nordamerikanischen Häfen in einen dreijährigen verlängert wird. 1829.

11. ———. Fasc. 6. Reklamation des hamburgischen Generalkonsuls Schumacher bei dem Schatzamte der Vereinigten Staaten von Nordamerika wegen traktatwidrig erhobenen Zolles von Kaffee, welcher direkt aus den Niederlanden in hanseatischen Schiffen nach New-York gebracht worden war. 1846, 1847.

12. ———. Fasc. 7. Akte, betreffend die mildere Auslegung einer Akte des Kongresses der Vereinigten Staaten von Nordamerika in Betreff der Passagierzahl der dort ankommenden (Auswanderer-) Schiffe, sowie in Betreff der Passagierabgabe in New York. 1847.

13. ———. Vol. 3 C. Fasc. 1. Fernere kleine Verhandlungen mit dem Konsul der Vereinigten Staaten von Nordamerika Cuthbert (Fortsetzung von Cl. VII. Lit. yb. Nr. 20. Vol. 18 gg). 1843, 1846.

14. ———.Vol. 4 a. Fasc. 1. Akten, betreffend das hamburgische Generalkonsulat zu Philadelphia, errichtet 1794; für die Vereinigten Staaten bis 1844, sodann für den Staat Pennsylvanien. Konsul John Ross, 1794, Generalkonsul 1796. Generalkonsul Carl Nicol. Buck, 1816. Korrespondenz bis 1846.

15. ———————. Fasc. 2. Ratsprotokollextrakte, betreffend eine Korrespondenz unter den drei Hansestädten über die projektierte Anstellung eines gemeinschaftlichen hanseatischen Agenten für die Vereinigten Staaten von Nordamerika. 1816.
16. ———————. Vol. 4 C. Fasc. 1 a. Errichtung eines hamburgischen Konsulats zu New-Orleans und Verleihung desselben an Vincent Nolte. 1816, 1817. Abgang von Vincent Nolte und Bestellung von F. W. Schmidt als Konsul. 1830.
17. ———————. Fasc. 1 b. Resignation des Konsuls Friedr. Wilh. Schmidt. Erwählung von Joh. Herm. Hagedorn zum Konsul. 1844, 1845.
18. ———————. Fasc. 1 c. Resignation von F. H. Hagedorn. Bestellung von Wilh. Vogel zum hamburgischen Konsul. 1846, 1847.
19. ———————. Fasc. 2 a. Errichtung eines hamburgischen Konsulats zu New-York und Ernennung von Joh. Wilh. Schmidt zum Vizekonsul 1819, zum Konsul 1837. Korrespondenz mit demselben 1842 bis 1844.
20. ———————. Fasc. 3. Anstellung von Cazenove als hamburgischer Vizekonsul zu Alexandria (Virginien). 1819. Entlassung desselben. 1852.
21. ———————. Fasc. 4 a. Ernennung von Friedr. L. Graff zum hamburgischen Vizekonsul in Baltimore. 1819. Sein Tod. Bestellung von Friedr. Rodewald zum hamburgischen Konsul für Maryland zu Baltimore. 1838, 1839.
22. ———————. Fasc. 5 a. Bestellung von Jacob Wulff als Vizekonsul, 1819, and 1835-1836; desgleichen von John Lawden als Konsul, 1836, 1837; desgleichen von Louis Trapmann als Konsul, 1838.
23. ———————. Fasc. 5 b. Korrespondenz mit dem Konsul Trapmann, betreffend J. H. Ingwersen und J. F. Brandt daselbst in Sachen seiner Ehefrau, geborenen Beinhauer. 1842-1844.
24. ———————. Fasc. 6 a. Notiz über die Bestellung von Carl Knorre zum Vizekonsul. 1834. Korrespondenz mit dem Verweser des Vizekonsulats. 1842.
25. ———————. Fasc. 6 b. Resignation des Vizekonsuls G. Carl Knorre. Erwählung von C. H. F. Möring zum Konsul. 1842-1844. Korrespondenz mit ihm. 1844-1847.
26. ———————. Fasc. 7 a. Hamburgisches Konsulat zu Richmond. Errichtung desselben und Bestellung von Henry Ludlam zum Konsul. Korrespondenz mit demselben. 1844, 1845.
27. ———————. Fasc. 9 a. Hamburgisches Konsulat zu Galveston. Errichtung desselben. Erwählung von J. W. Fockusch zum Konsul. 1844-1847.
28. ———————. Fasc. 13 a. Vorschlag, ein hamburgisches Konsulat zu Savannah in Georgia zu errichten, und Bewerbung um das Konsulat. 1845.
29. Cl. VII. Litt. Cc. Nr. 15 a. Vol. 81. Aufhebung des juris detractus und census emigrationis in Bezug auf die Nordamerikanischen Freistaaten, nebst den Verhandlungen darüber mit Amerika. 1822, 1823. Bestätigung der Aufhebung des decems durch eine Verhandlung im Jahre 1833.

Hamburg 269

30. Cl. VII. Lit. Ea. Pars 1. Nr. 5. Vol. 4 a. Hamburgische Kontentzettel von allen zu Wasser am Ober- und Niederbaum hier ankommenden Waren.
31. Cl. VII. Lit. Ea. Pars 2. Nr. 6 b. Vol. 7. Gesuch des Schiffsmaklers Clemenius um Erlass des Schiffszolls für das in Glückstadt gelöschte, nach Hamburg bestimmte amerikanische Schiff *Citizen*. 1820-1822.
32. Cl. VII. Lit. Yb. Nr. 1. Vol. 6 k. 1. Akten, betreffend Streitigkeiten mit dem amerikanischen Konsul Parish über die Befugnisse des Schouts, Matrosen in Haft zu nehmen. 1794.
33. Cl. VII. Lit. Yb. Nr. 20. Vol. 18 a. 1. Akten, betreffend die Annahme von John Parish als Konsul der Vereinigten Staaten von Amerika in Hamburg. 1793.
34. ——————. Vol. 18 a. 2. Kleine Verhandlungen des amerikanischen Konsuls Parish mit Syndikus Matsen, insbesondere wegen eines Matrosen, der seinen Schiffskapitän arretiren lassen, und dessen Bestrafung. 1794.
35. ——————. Vol. 18 a. 3. Akten, in Sachen des Konsuls Parish, den Betrug mit der amerikanischen Flagge betreffend. 1794.
36. ——————. Vol. 18 a. 4. Des Konsuls Parish Antrag wegen eines in Arrest gesetzten amerikanischen Steuermanns. 1795.
37. ——————. Vol. 18 a. 5. Von Konsul Parish mitgeteilte Akte des Kongresses, den Rückzoll betreffend. 1795.
38. ——————. Vol. 18 a. 6. Beschwerde des Konsuls Parish, über Misshandlung eines Amerikaners namens John Gregorie im französischen Schauspielhause. 1795.
39. ——————. Vol. 18 b. Akte, betreffend den Rücktritt des Konsuls John Parish von seinem Amte und Wiederbesetzung desselben durch Sam. Williams. 1796. Abberufung von Williams. 1798.
40. ——————. Vol. 18 c. Anstellung von Joseph Pitcairn als Konsul der Vereinigten Staaten. 1798.
41. ——————. Vol. 18 d. Korrespondenz mit dem amerikanischen Konsul Pitcairn, wegen einer Anzahl Malayen, die dem Colonel Bowen vom Schiffe genommen wurden. 1799.
42. ——————. Vol. 18 e. Akten, betreffend verschiedene mit dem Konsul Pitcairn verhandelte Sachen. 1798-1800.
43. ——————. Vol. 18 f. Annahme von John M. Forbes als amerikanischer Konsul. 1802. Substitution von Morewood und Kyng für Forbes. 1803.
44. ——————. Vol. 18 g. Beschwerde des Konsuls Forbes über eine Gewalttat der Besatzung der englischen Fregatte *Amethiste* auf der Reede zu Cuxhaven gegen das amerikanische Schiff *Astrea*. 1803.
45. ——————. Vol. 18 k. Beschwerde des Konsuls über Misshandlung des amerikanischen Kapitäns Kearny. 1802.
46. ——————. Vol. 18 l. Verhandlungen mit dem Konsul Forbes, betreffend das von den Franzosen zu Cuxhaven angehaltene amerikanische Schiff *Neuenstädten*. 1805-1806.
47. ——————. Vol. 18 m. 1. Anzeige des Konsuls Forbes, dass er während seiner Abwesenheit Dobson zum Vizekonsul und Hambroeck zum Kanzler bestellt habe. 1806.

Hamburg

48. ——————. Vol. 18 m. 2. Noten des Konsuls Forbes, in Betreff einiger zu Cuxhaven unter Quarantaine gestellter amerikanischer Schiffe. 1806.
49. ——————. Vol. 18 n. Korrespondenz mit dem Konsul Forbes wegen des amerikanischen Kapitäns Jesse Inglée. 1807.
50. ——————. Vol. 18 p. Anzeige der kreisausschreibenden Fürsten von der Legitimation des Konsuls Forbes als Konsul der Vereinigten Staaten Nordamerika beim Niedersächsischen Kreise. 1806.
51. ——————. Vol. 18 q. Varia, den Konsul Forbes betreffend:
   1. dessen Ersuchen, hier einen amerikanischen Post zu etablieren.
   2. dessen Beschwerde wegen der hier von französischer Seite geschehenen Belästigung amerikanischer Schiffe. 1807.
   3. dessen Erkundigungen wegen Herm. Lübbert. 1808.
52. ——————. Vol. 18 r. Anstellung von Vizekonsuln durch den Konsul Forbes während seines Aufenthalts in Kopenhagen. 1814-1817.
53. ——————. Vol. 18 s. 1. Anerkennung von Edward Wyer von Massachusetts als Konsul der Vereinigten Staaten in Hamburg und Anerkennung des von diesem während seiner Abwesenheit von hier im Dezember 1817 ernannten John Cuthbert als amerikanischer Vizekonsul ad interim. 1817. Verfügung über die Pässe, die denen zu erteilen sind, die sich als Amerikaner ausgeben.
54. ——————. Vol. 18 s. 2. Verhandlungen mit dem Konsul Wyer, dessen Requisition, dass niemand den amerikanischen Matrosen Kredit geben oder ihre Kleidungsstücke, etc., zu Pfand nehmen solle. 1818.
55. ——————. Vol. 18 t. Anzeige des Konsuls Wyer von seiner Beurlaubung und der Bestellung des Vizekonsuls Cuthbert zu seinem Vertreter während seiner Abwesenheit. 1819.
56. ——————. Vol. 18 u. Verwendung des Vizekonsuls Cuthbert in einer Privatforderungssache des amerikanischen Bürgers F. Krittmann wegen Zurückhaltung der ihm im Jahre 1811 während der französischen Herrschaft von dem Maire Röger zum Hohenfelde abgenommenen Effekten. 1820.
57. ——————. Vol. 18 w. Untersuchung gegen den Wirt Hastedt auf dem Baumhause wegen Auslieferung des vom Zehntenamte versiegelten Nachlasses des hier verstorbenen Schiffskapitäns Carvick an den Vizekonsul Cuthbert zur Beförderung nach Amerika. 1824.
58. ——————. Vol. 18 y. Verhandlungen mit dem Konsul Cuthbert 1822, betreffend:
   1. den Verkauf des amerikanischen Schiffs *Oriental*, Kapitän Swain;
   2. Beschwerde desselben über das Verfahren bei der Quarantaine gegen die Schiffe *Rising Sun* und *Amanda* von Philadelphia.

59. ——— ———. Vol. 18 z. Dem Konsulate der Vereinigten Staaten gestattete Befugnis, die Verlassenschaften hier verstorbener nordamerikanischer Schiffskapitäne und Seeleute ohne Mitwirkung des Zehntenamtes zu versiegeln. 1824.
60. ——— ———. Vol. 18 aa. Bestellung von John Cuthbert zum Konsul der Vereinigten Staaten und Anerkennung desselben in dieser Eigenschaft. 1826.
61. ——— ———. Vol. 18 bb. Ernennung von Chs. Dav. Tolmé zum Vizekonsul durch den Konsul Cuthbert. 1827.
62. ——— ———. Vol. 18 cc. Korrespondenz mit dem Konsul Cuthbert in Anlass der Tötung des Matrosen David durch den amerikanischen Matrosen Imbert am Bord des amerikanischen Schiffs *Arabella*. 1826, 1827. Nachweisung einer Untersuchungsakte wegen Misshandlung zweier Matrosen an Bord eines amerikanischen Schiffes auf der Elbe bei Stade im Jahre 1836.
63. ——— ———. Vol. 18 dd. Einzelne Verhandlungen mit dem Konsul Cuthbert. 1828, 1829, 1831, 1833, 1834.
64. ——— ———. Vol. 18 ee. Verhandlung, veranlasst durch Anträge des Konsuls Cuthbert
wegen Sicherung der in Cuxhaven überwinternden Schiffe;
wegen der Weigerung des dispacheurs Decker, die Havarie des Schiffs *Beaver*, Kapitän Francisco, ohne neue Taxation aufzumachen, obgleich diese Taxation schon in Ritzebüttel stattgefunden hat;
wegen einer an einem amerikanischen Schiffskapitän verübten Erpressung. 1830.
65. ——— ———. Vol. 18 ff. Anstellung von James Wilson als Vizekonsul an Stelle von Tolmé. 1831.
66. ——— ———. Vol. 18 gg. Einzelne Verhandlungen, veranlasst durch Anträge des Konsuls Cuthbert, betreffend.
Beschwerde des Kapitäns Johnson vom Schiffe *Marblehead* von Boston über den dänischen Lotsen Peter Wohlers, 1834-1835;
den an Bord der norwegischen Brig *Enigheden*, Kapitän Peterson, gelockten und zwangsweise hierher mitgenommenen Amerikaner Peter Morrison, 1838;
die Forderung des Schneiders Stoffers an W. G. Blecker aus New-Orleans, 1838;
das Gesuch um Bewilligung der Freiheit vom Sperrgelde an Todson, 1838;
die Forderung, eine Sache des amerikanischen Bürgers A. H. Gläser gegen I. L. Gläser vor die amerikanischen Gerichte verwiesen zu sehen, 1840;
die hiesigen Wiedertäufer, insbesondere ihren Vorstand J. G. Oncken, 1840.
67. Cl. VII. Lit. K a. Nr. 2. Vol. 11. Verhandlungen mit der Kommerzdeputation, die Errichtung und Besetzung verschiedener Konsulate betreffend, unter anderem der Konsulate zu Philadelphia, New-York und New-Orleans. 1814-1819.

68. Cl. VII. Lit. K a. Nr. 8. Vol. 3. Fasc. 8. Generalverzeichnisse sämtlicher Einfuhren der vorzüglichsten Waren, die seewärts in Hamburg und Altona angekommen sind, herausgegeben von J. C. C. Krausz. 1840, 1841.
69. Cl. VII. Lit. K d. Nr. 3. Vol. 1 c. Protokoll der Konferenzen zwischen Deputierten des Senats und des Kommerziums in Anlass der Kriegsereignisse des Jahres 1778 *et seq.*
70. ―――――. Vol. 4 b. Korrespondenz mit Lübeck, betreffend die Neutralität. 1778 *et seq.*
71. ―――――. Vol. 5 g. Akten in Sachen Fr. Klefeker and Paschen und John Parish, betreffend Schadensersatz für zwei im Jahre 1776 auf Requisition des englischen Ministers mit Arrest belegte Schiffe, weil sie in Philadelphia gebaut seien, den Insurgenten gehören und Kontrabande für sie geladen haben sollten. 1782-1783.
72. Cl. VII. Lit. K e. Nr. 7 b. Listen und Etats sämtlicher unter hamburgischer Flagge fahrenden Schiffe, ihrer Lastenzahl, Kapitäne und Reeder. 1798-1830.
    Tabellen über sämtliche im hiesigen Hafen angekommene und ausgegangene Schiffe und Waren.
73. ―――――. Nr. 7 c. Verschiedene Listen die hamburgische Schiffahrt und Reederei betreffend.
    1. Uebersicht der Hamburg-Altonaer Schiffahrt des Jahres 1840, von J. C. C. Krausz.
    2. Uebersicht der im Laufe des Jahres 1842 in Hamburg angekommenen Seeschiffe.
    3. Desgleichen der abgegangenen Seeschiffe. 1846-1847, 1849-1850, 1852-1854.
74. Cl. VII. Lit. K e. Nr. 9 b. Akten über die Revision der den Transport von Auswanderern betreffenden Verordnungen, insbesondere Erlass Verordnung von 27 Februar 1837 über die Verschiffung der über Hamburg nach andern Weltteilen Auswandernden und des Additaments dazu vom 11. August 1837. 1836-1838.
75. ―――――. Nr. 9 c. Drucksachen, insbesondere hamburgische, bremische und englische Gesetze über Verschiffung von Auswanderern; Prospekte hamburgischer und bremischer Beförderer (Reeder, Makler, Agenten) von Auswanderern; Statuten des Vereins Hamburgischer Reeder. 1837.
76. ―――――. Nr. 9 d. Fernere Akten, betreffend die Verordnungen über die Verschiffung von Auswanderern. Gesuche der hiesigen Reeder um Revision und Abänderung derselben, desfallsige Verhandlungen mit der Kommerzdeputation und Bekanntmachung des Senats vom 9. März 1842. 1839-1842.
77. ―――――. Nr. 9 e. Revision der Verordnung vom 27 Februar 1837 mit Nachträgen, den Transport von Auswanderern betreffend. Publikation der revidierten Verordnung in Betreff der Verschiffung der über Hamburg direkt nach andern Weltteilen Auswandernden vom 26 März 1845.
78. Cl. VIII. Lit. K e. Nr. 9 f. i. Akte, betreffend die für die durchpassierenden Auswanderern zu erbauenden Wohnungsschuppen. 1846.

79. ———. Nr. 108-125. Spezifikation aller in Hamburg angelangten See-schiffe mit ihren Ladungen. 1778-1801.
   No. 108. Specification derer Schiffe, so von Engeland, Schottland, Irrland, und deren Eylanden im Jahre 1778 an Hamburg mit Kaufmannsgüter gekommen. Valuable list of ships giving the names of the shipmasters, the date and port from which they sailed.
   No. 109. *Id.* 1779.
   No. 110. *Id.* 1780, including ships from other ports.
   No. 111. Specificatio aller im Jahr 1787 in Hamburg angelangten See-Schiffen nebst deren Ladungen. This is the beginning of a series of volumes continuing down to 1801, bound in leather and gilt. The following is a sample entry of the cargo of a ship from Philadelphia:

     1 Schiff von Philadelphia
     3 Pack Bäume
     1 Kist Blumenzwiebel
     1 Kist Bücher
     1 Kist China
     3 Fass Chorinten
     1 Fass Drogerey
     1 Fass Eisen Ware
     1 Parthey Farbe Holtz
     2 Pack Häute oder Fälle
     2 Fass Horn Spitzen
    18 Fass Kaufmannsschaft
    12 Pack dito
     4 Kisten dito
     1 Pack Leinen
     2 Parthey Mahagony Holtz
   498 Fass Mehl
     1 Fass Messer
     2 Pack Saat
    64 Stück Sagen (Lagen ?)
     1 Kist Schnupf-Toback
     9 Fass Terpentin Oehl
    64 Fass Toback
    39 Pack dito

   Volumes 112-125 relate, with similar details, to the years 1788-1801 respectively.
80. ———. Nr. 126-134. Verzeichnis der von der See hier angekommenen Schiffer. 1800-1811.
81. ———. Nr. 135-137. Verzeichnis aller angekommenen und abgegangenen Schiffe. 1801, 1802, 1804.

HAUPTMELDEAMT DER POLIZEI IN HAMBURG.

A most valuable collection of some 300 bound volumes of records relating to emigrants passing through Hamburg.

   Protocoll der Aufenthalt-Karten. 1834-1867. The first emigrants are entered Apr. 29, 1837, with the following details: Wohnung, Nr. d. Aufenthaltskarte, Dauer des Aufenthaltskarte, Bemerkungen, Wohin. Then begins:

Das Melde-Register, which continues to 1889. Before 1890 a separate sheet was used for each individual giving the particulars. These sheets are known as " Register-Blätter ".

Auswandererlisten, requiring the following data: Name, Geburtsort, Name des Schiffes und des Capitains, Wohin, Datum des Abganges. These lists continue from 1850 to the present time. There is a separate index of names for each year. From 1855 on the information is more detailed and includes the following items: Zu- und Vorname, Geburts- und Wohnort, Landes, Gewerbe, Alter, Geschlecht männlich und weiblich, Total, Recapitulation, Erwachsene u. Kinder über 8 Jahr, Kinder unter 8 Jahr, Kinder unter einem Jahr. There is also an Index of Proper Names giving the number and folio of the book.

In addition to this material, there is also a collection of passes for travelling Hamburgers giving the following details and continuing to the present time: Name, Stand, Geburtsort, Alter, Statur, Haare, Augenbrauen, Bart, Stirn, Augen, Nase, Mund, Kinn, Gesicht, Gesichtsfarbe, Besondere Kennzeichen, Unterschrift des Reisenden, Bürgschaft, Fernere Nachweisungen.

HESSE (DARMSTADT).
GRAND-DUCAL HESSIAN HOUSE AND STATE ARCHIVES.
(GROSSHERZOGLICH HESSISCHES HAUS- UND STAATSARCHIV.)

Located in the lower part of the Grand Ducal Palace in Darmstadt. Embraces certain old archives of Mainz and the Palatinate as well as of Hesse Darmstadt. Permission to consult the records is given by the Minister of State.

Hours: 8 to 1.

Acten des Geheimen Staats-Archivs.

XI. Abteilung. Bevölkerungspolizei. Ier Abschnitt.

Convolut 1. This Convolut contains older decrees and those of the eighteenth century of which the following have special bearing:

Important printed communication to the chancellor in Darmstadt (in French and German), giving a very emphatic account of the situation in England and Holland as regards the shipping of Palatines, etc. Leyden, May 14, 1709. (1 folio.)

Acta das Auswandern der Fürstlichen Unterthanen, und die dagegen erlassene Verfügungen und Verordnungen betr. 1630, 1643, 1658, 1692, 1722, 1766, 1767, 1770, 1772, 1779. (1692 relates to confiscation of property of emigrants.)

Die Auswanderung nach Russland betreffend. 1766.

Bericht über die Auswanderung nach Brasilien mit Anlagen Lit. A.-O., not dated.

Ex Resoluto Regiminis. Die von mehrern Unterthanen des Fürstlichen Amts-Battenberg nachgesuchte Erlaubniss nach Amerika auswandern zu dürfen, betr. Darmstadt, May 10, 1796.

Acta ministerialia, betreffend die Ausdehnung der Verordnung über die Auswanderung der Unterthanen de 1787 auf die Entschädigungs-Aemter, 1804.

Acta, betreffend Verfügungen wegen dem Emigriren der Fürstlichen Unterthanen, und zur Verbesserung deren Nahrung-Stands. 1766-1769.

Military matters of 1709.

Documents, relating to emigration to Hungary. Eighteenth century.

Documents, relating to Waldo and the New England Colony. 1753.

Decree against Johannes Wallrab's efforts to secure colonists. (*Cf.* also documents of Dec. 12, 1764, and others of the same year.)

Decree and other papers, relating to emigration to New England or Pennsylvania. Feb. 21, 1765.

Decrees relating to the Banat, " Vormauer der Christenheit ", especially matter of 1722 f., relating to Hungary, etc.

Convolut 2. Contains the following relevant fascicles:

Acta die Auswanderung nach Brasilien betr. Mense Mertz 1825. (Extends later into the year 1825.)

Acta die wegen Emigrirens der Unterthanen ergangene Verordnungen betr. 1785-1787.

Nachsteuer-Sachen. 1640-1780.
Verordnung wegen Nachsteuer, etc. 1725-1779.
Kriegsteuer, etc. 1802.
Acten des Grossherzoglich Hessischen Ministeriums des Innern und der Justiz betreffend die Aufhebung der in dem vormals Rheinpfälzischen Aemtern bestandenen Abgabe an Landesfundi Gebühren und insbesondere der Detracts-Gelder bey Auswanderungen und Vermögens-Exportationen. 1809-1818.

Grossh. Kreisamt Worms.

N. A. **782.** Bevölkerungspolizei.
   9. (35.) Auswanderungen. Agenten und Hauptagenten. 1846-1895. 3 Convolute.
  10. (36.) (a.) Die Beseitigung der bei Beförderung von Auswanderern bestehenden Missbräuche. 1854-1890. (1 fascicle.) (b.) Warnungen. 1825-1890. (1 fascicle.)
  11. (40.) Mennonitengemeinde Ibersheim. 1844-1857. (1 fascicle.)

Grossherzogliches Kreisamt Gross-Gerau.

4. II. **2.** Ueberschrift über aufgenommene und ausgewanderte Untertanen.
5. III. **1.** Alte Gestze und Verordnungen. 1763.

Grossh. Kreisamt Friedberg.

Ord. No.	Abteil.	Abschn.	
244.	X.	3.	Auswanderungen Nieder-Eschbach. 1827-1854.
			Id. Kirchgaus. 1843-1845.
			Id. Ziegenberg. 1843-1857.
			Id. Maibach. 1840-1857.
245.	X.	3.	*Id.* Holzhausen. 1822-1837.
			Id. Nieder-Mörten. 1837-1857.
			Id. Münzenberg. 1831-1854.
246.	X.	3.	*Id.* Ilbenstadt. 1843-1854.
			Id. Heldenbergen. 1824-1859.
			Id. Nieder-Erlenbach. 1854.
247.	X.	3.	*Id.* Klein-Karben, Klappenheim, Kaichen, Messenheim. 1832-1854.
248.	X.	3.	*Id.* Bad-Nauheim, Bauernheim, Beienheim. 1843-1854.
			Id. Bodenrod, Bönstadt, Bruchenkrücken. 1843-1854.
			Id. Assenheim. 1841-1856.
249.	XI.	1.	*Id.* Burg-Gräfenrod, 1836-1856. Büdesheim, 1836-1856. Mellbach, 1848-1857. Münster, 1848-1857. Fauerbach bei Fr., 1848-1857. Fauerbach v. d. H., 1848-1857.
300.	XI.	3.	*Id.* Hausen, Hoch-Wiesel, Werkesheim, Wieksbadt, Wisselsheim bis 1857.
301.	XI.	3.	*Id.* Pohl-Goens, Reichelsheim, Rockenberg, Rödgen, Schwalheim, Södel. 1857.
302.	XI.	3.	*Id.* Staden. 1857.

Hesse (Darmstadt)

303.	XI.	3. *Id.* Stammheim, Steinfurth, Trais, Münzenberg. 1857.
304.	XI.	3. *Id.* Wölfersheim, Wohnbach. 1857.
305.	XI.	3. *Id.* Ober-Wöllstadt, Ockstadt. 1857.
333.	XI.	3. *Id.* Gambach, Griedel. 1857.
334.	XI.	3. *Id.* Obermärlen, Ober-Rosbach. 1857.
335.	XI.	3. *Id.* Okarben, Retterweil, Oppershofen, Offenheim, Ostheim. 1857.
336.	XI.	1. *Id.* Rendel, Rodheim, Nieder-Florstadt. 1857.
337.	XI.	1. *Id.* Gross-Korben, Harheim Nieder-Wöllstadt, Ober-Erlenbach, Ober-Eschbach. 1857.
383.	XI.	3. *Id.* Varia. 1857.

LIPPE (DETMOLD).
HOUSE AND NATIONAL ARCHIVES OF THE PRINCIPALITY.
(FÜRSTLICHES HAUS- UND LANDES-ARCHIV.)

Located in the Government Buildings. Permission to consult the records for scientific purposes is given by the Director; for other purposes by the Governor. No matter found relating to America.

Hours: 10 to 1.

LÜBECK.

STATE ARCHIVES.

(STAATSARCHIV.)

Located Königstrasse 21, and contains the records of the government of the state of Lübeck and also the city archives of the earlier and later periods.

Hours: 9 to 2.

Bibliography. 1. Wehrmann, " Das Lübecker Archiv " (*Zeitschrift des Vereins für Lübeckische Geschichte und Altertumskunde,* Band 3, Lübeck, 1876). 2. Kretschmar, " Geschichte des Lübecker Staatsarchivs " (*Protokolle des achten deutschen Archivtages in Lübeck 1908,* Berlin, Mittler und Sohn, 1908).

The following list of papers relating to America has been supplied by the state archivist. The orthography has been modernized by the copyist.

A. VEREINIGTE STAATEN VON NORD-AMERIKA (AUCH TEXAS).

I. Handels- und Schiffahrts-Beziehungen.

Vol. A.

Fasc. 1. Acta und Correspondenz unter den Hansestädten den Abschluss eines Handels-Tractates mit den Nord-Amerikanischen Freistaaten betr. 1782-1784.

Fasc. 2. Acta betr. die intendirte Vereinbarung mit den Nord-Amerikanischen Freistaaten wegen der Schiffahrts-Abgaben. 1819-1820.

Fasc. 3. Acta betr. den Abschluss eines Handels- und Schiffahrts-Vertrages zwischen den Hansestädten und den Vereinigten Staaten von Nord-Amerika. 1827-1829.

Fasc. 4. Tractat mit Texas. 1844.

Publicationen des Texas Vereins. 1851.

Fasc. 5. Acta betr. den Handelsvertrag der Hansestädte mit Nord-Amerika, in sp. Vereinbarung eines Zusatz-Artikels über die Jurisdiction der Handels-Agenten und Consuln in Nordamerika. 1850-1853.

Fasc. 6. Acta betr. Verhandlungen wegen des Beitritts Lübecks zu dem zwischen Preussen pp. und Vereinigten Staaten von Nordamerika abgeschlossenen Vertrage wegen gegenseitiger Auslieferung von Verbrechern. 1853.

Fasc. 7. Acta betr. Reclamationen aus dem Kriege in den Vereinigten Staaten von Nordamerika und diesseits anzumeldende Schadenersatzansprüche. 1865, 1866.

Fasc. 8. Acta betr. die Zulassung der Schiffe des Norddeutschen Bundes in die Häfen der Vereinigten Staaten von Nordamerika unter denselben Bedingungen wie die einheimischen. 1868.

Fasc. 9. Varia.

II. Diplomatische Beziehungen.
  a. Hiesige Agenten, Consuln, etc., in Nord-Amerika.
    Vol. B.
      Fasc. 1. Allgemeine Verhandlungen wegen Bestellung hanseatischer Agenten und General-Consuls in Nord-Amerika. 1816—.
      Fasc. 2. Acta betr. die Bestellung des Hieronymus Daniel Wichelhausen zu Baltimore zum Lübeckischen General-Consul für Nord-Amerika; dessen Rücktritt; Correspondenz. 1820-1822.
          Ernennung des Hermann v. Kapff zum Consul. 1852.
      Fasc. 3. Consulat zu Neuyork.
      Fasc. 4. Consulat zu Neu Yersey.
      Fasc. 5. Consulat zu Boston.
      Fasc. 6. Consulat zu Nassau; desgl. zu Chicago; desgl. zu St. Louis.
      Fasc. 7. Consulat zu Galveston.
      Fasc. 8. Consulat zu Charlestown in Süd-Carolina.
      Fasc. 9. Consulat in Cincinnati für die Staaten Ohio, Illinois, Indiana und Wisconsin.
      Fasc. 10. Consulat in S. Franzisco.
      Fasc. 11. Consulat in New-Orleans.
      Fasc. 12. Consulat in Philadelphia.
      Fasc. 13. Errichtung von Consulaten des Nord-deutschen Bundes und Aufhebung der Lübeckischen Consulate. 1868.
    Vol. C. Ministerresidentur in Washington.
      Fasc. 1. Acta betr. die Errichtung einer hanseatischen Ministerresidentur in Washington und Ernennung des Dr. Schleiden zum Ministerresidenten. 1862.
      Fasc. 2. Berichte desselben und des Geschäftsträgers Dr. Rösing. 1862-1864.
      Fasc. 3. Acta betr. die Recreditirung des Dr. Schleiden und die Accreditirung des Dr. Rösing als hanseatischer Geschäftsträger; incid. betr. die Form der Ausstellung des Creditivs für den Geschäftsträger. 1865.
      Fasc. 4. Correspondenz mit der hanseatischen Gesandtschaft in Washington. 1865.
      Fasc. 5. Acta betr. die Abberufung des Dr. Rösing und die Aufhebung der Stelle. 1868.
      Fasc. 6. Ermordung des Präsidenten Abraham Lincoln. 1865. Attentat auf den Präsidenten Garfield. 1881.
  b. Nordamerikanische Consuln bei hiesiger Stadt.
    Vol. D.
      Fasc. 1. Acta wegen Accreditirung des Nordamerikanischen Consuls John M. Forbes beim Niedersächsischen Kreise. 1806-1808.
      Fasc. 2. Ernennung des Herrn F. H. Pauli jr. zum Vice-Consul bei hiesiger Stadt. 1814. Anspruch desselben auf Befreiung vom Dienst in der Bürgergarde.
      Fasc. 3. Ernennung des Herrn Clarck zum Consul hieselbst. 1824.

Fasc. 4. Ernennung des Herrn Sam. Ricker in Frankfurt a. M. zum General-Consul bei den freien Städten Deutschlands. 1857.
Fasc. 5. Ernennung des Hrn. Carl Hermann Schroeder zum Vice-Consul der Vereinigten Staaten hieselbst. 1859.
Fasc. 6. Ernennung des Hrn. Wilh. Coleman zum Vice-Consul der Vereinigten Staaten hieselbst. 1865.
Fasc. 7. Aufhebung des Consulats der Vereinigten Staaten in Lübeck. 1870.

B. MITTELAMERIKANISCHE STAATEN.

1. Vereinigte Staaten von Mexico.

I. Handels- und Schiffahrts-Beziehungen.
  Vol. A.
  Fasc. 1. Allgemeinere Verhandlungen in Betreff Sicherung und Feststellung der Handels- und Schiffahrts-Verhältnisse zu den neueren Staaten des südlichen und mittleren Amerikas, insbesondere zu Mexico, bis zur Eröffnung der Verhandlungen über den Abschluss eines Handels- und Schiffahrts-Vertrages. Apr. 7, 1825–May 9, 1827.
  Fasc. 2. Bevollmächtigung des General-Consuls Colquhoun zu London wegen Unterhandlung und Abschluss eines Handels- und Schiffahrts-Vertrages abseiten der Hansestädte mit dem Mexikanischen Gesandten zu London.
    Tractat vom 16 Juny,
    Additional Artikel vom 27 do,
    Separat-Artikel vom 12 July, 1827.
    Verhandlungen in Betreff der Ratification abseiten der Mexikanischen Regierung. Protest der Spanischen Regierung. May 10, 1827–Mar. 10, 1830.
  Fasc. 3. Verhandlungen von der verweigerten Mexikanischen Ratification des Tractates vom 16. Juny 1827 bis zur Ratification des neuen am 7. Apr. 1832 zu London zwischen den Hansestädten und der Mexikanischen Regierung abgeschlossenen Handels- und Schiffahrts-Vertrages. Mar. 30, 1830–Dec. 15, 1841.
  Fasc. 4. Acta betr. die von der Republik Mexico geschehene Kündigung des mit den Hansestädten am 7. April 1832 geschlossenen Vertrages, Verhandlungen wegen eines neuen und Abschluss desselben am 4 Juni 1856. Incid. ein dem Hanseatischen Bevollmächtigten, dem Bremischen Minister-residenten Schleiden in Washington gemachtes Ehrengeschenk. Sept. 9-13, 1854.
  Fasc. 5. Acta betr. Handelsverhältnisse mit Mexico, in specie Behandlung der in Hanseatischen Schiffen in die Häfen der mexicanischen Republik eingeführten Natur- und Fabrikerzeugnisse der deutschen Bundesstaaten. 1854.
    Das Verfahren des zum Präsidenten der Republik Mexico erhobenen Generals Felix Zuloaga gegen die dort ansässigen Staatsangehörigen der Hansestädte und deren Handelsinteressen. 1858-1860.

Fasc. 6. Fernere Verhandlungen einen mit Mexico abzuschliessenden Handelsvertrag betreffend. 1861-1863, 1865, 1866.
II. Diplomatische Beziehungen.
  a. Hiesige Agenten, etc., bei der Mexikanischen Regierung.
    Vol. B.
      Fasc. 1. Consulat zu Mexico:
        a. betr. die Bestellung des Kaufmannes Hermann Nolte zum Lübeckischen Handels-Commissair. Correspondenz desselben. 1825.
        b. betr. die Gerirung des Louis Sulzer als General-Consul der Hansestädte zu Mexico. 1831-1833. Interimistische Wahrnehmung des Hanseatischen General-Consulats durch den brem. General-Consul Färber und dessen Antrag auf Uebertragung dieser Functionen von Seiten Lübecks. 1833, 1834. Verhandlungen wegen Anstellung eines diplomatischen Agenten. 1844, 1845.
        c. Consulat des Herrn Johann Rudolph von Lübeck. Ernennung desselben. 1854.
        d. Rücktritt des Hrn. v. Lubeck vom Consulate und Ernennung des Herrn Aug. Christian Doormann zum Lübeckischen Consul, 1858; angeregte Ernennung desselben zum Generalconsul, 1859; Ernennung desselben zum General-consul, 1865.
      Fasc. 2. Consulat zu Veracruz. Bestellung des Kaufmannes Eduard Mahn zum diesseitigen so wie zum gemeinschaftlichen Hanseatischen Consul daselbst. 1832, 1834.
      Fasc. 3. Consulat zu Tampico.
      Fasc. 4. Acta betr. die in Anrege gekommene Begründung einer diplomatischen Vertretung der Hansestädte in Mexico. 1854, 1855, 1866.
      Fasc. 5. Consulat in Mazatlan.
  b. Mexikanische Geschäftsträger, etc., bei den Hansestädten.
    Vol. C.
      Fasc. 1. Accreditiring des Francisco de Facio als Mexikanischen General-Consul bei den Hansestädten. Dessen Abberufung. 1831-1833.
      Fasc. 2. Accreditirung des José Ignacio Valdicielso als Mexikanischen General-Consul. 1834.
      Fasc. 3. Wieder-Accreditirung des Francisco de Facio als Mexikanischen General Consul bei den Hansestädten. 1837.
      Fasc. 4. Ernennung des Herrn E. G. Kulenkamp zum Consul hieselbst. 1826, 1832. Entlassung desselben. 1835.
      Fasc. 5. Ernennung des Herrn Negrete zum General-Consul bei den Hansestädten. 1842.
      Fasc. 6. Desgl. des Hrn. Salvator Batres. 1854. Desgl. Hrn. Friedr. Hube. 1861.

2. Guatemala.

Vol. A. Consulate.
    Fasc. 1. Von der Regierung Guatemala's hieselbst beglaubigte Consuln.

Lübeck

    a. Ernennung des Herrn Ioh. Frederich Hinck in Hamburg zum General-Consul bei den Hansestädten. 1841. Entlassung desselben. 1846.
    b. Ernennung des Herrn Carl N. L. Weber in Hamburg zum General-Consul. 1847.
Fasc. **2.** Vom hiesigen Senate in Guatemala ernannte.
    a. Consulat des Herrn Carl Rudolph Klee zu Guatemala. Ernennung desselben für die Republik von Central-Amerika und für die einzelnen in derselben föderirten Staaten. 1842, 1843. Ernennung desselben zum General-Consul. 1844, 1845. Correspondenz. 1844-1846.
    b. Consulat des Herrn Hermann Gädechens. Ernennung desselben zum Vice-Consul. 1853. Zum Generalconsul. 1855.

Vol. **B.** Acta betr. den Abschluss eines Freundschafts-, Handlungs- und Schiffahrts-Vertrages mit der Republik Guatemala. 1844-1851.

3. Salvador.

Herabsetzung der Einfuhrzölle auf fremde Waren in San Salvador. 1884.

4. Nicaragua.

Fasc. **1.** Acta betr. den Abschluss eines Handelsvertrages zwischen den Hansestädten und der Republik Nicaragua. 1852-1856, 1860.
Fasc. **2.** Acta betr. den Nicaragua-Canal. Verhandlungen in Veranlassung eines bewaffneten Angriffs auf Kaiserliche Consularbeamte in Leon im October und November. 1876.

5. Costa Rica.

Fasc. **1.** Generalconsulat des Herrn Ed. Gorrissen in Hamburg. 1858.
Fasc. **2.** Abschluss eines Freundschafts-, Handels-, und Schiffahrts-Vertrages. 1848-1866.

6. Haiti.

Fasc. **1.** Handels- und Schiffahrts-Beziehungen. 1827-1829.
Fasc. **2.** Consulat auf Haiti. 1825-1826.
Fasc. **3.** Beabsichtigte Errichtung eines Consulates von Haiti in hiesiger Stadt. 1847, 1848.

C. SUDAMERIKANISCHE STAATEN.

1. Venezuela (1831 seq.).

Vol. **A.**
Fasc. **1.** Handels- und Schiffahrts-Beziehungen.
    Abschluss eines Freundschafts-, Handels-, und Schiffahrts-Vertrages der Hansestädte mit Venezuela. Incid.: Ertheilung des Bürgerrechtes an den Unterhändler Gramlich. Anstellung von Handels-Agenten. 1836-1839.

Acta betr. das von der Republik Venezuela erlassene aber demnächst wieder aufgehobene Gesetz über die Bewilligung von Moratorien für die Angehörigen der Republik durch die dortigen Landesgesetze. 1850.
Acta betr. Verhandlungen zwischen den Hansestädten und der Republik Venezuela wegen eines abzuschliessenden Freundschafts- und Handels-vertrages. 1850-1861.

Fasc. 2. Consulate.
  a. Zu Caracas und La Guayra, Consulat des Georg Blohm. 1837-1845. Anstellung desselben. 1837. Entlassung desselben. 1845. Correspondenz. Verhandlungen wegen Wiederanstellung eines Consuls nach dem Abgange des Herrn G. Blohm. 1845, 1850, 1851. Ernennung des Hrn. Georg Heinrich Blohm zum Consul. Correspondenz. 1860.
  b. Consulat zu Angostura (Ciudad Bolivar). Ernennung des Hrn. Ad. Wuppermann in Angostura (Ciudad Bolivar) zum Consul. Correspondenz. 1839. Abgang des Consuls Wuppermann und Ernennung des Hrn. Heinr. Aug. Carl Krohn zum Consul. 1856, 1857. Vertretung desselben. Correspondenz. 1858.
  c. Ernennung des Kaufmanns Louis Brandt zum Lübeckischen Consul in Porto Cabello. Correspondenz. 1861.

Fasc. 3. Consuln und Vice-Consuln Venezuelas bei den Hansestädten. Consul Sprotto in Hamburg. 1834. Vice-Consul Green hieselbst. 1835. Consul Louis Glöckler in Hamburg. 1850.

2. Columbia (Neu Granada 1831-1861).

Fasc. 1. Handels- und Schiffahrts-Beziehungen.
Acta betr. den Abschluss eines Handels- und Schiffahrts-Vertrages mit Neu-Granada. 1844-1849.
Acta betr. den Abschluss eines Freundschafts-, Handels- und Schiffahrts-Vertrages mit der Republik Neu-Granada. 1853-1857.

3. Ecuador.

Handels- und Schiffahrts-Vertrag mit Ecuador. 1839.
Ernennung des Hrn. F. C. Schaar zum Consul der Republik Ecuador bei den Hansestädten. 1846.

4. Peru.

Acta betr. den Abschluss eines Handelsvertrages mit Peru. 1860-1863.
Verhältnisse zu Spanien. 1864, 1866.
Ernennung des Hrn. F. L. v. Lindeman zum Consul in Lima. 1858, 1859.
Ernennung des Hrn. A. Warncke zum Consul in Arequipa. 1864.

Entlassung desselben. 1866.
Acta betr. die Errichtung von Consulaten des Norddeutschen Bundes zu Lima und Guatemala, sowie die Aufhebung der dortigen Lübeckischen Consulate. 1868.

5. Bolivia.

Ernennung des Hrn. Heinr. Joh. Lampe zu Bremen zum Consul bei hiesiger Stadt. 1846.
Ernennung des Kaufmanns Christian Julius Gustav Wolde zum Generalconsul der Republik Bolivia bei den Hansestädten. 1857.
Das Aufhören der consularischen Functionen desselben. 1887.

6. Chile.

Bewerbungen um ein Consulat in Valparaiso. 1841.
Gleichstellung der chile[a]nischen und der Lübeckischen Schiffe hinsichtlich der Schiffahrts- und Hafenabgaben. 1855.
Ernennung des Kaufmanns Herm. Friedr. Wilh. Lüdemann zum Lübeckischen Consul in Valparaiso. 1851.
Rücktritt des Consuls Lüdemann, einstweilige Wahrnehmung der Consulatsgeschäfte durch Herrn Th. Krook und Ernennung des Herrn Reinhard Behrens zum Lübeckischen Consul. Correspondenz. 1860-1865.
Auswärtige Angelegenheiten, Mecklenburg, die Vermittlung der Uebergabe einer Mecklenburgischen Reciprocitäts-Declaration bei der Regierung der Republik Chile. 1855.

7. Argentinien.

Fasc. 1. Handels- und Schiffahrts-Beziehungen. Verhandlungen betr. Einleitung eines Handels- und Schiffahrts-Vertrages mit Buenos Ayres. 1832.
Verhandlungen wegen eines mit der Argentinischen Republik abzuschliessenden Handelsvertrages. 1859, 1860.
Fasc. 2. Consulate in Argentinien. Bestellung des Kaufmanns Zimmermann zum Lübeckischen Consul in Buenos Ayres. 1840.
Ernennung des Herrn F. H. Hartenfels zum Consul. 1852.
Zum Generalconsul. 1860, 1861.
Errichtung von Consulaten des Norddeutschen Bundes zu Buenos-Ayres u. Montevideo, sowie die Aufhebung der dortigen Lübeckischen Consulate. 1868.
Fasc. 3. Argentinische Konsulate bei den Hansestädten. Ernennung des Hrn. E. W. Berckemeyer zum General-Consul von Argentina bei den Hansestädten. 1835.
Ernennung des Kaufmanns Friedr. Eduard Schütt zu Hamburg zum Consul der Provinz Buenos Ayres bei hiesiger Stadt. 1853.

8. Uruguay.

Fasc. 1. *a*. Handels-Schiffahrts-Beziehungen, Verhandlungen wegen eines Handels- u. Schiffahrts-Vertrags. 1841-1849.
  b. Acta betr. die von der Argentinischen Republik ergangene Anordnung wegen des Erfordernisses der Visierung der Schiffspapiere durch den Argentinischen Consul im Abgangshafen. 1852.
  c. Verhandlungen wegen eines abzuschliessenden Handelsvertrags. 1856, 1857, 1860-1862.
Fasc. 2. Consulat zu Montevideo. Anstellung des Herrn Rodewald. 1841. Berichte und Correspondenz desselben. Entlassung des Herrn Rodewald und Anstellung des Herrn Zimmermann. 1847. Berichte und Correspondenz desselben. Entlassung des Hrn. Zimmermann und Anstellung des Hrn. P. B. Möller. 1852. Berichte und Correspondenz. Entlassung des Hrn. Möller und Anstellung des Hrn. J. F. Crome. Berichte und Correspondenz. 1854, 1855.
Fasc. 3. Uruguay'sches Consulat bei den Hansestädten. Ernennung des Hrn. G. L. Forrer zum Viceconsul hieselbst. 1839.
  Ernennung des Bacilino Pereira Galvão in Hamburg zum Consul bei den Hansestädten. 1839. Beförderung desselben zum General-Consul. 1855.
  Abberufung desselben und Ernennung des Kaufmanns Hermann Rooten in Hamburg zum General consul von Uruguay. 1856.
  Ernennung des Kaufmanns Heinr. Julius Gustav Lilienthal zum Viceconsul von Uruguay hieselbst. 1858.
  Correspondenz mit dem Consulat der Republik Uruguay zu Hamburg. 1839, 1847.

9. Brasilien.

I. Handel u. Schiffahrt betreffend.
  Vol. A.
    Fasc. 1. Verhandlungen über einen von den Hansestädten mit Brasilien abzuschliessenden Commerz-Tractat. 1825-1828.
    Fasc. 2. *a.* Handelsverhältnisse mit Brasilien, insonderheit Aufkündigung des Tractates vom Jahre 1827 und Anknüpfung von Verhandlungen über Abschluss eines neuen Tractates 1838-1844.
      b. Verhandlungen über einzelne die Handlung und Schiffahrt betreffende Beziehungen. Schiffsabgaben und w. d. g. Gleichstellung der Flagge. 1844-1848.
  Vol. B. Varia. Commercielle und politische Beziehungen Brasiliens betr.
II. Diplomatische Beziehungen.
  a. Consulate der Hansestädte oder hiesiger Stadt in Brasilien.
    Vol. A.
      Fasc. 1. Consulat zu Rio de Janeiro.
        a. betr. die von Herrn Hoffmann nachgesuchte Bestellung zum Consul daselbst. 1815-1818.

  b. betr. die Ernennung des Herrn Caspar Friedrich Stuhlmann zum General-Consul in Rio und für ganz Brasilien. Correspondenz mit demselben. 1818, 1819. Niederlegung des Consulates und Bestellung des Herrn Joh. Fried. Bothe zum Vice-Consul. Correspondenz. 1820-1822.
  c. betr. Accreditirung des Herrn Hermann Christian Ten Brinck. Anstellung von Vice-Consuls durch denselben. Correspondenz. 1823.
  Ernennung des Kaufmanns Alexander Avé-Lallemant zum Lübeckischen General-Consul. 1853.
  Errichtung eines Lübeckischen Vice-Consulates zu Rio de Janeiro und Ernennung des Kaufmanns Wilhelm Boje zum Vice-Consul. 1857.
 Fasc. **2.** Consulat zu Bahia.
  a. Bewerbung des Herrn Meuron um das Consulat. 1817, 1820.
  b. Anstellung des Kaufmanns Pedro Peyke. 1826.
  c. Anstellung des Kaufmanns Christian Schriever. 1833. Entlassung desselben und Tod des Herrn Peyke. 1836.
  F. H. Wolters Consul. 1841. Entlassung. 1846.
  Ernennung des Herrn S. I. Luetjens. 1852.
  Entlassung des Hrn. Luetjens und Ernennung des Kaufmanns Johannes Matthias Meyer zum Consul zu Bahia. 1865.
  Correspondenz des Luetjens und seines Stellvertreters.
 Fasc. **3.** Consulat zu Pernambuco.
  Anstellung des Kaufmanns Joaquin Jozé d'Amorim. 1826.
  Ernennung des Kaufmanns Antonis Marques Amorim zum Lübeckischen Vice-Consul. 1843.
  Desgl. des Kaufmanns Wilhelm Otto. Correspondenzen, 1862.
 Fasc. **4.** Consulat zu Santos. Anstellung des Kaufmannes Friedrich Fomm. 1826.
 Fasc. **5.** Consulat zu Rio Grande de S. Pedro do Sul.
  Anstellung des Kaufmannes Ignacio Alves de Souza Pinto. 1828. Miguel Tito de Sâ. 1850.
 Fasc. **6.** Consulat zu San Luiz.
 Fasc. **7.** Consulat zu Porto Allegre.
 Fasc. **8.** Errichtung von Consulaten des Norddeutschen Bundes in Brasilien und Aufhebung der Lübeckischen Consulate. 1868.
b. Kaiserl. Brasilianische Agenten, Gen.-Consuls, Consuls etc. bei den Hansestädten.
 Vol. **A.**
  Fasc. **1.** Acta betr. die Accreditirung des Majors Georg Anton Schaeffer zum Kaiserl. Brasilianischen Agent des affaires politiques. Beabsichtigte Accreditirung des hiesigen Kaufmannes August Stolterfoht zum Kaiserl. Brasil. Consul bei hiesiger Stadt. 1826-1828.

Fasc. 2. Acta betr. die Accreditirung des Herrn Anton Joseph Rademacher zum Kaiserl. Brasil. General-Consul bei den Hansestädten. 1827-1829.
Fasc. 3. Acta betr. die Accreditirung des Herrn Antonio da Silva Caldeira zum Kaiserl. Brasil. General-Consul bei den Hansestädten. 1830.
Fasc. 4. Acta betr. die Anstellung des hiesigen Kaufmannes Johann Sigismund Mann, jr., zum Kaiserl. Brasil. Vice-Consul bei hiesiger Stadt; dessen Entlassung. 1830-1835.
Fasc. 5. Acta betr. die Accreditirung des Ritters Antonio de Menezes Vasconcellos de Drummond zum Kaiserl. Brasil. interimistischen Chargé d'affaires und General-Consul bei den Hansestädten. 1832.
Fasc. 6. Ernennung des Chevalier Marios Antoine d'Araujo zum Chargé d'affaires ad interim und General-Consul. 1834. Zum Ministerresidenten. 1852. Zum ausserordentlichen Gesandten. 1857. Dessen 25 jährige Amtsführung. 1859.
Fasc. 7. Acta betr. die Ernennung des Herrn Joh. Chr. Klügmann zum Kais. Brasilianischen Vice-Consul hieselbst. 1835.
Fasc. 8. Ernennung von Josá Lucio Correiá in Hamburg zum General-Consul bei hiesiger Stadt. 1852.
Fasc. 9. Ernennung des Kaufmannes Gustav Riebeck zum Brasil. Vice-Consul, an Stelle des verstorbenen Klügmann. 1861.
Fasc. 10. betr. die Versetzung des Brasilian. General-Consuls zu Hamburg, Ritter von Correā, und die Ernennung des Ritters Moniz des Aragão zu dessen Nachfolger. 1863.
Fasc. 11. Bestellung des Lübeckischen Staatsangehörigen Johann Friedrich Luetjens zum Kais. Brasil. Vice-Consul hieselbst in Stelle des verstorbenen Gustav Riebeck. 1888.

ACTA HANSEATICA.
D. Sclavenhandel.

Vol. D¹.
Fasc. 1. Acta betr. den Abschluss eines Accessionsvertrages der Hansestädte zu den Conventionen zwischen Frankreich und Grossbritannien wegen Unterdrückung des Sclavenhandels. Erlass der Verordnung wider den Sclavenhandel d: 26. July 1837. 1836, 1837.
Fasc. 2. Varia.
Fasc. 3. Acta betr. die Accession zu dem Vertrage zwischen Frankreich und Grossbritannien d: 28. Mai 1845 u. w. d. a. 1845-1846.
Acta ad litt. des Englischen Gesandten in Hamburg, in welchem verlangt wird, dass Lübeck den Sclavenhandel für Seeraub erkläre. 1851.
Abänderung der Vollmachten und Instructionen der Kreuzer. 1868.

Vol. D². Formulare zu den Vollmachten für die englischen und französischen Kreuzern, so wie die wegen Ertheilung oder Rücksendung solcher Vollmachten erwachsene Correspondenz. 1838-1846.

Vol. D³. Correspondenz bezüglich der Vollmachten für die englischen und französischen Kreuzer. 1847.

URKUNDEN (TRESE).

No. 3. Handels- und Schiffahrts-Vertrag zwischen den Vereinigten Staaten von Nordamerica und den Hansestädten. Dec. 20, 1827. Nebst Vollmacht vom 26. Novbr. 1827 für den Staatssecretair Clay zum Abschluss des Vertrages und der Ratificationsurkunde des Praesidenten Adams vom 8. Januar 1828. Mit Siegel in metallener Kapsel. In einem hölzernen Kasten.

No. 4. Freundschafts-, Schiffahrts-, und Handels-Vertrag zwischen den Vereinigten Staaten von Mexico und den Hansestädten Juni 16. 1827. Nebst Additional-Artikel vom 27. Juni 1827 und Separat-Artikel vom 12. Juli 1827.

No. 5. Handels- und Schiffahrts-Vertrag zwischen dem Kaiser von Brasilien und den Hansestädten Novbr. 17, 1827. Nebst der Ratificationsurkunde des Kaisers Pedro I. vom 17. Novbr. 1827 und dem Protokoll über die Auswechselung der Ratificationen vom 24. März 1828. Mit Siegel in metallener Kapsel. In einem hölzernen Kasten.

No. 11. Ratificationsurkunde des Vice-Praesidenten Carlos Soublette zu dem am 27. Mai 1837 zwischen den Vereinigten Staaten von Venezuela und den Hansestädten abgeschlossenen Freundschafts-, Handels-, und Schiffahrts-Vertrag. März 10, 1838. Nebst Protokoll über die geschehene Auswechselung der Ratificationen vom 19. März 1838.

No. 13. Mexicanische Ratificationsurkunde zu dem am 7. April 1832 zwischen den Vereinigten Staaten von Mexico und den Hansestädten abgeschlossenen Freundschafts-, Handels-, und Schiffahrts-Vertrage. April 30, 1841. Nebst Protokoll über die geschehene Auswechselung der Ratificationen vom 8. Novbr. 1841.

No. 19. Ratificationsurkunde des Präsidenten Fillmore zu dem zwischen den Vereinigten Staaten von Nordamerica und den Hansestädten am 30. April 1852 abgeschlossenen Vertrage, die gegenseitige Erweiterung der Jurisdiction ihrer Consuln betreffend. Septbr. 24. 1852. Nebst dem Original des Vertrags und dem Protokoll über die geschehene Auswechselung der Ratificationen vom 25. Febr. 1853.

No. 20. Ratificationsurkunde des Präsidenten der Republik Guatemala Rafael Carrera zu dem zwischen der Republik und den Hansestädten am 25. Juni 1847 abgeschlossenen Handels- und Schiffahrts-Vertrag. Juli 20, 1847. Nebst Protokoll über die geschehene Auswechselung der Ratificationen vom 1. Octbr. 1850.

No. 22. Ratificationsurkunde des Präsidenten von Neu-Granada, Manuel Maria Mallarino, zu dem von der Republik Neu-Granada mit den Hansestädten am 3. Juni 1854 abgeschlossenen Freundschafts-, Handels-, und Schiffahrts-Vertrage. Juli 20, 1856. Nebst Protokoll über die geschehene Auswechselung der

Ratificationen vom 28. März 1857. Mit Siegel in silberner Kapsel. In einem hölzernen Kasten.

No. 27. Ratificationsdocument des Präsidenten der Republik Costa Rica, Jose Maria Montealegre, zu dem zwischen der Republik und den Hansestädten am 10. März 1848 abgeschlossenen Freundschafts-, Handels-, und Schiffahrts-Vertrage. Septbr. 20, 1859. Nebst Protokoll über die geschehene Auswechselung der Ratificationen vom 28. Februar 1866.

MECKLENBURG-SCHWERIN (SCHWERIN).
GRAND-DUCAL PRIVY AND CENTRAL ARCHIVES.
(GROSSHERZOGLICHES GEHEIMES UND HAUPT-ARCHIV.)

Located in the basement of the Government Building in Schwerin, Schlossstrasse 2, but will soon be transferred to the new Archives Building now in process of erection.
Hours: 9 to 2.

1. Auswärtige Angelegenheiten, America:
    3. Berichte über Brasilien, La Plate Staaten, etc. 1817, 1818.
2. Ablieferung des Ministeriums des Innern:
    a. Auswanderung betreffend.
    b. Passgesuche für fremde Weltteile. 1863-1869.
3. Aus dem früheren Kriminal-Kollegium:
    Akten über Deportation von Sträflingen nach Amerika. 1824-1825, 1847.
4. Ablieferung des Grossherzoglichen Kabinets:
    a. Auswanderung nach Brasilien, 10 Fascikel. 1824-1829.
    b. Auswanderung nach Nord-Amerika. 1792.
    c. Auswanderung nach Peru. 1851.
    d. Auswärtige Beziehungen, Amerika, zwei Stücke, 1789 und 1844, betr. deutsche Ansiedlung in Neu-Schottland und Süd-Carolina.
    e. Auswärtige Beziehungen, Brasilien, sechs Stücke, 1824-1828, betr. (1) Konsulate und Gesandtschaften; (2) Verzeichnis von Mecklenburgern in brasilianischen Militärdiensten (1828).
Berichte der Mecklenburgischen Agenten in Hamburg.

MECKLENBURG-STRELITZ (NEUSTRELITZ).
GRAND-DUCAL CENTRAL ARCHIVES.
(GROSSHERZOGLICHES HAUPTARCHIV.)

Founded 1784; includes the archives of the Duchy of Stargard and the Principality of Ratzeburg. No matter relating to America was found, although there is a possibility that a search among the papers of the Duchess Charlotte Sophie, spouse of George III. of England, might yield something relating to America.

OLDENBURG (OLDENBURG).
GRAND-DUCAL HOUSE AND CENTRAL ARCHIVES.
(GROSSHERZOGLICHES HAUS- UND CENTRAL-ARCHIV.)

B. Staatsarchiv. I. Urkunden.
1. Staatsverträge:
    No. 101. Handels- u. Schiffahrtsvertrag mit Nordamerika. Mar. 10, 1847.
    No. 120. Auslieferungsvertrag mit Nordamerika. Mar. 21 (Dec. 30), 1853.
    No. 139. Handels- u. Schiffahrtsvertrag der Staaten des Zollvereins mit Mexico. July 10 (Oct. 15), 1855.
    No. 146. *Id.* Uruguay. June 23, 1856 (Apr. 3, 1857).
    No. 159. *Id.* Argentinien. Sept. 19, 1857 (June 3, 1859).
    No. 171. *Id.* Paraguay. Aug. 1, 1860 (Oct. 29, 1861).
    No. 179. Chili. Feb. 1 (June 14), 1862.

B. Staatsarchiv. II. Akten.
A. Staatsministerium.
   2. Kabinettsregistratur Oldenburg.
       IV. 34. 25. 1791, no. 129. Mädchen-Handel des amerik. Schiffs-Capitains Ebenezer Jenney.
       VI. 34. 1. 1801, no. 293, 309. Amerik. Consulat in Bremen.
       XII. 14. 7. 1822, no. 232. Schiffahrts-Abgaben in den Häfen von Nordamerika.
       XII. 6. 1. 1822, no. 526. Abschossrecht mit Nordamerika.
       XII. 46. 19. 1823, no. 177. *Id.*
       XII. 7. 22. 1827, no. 929. Auswanderung nach Amerika insbes. Brasilien.
B. Ressort. Ministerien.
   VI. Ministerium des Innern. 2. Innere Landesregierungs- u. Polizeisachen.
       No. 7. Amerikan. Consulat für Oldenburg in Bremen. 1805, 1806.
       No. 78. Auswanderung nach Amerika. 1805, 1806.

REUSS, ELDER LINE (GREIZ).
STATE ARCHIVES OF THE PRINCIPALITY OF REUSS, ELDER LINE.
(FÜRSTLICH REUSS-PLAUI. STAATSARCHIV.)

Located in the basement of the princely castle at Greiz, and consist of (1) the Hausarchiv, (2) the Regierungsarchiv, and (3) the Konsistorialarchiv. The secretary of the government is archivist.
Hours: 8 to 1 and 3 to 6.

Verwaltungssachen, Band II., Cap. XXVII b., Auswanderungssachen.
No. 3. Akta, die Uebersiedelung von Sträflingen, Correktionairs, und Landstreichern nach Amerika betreffend. 1837.
No. 4. Akta, der Christiane Friedrike verehel. Seifert geb. Rother hier Anwanderung nach Nordamerika betreffend. *Id.* Ferdinand Clemen. *Id.* Moritz Friedrich Hiermann. 1837.
No. 5. Akta, die auf öffentliche Kosten bewirkte Auswanderung des bisher in der hiesigen Zwangsarbeitsanstalt detinierten Buchdruckergesellen Ludwig Anton Schulz nach Amerika betr. 1840.
No. 6. Akta, die Ueberschiffung mehrerer Sträflinge und deren Kostenaufwand von hier nach Nordamerika betr. 1842.
No. 7. Akta, die unter Vermittelung Fürstlicher Regierung erfolgte Uebersiedelung verschiedener Individuen nach Nordamerika betr. 1847.
No. 13. Akta, das Gesuch Johann August Rüdigers zu Zoppoten und Genossen um Erteilung eines Auswanderungsscheines zur Uebersiedelung nach Nordamerika betr. 1852.
No. 16. Akta, die beabsichtigte Auswanderung der Kinder des nach Amerika ausgetretenen Fabrikanten Karl Friedrich Pfeifer von hier betr. 1854.
No. 19. Akta, die wegen Uebersiedelung entlassener Sträflinge nach Amerika in Vorschlag gekommenen Massregeln betr. 1856.

REUSS, YOUNGER LINE (GERA).
Archives contain the records of the government and the former consistory. No papers found relating to America.

SAXE-ALTENBURG (ALTENBURG).
DUCAL GOVERNMENT ARCHIVES.
(HERZOGLICHES REGIERUNGSARCHIV.)

Contain nothing relating to America. The state papers relating to emigration and kindred subjects are still deposited with the ministry.

SAXE-COBURG-GOTHA (COBURG).
DUCAL SAXON HOUSE AND STATE ARCHIVES.
(HERZOGLICHES SÄCHSISCHES HAUS- UND STAATSARCHIV.)

Nothing found relating to America; the same is the case with the separate archives in Gotha.

SAXE-MEININGEN (MEININGEN).
PRIVY STATE ARCHIVES.
(GEHEIMES STAATSARCHIV.)

The archives are under the direction of the Ministry of State, which decides what records may be consulted during the usual business hours.

A. Geheimes Archiv.

1. Errichtung eines Konsulates für das Herzogtum Sachsen-Meiningen in den nordamerikanischen Freistaaten. 1837-1869.
2. Convention mit den Vereinigten Staaten von Nordamerika wegen gegenseitiger Auslieferung flüchtiger Verbrecher. 1843-1847.
3. Verhältnisse mit Nordamerika insbesondere Berichte des Konsuls Adä in Cincinnati. 1861-1868.
4. Bestellung eines hiesigen Konsuls in Cincinnati. 1861-1868.
5. Thronbesteigung Seiner Majestät des Kaisers Maximilian von Mexiko und die Accreditirung eines Gesandten beim deutschen Bund resp. am hiesigen Herzoglichen Hof. 1864-1865.
6. Verhältnisse insbesondere die Bestellung eines hiesigen Konsuls in Milwaukee für die Staaten Wisconsin und Minnesota. 1864-1869.
7. Die Bestellung eines hiesigen Konsuls in Chicago. 1864-1870.
8. Die Anzeige von dem Präsidentenwechsel der Republik Paraguay. 1863-1867.
9. Errichtung eines Konsulats in San Francisco. 1866-1869.
10. Requisitionen deutscher Gerichte um Abhörung von Zeugen und Abnahme von Eiden in den Vereinigten Staaten von Amerika. 1869-1878.
11. Ablieferung von Verbrechern seitens der Vereinigten Staaten Nordamerikas. 1870-1884.

B. Archiv des Herzoglichen Staatsministeriums, Abteilung des Innern.

1. Die Leistung von Kautionen von Auswanderern wegen Ansprüche, die binnen Jahresfrist gegen sie geltend gemacht werden. 1841-1846.
2. Auswanderungen nach Amerika, insbesondere das Pressen hiesiger Untertanen zum Militär. 1864-1891.
3. Die Bundesanträge wegen der Auswanderung. 1858.
4. Auswanderungen nach Amerika. 1863-1879.
5. Die gewerbsmässige Beförderung von Auswanderern nach überseeischen Häfen. 1849.
6. Conzessionserteilungen zur Führung von Agenturen für Auswanderergeschäfte. 1849-1897.
7. Die Auswanderung nach Brasilien. 1858-1888.

SAXE-WEIMAR-EISENACH (WEIMAR).
GRAND-DUCAL AND DUCAL SAXON STATE ARCHIVES.
(GROSSHERZOGLICHE UND HERZOGLICHE SÄCHSISCHE STAATS-ARCHIVE.)

Located in Weimar, Alexanderplatz 3. The archives were organized in 1737 by the union of the " Kircharchiv " formed by Duke Wilhelm Ernst of Saxe-Weimar in 1693 and the " Brunnenarchiv " begun in 1697. The archives contain the most important earlier acts of the grand-ducal government and its several departments, treaties, official documents, and transactions relating to the ducal house and the like. In 1850 the " Geheimes Archiv " and the old " Kammerarchiv " of Eisenach were added to the collections. In 1866 the " Wartburg Archiv " and later the " Grossherzogliches Hausarchiv " were transferred to the Staatsarchiv.

Permission to use the archives is to be sought from the director, except that in the case of the Hausarchiv application must be made to the Staatsministerium, Dep. des Kultus, to obtain the Grand-Duke's permission.

Hours: 9 to 1 (Nov.-Mar. 9 to 2), and 3 to 5.

B. **5539 b.** Geheime Staats-kanzlei-Acten betreffend das Gesuch des Kaufmanns Leutloff zu Remde, um Erlaubniss zu Uebernahme einer Agentur zum Verkauf von Ländereien an Auswanderer nach Amerika, desgleichen die mehreren Grossherzoglichen Unterthanen erteilte Erlaubnis und Unterstützung zur Auswanderung nach Amerika. Vol. 1. Weimar, 1838-1844.
B. **5599.** Acten der Geh. Staatskanzlei betreffend die Erlaubniserteilungen zur Auswanderung nach Amerika und Texas. Vol. 2. Weimar, 1845-1849.
B. **5626.** *Id.* Vol. 3. Weimar, 1848-1849.
B. **5577.** Acten der Geh. Staatskanzlei betreffend die Auswanderung diesseitiger Unterthanen behufs der Niederlassung im Auslande. Weimar, 1843-1849.
F. **837.** (At the end.) T. C. Stöver, *Nachricht von einer evangelisch-lutherischen deutschen Gemeinde in dem amerikanischen Virginien* [Pennsylvanien]. (Printed, Hannover, 1737.)
D. **60.** Geh. Staatskanzlei-Akten betreffend den Krieg zwischen der Republik Paraguay und dem Kaiserreiche Brasilien. 1867.
D. **65 and 66.** Geh. Staatskanzlei-Akten betreffend Jahres- und sonstige allgemeine Handelsberichte des Konsulats zu Cincinnati: **65**, vol. I., 1855-1864; **66**, vol. II., 1865-1866.
D. **67.** Geh. Staatskanzlei-Akten betreffend generelle Berichte des Konsulats zu Philadelphia. 1858-1868.
D. **68.** Geh. Staatskanzlei-Akten betreffend allgemeine Berichte des Konsulats zu Chicago. 1859-1869.
D. **69.** Geh. Staatskanzlei-Akten betreffend verschiedene allgemeine Berichte des Konsulats in New-York. 1861-1868.

SAXONY (DRESDEN).
ROYAL SAXON CENTRAL STATE ARCHIVES.
(KÖNIGLICH SÄCHSISCHES HAUPTSTAATSARCHIV.)

Located in the Albertinum, Zeughausplatz. The records are accessible down to Sept. 4, 1831. Permission to consult the collections must be obtained from the Director.[1]

Hours: 9 to 1 and 3 to 6 (Saturdays 9 to 3).

Abt. III. Handelsschreiben Fol. 58. Bl. 288 fl 312. Entdeckung einer unbekannten Insel in Amerika: Ein Bruder des dortigen Königs in Spanien. 1561.

Abt. 310. Auswanderung.
  60. Die Ein- und Auswanderungen in und aus dem Warschauischen Gebiet, auch sonstigen Provinzen. 1808-1846.
  61. Die Verpflichtung einzelner hiesiger Einwohner, die Hinterlassenen der nach Amerika ausgewanderten oder wandernden hiesigen Einwohner zu ernähren. 1867-1872.

Abt. 329.
  309. Die nachgesuchten Auswanderungen. 1825-1864.

Abt. 335.
  1313, 1314, 1315 (relating to emigration).

Abt. 343-357.
  101, 102, 177, 178 (relating to emigration).

1885. (Loc. 27, no. 43.) Acta die für ein zu errichtendes theologisches Seminarium der deutschlutherischen Kirche in Nord-Amerika gesammelten Beyträge betr. Ober-Consistorien, 1827-1829.
  Letter of Hans Carl Alexander von Schönberg. Davidson County, N. C., Feb. 14, 1826.
  Letter from Benj. Kurz, Lutheran minister in Maryland and agent of the Lutheran church, dated Dresden, Feb. 27, 1827, and other official papers relating thereto.
  List of the collections made.

2249. (Loc. no. 815.) Die aus Thüringen auf die Englische Americanische Insul Carolina sich zu begebene gesonnene Hoch Teutsche Compagnie betrf. 1706.
  Documents relating to the plans and purposes of the Hochteutsche Compagnie von Langensalza, which is to go to America by way of England under the guidance of "eines grossen Quäckers der einer der 8 Lords Proprietaires von der Provinz Carolina in America, und als erneuter Gouverneur dahin abseegeln wird".
  Letters of Carl Christian Kirchner in London, dated March, 1706, relating to a report of Mathew Elliston and containing

---

[1] Other important collections relating to local matters are found in the Ratsarchiv, which is open from 9 to 1.30 and from 4 to 7, and can be consulted with the permission of the Council. Military records are found in the Königlich Sächsisches Kriegsarchiv, located Marienallee 3.

among other things the following: "Anfragen wegen Carolina so Ihrer Ezcell. John Archdal Proprietor von Carolina unterthänig übergeben werden, mit gehorsamster Bitte solche dergestallt zu beantworten, dass man sich darauff verlassen könne" (58 questions in all).

A son Excellence Monseigneur le Comte de Pflugk Grand Maréchal de la cour et premier ministre d'État de Sa Maj. le Roi de Pologne, etc., à la cour. A package of papers, 33 folios.

2420. Acta die Eröffnung eines unmittelbaren Handels nach Nordamerika und Errichtung einer diesfalsigen Handlungs-Societät betrf. 1783. A fair-sized folio volume, containing "notes" relating to the earliest commercial negotiations with the United States of America. The first "Nota" has the subscription, "Dresden, am 9 May 1783—Etranger Departement der Geheimen Cabinets-Canzley"; the papers in the volume continue till Apr. 12, 1803.

Paper dated Philadelphia, Apr. 12, 1784, and signed by Philipp Thieriot, "Handelscommissionaire", also an extract of a letter of Thieriot dated Philadelphia, May 31, 1784, relating to commerce and trade conditions in America. (Both in French. See W. E. Lingelbach, "Saxon-American Commercial Relations", in *American Historical Review*, April, 1912.)

Papers from the "Domestique Departement", relating to the organisation of a "Handels Societät" to facilitate commerce with America, and dealing with an important chapter in the commercial relations of Saxony and the United States. Dresden, Nov. 17, 1784.

2503. (Loc. 371. 9.) Acta die Elb-Amerikanische Compagnie betr. May 29, 1823-Dec. 12, 1829.

Erfolge der projectirten neuen Handels-Societät in Vergleichung mit denjenigen, unter denen die rheinischwestindische Gesellschaft entstand.

Elb West-Indische See-Handlungs Compagnie. Printed prospectus in 15 paragraphs signed: "J. G. Hoyer-Frauenstein, Voogt, Peters u. Cons."

Clippings of the *Dresdener Anzeigen* of Dec. 1, 1823, Jan. 8, 1824, and Feb. 14, 1824.

Among the important state papers relating to the matter are the following: A decree of King William I. of the Netherlands, dated Amsterdam, Mar. 29, 1824, relating to trade and to the "Entwurf der Statuten für eine in Dresden zu errichtende Seehandlungs-Compagnie" with the name "Elb-Amerikanische Compagnie". The Entwurf is of 54 paragraphs. "Statuten der Elb-Amerikanischen Compagnie in Leipzig." 27 paragraphs. Among the names in Leipzig is that of Jacob Heinrich Thieriot. 1824.

2610. Die Abschickung eines Sächs. Chargé d'Affaires nach Amerika betr. Project des H. v. Seckendorf. 1803.

2610. Vol. I. u. II. Acta den Nord-Amerikanischen Handel betrf.

Vol. I. Contains papers relating to the "Churfürstl. Commercien Deputation", etc.:

A French letter signed by Schönfeld, dated Paris, Sept. 21, 1778, and other related papers.
"Tarif des Droits d'Entrée que payent différentes marchandises de l'Europe, pour être vendues en France."
A number of "Pro Memoria" papers.
Communications from Schönfeld in Paris.
Papers in cipher with transliteration interlined, notably one addressed to Count de Gersdorff and dated Madrid, Jan. 10, 1783, relating to Saxon wares in America.
"Extrait d'une dépêche du Comte de Zinzendorf." Berlin, Mar. 7, 1783.
Paper in French with list of prices of manufactured stuffs. Mar. 9, 1783.
Despatches from Stockholm sent by the "Conseiller de Légation".
Papers relating to a consul of the Electorate of Saxony for America. 1783.
Letters from Stutterheim in Dresden to Thieriot in Philadelphia. 1783.

Vol. II. 1784-1801.
Papers of Stutterheim and Thieriot, and reports of the merchants Rasche and Shée in Philadelphia. 1784.
Important paper from Thieriot. Philadelphia, Apr. 12, 1784.

2610. Actes touchant l'état présent de l'Amérique septentrionale à Londres. Historical treatise in French, containing in all eight chapters, of which only three chapters are here given—130 pages. Important information concerning America. 1755.

2748. Des Kammerherrn von Schönfeld Negociation. Reports from the Saxon ambassador in Paris, containing the originals for much of the material in no. 2610.

Conv. **XXVII.**, fol. 227 e, 245 e, 269.
Conv. **XXVIII.**, fol. 62, 66, 80, 88, 92, 101, 109, 111, 117, 121, 124, 127, 142, 145, 157, 171, 198.
Conv. **XXIX.**, fol. 34, 198, 228, 332.

2750. Conv. **XXXV a.** Des Legationsraths Riviere an dem Königlichen französischen Hofe geführte Negotiation betrf. 1790. Reference to the anarchy in Santo Domingo (Bl. 269) and to the death of Franklin (Bl. 47).

Conv. **XXXV b.** *Id.* 1790. Ref. to St. Domingo, Bl. 228, 242 b, 252 b, 280, 291.

2751. Conv. **XXXVII a.** *Id.* 1792. Ref. to St. Domingo, Bl. 4, 6, 8, 10, 14, 15, 25, 31, 38, 45, 51, 120, 127,* 130.*

2754. Conv. **XLVI b.** Des Grafen von Bünau Abschickung an die Französische Republik und dessen daselbst geführte Negotiation betrf. 1801. Reference to St. Domingo, Bl. 114 b, 123 b, 126 *et seq.*

3003. Conv. **XII.** Loc. 422. Stutterheim à Berlin 1776. (Jan. 6–Dec. 27, 1776.) Colonie Angloise 5, 12, 16, 17, 44, 49, 50, 57. Important matter in cipher directed by Stutterheim to Count de Säken, Minister of State, dated Jan. 15, 1776, and dealing with the policy of the king of England in his relations to the king of Prussia. The volume contains a table of contents. Page 225 relates to Count de Zanowiz, his history, etc. (Berlin, July 12, 1776.)

3096. Acta Verwendungen für Chursächsische Unterthanen am Königl. Spanischen Hofe betrf. 1793-1807. (Bergleute, die nach Mexico gegangen 1787.)

3114. Papiere der Gesandschaft zu Madrid, die rückständigen Pensionen des Kurfürsten von Trier aus den mexicanischen Bisthümern betr. 1820-1825.

3285. Vermischte auf auswärtige Angelegenheiten und den Krieg bezügliche Papiere. 1759. 95 leaves. Contains papers of very miscellaneous character, such as:
Notizie aneddote dell'Anno 1755 sino all'Anno 1759, tanto in riguarda agl' Affari del Paraguay, quanto alla persecuzione de' Padri della Compagnia di Gesù nel Portogallo.

7441. Allergnädigst bewilligte Collection. Vol. I. 1709-1725. Papers relating to collections made for Lutheran pastors in the Palatinate, Mannheim, etc. 1708. The documents go back in some cases to 1689. There is a kind of index at the beginning of the volume and a list of " Rescripte " directed to the Oberconsistorium from 1689 to 1785. The volume contains a number of original papers relating to the several rescripts.

8510. Landgraf Philippi zu Hessen an Churfürst Augustum zu Sachsen abgelassene Schreiben. 1561-1562.
Fol. 288 refers to the brother of an Indian chief or king in the year 1561.
Fol. 311 et seq. refers to mission affairs of the year 1561. Cf. " Entdeckung einer unbekannten Insel in Amerika ", etc., first item under Saxony, above.

9905. Eine Langen Salzer Compagnie betr. so sich aus Thüringen hinweg nach der Provinz Carolina in America wenden wollen. Feb. 12/23-July 24, 1706. 49 folios.
Letters of Kirchner to Prince Fürstenberg.
A paper relating to Matthew Elliston with a list of 14 questions asking for information concerning Carolina and the plan of settlement by the Germans and referring to the " Hochteitsche Compagnie ".
Further letters of Kirchner dated London and a document entitled: Extrait Geführter Rechnung über aufgewandte Unkosten, etc. Jan. 31/Feb. 11-Apr. 6, 1706.
Papers from Polycarp. Mich. Rechtenbach to John Archdale, Proprietor and Governor of Northern Carolina in America. Langen Salza, Feb. 22, 1705.
Specificatio derjenigen Bürger, so de Ao. 1705 bis 1706 wegen entgangenen Gewerbe und verfallener Nahrung von hier gezogen.

30046. Vertrag zwischen den Vereinigten Staaten von Nordamerika und Russland den Handel der beiderseitigen Staatsangehörigen im Südsee betr. Petersburg, Apr. 5/17, 1824.
Notice sur l'Amérique Espagnole. 1819. (French translation of a manuscript in English by William Jacob.) An interesting account of the Spanish possessions in America. Dresden, Nov. 3, 1819. 14 pp.

Portugiesische Angelegenheiten Don Pedro und Don Miguel betr. 1826-1828. 24 pages containing among other things the following:
"Résumé d'une dépêche du Cte de Nesselrode au Pce de Lieven. Août 1826."
Letters of Earl Dudley to Sir F. Lamb, written from the Foreign Office in London, Mar. 19, 1828, and later.

30087. Schriften die Anerkennung des Kaiserreichs Brasilien betr. 1827.
31519 A. Emigrations Sachen betrf. [I Dept. 2. Exp. Rep. II. No. 291 a. Repos III. Loc. 9.]
    Vol. XIII. Feb. 12, 1788–Sept. 28, 1791. Matter relating to the following:
    Die von des Herzogs zu Sachsen-Meiningen Durchl. über den Commercien-Rath Langen geführte Beschwer, etc.
    The case of Peter Amthor and the ducal service sent by him.
    Vol. XIV. Dec. 12, 1791–Nov. 8, 1802.
    Important matter relating to Johannes Hennig's scheme of establishing a cotton factory in Sihlitz in the district of Fulda. Sept. and Oct., 1792.
    Papers relating to the removal of cotton workers from Chemnitz, Saxony, with a recital of the facts and motives relating thereto. 1793. These papers are valuable as evidences of the influence of American industry and trade in Germany, and particularly in Saxony at this early period, as well as of the conditions which led the Saxon emmigration to America. These papers are continued in a long series of volumes:
    Vol. XV. Aug. 27, 1803–Aug. 20, 1813.
    Vol. XVI. 1814-1818.
    Vol. XVII. 1818-1824.
    Vol. XVIII. 1824-1827.
    Vol. XIX. 1826-1828. Rep. VI. Loc. 29.
    Vol. XX. 1828-1829.
    Vol. XXI. 1829.
    Vol. XXII. 1830.
    Vol. XXIII. 1830.
    Vol. XXIV. 1831.

31716. Acta die Anstellung und Begläubigung des kgl. Consuls in Baltimore betr. 1826.
31719. *Id.* New York. 1826.
31720. *Id.* Philadelphia. 1826.

Schrank II. Fach **86.**
    Nr. **5.** Carton **C.** Karte von den Besitzungen der Engländer und Franzosen in N. America.
    Nr. **32.** Carton **F.** Karte von Amerika in 7 Blättern. 1787.
    Nr. **33.** Carton **F.** Karte von der N. W. Amerikanischen und N. O. Asiatischen Küsten. 1787.
    (*Cf.* the large collection of maps of America in the Königlich-Sächsische Hofbibliothek in Dresden.)

In addition to the numbers referred to above the following rubrics of the Staatsarchiv in Dresden may be mentioned:

Polizei-Sachen.
    Cap. Vorträge u. Verhältnisse zum Ausland. § mit der Schweiz, 1820-1834.

Landesregierung. Das Auswandern von Fabrikanten betr. Vol. I. 1827-1830.
Landesdirection 25. III. Depart. A. 96. Loc. 31479. Das Auswandern hiesiger Unterthanen betr. 1829-1830.
Landesdirection 506. I. Dep. 2. Exp. Rep. II. Loc. 1383. Religions-Sachen. *Auswanderungs-Revers Gesuche* betr. Arranged according to districts (Bezirke).

Another important source of information concerning the industrial and trade relations of Saxony and America is to be found in the American Archiv, formerly in Annaberg, but now in Chemnitz, and also the American consulates in Saxony. (*Cf. Staatshandbuch für das Königreich Sachsen*). The places of importance are Chemnitz, Dresden, Eibenstock, Glauchau, Leipzig, Markneukirchen, Plauen, Zittau.

SCHAUMBURG-LIPPE (BÜCKEBURG).

In the Archives of the Ministry of the Principality, no records relating to America are reported.

SCHWARZBURG-RUDOLSTADT (RUDOLSTADT).

In the Privy Archives of the Principality (Fürstlich Geheimes Archiv), no records were reported relating to America.

SCHWARZBURG-SONDERSHAUSEN (SONDERSHAUSEN).

In the Archives of the Principality (Fürstlich Schwarzburg-Sondershausensches Landesarchiv), located in the Castle, no records were reported relating to America.

WALDECK (AROLSEN).

The records of the Archives of the Principality of Waldeck relating to America are deposited for the greater part in the State Archives in Marburg. See, under Marburg, the list of documents on the III. English-Waldeck Regiment, and on the Wildunger Brunnen, pp. 144-149, *supra*. For special papers not yet handed over application can be made to the Landesdirektor der Fürstentümer Waldeck und Pyrmont in Arolsen.

WÜRTTEMBERG (STUTTGART AND LUDWIGSBURG).
ROYAL PRIVY HOUSE AND STATE ARCHIVES.
(KÖNIGLICH GEHEIMES HAUS- UND STAATSARCHIV.)

Located at Stuttgart, Neckarstrasse 4, and in the Branch (Filiale) in the Royal Palace at Ludwigsburg, the spacious residence built by Duke Eberhard Ludwig in rococo style in 1710-1720. The materials relating to America were deposited for the most part in the Royal Castle in Ludwigsburg. The Archives in Stuttgart were closed for repairs at the time of this search. The collections date back to the Dukes of Württemberg.[1]

Hours: 9 to 12 and 3 to 6.

STAATSARCHIV FILIALE IN LUDWIGSBURG.
Generalrescripte.

Band II. S. 647. General Rescript . . . . Wegen des Hinweg-Ziehens diesseitiger Unterthanen in Americam. Rescript of Eberhard Ludwig Herzog zu Württemberg, showing that the duke tried to nip the emigration in the bud by forbidding emigrants to sell their property. Stuttgart, June 25, 1709.

S. 867. Another copy of the same with certain passages underscored.

S. 931. Another rescript of the duke, stating that " Gantze Familien in zimmlicher Anzahl, und darunter nicht allein solche, die mit Schulden beladen, sondern auch, dem äusserlichen Vernehmen nach, vermögliche, die ohnbedachtsame und ihnen selbst sehr schädliche Entschliesung gefasst, aus Unserem Herzogthum und Landen hinweg, nach Pennsylvanien und Carolina in Americam zu ziehen ". The rescript shows that the authorities had made no particular effort to restrain the subjects of the duke from emigrating, and hence the rescript forbidding the sale of property. The rescript is directed particularly against the " unruhige fanatische Missionarios ". Stuttgart, Sept. 8, 1717.

Another rescript in manuscript, endorsed: " Hoch Fürstl. Befehl. Wie es mit denen Wttb. Unterthanen fortweg nach der Insul Missisippi zu ziehen vorhabens gehalten werden soll." Stuttgart, May 18, 1720. This is the sequel to the rescript of June 25, 1709. The text contains this interesting geographical passage:

" Von einem in hiesiger gegend befindlichen Commissario, sich bereden lassen wollen, nach der in Nord America ligenden Insul Missisippi zu ziehen." Reference is made to the rescript of Sept. 8, 1717, regulating the emigration to Carolina and Pennsylvania.

---

[1] Other valuable sources of Württemberg history are found in the Ständisches Archiv, Kronprinzenstrasse 2 a, containing materials from the sixteenth century on.

Rep. Geh. Rats Akten.

I. Ziff. 46. No. 86 b. Acta das Emigriren der Unterthanen betr. von 1750-1797.
Official papers relating to individuals and the permission to emigrate and the like. The papers are particularly numerous for the year 1780 and 1781. The statistics for the year 1750 show 2480 emigrants to America, 1512 to Pomerania, 57 to Hungary.
Papers describing the operations of the subjects who decoy their fellow burghers to emigrate and practically sell them into servitude: "diese selben Verkaufer verkauffen die Persohn gross und klein vor 3 gulden und da sie dan von denen Kaufleuthen in radertham [Rotterdam] wieder vor villes Geld nach dem neuen Engelandt und anderen Platz verkaufft werden". This document is dated Aug. 2, 1752, and signed: "Adolph Friedrich Blaufelder Bürger und Schreiner Meister aus Stuttgardt Wohnt auf dem Hüb vom Stillen Vier Gaei [Stille Veer Kaai] in Graffen Haag" [the Hague].
A paper stating that the rescripts have been so well enforced that emigration to America seldom occurs. July 7, 1768.
Papers relating to the emigration of Melchior Friz with wife and children to New England. 1771.

II. S. 32. No. 588. 1. Ueber die Frage, ob die in der Landes-Ordnung begründete Loskaufs Abgabe eines auswandernden Bürgers an die Gemeinde noch fortzudauern habe, oder allgemein aufzuheben sei? 1818-1819.

No. 685. Verordnungen in Auswanderungs-Sachen. 1803-1817. Contains among other papers the following:
Die Verordnung vom 15. Aug. 1817 für die künftige Behandlung der Auswanderungs-Angelegenheiten betr. (A bundle of printed and manuscript documents).
Auswanderungen. Massregeln wegen der Behandlung zurückkehrender Auswanderer. 1817.
Auswanderungen, insbesondere minderjähriger Kinder mit Stiefväter oder verwittweten Müttern betr. 1817.
Auswanderungen, insbesondere die Fragen:
1. Ob Militärpflichtige Söhne mit einer Mutter, die Witwe ist, oder mit einem Stiefvater auswandern dürfen?
2. Ob eine auswandernde Mutter ihre sämtliche minderjährige Kinder mit sich nehmen könne?
3. Ob die Ausfolge des Vermögens dieser Kinder gegen Bürgschafts Leistung eines Dritten zu gestatten sey?
5. Verordnung die Auswanderungen betr. Mar. 9, 1804.
Acta das Emigriren der Württembergischen Unterthanen betreffend. Official papers relating to the military and other conditions of emigration. 1803-1817.

No. 686. Die zu Anlegung von Colonien in Nord-Amerika errichtete Gesellschaften und das von einer derselben hier errichtete Comptoir betr. 1819. Reference to the "Nordamerikanische Colonisations-Gesellschaft in Stuttgardt", shedding important light on the operation of this and other societies.

MINISTERIUM DES INNERN IN LUDWIGSBURG.
Acten der vorm. Oberregierungs-Registratur v. 1806-1817.
Zimmer E. Schrank VIII.
Fach 50. A thick fascicle which is calendared or specially catalogued in the "Verzeichnis über die Akten der Oberregierungs-Registratur 1806-1817". This part of the catalogue contains 20 manuscript pages in folio. The material is arranged chronologically. Wegzug No. 1-27 de anno 1806-1813.
Fach 51. A bundle of similar papers also in the catalogue like Fach 50. It includes numbers 28-69, 1813-1817.

Ministerial-Acten.
Zimmer F. Schrank 20. Auswanderungen, Generalia.
Fach 40. Contains the following convolutes:
Conv. I. Monatslisten über die Verheirathung Weibl. Unterthanen im Ausland. Aug., 1811–Mar., 1815.
Conv. II. Auswanderungs Gesuche und Tabellen. Mar.-Dec., 1816.
Conv. III. Auswanderungs Gesuche und Tabellen. Apr., 1818–Dec., 1820.
Zimmer F. Schrank 21.
Fach 1. Berichte der Oberämter zu den Monatsübersichten über die Ausgewanderten vom Jahr 1849. These papers furnish names and other data of the emigrants according to the "Aemter" or districts, and relate to other countries as well as America.
Scattered material may be found also in the following, in Zimmer C, Schrank 1:
F. 7. No. 252. Geburtsscheine der im Auslande geb. Kinder. 1857-1870.
253. Trauscheine (Schweiz). 1874-1876.
254-255. Todesscheine von in Württemberg gestorbenen Ausländern. 1851-1881.
F. 71. 257. Todesscheine von solchen im Ausland gestorbenen Personen, deren Identität oder Heimatsangehörigkeit nicht ausgemittelt werden konnte. 1831-1877.
F. 72. 262. Todesscheine der in Amerika gestorbenen. Spez.-Akten. 1851-1876.
F. 77. 280. Ansprüche auf Erbschaften im Auslande.
281. Erbschaften im Auslande. 1822-1868.
F. 78. 282. 32 Unterfasz. 1806-1847.
283. 16 Unterfasz. 1848-1868.
284. Dispensationsgesuche (Dispens. von der K. Verordng. von 1817), Zurücklassung unmündiger Kinder btr. Spez.-Acten bis 1877 nach Oberämtern.
F. 79. 285. Unglücksfälle durch Schiffe, etc. Unterstützung der Verunglückten Spec.-Akten. 1848-1875.
286. Amerikanische Kolonisationsgesellschaft. Gründung einer Kolonie in Algier. 1819-1865.
287. Auswanderungen in gewisse Länder (Ungarn, Siebenbürgen, Surinam, Kalifornien, Türkei, Algier, etc.). 1839-1868.

	288.	Misshandlung von Auswanderern auf dem Schiffe *Michel Angelo*. 1853-1857.
F. 80.	289-290.	Auswanderungen nach Frankreich. (Spec.-Akten nach Namen.) 1858-1871.
	291.	Verein zum Schutz Württembergischer Auswanderer nach Amerika.
	292.	Nachweisungsbureau für Auswanderer in Bremen. 1851-1873.
	293.	Auswanderungsbureau (Württemb.). 1853-1858.
	294.	Beilagen zu den Generalakten über das Auswanderungswesen in Bremen, Hamburg, und Havre. 1867-1873.
	295.	Auswanderungen (Entlassungen aus der Württ. Staatsangehörigkeit). Spezialakten nach Oberämtern. 1855-1880.
F. 81.	296.	Mayer'sche Akten (Auszahlung von Unterstützungsbeiträgen an Württ. Auswanderer). 1860-1886.
	297.	Postportoauslagen des Oberreg. Rats Gessler in Auswanderungsangelegenheiten. 1853-1865.
	298.	Akten betr. die Verlegung der Auswanderungsgesuche nur alle Wochen in tabellarischer Form. 1816-1820.
	299.	Schiffbruch des Auswandererschiffes *Halcyon*. 1851-1865.
	300.	Uebersichten über den Gang der Aus- und Einwanderung. Spec. 1847-1850.
	301.	Uebersichten, etc. Gen. 1848-1873.
	302.	Oberamtliche Uebersichten. 1854-1871.
	303.	Statistische Uebersichten über die pro 1865-1867 beförderten Auswanderer. 1868.
	304.	Erhebungen über den Umfang der Auswanderung aus Württemberg. 1879-1880, 1880-1881. Gen. Ueberschiffs-Vermittlung zur Auswanderung nach Amerika (Verfügung vom 11ten Jan. 1847).
F. 82.	305.	Fasz. I. 1845-1854.
F. 83.	306.	Fasz. II. 1855-1864.
	307.	Fasz. III. 1865-1881. Agenten zum Betrieb des Transports von Auswanderern.
	308.	Fasz. I. 1847-1854. Spez. Akten nach Namen.
	309.	Ueberschiffahrts-Vermittelung. Koncessions-Gesuche. Fasz. II. 1865-1887. Spec. Akten nach Namen.
F. 84.	310.	Bezirks-oder Unteragenten. Min. Erl[aubnis] vom 17. October 1867. 1867-1870.
	311-348.	Auswanderungsagenten. A valuable list of names of ship agents.
C. IX.	39-48.	Auswanderungen. Spec. nach Oberämtern bis 1854.

Fasz. I. Aalen bis Hornberg.
Fasz. II. Kirchheim bis Rottweil.
Fasz. III. Saalgau bis Waiblingen.
Gen. Fasz. I. Mayer'sche Akten. 1854.
    Oberamtliche Uebersichten über den Gang der Ein- und Auswanderungen. 5 fascicles, one for each of the following years: 1851, 1852, 1854, 1855, 1856.

Auswanderungen mit öffentlicher Unterstützung nach Oberämtern.
   5 fascicles, one each for the following groups:
   Aalen bis Crailsheim;
   Ehingen bis Göppingen;
   Hall bis Ludwigsburg;
   Marbach bis Sulz;
   Tettnang bis Welzheim.
Ministerial Akten, welche in verschiedenen Zeitabschnitten von der Ministerialregistratur des Innern in das Archiv des Innern zur Verwahrung übergeben wurden.

MUNICIPAL AND OTHER LOCAL ARCHIVES.

In the course of the compiler's search the following local archives were examined, as most likely to contain matter relating to America.

COLOGNE.
HISTORICAL ARCHIVES.
(HISTORISCHES ARCHIV DER STADT CÖLN.)

Located Gereonskloster 12. Special permission to consult the collections not required.

Hours: 10 to 1 and 5 to 7.

Connected with the Historical Archives is the Archiv für Rheinisch-Westfälische Wirtschaftsgeschichte.

G[ymnasial] B[ibliothek]. No. **23**. Mundus Novus. A Latin account of the journey of Albericus Vesputius, 1505. The entire manuscript contains 16 leaves (32 written pages) 4¾ by 6⅜ inches in size, parchment paper, and is bound in vellum. The journey covers only the first 12 pages.

Akten der Kölner Handelskammer.

Mappe **4**. Navigation (B) entre Cologne et la Hollande. 1800-1814.
  Navigation entre Cologne et les Pays de Clèves. 1803-1813.
  13. Certificats et Manifestes I. u. II. (Correspondenzen, Beschwerden, Original Certificate, Liste, der von d. H. K. seit 1805 ausgestellten Ursprungszeugnisse.) 1803-1813.
  14. Renseignements individus sur les négociants et les fabricants de Cologne. (Im Auftrage der Regierung angestellte Nachfrage über Familie, Persönlichkeit, Vermögen der Kölner Kaufleute.) 1810.
  19. Fret en général et fiscation du fret sur le haut et le bas Rhin. Korrespondenzen mit Coquebert-Monsbret, dem Minister, dem Conseil général de commune in Paris, mit Eichhof, Daniels u. a. Frachtberechtigungen des Frankfurter Börsenvorstandes, der Handels-Kammer Mainz, Strassburg u. Cöln, Manifeste, Tarife, Zeitungsanzeiger u. s. w. 1805-1813.
  Fret entre Cologne et la Hollande, I. 1803-1806.
  Fret entre Cologne et la Hollande, II. 1806-1813.
  26. Duane. No. 5. Referring to " Plantage, Tabak, etc." (See also Mappe 22 and Mappe 59.) 1798-1803.
  27. Duane III. (Relating to Rotterdam, Amsterdam, Antwerp, and the Rhine.) 1811-1813.
  38. Dampfschiffahrt a. Korrespondenzen mit Rotterdam, Antwerpen, etc. (Compare 1824-1826 C. " James Watt, etc.") 1824-1826.
  65. Diverse b. Papers relating to " Handel mit Amerika ". 1816-1817.
  68. Vermischte Gegenstände IV. Handelsvertrag mit Brasilien. 1840-1842.

Cologne

79. IV. 1. a. Auswärtiger Handel u. Schiffarts-verträge. Zolltarif der Vereinigten Staaten. Brazilien .... Allgemeine Verfügungen an die Konsuln der Vereinigten Staaten u. a. 1843-1854.
IV. 1. b. Zolländerungen in den Vereinigten Staaten. (Handelsvertrag mit) Spanien, Mexico, Buenos-Aires. Kriegerische Konflikte in Nordamerika. 1854-1862.
IV. 2. a. Innerer Handel u. Gewerbe. Neues System des Flachsspinnens (John Madden). 1843-1853.
V. 3. Ein- und Durchgangsabgaben. Zusammenstellung der ausgeführten Zucker. 1842-1861.
V. 5. Eingabe der Zuckersieder Cölns an Flottwell. 1843-1859.
83. VI. 3. a. Auswanderungsgesellschaft (of Cologne). Berliner Kolonisationsgesellschaft. Centralverein für Auswanderung in Cöln u. Düsseldorf. 1843-1854.
VI. 3. b. Verhältnisse der Handelsgehülfen in Südamerika. 1854-1862.

Register (indexes for general reference in the Cologne archives).
1. Reichskammergericht. Prozesse Register IX.
2. Alphab[etisches] Rathsherren-Verzeichniss. 1396-1796.
3. Burgeraufnahmebuch Inventar. No. 82.
4. Alphabetisches Verzeichniss der Kölner Testamente im Düsseldorfer Staatsarchiv. Vol. I., A-G; vol. II., H-N; vol. III., O-Z.
5. Register zu den Kirchenbüchern.

FRANKFORT-ON-THE-MAIN.
CITY ARCHIVES.
(STADTARCHIV.)

Located in the same building with the museum opposite the Cathedral. Permission to consult the collections should be asked for by written communication to the Director.

Hours: 9 to 1 and 3 to 6.30.
Bibliography: Rud. Jung, *Das Frankfurter Stadtarchiv, Seine Bestände und seine Geschichte* (Frankfurt, Joseph Baer, 1909).

Ugb. A. 9. Nr. 3. A decree of the Senate of Frankfort, dated June 5, 1773, requiring information of Hofrat Bodo Wilhelm Stöcken and his efforts to enlist emigrants to South Carolina. Reference is made to a print entitled: *Freiheiten welche die Regierung zu Süd-Carolina unter Protection Sr. Königl. Grosbritt. Majestät denen dorthin von Hamburg kommenden und sich daselbst niederlassenden Personen auf 5 Jahre von 1773 allergnädigst angedeihen lässet*, etc. A copy of the pamphlet is enclosed. It contains 4 pages.

Nr. 4. Papers relating to emigration to America in the year 1773, of which the following are the most important:

An order of the Senate requiring that a shipmaster who has arrived at Wertheim with a shipload of emigrants for America and sent to Frankfort to buy bread, shall appear before the Senior Consul and take oath that he will take his passengers back to Wertheim, that is, not allow them to remain in Frankfort.

Paper manumitting Peter Diehm to emigrate to New England on the condition that, if he return, he shall together with his family resume his former condition of servitude.

Another paper relating to Leonhard Spielmann of Lendelbach, who wishes to emigrate with his three children to New England. Wertheim, Apr. 2, 1773.

Order of the Senate relating to emigration. May 10, 1773.

Decree of the Senate touching " die bey dem Gastwirth Lehn am Holzpförtgen ligierende beyde Philadelphianer ", who are summoned to give an account of themselves, viz.: " Jacob Schaffner, aus dem Canton Basel, der Schweiz, gebürtig, aber in der Provinz Pensilvanien in der vor 15 Jahren angelegten Stadt Libanon wohnhaft, 49 Jahr alt, Reformirter Religion; Andreas Glanschett, aus dem Maulbronner Amt im Würtembergischen gebürtig, dermalen aber in Philadelphia wohnhaft, 28 Jahr alt, Reformirter Religion ". The investigation here referred to shows that the persons in question were in Frankfort purchasing hardware: " Sensen, Sicheln, und dergleichen item in Büchern ". This is a most important document, showing the methods of dealing with suspect emissaries. May 8, 1773. 15 pp. folio.

Four papers addressed to the government at Wertheim, relating to a number of emigrants with the shipmaster Johann Jacob Kress on their way to America. May 8, 1773.

Nr. 8. A bundle of 4 papers dealing with the emigration to America, and relating specifically to the investigation of the case of " Baron Carl von Röder seiner Angabe nach aus Haduwam in Ungarn gebürtig, welcher Hauptmann in Königlich Grosbrittannischen Diensten gewesen, wegen Anwerbung teutscher Colonisten nach Amerika ". 1804-1805.

A bundle of 15 papers relating to emigrants to America, 1805, including the following:

Decree of the Senate of Frankfort, relating to emigrants passing en route for Louisiana. Mar. 29, 1805.

Decree of the Senate, referring to Lindheimer and Schlafmunter and Unger, as permitted to emigrate because they were " dem Staate lästig ".

Papers relating to emigrants from Wertheim to North America, especially to the North American provinces Louisiana and Florida, and relating also to secret efforts to secure recruits for Holland. April, 1805. Enclosed in this bundle is an interesting printed form of agreement of indenture, which reads as follows: *Freiwillige Verpflichtung der nach Nord-America bestimmten Colonisten*, etc. The passenger obligates himself to serve six years to pay " Wills und Compagnie " the passage money.

Papers relating to the two brothers Kilian and Cälestin Göller, " wegen Verführung der Unterthanen nach Amerika ". Apr. 26, 1805.

Order issued by the City Chancellery, relating to emigration to America, to Wills and Company, and to the shipping of emigrants to Louisiana. Apr. 20, 1805.

Nr. 10. Grossgünstige Gestattung der Durchreise für 200 aus dem Würtembergischen nach Amerika reisende Personen betreffend. A very important paper signed by Friedrich Carl Tausent, addressed to the Senate of Frankfort, June 5, 1805. These emigrants were furnished with the proper passports and other papers and met no obstructions on the part of the Senate. (*Cf.* the Rappisten ?)

Ugb. D. 42. Nr. 46. Two papers relating to the shipping of emigrants in the year 1773:

Pro Memoria, referring to the " selling of emigrants " (" den Schiffleuthen zum Transport nach America quasi verkaufft "). Mention is made of Emig of Rossdorff, who sold his own son and " noch neun junge Pursche " under such conditions. Frankfort, May 7, 1773.

Pro Memoria, referring to the said Emig of Rossdorff. Frankfort, May 10, 1773.

Repertorium. Tom. I.

H. 26. Nr. 3. Uebereinkunft zwischen den Zollvereins-Staaten und dem Nordamerikanischen Staatsverband wegen Auslieferung flüchtiger Verbrecher. 1843-1845.

M. 27. Deutsche Bundesversammlung.
    Nr. 7. Verhandlungen beim Bundestag über Auswanderung. 1856-1859.
M. 30. Gesandte hiesiger Stadt und Consuln.
    Nr. 6. America mit Ausnahme der Verein. Staaten v. N.-A.
        1. Mexiko.
        2. Chili.
        3. Buenos Ayres.
        4. Pernambuco.
        5. Peru.
        6. Rio Janeiro.
    Nr. 13. Vereinigte Staaten v. N. Amerika.
        1. New York.
        2. Philadelphia.
        3. Ohio u. Indiana.
        4. Illinois.
        5. Missouri.
        6. Washington (General Consulat).
        7. Wisconsin.
        8. Iowa.
M. 35. A. Gesandte dahier, Geschäftsträger, Residenten, und Consuln.
    Nr. 6. Vereinigte Staaten von Nordamerika. Consuln. 1829-1866.
    Nr. 19. (1.) Argentinische Republik und Buenos Ayres. 1857—.
    (2.) Bolivia.
    Nr. 21. Brasilien. General-Consulat. 1862-1864.
    Nr. 22. Mexiko. Consulat. 1865—.
M. 42. Gratulation und Condolenzen.
    Nr. 38. Peru.
    Nr. 39. Paraguay.
    Nr. 40. Nord-Amerika.
Repertorium. Tom. II.
    B. 118. Nr. 42. Auswanderung nach Amerika, durch die Niederlande. 1828-1832. (Stricken out in the Repertorium.)
    B. 120. Nr. 16. Gesuch von 13 Dcbr 1853, die Polizeiliche Ueberwachung der Gewerbmässigen Bevörderung von Auswanderern. Generalia. Tom. I., 1817-1854. Tom. II., 1855-1866. Tom. III., 1867.
        Fasc. spec. I. Agenten: deren Bestellung u. Consuln. 1854-1867.
Repertorium. Tom. III.
    A. 128. Nr. 7. Handelsverhältnisse zwischen dem Prss. Zollverein und den Nordamerikanischen Freistaaten. 1838, 1842, 1844-1846, 1857.
Repertorium. Tom. IV.
    A. 144. Nr. 5. Verhandlungen über den Anschluss des F. Th. und Taxischen Postgebiets zu dem Preussisch-Amerikanischen Postvertrag. 1853-1855.
I. Rathssupplicanten. 1600-1810.
II. Senatssupplicanten. 1814-1868.
    Two series of immense tomes of acta containing "Gesuche" of every imaginable kind brought before the Council and Senate

of Frankfort for consideration. The papers are arranged chronologically and divided into two classes as indicated by I. and II. above. To these series there is a " Namenregister ". Among these papers are to be found the " Auswanderungsgesuche ", which in other archives are usually arranged in separate groups. To find the names of the emigrants to America, one must either know the specific name to be looked for or look through these great tomes systematically.

HERRNHUT.

MORAVIAN ARCHIVES IN HERRNHUT.
(ARCHIVUM UNITATIS FRATRUM, ARCHIV DER EVANGELISCHEN BRÜDER-UNITÄT.)

Located in the Archive Building. Contains one of the most interesting religious collections in Germany. By a system of copying, much that is found in the Moravian Archives of Bethlehem, Pennsylvania, and Winston-Salem, North Carolina, and other Moravian settlements, is found in copy also at Herrnhut. The material is rich in matter relating to America and is well assorted and labelled, arranged in cases (Schränke), and easily accessible through the archivist. The old catalogue, made in 1838, has the title: "Repertorium zum Geschäfts-Archiv des Unitäts-Vorsteher Collegii gefertigt in Jahre 1838". It consists of five parts, but must soon be superseded by a new one based upon the recent arrangement of the records under the direction of the present archivist. In the following notes the orthography has been modernized by the copyist.

Hours: Specially arranged.

R. 14. A a. Missions in Pennsylvania.

1. Protokolle der Pennsylvanischen Helferkonferenz in Bethlehem (since 1851 has been called Provinzial Aeltesten Konferenz, Provincial Elders' Conference).

   a. 1785-1790.
   b. 1791-1797.
   c. 1798-1800.
   d. 1801-1804.
   e. 1805-1807.
   f. 1808-1812.
   g. 1813-1824.
   h. 1825-1833.
   i. 1834-1859.
   k. 1860-1872.
      (1873-1877 is lacking).
   l. 1878-1885.
   m. 1886-1894.
   n. 1895-1899.

2, a-f. Protokolle der Pennsylvan. Societas zu Förderung des Evangeliums unter den Heiden. 1791-1847.
3. Protokolle, Berichte, u. Correspondenzen der Predigerkonferenzen in Bethlehem 1851-1852, Nazareth 1853, Lititz 1854.
4, 1-3. Monatl. Berichte d. Pennsylvan. Helferkonferenz. 1801-1849.
5, a-z. Correspondenz d. Pennsylvan. Helferkonferenz. 1765-1899.
6. Kirchenbücher von Bethlehem. 1774-1817.
7. Kirchenbücher von Nazareth. 1774-1817.
8, a-b. Kirchenbücher v. Lititz u. den 8 dazu gehörenden Landgemeinden: Hope (Jersey), Lancaster, Yorktown, Hebron, Mountjoy, Heidelberg, Bethel/a. Swatara, Graceham. 1774-1817.
9. Kirchenbücher von Emmäus 1786-1817, Schöneck 1790-1817, Philadelphia 1774-1817, New York 1786-1814, 1816, Staten Island 1786-1817, Newport 1801-1814, Gnadenhütten am Mahoning 1805-1812, Gnadenhütten am Muskingum u. Bersaba 1800-1817.
10, 11. Diarium von Bethlehem. 1742-1744.

12. Diarium v. Bethlehem. 1745.
13. *Id.* 1746.
14. *Id.* 1747.
15. *Id.* 1748.
16. *Id.* 1749.
17. *Id.* 1750, 1751.
18. *Id.* 1752.
19. *Id.* 1753.
20. *Id.* 1754.
21. *Id.* 1755.
22. *Id.* 1756-1758.
23. *Id.* 1759-1766.
24. *Id.* 1767-1769.
25. *Id.* 1770-1776.
26. *Id.* 1777-1782.
27. *Id.* 1783-1787.
28. *Id.* 1788-1791.
29. *Id.* 1792-1796.
30. *Id.* 1797-1806.
31. *Id.* 1807-1810.
32. *Id.* 1811-1813.
33. Memorabilien (*i. e.,* Jahresberichte) v. Bethlehem. 1811-1822.
34. *Id.* 1823-1831.
35. *Id.* 1832-1847, 1849-1852, 1861-1898.
36. Diarium von d. Kinder Anstalten in Bethlehem, Nazareth, Salisbury. 1751-1761.
37. Diarium von den Besuchen bei den Kindern im Land. 1752-1763.
38. Diarium von Nazareth. 1751-1754.
39. *Id.* 1755-1761.
40. *Id.* 1765-1771 (1761-1764 under Nr. 23 with the Diarium of Bethlehem).
41, 42. *Id.* 1777-1790.
43. *Id.* 1791-1796.
44, a-b. *Id.* 1797-1806, Diarium v. Schöneck 1796-1799, 1802, v. Hope (Jersey), 1797-1806.
45, a-b. *Id.* 1807-1817, 1820, 1821, 1825-1834, 1839-1849.
46. Diarium von Lititz. 1763-1776.
47. *Id.* 1777-1786.
48, 49. *Id.* 1787-1795.
50. *Id.* 1796-1806.
51. *Id.* 1807-1821.
52. *Id.* 1822-1838, 1840-1849, 1853.
53. Diarien v. Pennsylvanischen Stadt- und Landgemeinden (Zusammengeschrieben). 1752-1759.
54. *Id.* 1765-1768.
55. *Id.* 1769-1776.
56, 57. *Id.* 1777-1786.
58. *Id.* 1787-1790.
59. *Id.* 1790-1794.
60. *Id.* 1795-1805.
61. *Id.* 1806-1810.
62. *Id.* 1811-1821.
63. *Id.* 1822-1839.

R. 14. B. Wachovia.

1. Akten zu den Verhandlungen mit Lord Granville über die Wachau. 1750-1754.
2 a. Berichte vom Anfang der Niederlassung in der Wachau. 1750-1754.
2 c. Akten betr. die Anfänge in der Wachau, von Spangenberg gesammelt. Vol. I., 1752-1755; vol. II., 1755-1762.
3. Die ersten Reisen nach der Wachau. 1753.
4, 6. Reisediaria nach der Wachau, 1755; Einige Hauptstücke die Anfänge in der Wachau betr., 1753, 1754.
7. Briefe u. Aufsätze die Einteilung u. Cultivierung der Wachau betr. 1752-1759.
8. Beschreibung des Landes, der Bäche u. Nachricht von Bethanien. 1759.
14-20. Historische Nachrichten von den Brüdergemeinen in der Wachau. 1754-1803.
21. *Id.* 1804-1811.
22-24. Nachrichten v. Bethanien, 1806, 1809; Levelys Reisen in Virginien, 1833-1841; Ordnungen v. Salem, 1850.
25. v. Marshalls u. Benziens Untersuchungsreise nach Süd-Carolina. 1790.

R. 14. B b. Wachovia and Southern Missions.

1. Wachauische Diaria. 1753-1758.
2. *Id.* 1759-1776.
3, 4. *Id.* 1777-1786.
5. *Id.* 1787-1789.
6. Diaria v. Salem. 1787-1795.
7. *Id.* 1797-1800.
8. *Id.* 1801-1803.
9. *Id.* 1804-1806.
10, 11. *Id.* 1807-1811 dabei die Diarien der Landgemeinen.
12, 13. *Id.* 1812-1822, dabei die Diarien der Landgemeinen.
14. Diarium v. Salem u. den Landgemeinen. 1823-1856.
15. Memorabilien v. Salem, etc. 1802-1809, 1887-1898.
16-17. Protokolle der Provinzial Aeltesten Konferenz des südl. Distrikts d. Vereinigten Staaten. 1773, 1785, 1786, 1802-1805, 1807-1810, 1813-1816, 1819-1857, 1858-1859, 1872-1873, 1877-1878.
18. *Id.* 1858-1859, 1872, 1873, 1877, 1878.
19. Protokolle d. Aeltesten Konferenz in Salem. 1773-1775, 1824-1882, 1884-1898.
20, 21, 22. Protokolle d. Wachauischen Heidensocietatis. 1801-1845, 1849, 1850, 1855.
24, 27. Korrespondenz d. Provinzial Helfer Conferenz (später Provinzial Aeltesten Conferenz in Salem. 1753-1824.
29. *Id.* 1826-1842.
30. *Id.* 1843-1858.
31 a-b. *Id.* 1859-1882, 1883-1898.
32. Kirchenbuch von Bethania 1760-1817, v. Bethabara 1756-1817.
33. Kirchenbuch von Friedberg 1801-1817, von Friedland 1801-1817, von Hope 1801-1817, von Salem 1771-1817.

R. 14. C. North American Provincial Synods.
1. Synodus von Friedrichstown. 1745.
2. Pennsylvanische Synodi. 1745, 1746.
3. *Id.* 1747.
4. *Id.* 1748.
5. *Id.* 1749.
6. *Id.* 1750, 1751.
7. *Id.* 1752, 1753, 1754.
8. *Id.* 1755-1759.
9. *Id.* 1760-1765.
10. Acta des Provinzial-Synodi gehalten zu Bethlehem. 1766. Tom. I.
11. David Nitschmanns Beilagen zu diesem Synodus. Tom. II.
12. Protokoll einer Conferenz gehalten in Bethlehem. June 11-14, 1786.
13. Verhandlungen wegen der in Hope (Indiana) zu haltenden Provincial Synode des nördlichen Bezirks. 1878.

R. 14. D. South America: Brazil.
1. Anfänge der Colonie Brüderthal in Brasilien. 1886-1893.
2. Correspondenz der Unitäts Aeltesten Conferenz mit Brüderthal. 1886-1894.
3. *Id.* 1894-1898.
4. Jahresberichte von Brüderthal. 1894, 1895.
5. Das Ende Brüderthals. Schlussverhandlungen. 1897.

R. 14. E. Bethel in Australia.
1. Statuten von Bethel, An Act to provide for the incorporation of institutions, etc. 1858.
2. Correspondenz der Unitäts Aeltesten Conferenz mit Bethel. 1852-1872.
3. *Id.* 1873-1894.
4. *Id.* 1895-1907.

KARLSRUHE.
CITY ARCHIVES.
(Städtisches Archiv.)

Located in the City Hall. Permission given by the Burgomaster. Hours by special arrangement. The following items are from the Stadtregistratur: Bürgerrecht, Heiraten und Wegzug.

Bürgerannahmen, Führung der Bürgerbücher.
    Jahr 1831. Die Fertigung des Bürger- und Schutzbürgerbuches für die hiesige Stadt. 1831.
Kast. I. Fach II. Band I. Jahr 1831. Bürgerannahmen, Heirathen, Wegzug. Bürger-Recognitionsgelder, Antritts- und Einkaufsgelder, etc.
    Heft 4. Die bei jeder Bürgerrecognition an die Stadtkasse zu ertheilenden Bürgerantritts- und Anerkennungsgelder btr. sowie die Beiträge zu Stiftungen.
Jahr. 1832-1835. Bürgerannahmen, Schutz und Schirm der Hofdiener, der Schauspieler und Hofmusiker. 1832-1835. Contains lists of persons, giving the name, home of the father, place of birth or home of the wife.
Kasten I. Fach II. Band 2. Heft 2. Die Ertheilung von Zeugnissen und Heiraths-Urkunden für solche, die auswärts heiraten und sich niederlassen. 1859.
Jahr 1853. Theil I. Bürgerannahmen. Schutz u. Schirm. Heimatsrechte verschiedener Personen, welche hier kein Bürgerrecht geniessen. 1838-1840.
    Theil II. Heimatsrechte, etc. 1832-1834.
    Theil III. Heimatsrechte, etc. 1853.
Jahr 1870-1873. Theil I. Gesuche um Geburts-, Ehe-, und Todtenscheine, etc. betreffend. 1870-1873.
    Fasc. 2. Auswanderungsagenten. 1895.

MANNHEIM.
CITY ARCHIVES.
(Städtisches Archiv.)

Located in the municipal Kaufhaus. Administered in connection with the Municipal Central Library. Hours specially arranged.

Verwaltungs-Sachen.

Rubr. V. Bürgerannahme. Wegzug.

Bestimmungen und Verordnungen über das Auswanderungswesen im Allgemeinen. 1817, 1855, 1862 (intervening years are also represented in many cases). Contains also printed matter such as reports, newspaper clippings, etc.

V. 3/1. Das Verbot der Auswanderung und die Massregeln gegen die sogenannten Werber betreffend. 1709-1804. Contains the following old matter:

A decree of the Elector Palatine, reiterating the prohibition of emigration " in die sogenannte Insul Pensylvaniam ", directed against the " heimliche Emigration ". Heidelberg, Apr. 25, 1709.

Decree of the same, beginning: " Nachdem die aus hiesigen und umbliegenden Landen bereits würcklich emigrirte und noch täglich zu emigriren gesinnte einfältige arme leuthe, so sich in die sogenandte Landschaft Pensylvaniam zubegeben willens, zu dieser langwiehrig-, gefahr-, und müheseeliger Reysz vermuthlich daher verleitet worden ", etc., continuing, that " etliche 1000 an der Zahl vor Rotterdam, auf denen so genandten Dycken, aus der Ursach, damit diese arme Leuthe auf der Ebene, vielen das gantze Land voller Wasser, nicht jämmerlich ertrinken möchten ", and to put an end to this " Miserie " the Verordnung is made. An important document giving much valuable detail. May 22, 1709.

Printed decree, issued by the " Chur Pfältzische Regierung ". Mannheim, June 21, 1752.

Decree against the emigration to Denmark. Mannheim, Mar. 4, 1760.

Decree against the emigration " in die neue französische Colonie und andere dergleichen frembde Landen ", stating that " auch vielmahlen ganze Haushaltungen und Familien Trouppen weisz abzieheten ". Mannheim, Mar. 3, 1764.

Decree against the emigration to Cayenne, " auf Veranlass nehmlicher Auswanderungen in die Insul Cajenne allschon unterm 3ten Martii, 14ten Maji, dann 9ten Junii und 27sten Novembre 1764 im Druck erlassenen General-Verordnungen ". Directed against the " Emissarii ". Mannheim, Apr. 29, 1766.

Decree against emigration to Russia, reiterating the decree of Apr. 21, 1766, and aiming at the " Emissarii ". Mannheim, May 27, 1766.

Bestrafung der ohne Landesherrlichen Vorwissen auswandernden Churpfältzischen Angehörigen, auch neuen Unterthanen. (Printed. Mannheim, Feb. 23, 1779.)

Verordnung die Erbschafts- oder Vermögens-Verabfolgungsgesuche aus den K. K. Erbstaaten betreffend. (Issued by General-Landes-Commissariat of the Palatinate). Mannheim, Sept. 26, 1800.

Decree of Maximilian Joseph. Nov. 16, 1801.

Auszug Kurbadischer Hofraths Protocolle I. Senats. Mannheim, Sept. 4, 1804.

Verzeichniss der im 17ten Jahrhundert ausgewanderten Wallonen. (On the new cover.) This is a very old manuscript list of names of burghers of Mannheim, residing in other places. The title inside on the original manuscript runs: " Verzeichnus der hin und wieder sich aufhaltend Bürger von Mannheim ". (No date.) The manuscript consists of 10 folios, 20 pp., written in some cases on both sides and in double columns. A most valuable list of names for the genealogist.

Protocollum Commissionale.

Gesuche um Erlaubniss zur Auswanderung nach Amerika. 1852, 1855, 1856, 1857, 1858, 1859, 1860, 1862, 1864.

V. 3/3. Gesuche um Entlassung aus dem Staats- und Unterthanen-Verbande Behufs der bürgerlichen Niederlassung und Verehelichung in anderen Staaten betr. 1852, 1856, 1857, 1858, 1859, 1862, 1864.

V. 3/4. A thick package of Gesuche. A number relating to America. 1870-1874.

V. 3/5. Gemeinderaths-Akten. 8 Gesuche relating to emigrants to America. Note particularly that of Joseph Alexander Geiger, 1855. A large parcel of papers (1852-1855).

Polizeisachen.

Rubr. **XXII.** No. **2.** Sicherheit.

Fasc. Die Zahlung der Unterhaltungskosten für die in der Polizeilichen Verwahrungsanstalt befindlichen hiesigen Individuen betr. 1855, 1856, 1863, 1864. The following fascicles contain, here and there, information of this sort respecting emigrants to America, the capital letters referring to the names of the individuals, which are alphabetically arranged.

XXII. 2. 11. A 1844-1861.
E 1842-1857.
F 1843-1853.
G 1844-1864.

XXII. 2. 12. H 1844-1860.
J 1852-1864.
K 1852-1860.
L 1850-1851.
O 1850.
P 1853-1855.
R 1843-1860.
U 1841-1852.

XXII. 2. 13. W 1837-1853.
W 1842-1866.
Also, without numbers:
B 1849-1862.
D 1841-1855.
S 1841-1862.
T 1856.
U 1843-1866.

NEUWIED.
ARCHIVES OF THE (MEDIATIZED) PRINCIPALITY OF WIED NEUWIED.
(Fürstliches Archiv zu Neuwied.)

Located in the castle, directly on the Rhine, and commanding a splendid view of the river to the west. The archives are repertorized and have recently been catalogued down to 1800 by Dr. Schultze of the State Archives of Marburg. The first part of the catalogue is in press. The papers are arranged in movable chests, which can be easily removed in case of high water from the overflow of the Rhine. Hours arranged by special appointment with the Director.

Schrank 2.
    Gefach 13. Fasc. 1. Graf Wilh. v. Schwerin in Fr. Kriegsdienste, etc. 1777, 1778.
        Fasc. 2. Acta die Correspondenz mit dem H. Grafen von Schwerin während der Campagne in Britannien und Amerika. 1779-1782.
        Fasc. 3. Acta Bezahlung eines Wechsels ad 1200 lb. oder 550 Fl. an die Kaufleute Heyder und Comp. zu Fort Louis, welchen H. Graf Wilhelm von Schwerin auf Celsmo ausgestellt ferner Bezahlung eines Wechsels ad 300 lb. an Mr. Cabanar.
           3. Ferneres Schreiben was derselbe vom Anfang der Campagne in America depensirt, und noch schuldig ist.
           4. Schreiben von dessen Wiederkunft aus America vom 17 Juny 1783 aus dem Hafen von Brest.
           5. Sammt Antwort darauf von Celsmo und
           6. Etat was dessen Militair-Dienst schon gekostet.
        (The following, 7, 8, and 9, relate to the payment of the prince's debts.)
        Fasc. 9. Acta relating to Graf von Schwerins " Patent " as captain in the Royal Deux Ponts.
        Fasc. 41. " Fremdenbuch " of the Princess of Nassau (lost for 30 years but found again).

Schrank 6.
    Gefach 5. Fasc. 2. Vertrag des Gr. Friedr. Alex. zu Wied-Neuwied mit Samuel Waldo, Esq., betr. die Ansiedlung von 1000 Familien in der Provinz Massachusetts. Westminster. (Original parchment, in English.)

Schrank 26.
    Gefach 8. Fasc. 4. Colonisten und Fremde. 1721.
    Gefach 10. Fasc. 6 u. 7. Fremde.
        Fasc. 8. Französische Colonisten. 1732, 1733.
        Fasc. 9. Colonisten. 1734.
        Fasc. 10. Menonisten Aufnahme. 1680.

Schrank 30.
    Gefach 2. Fasc. 8. Acta Hundert Tausend Morgen Land in Neu-Amerika (Massachusetts) betr. 1774. (Repert. no. 2985 in Dr. Schultze's Verzeichnis.)

Gefach 3. Fasc. 1. Acta betr. Landerwerb in Amerika. Korrespondenz mit Waldo und Palairet in England. 1757-1766. (Repert. no. 2987 of Dr. Schultze's Verzeichnis.)
Schrank 45. Gesetzgebung (Verordnungen), etc.
Schrank 65. Religions- und Glaubens-Sachen. Sekten.
Gefach 10. (a) Generalia und (b) Specialia.
Gefach 11. Fasc. 1. Die Mährische Brüder Gemeinde in Neuwied.
Fasc. 2. Die Mennoniten Gemeinde zu Neuwied.
Fasc. 3. Die Gemeinde der Inspierirten zu Neuwied.
Fasc. 4. Die Pietisten aus Teschen.
Fasc. 5. Die Pietisten aus Schweden.
Fasc. 6. Die Societät zur Vereinigung des Glaubens in der Grafschaft Wied-Neuwied.
Fasc. 7. Religions Sekten in der Grafschaft Wied-Runkel.
Fasc. 8. Die Joh. Christ Edelmanns-Sekte zu Neuwied (Antichristen).
Fasc. 16. Correspondenz mit Zinzendorf, etc. 1750-1754.
Schrank 70.
Gefach 5. Einzugsgeld neuer recipirter Unterthanen. Auszugsgeld. Nachsteuer oder sog. Zehntepfennig (*cf.* also Schrank 103, Gefach 97-98, for supplementary material relating to this; also Schrank 76-79).
Schrank 74, 75. Veräusserungen.
Schrank 82.
Gefach 4. Fasc. 3. Acta das Ableben und den Nachlas Seiner Durchlaucht des Prinzen Max zu Wied, betr. In diesen Akten sind auch die Verhandlungen enthalten betr.:
1. Schenkung der Bibliothek des Prinzen an die Universität in Bonn.
2. Verkauf der Naturaliensammlung desselben nach New-York. 1867-1870. (*Cf.* Schrank 107, Fasc. 38).
Zwei Verzeichnisse der Ornithologischen Sammlung (1869 mit dem Naturhistorischen Museum nach New-York verkauft).
Gefach 12. Fasc. 7. Acta des Prinzen Maximilian zu Wied Durchl. Reise nach Amerika betr. 1832-1834.
Schrank 106.
Fasc. XV. No. 24-32. Am. Krieg zwischen England und den 13 Provinzen, etc. Friedensstatue zu Philadelphia, etc.
Schrank 107. Fasc. 9. Tagebuch der Reise [des Prinzen Max zu Wied] nach Brasilien. 1815, 1816, 1817. 3 Bände. (Original.)
Fasc. 10. Tagebuch der Reise nach Brasilien. 1815-1817. 4 Bde. (Fair copy.)
Fasc. 11. Brasilianische Notizen. Naturgeschichtliches. Manuscripte. 1815 *et seq.*
Fasc. 12. Naturhistorische Zeichnungen von der Brasilianischen Reise. 1815, 1816, 1817.
Fasc. 13. Manuscripte des Werks über die Brasilianischen Vögel. 1820.
Fasc. 14. Einige Papiere von der Reise nach Brasilien. 1815 *et seq.* (Alphabetische Verzeichnisse von.)
Fasc. 15. Indianische Nationen von Süd-Amerika, 5 Abthlgn., jede in 1 Schachtel.

Fasc. 16. Indianische Sprachen. Sprachproben, Wortverzeichnisse aus Süd- und Nord-Amerika.
Fasc. 17. Tagebuch der Reise in Nord Amerika. 3 Bände. (Original.) 1832, 1833, 1834.
Fasc. 18. Reise nach Nord-Amerika. Verschiedene Papiere, Briefe, Notizen, Ausgaben, kleine Tagebücher, Davids Briefe.
Fasc. 19. Nordamerikanische Reptilien von der Reise. (Manuscript.) 1833, 1833, 1834.
Bearbeitung des Nordamerikanischen Thierverzeichnisses. Vögel und Amphibien.
Verzeichniss der auf der Reise nach Nord-Amerika beobachteten Reptilien, Amphibien, und Säugethiere.
Bemerkungen über Cassins [Catlin's] Werk über Nordamerikanische Indianerstämme.
Naturhistorische Notizen auf der Nord-Amerikanischen Reise. 1832, 1833.
Fasc. 20. Prinz Max zu Wied. Herausgabe seines Werks über die Amerikanischen Reise. Correspondenzen darüber. 1833-1835.
Fasc. 21. Naturhistorische Zeichnungen von der Amerikanischen Reise. 1832, 1833, 1834.
Fasc. 22. Nordamerika incl. Mexico. Sammlung von Zeichnungen und Ansichten.
Fasc. 23. Nordamerikanische Landschaftszeichnungen, etc.
Fasc. 24. Abbildungen von Ausländischen Fischen.
Fasc. 25. Nordamerikanische Zeitungen. Bound. 1832 *et seq*.
Fasc. 26. Nordamerikanische Schiffsankündigungen, etc. Bound. 1830 *et seq*.
Fasc. 27. Briefe an den Prinzen Max. 1808-1818.
Fasc. 28. Correspondenzen mit Verschiedenen, 1844 schon verstorbenen Naturforschern.
Fasc. 29. Briefe des Prinzen an seine Mutter u. Geschwister, including:
Briefe aus Brasilien. 1817.
Briefe aus Nordamerika. 1832-1833.
Verschiedene Briefe an den Prinzen auf der Nordamerikanischen Reise. 1832-1843.
Verschiedene Briefe an den Prinzen Max. 1840-1854.
Fasc. 31. Prinz Max zu Wied Correspondenzen über Aufnahme in wissenschaftlichen Vereinen. 1808-1865.
Fasc. 32. Diplome, etc.
Fasc. 39-48. Contains scattered material relating to America.
Fasc. 49. Briefe nach Brasilien an den Prinzen Max zu Wied. 1815-1817.
C. 13. Karten. Verschiedene Landkarten von Asien, Afrika, und Amerika. Nos. 12-21. Maps of America.

INDEX.

Aachen, emigration from, 95
Abbott, *Capt.* Edward, correspondence of, 250
Abensberg, *Landgericht,* emigration from, 207
Aberdeen, *Lord,* letter of, 189
Abrantes, *Vicomte* d', papers of, 55
Adā, Carl F., German consul in Cincinnati, 131, 172, 294
Adam, Johann, emigration of, 203
Adams, John, American commissioner at Versailles, 26; papers concerning, 30, 31; U. S. minister at the Hague, 30
Adams, John Quincy, correspondence, 33, 34, 40; Massachusetts petition for dissolution of the Union, brought by, 41; papers of, 50, 289
Adelnau, *Kreis,* emigration papers, 158
Adriane, ship, 162
Affleck, *Capt.* Edmund, correspondence of, 250
Agricultural Society of South Carolina, Notice of the, 238
Albany, Hessian troops in, 119
Albemarle, Va., auxiliary German troops in, 119
Alberthal, brothers, emigrants to New England, 85
Albrecht, Carl Johann, 164
Albrecht, Michael, emigration of, 198
Albus, *Lieut.* G., correspondence, 250
Alexander, margrave of Anspach-Bayreuth, *see* Anspach-Bayreuth
Alexander, *Maj.-Gen.* William, correspondence, 112
Alexandria, Va., Hanseatic consulate in, 242, 268
Allen, *Capt.,* letter of, 178
Allen, Julian, contract of, 61
Allgemeine Zeitung, extracts from, 54
Allgemeinen Zeitung, Abgedrungene Erwiederung auf die in den Beilagen der, 57
Allgemeines Organ für Handel und Gewerbe, 55
Alsace-Lorraine, archives of, 223-227; emigration from, 223, 224, 225, 226, 227
Alt, von, correspondence, 144
Altdorf, *Rentamt,* emigration from, 213
Altenburg, archives of Saxe-Altenburg in, 293
Altonaer Zeitung, copy, 74
Altonaischer Mercurius, extracts from, 50
Alvensleben, *Baron* Albrecht, correspondence and papers of, 43, 44
Alvensleben, *Count* Philipp Karl, correspondence and papers of, 34, 110
Alzenau, emigration from, 220
Alzevedo Barroso Bastos, de, Brazilian consul in Bremen, 244

Amanda, ship, 270
Amberg, Royal Bavarian Provincial (Circuit) Archives in, 201-203
Am Ende, F. W., petition of, 47
America, agriculture in, 70; arts and inventions, 69; coast survey, 99; diseases, 33; emigration from France, 53, 188, 224, 225, 226, 227; emigration from Germany, 1-4, 6-10, 35, 47-111 *passim,* 114, 132-141 *passim,* 150-172 *passim,* 181-222 *passim,* 229-245 *passim,* 265, 267, 272-277 *passim,* 291-313 *passim,* 318, 319, 320, 321, 322; emigration from Switzerland, 56; French dominions in, 192; geography, 70; gold production, 41; Indians in, 178, 299, 324; libraries, 190; manufactures, 69; maps, 100, 263, 300, 324; missions, 239, 299; Mormons in, 41; re-emigration to Germany from, 199, 209, 215; scientific notes concerning, 324; shipping, 19, 20, 41, 42, 46, 47, 50, 55, 59, 70, 98, 99, 161, 162, 166, 238, 241, 242, 269, 270, 271, 279, 292; shipping, Dutch, 51; shipping, French, 51; shipping, German, 35, 41, 42; trade, 20, 40, 42, 167, 297, 298, 300; trade, linen, 42, 80, 81, 134; trade, tobacco, 44, 71, 223, 238; trade with Belgium, 45; trade with England, 42, 81, 180; trade with France, 45, 223, 224; trade with Germany, 30-38, 40-48, 69, 70, 71, 72, 79, 80, 81, 82, 95, 98, 99, 107, 133, 134, 137, 150, 165, 166, 167, 171, 185, 186, 199, 205, 238, 239, 266, 267, 273, 279, 292, 295, 297, 298, 299, 300, 308, 309, 312; trade with Netherlands, 45; *see also* American Revolutionary War; Emigration; Germany; United States; names of particular countries, states, and places
American and Pacific Ship Canal Co., charter, 74
American Jewish Historical Society, Publications of, 36
American Revolutionary War, 37, 112-131, 180, 181, 182, 183, 217, 218, 271, 298, 299, 323; arms and supplies from Germany for, 21, 24, 25, 26, 27, 33, 36; auxiliary German troops in, 5-6, 23, 33, 35, 37, 76, 77, 102-106, 126-127, 142-143, 144-149, 204, 205, 217, 218, 248-265 *passim;* French troops in, 181, 182; Indians in, 183; maps and plans, 142; mutinies, 183; pensions, 77; Russia's attitude towards, 37; Spain's attitude towards, 37; *see also* Brunswick; Hesse; United States; names of particular countries and places
Amethiste, frigate, 269
Amherst, *Gen. Lord,* correspondence, 250

Ammer, Xaver, emigration of, 198
Amorbach, emigration from, 219, 220
Amorim, Antonio Marques, Lübeck consul in Pernambuco, 287
Amorim, Joaquin José d', Hanseatic consul in Pernambuco, 287
Amorsbach, *Gericht*, emigration from, 221
Ampfurt, G. A., 147
Amsterdam, emigration via, 231
Amthor, Peter, case of, 300
Anabaptists, 232, 233, 271
Ancillon. J. P. F., correspondence of, 40
André, *Maj*. John, case of, 114, 118, 183
Andreä, Heinrich and Ida, American emigrants, 162
Angelrodt, German consul in St. Louis, 48, 131, 196
Angostura, *see* Bolivar
Anhalt, Ducal House and State Archives of (at Zerbst), 228
Anhalt, *Gen. Maj*. W. von, 29; correspondence of, 37
Anhalt-Zerbst, troops of, in British service, 105
Anne, queen of England, 3
Anspach, troops in British service, 23, 105, 217, 218; *see also* Anspach-Bayreuth, Karl Alexander, margrave of
Anspach-Bayreuth, margraves of: (Friedrich Karl Alexander), contract of, 204; letters of, 116, 217, 218; order of, 205; soldiers of, in British service, 204, 205
Antwerp, emigration via, 55, 59, 61, 62, 74, 93; Prussian consul in, correspondence, 54
Arabella, ship, 271
Aragão, Francesco Moniz Bareto d', *see* Moniz Bareto d'Aragão, Francesco
Aranjo, Mario Antoine d', Brazilian representative in Hanse towns, 288
Arbuthnot, *Admiral* Marriot, correspondence, 250; *Declaration* of, 115
Archdale, *Gov*. John, of Carolina, papers relating to, 196, 197
Archdale, *Capt*. R., correspondence, 250
Arendt, *Col*., correspondence of, 27, 28, 37, 80, 81
Arequipa, Lübeck consulate in, 284
Arethusa, ship, 99
Arfeld, *Amt*, emigration papers, 151
Argentina, relations with German states, 132, 247, 285, 286, 292, 312; treaties with Germany, 133, 190, 309; treaties with United States, 239
Arms, 18, 24, 25, 26, 33
Arnim, correspondence of, 54
Arnold, *Gen.* Benedict, 183; correspondence, 250
Arnsberg, *Regierung*, emigration papers, 150-151
Arolsen, Waldeck, archives in, 302
"Articles of Capitulation" of Charleston, 114
Articles Préliminaires de Paix, entra sa Majesté Britannique et les Etats Généraux des Provinces Unies des Païs Bas, 1783, 183

Aschaffenburg, Circuit Archives of, 216-222; emigration from, 220
Aschersleben, *Kreis*, emigration petitions, 110
Asia, ship, 162
Assenheim, emigration from, 276
Astrea, ship, 269
Atlantic Ocean, observations, 125; *see also* Shipping, under particular countries and places
Aufruf und Warnung an Auswanderungs-Lustige in Deutschland, 60
Augsburg, emigration from, 187
Augsburger Ordinari Postzeitung, copies of, 194
Augustus I., elector of Saxony, 1 n.
Aurich, Prussian State Archives at, 17 n.
Aurojo, Marcos Antonio de, Brazilian representative in Hanse towns, 244
Ausländer in einzelnen Staaten von Nord-Amerika betreffend, Die Erbberechtigung der, 196
Australia, emigration to, 53, 54, 72, 101; Moravians in, 317
Austria, relations with Brazil, 190
Auswanderer, Die Deutsche Platz- und Schutzagentur für, 74
Auswanderer in Berlin, Mittheilungen des Vereins zum Schutze deutscher, 159
Auswanderer! Rath, Auskunft und Belehrung an, 73
Auswandern wollen, An Alle welche, 73
Auswanderungswesen, Die Inspection für das, 239
Auxiliary German troops, *see* American Revolutionary War
Avé-Lallemant, Alexander, Lübeck consul in Rio de Janeiro, 287
Avis aux Émigrants Français traversant la Grande Bretagne, 61
Axtell, *Col*. W., correspondence, 250

Baasch, *Dr*., letter of, 267
Bach, Joh. Mich., letters of, 120
Baden, emigration from, 54; emigration papers, 229, 230, 231, 232, 234, 236, 237; Grand-Ducal General National Archives of (at Karlsruhe), 229-237
Baden-Durlach, emigration from, 229, 236
Bader, Johann, emigration of, 210
Bad-Nauheim, emigration from, 276
Bäcker, from Magdeburg, emigration case of, 110
Bärtling, *Capt*. August von, correspondence, 250
Bahia, German consulates in, 189, 244, 287
Balles, Johann Michael, emigration of, 219
Baltic ports, trade with America, 167
Baltimore, German consulates in, 70, 131, 242, 268, 271, 280, 300; Germans in, 47; refugees in, 184; shipping, 59, 161; *see also* Maryland
Bamberg, Royal Bavarian Provincial (Circuit) Archives in, 204-206
Banat, decrees relating to, 275; emigration to, 85
Bardet, reclamation case of, 225

Index 327

Barker, J. N., comptroller U. S. treasury, papers of, 44
Barner, *Maj.* W., correspondence, 250
Barner, von, battalion of, 103
Barnes, *Capt.* John, correspondence, 250
Barrington, *Maj.-Gen.*, 178
Barros, José Marcelino de Moraes, *see* Moraes Barros, José Marcelino de
Barth, André and Jean, reclamation case of, 225
Barth, Robert, Hessian consul in St. Louis, 131
Bartholomäus, Carl, wife of, inheritance case of, 170
Bartram, Albert, Brazilian vice-consul in Bremen, 244
Bastos, *see* Alzevedo Barroso Bastos
Batres, Salvator, Mexican consul in Hanse towns, 282
Battenberg, emigration from, 275
Battersby, *Capt.* James, correspondence, 250
Bauer, Carl, journal of, 124-125
Bauer, E., paper by, 166
Bauernheim, emigration from, 276
Baum, *Capt.*, document by, 112
Baum, *Lieut.-Col.* Friedrich, correspondence, 250
Baum, Max, emigration of, 198
Bavaria, archives of, *Bestimmungen für die Benützer des Kgl. Bayer. Geheimen Staats-Archives*, 173; consulates in America, 188, 190-191, 205; emigration from, 48, 181, 185-213 *passim*, 218; relations with Great Britain, 175; relations with South America, 190; relations with U. S., 8; treaty with Great Britain, 178; treaty with U. S., 185; *see also* Bavarian Archives
Bavaria, electors of: Karl Albrecht, edict of, 192; Maximilian II. (Emanuel), edict of, 192; Maximilian III. (Joseph), correspondence of, 180, 181; edicts of, 192; Maximilian IV. (Joseph), decree of, 320
Bavarian Archives, 173-222; general information on, 173; circuit archives, 191-222; National Archives, 191; State Archives, 173-190
Bayreuth, *see* Brandenburg-Anspach and Bayreuth
Bayreuth, *Bezirksamt*, emigration from, 205
Bayreuther Zeitung, extracts from, 205
Beauséjour, capture of, 176
Beaver, ship, 271
Becher, in Elberfeld, correspondence, 150
Becker, *Lieut.*, 146
Becker, priest, correspondence, 250
Becker, A. L., correspondence, 250
Becker, August Julius, case of, 62
Beckwith, *Maj.* Ferdinand A., correspondence, 250
Beckwith, *Capt.* George, correspondence, 250
Bedford, L. I., Hessian troops at, 115
Bedingungen der Anwerbung, 57
Beer, Maria Anna, emigration of, 198
Behrens, Reinhard, Lübeck consul in Valparaiso, 285

Beienheim, emigration from, 276
Beilstein, *Amt*, emigration to America from, 170
Belair, Louis, post-master, correspondence, 250
Belgium, emigration companies, 53; trade with America, 45
Bell, *Serj.-Maj.* W., correspondence, 250
Bengal, ship, 47
Benning, *Col.*, correspondence, 120
Benning, von, regiment, 123
Bennington, auxiliary German troops at, 119
Beraldingen, of Stuttgart, correspondence of, 54
Berckemeyer, E. W., Argentinian consul in Hanse towns, 285
Berczy, William, emigration agent, 75
Berent, emigration from, 87, 88
Berg, duchy and grand-duchy of, emigration from, 92, 185; papers of, 92
Berger, A. W., 74
Berkewitz, *Quartermaster*, journal of, 121
Berlin, archives in, 17-77, general information about, 17-18, 76; emigration records, 10; State Archives, 17-76; War Archives, 76-77
Berlinische Nachrichten, extracts, 56
Bermudas, papers relating to, 243
Bernhard, Duke of Saxe-Weimar-Eisenach, visits America, 8
Bernstorff, *Count* Christian Günther von, correspondence, 42, 49, 150
Bersaba, Moravians in, 314
Bese, Louise, correspondence, 253
Beseler, Andreas von, proposition of, 266
Besseling, G. F., 147
Best, *Ensign* Konrad, correspondence, 250
Bethabara. N. C., Moravians in, 316
Bethania, N. C., Moravians in, 316
Bethel, Australia, Moravians in, 317
Bethel, Pa., Moravians in, 314
Bethlehem, Pa., Moravians in, 314, 315, 317
Bettmann, Leonhard, emigration of, 9-10
Beuschl, Peter, emigration of, 198
Bibby, *Dep. Adj.-Gen.* T., correspondence, 250
Bibra, of Neuwied, letter of, 73
Bickell, *Lieut.*, correspondence, 250
Bielefeld, I. M., papers of, 56
Billandes, letter of, 225
Birki, Andreas, emigration of, 198
Birnbaum, *Kreis*, emigration papers, 158
Bischausen, von, regiment of, 121
Bismarck, *Prince*, correspondence of, 60, 62, 63
Bissinger, *see* Kapp and Bissinger
Bittburger Intelligenzblatt, copy of, 60
Bland, *Col.* Theodoric, correspondence, 250
Blanfelder, Adolph Friedrich, paper by, 304
Blankenloch, emigration from, 229
Blecker, W. G., case of, 271
Block, *Gen.* von, 142, 143
Block, von, battalion of, 103, 129
Bloem, *Chevalier* de, papers concerning, 52
Blohm, Georg Heinrich, Hanseatic consul in Venezuela, 284
Bloomfield, letter of, 59
Blouet, Demetz and, papers of, 70

328　　　　　　　　　　　　　　　　　Index

Bluch, Jonas Hirschel, inheritance papers of, 34
Blum, Joseph, emigration of, 198
Blumenau, *Dr.* Otto, papers relating to, 56
Bochum, *Amt*, emigration papers, 150
Bodenrod, emigration from, 276
Bodingen, *Capt.* von, correspondence, 250
Böckling, Johann Thiel, property of, 172
Boedeker, F. B., emigration agent, 111
Boehm, case of, 7
Boehm family, case of, 155
Boele, *Amt*, emigration papers, 151
Börsch, Carl, papers of, 190
Boettiger, letters of, 224
Bogen, *Landgericht*, emigration from, 207
Boilan, *Capt.*, correspondence, 250
Boje, Wilhelm, Lübeck vice-consul in Rio de Janeiro, 287
Bolivar, Hanseatic consulate in, 246, 284
Bolivia, relations with Germany, 247, 285, 312
Bomster, *Kreis*, emigration papers, 158
Bonj, Andres, paper by, 236
Bonstädt, emigration from, 276
Bornemann, *Lieut.*, correspondence, 250
Borthwick, *Capt.* William, correspondence, 250
Boscawen, *Admiral*, fleet of, 176, 177
Bose, *Maj.-Gen.* Carl von, correspondence, 250; reports of, 115
Bose, von, regiment, 128, 143; journal of, 122
Boston, capture of, 249; German consulates in, 70, 242, 280; papers relating to, 180; shipping, 161, 271
Bothe, Johann Friedrich, Hanseatic vice-consul in Rio de Janeiro, 243, 287
Boudinot, Elias, letter of, 267
Boyd, *Capt.* William, correspondence, 250
Brachthäuser, Daniel, case of, 170
Braddock, *Gen.*, on the Ohio, 176
Bradfield, Jonathan, papers relating to, 35
Braditsch, adventures of, in Maine, 189, 198
Bramson, Steven John, petition by, 36
Brandenburg, *see* names of respective electors
Brandenburg-Anspach and Bayreuth, Margrave of, *see* Anspach-Bayreuth, Karl Alexander, and Anspach
Brandis, *Dr.* Hermann, application of, 241
Brandt, Louis, Lübeck consul in Porto Cabello, 284
Brandt, *Pastor*, 74
Brandywine, battle of, 122
Brangon, John, correspondence, 254
Brattelen, emigration from, 237
Braun, F. L., of Baltimore, 73; report of, 70
Brazil, Austrian emigration to, 50, 51; German consulates in, 108, 261; German emigration to, 8, 50, 51, 55, 56, 61, 73, 99, 102, 132, 135, 138, 152, 155, 159, 186, 187, 194, 197, 210, 212, 219, 231, 243, 244, 275, 291, 292, 294; map of, 55; Moravians in, 317; politics, 102; relations with Austria, 190; relations with German states, 57, 65, 131, 132, 243, 244, 286-288, 312; scientific papers concerning, 323; tobacco trade, 223; trade with Germany, 134, 244, 245, 308, 309; treaties with Hanover, 289; wars, 102, 295; *see also* Rio de Janeiro

Brazil, *Einige Nachrichten über*, 51
Brehm, *Capt.* D., barrackmaster general, correspondence, 250
Bremen, archives in, 238-247; consulates in U. S., 241, 242; emigration via, 10, 56, 57, 58, 59, 62, 73, 74, 101, 107, 111, 152, 156, 181, 238, 239, 241, 242, 243, 244, 245, 306; Hessian troops in, 104, Senate of, *Obrigkeitliche Verordnung*, 53, 56, 58; shipping, 53, 57, 134, 239, 240, 241, 242, 243, 247; trade with America, 238, 239, 240, 244; treaties with U. S., 185; *see also* Hanse towns
Bremen als Einschiffungsplatz für deutsche Auswanderer, 73, 108
Bremen Auswanderer Zeitung, extracts, 61
Bremen, Bericht des Nachweisungs-bureau in, 74
Bremen, Erster Bericht des Nachweisungs Bureau in, 57
Bremen, Erster Bericht über die Wirksamkeit des Nachweisungs-Bureau für Auswanderer in, 73
Bremen Gazette, 239
Bremer Zeitung, extracts from, 50
Breslau, City Archives in, 82-83; Royal State Archives in, 78-82; trade papers, 80, 82, 83
Bresslauer, R. or B., 73
Breunig, F. J., emigration of, 219
Breva, *Lieut.* A. W., correspondence, 250
Brewster, Gilbert, letters of, 69
Briesen, *Landratsamt*, emigration papers, 88
Brink, Johann Hermann Christen, Bavarian consul in Rio de Janeiro, 189
Bröder, Nikolaus, emigration petition of, 198
Brohm, E., emigration of, 219
Brown, *Col.*, correspondence, 250
Brown and Ives, of Providence, 162
Bruchenkrücken, emigration from, 276
Bruen, *Maj.* Henry, correspondence, 250
Brunswick-Lüneburg, consulates in America, 264; Ducal National Central Archives of (at Wolfenbüttel), 248-265; emigration from, 265; troops in British service, 23, 102, 104, 105, 116, 118, 126, 248-265
Brunswick-Lüneburg, dukes of: (Karl), correspondence, 248, 249; treaties, 261, 263, 264; (Karl Wilhelm Ferdinand), correspondence, 249, 260, 261; (Ludwig Ernst), correspondence, 249
Brunswick-Lüneburg-Oels, duke of (Friedrich August), correspondence, 249
Brust, Johann Caspar, 149
Bryan, Eduard, correspondence, 250
Buchanan, James, correspondence of, 45
Buck, Carl Nicol., consul of Hamburg in U. S., 267
Büchig, emigration from, 229
Bückeburg, Schaumburg-Lippe Archives in, 302
Büddecke, T. W., letter of, 60
Büdesheim, emigration from, 276
Bülow, Heinrich *Freiherr* von, correspondence, 54, 69, 150
Bülow, Ludwig Friedrich Victor Hans *Graf* von, correspondence, 42, 167

Bülow, von, battalion, 129
Bünau, *Col.* von, 143; letter of, 120
Bünau, von, regiment of, 104, 130, 143
Buenos Aires, emigration to, 189, 229; German consulates in, 189, 205, 247, 312; German trade in, 205; *see also* Argentina
Bütemeister, in the Hague, correspondence, 149
Buisson, Jean Baptiste, correspondence, 250
Buk, *Kreis*, emigration papers, 158
Bunde, D., Hessian chargé d'affaires in Brazil, 131
Burchardt, Prussian consul in Liverpool, correspondence, 58
Burckhard, *Fänrich*, letters of, 120
Burgau, emigration from, 209, 210
Burg-Gräfenrod, emigration from, 276
Burgoyne, *Gen. Sir* John, army of, 119; capitulation of, 24, 119; correspondence and papers of, 120, 250
Butte, *Dr.* Wilhelm, pamphlet by, 48
Buttlar, *Capt.* von, correspondence, 120, 250

Cabanal, de, correspondence, 251
Cabet, Étienne, president of "Icaria" colony, 164
Cadolsburg, *Rentamt*, emigration from, 213
Cadwalader, *Gen.* John, correspondence, 112
Calbe, *Kreis*, emigration petitions, 110
Caldeira, Antonio da Silva, *see* Silva Caldeira, Antonio da
Caldwell, *Col.*, correspondence, 251
Calhoun, John C., speech of, 43
California, German consuls in, 171, 191; German emigration to, 107, 305; land titles, 70
Callao, German emigration to, 62; Hanseatic consulate in, 246
Calonne, Charles de, letters of, 223
Calvinist Church, 2
Cambridge, Mass., auxiliary German troops in, 119, 121
Campbell, *Maj.* Alexander, correspondence, 251
Campbell, *Gen.* Archibald, correspondence, 251
Campeche, Hanseatic agent in, 246
Canacas Islands, shipping, 62
Canada, accounts of, 121; auxiliary German troops in, 116, 119, 126, 127, 142; boundaries, 176; finance, 225; French in, 223; German emigration, 60, 61, 189, 197, 199, 200; in the Revolutionary War, 183; trade, 199
Canitz, *Baron* de, minister of state, 45
Canitz, F. M. von, regiment, 143
Cape Fear River, Hessian troops at, 115
Cap Haitien, Hanseatic consulate in, 246
Caracas, Hanseatic consulate in, 284
Carl, *see* Karl
Carleton, *Maj.* Christopher, correspondence, 251
Carleton, *Maj.-Gen. Sir* Guy, correspondence, 115, 119, 120, 183, 251
Carleton, *Gen.* Thomas, correspondence, 251
Carlshafen, military papers, 76
Carmichael, William, correspondence of, 19, 20, 23, 24, 28

Carolinas, German emigration to, 4, 172, 236, 296, 297, 299, 303, 310; in the American Revolution, 182; *see also* South Carolina
Caroline, ship, 50
Carp, Prussian consul in Rotterdam, correspondence of, 56; papers of, 54
Carriole, sketch of, 126
Carter, *Maj.* T., correspondence, 251
Carvick, *Capt.*, case of, 270
Casenove, Hamburg consul in Alexandria, Va., 268
Casius, W. W., petition of, 221
Cass, *Gen.* Lewis, speech of, 98
Cassel, military pensions, 76
Casse-tete, sketch of, 126
Castens, Moritz, inheritance case of, 238
Castle Garden, conditions in, 63, 74
Castro, in Texas, 74
Catholics, 169
Cayenne, colonization of, papers relating to, 2 n., 235, 319
Ceará, Hanseatic consulate in, 244
Cella, ship, 61
Central America, 57, 74; colonization of, 98; German consulates in, 108, 247; German trade in, 133; maps, 53; *see also* names of particular countries and places
Ceres, ship, 46, 50, 75
Chambers, *Commodore* W., correspondence, 251
Chandler, K., correspondence, 251
Charles, *see* Karl
Charles King, ship, 161
Charleston, S. C., capitulation of, 182; Clinton's expedition against, 118; German consulates in, 70, 242, 280; Germans in, 47; Hessian troops in, 115
Charlotte A. Plimpton, ship, 162
Charlotte Sophie, queen of George III., papers of, 291
Charlottesville, auxiliary German troops in, 118, 119
Chatham, *Earl* of (William Pitt), 21; correspondence of, 22
Chemnitz, American Archives in, 301; U. S. consulate in, 301
Chicago, German consulates in, 241, 280, 294, 295
Chile, German consulates in, 108, 312; German emigration to, 56, 62, 72, 138; relations with German states, 133, 247, 285, 292; relations with Peru, 100
Choiseul, *Duke* de, correspondence, 223, 225
Cincinnati, German consulates in, 131, 172, 242, 280, 294, 295; trade, 71
Citizen, ship, 269
Civil War papers, 46, 60, 61, 63, 240, 279, 309
Clarck, U. S. Consul in Lübeck, 280
Clarke, Jon., commissioner, correspondence, 251
Clarke, *Gen.* Thomas, correspondence, 251
Clausenius, H., report of, 63
Clay, Henry, papers of, 289; speeches by, 43
Clemen, Ferdinand, emigration of, 293
Clemenius, ship-broker, petition of, 269
Clementine, ship, 239

Clerke, *Adj.* Francis Carr, letters of, 113, 251
Cleve, *Lieut.* Friedrich, correspondence, 251
Cleve, *Capt.* H. Urban, papers of, 251
Cleve, *Landratsamt,* emigration papers, 92
Clinton, *Gen.* Sir Henry, correspondence, 28, 115, 251; expedition against Charleston, 118; papers of, 115, 180
Clover, *Brig.-Gen.,* correspondence, 251
Coast Survey, Annual Report of the Superintendent of the United States, 99
Coblenz, emigration to U. S. from, 71; Royal State Archives, 84-86
Coburg, Ducal Saxon House and State Archives in, 293
Cochenhausen, von, correspondence, 120, 251
Cochrane, John, correspondence, 251
Cölnische Zeitung, extracts from, 45, 55
Coeper, correspondence of, 20
Colbert, Jean Baptiste, letter of, 216
Coleman, William, U. S. vice-consul in Lübeck, 281
Colima, Hanseatic agent in, 246
Collier, W., correspondence, 251
Colmann, *Dr.* Ludwig, report of, 55
Colmar, District Archives of Upper Alsace in, 223
Cologne, emigration to America from, 48, 56, 181; Historical Archives in, 308-309; trade, 308
Cologne, *Archbishop* of, letter of, 217
Colombia, emigration to, 72; map, 100; papers relating to, 97; politics, 102; Prussian legation in, 57; relations with Hanse towns, 246, 284; treaties, 69, 133, 290
Colquhoun, Hanseatic consul in London, negotiations with Mexico, 281
Colson, von, regiment, 130, 143
Columbia, ship, 62
Concepcion, Hanseatic consulate in, 247
Congress, Continental, minutes of, 27; resolutions of, 29
Congress, ship, 161
Connecticut, Germans in, 47
Conway, *Gen.* H. S., correspondence, 251
Copie du Traité Définitif de Paix, 179
Coquebert-Monsbret, correspondence, 308
Cornwallis, *Maj.-Gen. Lord,* correspondence, 183, 251; papers concerning, 180, 182; troops in charge of, 115
Correia, Jose Lucio, Brazilian consul in Hanse towns, 244, 288
Correspondenz für Deutschland, 159
Corry, James, correspondence, 251
Costa Rica, German emigration to, 57, 72; papers relating to, 100; relations with Hanse towns, 247, 283, 290
Courrier Politique et Littéraire, copies of, 182
Couwenhoven, *Capt.,* correspondence, 252
Crafft, Johann Daniel, papers of, 216
Cramahé, *Lieut.-Gov.* H. T., correspondence, 252
Cramer, A. B., petition of, 221
Cramer, E. H., petition of, 221
Cranz, *Krieges-Rath,* correspondence of, 28

Crause, of Herzberg, 99
Crefeld, trade with America, 95
Creutz, Gustave Philippe, *Comte* de, 30
Creuzbourg, *Col.* C. de, correspondence, 118, 125, 126, 252
Crosbie, *Col.,* correspondence, 252
Crown Point, French at, 178
Croxal, M., correspondence, 252
Cruse, *Lieut.* P. S., correspondence, 252
Cuba, German emigration to, 194; papers relating to, 69; relations with Hanse towns, 247
Cuff, *Maj.* W., correspondence, 252
Curral, Hanseatic consulate in, 247
Cusseau, *Major,* correspondence, 252
Cuthbert, U. S. consul in Hamburg, 97, 267, 270
Cuxhaven, *see* Hamburg

D'Aigrefeuille, letters of, 224, 225
Dalrymple, *Col.,* correspondence, 252
Dansard, Nikolaus, emigration to America of, 49
Danzig, emigration from, 87; Royal State Archives in, 87-91
Darmstadt, Grand-Ducal Hessian House and State Archives in, 275-277
David, sailor, case of, 271
Davis, Abel, correspondence, 252
Day, Nathaniel, commissary general, correspondence, 252
Deane, Silas, correspondence of, 20
Dechambault, correspondence, 252
Declaration of Independence, copy of, 123
De Cressener, minister plenipotentiary, letter of, 217
Deggendorf, *Landgericht,* emigration from, 207
Dehnhard, *General Sergeant-Major,* correspondence, 252
De la Clue, fleet of, 178
De la Motte, squadron of, 177
Delancey, *Adj. Maj.-Gen.* Oliver, correspondence, 252
Delbrück, papers of, 46
Delius, consul in Bremen, 58, 98
Delius, George. consular papers concerning, 47
Demerara, German emigration to, 52, 199; trade with Germany, 199
Demetz and Blouet, papers of, 70
Denmark, treaty with U. S., 238
Depaky, *Capt.* Rice, quartermaster general, correspondence, 252
De Puydt, report of, 53
Dernisch, claim by, 36
Descheneaux, *Capt.* Crevier, correspondence, 252
Desegner [De Segner], correspondence of, 21, 252
Dessauer, Franz, Bavarian consul in Buenos Aires, 205; emigration agent, 189, 219
Dessel, widow, pension of, 77
Detmold, House and National Archives of the Principality of Lippe in, 278
Detroit, Prussian consulate at, 48
Deutsche Auswanderer-Zeitung, 107, 158, 243; extracts, 159

Index 331

Deutsche Gesellschaft von New Orleans, 73
Deutschen Gesellschaft, Jahresbericht der, 63
Deutschen Gesellschaft in New York, Wohlgemeinter Rath der Vorsteher der, 51
Deutschen Gesellschaft von Maryland, Wohlgemeinter Rath der, 32
Deutschen Volks-Vereins in Stadt Neu-York, Jahresbericht des Direktoriums des, 56
Deutscher Einwanderer in Texas, Bericht des Vereins zum Schutze, 72
Deutsch-Krone, Landratsamt, emigration papers, 88
Deux-Ponts, see Zweibrücken
Dickson, *Capt.* H., correspondence, 252
Dieckmann, G. A., lawsuit of, 108
Diehl, *Capt.* John Justus, correspondence, 252
Diehm, Peter, emigration of, 310
Diemar, *Capt.* Friedrich *Freiherr* von, correspondence, 118, 144, 252
Diergardt, in Viersen, correspondence of, 43, 44
Dildey, Maria, estate of, case of, 7, 29
Dillenburg, *Regierung,* emigration to America from, 169-170
Dingisweiler, emigration from, 189
Dingolfing, *Landgericht,* emigration from, 207
Dinkelsbühl, *Bezirksamt,* emigration from, 211
Disunion and Its Results to the South, 46
Ditfurth, von, *Kammergerichtsassessor,* correspondence, 252
Ditfurth, von, assessor of the supreme court of judicature, correspondence, 252
Ditfurth, von, regiment, 129, 143
Dittmar, *Lieut.* Carl, letters, 120
Dobel, Moritz, wife of, inheritance case of, 170
Dobner, Wolfgang, emigration of, 202
Dodge, Joshua, letter of, 44
Döring, of Cassel, correspondence, 130
Dörnberg, correspondence of, 21
Dolby, ship, 162
Dominican Republic, papers relating to, 243; relations with Hanse towns, 246; treaty with Germany, 133
Dominque, *Capt.,* correspondence, 252
Dommes, *Capt.* August Friedrich, correspondence, 252
Donelson, A. J., papers of, 45
Donop, *Col.* Karl Emil Kurt von, correspondence, 112, 114; papers of, 114, 118, 142
Doormann, August Christian, Lübeck consul in Mexico, 281
Dortmund, *Kreis,* emigration papers, 150
Dougall, see McDougall
Douglas, Charles, letter of, 119
Dreier, Martin H., case of, 60
Dreppenstedt, of Hesse, 103
Dresden, Royal Saxon Central State Archives in, 296-301; U. S. consulate in, 301
Dresdener Anzeigen, extracts from, 297
Dresel, Werner, Hessian consul in Baltimore, 131
Drewitz, Anna Elizabeth, Conrad, and Johann Jacob, emigration of, 170

Droste, Franz Friedrich, Brazilian vice-consul in Bremen, 244
Drummond, Antonio de Menezes Vasconcellos de, see Menezes Vasconcellos de Drummond, Antonio de
Du Buy, *Lieut.-Col.* von, letter of, 252; reports of, 115
Duden, Gottfried, travels in Missouri, 8
Dudley, *Earl,* letters of, 300
Düsseldorf, emigration to America from, 56, 92; Royal State Archives in, 92-96
Dufais, letter of, 120
Duffing, Wilhelm, emigration case of, 171
Dufossey, *Sieur,* in London, correspondence, 184
Dumas, C. W. F., U. S. chargé d'affaires, correspondence of, 29
Dumford, engineer, correspondence, 252
Dunlop, *Capt.,* correspondence, 252
Dunn, *Ensign* Joseph, correspondence, 252
Duport, R., assistant quartermaster-general, correspondence, 252
Dupré, *Col.* George, correspondence, 252
Durlach, *Amt,* emigration from, 229, 232
Dutreil, Nadan, 178

Ebenezer, Georgia, immigration to, 33
Eberhard and Kramer, case of, 85
Eberhard Ludwig, Duke of Württemberg, rescript of, 303
Ebermaier, papers of, 49
Ebersberg, *Landgericht,* emigration from, 196
Ecclesiastical collections, iii; Moravian, 314-317
Echenique, José Rufino, document of, 62
Eckartsberg, Paul von, papers concerning, 64
Ecuador, relations with Hanse towns, 246, 284
Edelmann, Johann Christ, sect of, 323
Eden, Morton, 175
Edicts, Declaration des, de dato Berlin, 78; Erneuertes, 78
Edmonstone, *Capt.* A., jr., correspondence, 252
Edmonstone, Archibald, correspondence, 252
Edward, ship, 161
Effingham, *Countess* of, correspondence, 252
Eggenfelden, *Landgericht,* emigration from, 207
Egremont, *Lord,* 179
Ehrenkrook, *Maj.* Karl Friedrich von, correspondence, 252
Eibenstock, U. S. consulate in, 301
Eichhorn, K. F., councillor, correspondence of, 53, 54
Eichstädt, *Bezirksamt,* emigration from, 213
Eigner, Maria, emigration of, 198
Einzel-Abdruck aus den Mittheilungen von Nordamerika, 74
Elb-Amerikanische Compagnie, 297
Elberfeld, emigration from, 92
Elbing, city and *Landkreis,* emigration papers, 87
Elb West-Indische See-Handlungs Compagnie, prospectus of, 297
Electoral Palatinate, see Palatinate
Elizabeth, ship, 247
Elliston, Matthew, 299; report of, 296

Elphinstone, *Capt.* G. B., correspondence, 252
Emich, from Amorbach, emigration of, 220
Emig of Rossdorf, emigration case of, 311
Emigrants, Act to amend the Law relating to, 60
Emigrants, arrival of, 63; condition of, 62; forwarding of, 60; list of, 52, 53; papers relating to, 78, 79; protection of, 72; statistics of, 71, 88; treatment of, 61; *see also* Emigration
Emigration, early, 1-4; German trend towards southeastern Europe, 193; inheritance cases, 170, 229, 232, 238; laws, 60, 63, 75, 181, 189, 192, 193, 195, 199, 209-210, 214, 215, 218, 219, 221, 222, 233, 234, 235, 242, 243, 245, 272, 303, 304, 306, 310, 311; military duty, 187, 194, 219, 230, 242; *Rückwanderungen,* 63, 199, 209, 215, 304; statistics of, 71, 87, 88; societies for, 4, 8, 9, 47, 50, 51, 53, 54, 56, 57, 58, 59, 61, 71, 72, 73, 74, 75, 87, 88, 98, 101, 108, 111, 134, 197, 200, 216, 219, 226, 276, 296, 297, 299, 304, 306, 309; transportation, 139, 140; *see also* Emigrants; names of particular countries and places
Emigration of the State of New York, Annual Report of the Commissioners of, 74
"Emissarii," 4, 94, 109, 170 192, 219, 235, 310, 311, 319
Emmaus, Pa., Moravians in, 314
Endemann, J. W., correspondence, 114; journal of, 121
Engel, of Züllichau, papers of, 34
Engelmann, George, M. D., correspondence of, 48
England, shipping, 22, 225; trade with America, 40, 42, 81, 180; *see also* Great Britain
English-Waldeck Regiment, III., documents of, 144-149; in Hanover, 104-105; levies, 145, 146; statistics, supplies, 147
Engmann, case of, 7, 34
Enigheden, ship, 271
Equitable Life Insurance Co., 111
Erbprinz, Hessian regiment, 116, 117, 118, 121, 122, 127-128
Erie, Lake, boundary disputes concerning, 176
Erie, Pa., papers relating to, 52
Erie Canal, 69
Erkelenz, emigration from, 92, 93
Erlangen, *Bezirksamt,* emigration from, 213
Erlanger Real-Zeitung, extracts from, 205
Erlbach, *see* Markt Erlbach
Ernst, Friedrich, correspondence, 252
Ernst Ludwig, landgrave of Hesse-Darmstadt, orders of, 171, 172
Erthal, *Minister* von, papers concerning, 218
Esche, Pommer, paper of, 58
Eschenburg, Johann, Bavarian consul in Buenos Aires, 189
Eschwege, F. von, letter of, 120
Eschwege, von, battalion, 128
Essen, *Landratsamt,* emigration papers, 93
Estorf, *Col.,* quartermaster-general, correspondence of, 103, 104
Eulenburg, *Count* Friedrich Albrecht, correspondence of, 60

Ewald, *Capt.* Johann, correspondence, 115, 252
Exploration papers, 70
Exports, statistics of, 70

Faber, Hessian consul in N. Y., 131, 134
Fabrice, A. G. von, correspondence, 144
Facio, Francisco de, Mexican consul in Hanse towns, 282
Färber, Hanseatic consul in Mexico, 282
Fagel, von, agent in the Hague, correspondence, 144
Falk, *Dr.,* letter of, 72
Fantina, G., letters of, 182
Fatiasch, *Capt.,* papers relating to, 37
Fauerbach bei Fr., emigration from, 276
Fauerbach v. d. H., emigration from, 276
Fawcett, *Maj.-Gen. Sir* William, correspondence, 103, 113, 144, 253; overtures of, 123; papers of, 105, 204, 263
Feldwisch, Johann Heinrich, emigration papers of, 75
Ferguson, *Lieut.,* correspondence, 253
Feronee, von Rotencreuz, privy councillor, correspondence, 253
Fessel, Franz Xavier, emigration case of, 194
Feuchtwangen, *Bezirksamt,* emigration from, 212
Fieselmann inheritance case, 33
Fillmore, *President* Millard, document by, 289
Filzhofer, *Lieut.* von, correspondence, 253
Finkenstein, *Count,* correspondence, 21, 26, 27, 30, 31, 32, 33
Finley, Hugh, correspondence, 253
Firado, José Manuel, document of, 62
Fitzgerald, Elizabeth, correspondence, 253
Flatbush, sketch of, 114
Flatow, *Landratsamt,* emigration papers, 89
Fleckenstein, Johann, confiscated property of, 220
Florida, and the American Revolution, 184; German emigration to, 311
Flossenburg, emigration from, 9, 10, 203
Fockusch, J. W., Hamburg consul in Galveston, 268
Förster, *Maj.* G., correspondence, 253
Fomm, Friedrich, Hanseatic consul in Santos, 287
Fontain, *Col.,* correspondence, 253
Forbes, *Capt.* D., correspondence, 253
Forbes, John Michael, U. S. consul in Germany, 35, 162, 269, 270, 286
Forbes, Ralph Bennet, petition of, 47
Forcellado, *Don* Francisco, papers of, 58
Forrer, G. L., Uruguayan vice-consul in Lübeck, 286
Forster, Charles de, letter of, 72
Forsyth, John, correspondence of, 43
Fort Carillon, *see* Ticonderoga
Fortlage, *Senator,* commissioner of deeds in Missouri, 100
Fox, *Col.,* correspondence, 253
Fox, Francis, letter of, 56
Foy, *Capt.* Edward, correspondence, 253
Fränkel, Carl, Brazilian consul in Bremen, 244

Index 333

France, customs, 298; emigration from, 2, 53, 188, 224, 225, 226, 227; emigration laws, 188; pro-American sentiment in, 36; recognition of U. S. by, 24, 25; shipping, 51; trade with America, 45, 223, 224; territorial expansion in America, 192; treaties with Great Britain, 179; troops in Revolutionary War, 181, 182; war with Great Britain, 176, 177, 178, 179
Franck, *Capt.*, letters of, 120
Francken, *Maj.* von, correspondence, 253
Franconia, Circuit Archives of Lower, 216-222
Frankfort-on-the-Main, City Archives in, 310-313; commercial and diplomatic relations with America, 312; emigration papers, 181, 310, 311, 312, 313
Frankfurter Journal, extracts from, 52, 55
Frankfurter Oberpostamts-Zeitung, extracts, 55, 72
Franklin, Benjamin, correspondence of, 20; death of, 298; in Paris, 82; papers relating to, 30, 31, 32, 184
Frankschaller, *Col.*, article by, 63
Fransladt, *Kreis*, emigration papers, 158
Fraser, secretary to Foy, correspondence, 253
Fraser, *Brig.-Gen.* Alexander, correspondence, 253
Fraser, *Capt.* Thomas, correspondence, 253
Fraser, *Capt.* W., correspondence, 253
Frederick III., elector of Brandenburg (Frederick I., king of Prussia), edict of, 107
Frederick VI., king of Denmark, papers of, 161
Frederick the Great, correspondence, 18-23, 25-32, 36, 37, 81; edict of, 165; policy of towards United States, 6 ff., 24
Frederick William, of Brandenburg (the Great Elector), edict of, 107
Frederick William I., king of Prussia, edict of, 107, 192
Frederick William II., king of Prussia, documents of, 38; patent of, 81
Freeman, Quin John, aide-de-camp, correspondence, 253
Freemasons, Riedesel and, 263
Freiburg, Baden, emigration from, 231, 232
French Morning Post, copies of, 182
French War papers, 176, 177, 178, 179
Frensdorff, secretary, correspondence, 145; journal, 147; papers of, 144, 148, 149
Freudenthal, consul in New Orleans, report of, 172
Freytag, *Feldmarshall* von, correspondence, 103
Fricke, *Capt.* H., correspondence, 253
Friedberg, emigration from, 276
Friedberg, N. C., Moravians in, 316
Friedel, Bonifaz, petition of, 221
Friedland, N. C., Moravians in, 316
Friedrich, *Prince*, regiment of, 103, 122
Friedrich II., landgrave of Hesse-Cassel, *see* Hesse-Cassel
Friedrich Alexander, *Count, see* Wied-Neuwied
Friedrich *and* Friedrich Wilhelm, of Brandenburg *and* Prussia, *see* Frederick *and* Frederick William

Friedrich Kasimir, count of Hanau, *see* Hesse-Hanau
Friedrich Wilhelm, prince of Hesse, regiment of, 143
Friedrichsburg, Tex., plan of, 139
Friends, Society of, *see* Quakers
Friendship, ship, 162
Fritsche, H., emigration report of, 51
Fritze, August, Hessian consul in New York, 131
Friz, Melchior, emigration of, 304
Fuchs, von, correspondence, 120; reports of, 115
Fürstenwerther, diplomatic papers concerning, 241
Fugger, Heinrich, letter on Peru, 191
Fugger family archives, 1, 13
Fulda, emigration from, 141

Gademann, B., petition of, 221
Gädechen, Hermann, Lübeck consul in Guatemala, 283
Gärtner, Wilhelm, 116
Gailertsreuth, emigration from, 203
Gall, *Gen.* W. R., correspondence, 120, 125, 253
Galvão, Bacilino Pereira, Uruguayan consul in Hanse towns, 286
Galveston, German consulates in, 131, 242, 268, 280; emigration to, 55; shipping, 58
Galveston-Zeitung, extracts from, 62
Gambach, emigration from, 277
Gamble, *Lieut.* Moses, correspondence, 253
Gamble, *Maj.* Thomas, correspondence, 112, 253
Ganges, ship, 162
Gardelegen, *Kreis*, emigration petitions, 110
Garfield, *President*, assassination of, 280
Gargot, Nicolas, 2; commission of, 192
Gates, *Maj.-Gen.* Horatio, correspondence, 253; papers, 119, 123-124
Gaugette, Joseph, correspondence, 253
Gayot, correspondence, 225; order of, 224
Gazette de Cologne, see *Cölnische Zeitung*
Gebhard, *Lieut.* Theodor, correspondence, 253
Gebsattel, Franz von, letter of, 217
Gehrcke, brewer, of Stargard, petition by, 34
Geiselbach, emigration from, 220
Geismar, *Maj.* Friedrich Wilhelm von, letters of, 119, 120, 253
Geissler, claim of, 36
Geldern, *Landratsamt*, emigration papers, 93
Gemmingen, Charles de, document of, 204
Genesee district, German emigration to, 75, 160
George II., king of Great Britain, speeches of, 176, 177; papers concerning, 216
George III., correspondence, 106, 144, 180; proclamation, 179; rescript of, 105; treaties of, 263, 264
Georgia, German emigration to, 4, 197, 236, 237; inheritance cases, 238; in the Revolutionary War, 182; trade, 42
Georgia Weekly Telegraph, extracts from, 63
Gera, Reuss archives in, 293
Gerfen, Friedrich Wilhelm, death of, 64
Gerlach, *Capt.* J. D., correspondence, 253, 263

Germain, Lord George, correspondence, 253; discussion with Fox, 183
German-American Annals, 180
German archives, classification, organization, administration, and equipment of, 11-16
Germania, ship, 50
Germania Life-Insurance Co., 111
Germanic Confederation, consular relations with U. S., 133; extradition treaties, 134; *see also* Germany and Zollverein
Germann, von, letter of, 120
German Society of New York, Warning to the, 61
Germany, consuls in America, 6-10; emigration laws, 59, 75, 85, 87, 88, 90, 94, 99, 100, 101, 107, 109, 132, 133, 134, 135, 138, 169, 170, 171, 172; emigration to America, 1-4, 6-10, 48, 49, 50, 51, 53-56, 59-63, 72-75, 78, 79, 81, 84, 85, 87-102, 107-111, 114, 132-141, 150-160, 163-165, 169-172, 181, 185-190, 192-203, 205-214, 218-222, 229-232, 234, 236-239, 242, 243, 265, 267, 272-277, 291-297, 299-301, 303-307, 309-313, 318-322; emigration to other lands, 75, 192-198, 200-203, 207, 208, 213, 215, 216, 218-221, 231, 261, 275-277, 296, 304-306, 309, 311, 312, 319; *Freizügigkeit*, 134, 135, 136, 137, 171; internal trade relations, 185, 186; linen trade, 99; military duty regulations, 132, 134; passport regulations, 154, 155; press-censorship, 154; religious liberty, 209, 211, 232-235, 276, 296, 299, 301, 314-317, 322, 323; shipping, 41, 55, 56, 57, 70, 82, 97, 308, 310, 311; silk trade, 44; societies in America, 57, 58, 61, 62, 63; student movements, 185, 186; trade with America, 69, 70, 71, 72, 79, 80, 81, 82, 95, 98, 99, 107, 133, 134, 137, 150 165 166, 167, 171, 185, 186, 199, 205, 238, 239, 266, 267, 273, 279, 292, 295, 297, 298, 299, 300, 308, 309, 312; U. S. consuls in, 162, 187; *see also* America; American Revolutionary War; Emigration; Germanic Confederation; North German Confederation; United States; *Zollverein*; names of particular countries, states, and places
Gerolt, *Baron*, Prussian minister resident at Washington, correspondence of, 41, 45, 54, 57, 60, 63, 64, 70, 73; papers of, 46
Gerolzhofen, *Gericht*, emigration from, 221
Gesetz und Verordnung über die Durchreise, 60
Gessler, in Strassburg, communication of, 59
Gevekoht, paper of, 239, 241
Geyger, Gottfried, grenadier, papers of, 232
Gibson, William, papers of, 52
Giehne, Emil, emigration of, 231
Giengen, emigration from, 187
Giesing, emigration to America from, 198
Gildermeister, *Senator Dr.*, papers of, 245
Gill, John, correspondence, 253
Gillon, *Commodore* Alexander, correspondence of, 27
Girardot, Haller, and Co., maritime enterprise of, 24
Giuseppe Baccarcici, ship, 61

Gladbach, *Landratsamt*, emigration papers, 93
Gläser, A. H. and I. L., case of, 271
Glanschett, Andreas, suspected emissary, 310
Glauchau, U. S. consulate in, 301
Gleissenberg, *Capt.* von, correspondence, 253
Glöckler, Louis, Venezuelan consul in Hamburg, 284
Glover, *Gen.* John, correspondence, 253
Glückert, A. M., petition of, 221
Gnadenhütten, Ohio, Moravians in, 314
Gnadenhütten, Pa., Moravians in, 314
Gödecke, H., paymaster in chief, correspondence, 253
Göller, Cälestin and Kilian, emissaries, 311
Görne, von, correspondence of, 19, 22, 23
Görtz, von, Prussian envoy, correspondence, 143
Gohr, *Lieut.-Gen.* von, correspondence of, 103, 104
Golden Fleece, ship, 161
Goltz, *Baron* de, correspondence of, 20, 21, 22, 29, 36, 39
Gore, Jean, and Co., correspondence, 253
Gorges, Gottfried, grenadier, 165
Gorissen, Eduard, Costa Rican consul in Hamburg, 283
Gorostiza, de, chargé d'affaires, 102
Gossler, Gustav, correspondence of, 70
Gotha, archives in, 293
Gottschalk, J. A., petition of, 221
Grabow, *Baron* Guido de, Prussian chargé d'affaires, letters of, 60, 62
Graceham, Pa., Moravians in, 314
Graebe, Carl, U. S. consul in Hesse, 132, 137
Gräfe, *Cornet* August, correspondence, 253
Gräffendorf, von, regiment, 128
Graf, M. C., proposition of, 36
Grafenau, *Landgericht*, emigration from, 207
Graff, Caspar, case of, 61
Graff, Friedrich L., Hamburg consul in Baltimore, 268
Grant, *Ensign* J., correspondence, 254
Grant, *Col.* James, correspondence of, 112, 113; order of, 112
Grau, *Lieut.* C. W. F., correspondence, 254
Gravenbroich, *Landratsamt*, emigration papers, 93
Great Britain, auxiliary German troops in service of, 5, 6, 23, 25, 37, 102, 106, 112-131, 142-149, 204, 205, 217, 218, 248-265; dispute with U. S. concerning Oregon Territory, 41; legations in, correspondence, 38, 39, 143, 144, (Haslang) 176-184, 189; Prussian consulates in, 108; subsidies from, 126, 127; treaties with German states, 177, 178, 204; treaties with Russia, 177; treaties with U. S., 183, 184; war with France, 176, 177, 178, 179; war of 1812 with U. S., 165; *see also* American Revolutionary War; England
Greece, law regulating emigration to, 75
Green, Charles, aide-de-camp, correspondence, 254
Green, Venezuelan vice-consul in Lübeck, 284

Index   335

Greene, *Maj.-Gen.* Nathaniel, correspondence, 254
Gregorie, John, in Hamburg, 269
Greiz, State Archives of the Principality of Reuss, Elder Line, in, 293
Greuhm, Friedrich, Prussian minister-resident at Washington, 39; correspondence, 40, 50; reports, 42, 167
Greytown, Hanseatic consulate in, 247
Griedel, emigration from, 277
Griesbach, *Landgericht*, emigration from, 207
Grigsby, Mary, correspondence, 254
Groff, Jacob, Mennonite, 232
Gross, consul in Havre, report of, 231
Gross-Gerau, emigration from, 276
Grossherzoglich Hessischen Zeitung, extracts, 56
Gross-Korben, emigration, 277
Gross-Ostheim, emigration from, 220
Grozingen, emigration from, 229
Grünter, C. M., papers of, 42, 47
Grund, F. J., U. S. consul in Bremen, 98
Guerrero, Vicente, president of Mexico, 102
Guatemala, German consulates in, 282, 285; German emigration to, 98; papers relative to, 53; relations with Hanse towns, 247, 289
Güldin, H., paper by, 236
Guiana, papers relating to, 52
Guilford Court-House, action at, 115
Guillot and Co., Havre, colonisation agents, 51
Gummersbach, *Landratsamt*, emigration papers, 93
Gunn, *Maj.*, correspondence, 254
Gusshübl, emigration from, 198

Hagedorn, Clamor Friedrich, Hessian consul in Philadelphia, 131
Hagedorn, Johann Hermann, Hamburg consul in New Orleans, 268
Hagen, J. W. von, correspondence, 254
Hagen, *Kreis*, emigration papers, 151
Haidt, Joseph, case of, 188
Hairre, *Col.*, correspondence, 254
Haiti, relations with Hanse towns, 246, 283; tariff, 79
Halberstadt, *Kreis*, emigration petitions, 110
Halcyon, ship, 306
Haldimand, *Gen.* Frederick, correspondence, 254
Halifax, papers relating to, 243
Haller, Girardot and, maritime enterprise of, 24
Hambrunn, emigration from, 219, 221
Hamburg, consulates in U. S., 267, 268, 271; emigration via, 10, 52, 53, 57, 59, 73, 74, 101, 109-110, 181, 268, 272, 273, 274, 306; *Polizey-Bekanntmachung das Auswanderungswesen hierselbst betreffend*, 52; *Priv. wöch. gem. Nachrichten v. n. f.*, extracts from, 50; *Revidirte Verordnung in Betreff der Verschiffung der Auswandernden*, 53, 57; shipping, 63, 108, 269, 270, 271, 272, 273; *Staats und Gelehrte Zeitung*, copies and extracts, 43, 50, 58; State Archives in, 266-274; trade with U. S., 266-273; treaties with U. S., 185;
U. S. consuls in, 269, 270, 271; Uruguayan consulate in, 247; *see also* Hanse towns
Hamburg, *Erster Jahresbericht über die Wirksamkeit des Nachweisungs-Bureau der Auswanderer Behörde in*, 59
Hamburger Nachrichten, extracts, 72
Hamburger Vereins, Auswanderung: Erster Rechenschaftsbericht des, 73
Hamburger Zeitung, extract from, 204
Hamburgische Abend Zeitung, etc., copy of, 73
Hameln, transport, 146
Hamilton, *Brig.-Gen.* James, correspondence, 254
Hanau, emigration from, 141; troops in British service, 105; *see also* Hesse-Hanau
Hancock, John, 114
Handfield, W., correspondence, 254
Hanover, consulates in U. S., 97, 98, 156; emigration from, 100, 101, 102; Royal State Archives in, 97-106; treaties with U. S., 97, 102; troops in British service, 102-106
Hansa, copies of, 58, 73
"*Hansel a Jew Boy*", 35
Hanse towns, commercial and diplomatic relations with U. S., 238, 239, 240, 241, 242, 243, 267, 268, 269, 270, 271, 279, 280, 281, 289; relations with other American countries, 243, 244, 245, 246, 247, 281-288, 289, 290; shipping, 267, 269, 270, 271, 272, 273, 279, 280, 281, 282, 283, 285, 286, 289, 290; treaties, 289, 290; *see also* Bremen; Hamburg; Lübeck; Zollverein
Harbord, *Capt.*, correspondence, 254
Harburg, von, emigration of, 136
Hardenberg, *Field Marshal* von, papers of, 104, 105
Hardenberg, *Prince* de, letter of recommendation for, 40
Hardenberg, Karl August, *Prince* von, 157
Harheim Nieder-Wöllstadt, emigration from, 277
Harrassowitz, consul in La Guayra, reports of, 54
Harstall, *Lieut.* von, correspondence, 254
Hartenfels. F. H., Lübeck consul in Buenos Aires, 285
Harvie, *Col.* Jonathan, correspondence, 254
Hasenclever, merchant of Landshut, proposal of, 38
Hasenclever, Frantz Caspar, emigration agent, 94
Hasenclever, Peter, correspondence of, 27, 31, 81
Haslang, *Count*, correspondence and diplomatic papers of, 175, 176, 178, 179, 180, 181, 182, 183, 184
Hassard, *Capt.* Thomas, 254
Hasskarl, Julie, letter of, 62
Haugwitz, *Comte* de, correspondence of, 33
Hausen, emigration from, 276
Hausler, Klemens Joseph, emigration case of, 193-194
Hauss, Jobst Heinrich, widow of, correspondence, 254
Havana, bombardment of, 179

Havre, emigration via, 51, 57, 306
Hayn, von, regiment of, 104
Haynes, *Capt.* T., correspondence, 254
Heath, *Maj.-Gen.* William, correspondence, 254
Hebeler, Prussian consul in London, emigration papers by, 101; report of, 58
Hebron, Pa., Moravians in, 314
Hecht, Carl, emigration case of, 110
Heckenberg, von, correspondence, 120
Heerwagen, *Ensign* J. F., correspondence, 119, 120; journal of, 120
Heidelberg, Pa., Moravians in, 314
Heidenheim, emigration from, 187
Heilman, H., emigration of, 220
Heilsbronn, *Bezirksamt*, emigration from, 213
Heinemann, widow, pension of, 77
Heinrichsen, in San Francisco, 74
Heister, *Capt.* L. C. von, report by, 112
Heister, *Lieut.-Gen.* Philipp von, 114; correspondence and papers of, 103, 112, 113, 117
Heldenbergen, emigration from, 276
Heller, G. A., of Göttingen, 99
Hellespont, ship, 99
Helling, Carl Gottlob, paper of, 79
Henderson, *Capt.*, correspondence, 254
Hengersburg, *Landgericht*, emigration from, 207
Henkelmann, *Lieut.*, letter of, 117
Henny, *Col.* Mark, *see* McHenry, *Col.* James
Henry, *Gen.* James W., correspondence, 254
Herff, *Doctor* von, pamphlet of, 72
Hering, *Col.* von, letter of, 117
Herman, Jahns Reinhard, paper by, 233
Hermann, Heinrich Benedict von, colonization agent, 51
Hermann, *Prince* of Wied, *see* Wied
Hero, ship, 116
Herold, Chr., petition of, 221
Herold, J. P., petition of, 221
Herrnhüter, 81; in Hessian states, 135
Herrnhut, Moravian Archives in, 314-317
Hertel, Frederick, application of, 241
Hertz, Hendel, inheritance papers concerning, 35
Hertzberg, *Count*, correspondence, 29, 31, 32, 33
Herzer, correspondence of, 37
Hesler, *Lieut.* Curt von, correspondence, 254
Hess, Frederick, correspondence of, 63
Hesse, landgrave of (Philipp I.), letter of, 1 n., 299
Hesse-Cassel (electoral Hesse), consulates in, of U. S., 132, 137; consulates of, in U. S., 131, 132, 134; diplomatic papers, 131-134, 137, 143-144; emigration from, 53, 132-141; Jews in, 133; politics, 133, 138; press censorship, 133; relations with South America, 131, 132; trade with America, 137; treaties with Great Britain, 122, 177, 261; troops in British service, 23, 103-105, 112-131, 142-143, 176, 257, 258, 260, 261, 263
Hesse-Cassel, landgraves of: (William VIII.), 142, 143; (Friedrich II.),142; correspondence, 103, 112, 113, 129, 130-131; regiment of, 142; (Wilhelm IX.), 142, 143

Hesse-Darmstadt, grand duchy of, emigration from, 218; House and State Archives of (at Darmstadt), 275-277; laws of, 74, 275-277
Hesse-Darmstadt, landgrave of, 171, 172
Hesse-Hanau, troops of, in British service, 116, 117, 118, 121, 125, 126, 142, 249, 252, 254, 258, 261, 263
Hesse-Hanau, counts of: (Friedrich Kasimir), project of, 216; (Wilhelm), correspondence, 142, 143, 249; treaty of, 261
Hesse-Homburg, landgraviate of, emigration to America irom, 172
Hesse-Nassau, emigration to America from, 169, 170, 172
Heunisch, Marg., petition of, 221
Heus, *Licut.*, 145
Heusser, *Quartermaster*, journal of, 121
Hewlett, *Lieut.-Col.* Richard, correspondence, 254
Heydt, minister of trade, paper of, 79
Heye, Hermann, letter of, 239
Heyman, Henry, letter of, 238
Heymann, August Franz Friedrich von, Brazilian vice-consul in Bremen, 244
Hiermann, Moritz Friedrich, correspondence of, 293
Hiesland, Henry, papers concerning, 97
High German Company, for emigration, 296, 299
Hill, *Lieut.-Col.* J., correspondence, 254
Hilley, John P., paper by, 233
Hinck, Johann Friedrich, Gautemalan consul in Hanse towns, 283
Hinnigoffen, Leonardt, emigration case of, 171
Hintze, of Lilienthal, correspondence of, 104
Hinüber, Charles, correspondence, 254
Hippolstein, *Bezirksamt*, emigration from, 212
Hochheim, *Amt*, emigration to America from, 169
Hochteutsche Compagnie, for emigration, 296, 299
Hoch-Wiesel, emigration from, 276
Hocking, *Lieut.* R., correspondence, 254
Hoffman, in Philadelphia, letter of, 204
Hoffmann, Jeremias, papers concerning, 137
Hofheinz, Johann Jost, case of, 130
Hogel, Francis, correspondence, 254
Hohenzollern-Sigmaringen, *see* Sigmaringen
Holburne, *Admiral* Francis, squadron, 177
Holderness, *Lord*, letter of, 178
Holland, Samuel, correspondence, 254
Holles, Thomas, order of, 170
Holtzmann, from Magdeburg, emigration case of, 110
Holzhausen, emigration from, 276
Holzinger, Nathan, emigration of, 212
Homburg, duchy of, *see* Hesse-Homburg
Homœopathy, the Healing Art, 55
Hooke, *Capt.* G. P., correspondence, 254
Hooper, *Col.*, correspondence, 254
Hope, Col. Henryk, quartermaster-general, correspondence, 254
Hope, Ind., Moravians in, 317
Hope, N. J., Moravians in, diaries, 314, 315

Index

Hormayer, von, trade papers by, 186
Horstein, emigration from, 220
Houghton, *Lieut.* Rich., correspondence, 255
House of Commons, addresses, 177
House of Lords, address, 177
Howe, *Lieut.-Gen. Sir* William, correspondence and papers of, 25, 114, 181, 255
Hoyer, Wilhelm, correspondence, 255
Hoyer-Frauenstein, J. G., paper by, 297
Hoyes, Robert, correspondence, 255
Hube, Friedrich, Mexican consul in Hanse towns, 282
Huber, *Postmaster*, case of, 188
Hubert, *Col.*, correspondence, 225
Huff, *Maj.* Paul, correspondence, 255
Hughes, David, correspondence, 255
Hughes, James, agent, correspondence, 255
Huguenots, emigration of, 3
Humboldt, "Patriotische Vorschläge", 82
Hummel, A. M., petition of, 221
Hungary, emigration to, 85
Hunter, James and Adam, correspondence, 255
Huss, Johann, 2
Huyn, *Col.* von, 143; regiment, 123
Hygle, von, letter of, 217

Iburg, *Amt*, emigration papers, 155-156
"Icaria", German colony in Illinois and Iowa, 164
Ichon, Edward, paper by, 60
Ilbenstadt, emigration from, 276
Illinois, German colony of "Icaria" in, 164; German consulates in, 241, 280, 312; German emigration to, 198
Immigration, *see* Emigration
Imports, American, 42, 43, 45; statistics of, 70
Indiana, German consulates in, 241, 280, 312
Indianola, Tex., Hanseatic agent in, 242; plan of, 139; shipping, 58
Indians, 178, 299, 324; in the American Revolutionary War, 183
Indian War papers, 176
Ingersleben, correspondence of, 49
Inglée, *Capt.* Jesse, case of, 270
Instruction für Auswanderer nach Texas, 72
Insurance companies, 20, 22, 72, 111, 140
Intelligenz-Blatt für den Bezirk des Königlichen Oberlandesgerichts von Sachsen, copy of, 71
Iowa, German consulates in, 241, 312; "Icaria" in, 164
Irchenreuth, emigration from, 202
Ireland, linen industry, 79
Irving, *Maj.* Amelius, correspondence, 255
Isabel, Central America, Hanseatic consulate in, 247
Isenburg, *Count* von, papers concerning, 218
Isenburg-Birstein, *Gen.-Prince* J. C. von, 142
Iserlohn, *Kreis*, emigration papers, 151
Isis, ship, 119

Jacob, a Jew of Philadelphia, plan by, 28, 36
Jacob, William, paper of, 299
Jäger, Franz Ludwig, petition of, 221

Jamaica, earthquakes, 183; German emigration to, 53; papers relating to, 243
Janecke, *Lieut.* von, correspondence, 120
Jaritz, *Lieut.* Erasmus, correspondence, 255
Jefferson, Thomas, correspondence, 255; papers relating to, 30, 31, 34
Jefferys, Thomas, map by, 263
Jenifer, Daniel, correspondence of, 43
Jenison, Jean, correspondence, 255
Jenney, *Capt.* Ebenezer, 292
Jerichow, *Kreis*, emigration petitions, 110
Jessup, Eben, correspondence, 255
Jessup, *Col.* Edward, correspondence, 255
Jesuits, in Paraguay, 299
Jimenes, Jesus, president of Costa Rica, 100
Jockusch, J. W., in Galveston, 74
Johanna, ship, 50
John, ship, 116
John Drew, ship, 161
Johnson, *Capt.*, complaint of, 271
Johnson, *Maj.-Gen.*, letter of, 176
Johnson, *Lieut.* John, correspondence, 255
Jones, *Lieut.* David, correspondence, 255
Jones, *Capt.* John, correspondence, 255
Jones, *Commodore* John Paul, papers concerning, 182
Jordan, correspondence, 44
Jordan, Jacob, paymaster, correspondence, 255
Joseph II., emperor, edict of, 181; order of, 94
Jülich, *Landratsamt*, emigration papers, 93
Jülich-Berg, emigration papers, 93-94
Jüngsten, Johann Friedrich, wife of, case of, 170
Jung, Friedrich, emigration of, 49
Jungkehn, *Lieut.-Gen.* von, orders of, 116
Junken, von, of Hessen, correspondence of, 103

Kadolsburg, *Landgericht*, emigration from, 212
Kaichen, emigration from, 276
Kaiserl. Reichs-Post-Zeitung, extracts, 170, 214
Kalkmann, Ludwig Friedrich, Brazilian consul in Bremen, 244
Kaltenbrunn, emigration from, 202
Kaltmann, consul in Hanover, 102
Kapff, Hermann von, Lübeck consul in U. S., 280
Kapp and Bissinger, report of, 61
Karl, *Landgrave*, regiment, 143
Karl, *Prince*, regiment of, 120, 128
Karl I., duke of Brunswick-Lüneburg, *see* Brunswick-Lüneburg
Karl II., elector palatine, *see* Palatine
Karl III., Philipp, elector palatine, *see* Palatine
Karl Albrecht, of Bavaria, elector palatine, *see* Bavaria
Karl Theodor, elector palatine, *see* Palatine
Karl Wilhelm Ferdinand, duke of Brunswick, *see* Brunswick-Lüneburg
Karlsruhe, City Archives of, 318; emigration from, 55, 231, 318; Grand-Ducal General National Archives of Baden in, 2, 229-237
Karlsruhe-Augspurg, emigration from, 232
Karlstadt, emigration from, 218, 221
Karp, Georg, case of, 64

22

Karthaus, emigration from, 87, 88
Karwinsky, Wilhelm Friedrich, *Freiherr* von, emigration of, 194
Kay, William, correspondence, 255
Kearny, *Capt.*, case of, 269
Keating, John, emigration agent, 226
Kehlheim, *Landgericht*, emigration from, 207
Kehr, Johannes, indenture of, 52
Keller, F., paper by, 231
Kellerhoff, C. W., letter of, 184
Kelsick, Richard, correspondence, 255
Kempfer, letter of, 120
Kettner, Fr. von, correspondence, 143
Key West, Hanseatic agent in, 242
Kiel, U. S. consul in, 162
Kielmansegge, *Count*, 99
King's Bridge, Hessian troops at, 117, 118
Kingston, *Adj.* Robert, correspondence, 255
Kirchberg, *Oberamt*, emigration to America from, 85
Kirchgaus, emigration from, 276
Kirchhoff, *Capt.*, letters of, 120
Kirchner, Carl Christian, letters of, 296, 299
Kirchzell, emigration from, 219, 221
Klaener, D. H., communication of, 58
Klaest, *Baron* Jacob, correspondence of, 34
Klappenheim, emigration from, 276
Klee, Carl Rudolph, Lübeck consul in Guatemala, 283
Klein, Anton, petition of, 221
Klein-Karben, emigration from, 276
Kleinschmidt, *Quartermaster*, journal of, 123
Kleist, see Klaest
Klingenbach, *Gericht*, emigration from, 221
Klugmann, Johann Christoph, Brazilian vice-consul in Lübeck, 288
Knoblauch, H. von, journal of, 123
Knoblauch, von, regiment, 143
Knorre, G. Carl, Hamburg vice-consul in U. S., 268
Knyphausen, von, regiment of, 103, 112, 114, 117, 122
Knyphausen, *Lieut.-Gen.* Wilhelm von, correspondence, 113, 120, 255; papers relating to, 104, 117, 142; report of, 112
Koch, Andreas, letters of, 120
Köhler, *Col.* J. C., 143
Köhler, von, battalion of, 104
Köln, see Cologne
Königlich Preussischer Reise-Pass für das Ausland, 59
Königsberg, emigration from, 107; Royal State Archives in, 107-108
Könnecke, Heinrich, emigration petition of, 110
Körsching, emigration from, 198
Kötzting, *Landgericht*, emigration from, 207
Kohler, Anna Maria, *née* Kramer, emigration papers of, 85
Kohler, Johann Baptist, emigration of, 189
Kollmann, M., petition of, 220
Kolster, secretary of legation at Hamburg, 108
Konitz, *Landratsamt*, emigration papers, 89
Kospoth, *Maj.-Gen.* von, correspondence, 255
Kosten, *Kreis*, emigration papers, 158
Koszta, Martin, papers concerning, 239
Kotoschin, *Kreis*, emigration papers, 158
Kramer, Eberhard and, case of, 85
Kramer, Johann Martin, emigration papers of, 85
Krause, John Christoph, 51; correspondence, 255
Krausz, J. C. C., paper by, 272
Kress, Johann Jacob, shipmaster, 311
Kretzschmer, *Doctor*, connection with G. A. Schäfer of Brazil, 186
Krittmann, F., claim of, 270
Kröben, *Kreis*, emigration papers, 158
Krohn, August Carl, Hanseatic consul in Bolivar, 284
Krook, Th., Lübeck agent in Valparaiso, 285
Krumbhaar, Prussian consul in Philadelphia, 47
Kühne, Friedrich, Hessian consul in New York, 131; report by, 46
Küster, correspondence of, 50
Kuhn, Christoph, case of, 85
Kuhn, Johannes, case of, 85
Kuhr, of Amorbach, emigration of. 220
Kulenkamp, E. G., Mexican consul in Lübeck, 282
Kuntzsch, *Lieut.* T. F. von, correspondence, 255
Kurz, Benj., letter of, 296
Kutzleben, *Baron* de, correspondence of, 120
Kyng, U. S. consul in Hamburg, 269

Labonne, at Trois Rivières, correspondence, 255
Lafayette, *Marquis* de, correspondence, 255; operations of, 180
Lafitte, J. M., Baltimore colonization agent, 51
La Guayra, 58; German consulates in, 189, 246, 284
Lampe, Heinrich Johann, Bolivian consul in Hanse towns, 285
Lampman, John, correspondence, 255
Lancaster, Pa., Moravians in, 314
Lancastrische Zeitung, extracts, 170
Landau, *Landgericht*, emigration from, 207
Landgraf, regiment, 127
Landmesser, Jakob, petition of, 229
Landshut, emigration from, 207; Royal Bavarian Provincial (Circuit) Archives in, 207-208
Langemeyer, *Secretary*, correspondence, 255
Langen, *Capt.-Lieut.* von, report of. 103
Langensalza, Company of, for Carolina, 299
Langsdorff, *Legationsrath* von, papers concerning, 134
La Plata, German emigration to, 197; papers relating to, 55; war with Brazil, 102
Laporte, Ind., Prussian consulate at, 48
Larbusch, *Count* Arnold, correspondence, 115
Lawden, John, Hamburg consul in U. S., 268
Lawe, George, correspondence, 255
Lawrence, Abbott, correspondence of, 43
Leaver, Deal, correspondence, 255
Leda, ship, 247
Lee, Arthur, American agent abroad, 7; correspondence of, 20, 21, 22, 23, 24, 25, 27, 29

Index

Lee, William, American agent abroad, 23, 25; correspondence of, 17, 21, 22, 24, 25, 26, 27, 28
Lee, *Col.* William R., correspondence, 255
Legge, Henry B., chancellor of the exchequer, 177
Leibnitz, ship, 61, 159
Leigh, Charles C., letter of, 240
Leiningen, emigration papers, 218
Leipzig, U. S. consulate in, 301
Leland, *Brig.-Gen.,* correspondence, 255
Le Maische, *Adj.-Gen.* François, correspondence, 255
Lembke, Julius, papers concerning, 47
Lengerke, G. E. von, 142; journal of, 124
Lengerke, von, battalion, 124, 129
Lentz, battalion, 129
Lentz, *Lieut.-Col.* von, correspondence, 120, 255
Leonidas, ship, 47
Lerchenfeld, letters of, 183
Lernoult, *Adj.-Gen.* R. B., correspondence, 255
Leslie, A., correspondence, 112, 113
Le Suire, *Lieut.,* 145
Letter from a Resident of Washington to a Friend in South Carolina, 46
Lieber, *Professor* Francis, papers of, 56
Liebig, ship, 159
Lilienthal, Julius Gustav, Uruguayan vice-consul in Lübeck, 286
Lima, Hanseatic consulate in, 246, 284, 285
Lima, *Chevalier* Vianna de, *see* Vianna de Lima, *Chevalier*
Linckersdorff, *Lieut.* von, communication of, 113
Lincoln, Abraham, assassination of, 240, 280
Lincoln, *Gen.* Benjamin, correspondence, 29; orders of, 182
Lind, *Lieut.-Col.,* correspondence, 256
Lindau, von, letter of, 120
Lindemann, F. L. von, Lübeck consul in Lima, 284
Lindner, Franz Mathes, petition of, 221
Lindsay, William, correspondence, 256
Linen, industry of Scotland, 79; trade with America, 80, 82
Lingelbach, William E., article on Saxon-American commercial relations, 297
Lingen, *Amt,* emigration papers, 156
Link, G., order concerning, 219
Link, G. T., emigration of, 220
Linsing, correspondence, 115
Linsingen, *Col.* von, 142
Linsingen, von, battalion, 129, 143
Lippe, principality, House and National Archives of (at Detmold), 278
Liston, Robert, diplomatic papers concerning, 34
Lititz, Moravians in, diaries, 314, 315
Liverpool, shipping, 58
Löscher, *Dr.* H. Ludewig, 73
Löwenstein, von, 142; correspondence, 115
Löwenstein, von, battalion, 124
Lohr, emigration from, 220

London, plan of, 263
London *Gazette,* extracts from, 120, 182
London *Morning Post,* extracts from, 55
London *Times,* extracts from, 52
Long Island, auxiliary German troops in, 115, 117
Loos, *Col.* von, correspondence, 256
Lopez, *Don* Francisco Solano, president of Paraguay, 100
Lorck, Berent, U. S. consular agent in Königsberg, 108
Lorentz, J. G., councillor of war and commissary-general, correspondence, 256
Lorentz, Richard, paymaster, correspondence, 256
Lorenz, *Kriegsrath,* letter of, 117
Lossberg, *Lieut.-Gen.* von, correspondence and papers of, 114, 115, 120, 256
Lossberg, von, regiment, 103, 112, 121, 143
Lott, *Lieut.-Col.* Jeromus, correspondence, 256
Louis XIV., declaration of, 224; document of, 192; edicts of, 2, 225
Louis XV., edicts of, 225
Louisburg, blockade of, 176; siege of, 178
Louisiana, German emigration to, 239, 311
Loureiro, *Dr.* Jean Alves, Brazilian chargé d'affaires in Hesse, 131
Lucé, *Baron* de, correspondence, 225
Ludewig, *Quartermaster,* journal of, 123
Ludlam, Henry, Hamburg consul at Richmond, correspondence, 268
Ludlow, Daniel, correspondence, 256
Ludlow, Geo. D., correspondence, 256
Ludlow, G. G., correspondence, 256
Ludwig, Ernst, duke in Brunswick-Lüneburg, *see* Brunswick-Lüneburg
Ludwig Leopold, count palatine of Veldenz, *see* Veldenz
Ludwigsburg, Royal Privy House and State Archives of Württemberg in, 303-307
Lübbert, Hermann, 270
Lübeck, commercial treaty with U. S., 185; emigration from, 181; State Archives in, 279-290; U. S. consulate in, 280-281; *see also* Hanse towns
Lübke, George, emissary, 170
Lüdemann, Friedrich Wilhelm, Lübeck consul in Valparaiso, 285
Luedering and Co., emigration agents, 111
Lüdering, Traub, und Duntze, Notwendige Anzeige für Auswanderer sowie Entlarvung und Abfertigung der Bremer Schiffsmäkler, 53
Lüneburg, *see* Brunswick-Lüneburg
Luetjens, Johann Friedrich, Brazilian vice-consul in Lübeck, 288
Luetjens, S. I., Hanseatic consul in Bahia, 287
Lütkens, Heinrich, papers relating to, 64
Luna, ship, 161, 231
Lusi, *Count* von, correspondence of, 39
Lutheran Church, 2, 53, 296, 299
Lutterloh, *Col.* Henry Edmund von, correspondence and papers of, 32, 33, 38, 145

340   *Index*

Lutwidge, *Capt.,* correspondence, 256
Lyttelton, George, chancellor of the exchequer, 177

Maasen, Heinrich Joseph, and Co., contract of, 59
Macbean, *Lieut.-Col.* Forbes, correspondence, 256
Macdonald, *Maj.* John, correspondence, 256
McDougall, *Gen.* Alexander, correspondence, 252
Macdukel, *Gen.,* correspondence, 256
McHenry, *Col.* James, 254
Mackay, *Mrs.* Jannet, correspondence, 256
Mackenzie, *Maj.* Frederick, 115
McKinley, *President,* assassination of, 240
Madden, John, papers concerning, 309
Madeweiss, correspondence of, 29
Madison, *President,* declaration of, 188
Magdeburg, emigration to America from, 110, 111; Royal State Archives in, 109-111
Magusch, *Finanzrath,* 18; correspondence of, 19, 20, 23
Mahler, Bartholomée, emigration agent, 226
Mahn, Eduard, Hanseatic consul in Vera Cruz, 282
Maibach, emigration from, 276
Maibücher, Carl, article by, 60
Maierhöfer, Anna Maria, emigration of, 203
Maine, adventures of Braditsch in, 189, 198; German emigration to, 169, 275, 322
Mainz, electorate, emigration papers, 218, 219, 220
Malaga, ship, 117
Mallarino, Manuel Maria, president of New Granada, document of, 289
Mallersdorf, *Landgericht,* emigration from, 207
Malortie, *Maj.* von, reports of, 103
Maltzan, *Count* von, correspondence, 35, 38, 39
Manhattan Life Insurance Co., 111
Mann, A. Dudley, consul, papers of, 98, 239
Mann, Anton, correspondence, 144
Mann, Johann Sigismund, Brazilian consul in Hanse towns, 288
Mannheim, City Archives of, 319-321
Mannheimer Zeitung, article in, 186
Mansfeld, *Grafschaft,* emigration papers, 109
Manteuffel, Otto *Freiherr* von, correspondence, 45
Mantl, emigration from, 203
Manzanillo, Hanseatic agent in, 246
Marblehead, ship, 271
Marburg, Royal State Archives in, 112-149
Marc, Jacob, 148
Marc, Philipp, Waldeck commissary, 148, 149
Marienburg, *Kreis,* emigration papers, 87
Marienwerder, *Landratsamt,* emigration papers, 88, 90
Mark, Jacob, case of, 7, 34
Mark, Louis, U. S. consul in Bamberg, 187
Markt Erlbach, *Landgericht,* emigration from, 212
Marsh, *Col.* J., correspondence, 256
Marsh, William, correspondence, 256

Marshall, *Capt.,* correspondence, 256
Martin, Hans, letters of, 236
Martin, Maria, letter of, 237
Martini, Johann Peter, inheritance papers of, 85
Martinique, war papers concerning, 179
Martinstein, *Amt,* emigration to America from, 85
Maryland, German emigration to, 9; German societies in, 52, 58, 63; immigration laws, 58; tobacco trade, 238
Maryland, ship, 98
Masquinonge, auxiliary German troops at, 119
Massachusetts. enlistment of Germans in, for Union Army, 60; German emigration to, 47, 170, 225, 322; German troops in, 119
Mathews, *Capt.* R., correspondence, 256
Mathias, Prussian consul in Baltimore and Philadelphia, 47
Matthaeus, document by, 112
Matthäus, J., communication of, 114
Maudry, Abram and Fae, correspondence, 143
Maurer, *Capt.* J., correspondence, 256
Maximilian, emperor of Mexico, 132, 294
Maximilian, prince of Wied, acts, journeys, and letters of, 323, 324
Maximilian II. Emanuel, elector of Bavaria, *see* Bavaria
Maximilian III. Joseph, elector of Bavaria, *see* Bavaria
Maximilian IV. Joseph, elector of Bavaria, *see* Bavaria
Mayer, private secretary, document by, 189
Mayer, Hans, Mennonite, 232
Mazatlan, Hanseatic agent in, 246, 282
Mebius, Christian Friedrich, Hessian consul in San Francisco, 131
Mecklenburg-Schwerin, Grand-Ducal Privy and Central Archives of, 291; consulate in Brazil, 291; emigration from, 291
Mecklenburg-Strelitz, Grand-Ducal Central Archives of, 291
Meibom, *Maj.* de, correspondence, 256
Meier, consul, request of, 241
Meier, H. H., correspondence of, 43
Meinel, *Pastor,* 165
Meinhardus, Johannes, request of, 84, 85
Meiningen, Privy State Archives of Saxe-Meiningen, 294
Mellbach, emigration from, 276
Melvin and Wills, correspondence, 256
Melzheimer, field preacher, correspondence, 256
Mendonsa, Peter, correspondence, 256
Mendt, Hans, Mennonite, 232
Menezes, Vasconcellos de Drummond, Antonio de. Brazilian representative in Hanse towns, 102, 244, 288
Mengen, *Lieut.-Col.* Otto Carl Anton von, correspondence, 256, 263
Mennonites, papers relating to, 2, 135, 166, 169, 232, 233, 235, 236, 276, 322, 323
Mercer, *Capt.* Alex., correspondence, 256
Merry, Anthony, appointed minister to U. S., 34
Mersereau, Joshua, correspondence, 256

Mertgen, Jacob, emigration papers of, 49
Meseritz, *Kreis*, emigration papers, 158
Messenheim, emigration from, 276
Mettmann, *Landratsamt*, emigration papers, 94
Metz, District Archives of Lorraine in, 223-224
Metzner, *Maj. P.*, correspondence, 256
Mexican War, papers relating to, 41, 64, 65, 70, 139
Mexico, emigration to, 299; German consulates in, 57, 108, 189, 245, 282, 294, 312; papers relating to, 51, 70, 74; relations with German states, 132, 133, 245, 246, 281-282, 292; tariff, 82; trade with Germany, 51, 102, 133, 150, 245, 246, 281, 282, 292, 309; treaties, 69, 133, 289
Meyer, Johannes Matthias, Hanseatic consul in Bahia, 287
Meyer, Ludwig, death of, 64
Meyer, Valentine Lorenz, emigration agent, 111
Michel, ship, 306
Michelbach, emigration from, 220
Michigan, Bremen consulate in, 241; German emigration to, 63
Miguel, *Dom*, claimant of Portugal, 300
Miltenberg, *Gericht*, emigration from, 221
Milwaukee, German consulates in, 48, 241, 294
Minden, *Regierung*, emigration papers, 151
Minerva Smith, ship, 162
Minnesota, German consulates in, 241
Minnigerode, *Col.* von, 142
Minnigerode, von, battalion, 103, 143
Minuit, Peter, of Wesel, 1
Mirbach, von, communication of, 113
Mirbach, von, regiment, 103, 122, 128
Mississippi, "*Insul*", 303
Mississippi River, and the American Revolution, 183
Missouri, admission of, 42; consulate of Frankfort in, 312; German emigration to, 8; relations with Hesse, 137
Missouri, ship, 161
Mitterfels, *Landgericht*, emigration from, 207
Mobile, Hanseatic agent in, 242
Möller, Friedrich, consul of Argentina and Uruguay in Hesse, 132
Möller, P. B., Lübeck consul in Montevideo, 286
Möring, C. H. F., Hamburg consul in U. S., 268
Moers, emigration papers of, 95
Mörschell, Johannes, letter of, 120
Moniteur Belge, 53, 56
Moniteur Universel, Le, copy, 74
Moniz Bareto d'Aragão, Francisco, Brazilian agent in Hanse towns, 244, 288
Monroe, James, declaration signed by, 188
Monsell, *Maj.* William, correspondence, 256
Montealegre, José Maria, president of Costa Rica, document, 290
Montessuy, Prussian minister in Paris, 7; correspondence of, 18, 19
Montevideo, Hanseatic consulates in, 247, 285, 286
Montgolfier, correspondence, 256
Montjoie, *Landratsamt*, emigration papers, 94
Montreal, capture of, 178

Montresor, *Captain*, map by, 263
Moraes Barros, *Dr.* José Marcelino de, Brazilian vice-consul in Bremen, 244
Moravian Archives, 314-317
Moravians, emigration of, 4; missions in North and South America and Australia, 314-317; papers relating to, 81
Morewood, U. S. consul in Hamburg, 269
Morin, *Capt.* Jean, correspondence, 256
Mormons, papers relating to, 41
Morrison, Peter, case of, 271
Mosel, Fritz and Johann Heinrich, emigration of, 155
Moser, Fr. Carl von, correspondence, 144
Mosle, Alexander Georg, Hanseatic consul in Rio de Janeiro, 243
Mosquitia, emigration to, 55; Hanseatic consulate in, 247
Mostyn, *Vice-Adm.* Savage, squadron, 177
Motley, J. Lothrop, U. S. minister at Vienna, letter of, 191
Mott, J. B., passport of, 99
Mottern, case of, 7
Motz, *Lieut.*, correspondence, 114
Mount Independence, plan, 126
Mountjoy, Pa., Moravians in, 314
Müller, *Lieut.*, letters of, 114
Müller, Johann Jost, widow of, lawsuit of, 170
Müller, Johannes, lawsuit of, 170
Müller, Theodor, letter of, 62
Münchener Tageblatt, copy of, 198
Münchhausen, *Baron* von, papers concerning, 177
Münchhausen, *Capt. Baron* von, correspondence, 115, 182
Münchhausen, *Widow* von, 76
Münster, emigration from, 151-153, 276; Royal State Archives of the Province of Westphalia in, 150-153
Münzenberg, emigration from, 276, 277
Munich, Royal Bavarian Circuit Archives of Lower Bavaria in, 192-200; Royal Bavarian General National Archives in, 191; Royal Bavarian Privy State Archives in, 173-191
Municipal archives, iii, 308-313, 318-321
Murphy, *Don* Thomas, Mexican envoy to Hesse, 132
Murphy, William W., U. S. consul in Hesse, 132
Murray, Michael, correspondence, 256
Murray, Thomas, aide-de-camp, correspondence, 256
Mutual Life Insurance Co., 111

Nachweisungsbüreau, *Berichte* of, 108
Nagel, of New Orleans, report of, 70
Nagler, correspondence of, 51
Naigeon, emigration agent, 226
Nairne, *Maj.* John, correspondence, 256
Nantes, companies of insurance at, 20
Nantes, Edict of, revocation of, 3
Nassau, decree of the ducal government of, 56; duchy of, consulate in California, 171; emigration from, 169, 170, 172; Lübeck consulate in, 280

Nassau, *Princess* of, *Fremdenbuch* of, 322
Nassau Dreiserisch, *Amt*, emigration to America from, 171
Nassau Katzenellenbogen, emigration to America from, 171
Nassau Weilburg, emigration to America from, 169
Nativism, papers relating to, 63
Nazareth, Pa., Moravian mission in, diaries of, 314, 315
Negrete, Mexican consul in Hanse towns, 282
Nesselrode, *Count* de, despatch of, 300
Netherlands, colonial papers, 134; emigration laws, 101; emigration via, 50, 312, 319; royal decrees, 56; shipping, 225; trade with America, 45, 79
Neuburg, *Regierungsbezirk*, emigration from, 210
Neuburg, Royal Bavarian Provincial (Circuit) Archives in, 209-210
Neudi, *Director*, in Hamburg, correspondence of, 21
Neudorf, emigration from, 220
Neue Europäische Zeitung, extracts from, 125
Neuenbuch, emigration from, 221
Neuenstädten, ship, 269
Neuhaldensleben, *Kreis*, emigration petitions, 110
Neuhard, *Legationsrath*, correspondence, 144
Neuhausen, emigration from, 198
"Neuländer", 4
Neustadt, emigration from, 87, 88, 202, 203, 212
Neu-Strelitz, Grand-Ducal Central Archives of Mecklenburg-Strelitz in, 291
Neutrality, ship, 161
Neuwied, Archives of the (Mediatized) Principality of Wied Neuwied in, 322-324; information about these, 322; emigration from, 322, 323; religious papers, 322, 323; *see also* Wied-Neuwied
Neveusevertre, *Col.*, correspondence, 257
New Albany, Ind., Prussian consulate at, 48
New Bedford, Mass., Prussian consulate at, 48
New Braunfels, Tex., plan of, 139
New Brunswick, boundary disputes, 70
Newcastle, Thomas Holles, duke of, order by, 170
New England, emigrants to, 85; French emigration to, 224, 225; German emigration to, 275, 304, 310, 322; manufactures, 69; map, 263
Newfoundland, war in, 179
New Georgia, *see* Georgia
New Granada, *see* Colombia
New Hampshire, Germans in, 47
New Jersey, Bremen consulate in, 241; expedition in, 182
New London, in the Revolutionary War, 182
New Orleans, cotton trade, 46; finance, 185; German consulates in, 58, 70, 72, 100, 131, 191, 242, 268; German emigration to, 9, 47, 55, 73; German societies in, 57, 58, 62, 73; papers relating to, 58, 171; shipping, 58, 59; trade, 71

Newport, R. I., auxiliary German troops in, 125, 250; Moravians in, 314; papers relating to, 180
New Providence, papers relating to, 243
Newspapers, extracts from, 69; *see also* names of particular newspapers
New Utrecht, auxiliary German troops in, 250
New York, exhibitions, 71, 99, 239; finance, 185; German consulates in, 99, 131, 134, 242, 268, 271, 280, 295, 300, 312; German emigration to, 9, 55, 74, 93, 94; German societies in, 53, 56, 61, 62, 72, 74, 100, 139; immigration commission, 62; imports, 45; life-insurance societies in, 111; maps, 263; Moravians in, 314; papers relating to, 100, 180, 182; scientific notes, 323; shipping, 58, 60, 70, 71, 161, 238, 241, 242
New Yorker Handels Zeitung, extracts, 61
New-Yorker Staatszeitung, extracts from, 63
New York Gazette, 183
New York Life Insurance Co., 111
Niagara, papers relating to, 178
Nicaragua, relations with Hanse towns, 247, 283
Nicaragua Canal papers, 283
Nieder-Erlenbach, emigration from, 276
Nieder-Eschbach, emigration from, 276
Nieder-Florstadt, emigration from, 277
Niederhessen, emigration from, 141
Nieder-Mörten, emigration from, 276
Niederstetter, Prussian chargé d'affaires in Washington, correspondence of, 40, 43, 69
Niemeyer, of Hesse, 103; report of, 104
Niles' Register, extracts from, 45
Noezel, *Lieut.*, 146
Nolte, Hermann, Bavarian and Lübeck consul in Mexico, 189, 282
Nolte, Vincent, Hamburg consul in New Orleans, 268
Nootka Sound controversy, 238
Nordamerikanische Colonisations-Gesellschaft, of Stuttgart, 304
Norddeutsche Zeitung, extracts from, 165
Norden, H. H., 98
Norma, ship, 164
Northern Pacific Railroad, 240
North German Confederation, consulates in America, 281, 285, 287; shipping, relations with U. S., 277; *see also* Germany and Zollverein
North German Lloyd, correspondence, 62; papers of, 10
Norton, ship, 62
Norton, *Capt.* William, correspondence, 257
Notten, van, and Co., bankers, 127
Nuremberg, consul of, letter of, 181
Nuremberg, emigration from, 181; Royal Bavarian Provincial (Circuit) Archives in, 211-213

Oberdalling, emigration from, 198
Oberdorff, in Mannheim, letters of, 215
Ober-Erlenbach, emigration from, 277
Ober-Eschbach, emigration from, 277
Oberhessen, emigration from, 141

Oberhessisches Provinzial Wochenblatt, supplement to, 139
Obermärlen, emigration from, 277
Oberpfalz, *Regierungsbezirk*, emigration from, 201
Ober-Rosbach, emigration from, 277
Ober-Wöllstadt, emigration from, 277
Obornik, *Kreis*, emigration papers, 158
Observatory, naval, in Washington, 190
Ockstadt, emigration from, 277
Offenheim, emigration from, 277
Ohio, German consulates in, 280, 312
Okarben, emigration from, 277
Oldenburg, commercial and diplomatic relations with U. S. and other American states, 292; emigration from, 59, 101, 292; Grand-Ducal House and Central Archives in, 292
Olivier, Louis, correspondence, 257
Olympe, ship, 51
Oneida, ship, 159
Ontario, Lake, boundary disputes concerning, 176
Oppershofen, emigration from, 277
Oregon Territory dispute, papers relating to, 41, 70, 98
Organ zur Beförderung der Kolonisation, 73
Oriental, ship, 162, 270
Orkneys, Germans in the, 56
Osborn, Sir George, letter of, 113
Oschersleben, *Kreis*, emigration petitions, 110
Osnabrück, Royal State Archives in, 154-156
Osten-Sacken, *Capt.* von der, 145
Oster, Johann, petition of, 65
Osterburg, *Kreis*, emigration petitions, 110
Osterhofen, *Landgericht*, emigration from, 207
Ostheim, emigration from, 277
Oswego, garrison of, 177
Otterstedt, *Baron* von, paper of, 48
Otto, *Kurfürst*, order of, 94
Otto, Wilhelm, Lübeck consul in Pernambuco, 287
Ouvrier, *Professor* Ludwig Benjamin, correspondence, 257
Oynhausen, Hessian envoy at the Hague, correspondence, 144

Paget, Arthur, 175
Paine, *Dr.* W., correspondence, 257
Palatinate, *Bestrafung der ohne Landesherrlichen Vorwissen auswandernden Churpfältzischen Angehörigen, auch neuen Unterthanen*, 320; emigration from the, 3, 94, 185, 275, 319; emigration papers concerning, 214, 215
Palatine, electors: (Karl II.), edict of, 214; (Johann Wilhelm), decree of, 319; (Karl III. Philipp), edict of, 214; (Karl Theodor), correspondence, 184, 185; orders of, 94, 319
Paleske, Carl Gottfried, Prussian consul in America, 7, 32, 33, 79, 81, 107, 108
Panama, circular about, 61
Papendiek, H. H., consul for Bremen in Milwaukee, 241
Pará, Hanseatic consulate in, 244

Paraguay, conditions in, 299; papers relating to, 100, 294; relations with Germany, 247, 292, 312; treaties, 133; war with Brazil, 295
Paris, treaty of, 48, 49
Parish, John, merchant commissioner of the Americans, 21, 272
Parish archives, iii
Parker, *Dr.* Thomas, correspondence of, 34
Parnel, James, paper by, 233
Passau, emigration from, 207
Passern, Ludwig von, letter of, 120
Passports, *see* Emigration, laws
Patell, ship, 55
Paterson, *Brig.-Gen.*, correspondence, 257
Pattison, *Maj.* Jac., correspondence, 257
Pauli, F. H., jr., U. S. vice-consul in Lübeck, 280
Paulsen, G. H., petition of, 190
Pausch, *Maj.* G., correspondence, 120, 257
Peau de Buffle, sketch of, 126
Pedro I., emperor of Brazil, 102, 190, 300; treaty of, 289
Pedro II. of Brazil, 102
Peers, *Col.*, tries to enlist German officers for American service, 33
Pelz, Eduard, report of, 74
Penn, William, *Letter to the Committee of the Free Society of Traders of London*, 2, 3 n., 180; visits German Mennonites, 2
Pennsylvania, accounts of, 180; auxiliary German troops in, 125; coal mines, 60; constitution of, 20; German emigration to, 2, 3, 4 n., 9, 60, 84, 85, 170, 171, 198, 214, 226, 229, 234, 235, 236, 275, 295, 303, 310, 319; Hamburg consulate in, 267; inheritance cases, 229; legislature of, 55; maps, 263; Moravian missions in, 314-316; papers relating to, 52
Pennsylvania Central Rail Road, papers relating to, 63
Pennsylvania Gazette, 183
Pennsylvanien im Siebzehnten Jahrhundert, 180
Pennsylvanische Zeitung, extract from, 118
Pensacola, in the American Revolution, 183
Perlach, emigration from, 198, 200
Pernambuco, German consulates in, 244, 287, 312; papers relating to, 51
Perseverance, ship, 160
Peru, alliance with Chile, 100; consulate of Frankfort in, 312; German emigration to, 58, 62, 99, 291; papers relating to, 57, 100; relations with Hanse towns, 246, 284-285; relations with Spain, 284; treaty with Germany, 133
Petermann, *Regierungsrath* of Bayreuth, poem by, 205
Peters, Johanne Wilhelmine Elizabeth, case of, 65
Peyke, Peter, German consul in Bahia, 189
Pfärring, emigration from, 198
Pfaff, *Quartermaster* J. H., journal of, 120
Pfarrkirchen, *Landgericht*, emigration from, 207

344　　Index

Pfeifer, Karl Friedrich, emigration of, 293
Pflüger, widow, correspondence, 257
Pflügk, *Count*, of Poland, papers addressed to, 297
Pforzheim, emigration from, 229, 232
Philadelphia, accounts of, 180; emigration to, 73, 110; evacuation of, 180; German consulates, 69, 70, 79, 131, 191, 242, 267, 271, 280, 295, 300, 312; Germans in, 47; in the American Revolution, 183; mint, 240; Moravians in, 314; shipping, 59, 161, 270, 273
Philadelphische Zeitung, extracts from, 125
Philipp I., landgrave of Hesse, *see* Hesse
Philips, W. P., letter of, 120
Phillips, *Maj.-Gen.* W., correspondence, 257
Pietists, 2, 323
Pilgrim, ship, 161
Piper, *Capt.* John, quartermaster-general, correspondence, 257
Piracy, 238
Piret, Franz, chaplain of Anspach troops, 217
Pirkl, Andreas, emigration of, 200
Pirsch, *Col.* von, correspondence, 130
Pistor, Thomas Wilhelm, 147
Pitcairn, Joseph, U. S. consul in Hamburg, papers of, 268
Platen, von, of Mansfeld, papers of, 109
Plato, ship, 161
Platte, battalion, 124-125
Platzmann, H. C., circular of, 59
Plauen, U. S. consulate in, 301
Pleschen, *Kreis*, emigration papers, 158
Plitt, Georg, 190
Pöhlmann, commercial agent, petition by, 35
Pöllnitz, *Capt.* von, correspondence, 257
Pohl-Goens, emigration from, 276
Point Levis, auxiliary German troops at, 121
Pokrantz, Carl, and Co., emigration agents, 111
Poland, emigration to, 85
Polk, James K., message of, 98
Pomerania, emigration to, 85; emigration to America from, 164; shipping, 166
Porbeck, von, regiment, 129, 143
Port au Prince, Hanseatic consulate in, 246
Porto Alegre, Hanseatic consulate in, 244, 287
Porto Plata, Hanseatic consulate in, 246
Port Républicain, *see* Port au Prince
Port Smith Town, auxiliary German troops in, 250
Portsmouth, Va., Hessian troops at, 115
Posen, emigration papers, 157-159; Royal State Archives in, 157-159
Postal arrangements, for Waldeck soldiers, 149; of prince of Thurn and Taxis, 312; with Hamburg, 266
Potsdam, Amtsblatt der Königlichen Regierung zu, 73
Powhattan, ship, 231
Powl, *Brig.-Gen.*, correspondence, 257
Prätorius, Christian Julius, correspondence, 263
Prairie St. Magdelaine, auxiliary German troops in, 119
Prant, James, correspondence, 257

Preliminary Articles of Peace, between His Brittanick Majesty, and the Most Christian King, 1783, 183
President Adams, ship, 161
Preunschen, emigration from, 219
Preussisches Patent, Königlich, 78
Preussische Staats-Anzeiger, copy of, 74
Price, in Havre de Grace, emigration agent, 226
Prichsenstadt, *Amt*, emigration from, 221
Prill, Michael, emigration papers of, 87
Pringle, T., correspondence, 257
Pritchard, Agar, correspondence, 257
Providence, R. I., emigration to, 33
Prüschenck, *Lieut.-Col.* von, correspondence, 257
Prussia, arms sold to United States by, 24, 33, 36; army papers, 76, 77; consuls in, of U. S., 47, 108; consuls of, in U. S., 32, 33, 34, 36, 38, 39, 47, 48, 58, 59, 64, 69, 70, 79, 81, 107, 108; emigration to America from, 35, 48, 49, 50, 51, 52, 53, 57, 58, 59; government of, 17; inheritance question with U. S., 33, 33; linen trade, 42; means of transportation in, 22; negotiations with American agents abroad, 18-30; recognition of U. S. by, 24, 25, 28; relations with U. S., 7, 34, 40, 41, 82; Royal State Archives of, 17-172; shipping, 20, 26, 27, 31, 35, 41, 42, 62, 108; soldiers of, in America, 35, 64, 65 ff.; trade with America, 20, 30, 32, 33, 34, 35, 36, 38, 40, 41, 42, 43, 44, 46, 47, 48; treaties with U. S., 30, 43, 44, 45, 79, 81, 188; *see also* Germany; names of particular places; names of the respective kings
Prussian commercial treaty, importance of, 79; papers relating to, 81
Prussian Marine Insurance Co., 47
Puerto Cabello, Hanseatic consulate in, 246
Punto Arenas, Hanseatic consulate in, 247
Purchase of Public Lands, 63
Puttkammer, papers relating to, 57

Quakers, 2, 232, 233, 296
Quebec, auxiliary German troops in, 119; immigration office papers, 61; shipping, 59; siege of, 178
Quincy, *Col.* John, correspondence, 257
Quintal, *Capt.* Michael, correspondence, 257

Rademaker, Anton Joseph, Brazilian consul in Hanse towns, 244, 288
Railroads, U. S. transcontinental, 41
Rainsford, *Col.*, letter of, 118
Rall, Hessian brigade of, 112; regiment of, 103
Rall, *Col.* Johann Gottlieb, 142; correspondence, 112
Ramsay, George William, correspondence, 257
Rappists, 311
Raquette, sketch of, 126
Rasche and Shée, Philadelphia merchants, reports of, 298
Rauschenplat, *Lieut.-Col.* Georg von, correspondence, 257

Index

Ravenhorst inheritance case, 33
Rechberg, *Count* de, correspondence, 187
Rechtenbach, Polycarp Michael, papers of, 299
Reed, Joseph, correspondence, 112
Regen, *Landgericht*, emigration from, 207
Regensburg, emigration from, 181, 201
Reichelsheim, emigration from, 276
Reichert, Gottlieb Friedrich, inheritance claim by, 36
Reid, *Dr.* A., papers of, 56
Reiffurth, *Capt.*, correspondence, 114
Reinking, *Lieut.* F. C., correspondence, 257
Reinwald, Korbinian, emigration of, 198
Rendel, emigration from, 277
Repp, N., petition of, 221
Reppert, Georg, widow of, emigration papers, 85
Retterweil, emigration from, 277
Reuss, archives of principalities of, 293; emigration from, 293
Rheinbach, *Landratsamt*, emigration papers, 94
Rheinisch-Westindische Handels-Gesellschaft, papers of, 150; reference to, 297
Rheinkreis, emigration from, 207
Rheinländisch Westindisch Handels-gesellschaft, papers of, 167
Rheinpfalz, *see* Palatinate
Rhetz, *Lieut.-Gen.* August Wilhelm von, correspondence, 257
Rhetz, von, regiment of, 103
Rhine, French department of the, papers of, 92, 94
Rhine, Lower, emigration from, 49, 226
Rhine, Middle, emigration from, 230
Rhode Island, Germans in, 47; Hessian troops in, 118
Rice, *Capt.*, correspondence, 257
Richard, Clemens, papers of, 58
Richmond, Va., Hanseatic agents in, 242, 268
Ricker, Samuel, U. S. consul in German free cities, 280
Riebeck, Gustav, Brazilian vice-consul in Lübeck, 288
Riedeln, Dorothea Sophia, inheritance case of, 33
Riedesel, Charles von, brother of the general, correspondence, 257
Riedesel, D. R. von, sister-in-law of the general, correspondence, 257
Riedesel, *Maj.-Gen.* Friedrich Adolph von, correspondence and papers of, 118, 119, 120, 248-263
Riedesel, *Col.* Johannes Conrad von, correspondence, 257
Riedesel Papers, 248-263
Riensch, Rücker, and Co., claims of, 241
Rinteln, emigration from, 141
Rio de Janeiro, German consulates in, 55, 83, 189, 191, 243, 286-287, 312; German school in, 159; immigration, 55
Rio de la Plata, *see* La Plata
Rio Grande do Norte, Hanseatic consulate in, 244

Rio Grande do Sul, Hanseatic consulate in, 244, 287; laws of, 58
Rising Sun, ship, 270
Ristau, Johann, case of, 62
Ritter, *Lieut.*, journal of, 122
Ritter, C., letter of, 48
Ritter, J., papers concerning, 220
Ritter, J., wife of, emigration of, 220
Rives, William C., speech of, 43
Rivinus, *Dr.*, U. S. consul at Dresden, complaint of, 47
Robinson, Christopher, document of, 62
Rochow, von, correspondence of, 53, 54
Rockenberg, emigration from, 276
Rocque, John, map by, 263
Rodewald, Lübeck consul in Montevideo, 286
Rodewald, Friedrich, Hamburg consul in Baltimore, 268; letter of, 239
Rodheim, emigration from, 277
Röder, *Baron* Carl von, and emigration to America, 311
Rödgen, emigration from, 276
Römer, Emil, case of, 67
Rönne, *Baron* von, Prussian minister, correspondence and papers of, 40, 43, 44, 48, 70, 167
Roer, French department of the, papers of, 95
Rösch, Andreas, emigration of, 202
Rösing, *Dr.* Johannes, Hanseatic minister to U. S., 241, 242, 280
Rogers, *Maj.* Jac., correspondence, 257
Roman Catholic Church, 1, 2
Romrod, *Col.* Carl von, correspondence, 257
Roohr, deputy inspector-general, correspondence, 257
Rooten, Hermann, Uruguayan consul in Hamburg, 286
Ross, *Col.*, correspondence, 257
Ross, John, consul of Hamburg in U. S., 267
Ross, M. D., contract of, 61
Rothenburg, *Bezirksamt*, emigration from, 213
Rothenfels, *Gericht*, emigration from, 221
Rottenburg, *Landgericht*, emigration from, 207
Rotthalmünster, *Landgericht*, emigration from, 207
Rouen, insurance companies at, 20
Roussel, J. B., correspondence, 258
Royal Gazette, copies of, 115
Rudolph, Johann, Lübeck consul in Mexico, 282
Rudolstadt, *Allgemeine Auswanderer-Zeitung*, copy of, 59
Rudolstadt, Schwarzburg-Rudolstadt Archives in, 302
Rübel, Jacob, case of, 60
Rücker, Samuel, U. S. consul in Hesse, 132
Rücker, Riensch, and Co., claims of, 241
Rüdiger, Johann August, petition of, 293
Ruff, Johannes Conrad, correspondence, 258
Runkel, Dutch envoy, correspondence, 143
Runken, F. C. A., Brazilian vice-consul in Bremen, 244
Rupanus, Balthazar, paper by, 236
Russia, attitude of, towards the American Revolution, 37; emigration to, 319; papers

relating to emigration to, 235; relations with U. S., 8; treaties with Great Britain, 177; treaties with U. S., 99
Rust, Christian, complaints of, 63

Sá, Miguel Tito de, Hanseatic consul in Rio Grande de S. Pedro do Sul, 287
Saabye, Hans Rudolph, U. S. consul-general at Copenhagen, papers of, 67
Saarbrücken, emigration to America from, 51, 85
Sack, Count von, botanist, 46
Sack, Oberpräsident, correspondence, 167
Saile, Martin, 163
St. Augustine, plan of, 118
St. Barbara, lazaret of, military papers, 83
St. John, Isle of, 182
St. John, N. B., papers relating to, 243
St. John's, prov. Quebec, 250-260 passim
St. Lawrence river, boundary disputes concerning, 176
St. Lawrence, ship, 239
St. Leger, Col. Barry, correspondence, 255
St. Louis, description of, 48; German consulates in, 47, 131, 196, 242, 264, 280; German societies, 62; harbor of, 62; shipping, 59; trade, 71
St. Morris, Fort, plan of, 118
St. Onges, Gen., correspondence, 258
St. Thomas, expeditions to, 53; papers relating to, 243
Salem, N. C., Moravian mission in, diaries, 316
Salisbury, Pa., Moravians in, 315
Salvador, relations with Hanse towns, 283; treaty with Germany, 133
Salzburgers, 194, 196; emigration of, to Georgia, 4
Salzwedel, Kreis, emigration petitions, 110
Samson, consul of Brunswick in U. S., instructions for, 264
Samter, Kreis, emigration papers, 158
San Blas, Hanseatic agent in, 246
Sande, Mr., in the Hague, correspondence, 143
Sandwich, Earl, correspondence, 258
San Francisco, German consulates in, 131, 242, 280, 294; harbor of, 70
San José, Hanseatic consulate in, 247
San Juan de Puerto Rico, Hanseatic agent in, 242
San Luiz, Hanseatic consulate in, 287
San Roman, Don Miguel, president of Peru, 100
Santiago de Cuba, Hanseatic agent in, 242
Santo Domingo, conditions in, 298
Santos, Hanseatic consulate in, 244, 287
Santo Tomas, Hanseatic consulate in, 247
Saratoga, capitulation of, 262
Sardinia, treaty with U. S., 190
Sargent, speech of, 43
Sartorius, Lieut., journal of, 117; letters of, 120, 258
Sasse, G., papers concerning, 39, 40
Saucier, Louis, correspondence, 258
Sauer, Johann Georg, emigration papers concerning, 202

Saunders, A., correspondence, 258
Saur, C. H., correspondence, 258
Savannah, Hanseatic agents in, 242, 268; in the American Revolution, 182; plan of, 118
Saxe-Altenburg, Ducal Government Archives of (in Altenburg), 293
Saxe-Coburg-Gotha, Ducal Saxon House and State Archives of (in Coburg and Gotha), 293
Saxe-Eisenach, Prince of, decree respecting emigration, 84
Saxe-Gotha, Prince of, regiment, 128
Saxe-Meiningen, consulates in U. S., 294; emigration from, 294; Privy State Archives of (in Meiningen), 294
Saxe-Weimar-Eisenach, consulates in U. S., 295; emigration from, 295; Grand-Ducal and Ducal Saxon State Archives of (in Weimar), 295; see also Bernhard, duke of Saxe-Weimar
Saxony (kingdom of), emigration to America from, 48, 296, 297, 300, 301; relations with U. S., 297, 298, 300; Royal Saxon Central State Archives of (in Dresden), 296-301; U. S. consulates in, 301
Sayn Altenkirchen, emigration to America from, 84
Sayre, Stephen, correspondence of, 21, 22, 24
Schaabye, Andreas, ship of, 162
Schaar, F. C., Ecuadorian consul in Hanse towns, 284
Schachten, von, letter of, 120
Schäfer, from Magdeburg, emigration case of, 110
Schäfer, from Lohr, emigration of, 220
Schäfer, Carl, colonizer, 98
Schäffer, Georg Anton von, Brazilian agent in Hanse towns, 8, 102, 186, 244, 287
Schäffner, P. W., diary of, 116
Schaffner, Jacob, suspected emissary, 310
Schank, Johann, correspondence, 258
Schaumburg-Lippe, Archives of Ministry of (in Bückeburg), 302
Scheffer, document by, 112
Scheffler, Martin Ernst Gottfried, case of, 75; indenture by, 35; petition by, 35
Scheibler, Georg, papers concerning, 220
Scheither, Lieut.-Col., 105
Schellbass, Dr. Carl Julius, attaché at Washington, 241
Schellow, Friedrich, U. S. consul at Stettin, 108
Scherhammerin, Maria Magdalena, emigration case of, 85
Scheuermann, Franz Anton, petition of, 221
Schiedig, Franz, emigration of, 219
Schiel, K., emigration of, 220
Schiffahrts-Abgaben, Bericht der Deputation wegen Revision der Accise und, 239
Schildberg, Kreis, emigration papers, 158
Schlagenteufel, Capt., 258
Schleiden, Dr. Rudolph, Hanseatic minister to U. S., 241, 280, 281
Schleswig, Royal State Archives in, 160-162

Index 347

Schleswig and Holstein, emigration papers, 160; shipping, 161, 162
Schleswig-Holsteinische Blätter, copy of, 160
Schlieffen, *Lieut.-Gen.* von, of Hesse, correspondence, 103
Schlochau, *Landratsamt*, emigration papers, 90
Schlosser, emigration papers of, 232
Schmalkalden, emigration from, 141
Schmidt, *Capt.*, correspondence, 258
Schmidt, Andreas, emigration case of, 110
Schmidt, F. W., Hamburg consul in New Orleans, 268
Schmidt, *Hofmeister* Fr., correspondence, 258
Schmidt, Heinrich Carl, civil engineer, letter of, 61
Schmidt, Johann Jost, case of, 170
Schmidt, Johann Wilhelm, Prussian and Hamburg consul in New York, 47, 268; correspondence of, 41, 45, 55, 64; reports of, 70, 71
Schmidt, *Maj.-Gen.* Martin Conrad, 113
Schmied, Anton, emigration case of, 194
Schmitt, Bartholomäus, petition of, 221
Schneider, Anna Gottliebe, inheritance case of, 36
Schneider, Peter, emigration of, 220
Schneitler, C. P., papers of, 57
Schöle, von, Hessian officer, correspondence, 258
Schöll, von, letter of, 120
Schömckell, Georg Conrad, 147
Schömckell, Johann Conrad, 147
Schönberg, Hans Carl Alexander, letter of, 296
Schöneck, Moravians in, diaries, 314, 315
Schönfeld, letter of, 298
Schönning, *Cammer Präsident* von, 166
Scholtz, papers of, 49
Schriever, Christian, Hanseatic consul in Bahia, 287
Schrimm, *Kreis*, emigration papers, 158
Schroda, *Kreis*, emigration papers, 158
Schroeder, Carl Hermann, U. S. consul in Lübeck, 281
Schuckmann, letter of, 49
Schuckmann, von, letters of, 69
Schütt, Friedrich Eduard, Buenos Aires consul in Hamburg, 285
Schulenburg, *Baron*, Prussian minister, correspondence, 18, 19, 20, 21, 22, 23, 24, 25, 26, 27, 28, 29, 30, 31, 32, 38; negotiations with Lee, 7; papers of, 165, 166
Schultheis, paper of, 49
Schultz, *Captain*, of the *Ceres*, 46, 75
Schultze, J. E. C., German consul in Baltimore, 7, 34, 81, 82
Schulz, Ludwig Anton, emigration of, 293
Schulze, consul in New Orleans, offer of, 100
Schumacher, of Baltimore, letter of, 48
Schumacher, consul of Hamburg in U. S., 267
Schuyler, *Maj.-Gen.* Philip, correspondence, 258
Schwabach, *Bezirksamt*, emigration from, 213
Schwaben, *Regierungsbezirk*, emigration from, 210

Schwalheim, emigration from, 276
Schwarzburg-Rudolstadt, Privy Archives of (in Rudolstadt), 302
Schwarzburg-Sondershausen, Archives of (in Sondershausen), 302
Schweinfurt, emigration from, 221
Schwenckfelder, Edict wegen Unterbringung und Placirung der so genannten, 78
Schwenkfeld, Caspar, 2
Schwenkfelders, papers relating to, 4, 81
Schwerin, *Count* Wilhelm of, correspondence, 322
Schwerin, Grand-Ducal Privy and Central Archives of Mecklenburg-Schwerin in, 291
Schwertfeger, Johann Conrad, widow of, 147
Schwetz, *Landratsamt*, emigration papers, 90
Sclaven in Amerika, Die Befreiten, 240
Scotland, linen industry, 79
Scott, Edward, correspondence, 258
Scott, T. C. W., correspondence, 258
Seckendorff, H. von, plans of, 7, 297
Seckendorff, 47
Seddon, George, cabinet maker, correspondence, 258
Seebisch, *Maj.* von, 146
Seeland, Jacob, petition of, 229
Seibert, von, of Frankfort, protest of, 35
Seifert, Christiane Friedrike, emigration of, 293
Seitz, von, correspondence, 114
Seitz, von, regiment, 129
Senf, Christian, correspondence, 263
Separatists, papers of, 79
Seward, William Henry, secretary of state, complaint by, 191; correspondence, 60
Shée, Rasche and, Philadelphia merchants, reports of, 298
Shelburne, *Earl* of, correspondence, 258
Sherwood, *Capt.* J., correspondence, 258
Shipping, *see* under names of particular countries and places
Siegler, Sebastian, petition of, 220
Sigismund, archbishop of Salzburg, correspondence, 181
Sigmaringen, emigration to America from, 163; Royal State Archives of, 163
Silbermann, A. R., petition of, 221
Silesia, deserters, 78; emigration from, 78; military papers, 78; *Publicandum betreffend die den Ausländern bei ihrem Anzuge in Schlesien*, 78; trade with America, 80
Silva Caldeira, Antonio da, Brazilian consul in Hanse towns, 244, 288
Simbach, *Landgericht*, emigration from, 207
Sinde, E., correspondence of, 38
Skeenes, *Col.* Benjamin, correspondence, 258
Slade, in Havre, colonization agent, 51
Slavery papers, 132, 288-289
Smith, *Dr.* George, correspondence, 258
Smith, Reuben, arrest of, 161
Smith, Richard, paper by, 71
Snydacker, Gottfrey, application of, 241
Södel, emigration from, 276

Soest, *Kreis*, emigration papers, 150
Sohren, Alberthal von, case of, 85
Solingen, *Landratsamt*, emigration papers, 95
Solms, *Count*, papers of, 102
Solms, and Co., Strassburg and Philadelphia colonization agents, 51
Solms, von. regiment, 143
Sommer, John Jac., house of, papers relating to, 36
Sondershausen, Schwarzburg-Sondershausen Archives in, 302
Sotheron, *Capt.*, correspondence, 258
Soublette, Carlos, vice-president of Venezuela, document by, 289
South America, German consulates in, 108; German emigration to, 54; German trade in, 133, 150; Indians in, 323, 324; relations with Hesse, 131, 132; trade, 40; *see also* names of particular countries and places
South Australia, *Darstellung der neuen Colonie*, 53
South Australian Company, director of, report of, 52
South Carolina, agricultural society of, 238; Declaration of Independence of, 41; *Freiheiten welche die Regierung zu Süd-Carolina, etc.*, 310; German emigration to, 170, 291; Moravians in, 316; rice trade, 238; secession of, 99; trade, 42, 47; *see also* Carolinas
Souza, Ygnacio José Alves de, jr., Brazilian consul in Hanse towns, 244
Souza Pinto, Ignacio Alves de, Hanseatic consul in Rio Grande do Sul, at S. Pedro do Sul, 287
Spahrmann, Gottlob Friedrich, papers relating to, 63
Spain, ambassador to England, manifesto of, 182; attitude towards American Revolution, 37; relations with South America, 100; trade with Germany, 83
Spangenberg, garrison papers, 76
Spangenberg, *Lieut.* C. D., letters of, 120
Spanish America, accounts of, 299; German trade in, 79; *see also* names of particular countries and places
Specht, Anton, officer, correspondence of, 258
Specht, Anton Christoph, correspondence, 258
Specht, *Col.* J. H., correspondence, 258
Specht, von, correspondence, 263
Specht, von, regiment of, 103
"Spediteurs", 57
Spener, Jacob, 2
Speth, *Maj.-Gen.* Ernst Ludwig Wilhelm Friedrich von, correspondence, 258
Speyer, Royal Bavarian Provincial (Circuit), Archives of the Palatinate in, 214-215
Speyer, John, proposal by, 36
Spielmann, Leonhard, emigration papers of, 310
Spies, Anna Maria, emigration of, 219
Spiess, Philipp Ernst, 204
Splittgerber, gun-merchant, 24, 25, 26
Spörken, *Fieldmarshal* von, report of, 103, 104, 105

Sponheim Baden Sohren, emigration to America from, 84
Sprengelmeyer family, emigration to America of, 156
Sprotto, Venezuelan consul in Hamburg, 284
Sprotto, G. P., Bavarian consul in La Guayra, 189
Staden, emigration from, 276
Stadtseinach, *Bezirksamt*, emigration papers, 206
Stamford, *Capt.*, 114
Stammheim, emigration from, 277
Stapleton, John, deputy adjutant-general, correspondence, 258
Staten Island, Moravians on, 314
Statistische Notizen über den Handel der Vereinigten Staaten und Venezuela, 238
Stecker, *Dr.*, paper by, 52
Steffen, P. J., papers concerning, 60
Steffens, tries to buy cloth in Germany, 21
Steiger, *Capt.*, emigration papers concerning, 50
Steigerwald, Georg, petition of, 220
Stein, *Lieut.-Gen.*, 143
Stein, *Maj.* von, correspondence, 258
Steinfurth, emigration from, 277
Steinmetz, Prussian consul at Charleston, 47
Stendal, *Kreis*, emigration petitions, 110
Stetten, *Baron* von, letter of, 217; reports, 218
Stettin, Royal Prussian State Archives of the Province of Pomerania in, 164-167
Steuben, *Maj.-Gen.* Wilhelm von, papers of, 29, 66
Steuber, *Auditeur*, correspondence, 114
Stilke, *Baron*, director in Magdeburg, correspondence of, 28
Stillwater, auxiliary German troops at, 119
Stirling, *Lord*, *see* Alexander, *Maj.-Gen.* William
Stockmeyer, Christian, Hanseatic consul in Rio de Janeiro, 243
Stöck, Joseph, papers of, 59
Stöcken, Bodo Wilhelm, and emigration to South Carolina, 310
Stöver, T. C., book by, 295
Stohlman, Friedrich, papers by, 52
Stolterfoht, August, Brazilian consul in Lübeck, 287
Stono Ferry, in the American Revolution, 182
Stranger, ship, 162
Strangways, W. Fox, letter of, 132
Strassburg, District Archives of Lower Alsace in, 224-227; emigration from, 90
Straubing, emigration from, 207, 208
Strauch, T. C., paper by, 231
Strecker, *Dr.*, papers of, 52
Struensee, correspondence of, 29, 32, 38
Stuhlmann, G. E., Hanseatic consul in Rio de Janeiro, 243, 287
Stuhm, *Landratsamt*, emigration papers, 90
Sturmfelz, Johann Paul, letter of, 85
Stutterheim, in Dresden, letters of, 298

Stuttgart, emigration from, 304; Royal Privy House and State Archives of Württemberg in, 303
Stuttgarter Zeitung, copy of, 187; extracts from, 49
Stutzer, *Cornet* J. B., correspondence, 258
Suffolk, *Lord,* correspondence, 258
Sulzer, Louis, Hanseatic consul in Mexico, 282
Sunday London Gazette and Weekly Monitor, copy of, 184
Surinam, German emigration to, 231
Suscombe, John, correspondence of, 56
Susquehanna, emigration to the, 226
Sutherland, *Col.,* correspondence, 258
Swan, *Col.* James, commercial plan of, 34; lands of, 50
Sweden, treaty with U. S., 30
Swiss reformers, 2
Switzerland, emigration to America from, 49, 50, 56; *see also* names of respective cantons and towns
Sydow, papers of, 52

Tampico, Hanseatic agent in, 246, 282
Tanswell, Jacob, correspondence, 258
Tariff, 42, 43, 44, 45, 46, 81; *Commissions-Bericht über den Vereinszolltarif,* 44; *Gesetz der Ver. Staaten von Nordamerica,* 44; in Mexico, 82
Tausent, Friedrich Carl, paper by, 311
Tecklenburg, *Kreis,* emigration papers , 153
Telegraph, single-wire, 45
Tellkampf, *Dr.* Th. A., papers of, 57
Ten-Brink, I. H. Chr., Hanseatic consul in Rio de Janeiro, 243, 287
Tepic, Hanseatic agent in, 246
Tewitz family, case of, 155
Texas, German emigration to, 8, 9, 54, 58, 61, 62, 72, 73, 139, 164, 172, 219, 230, 231, 237, 295; German societies in, 62; papers relating to, 55, 59; relations with Hanse towns, 247, 279, 280; treaty with Lübeck, 279
Texas Verein, publications of, 279; settlements by the, 139, 230
Theobald, chaplain in Hessian army, letter of, 118
Theobald, Hesse-Hanau officer, correspondence, 258
Theodore, F., curé, correspondence, 258
Theremin, Prussian consul in Rio de Janeiro, report of, 55
Thiele, Richard, Hessian consul in New Orleans, 131
Thieriot, Jacob Heinrich, emigration agent, 297
Thieriot, Philipp, Saxon commissioner of trade in Philadelphia, 7; paper of, 297, 298
Thirty Years' War, 1, 2
Tholen, C., correspondence, 63
Thomae, *Capt.* A. J., correspondence, 259
Thomas Wilson, ship, 161
Thommen, Catharina, letter of, 236
Thommen, Durss, letter of, 236
Thommen, Joggi, letter of, 237

Thomson, Charles, papers of, 114, 267
Thon, Eduard, emigration agent, 111
Thorn, *Landratsamt,* emigration papers, 90-91; industries in, 91
Three Rivers, auxiliary German troops at, 117
Thürriegel, Johann Caspar, paper by, 235
Thulemeier, *Sieur* de, correspondence of, 30, 31, 32
Thurn and Taxis, *Prince* of, postal arrangements with America, 312
Ticonderoga, battle of, 23; Fort Carillon, plan, 125, 126; French at, 178
Tischler, from Magdeburg, emigration case of, 110
Tobacco, market of Cincinnati, 71; trade, 18, 19, 23, 31, 44, 45, 83
Tohlmann, Chr. Ad., Brazilian agent in Bremen, 244
Tolcahuano, Hanseatic consulate in, 247
Tolmé, Charles David, U. S. vice-consul in Hamburg, 271
Tonnacourt, George, correspondence, 259
Torriano, *Lieut.* Charles, correspondence, 259
Trade, *see* under names of particular countries and places
Trais, emigration from, 277
Transatlantic marine societies, 134
Trapmann, Louis, Hamburg consul in U. S., 268
Trappists, 195
Treasury Circular and Navigation Act, 238
Trendelenburg, *Quartermaster,* correspondence, 130
Trenton, battle of, 19, 112, 113, 118, 122; Hessian troops in, 117
Trevor, John, 175
Trier, electorate of, 86; emigration from, 48, 49; revenues of electors, 299
Trier, Amtsblatt der Regierung zu, 51
Trinidad, Hanseatic agent in, 242
Trötsch, Katharine, emigration of, 202
Trois Rivières, *see* Three Rivers
Trottig, *Capt.* Jean, correspondence, 259
Trümbach, von, regiment, 128, 143
Tunderfeld, *Capt.* Carl von, correspondence, 259
Turner Halls, closing of, 8
Tuttle, Stephen, correspondence, 259
Twiss, *Capt.* W., correspondence, 259
Tyler, *President* John, correspondence of, 44
Tyler, *Lieut.* W., correspondence, 259
Tzschoppe, letter of, 71

Ukersdorf, emigration to America from, 170
Ulloa, Juan José, 100
Ulm, emigration from, 181
Ulrici, C., and Co., letter of, 48
Ungar, S. A., journal of, 124
Unger, *Lieut.* von, correspondence, 259
United States, agents of, in Europe, negotiations of, 18, 19, 20, 21, 22, 23, 24, 25, 26, 27, 28, 29, 30; army papers, 35, 64, 65 ff., 69; Articles of Confederation, 20; arts, inventions, patents, 70, 71; boundary disputes, 70; commercial and diplomatic re-

lations with Germany, 6-10, 40, 41, 82, 238, 239, 240, 241, 242, 279-281, 294, 297, 298, 300; commercial and diplomatic relations with Great Britain, 40, 45; consulates in, German, 34, 36, 38, 39, 47, 48, 58, 59, 64, 69, 70, 79, 81, 97, 107, 108, 131, 132, 133, 134, 150, 171, 172, 188, 205, 241, 242, 264, 267, 268, 271, 280, 281, 312; consulates of, in Germany, 47, 108, 132, 137, 162, 187, 269, 270, 271, 292; extradition papers, 99, 134, 189; finance, 41, 42, 69, 70, 185, 238, 240; German ministers in, 160; immigration laws, 50, 58, 60, 62, 63, 98; inheritance question with Prussia, 35; lawsuits, 67 ff.; majority age in, 100; navy papers, 165; Oregon dispute papers, 41; politics, 33, 41, 45, 70, 98, 99, 114, 160, 239; postal papers, 239, 266, 311, 312; public lands, 41, 63; recognition of, 24, 25, 27, 28; relations with Russia, 8; secession movement in, 41, 46; slavery, 41, 42, 240; statistics, 38, 70; Supreme Court decisions, 42; tariff, 8, 42, 43, 44, 45, 46, 47, 79, 98, 239, 240, 267, 309; taxes, 42; trade-laws, 46; Treasury Bill of 1840, 70; Treasury reports, 43; treaty with Argentina, 239; treaty with Denmark, 238; treaties with German states, 36, 43, 44, 45, 81, 133, 185, 188, 289; treaties with Great Britain, 183, 184; treaty with Russia, 99; treaty with Sardinia, 190; treaty with Sweden, 30; *see also* America; American Revolution; Emigration; Germany; names of particular countries, states, and places
Upton, George, letter of, 189
Uruguay, Hanseatic consulate in, 244; relations with Hanse towns, 247, 286; relations with Hesse, 132; trade with Oldenburg, 292; treaty with Germany, 133
Uslor, von, Hanoverian trade agent in Mexico, 102
Utica, State Convention of Mechanics at, *Proceedings*, 52
Utz, George, papers relating to, 35

Valdicielso, José Ignacio, Mexican consul in Hanse towns, 282
Valdivia, Hanseatic consulate in, 247; settlement in, German, 62
Vallancy, *Capt.*, quartermaster-general, correspondence, 259
Valparaiso, Bavarian manufacturers in, 190; Hanseatic consuls in, 247, 284
Van Alstine, *Maj.* Peter, letters of, 250
Van Buren, *President* Martin, correspondence of, 44
Vanolles, de, correspondence, 224
Vaudreuil, *Marquis* de, French commander in America, 177
Veldenz, Ludwig Leopold, count palatine of, document by, 216-217
Velten, Peter, request of, 84, 85
Venezuela, German emigration to, 54; papers relating to, 99; relations with German states, 137, 246, 283, 284, 289; trade, 137; treaties with German states, 133

Venezuela, *Statistische Notizen über den Handel der Vereinigten Staaten und*, 238
Vera Cruz, Hanseatic agent in, 245, 282
Vera Paz, territory of, in Central America, 53
Verreau, Joseph, priest, correspondence, 259
Versailles, treaty signed at, 179, 183
Vesputius, Americus, journey of, 308
Vianna de Lima, *Chevalier*, Brazilian representative in Hesse and the Hanse towns, 131, 244
Victoria, British province in Central America, 53
Victoria, the New British Colony (Central America), 53
Viechtach, *Landgericht*, emigration from, 208
Vienna, congress of 1815, 7
Vilsbiburg, *Landgericht*, emigration from, 208
Vilshofen, *Landgericht*, emigration from, 208
Vincke, *Ober-Präsident* von, of Münster, correspondence of, 51, 150; paper of, 152
Virginia, Moravians in, 316; tobacco trade, 18, 19, 23
Völker, Joseph, emigration of, 200
Vogel, C. H., correspondence, 259
Vogel, Charles H., complaint of, 266
Vogel, Wilhelm, Hamburg consul in New Orleans, 268; Prussian consul there, 58
Voigt, registrar, correspondence, 259
Voigt, Joh. Andr., correspondence, 259
Volkeniers, Dutch envoy, correspondence, 143
Voogt, Peters and Cons., paper by, 297
Vultejus, in the Hague, correspondence, 143

Wachovia, Moravian missions in, 316
Waddington, B., correspondence, 259
Wätjen, Hermann, Brazilian vice-consul in Bremen, 244
Wagner, letter of, 117
Wagner, H., letter of, 130
Wagner, Philipp, emigration case of, 85
Wagner, Th., Hessian consul in Galveston, 131
Waitz, papers of, 52
Walch, Matthew, master, correspondence, 259
Waldbroel, *Landratsamt*, emigration papers, 95
Waldeck, see English-Waldeck Regiment
Waldeck, archives of, *see* Marburg
Waldeck, Eduard, 47
Waldenmeyer, Andreas, petition of, 229
Waldenses, 2
Waldo, Samuel, and the New England Colony, 169, 275, 322
Wallace, Hugh Alexander, correspondence, 259
Wallace, Moses Abraham, correspondence, 259
Walloons, in Mannheim, 320
Wallop, *Maj.* B. H., correspondence, 259
Wallrab, Johannes, colonizer, 275
Walpole, Thomas, 175
Wangerland, ship, 62
Wangermann, opinion of, 112
Wanzleben, *Kreis*, emigration petitions, 110
Ward, Richard, paper of, 238

Index 351

War Declared against Great Britain by the United States, 188
Warmholtz, agent in the Hague, correspondence, 144
Warncke, A., Lübeck consul in Arequipa, 284
Warner, Levi, correspondence, 259
War of 1812, papers relating to, 188
Washington, *Gen.* George, army of, 114, 180; correspondence of, 184, 259; letter of resignation, 184; papers concerning, 23, 25, 205
Washington, ship, 162
Washington *Madisonian*, extracts from, 45
Washington Monument, papers concerning, 240
Washington *National Intelligencer*, extracts from, 62
Wasmus, Johann Friedrich, surgeon, correspondence, 259
Wasmus, Julius Friedrich, paper by, 265
Watson, Brook, correspondence, 259
Watson, Josiah, correspondence, 259
Watterbach, emigration from, 221
Weber, Carl N. L., Guatemalan consul in Hanse towns, 283
Webster, Daniel, speech of, 43
Weckbach, emigration from, 219, 221
Wegener, O. A., document by, 119
Wegscheid, *Landgericht,* emigration from, 208
Weiden, *Landgericht,* emigration from, 202
Weilbach, emigration from, 219
Weimar, Grand-Ducal and Ducal Saxon State Archives of Saxe-Weimar-Eisenach in, 295
Weinschenk, G. C., emigration petition of, 110
Weise, *Capt.*, correspondence, 259
Weisskopf, emigration agent, letter of, 226
Welderen, von, agent in the Hague, correspondence, 144
Wellinghoff, H. F., letters of, 63
Wellmann, Jobst Heinrich, 155
Wells, David A., pamphlet of, on the tariff, 240
Welser family archives, 1, 13
Weltmann, Carl, Brazilian vice-consul in Bremen, 244
Wende, C., quartermaster, correspondence, 259; journal of, 120
Wendel, Ferdinand, emigration petition of, 154
Wenz, James, application of, 241
Werkesheim, emigration from, 276
Werneck, Louis Peixoto de Lacerda, Brazilian consul in Hesse, 132
Werner, Gottfried, correspondence of, 50
Werner, Prussian consul in Havre, correspondence, 55
Werner, von, emigration project of, 53
Wernigerode, *Kreis*, emigration petitions, 110
Wertheim, emigration from, 311
Werther, von, correspondence, 137
Wesel, emigration papers, passports, 95, 96
Weser-Zeitung, extracts from, 44, 45, 54, 56
Wessenbacher, Michael, emigration of, 229
Westensee, P. F. H., correspondence, 259
West Indies, German consulates in, 108; German emigration to, 164, 297; German trade in, 36, 79, 150, 166; trade with U. S., 42, 167; war in, 179
Westphalen, *Ensign* Georg Philip von, correspondence, 259
Westphalia, consulates in U. S., 150; emigration papers, 150-153; peace of, 1
Wettenhausen, emigration from, 210
Wettstein, paper of, 236
Wetzlar, Royal Prussian State Archives in, 168
Wheaton, Henry, U. S. minister at Berlin, 44; correspondence, 43, 44, 55, 97, 137, 239
White, Georg Christoph, property of, case of, 7, 29
Wichelhausen, F. Y., and Co., emigration agents, 111
Wicke, Wilhelm, soldier, correspondence, 259
Wickelhausen, Hieronymus Daniel, Lübeck consul in U. S., 280
Wider das Mord-, Raub-, und Diebs-Volk, 235
Wied, see Neuwied
Wied, Daniel, correspondence, 260
Wied, Hermann, prince of, document of, 73
Wiederhold, *Lieut.* William, 115
Wied-Neuwied, *Count* Friedrich Alexander, contract of, 322
Wiegand, *Quartermaster*, 148
Wieksbadt, emigration from, 276
Wiesbaden, Royal State Archives in, 169-172
Wiesenthal, emigration from, 221
Wieterscheim, *Capt.* von, correspondence, 260
Wieting, Johann Christoph, papers concerning, 34
Wilberforce, ship, 61
Wilcke, E. H. von, papers of, 129
Wilcke, von, regiment, 129
Wildunger Brunnen, the, documents on, 149
Wilhelm, count of Hanau, see Hesse-Hanau, counts of
Wilhelm, *Count* von Schwerin, see Schwerin
Wilhelm VIII., landgrave of Hesse-Cassel, see Hesse-Cassel
Wilhelm IX., landgrave of Hesse-Cassel, see Hesse-Cassel
Wilhelmine, ship, 50
William, ship, 161
William I., king of the Netherlands, decree of, 297
William Nelson, ship, 60
Williams, Samuel, U. S. consul in Hamburg, 269
Willmanns, Heinrich, papers relating to, 33
Willoe, Samuel, correspondence, 260
Wills, Melvin and, correspondence, 256
Wills and Co., emigration agents, 311
Wills and Co., of Amsterdam, papers concerning, 35
Wilmanns, A. G., Hanoverian consul of Milwaukee, 241
Wilmowsky, *Maj.* von, correspondence, 260
Wilseck, *Landgericht*, emigration from, 201
Wilson, James, U. S. vice-consul in Hamburg, 271
Winkelmann, correspondence, 260

352   *Index*

Winslow, Joshua, correspondence, 260
Winzingerode, *Col.* von, correspondence, 260
Wisconsin, German consulates in, 241, 280, 294, 312; German emigration to, 60
Wisselsheim, emigration from, 276
Wissenbach, von, regiment of, 104
Wisserbach, *Maj.-Gen.* von, 143
Wiszmann, insurance agent at Stettin, complaint of, 47
Witte, Heinrich Wilhelm, Brazilian consul in Bremen, 244
Wittgenstein, *Count*, in Berlin, correspondence, 150
Wittgenstein, *Kreis*, emigration papers, 151
Wittgenstein, Salomon, lawsuit of, 67
Wittlage, *Amt*, emigration papers, 155
Wittlage-Hunterburg, *Amt*, emigration papers, 155
Wittlicher Intelligenz Blatt, extract from, 60
Wittman, Bernhard, emigration of, 203
Wölfersheim, emigration from, 277
Wöllner, *Finanzrath* von, correspondence of, 38
Wölwarth, von, papers concerning, 112
Wörner, Daniel, 169
Wohnbach, emigration from, 277
Wolde, Christian Julius Gustav, Bolivian consul in Hanse towns, 285
Wolf, William, 100
Wolfe, *Gen.* James, debarkation of, before Quebec, 178
Wolfenbüttel, Ducal Brunswick-Lüneburg National Central Archives in, 248-265
Wolfstein, *Landgericht*, emigration from, 207
Wolmirstedt, *Kreis*, emigration petitions, 110
Wolters, F. H., Hanseatic consul in Bahia, 287
Wood, *Capt.*, correspondence, 260
Wood, Fernando, correspondence of, 62
Worms, emigration from, 276
Wrede, correspondence, 112
Wreschen, *Kreis*, emigration papers, 158
Württemberg, emigration to America from, 49, 51, 303, 304, 305, 306, 307; Royal Privy House and State Archives of (in Stuttgart and Ludwigsburg), 303-307
Württemberg, Regierungs-Blatt für das Königreich, 56
Württembergischen Auswanderer, Rechts-Verhältnisse der, 51

Würzburg, Circuit Archives of Lower Franconia and Aschaffenburg in, 216-222; emigration from, 220, 221
Würzburg, bishop of, letter of, 217
Wulff, Jacob, Hamburg vice-consul in U. S., 268
Wuppermann, Ad., Hanseatic consul in Bolivar, 284
Wurmb, *Lieut.-Col.* Ludwig Johann Adolph von, correspondence, 260; journal of, 125; letters of, 206; reports of, 115
Wuttginau, von, regiment of, 104, 127
Wyer, Edward. U. S. consul in Hamburg, 270
York, Pa., Moravians in, 314
Yorke, *Maj.-Gen. Sir* Joseph, British ambassador at the Hague, correspondence, 118, 149; negotiations, 179
Yorktown, battle of, 37, 115, 118, 123; seige of, 118

Zahn, Gerhard, papers concerning, 220
Zanowiz, *Count* de, papers relating to, 299
Zastrow, Prussian minister in Munich, correspondence of, 49
Zedlitz, von, correspondence of, 80
Zeitskofen, emigration from, 208
Zeitung der freien Stadt Frankfurt, copies of, 187
Zeller, B., emigration of, 219
Zerbst, Ducal House and State Archives of Anhalt in, 228
Ziegenberg, emigration from, 276
Ziegenhain, garrison papers, 76
Zimmermann, Lübeck consul in Buenos Aires, 285; in Montevideo, 286
Zincke, *Lieut.*, letter of, 120
Zinn, *Quartermaster*, journal of, 121
Zinzendorf, *Count*, despatch of, 298; letters of, 323
Zittau, U. S. consulate in, 301
Zollverein, commercial and other treaties with North, Central, and Southern American states, 133, 134, 137, 171, 190; extradition treaty with U. S., 311; *see also* Germanic Confederation; Germany; North German Confederation
Zuloaga, *Gen.* Felix, president of Mexico, 281
Zwackh, *Baron* von, papers of, 48
Zweibrücken, regiment, 322

2.

Guide to the Materials for American History in Swiss and Austrian Archives

By Albert B. Faust

Guide to the Materials for American History in Swiss and Austrian Archives

BY

ALBERT B. FAUST

PROFESSOR OF GERMAN IN CORNELL UNIVERSITY

WASHINGTON, D. C.
Published by the Carnegie Institution of Washington
1916

CARNEGIE INSTITUTION OF WASHINGTON
PUBLICATION NO. 220

PAPERS OF THE DEPARTMENT OF HISTORICAL RESEARCH
J. FRANKLIN JAMESON, EDITOR

The Lord Baltimore Press
BALTIMORE, MD., U. S. A.

INTRODUCTORY NOTE.

This descriptive inventory of the manuscript materials for the history of the United States contained in the various archives of Switzerland and Austria stands closely related, in the plans of this department, to a previous volume in the same series, Professor Marion D. Learned's *Guide to the Manuscript Materials relating to American History in the German State Archives* (Washington, 1912). Among the reasons for the preparation of the latter book, one, and on the whole the chief reason, is common to the two books, namely, the large part which emigration from German lands had in the populating of America. The records and other manuscript materials found in archives within the present German Empire are far from covering the whole history of that immigration, for a large part of it came from the German-speaking cantons of Switzerland, and a portion of it from the German parts of Austria. Therefore, after the preparation of Dr. Learned's book, it was natural to think of supplementing it by reasearches in the archives of these German lands outside of the German Empire, and for such a task it was natural to obtain the aid of Professor Albert B. Faust of Cornell University, author of a widely-known history of *The German Element in the United States* (Boston, 1909). But if a volume were to be published having as its main subject the materials in the archives of the German cantons, it should for the sake of completeness include also a treatment of the less important materials in the archives of the French cantons. These the undersigned examined in the summer of 1912; Professor Faust's researches, first in the Austrian archives and then in those of German Switzerland, occupied the spring and summer of the next year.

Besides those officials in Switzerland and Austria to whom Dr. Faust's thanks are expressed at the end of his preface, we are also very greatly indebted, for aid most kindly rendered in the general preparations for our expeditions, to their Excellencies, Dr. Paul Ritter, envoy of Switzerland to the United States, and Hon. Henry S. Boutell, envoy of the United States to Switzerland.

J. FRANKLIN JAMESON.

PREFACE.

The quest for materials relating to American history in the archives of German Switzerland and Austria extended through a period of about six months, from March to September, 1913. In Switzerland the search could not be confined to state (*i. e.*, cantonal) archives, since materials of equal importance were frequently hidden in municipal archives, or in city or private libraries. For this reason the number of repositories visited and examined became quite large.

In Austria the attempt was not made to visit all the archives, owing to specific directions that, within the limited period allotted, effort should be concentrated upon the archives of Vienna, Salzburg, and if possible Innsbruck. Six archives in Vienna were found to contain materials for American history. These showed that diplomatic and commercial affairs were in the foreground in the relations between the Hapsburg Empire and the United States before 1847, the date beyond which the archives are closed to investigators. Emigration was effectively checked in Austria before this time, and was not a problem, as it became for certain provinces at a later day.

On the other hand, the question of emigration is at the very centre of interest in the materials found in the Swiss archives. Ever since the beginning of the eighteenth century, America periodically attracted large groups of Swiss emigrants. Carolina and Pennsylvania, supposed to be West India islands under the British Crown, were names that between 1734 and 1750 conjured panic fears in the bosoms of patriotic councillors in nearly every canton of Switzerland. The Ratsherren met and pondered, they gave paternal warnings, issued severe mandates, and punished offenders, nevertheless the " rabies Carolina " continued its ravages. Overpopulation and bad economic conditions sought relief beyond the seas. Switzerland is therefore linked with America not by governmental policy, but by the bonds of blood, that go back, just as in the case of Germany, and for the same reasons, to the earliest colonial periods.

In preparing this Guide, care was taken to indicate, by a few descriptive words, the nature or contents of every document examined, and wherever possible to preserve the title given by the archivist (in the latter case quotation marks have been used). By this means investigators may be led directly to the material desired, or be spared vain inquiries. In many instances large abstracts of the contents of acta have been made, where important policies were outlined, or sometimes documents have been quoted in full, as in the case of some decrees against emigration. The purpose was to provide more than a mere calendar, to present some results to those who will not find the opportunity themselves to draw from the sources, and partially to reveal the valuable and fascinating record of human experience which these archives contain. In all quotations the original dialect and spelling have been preserved, so as to reproduce the characteristic color, personality, or social condition. A brief survey of the materials found in the archives is given in an Introduction preceding the Guide.

The following are lists of the archives visited and examined in Switzerland and in Austria respectively, which contain materials for American history:

Canton.	State (or cantonal) archive.	Municipal archive.	City library.	Other archives.
Zürich............	1	2 Zürich, Winterthur	1	—
Bern..............	1	—	1	3 Bundesarchiv, Auswanderungsamt, American Legation
Luzern...........	1	—	1	—
Uri...............	1	—	—	—
Schwyz...........	1	—	—	1 Einsiedeln
Obwalden	1	—	—	1 Engelberg
Nidwalden........	1	—	—	—
Glarus............	1	—	—	—
Zug...............	1	—	—	—
Solothurn........	1	—	—	—
Baselstadt........	1	—	—	—
Baselland........	1	—	—	—
Schaffhausen.....	1	—	—	—
Appenzell A. Rh...	1	—	—	—
Appenzell I. Rh...	1	—	—	—
St. Gallen........	1	2	—	2 Stiftsarchiv, Kaufmännisches Direktorium
Graubünden......	1	1	—	—
Aargau............	1	—	—	—
Thurgau...........	1	—	—	—
Ticino.............	1	—	—	—
Totals.......	20	5	3	7, together, 35

The archives of the French cantons: Fribourg, Vaud, Valais, Neuchâtel, Geneva, were examined by Dr. Jameson. See pp. 149-184, *post*.

Place.	State archive.	Municipal archive.	City library.	Other archives.
Vienna............	1	1	1	3 Kriegs-, Hofkammer-, Minist. d. Innern
Salzburg	1	—	1	1 Erzbischöfl.
Innsbruck........	1	—	1	—
Totals.......	3	1	3	4, together, 11

Total of archives examined, 40; libraries, 6.

An investigation of this kind could not be carried forward without constant help from those familiar with the contents of their archives and expert in bringing them into service. In gathering the material for this Guide the investigator was uniformly aided, in Austria and in Switzerland, by the most cordial coöperation of the archivists in charge and their assistants. His grateful acknowledgments extend to Hofrat Árpad von Károlyi, director of the K. u. K. Haus-, Hof- und Staatsarchiv of Vienna, and to Dr. Hanns

Schlitter, vice-director, whose valuable publications from the archives of Vienna and Washington are mentioned below; also in the same archive to Dr. Roderich Goos, Vizearchivar, and to Dr. Hans Prankl, who made the laborious search and prepared the outline in the section under the rubric "Länder". Similarly, to Oberstleutnant Ludwig Eberle, and Rittmeister von Lerchenau, of the K. u. K. Kriegsarchiv; to Professor Dr. Heinrich Kretschmayr, director, and Dr. Josef Kallbruner, secretary, of the Allgemeines Archiv d. K. K. Ministeriums d. Innern; to Archivdirektor Dr. Hermann Hango of the Archiv der Stadt Wien, and to Dr. Gustav Bodenstein, archivist of the Hofkammerarchiv. Likewise to Dr. Andreas Mudrich, director of the Archiv d. K. K. Landesregierung at Salzburg, and his assistant, Dr. Franz Martin; to Professor Dr. Michael Mayr, director of the K. K. Staatsarchiv, Innsbruck, and Dr. Otto Stolz, assistant.

In the three Swiss archives where the fullest harvest of American materials was gathered, at Bern, Zürich, and Basel, it was my good fortune to meet archivists who became deeply interested in the subject, who spared no efforts to strike into obscure recesses, often to be rewarded with nuggets of unsuspected richness and quality. I refer to Professor Dr. Heinrich Türler, archivist, and Mr. G. Kurz (to whom I am indebted for some of the most interesting materials), assistant archivist of the Staatsarchiv of Bern; to Professor Dr. Hans Nabholz, state archivist of the canton of Zürich; to Dr. Rudolf Wackernagel, state archivist, and Dr. August Huber, assistant archivist of the Staatsarchiv d. Kantons Baselstadt. I wish to give expression to my indebtedness for facilities provided and courtesies extended, also to Professor Dr. W. F. von Mülinen, chief librarian of the Stadtbibliothek of Bern, who also permitted me to use the Graffenried manuscripts in his private library; to Dr. Jakob Kaiser, archivist of the Confederation[1] in Bern; to Mr. J. Möhr, chief of the federal Auswanderungsamt in Bern; to Mr. J. Weber, assistant secretary of the American Legation; to Dr. F. von Jecklin, town archivist in Chur; to Dr. Robert Durrer, archivist of Stans, Unterwalden; to Dr. P. Odilo Ringholz, Stiftsarchivar, Einsiedeln; to Professor Dr. Johannes Dierauer, historian and librarian (Vadiana), Dr. Schiess, town archivist, and Dr. Hermann Wartmann, actuary of the Kaufmännisches Direktorium, in St. Gallen; to Dr. Hermann Escher, chief librarian of the Stadtbibliothek of Zürich; to Mr. Friedrich Frey, cantonal archivist at Glarus; Dr. H. Werner, archivist of the Staatsarchiv at Schaffhausen; Dr. A. Lechner, Staatsschreiber at Solothurn; and Signor Bustelli, archivist at Bellinzona. To all of these and many more it gives me pleasure to express sincere thanks for their valuable assistance in this work.

ALBERT BERNHARDT FAUST.

Cornell University,
Ithaca, July 1, 1914.

---

[1] Upon Dr. Kaiser's retirement in 1914, Prof. Dr. Türler, Staatsarchivar, was appointed director of the Bundesarchiv, while Mr. G. Kurz was advanced to the position of archivist of the Staatsarchiv of Bern.

TABLE OF CONTENTS.

	PAGE
INTRODUCTORY NOTE	iii
PREFACE	v
INTRODUCTION	1
Swiss Archives	1
History and Statistics	1
Survey of Materials found in Swiss Archives	2
Emigration	3
Diplomatic Correspondence	7
Trade Relations	7
Austrian Archives	7
Survey of Materials found in Austrian Archives	8
Eighteenth Century	8
Trade Relations	8
Austria during the Revolutionary War	9
Emigration	9
Nineteenth Century	10
Diplomatic Correspondence	10
Emigration	11
Police Records	11

SWISS ARCHIVES, GERMAN CANTONS.

CANTON ZÜRICH	13
Staatsarchiv, Zürich	13
Stadtarchiv, Zürich	27
Stadtbibliothek, Zürich	29
Stadtarchiv, Winterthur	31
CANTON BERN	33
Staatsarchiv, Bern	33
Bundesarchiv, Bern	63
Auswanderungsamt, Bern	69
Stadtbibliothek, Bern	71
American Legation, Bern	75
CANTON LUZERN	78
Staatsarchiv, and Bürgerbibliothek, Luzern	78
CANTON URI	83
Staatsarchiv, Altorf	83
CANTON SCHWYZ	84
Kantonsarchiv, Schwyz	84
Stiftsarchiv, Einsiedeln	84
CANTON UNTERWALDEN	86
Obwalden: Staatsarchiv, Sarnen	86
Stiftsarchiv, Engelberg	87
Nidwalden: Staatsarchiv, Stans	89
CANTON GLARUS	90
Staatsarchiv, Glarus	90
CANTON ZUG	95
Kantonsarchiv, Zug	95
CANTON SOLOTHURN (SOLEURE)	98
Staatsarchiv, Solothurn	98
CANTON BASEL	101
Basel-Stadt: Staatsarchiv, Basel	101
Basel-Landschaft: Staatsarchiv, Liestal	121
CANTON SCHAFFHAUSEN	122
Staatsarchiv, Schaffhausen	122

	PAGE
CANTON APPENZELL	126
Appenzell I. Rh.: Staatsarchiv, Appenzell	126
Appenzell A. Rh.: Staatsarchiv, Herisau	127
CANTON SANKT GALLEN	128
Staatsarchiv, St. Gallen	128
Stiftsarchiv, St. Gallen	129
Archiv der Stadtgemeinde, St. Gallen	129
Stadtarchiv, St. Gallen	130
Das Kaufmännische Direktorium, St. Gallen	130
CANTON GRAUBÜNDEN (GRISONS)	132
Staatsarchiv, Chur	132
Stadtarchiv, Chur	132
CANTON AARGAU	140
Staatsarchiv, Aarau	140
CANTON THURGAU	144
Staatsarchiv, Frauenfeld	144

ITALIAN CANTON.

CANTON TICINO	147
Archivio Cantonale, Bellinzona	147

FRENCH CANTONS.

INTRODUCTION	149
CANTON DE FRIBOURG	150
Archives d'État, Fribourg	150
CANTON DE VAUD	159
Archives Cantonales, Lausanne	159
Minor Archives, Lausanne	161
Yverdon	162
CANTON DU VALAIS	163
Archives d'État, Sion	163
CANTON DE NEUCHÂTEL	166
Archives de l'État, Neuchâtel	166
Archives de la Ville, Neuchâtel	173
Bibliothèque de la Ville, Neuchâtel	173
Compagnie des Pasteurs, Neuchâtel	173
CANTON DE GENÈVE (GENEVA)	175
Archives d'État, Geneva	175
Ecclesiastical Archives, Geneva	183

AUSTRIAN ARCHIVES.

VIENNA	185
K. u. K. Haus-, Hof- und Staatsarchiv	185
K. u. K. Kriegsarchiv	237
Allgemeines Archiv des K. K. Ministeriums d. Innern	247
K. u. K. Gemeinsames Finanzarchiv (Hofkammerarchiv)	252
Hofbibliothek	255
Archiv der Stadt Wien	256
SALZBURG	258
Archiv der K. K. Landesregierung	258
Fürst-Erzbischöfliches Consistorialarchiv	264
INNSBRUCK	265
K. K. Staatsarchiv	265
K. K. Statthalterei-Archiv	265
Ferdinandeum	266

INTRODUCTION.

A. SWISS ARCHIVES.

The cantons of Switzerland have had an independent development, though at various epochs some were bound together in confederacies without strongly centralized power. Naturally every canton is eager to preserve the records of its independent existence, and there has never been an attempt to gather in one place the large body of historical material deposited in the cantonal archives. The latter, called Staatsarchive, vary greatly in equipment and resources. Some are well supplied with a staff of archivists, copyists, cataloguers, etc., but in many cases the annual sum granted by the canton is not sufficient to pay the salary of one archivist, or to carry on the work of cataloguing and indexing the materials, or putting them in order, so that they may be used by investigators. Most of the archives of Switzerland are housed in old buildings, in some cases renovated so as to be serviceable, in others allowed to remain inadequate. These handicaps place a heavier burden upon the archivists, whose zeal, efficiency, and scholarship very generally make up for the lack of material equipment. In the systematic grouping of materials, in convenience of access, indexing, card-cataloguing, and various other helps, the Staatsarchiv of the city of Basel stands out pre-eminently. The Bundesarchiv of Bern is housed in the only really modern structure, built with attention to danger from fire. The Bundesarchiv was completed in 1899, built by the Federal State for the safe-keeping of materials that concern its own history, since its foundation in 1848, and also the records of the confederacies of the nineteenth century, going back to the Helvetic Republic (1798).[1]

History and Statistics.

The essential facts in the development of the Swiss confederation need to be borne in mind by the readers of this book, and help to explain its structure. At the end of the seventeenth century, when Swiss relations with America began, the league consisted of thirteen members: Zürich, Bern, Luzern, Uri, Schwyz, Unterwalden, Glarus, Zug, Fribourg, Solothurn, Basel, Schaffhausen, and Appenzell. This was its composition from 1513 to 1798. The members were united in a loose confederation lacking in executive power, and were represented in its Diet. The independence of Switzerland was proclaimed in the treaty of Westphalia in 1648, but the Confederation leaned heavily on France, and the country was a great source of supply of troops to that kingdom. The governments of the individual states had by the opening of the eighteenth century become highly oligarchical. In the course of that century movements of revolt against aristocratic rule occurred in many states. The agents and armies of revolutionary France broke up the old governments, and substituted for the Confederation in 1798 a Helvetic Republic, with a highly centralized government modelled on that of the

---

[1] On the Swiss archives in general, see Ch. V. Langlois and H. Stein, *Archives de l'Histoire de France* (Paris, 1891), pp. 823-840.

French Directory. In 1803 Bonaparte, by the Act of Mediation, set up in place of this a federal constitution, partially modernized, with the addition of six new cantons. After his fall in 1814, there was a recurrence to a system resembling that which had prevailed before 1798, but with the new cantons added, making twenty-two states instead of thirteen; and whereas before 1798 many portions of the Swiss territory were in somewhat abject subordination to the original states, now all cantons stood upon an equal basis in constitutional law. The Diet remained weak. The seat of government under it shifted every two years between Zürich, Bern, and Luzern (the three *Vororte*). The cantonal governments became once more reactionary, but by 1848 most of them had been liberalized. In that year, as the result of the brief war of secession with the Sonderbund (1847), a new federal constitution was adopted, instituting a strong central government, with its seat at Bern. The present, revised constitution, radically democratic, dates from 1874.

Of the additional cantons established in 1803, St. Gallen had before 1798 been an ally of the Confederation (or rather two allies, abbot and town). Graubünden (or the Grisons) had been an allied federal republic. Aargau, Thurgau, and Ticino had been dependencies of groups of the old cantons. Vaud had before 1798 been subject to Bern. Of the three cantons added in 1814, Valais had long been an independent republic, having relations more or less close with the Swiss Confederacy; Neuchâtel, an independent principality till 1814, was from 1707 to 1857 under the sovereignty of the king of Prussia as prince; Geneva had been till 1798 a separate republic with a famous history, then for fifteen years a part of France.

The order in which the cantons are treated in this volume is that followed in official publications of the Swiss federal government, except that the cantons of German, Italian, and French speech are treated in separate groups, the archives of the French cantons having been described by another hand than those of the German and the Italian. The official order gives precedence to Zürich, Bern, and Luzern, and presents the other cantons in their chronological order, Fribourg appearing next after Zug, and Ticino, Vaud, Valais, Neuchâtel, and Geneva after Thurgau.

The Federal State of Switzerland now consists of twenty-five cantons (including the three divided cantons Appenzell, Basel, Unterwalden, which are counted double), and has a population of 3,741,971 (Dec. 1, 1910). Classified according to speech, 69 per cent. of the population is German, 21.2 per cent. French, 8 per cent. Italian, 1.1 per cent. Romansch, 0.7 per cent. other stock. Nineteen cantons are dominantly German, five French (Fribourg, Vaud, Valais, Neuchâtel, Geneva), one Italian (Ticino). Graubünden contains almost all of the Romansch population (46 per cent. German, 38 per cent. Romansch, 14 per cent. Italian); Bern is 83 per cent. German, 15 per cent. French; Fribourg 68 per cent. French, 31 per cent. German; Vaud 81 per cent. French, 11 per cent. German, 5 per cent. Italian.

B. SURVEY OF THE MATERIALS FOR AMERICAN HISTORY IN SWISS ARCHIVES.

The material relating to American history found in Swiss archives may be discussed under three heads: I. Emigration; II. Diplomatic correspondence; III. Trade relations.

I. Emigration.

The earliest plan of a Swiss colony in America was that of H. Ritter, of Bern, concerning which there is a record as early as 1705 (Rats-Manuale, Bern, 18). The governing Ratsherren of Bern were willing to coöperate with Ritter, seeing their advantage in a scheme which was to eliminate what they considered undesirable elements of the population, Wiedertäufer (Mennonites, Anabaptists), and Landsassen (pauper squatters). In 1710 Ritter received 45 thalers a head for the deportation of Swiss Mennonites (R. M. 41), an expedition which ended in failure because of the determined opposition of Dutch Mennonites against forceful deportation of brothers in their faith. Some of the group returned to Switzerland, others found refuge in the Netherlands or in Prussia. In succeeding years considerable numbers of Swiss Mennonites reached Pennsylvania and Carolina.

In 1710 Christoph von Graffenried founded the colony of New Bern, N. C., and on his return in 1713 he wrote a description of the colony together with a narrative of his adventures. Three manuscripts of this " Relation ", two in French and one in German, were found, and two were subsequently published (see *German American Annals*, n. s., XI. 205-312, and XII. 63-190, 1913 and 1914). Descriptions of the new country soon began to awaken general interest, as is shown by the purchase on March 21, 1711, by the council of Bern, of 50 copies of the book of Ochs (Johann Rudolff Ochs, *Amerikanischer Wegweiser*, Bern, 1711, describing Carolina, based on Lawson's *New Voyage to Carolina*, London, 1710).

The records show that attempts were made in 1720 by Merveilleux (captain in the regiment Karrer) to win recruits for the Mississippi service, and that J. P. Pury and Company of Neuchâtel began as early as 1725 to advertise their colonial scheme, which culminated in the founding of Purysburg, S. C., in 1732. Both of these plans were strenuously opposed by the Ratsherren of Bern, who began to fear a exodus of their people. The emigration fever (" rabies Carolina ") reached its most critical stage in the years 1734-1750, and affected most the populous Protestant cantons Bern, Zürich, and Basel. Decrees (*Mandate*) were issued against emigration in 1720, 1735, 1736, 1738, 1749, 1753, 1754, 1771, and 1773, with ever increasing severity. Loss of landright and citizenship, not to be restored in case of return, restriction of sale of lands, severe punishment of those attempting to induce others to emigrate, were some of the terrorizing defensive measures adopted to restrain the flow of emigration.

Lists (*Rödel*) of those leaving the country go back to the seventeenth century and are very frequently found in the archives. The more valuable are those giving exact dates, and the destination of the emigrants. There is one in the Staatsarchiv of Zürich which gives a complete catalogue of all those that migrated to America from every district of the canton between the years 1734 and 1744. The total number is 2310. This document furnishes the only means of determining with some degree of accuracy what was the actual number of Swiss emigrants from Switzerland in the eighteenth century. It is also very valuable for genealogical purposes, and should be published entire. Decrees against migration to other countries than America also appeared, to Russia in 1765, to the Spanish colonies in 1767, to Prussian Pomerania in 1771. In the Ratsmanuale of Bern, which were searched very thoroughly and yielded rich returns, we find the statement in 1742, " ist die Auswanderung wieder lebhaft im Gang ", and in 1750 that the emigration fever had again taken hold. The periodic tides of emigration could not be stopped; the compelling force of overpopulation with bad economic conditions was behind it. The various cantonal governments made every effort to get at the causes of emigration. Their investigations appear in the form of examinations (*Verhöre*) of individuals and groups of people about to leave the country, reports (*Berichte*) of special committees, discussions, or statements of opinion (*Gutachten*), complaints and warnings (*Bedenken, Gravamina, Beschwerden*), all of them interesting and many of them valuable. A plan conceived in Bern to relieve the poor by providing opportunity for work at home on a large scale, and thus to remove one of the main causes of emigration (see Responsa Prudentum), was never carried into execution. Poverty, non-employment, small returns for labor, large families to provide for, no hope of improved conditions in the future, these were reasons commonly assigned by those wishing to leave. The unwary spoke of the expectation of improving their condition in the American colonies, and of favorable reports on this point. Such impressions were gained through letters from settlers in America, and through printed emigrant literature.

Favorable letters from emigrants settled in Carolina appeared in Bern as early as 1710 (see Graffenried Manuscripts, Bern), and undoubtedly such genuine records of actual experience were of determining influence. The archive of Basel contains the best collection of letters from Swiss settlers in Carolina, Pennsylvania, and other colonies. A large number of them were undoubtedly confiscated letters kept in the archive to remove the danger of their circulation. Records in the Ratsmanuale prove that letters were feared and hunted quite as much as emigrant agents. A consistent policy seems to have prevailed, that letters which reported unfavorable conditions should be published in the annual calendars and spread about in printed editions, while those containing favorable reports were captured and rendered harmless by safe-keeping in the archives. Not surprising therefore is the fact, which appears for the first time in these archives, that devices were used to conceal letters, such as that of Peter Huber, who brought letters from America in the false bottom of a wooden drinking-cup, which, he confessed when his captured baggage was examined, had been constructed by a German settler in Carolina. (See Thurn-Buch, Bern, 1740-1742.)

A complete collection of the interesting emigrant literature, pro and contra, published in Switzerland in the eighteenth century, nowhere exists. The best collection is found in the Simmlersche Sammlung in the Stadtbibliothek of Zürich, which, though by no means complete, contains some of the classics of emigrant literature, as: *Der nunmehro in der neuen Welt vergnügt und ohne Heim-Wehe lebende Schweitzer*; and the reply published in the same year, and given much encouragement by cantonal governments, *Neue Nachricht alter und neuer Merkwürdigkeiten, enthaltend ein vertrautes Gespräch und sichere Briefe von der Landschaft Carolina und übrigen englischen Pflanzstädten in Amerika, zufinden zu Zürich, Bern, Basel, Schaffhausen und St. Gallen* (1734).

Especially severe measures were taken to arrest and punish persons suspected to be emigrant agents, or to be in any way stirring up (*aufwiegeln*) a desire in the rural population to emigrate. The Swiss archives throw much new light on the methods by which such men proceeded, the manner in which they evaded detection, and the skill with which they defended themselves when caught. The two most interesting cases are those of Peter Huber (1742), and Peter im Aebnit (1744). The verbatim reports of their trials in Bern (Thurn-Buch) and Basel (Huber only), are unique documents, of historical, literary, and human interest. Peter Huber escaped from the hands of his judges, while Peter im Aebnit was less fortunate. Though escaping from torture with which he was threatened, he made an unsuccessful attempt at flight from the prison tower at Bern, in which he lost his life. Conspicuous figures in emigration matters, though of a different type, were also Pfarrer Göttschi, and his son (see Zürich archives), and Michael Schlatter (see Bern, St. Gallen, etc.).

Though most emigrants were poor and not able to pay for their passage, a large number of others had possessions large or small in amount, which were taxed before leaving the country. The Staatsarchiv at Basel contains very many lists of property belonging to departing emigrants. Permission had to be obtained to sell their property (*Vergantung*), which was taxed ten per cent. (*Abzug*) for emigration; and if the emigrant was a serf who had property, about eight per cent. in addition was exacted for the purchase of freedom (*Manumission*). In this way the canton attempted to insure itself against too great a loss of property through emigration. Often, to evade the taxes, emigrants disposed of their property secretly, and left without permission or passes. They sometimes left pathetic letters behind, taking leave of their friends, whom they did not wish to implicate with a knowledge of their flight before it was accomplished. (See archive of Basel: " Heimliche Emigranten ".)

The larger number of emigrants came from the mountain districts, *e. g.,* from the Berner Oberland, rather than from the city of Bern, or from the country districts of Zürich rather than from the cities of Zürich and Winterthur; this seems to indicate better conditions in the cities than in the country. The Protestant contributed more emigrants than the Catholic cantons. The Benedictine monasteries Einsiedeln and Engelberg established branches in the United States during the nineteenth century.

The embargo placed upon emigration was removed in the nineteenth century, when conditions of overpopulation, famine, failure of crops, hard times, etc., periodically recurred in many districts. Paternal authority began to see some advantages in emigration, provided the emigrants prospered in their new abode. The complaints from the governments of France, the Netherlands, and Prussia, in the second decade of the nineteenth century, concerning the congregating of large numbers of Swiss paupers at the seaports, hopelessly waiting for an opportunity to embark for America, brought about the beginnings of the regulation of emigration from Switzerland. The money for the trip had to be vouched for before an emigrant was furnished with a pass. The policy was adopted, neither to encourage nor to discourage emigration, but to let it take its course, and to protect the emigrant as far as possible against the selfishness of speculators. The business of transporting emigrants was left in the hands of agencies, who were soon required to secure a license and obey the laws protecting the emigrant. In 1880 the Federal Emigration Bureau (Eidgenössisches Auswanderungsamt) was established at Bern, to watch the licensed emigration bureaus, to distribute literature furnishing all needed information, to advise emigrants personally, and to keep statistics of emigration.

A phase of the emigration problem which hastened regulation was the tendency, which arose in Switzerland about 1848, to ship undesirables to the United States, *i. e.,* criminals, paupers, and defectives. For instance, when a criminal was about to complete his term of sentence in the penitentiary, he would plead for a sum of money to pay his transportation to America. Town, parish, canton, and friends made contributions for the necessary sum to rid the community of the undesirable person. The United States complained through its first minister to Switzerland, Theodore S. Fay (see archives of American Legation, 1855, etc.). The central government at Bern acted promptly in an effort to prevent the continuance of this abuse, but its power was not great enough to prohibit the deportations. Some cantons (see, *e. g.*, archives of Frauenfeld, Canton Thurgau) continued the practice until the United States shipped back persons of the undesirable classes at the expense of those that sent them. The deportations then came to an end.

The Federal Emigration Bureau issues annual statistics of Swiss emigration, giving the home canton and the destination. In the section devoted to its archive will be found a list of places in the United States where larger numbers of Swiss settlers have gathered. As a rule the Swiss do not isolate themselves in colonies. Even at New Glarus, Wisconsin (see *Neues Archiv d. Kantons Glarus*), many Swiss settlers have left, being most content and successful when becoming assimilated.

The Swiss official statistics of the last fifty years show an average emigration of 8000 Swiss per annum, of whom on an average 4500 per annum are stated to have come to the United States. The United States statistics as to Swiss immigration run back to 1820, and show a total of nearly 520,000. The rate in recent years has exceeded 3000 per annum. The number of inhabitants in the United States who were born in Switzerland was reckoned at 124,848 in the census of 1910. Of these, 16,315 were found in the state of New York, 14,521 in California, 10,988 in Ohio, 8661 in Illinois, and from eight to six thousand in Wisconsin, New Jersey, Pennsylvania and Missouri; no other state contained more than four thousand. Of the total number, 103,652 had German for their mother tongue, 11,170 French, and 7835 Italian.

Bibliography: J. Dreifuss, *Émigration*. Élaboré par J. Dreifuss, Chef du Bureau Fédéral de l'Émigration. Fasc. V9g< of *Bibliographie Nationale Suisse* (Berne, 1905, pp. viii, 68).

L. Karrer, *Das Schweizerische Auswanderungswesen und die Revision und Vollziehung des Bundesgesetzes betreffend den Geschäftsbetrieb von Auswanderungsagenturen*. Bericht im Auftrage des schweiz. Handels- und Landwirthschaftsdepartementes erstattet von L. Karrer, Nationalrath. (Bern, 1886, pp. 318.)

Id. (French edition of the above.) *L'Émigration Suisse et la Loi Fédérale sur les Opérations des Agences d'Émigration.* Rapport, etc. (Berne, 1887, pp. 286.)

Ratgeber für Schweizerische Auswanderer nach den Vereinigten Staaten von Amerika. Verfasst vom Schweizerischen Auswanderungsamt in Bern. (Bern, no date, but since 1906.)

Ernest Röthlisberger, " Die Internationale Bedeutung der Schweiz, III. Die Schweizer in der Fremde ", in Paul Seippel's *Die Schweiz im Neunzehnten Jahrhundert*, I. 577-596 (Bern, 1899; French ed., *La Suisse au Dix-neuvième Siècle*).

N. Reichesberg, *Handwörterbuch der Schweizerischen Volkswirtschaft, Socialpolitik, und Verwaltung* (Bern, 1903), I. Band, pp. 380-399: " Auswanderungswesen ", I. Allgemeines; II. Geschichtliches; III. Auswanderungspolitik, 1. Politik der Kantone, 2. Politik des Bundes; IV. Statistisches; V. Ursachen der Auswanderung; VI. Literatur.

Dr. Adelrich Steinach, *Geschichte und Leben der Schweizer Kolonien in den Vereinigten Staaten von Nord-Amerika* (New York, 1889). Many documents and reports respecting the matter may be found in the weekly *Bundesblatt der Schweizerischen Eidgenossenschaft (Feuille Fédérale de la Confédération Suisse)* from 1848 down. An account of the earlier history of the Swiss migration to America, by the writer of this book, appears as an article in the *American Historical Review* for (probably) July, 1916 (vol. XXI).

II. Diplomatic Correspondence.

This material is of the nineteenth century and is found in the Bundesarchiv at Bern. The general letters, *Kreisschreiben*, of which the originals are at Bern, are found also in the cantonal archives. Subjects included are: the establishment of consulships in the United States, *e. g.*, at New York, Alexandria, Philadelphia, New Orleans, Madison, Galveston, Louisville, etc.; the reports of consuls on American conditions, on property of individuals, answers to the questions of the Comités d'Émigrations des Sociétés d'Utilité Publique des Cantons de Vaud et de Genève; correspondence of the United States consul general in Switzerland; and acta concerning emigration and extradition treaties with the United States. The first treaty, concerning rights of domicile (" Freizügigkeitsvertrag ") was rejected by the United States Senate June 11, 1836, taken up again and carried May 18, 1847.

The diplomatic correspondence after 1848 is not accessible, but adequate reports upon the action taken by the Bundesrat can be found in the *Bundesblatt*, and the *Amtliche Sammlung*. Interesting legislation can be followed there on the establishment of emigrant agencies and the central emigration bureau (laws of 1880 and 1888). Other questions are matters concerning the postal union, the pensions of Swiss who served the Union in the Civil War as volunteers, etc.

The archive of the American Legation at Bern, very well kept, and accessible to students of history, fills the gap between 1848 and the present. Its most interesting material is that on forced emigration, *i. e.*, deportation of criminals, defectives, etc., referred to above. In 1879 the activities of Mormon preachers who were endeavoring to induce Swiss peasants, especially women, to emigrate, becomes a subject for diplomatic correspondence.

III. Trade Relations.

Consular reports on trade are found most complete in the Bundesarchiv, yet are also scattered in many other places, notably Zürich, Basel, Zug, and St. Gallen. The archive of the Kaufmännische Direktorium in Sankt Gallen is one of the best sources for the study of Swiss-American trade relations. The retiring actuary, Dr. Hermann Wartmann, pioneer in the study of the history of Swiss trade, is inclined to see an American influence on Swiss trade, viz., in the matter of centralization, systematization, and largeness of view (*Grosszügigkeit*). This would apply, *e. g.*, to the development of Swiss manufacture and trade in laces at St. Gallen, and the milk industry at Zug.

C. AUSTRIAN ARCHIVES.

The archive material of Austria-Hungary has not been centralized. The three crown lands have somewhat jealously guarded the records of their past, resulting in three principal stations for state archives, viz., Vienna, Budapest, and Prague. There are ten provincial archives, at Brünn (Moravia), Graz (Styria), Innsbruck (Tyrol), Klagenfurth (Carinthia), Cracow (Austrian Poland), Laibach (Carniola), Lemberg (Galicia), Prague (Bohemia), Salzburg (Salzburg), and Troppau (Silesia). *Cf.* Langlois and Stein, *Les Archives de l'Histoire de France,* pp. 645-655. An attempt at centralization has been made in the K. u. K. Haus-, Hof- und Staatsarchiv in Vienna, for which copies of the most important historical documents were made, the originals of which could not be obtained from the country or province of their origin. For students of history, therefore, this archive is the principal source, in which investigation should begin. It contains also the most abundant store of materials pertaining to American history. Other archives of Vienna examined and found to contain American materials, were: the K. u. K. Kriegsarchiv, Archiv der Stadt Wien, Allgemeines Archiv d. K. K. Ministeriums des Innern, K. u. K. Gemeinsames Finanz-Archiv (Hofkammerarchiv), K. K. Hofbibliothek. The archives of Salzburg and Innsbruck were found to contain interesting but not abundant American material.

The archives visited were provided with large and able staffs of archivists, many of whom were engaged upon historical investigations. The buildings, with the principal exception of the K. u. K. Haus-, Hof- und Staatsarchiv, were generally old and inconvenient, and the work of indexing, cataloguing, and arranging the material had not always been completely or adequately carried out. The date beyond which manuscript materials are not accessible is fixed at 1847.

Diplomatic correspondence with a view to cultivating better understanding between the two nations, Austria-Hungary and the United States, and establishing trade relations favorable to both, forms the centre of interest in the Austrian archive material discovered. Emigration to the United States, while it occurred sporadically, seems never to have been frequent enough before 1847 to attract governmental attention. Indications of increased emigration in printed records begin after 1848; only within recent times and in certain provinces has it grown so as to become a problem.

D. SURVEY OF THE MATERIALS FOR AMERICAN HISTORY IN AUSTRIAN ARCHIVES.

The material relating to American history found in Austrian archives may be grouped as follows:

I. Eighteenth century: (a) Trade relations; (b) Austria's attitude during the American Revolutionary War; (c) Emigration.

II. Nineteenth century: (a) Diplomatic correspondence; (b) Emigration; (c) Police records.

I. Eighteenth Century.

(a) trade relations.

Voluminous reports were sent home to the Belgian government by the first agent (Handelsrat) to the United States, Baron Beelen-Bertholff, 1784-1789. These interesting reports have been published in full by Dr. Hanns Schlitter: *Die Beziehungen Österreichs zu den Vereinigten Staaten, 1778-1787* (Innsbruck, 1885); and *Die Berichte des ersten Agenten Österreichs in den Vereinigten Staaten von Amerika, Baron de Beelen-Bertholff, an die Regie-*

rung der Österreichischen Niederlande in Brüssel, 1784-1789 (Vienna, 1891), vol. XLV. in the second series of the *Fontes Rerum Austriacarum*.[1] The material in this section includes the draft of a treaty of commerce between Austria and the United States, a letter of Benjamin Franklin (1784) regarding this treaty, and notes and criticisms of the articles of the treaty by Count Mercy.

In the Hofkammerarchiv the earliest reference to America is a fantastic scheme for a world-wide expansion of trade, by Filippo Fabrini; there is another plan of trade with America in 1776 by Christoph Beller; in 1783 the sending of Beelen-Bertholff is noted. The Kriegsarchiv shows a record of an offer of grain for sale from America in 1789.

(B) AUSTRIA'S ATTITUDE DURING THE REVOLUTIONARY WAR.

The earliest record in the Kriegsarchiv at Vienna shows that some few (20) men from Austrian domains in 1780 slipped away to join the troops of the Anspach contingent which was used by England against her revolting American colonies. In 1780-1781, auxiliary troops to the number of 3300 passed through Höxter on the Weser on their way to the British American service. They were not Austrian subjects, and were stopped at Höxter long enough for the arrest of deserters and Austrian subjects who might be found in the ranks. By Austria's action in preventing her own subjects from entering this service, the cause of the American colonists was greatly benefited. Had Prussia and Austria, the two most populous and powerful German states, allowed recruiting in their territories, the number of auxiliary troops that England could have put into the field against the American colonies would have been greatly increased, perhaps with crushing force.

The division " Länder " in the K. u. K. Haus-, Hof- und Staatsarchiv tells us that in 1781 there was a secret attempt on the part of one Gerstenberg, secretary of legation to the English ambassador at Vienna, to secure recruits for England from among Austrian subjects, and in 1782 there is a record that there was some success. When this was reported, measures were taken to prevent its recurrence (see Kriegsarchiv, 1781-1783).

The Staatsarchiv records the arrival of William Lee in Vienna, May, 1778; he was not received and his mission was unsuccessful, because the court did not wish to antagonize England. Franklin's arrival in Paris is noted in 1776 and his appointment as minister to France in 1779. Traces of a plan of mediation on the part of Prussia and Russia, between England and France and the American colonies, appear in 1779. Between 1774 and 1784 frequent complaints are made on the part of England concerning shipments of arms and supplies to the American army by way of St. Eustatius (West Indies), principally by Dutch vessels.

(C) EMIGRATION.

Decrees were issued against emigration, not so much from any fear of losing population to America, or any other country, but as a protective measure against desertion from the army, or the loss of recruits for military service. The old tradition placed emigration on the same level as desertion; it was morally wrong. The prohibition of emigration brought a complaint (in 1794) from a district under Austrian rule wedged into Swabia, where it

[1] See also *American Historical Review*, XVI. 567-587.

was difficult to obey the emigration law. A lenient policy prevailed, so long as the emigration did not exceed the immigration. The Salzburg archives do not mention the name America, though this Austrian province furnished an influential group of sturdy pioneers in the earliest settlement of Georgia. Nevertheless in the Staatsarchiv of Salzburg can be found excellent material for the study of the steps that led up to the cruel expulsion of the Salzburg Protestants from the archbishopric of Salzburg in 1731. The inquisition of heretics for breaking fast, for reading a Lutheran tract, or owning a Lutheran Bible, the dangers of being under suspicion of concealing a Protestant book, can be authentically followed in these records. The adjustments of property claims, forced by the action of King Frederick William I. of Prussia (1734), continued until 1764, thirty-three years after the publication of the famous edict of expulsion, Emigrations Edikt vom 31. Oktober, 1731.

II. NINETEENTH CENTURY.

(A) DIPLOMATIC CORRESPONDENCE.

The K. u. K. Haus-, Hof- und Staatsarchiv contains the complete reports of the diplomatic agents sent by the court of Vienna to the United States, beginning with Graf von Stürmer in 1819, succeeded in the following year by Freiherr von Lederer, consul general, and in effect chargé d'affaires until the appointment in 1838 of Baron Mareschal as first minister plenipotentiary of Austria to the United States, the same year in which Henry Augustus Mühlenberg was sent as first United States minister to the Dual Empire. The reports of Baron Lederer to Prince Metternich were carefully prepared and gave detailed information on current events in the United States, they reviewed the action of Congress and the messages of presidents (with comments), and attempted also to give an impression in regard to the state of public opinion, illustrating with numerous clippings from newspaper editorials, and public addresses. The inquisitorial mind of Metternich was observing America through his agent's eyes. Baron Lederer's principal achievement was the successful negotiation of the commercial and navigation treaty between Austria and the United States, which failed to meet the approval of Henry Clay as Secretary of State, but was safely carried through under his successor in the same office, Martin Van Buren, in the following year, 1829. Interesting items in the correspondence are a statement on Austria's position in regard to slavery (1830), on the Austro-Italian political refugees, comments on the Mexican situation, and on the condition of Catholics in America. Occasional characterizations of public men appear, as of Randolph in 1830, when about to visit Vienna—" an extraordinary envoy, not an envoy extraordinary"; " die Menge seiner Ideen war er nie im Stande in Ordnung zu bringen ".

The reports of the minister, Baron Mareschal (1838-1841), are not as full as those of Lederer and contain more matters of routine. The best part are the enclosed reports of the secretary of the legation, von Hülsemann (Chevalier de Hülsemann), who was sent on numerous trips throughout the country, and required to submit his observations and results. This was accomplished by Hülsemann in a thorough and able manner, e. g., in his paper on the written constitution and the rights of neutrals on the sea ; report on a trip to the Southern States (products and commerce of Virginia ; relation of white and black labor ; leading cities, Norfolk, Charleston, Savannah, etc.) ; report on a trip to New England (factories at Lowell, railroads of Belgium compared with those of the United States, 1839); pen-portraits of the principal members of Congress, Nov. 22, 1839; report on the Whig convention of 1839 and the Democratic convention held at Baltimore, May 4-5, 1840. Hülsemann was rewarded for his zeal and industry with the position of chargé d'affaires at Washington after Baron Mareschal left the post for that of Lisbon in 1841. The reports of Hülsemann to Metternich continue from 1841 to 1847. He negotiated an extradition treaty in 1856.

In the archives of the War Department some interesting American influences are noted. In 1819, when new frigates are to be constructed for the Austrian navy, the newest type of frigate in the American navy is to be taken as a model. After 1820 a number of American marine inventions, and the use of cotton duck for sails (instead of flax or hemp), are earnestly inquired into. Travels in America, as the journey of Duke Bernhard of Saxe-Weimar (1825-1826), are watched with interest.

(B) EMIGRATION.

Edicts against emigration continued in force in the nineteenth century. They seem not to have been a cause of hardship, however, as in the case of Switzerland or Germany, hemmed in on all sides by vigorous peoples. The great incentive for the ambitious emigrant, free land, could be had at home for the Austrian. There were still unsettled areas in the plains of Hungary, the mountains of Transylvania, and the Galician territory on the other side of the Carpathian range. These favorable conditions prevailed for the greater part of the nineteenth century. The records at Innsbruck show that emigration for America was not of moment in Tyrol before the middle of the nineteenth century. Only one other province seems to show a greater proclivity toward emigration, viz., the crown land Bohemia. It is possible that the records of Bohemia if carefully searched might show an earlier migration to America. The country is populous, and the friction between Slav and German is not of recent date; it might have acted as an incentive to either race-stock to leave a district where it was outnumbered.

(C) POLICE RECORDS.

In the archive of the Department of the Interior (Allg. Archiv d. K. K. Ministeriums d. Innern) in Vienna are deposited the records of the police department under Metternich. They constitute a great mass of material poorly indexed, and consequently the progress of work in them is slow and difficult. Knowing the name of a particular refugee it is possible to find the acta concerning him, but to collect the whole body of material relating to America would be a huge task. Several great bundles of acta are found on the Lombard-Venetian conspirators of 1835, deported subsequently to America, and on another group of revolutionists from Galicia deported in 1836; acta are found (1823) on the refugee Carl Postl (the novelist Charles Sealsfield), author of *Austria as it Is* (*i. e.*, under the Metternich system); on the religionist Bernhard Müller, *alias* Proli, of Offenbach (1830); on P. Szirmay's plan of emigration in 1835, concerning which he writes to Gottfried Duden, author of the book of travel in the Middle West, which brought great numbers of settlers to Missouri; on Friedrich Baraga (1841), the Indian missionary of Michigan and Lake Superior; on the merchant Leopold Förstl (Ferstl), 1846; on Friedrich Wilhelm Bornemann (1847), an emigrant agent for North America; on Karl Heinzen, the revolutionist of 1848, author of " der teutsche Tribun ", who is reported as " aus der Schweiz gewiesen ". It is very regrettable that the accessibility of the archives ceases with 1847, for the period of 1848 and thereafter would unquestionably furnish the most interesting material from the American point of view. Acta on the career of Hans Kudlich, the liberator of the Austrian peasantry, leader of the revolutionists in Vienna in 1848, sentenced to death, refugee in America (where he lived in retirement from politics), and of many other brilliant men of this epoch, would undoubtedly appear in this archive.

CANTON ZÜRICH.

ZÜRICH: STAATSARCHIV.

Location: The "Staatsarchiv des Kantons Zürich" is located on the second floor of the Obmannamt, which faces the Hirschengraben.

Hours: 8 a. m. to 12 m.; 2 to 6 p. m.

Bibliography: Paul Schweizer, "Geschichte des Staatsarchivs Zürich", in *Neujahrsblatt des Waisenhauses Zürich* (Zürich, 1894). Paul Schweizer, "Inventar des Staatsarchivs des Kantons Zürich", in *Inventare Schweizerischer Archive,* Beilage to the *Anzeiger für Schweizerische Geschichte,* II. 1-110 (Bern, 1899.)

A. 103. Auswanderungsverzeichnis. 1651, 1661, 1680. A large bundle of acta. Destinations of emigrants: the Palatinate, Netherlands, Swabia, French and Dutch service. Some of these probably migrated to America, though the American colonies are not named as a destination.

E. II. 269. "Rödel aus allen Capiteln, namentlich der nach der Pfalz, dem Elsass und Würtemberg Ausgewanderten, nebst Mandaten und Rathserkenntnissen seit 1651, mit Index." 1657.

E. II. 270. "Rödel (a) nach Gemeinden sämtlicher Capitel der nach der Pfalz, der Markgrafschaft Baden und Würtemberg Ausgewanderten, mit Index." 1657, 1663.

(b) "Rödel der aus dem Capitel Regensberg in den Vilmerger Krieg zu Feld gezogenen." 1656.

(c) "Gemeinderödel v. Dielstorf, Dietikon u. Regensberg." 1649.

E. II. 270 a. "Rödel der 1661 ausser Landes befindl. Züricher Landleute." 1661.

E. II. 268. "Gemeinderödel der Stadt Eglisau." 1767.

A. 8. "Visitation- und Undersuchung, wie selbige in Ao. 1702 ist vorgenommen worden, von derjehnigen Mannschafft ausz mr. Gn. Hrn. Bottmäszigkeit, welche sich theils in Frömbden Kriegsdiensten, theils sonsten auszert Lands befindet, wie solches von dem Hrn. Decanis einkommen." This is a list of names of persons who were not at home in the year 1702. The place whence they were last heard from is given wherever possible. Many undoubtedly found their way from Alsace to the American colonies.

A. 90. 2. (XVII. 75. 2.) "Herr Jacob Christ. Zollikofer, Bürger von St. Gallen; dermahlen Einwohner und Handelsmann zu Virginien in America; alsz zu dieser Affaire bevollmächtigter, bittet um gnädige Beisteuer zum Kirchen und Schulbau für die Deutschen in Virginien." Zürich, Aug. 28, 1720. (3 Stück.) "Virginia Gemeinde besteht aus 12 Familien Reformierter und 20 Familien Lutherische." This was the German colony founded by Governor Spotswood in Virginia, "Germanna", and its offshoots, Germantown, Hebron Church (Madison County), etc. Letter dated June 18, 1720.

A. 128. 10. "Akten betr. Auswanderung in Carolinam et Pensylvaniam." Vogtei Knonau. 1729, 1734-1735. (12 Stück.)
Inquiry for advice concerning emigration. Mar. 29, 1729.
Reply and plan suggested. Apr. 2, 1729.
Description of Pennsylvania. "Verhör einiger Mannspersonen welche nacher Pensylvaniam reisen wollen." Reasons for emigration. Apr. 4, 1729.
"Drei treue Hausväter" wollen reisen. Apr. 11, 1729.
Passes given. July 27, 1734.
Attempt to dissuade emigrants from going to Carolina. Aug. 4, 1734.
Other acta dated Aug. 5, 20, Sept. 15, 25, Oct. 5, 1734; Apr. 13, 1735.
A. 131. 25. Akten. Kieburg. (6 Stück.)
"Verhör." Aug. 18, 1734.
List of emigrants. Apr. 3, 1737.
Request to emigrate. Oct. 8, 1734.
Returning emigrant. Sept., 1738.
A. 169. 2. Akten. Verhör Götschi, etc. Briefe von Emigranten aus London. The letters are dated Oct. 4, 20, 25, 1734. They describe the journey through France and the long delays before embarkation at London. They give a favorable picture in the main, describing hardships as possible to endure or overcome. (8 Stück.)
A. 44. 1. Mandate auszuführen vs. Emigration. Dec. 7, 1739. (1 Stück.)
A. 174. "Verzeichnisse der Ausgewanderten nach Carolina und Pensylvanien." 1734-1744. Nos. 1-98. This is a complete list of emigrants from every district of the canton of Zürich during the period of greatest migration to the American colonies. It is invaluable for genealogical purposes, and should be printed entire. It is the only source which gives complete statistics on which we can base an accurate estimate of the number of persons that came to America from Switzerland during the great exodus of 1734-1744. During this decade, in spite of repressive measures of all kinds, the number of emigrants that came from the "Zürich-Gebiet" and journeyed to the American colonies was 2310. The record made by the district Eglisau was 680. The country districts furnished more emigrants than the cities Zürich and Winterthur. Many names that have become familiar American family names are found in these lists, as Frik (Frick) from Knonau (also from Aargau), migrating to Carolina in 1739.
"Protokoll über ausgefertigte Mannrechts-Patente für hiesige Bürger und Angehörige so ihr Bürger- und Landrecht aufgeben; angefangen von Hans Wilgert Zoller, Staatsschreiber, Ao. 1720, revidiert und registriert von Johann Conrad Hirzel, Staatsschreiber, Ao. 1785."
A. 26. 18. Zürich, Stadt und Landschaft. Criminalsachen, Diverse Personalien, 1741-1755.
X. 135. 6. "Acta u. Verhör der nach Pensylvania abreisenden Landleuthe." Apr.–May, 1743. (10 Stück.) Incl. letter of Johann. Mauritius Goetschius, Amsterdam, Aug. 8, 1743.
B. VII. 13. Tom. XIII. 4. Auswanderungen, pp. 86-105.
Printed pamphlet, *Glückshafen*, etc. Spanish emigration, 1767. Acta concerning this, and also Pomerania (Preussisch Pommern).

B II. RATHS MANUALE.

1734. Unterschreiber Manual (UM) II. " Caroliner Sachen." (21 references; see index at end of volume.)
Stadtschreiber Manual (SM) II. " Carolina, hinwegziehen dahin." (4 references.)
1735. UM I. " Ein Mann von Walliszellen kommt zurück ", p. 45.
1736. UM I. " Caroliner Sachen ", p. 41.
1737. UM I. " Carolina ", p. 187. A group of people from two districts planning to go to Carolina. They are to be reasoned with; dangers of the voyage to be urged; and loss of " Landrecht ".
1738. UM I. " Das Reisen nach Carolina und Pensylvania verboten." (3 references.)
UM II. " Carolina, Reisen dahin." (8 references.)
" Carolina, Wiederheimkunft aus." (4 references.)
" Pensylvanien, Reisen dahin." (2 references.)
1739. UM I. " Carolina, Reisen dahin." (5 references.)
" Carolina, Mandat deswegen." (2 references.)
1740. UM II. " Carolina, Colonie in America." (2 references.)
1741. UM I. " Carolinam, Reisen in." (14 references.)
1743. UM I. " Carolina, dahinziehendes Landvolk." (4 references.)
" Pensylvania, dahin ziehende Landleuth." (2 references.)
UM II. "Pensylvania, dahin zu verschicken parat gelegene Quart Biblen ", p. 54.
1744. UM I. " Carolina, dahin verlangende Landleuth ", p. 66.

MANDATE.

III. Landwirtschaftliche Sachen.
I. Emigration; Lands-Verlassung.
1652, Aug. 2. " Dass niemand mehr ohne Erlaubnis aus dem Land wegzeuche; sonderlich nicht an papistische Ohrt; noch zu den Widertäufferen." CXL.
1734, Nov. 3. " Verbot nach Carolinam zu reisen." DCVII.
" Wir Burgermeister und Rath der Stadt Zürich entbieten allen u. jeden Unseren Angehörigen auf Unserer Landschaft Unseren gnädigen Grusz, und darbey zuvernemmen: Demnach wir zu Unserem nicht geringen Bedauern und Miszfallen sehen und erfahren müssen, wie dasz einerseiths die Zeithero eint und andere, Uns zum Theil bekannte Persohnen sich understanden, hin und wider auf Unserer Landschafft viel von Unseren Angehörigen, unter allerhand, meistens gantz und gar unwahrhafft, nichtig- und boszhaftersonnenen Auszstreuw und Vorgebungen zu überreden, und zu vermögen, dasz sie würklich in die Viel Hundert Meilen weit von hier in West-Indien gelegene, theils der Bottmässigkeit Ihro Königlichen Majestät von Grosz-Brittanien, theils aber dem unsicheren Gewalt allerhand wilder und unchristlicher Nationen unterworffene Landschafft Carolinam abgereiset; anderseiths aber, dasz vil-ermeldt-Unserer Angehöriger sich durch allerhand verführische Büchlein, und ihren Eigensinn so stark einnemen lassen, dasz selbige weder denen auf Unseren Befehl von Oberkeitlichen, noch denen von Privat-Persohnen gegen ihnen ausz aufrichtiger Wolmeynung geschehenen Abmahnungen Gehör

geben wollen, dieselbe unwüssende und unbesinnter Weise verachten, und gäntzlich in den Wind schlagen, ja gar einiche, als wann man ihnen an ihrem Wohlstand verhinderlich seyn wollte, sich leichtsinniger Dingen einbilden dörffen; als haben Wir ausz Lands-Vätterlicher, für den Wohlstand der lieben Unserigen, aufrichtig tragender Vorsorg und ausz habender Überzeugung, nicht allein was grosser Mühe, Kosten und Gefahr die Reise, sonderlich für kleine Kinder, in ein solch-entfehrntes Land unterworffen, sonder auch mit wie vielem Ungemach und allerdings unübersteiglichen Schwierigkeiten eine neue Einrichtung in diesem Land unausweichlich begleitet, und annoch, ob die würklich Abgereiseten in dieses Land übergeführt, oder zuruck gewisen werden, gantz ungewüsz seye, Unsere Oberkeitliche Pflicht und Schuldigkeit zu seyn ermessen, durch offentliche Verkündigung dieses Unsers best-gemeynten Mandats, jedermänniglichen mit Vorstellung vor auszgeführtem, der Sachen wahrer Beschaffenheit von solch leichtsinnig, unbegründetem und sehr grossen Gefahren begleitetem Vornemmen treuhertzig abzumahnen und zu verwahrnen, und hingegen, wie hiermit geschihet, alles Ernsts für diszmal zugebiethen, dasz bisz auf Unsere weitere Verordnung niemand, weder Mann, Weib noch Kinder ausz dem Land gehen, sondern in demselben verbleiben, und mittlest des Allerhöchsten mitwürkenden und verheiszenen Segens durch fleiszig und ehrliche Arbeit, sich und die seinigen redlich zu ernehren trachten thue, und wollen dahero, dasz Unsere Ober- und Land-Vogt, und dero nachgesezte Beamtete, dergleichen Leuthen ligend- und fahrend-Gut zu verkauffen keineswegs mehr gestatten, die würklich beschehene Kauff und Verkauff auf Verlangen der Verkäufferen, wenn sie den Kauff-Schilling wider erstatten können, wider aufheben, auf die Auszstreuer dergleichen verführischer Büchlenen und die Aufwigler zu Statt und Land geflissene Achtung gegeben, selbige auf Betretten gefänglich anhero geschickt, und von der hierzu verordneten Commission exemplarisch abgestrafft; und wann über all dise Unsere, so wohl und Vätterlich-gemeynte Verwahrungen und Gebott, dannoch der eint oder andere sich erfrechen, und heimlich darvon ziehen thäte, dem ald [=oder] denenselben nicht allein das hiesige Land-Recht auszhingegeben, sondern auch, wann ein solcher ausz Armuth getrieben, darinnen er sich auf dise Weise muthwillig gestürtzet, wider in sein Heymath käme, von denen Beamteten Unseren Ober- und Land-Vögten angezeiget, mit Weib und Kinderen, von Stadt und Land verwisen, und zu keinen Zeiten mehr darinnen geduldet werden solle. Wornach sich jedermänniglich zurichten, und vor Straff und Ungnad zuverhüten wohl wüssen soll und wird.

"Geben, den dritten Tag Wintermonats, nach Christi unsers lieben Herrn und Heylands Geburth gezelet, Ein Tausend, Siben Hundert, Dreyszig und Vier Jahr. Kantzley der Stadt Zürich."

1735, Jan. 29. "Dto. wie 1734." **DCX.**

"Wir Burgermeister u. Rath d. Stadt Zürich entbieten allen und jeden Unseren Angehörigen zu Stadt und Land Unseren Gnädigen Grusz und darbey zuvernehmen: Demnach Wir zu Unserem nicht geringen Bedauern sehen und erfahren müssen dass ungeachtet all Unserer vorgewandt-Lands-Vätterlicher Sorgfalt und des unterm 3ten Winter-Monat letst-verwichenen Jahrs ab allen Cantzlen zu Stadt und Land verlesenen wohlgemeinten Mandats, dennoch viel der Unsrigen auf eine muhtwillige Weisz ihr Vaterland verlassen mit ihren Weibern und vielen ohnschuldigen Kindern in der Meynung verreiset in dem so weit entlegenen Carolina ihr Leben besser durchzubringen, einestheils; Anderseits aber verlauten will, als wann durch Aufwiegelung ohntreuer Leuthen annoch eint- und andere in gleiches Unglück verleitet werden möchten; Als haben Wir Uns zu wahrem Nutzen samtlicher Unserer lieben Angehörigen veranlasset gesehen, obvermeldt-Unser-Hoch-Oberkeitliches Mandat zuwiederholen, und dahin zuvermehren, dasz hiermit männiglichen das Verreisen in Carolina gänzlichen und so verbotten seyn solle, dass derjenige, so sich hierauf erfrechen wurde, heimlich ald offentlich wegzuziehen, hardurch sein Burger- und Land-Recht solle verlohren haben, und weder er noch die Seinigen zu keiner Zeit mehr dazu gelangen mögen; Und damit dieser Unbesonnenheit der Riegel noch mehrers gestossen werde, so sollen Unsere Ober- und Land-Vögte fleissigste Achtung geben, dasz dergleichen Leuthen keine Verkauff mehr, es seye von Ligend- oder Fahrendem zugelassen, sondern selbige behindert, und je nach Beschaffenheit der Sach die Käuffere, als die meistentheils hardurch ihren unbilligen Eigennutz suchen, mit ernsthafter Straff zur Verantwortung gezogen werden. Auch werden sie so wohl als ihre nachgesetzte Beamtete, wie dann in Unserer Stadt von den eigens hierzu verordnetgeliebten Mit-Rähten auch beschehen wird, auf obvermeldte Aufwieglere eine genaue Aufsicht haben, und selbige auf Betretten zu ernstlich und exemplarischer Abstraffung ohngesäumt allhero schicken. Alles um so mehr, weilen Wir sint der Zeit die betrübte Nachricht ganz Stand- und wahrhaft erhalten, dasz obgleich keiner von diesen elenden Leuthen in das sogenannte Carolina kommen wird, dennoch eine grosze Anzahl meist Unserer vormahligen Angehörigen zwar in Engelland angekommen, sich aber in dem gröszten Elend und Erbarmungswürdigsten Zustand befinden, so dasz zubesorgen, sie werden, als die sich selbst in äusserstes Elend gestürzt in Ermangelung nöthiger Lebens-Mittlen, so wohl als der Kleidern, ihre Ohnbesonnenheit und den ihrem Vaterland bewiesenen Ohndank, in ihrem Verderben bedauren müssen; Welches Wir hierdurch jedermänniglichem zuwüssen thund, und also auch ein jeder sich vor Unglück, Straff und Ungnad zuverhüten wohl wüssen wird.

" Geben Samstags den Neun und Zwanzigsten Jenner, Eintausend Siebenhundert Dreyszig und Fünf Jahr. Kantzlei der Stadt Zürich."

1736, Feb. 3. " Dto. wie 1736." **DCXV.**
1739, May 13. " Verbott in Süd-Carolinam, Pensilvaniam, Georgien u. andere Oerther zu ziehen, conf. 1736." **DCXXXVII.**
1741, Feb. 4. " Dto. wie 1739." **DCLIII.**
1744, Mar. 18. " Dto. wie 1741." **DCLXXIII.**

1767, Dec. 10. " Mandat wider die Emigration in die spanische Colonien, für das Thurgau. Idem für das Rheinthal; Sargans; O. fr. (frei) Ämter; Gr. Bad. u. fr. Ämter; alle gleichlautend." DCCCLV.
1770, Nov. 29. " Verbott in das preussisch Pommern zu ziehen. Conf. 1767." DCCCCVII.
E. II. 43, 44. Protokollum Actorum Ecclesiasticorum ab Anno 1731-1749, 1749-1757.
E. II. 43. p. 271. Zell: " Gravamen [*i. e.*, Beschwerde] Begird in Carolinam zuziehen. Wird vielleicht im Prosynodo der HHrn. Decanorum vorkommen." Oct., 1734.
p. 410. " Hr. Decan berichtet am end, dass in dem den 14 Sept. gedruckten Nachrichtsblättlein enthalten, dass viel aus dem Canton Appenzell und Grafschaft Toggenburg nacher Carolina reisen. Dieses und dergleichen, um unser Volck nicht auf das neue gelüstig zumachen, sollte nicht gedruckt werden. Einer der Ihr. Censorum berichtete, dass ob er es gleich improvirt, der Drucker es dennoch auf seinen Kopf gedruckt: worüber er zu reden gestellt worden." Oct., 1736.
p. 736. " Carolina. Schweizerische Colonisten, die sich dort niederlassen. Um dieser .... als Prediger Indianer begehrte (1734) ein gr. [*i. e.*, gewisser] Mawritz Göttschi von .... ein Attestat von hier. Acta 260, 263, welches ihm auch gegeben ward. Sein Sohn Heinrich schrieb aus Pensilvanien (p. 581) begehrt ad S. Minist. ordinirt zu werden; was man zu thun bedenklich fand. Schreibt wieder aus Holländ. America (p. 736) u. verlangt, ein Membrum Synodi nostra zu seyn, und dass man auch seinen aus Carolina hergekommenen Bruder zum Ministro mache, damit er hernach die Gemeinde der Schweizer-Colonisten in America bedienen könne. Auf das erste wurde geantwortet—' Einen Abwesenden und bey uns nicht ordinirten in Synodum auf zunehmen, reime sich nicht mit unserer Verfassung. Seinen Bruder betreffend, wird selbiger aus S. Allmosenamt adsistirt, dass er Chirurgie erlehrnen kann. MGn. HHrn. haben seinethalben expresse erkannt, dass er bey uns ad S. Minist. nicht adspiriren solle, aus landesväterlicher Sorg, dessen er nicht nach der Hand viele von unserm Volk zu emigriren lüstern mache'."
" Späterhin (1747) liess ersterer, durch eben diesen seinen Bruder bitten, dass man ihm im Sackcalender unter unsern Ministris in der Fremde mit einrücken mögte. Erk[annt] Nein; er solle ein Patent einschicken, wann, wo und wie er ordiniert worden sey", p. 828.
p. 283. " Schulmeister Kuhn von Grafstal der Pfarr Lindau, so wegen Carolina sein Sächli verkauft, von der Gemeind seinen Dienst aufgegeben, und ein Abschiedszeugnisz bekommen, jezo aber den reuen spilt, bittet MHHrn mit einem für ihne mitgekommenen Kirchenpfleger demüthig, ihne wider in seinen Schuldienst einzusezen. Ward ihme in seiner angelegenlichen Bitt gnädig willfahret, und deszen zum Urkund ein Schrn. an seinen Hrn. Pfarrer, Hrn. Camerarium Wysz, mitgegeben."
pp. 286-287. "Hans Heinrich Maag, der in Carolinam ziehen wollen, und ein extra guter angenehmer Sänger ist, zu Schulmeistern gesezet und erwehlet worden." Nov., 1734. Beylag 553.

p. 287. " Schulmeister zu Ellikon hat in Carolinam ziehen wollen."
(Received an inducement to stay.) Nov., 1734.
p. 345. " Emigratio in Carolinam. Elsau: Bericht Hr. Decani von
16 Emigranten seiner Gemeinde. Ist gut wann die fata und elend
dieser zurückgekommenen leuthen unserm Landvolk bekannt, und
dadurch andere vom emigriren abgehalten werden." Oct., 1735.
p. 385. " Elgäuer Capitel. 2. Bericht wegen Carolina (nicht vorhanden)." Apr., 1737.
p. 518. " Emigrirte aus diesem Capitel [Eglisau] in Carolinam sind
291 Seelen; die mit weggenohmen 4321 fl. [Gulden] nur was
man weiszt; noch vieles unwiszend." Nov., 1738.
p. 593. " Vorhabendes Emigriren in Carolinam. Weyach: Da und
in der Nachbarschaft grosse Bewegung und Anstalten, könftige
Frühling in Carolinam wegzuziehen. Hierüber kann man sich bey
der Commission, die MGHHrn geordnet, anmelden. Diesmalige
Kriegs-Conjuncturen in selbigem Lande sollten unseren Landen
den appetit vergehen machen." Oct., 1740.
p. 638. " Weiach: Gravamen wegen des Leuthverführer Bersinger,
nach Carolinam." Oct., 1741.
p. 639. " Märsteten: grav. dasz 3 Haushaltungen in 19 Personen
bestehend, nacher Carolinam emigrirt. Wollten sich nicht hinterhalten laszen." Oct., 1741.
p. 712. " Jägerlen (Steinercapitel) lamentirt, dasz nur aus seiner
Pfarr. 53 Personen in Carolinam emigrirt." Nov., 1743.
pp. 276, 714. "Auswanderer nach Carolinam. Ein Gravamen Synodale."
pp. 618, 699. " Das Emigriren nach Pensylvanien. Ein Gravamen
Synodale."
E. II. 434. Litterae et acta varia; ab anno 1737 et deinceps ecclesia; speciatim Americanas, Palatinas, Polonicas, Lithuanicas, Rhaeticas,
et Wetzsteinianas lites concernentia.
A large number of letters concerning contributions to churches in Pennsylvania and Carolina, e. g., Schlatter's attempt to secure contributions (1751); letter of Balthazar Pfister (1752) explaining
why no contribution was possible from Schaffhausen; Götschi's
letter in Dutch; a request for 50 copies of the Bible refused.
A copy of Schlatter's book: *Wahrhafte Erzehlung von dem wahren
Zustand der meist Hirtenlosen Gemeinden in Pensilvanien und
denen angrenzenden Provinzen, von Michael Schlatter, Evangelisch Reformirten Prediger zu Philadelphia, denen Hoch-Ehrwürdigen Christlichen Synoden in den Niederlanden, wie auch
andern mildthätigen Christen in Holländischer Sprache vorgestellt. Nunmehro aber von dem Verfasser selbst in die deutsche
Sprache übersetzet, und zugleich an die löbliche Reformirte Eidgenoszschaften und Ministeria in der Schweitz dediciret, nebst einem
Vorbericht der Verordneten von der Classe zu Amsterdam*
(Frankfurt a. M., gedruckt bey Ph. W. Eichenberg, d. Jüngern,
1752).
E. II. 44. p. 65. " Obrigkeitliche Veranstaltungen die Auswanderung nach
Carolina zu verhindern." Apr., 1750.

E. II. 66. Beylagen zu dem Protokoll Actorum Ecclesiasticorum ab anno
1731 ad ann. 1749. (A large number of references.)
No. 516 ad p. 260. " Supplication Hrn. Moritz Götschis."
No. 524 ad p. 263. " Erlaubnis dass Götschi als Prediger der Schweizer
Colonisten in Carolina diene." Aug. 29, 1734.
Das Hochoberkeitliche Staats Archiv zum Frauen Münster von Alten her
bis auf das Jahr 1740. Register von Salomon Wolf 1778. Entries under " America ".
1726. " Reisen in Ost- und West Indien, in Carolinam, in Pensilvaniam."
1734. " Löblichen Stands Bern Anzug, wegen der in Carolinam häufig
reisenden Leuthen." XXX. 552. 2.
" Junker Landvogt Zoller zu Kyburg berichtet, es wollind viele
Leuth in Carolinam reisen." IX. 663. 24 b.
" Item Hr. Pfr. zu Altorf, dass Jacob Schenkel mit Weib und
Kinder dahin wolle." IX. 663. 24 b.
" Mandat wieder das Reisen in Carolinam." XXX. 553. I.
" Basel bittet, dass man die Caroliner mit Pässen versehe, damit
sie ihnen mit Bettlen nicht beschwerlich fallen." V. 731. 18.
1737. " Hr. Landvogt Leu zu Kyburg berichtet seine vergebens gehabte
Bemühungen zwey von Billikon und Ernst von ihrer Reisz in
Carolinam abzuhalten." IX. 668. 32.
1738. " Relation eines von hoher Verordnung verhörten und aus Carolina zurückgekehrten Elggauers." IX. 670. 9.
" Johannes Schweizers vorhabende Entführung seiner Ehebrecherin, in Carolinam." XXIII. 709. 5.
" Rahts Begehren Hrn. Landvogt Wolfen zu Greyffen See, wegen
einicher aus seiner Herrschaft in Carolinam zu reysen entschlossener Haushaltungen." X. 563. 33.
" Item Jkr. Landvogt Grebel." X. 704. 16.
" Hrn. Landvogt Stockers Amts Bericht, auch deswegen." X.
878. 29.
" Idem begehrt Befehl, wie er sich der zurückgekommenen Carolinern halben zu verhalten habe." X. 878. 30.
" Die Gemeind Boppelsen beschwährt sich über die Ihro zugemuthete Wieder Annahme eines nacher Carolinam verreisten
Heinrich Mathisen, oder dessen Kinderen Versorgung." X.
704. 17.

America. 1741-1756.

1741. " Hr. Landvogt Streif zu Frauenfeld berichtet das Vorhaben vieler
seiner Angehörigen in Carolinam zu ziehen." V. 4. 18.
1752. " Abgeschlagene Steuer für die Kirchen in Pensilvanien." I. 273. 14.
" Einfrag bei Mr. de Vermont ob man zu Hünigen in der Schweiz
herumvagierende Bürsch annehmen [=verhaften], und in die
americanischen Insuln schicken würde." I. 271. Beilage C, D.
" Französische Antworten betr. den Eidgenöss. Vorschlag wegen Verschickung der Vaganten in die französ. Colonie in America." I.
107. 9, 10.
1756. " Gottlieb Mittelberger übersendet aus Stuttgart einiche Exemplar
seiner Beschreibung von Pensilvanien." I. 711. 10.

Emigrationen.

1729. "Resolution etwelcher junger Mannschaft aus der Herrschaft Knonau in das Neu Engellend in America zu ziehen, und Rathsbegehren, ob sie nicht von dem mitnehmenden Gelt den Abzug liefern sollen." **XI.** 164. 10.

"Verhör einicher Manns Personen, aus der Herrschaft Knonau, welche nacher Pensylvanien zu reisen gesinnet." **XI.** 165. 11.

"Aus der Herrschaft Knonau in Neu England Abzug von dens." See A. **128.** 10, above, p. 14.

1734. "Hr. Landvogt Scheuchzers Bericht, dass einiche von denen in Carolina zu reisen gesinnten sich abhalten lassen, und die Päss zurückgeben." **XI.** 173. 17 a.

"Hr. Landvogt Scheuchzer berichtet, dass Heinrich Näf von Hausen (ein ziemlich bemittleter Paur) verschiedene (Pietisten) zur Reisz in die Insul Carolinam animiert und entführt." **XI.** 173. 17 b.

"Hr. Land Schreiber zu Knonau berichtet, die Namen der 11 Personen, so in Carolinam verreiszt, der Abzug werde genohmen von dem Gut, so aus dem Land gezogen werde, der Näfen Bruder wolle die 605 fl. nicht verabzügen." **XI.** 173. 17 c.

"Hr. Landvogt Scheuchzer bittet um befehl, wie er sich wegen der Näfen aus der Graben, der Pfarr:Hausen, verweigernden Abzug ihrer Brüdern in Carolina gezogener Mittlen zu verhalten." **XI.** 173. 18.

"Verhör der nach Carolina ziehenden Alt Pfarrer Götschis und Meister Wüsten des Metzgers, samt einigen Berichten von abgereisten Carolinern aus der Herrschaft Knonauw, von London." **XIX.** 1049. 26.

"Verdacht auf Ludwig Herder und Heinrich Kambli wegen des Caroliner Geschäfts." **XXIII.** 668. 8.

1735. "Des Metzger Wüsten schlecht Aufführung in dem Caroliner Geschäft." **XXIII.** 689. 4.

1738. "Johannes Schweizers vorgehabte Entführung s. Ehebrecherin in Carolinam." **XXIII.** 709. 5.

1739. "Emigrationen. Gutachten deswegen." **XIV.** 280. 12.

Emigrationen, 174 -90.

1740. "Gutachten betr. den Streit zwischc Hrn. Landvogt Öris sel[igen] Erben, und den Verwandten der in Pensilvanien sich befindenden Hagemanns von Herziken." **VI.** 513. 4 a.

1741. "Ulrich Hubers und Heinrich Weidmanns von Süniken beharrliches Vorhaben mit ihren Haushaltungen in Carolina zu ziehen." **VI.** 546. 5.

"Verhör mit 31 Emigranten in Carolina aus dem Zürichgebieth." **VIII.** 357. 8.

"Hr. Landvogt im Thurgau bittet um einen Provisional Befehl d. L[öblichen] St[adt] Zürich, wegen vieler Thurgauer Vorhabender Emigranten in Carolina." **V.** 4. 18.

1743. "Der nach Pensilvanien abzureisen vorhabender Landleuten Verhör." **X.** 135. 6. (With lists of names.)

"Bericht der Hrn. schirm Vögten betr. den von Zürich abreisenden Solomon Nüscheler." **VIII.** 338. 11 b.

" Bittschrift Moritz Götschis aus Pensilvanien." XII. 40. 20.
" Basel berichtet betr. ein nach Carolina gereistes und zu Mumpf gestorbenes Töchterlein." III. 450. 12.
1743 u. 1744. " Acta betr. emigrirte Landleute in Carolina." VII. 257. 1 a.
1749. " Drei Männer von Ryken wollen in Pensilvanien ziehen." VI. 142. 4.
" Bern klagt über Jacob Walder von Knonau, wegen Verlockens in Pensilvanien." III. 12. 10.
1750. " Weisung betr. den aus Carolina zurückgekommenen, und während sr. Abwesenheit Verauffalten [*i. e.*, in Concurs geratenen] Küfer Öri von Zürich." VIII. 110. 7.
1751. " Weisung betr. Seckelmeister Bären Sohn, ab den Hirzel, der aus Pensilvanien zurückgekommen." VII. 165. 10.
" Bern berichtet dass sie Hrn. Pfarrer Schlatter wegen einer Steuer zur Reise in Pensilvanien abgewiesen haben." III. 18. 17.
1752. " Weisung betr. die Erbs-Extradition der in Pensilvanien sich aufhaltenden Elisabeth Bleuler von Zolliken." VII. 227. 17.
1759. " Verena Üelin von Andelfingen, kommt aus Carolina zurück." X. 159. 13.
1765. " Bern berichtet, dass in der Eidgenossenschaft Verlocker in die Russischen Colonien herumschleichen." III. 37. 18-20.
1767. " Solothurn notificirt betr. Lockungen in Spanische Colonien." II. 262. 9.
Wegen emigranten in Spanische Colonien. Mandate, etc. III. 42, 12-23.
" Bern consentirt zu den Anstalten in untern freien Aemtern wegen der zurückkehrenden Colonisten." III. 42. 25.
" Glarus consentirt auch deswegen." III. 42. 26.
" Gutachten betr. die emigrationen in Spanishe Colonien." VIII. 319. 1, 2, 6.
1768. " Wegen Verlockung in Spanische Colonien." II. 262-3. 10-15. " Emigrationen dahin." VIII. 319. 7. " Anstalten dagegen." VIII. 320. 4-6; VIII. 321. 6, etc.
" Verhör mit dem nach Pensilvanien zu reisen vorhabenden Heinrich Huber von Metmenstätten." VI. 717. 11.
1769. " Vollmacht auf Heinrich Grob Übernehmung der Mittlen, des in Pensilvanien sesshaften Heinrich Syzen von Knonau." VI. 718. 2.
1770-1771. " Acta betr. die Mittel Extradition Zwyer in Pensilvanien sesshaften Angehörigen von Wädenschweil und Knonau." VI. 767. 7.
1773. " Knonau berichtet betr. die Erbs Theilung des in Carolina verstorbenen Christian Groben von Maschwanden." VI. 726. 14.
" Mittel Extradition des in Pensilvanien sesshaften Heinrich Schweizers von Opfikon." VI. 209. 9.
1778. " Appellation zwischen Rudolf Rütschi von Dällikon einer-, dann Kirchenpfleger Bersinger, Müller zu Weyach und Mitintressierten Erben, der in Pensylvanien verstorbenen Margaretha Bersinger anderseits,—betr. eine Schuldforderung von Fl. 715 Capital, nebst Zinsen, welche lestere an Erstern machen." VII. 105. 3.
" Commisionalacta über obig bersingerische Schuld- und Erbstreitigkeit." VII. 105. 4-8.

America. 1790-1798; 1803-1814.

1791. "Angesuchte Mittel und Landrechts Extradition der zu Albanien sich aufhaltenden Huberischen Familie von Unter-Mettmenstetten." IX. 341. 52.

1794. "Amts Bericht des Landvogtey Amts Knonau, wegen einem dem in America sich aufhaltenden Jacob Buchmann v. Dachelsen zufallenden Erb." IX. 346. 48, 50.
1803. "Anzeige und Bericht von vorhabender Auswanderung einiger Familien von Hesserschweil nach Nord America." IX. 426. 2, 4, 5.
"Raths Erlaubnis und Auftrag deswegen an die Commission des Innern." IX. 426. 3.
1804. "Antrag wegen Versendung des Staatsgefangenen Hauptmann Hanharts von Pfeffikon nach dem Spanischen America." XIII. 929. 133; XIII. 936. 79.
"Acta betr. Masznahmen in Absicht d. i. span. America ausgebrochenen gelben Fiebers." XI. 3 u. 4.
1805. "Gutachten betr. die Versorgung des inhaftirten Staatsverbrechers J. Jacob Hanhart von Pfäffikon nach Nord America." VI. 995. 1.
"Antwort der Regierung des Cantons Basel auf die diesfällige Recharge." Ibid., 4.
"Ob die hinterlassene Tochter d. nach America emigrirten Hr. Ulr. Hinderling von Waltenstein daselbst als Gemeinde Bürgerin aufgenommen werden müsse." IX. 443. 83.
1806. "Schuldstreitigkeit einiger von Alfoltern mit dem in America sich aufhaltenden Heinr. Schneebeli, und der Kinderen des dorten verstorbenen Schrepfers E. Schneebeli sämtl. von Alfoltern." XIV. 63. 24.
1807. "Einfrage: Ob Bürger, so aus einer Gemeinde wegziehen, eine Tröstung zurücklassen müssen, oder nicht." IX. 339. 112.
"Gutachten deswegen." IX. 445. 69.

America. 1814-1827.

1815. "Die Berner Polizeidirektion meldet den Aufenthalt von Joseph Buonaparte in America." XVI. 511. 43.
1815-1816. "Acta betr. das Vermögens Extraditions Begehren der zu Harmonie in Nord Amerika befindl. Joh. Meyer von Winkel." VI. 76. 11-15.
1816. "Die eidgenöss. Canzley übermacht verschiedene Berichte über die gute Behandlung der nach America ausgewanderten Schweizer." IX. 503. 28.
1817. "Anzeige dass G. Bader, Schuldner, nach Nord Amerika ausgewandert sey." I. 729. 7.
"Der eidgenössische Vorort communiciert eine k. niederländische Verordnung dass alle nach Holland kommende Auswanderer nach America Bürgschaft leisten sollen, dass sie dort bis zur Abreise ihren Unterhalt finden können." IX. 509. 13; IX. 507. 25, 26.
1819. "K. span. Decret welches Todesstrafe und Ausschliessung von Amnestie gegen diejenigen ausspricht, welche den südamerikanischen Insurgenten durch Kriegsdienste oder Lieferung von Waffen, Munition und soweitere Hilfe leisten." I. 429. 36.
"Der eidgenöss. Vorort berichtet dass der k. preuss. Gesandte laut k. Verordnung nur denjenigen Auswanderern nach America die Pässe visiere, welche die Reisekosten vorweisen können." I. 556. 4, 5.

"Der eidgenöss. Vorort erinnert an die Verordnung der k. holländ. Regierung, dass Auswanderer nach America für ihre Aufenthaltskosten in Holland Bürgschaft leisten müssen." XVII. 512. 43.
"Acten betr. Erbschaften." IV. 474. 31, 32; VI. 82. 18, 20.
1820. "Rathsbeschluss betr. die zu beobachtenden Maasnahmen wegen Auswanderungen nach America und Brasilien." XVII. 690. 39.
"Deposition Hr. Schiffmeisters Reutlinger über den bey Goldbach verunglückten Hr. F. W. Goddard von Poston [Boston] in America, nebst Auskunft des Schiffknecht Rud. Gimpert von Küssnacht." XVI. 746. 96.
1821. Acten betr. Erbschaften. IX. 380. 31, 32; XVII. 529. 1; XVII. 530. 8.
1823. Acten betr. Vermögens Extradition. V. 833. 38; XVII. 588. 13.
"Der eidgenöss. Vorort berichtet die Anerkennung des schweiz. Handelsconsuln zu New York und Alexandria." VIII. 268. 44.
"Ansuchen des Herrn von Mater aus America um Ratification seines Kaufs des Gutes Goldenberg im Oberamt Andelfingen und um Gestattung seiner Niederlassung." VI. 735. 63; XVIII. 24. 32, 33.
1824. "Acten betr. d. Nachfrage wegen Johann Meyer in Harmonie in Nordamerika und Bericht über das Absterben dieses Meyer, von Heisch gebürtig, in Paris." I. 348. 27-32.
"Gutachten d. Commission des Innern betr. die Erblassung der in Virginien in Amerika verstorbenen Carl Frey von Weisslingen." V. 685. 4.
"Bitte des Jacob Meyer von Winkel, dass auf diplomatischem Wege in Erfahrung gebracht werde, ob seinem Bruder in Amerika die Ao. 1816 übersandten 100 Ldors zugekommen und ob er noch am Leben seye." VI. 88. 49, 50.
"Rathsbeschluss betr. die Mittheilung der Eröffnungen d. Hr. A. Sg. Cazenova, Consul in Alexandria, wegen Betreibung der Verlassenschaftsangelegenheiten der in Amerika mit Tod abgehenden Schweizer." IX. 384. 31.
"Die Berner Polizeidirection übermacht eine Publication rücksichtlich der nach Nordamerika auswandernden Schweizer." XVIII. 216. 99.
1826. "Der Kirchenrath empfiehlt den Wunsch des amerikan. Geistlichen Hr. James R. Reily zu Errichtung eines theologischen Seminariums für die deutsch-reformierten Gemeinden in den Vereinigten Staaten milde Beiträge zu sammeln." XI. 356. 2.
1824, 1826. "Verschiedene Acten betr. Erbschaft von Barb. Frey verstorben in Little York in Amerika."

America. 1827-1848.

1827. "Bericht d. Eidgenöss. Vorort, dass die Nachforschungen über Leben u. Tod eines Ao. 1805 nach Amerika ausgewanderten Joh. Meyer von Winkel bisher fruchtlos geblieben; und Auszüge aus den Protokollen der Commission d. Innern betr. den diesem Meyer 'als Colonist in Harmonie in Nord Amerika' übersandten Vermögensbetrag von Fl. 1000." VI. 93. 32, 33; VI. 95. 14.

1828. "Ansuchen des Obrmt. Embrach betr. d. Verlassenschaft eines zu Philadelphia verstorbenen Georg Friedrich Haga." I. 652. 2.
" Wegen angeblicher Erbverlassenschaft Barba. Frey." V. 695. 6.
1828-1829. Erbschaftsangelegenheiten. IV. 574. 47; XVII. 723. 12.
1830. " Verschiedene Akten betr. die Ankunft d. Hrn. J. G. Böcker als General Consul d. Nord Amerikanischen Freystaaten i. d. Schweiz." II. 631. 35, 36.
" Vorörtliches Kreisschreiben betr. die Form d. eidlichen Beglaubigung von Waarenfacturen die aus der Schweiz nach Nordamerika gehen." *Ibid.*, 37.
" Ratherkanntnusz betr. die Einfragen des Nord Amerikanischen General Consuls auf welche Weise die Angaben des Werthes von Waaren Sendungen in die Schweiz erhärtet werden; diesf. Auskunft der l. Staatskanzlei ", etc. *Ibid.*, 38-41.
Erbschaftsangelegenheiten. IV. 575. 12, 33-35.
" Antrag Hrn. F. L. Guyot in Paris die aus Frankreich zurückkehrenden Schweizertruppen zur Colonisation nach Columbia zu senden." XVII. 492. 7.
1831. " Der Consul der Ver. Staaten i. Nord Amerika erkundigt sich nach dem Werte des spanischen Thalers auf hies. Platz." I. 439. 71.
" Vorörtliches Kreisschreiben betr. d. Anweisungen, welche die durch Frankreich Auswandernden zu leisten haben." II. 308. 5.
Id. " betr. ein Ansuchen d. vereinigten Nord Amerikanischen Staaten um Mitteilung d. schweizerischen Handelsgesetze." II. 639. 152.
" Akten betr. das abgelehnte Ansuchen d. Hr. Pfarrer Schinz in Fischenthal seinem in Kulm Ct. Aarau sesshaften Jakob Furrer, Spengler, um eine Unterstützung an die Kosten seiner beabsichtigten Reise nach Nord Amerika zu geben." II. 885. 11, 12.
" Das Nord Amerikan. Handelsconsulat bittet um Mitteilung d. hiesigen Handelsgesetze; Bericht d. kaufmännischen Directorii." XIII. 712. 16, 17.
" Bericht d. Regierungsrath löblichen Stands Luzern wegen Gebrüder Yedy von Bern, dato in Amerika." XVIII. 495. 25.
" Auftrag d. Regierungsrath betr. das Auswandern schweizerischer Angehörigen nach Amerika." XVIII. 496. 39.
1832. " Akten betr. eine Vorörtl. Zuschrift an die handeltreibenden Stände über das schweizer. Handelskonsulat und die Grundlagen der mit Mexiko und Nord Amerika anzubahnenden Unterhandlungen und Bekanntmachung einer Note des Consuls." XV. 751. 1-4.
" Akten betr. die Mitteilung einer französ. u. holländ. Note über die Auswanderer nach Amerika." XV. 751. 5, 6.
" Der eidgenöss. Vorort theilt die holländ. Verordnung betr. die Auswanderung durch die niederländ. Staaten mit." XIX. 266. 51.
" Die österr. Gesandtschaft ersucht um Bekanntmachung des von ihrem Hofe erlassenen Gesetzes über die Auswanderung aus dortigen Staaten." VIII. 911. 11.
1833. "Vorörtliches Kreisschreiben betr. die Visirung der Pässe zur Auswanderung." Sch. 591. M. 1. 11.
1836. " Akten betr. d. Freizügigkeitsvertrag mit d. Ver. Staaten v. Nordamerika." F. 1. A. 2. M. 1. 15.
1837-1839. " Akten betr. d. Verhältnisse d. schweizer. Handelsconsulate daselbst." F. 1. A. 5. M. 1. 1, 2.

1839. "Einsendung d. Berichtes d. Staatssecretairs d. Finanzen an d. amerikanischen Congress." F. 1. A. 1. 32. M. 1. 1.
1845. "Vorörtliches Schreiben betr. d. Vertrag mit den Ver. Staaten über gegenseitige Auslieferung der Verbrecher." F. 1. A. 2. M. 2. 20-21.
"Akten betr. die Handelsverhältnisse mit Obigen." F. 1. B. 10. 2. M. 1. 40.
"Schreiben d. Consuls in New York betr. d. Auswanderungen nach d. Ver. Staaten." F. 3. D. 3. M. 1. 8.
1846. "Anerbieten d. Consuls über Einrückung von Inseraten in nordamerikanische Blätter." F. 1. A. 1. 32. M. 1. 12.
1847. "Vorörtliche Kreisschreiben betr. d. Handelsverkehr aus der Schweiz nach d. nordamerikan. Freistaaten." F. 1. B. 10. 2. M. 2. 2, 6.
"Bericht d. glarnerischen Vereins für Auswanderer über die Kolonie Neu Glarus." F. 3. D. 3. M. 1. 10.
"Vorörtl. Kreisschreiben betr. d. Auswanderung nach d. Vereinsstaaten." F. 1. A. 2. M. 2. 27, 28.
Id. "Erhebung von auswandernden Schweizern dahin. F. 3. D. 3. M. 1. 13.
Id. "Überfahrt dahin." F. 3. D. 3. M. 1. 16, 17.
O. 61. I. Handelsverhältnisse mit dem Ausland.
(13) Vereinigte Staaten von Nordamerika. 1841-1853. Contains: Acta concerning commercial treaty with U. S. 1845.
Id. concerning changes in tariff.
Id. concerning consular fees.
Id. concerning improvement of trade facilities between Switzerland and the United States.
Id. betr. Eidesleistung für Verification von Facturen.
Id. betr. Gesuch, Zürich: Seidefabrikanten um diplomat. Verwendung.
Id. betr. Generalkonsulat in Washington: Beschlagnahme von Seidenwaaren in New York. 1867.
Id. betr. Sequestration Schweiz. Seidenwaaren. 1867.
O. 60. I. Ausstellungen im Ausland.
No. 2. Acta über Ausstellung in New York. 1854.
No. 12. *Id.* Philadelphia. 1876.
No. 22. *Id.* Chicago. 1892.
L. 2. 1. Schweizerische und ausländische Angelegenheiten.
Ausland. Allgemeines II. Geschäftsträger und Consulate, 1804-1873. Vereinigte Staaten von Nordamerika 1823 f.
Consulate in den Ver. Staaten: Cincinnati, Chicago, New York, New Orleans, Philadelphia, Washington, St. Louis, Louisville, Charleston, Milwaukee, Highland, San Francisco.
Consulate in Centralamerika, Mexico, Panama, Brasilien, Peru, Chili.
L. 2. 2. Geschäftsträger und Consulate im In- und Ausland. 1874- .
L. 33. Schweizerische und ausländische Angelegenheiten. Ausland. Amerika. Vereinigte Staaten. 1832-1854. (Mostly federal circulars relating to arrival and recognition of American consuls general in Switzerland.)
L. 33 a. Dasselbe. Brasilien, Mexico, Argentinien, Chile, etc.

Stadtarchiv

L. 104. 1. Auswanderungswesen. Allgemeines. 1843-1901. Gesetze, Verordnungen, Kreisschreiben, Gutachten, Massregeln, Mitteilungen, etc.
Allgemeines. 1880-1890. Agenturen.
Allgemeines. 1891-1901. Agenturen.
L. 104. 2. Allgemeines. 1902. Agenturen.
L. 104 a. Spezielles. 1837-1848. Auswanderung nach New Orleans. Kreisschreiben des Bundes.
1837-1846. *Id.* Algier. The same.
1856-1858. *Id.* Brasilien. The same.
1889-1901. Verschiedene Akten, darunter Fall einer Verletzung der Vorschriften seitens der Auswanderungsagentur Zwilchenbart, mit Bundesbeschluss, Jan. 13, 1893.

Bevölkerung.

N. 35. I. Auswanderung. Allgemeines, 1847- . *Cf.* L. 104.
Gesetze, Verordnungen, Kreisschreiben, Gutachten, Verzeichnisse von Agenturen, etc.
N. 35 a. I. Auswanderung. Spezielles. *Cf.* L. 104.
Anfragen, Auskünfte, über einzelne Agenturen, etc. 1838- ; 1881- .
Berichte, Correspondenz, Regierungsbeschlüsse, Briefe, etc., betr. die Auswanderung nach Brasilien.

Innere Angelegenheiten.

N. 74. I. Armen- und Unterstützungswesen. 1854-1877.
Verpflegung Angehöriger des Auslands. Amerika, 1861. (2 cases of support of children.)
N. 76. 1 and 2. Armen- und Unterstützungswesen. Schweizerische Hilfsgesellschaften im Ausland.
Allgemeines, u. a. Quittungen über die Beiträge an die schweizerischen Hilfsgesellschaften im Auslande: Boston, 1868-1888; Cincinnati, 1880- ; New Orleans, 1837-1862; New York, 1851-1873; Philadelphia, 1864-1880; San Francisco, 1886- ; Washington, 1867-1879; Chicago, 1873- ; St. Louis, 1874-
P. 214. I. Zustellung von Akten aus dem Ausland. 1836-1858.
Matters concerning the affairs of several immigrants to the U. S.

Kirchenwesen.

T. 59. Verschiedene freie Gemeinschaften resp. Sekten. 1817-
No. 5. Methodisten. (A large number of acta.) 1858-1874.
No. 6. Mormonen. (A large number of acta.) 1854-1863.
No. 8. Separatisten ohne besonderen Charakter. 1830-1889.
T. 59. 2. Wiedertäufer (Baptisten) und Neutäufer (Fröhlianer). 1829-1896.

ZÜRICH: STADTARCHIV.

Location: The city archive of Zürich is located in the Stadthaus, opposite the post-office.
Hours: By arrangement with the city archivist.
Bibliography: Theodor Usteri, " Inventar des Archivs der Stadt Zürich ", in *Inventare Schweizerischer Archive,* Beilage to the *Anzeiger für Schweizerische Geschichte,* II. 111-117 (Bern, 1899).

Zürich

G. Meyer von Knonau, *Der Kanton Zürich* (St. Gallen and Bern, 1844), I. 222.

Das Archiv der Stadt Zürich (Zürich, 1900, pp. 19).

STADTRATSPROTOKOLLE.

Acta Nr. 350. " Verabfolgung einer Reiseunterstützung an Joh. Schweizer, Kammacher, zur Übersiedelung nach Amerika." S. had been sentenced to imprisonment for two years, had served two-thirds of the time, and now petitioned for permission to emigrate and for partial payment of his transportation. Decision: " Es seie die Polizeicommission eingeladen, den Petenten für den Fall seiner Abreise nach Amerika ein Reisegeld v. Fr. 100 zu verabfolgen und dasselbe auf den Titel der ausserordentlichen Polizeiausgabe zu nehmen. Diese Schlussnahme wird der Direktion d. Strafanstalt zu Handen des Schweizer mitgeteilt." May 6, 1848.

No. 609. " Abweisung des Gesuches d. Hrn. Zimmermann, um Reisemittel zur Übersiedelung dahin." (Südamerika.) July 18, 1848.

Nos. 672-674. " Verhandlungen betr. Unterstützung an nach Amerika auswandernde Stadtbürger u. diesfällige Bestellung einer Spezialcommission." Aug. 15, 1848.

No. 742. " Bestimmung der zu befolgenden Grundsätze bei der Behandlung der Unterstützungsbegehren von verbürgerten Auswanderern nach Amerika." Sept. 5, 1848. Decision of the special commission: " Stelle sich die Auswanderung als ein durch die Verhältnisse begründetes Gemeindebedürfnisz dar, so seie die Gemeindebehörde nach § 1 des Gesetzes über die Verwaltung der Gemeindegüter befugt, unter Umständen sogar verpflichtet, das Gemeindegut zur Unterstützung dieses Bedürfnisses in Anspruch zu nehmen. Im entgegengesetzten Falle aber, wo die Auswanderung nicht als Gemeindebedürfnisz, sondern als individuelles Bedürfnisz erscheine, seie die Befugnisz, das Gemeindegut hiefür in Anspruch zu nehmen, nur in den seltensten Fällen vorhanden, wo gleichzeitig neben dem individuellen Grunde zur Auswanderung noch ein öffentliches Bedürfnisz, die betreffenden Personen aus hiesiger Gegend zu entfernen, damit verbunden seie. In allen andern Fällen erscheine die Unterstützung der Auswanderung als Gegenstand persönlicher Vorsorge, für welche der hiesigen Gemeindeverwaltung keine bestimmten Güter oder Stiftungen zugewiesen seien. Es müszte sich somit in allen diesen Fällen einfach fragen, ob die städtische Armenverwaltung Interesse oder Veranlassung habe, seie es vorsorgend oder unterstützend sich bei einem Auswanderungsprojecte zu betheiligen; und somit alle Gesuche in dieser Richtung, bei welchen nicht ein öffentliches Interesse die betreffende Person aus hiesiger Gegend zu entfernen vorliege, ausschliessend in die Behandlung der Armenbehörden zu weisen. Nach Anhörung und Prüfung dieses Gutachtens werden die in demselben aufgestellten Grundsätze von dem Stadtrathe für alle in nächster Zukunft erscheinenden Auswanderungsbegehren einstimmig als maszgebend erkannt." Sept. 5, 1848.

Nos. 673, 674, 743. "Demgemäsz werden: die Gesuche von J. Körner, Commis, vom 25. Juli, Johannes Brunner, Mahler (v. 7. Aug.), und ein ähnliches neu eingegangenes Gesuch gleicher Art von J. Jakob Maurer, Schneider, abgewiesen, mit dem Bemerken, dass sich die Petenten hierüber an die städtische Armenpflege zu wenden haben." Sept. 5, 1848.

Nos. 761, 798, 799. A number of similar cases. Sept.–Oct., 1848.

1854, p. 138. " Das Statthalteramt erlässt unterm 26. Merz ein Kreisschreiben an die Gemeinderäthe, in welchem diese erinnert werden, dazu keinerley Hand zu bieten, dasz ganz mittellose Leute, oder gar Verbrecher zur Auswanderung nach Amerika veranlaszt oder unterstützt werden, in dem die Kosten für deren Rücktransport auf die Gemeinden fallen müssten. Nach Einsicht dieses Kreisschreibens wird beschlossen: es seye die Kanzley beauftragt, in dem Falle, wo eine Paszempfehlung zur Reise nach Amerika für eine mittellose hiesige Bürgerperson verlangt würde, vor deren Ausstellung dem Stadtrathe hievon Kenntnisz zu geben." Apr. 3, 1855.

1857, no. 619. " Bericht an's Statthalteramt über die Zahl der von 1854 bis incl. 1856 nach Nordamerika Ausgewanderten." Aug. 25, 1857.

ZÜRICH: STADT-BIBLIOTHEK.

Location: Adjacent to the Münster-Brücke, in the same ancient building (Wasserkirche) with the Zwingli Museum and Gottfried Keller rooms.

Hours: 10 a. m. to 12 m.; 2 to 6 p. m., except Saturdays.

This library contains one valuable collection of manuscripts and early prints of the eighteenth century, relating to early Swiss settlers in Pennsylvania and Carolina. It is found in the extensive series of 190 manuscript volumes called the Simmlerische Sammlung.

" Extract aus einem Brief, der den 9/20 Febr. in Charleston, dem ersten Orth u. Anlandungs-Hafen in Georgien [*sic*] geschrieben, und den 20/31 May in Sankt Gallen angelanget." References to Purysburg and Sebastian Zuberbühler (who is expected to arrive in Charleston with 50 or 60 families to settle in Carolina). Year not given. [1731-1740.]

" Verbote gegen Auswanderung." 1734, 1735, 1736, 1739, 1741, 1744.

" Abschiedsgebet bey Einschiffung der Züricherischen Colonie nacher Carolina, 1734." (Three manuscript pages.)

Neu-Gefundenes Eden, oder aussführlicher Bericht von Süd und Nord Carolina, Pensilvania, Mary Land und Virginia. In Truck verfertiget durch Befelch der Helvetischen Societät (1737).

Hans W. Trachsler, *Kurtz verfasste Reisz-Beschreibung eines neulich aus Carolina in sein Vaterland zurückgekommenen Lands-Angehörigen.* (Zürich, Bürkli, 1738, pp. 13; unfavorable.)

Nöthigste Nachricht, betreffend Carolina, aus den Weitläuffigern kurtz gefasset, für den gemeinen Mann. (1734, pp. 2; warning.)

Johann Tobler von Appenzell, *Eine ausführliche Relation aus Carolina, Gedicht.* (Bern, 1742.)

" Merkwürdige Beschreibung von Süd-Carolina." In J. Tobler's *Alter u. verbesserter Schreib-Kalender.* (St. Gallen, 1754, pp. 11; favorable.)

Copia eines von einem Sohne N. N. an seine Eltern ausz America abgelassenen Briefes, sub dato Philadelphia, d. 7. Martii, 1684. Next page: *Sichere Nachricht ausz America, wegen der Landschafft Pennsylvania, von einem dorthin gereiszten Teutschen, de dato Philadelphia, d. 7. Martii 1684.*
> (The author of this printed document of 8 pages was undoubtedly Pastorius, the founder of Germantown, Pa. See M. D. Learned, *Life of Francis Daniel Pastorius*, Philadelphia, 1908, in which will be found photographic facsimiles of the *Copia* and of the *Sichere Nachricht*, facing respectively p. 124 and p. 128. A translation of the latter will be found in A. C. Myers, *Narratives of Early Pennsylvania*, in the "Original Narratives" series, at pp. 392-411.)

Königlich Englisch in Teutschland verschickte Erklährung oder Abmahnungs-Schreiben (Dec. 31, 1709).

Eine leyder wahrhaffte Traurige Geschicht u. Beschreibung, wie im nächst abgewichenen Monat Julii, 1754, ein grosses Schiff nach West Indien mit 468 Personen, ein lamentables Ende genommen (1754). Poem at the end.

Christholds Gedanken, bey Anlasz der Bewegung, welche die bekannte Beschreibung von Carolina, in America, in unserm Land verursacht, und der vor etlichen Tagen dahin geschehenen Abreisz verschiedener von unserm Volck (pp. 12). Argument: The Kingdom of Heaven is superior to the New Eden; a beautiful voyage thither without sea-sickness; eternal peace instead of wars; no savages, no wild beasts, and a great and just king, better than the king of England, however good.
> (The book in question, the "bekannte Beschreiben", is perhaps that named above: *Neu-Gefundenes Eden oder ausführlicher Bericht von Süd und Nord Carolina*, etc. 1737.)

Warhaftige und gantz zuverlässige Gute Zeitung von der Königlich-Englischen Provintz Carolina, hergebracht von glaubwürdigen Männern die vor 4 Jahren hineingereiset, anjetzo glücklich wiederum zurück gekommen u. aufs neue dahin sich zuverfügen entschlossen. (St. Gallen, 1740, pp. 15.) Signed by 31 heads of families living in Saxe-Gotha, S. C., in 1740.

Der Hinckende Bott von Carolina, oder Ludwig Webers von Wallisellen Beschreibung seiner Reise von Zürich gen Rotterdam, mit derjenigen Gesellschaft, welche neulich aus dem Schweizerland in Carolinam zu ziehen gedacht (Zürich, 1735, pp. 32).
> (The author went with the group, 194 persons, under the leadership of Pfarrer Götschi of Zürich; he went as far as Rotterdam, and then turned back. On his return, he explains his reasons for returning home, to a schoolmaster—the form of the "Gespräch", question and answer, was popular in books of this kind, and very effective. The story told of the difficulties encountered by Götschi is probably authentic. Götschi was obliged to take a ship for Philadelphia instead of Carolina. Many returned, fearing the redemptionist system. The leader Götschi died soon after landing in America. His son, whose name appears in records quoted on previous pages, subsequently became a minister in the Dutch Reformed Church of America. Cf. James I. Good, *History of the Reformed Church*

in the United States, 1725-1792; based on researches in archives made by W. J. Hinke.)
Der nunmehro in der Neuen Welt vergnügt und ohne Heim-Wehe lebende Schweitzer. Oder: Kurtze und eigentliche Beschreibung des gegenwärtigen Zustandes der königlichen englischen Provinz Carolina, aus den neulich angekommenen Briefen der Alldorten sich befindenden Schweitzeren zusammengetragen von J. K. L. (Bern, getruckt bey Joh. Bondeli, 1734, pp. 46).
Neue Nachricht alter und neuer Merkwürdigkeiten, enthaltend ein vertrautes Gespräch und sichere Briefe von der Landschafft Carolina und übrigen Englischen Pflantz-Städten in Amerika. Zufinden zu Zürich, Bern, Basel, Schaffhausen u. St. Gallen in den Bericht-Häusern gegen Ende des Jahres 1734 (pp. 80).
(The latter work was published and freely distributed to counteract the effects of the former. *Cf.* L. Hirzel, " Nach Amerika aus dem Anfang des 18. Jahrhunderts", *Sonntagsblatt des Bunds*, Bern, Nov. 8, 15, 22, 29, and Dec. 6, 13, 20, 1896.)
Another booklet published to counteract the influence of immigration literature, in an earlier period, was the one entitled: *Das verlangte, nicht erlangte Canaan bei den Lust-Gräbern; Oder, Ausführliche Beschreibung von der unglücklichen Reise derer jüngsthin aus Teutschland nach dem Engelländischen in America gelegenen Carolina und Pensylvanien wallenden Pilgrim, absonderlich dem . . . . Kocherthalerischen Bericht wohlbedächtig entgegen gesetzt* (Frankfurt and Leipzig, 1711, pp. xvi, 127).
(It is found in the Stadtbibliothek—not in the Simmlerische Sammlung—which contains a good collection of printed books on America. The *Ausführliche Beschreibung* also opposed the following very widely distributed and influential book of J. R. Ochs on Carolina.)
Amerikanischer Wegweiser oder kurtze und eigentliche Beschreibung der englischen Provintzen in Nord-America, Sonderlich aber der Landschafft Carolina, mit Grossem Fleiss zusammen getragen und an Tag gegeben durch Joh. Rudolff Ochs neben einer neuen u. correcten Land-Karten von Nord- und Süd-Carolina (Bern, 1711).
(50 thalers were voted to the author, by the Berner Rath, for this work. See *Ratsmanuale* of Bern. A copy of this work is to be found in the Stadtbibliothek of Bern; one is in private hands in Bern. There seem to be no other copies.)
Among books of curious interest in the Stadtbibliothek of Zürich referring to American conditions, are the works of the local celebrity Karl Bürkli, socialist and idealist, *e. g., Das Evangelium der Armen, Chiridonius Bitter Süss* (1861), etc.

WINTERTHUR: STADTARCHIV.

On application, the materials in this archive may be sent to the Staatsarchiv in Zürich, and used there.
Akten. Kasten I., No. 15.
1734, Sept. 4. " Begehren des Rathes v. Zürich um Einvernahme des Goldschmid Sulzer, von hier, wegen Verleitung zürcherscher Angehöriger zur Auswanderung nach Carolina."

Nov. 5. " Begleitschreiben des Rathes von Zürich zu seinem Mandat wider die Auswanderung nach Carolina." (Beigelegt sind das gedruckte Mandat vom 3. Nov. und die behufs Verlesung in der Kirche zu Winterthur verfasste schriftliche Ausfertigung.)

1735, Jan. 29. " Züricherisches Mandat gegen die Auswanderung nach Carolina, verlesen in der Kirche zu Winterthur am 13. Februar."

1736, Feb. 15. " Begleitschreiben des Rathes von Zürich zu seinem Mandat gegen die Auswanderung nach Carolina." (Beigelegt sind das gedruckte Mandat vom 3. Februar und die schriftliche Ausfertigung, welche am 26. Feb. in der Kirche zu Winterthur verlesen wurde.)

1739, May 13. " Begleitschreiben des Rathes von Zürich zu seinem Mandat wider die Auswanderung nach Amerika." (2 Beilagen.)

1768, Apr. 1. " Begehren des Rathes von Zürich, dass den schwäbischen Auswanderern nach den spanischen Colonien kein Durchzug gestattet werde."

1848, Aug. 2.
1850, July 24. } " Gewahrungen von Unterstützung behufs Auswanderung nach Amerika. Übernahme der gesamten Kosten."

1850, Jan. 7. " Gesuch um Erhöhung des Beitrages der Stadt Winterthur von 80 Fk auf 150 Fk für den Sträfling Stoll zur Auswanderung nach Amerika." Vormund der Bruder: C. Stoll, Eichmeister.

1862, Dec. 9. " T. Barbe, Auswanderungsagent in Basel, wiederholt gegenüber der Waisenkommission Winterthur die Forderung von fr. 265 für Verpflegung der nach Amerika ausgewanderten und nun im Spital zu New-York weilenden Marie Hardmeyer von Winterthur."

1869, Jan. 18. " Kreisschreiben der Direktion des Innern in Zürich betr. die Einführung einer Auswanderungsstatistik."

CANTON BERN.

BERN.

The "Staatsarchiv" of Bern is the repository of the historical materials of the canton of Bern, the most populous and at many periods the strongest of the Swiss cantons. The "Bundesarchiv" contains only materials of the nineteenth century, concerning the Helvetic Government (1798-1803), the Federation (1803-1814, 1814-1848), and the Federal State since 1848. Materials relating to American history were also found in the Eidgenössisches Auswanderungsamt, the Stadtbibliothek, and the archive of the American Legation.

BERN: STAATSARCHIV.

Location: In an old building, Postgasse 72, adjoining the picturesque old Rathaus. New quarters are soon to be prepared.

Hours: 8 a. m. to 12 m.; 2 to 6 p. m., except Saturdays and holidays; on Saturdays, closed at 5 p. m.

Bibliography: Heinrich Türler, *Uebersicht über den Inhalt des Staatsarchivs des Kantons Bern* (Bern, 1889, pp. 36).

Id., "Inventar des Staatsarchivs des Kantons Bern", in *Inventare Schweizerischer Archive*, Beilage to the *Anzeiger für Schweizerische Geschichte*, I. 37-64 (Bern, 1895).

Dr. E. Lerch, *Die Bernische Auswanderung nach Amerika im 18. Jahrhundert*. Separate print from the *Blätter für Bernische Geschichte, Kunst, und Altertumskunde*, Jahrgang V., Heft 4, December, 1909. 32 pp. (Based on archive study.)

E. Rodt, *Bern im XVIII. Jahrhundert* (Bern, 1901). Pp. 86-88 contain a brief account of Bernese emigration in that century.

MANDATEN-BUCH.

1641, Mar. 12. "Emigranten um sich anders wo zu sezen, werden nicht nur nicht bey ihrer Rückkunft wieder als Unterthanen annehmen, sondern habend auch ihr Hab und Guth verwürkt." **6**, 270, 332; **7**, 660.

1643, Feb. 28. "Emigranten, an den Pässen anzuhalten." **6**, 332 b; **7**, 660.

1660, Jan. 13. "Denen aus dem Land reisenden noch darein zurückkommenden, keine Scheinen, noch Extracten, ohne Einwilligung zu ertheilen." **8**, 77.

1710, Jan. 18. "Emigrationen nach Danzig und Pennsylvanien. Abmahnung. Einerseits Pest, anderseits Desert." **11**, 338, 339.

1717, July 8. "Verbot der Emigration, und wie zu hintertreiben." (Opposition to emigration based on religious grounds, loss of souls for church.) **12**, 203-205, 585.

1720, Apr. 10. Merveilleux, oder Wunderlich, has sent out printed circulars, recruiting soldiers for service across seas, in Mississippi or Louisiana. Placards (*affiches*) to be set up against him. (Opposition also on religious grounds; service under Catholic régime.)

May 28. Mandate against Merveilleux of Neuchâtel not being observed, and the recruiting continuing, a reward of 30 thaler is offered for catching him. (Merveilleux was probably securing recruits for the regiment Karrer-Hallwyl.) 12, 572-574.

1735, Jan. 12. "Die dahin abreysenden, sollen abgemahnet werden." 15, 37-40.

"An etwelche Oberländische Ambtleuth, als Thun, Oberhofen, Wimmis, Underseen, Interlaken und Oberhassli. Ihnen befehlen, diejenigen so auss Ihren Aembteren annoch entschlossen, in Carolina Ihr Glük zu suchen, von dieser Reyss nochmahlen kräfftigster massen abmahnen, und selbigen mit allem nachtruk die vorschwebende gefahr und andere zu befahren habende ohngemach vorstellen.

Schultheiss und Rath der Statt Bern.

"Nachdemme Wir durch einen Auszschuss aus Unsern Ehrenmitteln dein Schreiben samt Verzeichnuss und Bericht, ansehend diejenigen, so sich entschlossen, die Reyss in Carolinam anzutretten, und alldorten Ihre Fortun zu suchen, reyfflichen erdauren und das befinden Unss referieren lassen ; so habend wir gut funden, dir in antworth zu befehlen, denen, so noch auff dieser vorhabenden Reyss in Carolinam verharren, nochmahlen die beweggründt hierwider mit allem ernst und nachtruk dahin vorzustellen:

"(1) dass die in offentlichen Truk aussgangene und andere berichten von Carolina nicht allerdings richtig ; hingegen

"(2) viel gewüsser, dass sothane Reyss über Meer von hier sehr weith entfehrnt seye, und die meiste, sonderheitlichen die Schweitzer, die grosse veränderung der lufft, die auf der See gewohnliche, aber sonst ohngewohnte nahrung, der mangel süessen wassers, und andere dergleichen zustossende noht und ohngemach nicht vertragen können, sonder darvon erkranken, ja gar sterben müssind ;

"(3) Ferners seye diese Reyss in ansehen der See-Räuberen gefährlich, da nun Sie in dero handen gerahten thäten, wurde mann Sie in die Sclaverey verkauffen, annebens obschon selbige Reyss wohl von statten gehet, sehr kostbahr, und fallen ohngewitter ein ; oder tragen sich andere dergleichen ohnversehene zufähl zu, so wirdt die überfahrt entweders umb viel verlängert, oder gehet gar alles zu grund. Und

"(4) Wurden sie nun in Carolina oder der Enden also anlangen, dass Sie erkranket und presthafft worden und Ihre bahrschafft oder andere effecten verbraucht, müssten Sie dem Allmoossen nachziehen, oder wurden villicht gar um Ihre freyheit kommen, dass sie als Sclaven dienen müessten, etc.

"Solten aber diese so Landsvätterliche und treüwe Vermahnungen nicht erheblich, sondern ohnverfänglich seyn, die vest entschlossenen nach Carolina, von dieser Ihrer vorhabenden Reyss abwendig zu machen, So wollen wir selbige jehdenoch durch gewalt nicht hinderen, wohl aber Ihres vermeinendes glük suchen lassen, ohne sie mit einicher ungnad anzusehen, aussert denen jenigen, so sich hier Landts wohl erhalten können, und über fünffhundert

Pfund mittel besizen, dass dieselben, fahls Sie so viel vermögen, auss dem Landt zu ziehen gesinnet wären, selbige auch zugleich gehalten seyn sollen, Ihres Landt- und Mannrecht auffzugeben, oder sonsten dasselbe verwürkt haben wurden. Welch-Unsseren bestgemeinten willen du denen Interessierten zu eröffnen wohl wüssen wirst. Datum 12. Jan. 1735."

Jan. 12. " Ihnen auch keine Päss gegeben werden." **15**, 63-67.
Feb. 24. " Den Schiffleuthen verbothen dieselbigen abzuführen." **15**, 65.
Mar. 2. " Etlichen die Abreisz (nach Carolina) gestattet." **16**, 66.
Mar. 17. " Desshalb getruktes Gespräch den Ambtläuthen zur Publication zugetheilt." **15**, 73.
Mar. 17. " Dass die Aufwükler, so die Leuth zu dieser Reysz bereden, soll geachtet [beobachtet] werden." Sollen als falsche Werber bestraft werden. **15**, 74-78.
July 13. " Denen, so sich von diser Reyss haben lassen abmahnen, wird zur Erhaltung ihrer Kinder gesteuert." **15**, 100.
Sept. 26. " Anstalten zu nochmaliger Verhinderung der Abreysz." **15**, 110-111.
Apr. 10. " Wer solche dahin Abreyssende und die ihre Mittel heimlich wegziehen wollen entdeckt, soll belohnt werden." **15**, 292-293.

MANDATEN-BUCH.

1739-1744.

" Carolina, reysen dahin verboten. Auf die Locker zu achten." **16**, 230, 332, 349, 359, 363, 365, 367, 390, 399.
Mandate: " Wiederholte Verbote nach Carolina zu reysen."
12. Januar 1735.
10. April 1738.
19. Januar 1742.
26. April 1742.
" Auf den Missionarium Riemensperger soll geachtet werden." **16**, 229, 231, 233, 234.
" Von Geburt ein Toggenburger, der sich verpflichtet hat einhundert Familles aus unseren Landen, sowohl als aus dem Zürich-Gebieth und Toggenburg den einten halben Theil nach Carolinam, den anderen halben Theil aber nacher Georgien zu transportieren. Falls er das Land betreten, solle selber und sein Knecht in Gefangenschaft gesetzt werden. Wir für jede dieser Beyden eine Recompens von 50 Thalern entrichten lassen werden für solche die indicieren wollen, dass selbe in Gefangenschaft gebracht werden."
" Carolina. Peter Huber mit Weib und Kindern dorthin zu ziehen erlaubt." **16**, 3-5-330, 363, 365. See pp. 55, 111, *post*.
" Peter und Jakob Nägely, so dorthin zu ziehen in Verdacht, ihre Mittel und Land Recht wegzuziehen, abgeschlagen." **16**, 327, 352.
" Ihre Mittel sequestrirt." **16**, 355-357.
" Dem Peter Stoker sollen seine aus Carolina gekommenen Briefe abgefordert werden." **16**, 358.
" Den Hans Brunner, so hier zu bleiben sich entschlossen, sollen seines Kindes Mittel zugestellt werden." **16**, 388.

"Anna Brunner, Peter Wysen sel. Wittib soll ihr Gelt restituirt werden." **16,** 388.

"Die dahin reysende banisirt." ("Eine Zeit von drei Monaten angesetzt, in welcher diejenigen so verreyset, ohngehindert sich wieder im Land setzsen mögen. Nach Verfliessung dieser Zeit aber soll die Bannisation ihre völlige Würkung erreichet haben." Mar. 17, 1742.) **16,** 390.

"Wie ratione ihres Erbrechtes zu halten." **16,** 399-403.

"Auf die wiederkommende soll geachtet werden." **16,** 724. (In Verhaft zu setzen bis zu fernerer Verordnung.)

1749, May 6. "Carolina, Pennsylvania und Neu Schottland. Dahin zu reysen verboten." **18,** 10-14.

1751, May 13. "Emigration nach Neu-Schottland verboten." (Recompens von 100 Thalern Verführer und Anlocker einzufangen.) **18,** 144-146.

1753, May 21. "Neues Auswanderungsverbot." **18,** 434.

1754, May 18. "Nachricht, dass eine grosse Anzahl unserer Unterthanen nach Pennsylvanien gezogen, Entvölkerung unserer Landen zu besorgen. Kein Wegzug ohne Erlaubnis. Verbot auch denen Unterthanen so im Erguel auf Lehen sitzen." **18,** 515.

"Emigration. Auf die Emboucheurs eine Summe von 100 Thalern gebothen." **18,** 14.

1756, Jan. 2. "Carolina. Wie die Emigrationen zu hinterhalten." **19.**

"Carolina. Einen Emboucheur proscribirt." **19.**

Jan. 7. "Carolina. Wie wegen denen wiederkommenden zu procediren." **19.**

1765. "Emigrationen, Verbot, besonders nach Russland." **21,** 534, 538, 541, 569.

1767, Nov. 23. "Emigration, Verbot in die spanischen Colonien." **22,** 308-310.

1768, Mar. 31. "Emigration, Verbot in die spanischen Colonien." **23,** 419, 421.

Dec. 21. "Vorsorge wider die Verlockung hiesiger Angehörigen nach Spanien. Das ganze Land wird verwahrnet, dass sich nicht jemand nach Sierra Morena verlocken lasse." **23,** 50.

1770, Feb. 13. "Das Welschland besonders, wegen denen Einladungen nach dem Captalat de Buch und der Teich en Guiêne." **23,** 322.

1771, Nov. 29. "Das ganze Land wird verwahrnet wegen Preussisch Pommern." **24,** 71, 160.

TEUTSCHE MISSIVEN BUCH DER STADT BERN.

Wiedertäufer.

1599-1600. "Confiscationen gehören den Twingherren nicht, und die zu Sumiswald gehören nach Trachselwald." **22,** 168, 381.

"Zu Sumiswald mag der Landvogt zu Trachselwald fangen lassen." **22,** 378, 380.

1602. "Die ungehorsamen [Wiedertäufer] hieher zu liefern." **22,** 898.

1616. "Ein ihnen günstiges Tractätlein von Poll—zu unterdrücken. Poll selbst in Zürich verhaftet." **1,** 261, 314.

1644. "Derselben—sowohl eingebornen, als fremden—will man sich hier (und in Zürich) entladen." **12,** 655.

1648. " Ernstliche Nachstellung gegen solche irrige Leute, die dann ' aufs Meer nach Venedig' zu Kriegs- oder Soldatendienst verschicket werden sollen." **14**, 512.
1660. " Ihrer hierseitigen Behandlung und Landesverweisung halb—Erklärung an die für sie intercedirenden Staaten, von Holland, auch Städte Amsterdam und Rotterdam." **20**, 307.
1668. " Intervension der Stadt Amsterdam für dieselben abgelehnt." **23**, 56.
1671. " Werden ' in Eisen gefesselt ' unter bewaffnetem Geleit über Lauis an Venedig abgeliefert zu zweijähriger Ruder-Arbeit—ungesöndert auf einer Galeere." **24**.
1676. " Hier fortgewiesen [Wiedertäufer] solle auch Solothurn ausmustern helfen." **25**, 295.
1683. " An einige [W.] in der pfalz Vermögens-Ablieferung halb." **27**, 20, 154.
1699. " Ihr Lehrer, Isaac Kaufmann, der ostindischen Compagnie in Amsterdam überliefert zur Versendung: Für Mehre bestellen MeGnHn. [Meine Gnädige Herren] Platz." **34**, 822.
1705. " N. Testament, Basel, bey Genath, 1702, soll Basel wegen ' wiedertäuferischen Version' unterdrücken helfen." **38**, 277.
" An Hn. Angliombi [Aglionby], Englischen Envoyé. (Hr. Ritter und seine in Americam zu führen vorhabende Colonie recommendieren.)
" Hochwohlgebohrener, etc.—Unser liebe und getreuwe Burger Georg Ritter hat uns in mehrerem zu vernemen gegeben, welcher massen er und mit Interessierte auf unsere Bewilligung bedacht wären, eine Colonie in diesen schweizerischen Landen von vier- bis in fünfhundert Persohnen stark aufzubringen und under Ihro Königl. Mayst. in Engelland Gebiete in West Indien etwan in Pensylvania, oder der Gegend Virginien zuführen und zusetzen, zu welchem Ende er beykommendes Placet an hochbsagte Ihro Königl. Mayst. gestellet, und uns in Demuht ersuchet, dass Wir dasselbe dem Herren zulangen lassen und mit unser Vorschrift begleiten wolten, damit durch dessen Mittel dieses Placet Ihro Mayst. behändiget, und darüber dero gnädigster Entschluss vernommen werden möchte; womit Wir Ihme unserem Burger Ritter in willfahr geantwortet, den Herren also durch disz wenige fründtdienstlichen ersuchende, demselben mit seinen vielgültigen Officien und Favorn zunderstützen, damit dafern Ihro Königl. Mayst. diese Colonie ebenmässig belieben thäte, dieselbe deszfalls Ihro Mayst. Gnade und allen müglichsten Vorschiebs sich zugewarten und zubefreüwen hätte; zugleich auch erforschen, ob im Fahl allhiesiger Stand mit der Zeit under einigen gedingen auch eine Colonie dahin verschaffen wolte, allda zu einem gewüssen Bezirk landts hoffnung gemacht werden könnte: Für die Mühwalt und Officien, die der Herr übernemen wirdt, ermanglen wir mit neben gezimenden Dank denselben in allerley begegnussen mit unsern Fründdienstgefälligkeiten, zu reciprocieren, undt erlassen damit den Herren der starken Obhut des Allerhöchsten. Dato 19. Martii, 1705. Schultz und Raht der St. Bern."
1707. " Vermehrung derselben [Wiedertäufer] im Bucheckberge." **39**, 513.

1710. "Abführung einiger [W.] in America, den Rhein hinunter, mit 120 freywillig in West Indien Reysenden." **41**, 397, 413, 414, 430, 468, 607.
"Aufnahme von 400 an der Zahl in die Preussischen Staaten wird negotiiert." **41**, 594, 666, 702.
1711. "Und ferner 550 Männer, Weiber, Kinder—unter Führung Georg Riedens, Negt." **41**, 949, 985, 990, 994.
1712. "Von hier in Holland Vermögens-Verabfolgung an dieselben." **42**, 261.
1715. "In Holland verwiesen, schleichen sich wieder ein; zur Galeere verurtheilt; Hollands Fürsprache." **45**, 226, 237, 660, 664.
1717. "Wiedertäufer und Pietisten: Unterdrückung der ihnen dienlichen Bücher, wie des Froschauer N. Testament." **47**, 206.
1725. "Lehrer—Grimm und Brechbühl—zu behändigen; Lucern verfolgt sie auch." **52**, 433, 445, 463, 531, 564.
1726. "Vermögens- und Erbschaften halb." **52**, 941.
1728-1731. "[Wiedertäufer] auch Wiedertäuferinnen werden verfolgt—durch 'Täufer-Jäger'—bis ins Lucern Gebiet." **54**, 139, 173, 329, 429, 529; **55**, 19.
[W.] "daheriger Grenzmarch- und Jurisdictions Zwist" (see Luzern). **56**, 83, 91, 486, 616.
1729. "Versammlung im Schlössli zu Mett." **55**, 213.
1732. "Erbschafts Angelegenheiten zwischen Holland und Bern." **57**, 510.
1734-1735. "Wegen Fortschaffung derselben hinter Valengin, Unterhandlung mit Preussen und Neuenburg." **60**, 73, 76, 100, 112, 189, 311, 319, 338, 346, 356, 397, 404, 423.
1739. "Ihrethalben Beschwerden von Valenzin." **62**, 707, 708, 730, 731.
"Ihrethalben Königl. Preuss. Rescript." **63**, 8, 93.
1756-1757. "Abwesende [W.], als Ansprecher in einem Bucheckbergischen Geldstage für hierseitige Angehörige erklärt." **75**, 500, 519.
1760-1761. "Hans Farnis, von Steffisburg, Nachlass, von abwesenden Enkeln reclamirt, nicht verabfolgt, sondern der Kirche daselbst zugesprochen." **77**, 500, 702, 853.
1762, 1766, 1772. "Ihnen wird kein Vermögen aus dem Kantone verabfolgt." **78**, 359; **80**, 653; **85**, 313.

TEUTSCHES MISSIVEN-BUCH DER STADT BERN.

Carolina.

1735. "Auswanderung dahin wird zu verhindern gesucht" (Pury). **60**, 279, 291, 478, 510.
"Auswanderer dahin wird Neuenburg zurückzuweisen ersucht (keine Pässe zu erteilen", etc.). **61**, 3.
1740. "Gegen Anwerbung und Auswanderung dahin strenge Maassregeln." **63**, 308.
1741-1742. "Dahin und nach Georgien wirbt Hans Riemensperger und Peter Huber: sollen verhaftet werden." (Peter Huber wird von Basel ausgeliefert.) **64**, 110, 566, 574, 577.
1742. "Basel. Wegen behändigung eines gewüssen Hubers, der die Leüth in Carolinam verlocket.
"Tit. Schon sinth geraumer Zeith dahar ist Peter Huber, einer unser Unterthanen von Oberhasli in starkem Verdacht gewesen, ob

habe derselbe im Oberland und der Enden viele Unserer
Angehörigen angetrieben, sich in das entfernteste Land nacher
Carolina zu begeben, da nun erst under gestrigem Dato Wir die
zuverlässige Nachricht erhalten, was gestalten etwelche Haushaltungen von Oberhaszli und Interlaken, bestehend in 20 bis
mehr Persohnen theils zu Wasser, theils über Land aus Basel zu
nacher Carolina verreyset, welche alle von erwehntem Peter
Huber hierzu verleitet und aufgewiklet worden sein sollen, und
nun uns daran gelegen sein will, dass sothaner Peter Huber zu
gebührender Verantwortung auf allfählig in die behörige Straf
gezogen werde, als haben auch vernomen, dass derselbe über den
Brünig nacher Basel verreyst seyn und dorten diesen Leuthen
warten solle,—Wir nicht umhin mögen, Euch dessen allesen hiemit zu benachrichtigen, mit dem beyläufigen freundteydtgenössischen Ersuchen, Ihr beliebt sein wollet, die fürdersame ohnbeschwehrte Anstalt, in Euwerer Hauptstadt und Pottmässigkeit
dahin ergehen zu lassen, dass dieser Huber, als welcher unsre
Underthanen, auf eine so gefährliche Weiss entführt, auf betretten angehalten, und in gefängkliche Verhaft gebracht, Wir aber
dessen nachrichtlich verständiget werden; Wir wollen an geneigter Willfahr keines Wegs und umb so da minder zweifeln als
einerseiths uns höchstens daran gelegen, dass dergleichen landschädliche Leuth und Entführer der verdienten Bestrafung nicht
entgehen; anderseits dann wir ein solches in gleichen und andern
Begebenheiten zu erwiedern nicht ermangeln werden, in dessen
Erwartung Wir in, [etc., etc.]. Dato 1 Martii, 1742. Schultheisz
und Raht der Stadt Bern."

1741-1742. "Carolina—die dahin reysen soll Basel abmahnen." 64, 586.
1744. "Verführer dahin Peter in Aebnit [Amt Interlaken] ausgeschrieben,
von Basel ausgeliefert." 66, 183, 202, 209, 211, 233, 574, 577.
1749. "Verführer dahin und nach Pennsylvanien zu bestrafen" (Walter).
70, 105, 139.
1750. "Auswanderung nach Carolina und Pennsylvanien eidgenössisch zu
verhindern, Verführer zu bestrafen." 71, 20.
"Vermögens-Abzug dahin à 5 per cent. bezogen."[1] 71, 371.
"Deutsche Prediger dahin nicht zu bewilligen" (Schlatter). 72, 97.
"Fryburg. Wegen Abzug des Christen Gilgiano Mitlen."
"Unser freundlich willig Dienst, samt was wir ehren liebs und guts
vermögen zuvor, Fromb, Fürsichtig, Ehrsamb, Weiss, sonders
gut Freund, getreuw lieb Eydgenossen Mitburger und Brüder.
"Euer Schreiben vom 4. abgewichenen Monats Junii, über die Bittschrift
der Anverwanten des in Carolina verstorbenen Christen Gilgiano,
dass nämlich denenselben, von denen 572 Kr. so sie in Carolinam
zusenden gemüssiget, der Abzug nachgelassen werden möge, etc.;
haben wir in U berlegung nemen lassen, und auf uns erstattete
Relation hingleich Euch, etc., billich befunden, dass von diesen
572 Kr. Ihnen der Abzug, aus milten Considerationen jehdoch
höher nicht als auf 5 per cent. gefordert werden solle, in massen

---

[1] Kaspar Hauser, "Ueber den Abzug in der Schweiz", in *Jahrbuch für Schweizerische Geschichte*, herausgegeben auf Veranstaltung der Allgemeinen Geschichtsforschenden Gesellschaft der Schweiz, Bd. XXXIV. (Zürich, 1909.)

desshalb Wir an Unseren gemeinen Amtsmann zu Schwarzenburg befelchlich—abgeben, was aus Copeyl. Anschluss [copy enclosed] zu ersehen; welches Euch hie anmit, freund eidgenössisch participieren, etc. Dato den 26. Dec., 1750. Schultheisz und Raht." **71.**

1751. " Wegen Michael Schlatter, Prediger der teutschen Gemeind zu Philadelphia in Pennsilvanien." **72,** 96-97.

"Bei einem Ehrwürdigen Convent allhier hat sich angemeldet Michael Schlatter, Prediger der teutschen Gemeind zu Philadelphia in Pennsilvanien, und den Zustand der daselbstigen Teutsch Reformierten zum Theil aus Schweizern bestehenden Colonie vorgestelt, auch mit Attestates versehen, dargethan, dass Ihme aufgetragen seye, 5 oder 6 tüchtige teutsche Prediger für Pennsilvanien aufzusuchen, und eine milte beysteuer zu diesem Vornehmen zu begehren und dahero sich bey den evangelischen Kantonen der Eydgenossschaft und zugewanten Orten anzumelden; Wann aber Wir betrachtet, was für Bedenklichkeiten hier unterlaufen, da oft unter dergleichen Vorwand unsere Angehörigen und Unterthanen in diese entfernte Land verlocket, und in Unglück gestürzt werden; haben Wir in dieses Pfarrers Begehren auch im Wenigsten nit eintreten wollen, sondern hierbey sorgfältigst ausgemitten [gemieden], was etwan unseren Unterthanen Anlas geben möchte, wider Unsere Verbot in diese Land zu gehen, und haben von dieser Unser Gesinnung und Entschluss Euch die Vertraute Nachricht hiemit geben, und inmitlest, in, etc. Dato den 25. Nov., 1751. Schultheisz und Raht."

RATHS-MANUALE DER STADT BERN.

1701.

" Auswanderer bezahlen 10 per cent. Vermögenabzug." R. M. **1,** 359.
" Auswanderer Errichtung einer Kontrolle." R. M. **2,** 229.
(See Rödel Weggezogener Mannrechten, 1694-1754, Alphabetisches Verzeichnis der Namen.)

1702.

" Nach Brandenburg Untersuchung." R. M. **8,** 135, 139.
" Vertheilung geistlicher Bücher an die Auswanderer." R. M. **9,** 86.
" Abzugsbefreiung für Auswanderer." R. M. **9,** 100.

1703.

" Mit Wegzug des Vermögens geht auch das Landrecht verloren." R. M. **11,** 203.

1705.

" Colonien Gründung aus hiesigen Landsassen in Pennsylvanien." **18,** 196, 475; **19,** 12; **24,** 461, 496.
Herr Georg Ritter, Specierer (Kleinhändler), plans to found a colony in Pennsylvania. A commission appointed and the English envoy in Switzerland consulted. This is an actual attempt on the part of the government of Bern to found a colony in America. The desire was to send off "Landsassen", an undesirable element from the government's point of view.

1709.
"Beabsichtigte Ansiedlungen in Amerika." R. M. 40, 238; 46, 346.

1710.
"Nach Danzig und Pennsylvania, Warnung davor." R. M. 40, 392. (See Mandaten-Buch, Jan. 18, 1710.)
"Abschiebung der Täufer nach Amerika durch H. Ritter, welchem für die Person 45 Thl. von der Regierung bezahlt wird." R. M. 41, 229, 281, 285, 301, 306, 307, 323, 437, 488.
"Landankauf in Amerika behufs Abschiebung der lästigen Unterthanen." R. M. 41, 408.

1711.
"Von Zweysimmen (arme Leute dort, im Oberland), Warnung vor Auswanderung unter Hülfsversicherung durch die Regierung." R. M. 46, 345.

Mar. 21. "Die dem Rathe dedicierte gedruckte Beschreibung 'der amerikanischen Inseln', speciell Carolina, dafür 50 Thaler verordnet Recompens." (The author of this was Rudolff Ochs.)
"Zedel, was massen Hr. Rudolff Ochs gesinnet wäre etwelche MGH. Unterthanen mit sich in Americam zu nemen; Vorschläge anhören."

1712.
"Auswanderung nach Preussen, Abmahnung davor." R. M. 50, 321; 51, 86, 162.

1716.
"Auswanderung soll nur solchen gestattet werden, die bescheinigen können, dass sie in der Religion wohl unterrichtet, und arm seyen." R. M. 68, 36.

1720.
"Anwerbungen nach Mississippi durch H. Wunderlich (Merveilleux) von Neuenburg." R. M. 84, 94.
"Dahin die Recroutirung verboten." R. M. 61, 94, 311.
"Merveilleux." R. M. 61, 311, 378.
"Vermahnung sich nit in die Companey des Mississippi zu lassen." R. M. 84, 61. (See also Mandaten-Buch.)
"Erlach. Wunderlich-Merveilleux." R. M. 84, 94.
"Klage des Merveilleux wider das Verpot seiner Mississipianischen Werbungen, zu erdauern und referieren." R. M. 84, 311.

May 28. "Iverten. Ueber Begehrte Wegweisung, wie er sich, wegen von N: Merveilleux Haubtmann über 200 nach Mississippi angeworbener Männer empfangene Verweis Schreibens—darin Er sich desz sub 10. Aprilis lesthin wider Ihne auskündeten Mandats beschwährt etc. zu verhalten habe; wollendt Ihro Gn. Ihme hiemit befohlen haben, dasz Merveilleux Schreiben für unempfangen zu achten, mithin dann Ihne Merveilleux durch Affiches an die Gränzen zu proclamieren; übrigens aber umb so da geflissener, ob Ihr Gn. jetzgemeltem Mandat so eyfferen, weilen gefallenen Bericht nach eint und anders Ihr Gn. Unterthan under allerhandt Vorwand auf die Grenzen angelocket, nachwertz mit Gewalt weggenommen und bis auf allgemeinen Abmarsch eingespehrt werdindt." R. M. **84**, 378. See also M. B. **12**, pp. 572-574 (April 10, 1720), 585-586 (May 28, 1720).

Apr. 15. "Erlach: Aus seinem Schreiben habend Ihr Gnaden verstanden, dass durch ein gewissen Hr. Wunderlich von Neuwenburg verschiedene arme gantze Familles es seye durch gute Wort oder Gelt verlocket und angedinget worden, etc. Nun stehend Ihr Gn. in denen Gedanken, dass er dergleich Sachen wegen Ihr Gn. Befelch und Willen werde vernommen haben, welchem nach Er sich zurichten müssen werden. Indessen solle Er Ihr Gn. berichten, wasz für Leüth sich nach Mississippi zugehen gegen Hrn. Wunderlich verbunden, wer sie verlocket, und was Qualitet und von wannen sothane Unterthane seyen." Erlach Buch D., p. 661.

1723.

"Auswanderung ins Niderlandt, wie zu hinterhalten soll untersucht werden." R. M. **93**, 178.

1725.

"Errichtung einer Colonie in Amerika durch H. Pury et Cie. in Neuenburg." July 30, 1725. R. M. **102**, 295.

"Erlach: Aus seinem Schreiben und beygefügt gewesenes gedrucktes advertissement habend Ihr GnH. ersehen wie die H. Pury et Cie. von Neuwenburg von Ihr GnH. Unterthanen suchend in die Americanische Insul Carolinam zu verlocken; wie nun Ihr GnH solches als ein ohngewüsses und den Ihrigen nachtheiliges Etablissement ansehen, als wollend sie Ihme gleich gegen verschiedenen Anderen Ambtleüthen auch beschicht hierdurch befohlen haben, seine Ambtsangehörige zu verwahren, dass sie sich ohne Ihr GnH. Vorwüszen und Bewilligung nicht dahin begeben thüyend; fürs Einte [*illegible*] fürs Andere dann wollend Ihr GnH Ihme hiemit aufgetragen haben, Nachforschung zehalten, durch wen die H. Pury et Cie. solche Advertissement ausstreuwen lassind? Und von weme er der Herr Ambtsmann das allhar communicirte Exemplar bekommen haben und dessen Ihr GnH. zuberichten, wie zethun er wissen werde."

1729.

Mar. 24. "Zwei Brüder Schwarz, der eine mit 4 Söhnen, erhalten die Erlaubnis, gegen die Erlegung des Abzuges von 10 Prozent nach Pennsylvanien auszuwandern. Die Leute stammen von Langnau im Emmental." R. M. **121**, 291.

1731.

Nov. 5. "Im Rat taucht die Frage auf, ob nicht das bäuerliche Erbrecht zu ändern sei. In gewissen Gegenden waren dadurch die jüngern Kinder benachteiligt, weswegen viele auswanderten. Ziel der Auswanderung war um diese Zeit auch Nassau-Saarbrücken, wie 20 Jahre früher Ostpreussen." R. M. **133**, 35.

1732.

Dec. 17. "Der Grosse Rat verwirft den Antrag, es seien mit der Krone England oder 'Indianischen Compagnien' Verhandlungen anzuknüpfen, um Verbrecher nach Kolonien zu verschicken." R. M. **137**, 482.

1733.

Mar. 19. "Die Regierung gestattet dem aus Münchenbuchsee stammenden, in Philadelphia angesiedelten Johannes Bartlome, sein Muttergut unter Erlegung des Abzuges aus dem Lande zu ziehen. Sie lehnt eine Beitragsleistung für Kirchen und Schulen in Pennsylvanien ab." R. M. **138**, 591-592.

1734.

Jan. 21. "Die Gemeinde Thierachern wird von der Regierung angewiesen, dem Christian Küntzi soviel von seinem Vermögen auszuhändigen, als zur Reise nach Pennsylvanien enforderlich sei." R. M. **142**, 95.

June 22. "Alle Amtleute erhalten Weisung, von der Auswanderung nach Carolina abzumahnen. Der Schultheiss wird angewiesen, nur noch Heimatlosen und Proselyten Reisegeld zur Auswanderung zu bewilligen." R. M. **144**, 8.

June 28. "Die Regierung verlangt von der Vennerkammer ein Gutachten über die Anwerbungen durch Herrn Pury und andere." R. M. **144**, 43.

June 29. "Der am 22. Juni beschlossene Befehl an die Amtleute wird vorläufig noch nicht ausgegeben." R. M. **144**, 47.

July 6. "Dieser Befehl wird nun doch erlassen." R. M. **144**, 106.

"Der Amtmann von Unterseen wird angewiesen, den Auswanderungslustigen zu erklären, das 'gedruckte Büchlein' enthalte unwahre Angaben. Unbelehrbare können abreisen, müssen aber 5 Prozent Abzug zahlen." R. M. **144**, 111.

July 12. "Ein neues Mandat zur Warnung vor Auswanderung wird vorläufig noch aufgeschoben." R. M. **144**, 162.

Aug. 16. "Bern setzt Zürich auseinander, warum man bezüglich der Auswanderung nach Carolina eine abwartende Haltung einnehme. Bericht über den bisherigen Verlauf der Dinge." R. M. **144**, 259.

Oct. 4. "Ein Auswanderungsagent Stryger zu Steffisburg soll verhört werden." R. M. **144**, 508.

Oct. 14. "Der Agent Striker [= Stryger], der aus Graubünden stammt u. in Steffisburg als Büchsenschmied wohnt, soll zur Aushändigung der Verzeichnisse der Auswanderungslustigen veranlasst werden." R. M. **145**, 1.

Nov. 10. "Die Auswanderungsangelegenheit soll an der Tagsatzung behandelt werden. S. Instruktionenbuch. Der Agent Striker soll seine Tätigkeit einstellen. Die Regierung werde die Sache selber an die Hand nehmen." R. M. **145**, 85.

Nov. 27. "Abzug auf 10 Prozent bestimmt. Warnung an die Untertanen. Erkundigung was man in Zürich gegen das Auswanderungsfieber tue." R. M. **145**, 172.

Dec. 7. "Eine Untersuchung über die Verhältnisse und Beweggründe der Auswanderungslustigen wird angeordnet." R. M. 145, 256.
Dec. 11. "Der Agent Striker wird ausgewiesen." R. M. 145, 284.

1735.

Jan. 3. "Eine Kommission wird beauftragt, ein Gutachten über die Auswanderungssache auszuarbeiten." R. M. 145, 415.
Jan. 12. "Warnung ins Oberland vor der Auswanderung." R. M. 145, 475.
Jan. 18. "Die Kommission erhält zwei Briefe aus Landau mit Berichten über Carolina, ferner das zürcherische gedruckte Mandat gegen die Auswanderung." R. M. 145, 507.
Feb. 14. "Die Auswanderung ist zwar nicht zu verbieten, aber tunlich zu verhindern und zu erschweren. Die Kommission erhält Auftrag, ihr Gutachten zu entwerfen. Die Gemeinde hofft man gegen die Auswanderung zu stimmen, indem man Zwangseinbürgerung von Heimatlosen an Stelle der Ausgewanderten in Aussicht nimmt." R. M. 146, 138.
Feb. 23. "Zürich wird um Auskunft ersucht, ob man dort Nachrichten über Carolina habe." R. M. 146, 212.
"Es sollen an Auswanderer keine Pässe mehr verabfolgt werden." R. M. 146, 215.
Mar. 2. "Wiedererwägungsgesuch der Auswanderungslustigen gegen das Passverbot." R. M. 146, 262.
"Die Abreise wird 322 Personen gestattet. Beschluss des Gr. Rates." R. M. 146, 266.
Mar. 3. "Weitere Auswanderer aus dem Oberhasle dürfen ebenfalls abreisen. Jeder soll aber 500 *lb*. Mittel besitzen. Zurückbleibende Kinder müssen sichergestellt werden." R. M. 146, 270.
Mar. 8. "Das Zürcher Mandat gegen die Auswanderung soll in das 'Ordinari Sambstagsblätlin' eingerückt werden." R. M. 146, 298.
Mar. 13. "Für die Abfahrt des Hauptschwarms der Auswanderer sind 3 Schiffe bestimmt." R. M. 146, 337.
Mar. 16. "Die Kommission hat ihr Gutachten eingereicht." R. M. 146, 351.
Mar. 17. "Mandat an die Untertanen gegen die Carolina-Reise." R. M. 146, 366.
"Beschluss, den in Bern versammelten Auswanderern den bezahlten Abzug zu schenken, d. h. wieder zu geben. Wer jetzt noch heimzieht, darf s. verkauften Güter wieder lösen. Wenn Kinder nicht mit den Eltern ziehen wollen, müssen letztere ihnen einen Teil des Vermögens hinterlassen." R. M. 146, 368/70.
Mar. 18. "Ein Gespräch gegen die Auswanderung soll nachgedruckt, ins Französische übersetzt und verbreitet werden." R. M. 146, 371.
"Der Grosse Rat genehmigt die gestrigen Beschlüsse der Regierung. Der Agent Striker sei der Anführer der Gesellschaft. Allfällig von Auswanderern ihm anvertrautes Geld soll er hergeben." R. M. 146, 375/377.
Mar. 19. "Die Kommission soll über die Regelung der Verhältnisse der Umkehrenden Bericht geben, letztere erhalten Reisegeld." R. M. 146, 379.

Mar. 21. "Mandat zur Abmahnung vor Auswanderung nach Carolina und andere entfernte Gebiete." R. M. 146, 385.

Mar. 23. "Von dem bernischen Kommissär May in England (Er verwaltete dort die in England angelegten Schatzgelder Berns) sind betrübliche Berichte über den Zustand der nach London gelangten Auswanderer angekommen. Es sind solche aus Bern, Zürich, und Graubünden. Diese Nachrichten sollen deutsch und französisch gedruckt werden. Die Kommission soll Vorschläge machen betr. Rückschaffung der in London liegenden Leute." R. M. 146, 395.

Mar. 29. "Die Kommission erhält Vollmacht, die in London zurückgebliebenen Auswanderer mit Reisegeld zur Rückkehr zu versehen. Einer Witwe Christen aus Aarburg u. ihren Kindern—die man nicht zurückwünscht—soll per Kopf 1 Guinée bezahlt werden zur Fortsetzung der Reise." R. M. 146, 433.

Mar. 31. "Massregeln zur Unterztützung der umgekehrten Auswanderer." R. M. 146, 444.

"Gesuch an den kaiserlichen Botschafter in Basel um Ausstellung eines Passes an die Fortziehenden." R. M. 146, 447.

Apr. 25. "Auswanderer aus der Gegend von Oberhasle und Interlaken, 'so sich vorgenommen, ihr vermeint besser Glük in der entfernten Insul Carolina zu suchen', konnten z. T. wieder abwendig gemacht werden. Die Amtleute erhalten nun Auftrag zu berichten, wie diesen armen Leuten geholfen werden könne und ob ihre Klagen begründet seien." R. M. 147, 12.

Sept. 26. "Massregeln gegen einen gewissen Quinche von Neuenburg, der neuerdings Leute zur Auswanderung nach Carolina veranlassen will." R. M. 148, 387.

Nov. 21. "Der bernische Kommissär in London meldet, dass dort verschiedene Berner angekommen seien, die nach Georgien auswandern wollen." R. M. 148, 547.

The following note in the D. Sekelmeister-Rechnung, refers to the above action of the Berner Rat:

"Auf Befehl des Rates wurde mehreren Carolina-Emigranten der an die Amtleute bezahlte Abzug mit zusammen 237 Kronen 16 Batzen 2 Kreuzer rückvergütet. Die Auswanderer stammten von Schwarzenburg (Bücher, Gilgen, Wäber, Stäbli, Mischler, Zwahlen), Güggisberg (Wänger), Interlaken (im Äbnit), Oberhasle (Rüdler, Meiden, Egger, Rübi, Zäuger, Horger).

"An Auswanderer, die von ihrem Vorhaben abwendig gemacht werden konnten, wurden als Reisegeld nach Hause 226 Pfund 13 Schilling 4 Pfennig ausbezahlt."[1] D. Sekelmeister-Rechnung, 1735, p. 76.

1736.

Oct. 8. "Da das Avis-Blättlin neulich einen Artikel über Carolina gebracht hat, wird der Herausgeber angewiesen, zukünftig keine Nachrichten über Carolina und den Zustand der dorthin Ausgewanderten zu veröffentlichen. Jedenfalls soll nichts Vorteilhaftes über Carolina gedruckt werden." R. M. 152, 224.

---

[1] A pound at that time was equivalent to about 4-5 francs, a crown to about 13-15 francs.

1737.

Feb. 27, Mar. 5. " Hans Georg Striker hat von Carolina aus an Leutnant Rubi in Thun einen Bericht über dieses Land geschickt. Der Brief wird beim Empfänger konfisziert und der Regierung vorgelegt." R. M. **153**, 403-443.

1738.

Feb. 6. " Da neuerdings von Neuenburg aus für Carolina und Pennsylvanien Stimmung gemacht wird, erhalten die Avisblätter in Lausanne und Bern Befehl, über diese beiden Länder keine Nachrichten ins Publikum zu tragen." R. M. **157**, 122.

Mar. 12. " Neuerdings Auswanderungslust in der Gegend von Bern." R. M. **157**, 370.

Apr. 10. " Mandat betr. Auswanderung beschlossen." R. M. **157**, 531.

May 20. " Der Antrag, es sei der Abzug für Auswanderer nach Carolina zu erhöhen, wird fallen gelassen." R. M. **158**, 307.

1741.

Mar. 30. " Befehl, den Agenten Hans Riemensperger aus dem Toggenburg, der Leute nach Carolina und Georgien anlocken will, zu verhaften. Neuenburg wird vor dem Manne gewarnt. An Zürich werden Nachrichten über Carolina geschickt, die Bern aus London erhalten hat." R. M. **169**, 383.

Apr. 5. " Neue Vorkehren gegen Riemensperger." R. M. **169**, 408.

1742.

Jan. 19. " Ein Mann aus Oberhasle Peter Huber, der nach Carolina ausgewandert war, holt Weib und Kinder. Andere Oberländer wollen auswandern."

" Die Regierung verlangt ein Gutachten, wie armen Leuten, die sonst auswandern, Arbeit verschafft werden könnte." R. M. **173**, 275.

Feb. 10. " Vorkehren gegen die sich wieder regende Auswanderungslust." R. M. **173**, 403.

Feb. 13. " Peter Huber soll sich ' ohne Verzug mit Weib und Kind fortpaken '. Man sucht zu verhindern, dass er nicht Leute zur Auswanderung verleite." R. M. **173**, 432.

Feb. 22. " Weitere Verfolgung Hubers. Er hat zahlreiche Leute auswanderungslustig gemacht, sogar einen 75 jährigen Mann." R. M. **173**, 498.

Mar. 1. " Die Auswanderung wieder lebhaft im Gang. Leute aus Oberhasle und Interlaken ziehen über den Brünigpass. Man sucht Huber zu erwischen." R. M. **173**, 552-554.

Mar. 3. " Polizei soll auf Auswanderer fahnden." R. M. **174**, 8-9.

" Man soll ihnen keine Pässe mehr geben." R. M. **174**, 12-13.

Mar. 6. " Huber ist in Basel erwischt worden." R. M. **174**, 29.

Mar. 7. " Meldung aus Basel, man habe Huber verhaftet und halte die Auswanderer an." R. M. **174**, 34.

Mar. 8. " Ein aus Carolina kommender, an Daniel Kissling in Wattenwil adressierter Brief soll ausgehändigt werden." R. M. **174**, 54.

Mar. 9. " Massnahmen gegen die Auswanderung." R. M. **174**, 63.

Mar. 10. "Massnahmen gegen die Auswanderung. Man teilt den Leuten mit, Huber sei verhaftet worden." R. M. **174**, 68-69.
Mar. 12. "Man bringt verschiedene Auswanderer dazu, statt nach Carolina in den franz. Kantonsteil zu ziehen, um dort Arbeit zu suchen. Diese Leute werden unterstützt und sollen den Abzug wieder erhalten." R. M. **174**, 78-80.
Mar. 13. "Man verschafft ihnen das beschlagnahmte Gepäck wieder." R. M. **174**, 88.
"Vorbereitung einer Druckschrift zur Warnung vor Carolina." R. M. **174**, 89.
Mar. 14. "Man will die Auswanderung radikal verbieten, dagegen für Arbeit im Lande sorgen." R. M. **174**, 100-102.
Mar. 17. "Mandat betr. Auswanderer." R. M. **174**, 129.
Apr. 2. "Die Basler Polizei stellt Rechnung für ihre Bemühungen zur Anhaltung der Auswanderer." R. M. **174**, 184.
"Der Grosse Rat beschliesst: 'Die Auswanderung bernischer Untertanen nicht nur nach Carolina, sondern nach Amerika überhaupt ist verboten!'" R. M. **174**, 187.
Apr. 26. "Dieser Beschluss wird als Mandat veröffentlicht." R. M. **174**, 383.

1744.

Jan. 18. "Peter Inäbnit ist aus Carolina nach seiner alten Heimat Grindelwald heimgekehrt und wirbt Auswanderer an. Er soll verhaftet und nach Carolina abgeschoben werden." R. M. **181**, 103-104.
Jan. 22. "Inäbnit ist verhaftet. Grosse Untersuchung. Er hat an den englischen Residenten geschrieben. Brief beschlagnahmt." R. M. **181**, 127-128.
Feb. 4. "Der gefangene Inäbnit soll schärfer ausgeforscht und mit der Folterung bedroht werden, wenn er nicht Auskunft geben will." R. M. **181**, 212.
Feb. 17. "Er gesteht nichts, kommt für zwei Stunden an den Pranger und wird an die Grenze geführt." R. M. **181**, 305.
Feb. 20. "Ein Brief von Philipp Friedrich Wild aus Rotterdam an Inäbnit wird beschlagnahmt. Es stellt sich heraus, dass Inäbnit etwa 70 Familien auswanderungslustig gemacht hat. Die Post wird angewiesen, verdächtige Briefe auszuliefern. Inäbnit soll wieder verhaftet werden." R. M. **181**, 322-325.
Feb. 27. "Trotz aller Anstrengungen der Regierungen 'ziehen oberländische Landleute haufenweise nach Carolina'. Man lässt sie ziehen. Befehl, aus Carolina zurückkehrende Leute in Gefangenschaft zu nehmen. Auftrag an den Kommerzienrat, für Abhilfe zu sorgen." R. M. **181**, 357-359.
Mar. 4. "Polizeimassnahmen, um die Anwerbung von Auswanderern durch Briefe zu verhindern." R. M. **181**, 397.
"Basel wird ersucht Inäbnit zu verhaften und auszuliefern." R. M. **181**, 399.
Mar. 9. "Die Regierung sucht die jungen Leute zurückzuhalten, damit sie nicht mit den Eltern abreisen. Man sucht die Auswanderer damit zu schrecken, ihr Führer Inäbnit sei verhaftet." R. M. **181**, 421-425.
Mar. 16. "Die Auswanderer erhalten Pässe, verlieren aber das Landrecht." R. M. **181**, 466.

Mar. 17. "Heute passieren 80 Auswanderer, die den Abzug bezahlt haben, die Stadt per Schiff." R. M. 181, 475.
"Inäbnit ist nun wieder in der Gewalt der Berner Regierung, Verhör." R. M. 181, 478.
Apr. 2. "Bei einem Befreiungsversuch stürzt Inäbnit vom Turm herab zu Tode. Leichnam wird unter dem Hochgericht verscharrt." R. M. 181, 537.

1749.

Apr. 21. "Hans Curt aus dem Amt Wangen will nach Pensylvanien ziehen. Man geht damit um den Abzug von 10 auf 20 per cent. zu erhöhen." R. M. 201, 312.
Apr. 24. "Befehl an die Amtleute, auf die Amerika-Werber zu achten. Die Kanzlei soll einen Bericht erstatten, was bisher in der Auswanderungssache vorgekehrt worden sei." R. M. 201, 351, 358.
"Befehl an alle Amtleute des ganzen Kantons, insgeheim auf die Verführer zu achten, welche bernische Untertanen verlocken, ' ihr vermeint besseres Glück in America und Pensilvanien zu suchen '. Die Agenten sind zu verhaften, sobald sie sich verdächtig machen." Geheimes Missivenbuch C, 532.
Apr. 28. "Auswanderungsfieber im Aargau. Agent Jakob Walder aus dem Kanton Zürich." R. M. 201, 386.
May 3. "Abzug wird vorläufig nicht erhöht." R. M. 201, 444.
May 6. "Massregeln gegen die Auswanderung aus dem Aargau." R. M. 201, 480-483.
May 12. "Zwei Basler werben in der Gegend von Büren für Carolina und Pennsylvanien." R. M. 201, 535-536.
May 13. "Erwägung der Frage, ob den zahlreichen Heimatlosen die Auswanderung zu gestatten sei." R. M. 201, 551.
May 19. "Die beiden Basler, die aus Pennsylvanien zurückgekehrt sind und nun Leute anwerben, heissen Jakob Joner von Prattelen, M. Spänhauwer von Muttenz. Befehl sie zu verhaften." R. M. 202, 11-12.
June 26. "In Zeitungen erscheinen Berichte, dass in Basel viele Tausende sich sammeln, um nach ' Amerika und Neu Schottland ' auszuwandern. Bern sucht in Basel, Zürich, etc., zu bewirken, dass solche Zeitungsmeldungen unterdrückt würden." R. M. 202, 377-378.

1750.

Feb. 24. "Auswanderungsfieber in der Gegend von Interlaken. Die Vorbereitungen zur Abreise werden heimlich getroffen." R. M. 205, 88-90.
Feb. 26. "Der Redakteur der in Bern erscheinenden französischen Zeitung de Morancour erhält einen Verweis, weil die gestrige Nummer einen Artikel über Carolina und Pennsylvanien brachte, wo ' die Leute ihr Glück finden '." R. M. 205, 105.
Mar. 6. "Empfang eines Schreibens von Basel betr. Zeitungsmeldungen." R. M. 205, 164.
Mar. 9. "Konfiszierte Briefe aus Amerika für bernische Untertane." R. M. 205, 185.

Apr. 10. "Auswanderer aus dem Oberland sind von Yverdon (am Neuenburgersee) aus zu Schiff abgereist. Den Schiffern von Yverdon wird verboten, Leute, die nach Carolina, Pennsylvanien und Neu-Schottland reisen wollen, mitzunehmen." R. M. 205, 412-413.

1751.

Mar. 27. "Jakob Joner aus Pennsylvanien versucht das Vermögen Ausgewanderter herauszubekommen. Seine Vollmachten werden aber nicht für genügend erachtet. Er wird ausgewiesen." R. M. 209, 440.

Apr. 16. "Man ratschlagt wieder einmal, wie die Auswanderung in 'americanische Colloneyen' verhindert werden könne." R. M. 209, 545.

Apr. 21. "Auswanderer nach Pennsylvanien werden verhört." R. M. 210, 5.

May 5. "Dupaquier von Neuenburg Agent für Neu-Schottland." R. M. 210, 143.

May 24. "Eine arme Familie namens Bernhart aus dem Städtchen Wiedlisbach wird ziehen gelassen. Nachforschung, wer sie 'franko bis ans Meer' liefern wolle." R. M. 210, 281.

June 26. "Drei Agenten: Joner, Tschudi, und Bratteler, werden proskribiert. Sie kommen gewöhnlich im Monat März ins Land, um Auswanderer zu holen." R. M. 210, 540-541.

(1751.)

"Zedel an Hr. Groszweibel: indeme Hr. Michael Schlatter Prediger der Teutschen Gemeind zu Philadelphia in Pennsilvanien sich bey allhiesigem E. Convent angemeldet, und den Zustand der alldort etablirten zum Theil schweizerischen Religionsgenossen vorgestellet, mit dem Beyfügen, dass die holländischen Sinodi Ihne Pfarrer mit Beglaubigungsbriefen an die Reformirte Ministeria vorgehen, und Ihme aufgetragen, etwelche Prediger für Pennsilvanien auszusuchen, und auch milte Bëysteuer zu suchen, haben MeGnHn in Bedenken der bösen Folgerungen so aus dergleichen Sachen entstehen, in dieses Pfarrers Begehren gar nit eintretten können, sonderen befehlens Ihme Hn. Groszweibel demselben zu bescheiden, Ihme das Consilium Abeundi von hier zu ertheillen, mit der Vermahnung hierlands von seinem Vorhaben mit niemand zu reden, sonsten er sich in schwäre Verantwortung setzen würde. Ubrigens haben MeGnHn Ihm bisz zu heutigem dato (inclusive) Ine für seinen Aufenthalt allhier kostfrey halten und vom Wirthen lösen wollen, massen Hr. Ammann den Conto unterschreiben solle." R. M. 212, 78-79.

1752.

Apr. 29. "Briefe * aus Pennsylvanien werden von der Polizei geöffnet und abgeschrieben. Die darin enthaltenen ungünstigen Nachrichten sollen im nächstjährigen Kalender † erscheinen." R. M. 214, 9.

* Nacher werden sie den Adressaten zugestellt.
† S. *Hinkender Bote*, 1749-1756. Confiszierte Briefe, 1752.

Auszug aus einem Brief von Johannes Storker aus Pennsylvanien.
Ein anders Schreiben eines Land-Manns aus dem Oberland.
Brief aus Pennsylvanien an Weib und Kinder.
Brief eines bekannten Schweizers aus Philadelphia.

June 4. "Der Kirchenkonvent beschliesst, das Gesuch zu unterstützen, 'zu Errichtung fernerer Kirchen und Schulen und Salarierung Prediger und Schulmeister in Pensilvanien' sei von Staatswegen eine Beisteuer zu geben. Das Gesuch von den holländischen Synoden an die evangelischen Orte der Eidgenossenschaft." Akten des Kirchenkonvents, IV. 12.

1753.

Feb. 19. "Briefe zur Verlockung nach Carolina und Pennsylvanien in der Gegend von Interlaken." R. M. **217**, 185.

Feb. 20. "Ihre Überbringer Hans Zurflüh von Oberried und Hans Wyss von Isenfluh werden auf 24 Stunden eingesperrt und sollen in 8 Tagen das Land räumen. In der Regierung wird der Antrag gestellt, es sei den Auswanderern das Erbrecht auf Vermögen in der Heimat zu nehmen." R. M. **217**, 202.

Feb. 24. "Überweisung des Antrages an eine Kommission." R. M. **217**, 233.

May 21. "Das Mandat vom 26. Apr., 1742, wird bestätigt. Von einer Verschärfung wird Umgang genommen." R. M. **218**, 345.

1754.

May 18. "Die Regierung nimmt hinterlassenes Gut von Auswanderern in Verwaltung. Aus der Landschaft Erguel, die dem Bischof von Basel untertan war, wo aber viele Berner als Pächter wohnten, sind solche nach Pennsylvanien abgereist. (Es waren meist Wiedertäufer.) Sie durften nach Befehl des Bischofs nur abreisen, wenn sie andere vermögliche Leute als Pächter stellten. Die bern. Regierung sucht eine Abwanderung nach dem Erguel zu hindern." R. M. **223**, 45.

1755.

Sept. 25. "Herr Gasser, Prediger bei der reform. Gemeinde Sandyvarck[1] in Süd-Carolina bewirbt sich um eine Beisteuer in Geld, Bibeln oder Psalmenbüchern. Der bern. Kirchenkonvent empfiehlt das Gesuch. Die Regierung weist Gasser ab, gibt ihm ein Viaticum von 6 Dukaten und zugleich das Consilium Abeundi." R. M. **228**, 411.

1756.

Jan. 2. "In der Gegend von Interlaken Auswanderungslust. Befehl, den Prediger Gasser, der Leute anwerbe, zu verhaften. Er stammte von Steckborn im Thurgau." R. M. **229**, 339-341.

Jan. 15. "Einer Familie von Interlaken (10 Köpfe) wird das Vermögen gesperrt, damit sie nicht auswandern könne." R. M. **229**, 425.

Jan. 24. "Zwei aus der Gegend stammende Männer Hans Moser und Heinrich Ritschard, die von Carolina zurückgekommen und als Agenten verdächtig sind, kommen unter Polizeiaufsicht." R. M. **229**, 481.

---

[1] This is undoubtedly Santee Forks. Cf. Wm. J. Hinke, "The Origin of the Reformed Church in South Carolina", *Journal of the Presbyterian Historical Society*, III. 387 (Dec., 1906).

Apr. 24. "Ein gewisser Gottl. Mittelberger, gegenwärtig zu Stuttgart, sendet an die Regierung einige Exemplare seiner gedruckten Reisebeschreibung von Pennsylvanien."[1] R. M. 230, 504.

1763.

Apr. 28. "Johannes Christen, aus dem Kt. Basel, sucht das Vermögen des in Pennsylvanien befindlichen Hildebrand Inäbnit herauszubekommen." R. M. 265, 199.

May 17. "Nach dem Mandat vom 16. Apr., 1742, verfügt die Regierung, dieses 1200 Kronen ausmachende Vermögen sei nicht auszuhändigen, sondern unter vormundschaftliche Verwaltung der Gemeinde Grindelwald zu stellen. Inäbnit war ein Leineweber." R. M. 265, 355.

Dec. 28. "Auch 400 Kronen Schulden des Inäbnit werden aus dessen Vermögen nicht bezahlt. Mittel, die Auswanderung im Volk verhasst zu machen." R. M. 268, 71.

1764.

Jan. 23. "Um diese Zeit werden vielfache Klagen über die Entvölkerung des Kantons laut. Zahlreiche Gegenmassnahmen werden vorgeschlagen, und es wurde auch die erste Volkszählung nach neuzeitlichen Grundsätzen vorgenommen.

"Als Grund der Entvölkerung wird auch die Anwerbung von Männern und Frauen nach England und Amerika, 'in die neuw angelegten Plantationen' angegeben." R. M. 268, 269.

Mar. 27. "Eine abschreckende 'Relation von Philadelphia' von einem gewissen Pfarrer Rottenbühler (vermeintlich in Amerika) verfasst, soll durch den Druck verbreitet werden." R. M. 269, 158.

1765.

Dec. 4. "Massnahmen gegen die Entvölkerung des Landes sollen von einer besondern Kommission vorgeschlagen werden." R. M. 277, 460.

1766.

Jan. 23. "Bern erkundigt sich bei mehreren anderen Kantonen, was man dort gegen die Auswanderung vorkehre." R. M. 278, 367.

1767.

Nov. 1. "In Bern ist ein nach der Meinung des Kirchenkonvents irreligiöses Buch: *Sur la population de l'Amérique* erschienen. Theologieprofessor Stapfer soll es näher prüfen." Akten des Kirchenkonvents, IV. 328.

[1] Gottlieb Mittelberger, *Reise nach Pennsylvanien im Jahr 1750 und Rückreise nach Teutschland im Jahr 1754* (Stuttgart, 1756). This book, appearing in 1756, was welcomed by those that opposed emigration. The full title literally translated is as follows: *Gottlieb Mittelberger's Journey to Pennsylvania in the Year 1750 and Return to Germany in the Year 1754, containing not only a Description of the Country according to its Present Condition, but also a Detailed Account of the Sad and Unfortunate Circumstances of most of the Germans that have emigrated, or are emigrating to that Country.* It has been translated from the German by C. T. Eben (Philadelphia, 1898, pp. 129).

1768.

Jan. 10. "Das Buch bestreitet die Inspiration der Bibel. Das Gutachten Stapfers geht dahin, wenn man das Buch verbiete, werde es begierig gelesen. Es soll also mit Schweigen übergangen werden." Akten des Kirchenkonvents, IV. 334.

1769.

May 24. "Die Synode von New York (Novum Eboracum) und Philadelphia schreibt an die schweiz. ref. Kirche in lateinischer Sprache und gibt Auskunft über ihre Verhältnisse seit 1729." Akten des Kirchenkonvents, IV. 418.

1771.

Mar. 10. "Der bernische Konvent lässt ebenfalls lateinisch durch Prof. Joh. Stapfer antworten. Hoffnung auf Bekehrung der heidnischen Eingeborenen." Akten des Kirchenkonvents, IV. 420.

1779.

Nov. 24. "Jakob Philadelphia aus Amerika erhält die Erlaubnis während der Messe seine 'mathematisch-physikalischen Künste' dem Publikum vorzuführen." R. M. **350**, 161.

1780.

June 2. "Die Regierung lässt die Einführung von Blitzableitern prüfen." R. M. **353**, 296.
Aug. 25. "Man will nächstes Jahr damit einen Versuch machen." R. M. **354**, 377.

1781.

"Es sind Werbungen für die ostindische Kompanie im Gange. Bern hält seine Angehörigen zurück und verfolgt die Werber. (S. auch R. M. 360.)"
(Summer.) "Der franz. Gesandte reklamiert wegen Werbungen für den Königl. Grossbrit. Dienst in Amerika." R. M. **359**, 395, 408, 433.
Aug. 13. "Nach dem Ergebnis einer grossen Untersuchung über unerlaubte Werbungen wurden diese vorgenommen:
1. für die englische-ostindische Kompanie.
2. für die holländische-ostindische Kompanie.
Dagegen wurde festgestellt, dass es sich *nicht* um Werbungen für den K. Grossbrit. Dienst in Amerika handle." Manual der Rekruten-Kammer, **35**, 157.

1796.

Mar. 14. "Der bernische Kaufmann Rudolph Tillier ersuchte die Regierung um die Erlaubnis, 24-30 freiwillige Arbeitsleute nach Amerika anwerben zu dürfen. Er wurde mit seinem Begehren an den Grossen Rat gewiesen (scheint aber von der Sache abgestanden zu sein). Tillier hatte den Auftrag aus Amerika bekommen. Rud. Tillier geb. 1754, war mit einer Engländerin verheiratet." R. M. **445**, 70.

July 7. " Die Regierung erwägt den Verkauf englischer Fonds und die Erwerbung amerikanischer Fonds." N. B. Der bernische Staatsschatz besass 1790: 440,960. 16. 10 Pfund in englischen Fonds. Durch Spekulation in Mississippiaktien gewann s. Z. das bernische Bankhaus Malacrida und Co. 150,000 Kronen; aber durch den Mississippi- und Südsee-Krach um 1720 verloren der Staat Bern und bernische Privatleute: 513,611. 20. 3. Taler+85, 445. 12. 5 Pfund. Bankiers: Malacrida und Co. (Bern), Müller und Co. (London)." R. M. 447, 194.[1]

1820.

Apr. 4. " 1. Bericht des Hauptmanns Rudolph May über die Anwerbung von Züchtlingen für die Kolonie des Lord Selkirk am Roten Fluss (Hudson Bay Distrikt)." R. M. 52, 56, 57.

1821.

Jan. 26. " Mehrere (etwa 30) sich bereit erklärt nach der Colonie am Rothen Fluss in Nord Amerika für welche Hr. Hauptmann May (von Utzendorf) Colonisten sucht; mehrere ihre Reisekosten ganz zu bezahlen vermögen; Strafumwandlung, Deportation. Verneint: (1) weil Colonie von Selkirk noch keineswegs so weit gediehen ist; (2) weil keine Sicherheit gegen das Entlaufen und Rückkehr. Beschluss: Werden Sträflinge nicht freigegeben." R. M. 54.

TÄUFER.

Manual der Täufer-Kammer (special court established). 4 vols. 1721-1743.

RODEL.

Rodel Weggezogener Mannrechten. 1694-1754. Alphabetical list of persons who withdrew their home-rights. The destination of the emigrants is unfortunately never mentioned.

RECROUTEN KAMMER.

Manual MHHRN der Recrouten Kammer der Statt Bern. Nr. 8. 1720-1724.
p. 7: " Entführung dahin Daniel Müllers " (case of a father and 2 sons kidnapped for service in Mississippi). Evidences of the successful recruiting of Merveilleux.
pp. 25-26: " Friedrich Vannaz, wegen seiner Entführung nach Mississippi." The following droll entry appears: " Bomont. Praef.: Ihme befehlen, den Friedrich Vannaz von Gingins, so wider Verbott, für das Mississippi Dienst genommen, hernach sich wieder los gemacht und ins Land kommen, vor sich zu beschicken, und ihme verdeuten, dass er das Schallenwerk [Schellentragen, i. e., Zuchthaus, penitentiary] verdient hätte; weihlen er aber sehr einfältig, und wenig Verstand habe, so seye er pardoniert, und wollind MHWH die Sach dahin gestellt seyn lassen." Jan. 9, 1722.

[1] Cf. Landmann: "Die auswärtigen Kapitalanlagen aus dem Berner Staatsschatz im 18. Jahrhundert", in Jahrbuch für Schweiz. Geschichte, XXVIII.

Erlach D., p. 661. "Demnach ich vernommen, wie dass sich einige arme gantze Familien etc. sich in die neuerfundene Insull Mississippi zubegeben und von einem gewüssen Hr. Wunderlich von Neüwenburg auf gute vorgebente Wort und Gelt dorthin engagirt worden. Als habe ich dise Leuth, umb selbige von ihrem Vorhaben abwendig zu machen vor mich beschieden, allein nichts bey ihnen ausrichten können, allemaszen sie, wie mir der Bericht abgestattet worden kurtz darauf verreiset. Wann ich dises nun von groszer Consequentz erachte in Betrachtung man nicht weiss, wo dise Leuth hinkommen und wie es ihnen in Ansehen der Religion oder sonsten ergehen möchte, Als habe Ew. Gn. dessen in aller Gebühr verständigen, dero Hochweyssen Guthfinden hierüber erwarten mithin dieselben göttlichem Machtschirm wohl erlassen wollen, verbleibe, Euer Gnaden, etc. Hier [onymus] Huser, Ambtsmann zu Erlach." Apr. 13, 1720. See action of Berner Rat.
Rats Manuale, Apr. 15, 1720.
Erlach D. Printed advertisement of "Messieurs Purry et Compagnie", "ayant besoin de trois ou quatre cents hommes ouvriers de differentes professions, pour aller faire bon Etablissement en Amérique dans la Caroline Méridionale etc." Neufchâtel, June 28, 1725.
Neuenburg Bücher. 1735, pp. 599-610. Capitaine Quinche accused of luring Bernese to Carolina. His denial and defense. As Maitre des Clefs in Neufchâtel, which gave Capt. Quinche military power, he probably succeeded in getting people off. See also Missiven Buch, Sept. 16, and Nov. 22, 1735: the Bernese Council insists on the correctness of its information, which Quinche denies.
Frütigen D., pp. 1061-1072. Concerning the legacy of Hans Schrantz, who in 1749 emigrated to Carolina, and subsequently became a well-to-do man in Canastoga (probably Conestoga, Pa.).
Hasle-Buch D. Typical case: "Barbara Horger, so in Carolinam ziehen will, haltet um Verabfolgung ihrer Mittel an." (Vermögen 90 K. 10 per cent. Abzug.)

SÄCKELSCHREIBER PROTOCOLLE.

W. Protocollum vom 1. Februar, 1735, bis 1. August, 1736.
pp. 57-61. "Vortrag MrHwH der Committirten wegen Versorgung deren, so nacher Carolinam emigrirt waren." All those stranded at foreign ports to be brought back, transportation paid, "damit sie desto sicherer ankämen, und durch Erzählung ihres überstandenen Elends die anderen desto mehr von der Nachfolg abschrecken thäten, dann es ist zu besorg, dass diese Sucht der Emigration je mehr und mehr überhand nehmen werde, also allerhand gelind Mittel dar wieder vorzukehren nit undienlich." Mar. 28, 1735.
Y. Protocollum, Aller von mir Beath Ludwig May diszmahligem Teutschen Sekelschreiber, expedierten und signierten Instrumenten, Bedäncken, Vorträgen, etc., angefangen d. 13. Januarii 1738 und endet d. 13. Marty 1739.
"Gutachten: Ob der Abzug von denen so nacher Carolinam emigriren zu erhöhen seye. Acte 5 May, 1738." Conclusion: that the tax on emigrants should not be increased, first, because of attention

and dissatisfaction aroused, and secondly, emigration was now less frequent. Characteristic passage: "Anderseits dann ist nunmehr die RABIES CAROLINAE [*sic*] zu gutem Glück allerdings verschwunden, und haben sich die Unterthanen durch das Traurige Fatum der angesehensten von den Emigranten ein mehrers belehren lassen, als durch alle MeGH Ihnen gethane so väterliche Vermahnung . . . ."

RESPONSA PRUDENTUM.

VI., pp. 155-187. " Ohnmaszgebliche und Wohlmeinentliche Gedanken Wie die von der Carolinischen Reyse abgehaltene Oberländische Hauszhaltungen, samt übrigen dortigen Armen in einen besseren Nehrstand gesetzet werden könnten." (Addressed to Commercien Räthen.)

pp. 189-191. " Wegen der Armen im Oberland." Advice to establish manufactures. Mar. 3, 1744.

pp. 193-210. " Wie der Armut im Oberlande abgeholfen werden könnte." Mar. 5, 1744.

pp. 215-235. Abstract of all suggested plans, Memoriale, on the subject. Proposal of " Arbeitshaus ". None of the plans were carried out. For a brief account, *cf*. E. Lerch, *Die Bernische Auswanderung nach Amerika im 18. Jahrhundert* (1909).

VII., pp. 823-833. " Gutachten zu Behinderung der amerikanischen Emigrationen." May 6, 1749.

THURN-BUCH DER STATT BERN.

1740-1742.

The Thurn was the tower, used as a prison, and the Thurn-Buch the record kept of the examinations of prisoners confined in the tower (now an archive) in Bern. The questions and answers of these searching court-examinations are carefully recorded in the Thurn-Buch, and afford a most realistic picture of social and moral conditions of the period. Two of these " Verhöre " concern American history, inasmuch as the prisoners examined are suspected of being emigrant agents, who have been inciting Swiss people to immigrate to Carolina. Their names are Peter Huber and Peter Im Aebnit, both born in the Berner Oberland. These " Verhöre " will be published in full in the *American Historical Review*; abstracts only follow here:

1740-1742, p. 479 f. (41 pp.). " Peter Huber, 36 Jahre alt, gebürtig von Ober-Hasli, Schuhmacher, Weib und 3 Kinder, davon eines in Carolina.

" Der zu Basel arrestirte Peter Huber wegen Verdachts ob hätte er Leuthe in hiesigen Landen angeworben, nach Carolina in America zu führen, auf Ihr. Gn. Befehl anhero gebracht worden—habend dato 21. März, 1742, folgendes Examen mit demselben gehalten " : (Huber denies having induced anyone to go; claims to have represented facts as they were, calling attention to dangers and difficulties; has appointed no meeting-place at Basel or elsewhere; has had nothing to do with crowds of emigrants gathering at Basel.—See notes on Basel archive below, p. 111.)

F. " Ob er nicht ein hölzernes Geschirr habe, da man obenher Getränk, unden her aber Briefen darinn thun könne?"

A. "Ja ein solches habe Ihme ein gewisser Hans Rodt in Carolina gemacht und werde man solches under seinem Plunder wohl finden."
F. "Er habe nun alle an Ihne gethane quaestiones ziemlich hartnäckig geläugnet und darbey versichert, dass er gern alles bekennen wollte was wahr seye, nun wolle man anoch eine frische ganz wahrhafte frag an Ihne truken und darbey sehen, wie sehr er die Wahrheit liebe? Ob er nicht vorgestern ein Papeyr aus Gefangenschafft einem Weibe von seinen Lands Leuthen zu geworfen darauf geschrieben gestanden, das diejenige so auch Lust haben möchten mit Ihme zu reisen, trachten sollind, in das Neuenburgische zu gehen und sich dorten eine Weil aufhalten, Er hoffe seine Sachen seyen noch nicht so schlimm beschaffen, dass er nicht Hoffnung haben sollte bald loos zu werden, wenn er dann loos seye, wolle er hinkommen und im Vorbey gehen Sie mit Ihme nemen, sie seyind als dan grad in Burgund, und könnind Ihren Weg ohngehindert vortsezen?"
A. "Über diese quaestion schienen Er ganz erschrocken zu seyn, schauete hin u. her, wusste ein Weile nicht was er sagen sollte, und schosse Ihme das Wasser in die Augen. Endlich sagte er. Ja! Er könne dieses nicht läugnen, Er habe vermeinet, wan er einmal ledig werden könte und diese Leuthe auszert Er. Gndl. Bottmässigkeit antreffen wurde, er selbige, ohne dann Übels zu thun, mit sich nemen könte, er gestähe aber auch, hierinnen gröblich gefählet zu haben, seye Ihme wohl herzlich leid, er bitte Bott. und Er. Hoh. Gn. in dehemuth um Verzeihung u. Gnad."
"Worauf er wieder in seinen Orth geführt worden." Mar. 21, 1742.
Examination of numerous persons who were to go with Huber (same method pursued at Basel). Attempt made by the court to get witnesses to declare that they were encouraged by Huber to emigrate. Peter Scherz is determined to emigrate, he sought Huber, not Huber him; poverty was the cause. Ulrich Müller induced by encouraging letters from America. Jacob Ritschard, with family of seven, long determined to go. Hans Poster induced by poverty, Christ. Oehrli by relations in Carolina. Hans Egger declared Huber had said he would get 50 acres of land and cash money on arrival in Carolina (large inducements were made at that time for colonists).

KLEIN THURN-BUCH DER STATT BERN.
1743-1744.

1743-1744, pp. 132-149. "Peter Im Aebnit aus Grindelwald, bey 25 Jahren alters, vor neun Jahren mit Vater, Mutter, Geschwistern und vier Landsleuthen nach Carolina ausgewandert." When asked to explain his reappearance in Switzerland, he declares that he was sick all but two years in Carolina, and therefore wished never to return thither. Questioned about his visit to the English minister at Reichenberg; about the crowds gathering about him at Grindelwald; the letters he had carried with him (8 in number), etc.
List of 20 adults and 44 children who are resolved to go to Carolina.
pp. 153-160. "Da er nun ohngeachtet alles ernstlichen Zusprechens, Antrohung der Marter, und da der Scharfe Richter Ihme vorge-

stellet worden, ein mehreres nicht bekennen noch eingestehen wollen, ward derselbe hinauf und zu der Folter-Bank geführt, Ihme nochmalen äussersten Ernsts zugesprochen und die Marter anzuwenden angetrohet, dessen ohngeacht verbliebe derselbe durchaus bey seiner hiervorigen Aussaag, und dass er gar nicht gekommen, jemand nach Carolina zu verleiten, noch dass er gewusst was in denen mitgebrachten Briefen enthalten gewesen, er seye selbsten nicht gesinnet wieder hinein zu gehen, und werde niemand zeugen können, dass er jemanden dahin verlocket, in dem Gegentheil habe er mehr abgewerth als angerathen; im übrigen seye er in seiner Hohen Oberkeit Banden, man könne mit Ihme machen was man wolle; er bäte aber um Gnädige Looslassung." Actum, 10. Feb., 1744.
"Wird an den Pranger gestellt, und ewig banisirt."
In answer to the question, how many went with Peter Huber, he said, nine to ten persons arrived with him in Carolina. Huber derived no profits from them, he declared.

pp. 206-215. After this punishment with the stocks and subsequent banishment, Peter Im Aebnit was implicated again and imprisoned in the Kefi-Thurn (Käfig-Turm, still standing) in Bern. From this tower Peter Im Aebnit tried to escape by means of a rope which his friends had brought him. The rope broke and Peter lost his life. His body was picked up in the morning, and the following record appears in the book: "Wegen der am Tag liegenden, und z. Theil gestandenen Verbrechen" wurde "der tote Körper unter dem Hoch-Gericht verscharrt."

Die Eidgenössischen Abschiede aus dem Zeitraum von 1712-1743.

Printed volume (Zürich, 1860, VII. 1 of the series), prepared by D. A. Fechter, containing the minutes of congresses of the thirteen cantons.

p. 506 b. " Bern ersucht die Gesandten Zürichs, mitzutheilen, was für Maszregeln ihre Gn. Herren und Obern gegen die in so groszer Zahl nach Carolina 'in Westindien' reisende Leute getroffen hätten. Diese antworten, dass dieselben in Folge der zu Bern u. Neuenburg eingezogenen Berichte den Verkauf des Büchleins von Herrn Pury von Neuenburg im Lande verboten hätten. Wie nun aber gegen den Herbst trotz aller Abmahnungen dennoch über 200 Personen dahin verreist seien, so habe man durch ein Mandat die fernere Auswanderung verboten. Da jedoch ' diese Krankheit' dergestalt überhand genommen habe, dass seither noch mehr verreist seien, und im Frühlinge noch mehr wegziehen wollen, so hätten sie die Untersuchung dieser Sache einer Commission übergeben. Es wird einmütig befunden, dass man auf die Rädelsführer Acht haben und sie zur Strafe ziehen solle; ferner, dasz man niemanden mit Pässen oder Geld für die Abreise Vorschub thun, im Gegentheil dieselbe auf alle Weise hindern solle." Dec., 1734.

p. 696. Auswanderung. Mandat: "Die Gemeinden sollen dem Landvogt anzeigen, wenn jemand ausziehen will." Oct. 16, 1728.

Acta Conventus Ecclesiastici Bernensis, MS.

III. 671 f. Praeside Hr. Decan Kilchberger.
Acta: "Erschinne Hr. Michael Schlatter prediger göttlichen worts zu Philadelphia in Pensilvania vorweisende ein recommendatorium von dem allgemeinen Synodo der Hollendischen Kirchen an die Reformirten Kirchen in der Eydgenossschafft, in welchem gezeiget wird, mit wass mühe und vielem seegen dieser Hr. Schlatter, sonst gebürtig von St. Gallen, dortige Colonien der Reformirten, deren Anzahl sich auff 30,000 belaufft, under welchen die Helffte Emigranten aus der Reformirten Eydgenossschaft, in eine kirchliche Verfassung gebracht, in verschiedenen Kirchspielen eingetheilt, und alles also angeordnet, dass wofern ihme mit kreftiger Hülffe under die armen griffen werde, zu hoffen, dass under Gottlichem Beystand das Evangelium mit grossem seegen alldorten werde fortgepflanzet werden. destwegen schon albereit ihr Hochmögenden für 5 Jahr jedes Jahr zu steuern erkent 2000 Gulden, sonder ess haben die Synodi erklärt, hierzu ansehenliche Collecten zu samlen, wie dan ihr Vorwort an alle Reformirten stenden der eidgnossschaft dahin gehet, dass auff eine gleiche weise der aufnahm der Reform: Kirchen in america durch thätliche liebe beherziget werde. die gantze nachricht von dieser Reform: Colonie ist getruckt in Hollendischer Sprach, wie zu sehen in den authenticis zu disem Manual."
"Erkent: (1) wurden Hr. Prof. Altmann und Hr. Theologus Wytenbach verordnet, Hrn. Schlatter für die audientz zu Ihren Gnaden zu begleiten, sein begehren im Namen eines E. E. [ehrwürdigen] Convents kreftig zu understützen. (Zusatz: ware aber vollkommen abgewiesen.)
"(2) war Hr. Theologo Wytenbach aufgetragen, entweders an die H. Representanten des General Synodi im Haag oder an den Synodum in Amsterdam zu schreiben, mit verdeuten einerseits, wie dass wir diss christl. werck nach unsserem vermögen werden zu understützen und befördern trachten, anderseits anzurühmen den lobl. Eifer Hrn. Schlatters, nach welchem er ihme die beförderung der Ehre Gottes in fortpflanzung seines evangelii höchst angelegen sein lasset." Nov. 21, 1751.

Evangelische und Drey-Oerthische Abscheiden.
1746-1752.

AA, p. 883 f. "Der Synodus der Reformierten Kirche in der Republik Holland hat die Löbl. Eidgenossenschaft um ihre Milte Concurrenz zu gemeinsamem Handeln zu gunsten des wahren Gottesdienstes in Pennsylvanien, Besoldung der nötigen Lehrer und Schulmeister" gebeten. (Bitte des Hrn. Michael Schlatter, gebürtig in St. Gallen.) "Verneint." Denied to discourage emigration. "Diese Leuthe sind wider sorgfältige Einrathung und Vermahnung weggezogen", "jetzt auch darauf angewiesen sein sollen".

Emigration. Sammlung verschiedener Verordnungen und Mandaten, die Grafschaft Baden, das Thurgau und die Freyen-Ämter betreffend. 1770.
Emigrationen nach Spanien und spanischen Colonien. 1767.

Allgemein Eidgenössische Bücher. Special Heft: Verordnungen gegen die Auswanderungen, 1765-1770. Especially concerned with Spanish American colonies. Most interesting collection of letters, pamphlets, circulars, printed advertisements, e. g., *Glücks-Hafen, oder Reicher Schatz-Kasten, welchen der Spanische Monarch als einer der reichsten Königen zum Trost und Nutzen aller Teutschen und Niederländischen Bauersleuten, Taglöhnern, Handwerk-Männern, Burschen oder Gesellen, Jungen und Alten, Ledig- und Verheuratheten Manns- und Weibs-Personen und kleinen Kindern aufgeschlossen hat; aus welchem sie allezeit Treffer, als Geld, Rindviehe, Schafe, Geissen, oder Ziegen, Schweine, Flügelwerk, Waizen, Korn, Gersten, und andere erdenkliche nothwendige Lebensmittel; ingleichem Häuser, Aecker, Wiesen, Waldungen, wie auch allerley nöthigen Handwerkzeug und sonst Instrumenten, heraus ziehen können; wenn sie nachstehende Nachricht und Vortheile sich zu Gemüth führen, und der angehängten Vorschrift folgen wollen* (1767).

Engelland-Buch. D.

1772. Gebr. Fiess in Nordamerika, Vermögenssache. p. 493.

1772. Franz Spring, Verlassenschaft, Überlassung an Dan. Kahn, Lancaster, Pa. pp. 499-514.

1773. Vermögenswegzug, Erbschaft von Anna Barbara Schmidt, geborene Küntzlin. pp. 551-566.

A document conveying power of attorney, printed in German. Michael Schmidt of Boxborough (Philadelphia County), conveys power to Joh. Jakob Pfister of Reading (Berks County).
A document, signed by Rev. A. Helffenstein, testifying that Anna Barbara Schmidtin and her husband Michael Schmidt are members of the Reformed Church. Inheritance divided into shares, one-fifth to Anna Barbara Schmidt; 10 per cent. Abzug.

1775. Jakob Plüss. Verlassenschaft in Amerika. p. 587.

1776. Künzli. Schwestern in Amerika. Vermögenssache. pp. 591-610.

Frankreich-Buch. NNN. 231.

1781, July 13. " Der französische Gesandte de Polignac antwortet nach Weisung von Paris der bernischen Regierung ablehnend auf ihre Beschwerde, weil Waren, die bernischen Kaufläuten gehörten, auf englischen Schiffen weggenommen worden waren. Es handelte sich um folgende Fälle.

" (a) Mr. de La Mothe Piquet (franz. Anführer) hatte englische Schiffe weggenommen, die auch schweizerische Waren führten. Der König erklärte diese Waren nicht freigeben zu können, weil keine Ausnahme möglich sei.

" (b) Ein englisches Schiff *La Lady* war von einem amerikanischen Korsaren genommen und nach Frankreich geführt worden. Der König wies darauf hin, in diesem Falle könne er erst recht nichts zu Gunsten der bernischen Kaufleute tun."

Frankreich-Buch. NNN. 441-448.

1784. " Der bernische Angehörige Moïse Roch von Chateau d'Oex war als Kaufmann im Dienste eines Hamburger Hauses nach San Domingo gekommen und dort gestorben. Der franz. Fiskus wollte die Erbschaft an sich ziehen, weil die Abzugsfreiheit zwischen Frankreich und der Schweiz sich nicht auf die Kolonien erstrecke. Auf Beschwerde Berns gab der König aus besonderer Gunst das Erbe aber doch frei."

Procedur zwischen dem Edelgebohrnen Mmwghrn. Fürsprech Wysz, als Vogt des in Virginien verstorbenen Christoph von Grafenrieds hinterlassenen Mannesstammes, gegen den wohledelgebohrnen MnHhrn. Ohmgeldner Ryhiner, als rechtsgeordneten Vogt der Hochgeehrten Frau Landvögtin von Grafenried von Boaden, und allfällige Erben des sel. verstorbenen Hrn. Alt Landvogt von Grafenried von Nydau, gewesenen Herrschafts Herrn auf Worb. Rechtsfrage: "Ob die Herrschaft Worb, in Kraft des i. J. 1683 aufgerichteten Kaufbriefs einer ewigen Substitution unterworfen seye?—und daher dem Herrn Kläger zu Handen des von Herrn Christoph von Grafenried so in Virginien verstorben, hinterlassenem Mannsstamm, um die in dem Kaufbrief bestimmte Summe der 42,000 Pf. abgetreten werden müsse?" (Printed pamphlet, Bern, 1781.)

Note: The Graffenried family, the most numerous among the members of the old Bernese aristocracy, dates back to the thirteenth century. The estate Worb, a few miles distant from the city of Bern, was by will, in 1683, not permitted to depart from the male heirs of the Graffenried family. In 1780 the widow of Karl Emanuel Graffenried received permission from the government to sell the property, against the claim of the male descendants of Baron Christoph v. Graffenried in America. The lawsuit that arose is described in the records cited above.

The son of the founder of New Bern, also named Christoph Graffenried (b. 1691), remained in America after the departure of his father. The son seems not to have remained long in Newbern, N. C., but he and his descendants lived in other states. Hon. Reese Calhoun de Graffenried (b. 1853, d. 1902) was a member of Congress, 1897-1902, from Texas. For the Graffenried manuscripts, descriptive of the New Bern settlement in North Carolina, see below.

Auswanderung. Schriften betreffend die Auswanderung nach Brasilien und Nord Amerika in den Jahren 1810 bis und mit 1821.

A large volume of letters, reports, and memoranda, mostly on Brazil. No index in back of volume. Several letters complain of large number of paupers at French and American ports, and urge government action to prevent the evil.

AKTEN DES DIPLOMATISCHEN DEPARTEMENTS DES CANTONS BERN.

1831-1846. Ausland. Amerika.

1833. " Landschafts Commission von Ober-Simmenthal bittet Beitrag an die Kosten, welche Reise eines oder mehrerer Männer zur Folge hätten, Colonie zu gründen, Ländereien in Nordamerika auszusuchen. Überhandnehmende Verarmung, Arbeit suchende und keine zu finden." p. 19 f.

Apr. 15. "Ablehnung des Gesuches " . . . . Manual des Diplomat. Departements, Nr. 3, pp. 121-123.

Aug. 21. "Le département diplomatique" announces that whereas the sun. of 850 fr. was necessary heretofore to pass through France to Havre for emigration, now only 300 fr., in U. S. paper money or equivalent, are required. Manual, Nr. 4, pp. 283-284.

1836. "Anfrage wegen Texas, über Auswanderung dahin. Man soll warten, weil Mexico und Texas Krieg führen." Manual, Nr. 9, p. 65 f.

1846, Jan. 26. Plan of colonies in America. No results.

DIREKTION DES INNERN.

Auswanderungswesen: Akten der Direktion des Innern in den 40er und 50er Jahren. Contain many petitions from criminals for financial assistance to pay expenses of emigration; destination mostly North and South America.

Auswanderungswesen: Ao. 1855-1861. A large volume containing correspondence, agreements, reports, etc. Wholesale deportation of paupers and criminals. In 1855 the sum of 30,000 francs was distributed among the "Gemeinden" for deportation (mostly to America) of paupers and criminals.

Auswanderungs-Steuer-Begehren. 1855.

Correspondenzen. Vorträge. Thorberg-Sträflinge. Large number of pleas for assistance to emigrate, before or at time of completion of sentence.

Id. Zuchthaus-Sträflinge.

Id. Abgewiesene Auswanderungs-Steuerbegehren pro 1855.

JUSTIZ RATH.

1820. Private advertisement of May's colony on Red River, Hudson's Bay district. Pp. 226-227.

1803-1846. Akten des Justiz Rathes. **119.**

1817. Ueber Auswanderungen aus dem Kanton vorzüglich nach Amerika. Great increase of emigration reported. Policy to let the poor go without any restrictions (no loss of home right). Reference to Polizei Verordnung, June 11, 1804, §5. Also to Mannrechtsordnung vom Jahre 1765 (restriction on fathers of families, etc.).

Causes of increase of emigration: Overpopulation, and "Verstückelung des Grundeigenthums". Emigration "in einigen Theilen so eingerissen, dass es eine eigentliche Angelegenheit der Regierungen wird, sich damit zu befassen". Policy to favor emigration in order to relieve poverty and consequent burdens on the community. Passes to be provided without trouble.

Dangers of redemptioner system described. Care of emigrants, means of getting across; fathers of children, how latter are to be provided for.

Zürich also adopts liberal policy toward emigrants. In response to inquiry: "Eine Caution von 15-18 Ldrs. soll hinterlegt werden, welche alsdann dem schweizerischen consul in Amsterdam übersandt wird." Policy of Aargau also liberal. A large number go by way of Havre de Grace, France. Swiss consul there directed to take care of them.

A reported communication of Gallatin from U. S. Gallatin suggests that consuls look into the matter of the terms on which the ship-owners transport the immigrants. Reported answers of Gallatin, as: " Il n'y a en général point de taxe fixe pour le passage—mais Mr. Gallatin suppose l'on doit demander à peu près 300 francs par tête (alors on a le pain, l'eau et la viande salée) et environ 1200 francs par famille."
Remarks on redemptioners, passports of various tradesmen, etc. Most arrivals are Germans. Government has established a magistracy for protection of arrivals, called: Register of German passengers. For a husband and wife and two children it takes four years to get clear of expenses of passage. A four-page well-written letter by Tschann, Paris, July 15, 1817.

1831. Several letters concerning passports, dated 1831 and 1832. This is a period of increased immigration by way of France and Holland.

Neue Offizielle Gesetzessammlung des Kantons Bern.

1715-1861. Ten printed volumes.

On the subject of emigration there is the following:
Auswanderung: Reisesteuern der Gemeinden an arme Angehörige. Vorschriften, II. 49; VIII. 145.
Beschlusz über das Auswanderungswesen, Staatsschutz. V. 22.
Dekret (mit Citation darauf bezüglicher Erlasse). VII. 265.
Förmlichkeiten, die vorher zu erfüllen sind. VII. 519.
Amerikanische Inlandfahrbillets, Verbot des Verkaufs. IX. 337.
Pässe, Requisite zur Ausstellung. IV. 120, 121.
Pässe, Unentgeltliches Visa der französischen Gesandtschaft. VIII. 335.
Auswanderungs-Agenten. Pflichten, Bürgschaft. VII. 307.
-Commissair. Ermächtigung der Regierung zu Ernennung eines solchen. Dekret VII. 265.
-Steuern. Gegen einseitigen Bürgerrechtsverzicht ist unzulässig. II. 49.

Repertorium der Abschiede der Eidgenössischen Tagsatzungen aus den Jahren 1814-1848, bearbeitet von Wilhelm Fetscherin (Bern, 1874-1876).

Auswanderungswesen, als Sache der Kantonsregierungen, nicht des Bundes. II. 582, 583.
Auswanderungswesen.
1817. " In Folge der furchtbaren Nothstände des Jahres 1817, Auswanderung bedeutend zugenommen, ohne Erleichterung zu schaffen."
July 17. " Gesandte von Appenzell a. Rh. legte Frage vor, ob das Auswandern in fremde Welttheile zu begünstigen oder einzuschränken sei. Kanton Glarus mehr als ein Viertel der ganzen Bevölkerung ohne eigene Nahrungsmittel."
1818. " Am 29. Juli Gesandte von Luzern zum Schutz der Auswanderer Errichtung schweizerischer Konsulate. 20 Stände beschliessen, Vorort möge nähere Berichte einziehen, über günstige Länder, passende Art der Reise, etc."

1819, Aug. 9. " Auswanderung Sache der Kantonsregierungen, nicht des Bundes. Nur in seltenen Fällen Bundesunterstützung."
1848, Sept. 19. " 130 im Grossherzogt. Baden wohnende Schweizer Bittschrift: dass die Tagsatzung die Auswanderungsfrage näher reguliere; zur Berücksichtigung dem Vorort überwiesen."

EHEMALIGES FÜRSTBISCH.-BASELSCHES ARCHIV
im Staatsarchiv Bern.

Location: Käfigturm, Bärenplatz. For admission apply at Staatsarchiv, Postgasse 72.

One fascicle on emigration. " Ab- und Freyzug der Obern Aemter des Fürstenthums Basel, auswärts." II. Theil, 1730-1791. Concerning a large number of inhabitants of Erguel, mostly Anabaptists, who propose to depart for America. Bern complains and wishes to prevent it. Discussion as to amount of tax, 10 per cent. Abzug. Settlement in Lancaster Co., Pa. Mar. 11, 1754. Also correspondence of 1786-1787.

Landesfürstliche Verordnung, oder Emigranten betreffend. (Auswanderungsverbot.) " Simon Nicolaus, Bischof zu Basel, des Heil. Röm. Reichs Fürst." May 4, 1771.

BERN: BUNDESARCHIV.

Location: Kirchenfeld, Archivstrasse. A new building, completed in 1899; modern fire-proof construction. This archive contains only materials beginning with the nineteenth century. It is the archive of the Federal State, founded in 1848.

Hours: 8 a. m. to 12 m., 2 to 6 p. m. Closed Sundays and holidays.

Bibliography: Reglement und Plan für das eidgenössische Archiv, nebst dazu gehörender Instruction vom 14. September, 1864 (Bern, 1864).

Das eidgenössische Archiv, or Bundesarchiv, embraces:
 A. Das Helvetische Archiv, including the period 1798-1803.
 B. Das Tagsazungsarchiv, for the period 1803-1848. This section is divided into: Die Mediationsperiode, 1803-1813; Die Restaurations- und Regenerationsperiode, 1813-1848.
 C. Das neue Bundesarchiv, for the period since Nov. 6, 1848.

EIDGENÖSSISCHES ARCHIV, PERIODE 1813-1848.
AUSWÄRTIGES: NORDAMERIKANISCHE FREISTAATEN.

1978. HANDELSKONSULATE.
Schweizerisches Handelskonsulat in New York.

1823-1832.

Reports of H. C. de Rham, Swiss consul in New York (whose territory included New England, New York, New Jersey, Pennsylvania, Delaware, all the states to the north of the Ohio River, and Missouri).

1833-1842.
Reports and routine matters, settling of estates, etc.

Bern

1842-1848.

L. Ph. de Luze, consul at New York from 1842.

Reports, routine matters, legacies, passports, immigration statistics at the port of New York, Swiss commerce with the U. S. during the year 1843.

1843. Answers to questions of the Comités d'Émigrations: For a number of years there has been a decline in the number of Swiss immigrants. In the years 1816-1819 there was a larger number. Most Swiss immigrants come from the canton of Bern, some from the canton of Aargau, also from the cantons Schwyz, Uri, and Unterwalden. They are mostly farmers, some merchants, and watchmakers from Geneva and the mountains of Neuchâtel.

"Je crois que petit à petit ils perdent leur nationalité, et se font dans la nation américaine et leurs descendants finissent souvent par oublier même la langue de leurs parents."

The laws of the U. S. neither favor nor discourage immigrants. Existence of a society in New York for the benefit of Swiss immigrants. Immigrants more easily take fevers and diseases than those acclimated. Those well established in the country exert a strong influence on the coming of friends and relatives from the old country.

"La grande Bretagne, l'Allemagne, principalement l'Allemagne méridionale et les provinces Rhénanes, Prussiennes et Bavaroises et l'Alsace, fournissent les plus grands nombres d'émigrants aux États-Unis. Je crois que ce sont les émigrants allemands et suisses qui réussissent généralement le mieux dans ce pays. La France, outre l'Alsace, fournit peu d'émigrants aux États-Unis et des pays du nord et du sud de l'Europe nous en voyons arriver fort peu."

Trade reports, passports of 1845, etc.

Great increase of Swiss immigrants announced in a letter of Sept. 8, 1848, from consul de Luze, who suggests the appointment of an able lawyer as general agent at Bern to guard their interests. Many difficulties arising daily from the great increase in the number of immigrants, many of whom are destitute, uninformed, or badly advised.

Handelskonsulat in Alexandria bei Washington.
1823-1848.

Very elaborate reports by consul Anthony Charles Cazenove.

1843. Very complete answers to questions of the Comités d'Émigrations.

"Les Suisses sont probablement de tous les émigrés, eux qui reste[nt] le plus attachés à leur nationalité, puis les Écossais, et généralement, les habitants de pays montagneux, mais les pères émigrés ne peuvent pas se cacher que leurs enfants, des deux sexes, n'importe de quel pays ils sont sortis eux-mêmes, montrent une impatience d'être fondus dans la masse du pays; en sorte qu'il est difficile de leur faire bien apprendre et encore plus parler la langue de leurs pères, si elle est autre que la langue anglaise."

Routine matters reported in great detail.

1979. HANDELSKONSULATE, CONTINUED.

"Handelskonsulat. Korrespondenz der schweizerischen Konsulate in New Orleans, Philadelphia, Madison, Galveston, und Louisville." 1829-1848.

Handelskonsulat in New Orleans.

In 1829 a group of about 30 Swiss residing in New Orleans request the Swiss diet to appoint a consul at New Orleans. Theodore Nicolet was appointed first consul in the same year. Henri Chatelanat, secretary, in charge of consulship for 3 years. John A. Merle, second consul, 1839-1844.

Papers mostly concerning routine matters of business, reports on inquiries about prisons and conditions, deaths, legacies, etc.

Printed pamphlet: *Compte Rendu de l'Assemblée Générale de la Société de Bienfaisance de la Nouvelle-Orléans tenue le 12 mars 1838* (1 année).

Passports delivered at the Swiss Consulate, 1842. (34 names, about one-half German, the other half French and Italian.)

1843. Answers to questions by the committee on emigrations of the Society of Public Utility of the cantons of Vaud and Geneva.

"Les émigrants suisses qui arrivent ici [New Orleans] ne restent que le temps de sortir du navire qui les amène d'Europe pour se mettre à bord des bateaux à vapeur qui les conduisent dans l'Ouest. Ils ne se présentent ni au consulat, ni à la mairie, n'ayant aucune formalité à remplir, pas plus à leur arrivé qu'à leur départ. Ils viennent et vont sans que personne s'enquière ou connaisse leur nationalité ou leur nombre, et comme la plupart sont des cantons-allemands et italiens, ils passent généralement pour Allemands ou Italiens, de même que le peu de Suisses qui sont des cantons français sont généralement pris pour Français.

"Ils s'adonnent surtout à l'agriculture, et presque toujours se fondent dans la nation." (The latter in answer to the question: "Tendent ils à conserver leur nationalité ou à se fondre dans la nation?")

"Les émigrés prospèrent très généralement.

"Les lois des États-Unis protègent l'émigrant autant qu'un national, et comme dans ce pays on a toujours besoin de bras, les émigrants sont bien acceuillis quand ils sont industrieux.

"Question: Quelle condition ou garantie le gouvernement exige-t-il des émigrants à leur arrivée? Réponse: Aucunes.

"Ceux qui ont des métiers les suivent, ceux qui n'en ont pas travaillent la terre ou se font manœuvres. Avec de faibles resources ils peuvent acheter un morceau de terre, des outils, et accumuler par la suite des capitaux considérables. Ils trouvent dans presques toutes les industries un bon intérêt. Ceux sans moyens se mettent charretiers, laboureurs, manœuvres, etc.

"Question: Comment la propriété foncière est-elle acquise? Réponse: Par achat.

"Les émigrants peuvent acheter comme tout citoyen de qui bon leur semble.

"Le prix des terres du gouvernement qui sont naturellement vierges est de $1.25 l'acre. Les cultivées ou défrichées varient de $2.50 à $7.00, selon le plus ou moins d'éloignement des points centraux.

" Les cultures les plus productives sont celles du coton, sucre, tabac, blé, mais, chanvre, et gros légumes.—Quelques Suisses avaient entrepris la vigne à Vevay [Indiana], mais le climat s'y est montré peu propice, et ils en ont presque entièrement abandonné la culture.

" Toutes les religions sans exception aucune sont tolérées aux États-Unis et jamais pays n'a offert une aussi grande variété de sectes. La seule qui n'y existe pas, est celle fondée sur l'Alcoran.

" Le climat à la Nouvelle-Orléans n'est pas sain, mais dans l'intérieur du pays où se rendent les émigrants, latitude de 35 à 46, il y a parfaite salubrité.

" Toutes les professions sont bien rétribuées pour le travailleur consciencieux.

" Question: Comment les Suisses établis dans le pays ont-ils été poussés par cette émigration? (Par publications, emboucheurs, etc.?)

" Réponse: Rien à dire à ce sujet.

" Pour tout individu qui se trouve trop serré dans la vieille Europe, qui ne peut y gagner que difficilement sa vie, ce pays-ci offre d'immenses régions où certe il se trouvera au large et son travail sera bien rémunéré.

" La meilleure époque de l'année pour arriver ici et repartir pour l'intérieur, est le printemps. Plus tard que juin il y a danger de fièvres malignes, fièvre jaune et al. De décembre à juin il n'y rien à craindre.

" Question: Si vous désapprouvez l'émigration, quels moyens croyez-vous les plus propres pour éclairer les émigrants et y mettre un terme?

" Réponse: Rien à répondre, si ce n'est que tout homme qui est heureux dans son pays a toujours tort de le quitter.

" Toutes les nations d'Europe—les Allemands, Irlandais, Français, Suisses forment le plus grand nombre [des émigrants à New Orleans], et tous réussissent au moins à se procurer le nécessaire et quelquefois arriver à la fortune quand ils ont santé, industrie, économie et capacité."

List of passports, 1843-1848.

Explanation of purpose of " Die Deutsche Gesellschaft und deren Agentur " (foundation for the benefit and assistance of emigrants). Letter signed by William Vogel, president.

Handelskonsulat in Philadelphia.
1842-1847.

Exequatur of consul Johann Georg Syz, who was followed by Jean Syz, 1845-1847.

1844. Answers to questions of the Comités d'Émigrations des Sociétés d'Utilité Publique des Cantons de Vaud et de Genève.

" D'après tous les renseignements que j'ai pu obtenir sur ce sujet, je suis d'opinion qu'elles [nombre des familles] ont été plutôt réduites qu'augmentées et que le nombre sorti de la Suisse française compare avantageusement avec celui de la Suisse allemande, c'est-à-dire que comme la population de cette dernière est plus nombreuse en Suisse, il en résulte que le nombre des émigrants de la Suisse

allemande arrivé aux États-Unis, est dans la même proportion plus numérique."
Swiss emigrants are declared to be for the most part agricultural, preferring the country and village to the city; their success depends upon themselves. " Se fondre dans la nation."
Treatise on the potato disease. Two printed pamphlets by Thomas Croft, Wilkesbarre, Pa.

Handelskonsulat in Madison, Indiana.
1843.

Consul A. Ott. Territory: Ohio, Indiana, Kentucky, Illinois, Michigan, and territories of Wisconsin and Iowa.
Answers to questions of the Comités d'Émigrations: Swiss immigrations not large in this territory. Oldest settlement at Vevay. In general most Swiss emigrants from canton of Bern. " Généralement ils tendent à maintenir leur nationalité; même leurs descendants qui sont nés dans ce pays—retiennent leur caractère national et rarement un descendant Suisse se fondra aisement dans la nation."[1]
Comments on laws favoring immigrants, rapid naturalization, etc.
Letters written home by successful immigrants have had a stimulating effect upon immigration.
" Les Ro; aumes de Prusse, Bavière, Würtemberg, Hanover, Angleterre, Écosse, Irlande, Wales, les Duchés de Hesse-Darmstadt, Hesse-Kassel et Baden "—ont le plus grand nombre d'émigrants. " Un nombre très limité d'Hollande, Belgique, Italie, France, et l'Espagne se trouve dans nos états." " Parmi la masse des émigrants les plus destitués sont les Irlandois, les Badois, et les Espagnols, moins les autres plus actifs et moins indolents."

Schweizerisches Handelskonsulat in Galveston.
1846.

T. C. Kuhn appointed consul of the Swiss Confederation for the state of Texas.
Application of 15 Swiss citizens for consul in Galveston, Mar. 3, 1845.

Schweizerisches Handelskonsulat in Louisville.
1845-1848.

N. J. Basler succeeds consul Ott (after the latter's death), who was located at Madison, Ind.
Clippings from Cincinnati *Volksblatt*, 1846.
Routine matters.

2123. VERHANDLUNGEN AUSWÄRTIGER STAATEN MIT DEN BUNDESBEHÖRDEN.

Nordamerika. Korrespondenz des Generalkonsuls der Vereinigten Staaten von Nordamerika in der Schweiz, 1830-1848.
Exequatur of John G. Boker, consul general.
Appointments of consuls in various places in Switzerland.

---

[1] This statement is contradictory to the reports from other localities.

Gerard Koster's defalcations (1844) instrumental in advancing negotiation in matter of extradition treaty.
Printed pamphlet on Oregon question; routine matters.

2124.

Akten betreffend die Unterhandlung eines Freizügigkeitsvertrags und eines Vertrags über Auslieferung der Verbrecher zwischen der Schweiz und den nordamerikanischen Freistaaten. 1834-1848.

2125. FREIZÜGIGKEITSVERTRAG.

Treaty rejected by Senate June 11, 1836. Taken up again, and carried May 18, 1847.
Vertrag über Auslieferung der Verbrecher (correspondence). 1844-1847.
The diplomatic correspondence after 1848 is not accessible.

EIDGENÖSSISCHES ARCHIV, 1848—
AKTEN DES BUNDESRATS ÜBER AUSWANDERUNG.

III. ABTEILUNG: AUSWANDERUNGSWESEN.

Fasz. 1. Verhandlungen der Bundesbehörden über das Auswanderungswesen. (I. Bd.)
Fasz. 2. Auswanderungswesen im Allgemeinen. 1848-1853.
Fasz. 3. Auswanderungswesen im Allgemeinen. 1854-1870.
Fasz. 4. Gesetzliche Bestimmungen des Auslandes über das Auswanderungswesen.
Gesetzliche Bestimmungen der Kantone über das Auswanderungswesen.
Gesetzliche und reglementarische Bestimmungen der Kantone über die Auswanderungsagenturen und daherige Konzessionen.
Auskunft über das schweizerische Auswanderungswesen an das Ausland.
Massnahmen zum Schutze von solchen, welche ohne bestimmtes Ziel auswandern.
Kolonieprojekt Joos [Costa Rica, 1859-1863].
Petition des schweizerischen Auswanderungsvereins. 1867.
Auswanderungsstatistik.
Unterstützung der Auswanderungs Zeitung von Jäggi-Gyger in Bern.
Verschiedenes.
Ordnung der Kautionen.
Fasz. 5. Bundesgesetze betr. den Betrieb von Auswanderungsagenturen vom 23. Dezember 1880 und 22. März 1888. Schweizerisches Auswanderungs Bureau. Vollziehung und Interpretation. Patentierung von Auswanderungsagenturen.
Fasz. 6. Organisation und Personal. Enquête über das schweizerische Auswanderungswesen. 1886.
Fasz. 7. Klagen und Beschwerden gegen und von Auswanderungs Agenturen.

Auswanderung nach den Vereinigten Staaten von Nordamerika.

Fasz. 1. Allgemeines, 1852 bis 18—.
Fasz. 2. Californien.
Untergang des Schiffes *Royal Charter*, 1859, und des *William Nelson*, 1865.
Verkauf von Inlandfahrbillets.

Beschwerde der Regierung des Kantons Aargau gegen den nordamerikanischen Konsul Wolff in Basel wegen Erschwerung der Auswanderung.
Landschenkungen in Florida und Texas.
Kolonisationsprojekt Plümacher in Tennessee.
Beschwerde der Auswanderungs Agentur Stössel und Cie. in Basel, gegen den schweizerischen Konsul Wanner in Havre.
Kolonieunternehmung in West Virginien.
Kolonie Bernstadt in Kentucky.
Fasz. 10. Auswanderung nach den Vereinigten Staaten von Nordamerika.
Abschiebungen von Mittellosen, Krüppeln, und Verbrechern.
Fasz. 11. Auswanderung nach Zentral- und Südamerika, Magellenstrasse, und Feuerlandsinseln, und projektierte Gründung einer Kolonie daselbst, Mexiko, Neu Britannien (Port Bretton) im Stillen Ozean, Uruguay, Venezuela, etc.
Fasz. 12. Auswanderung nach Argentinien.
Fasz. 13, 14, 15. Auswanderung nach Brasilien. 1850-1860. Mission Tschudi. Prozess Vergueiro.
Fasz. 16. Auswanderung nach Brasilien. 1870.
Fasz. 17. Auswanderung nach andern Ländern.
Frankreich und französische Kolonien.
Russland, Ungarn, Alexandrien in Aegypten.
Kleinasien, Ostindien, Australien.

The Eidgenössisches Archiv contains sets of three printed series which, though also to be found elsewhere, and, for instance, in some American libraries, may well be mentioned here, because they contain much material relating to Swiss relations to America. These are:

1. The *Amtliche Sammlung der Bundesgesetze und Verordnungen der Schweizerischen Eidgenossenschaft* (1848-), containing treaties and federal laws and decrees, and of course all those respecting America and emigration.

2. The weekly *Bundesblatt der Schweizerischen Eidgenossenschaft* (the French edition is entitled *Feuille Fédérale de la Conféderation Suisse*, see above, p. 7), which, from 1848 down, has contained many reports and other documents on these subjects, such as diplomatic papers, reports of Swiss consuls in America, and reports on Swiss emigration, monthly from 1887 on, less frequent before that date. For references in detail, to both collections, for 1874-1893, see F. Widmer, *Alphabetisches Sachregister zum Bundesblatt und zur Amtlichen Sammlung der Bundesgesetze und Verordnungen der Schweizerischen Eidgenossenschaft, Jahrg. 1874-1893*, pp. 37-39.

3. *Berichte des Schweizerischen Bundesrates an die Bundesversammlung über seine Geschäftsführung vom Jahre* —(1848-). Reports of the executive to the legislature, continuing to the present time. Each volume is furnished with an adequate index.

BERN: EIDGENÖSSISCHES AUSWANDERUNGSAMT.

Location: Bollwerk 27, Bern.

This federal emigration bureau was founded in 1880, by a law of the Bundesrat passed Dec. 24, 1880. The chief business of the federal bureau is the regulation and watching of the activities of the various emigration bureaus, required in every case to procure a license; in addition to this to keep accurate statistics of emigration, and to render service to prospective emigrants by furnishing accurate and useful information concerning conditions and prospects in foreign countries.

The Auswanderungsamt contains an extensive archive, including reports from the numerous Swiss emigration bureaus, statistics in detail, acta concerning various Swiss colonies in foreign countries, etc. Since 1881 annual reports have been published on the emigration from each canton, *Die überseeische Auswanderung aus der Schweiz,* the destination also being tabulated in these thoroughgoing reports. For a bibliography of Swiss emigration, see above, pp. 6-7.

The following are Swiss settlements, at least in origin, upon which there are (incomplete) acta in the archives of the Auswanderungsamt. The bureau acknowledges a debt to the *New-Yorker Staatszeitung* in compiling this list:

Alabama:
1. Cullman, Cullman Co.
2. Newbern, Hale Co.

Arkansas:
3. Pocahontas, Randolph Co.

Dakota:
4. Seelisberg, Spink Co.

Florida:
5. Monticello, Jefferson Co.

Georgia:
6. New Switzerland, Habersham Co.
7. Stuckey, Montgomery Co.

Illinois:
8. Eberle, Effingham Co.
9. Highland, Madison Co.
10. Newberne, Jersey Co.

Indiana:
11. Vevay, Switzerland Co.
12. Tell City, Perry Co.
13. St. Meinrad (Einsiedeln), Spencer Co.
14. Switz City, Greene Co.
15. Bremen, Marshall Co.
16. Berne, Adams Co.
17. Newbern, Bartholomew Co.

Iowa:
18. Luzerne, Benton Co.
19. Newbern, Marion Co.
20. Zwingle, Dubuque Co.

Kansas:
21. New Basel, Dickinson Co.
22. Enterprise, Dickinson Co.
23. Newbern, Dickinson Co.
24. Zürich, Rooks Co.

Kentucky:
25. Bernstadt, Laurel Co.
26. White Lily, Laurel Co.
27. Pine Hill–Salzburg, Rockcastle Co.
28. Grünheim, Lincoln Co.
29. Highland, Lincoln Co.

Michigan:
30. Berne, Huron Co.
31. Luzerne, Oscoda Co.

Minnesota:
32. Newbern, Dodge Co.
33. Helvetia, Carver Co.

Missouri:
34. New Engelberg, Nodaway Co.
35. Coppeln, St. Charles Co.
36. Swiss, Gasconade Co.
—. (Swiss Colony Ozark)

Nebraska:
37. Zürich, Hall Co.
38. Grütli, Platte Co.
—. (Steinauer, Pawnee Co.)

North Carolina: 39. Ridgeway, Warren Co.
40. Asheville, Buncombe Co.
41. Newbern, Craven Co.
New York: 42. Berne, Albany Co.
43. Zürich, Wayne Co.
Ohio: 45. Switzer, Monroe Co.
46. Basil, Fairfield Co.
47. Tell Cottage, Hamilton Co.
48. Berne, Noble Co.
49. Geneva, Ashtabula Co.
Oregon: 50. Cedar Mill, Washington Co.
51. Engelberg, Marion Co.
Pennsylvania: 52. Biehl, Union Co.
53. Brunnerville, Lancaster Co.
54. Benzinger, Elk Co.
55. Berne, Berks Co.
56. Geneva, Crawford Co.
57. Baumgardner, Lancaster Co.
58. Luzerne, Luzerne Co.
59. Tell, Huntingdon Co.
60. Stauffer, Westmoreland Co.
61. Brodbecks, York Co.
62. Eberly's Mill, Cumberland Co.
63. Swissvale, Allegheny Co.
Tennessee: 64. Warburg, Morgan Co.
65. Winchester, Franklin Co.
66. Grütli, Grundy Co.
67. South Pittsburg, Marion Co.
68. Newbern, Dyer Co.
Texas: 69. New Baden, Robertson Co.
70. Seguin, Guadalupe Co.
71. Swiss Alp, Fayette Co.
72. Cheesland, Angelina Co.
Virginia: 73. Newbern, Pulaski Co.
West Virginia: 74. Helvetia, Randolph Co.
75. Alpena, Randolph Co.
76. Kendalia, Kanawha Co.
77. New St. Gallen, Webster Co.
78. Cotton Hill, Fayette Co.
Wisconsin: 79. New Glarus, Green Co.
80. New Elm, Winnebago Co.
81. Interlaken, Price Co.
82. Burkhardt, Saint Croix Co.
83. Helvetia, Waupaca Co.

BERN: STADTBIBLIOTHEK

Location: Old, spacious building, entrance on the Kesslergasse, not far from the cathedral.
Hours: 9 a. m. to 12 m.; 2 to 7 p. m.
Catalogue: Katalog der Handschriften zur Schweizergeschichte der Stadtbibliothek Bern (Bern, 1895).

Manuscripts relating to American History.

MSS. Hist. Helv., III. 81 (4) : "Momente aus der Geschichte von Amerika. Auszüge aus Bancroft." (A chronological table derived from Bancroft's *History of the United States*.)

MSS. Hist. Helv., III. 245 (92) : "Aus Bancrofts Geschichte von Nordamerika. Auszug aus dem 24. Kapitel."

MSS. Hist. Helv., VII. 113 (52) : "Wunderbare Nachricht aus Amerika. Stück einer geographischen Beschreibung." Pp. 393-399. (Descriptions of some fabulous beasts in America.) Aus Hallers Sammlung (son of the great anatomist of Bern).

MSS. Hist. Helv., X. 152 : Franz Ludwig Michels Reisebeschreibung, 1701-1702. A quarto volume, bound in half-vellum, with 73 numbered leaves, some armorial drawings, and several illustrations of remarkable interest. The manuscript contains: ff. 1-61, narrative of voyage to America, then of travels, chiefly in Virginia; f. 63 recto, pen-and-ink drawing, " Collegium zu Willemsburg stehend, worin der Gouverneur seine Wohnung hat ", *i. e.*, the first building of the College of William and Mary, planned by Wren, begun in 1694, burned in 1705, of which, as of the two other buildings mentioned below, no other picture is known; also, a typical " Kaufmanshausz ", " Ein Baurnhausz ", " Das Fundament des Rathauses ", " Das neuwe Rathausz so man dis Jahr 1702 angefangen zu bauen ", *i. e.*, the half-finished Capitol of Virginia, erected at this time and standing till 1746, and " Die Kirche so zu Willemsburg stehet ", *i. e.*, Bruton Parish Church, finished in 1683, and replaced by the present structure in 1715;[1] f. 64 recto, a waterspout, three Indians and their house; f. 64 verso, a rude map of Chesapeake Bay; ff. 65-70, two or three letters from America, preserved by Michel's brother, from whom the book comes down; ff. 72, 73, George Ritter to Queen Anne. The following note shows that Michel made a second trip to Carolina before Graffenried: " Mein elterer Bruder Frantz Ludwig ist den 14. Februar 1703 wieder von Bern nach Amerika verreiset, und den 16. Jan. 1704 glücklich aldort wieder angelanget. Wie aus seinem Schreiben zuersehen." Much of the text of this manuscript, though with paraphrasing in parts, and with explanations instead of text in parts, is given in an article by J. H. Graf, entitled " Franz Ludwig Michel von Bern und seine ersten Reisen nach Amerika 1701-1704; ein Beitrag zur Vorgeschichte der Gründung von New-Berne ", in the *Neues Berner Taschenbuch* for 1898, pp. 59-144. This printed narrative is of about two-thirds the length of the original journal.

MSS. Hist. Helv., XI. 8. Folio volume. Among the contents are, (10) " Auswanderungen ":

(a.) " Colonie Brandenburg (Preussen), 1704-1707; Hrn. A. M. d'Arnay's nach St. Domingo; von bernischen Täuffern nach Amerika, 1710-1711." 7 ff.

---

[1] Photographs of these drawings, of unique interest, are in the possession of Dr. J. F. Jameson. A translation of Michel's journal into English by Professor William J. Hinke appears in the *Virginia Magazine of History*, beginning in January, 1916.

(c.) " Relation de l'Établissement d'une Colonie française réfugiée en Pensilvanie." [This is a letter of 1700, written not from Pennsylvania but from New Oxford, Mass., by a minister established there (Rev. Jacques Laborie) to the widow of a French minister in London, Madame Favin. J. F. J.]
Lettre de Mr. Michel de Carolina, 1703 (French), und vom nemlichen an Herrn Ochs aus Maryland, von 1704 (German). The latter also found in the manuscript Hist. Helv., X. 152.
Auswanderung des Herrn G. Ritter, Spezierer von Bern, 1705-1708, various writings. 12 ff.
Ibid., (15). Auswanderungen, aus dem Kanton Bern. A general account, the beginning of which is printed in the *Berner Monatschrift*, p. 77 ff. (fragment), and which is here continued, 1692-1805. 12 ff. This is for the most part an abstract based on the materials found in the " Mandatenbücher " of Bern. (See record of this material under " Staatsarchiv " of Bern.)

MSS. Hist. Helv., XIV. 116. A quarto volume, 104 pp., half-vellum binding, nineteenth century.

(10.) Schweizerische Hülfsgesellschaften im Ausland, Nordamerika und Auswanderung, pp. 70-88. (One interesting point brought out: Proletariat of Europe now entering America, too great leniency; no restriction. " Trop de bonté est bêtise! ")

The Stadtbibliothek of Bern (located on the Kesslergasse), and the Schweizerische Landesbibliothek (located in the same building with the Bundesarchiv, *i. e.*, Archivstrasse, Kirchenfeld), each contains a collection of printed books descriptive of American colonies, and of travels in America, some offering advice and information to immigrants. The rarest prints, those of the eighteenth century, are nowhere grouped together, and are mostly scattered in private libraries.

The Graffenried Manuscripts.

A series of manuscripts of which Christoph von Graffenried, the founder of the colony of New Bern, N. C., was the author. Four of them (A, B, C, D) describe his successes and mishaps in America, two (E, F) are autobiographical, relating to other periods of their author's life.[1]

A.

This manuscript was written in the French language, between 1710 and 1714. It consists of 105 folio pages, and is preserved in the library of the city of Yverdun (No. 3110). It contains a series of detached chapters or adventures, written by various hands, but corrected in the handwriting of Graffenried. A good description of the manuscript is to be found in the *Revue Historique Vaudoise*, reprinted under the title *New Berne*, by John Landry (Lausanne, 1907). A translation of this manuscript appeared in the *Colonial Records of North Carolina* (1886), I. 905-985.

[1] For a fuller account of these manuscripts, including my comparison of their merits, see *German American Annals*, n. s., XI. 205-210 (1913). Of the manuscripts named above, B and C are printed for the first time, in the original languages, in *German American Annals*, n. s., XI. 210-302; and XII. 63-190.

B.

Written in the German language, about the same time as manuscript A, though probably begun later; preserved in the private library of W. F. von Mülinen,[1] in the city of Bern. This manuscript consists of 154 pages, as follows:

(a) A large map of the colony of New Bern, N. C.
(b) Letter descriptive of Carolina, dated: Carolina, Neu Bern d. 6 May 1711. Also bills of expenditures. pp. 1-20.
(c) Handlungs Contract zw. Michel, Graffenried, und Georg Ritter und Co. May 18, 1710. pp. 21-27.
(d) Memorial über Eint und andere Puncten Carolina betreffend, aus dem Englischen übersetzt. pp. 28-47.
(e) Copia unterschiedlicher Briefen ausz Nord Carolina. pp. 47-67.
(f) Vorbericht und Relation meines amerikanischen Unterfangens. Description of Graffenried's adventures in America, settlement of New Bern, capture by the Indians, etc., as in manuscript A. pp. 68-154.

C.

Written in the French language, about 1716; a revision of manuscript A, surpassing it in style and in the order of arrangement of events, and containing a large number of additions in material. This manuscript is preserved in the private library of W. F. von Mülinen, in Bern. It was written in Graffenried's own hand.[2] Title: "Relation du Voyage d'Amérique que le B. de Graffenried a fait, en y amenant une Colonie Palatine et Suisse; et son Retour en Europe".

D.

A small manuscript written in French, 10 folio pages; preserved in the state archive of the city of Bern. The titles describe the contents: (a) "Copie d'une Lettre écrite sous date New-Berne en North Caroline le 4ème Janvier 1712 par le Baron de Graffenried, Gouverneur des Palatins en North Caroline, à Msr. Ed. Hyde, Gouverneur des Colonies et Provinces de la North Caroline"; (b) "Copie d'un Traité conclu sous date du mois d'Octobre 1711 entre le Baron de Graffenried et les Indiens de Tuscaroro", etc., etc.; (c) "Copie d'une Lettre écrite sous date 8ème Octobre 1711 par Alexandre Spotwood, Lieutenant Gouverneur et Commandant en Chef des Colonies et Provinces de Virginie, à la Nation des Indiens qui tiennent le Baron de Graffenried prisonnier".

---

[1] W. F. von Mülinen, librarian of the city library of Bern, has written the authoritative account of the life and career of Christoph von Graffenried, based throughout on the original manuscript material given him by the Graffenried family. Cf.: *Christoph von Graffenried, Landgraf von Carolina, Gründer von Neu-Bern,* zumeist nach Familienpapieren und Copien seiner amtlichen Berichte, von Wolfgang Friedrich von Mülinen, *Neujahrsblatt hrg. v. Historischen Verein des Kantons Bern für 1897* (Bern, 1896). A trustworthy and very readable account in English of Graffenried's settlement of New Bern has appeared in the *Jahrbuch der Deutsch-Amerikanischen Historischen Gesellschaft von Illinois,* Jahrgang 1912, by Vincent H. Todd: "Christoph von Graffenried and the Founding of New Bern, N. C."

[2] For the proof of this statement, see *German American Annals,* XI. 205 f. The C manuscript is printed in full in the same journal, XII. 63-190.

E.

Written in German; preserved in the private library of W. F. von Mülinen, Bern. Title: "Fataliteten Hrn. v. Graffenriedt Alt Landvogt v. Yverdun und Herrschaft Herrn zu Worb, in seinen jüngeren Jahren". I. Teil, 149 pp.; II. Teil, 123 pp. This is the story told by Graffenried, after 1716, of his early experiences and escapades in England, France, and at Yverdun.

F.

A series of family letters, written partly in French, partly in German, many of them addressed to the writer's father, Anton Graffenried. These letters also belong to the private library of W. F. von Mülinen, Bern.

BERN: ARCHIVE OF THE UNITED STATES LEGATION.

Location: Hirschengraben 6.
Hours: By appointment, archive open to scientific investigation only.
The most interesting portion of the diplomatic correspondence is that concerning forced emigration, *i. e.,* the deportation of paupers and criminals, and that concerning the Mormon missionaries seeking Swiss colonists. This material may also be found in Washington, D. C., in the archives of the Department of State.
Under the former head, the following dispatches are noted:

No. 108. Theodore S. Fay (first minister to Switzerland, appointed 1853). Protest against shipment of four Unterwalders to America; shown not to be deported criminals, and protest withdrawn. Suggestion of agreement between U. S. and European countries on matter of deportation. Feb. 22, 1855.
111. Protest against shipment of paupers and criminals produced considerable attention on the part of the public press of Switzerland.
120. Abuses in emigration looked into by cantons.
226. Circular No. 17 on emigration. Mar. 3, 1857.
243. Emigration abuses. June 11, 1857.
247. June 23, 1857.
248. July 7, 1857.
251. July 17, 1857.
258. Correspondence on emigration. Concerning Castle Garden. Oct. 10, 1857.
269. Since 1834 the annual emigration from Switzerland has averaged 6000-7000. Total to U. S. since 1834, 168,000. During last three years greatest number from Solothurn, Aargau, Glarus, and Schaffhausen. Thirteen licensed emigration bureaus, of which two occupy themselves with South America. Havre is the port usually proposed. Attempt to prevent inland booking. Dec. 15, 1857.
341. Mar. 14, 1859.
25. Oct. 25, 1862.
7. Feb. 17, 1866.
36. Shipment of criminals. Aug. 13, 1867.
63. Aug. 1, 1868.
71. Oct. 7, 1868.
83. Jan. 22, 1872.

78. June 3, 1878.
81. June 10, 1878.
82. June 16, 1878.
83. June 16, 1878.
84. June 18, 1878.
101. Sept. 20, 1878.
108. Sept. 23, 1878.
160. Mar. 10, 1879.
180. May 26, 1879.
181. May 26, 1879.
201. July 24, 1879.
202. July 30, 1879.
204. Aug. 16, 1879.
226. Nov. 15, 1879.
246. Feb. 10, 1880.
261. Apr. 16, 1880.
265. Apr. 30, 1880.
266. May 5, 1880.
269. May 11, 1880.
297. Proposed Swiss federal law concerning emigration agencies. Discussion in the National Council; its adoption and modification by that body. Strong opposition. The clause forbidding the deportation of pardoned criminals struck out in opposition to the Federal Council. Postponement of its consideration by the Council of States. Necessity of our legislation (Nicholas Fish, minister). Sept. 18, 1880.
298. Colonization scheme of the Grütli Verein. Their petition is referred without comment to the Federal Council. Sept. 18, 1880.
300. Swiss law respecting emigration agencies. Sept. 24, 1880.
319. Dec. 9, 1880.
321. Dec. 15, 1880.
326. Jan. 10, 1881.
328. Jan. 10, 1881.
330. Jan. 15, 1881.
331. Jan. 20, 1881.
332, 333. Jan. 24, 1881.
334, 335. Jan. 26, 1881.
338. Feb. 10, 1881.
343. Feb. 16, 1881.
371. Mar. 20, 1881.
372, 373. Mar. 23, 1881.
375. Mar. 25, 1881.
376. Mar. 26, 1881.
377. Mar. 27, 1881.
383. Mar. 31, 1881.
384. Apr. 4, 1881.
385. Apr. 5, 1881.
386. The return of several of criminal class by the U. S. announced to the federal government. Comments of the Swiss press thereon. Apr. 8, 1881.

387. Quotation from an article in the *Journal de Genève*, defending the position, that "the U. S. is the reformatory (Botany Bay) of Europe, and comparable to the British penal colonies ". " It will be news to some portions of our press, that their Genevan colleague considers that Switzerland has a vested interest in the U. S. as a reformatory for Swiss delinquents " (Nicholas Fish) Apr. 9, 1881.
391. Apr. 16, 1881.
392, 394. Apr. 18, 1881.
398. Apr. 28, 1881.
400. Apr. 29, 1881.
403. May 8, 1881.
409. May 13, 1881.
496. July 12, 1881.
68. July 5, 1883.
183. Nov. 26, 1884.
188. Dec. 18, 1884.
254. Jan. 24, 1889.
101. Feb. 3, 1895.
10. Mar. 6, 1896.

After this date there appear no more cases of assisted or forced emigration.

Secondly, as to Mormon emigration. Mormon preachers visited Swiss cantons with the purpose of soliciting emigrants, mainly women. Instruction No. 107 received from U. S., Wm. M. Evarts to Nicholas Fish, Washington, Aug. 9 (received Aug. 28), 1879: wishes that the government of Switzerland shall take measures such as to prevent Mormon emigration; encouragement of bigamy thereby, against laws of U. S. Dispatches:

No. 213. Aug. 29, 1879.
220. Oct. 21, 1879.
229. Nov. 27, 1879.
262. Apr. 16, 1880.
319. Dec. 9, 1880.
13. May 13, 1882.
225. May 8, 1885.
61. May 25, 1886.
66. June 23, 1886.
168. Oct. 24, 1887.

CANTON LUZERN.

LUZERN: STAATSARCHIV.

Location: In the Jesuitenkollegium (1894), Bahnhofstrasse 18.
Hours: 8 a. m. to 12 m.; 2 to 6 p. m. In winter the archive closes earlier.
Permission to use the archive is given on application to the Regierungsrat.

ACTA.

1793, Nov. 17. " Dekret des Nationalkonvents, die Neutralität zusichernd der Eidgenossenschaft und Amerika."
Fach II. Kreisschreiben des schweizerischen Bundesrats an sämtliche eidgenöss. Stände. (1848-1902.) Ausland. III. Amerika. A. 1848-.
1859. " Über den zum Vice-Consul vorgeschlagenen John [Joseph] Suppiger von Sursee in Highland [Illinois]. Schultheiss u. Regierungs Rath des Kantons Luzern an das Titl. Schweiz. Handels u. Zolldepart. in Bern, und das Stadthalteramt Sursee an d. Eidgenöss. Depart. d. Äussern d. Kantons Luzern."
Contains two interesting letters of recommendation respecting Joseph Suppiger, telling of his affairs, *e. g.,*
§ 4. " Im Jahre 1830 wanderte er mit seinem Vater, der ein Vermögen von 30,000 Gl. mitnahm, aus, baute in Highland eine Dampfmühle, welche er mit seinen Geschwisterkindern betreibt. Aus einem [mir] vorgewiesenen Briefe ergiebt sich, dass er erst das verflossene Jahr an derselben Verbesserungen im Bauwerte von 20,000 Dollars vornahm."
§ 5. " Er wurde daselbst zum Friedensrichter erwählt, und soll diese Stelle freiwillig abgegeben haben."
§ 6. " Gegen die Familie Köpfli, mit denen er verwandt ist, und welche ihr Vermögen durch Landankauf und Wiederverkauf bedeutend vergrössert, wurden vor mehreren Jahren Klagen laut, die sich darauf mögen bezogen haben, dass sie vielleicht die Einwanderung zu hoch anpriesen, um Land verkaufen zu können, und dieses theurer verkauften, als sie den Wert in einem gedruckten Buche angaben." (See titles of works below, in Bürgerbibliothek.)
§ 8. " Ich kenne in Highland noch mehrere Luzerner, worunter viele Sursee'r, aber keinen dem Herrn Suppiger für die Stelle vorzuziehen; er gilt für den geachtetsten Mann in Highland."
1861, May 20. " Todesanzeige des Joseph Suppiger, Vize-Konsul in Highland."
1865, May 4. " Schreiben an den Schweiz. Bundesrat mit Beileidsbezeugung in Betreff der Ermordung des Präsidenten Abraham Lincoln."
1882, May 2 and 6. " Oberst Emil Frei in Arlesheim, Kanton Baselland, Ernennung zum ausserordentlichen Gesandten und Bevollmächtigten Minister der Schweiz. Eidgenossenschaft bei der Regierung der Vereinigten Staaten in Washington."

Fach II., Fascikel 1. Amerika. 1830-. Gesandte auswärtiger Mächte und Staaten.
Nordamerika: Freistaaten, Mexico, Kolumbia.
Freistaaten: Consulate in der Schweiz. 1830-1846.
Schweiz. Consulate in d. Ver. Staaten. 1823.
Auslieferungsvertrag. 1845.
Freizügigkeitsvertrag. 1836.
Erbwesen. 1824.
Andere Kreisschreiben. 1846.
Mexico. Kreisschreiben.
Kolumbia. Anerkennung der Republik. 1822.
Südamerika: Brasilien.
Rio de Janeiro.
Pernambuk.
Fach III. Ausland III. Amerika. A.
" Geschenk von Militärpapieren (Bürgerkrieg, 1861-1865) durch Casimir Muri", (Gotthardbahn Beamter). Nov. 6, 1907.
" Kreisschreiben betr. Ausbezahlung von Nachtragsvergütungen an gewesene Soldaten der Union oder deren Erben."
" Kreisschreiben betr. Kriegsdienstvergütungen (bounties)."
" Reklamation des Johann Baptist Minder von Flühli (Luzern), gewesenen Soldaten in den Ver. Staaten für Ausrichtung von Nachtragsbounty." 1867-1869.
" Verwendung für Entlassung des Joseph Mahler von Kriens aus dem Heere der Ver. Staaten." June 3, 1870. *Vide* Personalia.
" Pensionsangelegenheit betr. Kasimir Muri von Schlötz." 1872. *Vide* Personalia.
" Vinzenz Schärli, Soldatenangelegenheit." 1880.
" Kreisschreiben."
Fach IV., Fascikel 48. Auswanderung. 1798-1848.
" Dekret gegen die Auswanderung, 1799." (Printed decree, prohibiting emigration under heavy penalties; men needed as defenders of the country against foreign invaders.) Feb. 22, 1799.
" Warnung vor der Auswanderung vorzüglich aber nach Dänemark." June, 1801.
" Koncessionen der Kais. russischen Regierung für die Kolonisten in ihren Staaten (nach der Krim)." Sept., 1806.
" Bericht der Regierung von Basel über die Auswanderung nach Amerika." Apr., 1816.
" Massregeln in Amsterdam gegen Auswanderer." Apr.–June, 1817.
" Auswanderung einer Anzahl Luzerner nach den Nordamerikanischen Staaten." 1817. (Eleven cases, certificates, letters, etc.)
" Verfügungen der Königl. preuss. Regierung wegen der schweizer. Auswanderer nach Amerika oder Polen." (Gegen Mittellose, etc.) May, 1819.
" Verordnung der Königl. niederländ. Regierung betreffend die truppenweise Durchreise der Auswanderer durch dieses Königreich." Feb. 28, 1828.
" Schiffbruch einer Abteilung nach Chili Auswandernder. Unterstützung der Familie Glanzmann von Marbach behufs Rückkehr." 1828.

"Beschluss über Verabfolgung der Mittel der Auswanderer." Mar. 16, 1831.
"Anfrage des Gemeinderats Escholzmatt, ob man die Auswanderung nach Nordamerika verhindern solle oder könne?" Apr., 1832. (Two families, including about twenty individuals, made preparations to emigrate, selling their property, and procuring passes without stating definitely that they intended going to America. It was known that a member of the family had been in America, visiting an uncle, and returned with very favorable reports. Reply: that nothing could be done to stop them, and since their property was exclusively theirs—"Verfügungsrecht ausschliesslich"—they could dispose of it as they saw fit.)
"Ansuchen die Auswanderung nach Nordamerika zu verschieben, bis die in Havre angehäuften Auswanderer weitergeschifft wären." May, 1832.
"Weisung jenen Auswanderungslustigen, die wenigstens 25 Louis d'or auf den Kopf vorweisen können, die nötigen Reiseschriften zu verabfolgen." Feb. 25, 1833.
"Anzeige, dass künftighin alle schweizerischen Auswanderer nach den Vereinigten Staaten Nordamerikas ihre Reisepässe bei dem nordamerikanischen Vizekonsul in Basel zu visieren haben." Feb. 28, 1833.
"Bericht des schweizerischen Handelskonsuls in New Orleans, in betreff der kommerziellen Beziehungen und über die Verhältnisse der Einwanderer in die südlichen Staaten der Union." Mar. 30, 1835.
Antrag zur Aufnahme schweizerischer Colonisten in der zum Staate Mexico gehörigen Provinz Texas im westlichen Nordamerika. (Printed circular.) 1835.
"Berichte über Auswanderung nach Nordamerika, und Kreisschreiben." 1844-1847.
Das Für und Wider der Auswanderung nach Amerika (pamphlet, Sursee, 1835). Contains a discourse against emigration addressed by Sonnenwirth Johann Lanz of Huttwyl to Schlosser Bandtli of Willisau. Part I., sheets I.-V. (IV. is lacking). Part II., Blatt VI., contains the answer of Bandtli. Motto of Blatt I.: "Einst hörte ein Savoyarde von einer Meerreise erzählen; am Ende sprach er: ' Ig willen lieber marschier, wo Kuh spazier, als Fisch spazier.'" Motto of Blatt VI.: "Ich liebe mein Vaterland vor jedem andern Land auf Erden, so lange ich darin frei und unabhängig sein kann. Ich liebe und ehre die Priester, wenn sie das Volk lieben wie sich selbst. Ich hasse aber und verachte die Pfaffen, die unser Vaterland bald zum Narrenhaus gemacht, und dasselbe als solches gerne an das Ausland überliefern möchten. Bei diesen beichte ich nicht, denn sie sollten bei mir beichten." Cf. also Dr. Theodor Liebenau, *Geschichte der Stadt Willisau*, p. 91, etc.

Fach IV., Fascikel 49. Auswanderung. 2(1798-1847).
1819. Auswanderung nach Brasilien. (Large bundle of papers.)

Fach IV., Fascikel 66. Auswanderung im Allgemeinen. Verträge. 3(1848-———).
"Versuch einer Gesellschaft aus Genf die schweizerische Auswanderung nach Amerika zu organisieren und zentralisieren." 1848.

"Gesuch einer Anzahl Bürger des Kantons Luzern das Auswanderungswesen durch die Regierung zu organisieren." 1848.
"Einstweiliges Verbot des Durchpasses aller und jeder Auswanderer durch Frankreich." (Anhäufung in Havre der Auswanderer.) Mar. 24, 1849.
"Warnung vor den Auswanderungsagenten der kalifornischen Gesellschaft." Dec., 1850.
"Statistische Erhebungen über die Auswanderung aus dem Kanton Luzern in den Jahren 1854, 1855, 1856." 1857.
"Verunglückung des Auswandererschiffes *William Nelson* auf der Reise Antwerpen nach New York. Daherige Entschädigungsklagen und Untersuchungen." 1865-1866.
Two printed pamphlets: *Ratgeber für die schweizerischen Auswanderer in den Vereinigten Staaten von Nordamerika* (Bern, 1893). Official publication. *Die materiellen Verhältnisse und Vortheile für Einwanderer im Staate Kentucky* (Frankfort, Ky., 1880). A publication of the "Kentucky Bureau für Geologie und Immigration ", John R. Proctor, Director.
"Erkundigungen betreffend die Heimat verschiedener auf der *Bourgogne* angeblich ums Leben gekommene Schweizer." Nov. 2, 1898.
"Auswanderungsverträge 1862-1889." (Large bundle.)
Fach IV., Fascikel 67. Statistik der überseeischen Auswanderung. 1873-1899.
Fach IV., Fascikel 68. Auswanderungsagenturen. 1888-1896.
Fach IV. Kreisschreiben. 1860-1871. Verträge, Auswanderung, Gesetze, etc.
Fach VII. und VIII. Consulatsberichte und Schreiben, betr. Handel, Zolltarif, etc.

LUZERN: BÜRGERBIBLIOTHEK.

Location: In the same building with the Stadtarchiv, Münzgasse.

This library is the government repository of books on Swiss history before 1848 (Eidgenössische Sammelstelle für Helvetica vor 1848), the Landesbibliothek in Bern containing the works on the period after that date. The Bürgerbibliothek contains a very good collection of books, pamphlets, and articles written on America in the first half of the nineteenth century, mainly by Swiss settlers or travellers, and bearing on the questions of emigration, e. g.:

Der Waldstätter-Bote (Luzern, 1828-1844), contains a number of articles on America, as nos. 13, 14, 15, in the year 1828. (Story of shipwreck.)

Reisebericht der Familie Köpfli und Suppiger nach St. Louis am Mississippi und Gründung von New-Switzerland im Staate Illinois (Sursee, 1833).

Kaspar Köpfli, Vater, Arzt, *Licht und Schattenseite von New-Switzerland in Nordamerika*, 2te Aufl. (Sursee, 1833).

Franz G. Rüegger. *Kurzer Reisebericht von Havre bis Highland (New-Switzerland in Nordamerika)* (Luzern, 1846).

Salomon Köpfli, *Geschichte der Ansiedlung von Highland, Illinois* (Highland, 1859).

Id., *Neu-Schweizerland in den Jahren 1831 und 1841* (Luzern, 1842).

Id., Spiegel von Amerika: Praktische Grundsätze, Belehrungen und Warnungen für Auswanderer nach Amerika (Luzern, 1849).
Theil von einem Schreiben eines Landmanns aus Pennsylvanien, an den Lands-Venner Martin von Sarnen, welches von des Hrn. Pfarrherrn Rothenbühler eigner Hand geschrieben, und von dem in Bern befindlichen Hrn. Pfarrherrn Rothenbühler, als die Hand seines Bruders erkannt worden (no date, 4 pp.).

The following manuscripts were found in the Bürgerbibliothek:
" Beschreibung der Meerfahrt, und der übrigen Schicksale der Schweizer-Kolonisten, die nach Brasilien wanderten samt einer kurzen Darstellung der Beschaffenheit des Königreichs Brasilien, der Sitten und Gebräuche der Einwohner, der Behandlungsart der Neger und anderen Merkwürdigkeiten, verfasst durch einen Privatmann im Jahre 1822 heimgekehrten Schweizerkolonisten." (Joseph Hecht, Canton Luzern.) Im Jahre 1823. (A manuscript of 216 pp.)

Manuscript No. XXIII. " Traitement que les Bataillons Suisses auront en Amérique." (*I. e.*, in South America. Manuscript of 4 pp., probably of eighteenth century.)

CANTON URI.

ALTORF: STAATSARCHIV.

The Staatsarchiv (Cantonal Archive) is located in the town of Altorf, and kept in the Rathaus. During the French invasion, Apr. 5, 1799, fire destroyed all records of the earlier periods. The archive therefore contains only materials of the nineteenth century. One of the earliest notices respecting emigration from Uri may be found in the *Anzeiger für Schweizerische Geschichte*, n. F., Bd. XI. (1911), no. 4, p. 190, from the autobiography of the Uri historian Franz Vincenz Schmid: "1776 im Frühjahr kehrte ich zum Regimente auf Verdun zurück. Mich wandelte die Lust [an], in königlich englische Dienste zu treten und den Feldzug in Amerika mitzumachen [Nordamerika, Unabhängigkeitskrieg], allein meines dringlichsten Bittens ungeachtet, mochte ich die Bewilligung hierzu von meinem Herrn Vater nicht auswirken."

Faszikel I. C. 5-9.
> Verhältnisse zur auswärtigen Gesandtschaft. Kreisschreiben. 1848.
> Tarif-Verhältnisse u. Handelsverhältnisse zu den verschiedenen Staaten Amerikas. 1847-1851.
> Auslieferungsvertrag mit der Republik Salvador, Amerika. Kreisschreiben, 1884.

Faszikel: Auswanderung, überseeische. Meist nach Nordamerika. Kreisschreiben. 1875-1883.

A number of petitions of individuals desiring passes for emigration.

Faszikel: Pässe, Heimatscheine, und Wanderbücher.
> Several volumes. 1807 to present time. In the years 1867-1872 a large number of emigrants came out of the district Wassen, in the Meienthal, canton Uri, reduced to poverty on account of bankruptcies, inebriety (Schnapspest), and intemperance (coffee and liquor habit).

From a manuscript chronicle, in the manuscript collections of Dr. Karl Franz Lusser, landammann and physician, which are now a part of the archives: Aug. 29, 1806, " Wandert Vinz. Good heimlich nach Amerika, von wo er nicht wieder kam, aus, und entzog so dem Lande und den Armen sein bed[eutendes] Vermögen."

CANTON SCHWYZ.

SCHWYZ: KANTONSARCHIV.

Location: Cantonal archive in the town of Schwyz, located in an old tower-like building very near the Rathaus.
Hours: 9 a. m. to 12 m., or by appointment.
Bibliography: J. C. Benziger, "Das Schwyz. Archiv", in *Mitteilungen des Historischen Vereins des Kantons Schwyz,* Heft 16.

The material of the eighteenth century is not in condition for investigation; that of the nineteenth century is being put into order. That relating to American history of the nineteenth century seems confined to the circular letters (Kreisschreiben der Vororte), which are preserved, more or less completely, in most of the cantonal archives. The following will serve for illustration: Faszikel " Amerika ", containing acta on North America, Mexico, South America.

1817. " Schreiben des Königs der Niederlande, Klage über unbemittelte Schweizer in den Häfen der Niederlande, die nach Nordamerika abreisen wollen."
1819. Inquiry as to estimated cost of immigration to Brazil, etc.
1830. Consul Boker, and other consulships.
1838. " Der Schweizer Verein zum Wohlthun in New Orleans an d. Herren Glieder der Regierung d. löblichen Staats zu Schwyz." Jan. 22, 1838.
1838-1847. Kreisschreiben an sämtliche eidgenössische Stände.
Faszikel " Auswanderung ". 1846-1847.

EINSIEDELN: STIFTSARCHIV.

The archive of the Benedictine Abbey of Einsiedeln contains records of the founding of branch institutions in the United States, *e. g.*, St. Meinrad Abbey, St. Meinrad, Spencer Co., Ind.; New-Subiaco Abbey, Spielerville, Logan Co., Ark.; St. Mary's Abbey, Richardton, Stark Co., N. D. *Cf.* the following:
P. Franz Züricher, " Die Benediktiner in Amerika ", in *Katholische Studien,*
    Heft II., 37 pp. (Würzburg, 1875); this article gives an account of the settlements of the Benedictine order in the United States, beginning with St. Vincenz, in Westmoreland Co., Pa.
Annalen der Verbreitung des Glaubens, arts.:
" Missionen in Amerika; Überblick der acht ersten Jahre der Benediktinermissionen in Indiana; aus einem Schreiben des Pater Martin an seine Oberen und Mitbrüder in Einsiedeln in der Schweiz. Sankt. Meinrad (Indiana) d. 1. Januar, 1861." No. 199, p. 428 f.
" Schreiben Sr. Gnaden d. hochwürdigsten Herrn Baraga, Bischofs von Sancta Maria v. Obernsee (Lake Superior)." No. 199, pp. 75 f., 462 f.
" Bericht des P. Beda Conner. Indianastaat im September 1853." No. 125, p. 225 f.

Dr. P. Odilo Ringholz, *Geschichte des Fürstlichen Benediktinerstiftes U. L. Frau von Einsiedeln.* Die Kulturarbeit des Stiftes Einsiedeln, p. 11. ("1852, 21. Dezember, verreisen P. Ulrich Christen, und P. Beda O'Connor nach Amerika zur Gründung des neuen Klosters St. Meinrad in Indiana." Ringholz.)
The Catholic Church in the United States of America (New York, 1912), I. 58.
Die katholischen Missionen im nordöstlichen Arkansas und das Benediktiner-Frauenkloster Maria Stein, bei Pocahontas, Randolph Co., Ark. Eine Festschrift zum goldenen Jubiläum der Diözese Little Rock und zum Silberjubiläum der Mission Nordost-Arkansas (Little Rock, 1893, pp. 110). An historical account of the Catholic missions in the northeastern part of Arkansas, since their foundation by Bishop Fitzgerald in 1868.

EINSIEDELN: BEZIRKSARCHIV.

This archive contains records of emigration; *cf.*:
Meinrad Kälin, " Einsiedler in der Fremde ", in *Einsiedler Anzeiger*, 1909, 6tes Blatt. This is based upon the records, and adds some information drawn from the immigrants settled in the U. S.
Id., " Vom Geisbuben zum Städtegründer ", in *Alte und Neue Welt*, 42. Jahrgang, 1907-1908, 9. Heft, pp. 336-338. (Steinauer, Neb., founded by the Swiss settler J. A. Steinauer.)
Kälin estimates that over two thousand settlers from Einsiedeln are living in the United States.

CANTON UNTERWALDEN.

Divided politically into two half-cantons, Obwalden and Nidwalden.

OBWALDEN.
SARNEN: STAATSARCHIV.

The cantonal archive is located in the town of Sarnen, and in the Rathaus.

AKTEN ÜBER AUSWANDERUNG.

Kreisschreiben von 1850 bis 1909.
Verzeichnis der anno 1852 ausgewanderten Alpnachter Familien, und was sie bei ihrer Abreise schuldig geblieben (about 5200 francs). Their destination was Brazil. Six cases. Similar record of 7 cases in 1854, indebtedness 11,000 fr.
Protokoll der Konferenz der eidgenössischen Stände Zürich, Unterwalden, Glarus, Schaffhausen, Graubünden, und Aargau, betreffend die Lage der schweiz. Kolonisten in Brazilien.
Brief eines Ausgewanderten in Brasilien, d. 5. Nov., 1854, an den Herrn Anton Britschgi in Alpnach, Canton Obdenwald.
Query about Alois Britschgi, who left with indebtedness of 900 fr.
Letters of immigrants to Brazil, mostly lamenting their departure.
Printed report of Dr. Heusser (a trusted teacher, sent to investigate), "an die Direktion der Polizei des Kantons Zürich" (Zürich, 1857): *Die Schweizer in St. Paolo in Brasilien* (printed 1860, Tschudi).
Zuschrift an den Bundesrat über die Auswanderung nach Brasilien. (Stirring complaint.) Dec. 1, 1857.
Brief von 11 Familien um Contract bittend, aus Sarnen, Sachseln, und Alpnach.
Bericht des Dr. Heusser v. 28. März, u. 6. April 1857, betr. die Colonie in Brasilien.
Answer to inquiry, how many went to Brazil from Obwalden, 1852-1854, viz.: 33 persons over 8 years, 9 under 8 years; five families were given help to emigrate.
Letter of complaint from Brazil to the President of the Swiss Confederation. Rio de Janeiro, Mar. 8, 1858.
Protokoll der Konferenz der eidgenöss. Stände Zürich, Bern, Ob dem Wald, Glarus, Schaffhausen, Graubünden, und Aargau, betr. die Lage d. schweiz. Kolonisten in Brasilien. (22 pp.) 1., 2., 3. Sitzung, etc.
1866. Complaint of Schweiz. Wohltätigkeitsgesellschaft concerning immigrant paupers.
1868. Vermögensangelegenheiten der Theresia von Deschwanden in St. Louis, Amerika.
1876. Warnung vor Auswanderung nach Bolivar, S. A. Kreisschreiben von Bern.
1881-1900. Auswanderung X. 12. Statistiken über Auswanderung, und Kreisschreiben.

1900-1912. Auswanderung X. 12. Kreisschreiben über Auswanderungsagenturen. Statistiken der Auswanderung.
   The names of all emigrants between 1854 and 1894 from the half-canton
Obwalden are printed in the *Amts-Blatt des Kantons Unterwalden ob dem
Wald*. The custom of printing their names originated in the desire to enable
creditors to collect debts before the emigrants' departure. Typical entry:
" Nach Amerika wollen auswandern :
   " 1. Joseph Andermatt und dessen Frau und drei Kinder, von Alpnacht.
   " 2. Franz Wallimann, mit Familie, von Alpnacht.
   " Etc., etc.
   " Allfällige Einsprache gegen Aushingabe von deren Reiseschriften sind
       sogleich bei der unterzeichneten zu machen.
   " Sarnen den 14. März, 1855.   Die Standeskanzlei."
   Many interesting items under the rubric " Auswanderung " can be found
in the pages of the *Amts-Blatt*. Since 1900 a larger number of emigrants left
Obwalden than Nidwalden. The larger part settled in California; many in
Washington (Tacoma).

SARNEN: FRAUENKLOSTER ST. ANDREAS.

   Archives not accessible. Two printed pamphlets on branches founded in
the United States:
Nach dem fernen Westen. Reise-Notizen der Klosterfrauen von St. Andreas
       in Sarnen, O. S. B. Sechste Auflage mit 27 Abbildungen.
       (Printed in Einsiedeln; Verlag des Frauenklosters St. Andreas
       in Sarnen, 1886, pp. 94.)
Verzeichnis der Benediktinerinnen zur Hl. Gertrud. der Grossen, O. S. B.
       (Cottonwood, Idaho, U. S. A., 1911, pp. 20.)

ENGELBERG: ABTEI.

   The archive of the monastery of Engelberg contains the following material
relating to America:
   1. P. Adalbert Vogel, *Die Benediktinerkolonie in Neuengelberg bei Concep-
       tion*. Separatabdruck aus der Zeitschrift *Studien und Mitthei-
       lungen aus dem Benediktiner- und Cistercienserorden*, Bd. LV.,
       pt. III. (1882), erschienen bei L. Wörl in Würzburg. (" Es ist
       eine Schilderung der Klostergründung von Conception im Staate
       Missouri. Das dortige Kloster wurde im Jahre 1873 von Engel-
       berg aus durch P. Frowin Conrad gegründet und im Jahre 1880
       zur Abtei erhoben." P. B. E., Stiftsarchivar.)
   2. Ein Gesuch an den Papst um Erhebung Neuengelbergs zur Abtei, mit
       einigen historischen Notizen.
   3. Personallisten dieses Klosters aus verschiedenen Jahren mit Heimats-
       angabe.
   4. Zeitungsberichte über die Niederlassung, welche P. Adelhelm Odermatt
       von Engelberg aus im Staate Oregon gründete und Mount Angel
       nannte. (" Diese Gründung fand im Jahre 1882 statt. Für sie
       mag eine Bemerkung im *Bote der Urschweiz*, no. 100 (1882), von
       Belang sein; es heisst nämlich da, dass mit den Patres fünfzig
       Urschweizer ausgezogen seien." P. B. E., Stiftsarchivar.)

5. Prospekte und Jahresberichte des im Jahre 1887 eröffneten Mount Angel College.
6. Bulletin mit kurzer Schilderung des Brandunglückes, durch welches am 3. Mai, 1892, das ganze Kloster Mount Angel in Asche gelegt wurde.
7. Baupläne von Mount Angel.

More material relating to these monasteries founded in America may be obtained by addressing the Rev. Abbot of the abbey of Conception, Missouri, and of Mount Angel, Oregon. The archives of these American monasteries may also throw light on the question, whether Swiss immigrants settled around the monasteries to any considerable extent.

CANTON UNTERWALDEN.

NIDWALDEN.

STANS: STAATSARCHIV.

The Staatsarchiv (Cantonal Archive) is located in the town of Stans, and in the Rathaus.

Bibliography: Adalbert Vokinger, " Inventar des Staatsarchives des Kantons Unterwalden nid dem Wald in Stans ", in *Inventare Schweizerischer Archive,* Beilage to the *Anzeiger für Schweizerische Geschichte,* I. 153-168 (Bern, 1895).

Registration of emigration since 1848, in the Ratsprotokolle.

Names of emigrants printed, for the benefit of creditors, in the *Amts-Blatt des Kantons Unterwalden Nid dem Wald.* This begins with the first recorded case in 1854 and ends in 1895. The following is a typical case:

" (1) Geschwister Franz und Anna Ackermann, Kinder des Goldschmid Felix und der A. M. Ackermann sel., von Buochs, ledig, ersterer 26 und letztere 31 Jahre alt;

" (2) Alois Hug, Sohn des Alois und der A. M. Christen, von Buochs, ledig, 21 Jahr alt "; etc., etc.

" Dieses wird in der Absicht zur öffentlichen Kenntnis gebracht, damit allfällige Einsprachen gegen die Aushingabe der Reiseschriften binnen nächsten 3 Wochen beim Titl. Polizeiamt erhoben werden können. Stans, den 20. Hornung [Feb. 20], 1860. Die Standeskanzlei."

The Stammbuchamt is also in the Rathaus at Stans, and contains " Obrigkeitliche Stammbücher " (official genealogies), back into the fourteenth century. This official bureau of genealogies was established in the eighteenth century.

CANTON GLARUS.

GLARUS: STAATSARCHIV.

Location: " Neues Archiv des Cantons Glarus ", in the Gerichtsgebäude, Hauptstrasse.
Hours: 8 a. m. to 12 m.; 2 to 6 p. m.
No material was found belonging to the eighteenth century, and none relating to the nineteenth, before 1837.

ACTA. T. 22.

Rubrik 73. Auswanderung. Vermögenszug.
    Fascikel 1: Vermögenszug: Jahre 1837-1867. (A considerable number of cases of transfer of property to persons in America.)
    Fascikel 2: Auswanderung: Jahre 1837-1852.
        No. 1. " Der Interims-Präsident des Auswanderungs-Vereins macht Mitteilung vom Auswanderungs-Plan, von den sich beteiligenden Gemeinden und ersucht um Unterstützung durch die Regierung." May 28, 1844.
        No. 2. " Der Vorstand des Auswanderungs-Vereins ersucht um Beförderung der Vorlage des Schreibens vom Interimspräsidenten vor Rath." May 31, 1844.
        No. 3. " Gemeindebeschlüsse über den Beitritt zum Auswanderungs-Verein und über die zu gewährende Unterstützung." June 3-12, 1844.
        No. 4. " Landammann u. Rath: Circular an sämtl. Gemeinedräthe über Unterstützung u. Betheiligung des Landes am Auswanderungsverein." June 12, 1844.
        No. 5. " Standeskommission: Circular an die eidgenöss. Consulate in Nord-Amerika über die Auswanderungsfrage." June 14, 1844.
        No. 6. " Der Präsident des Auswanderungs-Vereins setzt die Wichtigkeit der Auswanderungsfrage und die Dringlichkeit der Beförderung derselben auseinander." July 23, 1844.
        No. 10. " Abschrift eines Briefes von W. Blumer von Allentown in Pennsylvanien, Auswanderungs-, Untersuchs- und Landankaufs-Reise betreffend." Nov. 8, 1844.
        No. 11. " Der Vorstand des Auswand.-Vereins macht Mitteilung einer stattfindenden Versammlung, und ladet die Regierung zur Teilnahme durch Abgeordnete ein." Nov. 29, 1844.
        No. 12. " Der Vorstand teilt die Beschlüsse der Versammlung des Auswand.-Vereins vom 30. November mit." Dec. 13, 1844.
        No. 13. " Hr. Peter Jenny v. Schwanden macht Mitteilung eines Plans zur Bildung einer schweiz. Unterstützungs- u. Schutz-Gesellschaft für Auswanderer." Jan. 17, 1845.
        No. 14. " Nachträgliche Erklärungen des Gemeinderaths betr. die Auswanderer auf die Anfrage vom 22. Januar, 1845." Jan., 1845.

No. 15. "Der Vorstand des Auswand.-Vereins: Einladung an die Regierung, sich gutächtlich über die, von den resp. Tagwen (Bürger der Gemeinde, die besitzen) zu leistenden Beiträge auszusprechen." Jan. 22, 1845.

No. 16. "Einladung des Auswand.-Vereins Vorstands zur Beschickung der Versammlung der Abgeordneten der betreffenden Gemeinden durch Mitglieder der Regierung." Jan. 31, 1845.

No. 17. "Landammann u. Rath: Circular. Mitteilung der gefassten Beschlüsse über die Unterstützung der Auswanderer von Seite des Landes, der Gemeinden und durch Liebessteuern." Feb. 5, 1845. (100 fr. for each Bürger, 25 fr. for each minor.)

No. 18. "Protestation einer Minderheit des Tagwens Reuty gegen einen Tagwens-Beschluss, die Unterstützung d. Auswanderer betref." Feb. 5, 1845.

No. 19. "Protokoll über die Versammlungen u. Comite-Sitzungen des Auswand.-Vereins." Feb. 5, 1845; May 19, 1847.

No. 20. "Einladung an die Regierung zur Teilnahme an der Versammlung d. Auswand.-Vereins. Bezeichnung der 2 Experten zur Genehmigung." Feb. 18, 1845.

No. 21. "Übersendung eines königl. Dekrets, betr. schützende Bestimmungen für durch die Niederlande reisende und dort einschiffende Auswanderer." Feb. 21, 1845.

No. 22. "Übersendung der Statuten, Anzeige und Ursache des Wechsels des 2ten Experten." Mar. 18, 1845.

No. 23. "Standeskommission: Einladung an die Polizeikommission, betr. Verhinderung der Kollektionen unter dem Titel der Auswanderung." Mar. 19, 1845.

No. 26. "Eidgenöss. Vorort Zürich: Mitteilung einer Warnung d. schweiz. Consuls in New York vor dem Auswandern armer Personen." Oct. 24, 1845.

No. 27. "General-Consul d. Ver. Staaten für d. Schweiz: Mitteilung eines Gesetzes des Staates New York, die Auswanderer betreffend." Mar. 13, 1846.

Nos. 28, 29. "Eidgenöss. Kanzlei in Zürich: Kreisschreiben über die Auswanderung nach Amerika." 1846.

No. 30. "Der Vorstand d. Auswand.-Verein: Übersendung eines Berichts von Neu-Glarus; Comité-Beschluss über denselben; Wunsch d. Erwähnung d. Verteilung der Vorschuss-Summe vor d. Rathe." Jan. 12, 1847.

No. 31. "Der Glarnische Auswand.-Verein und die Colonie Neu-Glarus in Wisconsin. Hauptbericht d. Auswanderungs-Comités." 6. Hornung (Feb. 6), 1847.

No. 32. "Stadtrat Winterthur: Anfrage über den Schutz d. Auswanderer durch die Regierung u. die Gemeinden und über Anschluss an den Auswand.-Verein und die Colonie Neu-Glarus." Mar. 3, 1847.

Nos. 33, 34. "Kreisschreiben (Vorort Bern) über die Auswanderung." 1847.

No. 35. "Übersendung von Unterrichtsmitteln u. Schulmaterialien an die Colonie Neu-Glarus." May 19, 1847.

No. 36. "Landammann u. Rath: Kreditbewilligung von 100 fr. zu Schulzwecken für Neu-Glarus." June 15, 1847.

No. 37. "Gemeinde-Berichte über den Stand der Auswanderung und tabellarische Zusammenstellung derselben." Aug. 13, 1847.
Nos. 38, 39, 40. Emigration of a number of individuals.
No. 41. "Hr. Adv. Rud. Gallati ersucht im Namen mehrerer um Obrigkeitl. Aufhebung der Gemeindebeschlüsse von Mollis über die Unterstützung der Auswanderer." Feb. 1, 1848.
No. 42. "Antwort von Glarus, Kerenzen, und Filzbach auf ein Circular, betreffend die Beitragsleistungen der Gemeinden." Mar. 23, 1848.
No. 43. "Gemeinde Mollis: Nachsendung des Reisegeldes für die in Mainz zurückgehaltenen Auswanderer." Apr. 14, 1848.
No. 44. "Akten über die Allgemeine Gesellschaft gegenseitiger Unterstützung für Auswanderer in Genf." Apr. 14, 1848; Jan. 12, 1849.
No. 45. "Preislisten verschiedener Agenten zur Spedition von Auswanderern und vergleichende Zusammenstellung derselben." 1848-1849.
No. 46. "Eidgenöss. Consulat in Brüssel u. Antwerpen: Empfehlung d. Auswanderung über Antwerpen." Feb. 9, 1849.
No. 47. "Die Agentur für glarner Auswanderer in Basel betr." Feb. 15, 1849.
No. 47 a. "Tabellarische Darstellung d. Auswanderung im Kanton Glarus 1845-1848 und Beleuchtung derselben." Feb. 21, 1849.
Nos. 48, 49, 51. Auswanderungsagenturen betr. 1849.
No. 50. "Gesetz über den Durchzug d. Auswanderer durch Belgien." June 28, 1849.
No. 52. "Bericht über die Zustände der Kolonie Neu-Glarus." May 7, 1850.
No. 53. "Königl. belgischer General Konsul i. d. Schweiz: Mitteilung eines kön. Dekrets die Sicherheit d. Auswanderer auf ihrer Reise betr." June 5, 1850.
No. 54 "Bericht über die Verwendung d. Kirchensteuer für Neu-Glarus." Sept. 18, 1850.
No. 56. "Anzeige über die Errichtung eines Post-Bureaus in Neu-Glarus." Dec. 27, 1850.
(1851. Collekte für Neu-Glarus, s. in Rubr. 160.)
Nos. 57, 57 a, 58, 58 a. Details. 1851.
No. 59. "Einsendung eines eingegangenen Berichts über Neu-Glarus (Copie). Vorschlag zu weiterer Unterstützung des Kirchengutes u. s. w. dieser Gemeinde." Jan. 21, 1852.
Nos. 59 a, b, c, d, 60, 61. Details. 1852.
Fascikel 3. Auswanderung. Jahre 1853-1866.
Nos. 1-12, 14-17. Details.
No. 13. "Gemeinderat Glarus: Tagwensbeschluss betr. Unterstützung d. Auswanderer in Nord-Amerika." Sept. 30, 1853.
No. 18. "Gemeinderath Elm: Beschluss betr. Unterstützung d. Auswanderung nach Amerika." Jan. 27, 1854.
Nos. 19-28. Details. 1854.
No. 29. "Gemeinderath Netzthal: Bericht über die 1854 nach Amerika ausgewanderten Personen." Jan. 10, 1855.

No. 30. " Bundesrath: Warnung vor Absendung mittelloser Auswanderer oder Verbrecher nach Amerika." Mar. 2, 30, 1855.
Nos. 31, 32. Details. 1855.
No. 33 a. " Glarnischer Auswanderungs-Verein. Schlussbericht, Schlussrechnung, Liquidation des Vereins." Nov. 25, 1855.
No. 35. " Bericht der Gemeinden über die Auswanderung 1854-1856. Schreiben."
Nos. 36-62. Details on emigration, 1857-1866, including consular reports, statistics on emigration from canton Glarus, prevention of transportation of paupers and criminals. (No more forced emigration.)
Fascikel 4. Auswanderung. 1867-1875.
Nos. 1-26. Annual statistics, property settlements, immigration agencies, etc. Immigration to South American states (Neu Helvetia, Uruguay; La Plata states).
Fascikel 5. Auswanderung. 1868-1883.
Nos. 1-39. Vermögenszug, Erbschaftsangelegenheiten.
Fascikel 6. Auswanderung. 1876-1890.
Nos. 1-46. Emigration statistics, licensed emigrant agencies, increase of emigration. Not all to United States. Chili, etc.
No. 20. " Auswanderung aus der Schweiz im Jahre 1884 und 1885 resp. seit 1879, und speziell im Jahre 1885."
Fascikel 7. Auswanderung. Vermögenszug. Akten aus den Jahren 1884–.
Nos. 1-32. Individual cases.
Fascikel 8. Auswanderung. Akten aus den Jahren 1891–.
Überseeische Auswanderungen aus der Schweiz. Statistik.

Amerika.

Rubrik 1. A1. Fascikel 1. 1837-1856.
Acta 1-44. Consular reports, communications, and abstracts of messages delivered to all the cantons by the " Vorort ", and after 1848 by the " Bundesrat ", concerning the United States, Mexico, and the South American states.
Fascikel 2. 1857-1895. Material as above.

Registratur. Vereinigte Staaten von Nord Amerika. 1901-1909.

(Kreisschreiben von Bern.)
Landammannamt No. 926. " Auszug aus dem Protokoll des Regierungsrates des Kantons Glarus v. 27. Juli, 1905. § 826: Feier des 60-jährigen Bestandes der Kolonie Neu-Glarus in Nordamerika." Congratulatory message to New Glarus, Wis., and correspondence.
Memorial für die ordentl. Landsgemeinde des Jahres 1874 (printed), pp. 13-18: § 8: " Erwerbung eines Landkomplexes in Amerika." The " Kantonale Arbeiterbund " in 1873 addressed to the " Dreifache Rath " a plea for the purchase of a large tract of land as a permanent place of refuge for the unemployed (encouraged by the success of New Glarus colony in Wisconsin). Long argument presented, and conclusion as follows: " dass der Staat die Auswanderung weder hemmen noch fördern, sondern dass er sie frei gewähren lassen soll ".

Bibliography of printed material: Katalog der Landesbibliothek in Glarus (Näfels, 1903).
Berichte der Schweizerischen Consular Agenten, mit Anmerkungen der Auswanderungs-Commission der Gemeinnützigen Gesellschaft (Glarus, 1845).
Der Glarnische Auswanderungs-Verein und die Colonie Neu-Glarus: Hauptbericht des Auswanderungs-Comité, mit 2 Karten (Glarus, 1847).
Zweiter Bericht über die Colonie Neu-Glarus (Glarus, 1851).
The Planting of the Swiss Colony at New Glarus, Wisconsin, by John Luchsinger. Reprinted from *Wisconsin Historical Collections,* vol. XII. (Madison, Wis., 1892).
The Swiss Colony of New Glarus, by John Luchsinger, with additional notes by J. J. Tschudy. From vol. VIII. of *Wisconsin Historical Collections* (1879).
D. Dürst, Die Gründung und Entwickelung der Kolonie Neu-Glarus (Wiskonsin, N. A.) umfassend den Zeitraum von 1844-1892, nebst einer Reisebeschreibung, mit 3 Plänen (Zürich, 1894).
Andreas Baumgartner, *Ein Besuch in Neu-Glarus.* Separate reprint from the *Glarner Nachrichten* (Glarus, 1906).
Id., Erinnerungen aus Amerika (Zürich, 1906), pp. 86-125. " Besuch in Neu-Glarus."

CANTON ZUG.

ZUG: KANTONSARCHIV.

Location: In the Regierungsgebäude, on the Postplatz.
Hours: 8 a. m. to 12 m.; 2 to 6 p. m.
The materials of the eighteenth century are not put in order; a governmental appropriation is expected for this purpose. The nineteenth century material is well grouped, arranged, and indexed.

AUSLAND. AMERIKA. THEKE I.

A. Schweizerische Konsulate in Amerika. 1823-1847.

1824. " Bericht über Erhebung von Verlassenschaften verstorbener Schweizer."

B. Amerikanische Konsulate in der Schweiz. 1830-1845.

1831. " Bericht über Handelsverhältnisse mit Mexiko."
1832. " Handels- und Freundschaftsvertrag mit Mexiko."
1833. " Französische Verfügung zur Durchreise von Auswanderern nach Amerika."
" Freundschaft- u. Handelsvertrag mit den mexikanischen Staaten."
1834. " Übereinkunft zum freien Vermögensbezug zwischen der Schweiz u. Amerika."
1836. " Ermordung des schweizerischen Handelskonsuls (Marret) in Mexiko." Nov. 8, 1835.
1843. " Bericht über die Handels- u. Douanen-Verhältnisse in Mexiko."
" Verbot des Detailhandels für die Ausländer in Mexiko."
" Weisung über Beibringung von Todesscheinen u. Nachlass-Liquidationen in überseeischen Ländern."
1846. " Vertrag über Auslieferung der Verbrecher mit Nordamerika."
" Verhaltungsmassregeln für Auswanderer."
" Auskündigungen in amerikanischen Zeitungen " (Erbschaften, etc.).
" Verhaltungsmassregeln für Auswanderer nach Amerika vom amerikanischen Consul Goundie in Basel."

INNERES. AUSWANDERUNG. 1803-1847.

1817. " Warnung vor der Auswanderung nach Amerika."

AUSLAND. ARCHIV AKTEN 1848-1873. THEKE I.

Amerikanische Freistaaten, Verträge mit der Schweiz, über:
1848. " Aufhebung des Heimfallrechts und der Auswanderertaxen."
" Urlaub des Konsuls der Vereinigten Staaten (Goundie)."
1855. " Freundschafts-, Niederlassungs-, Handels-, u. Auslieferungs-Vertrag."
1858. " Verhältnisse der amerikanischen Israeliten in der Schweiz."
1859. " Legalisation von gerichtlichen Akten."

1860. " Bürgerrecht für Schweizerinnen, die sich mit Amerikanern verheiraten."
1861. " Reisevorschriften."
1865. " Sympathie- u. Beileids-Adresse an die amerikanische Union." (Lincoln's death.)
1866. " Nachtragsvergütungen an Soldaten der Vereinigten Staaten."
" Vorschriften über Sendung von Waaren und Briefen, 1851-1863."
1868. " Beschwerde über Spedition von Vagabunden und Verbrechern nach den Vereinigten Staaten."
" Austausch der amtlichen Publikationen."   " Mittel gegen die Trauben-Krankheit."
" Statistik der Vereinigten Staaten."
1869. " Geld-Auswechselungsvertrag."
1872. " Nachtrags-Artikel zum Postvertrag über Postanweisungen."

INNERES.   1848-1873.   THEKE 81.

K. I. AUSWANDERUNG.

Gesetze und Verordnungen über das Auswanderungswesen.
Auswanderung in Unteregeri: Vertrag mit der Korporation.
Statistik von Zug, 1867-1873.
Statistik: Überseeische Auswanderung aus der Schweiz im Jahre 1871.
Auswanderungs-Literatur. *Schweiz. Auswanderungs-Zeitung,* etc. Unterstützung für Auswanderer und Kolonisation, etc.
Bureau für Auswanderung in New York.
Eidgenössische Organisation der Auswanderung. Konferenz hierüber. Protokoll.
Nachweisungsbureau in Bremen.
Anweisung für Auswanderer.
Konferenz-Protokolle.
Auswanderung nach Algerien, Brasilien, Polen.
Auswanderungs-Agenturen. Anzeigen.
Untergang des Auswanderer-Schiffs *William Nelson* (1865).
Bedingungen zur Auswanderung nach Algerien.
Mitteilungen bezüglich der Auswanderung nach Amerika; Brasilien.
Auswanderer aus dem Kanton Zug. (25 individual cases.)

AUSWÄRTIGE ANGELEGENHEITEN.   1874-1893.   A. THEKE I.

I. VERTRÄGE UND ABKOMMEN.

a. Mit Amerika.

1. " Nachtragsartikel zum Postvertrag zwischen der Schweiz und den Ver. Staaten v. Amerika, betr. den gegenseitigen Austausch von Korrespondenzkarten." Mar. 31, Apr. 21, 1874.
2. " Bundesbeschluss betr. Vertretung der Schweiz in Washington." Jan. 28, 1882.
3. " Freundschafts-, Niederlassungs-, u. Handelsvertrag mit der Republik Salvador." Oct. 30, 1883.
6. Ditto, mit Ecuador. June 22, 1888.
7. " Gegenseitige Auslieferung von Verbrechern und Vollzug von Requisitorien. Übereinkunft v. 22. Juni, samt Begleitschreiben." July 18, 1889.

8. "Auswechselung von Geldanweisungen-Vertrag mit den Vereinigten Staaten." Oct. 18, 1881.

      6. AUSWANDERUNG. THEKE 77 II. Q. 6.
a. Auswanderungskommissariat.
    I. Aufgabe des Kommissariats. Kreisschreiben des eidg. Departments für Auswanderung. Sept. 26, 1888.
    II. Geschäftsbericht. Kreisschreiben des eidg. Depts.
b. Agenturen. (Complete material accessible in Bundesarchiv, and Eidg. Auswanderungsamt, Bern.)
c. Statistik. (As above.)
d. Verschiedenes.
    I. Iten Bländus, Oberägeri, Auswanderung nach Canada. Reklamation des schweiz. Konsulats in Philadelphia betr. zu geringer Subsistenzmittel. Nos. 1-10, 1871, 1874.
    II. Röllin Johannes. Auswanderungsgesuch. (1) Schreiben des Gemeinderats Menzingen; (2) Agentur Baumgarten, Basel, an Menzingen, Feb. 12, 1879.
    III. Auswanderung nach Uruguay, Südamerika. 1879.
Schweiz. Auswanderungszeitung. Jäggi an Reg. Rat. June 24, 1880.
    VI. Auswanderung nach Chile. Schreiben d. eidg. Depts. Dec. 11, 1883.
Übermachung des Auswanderungswesens. Auszug aus dem Protokoll der Commission des Innern. Mar. 27, 1884.

CANTON SOLOTHURN (SOLEURE).
SOLOTHURN: STAATSARCHIV.

Location: In the Rathaus, a good building with annex.
Hours: 8 a. m. to 12 m.; 2 to 6 p. m.

MANDATEN.

Auswanderung. "Ausser Land ziehen, den Unterthanen verboten." Year 1491, p. 3.
Auswanderung. "Ausser Land ziehen, unter fremde Fürsten." 1537, p. 284; 1577, p. 436; 1585, p. 445.
Auswanderung. "Ausser Land ziehen, ohne Billigung der Obrigkeit bei Verlust von Bürgerrecht und Hab und Gut" [verboten]. 1647, p. 825.
Auswanderung. "Mittel (Vermögen) soll keiner ausser Land ziehen ohne Vorwissen und Billigung der Obrigkeit." 1706, p. 164.

RATSPROTOKOLLE.

1767. Auswanderung. Spanische Kolonien. (18 documents.)
1768. Auswanderung. Spanische Kolonien. (27 documents.)
1769. Auswanderung. Spanische Kolonien. (11 documents.)

RATSMANUALE. IV. STAATSSACHEN. INNERES.

1837. "Für den nach Amerika reisenden Benedikt Schwaller von Oberdorf darf ein Pass ausgestellet werden."
"Dem Benedikt Bättiger von Schnottwil wird die Auswanderung nach Amerika auf verpflogenen Rechnungstag bewilligt."
1838. "Weisung wegen Abzugsgebühr von 10 per cent."
1839. Three requests for passes for emigrants granted, two refused, one inquired into.
1840. One family refused permission to emigrate; a number of other individuals allowed to go.
1841–1845. Emigration, also to Algiers and Russia.
1846. "Die Mitteilung der eidgenöss. Kanzlei betreffend die Auswanderung nach Amerika wird überwiesen."
1850. "In das Gesuch der Gemeinde Sumiswald den Johann Tschan, Schuster von hier, welcher mit Frau und Kindern nach Amerika auszuwandern wünscht, zu verhindern, wird nicht eingetreten." No. 28, a. b.
"In das Gesuch des R . . . von A . . . um eine Staatsunterstützung nach Amerika, wird nicht eingegangen."
1852. "Den Gemeinden Breitenbach, Büsserach, Erschwil, Himmelrid, und Kleinlützel wird die Verwilligung zu Geldaufbrüchen für Unterstützung auswandernder Familien nicht ertheilt."

"Von H. Turnlehrer Hängi werden 150 Copien seiner Denkschrift über die nordamerikanischen Verhältnisse @ 1 fr. angekauft und jeder Gemeinde eine Kopie zugeschickt." (Copy found in Staatsarchiv.)

1852. "Walterswil Gemeinde. In das Ansuchen, zur Unterstützung der Auswanderer Fr. 1000 aus dem Armenfond zu entheben, und um einen Beitrag von Seite des Staats, wird nicht eingetreten."

1853-1857. Detailed information about individual cases of emigrants; taxation of emigrants; some few cases of contributions to aid emigrants.

1855. "Auswanderung mittelloser Personen." Applications for assistance.

"Von einer Mitteilung des Bundesrats vom 19. dies bezüglich Auswanderung gänzlich mittelloser Personen und selbst Sträflingen nach Amerika wird vom Departement des Innern in Abschrift Mitteilung gegeben." No. 325.

REGISTRATUR ZU DEN RATSPROTOKOLLEN.

1847. Ausland B. 355. "Der vom Vorort übermachte Auszug einer Depesche des schweizer. Konsuls zu Amsterdam betreffend ein in Amerika wild wachsendes Knollengewächs, welches geeignet wäre die Kartoffeln zu ersetzen, wird überwiesen."

A number of property claims; inquiries as to persons; consular reports, etc.

AUSWANDERUNGSWESEN. 1837-1857. ACTA.

Rub. 229. No. 124. Bound volume of papers, mostly manuscripts; some few printed pamphlets; all pertaining to emigration, not all, however, concerned with the United States.

FRANKREICH.

During the period before the French Revolution the ambassadors of the King of France to the Swiss Confederation customarily resided at Solothurn. Therefore the archives of this canton contain, in a section entitled Frankreich, a collection especially devoted to Franco-Swiss relations, and containing correspondence with the ambassadors, correspondence of Swiss officers in the French service under the many contracts successively made by France for auxiliary Swiss troops, correspondence respecting the regiments, rolls of regiments, etc.

Of correspondence of Swiss soldiers in the Swiss archives there are some ten manuscript volumes, belonging to the eighteenth century. These volumes are not paged or indexed. Some of them have been gnawed by rats, others damaged by moisture. It was not possible in a rapid search to discover in them any reference to Swiss soldiers employed in the French service in America.

Bibliography: Emanuel May, *Histoire Militaire de la Suisse, et celle des Suisses dans les différens Services de l'Europe* (Lausanne, 1788, 8 vols.).

Baron Zur-Lauben, *Histoire Militaire des Suisses au Service de la France* (Paris, 1751, 8 vols.).

Abbé François Girard, *Histoire Abrégée des Officiers Suisses qui se sont distingués aux Services Étrangers aux Grades Supérieurs* (Fribourg, 1781, 2 vols.).

R. von Steiger, " Coup d'Oeil sur l'Histoire Militaire des Suisses aux Services Étrangers ", in *Archiv für Schweizerische Geschichte*, XVII. (1871).

I. E. Kilchenmann, " Schweizersöldner im Dienste der Englisch-Ostindischen Kompanie um die Mitte des 18. Jahrhunderts ", in *Neues Solothurner Wochenblatt*, I. Jahrgang, no. 34 (Solothurn, May 19, 1911).

CANTON BASEL-STADT.

BASEL: STAATSARCHIV.

Location: The cantonal archive of Basel is well housed in a special building on the site of the old Rathausgarten. The building is described in *Archivalische Zeitschrift,* n. s., XI. 237-252 (1904). The entrance is at Martinsgasse 2; the initiated may also enter from the Marktplatz by way of the stairways and galleries of the picturesque old Rathaus, with which the Archivgebäude is connected.
Hours: 8 a. m. to 12 m.; 2 to 6 p. m.

For conveniences for work and for accessibility of material, the Staatsarchiv of Basel is a model of its kind. The card index and the exhaustive catalogue, *Repertorium des Staatsarchivs zu Basel* (Basel, 1904, pp. lxviii, 834), are of very great service. The *Repertorium* contains a history of the archive, the regulations, a description of the building, etc.

The Schweizerisches Wirtschaftsarchiv is connected with the Staatsarchiv, and is under the same head, the state archivist.

The materials in the Staatsarchiv relating to America are chiefly to be found in the journals (Protokolle) of the Kleiner Rat and of its committee the Dreizehnerrat, in the section Nordamerika, and in the section Auswanderung. The latter consists of two divisions: Auswanderung A, Allgemeines und Einzelnes, 1732-1885, and Auswanderung B, Auswanderungsstatistik, 1817-1885.

Protokolle des Kleinen Raths.

No references to Carolina, Pennsylvania, or other American colonies until 1734.

Vol. 106. 1734-1735.

p. 144. "Hans Heinrich Breitenstein um Reisegelt in Carolinam." Oct. 23, 1734. (4 Gulden were voted to be given him when aboard ship.)

Jacob Müller (informator, Lehrer) begs to go to Carolina with wife and 3 children, and asks for help (Reisegelt). Nov. 17, 1734. Kl. R. Beschluss: "Ist abgewiesen, und solle weder er, noch andere, die in Carolinam reisen wollen, oder reisen zu wollen vorgeben, nicht weiter angehört werden."

p. 146. "In Carolinam reisende arme leut aus d. Zürich Gebiet" (ungefähr 100 Personen). Oct. 27, 1734.

"Solle diesen Leuten, ihre Reisz, wie sie es gut befinden fortzusetzen überlassen, doch das Betteln in der Stadt verbotten, und wan ihnen wegen Almosen etwas angelegen, sie an die arme Herberg verwiesen, übrigens nacher Zürich, dass man dergleichen leut mit erforderlichen Pässen versehe, geschrieben werde."

p. 154. Zürich writes, that these people left without permission, "gegen ihren willen, werden aber solche Anstalten vorkehren, dass diese reisende hiesiger Stadt nicht mehr beschwerlich fallen." Nov. 6, 1734.

Kl. Rath.: "bleibt dabei und wollen MGnHerrn den Erfolg erwarten."

p. 187. " Hans Giegelmann von Bubendorf mit Frau und 6 Kindern willens in Carolinam zu reisen, bittet sie der Leibeigenschaft gegen Gebühr zu entlassen und die Gebühr in etwas miltern." Dec. 1, 1734.
Kl. R.: " Sollen MGnHn die XIII wie dergleichen Reisen in Carolinam zu verhindern Rathschlag abfassen und eingeben."
p. 208. Mention of a book that instigates to immigration for Carolina. Several cases mentioned. Dec. 15, 1734.
p. 228. Zürich sends request to check fever of immigration to Carolina. Jan. 3, 1735.
p. 229. MGnHn XIII.: " In Betrachtung, dass die dahin sich begebenden Personen ihrem Verderben, grossem Elend und Sklaverey entgegen laufen, vorgeschlagen, dass zu Stadt und Land zu Verhinderung einer solchen reisz eine ernstliche Warnung gethan, die Aufwickler oder Anwerber angehalten, den Underthanen aus dieser Absicht keine Ganten [*i. e.*, Versteigerungen, freiwillig oder unfreiwillig] bewilliget, auch sonsten sie von dergleichen Undernehmung mit nachtruck abgehalten werden sollten." Jan. 5, 1735. See below: XIIIer Raths-Protokoll.
p. 345. " Gebrüder Giegelmann und noch einige andere Underthanen, welche umb in Carolinam zu reisen, ihre Güter und Mittel vergantet, sich immer anmelden, dass die Reiss und Päss bewilligt ", etc. Mar. 12, 1735.
Kl. R.: " Weil vor dem Verbott ihre Güter vergantet, soll Pass ertheilt werden."
p. 346. " Gant umb in Carolinam zu reisen, abgeschlagen. Ferner nicht erlaubt." Mar. 16, 1735.
p. 380. " Mandat soll getruckt, zu Stadt und Land publiciert, und auf der Landschaft drey Sonntag nach einander ob den Kantzlen abgelesen werden." Apr. 16, 1735.
p. 389. Seven families, 42 persons, given passes for journey down the Rhine, on way to Carolina. Apr. 23, 1735.
" Solle die Manumissions und Abzugsgebühr von sämtlichen bezogen, deswegen auf ihre in dem Land besitzende oder noch zu erben habende Güter Achtung gegeben werden."

Vol. 107. 1735-1736.

p. 324. About 80 persons, desirous of emigrating (destination Pennsylvania or Carolina), on examination declare, that poverty is the cause of their desire to emigrate, that the country is overpopulated, and that the soil cannot support them. When the hardships and dangers of the journey were described to them, they still insisted on going, and desired passes. Feb. 15, 1736.
Kl. R. addresses " Oberbeamten und Geistliche " to do all in their power to exert a restraining influence.
p. 334. A few of the above group persuaded to remain, but others take their places, making more than before asking to leave, for Carolina and Pennsylvania. Feb. 22, 1736.
Kl. R.: " Ein Bedenken abfassen."
p. 349. Compelled to let immigrants for Pennsylvania go. Provision made for children who were left behind. " Vergantung " permitted. " Abzug und Manumission " both deducted. Mar. 3, 1736.

p. 355. Another group, for Pennsylvania. Emigration and "Vergantung" permitted. Women and children asked whether they wanted to go; if not, provision for them taken out of the goods and property of the immigrant male relatives. Manumission und Abzug. Mar. 10, 1736.

pp. 368, 372, 373, 383. "Abreisz gnädig bewilligt." Mar., 1736. Four weeks period for "Vergantung". Some leave without giving notice.

p. 387. One case of refusal, another of granting permission to emigrate. Apr. 4, 1736.

p. 409. A large number of cases of emigration. Sales of property, deductions, accounts. Apr. 18, 1736.

p. 414. " Schreibern von Liechstal berichtet, dass dem Hans Joggi Bohni von Franckendorf, welcher mit Weib und 8 Kindern in Carolinam zu ziehen willens, nach beschehenen Gant 701 Pf. im Vermögen bleibe: indessen wolle seine zweite 23 jährige Tochter Eva Bohni nicht mit ihm wegziehen." Apr. 21, 1736.

Kl. R. Beschluss: " Kann die Tochter hierbleiben und solle bevögtiget, auch ihro so viel als wann die Eltern todt wären, von den Mitlen hinderlassen, und von dem Überrest der Abzug, samt denen Manumissionsgebühren von den Alten bezogen, die Kinder aber deswegen frey gelassen: übrigens von den Herren Deputierten veranstaltet werden, dass diesen wegziehenden Leuten über die Gebühren nichts abgenommen werde."

p. 421. A list of ten heads of families. Apr. 25, 1736.

Kl. R.: " Solle der Abzug schon erkanntermaszen von den wegziehenden Geldern und die Manumissionsgebühren von denen Häubtern der Hauszhaltungen, Vatter und Mutter abgestattet, doch denen welche weniger als 100 Pfund besitzen mit beiden Forderungen verschont werden."

p. 425. " Die Herren Deputierten haben wegen denen Unterthanen, welche in Carolinam ziehen wollen, ihre ferneren Berahtschlagungen gehalten, verschiedene angehöret und von denselben keine andere Ursach ihres Vorhabens um wegzuziehen vernommen, als dass sie in hiesigem land ihr nahrung nicht finden können." Apr. 25, 1736.

Vol. 109. 1737-1738.

p. 355. " Schreiben von Zürich: Brief v. 24. November, 1736 aus Philadelphia, aus welchem zu ersehen, in was elenden Stand sich die dahin reisenden personen stürtzen."

Beschluss: " Solle diese Abschrift getrucket, auf die Landschaft in alle ämter übersannt, denen Herrn Predigern in allen Gemeinden zugestellet, und absonderlich denen Unterthanen, welche aus dem Land zu ziehen und in Pennsylvaniam zu reisen lust bezeugen, mitgetheilet und kund gemacht werden." Apr. 2, 1738.

Vol. 111. 1739-1740.

p. 329. "Hans Joggi und zwei andere bis nach London gekommen und zurückgekehrt zu ihren Weibern in Läufelfingen." Nov. 28, 1739.

Beschluss: " Die Vögte der Weiber entlassen, das nöthige zugesprochen. (In Gnaden aufgenommen.)"

p. 453. New cases of emigrants; a considerable number.
A letter of H. Riggenbacher, who writes from Carolina, to be confiscated. Feb. 13, 1740.
p. 457. "Lockbrief soll verlesen werden." Feb. 17, 1740.
p. 464. "Brief von H. Riggenbacher aus Carolina an seinen Bruder verlesen." Attempt to get information concerning damage the letter has done. Feb. 20, 1740.
p. 473. The letter taken up again. Feb. 27, 1740.

Vol. 112. 1740-1741.

p. 21. Of a group of persons desirous of emigrating, some are persuaded to change their minds, and remain. Mar. 19, 1740.
pp. 27, 35, 41. Emigrants. Mar., 1740.
p. 65. A group of emigrants permitted to go. Some of them well-to-do. Apr. 20, 1740.
p. 76. More permitted to go, to Pennsylvania and Carolina. Apr. 27, 1740.
p. 81. Three heads of families destined for Pennsylvania. Property 4712 Pfund.[1] Apr. 30, 1740.
p. 84. Twelve persons, permitted to go to Pennsylvania or Carolina, property aggregating 12,370 Pf. 9 Sch. 2 R. Apr. 30, 1740.
Beschluss: "Neben Abzug, die Manumissions-Gebühren also bezogen werden, dass ein Vatter, Mutter oder die eigene Mittel haben, die Gebühr gantz, die Kinder jedes ein halbe Gebühr und jenige so nicht einmal hundert Pfund wegziehen, nichts abrechnen sollen."

Vol. 121. 1747-1748.

p. 51. "Colonie Holländisch Surinam" (Guiana).
p. 284. "Emigranten, wie selbige verhindern."

Vol. 122. 1748-1749.

pp. 151-168. "Emigrierende Unterthanen."
Ten cases or more requesting permission to emigrate with families (destination Pennsylvania), and to sell their property. Reason urged: "Weilen ihr Handwerk gering sei." Referred to Herren Dep. in Landsachen. Feb. 20, 1749.
A number of additional cases. Mar. 1, 1749.
A large number of additional cases. Mar. 5, 1749.
Four more cases. Mar. 7, 1749.
p. 169. "Bedenken." 5 pp.
Decree: Everything to be done to dissuade emigrants, by persons in authority, and sermons to be preached in all churches on the evils and dangers. Of those that persist, the following class permitted

---

[1] The following table, from Hannauer, *Études Économiques*, I. 501, will give a clue to the value of the Basel (and Swiss) coinage. The basis here is the franc.

Année.	Rappen (pence).	Schilling.	Pfund.	Gulden.	Batzen.	Kreutzer.	
1728	0.018	0.11	2.12	2.65	0.18	0.045	francs
1744	0.017	0.10	2.04	2.55	0.17	0.042	"
1756	0.016	0.10	1.96	2.45	0.16	0.04	"
1798	0.015	0.075	1.50	2.25	0.15	0.038	"
1820	0.0143	0.071	1.43	2.14	0.143	0.036	"

to emigrate: those that have no children and the unmarried persons; permitted also to sell their lands (at auction, Ganten), and leave after paying all taxes (Gebühren), Abzug (10 per cent.), and Manumission (10 Pfund a head); their landright (Landrecht) forfeited, and not allowed to return and resettle except by special permission. Mar. 8, 1749.

pp. 172-380 (26 references). " Emigrierende Unterthanen."
A large number of additional applications. Mar. 12, 1749.
Ruling of March 8 upheld. Persons with children not permitted to leave. Government feels responsible for safety of children; fear expressed, that if children were left behind by their parents, they would go to the bad, and become objects of charity. (Mortality of children on sea-voyage also probable consideration.) Reward set for discovery of emigrant agents at work among the people, " Werber ".
A large number of additional cases. Mar. 15, 1749.
March 8, 12, 15, 1749, total number applying for permission to emigrate: 85 men, 73 women, 224 children (382 persons).
Joner, suspected of being a " Werber ", notified to leave the country within twice 24 hours. All " Werber " to be taken into custody.
More petitions for permission to emigrate. Mar. 19, 1749.
Permission granted to several couples without children. Mar. 22, 1749.
More petitions granted to couples without children. Mar. 26, 1749.
Permission granted to several couples with children. Mar. 29, 1749.
Announcement made that no more would be granted.
A few more petitions granted. Apr. 2, 1749.
" Emigranten in dem Land zufallende Erbschaften." Bedenken, 4 pp. Apr. 12, 1749.
" Manumissions-Gebühren betr." Not taxed, if not possessed of property.
" Landesflüchtige Emigranten." Three cases of emigration without permission, two men with wives and children, one without wife. May 14, 1749.
Beschluss: " Sollen die Hrn. Ober Beamten genau vigiliren, dass dergleichen clandestine Emigrationen künftigs nicht mehr beschehen, die also weggezogene Emigranten aber wenn sie wieder ins Land kommen beygefängt werden."
" Bernische Angehörige nach Pensylvanien zu reisen verführet." May 14, 1749.
" Leonhard Bientzen Sohn soll verleitet worden sein, zu emigriren. Soll in Basel verhört werden." May 14, 1749.
" Verhör des Rudolf Bientz." (Father caught him at Strassburg and brought him back.) May 21, 1749.
" Verhör giebt nicht viel an Tag." Beschluss: " Bleibt dabei." May 24, 1749.
" Projekt des Mandats." August 13, 1749.

pp. 308, 331, 332, 333. " Erbschaften die Emigranten betreffend."
" Alle welche vor dem 22. Mertz 1849 [see Mandat below] aus dem Land in Americam gezogen auf keine Weiss etwas erblich beziehen dürfen, sondern als tod angesehen werden." Aug. 13, 1749. (Their inheritance to go to nearest relatives, or if none, then into " Armen-Seckel ".)

Vol. 123. 1749-1750.

p. 185. Jacob Joner Verhör (suspected of being a "Werber"). Feb. 25, 1750.
pp. 190-361. (15 references.) "Emigrationes."
"Emigration in Neu Schottland, Carolinam u. Pensylvaniam." Mar. 4, 1750.
"Jacob Joner betr." Mar. 7, 14, 1750.
After his business completed (collecting inherited money for a friend), banished from land ("zum Land hinaus geführt").
"Jacob Joner Vollmacht in Erbschaft." Mar. 21, 1750.
Case of protection of children of emigrant. May 6, 1750.
"Emigranten ohne obrigkeitliche Erlaubnusz." May 9, 1750.
Petitions for emigration. June 30, 1750.

Vol. 124. 1750-1751.

p. 174. Johannes Tschudi, returned from America, suspected of "werben". To be taken into custody, if possible to catch him. Mar. 6, 1751.
p. 181. Reward of 4 Neue Thaler offered to anyone who captures Joner ("Werber"). Mar. 10, 1751.
p. 214. "Heimlicher Emigrant, Konrad Weyser, mit Weib und Kind, und 1000£ bar Geld" (Gut vergantet). Apr. 7, 1751.
p. 216. Applications for permission to emigrate. Apr. 7, 1751.
Policy of "Mandat" (1749) to be adhered to.
p. 227. Increased emigration. Large number of applications. Complaint made against "Frondienst". Examination of emigrants recommended, and strict carrying out of the policy of the "Mandat" of 1749. Apr. 21, 1751.
p. 246. Inquiry about Weysz. Friends and neighbors assert they did not know that he was going to emigrate. May 1, 1751.
"Jacob Schaub, ein liederlicher Mensch, erlaubt nach Pennsylvanien zu ziehen." May 22, 1751.
p. 363. "Emigrirensverdächtige." July 28, 1751.

Vol. 125. 1751-1752.

p. 65. "Pensylvanische Reformirte Gemeinde: Memoriale d. Süd Holländischen Synodi an sämtl. evangel. Cantonen gerichtet, Beistand für reform. Gemeinde in Pensilvanien; Pfarrer Schlatter von St. Gallen berichtet 40 Gemeinden Pfarrer und Lehrer nötig."

Vol. 140. 1767.

pp. 139-382. "Emigrationsgeschäfte." 18 references.
pp. 139, 145, 164. "Martin Schäublins Wegziehen." Verhöre, etc. Apr. 8, 1767.
pp. 211, 213. Petitions for emigration. May 27, 1767.
pp. 232, 233. Some petitions granted. June 10, 1767.
"Zwei heimliche Emigranten." June 11, 1767.
pp. 280, 283. "Heimliche Emigranten." Additional cases. July 15, 1767.

Vol. 142. 1769.

pp. 141, 200. " Emigrationes nacher Spanien."

Vol. 143. 1770.

pp. 154, 159. " Heimliche Emigrationes." " Fabrique-arbeiter debauchieren." June 2, 1770.

Vol. 144. 1771.

pp. 31-414. " Emigrationes." 38 references.
pp. 159, 414. " Emigranten, wegen Veräusserung ihrer Güter."
pp. 191, 193. " Ganten und Käufe."
pp. 195, 218, 224. " Wegen heimlichen Wegziehens."
p. 202. " Minderjährige Emigranten."
p. 220. " Armer Emigranten Manumissions-Gebühren."
p. 31. " Bedenken der Landcommission über die Auswanderungen." Jan. 26, 1771.
p. 104. " Mandat." Mar. 25, 1771.
p. 118. Petitions of emigrants, destination Virginia (Junt, Rieger), with wives and children. Permitted. Apr. 10, 1771.
A large number of additional petitions, destinations mostly Pennsylvania.

Vol. 145. 1772.

pp. 2-124. " Emigrationes." (22 references.)
pp. 73, 145. " Emigranten, ob nicht Einhalt zu thun."
p. 147. " Emigranten, so wieder zurück kommen."
p. 282. " Emigrant, um Begnadigung."

Vol. 146. 1773.

pp. 82, 86, 94, 102, 121. Petitions of emigrants.

Vol. 159. 1786.

p. 70. " Emigranten und Emisarii. Mandate sollen wieder verlesen werden." Mar. 1, 1786.
p. 373. " Heimlicher Emigranten Erbrecht." Sept. 2, 1786.

Vol. 160. 1787.

p. 206. " Verdächtige Emigranten."

Vol. 161. 1788.

p. 246. " Emigrant zurückgekommen " (nur bis Holland gekommen). Begnadigt.

Vol. 162. 1789.

p. 88. Petitions for emigration. Mar. 24, 1789.

Vol. 165. 1792.

A few cases of emigrants.

Vol. 185. 1816.

pp. 7-372. 16 references to immigration to United States. This was a period of famine (Das Hungerjahr, as Wackernagel calls it). A very large number of people from the canton Basel immigrated to the United States.
Letters: " Briefe von Verwandten in Amerika ". Jan. 31, 1816. Letters of Dürring, Vogt, Hofmann, Breitenstein, etc.

Vol. 186. 1817.

pp. 72-286. Some 30 references to emigration. Large emigration to the United States. Measures taken to prevent paupers from gathering at shipping ports.

Vol. 187. 1818.

A few cases of emigration.

Vol. 199. 1830.

Two cases of emigration.

Vol. 200. 1831.

Nineteen cases of emigration.

Vol. 201. 1832.

Thirty-five cases of emigration. Names recorded.

Vol. 202. 1833.

Three cases of emigration.

Vol. 214. 1845.

Two cases of emigration.

Vol. 215. 1846.

Proposals of Graubünden concerning emigration.

Vol. 216. 1847.

" Auswanderung aus Glarus nach Amerika."

Vol. 217. 1848.

pp. 173, 194, 217, 339, 403. " Auswanderer nach Amerika. Warnung und Anweisungen."

p. 405. " Andr. Suter in der Strafanstalt. Er habe in Californien einen Oheim, der ihm wohl behülflich sein werde."
Stadtrath gives him 80 fr., making 800 fr. in his possession. Permission to emigrate granted.

Vol. 218. 1849.

A number of " Unterstützungsgesuche um nach Amerika auszuwandern."

Staatsarchiv

DREIZEHNER RATHS PROTOKOLL (AUSSCHUSS DES KL. RATHS). C 1.
Vol. 3. 1735-1758.

"Weilen so viel Landsleut in Carolinam gereiset, auch dem Verlaut nach einige MGnHrn Underthanen die Begierd hegen, solche reisz vorzunemen, als ward, wie solche liederliche Sehnsucht zu hemmen die Berahtschlagung vorgenommen, darbey reflectieret, dasz diese leut sich in das gröste Elend werfen:"
Beschluss: "Sollte zu Stadt und Land zu hinderung dieser Reisen die erforderliche befehl publicieret und morgen meinen Gn. Hrn. vorgelegt werden." Jan. 4, 1735.
"Soll ein Mandat, diese leut abzuhalten, concipieret und nächsten Rahtstag MnGnHrn vorgelegt werden." Apr. 14, 1735.
"Weilen sich noch immer viele underthanen anmelden, die aus dem Land ziehen und in Carolinam reisen wollen, die Herren Deputierte zu denen Landsachen auch denenselben, um sie abzuhalten, all mögliches vorgestellet, und dennoch nichts ausrichten können, indessen jenige, welche diesen Entschluss gefasset, und sich solches in den Kopf gesetzet, nichts mehr arbeiten, sondern nur herumziehen, darbey verlautet, dass sie ob verschiedenen Beschwärden, Frohnen, Zinsen, Strafen etc. klagen, als ward, was vorzunemmen, deliberieret:"
Beschluss: "Sollte MGnHrn angerahten werden, dass man jenige, die sich diesmalen angemeldet und auf 120 Seelen belaufen, gegen Abstattung der Gebühr, könne laufen, doch keine weitere, bis man von diesen werde bericht haben, gehen lassen." Mar. 3, 1740.

MANDATE.

EMIGRATIONEN, AUSWANDERUNGEN DER UNTERTHANEN.

1649, June 2. "Emigriren verboten." (After Thirty Years' War.) V. n. 39.
1735, Jan. 29. "Züricherisches Auswanderungsverbot."
1735, Apr. 20. "Emigrations Mandat" (vs. Carolina). IV. n. 129.
1738, Apr. 2. "Emigrations Verbott, samt Brief aus Carolina." I, VII, § 2 n. 4.
1749, Aug. 13. "Erbschaften der Wegziehenden" (since Mar. 22, 1749, no inheritance could be collected by emigrant). V. n. 67.
1771, Mar. 25. "Emigrations Mandat" (repetition of above). V. n. 138.
1773, Jan. 30. "Anhang zum Emigrations Mandat." V. n. 159.
(Particularly severe against agents, "Werber", here also called "Neuländer", who pretended to collect inheritance for friends in America.)

NORD-AMERIKA.

ALLGEMEINES UND EINZELNES. 1844-1885.

A 1. Meist Kreisschreiben von den Vororten, dann von Bern.
Auslieferungen, 3B. Millionen-Dieb: Gerh. Koster. 1844.
Acta über die Auslieferung des Amerikaners J. M. Shrok und für dessen Anhaltung ausgesetzte Prämie. 1855-1856.
Kreisschreiben meistens Auslieferungen von Betrügern betr. 1855-1885.
A 2. Auslieferungsvertrag der Schweiz mit Nordamerika. 1845-1846.
Kreisschreiben von Bern.

A 3. Freizügigkeitsvertrag der Schweiz mit Nordamerika. 1834-1848. Kreisschreiben.
A 4. Freundschafts-, Niederlassungs-, Handels-, und Auslieferungsvertrag der Schweiz mit Nordamerika. 1855.
B 1. Schweizer in Nordamerika. 1753-1886.
  1753, 1772. Vermögenssachen betr.
  1774. Hinterlassenschaft von Adam Fluebacher in Pennsylvanien.
  1797, Feb. 21. Brief (Copia) des Hrn. Pfarrer Hantz über Vermögen (700 Pf.) des verstorbenen Meyer.
  1807. Die vermeintliche Erbschaft eines gewissen Hrn. Peter aus Amerika.
  1816. Erbschaft Häfelfinger mit Einlage eines Briefes von Verena Plattner aus Baltimore, geschrieben d. 16. Juni, 1815.
  1824, 1838, 1839, 1841, 1846-1886. Acta betr. Hinterlassenschaften, Auskünfte, Berichte, Nachforschungen, Todesscheine etc.
B 2. Schweizer in Nordamerikanischen Diensten. 1865-1878. Erkundigungen, Nachforschungen wegen Schweizer im Bürgerkrieg.
C 1. Nordamerikanische Konsulate in der Schweiz. 1830-1855.
C 2. Nordamerikan. Konsulat in Basel. 1830-1883.
C 3. *Id.* Zürich. 1843-1844.
C 4. Schweizerische Konsulate in Nordamerika. 1823-1841.
C 5. Schweiz. Konsulat in Charleston. 1854.
C 6. *Id.* Chicago. 1859-1880.
C 7. *Id.* Cincinnati. 1864-1866.
C 8. *Id.* San Francisco. 1858-1867.
C 9. *Id.* Highland. 1856-1859.
C 10. *Id.* St. Louis. 1867.
C 11. *Id.* Madison. 1845-1853.
C 12. *Id.* New York. 1842-1867.
C 13. *Id.* New Orleans. 1837-1870.
C 14. *Id.* Philadelphia. 1841-1857.
C 15. *Id.* Texas. 1846.
C 16. *Id.* Washington. 1864.
C 17. Schweiz. Gesandtschaft in Nordamerika. 1882.

AUSWANDERUNG A. ALLGEMEINES UND EINZELNES.

1732-1738.

"Acta wegen Emigration einiger Baslerischer Underthanen in Americam so die Memorialen, Bedenken, Verordnungen, Schreiben und Specificationen der Weggereisten enthalten. Vom 16. April 1732, bisz 29. Mertz 1738."

Large bound volume of manuscript acta, including answers to request sent to various parts of the canton for information concerning the reasons for emigration to Carolina and Pennsylvania. One examination, dated Mar. 6, 1738, proved, that of 17 persons questioned, 6 emigrated because of poverty, 6 of inability to find work, 3 in hope of finding good land, 2 without assigned reasons. Several discussions of question of emigration. Many lists of persons desiring to emigrate to Carolina. Accounts of property. Deductions: for manumission 5-8 per cent.; tax for emigration 10 per cent. Certificates of character by preachers.

1738. " Waldenburg sagt, die Unterthanen arbeithen nicht gern, seyen zu viel dem Wein ergeben, und funden Arbeit genug wenn sie wollten, könten nunmehro zum Weg bey Höllstein gebracht werden."
1738. " Homburg vermeint die Bauern ziehen meistentheils aus Bosheit aus dem Land und vermeint wenn sie arbeiten wollten, so könnten sie sich durchbringen."
1738, Mar. 25. " Bedenken des Herrn Deputirten wegen denen Emigranten." (10 pp.)
  Advice: The very poor have reason to go, the well-to-do should not go, in consideration of the danger.
  Two other " Bedenken." (7 pp.)

1740-1748.

1740, Feb. 27. " Information wegen einem aus Carolina geschriebenen und in dem Land ausgebreiteten Brief."
  Feb. 20. " Relation der Herren Deputaten wegen vorhabender Emigration (nach Carolina) einiger Unterthanen von Muttents." Long lists of emigrants' names.
  Mar. 19. " Einige von Muttents, so ihre Resolution (nach Carolina) zu emigriren geenderet."
  Apr. 20. " Status über die Habschaft einiger Emigranten."
  May 11. " Relation der Herren Deputaten in Landts Sachen, wegen Daniel Meyer, welcher aus Amerika alhero gekommen, und denen von Ihme und Springen mit sich alhero gebrachten Brief."
  Enclosure: letter, Dec. 3, 1737.
  Apr. 23. " Bericht über den Zustand der Länder Carolina, Pennsylvanien, und dgl.
  Apr. 4. " Hans Spring[en] von Reutingen, Berner-Gebieths, wegen Werbung in Carolina."
  Apr. 2. Id.
  Apr. 30. " Letztes Verhör von Spring[en]." Skilful answers by Spring.
  May 14. " Verrichtung der Herren Sieben (HHR VII) bey Mattis Singeisen von Liechstal, welcher ausz seinem Accord [contract of service] und in Pennsylvaniam ziehen wollen." The HHR. is a " Gerichtsbehörde ", a police-court.
1741, Apr. 8. " Bedenken der Deputaten in Landts Sachen, wegen Barbara Boerlis Mittel, so nunmehr in Pensylvania."
  May-June. " Bedenken d. D. in L. S. wegen einiger nach Pensylvania ziehen wollenden Unterthanen."
1742. " Acta betr. Peter Huber von Oberhaszli, Bern, so die Leuth in Carolinam zu reisen verleitet."
  Gefangennahme. Verhör Hubers und der Berner Emigranten. (This is a most fascinating series of documents.)
1746. " Bericht der Herren Deput. zu den Fabriques wegen Jacob Dürrenberger von Lupsingen." Acta, 7 Stücke; including Verhör, and a French passport.
1747, Dec. 20. " Schreiben von Amsterdam wegen Kolonisten zu Surinam " (Dutch Guiana, South America).
1748, Jan. 28. A list of about 100 persons willing to go.
  A large number of acta on Surinam emigration, written in Dutch, French, and German.

1749.

A large fascicle, containing important and very interesting materials, which may be grouped under the following heads:
(1) Petitions of large numbers of subjects (of Basel) for permission to emigrate. Reasons stated for their desire to leave. (Poverty, lack of work, letters from relatives and friends, hope of bettering their condition.)
(2) Certificates of character, and written testimonials by ministers of the respective parishes, on the religious and moral standing of petitioners.
(3) Lists of names of petitioners, and number in family of each, with age of each member.
(4) Statements of the means of those permitted to emigrate, with deductions made by government. For "manumission", *i. e.*, release from serfdom (when still in bondage), eight per cent. of total amount of property. For "Abzugsgebühren", deduction for privilege of leaving the country with property, ten per cent. of total valuation. Thus, many emigrants were taxed 18 per cent. of their property, before receiving permission to leave.
(5) "Verhöre der Behörden, der Deputaten, der VII", etc. Examinations of emigrants before various courts. Reports of questions and answers.
(6) "Bedenken der Behörden." Reports on conditions. Pros and contras concerning emigration. Before 1749 the destination was mostly Carolina, especially in the thirties; in 1749 Pennsylvania received the larger number of emigrants from this section of Switzerland.
(7) Emigrants returning and claiming property. Arrested and examined before court. Emigrants not returning, but claiming property, usually by proxy.
(8) "Emigranten-Manumissions-Gebühren betreffend."

1750-1770.

1750, Feb. 25. "Jacob Joner aus Pensylvanien, und dessen Stifbruder Johannes Schwab betr." (Very interesting "Verhör" before the HHR. VII.) Vollmacht zur Einziehung einer Erbschaft.

Feb. 28. "Riggenbagherische Geschwisterte in Pensylvanien, um Beziehung eines Erbs."

Acta. Emigranten aus Surinam, etc.

Dec. 19. "Bedenken lobl. Waisenamts wegen Heini Wagners Verlassenschaft, dessen Tochter in Americam gezogen."

1751, May 10. "Besprechung MGH. VII wegen aus Pensylvanien zurückgekom. Johannes Tschudi und übrigen Personen" (Verwandten). "Tschudi nicht mehr vorhanden." Is quoted as having said: "Wer aber nicht wolle arbeiten, der solle nur zu Hause bleiben, und wer gern Wein trinken wolle, solle auch nicht hierin gehen, denn sie haben nichts anders als Klein-Bier und Aepfelwein."

May 26. Briefe aus Pensylvanien.

1750-1770. Verhöre von Wegziehenden, Erbschaften, zurückgelassene Briefe von Emigranten an Freunde Abschied nehmend, Meldungen über Ausgewanderte ohne Abschied, Gesuche zur Auswanderung, Abhörung von Eingefangenen oder abgehaltenen Emigranten. Heimliches Wegziehen.

1765. Werbungen in russische Colonien Gedruckte Formulare der Engagements.
1767, Apr. 6. Johannes Tschudi. He emigrated with his wife in 1749, reappeared in 1751 in company with " dem berüchtigten James Joner von Brattelen "; has after many years' absence appeared again, and is reported to be spending many English guineas luring people for the purpose of emigration.
" Verhör von J. J. Tschudi." A large number of acta on Tschudi (" er ist von der väterlichen Erbschaft ausgeschlossen "). Several others of the same family name: Nicolaus und Martin Tschudi. Johannes Tschudi is called a " Neuländer "; attempts to catch him. Jacob Würths Verhör.
Apr. 14. " Gutachten des Hochw. Kirchenrathes wegen Wegziehung nach Neu-Wied (Herrnhuter, Niederrhein) und Versendung der jungen Leute dahin zur Erziehung."
1767-1769. Acta betr. spanische Colonien. (In Spanien.)
1768. " Der Emigration verdächtige Personen " (large number of acta), " mit einem Brief aus Amerika ".
1769. Verhöre, etc.
1770. Züricher Verbot gegen Emigration nach Preussisch Pommern. (Printed.)

1771-1798.

1771. " Bedenken und Verbot wegen Auswanderungen." Also one in 1772. Emigration und Werber. Mit Brief aus Lebanon, 1769. Viele Acten.
Bittschriften um Entlassung von Leibeigenschaft, und zur Auswanderung.
" Memoriale der Canzley wegen unvermöglichen Unterthanen."
" Heimliche Emigranten." Large number of acta, proving that emigration without permission or passes was very frequent.
" Einige Emigranten." Numerous acta.
1771-1772. Auswanderungsgesuche. Very many cases, mostly of very poor people. Accompanying certificates of character by minister. A large number ask for release from Leibeigenschaft.[1]
1772. " Bewilligungen für Auswanderer." About 60 heads of families, 285 persons.
" Freylassung und Abzug der ausgewanderten Unterthanen im Jahr 1772." Total taken from them 2595 Pf. 3 Sch. 4 R.[2]
1784-1787. Renewed petitions for permission to immigrate to America.
1786, Nov. 22. " Emigranten um Auslieferung von Mitteln, nach Amerika."
1791, Feb. 26. *Id.*
1794, June 18. *Id.*
1798. " Gesetz die Auswanderung verbietend." " Im Namen der helvetischen einen und untheilbaren Republik." This decree was made largely to prevent emigration of able-bodied men, who were needed in defense of the country. Penalty: " 10 Jahre in Ketten, Verlust der Bürgerrechte."

---

[1] Leibeigenschaft continued until 1790. *Cf.* P. Ochs, *Geschichte der Stadt und Landschaft Basel* (Basel, 1832), VIII. 110, note: " Die Freylassungs- oder Manumissions-Gebühren waren von 10 Pfund, ausser den Kanzlei-Sporteln für den Manumissionsbrief selber."
[2] See p. 104, note 1, *ante.*

114   Basel-Stadt

1801-1808.

1803, Jan. 15. " Wegen d. Abzug v. Erbschaften an nach Amerika ausgewanderte hiesige Landbürger."
"Verzeichnis derjenigen Personen, grössentheils aus d. Canton Basel, welchen im Januar u. Hornung d. Jahres 1803 auf dem Bureau d. Unter-Statthalters d. Cantons Basel Pässe nach Amerika ertheilt worden sind." Total 278 persons; 84 heads of families.
"Verzeichnis über diejenigen Personen welche aus d. Gemeinden des Distrikts Gelterkinden (Baselland) unterm 3ten März 1803 nach Nordamerika ausgewandert sind." Personen ausgewandert, 84; Personen die sich noch dazu vorbereiten, 77; total (Pässe erhalten), 161.
Causes assigned for emigration, on being questioned:
 (1) Verdienstlosigkeit.
 (2) Unerträgliche Abgaben, und andere Lasten.
 (3) Hoffnung Glück zu finden, wo Bekannte sich niedergelassen haben. Günstige Berichte von solchen.
 (4) Aussichtslosigkeit im Vaterland.
 (5) Stehen dem Bettel bevor.
Mar. 4. District Waldenburg, in answer to inquiry, reports that 26 persons emigrated for North America, and 9 more are desirous of going. Reasons for emigration stated to be impoverishment, the result of the foraging of French troops since the Revolution. The latter left in their hands " nur lehre [leere] Bongs " (a Bon is a receipt for goods or supplies furnished to the soldiers and a promise to repay), which were never redeemed by the French government. As a result the people got deeper and deeper into debt.
Mar. 5. Eight more persons destined for North America.
Auswanderer aus dem Distrikt Liestal....44 Personen.
Auswanderer willens im Monat Mai zu ziehen....27 Personen.
1804. Acta betr. Auswanderer nach Nordamerika. Schuldverzeichnisse; Zeugnisse; Bescheinigung des Verzichts auf das Bürgerrecht; Auskündigung der Auswanderer (dass Gläubiger sich melden) auf vier Wochen; gewöhnlich freiwillige Auskündigung.
Auskündigungs-Protokolle. Extractus. Nos. 437-459, etc.

1816-1817.

1816, Jan. Inquiry of Bürgermeister u. Rath d. Cantons Basel an Statthalter d. Untern Raths, as to causes of renewed emigration to the United States.
Jan. 24. " Schreiben von Sissach wegen Emigration."
" Ankunft eines Haufens Briefe aus Nordamerika, günstig lautend ", etc.
Feb. 7. " Gutachten löbl. Justiz und Polizey Colleg. über Auswanderung nach Amerika."
" Zwei Briefe aus Amerika ", eingefangen d. 29. Januar, 1816. Beide: Jakob Schweitzer aus Frankendorf. Philadelphia d. 29. Juni, 1809; und 16. Mai, 1815.
Mar. and Apr. Acta wegen Auswanderung.

Apr. 18. Luzern speaks of " Aufmunterung zur Auswanderung nach Nordamerika und Werbungen zu dem Ende vom Canton Basel ". (Stadtrath der Stadt u. Republik Luzern an Bürgermeister u. Rath d. Standes Basel.)
" Verzeichnis derjenigen Angehörigen des Bezirks Waldenburg welche nach Amerika ausgewandert. 1816." 19 Personen.
" Schriften von H. Halter und General Consul de Planta, etc., wegen Verdächtigungen hinsichtlich d. Transports der Auswanderer nach Amerika."
Überfahrtskosten Verzeichnis. (Printed.)
1817, Jan. 19. Permission to emigrate given to a family, " denn sie sind in keinem guten Ruf ". (Shipment of paupers and undesirables brings about a complaint from the ports.)
" Auswanderung von Bevogteten." (Minors, boys and unmarried girls, and widows. A " Vogt " appointed as protector.)
Jan. 21. Complaint from Amsterdam, including letter of Consul General de Planta, Jan. 11, 1817, on the condition of large numbers of indigent Swiss emigrants in Amsterdam who expect to be transported to America.
Jan. 29. " Wegen Auswanderung nach Russland."
" Gutachten löbl. Justiz u. Polizey College über Auswanderung von Minderjährigen."
Feb. 15. " Verordnung in Betreff der Auswanderung." (No passes to paupers.)
Feb. 18. " Verlockungen von Werbern zum Auswandern."
Large number of acta, granting permission to individuals to emigrate; their names and conditions, with " Gutachten "."
" Verordnungen über das Auswandern nach Amerika. Vom. 14. Sept., 1816; 15. Feb., 1. Mai, 16. Mai, 7. Juni, 1817."
Feb. 28. Ship contract, including rate and daily menu.
Cases of emigrants returned from Holland, who had not the means for passage across.
Lists of emigrants. " Verzeichnis der Angehörigen des untern Bezirks, welche Anno 1817 ausgewandert sind." 31 cases.

1819-1847.

1819. Kreisschreiben, Luzern. " Vorschriften für Auswanderer durch die preussischen Rheinprovinzen, d. 22. Mai, 1819." (Against paupers.)
Kreisschreiben, Luzern. *Id.* durch Holland.
Acta concerning individuals or groups of individuals emigrating to United States, 1819, 1822, 1825, 1832, 1833, 1834, 1837, 1838, 1845, 1846.
1820. " Acta und Druckschriften die Kolonie des Rothen Flusses in Nordamerika betreffend." Pamphlet: Capt. Rudolf von May, *Kurze und wahre Uebersicht* (Bern, 1820). Verhör eines Werbers in Basel (claimed that he received 6 francs a head). Letter from London in answer to inquiry concerning the Hudson Bay Colony.
1828. " Holländische Verordnung wegen Auswanderung."
1829. " Auswanderung nach Buenos Ayres."
1831. " Vorschriften der Auswanderung durch Frankreich."

1832, May 24. Report that many Swiss, Baden, and Württemberg emigrants are lying at port of Havre, and that cholera morbus has broken out among them.
May 27. Kreisschreiben from Luzern, concerning emigrants in France.
1833. Kreisschreiben von Zürich. "Visirung der Pässe."
"Vermögensauslieferung. Verfügen für Auswanderer nach Amerika."
1837, Nov. 11. "Abmahnung vor Auswanderung nach Neu-Orleans."
1843. Kreisschreiben von Luzern. Auswanderung nach Algier.
1844, Feb. 17. "Erleichterung für Auswanderer nach Amerika."
1845, Aug. 10. "Christ. Schauenburg, Schuhmacher von Wolfenbüttel, bittet um Unterstützung zur Auswanderung nach Amerika, verlobt mit Wittwe Mohl, Basel."
Aug. 22. "Christoph Lehmann, Zimmergeselle, bittet um Mittel z. Auswanderung."
1846. "Vorschriften für Auswanderer nach Amerika." Kreisschreiben Zürich.
Apr. 8. "Unterstützungsgesuch zur Auswanderung."
May 2. "Unterstützungsgesuch zur Auswanderung nach Texas." Another, May 27.
May 6. "Vorschläge des Consuls in Havre zum Schutz d. Auswanderer." Kreisschreiben Zürich. Also May 28.
"Gesammelte Notitzen in betreff d. Auswanderungen."
"Protokoll einer am 8ten Herbstmonate 1846 zwischen den Abgeordneten der Kantone Zürich, Bern, Glarus, Basel Stadttheil, Schaffhausen, Appenzell AR., Graubünden, Aargau, Thurgau, Tessin, Waadt, und Neuenburg abgehaltenen Konferenz, betreffend die Auswanderung aus der Schweiz." (Policy: Neither to encourage nor to discourage emigration; no subsidies to be granted by state for paying expenses of emigrants; limited support might be extended by "Gemeinden"; concentration in colonies not good for Swiss.)
Nov. 9. Kreisschreiben Zürich. Meeting on question of emigration.
1847, Jan. 16. "Unterstützungsgesuch zur Auswanderung nach Nordamerika." Joh. Schultz. Thirteen other similar cases, extending to December.
Apr. 21. Kreisschreiben Bern. Report on recommendation of Graubünden. "Wertvolle Aufschlüsse von Consulaten."
May 8. Über Auswanderung.
Sept. 24. "Gesuch des Speditors K. Fischer in Basel v. 18 d. M. um Erlaubnis zur Vermittlung des Transports von Auswanderern betreffend."

1848-1853.

1848. "Bittschriften um Unterstützung zur Auswanderung nach Amerika." 15 cases. Letter from St. Louis, Mar. 15, 1848.
Jan. 28. "Beiträge zur Auswanderung in der Stadt Aarau." Answer to inquiry was, that they handled cases as individuals (not by any law or rule). Similar answer from Glarus. Conditions in Basel.
"Kreisschreiben von Bern über Auswanderungsverhältnisse." Schaffhausen recommends united action, a uniform policy.

Oct. 18. " Übersiedlung des wegen Diebstahls in der Strafanstalt befindlichen Martin Schaffner." Basel gives 60 fr., *i. e.,* half of sum requested.
Dec. 27. Another case. (Suter.) Out of Strafanstalt.
4 Kreisschreiben.
1849-1852. Unterstützungsgesuche. 38 cases of persons of good character.
1849, Mar. 21. Case of woman of criminal class, plea for support for transportation to America, on ground of being undesirable and little hope of improvement.
Similar plea for a family of undesirables.
1850, Feb. 20. " An Bürgermeister und Rath d. Kantons Basel-Stadt vom Departement des Innern wegen Unterstützung von Auswanderern." 5000 francs voted by the Swiss " Bund "; of this 2720 fr. paid in support of agency in Havre, 1000 fr. to the " Schweizerische Hilfsgesellschaft in New York ", 1280 for Basel and New Orleans.
Numerous papers relating to the beginnings of the emigration agencies.
Apr. 5. " Brief an Gebrüder Iselin, Basel, Beschreibung der ' Accomodations ' auf den transatlantischen Schiffen von Havre aus."
1852, Feb. 13. " Schreiben des Agenten V. Klenk wegen Fortschaffung von Flüchtlingen."
Acta concerning individual cases of emigrants (4).
" Die Auswanderer Familie Friedrich Vogt von Riehen." Subscriptionsliste [545 fr., 37 names of contributors] zu ihrem Transport. Auswanderungsbureau Beck u. Herzog, Basel."
" Acta betr. Auswanderungsagenturen. Gutachten. Beschwerden, etc. Gesetze."
" Acta betr. Besprechung der Vorschläge des Kantons Aargau wegen Auswanderungsbehörde. Entwurf eines Gesetzes."
1853, Mar. 30. " Missbrauch beim Abschluss von Auswanderungsaccorden."
Apr. 20. " Gegen das Auswanderungsbureau Beck u. Herzog in Basel."

1854-1863.

1854. " Gesuche zur Unterstützung zur Auswanderung nach Amerika." 32 cases.
1854-1855, 1857-1859. Kreisschreiben betr. Auswanderung. Anfragen, Gutachten, Agenturen betr., Aargau betr., etc.
1855. Acta über Auswanderung, Agenturen, Gesetze, etc.
Missbräuche: Anhäufung der Auswanderer in den Hafenstädten Amerikas. Beschwerde der Vereinigten Staaten über Sträflinge u. mittellose Personen. Kreisschreiben d. 19. Februar. Ermahnungen.
1855-1863. Auswanderungs-Agenturen.
1856. Auswanderungsunterstützungsgesuche; 7 cases. In 1858, 3 cases.
1857. " Zweite Warnung der amerikanischen Gesandtschaft an Auswanderer."
1857-1858. " Das Justizkollegium des Kantons Basel-Stadt in Sachen der Agenturen."
1858, June 11. " Joh. Dettwyler aus der Sträflingsanstalt, Gestattung zur Auswanderung nach Amerika, anstatt Versorgung nach Kalchrain (Thurgau)."

1860. "Beschwerden von Auswanderern nach Buenos Ayres gegen das Haus Beck u. Herzog und Barbe."
1861. "Beschwerden gegen Auswanderungsagenturen."
1862. "Fahrten Billets nach dem Innern von Amerika."

1864-1869.

1864. Acta. "Unterstützungsgesuche zur Auswanderung nach Amerika."
1864-1869. Auswanderungsagenturen: Zwilchenbart, Rommel, etc.
1864-1865. Polizeidirektion. Auswanderungswesen. Agenturen, etc.
1865. "Auswanderungsschiff *William Nelson* verbrannt." Liste der umgekommenen Schweizer.
1866. "Auswanderer-Reisekosten nach Buenos Ayres."
"Cholera auf den Dampfern *England, Virginia,* und *Helvetia.*"
1867. "Kreisschreiben über Auswanderungswesen", e. g., Sträflinge nach Amerika.
June 12. Rathsschreiben No. 201 (1867).
1869. "Deutsche Gesellschaft von New York bietet ihre Dienste auch Schweizern an." Verlesen d. 20. Januar, 1869.

1870-1880.

1870-1880. Auswanderungsagenturen. Anzeige der Namen; der Zeit d. Abreise. Printed material used by agencies: Zwilchenbart, Rommel, Baumgartner, Schmid, Werdenberg, Schneebeli, Brown and Co., etc. Klagen über Auswanderungsagenturen. *Auskunft für beabsichtigende Auswanderer; auf Befehl d. Canadischen Regierung herausgegeben* (printed pamphlet, without date). *Bericht und Anleitung betr. die verschiedenen Reiserouten der Auswanderer nach allen Landungsplätzen* (pamphlet, Basel, Zwilchenbart, 1864).
1870-1880. Polizei-Direktion. Auswanderungsacten. Agenturen, Anzeigen.
1873. Kreisschreiben, etc. Warnung gegen Auswanderung nach Bahia.
1870-1880. Kreisschreiben über Auswanderungswesen. Agenturen, Gesetze. Entwurf eines Bundesgesetzes betr. Auswanderungsagenturen (1875). Auswanderung von Krüppeln und Arbeitsunfähiger.
1879. "Auswanderung nach Uruguay."

1881-1884.

1881-1884. Polizeidepartement des Kantons Basel-Stadt. Acten: Auswanderungswesen, Anzeigen, Agenturen, Übertretungen der Gesetze, Klagen, etc.
1881, Apr. 5. "Amerikanisches Konsulat contra Verbringung von Dirnen nach Amerika." (Gemeinde Böttstein, Kanton Aargau, auf ihre Kosten 2 Dirnen nach Amerika spedirt.)
1881-1884. Kreisschreiben. Agenturen. Gesetze. Übertretungen d. Gesetze. Klagen des Bundesrates gegen Agenturen, 1882.
1882. Polizeidepartement Basel-Stadt. Objection to K. K. Kennan's methods of advertising emigration to Wisconsin. Acta: Question whether a violation of law against advertising emigration schemes. The following clipping illustrating K.'s method is taken from *Der Volksfreund aus Schwaben* (Tübingen, Feb. 13, 1883):

"Auswanderer! Die *fünfte gemeinschaftliche* Reise nach dem Staate Wiskonsin (Nordamerika), findet von Bremen aus, am 4. April, mit dem neuen Expressdampfer *Elbe* statt. Überfahrt von Bremen nach New York nur neun Tage. Auskunft betreffs Reisekosten ertheilt die *Direktion des Norddeutschen Lloyd in Bremen.* Werthvolle Karten und Broschüren über Wiskonsin sendet auf Verlangen gratis und portofrei der Commissär der Einwanderungsbehörde genannten Staates: K. K. Kennan in Basel, Schweiz."

1881-1884. Handels- und Landwirthschaftsdepartement. Verzeichnis der Agenten und Unteragenten, vom Bundesrat genehmigte Agenturen. Auswanderungsursachen.

1885-1896.

Kreisschreiben vom Bundesrat über Auswanderungssachen. Agenturen, Gesetze, Übertretungen der Gesetze, Strafen. II. Abth. Auswanderer. Auswanderungswesen.

Handels- und Landwirtschaftsdepartement, über Agenturen, Beschwerden, etc.

Polizeidepartement d. Kantons Basel-Stadt. Berichte, Agenturen, Übertretungen der Gesetze. Report of Mar. 22, 1889.

Schweizerisches Departement des Auswärtigen. Abtheilung: Auswanderungswesen. Übertretungen der Gesetze. Verzeichnis der Agenten. Large number of acta. Last accessible ones, of 1896.

Auswanderung B.

Auswanderungsstatistik, 1817-1885.

" Nach Amerika ausgewandert ": Lists of emigrants; names and birthplaces of men, women, and children; ages of each; date of permission to emigrate; amount of money in hand after deduction of debts; destination; date of leaving. Totals. Emigrants enumerated from each district of canton Basel.

" Summation der im Jahre 1816 nach Amerika Ausgewanderten."

"Anregung vom Bundesrath, 21 August, 1867, zu Tabellen der Auswanderungen."

Handel und Gewerbe.

V 10. Handel mit Nordamerika. 1828-1880. Handelsverhältnisse, Zölle, Verträge, Berichte, Gebühren, Waarenausfuhr, etc.

1843, Sept. 15. " Visirung d. Fakturen aller nach Nordamerika versandten schweizerischen Waaren durch die amerikanischen Konsuln in der Schweiz."

Kirchen.

K 25. Deutsch-Reformierte Kirche in Amerika. 1826.

1826, Jan. 21. " Collecte für die Nord-Amerikanische Reformierte Kirche." 5 documents.

K 26. Reformierte Gemeinde in Carolina. 1755.

"Memoriale E. E. Ministerii wegen Anschaffung einiger Christl. Bücher für eine Reformierte Gemeinde in Carolina." One document; read Oct. 22.

MILITÄR.

G 82. Militärpflichtersatz. 1870-1880.

NIEDERLASSUNG.

L 10. Nordamerika.
" Angehörige von Nordamerika und deren Heimatschriften überhaupt." 1869-1882.
1880, Feb. 20. " Militärpflicht der niedergelassenen Amerikaner."
R 2. Pässe nach Amerika. 1854-1861. Passrevision der amerikanischen Consuln.

POST.

S 6. Postverhältnisse mit Amerika. Amerikanische Correspondenz. 1803-1874.

ABTEILUNG EHE- ODER WAISENGERICHT.[1]
WAISENGERICHT AKTEN.

1818. " Erbschaften betr., mit vielen Schriften von und über schweizerische Ansiedler in America." From Philadelphia, 1817; Lancaster, Ohio, 1818; Charleston, S. C., 1819.
Letters: 1818, May 11, from Swiss settler about 50 miles from Baltimore.
1819, Mar. 20, from Swiss settler near Hanover, Pa.
1826, Oct. 12, from Swiss settler 4 miles from Hanover.
1826, June 12, from Swiss settler near Cincinnati, O.
1827, Mar. 1, from Swiss settler in Pennsylvania, 7 pages.
1829, Feb. 26, from Swiss settler in Schöneck, near Nazareth, Pa.
1829, Feb. 26, from Swiss settler, Lancaster, O.
All these letters speak very favorably concerning conditions in America.
Documents relating to inheritances; certificates of death; accounts of property; relationships established; power of attorney given.

The emigration bureaus of Basel, such as the long established houses Zwilchenbart, and Rommel and Co., have not preserved their archive materials. The Iselin family of Basel (originally from Rosenfeld, Württemberg) has several important branches, among them the American, of which Adrian Georg Iselin (1818-1905) was the founder. *Cf. Heinrich Iselin von Rosenfeld, und sein Geschlecht,* zusammengestellt und bearbeitet von Fried. Weiss-Frey (Basel, 1909).

[1] Not yet arranged.

CANTON BASEL-LANDSCHAFT.
LIESTAL: STAATSARCHIV.

Location: The " Staatsarchiv des Kantons Basel-Landschaft " is located in the " Regierungsgebäude " of the city of Liestal, the capital of the half-canton.

After the separation in 1832 of the country from the city, the records and documents which concerned Basel-Landschaft alone were brought to Liestal, constituting the " Altes Archiv " ; the materials collected since then make up the " Neues Archiv ". A good summary of the contents of both has been published: *Das Staatsarchiv des Kantons Basel-Landschaft, Archivplan* (Liestal, 1907, pp. 34). The materials relating to American history are scant and unimportant. In the Neues Archiv, B 4: Justiz und Polizei, see under " (d) Auswanderungen: Werbungen ".

CANTON SCHAFFHAUSEN.

SCHAFFHAUSEN: STAATSARCHIV.

Location: Staatsarchiv (cantonal archive) in the Rathaus of Schaffhausen.
Hours: 8 a. m. to 12 m.; 2 to 6 p. m.
Bibliography: Register zu den Akten der Gesetzgebungs- und Verwaltungsbehörden [to 1890] (Schaffhausen, 3 vols., 1882-1892).

RATHS PROTOKOLLE.

1734, Oct. 8. Henrich Vogel, Küster, Weib und 2 Kinder. Auswanderungsgesuch (Arbeit und Nahrungsorge) erlaubt, und Beysteuer von 20 fl. aus Säckelamt erlaubt, " solche ihne aber erst in einer Statt in Holland zugestellt werden solle ".

1735, Jan. 3. Carolina Engl. Provintz. " Von diesem Orth nichts zu drucken oder zu verkaufen."

" Dass nichts in die Zeitungen komme, welches die Leuth dahin zu gehen gelüstig machen möchte."

1735, Mar. 14. " Dahin begehrende Landleuth abzumahnen."

1735, June 20. " Jacob Pfeiffer von Neunkirch, welcher vor etwas Zeit den Forstknechtdienst aus unbegründeter Hoffnung in Carolina sich glücklich zu machen, aufgegeben, nun aber ihme solchen wider in Gnaden anzuvertrauen gebetten, ist hierin zwar in Gnaden entsprochen, er aber auf ein halbes Jahr der Besoldung verlustig erkannt."

1737, Jan. 2. " Hans Conrad Speiszegger, Orgelmacher, von seiner vorhabenden Reise nach Carolina zu dehortieren."

Oct. 3. " Nachdem H. Göpfert und Thebis Rüger von Meriszhausen, wie auch Jakob und Andreas Steinimann von Opfershofen, um permission in die Provinz Carolinam ziehen zu dürfen, bittlich angehalten; ist ihnen in bescheyd ertheilt, dass ausz vielen bedenklichen u. mehrentheils ihnen selbst eröffneten Ursachen die permission nicht gegeben werden könne, sollten sie aber dessen ohngeachtet fortgehen, so seyen sie eo ipso ihres Landrechts verlustig, auch vorhin der Abzug zu bezahlen, und ihre Creditores zu befridigen, gehalten."

Oct. 29. " Derjenige Kauf, welcher dato zwischen Hans Göpfert von Meriszhausen und Hans Weber daselbst vorkommen, ist zwarn Rechtl. gefertiget: weilen aber Verkäufer nach Carolina zu ziehen, ohnerachtet allen abmahnens, resolviert bleibet, dem Käufer den Kaufschilling an Hrn. Ober Vogt Hardern zu bezahlen, anbefohlen, ermeldtem Hrn. Ober Vogt aber aufgetragen worden, die Veranstaltung zu machen, dass vor allen Dingen des Göpferten Creditoren befriediget, die auf dem Lehen stehende Restanz entrichtet, und von seinem übrig habenden Mittlen, welche er ausz dem Land ziehet, der Abzug erstattet werde."

1738, Nov. 7. "Nachdem Hr. Ober Vogt Harder berichtet, wie denen nach Carolina reisen wollenden Meriszhausern u. zwar dem

> Thebis Rüger, Wagner, etwa zu................ 300 fl.
> dessen Sohn .... 50 "
> Hans Dunklen .... 105 "
> Peter Straaszer .... 234 "
> und Hans Göpferten, dessen Kauf, weil Käufer, nicht bezahlen können, aufgehoben und das Lehen einem andern überlassen werden müssen, wan er von einem andern gleichviel löste.............. 275 "

nach bezahlung ihrer passivorum (Schulden) übrig bleibe, welche aber sammtl. um. Gnl. Nachlasz des Abzugs bitten, ist diszfalls sie ohne Erkanntnusz conivendo zu entlassen resolviret worden."

1741, Mar. 15. "Weillen Hans Jakob Pfeiffer von Neunkirch, in Pennsylvanien zu ziehen nicht nur resolviert, sondern auch auf Vorbieten anstatt künftigen Kreuztag zu erscheinen, sich heut morgen mit Weib und Kindern würklich auf und davon gemacht, alsz solle er für sich und die seinigen desz gehabten Landrechts verlustig sein, sein Name in der Bürger Rodel zu Neunkirch ausgestrichen, und wann noch etwas von seinem Vermögen daselbst zu finden, solches von Hrn. Landvogt zu weiterer Versorgung in Verwahr genohmen werden."

MANDATENBUCH.

1738, Sept. 8. Actum vor gesessenem Rath.
Mandat betreffend die nach Carolina ziehen wollende Unterthanen. (Loss of Landrechts, refusal of readmission in case of return.)

1748, July 12. Actum.
Mandat wegen der vilen Emigranten. (Threat of refusal of permission to dispose of property before emigration, loss of Landrecht, refusal of readmission on return.)

1751, Jan. 25. Actum.
Mandat auf die Landschaft. "Keinen ausz Carolina oder Pennsylvania kommenden hiesig gewesenen Underthanen noch freunden underschlauf (Herberge) zu geben."

GUTACHTEN U. BERICHTE VON ANNO 1815 BIS 1817.

No. 79. "Die Behandlung der Auswanderer nach Amerika betreffend." June 5, 1817. If emigrants insist on going, they must show that they are in possession of the means to make the journey, *i. e.*, for a person between 4 and 14 years, 85 fl., and for adults 175 fl. This to prevent paupers gathering at the seaports.

PROTOKOLLE DES KLEINEN UND GROSSEN RATHS, 1816-1817.

Acceptance of "Gutachten" above. June 6, 1817. P. 341.

III. AUSWANDERUNG UND NIEDERLASSUNG. 1870-1874.

1870. No. 2. Auswanderung der Elisabeth Waldvogel.
No. 5. Entziehung d. Patente von Auswanderungsagenturen.
No. 6. Agenturen in Basel. Brown und Co.

1871. No. 2. Auswanderungsagenturen. Rommel und Co., Basel.
No. 6. " Controle " über die Auswanderung.
1872. No. 4. Gegenstand: Brasilien. Warnung vor der Auswanderung.
No. 12. Auswanderungsagentur des Hauses Andr. Zwilchenbart in Basel.
No. 16. Controle über die Auswanderung.
Nos. 6, 8, 9, 12. Auswanderungsagenturen.
1874. No. 5. Controle über die Auswanderung.

III. AUSWANDERUNG UND NIEDERLASSUNG.

1875-1878, 1879-1880, 1881-1883.

Auswanderungsbewilligungen, Agenturen, Controle über die Auswanderung, Ausweisungen ausser Landes.
1876. No. 2. Auswanderung nach Brasilien. Warnung vor Auswanderung nach Venezuela.
1877. No. 2. Reisebeitrag nach Amerika für Schreiner Lang.
1878. No. 5. Protest gegen die Spedition des Jakob Zimmermann nach Amerika. (Large number of acta.)
1879. No. 1. Auswanderung der Familie des (Sträflings) Martin Bächthold. Unterstützung und Rückkehr. Ausweisungen ausser Landes.
No. 6. Controle der Auswanderung.
1880. No. 8. Tabellen für 1880.
1881-1883. Ausweisungen, Controle der Auswanderungen.

AMERIKA. 1880-1889.

No. 1. 1880-1883. Gegenstand: Amerikanische Pensionen. (8 cases.)
No. 2. 1881. Erbschaftssachen und Informationen betreffend.
No. 3. 1882. *Id.*
No. 4. 1883. *Id.*
No. 5. 1884. Erbschaften und Unterstützungssachen betreffend.
No. 6. 1884-1889. " Pensionsbezüger." (7 cases.)
Among items derived from printed materials may be mentioned:
Offizielle Sammlung der Gesetze und Obrigkeitliche Verordnungen des Kantons Schaffhausen, VII. Heft (1824), pp. 11-12.
  IV. Verbott gegen das leichtsinnige Auswandern (ohne Hülfsmittel). Gegeben d. 13. Juni, 1817. Canzley des Kleinen Raths.
Offizielle Sammlung der für d. eidgenöss. Stand Schaffhausen bestehenden Gesetze, Verordnungen, und Verträge, N. F., I. 441-442. " Verordnung, die Agenturen betreffend." Schaffhausen, Aug. 23, 1854.
  N. F., IV. 17-18: " Regierungsbeschluss, betreffend die staatliche Controle der Auswanderung." Schaffhausen, Sept. 25, 1867.
Chronik der Stadt Schaffhausen, called Harder Chronik (Schaffhausen, 1844). See V. 120, 126, 127, 139.
  1738, Sept. 8. " Im Juni wanderten viele arme Leute aus den umliegenden Orten, namentlich von Merishausen und vom Reiat nach Carolina in Nord Amerika aus. Als sodann auch ' einige Unterthanen zu Rüdlingen und Buchberg den unzeitigen Schluss gefasset, aus ihrem Vaterlande hinweg und in weit entlegene Länder zu ziehen und sich also vielem Ungemach, ja dem äussersten Elend auf eine unbesonnene Weise und zu ihrer allzuspäten

Reue zu exponiren', schritt die Regierung ein, und verbot das Auswandern bei Verlust des Landrechts."

1748, July 12. " Gegen das Auswandern ' in weit entlegene Länder ' erliess die Regierung wieder ein Mandat, und zwar insbesondere zu Handen der Gemeinde Unterhallau."

1751, Jan. 25. " Die auf die Auswanderung gesetzte Strafe des Landrechts-Verlustes wird über mehrere aus Karolina und Pennsilvanien zurückkehrende frühere ' Landeskinder ' verhängt."

1751, Mar. 5. " Am 5. März wurde verboten, den Auswanderungslustigen ihre Liegenschaften abzukaufen."

1770. " Der grossen Noth wegen waren einige Familien von der Landschaft nach den preussischen Ländern ausgewandert und eine grosse Anzahl schickte sich an, ihnen zu folgen, wurde aber durch obrigkeitliche Maszregeln gezwungen zu bleiben."

CANTON APPENZELL INNER-RHODEN.
APPENZELL: STAATSARCHIV.

Location: The cantonal archive is located in the church.

In the cantonal archive of Appenzell Inner-Rhoden, the manuscript material is indexed from the fourteenth to the sixteenth centuries, but not beyond. By a decree of 1597 Appenzell I. Rh. was to accept as citizens all the Catholics of the other half-canton, Appenzell A. Rh., while the latter agreed to take all the Protestants of Appenzell I. Rh. The emigration from Appenzell has not been large. Some few families are known to have come to the United States, *e. g.*, families of the names Linherr, Signer (1850-1851), Kolbener, and Hershey. The ancestor of the Hershey family (who settled in Lancaster Co., Pa., in the eighteenth century), was Hans Hersche, a Mennonite, of Appenzell. *Cf. History of the Hershey Family from the Year 1600,* by Scott Funk Hershey (New Castle, Pa.). Representatives of the family in Appenzell preserve the original spelling of the name.

Several volumes of lists of " Heimatscheine " exist, but give no clue as to possible emigration to America. A curious circumstance is the recording not only of the family and surname, but also of the familiar name (Spitzname), as: Unterhuslebube, Zünglershanesli, etc.

CANTON APPENZELL AUSSER-RHODEN.

(TROGEN.) HERISAU: STAATSARCHIV.

The cantonal archive is divided between the two towns Trogen and Herisau. The materials pertaining to the courts (Gerichtssachen) are deposited in Trogen, as also the old historical materials, which, however, are not indexed, and are not in condition to be examined. The materials pertaining to the administration of cantonal affairs (Verwaltungssachen) are deposited in the capital city, Herisau. They are located in the city church. The archive is the proud possessor of one of the two extant copies of the *Sachsenspiegel*. The material pertaining to American history is all recent, *i. e.*, since 1850, and consists for the most part of circular letters sent from the Bundesrat at Bern.

FASCIKEL I. AUSLÄNDISCHE STAATEN.

A. Amerika. 1861-1893. Kreisschreiben von Bern, Bundesrat u. Departement des Auswärtigen.

FASCIKEL XXXVII. AUSWANDERUNGSWESEN. No. 114.

Walzenhausen. " Pfarrer Keller empfiehlt die Einführung von Auswanderungsbüchern." June 27, 1850.
Bemerkungen darüber. Aug., 1850.
Auswanderungsagenturen. June 1, 1852.
Aarau. Gutachten über Auswanderung. June 2, 1854.
Bundesrat. Warnung über Auswanderung. Mar. 2, 1857.
Memmingen. " Der Stadtmagistrat ersucht das Polizeiamt Herisau, einer dortigen Betrügerin für Weisung und Beistand bei ihrer Auswanderung nach Amerika zu sorgen." Apr. 6, 1857.
Bundesrat, Bern. Mitteilungen über das Auswanderungswesen. June, July, 1857.
" Erhebungen in den Gemeinden betr. Auswanderung in den letzten 3 Jahren." Aug., Sept., 1857.
Gais. " Synode des Kantons Appenzell A. Rh. über die Führung des Auswanderungsbuches." (Controlle.) Nov. 22, 1858.
Kreisschreiben des Bundesrats in Bern über Auswanderungssachen. 1865-1885.
Herisau. Bericht v. Etzweiler-Merz, über Auswanderungsagentur. July-Aug., 1881.
Herisau. Ratsschreiber Engwiller. Bericht und Antrag über Aufsicht über die Auswanderungsagenturen. Aug. 2, 1888.
Kreisschreiben des Bundesrats in Bern über Auswanderungssachen. 1889-1898.
Printed Matter: Amtsblätter des Kantons Appenzell A. Rh., since 1834. (With index.)
Rechenschaftsberichte des Regierungsrats an den Kantonsrat von Appenzell A. Rh. (Fifty-third report in 1911-1912; see index.)

CANTON SANKT GALLEN.

SANKT GALLEN: STAATSARCHIV.

Location: The cantonal archive is located in the Regierungsgebäude (bei der Stiftskapelle), in the same quarters as the Staatsbibliothek des Kantons Sankt Gallen.
Hours: 9 a. m. to 12 m.; 3 to 6 p. m. Permission for use is obtainable from the state archivist.
The archive contains material since 1803, the date of the founding of Sankt Gallen as a canton.

RUBRIK 45. FASCIKEL: AMERIKANISCHE STAATEN.

Argentinien (La Plata Staaten mit Paraguay u. Uruguay). 1858-1908.
Brasilien. 1825-1833; 1840-1844; 1905.
Chile und über Spanisch Amerika. 1867-1881.
Hayti. 1857.
Mexiko und Central Amerika. 1825-1884.
Vereinigte Staaten von Nordamerika. 1824-1908. Kreisschreiben der Vororte und später vom Bundesrat, Bern. Consularberichte, Erbschaften, Handelsverkehr mit Nordamerika, Handels- und Auslieferungsvertrag, etc.

RUBRIK 100. FASCIKEL 1. ZEITRAUM 1803- .

1. Auswanderungswesen im Allgemeinen.
2. Auswanderung nach Algerien.
3a. Auswanderung nach Nordamerika.
   1817. Warnung gegen Auswanderung nach Nordamerika.
   1817, Feb. 28. Typical contract for transportation, of 587 emigrants, on 3 ships, Amsterdam to Philadelphia. Rates:

	Those who pay in full at Amsterdam.	Those who pay ½ at Philadelphia, ½ at Amsterdam.	Those who pay in full at Philadelphia.
Adults, men or women:	170 francs	185 francs	190 francs
Children under 4:	...	...	...
" from 4 to 14:	85 "	92.10 "	95 "
" 14 and over:	170 "	185 "	190 "

Daily bill of fare given in detail in the contract.
   1820, Oct. 9. "Regierung über die Colonie in Amerika so Hauptmann May zu errichten sucht. Über Colonisten Werbung an dem Rothen Fluss. in Nordamerika durch Hrn. Hauptmann May von Bern. Antrag d. Hauptmanns abgelehnt, Werbungen in diesem Kanton auszuüben. (Ungewissheit der Erfüllung der Versprechen; zu weit nördlich, d. i. Hudson Bay; wenn indessen Kantonsbürger aus eigenem freien Willen Lust und Neigung haben, dahin zu ziehen, so soll denselben keine Hindernisse gemacht werden.)" See under Neuchâtel.

1832. Sämtliche Kreisschreiben von den Vororten Luzern, Zürich, Bern.
1869, Mar. 12. " Auswanderung nach Chicago, trügerische Verlockung durch Inserat im *Tageblatt St. Gallen* v. Casper Pfeiffer." (A copy of his article, which contains statement concerning high wages paid in Chicago.)
1880, Dec. 15. Neues Auswanderungsprojekt. Harlan u. Bell counties. Kentucky.
3*b*. Auswanderung nach Brasilien u. Süd Amerika. 1818-1888.

FASCIKEL 2. AUSWANDERUNGSAGENTEN.

No. 1. Allgemeines. Zeitraum 1849- .
No. 2. Individuelles. Zeitraum 1849- . Kreisschreiben. Processacten.
1854. " Processacten gegen Joseph Rufli von Siszeln, Kanton Aargau. (Rufli, Spediteur, der 24 Auswanderer nach Amerika befördern sollte, in folge dessen Insolvenz ein Theil der Überfahrtskosten vom Staat bestritten worden.)"
Auswanderer aus dem Kanton Sankt Gallen.
Auswanderer aus dem Bezirk Werdenberg—in Havre, Unterstützung.
Auswanderer aus dem Bezirk Werdenberg—in Havre, Unterstützung zur Überfahrt.
Auswanderer aus dem Bezirk Grabs, Rückvergütung für Reiseunterstützung.

SANKT GALLEN: STIFTSARCHIV.

Location: In the same building as the famous library of the abbey (Stiftsbibliothek), *i. e.,* in a wing of what is now the cantonal Regierungsgebäude. The privilege of using the materials is granted on application to the archivist. The materials desired may be sent to the Staatsarchiv, where it is more convenient to work.
Rubrik X. Gemein-eidgenössische Bundesangelegenheiten.
Polizeiliches. Zeitraum 1767-1769, 1770.
Fascikel 15. " Im Schwabenland angeworbene Emigranten für die neuen spanischen Kolonien." Swabian emigrants seeking passage through Zürich are refused permission to pass through that territory. Bürgermeister and Rath of the town of Zürich address Abbot Beda of St. Gallen, asking whether it be not desirable to give them no advantage and to send them back. Apr. 1, 1768.
Printed circular from Bern repeating order of Feb. 24, 1769, forbidding passage of recruits through country. Mar. 6, 1770.
Printed circular from Luzern. Passage allowed only under restrictions ; danger of citizens being carried along. Mar. 26, 1770.

ST. GALLEN: ARCHIV DER STADTGEMEINDE.

Location: In the Rathaus (St. Leonhardstrasse).
" Notizen oder Verzeichnis hiesiger bürgerlicher Personen, die grössentheils unter meiner (*i. e.*, J. M. Scheitlin, Präsident d. Verwaltungsrates) Mitwirkung nach Amerika ausgewandert sind." 1846-1853.

"Verzeichnis der im Jahre 1854 aus der Stadt Sankt Gallen ausgewanderten
     Personen." (28 persons, all to America.)
Id. 1855. (15 persons.)
Id. 1856. (8 persons.)
Id. 1857. (14 persons.)
Id. 1858. (6 persons.)
Id. 1859. (4 persons.)
Id. 1860. (9 persons.)
Id. 1862. (9 persons.)
Another rise in the number of emigrants from St. Gallen occurred after 1880.

SANKT GALLEN: STADTARCHIV.

Location: In the new building of the Stadtbibliothek (Vadiana), on the
     Notkerstrasse.
Hours: 8 a. m. to 12 m.; 2 to 4 p. m.
   The older section of the "Archiv des Kaufmännischen Direktoriums Sankt
Gallen" (beginning with 1830) is deposited here.
        Handlungs-Sachen überhaupt. 1830.
        Handlungs-Sachen überhaupt, Amerika betreffend. 1831-1835,
          1836-1838.
See also "Archiv des Kaufmännischen Direktoriums", below.
"Verzeichnis der hiesigen Ministerii, d. i. aller Herren Prediger der Stadt
     Sankt Gallen von Zeit der Reformation bis zum Jahre 1799, nebst
     alphabetischem Register."
   This valuable collection of records and biographical material on the
     Protestant ministers of Sankt Gallen, containing also a large
     quantity of letters of the Swiss reformers, including Zwingli, was
     removed from the church to the safe-keeping of the Stadtarchiv.
     No. 180, etc., contain records concerning Michael Schlatter, in
     detail: birth (1716), education, graduation (1739), vicarship in
     Thurgau, flight to America (1746); visit to Sankt Gallen (1750);
     attempt to procure ministers of the Reformed Church for Penn-
     sylvania; return to America (1751).
   The Stadtbibliothek contains a collection of books (mostly not rare) on
     America, among them a copy of Michael Schlatter's *Wahrhafte
     Erzehlung* (Frankfurt a. M., 1752), for full title of which see
     p. 19, above.

SANKT GALLEN: ARCHIV DES KAUFMÄNNISCHEN DIREKTORIUMS.

Location: Near the Stiftskirche. Permission to use the materials of the
     archive can be obtained on application. The publications of the
     Direktorium are thoroughgoing, the principal ones being the
     following:
(a) Dr. Hermann Wartmann (Aktuar des Kaufmännischen Direktoriums,
     1863-1913), *Industrie und Handel des Kantons Sankt Gallen auf
     Ende 1866 in geschichtlicher Darstellung* (St. Gallen, 1875).
   This is the pioneer work, which stimulated similar efforts in other can-
     tons, e. g., Jenny-Trümpy, *Handel und Industrie des Kantons
     Glarus* (Glarus, 1898); *Berichte des Schweizerischen Handels-
     und Industrie-Vereins* (Zürich, new series from 1874); T. Geer-

ing, *Handel und Industrie der Stadt Basel: Zunftwesen und Wirtschaftsgeschichte bis zu Ende d. 17. Jahrhunderts, aus den Archiven dargestellt* (Basel, 1886).

(b) *Berichte des Kaufmännischen Direktoriums über Handel, Industrie und Geldverhältnisse des Kantons St. Gallen.* These reports are annual, and go back to 1844. The exports of embroideries, laces, and cotton and silk weavings are largest to the United States, though there has been a falling off in the last years.[1] Even so, the U. S. is St. Gall's best customer. In 1910 the exports to the U. S. amounted to over 83,000,000 francs, in 1911, over 79,000,000 francs.

(c) *Die Kaufmännische Corporation und das Kaufmännische Directorium in St. Gallen in den Jahren 1901-1910* (St. Gallen, 1913).

(d) *Verwaltungsberichte des Kaufmännischen Direktoriums an die Kaufmännische Corporation in St. Gallen,* 1891-1900, pp. 22-27; 1897-1898, pp. 1-8; " Zollkrieg mit New York " (Dingley Bill). These reports are published annually.

[1] *Cf. Schweizerische Blätter für Handel u. Industrie,* XX. Jahrgang, pp. 278-280; Dr. H. Beerli, " Der Stickerei-Export im ersten Quartal 1913."

CANTON GRAUBÜNDEN (GRISONS).

CHUR: STAATSARCHIV.

Location: The " Staatsarchiv des Kantons Graubünden " is located in the Regierungsgebäude (Regierungsplatz) of the capital city, Chur. The archive is not in good condition, but the work of rearranging the large stores of manuscripts, indexing them, and making them accessible, has been begun. Judging from the large amount of material on emigration found in the Stadtarchiv in Chur, it would seem likely that more material relating to American history is contained in this cantonal archive than is accessible at present.

Hours: 9 a. m. to 12 m.; 3 to 6 p. m.

ACTA.

Freizügigkeitstraktate mit dem Nordamerikanischen Freistaate. Kreisschreiben an sämtliche eidgenössische Stände. 1833-1834.
Italienische Flüchtlinge von 1848, 1849, 1850.
Politische Flüchtlinge und Conscribierte aus Italien. 1870-1873.
Auswanderung nach überseeischen Ländereien und den erlebten Erfahrungen mehrerer Bündnerfamilien. (Bundle of papers.)
Nach Brasilien, 1857-1859. Die Schweizer auf der Kolonie in St. Paolo in Brasilien. Auswanderung nach Brasilien betr. Überfahrtsverträge. Vorschüsse an die Halbpachtkolonisten des Hauses Vergueiro et Cie. in Brasilien betr. Anzeige und Weisung betr. Oct., 1860.

CHUR: STADTARCHIV.

Location: The Stadtarchiv is located in the Rathaus (Obere Reichsgasse), an old building in the oldest section of the city.

Hours: 8 a. m. to 12 m.; 2 to 6 p. m.

B. 3. AUSWANDERUNG: 1844-1852; 1853-1867.

Two bundles of acta, mostly petitions for financial aid in defraying transportation expenses incident to emigration. A number of typical examples are given below, the minutes pertaining to them being quoted in full:

RATSPROTOKOLLE. "GESUCHE UM UNTERSTÜTZUNG ZUR AUSWANDERUNG NACH NORDAMERIKA."

1845, July 3 (pp. 400-401): " Es wird eine Einlage von Andr. Kron, Sohn, hiesigem Angehörigen, verlesen, womit derselbe die Absicht ankündigt, samt Kindern, Vater, Schwester, und Stiefmutter (11 Personen) nach Amerika auszuwandern u. damit das Gesuch um ein angemessenes Reisegeld verbindet. Der Herr Amtsbürgermeister fügt bei: er habe vernommen, dass je nach dem Schick-

sal, welches diese Bittschrift haben werde, noch eine Anzahl anderer Angehörigen dem Beispiel des Petenten folgen würde.
"Die Versammlung, zumal im Hinblick auf die Eröffnung des Präsidiums, die Wichtigkeit der Angelegenheit erkennend, beschlossen: dieselbe, und zwar insbesondere in *dem* Sinne vor die Behörde von Rath und Gericht zu bringen, dass darüber die Berathung gepflogen werde, wie namentlich auch die katholischen Angehörigen zum Fortreisen bewogen werden könnten? Zugleich wurde, um den diesfälligen Berathungen besagter Behörde eine Grundlage zu geben, die Vorberatungs-Kommission beauftragt, vorerst nachzuforschen, welche Angehörige sonst noch nachzureisen Willens wären."

July 25. Wurde erkannt: "Eine besondere Commission von 3 Mitgliedern auszuschiessen und zu beauftragen, die Verhältnisse der betreffenden Auswanderungslustigen näher zu untersuchen und sowohl mit den Übernehmern als mit andern zuverlässigen Personen, die mit der Lage und andern Umständen in Nordamerika bekannt sind, Rücksprache und Correspondenz zu pflegen und sich über alles darauf bezügliche hinlängliche Auskunft zu verschaffen, —sodann einen umfassenden Bericht nebst Gutachten einzureichen." Zur Commission wurden ernannt: (1) Herr Bürgermeister, (2) Stadtrichter, (3) Altstadtvogt.

RATHSPROTOKOLLS-SBOZZO [1] VON 1844-1845.

729. "Aufstellung einer Commission für die Auswanderung nach Nordamerika."

752. Bericht: "Zur Auswanderung hätten sich 51 Individuen gemeldet, wovon 30 ausgewachsene, 21 unausgewachsene, 11 bürgerliche u. 40 angehörige, unter welchen letzteren 2 katholische Familien seien. Die Vermögensverhältnisse aller seien derart, dass sie nach Abzug der Schulden, sämtlich nichts behielten, ausser das Guthaben, das mehrere Angehörige an ihrer Versorgungskasse haben. Unter solchen Umständen, da die Auswanderungslustigen nicht nur für die Reise, sondern auch für die Ansiedelung und das weitere Fortkommen in der neuen Welt, wofür man dann doch auch zum Voraus besorgt sein sollte, so zu sagen, nichts beitragen könnten, sei die Commission eben im Begriff gewesen, einen abmahnenden Antrag an die Behörde zu bringen, als dieser Tage eine Abordnung der Tennessee Colonisationsgesellschaft, welche mit Gründung einer Colonie im nordamerikanischen Staate Tennessee umgehn, erschienen sei und, unter Vorweisung eines diesfälligen Prospekts und sehr vorteilhafter Zeugnisse, äusserst günstige Anträge, sowohl bezüglich des Transports als der Ansiedlung selbst gemacht hätte, wonach die Transportkosten für eine erwachsene Person bis auf Ort und Stelle circa fl. 108 R. W., für Kinder noch billiger, zu stehen kämen, und jede Familie unbebautes Land bis zum Belauf von 200 Acker zu 37½ Kreuzer per Acker erhalten könnte. Nach den Eröffnungen jener Abgeordneten wäre die Kolonisationsgesellschaft zudem erbötig, den Auswandernden den Kaufpreis fürs Land bis zu dem 5ten Jahre

[1] *Sbozzo*, from Ital. *sbozzare*, to outline; Protokolls-Entwurf.

zu kreditiren, sowie den Auswandernden, sei es zur Überfahrt, sei es zum Bodenankauf von der Stadt gemachte Vorschüsse durch ihre Agenten später wieder einzuziehen, sodass es dannzumal der Stadt frei bliebe, das zurückbezahlte, wenigstens teilweise, zu beliebigen Auswanderungszwecken zu bestimmen.—Was die Auswanderungslustigen selbst betreffe, so seien die meisten von ihnen im Falle, durch ihre Arbeit, sei es als Handwerker, sei es als Landbauer, fortzukommen. Da nun die von dieser Tennessee Kolonisationsgesellschaft gestellten Bedingungen billiger seien, als sie sonst anderswie erhältlich wären und überdies den Vorteil gewährten, dass damit für das weitere Fortkommen des auswandernden Individuum gesorgt würde, auch nach dem persönlichen Eindrucke der hier anwesenden Herren Abgeordneten sowohl, als nach ihren Ausweisschriften, durchaus Grund sei, an die Solidität der Gesellschaft zu glauben, habe die Commission geglaubt, darauf antragen zu sollen, dass vorerst beschlossen würde, auf die Anträge der besagten Gesellschaft einzugehen, und die Auswanderung in diesem Sinne möglich zu machen und sodann eine Commission damit zu beauftragen, unter Ratifikationsvorbehalt, das genauere sowohl mit der Gesellschaft als mit den auswanderungslustigen Individuen festzusetzen. Beschlossen: " Den Antrag der Commission zu genehmigen und zwar so, dass schon diesen Herbst einige wenige gleichsam versuchsweise nach Tennessee abreisen sollen, um bis nächsten Frühling das genauere darüber berichten zu können, auch solle, was die Angehörigen in der Versorgungskasse besitzen, nicht zu Bestreitung ihrer Reisekosten, sondern zum Ankauf von Land verwendet werden. Mit der zweiten Ausführung dieser Sache nach dem Antrage der Commission immer aber unter Vorbehalt der Ratification wurde sodann die bestehende Commission beauftragt," etc. Aug. 15, 1845.

763. " Dem ihr gewordenen Auftrage nachkommend, habe die Commission vorerst die Auswanderungslustigen gefragt, wer von ihnen zur Abreise mit dem ersten Transport (v. 1-10. Sept., 1845) bereit wäre? Und als sich hierzu beinahe alle bereit erklärt, habe die Commission unter ihnen eine Auswahl treffen müssen, welche sie denn teils auf diejenigen Individuen zu lenken gesucht, welche den Bodenankauf möglichst aus eigenen Mitteln, nämlich aus ihrem Guthaben an der Versorgungskasse zu bestreiten vermöchten, teils auf diejenigen, welche während des Winters, besonders wegen zahlreicher Kinder, hier am schwersten fortkommen könnten. Hiernach habe sich dann für die sofortige Auswanderung eine Anzahl von 5 Familien bestehend aus 24 Individuen gefunden, nämlich, die Familie von Andreas Kron, Sohn, bestehend aus 9 Köpfen, diejenige von Joseph Vollmer best. aus 6 Köpfen, kathol. Confession, diejenige von Christ. Brei, best. aus 3 Köpfen, diejenige von Simon Schmid, best. aus 3 Köpfen, und endlich diejenige von Ciprian Fischer (Färber), ebenfalls 3 Köpfe zählend. Dem letzteren aber, der nur auf sehr dringendes Verlangen mitgelassen worden, habe man, in betracht der höchst geringen persönlichen Gewehr, welche er zu bieten im Fall ist, erklärt, es geschehe dieses nur unter der Bedingung, dass

er eine genügende Bürgschaft stelle, welche im Fall, dass er zurückkehren sollte, den ihm gemachten Vorschuss wieder erstatte. Überdies mache die Commission den Antrag, dass insofern ein diesfälliger Grundsatz von der Bürgerversammlung beliebt würde, dass durch die Abreise des Simon Schmid ledig werdende Gemeingut von der Stadt etwa 5 Jahre lang beibehalten werde, um mit dessen Erlös sowohl die dem Schmid als dem Fischer gemachten Vorschüsse zu Ankauf des Bodens zu decken. Was die mit diesem Transport abreisenden betreffe, so besässen sie sämtlich in der Versorgungskasse so viel als zum Ankauf des Bodens erforderlich seie, nämlich

    Andreas Kron, Gulden 51. Kr. 50.
    J. Vollmer   " 30. " 54.
    Chr. Brei   " 43.

" Auf solche Weise belaufe sich die gesamte der Stadtkasse zur Last fallende Ausgabe zu gewusten obigen 24 auswandernden Individuen, sowohl für die Reise als für den Bodenverkauf, auf Gulden 2304, Kr. 15, R. W. Den Transport derselben übernehme die Kolonisationsgesellschaft von Wallenstadt weg bis an Ort und Stelle, worüber die hier anwesenden Agenten bereits einen Schiffsakkord entworfen hätten. In Gemässheit des ihr gewordenen Auftrages habe dann die Commission auch den zwischen löblicher Stadt und der Colonisationsgesellschaft abzuschliessenden Vertrag entworfen, worin als Hauptgrundsätze aufgenommen worden: es sollen die Überfahrtskosten zur Hälfte gegen Ausweis der Einschiffung der Auswandernden in Antwerpen, und zur Hälfte gegen Ausweis ihrer Ankunft in Charleston oder New Orleans, und der Kaufpreis des von ihnen zu okkupierenden Bodens bei Übergabe des förmlichen Verkaufsaktes in beglaubigter Abschrift an die hiesige Obrigkeit, ausbezahlt werden. Es solle das diesen Colonisten angewiesene Land insofern sie es verlassen würden in das Eigentum der Stadt übergehen. Es soll ferner der Agent der Gesellschaft in Tennessee die von der Stadt für die Colonisten ausgelegte Summe von den letztern vom 5ten Besitzesjahre an, während der nächst folgenden 5 Jahre ratenweise zu Handen der Stadt einziehen und endlich sei die Colonisationsgesellschaft verpflichtet im Laufe des Jahres 1846 noch weitere 250 Acker gleichen Bodens zu gleichem Preise behufs fernerer Ansiedlung abzutreten, welch letzterer Punkt deshalb aufgenommen worden sei, weil die Bodenpreise vom nächsten Jahr an um die Hälfte steigen. Ausserdem bliebe dann noch der Vertrag mit den Auswanderern selbst abzuschliessen. Schliesslich bemerkte der Referent, es hätten die letzteren den Wunsch geäussert, man möchte ihnen, da sie sich laut Schiffsakkord bis Mannheim selbst verköstigen müssten, etwas weniges auf die Hand zu geben. Nach Verlesung des Entwurfs zu dem Schiffsakkord sowohl als zu einem Vertrag mit der Gesellschaft und hierüber gewalteten Diskussion, während welcher sich die Versammlung von der Zuverlässigkeit obiger Bestimmungen überzeugte, wurde beschlossen:

" Die Vorschläge der Commission unter Verdankung ihrer Bemühungen zu genehmigen, auch den Auswanderern eine auf die Köpfe zu

verteilende Summe von Gulden 50 als Viaticum mitzugeben."
Aug. 19, 1845.
Vouchers for these transactions are to be found in the Kassenbuch, under date of Oct. 16, 1845, and May 2, 1846.
The " Register zu den Ratsprotokollen " show a large number of applications for aid in defraying the expenses of emigration. In the years 1846-1847 at least 9 are noted ; 14 in 1848, 6 in 1849, 14 in 1852, 6 in 1853, 10 in 1854, fewer after that. A great many of these applications were favorably received ; for a time there were many " undesirables " among them, including criminals and paupers, some of whom were transported to America. Some typical cases are the following :

PROTOKOLLE. RATH UND GERICHT.

1845, July 25. " Sodann trug das Präsidium vor : Es sei nun schon zu wiederholten Malen der junge Christian Heinz, Sohn des Chirurgen Johann Martin Heinz, auf den Schub hierher geführt und an das Kantonsverhöramt abgeliefert worden. Da nun dieser junge Mensch sich ungeachtet aller Ermahnungen und Drohungen nicht bessern zu wollen scheine, sondern sich immer noch dem Müssiggange und einem liederlichen herumvagierenden Leben hingebe, und seinen Eltern schon so viel Kosten, Kummer und Verdruss verursacht habe, so sei bei seinem Vater der Wunsch rege geworden, diesen seinen Sohn entweder nach Fürstenau (Correctionsanstalt) oder nach Amerika zu schicken, doch trage er einiges Bedenken denselben nach Amerika geben zu lassen aus Besorgnis, dass sein Sohn bald wieder von dort zurückkehren, grosse Kosten verursachen, und neue arge Streiche machen könnte. Es frage sich nun, was die Behörde hinsichtlich dieses Subjekts, welches seit einigen Tagen hier auf dem Rathause verhaftet sei, beschliessen wolle. Nach Vorbescheiden und Einvernehmung des jungen Heinz wurde erkennt : denselben auf unbestimmte Zeit nach der Zwangsanstalt in Fürstenau zu versetzen und die löbliche Kantonalarmenkommission um dessen Aufnahme daselbst ersuchen."

Aug. 15. " In einem v. 20. Juli dat. Schreiben stellt Herr Chirurgus J. M. Heinz das Gesuch, man möchte seinen entarteten Sohn Christian statt ihn nach Fürstenau in die Zwangsarbeitsanstalt zu thun, nach Amerika auswandern lassen. Er der Vater wolle zu diesem Behufe die Hälfte der Reisekosten übernehmen, wenn die Stadtkasse in Berücksichtigung seiner bedrängten ökonomischen Verhältnisse die andere Hälfte bestreiten wolle. Mit dem Aktuar der Kantonalarmencommission wurde (auf Beschluss v. 25. Juli) Rücksprache genommen und von demselben erfahren, dass die Versetzung schwerlich sogleich bewerkstelligt werden könne, indem in jener Anstalt bereits sozusagen alle Plätze besetzt seien.
—In Berücksichtigung sowohl der letzterwähnten Umstände, als des von dem Vater ausgesprochenen Wunsches, beschloss die Versammlung :
" Dem jungen Heinz aus der Pflegschaft einen unverzinslichen Vorschuss von f. 50 als beiläufig der Hälfte der erforderlichen Reisekosten zum Behufe seiner Übersiedelung nach Nordamerika zukommen

1846, Mar. 30. zu lassen, jedoch unter der Bedingung, dass der Vater Herr Chirurgus Heinz auf den Fall dass sein Sohn zurückkehren sollte, sich zur Erstattung des obigen Vorschusses verpflichte."

1846, Mar. 30. " Gesuch der Frau Verena Camenisch um Unterstützung ihrem Manne nach Amerika zu folgen, der sich früher dort angesiedelt hatte. Ihm war eine Unterstützung von f. 150 gegeben, Entschädigung für seinen Anteil am Gemeingut. Der Frau wird f. 100 gegeben als Entschädigung für ihr. Anteil, und dass die Vereinigung der beiden Eheleute, die ja sonst getrennt blieben, erzweckt werden sollte."

Mar. 30. " Mit Einlage v. 19. d. M. bittet Andreas Büchele, hiesiger Angehöriger, theils auf seine schwächliche Gesundheit, theils auf seinen dürftigen, ausschliesslich auf Handlangerdienst beschränkten Erwerb hinweisend, um eine Unterstützung zur Auswanderung nach Nordamerika :—welchem Gesuche, in Betracht dass der Petent ein junger Mann ist, der sein Brod erwerben kann, nicht zu entsprechen beschlossen wurde."

1847, Mar. 18. " Schwestern Maria und Susanna Fehre hiesige Angehörige unter Hinweisung auf ihre z. Theil durch verschiedene Unglücksfälle herbeigeführte Mittellosigkeit, Schwächlichkeit und Kränklichkeit, das Gesuch ihnen zum Behuf der Auswanderung nach Nordamerika, welche sie in Gemeinschaft mit ihrem wackern Schwager dem Schuhmachermeister Heinr. Schuler von Zürich zu unternehmen gedachten, Unterstützung angedeihen zu lassen. Beschluss : Angelegenheit an die Auswanderungscommission zu weisen und sie zu ermächtigen, die von der Stadt aus zu leistende Unterstützung bis auf f. 100 für jede von beiden Schwestern festzusetzen."

Mar. 18. " Mit Einlage v. 23. Feb. abhin, bittet der hiesige Angehörige Mathis Plöckli zum Behufe der Auswanderung nach Nordamerika, wohin er auch seinen blödsinnigen Bruder Peter mitzunehmen gedächte, sowohl um Nachlass seiner rückständigen Besitzsteuer in Betrag v. f. 50 als um Leistung einer anderweitigen Unterstützung. Da die Behörde es für den Peter Plöckli sehr bedenklich fand mit seinem Bruder auszuwandern, da derselbe einerseits dem Mathis in seiner Ansiedlung nur hinderlich sein könnte, und anderseits wenn ihm einst aus welchen Gründen immer der Beistand des letzteren abgehen sollte, hülflos allem Elend preisgegeben werde, wurde beschlossen : dem Mathis Plöckli zwar behufs Unterstützung seiner Auswanderung sowohl die rückständige Beisäszsteuer nachzulassen, als darüberhin ihm aus der Stadtkasse einen Beitrag v. f. 50 zukommen zu lassen, jedoch ihm zugleich die Bedenken der Behörde bezüglich seines Vorhabens seinen Bruder Peter mitzunehmen zu eröffnen, und ihn womöglich von diesem Gedanken abzubringen suchen."

1848, June 14. " In einer andern Einlage wird Vorstellung gemacht namens der hiesigen Lucia Meyer, dass derselben in ihrer bedrängten Lage zur Sicherung ihrer eigenen Existenz und jenes ihrer 2 ausserehelichen Kinder kein anderer Ausweg übrig bleibe als die Auswanderung nach Amerika. Wo dann ihr Verlobter, der Vater des jüngeren Kindes, ein Bürger des Kgr. Württemberg für ihr und ihrer Kinder Fortkommen sorgen würde, während hingegen ihrer Verehelichung mit demselben hierzulande die Schwierigkeit sich entgegen stelle, dass sie das dazu erforderliche Vermögen nicht aufweisen und auch den Einkauf in die Heimatgemeinde ihres Verlobten nicht zu bestreiten vermöge. Da jedoch die Bittstellerin dermalen nicht im Stande sei, die zu ihrer Auswanderung nach Amerika benötigte Summe näher zu bezeichnen, so gehe ihre geziemende Bitte einstweilen nur dahin, es möchte aus der Mitte dieser titul. Behörde eine Commission mit Untersuchung und Begutachtung dieser Angelegenheit beauftragt werden. Hierüber wurde in Betrachtung dass es nicht nur nicht in der Pflicht der hiesigen Behörden liegen könne, sondern vielmehr in moralischer Hinsicht und des Beispiels wegen von den schlimmsten Folgen für das Gemeinwesen sein würde, wenn hiesigen Bürgerinnen oder Angehörigen, welche sich in Umständen wie die der Petentin befinden, etwelchen Vorschub behufs Auswanderung geleistet werden wollte, erkennt das vorliegende wie auch künftige ähnliche Gesuche abzuweisen."

July 14. "Frau D. Ursula Gubler (geb. Braun) mit 3 Kindern, Bitte ihr in Betracht angeführter Umstände (Rechte auf Anteil an unverteiltem Zunftvermögen) die Summe von f. 500 aus der Stadtkasse zukommen zu lassen, um Reisekosten zur Auswanderung nach Amerika zu bestreiten. Genehmigt."

1849, Aug. 15. "Antrag v. Hr. A. Passett auf sein hiesiges Bürgerrecht zu verzichten zu wollen, unter der Bedingung einer Unterstützung von f. 700 behufs seiner Auswanderung nach Amerika und zwar nach dem Goldlande Californien nachgesucht, worüber beschlossen: da dem Petenten seither diejenige Unterstützungssumme, welche ihm teils von dieser Behörde aus zuerkannt, teils von seinen Anverwandten zu gedachtem Zwecke zusammengeschossen, verabreicht worden sei, so könne sich die Behörde zu keinem weiteren Opfer zu Lasten der Stadt verstehen, und werde daher das gestellte Begehren abgewiesen."

Aug. 15. "Zwei andern schriftlichen Gesuchen der hiesigen Bürger F. Moritzi, Schreiner, und Jeremias Hatz, Schmied, um Unterstützung zur Auswanderung nach Amerika, wurde ebenfalls nicht entsprochen, weil die Petenten, zumal bei ihrer Arbeits- und Berufsfähigkeit sich hier eine eben so sichere Existenz als anderswo verschaffen können, wenn sie nur *arbeiten* wollen."

AUSWANDERUNG. ACTA.

B. 3. 1853-1867. (Complete fascicle.)

Bittschriften an den Amtsbürgermeister der Stadt Chur im Kanton Graubünden um Unterstützung der Auswanderung (1) nach Nordamerika, (2) nach Brasilien.

1854, June 1. "In sehr bescheidenem Ton anher gerichtetes Gesuch des in der Zwangsarbeitanstalt von Fürstenau befindlichen Bürger Joh. Rohner Sohn um seine sofortige Freilassung aus der genannten Anstalt sowie um Zuerkennung resp. Rückerstattung der Hälfte des von ihm 1849 ohne etwelche seitherige Genutzniessung bezahlten Bürgereinkaufs behufs seiner nochmaligen Auswanderung nach Nordamerika, wurde erkennt: dem Petenten die nachgesuchte Freisprechung innert Jahresfrist in Aussicht zu stellen, sofern es sich fortan durch folgsames und ordentliches Betragen die Zufriedenheit der Anstaltsdirektion sich zu erwerben beflissen sein wird, mit dem Bemerken jedoch, dass auf sein weiteres Ansuchen um materielle Unterstützung zu dem angegebenen Zweck hierorts nicht eingetreten werden könne, sondern man vielmehr darauf halten müsse, dass er sich alsdann über die ihm zu Gebote stehenden Mittel zu beabsichtigter Auswanderung des näheren ausweise, welcher Beschluss dem Herrn Direktor der mehrgenannten Anstalt zur Kenntnis gebracht werden soll."

The Stadtarchiv contains files of the following newspapers, which contain frequent references to emigration: *Churer Wochenblatt*, 1839-1850; *Churer Zeitung*, 1814-1856; *Bündner Zeitung*, 1830-1856; *Morgenstern*, 1842-1843; *Der liberale Alpenbote*, 1848-1860; *Der Freie Rätier*, 1843-1848, 1868– ; *Bündner Tageblatt*, 1852– ; *Rheinquellen*, 1856-1860.

CANTON AARGAU.

AARAU: STAATSARCHIV.

Location: The old " Staatsarchiv des Kantons Aargau " is located in the same building as the Cantonal Library (Kantonsbibliothek), *i. e.,* behind the Regierungsgebäude. Nothing relating to American history was accessible in the old Cantonal Archive. The Cantonal Library (about 100,000 volumes) contains about 500 manuscripts. There is an index for the latter, but this does not describe the manuscripts, some of which, such as the large group of the Hallwyl manuscripts, may in their great bulk contain some reference to America. The material for the nineteenth century is contained in the Registratur, located in the neighboring Regierungsgebäude. There is interesting evidence here of a large emigration from Aargau in the nineteenth century.

Hours: The state archivist, who is also cantonal librarian, must be consulted for permission and hours for work.

AARAU: REGISTRATUR.

Protokolle des Regierungsrates.[1]

1803-1809.

" Valentin Jäggy von Siszlen nach Amerika." Protok. No. 2, pp. 87, 181. (Auswanderung gestattet, 10 per cent. Abzug, 1803.)
" Joh. Jakob Urech von Othmarsingen nach Amerika." Prot. No. 7, p. 317. (Erlaubt. 10 per cent. Abzug. Verlust des Bürger- und Landrechts. 1806.)

1810-1819.

" Amerika, Auswanderung." Nos. 10, 11, 16, 17, 18, 19.[2]
" Grundsätze und Regeln darüber." No. 16.
" Anordnungen und Berichte." No. 17.
" Abzugsgebühren von Auswanderern." No. 17.
" Anwerbungen durch Hüber, Märk und Wasmer." No. 17.
" Auswanderungswerber." No. 16.
" Aus den Bezirken Baden und Brugg." No. 16.
" Bürgschaft und Geldhinterlagen der Auswanderer." No. 17.
" Bürgschaft der Gemeinde Wallbach für ihre Ausgewanderten." No. 17.
" Bürgerrechtsverzichtleistungen." No. 17.
" Heimatlose, Beförderung ihrer Auswanderung." No. 17.
" Masznahmen von Preussen, Holland und Baden gegen die lästigen Auswanderungstransporte." No. 19.
" Rückkehr von Ausgewanderten in traurigem Zustande." No. 17.

---

[1] Called " Kleiner Rat " until 1840, and elected by the " Grosser Rat ".
[2] The numbers here correspond to the years, *e. g.,* 19 means 1819.

" Planta, Handelskonsul in Amsterdam, Geldvorschüsse-Rechnung." Nos. 17, 18, 19.
" Siggenthaler, auswandernde, Unterstützungsgesuch." No. 16.
" Totenscheine der Ausgewanderten." No. 17.
" Auf der Reise verstorbener." No. 19.
" Weibergutsversicherung auswandernder Bürger." No. 16. (Emigrant compelled to insure property of wife.)

SPEZIALIA.

Thirty-seven cases, between 1816-1819, of individuals on record, some with families, emigrating to America.

1820-1829.

Amerika. " Aufstellung zweier schweiz. Gesandten in d. Ver. Staaten." 1823.
" Auskundschaftung der Ausgewanderten: Johann Jakob Märlis Familie. von Rufenach." Nos. 24, 27, 28.
" Auswanderung nach Amerika." 9 cases, some with families. Nos. 20, 21, 24, 27, 28, 29.
" Bürgschaftsleistung bei Auslieferung von Erbschaften." No. 24.
" Geldvorschüsse an die Auswanderer nach Nordamerika aus der Staatskasse, Rechnung darüber." Nos. 20, 21. (48 persons, total of over 2600 fr.)
" Holland: Klage wegen der Zudringlichkeit der Auswanderer." No. 20.
" Holland: Formalitäten für die einzuschiffenden Auswanderer." No. 28.
" Rechnung des schweiz. Consuls über die Auswanderer." Nos. 20, 21, 22.
" Verrechnung der Depositengelder von den im Jahre 1817 Ausgewanderten." No. 29.

1829-1840.

" Auskunft über bestehende Handelsgesetze." No. 31.
" Formalitäten für die Reisenden über Holland." No. 32.
" Requisiten der Auswanderer durch Frankreich." No. 33.
" Unglückliche Lage der Auswanderer in New Orleans." No. 37.
" Unterstützung der schweiz. Hülfsgesellschaft in New Orleans." No. 38.
" Visirung der Pässe der Auswanderer." No. 33.
Kreisschreiben. Matters pertaining to consular business. See Bern archives.
Auswanderung: Besonderes. About 50 individual cases of emigrants.

1840-1849.

Amerika. " Auslieferung des Gerhard Koster." No. 44.
" Auslieferungsvertrag mit den Vereinigten Staaten." No. 45.
" Auswanderung dahin, diessfällige Gefahren für Unvorsichtige." No. 45.
" Andreas Dietsch in Aarau, Kapitalfond d. Auswanderungsgesellschaft betr." No. 44.
" Eingangszoll für Seidenstoffe." No. 44. Other consular business.
" Rathanerbieten für die Auswanderer." No. 46.
" Consule und Vice-consule." Nos. 43, 44, 45, 46.
" Handelsvertrag mit der Schweiz." Nos. 44, 45, 46.
" Privilegiengesuch eines Bürgers der Ver. Staaten für die Erfindung einer Doppelzunge auf Feuerspritzen." No. 40.

Aargau

"Unterstützungsgesuch des J. P. Meier von Wohlen zur Auswanderung." No. 45.
"Zuschrift von Ellion Cresson in London über den Vorzug der Auswanderung nach den Ver. Staaten, statt nach Afrika." No. 41.
"Auswanderung-Unterstützungen (Beisteuern) und Gesuche." 38 cases, 1848-1849.
Kreisschreiben. See Bern archives.
"Versammlung von Auswanderern zu Degerfelden." No. 48. "Zu Windisch." No. 48.

1850-1859.
"Steckbriefe gegen Verbrecher. Versendungsart." No. 50.
"Requisite der Bürgerbriefe." No. 53.
"Wechselsendungen, erforderliche Verfallzeit bei Sicht." No. 59.
"Auswanderung—Staatsbeisteuern."
Several hundred cases, men and women, mostly from 1851 to 1854, fewer 1855 to 1857. A typical case is the following:
1854. "Oberlehrer Kaspar Bächli: Gesuch mit Frau und 6 Kindern um Staatsbeisteuer." Protokoll: "Der Hr. Direktor des Innern referirt mündlich über das von Oberlehrer Kasp. Bächli in Würenlingen an die Erziehungsdirektion gerichtete und von dieser der Direktion des Innern zur Entsprechung empfohlene Gesuch um Verabfolgung einer Unterstützung, um ihm, seiner Ehefrau, und seinen 6 Kindern die Auswanderung nach Nordamerika möglich zu machen, da nur dieses Mittel ihm übrig bleibe, dem drohenden Geldstag und dem drückenden Elend zu entgehen." Nach Antrag wird beschlossen: "In Anbetracht des 30jährigen Lehrerdienstes des Benannten, die Direktion des Innern zu ermächtigen, demselben einen ausserordentlichen Beitrag von Fr. 50. verabfolgen zu lassen."

1860-1869.
"Beschwerde über die Abschiebung von Vagabunden, Angeklagten, und Verbrechern nach Nordamerika." No. 68.
"Bürgerrechts-Erwerbung durch Schweizerinnen infolge Heirat mit einem nordamerikanischen Bürger." No. 60.
"Emigrations-Bureau-Errichtung zu Schutzen der Auswanderer." No. 64.
"Schenkung eines Lincoln-Albums." No. 68.
"Staatliche Verhältnisse-betreffende Broschüre von Stiger." H. No. 64.
"New York. Schweiz. Wohlthätigkeits Verein, Beschwerde über Spedition hülfloser Auswanderer durch viele Gemeinden." No. 66.

1870-1879.
"Statistik der überseeischen Auswanderung vom Jahr 1873 bis 1879."
"Angebliche Nötigung zur Auswanderung der Anna Büchi von Unterehrendingen nach Nordamerika." No. 77. (Beschwerde des Consuls in Philadelphia.)
"Angebliche Abschiebung der Marie Wehrli. von Küttigen, nach Nordamerika." No. 77. (Pflichtwidriges Verfahren gewisser Agenturen in Basel.)
"Beschwerde in Einwanderungssache."
"Militärpensionen aus Nordamerika." Nos. 70-79. Very many cases.
"Philadelphia Weltausstellung." Nos. 75, 76.

Registratur 143

1880-1889.
" Mormonenstaat Utah. Warnung." Kreisschreiben. No. 86.
" Statistik." Nos. 80-89.
Spezielles unter den Namen der Auswanderer.

AUSWANDERUNGEN, 1840-1851.

" Bezirksweise Übersicht der Auswanderungen während der letzten 11 Jahre (1840-1851)." A most interesting table of statistics showing the number of emigrants from every district of the canton of Aargau, men, women, and children, also the amount of their property (both that which was carried away and that which was left behind), and also the amount paid in support of those needing financial aid for emigration. During this period there were 3343 emigrants, of whom 2112 were adults, 1231 children; 1990 were males, 1353 females. The value of the property taken away amounted to over 588,530 francs, that left behind 196,220 francs; the home districts (Gemeinden) furnished 198,998 francs in support of these emigrants, the state gave 25,940 francs. The state (*i. e.*, the canton) made a practice of giving 30 francs per head to those emigrating poor persons to whom their own districts also gave aid (for the defraying of the expense of transportation to the foreign land). " Eine hergebrachte Unterstützung von Fr. 30 per Kopf für Arme von ihrer Gemeinde gleichfalls unterstützte Auswanderer."

Printed Reports: Rechenschafts-Berichte des Kleinen Raths (Regierungsrates) an den Grossen Rat des Kantons Aargau, 1837-1913.
Berichtliche und Statistische Notizen über Auswanderung vom Kanton Aargau.

CANTON THURGAU.

FRAUENFELD: KANTONSARCHIV.

Location: The " Thurgauisches Kantonsarchiv " is located in the Regierungsgebäude of the capital city, Frauenfeld.

Hours: 9 a. m. to 12 m. ; 3 to 6 p. m.

Serfdom (Leibeigenschaft) existed in the canton of Thurgau until 1760, rendering emigration practically impossible before that time. As a result of the hard times of 1798, when the Thurgau became the scene of war between the French, Austrians, and Russians, there arose a desire to emigrate, but the difficulties existing or imposed prevented emigration. No records on America appear before the nineteenth century.

The " Thurgauisches Kantonsarchiv, Alteidgenössische Abteilung " contains the " Archiv des Schlosses Arenenberg."

Rubrik IX. 221. Polizeiwesen. Sicherheitspolizei.
  Auswanderung, 1803-1804. Nach der Krim.
  Auswanderung, 1817. Nach Russland.
  Beschwerde des Königs d. Niederlande gegen (mittellose) Auswanderer nach Nordamerika. Kreisschreiben. 1817.
  Gesuche um Bewilligung zum Auswandern nach Amerika. 1828-1830.
  Gesuche um Unterstützung zum Auswandern. 1848, 1851, 1852.

Rubrik IX. 222. Auswanderungsangelegenheiten. Polizeiwesen, Flüchtlinge, Auswanderung.

1860-1863. Verhältnisse der schweizerischen Auswanderer in Brasilien.

1860, Nov. 3. " Auf die Mitteilung des Polizeidepartements, dass der Schutzverein für entlassene Sträflinge in Verbindung mit der Gemeinde Landschlacht beschlossen haben, dem Reinhard Schilling, Schlosser von Landschlacht, gegenwärtig 30 Jahre alt, die Reisekosten nach Amerika zu bestreiten, falls auch vom Staate hierfür ein Beitrag geliefert werde, in Betracht:

" (a) dass Schilling seit dem 24. Juni 1848, wo von begangener Betrügereien zum ersten Mal mit 6 Wochen geschätztem Arrest belegt wurde, 6 weitere Verurteilungen wegen Diebstählen und Betrügereien erlitt und in Folge dessen während diesem Zeitraum $7\frac{1}{2}$ Jahre theils im Arbeitshause, theils im Zuchthause zubringen musste——

" (b) dass Schilling laut den aufgenommenen Verhörakten bereits Bekanntschaft mit den gefährlichsten Verbrechern in mehreren Strafanstalten gemacht und selbst in ihrer Gesellschaft Verbrechen verübt hat——

" (c) dass unter diesen Umständen kaum gehofft werden darf, dass der gesunde, kräftige und auch geistig begabte junge Mann genug Kraft in sich fühle, von dem bisherigen verbrecherischen Lebenswandel abzugehen, so lange er mehr oder weniger in Verbindung mit den Genossen seiner Verbrechen steht——

" (d) dass Schilling als geschickter Arbeiter, sowohl als Schlosser als auch als Rothfärber mit Leichtigkeit überall sein redliches

Auskommen finden kann,—und dies natürlich da um so mehr, wo seine früheren Lebensverhältnisse gänzlich unbekannt sind——

" (e) dass nach den Akten dem Schilling bei seiner Verhaftung in Gossen eine ihm eigentümlich zugehörende Uhr abgenommen und an das Verhöramt dahier eingesandt wurde, die laut Bericht dieser Behörde nicht mehr aufgefunden werden könne, daher der Staat demselben hiefür einen Ersatz zu leisten hat——

" (f) dass in Besichtigung aller dieser Thatsachen es vollkommen sich rechtfertigt, wenn auch der Staat das Bestreben des Schutzvereins für entlassene Sträflinge und der Gemeinde Landschacht in concreto durch einen Beitrag unterstützt—auf den Antrag des Polizeidepartements: beschlossen:

" (1) Sie dem Schutzaufsichtsverein ein Beitrag an die Auswanderungskosten des Reinhart Schilling nach Amerika von f. 80 zu verabreichen, in der Meinung, dass damit auch die Angelegenheit wegen der obberührten Taschenuhr ihre Erledigung gefunden habe und dass der Schutzverein dafür besorgt sei, dass Schilling wirklich nach Amerika auswandere.

" (2) Mitteilung dieser Schlussnahme an die Finanzverwaltung behufs Ausbezahlung des fraglichen Beitrags."

1861, Mar. 13. 50 f. granted to Schutzaufsichtsverein in connection with another thief named Huber.

Aug. 13. 100 f. granted to Ulrich Früh, thief, similarly for emigration.

1864, July 1. 430 f. granted to J. Ruckstuhl, thief, similarly for emigration.

July 23. 125 f. granted to Lisette Klein, mother of 2 illegitimate children, for expenses of emigration.

1865. List of 176 Swiss who went down on the *William Nelson,* which was burned at sea June 26, 1865.

1867. Kreisschreiben. Untersuchung über Auswanderung.

Gesuche um Unterstützung zur Auswanderung.

1868, Apr. 11. Basel, Consulat der Vereinigten Staaten v. Nordamerika. Tit. " Auf ihr verehrliches Schreiben v. 16 d. M. mittelst welchem Sie uns mitteilen, dass die Regierung d. Vereinigten Staaten Ursache habe, zu glauben, dass eine Combination in fremden Ländern bestehe, die den Zweck habe, Vagabunden, Angeklagte, und Verbrecher von Verhaftung und Einkerkerung zu befreien, um sie nach den Vereinigten Staaten zu senden, beehren wir uns Ihnen zu erwidern, dass es im herwärtigen Canton laut diesfalls eingezogenen Berichten hie und da vorkommt, dass einzelne arbeitsscheue, jedoch arbeitsfähige Individuen, welche sich aus freien Stücken zur Auswanderung nach Amerika verstehen, hiefür aus Gemeindemitteln Reiseunterstützungen erhalten, dass uns dagegen durchaus keine Fälle bekannt sind wo Angeklagte oder Verbrecher, um sie vor Verhaftung und Einkerkerung zu befreien, nach Amerika geschickt worden wären." (Large number of papers on this matter, including replies from various districts of the canton.)

June 10. " Gesuch der Schwestern Maria Müller und Emilie Vollenweider, um Unterstützung zur Auswanderung nach Amerika. Abgeschlagen."

Statistik der Auswanderung aus dem Thurgau im Jahre 1870. Aus verschiedenen Bezirken.

1873. Warnung vor der Auswanderung nach brasilianischen Kolonien. Kreisschreiben.

1874, Apr. 17. "Auf das Gesuch der katholischen Kirchenvorsteherschaft Leutmerk[en] v. 9. April, dass dem verwahrlosten und wegen Diebstahls schon wiederholt bestraften Adolf Schönauer v. Leutmerk (geb. 10. Mai 1856) die Auswanderung nach Amerika durch Zuwendung eines Staatsbeitrags ermöglicht werde, sowie in Hinblick auf das unterstützende Begleitschreiben des Bezirksamts Weinfeld v. 31. Mai, und die vorausgegangenen Präcedenzfälle (Konrad Huber, 1861, und Reinhart Schilling, 1860[1]) wird zufolge des Antrags des Armendepartements, beschlossen:

"(1) Sei der kathol. Kirchgemeinde Leutmerken an die Kosten der Auswanderung des Adolf Schönauer aus dem Hülfs- und Armenfonds ein Beitrag v. fr. 100 bewilliget.

"(2) Sei dieser Beitrag an die kathol. Armenpflege L. aushinzubezahlen, sobald sie den Nachweis der erfolgten Einschiffung des Adolf Schönauer geleistet haben wird.

"(3) Mitteilung an die kathol. Armenkasse Leutmerken."

1875, Nov. 5. Refusal of an application for support of emigration. Statistics on emigration.

1881, Sept. 5. A case of support for an emigrating family. (Not of undesirable class.)

1883. "Auswanderung nach Chili betreffend." Kreisschreiben.

Printed Material: Amtsblatt des Kantons Thurgau. Rubrik Auswanderungswesen, especially 1888, 1889, 1892-1898, 1904.

Sonntagsblatt der Thurgauer Zeitung, Mar. 9, 1913: "Eine Schweizerkolonie im Ausland." Neu-Helvetia in Uruguay (Jakob Nater).

---

[1] Statement is made that these, on hearsay, are doing well in America.

CANTON TICINO.

BELLINZONA: ARCHIVIO CANTONALE.

Location: The " Archivio Cantonale in Bellinzona " is located in the government building, " Guberno ", Piazzo Giardino.
Hours: 8 a. m. to 12 m.; 2 to 6 p. m.
The manuscript material relating to America is very scant and unimportant. The archivist reports that under his predecessors the custom prevailed of lending manuscripts to private persons without proper security for their return. As a result of this custom the archive has been deprived of some of its most valuable materials.

Manuscripts: " Emigrazione ".

Bern, June 2, 1817. N. Direttorio Federale: " Communica nota importante, concernente quegli individui, che intendono emigrar per l' America, e sono privi di sustenenza per la loro dimora nei Paesi Bassi, e per far fronte alle spese per imbarcassi sul mare."
Bellinzona, Apr. 17, 1819. Communication in regard to the establishment of a colony of Swiss in Brazil, under the name of Nouvelle-Fribourg; also terms offered officers and underofficers in this service.
London, Oct. 12, 1821. " Il sg. Pietro Schmidtmeyer trasmette un rapporto in francese ed altro in inglese sull' infelice stato delle Colonia Svizzera a Conta-Gallo nel Brasile, e fa conoscere i soccorsi destinati a quella populazione."
Zürich, Nov. 9, 1846. " Trasmette il prodocollo d' una conferenza tenuta nell' 8. sett. 1846 concernente l'emigrazione dalla Svizzera."

Printed Material.

Emilio Bontà, " L' Emigrazione nel Cantone Ticino ", in *Almanaco del Popolo Ticinese* (Locarno, Scuola Normale, edito per cura della Società degli Amici dell' Educazione e di Utilità Pubblica), No. 68, 1912, pp. 104-123.
Bollettino Storico della Svizzera Italiana (ed. Emilio Motta [1]), 1888, pp. 276-277; 1891, p. 120; 1906, p. 16.
Conto Reso del Consiglio di Stato della Repubblica e Cantone del Ticino per l' Amministrazione dello Stato dal 1. Gennaio al 31. Dicembre 1855 (Bellinzona, 1856). These publications (accounts rendered) continue to the present time.
Il Dovere: Giornale dei Liberali Ticinesi, No. 34 (Locarno, Mar. 1, 1884). Feuilleton: " I Fratelli Delmonico: La storia dei più famosi Trattori d' America." (The story of the founding of the Delmonico restaurant of New York City; the Delmonico brothers came originally from Ticino.) This article is taken from a San Francisco paper, *Voce del Popolo di S. Francisco*.

---

[1] Signor E. Motta, archivist in Milan, is regarded as the leader in collecting the materials for the history of Italian-Swiss emigration. The bibliography here given was compiled with the aid of his suggestions.

Patria e Progresso: Organo dell' Emigrazione Ticinese, No. 16 (Bellinzona, 1888). La Festa annuale della Società Demopedenta e la Storia dell' Emigrazione Ticinese. (Emilio Motta proposes a plan of gathering all available extant material for a history of emigration from the Canton Ticino.)

Patria e Progresso, 1885-1886, various numbers.

L'Agricoltore Ticinese: Organo della Società Cantonale di Agricoltura e Selvicoltura (Lugano, 1897). L'Emigrazione in rapporto alla Prosperità del Cantone. Signed, Gallachi.

Brenno Bertoni, " Plan d'une Statistique de l'Émigration Tessinoise ", in Zeitschrift für Schweizerische Statistik (Bern, 1892), pp. 284-297.

Le Colonie Svizzere di California alla fine del Secolo Decimonono, 1900-1901 (San Francisco, Geo. F. Cavolli, 1901), pp. 10-40. Reprinted in the Nuovo Secolo dell' Elvezia, Nos. 3-4 (1905).

Schweizerisches Bundesblatt, 1849, II. 348; 1853, II. 447, 654; 1854, I. 604-615; 1868, II. 571; 1869, II. 108, etc.

T. Hardmeyer, " Ticinesi in California ". Dal Dovere di Locarno, 1885. In N. Züricher Zeitung, Nos. 172-174 (1885).

G. Preziosi, Gl' Italiani negli Stati Uniti del Nord (Milano, Libreria editrice Milanese, 1908).

In the absence of adequate manuscript and printed materials, the student of Italian-Swiss (i. e., from the canton Ticino) emigration would do well to consult native or resident observers of emigration. The compiler received, e. g., from Professor Eligio Pometta (author of the history of Ticino in its relations with Switzerland and Italy, in 3 vols.), the following interesting information: Some sections of Ticino are almost depopulated by emigration, as the Val Maggia and the Val Verzasca, similarly Broglio and sections near Locarno. The destination is mostly California; a few go to Argentina. The emigrants from Ticino are mostly successful in California and remain there. They are liberal in supporting needs at home with money. There is a new-built church in the village of Brontallo which bears the inscription: " cum auro Californiae ". Some of the few that return bring 10,000 to 20,000 francs with them, and build villas. The returning emigrants are called Californians (Californese), not Americans. Most of those that revisit their homes in Ticino (and the most desirable class) return to California. The climate of California and the means of livelihood correspond most closely to conditions at home. Two of the Italian newspapers, one in New York and one in San Francisco (Novella Helvetia) are published by Ticino-Americans.

THE FRENCH CANTONS.[1]

The French cantons of Switzerland, named in the order fixed by Swiss law, are Fribourg, Vaud, Valais, Neuchâtel, and Geneva. Of these Fribourg, the least completely French and the only one predominantly Catholic, is the only one which belonged to the old Swiss Confederation. In the official order of cantons it stands between Zug and Solothurn, while Vaud, Valais, Neuchâtel, and Geneva, added as cantons in 1803 (Vaud) and in 1815, stand, in the order named, as the last four of the twenty-two cantons. The archives of the five are treated below in the order indicated.

The French cantons of Switzerland hold a much less important relation to American history than the German. The emigration from them to America has been much less. Since 1878, when full Swiss statistics begin, the number annually migrating from the French cantons to America (to North America as a whole down to 1886, to the United States, separately enumerated, since then) has averaged only about 30 from Fribourg, 120 from Vaud, 100 from Valais, 200 from Neuchâtel, and 80 from Geneva. Though America has owed to French Switzerland some very eminent persons—Bouquet and Haldimand, Gallatin and Agassiz and Guyot—the total emigration has not been of such dimensions that we could expect to find in the archives of these cantons much material bearing on American history.

The amount of such material has been lessened by the fact that the emigration from these regions has in very few instances been organized emigration, almost always individual. Moreover, the governments of these cantons have not usually prescribed for their subjects a formal governmental permission to emigrate, as the governments of the states of Germany have usually done (see Mr. Learned's *Guide to the German State Archives, passim*); and when the emigration was the result of revolution or of political disturbance, as it often was, it naturally took place without passports, and left little or no trace in the governmental records.

Each of the cantonal archives of French-speaking Switzerland has a library, sometimes of moderate extent (best in the cases of Neuchâtel and Geneva), containing the local and other publications most needed for consultation by persons working in the archives.

---

[1] The archives of these cantons were examined, and the following accounts of them written, by J. F. Jameson; see the preface.

CANTON DE FRIBOURG.

FRIBOURG: ARCHIVES D'ÉTAT.

Location: Chiefly in the Chancellerie, but see below.
Hours: 9 a. m. to 12 m.; 2 to 5 p. m. (in winter, 2 to 4).

Down to 1902 the bureau of the archives was a portion of the Chancery, or office of the secretary of the Council of State. By *arrêté* of January 27, 1902, the archives of the canton are made a subdivision (*département*) of the Ministry (*Direction*) of Public Instruction and Archives. The Department of Archives was by this law given charge of the administration of the archives of the state, and of the control and supervision of the archives of the various executive ministries and offices, and also of the archives of the communes, parishes, and state institutions.

A *règlement* of September 20, 1867, respecting the organization and employees of the Chancery of State, still holds good in respect to details in spite of this transfer.

Reports on the archives, fuller than is usual in other cantons, are to be found in the annual *Rapports du Conseil d'État sur sa Gestion*. Before 1902 these are to be found in the section " Chancellerie "; after that date in the section devoted to the Ministry of Public Instruction and Archives.

The offices of the archivist, and the archives with the large exceptions noted below, are in the building called the Chancellerie, the main seat of the cantonal government. They have indeed always been kept there since that edifice was built, in the seventeenth century. For some time, however, it has been necessary, besides the two basement rooms in the Chancellerie now devoted to the archives, to make use of two others in a building called the Grenette, close by the Church of Notre Dame. A fifth large room at the Convent of the Cordeliers was also used until 1903; but in that year the manuscripts contained in it were removed to rooms in the basement or ground floor of the Hôtel de Ville (Hotel Cantonal, Rathaus).

The archives of Fribourg are extensive, amounting to some 15,000 volumes and nearly 20,000 parchments, the oldest being the will of Queen Bertha of Burgundy, A. D. 961. There are many special inventories or indexes, and a general manuscript Inventaire des Archives, made carefully in 1841. The last is long since out of date, and the present archivist has begun a new general and complete inventory. The following are the most important of the series in the archives: the Manuaux du Conseil or journals of the Council of State, the chief executive body of the canton, extending from 1438 and now (1912) amounting to 465 volumes; the Mandaten-Bücher or books of their ordinances, extending, in 11 volumes, from 1498 to the beginning of the nineteenth century; the Missiven-Bücher or letter-books of the council, which for the period from 1449 to 1814 extend to 104 volumes; the Correspondance Extérieure, beginning in 1800 (37 volumes); the correspondence with the other cantons; various record books of the administrative boards, and papers turned over from time to time by the executive ministries (no regular periods for this); the Abschied-Bücher or copies of the proceedings of the federal diets, filling about 250 volumes, from 1498 to 1848; the Livres de la Bourgeoisie of the town of Fribourg, for various periods from the fourteenth to he eighteenth century, 13 volumes (the registers of bourgeoisie since 1798 are in the archives of the town of Fribourg, those of other towns are preserved locally) ; a certain number of judicial and family records ; and a great variety of financial accounts. Chief among the latter are the accounts of the treasurers, extending from 1376 to the present time, in nearly 700 volumes. It is in the Manuaux and in the Correspondance Extérieure that materials having any bearing upon the history of America might be found (see the list which follows). Each of the volumes in these series has its own index, but there is no general repertory of these series. Since 1902 the protocols (journals) of the Conseil d'État have been printed (printed as manuscript, in three copies only), and are fully indexed.

The deposit at the Hôtel de Ville or Hôtel Cantonal consists of the conventual, feudal, and other medieval documents which have fallen into the possession of the cantonal government. That at the Grenette consists chiefly of the registers and papers of notaries, and of land papers. M. Joseph Schneuwly, for a long time (1867-1908) state archivist of Fribourg in the last generation,[1] displayed especial activity in the gathering and preservation of notarial papers, and the collection now numbers some six thousand volumes, running from the fourteenth century down. A guide to it may be found in a printed list prepared by him, *Tableau Alphabétique des Notaires qui ont stipulé dans le Canton de Fribourg antérieurement à 1868* (Fribourg, Imprimerie de Ch. Marchand, 1868, pp. 103), which gives each notary's name, domicile. date of patent and of death, the dates and number of volumes of his registers and where they are preserved—but all in this list are now in the archives of state.

The registers of *état civil* are kept in the communes solely. Births, marriages, and deaths have been registered by the communes since 1876; baptisms, marriages, and deaths have long been registered by the ecclesiastical authorities of the parishes, in accordance with the decrees of the Council of Trent. There is no sending of duplicates of registers of *état civil* to a central or cantonal deposit, as in certain other cantons.

Each commune has its archives. There is no fixed relation between the cantonal archives and those of the communes, no *service d'inspection*, for example ; but Mr. Schneuwly in his time classified all the communal archives on a uniform system.

After the death in 1897 of Abbé Grenaud, professor in the University of Fribourg, his manuscripts were bought by the cantonal government and these now form a special collection in the cantonal archives. Of this section there is a catalogue prepared by M. Paul E. Martin, formerly subarchivist of Fribourg, now archivist of Geneva, *Catalogue des Manuscrits de la Collection Grenaud aux Archives d'État de Fribourg* (Fribourg, 1911, pp. 68). For the most part these papers relate to the earlier periods of Fribourg history. One notes, however (p. 45 of the *Catalogue*) : " Projet d'un mémoire sur l'Atlantide, ou la connaissance qu'avaient les anciens d'Amérique, de la forme et du mouvement de la terre."

Regulations of the canton concerning emigration, 1848, 1852, 1854, and especially Nov. 25, 1862, may be found in their proper chronological places in the *Bulletin Officiel des Lois, Décrets, etc.*

[1] See the article, " Joseph Schneuwly, Archiviste d'État ", in *Revue Historique l'audoise*, XVI. 344-349, copied from articles in the local newspaper, *La Liberté*, issues of Oct. 5 and 17, 1908, by his successor, Mr. Tobie de Raemy. Substantially the same article appears, in German, in *Freiburger Geschichtsblätter*, XV. 140-144.

152   *Fribourg*

There are also at Fribourg the following archives: archives of the commune, naturally less important than those of the canton, at the Maison de Ville, next door to the (now cantonal) Hôtel de Ville; archives of the bishopric, relating to the period since the bishop removed his residence from Lausanne to Fribourg—that is to say, mostly modern—kept at the Évêché, and very well arranged; also archives of the convents (6), and of private families.

The following list of data as to relations between the canton of Fribourg and America, more especially the United States, was prepared by Mr. Georges Corpataux, under the direction of Mr. Tobie de Raemy, state archivist of the canton.

Manuaux du Conseil d'État.
Manual for 1817.

ff. 105, 154, 257. Concernant l'émigration pour l'Amérique.
f. 358. On ne prendra point de mesure pour empêcher l'émigration.

1819.

f. 66. Émigration d'une colonie Suisse au Brésil.
ff. 265, 281. Mesures prises par la cour de Baden au sujet des émigrants.

1820.

f. 240. Concernant l'émigration des Suisses pour l'Amérique.

1831.

f. 132. Mesures au sujet des émigrants pour l'Amérique.

1832.

ff. 171, 596, 673, 862, 863, 884. Émigration pour l'Amérique.
f. 777. États-Unis: Droits d'aubaine et de traite foraine.
ff. 862, 863. Émigrants pour l'Amérique: Émoluments pour expédition de passeports.

1833.

ff. 147, 626. Émigrations pour les États-Unis.
f. 273. Émigration pour le Brésil. Manière d'obtenir l'indigénat.

1834.

f. 219. Mr. Charles Ryhiner renonce à sa place de vice-consul des États du Nord de l'Amérique; et son remplacement.

1835.

f. 545. Mémoire de Mr. Bühler sur les émigrations au Brésil.

1836.

f. 15. Négociations avec le gouvernement du Brésil pour une émigration.

1839.
f. 196. Nomination du consul aux États-Unis.
Nomination de Powers comme consul.

1842.
f. 242. Petition adressée par un certain nombre d'émigrés.

1843.
f. 255. Émigrés: Mémoires des Argoviens.

1844.
f. 86. Émigrants: Transport gratuit jusqu'à Anvers de leurs effets.
f. 148. États-Unis d'Amérique: Nomination du consul.
f. 559. Démission du consul des États-Unis d'Amérique en Suisse.

1845.
f. 210. États-Unis: Remplacement du consul général.
f. 314. Présentation pour le sixième consulat.
f. 366. Projet de traité entre la Suisse et les États-Unis concernant l'extradition des criminels.
f. 522. Nomination du consul de commerce des États-Unis à Bâle.
f. 504. Dangers auxquels s'exposent les émigrants en Amérique.

1846.
f. 54. Déclaration pour les marchandises à destination de l'Amérique.
f. 113. Annonce du consul des États-Unis de l'Amérique de faire les publications des émigrés en Amérique.
f. 288. Circulaire sur les avis dans les contrats des émigrants en Amérique.

1847.
f. 113. Annonce du consul des États-Unis de faire les publications pour les émigrés.
f. 268. Les Grisons demandent que la question des émigrations soit traitée à la diète.
ff. 527, 572. Rapport de la conférence sur les émigrations.
f. 561. Enquête au sujet des émigrations de Gruyères.

1848.
f. 117. Émigrations en Amérique, projet.
ff. 209, 226, 440, 593. Émigrations en Amérique, renseignements.
f. 313. Émigrants sans ressources: plainte du consul suisse au Havre.
f. 419. Émigration: Circulaire de l'État de Schaffouse.
f. 451. Avis à la *Feuille Officielle* concernant l'émigration.
f. 792. Instructions aux émigrants en Amérique.

1849.
f. 212. Émigrants.

1850.
- f. 382. Mesures prises par la Belgique concernant le passage des émigrants.
- f. 788. Les mandats d'arrêts à envoyer en Amérique du Nord, doivent être expédiés par Liverpool.
- f. 864. Publications signalant les menées de quelques agents pour recruter des émigrants en Californie.

1851.
- f. 401. Émigration : Bureau de renseignements à Brême.
- f. 512. Émigrations : Propositions pour projet de loi.

1852.
- f. 210. Émigrants : Mesures prises concernant les subsides communaux.
- ff. 301, 387. Agence fédérale d'émigrations.
- f. 395. Conférence.
- f. 470. Renseignements sur les mesures de précautions à prendre par les émigrants en Amérique.
- f. 470. Émigrants : Précaution à prendre pour se rendre en Amérique.

1853.
- f. 101. Émigrants en Amérique, précautions.

1854.
- f. 131. Circulaire aux communes concernant les formes à suivre en cas de demande de subside pour émigrations.
- f. 140. Émigrations : Renseignements sur demandes.
- f. 145. Émigrations : Défense de viser des passeports sans déclaration du préfet.
- f. 177. Émigrations : Avis au public concernant les subsides des communes.
- f. 217. Plainte du consul Suisse au Havre sur les nombreuses missions et demandes en matière concernant émigrations.
- f. 330. Rapport d'Argovie sur la question d'émigrations.
- f. 365. Émigrations : Circulaire d'Argovie concernant un concordat à établir.
- f. 481. Mesures à prendre concernant les émigrants pauvres à New-York.

1855.
- f. 104. Émigrations : Le ministre des États-Unis fait des observations.
- f. 181. Émigrations : Surveillance.

1856.
- f. 8. Traité de commerce et d'extradition en Amérique.
- f. 199. Émigrants : La légation de France de visa gratis sur attestation de pauvreté.

1857.
- ff. 90, 455. Journal général sur l'émigration.
- f. 133. Nouvel avis du Conseil Fédéral concernant les mesures à prendre pour l'émigration.
- f. 357. Trafic dans les billets de voyage des émigrants.
- f. 444. Amérique : Émigrants, billets de voyage.

f. 455. Amérique: Émigrants, statistiques.
f. 559. États-Unis demandent par l'entremise du Conseil Fédéral la loi sur les incendies.
f. 610. Statistiques des émigrés en Amérique.

1858.

f. 246. Émigrés au Brésil: Projet de réponse sur la part du remboursement des avances faites.
f. 906. Mesures contre les abus qui se pratiquent à l'occasion de la vente de billets de transport pour les émigrations dans l'intérieur des États-Unis.

1859.

ff. 125,595. Émigrants: Billets de transport.
f. 125. Renseignements sur la position des émigrés au Brésil.
f. 493. Billets de transport pour les émigrants aux États-Unis; renseignements.

1860.

f. 221. Visa gratuit de la légation française en faveur des émigrants traversant la France.
f. 242. Circulaire fédéral concernant la législation de l'Amérique du Nord.
f. 539. Renseignements demandés sur la convention de 1818 sur l'émigration au Brésil.

1861.

f. 40. Précautions à prendre pour empêcher l'enrôlement pour l'Amérique.
f. 356. États-Unis: Réclamations au sujet de Pierre Hermann.
f. 459. Amérique du Nord: Correspondance.

1862.

ff. 807, 842, 942, 986. Entreprise d'émigration: Maison Barbe, plainte de Chaney.
ff. 942, 986. Émigration: Zwilchenbart à Bâle, cautionnement.
ff. 986, 1018, 1036, 1053. Compagnies d'émigration; projet de sécret sur garantie.

1863.

f. 725. Dr. Joos, projet d'émigration dans l'état de Costa Ricca.

1864.

f. 206. Amérique du Nord. Brochures de Mr. Stiger.

1866.

f. 657. Émigration: Plaintes du Conseil Fédéral, avis au public.

1867.

ff. 13, 34. Amérique, États-Unis: Règlement concernant allocation de bonifications supplémentaires aux ex-soldats de l'Union.
f. 384. Amérique: Envois de malfaiteurs, réponse au Conseil Fédéral.
f. 772. États-Unis: Demande d'échange des publications officielles.

1868.
f. 25. Émigrations: Tableau à fournir au Conseil Fédéral.
f. 193. Amérique: Réclamation concernant envoie de criminels.
f. 273. Amérique: Liste des réclamations liquidées, pour solde, pensions, etc., des ressortissants Fribourgeois.
f. 366. Lois concernant l'émigration, envoi au gouvernement d'Italie.

1869.
f. 6. Réponse à la circulaire du Conseil Fédéral au sujet du nombre des émigrants.

1870.
f. 75. Amérique du Nord, statistique des terres de l'état.

1871.
f. 82. Émigration dans la République Argentine, brochure.
f. 286. Amérique: Brochure concernant l'instruction publique.

1872.
f. 193. Envoi de la *Gazette d'Émigration*, par Allemann.
ff. 273, 347, 473. Émigration de Fribourgeois, renseignements.
f. 742. États-Unis, paiement de pension.

1873.
Jan. 24. Brochure sur l'émigration.
Jan. 31. Émigration: Renseignements sur le Brésil.
Nov. 8. Émigration pour la colonie de Monitz au Brésil, circulaire fédéral.

1874.
June 20. Émigration: Lettre au Conseil Fédéral.

1875.
Apr. 2. Émigration de mineurs, convention internationale.
Apr. 16. *Id.*, conférence.
Apr. 19. *Id.*, projet de concordat.
Apr. 26. Concordat projeté.
May 10, 28, Aug. 27 (*bis*), Sept. 3. Concordat.
Dec. 18. Concordat approuvé.
Dec. 31. Émigration de mineurs, conférence.

1876.
Jan. 5, 7. Émigration de mineurs, conférence.
Mar. 15. Opération des agences d'émigration.
July 15. Agences d'émigration: Observations.
Sept. 22. Avis concernant Société d'Émigration.
Nov. 15. Émigrants: Projets de loi (premiers débats).

1877.
Mar. 2. États-Unis: Envoie de rapports de question.
Dec. 11. Émigrants à Punta Arena, demandes de rapatriement.

1878.
Jan. 23. Émigrants à Punta Arena, demandes de rapatriement.

1879.
Feb. 7. Rapport sur l'émigration.
Apr. 7. Émigration: Envoi de tableau au Conseil Fédéral.

1880.
Jan. 12. Émigration, statistique.
Apr. 26. Émigration: Envoi de formulaire au Conseil Fédéral.
June 29. Émigration: Envoi de journal.

1881.
Jan. 17. Statistique des émigrations.
Apr. 15. Émigration: Entrée en vigueur de la loi fédérale.
May 11. Émigration: Promulgation de la loi fédérale.
June 3. Émigration: Tableau des agents patentés.
Sept. 30. Émigration: Modifications à la loi sur agences.

1883.
Dec. 15. Émigration: Suspension pour le Chili.

CORRESPONDANCE EXTÉRIEURE.
Volume for 1818-1820.[1]

f. 146. Amérique, insurrection.
ff. 106, 111, 112, 143, 147, 150, 154, 162, 165, 168, 169, 170, 179, 186, 187, 188, 189, 190, 193, 195, 197 (*bis*), 199 (*bis*), 229, 233, 234, 237, 242 (*bis*), 321, 324, 361, 393. Émigration de Fribourgeois au Brésil.
ff. 224, 234, 324. Planta, consul d'Amsterdam.
f. 229. Amsterdam, émigration suisse pour le Brésil.
f. 357. Réponse à une plainte du consul suisse à Amsterdam.

1824-1826, June 30.

f. 9. États-Unis d'Amérique. Succession des Suisses y décédés.
f. 56. Manière d'obtenir un acte authentique du Brésil.
ff. 316, 351. Brésil: Déclaration d'indépendance; avènement de Dom Pedro: traité de paix et alliance avec le Portugal.

1826, July 1-1829, June 30.

f. 249. Émigration en Amérique par les Pays-Bas; condition.

1829, July 1-1831, Mar. 7.

ff. 198, 209. États-Unis: Lettres de créance de Böcker comme consul général de commerce en Suisse.
f. 215. Lettres de créance de Charles Ryhinner comme vice-consul des États-Unis.

---

[1] These dates in the titles of the volumes are inclusive.

1831-1832.

ff. 40, 454. Passage par la France d'émigrants en Amérique.
ff. 454, 462. Passage par les Pays-Bas d'émigrants en Amérique.

1833-1835.

f. 26. Amérique: Visa des passeports pour les États-Unis.
f. 153. États-Unis: Agents de voyage des émigrants suisses.
f. 268. Amérique du Nord: Nomination d'un vice-consul.
f. 467. Relations commerciales avec les États-Unis; situation des émigrés.

1836-1838.

f. 4. Émigration au Brésil: Négociations.

1839-1840.

f. 53. Exequatur donné à Mr. de Powers, consul général suisse aux États-Unis.

1847-1850.

f. 168. On remercie le consul belge en Suisse des renseignements donnés sur les mesures prises en Belgique pour le transport des émigrants pour l'Amérique.

1857-1860.

f. 98. Tableau des émigrés en Amérique.
f. 195. Réclamation au sujet des juifs des États-Unis.

1864-1865.

f. 289. Procès des communes suisses avec la maison Vergueiro d'Amérique.

1866-1867.

f. 258. Émigration au Brésil: Difficulté entre les communes suisses et les agents d'émigration Vergueiro et Cie.
f. 277. Amérique: Pensions militaires.
f. 294. Amérique: Pension réclamée par la veuve Ruffener.
f. 428. Amérique: Pension d'Elise veuve Ruffener née Stettler.

CANTON DE VAUD.

LAUSANNE: ARCHIVES CANTONALES.

Location: In the tower of the Cathedral.
Hours: 8 a. m. to 12 m.; 2 to 6 p. m.
Bibliography: Maxime Reymond, article "Archives" in the *Dictionnaire Historique, Géographique et Statistique du Canton de Vaud,* ed. E. Mottaz (Lausanne, 1911), pp. 79-81.
Antoine Baron, " Notices sur les Archives du Canton de Vaud ", in the *Journal de la Société Vaudoise d'Utilité Publique,* XIII. 311-318 (1845).

The region now embraced in the canton of Vaud consisted in the Middle Ages of a variety of jurisdictions, subject to the Bishop of Lausanne, to other feudal lords, and to municipalities. From 1536 to 1798 this region of " Suisse Romande " was subject to the authorities of the canton of Bern. From 1798 to 1803 it was a part of the Canton du Léman, in the Helvetic Confederation; from 1803 to 1814, of the French Empire and of the Département du Léman. It is only since 1815 that it has been a canton of the Swiss Republic.

In the Middle Ages the Bishop of Lausanne, the feudal lords, and the municipalities each kept their own archives. The Bernese on taking possession of the land transferred to Bern a vast number of parchments, chiefly ecclesiastical, as being useful for the administration of the land, and at Bern they were classified, in some cases copied into record books, and listed in inventories of various sorts—Inventaires Blanc, Rouge, and Vert, large parts of which have recently been consolidated into the Inventaire Bleu. In 1798 the short-lived République Lémanique claimed from Bern the archives relating to the Pays de Vaud. At various times from that date to 1843 the Bernese government sent to Lausanne some 50,000 parchments relating to Vaud, and also several thousand volumes covering the Bernese administration of Vaud in the period from 1536 to 1798. These the government of the canton of Vaud installed in the belfry of the cathedral at Lausanne. In 1829 it appointed a cantonal archivist, Antoine Baron, who served from 1829 to 1861; his successor, Aymon Crousaz, from 1861 to 1909.

Besides the documents thus transferred from Bern, the cantonal archives embrace the minutes of the notaries of the Pays de Vaud from the fourteenth to the eighteenth century, the *cadastres* and accompanying blanks from the seventeenth century down, the registers of *état civil* from about 1560 to 1821, and the governmental papers of the period since 1798, in so far as these have been turned over by the executive departments to the cantonal archives. Such deposits have been made at various times by the seven executive ministers, but it may in general be said that the latter retain the papers which have arisen in their business since about 1870.

At first the cantonal archives were subject to the Commissaire Général, after 1837 to the Chancery of State; now they are subordinate to the Department of Public Instruction. Their administration is governed by a law of November 24, 1905, in accordance with which the Council of State appoints the archivist and subarchivist for terms of four years.

Further particulars respecting the history of the cantonal archives may be found in the articles mentioned in the bibliography above.

The office of the archives is in an ancient building opposite the northwest corner of the cathedral. The archives themselves are kept in the cathedral tower, in which they fill three large, high rooms, one situated over the other, and each having one or more galleries.

The highest apartment, in the third story, is, with its galleries, mainly occupied with the records of the Bernese and earlier periods. Its main room contains many volumes of mandates and ordinances ("Obrigkeitliche Mandaten und Verordnungen") of the Bernese government for the various *bailliages* of which the Pays de Vaud consisted under the Bernese administration; the *onglets* or letter-books of the *bailliages*, some 200 volumes, and many portfolios of unbound correspondence; several hundred, perhaps a thousand, volumes of their financial accounts; and several hundred volumes of the decrees and other documents of the Cour d'Appellation Romande, of the Chambre des Bannerets, of the Chambre Économique, of the Commissariat, and of the criminal courts—the general administrative bodies maintained at Bern for the government of the Pays de Vaud. One likewise finds here registers of the church and of the Academy, and a certain number of books of the consistory, and other ecclesiastical records. This chamber also contains the registers of *état civil* (births, marriages, and deaths) down to 1821.

The records of births, marriages, and deaths in the Pays de Vaud begin practically with the Reformation. From that time the pastors kept registers of baptisms and marriages, though with some irregularity. The Bernese government in 1707 required the recording of births and baptisms, and in 1708 registration of deaths. Under the Helvetic Confederation, from 1799 to the beginning of 1801, the registers of *état civil* were kept by the municipal authorities, but the function then returned to the hands of the pastors. The *Dictionnaire Historique, Géographique et Statistique du Canton de Vaud* gives (pp. 272-274 of the supplement of the old edition) a conspectus for each of the 107 *arrondissements d'état civil* showing from what dates registers of births, marriages, and deaths have been preserved. These are the primary materials for genealogical researches anterior to 1821. Since that date a system of registration on official blanks has been followed, in accordance with which one set of registers of *état civil* is preserved in the local *arrondissements,* while a duplicate set is to be found at the Department of Justice and Police.

The first gallery of this highest apartment contains the 50,000 medieval parchments already alluded to, the copies made from them, and their inventories. The second or highest gallery contains the *cadastres* of the period before 1798.

The apartment on the second or middle floor contains the *cadastres territoriaux* for the various districts and communes of Vaud in the nineteenth century, with many maps and plans. In the gallery are a part of the notarial documents mentioned above. These notarial documents, some 6000 volumes in number, were for a time kept in the castle of Chillon, but a few years ago were incorporated with the cantonal archives at Lausanne.

The lowest of the three apartments consists of a main floor and a gallery floor. The former is devoted chiefly to documents concerning births, marriages, and deaths, down to the latest times, but contains also the journals and letter-books of the administrative bodies and tribunals of the Canton du Léman under the Helvetic Confederation, 1798-1803. The gallery floor contains the archives of the departments of the canton from 1815, and indeed from 1803 (Canton du Léman). In this section, in one of the cartons of the Conseil d'État, lettered " L, Agriculture, Industrie, Commerce, etc.", is found a *dossier* of papers of dates from 1822 to 1856, relating to emigration, and containing administrative circulars, reports, petitions, and correspondence with other cantons, with emigration societies, and with foreign officials respecting migration to the United States and other countries. Upon this gallery floor are also volumes of registers of the diet of the Confederation and papers arising from the relations of the government of Vaud with the federal government; a part of the collection of notarial registers; and a part of the journals, letter-books, and account books of the *bailliages* under the Bernese. For one important section of this material, the *plumitifs* (journals) of the Council of State in the nineteenth century, there is a general index: the original of the *plumitifs* is at the chateau or government building of the canton, but a duplicate set is in the archives. It should be mentioned also that there is a general inventory for the Décrets Romands, an important series of the Bernese period; that many other of the Bernese volumes, especially of the eighteenth century, have individual indexes ; and that a repertory of the *onglets* has been begun. There is no general inventory of the whole archive.

The oldest document in the archives is a grant to the abbey of Payerne from Queen Bertha of Burgundy, A. D. 962.

The canton of Vaud contains 388 communes. The communal archives are from time to time inspected by the cantonal archive officials, and at the request of the local authorities are classified.

It could not be expected that much material bearing on American history should be found in the archives of Vaud. Such emigration as has taken place has mostly been individual. A few instances of organized emigration can, however, be cited.[1] In 1796 Jean-Jacques Dufour, of Montreux, migrated to America, where he took up land on the Kentucky River, and in 1801 was joined by seventeen other emigrants from Montreux and Blonay, who founded the colony of Firstvineyard. Others, joining them in 1803, went forth to found Switzerland, Dearborn County, Ohio, and Vevay, Switzerland County, Ind., just across the Ohio. About the same date others went with Genevese to Geneva, N. Y., while in the middle portions of the century others went to Highland, Ill., Alpina, Pa., Leopoldina in Brazil, and Esperanza in Argentina. Some data respecting these may be found in the carton " Émigration " mentioned above, in the *onglets* for the *bailliage* of Vevey, and elsewhere. The papers relating to the colony of Vaud on the Pecos River in New Mexico, being of late date (1892), will be found rather in the offices of the departments than in the cantonal archives.

LAUSANNE: MINOR ARCHIVES.

Besides the cantonal archives and those of the departments, Grand Council, and courts, there are also at Lausanne the archives of the synod of the National (Protestant) Church, kept in a building close by the office of the cantonal archives, and those of the city of Lausanne, kept in the Hôtel de Ville.

[1] See the article " Émigration ", in the supplement to Martignier and Crousaz, *Dictionnaire Historique du Canton de Vaud* (Lausanne, 1887), p. 265; the article by Dean Bridel, " Colonies Suisses sur l'Ohio ", in *Le Conservateur Suisse*, VII. 237-254 (Lausanne, 1856), based on manuscripts of Dufour; and that of Miss Julia L. Knox, " Vevay and Switzerland County ", in *Indiana Magazine of History*, XI. 216-230 (Sept., 1915).

YVERDON.

The library of Yverdon possesses one of the manuscripts of Christoph von Graffenried's memoirs of his American experiences, the one of which an English translation is printed in the *North Carolina Colonial Records*.[1]

General Frederick Haldimand came from Yverdon,[2] but it is reported that no manuscript materials relating to him are to be found there.

[1] I. 905-985. See Faust in *German American Annals*, n. s., XI. 206, and John Landry, "New Berne" in *Revue Historique Vaudoise*, XV. 83-94 (1907); and above, pp. 3, 73. Graffenried was at one time bailiff of Yverdon.

[2] Born in 1718. In the list of notaries given in *Revue Historique Vaudoise*, XII. 299-301, from a manuscript "Livre des Notaires du Bailliage d'Yverdon", one finds an F. Haldimand signing in 1698, and an F. L. Haldimand in 1732. Bouquet was also a native of the Pays de Vaud (b. Rolle, 1719), but I was not so fortunate as to find anything about him in the cantonal archives. See A. Burnand, "Le Colonel Henry Bouquet, Vainqueur des Peaux-Rouges", in *Revue Historique Vaudoise*, XIV., five articles (1906).

CANTON DE VALAIS.
SION: ARCHIVES D'ÉTAT.

Location: In the Lycée-Collège.
Hours: 8 a. m. to 12 m.; 2 to 5 p. m.

The archives of the canton of Valais are in the care of the Archiviste d'État, whose office since 1910 has been attached to the Ministry of Public Instruction of the canton, having before that time been attached to the Ministry of the Interior. The archives are administered under a *réglement* of the Council of State of September 12, 1873, for which, however, a more modern regulation may soon be substituted. The present archivist is also librarian of the cantonal library (and of the society of natural history and Alpine Club), and the archives are kept in the building called the Lycée-Collège, of which the wings are occupied respectively by the cantonal college and the normal school, while the central portion of the building contains the library. Five rooms, situated in the basement, but dry and light, are devoted to the cantonal archives, together with a large closet containing the very curious archives of the family of Torrenté. Of these rooms, one is the study room and the archivist's office, containing also the documents which are in process of classification and the local registers of *état civil*, which not long ago were transferred to the cantonal archives from their local repositories. Another room contains, first, a special collection made up of the individual volumes and documents, medieval and modern, which have the greatest interest for historical purposes. This section is of great interest and value but contains nothing for the purposes of the present volume. In the same room are preserved the registers of the Council of State and Grand Council, papers relating to them, and copies of the proceedings of the diet of the Confederation. A third large room is mainly devoted to volumes and portfolios of documents originating in the executive departments of the government of Valais and those resulting from judicial proceedings in earlier and later times. A small room is occupied with printed books, while a fifth contains the archives of the family de Rivaz, valuable for many periods of the history of Valais but apparently having no relation to American history, except for the possibility that the two volumes of the journal of Charles Emmanuel de Rivaz as prefect under the Helvetic and eight volumes of his letter-books for the same period may contain material on Turreau, commander of the troops stationed in Valais from July, 1798, to September, 1802, and afterward (1803-1810) minister of France in the United States. There is also a special volume of documents relating to Turreau ("Recueil de diverses Pièces", etc.), but its table of contents shows nothing concerning America. The chief authority for his régime in Valais is the *Mémoires* of Rivaz (Sion, 1890). Mangourit, consul at Charleston 1792-1794, also played an important part in Valais as resident of France, 1797-1798.

The cantonal archives of Valais comprise those still remaining from the period of the sovereignty of the bishops, those of the period of the republic, from 1628 to 1798, those of the period of government under the Helvetic Confederation, 1798-1802, those of the second period of independence of

Valais (République Rhodanique), from 1802 to 1810, those of the period of the French government, 1810-1815, including the period of the mediation of 1814, and, finally, those which are of date subsequent to the incorporation of Valais into the Swiss Confederation in 1815. For the period since 1815 the documents are or are to be arranged in accordance with the following categories: I. Diet and Great Council; II. Council of State; III. Departments. The first embraces the journals, laws, bills, and miscellaneous documents of the legislature. Those of the second division include the proceedings and decrees of the council, the domestic and foreign correspondence of the canton and documents relating to its courts, its relations with other countries and cantons, the Sonderbund, ecclesiastical affairs, etc. The papers belonging to the third class are, naturally, classified under the respective departments: finance, interior, public instruction, justice, militia, and public works.

Besides papers emanating from governmental sources, the archivist is authorized to acquire archives of individual families and has gathered several extremely interesting collections of this sort.

The canton of Valais has developed much more completely than most governments its system of dealing with local records, and this, especially for the value of its example to American states, perhaps deserves special mention. The canton maintains two inspectors who upon a uniform system of printed instructions have examined the local archives in most of the 171 communes into which the canton is divided. Their reports, which in the case of separate documents and especially the earlier papers, amount to a full calendar, are made out upon uniform blanks and preserved in a series of thirteen portfolios corresponding to the districts of the canton. For each commune there are or may be reports upon the respective archives of the *municipalité*, of the *bourgeoisie* (the distinction is like that between town records and proprietors' records in early New England), and of the ecclesiastical parish, though reports of the latter, in view of the separation between Church and State, cannot be insisted upon by the cantonal government. These reports by the inspectors are made out in duplicate, one copy being preserved in the cantonal archives and the other in the local archives, which retain possession of the original documents.

As to registers of births, marriages, and deaths, and the genealogical information which can be obtained from them, they must, for the period before 1853, be sought in the ecclesiastical archives of the parishes, though information respecting such volumes of parochial registers may frequently be found in the reports mentioned in the preceding paragraph. From 1853 to 1874 the curés of the parishes had a quasi-public function in respect to the matter, and records of *état civil* sent in by them are preserved in the cantonal archives. Since 1874 the records of *état civil* have been a federal affair, and complete sets of them, sent in on blanks from the communes, are preserved in bound volumes in the cantonal archives.

It should be mentioned that the cantonal library contains a large collection of files of newspapers published in Sion and other places, and these newspapers, which of course have nearly the rarity of manuscripts, sometimes in the earlier periods contain letters from emigrants to America. The first newspaper of Sion was the *Écho des Alpes*, which began publication in 1839. There is a *Bulletin Officiel*, published by the cantonal government from 1803 to the present time, giving official acts, and there is a section on emigration and on the cantonal archives in each *Rapport du Conseil d'État*, a printed series beginning in 1851.

The executive departments of the canton retain possession of their recent papers, turning over to the cantonal archives those which are no longer in current use. In many cases this happens after three or four years, in other cases papers for as many as thirty years back are retained.

Of other archives in Sion, the archives of the bishopric were almost entirely destroyed in the great fire of 1788. There are interesting municipal archives in a building near the old college, with a good manuscript inventory made in 1750; and there are archives of the chapter, kept in a building adjoining the old cathedral (de Valère), but they are reported to contain nothing whatever for American history.

CANTON DE NEUCHÂTEL.
NEUCHÂTEL: ARCHIVES DE L'ÉTAT.

Location: In the Château.
Hours: 8.30 a. m. to 12 m.; 2 to 4 p. m.

It is necessary to remind the reader of the peculiar history of Neuchâtel. Throughout the Middle Ages it was governed by its counts, usually allies of the Swiss Confederation. From 1503 to 1707 was the period of the (usually non-resident) counts or countesses of the French house of Longueville, who habitually maintained the same alliance. Under the counts, though they were Catholics, Neuchâtel became Protestant, the government of the church passing into the hands of the Company of Pastors, or Venerable Classis (for which in 1848 was substituted a synod, two-thirds laymen). In 1707 the King of Prussia became Prince of Neuchâtel, and he and his successors remained its sovereigns until 1857, except that from 1806 to 1813 it was placed by Napoleon in the hands of Marshal Berthier, as prince of Neuchâtel. In 1814 it became a canton of the Swiss Confederation, the King of Prussia still remaining its sovereign. This anomalous position caused two insurrections in September and December, 1831, and a revolt in 1848; and the Prussian rule was ended in 1857.

Under the counts the Audience du Comte was the highest administrative and judicial court and also had legislative attributes. Toward the end of the Middle Ages its judicial functions passed into the hands of the Tribunal des Trois États, while the Audiences Générales (three estates) became the legislative body, but were not convoked from 1618 to 1814. After existing actively from 1815 to 1831, this body was superseded by a more popular Corps Législatif, and this in 1848 by the present Grand Council. Under the Prussian rule, or at any rate from 1707 to 1848, Neuchâtel, still in alliance with the Swiss Confederation, and from 1815 a member of it, was ruled chiefly by its (native) Council of State, though with a Prussian governor.

The archives of Neuchâtel existed from medieval times, in the charge of the Chancellerie or of the Secretary of State. In the course of the eighteenth century a Commissaire Général was appointed, whose functions included those of an archivist. A cantonal archivist was substituted in 1848 and he continued until 1898. In that year the archives were reorganized. Down to that time there had been two deposits. The Commissaire Général and Archiviste Cantonale just referred to had had charge of all of the earlier papers, of date previous to 1707, while the papers of date subsequent to 1707 had been in charge of the Chancery of State. In 1898 an Archiviste d'État was appointed to take charge of the later series, as well as of the judicial documents brought together from the whole canton, and for four years (1898-1902) there were thus two archivists. In 1903 the two offices were combined by an *arrêté* of the Council of State. Except for the changes made in that year, the archives are governed by a *règlement* of the Council of State of February 7, 1899.

The archives of the canton of Neuchâtel have for centuries been housed in the ancient château of the counts. The general office and consultation room is in the southwestern tower, which forms the most ancient portion now existing of the castle, dating from about 1190. Several rooms along the south curtain of the fortification and near its southeast corner have for many years been occupied with the archive materials. In 1902 a plan was formed for a new building. In 1908, however, the Council of State resolved instead to make larger provision for the archives within the walls of the castle. Accordingly a large four-story stack has been built in an old court-yard at the north of the present quarters. This, with the space afforded by the present storage rooms (also converted into stacks) makes an ample provision of a most modern character for the installation of the archives. The additions are estimated to amount to 8000 metres of shelving. A well-catalogued library of 7000 or 8000 titles, made up partly of the books most appropriate for a cantonal archive, and partly by a recent concentration of the small and miscellaneous libraries of executive departments, and a good photographic apparatus, complete the equipment.

The archives are at present classified into three major sections, corresponding respectively to the periods of Neuchâtel history previous to 1707, from 1707 to 1848, and from 1848 to the present time. There are two classifications of the archives, one for the period previous to 1707, the other for the period from 1707 to 1848. The papers since 1848 are of course classified according to executive departments, which turn them over to the archives from time to time, retaining in general those of the last twenty-five years. For the papers of the first period there is an inventory, practically complete; for the latter the inventory is only partially completed. For this latter period, the only one which in any way concerns America, the most important section of the archives consists of the papers of the Council of State, which from the sixteenth century to the institution of a legislative body of modern form was by far the most important institution of the land, having both administrative and judicial functions and taking cognizance of all sorts of events and details of business. The most important portion of its archives consists of the Manuaux, *i. e.*, its journals, extending from 1514 to the present time— 298 great volumes.

Closely related to this are the Pièces Annexes, arranged in two sections, one anterior to 1707, the other posterior, and containing the papers on which the action of the Council was based, such as reports, petitions, letters from subjects, addressed to the Council of State, etc. The former series has an inventory in four large volumes; for the latter, there is a less perfect inventory in some ten volumes, amounting to little more than a chronological list of these papers. The Pièces Annexes for the period from 1707 to 1848 are classified in bundles, according to the subject-matter, such as, to name the *dossiers* most likely to contain American materials: Archives, Bourgeoisie, Chancellerie, Cultes-Général, Cultes-Pasteurs, Émigration (also the separate groups of documents made for each period of political revolution may contain papers respecting persons expatriated by reason of them), État Civil (several), Marchandises Anglaises (1806), Militaire (Service à l'Étranger), Naturalisation, Passeports, Relations Extérieures, and Successions. These *dossiers* or cartons are numbered; in each there is a chronological arrangement. Each document possesses its own number, by which it may be found through the general inventory of the Pièces Annexes.

There are tables of contents, for each ten years, of the Manuaux, also indexes of names for the Manuaux for the period from 1820 to 1850. For the volumes of correspondence there are merely tables of contents in each volume.

Other series are: "Missives" (general correspondence, from 1560 to the present time), Letters to and Rescripts from the King of Prussia (1707-1848), Lettres à la Suisse, and Lettres de la Suisse (to and from the other cantons and the federal authorities, since 1815); also laws, decrees, and the record books of administrative and financial boards and of tribunals. Among the boards, special mention may be made of the Chambre Économique, which administered ecclesiastical property.

For the journals of the nineteenth-century Audiences Générales, see the recent official publication, *Procès-Verbaux des Audiences Générales de Neuchâtel, 1816-1830* (Neuchâtel, 1904), edited by the present archivist, M. Arthur Piaget. The only American item in them appears to be that on June 25, 1819, Count Portalès-Gorgier made a proposal, which was merely referred to the Council of State, that the deputation of Neuchâtel should be charged to submit to the diet the propriety of negotiating with some American state to assure better protection to Swiss emigrants in respect to property and other rights (*Procès-Verbaux*, I. 344-345). The archives of the Corps Législatif, and of its successor (since 1848), the present Grand Council, consist of but little save the journals and the petitions and other papers upon which legislative action was founded.

The present archivist has obtained from Berlin a considerable mass of copies of documents of the Prussian administration of Neuchâtel, and a selection of these will be printed.

There is also a series of large volumes containing the Reconnaissances des Biens de Rentiers, drawn up from time to time and corresponding to *cadastres*. The archives have also a collection of newspapers of the canton, extending from 1830.

There are ten or twelve thousand volumes of registers and *minutaires* of notaries of the period before 1873, and others for the period since that date, at which time some modifications of the law respecting notaries were decreed. There are notarial documents from the fourteenth century. In 1905 the Conseil d'État decreed that the notarial registers of earlier date than 1848, preserved by the communes in their archives and clerks' offices, should be turned in to the archives at the Château. A detailed repertory of the notarial archives is in progress, and there is a card catalogue of the notaries. Of 1200 known to have exercised their functions in Neuchâtel, there are some 800 whose registers and *minutaires* are in the archives—indeed practically all those of the eighteenth and nineteenth centuries.

The earliest registers of *état civil* date from about 1560, and were kept by the pastors. The registers of *état civil* have continuously remained in the hands of the local authorities; but, beginning in the eighteenth century in some cases, in the nineteenth in others, there are duplicates made by the local and transmitted to the cantonal authorities, and these are now in the cantonal archives. The local subdivision for such purposes is not precisely the commune; the canton is divided into 47 *arrondissements d'état civil*, whereas there are 63 communes.

The law requires communes to keep their archives carefully and to have a place for them that is secure, dry, and safe from fire. By an *arrêté* of June 10, 1905, the Conseil d'État decreed that, except in case of communal archives already systematically arranged and classified, communal authorities should proceed upon the plan of classification annexed to the *arrêté*. A detailed classification under fifteen general headings is provided. The archivists of communes are permitted for special reasons to make different subdivisions in their particular cases.

In 1911 the archivist on request of the Council of State made a general inspection of all the communal archives. It appeared that of the 63 communes of the canton six had their archives completely classified, 13 partially, while six are classifying them in accordance with the plan of 1905, and 38 have neither classification nor inventory. Several communes have insufficient or dangerous places. The Council of State urged them to take proper measures. Some communes, however, have preferred to deposit their pieces of the old régime in the archives of state.

By search of indexes for most of the period from 1700 to 1848 the following items relative to American history were obtained:

From the Manuaux du Conseil d'État.

Oct. 7, 1720. The chancellor is to write a circular letter to all the châtelains and maires, to be read in open court, forbidding any person to solicit subjects and inhabitants of this city to go to Mississippi.

Feb. 11, 1732. The Council being informed that M. Pury, formerly maire of Lignières, is engaging people in this country to go to Carolina and that a certain number of families subject to this state have already engaged with him, voted that orders be sent to the châtelain of the barony of Vautravers (Val-de-Travers), where the said Pury is, to collect and transmit information as to the truth of this affair, and what sort of engagements Pury is making. This is the only item found, relating to Jean Pierre Purry or his settlement in South Carolina. Prolonged search might have developed more. Judge H. A. M. Smith, in his article " Purrysburgh ", in the *South Carolina Historical Magazine*, X. 187-219 (1909), the authoritative account of the colony, gives lists of two or three hundred names, many of which are of Neuchâtel families.

From the Rescrits de sa Majesté.

July 8, 1754. The King has been informed that many subjects of his principality of Neuchâtel and Valangin are allowing themselves to be engaged by all sorts of promises to quit their country to migrate to the English colonies of America. " Though we remember well that the third of the Articles Généraux provided that all subjects of the state may freely leave the country for travel or other purposes, we do not think that such a liberty ought to extend to wholesale enticing away of our subjects; also consider it our paternal duty to warn our subjects not to be deceived. Even the King of Great Britain has given his German subjects a warning of this sort, and we have refused such poor people permission to pass through our duchy of Cleves. Therefore you are to issue warnings and orders respecting such enticements." In the same volume is the rescript of Aug. 24, approving the action of the Council.

July 29, 1754. A rescript from the king having been received, ordering that everything possible be done to prevent the enticing away of his subjects in this state to go to the English colonies in America, it is ordered that a decree be drawn up forbidding such enticement and such emigration under the severest penalties.

MANUAUX.

Mar. 21, 1797. Col. Chambrier de Travanet recommended to the authorities of Philadelphia in a matter of collecting monies due him from Jean Antoine Guyenet of Couvet, who has died there.
June 7, 1817. Measures taken by the King of the Netherlands, because of the extraordinary number of Swiss emigrants crossing his country to go to America. See note from *dossier* " Émigration " in Pièces Annexes.
June 19, 1817. No. 45. Resolved, to see if emigration should be regulated and direction given to it.
June 7, 1819. Notification from the Federal Directory, dated May 27, reminding the cantons that emigrants cannot go through the Netherlands without passports.
June 29, 1819. Instructions to the deputies to collect information as to what other cantons have done to direct and protect emigrants to America, and to see if concerted action is possible or advisable.
Feb. 20, 1821. The mayor of Valangin having reported on the efforts to obtain recruits for the colony on the Red River, and suggesting measures to prevent the communes from ruining themselves by advancing money to such emigrants, the Council votes not to adopt the measures he proposes. See pp. 171, 172, *post*, and note.
May 11, 1831. The Council in pursuance of a circular from the Directory, dated Apr. 29, ordains the publication of a warning to persons intending to go to America, that the prefects of the French frontier departments will not hereafter grant passage through France to any who are not provided with the necessary papers and sufficient pecuniary means for the voyage.
June 11, 1832. Circular of the Federal Directory of May 27, transmitting the request of the ambassador of France that no emigrants for America be allowed to go out until those now in French territory, especially at Havre, have sailed. The Federal Directory has been notified that similar conditions also existed in the Netherlands.
Mar. 31, 1828. Circular of Mar. 20, from the Federal Directory, transmitting an ordinance of the King of the Netherlands as to the formalities to be followed by emigrants going through his dominions to America.
Nov. 20, 1837. Circular of the Federal Directory of Nov. 11, informing that the consul at New Orleans represents the situation of Swiss emigrants there as so unfortunate that advice is given to stay away until the financial crisis in America is over. The Council orders the communication to be sent to each local jurisdiction, to be read in open court.
Oct. 20, 1845. Federal circular of Oct. 16, transmitting report from the Swiss consul at New York on the dangers surrounding emigrants arriving there. The Council sends it to the Chancery for publicity.
Mar. 16, 1846. Similar warning from New York.
May 11, 1846. Circular from the Federal Chancery of May 6, on the difficulties surrounding intending emigrants at Havre. Publicity decreed.
Sept. 9, 1846. Warnings from America.

Some items may also be found in the indexes under " Commerce ". There are lists of passports since 1796.

Pièces Annexes.

" Émigration ": This *dossier* contains some 38 documents. Among them are the following relating to America:

Certificate of Jean Jaques le Roy, commissary on behalf of the King of Great Britain for colonists emigrating to Pennsylvania. In relation to a family whose transportation he had undertaken, the Sieur Friederich Guie, Marguerite Pewelef, his wife, Samuel Péter and Jean Friederich Péter, her children by a former marriage, and Jean Friederich Guie and Jeanne Marie Guie, children of this second marriage, all of Verrières in the county of Neuchâtel. Le Roy makes himself responsible for transfer to the stepchildren of any property belonging to them. Dampierre, outre les Bois, Feb. 2, 1754.

Letter of Lieut.-Col. Montjou to some one whom he endeavors to engage to collect colonists in Savoy and France and bring them to Basel to be taken down the Rhine to Amsterdam. Frankfort a. M., Nov. 20, 1765.

Letter of Savary, duc de Rovigo, Minister of Police, to Berthier, prince of Neuchâtel, informing him that Huguenin, the civil lieutenant at Locle, had written to a London house for information as to the protection of Swiss who wish to emigrate to America. Paris, Mar. 13, 1812.

Letter of Alexandre (Berthier), prince of Neuchâtel, to the president of the Council, ordering that Huguenin be questioned. Paris, Mar. 14, 1812.

Printet *arrêt* communicating a recent decree of the King of the Netherlands, who in view of the increasing number of Swiss and Germans passing through the Netherlands to go to America forbids any bodies of such emigrants to pass through the Netherlands unless citizens of the latter will be responsible for them. Neuchâtel, June 7, 1817.

Printed circular in German, three pages, put forth by Captain Rudolf de May. [May 24, 1820?]

Letter of A. de Chambrier, mayor of Valangin, calling attention to Captain May's circular of May 24, 1820, making brilliant promises to colonists on Lord Selkirk's land, and suggesting that while Article III. of the Charte may make it impossible to forbid single men to emigrate, the communes might be forbidden to give assistance to emigrants, especially to the heads of families. Valangin, Feb. 12, 1821. See above, pp. 128, 170.

Letter of Major E. May, brother of Captain Rudolf A. de May (of the Régiment de Meuron), to a correspondent in Neuchâtel, recommending Lord Selkirk's Red River proposals and referring to Mr. Hauser, who took out the expedition of the preceding spring from Rotterdam to Fort York, to Mr. Colville, and to Captain Mathey as probably now at Neuchâtel. Also to the recent union of the Hudson's Bay Company and the Northwest Company. Bern, Feb. 28 [1822?].

[These items require further explanation. Lord Selkirk's first experiment in colonization of the Red River of the North (1811-1816) not having succeeded, he or his agents distributed proposals in Neuchâtel, Vaud, Geneva, and Bern, and some 200 colonists, mostly French-speaking, agreed to set out in the spring of 1821. They went *via* Basel and Rotterdam, by sea to Fort York on Hudson Bay, and to Fort Douglas and to Pembina. Meanwhile Lord Selkirk had already, in 1816, secured 80 colonists from the Régiment de Meuron and 20 from the Régiment de Watteville. Charles Daniel de Meuron (1738-1806), after French service in the Régiment de Hallwyl and in the guards, agreed in 1781 to raise for the Dutch East India Company a regiment two-thirds Swiss. In 1795, at Ceylon, he and his proprietary regiment passed into the English service. After various service in the Napoleonic wars (during most of which it was about one-third Swiss), and under various Colonels de Meuron, the regiment went to Canada in 1814. Major Emmanuel May and Captain Rudolph May were of this regiment. After much suffering, many of the Swiss colonists withdrew in 1823 to St. Louis, in 1826 and after to Galena. See Th. de Meuron, *Essai Historique sur le Régiment Suisse de Meuron* (Neuchâtel, 1885); the same writer's articles on " Charles Daniel de Meuron et son Régiment ", in the *Musée Neuchâtelois,* XVII.-XXI.; Gen. A. L. Chetlain of Chicago, " Une Colonie Suisse dans l'Amérique du Nord ", French translation from an article in the *Chicago Tribune,* in *Musée Neuchâtelois,* XVI. 36-43 (1879); General Chetlain's *The Red River Colony* (Chicago, 1893, pp. 60), an expansion of his article. " The Settlement on the Red River ", in *Harper's Monthly Magazine,* LVIII. 47 (December, 1878); and Dr. Châtelain, " Les Neuchâtelois à la Rivière Rouge, 1821-1826 ", in *Musée Neuchâtelois,* XXXIII. 7-12, 38-44 (1896).]

To the *avoyer d'état* of the canton of Neuchâtel: letter of Joseph Paquier of Bulle in the canton of Fribourg. Hearing that this spring a colony is to go out to the United States, and that one should address one's self to the advocate of Neuchâtel, he and others request full information. Bulle, Feb. 4, 1828.

Arrêt of the Council transmitting warning from the Federal Directory as to unfortunate situation of emigrants as represented by the Swiss consul at New Orleans. Neuchâtel, Nov. 20, 1837.

Letter of Jacques Vuagneux, notary, concerning his son Charles, sworn notary in Porto Rico, asking letter of recommendation to the captain-general of the island. Neuchâtel, May 22, 1841.

Report of deputation to the diet. By vote of June 1, 1846, the Council had charged the deputation to take part in a discussion invited by Graubünden as to the safeguarding of emigrants. This conference took place Sept. 8, 1846, twelve cantons or half cantons participating. The propositions of Graubünden are quoted. The deputies at the conference being without instructions, the conference voted that its minutes should be sent to all the cantons with a request for consideration and instruction before the next diet. Zürich, Sept. 9, 1846.

There are other documents in the *dossier* relating to emigration to Russia under Catherine II.

The documents of the Council of State seem to contain nothing respecting Alpina, or the projects of Suchard and Favarger there. See below, Bibliothèque de la Ville.

NEUCHÂTEL: ARCHIVES DE LA VILLE.

The archives of the city of Neuchâtel are kept at the Hôtel de Ville, in the charge of the secretary-archivist. They consist of the journals (*procès-verbaux*) of the city council (Quatre Ministraux) from the sixteenth century; of the journals of the Great Council; of the correspondence of the Quatre Ministraux with Bern and the other confederated states, with the Confederation itself, with Prussia, with France, etc.; and of voluminous financial accounts. The journals of the Quatre Ministraux for 1731 seem to contain nothing respecting J. P. Purry's colonial enterprise.

NEUCHÂTEL: BIBLIOTHÈQUE DE LA VILLE.

A lithographed manuscript: Ph. Suchard and Ch.-L. Favarger, " Société en Commandite par Actions pour Achat de Terrain dans l'État de New York (Colonie d'Alpina) ", made at Neuchâtel in 1845, apparently.

Philippe Suchard (1797-1884), the eminent manufacturer of chocolate and of confections, had visited America in 1824; Heinrich Zschokke made from his notes a little book entitled *Ph. Suchard, Mein Besuch Amerikas im Sommer 1824* (Aarau, 1827). In 1834 Suchard established the first successful steamboats on Lake Neuchâtel. Coming over to America again in 1845, he took up lands apparently rich in iron in Lewis County, New York, and established there a colony, Alpina, with a stock company to exploit the iron mines. Charles Louis Favarger (1809-1882), afterward prominent in Neuchâtel politics, went out as manager of the company. The colony prospered for five years, then was given up. See Ph. Suchard, *Un Voyage aux États-Unis d'Amérique il y a quarante ans* (Neuchâtel, 1868, a revised version, in French, of *Mein Besuch*, above); *Notice sur Alpina, Terres situées dans les Comtés de Jefferson et de Lewis, État de New York* (Neuchâtel, 1847, pp. 64, three maps); *Le Véritable Messager Boiteux de Neuchâtel*, 1883, p. 41, 1885, p. 47; F. B. Hough, *History of Lewis County*, I. 73, 99.

NEUCHÂTEL: COMPAGNIE DES PASTEURS.

The archives of the Classis or Company of Pastors are in a building in the Rue Collégiale, now occupied by the independent faculty of theology. They date from the Reformation.

These archives contain, first, the registers of deliberations (minutes of meetings) of the Company of Pastors from 1560 to 1848, the chief records of the administration of the Church. There are eighteen volumes of these registers, quarto and folio. With 1848 begin the registers of the synod, whose records are kept in the Archives of State.

Secondly, the archives of the Company of Pastors contain the correspondence of the Classis, as follows:

(1) For the period of the Reformation and of the sixteenth century in general, ten portfolios of letters classified by authors, and two large *cahiers*

of letters stitched together without strict classification. One of the latter contains some letters of the seventeenth century.

(2) Two large registers of copies of letters written by the Company of Pastors, from about 1700 to 1848. These represent only a part of the correspondence; the registers described above mention many letters not thus preserved.

(3) Letters received by the Company of Pastors since the seventeenth century. These have been brought together in portfolios, but with only a rough classification.

(4) Miscellaneous papers.

Rev. Joseph Bugnon, minister of Purrysburgh, S. C., was not consecrated at Neuchâtel, and there seems to be in these archives no information respecting him.

There are also archives of the independent Protestant church of Neuchâtel, established in 1873. These are at the Bâtiment des Conférences.

CANTON OF GENEVA.

GENEVA: ARCHIVES DE L'ÉTAT.

Location: In the Hôtel de Ville, but see below.
Hours: 8 a. m. to 12 m.; 1.30 to 3.30 p. m. Thursday is reserved, but usually the archive is open on that day also.

Bibliography: Louis Dufour-Vernes, " Les Archives de l'État de Genève ", in *Bulletin de la Société d'Histoire et d'Archéologie de Genève,* II. 19-41 (1898).

F. Turrettini, *Les Archives de Genève: Inventaire des Documents contenus dans les Portefeuilles Historiques et les Registres des Conseils, 1528-1541* (Geneva, 1877, pp. iv, viii, 332, 19). Pp. i-viii form a " Notice sur les Archives de Genève ", by Théophile Heyer, at that time director of the archives.

Alfred L. Covelle, *Le Livre des Bourgeois de l'Ancienne République de Genève, publié d'après les Registres Officiels, 1339-1792* (Geneva, 1897, pp. xvi, 562).

Grenus-Saladin, *Fragmens Biographiques et Historiques extraits des Registres du Conseil d'État de la République de Genève de 1535 à 1792* (Geneva, 1815).

Herbert D. Foster, notes in article " Geneva before Calvin ", *American Historical Review,* VIII. 218-219.

Geneva, which in the Middle Ages had been an imperial city, under a bishop who was a prince of the Empire, was from 1530 to 1798 an independent republic, allied with the Swiss cantons. In 1798 it was annexed to France, and became a part of the Département du Léman (to be distinguished from the contemporary Canton du Léman = Vaud, in the Helvetic Confederation); in the last days of 1813 it resumed its independence, in 1815 it became a member of the Swiss Confederation.

The state archives of the canton of Geneva, which for centuries have been kept in the Hôtel de Ville, consist in the main of the archives of the old republic and of the period of French domination. They extend only to 1814, except that they contain the registers of the Conseil d'État down to 1830. Documents subsequent to 1814 are in the Chancellerie, if they are documents of the Conseil d'État, but in the offices of the executive departments if they originated in the latter. The whole collection in the archives amounts at present to at least 14,000 or 15,000 volumes and 400,000 detached pieces. The oldest document is of A. D. 912.

Provision for historical use of the archives by the public began in 1814. M. Louis Sordet, archivist from 1839 to 1851, began a classification of which the leading feature was the making of a series of " Portefeuilles des Pièces Historiques ". Some 40,000 documents were brought together into this collection of pieces classed as " historical " *par excellence,* by a process of segregation which would not now be approved. M. Louis Dufour-Vernes, state archivist from 1885 to 1909, introduced a more scientific classification, whose categories rested on the outlines of the old Genevese constitution, and made many new inventories, indexes, and calendars.

The state archives of Geneva are installed in eight rooms in the Hôtel de Ville, in one large room at no. 11 rue Calvin, and in seven rooms at no. 1 rue du Puits St. Pierre. In the Hôtel de Ville itself we have first the Salle des Fiefs, in the west corner of the building, on the ground floor. This room, which is used as the office of the archivist and as the search room for investigators, contains also the various inventories and indexes, the library of printed books, the collection called "Portefeuilles des Pièces Historiques", and a "Collection des Manuscrits Historiques", a certain number of maps and plans, the registers of baptisms, births, marriages, and deaths for the city and for the country districts of the canton (brought in by edict of 1902), and the registers of the Council of State from 1815 to 1830, with a collection of accompanying documents.

Half-way down a staircase that leads from this room is found the Salle des Annexes, which contains a large mass of papers auxiliary to the proceedings of the Council, such as financial accounts, reports of committees, and miscellaneous documents; and a collection of maps and plans connected with the system of administration and taxation of real estate. At the foot of the staircase is the Grande Grotte, which is the lowest story of the ancient square tower of the Hôtel, called the Tour Baudet, looking out upon the Treille.[1] This room contains the registers of the Council, 322 volumes, 1409-1798, with some gaps in the fifteenth century (this may perhaps be regarded as the most important series in the archives), petitions to the Council, publications of the Council relating to the affairs of individuals, called Livres des Particuliers, the accounts of the treasurer, and other financial documents of the Council, the letter-books of its correspondence, and the volumes, nearly 3500 in number, of the minutes and protocols of notaries.

The remaining rooms upon the lowest floor are still called the Salles Papon, from the name of a restaurateur who in 1822 was dislodged from the Hôtel de Ville to make additional space. They lie along the northwest side of the basement and are designated as the Grande Salle Papon (directly under the Salle des Fiefs), and the First, Second, Third, and Fourth Petites Salles Papon. In general it may be said that the large room contains the record books and portfolios of documents of administrative boards of the Genevese government and a considerable part of the judicial papers, especially those relating to criminal trials; the first small room mostly those of civil courts, the second those of the outlying jurisdictions in the environs of Geneva, and the third and fourth, mostly record books and rolls containing the *titres et droits de la seigneurie,* evidences of property chiefly ecclesiastical, given to the bishop, the chapter, or the churches, and turned over to the state at the time of the Reformation. The collection embraces a wide variety of auxiliary materials, such as those relating to tithes and episcopal visitations. In the third small room are also the registers of the Communauté, 1364-1386, which disclose the municipal business in the period before the registers of the Council begin.

At a short distance from the Hôtel de Ville, at no. 11 rue Calvin, in the building called Maison de Calvin, because it stands on the site of Calvin's dwelling, one very large room in the basement is filled with the documents

---

[1] The Tour Baudet dates from the fifteenth century, and its lowest story has remained unchanged since then. The Grande Grotte has been devoted to archives since 1561. See C. Martin, "La Maison de Ville de Genève", in *Mémoires et Documents de la Société d'Histoire de Genève,* third series, III. (1906, pp. xvi, 139).

for the French period, 1798-1814, chiefly the administrative documents of the department and prefecture of the Léman. These were installed in their present location in 1893, are partially reduced to systematic arrangement, and are listed in a separate manuscript inventory called "Inventaire des Titres, Pièces et Registres mixtes de l'ancienne Préfecture ou ci-devant Département du Léman, de l'Arrondissement de Genève, et autres administrations, dressé par Monsieur Constantin de Magny, dépositaire royal nommé par Sa Majesté le Roi de Sardaigne, et Monsieur Martin Servand, dépositaire pour le Canton de Genève, en exécution de l'article 20 du Traité de Turin du 16 Mars 1816."

Still another portion of the archives is kept at no. 1 rue du Puits St. Pierre, some two hundred yards from the Hôtel de Ville, in a suite of seven rooms which formerly constituted the Salle des Hypothèques, but which since 1911 has been under the jurisdiction of the archivist. Here are kept the archives of the Bourse Française, 1550-1849, an institution administering funds and charities of Huguenot refugees; those of the Hôpital Général, 1535-1868, archives turned over to the state in 1911; and those of the courts of justice of the nineteenth century.

To all this mass of archive material there is a general guide, in the form of a manuscript inventory prepared by the present archivist, M. Paul Martin, a large volume of 213 pages, bearing the title "État Général et Sommaire des Fonds, 1911". It does not include in its scope the archives of the Department of the Léman, for which there is the special inventory mentioned above. Its plan is, while listing all subdivisions, to enlarge upon those only which are not covered by any existing inventory; where a series has already been described in one of the ten partial inventories noted below, it refers to that book. Thus it supplements, and places in their general setting, in a classification corresponding to that of the old Genevese administration, the following bound volumes, all in manuscript:

Inventaire No. 1. Archives de Genève: Répertoire de la Partie Politique, par M. Ad. C. Grivel (a former archivist). Quarto, 85 pp. This presents an inventory of the documents of the chapter of St. Peter, of the registers and papers of the Council, of the Portefeuilles des Pièces Historiques, and of the registers of the treasurer.

Inventaire No. 2. Inventaire des plans et registres y relatifs déposés aux Archives de Genève, par M. Ad. C. Grivel. Small quarto, with parchment back, 93 written pages. This lists the various maps and plans of the earlier and later periods and the books of surveys and other books which accompany them, including the French land surveys.

Inventaire No. 3. Index des Chambres, par M. Dufour-Vernes. Quarto, 72 written pages. An inventory of the record books of various administrative chambers, such as the Chambre des Blés, Chambre des Comptes, Chambre du Vin, Département des Arts, de l'Industrie, du Commerce, et des Monnaies, Consistoire de Genève et des environs, Chambre de la Réformation (du Luxe), and some societies like the Société des Catéchumènes.[1]

Inventaire No. 4. Militaire, Justice, et Police, par M. Dufour-Vernes. Small quarto, with cloth back, 72 written pages. This is a guide to the records of the various military boards and councils, and to those of various civil and criminal courts.

---

[1] See Dufour-Vernes in *Bulletin de la Société de l'Histoire*, III. 23.

Inventaire No. 5. Catalogue des Minutes des Notaires déposées dans la Grotte des Archives, par M. Dufour-Vernes. Small quarto, parchment back, 35, 45 written pages. Part I. of this is a list of notaries—some 220, in chronological order, from 1373 to 1857, followed by an alphabetical list of the same, showing the number of volumes, from 1 to 90, coming down from each. Part II. is a list of former notaries of Geneva and its environs who are known to have existed but whose minutes are not in the archives.

Inventaire No. 6. Inventaire des Sceaux, Timbres, et Cachets, par MM. Grivel et Dufour-Vernes. Large quarto, 111 written pages. This includes both Geneva and its environs.

Inventaire No. 7. Inventaire des Titres et Droits de la Seigneurie de Genève, rédigé de 1888 à 1891, par M. Dufour-Vernes. Large quarto, in two parts, bound in cloth, with parchment back, 656 written pages. This inventory, carefully made, describes each roll, volume, or separate document contained in the series relating to the property rights of the bishopric, of the community, of the chapter and prévoté of St. Peter, of the priory of St. Victor, and of various minor and civil jurisdictions ; secondly, those of the churches, chapels, convents, and hospitals of the city and bishopric ; and thirdly, of particular fiefs belonging at one period or another to Geneva.

Inventaire No. 8. Inventaire des titres, registres, papiers, et plans de la Société Économique. Large quarto, with parchment back, 60 written pages. The archives of the Société Économique were turned over to the archives of the state in 1868 and 1869.

Inventaire No. 9. Catalogue des Archives de l'Hôpital Général de Genève. Small quarto, about 50 written pages. These archives were turned over to the archives of state in 1911.

Inventaire No. 10. Inventaire Général et Topographique des Archives de l'État, par M. Dufour-Vernes. Small quarto, bound in cloth, 28 written pages. This is an inventory by the late archivist, not quite finished, which proceeds in a methodical order around the various rooms devoted to the archives, both at the Hôtel de Ville and in the rue Calvin, and sets forth the order of arrangement, case by case and shelf by shelf. The order is not signally different from that maintained at present.

There are various other inventories ; the above are the most general. The data which follow are arranged in the order pursued in M. Martin's " État Général et Sommaire des Fonds ". Its first section relates to inventories, its second to the :

Portefeuilles des Pièces Historiques. A factitious collection, as mentioned above, filling some 6000 cartons. For the modern period it is derived mostly from the general correspondence received by the Council of State. There is a chronological inventory in two large folio volumes, and an alphabetical index of names and subjects. The only American pieces found by means of these were the following :

P. H. no. 3687. Long letter, of about a thousand words, of Jean Noblet, citizen of Geneva, dwelling at Amsterdam, to his cousin F. Duhamel, setting forth his design of colonizing three islands in the seas of America, to be a refuge for the Reformed and for those wishing to escape the wars of Europe. Others will help him, but

Archives de l'État

he would like further subscriptions from the Genevese. Also, to insure neutrality, he wishes the Republic of Geneva to assume the sovereignty of these islands and grant them to him as a fief. It is not expedient to name the isles yet, lest he be anticipated; but they are fertile, of warm climate, not near the dominions of France or of Great Britain, uninhabited, and as good as the Antilles or Carib Islands. He wishes to know if preachers and rulers can be had from Geneva; states the terms for settlers; declares that the islands can be cultivated by indentured servants, and that negro slaves can be brought thither more cheaply than to the Antilles or Carib Islands. Amsterdam, May 2, 1680.

Petition of Jean Noblet to the Council, in which he says that during his years of absence he has sailed the seas of America. May 2, 1680.

Draft of a patent to him: the islands "several hundred leagues from the French and English colonies"; the patentee to have powers of sovereignty "like those of the Dutch West India Company". Its full text is quoted in the *Histoire de Genève des Origines à l'Année 1690*, par Jean-Antoine Gautier, Secrétaire d'État, VIII. 211-212 (Geneva, 1911).

P. H. no. **5416**. In this carton, which consists of extracts from the registers of the central committee of the "Clubs Insurgés", containing votes of that body on various subjects, was found the following. It should be premised that on Aug. 23, 1794, soon after its dramatic reception of Monroe, the French Convention, after an oration by Reybaz as minister of Geneva, had decreed that the Genevese flag should be hung up in their hall alongside those of the French and the American republics. See also, below, p. 180, the Council entries of Aug. 30, Sept. 5, 11, 1794, and *Writings of James Monroe*, II. 34, 54.

"Extrait des Régitres du Comité Central du 3e 7'bre 1794 l'an 3 de l'égalité Genevoise.—Les Clubs Révolutionnaires s'étant occupés d'une proposition tendante à ce que l'Administration soit chargée d'écrire au Congrès des États Unis d'Amérique pour l'informer de l'évènement qui a donné lieu à l'arboré du Drapeau Américain en leur demandant alliance et fraternité, Cette proposition a été acceptée par 1731 suffrages contre 651. En conséquence le Comité Central arrête d'expédier le présent extrait de Régitres aux Syndics et Conseil; pour qu'ils fassent droit au vœu des Révolutionnaires.—Ant[oin]e Biveleux, Président du Comité Central. François Turc, Secrétaire."

Manuscrits Historiques. Another factitious collection. Manuscript inventory in order of subjects, one volume; alphabetical index, one volume. Apparently nothing American.

Archives d'État proprement dite.

Conseils. This large series, which precedes the subdivisions alphabetically arranged, embraces the Registers of the Council, 1409-1798, in 322 volumes,[1] and the Registres des Particuliers, 1643-1798, containing votes respecting individuals. The volumes of the

---

[1] The Société d'Histoire has published five volumes of the earlier registers, 1409-1499 (Geneva, 1900-1914).

former have individual tables of contents, but there is no general inventory or index (therefore no general search was made), though there are chronological and alphabetical *répertoires* of the *pièces annexes*. The Registres des Particuliers present many volumes of letters, acts, and proclamations of the Council and of the bodies which successively took its place during the revolutionary period.

Registers of the Council, vol. **180**, f. 67. May 4, 5, 1680. The Council confers citizenship on Lord Cornbury, son of the Earl of Clarendon, who had been in Geneva for some time and had so distinguished himself in archery as to be crowned King of the Archers. The Council also ordered extraordinary honors to his kingship. See *Récit de ce qui s'est passé à Genève, le 3me de May M.DC.LXXXI, à la feste des Nobles Chevaliers Archers, en reconnaissance de l'honneur extraordinaire qu'ils ont receu, d'avoir pour leur Roy, Très Illustre et Très Généreux Seigneur, Messire Hyde, comte de Cornbury* (Geneva, " par le Chappuzeau, chez Jean Herman Widerhold ", 1681, pp. 15, quarto).

Registers of the Council, vol. **305**, p. 603. " Le Cit. Syndic [Esaïe] Gasc a rapporté que conformément à la commission qui lui en avoit été donné ce matin il s'etoit rendu au près de la commission révolutionnaire pour lui soumettre le préavis du conseil relativement à la solemnité à donner à la publication des nouvelles officielles attendues de notre envoyé à Paris ; que la commission avoit écarté du plan proposé la jonction des Drapeaux des deux cantons non alliés à ceux des Républiques Française et Genevoise et leur avoit substitué celui des 13 États-unis d'Amérique, motivant cet arrangement sur la fraternité des principes qui doit unir les trois nations, et exclure toute adjonction qui ne seroit fondée que sur des rapports purement diplomatiques." Aug. 30, 1794. (Illumination ordered, etc. See above, p. 179, and Monroe to Reybaz, Sept. 15, 1794, in *Writings*, II. 64. Geneva and the United States were at this time the only states having diplomatic representatives in Paris.)

Registers of the Council, vol. **305**, p. 624. The Council voted that such a letter as the revolutionary clubs had demanded (see above, p. 179) should be sent to the United States Congress, and charged Citizen [Jean-Lazare] De la Planche to prepare it. Sept. 5, 1794.

Registers of the Council, vol. **305**, p. 1007. Under date of Dec. 11, 1794, the Council records with expressions of vivid regret the announcement of P. A. Adet that he is recalled as resident of France with only twenty-four hours' notice to go as minister to the United States.

Registres des Particuliers: Pièces Annexes. In an unnumbered carton, along with a document on the nobility of the house of Gallatin, are found several letters of 1786, relating to a rumor of Albert Gallatin's death. They are mostly copies of letters addressed to Secretary Jay, in response to an advertisement inserted by him in the Philadelphia newspapers, early in May, 1786, at the request of Gallatin's friends, made through Jefferson,[1] who it

---

[1] Adams, *Life of Gallatin*, p. 64; Jefferson to Jay, Jan. 27, 1786, in the former's *Writings*, ed. Washington, I. 525.

seems is quoted in the advertisement. The letter of Jefferson to Tronchin, Aug. 1, 1786, is, however, an original. The others are from Terrasson, French consul, Robert Morris, H. S. Charton, Peter S. du Ponceau, Andrew Dunscomb, Henry Banks (register of the Court of Appeals in Cases of Capture), and Savary de Valcoulon. It will suffice to give extracts from those of Charton and du Ponceau.

(H. S. Charton.) " I am perfectly acquainted with Mr. Albert Galatin who was reported some time ago to have met with so terrible a Fate, and I have the satisfaction to assure that he is still living; what gave rise to such a Report I don't know, but I was lately at Richmond with Mr. Savary de Valcoulon who was all the Time with Mr. Galatin in the back parts of Virginia, and who has told me, that none of their Party had received or likely to receive the least Alarm from the Indians.

" Mr. Galatin only went back to George Creek, the Place of his Settlement, in March last, and I have no Doubt has written to his Family, to contradict the News that had given them so much Pain."

(P. S. du Ponceau.) " Having seen the Advertisement you have caused to be put in the public Papers respecting Mr. Gallatin, I think it my Duty to inform you that on the 20th February last, the same Person was at my Office, and executed a Letter of Attorney to Messieurs Colladon and Hentsch of Geneva to transact his business for him in that commonwealth. He called himself Abraham Alphonse Albert Gallatin, Citizen of Geneva, and told me he was the same Man who had been killed by the Savages in the Fredericksburg Gazette. I believe he is now returned to the back Counties of Virginia, tho' I cannot well assert it. I shall be happy if this information proves any ways satisfactory to the Family of that young Gentleman, tho' I believe it probable that they have by this Time received more direct Intelligence respecting him."

Archives: Old inventories and the like.
Assistance.
Assurance.
Bourgeoisie: Lists of citizens, embracing especially the " Livres des Bourgeois ", rolls extending from 1442 to the end of the republic. See the book by M. Covelle, mentioned in the bibliography above, p. 175.
Cadastre.
Commerce.
Constitutions.
Douane.
Elections: This section includes the printed registers of electors from 1820 to 1911.
État Civil: This includes, first, the " Livres des Morts ", 1548-1798, consisting of 69 registers, with an index in ten volumes. The records of baptisms and marriages before 1798, approximately complete from 1550, were formerly kept in the churches of the city, including, besides the parish churches of the established faith, the

Italian, English, German Reformed, and German Lutheran churches, and in the latter part of the period the Catholic chapels. They are now in the state archives. The same is true of the country parishes, though in general their registers begin at later periods. The civil registers, kept by the municipalities, begin in the Pays de Gex in 1792, in the Savoyard communes after the French occupation in 1793, in the city of Geneva in 1798. These civil registers, to 1815, are preserved in the archives of state. For the period since 1815, the records of the births, marriages, and deaths are kept at the Bureau de l'État Civil Cantonal, 2 rue Étienne Dumont, with some additional local registers in the Catholic and other parishes. But the " répertoires " of the registers of *état civil* are at the Chancellerie d'État in the Hôtel de Ville. Neither this nor the Bureau d'État Civil Cantonal has any *salle de consultation* open to the public. But the archives of state has a duplicate of the " répertoires " for the period from 1814 to 1870. It now also has the registers for the earlier periods (1550-1798 and 1798-1815, as above). It also has guides, generally speaking some 220 volumes of alphabetical indexes of various sorts, to this whole great mass of records of births or baptisms, marriages, and deaths from 1550 to 1870. It also has by exception some Catholic parish registers.

Étrangers: Mostly registers of *permis de séjour*.
Feu.
Fiefs.
Finances.
Habitants: Most of these documents, relating to the refugees at Geneva, have been copied and indexed by M. Alfred L. Covelle.
Hygiène, and so on in alphabetical order, of series not likely to interest the American student.
Archives de la Société Économique. This was a group of fifteen Genevese citizens established in 1798 to administer the communal property for the benefit of educational establishments, of the Reformed worship, and of the maintenance of industries.
Archives Judiciaires. Records and papers of a great variety of judicial courts, of various periods.
Archives Notariales. There are 3474 volumes of minutes and protocols of the notaries from 1373 to 1878. For a list of these notaries, see Inventaire no. 5. The series embraces a great number of deeds, marriage contracts, and wills. Besides analyses of the Latin documents in this series, extending to about 1535, and preserved at the archives, there are analyses of the French documents of the sixteenth, seventeenth, and eighteenth centuries in the possession of the Société d'Histoire et d'Archéologie de Genève.
Archives de Familles. This section seems not to include any names which have been of note in American history.
Archive de l'Église. Mostly elsewhere; see next section, pp. 183-184.
Archives des Sociétés. This embraces books of the Noble Exercice du Canon, of the Exercices de l'Arcquebuse, of the Société des Catechumènes, etc.

GENEALOGICAL.

For the benefit of those who may have occasion to make genealogical researches, the following account of the resources of Geneva in this respect has been drawn off from notes made by Mr. C. Roch, attaché of the archives of state.

For the period before 1550, one has the *minutaires* of notaries (see above), the registers of the councils, the *grosses de reconnaissance,* etc. By the study of the sections entitled " Titres et Droits de la Seigneurie " one may even go back to the tenth century. See the *Regeste Genevois,* published by the Société d'Histoire.

For the period from 1550 to 1798, one has, primarily, the parish registers of *état civil,* Genevese, French, Savoyard, and the indexes to them, as described above. One has also, at the Archives d'État, the Registres des Habitants, the Registres des Bourgeois (see Covelle's *Livre des Bourgeois,* mentioned in the bibliography), the minutes of notaries (of which there are analytical indexes at the rooms of the Société d'Histoire), the wills and inventories, the *grosses de reconnaissances,* the judicial papers, the Registers of the Council, the Registres des Particuliers, the documents of the Bourse Française, etc., and at the Chancellerie the " Registre Unique de Citoyens, 1794 " (index at the Archives). These for the Protestants of Geneva; for the Catholics, the communes added from Savoy and the Pays de Gex, there are the *grosses,* the minutes of notaries, and the documents of the *tabellion* of Carouge and St. Julien.

For the period from 1798 to 1814, one has the Registres d'État Civil, at the Archives, with indexes in duplicate, at the Archives and at the Chancellerie; some parish registers, in the parishes, at the Archives, or at the Bureau Cantonal de l'État Civil; the papers of the Département du Léman; and some minutes of notaries.

For the period since 1814, one has the Registres, with indexes at the Chancellerie and (to 1870) at the Archives; and various parish registers, kept in the parishes, with indexes at the Archives and at the Bureau Cantonal.

The fees for copies of entries vary from two to three francs. Full name, and age at a given date, are generally prerequisite to successful search.

The genealogies of some seven hundred Genevese families have been published in the *Notices Généalogiques sur les Familles Genevoises* (Geneva, Jullien, 7 vols.), and in vols. I. and II. of the *Recueil Généalogique Suisse.* The Archives d'État possess a set of the former collection annotated in manuscript by the former archivist, M. Louis Dufour-Vernes.

GENEVA: ECCLESIASTICAL ARCHIVES.

From Calvin's time the Church of Geneva has been governed by two bodies, the Consistoire and the Compagnie des Pasteurs et Professeurs. See Eugène Ritter, *Les Archives de l'Église de Genève* (Geneva, 1886, pp. 15). The archives of the Consistoire are kept at the Auditoire, a building opposite the cathedral. This is not a public archive, but it is accessible to scholars. The secretary of the Consistoire, who has charge of it, is present during most of the day. It consists of from eighty to a hundred large volumes of registers, in which are recorded the proceedings and judgments of the consistory, matter abounding in data for the history of manners and morals in Geneva. There are some gaps, but none after 1605. The syndic August Cramer, who was apparently the only man who had ever read them through, furnished a large specimen of what they contain, in a volume produced by lithographic (?) process (and difficult to read) entitled *Notes extraites des Registres du Consistoire de Genève* (Geneva, 1853, pp. xvii, 459). The present secretary believes that the registers contain nothing for American history, and an examination of Mr. Cramer's book revealed nothing. The archive contains no correspondence. Since 1814 both Consistoire and Compagnie have kept their papers with great care.

The archives of the Compagnie des Pasteurs et Professeurs are also kept at the Auditoire, so far as their registers are concerned. These records of their meetings, extending to fifty or sixty volumes, were not kept with great carefulness. Something of their history may be read in an article by H. V. Aubert, " Nicolas Colladon et les Registres de la Compagnie des Pasteurs et Professeurs de Genève " in the *Bullétin de la Société d'Histoire et d'Archéologie de Genève*, II. 138-163 (1905). They abound in necrological notices, of which three specimens are printed as an appendix to M. Ritter's pamphlet noted above, pp. 10-15.

The earlier part of the correspondence of the Compagnie des Pasteurs et Professeurs has been deposited at the Bibliothèque Publique et Universitaire, where it can be consulted in the same manner as the manuscripts possessed by the University. It begins with the correspondence of the Company with foreign churches in the times of Calvin and Beza, and extends from 1550 to 1760. Calvin left his papers to Beza. What remains of them, and of the letters from his death on, is in the public library, as are also the papers of Antoine Court. Several families, descendants of the old pastors, have turned over their papers to the archives of the Venerable Company.

The correspondence of the Company is bound in 43 volumes. There is an old-fashioned manuscript " Inventaire de la Correspondance ", and a carefully made card-catalogue, arranged alphabetically by authors and taking note of each letter. Nothing American was found, despite the hopes raised by the entry in Cotton Mather's Diary, under date of Apr. 6, 1721, " Enter into a Correspondence with Geneva, whereto I am invited."

The papers of Genevese eminent in church or university affairs have of course often been preserved even till now by their families. Thus, it is in the correspondence of Professor Marc Antoine Pictet, privately preserved, that Professor Charles Borgeaud found some of the significant papers relating to the proposals discussed in 1794 by Jefferson, Adams, and Washington for the bodily transfer of the University of Geneva to America—one of the origins of the University of Virginia. See Professor Borgeaud's admirable *Histoire de l'Université de Genève*, I. 612-613 (1900) ; and Edwin D. Mead, " The Proposed Removal of the Academy of Geneva to America in 1794 ", in the *Educational Review*, April, 1910.

AUSTRIAN ARCHIVES.

The archives of Austria (see Introduction) searched for materials relating to American history were those of Vienna, Salzburg, and Innsbruck. In Vienna the following were found to contain materials bearing on the subject: the Kaiserliches und Königliches Haus-, Hof-, und Staatsarchiv; the K. u. K. Kriegsarchiv (archive of the Ministry of War); the Allgemeines Archiv des K. u. K. Ministeriums des Innern (archive of the Ministry of the Interior); the K. u. K. Gemeinsames Finanz-Archiv (Hofkammer-Archiv); the Archiv der Stadt Wien (archive of the city of Vienna); and the K. u. K. Hofbibliothek (Imperial and Royal Library).

VIENNA.

K. U. K. HAUS-, HOF- UND STAATSARCHIV.

Location: Wien I., Minoritenplatz 1. Very near the Hofburg; a modern building, constructed 1899-1902, for the archive solely.

The idea of gathering all the archive material of the House of Hapsburg under one head and at a single station was probably conceived by the Emperor Maximilian I., but the plan was not carried into execution until the age of Maria Theresia, and under her special patronage. In 1749 she appointed Theodor A. T. von Rosenthal, who became the scientific founder of the archive. He attempted to centralize the material and enlarge the scope of the archive by copying on a large scale all documents of importance the originals of which could not be removed to Vienna. The leading position of the House of Hapsburg in Central Europe, continuous through centuries, the service of Austria as the bulwark against the invasion of the Turks, the resistance of Austria during the Napoleonic wars, have contributed to make this archive one of the most valuable in existence. Many losses also have been sustained, as when with the forfeiture of her Italian provinces Austria had to give up also from her archive the documents relating to the history of Lombardy and Venetia.

The K. u. K. Haus-, Hof-, und Staatsarchiv is divided into the following large groups:
1. Das Haus- und Familienarchiv;
2. Das Staatsarchiv;
3. Das Archiv der Kais. Reichshofkanzlei und des Kais. Reichshofrats;
4. Das Italienische;
5. Das Niederländische oder Belgische;
6. Das Herzoglich-Lothringische;
7. Das Salzburgisch-Erzbischöfliche und Domkapitelarchiv;
8. Das Mainzer (Reichskanzlerische);
9. Das Archiv des ehemaligen Staatsrats;
10. Urkunden.

There is also a special collection of about 2000 manuscripts (for guide see bibliography), and a library of about 20,000 volumes. There is at present no complete guide to the materials in the K. u. K. Haus-, Hof-, und Staatsarchiv, though the arduous labor of preparing such a guide has been begun.

Hours: On week-days, 9.30 a. m. to 7 p. m. Sundays and holidays, 10 a. m. to 1 p. m. Closed on Saturdays after 4 p. m., and for several days at Christmas, New Year, and Easter. Application for use of documents should be made before 11 a. m. for use on the same afternoon, or in the afternoon for use the next morning. If the investigator is pressed for time, he will often find however that the courtesy of the officials extends beyond their rules. An exhibition of historical manuscripts, seals, etc., takes place every Wednesday, 10 a. m. to 1 p. m.

Bibliography: Gerson Wolf, *Geschichte der K. K. Archive in Wien* (Vienna, 1871). Treats the history of the three following archives, as well.

Gustav Winter, *Die Gründung des Kaiserlichen und Königlichen Haus-, Hof- und Staatsarchivs, 1749-1762* (Vienna, 1902).

Id., Das neue Gebäude des K. u. K. Haus-, Hof- und Staatsarchivs zu Wien (Vienna, 1903).

Langlois und Stein, *Les Archives de l'Histoire de France* (Paris, 1891), pp. 645-655.

Constantin Edler von Böhm, *Die Handschriften des Kaiserlichen und Königlichen Haus-, Hof- und Staatsarchivs* (Vienna, 1873). Supplement (Vienna, 1874).

Gustav Winter and Árpád von Károlyi, *Katalog der Archivalien-Ausstellung des K. und K. Haus-, Hof- und Staatsarchivs* (Vienna, 1905).

Joseph Cuvelier, " Les Archives Autrichiennes ", in *Revue des Bibliothèques et des Archives de Belgique*, V. 178-200 (1906).

G. Des Marez, " Les Archives Royales et Impériales de Vienne ", in *Revue de l'Université de Bruxelles*, April, 1905.

See also the publications of Dr. Hanns Schlitter mentioned below.

STAATSKANZLEI.

Fasc. 62. Noten von der Hofkanzlei.

" Die Errichtung eines Handlungs-Vertrags mit den Vereinigten Amerikanischen Staaten." Nota der Vereinigten Hofkanzlei. Mar. 31, 1785.

" Die sich zu Triest formierende Oesterreichisch-Amerikanische Handlungsgesellschaft betr." Nota der Vereinigten Hofkanzlei. Sept. 5, 1785.

DAS BELGISCHE ARCHIV.

The materials relating to American history contained in this section have been published by the archivist, Dr. Hanns Schlitter, in his two works: (1) *Die Beziehungen Oesterreichs zu Amerika, I. Teil,* . . . *zu den Vereinigten Staaten, 1778-1787* (Innsbruck, 1885) (for the preparation of this work Dr. Schlitter also searched American archives) ; and (2) *Die Berichte des ersten Agenten Oesterreichs in den Vereinigten Staaten von Amerika Baron de Beelen-Bertholff an die Regierung der Oesterreichischen Niederlande in Brüssel, 1784-1789,* herausgegeben von Dr. Hanns Schlitter (Vienna, 1891), published in *Fontes Rerum Austriacarum: Oesterreichische Geschichtsquellen,* herausgegeben von der Historischen Commission der Kaiserlichen Akademie der Wissenschaften in Wien, Zweite Abteilung, Diplomataria et Acta, XLV. Band, Zweite Hälfte, pp. 225-892. See also Hubert Van Houtte and Edmund C. Burnett, " American Commercial Conditions, and Negotiations with Austria, 1783-1786 ", in *American Historical Review*, XVI. 567-587.

B. Vereinigte Staaten von Nordamerika.

Aus Verträge betr. Acten, Fasc. 9. Report zu Abth. IV. 1784. " Den beabsichtigten Abschluss eines Freundschafts- und Handelsvertrags zwischen dem Kaiser und den Vereinigten Staaten von Nordamerika betref. Actenstücke." 1784. Namely:
1. " Orig. Schreiben des bevollmächtigten Ministers der Vereinigten Staaten in Paris Benjamin Franklin an den kaiserl. Botschafter Graf Mercy über die Bereitwilligkeit der Freistaaten einen Freundschafts- und Handelsvertrag abzuschliessen." Passy, July 30, 1784.
2. " Antwortsconcepte des Grafen Mercy." Paris, July 30, and Sept. 28, 1784. " Bemerkungen über den Vertragsentwurf zwischen dem Kaiser und den Vereinigten Staaten von Nordamerika."
3. " Vertragsentwürfe und Bemerkungen über den Vertragsentwurf zwischen dem Kaiser und Nordamerika."

A large fascicle containing documents relating to the trade of Belgium with America and the negotiation of a commercial treaty, viz.:
1. " Berichte des Handelsrathes Baron Beelen Bertholff aus Amerika an das Belgische Gouvernement ", etc. Aug., 1784–Apr. 30, 1789.
2. " Berichte eines Committees über diese." Aug., 1784–May 6, 1786.
3. " Original Noten des Gr. Belgiojoso an Gr. Mercy." Oct. 28, 1784–June 10, 18, 1785.
4. " Copie eines Schreibens des Gr. Trautmannsdorf an Gr. Proli." July 14, 1789. (An appendix to the following.)
5. " Original Schreiben des Grafen Proli an Brüssel (den Gouverneur), 14. Sept. 1792, wurde als zu Belgien gehörig in das Filiale B. abgegeben."

Belgien DDB 182 a. " Berichte Beelen-Bertholff's an Belgiojoso, ministre plénip. à Bruxelles." 1784, 1785, III.
Belgien DDB 182 b. "Berichte Beelen-Bertholff." 1785, IV-XII.
Belgien DDB 182 c. " Berichte Beelen-Bertholff." 1786.
Belgien DDB 182 d. " Berichte Beelen-Bertholff." 1787.
Belgien DDB 182 e. " Berichte Beelen-Bertholff." 1788-1789.
Belgien DD 6, 1, 182 e. " Berichte des Comité de Commerce." 1783-1785. 6/5. Relate to the reports of Beelen-Bertholff. Accompanying them are original letters of Starhemberg to Delplancq, drafts of instructions to Beelen, memorials respecting commerce, etc.
Belgien Rep. DD. Abth. B. Fasc. 182 e. " Proli an Cobenzl." 1792, 19/9. Among the accompanying documents, one, designated as B, " Observations concernant la correspondance du gouvernement des Pays-Bas Autrichiens avec le conseiller de commerce Baron de Beelen depuis l'arrivée de celui-ci en Amérique en 1783 jusqu'à la fin de 1787 ", gives a general conspectus of the matters treated by Beelen in his reports.
Nr. 20. Vorträge an den König. Kaunitz an Joseph. Département des Païs-Bas. " Très humble Raport du Chancelier de Cour et d'État, par lequel en présentant à la Rle Signature de Votre Majesté un Acte de Plein Pouvoir qui autorise le Cte. de Mercy à negocier et à conclure un Traité de Commerce avec les États-Unis d'Amérique." Mar. 8, 1786.[1]

---

[1] No. 13. Kaunitz to Joseph, Feb. 27, 1786, is printed in the *American Historical Review*, XVI. 576-578.

STAATS-RATH.

The Staats-Rath Indices begin with the year 1761 and continue into the nineteenth century. The material bearing on America and emigration is not abundant; the acta preserved, relating to America, are as follows:

1771. Nr. 1864. "Auswandern, ist den gemeinen Handwerkern einzuschränken."
1773. Nr. 340. "Auswandern, oder Reisen ausser Landes, das desfalls bestehende Gesetz ist auch in den Militär-Gränzen einzuführen."
1774. Nr. 2927. "Auswanderungen an den Gränzen sind nicht allgemein, sondern nur in gewissen Fällen zu gestatten."
1777. Nr. 1955. "America wird in einem Buch beschrieben, so zwahr von der Censur in Anstand gezogen, dannoch aber passiret wird." Title of the book: *Erdbeschreibung von ganz Amerika,* 1 u. 2 Theil.
1782. No. 4095. "Amerikanische Colonien. Dahin wird eine Schiffahrt von dem Consul zu Cadix eingeleitet." (Spanish-American colonies.)
1783. Nr. 1467. "Amerikanischer Handel: In Absicht auf denselben wird eine Consignation der Hung. und Siebenbürgischen Naturprodukten und Manufakturen, und deren Preys überreicht." (North America.)
1784. Nr. 375. "Womit der Entwurf der aus 96 einzeln zerstreuten Verordnungen in ein Auswanderungspatent zusammengefasst wird." Vortrag, Jan. 28, 1784.
Nr. 2304. "Im allgemeinen ist niemanden erlaubt weder selbst auszuwandern, noch jemand von seinen Kindern, oder von denen, welche unter seiner Gewalt und Aufsicht stehen, in fremde Landen zu senden." (Punishment, confiscation of property, or, if caught, hard labor; children of an emigrating father not deprived of property.) "Obrigkeitlicher Beamter oder Vorsteher der überführt wird, einem Auswanderer Hilfe zu leisten, Geldstrafe oder 6 Monate öffentliche Arbeit." Vortrag, June 4, 1784. (This law applied to emigration to any foreign country.)
1785. Nr. 3489. "Amerikanische, und in Triest sich formierende Handlungs Societät."
Nr. 1864. "Auswanderungs-Verordnung. Strafe eines Buchhändlers."
Nr. 4733. "Auswanderungspatent." Erbschaft.
1792. Nr. 2184. "America, dahinsiger Leinwandhandel." (Bohemia and South America.)
1794. Nr. 1872. "Die ständigen Deputirten stellten vor: dasz das bestehende Auswanderungsverboth den Unterthanen in Schwäbisch-Oesterreich bei der in fremden Territorien vermischten Lage des Landes sehr beschwerlich falle, und baten daher um Aufhebung dieses Verboths sowohl als der gewöhnlichen Auswanderungs-Bewilligungstaxen."
Regierung vermeint: "Es könnte diese zweyfache Bitte zur Probe bewilliget werden, wo sodann, wenn aus den jährlichen Berichten und Tabellen die Zahl der Auswandernden wider Vermuthen jene der Hereinziehenden übersteigen sollte, diesfalls immer Schranken gesetzet, und die Auswanderung wieder verbothen werden könnte." Vortrag gehalten, Apr. 16, 1794.

DIPLOMATIC CORRESPONDENCE.

NORDAMERIKA.

Under this rubric is found the entire correspondence between the Austrian agents in the United States and the home government under Metternich from 1819 to 1847. The material is divided into the groups: (1) Berichte (Despatches), Faszikel 1-6; (2) Weisungen (Instructions), Noten, Varia.

BERICHTE.

Faszikel I.

Stürmer to Metternich.

1819.

Four communications of: Barthol. Freyherr von Stürmer, k. k. General-Consul in den Vereinigten Staaten von Nord-Amerika.[1]

Mar. 5. Vienna. Claim of 300 pounds sterling for expenses of return trip from island of St. Helena, advanced by English governor.

Mar. 7. Vienna. Concerning two carriages left at Calais, belonging to the royal stables.

Apr. 8. Vienna. Offer of a substitute for a lost chart.

July 11. Vienna. Expenses of a trip from London to Milan, Dec. 25, 1815, to Feb. 20, 1816.

Lederer to Metternich.

1820-1823.

Portrait of Lederer, with following note:

"Alois, Freiherr von Lederer, K. k. Oest. Generalconsul in Nord-America, wurde im Jahre 1819 mit der Anknüpfung des diplomatischen Verkehrs mit der Republik der Vereinigten Staaten betraut. Er fand New York als den passendsten Centralpunkt zur Erfüllung seiner Aufgabe und versah da sein Amt daselbst bis 1838, wo dann seitens beider Staaten die Gesandschaftsposten creirt wurden. Am 27. August 1829 unterzeichnete er den ersten Handels- und Schiffahrtsvertrag mit den Vereinigten Staaten von America."

(Most of the communications of Baron Lederer were written in German, a few in French.)

---

[1] Bartholomäus Graf von Stürmer (b. 1787) was sent to the island of St. Helena in 1816 on special mission, as one of the commissioners kept there by the Allied Powers, to keep watch over Napoleon as a prisoner on the island. Unsatisfactory in this capacity, he was recalled after two years' residence on St. Helena, and appointed Austrian consul-general in the United States. He left St. Helena in July, 1818, eight months after the date of his new appointment. His reports, from Philadelphia, were directed to the Commerz-Hofkommission, not to Prince Metternich. After two years of service, which did not satisfy the home government, he was sent to Rio de Janeiro, in 1820, but his mission in Brazil terminated after five months, with the outbreak of the revolution. After these failures he seems to have lost favor, and did not receive a diplomatic post again until 1832, when he distinguished himself at Constantinople (1832-1850), being very successful in establishing an Austrian steamship service with the Orient.

No. 1. Report (in French). Exequatur; audiences with President Monroe and Secretary J. Q. Adams. Treatment of Austrian merchantmen in accordance with principle of reciprocity. Political conditions in U. S. Struggle between East and West. General ignorance of American newspaper editors concerning German and Austrian affairs. Large number of German immigrants contribute more to winning the soil for civilization than producing a favorable impression of the civilization of their native country. " In the National Library at Washington, containing 20-30,000 vols. in living and dead languages, I had difficulty in finding a single German book." New York, Dec. 9, 1820.
2. Report (in French) on political affairs. Outline of the constitution of Missouri. The exiled French. Joseph Bonaparte. Difficulty in choice of duty among so many duties devolving upon the first and sole representative of his country (Austria) in America. New York, Dec. 30, 1820.
3. Report. (a) Political news concerning the insurgents in the Spanish colonies; reported truce between Generals Morillo and Bolivar. (b) Expedition of Vice-Admiral Cochrane against Peru. New York, Jan. 6, 1821.
4. Report on current events. England's attitude toward U. S. Missouri and slave-trade. Newspaper clippings. New York, Feb. 24-25, 1821.
5. Remarks on the attitude of American papers (*National Gazette* and *National Intelligencer*) in reference to political events in Europe. Acquirement of Florida. May 13 and 15, 1821.
6. " Nachrichten über die revolutionären Umtriebe im südlichen Amerika." June 10, 1821.
7. The Floridas not yet given over by Spain. Current events. July 10, 1821.
8. Cession of the two Floridas. J. Q. Adams probably the next president. Sept. 10, 1821.
9. Lederer applies for Tuscan consul-generalship in addition to present position. Same date.
10. Report on various political events. Oct. 9, 1821.
11. Report on current events. Governor Jackson and the Spanish Colonel Callava, at Pensacola. Boundary questions with England and Spain. Oct. 19, 1821.
12. General Jackson and the Spanish Colonel Coppinger, governor of East Florida. (Baggage forced open to get documents that ought to have been given to U. S. government.) Nov. 12, 1821.
13. Current events. President's message. Dec. 10, 1821.
14. " Die nordamerikanische Regierung bedarf dieses Jahr keines Anlehens." Ukase of Russian Emperor claiming Northwest Coast, Behring Strait south to 51°. Impression in U. S. Jan. 9, 1822.
15. Report on census. Feb. 10, 1822.
16. Action of Congress. Mar. 15, 1822.
18. Northwest boundary question. Apr. 30, 1822.
19. Recognition of independence of South American states. May 5, 1822.
20. Current events. May 31, 1822.
21. Diplomatic relations between U. S. and South American states. June 28, 1822.

22. Commercial treaty with France. July 5, 1822.
23. Yellow fever in New York. Aug. 8, 1822.
25. Comprehensive report descriptive of conditions in U. S., relations to other countries, and suggestion of improvement of commercial relations between Austria and U. S. Sept. 9, 1822.
26. Current events. Oct. 15, 1822.
27. Newspaper clippings (*National Gazette*, Phila.). Nov. 6, 1822.
28. President's message. Dec. 5, 1822.
29. Cuba. Clipping from *National Intelligencer*, Washington. Dec. 9, 1822.
30. Appropriation to stop piracy in West Indies. Dec. 23, 1822.
31. Cuba; current events. Jan. 15, 1823.
32. Treaty between U. S. and Great Britain. Jan. 31, 1823.
33. Current events. Feb. 15, 1823.
34. No reliable information obtained on Bernhard Rauch, merchant. Feb. 15, 1823.
35. Current events. Mar. 7, 1823.
36. Current events. Mar. 31, 1823.
37. Current events; references to South America. Apr. 29, 1823.
38. Current events. Same date.
39. Jackson proposed for next President. May 18, 1823.
40. Current events. June 28, 1823.
41. Diplomatic and consular service. Aug. 23, 1823.
42. Current events. Slave-trade. Sept. 27, 1823.
43. " Ackerbaugesellschaft in New York." Sept. 27, 1823.
44. Remarks on President's message. Dec. 6, 1823.

1824.

45. Import duties. Jan. 6, 1824.
46. Current events. Jan. 7, 1824.
47. Translation of law governing duties and tonnage taxes of foreign vessels in American ports. Jan. 26, 1824.
48. Current events. Feb. 24, 1824.
49. Change of tariff on tonnage of vessels proposed in Congress. Apr. 27, 1824.
50. New tariff decided on. £6600 as present to Greeks. May 25, 1824.
51. Current events. June 21, 1824.
52. Copy of treaty between U. S. and England. June 27, 1824.
53. Current events. July 28, 1824.
54. Treaty between Russia and U. S. Aug. 23, 1824.
55. " Bitte um Urlaub: Der Wunsch meiner zwei Söhne in ihren gegenwärtigen zarten und kritischen Altern von 8 und 10 Jahren von den hier herrschenden Grundsätzen zu bewahren, sie in einer Erziehungsanstalt unterzubringen, in welcher sie eine dem allerhöchsten Dienste unseres gnädigsten Monarchens angemessene Erziehung geniessen könnten, sind die Beweggründe, welche mich bestimmten, diese Bitte zu tragen." Aug. 30, 1824.
56. Appointments in diplomatic service. Sept. 26, 1824.
57. Prognostications concerning the next president. Nov. 16, 1824.
58. President's message. Dec. 10, 1824.
59. Case of Joseph Hisky and his mother. Same date.
60. No information on Peter Cristofori. Dec. 20, 1824.

1825.

61. "Der Consul berichtet die Zunahme des Verkehrs mit Triest, welche ihm eine günstige Gelegenheit zur Ausführung solcher Massregeln anzubieten scheint, die die Gleichstellung der beiden Flaggen in diesen Staaten beabsichtigen." Jan. 3, 1825.
62. Concerning the business of Count Barzizza. Feb. 14, 1825.
63. The election of J. Q. Adams and J. C. Calhoun. Feb. 15, 1825.
64. Current events. Mar. 9, 1825.
65. The consul shows that in case of war between Spain and U. S., Austria would have advantages if her ships were treated on any equality with those of some other nations in American ports. Apr. 10, 1825.
66. Letter of Von Kapff and Brune in Baltimore showing expensive process of following up land claim of Count Barzizza in Williamsburg, Va. Apr. 24, 1825.
67. Probability of war with Spain. Additional reasons (see no. 66 above). Apr. 25, 1825.
68. Austrian signal for pilots decided on. May 20, 1825.
69. Current events. Indians. June 15, 1825.
70. Copy of treaty between U. S. and republic of Colombia. July 5, 1825.
71. Report of a committee of the house of representatives of the legislature of Georgia threatening secession. Lederer thinks the matter harmless for the present. July 6, 1825.
72. News of death of Peter Cristofori. July 15, 1825.
73. Current events. Aug. 12, 1825.
74. Visit of French fleet. Aug. 19, 1825.
75. Remarks on difficulties between federal government and state government of Georgia. Sept. 20, 1825.
76. Current events. Nov. 15, 1825.
77. Message of President Adams. Dec. 12, 1825.
78. Copy of letter of Henry Clay (Dec. 20, 1825) to Baron Lederer in reference to some arrangement to facilitate negotiation of a treaty between Austria and U. S. Table of exports and imports between U. S. and Triest for the year 1825. Dec. 27, 1825.

1826.

80. Leave of absence to begin in May. Jan. 20, 1826.
81. Reciprocity navigation bill passed in Congress. Mar. 28, 1826.

Sept. 23, 1826. Letter written from Vienna. "Bittet die Ernennung zum korrespondierenden Mitglied zweier wissenschaftlichen Gesellschaften annehmen zu dürfen." (Linnæan Society in New York, and Society of Natural History, Amherst, Mass.)

Oct. 19, 1826. Letter written from Vienna. "Hinsichtlich des Landeigentums des David Parish." C. C. Peterson, consular agent, left in charge in New York.

Dec. 11, 1826. (Report sent from Vienna.) "Denkschrift, einige Ansichten von den politischen Verhältnissen der Nordamerikanischen Vereinigten Staaten enthaltend." 17 pages. "Ich bin weit entfernt, ihre Staatsverfassung als dauerhaft anzusehen, sie scheint aber ihren gegenwärtigen Bedürfnissen, ihren Lokalumständen und anderen Verhältnissen angemessen zu sein, und so lange diese bestehen, wird sie wahrscheinlich keine Aenderung leiden."

Dec. 11, 1826. (Written during his brief stay in Vienna.) " Denkschrift über die Wichtigkeit eines Handelsverkehrs mit den Nordamerikanischen Vereinigten Staaten, und die Möglichkeit den mit der Oesterreichischen Monarchie schon bestehenden Verkehr mittelst eines Handlungs-Traktates auszudehnen." 70 pages. Mit 5 Beilagen (A. and D. lacking).
  B. Tabelle der Ausfuhr eigener Produkte aus den Nordamerikanischen Staaten im Jahr 1825.
  C. Tabelle der Einfuhr der vorzüglicheren Fremdenprodukte in die Nordamerikanischen Vereinigten Staaten im Jahre 1825.
  E. Abschriften der Handlungs-Konvenzionen der Nordamerikanischen Vereinigten Staaten mit Frankreich, Dänemark und der Republik Colombia.

1827-1828.

Mar. 22, 1827. Keine Nachricht über Dr. Nikolaus von Niederberg aus New York erhalten. (Letter written from Vienna.)

Apr. 30, 1827. Keine Nachricht über Philippo Ignazio Barzizza. (Letter written from Vienna.)

1. General report. (This and the succeeding numbers written from New York.) Dec. 10, 1827.
2. " Erbschaft des Anton Marschner von Lebanon, Dauphin County, Penna." Dec. 17, 1827.
3. Commercial and navigation treaty between U. S. and Sweden. Jan. 26, 1828.
4. Georgia preparing for secession. Article on Austria and the Porte. Mar. 3, 1828.
5. Current events. Apr. 30, 1828.
6. Property of David Parish. May 22, 1828.
8. Treaty between Great Britain and U. S. May 26, 1828.
9. Prussia and reciprocity. May 28, 1828.
10. Close of Congress. May 30, 1828.
11. Concerning Franz Anton Terzi of New Orleans. June 3, 1828.
12. Navigation treaty between U. S. and Hansa cities. June 5, 1828.
13. Navigation treaty between U. S. and Prussia. June 10, 1828.
14. Certain privileges to kingdom of Hannover. July 5, 1828.
15. Newspaper clippings (*National Intelligencer*). July 6, 1828.
17. Receives commission to negotiate commercial and navigation treaty with U. S. July 24, 1828.
18. The President appoints Henry Clay to confer with Baron Lederer. Aug. 8, 1828.
19. Legacy of Anton Marschner. Aug. 9, 1828.
20. Affairs of F. A. Terzi. Sept. 4, 1828.
21. Personal matters. Same date.
22. Navigation treaty between U. S. and Mexico. Same date.
25. Two interviews with Clay about treaty. First draft and memoranda. Beilage A, B, C. Washington, Oct. 30, 1828.
26. Newspaper clippings. Washington, Oct. 30, 1828.
27. " Lederer berichtet, dass Herr Clay die Unterhandlungen abgebrochen habe." Lederer's remarks on probable reasons. Washington, Nov. 18, 1828.

28. Declarations of Austria's willingness to abolish discriminating duties. Clay's explanation of the limitations of his power. Washington, Nov. 28, 1828.
29. Prospective treaty with Austria mentioned in President's message to Congress. Washington, Dec. 3, 1828.
30. No information concerning Johann M. Weisz (oder Deisz). New York, Dec. 22, 1828.

1829.

31. Concerning Georgio Jovovich in Porto Rico. Jan. 12, 1829.
32. Report on international relations of U. S. Jan. 15, 1829.
33. Copy of treaty of U. S. and Hansa cities. Jan. 20, 1829.
34. General Jackson's probable appointments. Feb. 28, 1829.
35. His inaugural address. Mar. 6, 1829.
36. Lederer goes to Washington. Mar. 28, 1829.
37. Report on results of trip. Apr. 12, 1829.
38. Commercial treaties. Apr. 13, 1829.
39. Routine matters. Same date.
40. Concerning Count Barzizza. Same date.
41. Concerning Jacob Werdtman. Apr. 15, 1829.
42. Routine matters. Same date.
44. Routine matters. May 12, 1829.
45. Concerning Michael Holzhofer. Same date.
46. Proposed visit to Washington on account of treaty. May 18, 1829.
47. Proclamation of President of U. S. abolishing discrimination against Austrian vessels. May 20, 1829.
48. News of six or eight weeks' delay in matter of treaty. June 9, 1829.
49. Routine matters. Same date.
50. Routine matters. June 15, 1829.
51. Routine matters. June 21, 1829.
52. Routine matters. July 9, 1829.
53. Copy of letter of Van Buren, stating that he is not quite ready to take up matter of treaty (Lederer: In spite of the fact, that Austria has long ago abolished discriminating duty). July 16, 1829.
55. Concerning Terzi, and Simon Cuculli. July 31, 1829.
56. Not yet invited by Van Buren, though envoys of England and France already received. Same date.
57. Van Buren invites Lederer to Washington. Aug. 11, 1829.
58. Lederer reports agreement with Van Buren. Aug. 22, 1829.
59. Treaty between Austria and U. S. signed Aug. 29, 1829. Sept. 2, 1829.
60. Routine matters. Sept. 29, 1829.
61. Legacy, Terzi-Cuculli. Sept. 30, 1829.
62. Routine matters. Oct. 7, 1829.
63. Cotton duck instead of hemp used in American sails. Oct. 7, 1829.
65. Routine matters. Nov. 9, 1829.
66. Routine matters. Same date.
67. Routine matters. Nov. 19, 1829.
68. On some Catholic institutions in U. S. Nov. 30, 1829.
69. President's message. Dec. 9, 1829.
70. Remarks on the message. Same date.

Haus-, Hof- und Staatsarchiv 195

Faszikel 2. A. 1830-1831.
71. Conditions in Mexico. Jan. 15, 1830.
72. Report of U. S. Secretary of War. Jan. 18, 1830.
73. Report of U. S. Secretary of Navy. Same date.
74. Legacy of Terzi, New Orleans. Jan. 31, 1830.
75. Concerning Anton Marschner. Same date.
76. Duty on Austrian wines. Feb. 14, 1830.
79. Concerning Terzi. Feb. 28, 1830.
80. American learned societies. Mar. 3, 1830.
81. On percussion-locks. Mar. 23, 1830.
82. Diplomatic agents of Portugal. Mar. 26, 1830.
83. Concerning Terzi-Cuculli. Apr. 8, 1830.
84. Controversy between diplomatic agents of Portugal. Apr. 4, 1830.
85. Concerning Terzi-Cuculli. Apr. 19, 1830.
86. Concerning Portugal. Apr. 30, 1830.
88. Movement against Masonic orders in U. S. May 1, 1830.
89. On change of tariff. May 3, 1830.
90. Plan of lowering import duties. May 9, 1830.
91. Report of Secretaries of War and Navy. May 12, 1830.
92. On abolition of negro slavery. Same date.
93. Routine business. May 31, 1830.
95. Portuguese diplomats, Barrozo *vs.* Torlade. June 17, 1830.
97. Report of Secretary of Navy. June 21, 1830.
98. Treaty between U. S. and Denmark. June 23, 1830.
99. Routine matters. June 30, 1830.
101. Routine matters. July 8, 1830.
105. American Philosophical Society of Philadelphia. July 30, 1830.
106. Concerning Randolph, who is to visit Vienna. Characterization: " Die Menge seiner Ideen war er nie im Stande in Ordnung zu bringen." " An extraordinary envoy, not an envoy extraordinary." July 31, 1830.
107. Routine matters. Same date.
— (no number). Routine matters. Aug. 9, 1830.
113. Routine matters. Sept. 13, 1830.
114. Routine matters. Sept. 14, 1830.
115. Routine matters. Sept. 30, 1830.
116. Newspaper clipping, article written by Joseph Bonaparte, Point Breeze. Oct. 14, 1830.
117. U. S. and British colonies. Oct. 15, 1830.
118. Exequatur (President Jackson). Same date.
119. Austria's position on slavery, published in *Daily Advertiser* of New York, and *National Gazette* of Philadelphia, regulating ships visiting the port of Triest. Oct. 31, 1830.
120. Austria has recognized new government of France, announcement in New York. Nov. 15, 1830.
122. President Jackson's message. Dec. 8, 1830.
123. Remarks on a message. Dec. 15, 1830.
124. Routine matters. Dec. 31, 1830.
125. Routine matters. Jan. 10, 1831.
127. Treaty between U. S. and Turkey. Feb. 10, 1831.
130. Routine matters. Feb. 28, 1831.

132. Terzi-Cuculli. Mar. 5, 1831.
133. Marschner. Same date.
135. Copy of convention between U. S. and Emperor of Austria concluded Mar. 28, 1830. Mar. 7, 1831.
136. Concerning increase of salary. Mar. 9, 1831.
137. Routine matters. Same date.
138. Marschner. Mar. 23, 1831.
139. Maine objects to boundary decision. Apr. 7, 1831.
140. Report on internal affairs in U. S. 35 pages. Apr. 10, 1831.
141. Resignation of members of the Cabinet. Apr. 22, 1831.
142. Northeastern Boundary question. Apr. 23, 1831.
143, 144. Routine matters. May 3, 1831.
148, 149. Routine matters. May 9, 1831.
151. Routine matters. May 23, 1831.
152. Prinz Paul von Württemberg in Mexico. May 31, 1831.
153. Routine matters. June 10, 1831.
154. Van Buren's proposed trip to England, and Portugal. June 19, 1831.
155. Frigate *Potowmac*. June 28, 1831.
156. Routine matters. July 5, 1831.
157. Routine matters. July 13, 1831.
158. Attitude of government toward Austria. July 30, 1831.
159, 160, 162, 163. Routine matters. July 30, Aug. 12, 27, 29, 1831.
164. Legacy of Anton Marschner ($1360). Aug. 29, 1831.
167. Arrival of Prince or Count Leon, who contemplates founding a colony of Germans and Netherlanders, with over 50 followers. Sept. 30, 1831.
Note by Lederer: " Vor einigen Tagen ist hier ein Individuum von Bremen angelangt, das die Aufmerksamkeit des Publikums auf sich gezogen hat, und sich nach einigen Fürst, nach anderen Graf Leon titulirt. Er bringt ein Personale von mehr als 50 Individuen mit sich, die er theils wie Bediente, theils wie Kolonisten behandelt. Man ist nicht über sein Vaterland einig, das nach einigen Belgium nach anderen Deutschland sein soll. Er scheint mit sehr beträchtlichen Summen versehen zu sein. Er hat sich nur wenige Tage hier aufgehalten und sich dann über Albany nach dem Innern begeben, wo er eine Colonie zu stiften die Absicht haben soll, in welchem Falle er, seiner Aussage zu Folge, eine grosse Anzahl seiner Landsleute zu sich zu berufen gedenkt. Die Verschiedenheit dieser Gerüchte scheint sich auf die Verschiedenheit seiner eigenen Erklärungen zu gründen." [1]
169. Return of Randolph. Oct. 30, 1831.
170, 171. Routine matters. Oct. 31, Nov. 29, 1831.
173. Report on internal conditions and foreign relations of U. S. Nov. 30, 1831.
174. President's message. Dec. 7, 1831.
175. Remarks on the message. Dec. 29, 1831.
176. Last report of directors of National Bank, with some remarks. Dec. 31, 1831.

[1] *Cf.* J. Hanno Deiler, *Eine Vergessene Deutsche Colonie: eine Stimme zur Verteidigung des Grafen de Leon, alias Proli, alias Bernhard Müller* (New Orleans, 1900).

Faszikel 2. A. 1832.

178. Routine matters. Jan. 17, 1832.
179. Jewels of Princess of Orange found and claimed. Certain international questions arising from the incident. Jan. 30, 1832.
180. Anton Marschner. Same date.
181. Routine matters. Jan. 31, 1832.
182. U. S. and the Porte. Feb. 13, 1832.
184. Prevention of appointment of Van Buren as minister to England. Feb. 20, 1832.
187. Routine matters. Mar. 15, 1832.
188. Current events. Mar. 31, 1832.
191. Concerning Terzi. Mar. 28, 1832.
192. Current events. Mar. 31, 1832.
193. Current events. June 15, 1832.
195. U. S. and the Porte. Written from Newburgh, July 15, 1832.
197. Legislation of Congress. 18 pages. Newburgh, July 26, 1832.
198. Current events. Newburgh, July 27, 1832.
203. Routine matters. Newburgh, Sept. 5, 1832.
204. Routine matters. New York, Sept. 28, 1832.
205. Anton Marschner. Newburgh, Oct. 16, 1832.
206. Cholera in New York. Newburgh, same date.
207. Routine matters. New York, Oct. 20, 1832.
208, 209, 210, 211. Routine matters. New York, Oct. 20, 30, 31, Nov. 6, 1832.
212. Review of political situation in U. S. New York, Nov. 29, 1832.
214. Duty on French wines. Nov. 30, 1832.
215. South Carolina Convention. Same date.
216. President's message with comments. Newburgh, Dec. 7, 1832.
217. Duplicate of note on French wine. Dec. 14, 1832.
218. Proclamation of President on nullification. Same date.
219. Current events. Dec. 31, 1832.

1833.

221, 222. Current events. Newburgh, Jan. 7, 10, 1833.
223. Report of Secretary of State. New York, Jan. 10, 1833.
224. Reciprocity. Jan. 17, 1833.
225. Routine matters. Same date.
227. Jackson and Van Buren in office. Feb. 17, 1833.
228, 229, 230. Current events. Mar. 7, 12, 18, 1833.
231. South Carolina and U. S. government. Mar. 19, 1833.
232. Duty on wines. Mar. 24, 1833.
234. Legacy of Dr. Spurzheim of Boston. Apr. 12, 1833.
235, 236, 237, 238, 240, 242, 243. Routine matters. Apr. 12–June 1, 1833.
246. Reciprocity. June 29, 1833.
248. Reciprocity. Aug. 15, 1833.
250. Current events. Aug. 20, 1833.
251. Reciprocity. Aug. 30, 1833.
252. Kingdom of the Two Sicilies and U. S. Sept. 5, 1833.
253. Routine matters. Oct. 1, 1833.
254. National Bank. Oct. 14, 1833.
256. American Zwieback. Nov. 1, 1833.
257, 258, 259. Routine matters. Same date.

262. Report on condition of U. S. before opening of Congress. Nov. 23, 1833.
263. Message of President. Comments. Matter of import duties with Austria regarded as settled. Dec. 6, 1833.

1834.

265, 266. Routine matters. New York, Jan. 10, 1834.
271. National Bank question. Feb. 27, 1834.
274. Current events. Mar. 23, 1834.
279. Current events. Apr. 21, 1834.
280. American Government *vs*. National Bank. Apr. 22, 1834.
281. Salute in harbor by mistake. Apr. 24, 1834.
285. Treaty with Russia. June 20, 1834.
286. Treaty with Naples. Same date.
287. Treaty with Chile. Same date.
288. Current events. July 3, 1834.
289. Adjournment of Congress. Comments. 27 pages. July 4, 1834.
290. Evil influence of contest between government and National Bank. July 15, 1834.
291. Riots (Volksaufläufe) in New York. Slight causes. July 15, 1834.
299. Report on general condition, preceding convening of Congress. Nov. 23, 1834.
300. Message of President and comments. Dec. 7, 1834.
301. Learned society of Philadelphia. Dec. 12, 1834.
302. Concerning Maria Rosalia Gruner. Same date.
304. Concerning Pietro Maroncelli. Dec. 15, 1834.
—. Appointment of consular agent by Baron Lederer, letters dated Dec. 10 and 26, 1834.

1835.

311. Attempted assassination of Jackson. J. Q. Adams's eulogy of Lafayette. Feb. 7, 1835.
312. Current events. Feb. 15, 1835.
314. France and U. S. Indemnity treaty. Feb. 23, 1835.
316. Action of Congress. Mar. 15, 1835.
318. Routine matters. Mar. 23, 1835.
319. Plan of treaty. K. K. Porzellanfabrik. Apr. 23, 1835.
320. Concerning Richard Harland. Same date.
322. Copy of monograph *Foreign Conspiracy*. May 9, 1835.
—. Bill for mahogany for Metternich. May 30, 1835.
327. More concerning the pamphlet, *Foreign Conspiracy*. May 30, 1835.
329, 330. Routine matters. June 7, 1835.
331. Riots and comments. June 30, 1835.
333. Routine matters. July 31, 1835.
—. Letter asking permission to introduce to Metternich Madame [Robert Goodloe] Harper, daughter of Mr. Charles Carroll of Carrollton, last surviving signer of the Declaration of Independence. Fact mentioned that they are a Catholic family. (French, signed by J. G. Schwarz). Nov. 4, 1835.
338. Observations on existing political conditions. 19 pages. Nov. 16, 1835.
341. Comments on President's message. Dec. 4, 1835.

1836-1837.

344. Statistics of commerce. New York, Jan. 9, 1836.
345, 346, 347. Current events. Jan. 16, 19, 23, 1836.
349. U. S. and France. Jan. 25, 1836.
351. President's message. Feb. 15, 1836.
352. Current events. Feb. 29, 1836.
353. Question of leave of absence. Mar. 18, 1836.
355, 356. Routine matters. Mar. 23, 31, 1836.
357. Hermann Czech, professor in the Royal Academy for the Deaf and Dumb in Vienna, offers his method to U. S. (John Forsyth, Secretary of State, letter to Lederer). Apr. 7, 1836.
358, 359, 360. Current events and routine matters. Apr. 20, May 1, 1836.
361. Florida. Texas. May 15, 1836.
362. Texas. Indians in the South. May 30, 1836.
363. Texas. Florida. June 10, 1836.
365. Suggestion to institute diplomatic post in U. S. July 9, 1836.
366, 368, 369, 370, 372, 377. Routine matters. July 30, Aug. 7, 15, 31, Oct. 15, 1836.
379. Texas. Van Buren probably unsuccessful for presidency. Oct. 23, 1836.
381. Pietro Maroncelli. Oct. 31, 1836.
382. Report on political situation before opening of Congress. 11 pages. Nov. 15, 1836.
385. Texas. Dec. 6, 1836.
389. Routine matters. Jan. 1, 1837.
391. Santa Anna. Jan. 23, 1837.
395. Van Buren elected. Feb. 11, 1837.
396. Called to Washington. Same date.
399. Congress decides to send U. S. minister to Vienna. Mar. 3, 1837.
400, 402. Routine matters. Mar. 7, 10, 1837.
406. Forsyth and Van Buren. Question about minister to Austria. Mar. 31, 1837.
408. " Bedrängte Zustände im hiesigen Handelsstande." Same date.
410. " Bedrängte Zustände im hiesigen Handelsstande." May 23, 1837.
411. Anthracite coal. May 30, 1837.
415. Delay in appointment of minister to Austria. June 18, 1837.
416. Mr. [Nathaniel] Niles sent on diplomatic mission to Austria, not as minister. June 19, 1837.
418. Purpose of the agent to pave way for a minister. June 30, 1837.
420. Mr. Niles has sailed. July 15, 1837.
423. Report on political situation before convening of Congress (extra session). 11 pages. Aug. 23, 1837.
—. Routine matters. Aug. 31, 1837.
425. President's message to Congress. Sept. 7, 1837.
428. Note of Secretary of State: No minister to be appointed in extra session; minister to proceed on his mission in spring. Sept. 30, 1837.
—. Original letter of Nathaniel Niles to his Highness Prince Metternich informing him of his appointment and his desire to present credentials. Oct. 20, 1837.
429, 430. Routine matters. Oct. 3, 19, 1837.

431. Asks permission to accept membership in Brooklyn Naval Lyceum. Oct. 19, 1837.
432. John J. Boyd made consular agent during Lederer's absence. Oct. 23, 1837.
433. Carl Christ. Hohenberger made temporary consul in New Orleans. Nov. 6, 1837.
434. Report on political situation before convening of Congress. Nov. 23, 1837.
435. Message of President. Dec. 7, 1837.
436. Clippings with reports of Secretary of State. Dec. 15, 1837.
437. Disturbances in Canada. Dec. 23, 1837.
—. Beilage B 1-5 Amerika [found in fascicle 1838] zu einem Berichte des K. K. General-Consuls in New-York Freih. Al. Lederer. (Newspaper clippings, Dec., 1837.)

Mareschal to Metternich.
Faszikel I. 1838.

Wenzel Philipp Freiherr von Mareschal. Gesandter in Washington, an Seine des k. k. Staats- und der auswärtigen Geschäfte Ministers Herrn Clemens Wentzel Lothar Fürsten von Metternich Winneburg, etc., etc., Durchlaucht. (À son altesse le Prince Clément Wenceslaus de Metternich Winneburg . . . Minister Directeur des Affaires Étrangères de S. M. l'Empereur et Roi à Vienne.)
The correspondence of Baron Mareschal is written in the French language, with very few exceptions.
June 4, 1838. Paris. Appreciation of the honor of the appointment.
July —, 1838. Paris. Acknowledgment of receipt of letter brought by Mr. de Friedrichsthal.
Aug. 23, 1838. Vienna. Claim of Franz Maurer vs. Ed. Lammer.
Aug. 31, 1838. New York. Announces arrival in New York, and makes some observations on the country.
Sept. 14, 1838. Letter from Washington. Marginal note of Metternich: " N. B. Voici le second rapport, qui arrive sans signature. M."
Sept. 26, 1838. New York. " Le G'l Baron de M. rend compte de l'impression produite à Washington, par le désaveu des mesures prises par L. Durham pour la pacification du Canada."
Sept. 28, 1838. New York. " Considérations sur l'établissement et les résultats des chemins de fer aux États-unis."
Oct. 2, 1838. Philadelphia. " Résignation de L. Durham."
Oct. 9, 1838. Philadelphia. " M. transmit un mémoire rédigé par M. de Hülsemann, avec quelques observations." Hülsemann's report (on written constitution, and rights of neutrals on the sea) in German, 12 pp.
Oct. 18, 1838. Washington. " Affaires du Canada. Blocus des côtes du Mexique. Elections."
Washington. " M. rend compte de la difficulté élevée par le gouvernement des États-Unis de recevoir la lettre de créance sans la remise préalable d'une copie d'office et de la manière dont cette difficulté a été tranchée." (With one postscript and two enclosures.)
Washington. " M. rend compte de la remise de sa lettre de créance à Mr. Martin van Buren Président des États-Unis." (Two enclosures.)

Oct. 23, 1838. Washington. " M. transmet deux brochures, le rapport du comité des ouvrages hydroliques au conseil municipal de la ville de Philadelphia, et celui des commissaires pour les eaux de celle de New York."
Washington. " M. transmet un article du *Globe*, organe du Gouvernement, annonçant que le Ministre du Texas a retiré la demande de ce pays d'être reçu dans l'Union fédérative des États-Unis ; cause de cette démarche."
Washington. " Sur Lord Durham, ses projets et la situation du Canada, nouvelles courantes."
" M. bestätigt den Empfang der Depesche v. 17. Juli d. J. die Aufstellung von provisorischen Consuln in den Hafenplätzen der nordamerikanischen Freistaaten betreffend."
" M. gibt die verlangten Auskünfte über Herrn Alexander Dallas [Bache] vom Girard College in Philadelphia."
" M. bestätigt den Empfang der Depesche vom 30. Juli d. J. den Herrn Ritter von Friedrichsthal betreffend."
Oct. 28, 1838. Washington. " Le général Bon. de Mareschal accuse la réception de la dépêche du 6 sept. annonçant le couronnement de sa Majesté l'Empereur à Milan."
Washington. " Le général Bon. de Mareschal accuse la réception des deux circulaires datées de Milan le 6 sept. concernant l'amnestie et transmet une lettre que lui a adressée Felice Argenti ainsi que sa réponse. Entretien avec Luigi Tinelli à New-York." (Two enclosures.)
Nov. 13, 1838. Washington. " Départ de L. Durham pour l'Europe. Nouveaux troubles éclatés au Canada." (Postscript and two enclosures.)
Nov. 23, 1838. Washington. " Freiherr von Mareschal berichtet über den Zustand der K. K. Gesandtschaft in Washington, die Theurung des Landes und die Unzulänglichkeit des ausgeworfenen Gehaltes [von 30,000 Gulden], um mit dem Anstande welchen der Rang des allerhöchsten Hofes erheischt, hier zu leben und den Zweck der Errichtung dieser Gesandtschaft zu erreichen."
Washington. " M. transmet une proclamation du Président des États-Unis à l'occasion des nouveaux troubles éclatés dans le Canada." (One enclosure.)
Dec. 2, 1838. Washington. " Affaires du Canada ; blocus des côtes du Mexique par l'escadre française ; nombreuses et fortes défalcations des agents de l'administration aux États-Unis." (One enclosure.)
Dec. 7, 1838. Washington. " Message du Président au Congrès avec quelques observations."
" Nouvelles courantes."
Dec. 11, 1838. Washington. " M. transmet une copie de la Convention conclue en date du 25 Avril 1838 entre les États-Unis et la République du Texas pour fixer les limites des deux États."
" Copie de la convention générale de paix, d'amitié, de commerce et de navigation conclue (Nov. 30, 1836) entre les États-Unis et la Confédération Peru-Bolivienne, et y ajoute l'observation, que les art. 11-22 se rapportent au principe, que le pavillon couvre la cargaison." (One enclosure.)

Washington. " Copie du traité de commerce et de navigation conclu (Dec. 22, 1837) entre les É.-U. et la Grèce, et fait observer, que l'article 16 contient une stipulation sur le blocus des ports respectifs." (One enclosure.)
Dec. 29, 1838. Washington. " Prise du château de S. Jean d'Ulloa par l'escadre française; capitulation de la Vera Cruz; position du gouvernement mexicain."
" Sur les affaires du Canada."
" Commotions civiles et désordres à Harrisburg en Penna. à l'occasion de l'ouverture de la législature de cet État." (One enclosure.)
" Nouvelles courantes."

Faszikel I. 1839, January to April.

Jan. 13, 1839. Washington. " Observations sur la partie du message du Président, faisant le panégyrique des institutions de l'Union américaine."
Washington. " Le Général Baron de Mareschal transmet des résolutions proposées dans la chambre des représentants par Mr. Cushing, apparemment dirigées contre l'Angleterre et la France, en y joignant l'observation, qu'elles n'ont aucune valeur pratique." (One enclosure.)
Washington. " Le Général Bon. de Mareschal transmet un pamphlet et deux projets de lois ayant rapport à la situation financière des États-Unis." (Three enclosures, including reprint from daily newspaper, " The Causes of the Present Crisis ", shown by an examiner.)
" Transmet le rapport annuel du Sécrétaire d'État du trésor au Congrès." (One enclosure.)
" Transmet un acte de la législature de l'État de New York en date du 18 avril 1838 sous le titre de ' Act to authorize the Business of Banking '." (One enclosure.)
Washington. " Affaires du Canada ; nouvelles du Mexique ; peu d'intérêt, que présentent les débats du congrès fédéral." (One enclosure.)
Jan. 29, 1839. Washington. " Affaires du Canada."
" Le Général B'on de Mareschal rend compte de l'échec éprouvé par l'administration dans la chambre des Représentants."
" Affaires du Mexico."
" Reprise des hostilités contre les Mexicains et les Français le 5 Dec. à la Vera Cruz; proclamation de l'admiral Baudin du 22 du même mois, déclarant le port de la Vera Cruz ouvert pour l'entrée des bâtiments, mais non pour le débarquement des marchandises, et celui de Tampico et du reste de la côte en état de blocus." (Postscript and one enclosure.)
" Rend compte de l'arrivée de Mademoiselle Ma. Ea. Ameriga dei Vespucci florentine, et de ses prétensions à un bienfait du Gouvernement des États-Unis à titre de descendante directe de celui, qui a donné son nom à ce Continent."
Feb. 4, 1839. Washington. " Nouvelles courantes."
Feb. 15, 1839. Washington. " Freiherr von Mareschal berichtet hinsichtlich des Rescripts der K. K. Geh. Haus-, Hof-, und Staatskanzlei vom

14ten Mai 1838, den Taufschein der Aloysia Dür von Halifax in Neu Schottland betreffend, dass er denselben zu verschaffen von hier aus nicht im Stande war, und dennoch [demnach] die betreffenden Papiere an die K. K. Botschaft in London übermacht hat."

Feb. 19, 1839. Washington. " État des affaires sur les côtes du Mexique; négociation entre l'admiral Baudin et le Gouvernement du Mexique par l'intermédiaire de Mr. Packenham, Ministre d'Angleterre." (With postscript.)

" Correspondance du Ministre des États-Unis, Mr. Stevenson, avec Lord Palmerston au sujet de la destruction du bateau à vapeur la *Caroline*." (One enclosure.)

" Transmet une lettre d'un nommé Smolinkary avec un paquet pour Sa Majesté l'Empereur." (Two enclosures.)

" Rapport du comité des affaires étrangères à la Chambre des Représentants sur le territoire de l'Oregon et proposition d'autoriser le Président à pourvoir à la protection des citoyens des États-Unis dans ce territoire ou trafiquant sur la rivière Colombia et ses affluens." (Two enclosures.)

" États des finances du gouvernement fédéral; augmentation rapide et disproportionée du nombre des banques sous le système de free banking, et resultat probable de l'expansion commercielle, qui doit en resulter." (One enclosure.)

" Nouvelles courantes."

Feb. 24, 1839. Washington. " Difficultés graves sur la frontière de l'État du Maine et de la province anglaise de New Brunswick; violation du territoire; abduction de l'agent territorial américain par des sujets anglais; mesures hostiles et proclamations des deux gouverneurs." (One enclosure.)

Feb. 25, 1839. Washington. " Frontières de l'État du Maine; communication du gouverneur de New Brunswick à celui du Maine; second message de celui-ci à la législature de l'État; arrestation de l'agent territorial anglais Mr. McLaughlin par les américains; armement de l'État du Maine; appel au Gouvernement fédéral de soutenir les droits de l'État du Maine." (One enclosure.)

Feb. 26, 1839. Washington. " Mesures prises à Washington pour mettre un terme aux actes hostiles, sur le territoire en litige entre l'État du Maine et la Province de New Brunswick."

Feb. 27, 1839. Washington. " États des choses au Mexique. Le Général St. Anna Président."

Mar. 4, 1839. Washington. " Issue des prétentions de Mlle. Ameriga dei Vespucci à la générosité du Congrès des États-Unis." (Three enclosures.)

" Freiherr von Mareschal berichtet, in Erledigung des hohen Rescriptes vom 6. Dez. 1838, das Gesuch des Joseph Svilovich um Beschaffung des angeblich von dessen verstorbenen Bruder Peter Svilovich in Savannah in Georgia hinterlassenen Testamentes betreffend, dass derselbe intestat und ohne Vermögen gestorben; und remittiert die betreffenden Dokumente." (Five enclosures.)

" Berichtet den Empfang des hohen Rescripts vom 10. Nov. 1838, wodurch ihm die Eröffnung eines Credites von 4200 Pf. Sterl. für das Verwaltungsjahr 1839 bei dem Hause Rothschild in London angezeigt wurde."

Mar. 6, 1839. Washington. "Affaires de la frontière du Maine. La correspondance du Secretaire d'État avec Mr. Fox sur l'affaire du Maine ainsi que la communication du premier au gouverneur de l'État du Maine." (One enclosure.)
"Clôture de la 3me et dernière session du 25me Congrès des États-Unis; ses travaux."
Mar. 7, 1839. Washington. "Affaires de la frontière du Maine; considérations ultérieures."
Mar. 13, 1839. Washington. "Cirkular des Finanz-Departementes, so wie die Abschrift einer darüber, sowie über die Suspension einiger Banken an den Gouverneur von Triest gerichteten Mitteilung."
"Affaires du Mexique; suspension de payements de deux banques."
"Affaires de la frontière du Maine."
Mar. 16, 1839. Washington. "Divers documents sur l'état des relations territoriales entre l'Angleterre et les États-Unis, le blocus des côtes du Mexique et du Rio de la Plata, ainsi que sur la navigation, et les machines à vapeur et les causes de leurs fréquentes explosions."
Mar. 17, 1839. Washington. "Affaire du Maine."
Mar. 20, 1839. Washington. "Berichtet den Legations-Secretair, Herrn v. Hülsemann nach Norfolk, Charleston und Savannah im Dienste abgeschickt zu haben."
Mar. 21, 1839. Washington. "Affaires du Maine."
"Nouvelles courantes."
Mar. 28, 1839. Washington. "Handels- und Schiffsvertrag zwischen Sardinien und den Ver. Staaten."
"Exequatur des Herrn Hohenberger." (Consul at New Orleans; three enclosures.)
Mar. 30, 1839. Washington. "La signature d'un traité entre la France et le Mexique, ajournement de la législature du Maine, ses derniers actes, embarras financiers aux États-Unis." (One enclosure.)
Apr. 8, 1839. Washington. "Nouvelles courantes." (Three enclosures.)
Apr. 19, 1839. Washington. "L'Autriche et la Belgique."
"Arrivé du *Great Western*; aspect pacifique des relations entre l'Angleterre et les États-Unis; effet produit sur le commerce et les fonds publics, situation présente de la question de juridiction dans le territoire en litige, esprit public sur la frontière du Canada."
Apr. 28, 1839. Washington. "Legations Secretair Hülsemann berichtet über die Produkte und den Handel in Virginien; Verhältnis der Arbeit der Weissen und der Negersklaven; die Städte Richmond und Norfolk; Nord Carolina; Süd Carolina und die Stadt Charleston; Commercial Convention; Georgien und die Städte Savannah und Augusta; Oesterreichische Produkte, für die sich dort ein Absatz erwarten liesse." (One enclosure.)

Faszikel II. 1839, May to December.

May 16, 1839. Washington. "Le Général B'on de Mareschal transmet 5 rapports, que Mr. de Hülsemann lui a adressés en suite de son voyage dans la Virginie, les deux Carolines et la Géorgie." (The five enclosed reports are written in German.)

May 31, 1839. Washington. " Freiherr von Mareschal übermacht eine Liste der unter gleichem Datum durch das Schiff *Gustav* über Bremen eingesandten Dokumente." (One enclosure.)
" Ueber den Handel und die Schiffahrt der Vereinigten Staaten im Allgemeinen, und besonders über jene zwischen den Vereinigten Staaten und Triest."
" Ueber die Mittel einen Absatz für unsere Weine in den Vereinigten Staaten zu finden."
June 8, 1839. Washington. " Vorschreiben für Herrn G. Plitt " (Europareise zum Studium des Postwesens).
June 10, 1839. Washington. Letters of introduction for Mr. George Plitt.
" Traité de commerce conclu entre S. M. Néerlandaise et les États Unis."
" Le Général B'on de Mareschal rend compte des formes observées par les Cours de Russie, de France, d'Espagne et d'Angleterre dans leurs communications avec le Président des États-Unis, et rappelle la difficulté qui s'est elevée à la remise de sa lettre de créance, laquelle n'a point encore été levée."
" Nouvelles politiques."
" Den genannten Braditsch, alias Cliovitsch, alias Baron Fridolin, aus Triest gebürtig, betreffend."
Sept. 13, 1839. Vienna. " Al. Baron v. Lederer (Generalconsul in New York) bittet, falls die Sendung eines Agenten nach Mexico beschlossen werden sollte, auf ihn gnädige Rücksicht nehmen zu wollen."
Sept. 25, 1839. Washington. " Legations Sekretair Hülsemann berichtet über die von ihm nach den Staaten von Neu England unternommene Reise im Allgemeinen, sich die Entwerfung detaillierter Berichte vorbehaltend."
Sept. 28, 1839. Washington. " Le Général B'on de Mareschal :· État du crédit public et de la circulation, currency, embarras du commerce."
" Nouvelles politiques."
" Freiherr von Mareschal berichtet, in Folge des ihm durch Rescript v. 21. Mai gewordenen Auftrages, die Mitteilung der von den Gebrüdern Grant et Comp. gegen Cornelius Specht zu St. Jago de Cuba erhobenen Klage an letztere, vermittelst des nordamerikanischen Consuls alldort, betreffend, dessen Auftrag vollzogen zu haben, und sendet den Empfangsschein des Cornelius Specht ein."
" Le G'l B'on de M. rend compte du voyage qu'il vient de faire dans l'Ouest et le Nord de l'Union. Ainsi que de celui de Mr. de Hülsemann dans l'Est."
" Accuse réception des hautes dépêches."
" Gesuch des Ferdinando Antonio Anelli aus Dessenzano in der Provinz Brescia, gegenwärtig in New York, um Erteilung eines Passes zur Rückkehr ins Vaterland."
Oct. 3, 1839. Washington. " Le G'l B'on de M. transmet trois rapports [written in German] de Mr. de Hülsemann, l'un sur la législation les chemins de fer dans l'État de Massachusetts, les deux autres contenant des notions statistiques sur les fabriques de Lowell et l'État de Massachusetts en général. Observations sur la législation des railroads aux États Unis, et sur les lacunes, qui s'y trouvent."

Oct. 8, 1839. Washington. " M. transmet les réglemens de l'académie militaire de West Point." (One enclosure.)

" M. berichtet den Tod und etwaigen Nachlass des Johann Mölzel, Verfertigers des bekannten schachspielenden Automaten, betreffend, dass derselbe am 19ten Juli 1838, auf der Ueberfahrt von Havanna nach Philadelphia gestorben ist, u. kein Vermögen hinterlassen hat."

" Ueberschickt den Report des Secretary of the Treasury über Handel und Schiffahrt, v. 30. Sept. 1837–30. Sept. 1838."

" Canal de Pennsylvania."

" Unsern Handelsvertrag mit d. Ver. St. betreffend."

Oct. 8, 1839. Washington. " Général B'on de Mareschal sur la crise financière et commerciale."

Oct. 17, 1839. Washington. " M. transmet une publication de Mr. le Chevalier de Gerstner " (*Railroads in the Kingdom of Belgium compared with those in the U. S.*) " avec quelques observations ". (One enclosure.)

" Indian Rubber oder gomme élastique Pontons." (Two enclosures.)

" Suspension des payemens en espèces par la Banque des États Unis et les autres banques de Philadelphie, suivie de celle de la plupart des banques du Sud." (Two enclosures.)

" M. meldet, dass der von ihm unter d. 16. Mai 1839 zum Vice Consul in Savannah vorgeschlagene Louis Ganalh, infolge eines Fallimentes nach Europa abgegangen sein soll."

Routine matters.

Oct. 22, 1839. Washington. " M. transmet la copie d'une lettre datée de Llanos de Santa Rosa in Guatemala 29 Juillet 1839, communiquée confidentiellement par le Secrétaire d'État." (Two enclosures; the confidential letter, copy, is written in English, on conditions in Central America.)

" Suspension des Banques—crise du commerce."

" M. rend compte de la manière dont le gouvernement fédéral a répondu à la protestation du gouvernement de Lisbonne contre le dernier Bill du Parlement anglais relatif à la traite des nègres. Envoi d'une croisière américaine sur la côte d'Afrique." (One enclosure.)

Nov. 5, 1839. Washington. " Nouvelles courantes."

Nov. 22, 1839. Washington. " M. berichtet, den Freiherrn Carl von Luzenberg betreffend, dass derselbe am Leben und einer der ersten ausübenden Aerzte in New Orleans ist."

" Fabriques de Pittsburg."

Washington. " M. transmet un travail de Mr. de Hülsemann sur les principaux membres du Congrès." 41 MS. pages in French; pen portraits of Col. R. M. Johnson, Silas Wright, Buchanan, Benton, Clay, Calhoun, Jackson, Van Buren, Preston, Crittenden, Webster, Rives, Tallmadge, Polk, Howard, Legaré, Cushing, J. Q. Adams, etc.

Pension of Frau Antonia von Höffern.

" Navigation des rivières aux États-Unis; celles de l'Est et celles de l'Ouest."

Nov. 27, 1839. Washington. " M. rend compte de la difficulté, où se trouve la Légation résidente à Washington de suppléer à l'absence prolongée du Consul Général à New York."
" Rend compte de la prétention élevée par les consuls brésiliens, de munir les bâtimens, qui se rendent dans les ports du Brésil, de documens consulaires brésiliens."
" Exposé de la situation des États-Unis dans le rapport des finances et de la politique intérieure au moment de l'ouverture de la première session du 26ème Congrès."
Dec. 11, 1839. Washington. " Nouvelles courantes."
Dec. 21, 1839. Washington. " Nouvelles courantes."
Dec. 28, 1839. Washington. " M. transmet le message du Président au Congrès, avec quelques observations."
" Rapport annuel du Sécrétaire du Trésor au Congrès."

Faszikel 4. 1839-1840.

This bundle of manuscripts contains letters and reports of Baron Mareschal to Prince Metternich from Feb. 4 to Oct. 8, 1839, and from Jan. 28 to Dec. 28, 1840. They are concerned with routine matters of business, current events, deportation of political refugees from Lombardy, and a few reports of Mr. Hülsemann.

Feb. 4, 1839. Washington. " Supplique de Felix Argenti, l'un des déportés."
May 16, 1839. Three reports, one containing: Prayer of Alessandro Bargnani, political refugee, asking permission to return home to Lombardy, and then to live in some country in Europe. (" Avocat de profession, il a moins qu'un autre trouvé le moyen de s'occuper et de gagner sa vie, et se trouve donc dans un plus grand dénuement, et plus malheureux que ses compagnons.")
May 22, 1839. Washington. Two reports, one containing: " Une supplique de Felix Foresti, déporté, demandant la permission de rentrer au sein de sa famille."
May 31, 1839. Washington. " Supplique de Luigi Tinelli, déporté, afin d'être gracié, rétabli dans les droits civils et placé dans la position, dans laquelle se trouvent les émigrants, ayant formé ici un établissement commercial." (Tinelli's plea is to be found among the " Polizeiakten ".)
" Le déporté Felix Argenti."
June 13, 1839. Washington. " Achille Murat. Situation et intentions."
Oct. 8, 1839. Washington. " La commission verbale envers le sieur Bargnani."
Oct. 17, 1839. Washington. " Mareschal rend compte de la manière dont il s'est acquitté des ordres contenus dans les trois hautes dépêches, datées Vienne le 31 juillet, concernant les déportés Luigi Tinelli, Felix Foresti, et Alessandro Bargnani."
Jan. 28, 1840. Washington. " Mareschal transmet une lettre d'Alessandro Bargnani, déporté, demandant l'appui et l'intervention du gouvernement afin d'amener à un terme la liquidation de ses intérêts en Lombardie."
Mar. 16, 1840. Washington. " M. transmet une supplique de Luigi Tinelli, demandant copie officielle de sa sentence à la peine capitale prononcée contre lui par le tribunal de Milan, ainsi que celle de la

Révolution Impériale de l'an 1835 et du procès verbal, par lequel il a accepté la déportation en Amérique, enfin copie de la déclaration de dame Anne Tinelli, née Baronne Zanini, de ne vouloir point le suivre dans l'exil."
" M. transmet une lettre de Msgr. Rosati, Évêque de St. Louis, à Msgr. l'Archevêque de Vienne, demandant des secours de l'Institution Léopoldine pour son diocèse."[1]

Apr. 10, 1840. Washington. Current events.
" Mr. Hülsemann: rapports peu satisfaisants d'une partie des Indiens émigrées à l'Ouest du Mississippi avec le Gouvernement des États Unis."
Apr. 28, 1840. Washington. Luigi Tinelli. Divorce case before Senate. (Contains interesting American newspaper clipping.)
May 29, 1840. Washington. Luigi Tinelli. Bittschrift in den Polizeiakten (Ministerium des Innern).
June 6, 1840. Washington. Bittschrift des Deportierten Giovanni Albinola (Polizeiakten).
" M. rend compte d'une conversation avec Mr. Forsyth, que Mr. Mühlenberg [U. S. minister to Austria] venait d'obtenir le congé qu'il souhaitait depuis longtemps."
" M. transmet un rapport de Mr. de Hülsemann sur le comité provincial catholique tenu à Baltimore le 7 mai, avec quelques observations sur l'Église Catholique aux États Unis."
" M. annonce le départ de Mr. de Hülsemann pour visiter l'Ouest et le Nord des États Unis, avec une copie de ses instructions."
June 22, 1840. Washington. Concerning Alessandro Bargnani.
Washington. Concerning Felice Argenti.
July 28, 1840. Washington. Current events. Seven communications, the last one on Giuseppe Vannoni, and the political refugees.
Aug. 4, 1840. Washington. Alessandro Bargnani.
Sept. 2, 1840. Washington. Felice Argenti.
Oct. 13, 1840. Washington. " M. transmet quatre reports de Mr. de Hülsemann, ensuite de son voyage dans l'Ouest, le Canada et le Nord de l'Union." (Four enclosures.)
Oct. 29, 1840. Washington. Current events.
Washington. " M. rend compte d'une visite de Mr. Achille Murat et de son intention d'aller en France et d'attaquer son oncle Joseph Bonaparte pour obtenir sa part de l'héritage de l'Empereur Napoléon."
Giovanni Albinola; Luigi Tinelli.
Nov. 6, 1840. Washington. " Mareschals Bericht über die nach den Staaten von Neu England und Boston im Laufe der Monate August und September letzten Jahres gemachte Reise."
Nov. 27, 1840. Washington. Current events, three communications, last one on Alessandro Bargnani.
Dec. 15, 1840. Washington. Routine matters.
Dec. 16, 1840. Washington. Alessandro Bargnani.
Current events.
Dec. 28, 1840. Washington. Convention of tobacco planters, Dec. 15, 1840 (with clipping from *National Intelligencer*).

[1] See *Catholic Historical Review*, I. 51-63, 175-191.

Faszikel 2. 1840.

Jan. 21, 1840. (All the following reports come from Washington.) Routine matters.
Jan. 28, 1840. Eight communications. Routine matters and current events.
Jan. 29, 30, 1840. Two communications. *Id.*
Feb. 7, 1840. Two communications. £4200 sterling received for expenses of the year 1840.
Feb. 26, 1840. Three communications. "Le général Baron de Mareschal remarque que le 10 Février 1840, terme auquel d'après l'article 12 de notre traité de commerce avec les États Unis les deux parties sont autorisées à le dénoncer, est passé sans notification quelconque à cet effet."
Mar. 5, 1840. One communication. Nouvelles courantes.
Mar. 16, 1840. Four communications. *Id.*
Mar. 28, 1840. Four communications. *Id.*
Mar. 30, 1840. Two communications. *Id.*
Apr. 14, 1840. Two communications. *Id.*
Apr. 28, 1840. Seven communications. *Id.*
May 6, 1840. Death of Professor François Antoine de Gerstner.
May 9, 1840. Report of Hülsemann on the two conventions (Whig and Democratic) held in Baltimore May 4 and 5. (12 pages in French.)
May 22, 1840. Comments on the political conventions.
May 29, 1840. " Nouvelles courantes."
June 22, 1840. Two communications. *Id.*
June 28, 1840. Three communications. *Id.*
July 28, 1840. Two communications. *Id.*
Aug. 30, 1840. One communication. *Id.*
Sept. 1, 1840. One communication. *Id.*
Sept. 24, 1840. Five communications. *Id.*
Oct. 28, 1840. Routine matters.
Nov. 4, 1840. *Id.*
Nov. 25, 1840. *Id.*
Nov. 26, 1840. *Id.*
Dec. 15, 1840. *Id.* Alessandro Bargnani.
Dec. 16, 1840. Three communications, one concerning replacement of Henry Augustus Mühlenberg in Vienna.
Dec. 28, 1840. " Nouvelles courantes."

Faszikel 2. 1841.

Jan. 5, 1841. Two communications. The McLeod affair and relation between England (Canada) and U. S. are the subject of a great many reports in this year.
Jan. 27, 1841. Three communications. " Nouvelles courantes."
Feb. 10, 1841. Three communications. *Id.*
Feb. 18, 1841. Routine matters.
" M. transmet un travail du Baron de Roenne, ministre de Prusse, sur une loi uniforme de banqueroute aux États Unis, qui se trouve devant le Congrès." (German manuscript of 32 pages.)

Mar. 7, 11, 1841. Eight communications. " Nouvelles courantes."
Mar. 27, 1841. Six communications. *Id.*
Apr. 5, 8, 13, 1841. Six communications. *Id.*
May 3, 1841. Seven communications. *Id.*
May 19, 1841. One communication. *Id.*
May 27, 1841. Three communications. *Id.*
June 12, 1841. Eight communications. *Id.*
July 11, 1841. One communication. *Id.*
July 13, 1841. Three communications. *Id.*
July 14, 1841. One communication. *Id.*
July 24, 1841. New York. " Baron von Lederer, Generalkonsul in New York, bittet um die Geschäftsträgerstelle im nordamerikanischen Freistaate."
July 26, 1841. Four communications. " Nouvelles courantes." The last one instructions for trip of the secretary of legation, Hülsemann. Mareschal receives post to Lisbon, and writes letter of thanks to Prince Metternich.
Aug. 5, 1841. Three communications. " Nouvelles courantes."
Aug. 12, 1841. Two communications. *Id.*
Aug. 27, 1841. Three communications. *Id.*
Sept. 11, 1841. Daniel Jenifer of Maryland, envoy extraordinary and minister plenipotentiary to Austria (successor to H. A. Mühlenberg).
Sept. 22, 1841. Three communications. " Nouvelles courantes."
Sept. 27, 1841. Two communications. *Id.*
Sept. 28, 1841. " Tournée de S. A. R'le le Prince de Joinville aux États Unis."
Sept. 29, 1841. (Written from New York.) Lederer to Metternich (concerning Joseph A. Menzel).
Oct. 7, 1841. One communication. Routine matters.
Oct. 12, 1841. Two communications. " Nouvelles courantes."
Oct. 15, 1841. " Hülsemann berichtet, dass Baron Mareschal am 14. Oktober dem Präsidenten sein Zurückberufungsschreiben übergeben hat; und er als Geschäftsträger präsentirt worden ist."
" Hülsemann annonce le départ de Baron de Mareschal de New York le 19 octobre, et transmet le discours adressé par le Baron au Président, aussi bien que la réponse de Mr. Tyler."
Oct. 24, 1841. Two communications: (1) Le procès de McLeod terminé; (2) Pétition de Mr. Bernardino Castelli.
Oct. 25, 1841. Routine matters.
Nov. 12, 1841. *Id.*
Nov. 18, 1841. " Hülsemann transmet une pétition d'Alessandro Gambato de Rovigo de rentrer en Autriche."
Nov. 21, 1841. " Nouvelles courantes."
Dec. 2, 1841. Bernardino Castelli.
Dec. 11, 1841. Three communications. " Nouvelles courantes."
Dec. 20, 1841. One communication. *Id.*
Dec. 26, 1841. " Hülsemann berichtet den Empfang des hohen Rescripts vom 11. November d. J. und des Credits für die K. K. Mission von 1200 £ Sterling für das Verwaltungsjahr 1842."
Dec. 27, 1841. Three communications. " Nouvelles courantes." The last, " affaire de la *Créole* ".

Hülsemann[1] to Metternich.

Faszikel 5. Convolut 1. 1842.

Jan. 23, 1842. "Bemerkungen über das Bankwesen in den Vereinigten Staaten." (Most of Hülsemann's communications were written in the German, the others in the French language.) Three communications. Current events.
Jan. 27, 1842. Six communications. Current events.
Feb. 6, 1842. Four communications. Current events, including a petition of Alessandro Luigi Bargnani (see Polizeiakten).
Mar. 12, 1842. One communication. Current events.
Mar. 15, 1842. Routine matters. " H. berichtet, in Erwiderung des hohen Rescripts vom 12. September vorig. J., Karl Bozzachi betreffend, dass es ihm nicht möglich gewesen, etwas über dessen Leben oder Tod zu erfahren."
Mar. 27, 1842. Six communications. Routine and current events.
Apr. 4, 1842. One communication. Routine matters.
Apr. 5, 1842. One communication. Current events.
Apr. 14, 1842. " Lederer berichtet dem Hauptmann Moering Verlängerungsurlaub übermacht zu haben."
Apr. 15, 1842. Two communications.
Apr. 18, 1842. Ankunft des Ingenieur Ghega.
Apr. 26, 1842. Two communications. Current events.
May 7, 1842. Two communications. Routine matters.
May 8, 1842. Two communications. *Id.*
May 9, 1842. One communication. *Id.*
May 10, 1842. One communication. Current events.
May 22, 1842. One communication. *Id.*
May 27, 1842. Two communications. *Id.*
June 13, 1842. Three communications. *Id.*
June 28, 1842. Two communications; the last contains a letter of the deported Felix Argenti.
Two communications. Routine matters.
June 29, 1842. One communication. Current events.
July 12, 1842. Three communications. *Id.*
July 13, 1842. One communication. *Id.*
July 28, 29, 1842. Three communications. *Id.*
Aug. 13, 1842. Three communications. *Id.*
Aug. 18, 1842. Petition of Alessandro Bargnani.
Aug. 29, 30, 31, 1842. Four communications. Current events.
Oct. 13, 1842. Three communications, including a request of Baron Lederer, consul-general of New York, for leave of absence for six months.
Oct. 14, 1842. One communication. Routine matters.
Oct. 22, 1842. (From Philadelphia.) *Id.*
Nov. 2, 1842. Report that Pietro Pelizcaro lives in Havana.
Nov. 11, 1842. Two communications. " Hülsemann übermacht ein Schreiben des Herrn K. K. Ingenieurs Hauptmann Carl Moering und 2 Hefte von dessen Werk über die Eisenbahnen, sowie 2 Berichte an Se. Kais. Hoheit dem Erzherzog Johann."

[1] The Chevalier Hülsemann was Austrian chargé d'affaires in Washington from 1841 to 1855, minister resident from 1855 to 1863.

Nov. 15, 27, 1842. Two communications. Current events.
Dec. 12, 1842. One communication. *Id.*
Dec. 27, 1842. Two communications. Routine and current events.

Faszikel 5. Convolut. 2. 1843.

Jan. 4, 5, 27, 29, 1843. Seven communications. Current events.
Feb. 24, 26, 1843. Five communications. *Id.*
Mar. 15, 18, 20, 1843. Three communications. Routine and current events.
Apr. 7, 27, 28, 1843. Six communications. *Id.*
May 7, 9, 11, 26, 1843. Six communications. *Id.*
May 16, 1843. Ingenieur Carl Moering in U. S.
June 15, 1843. "Das K. K. General Consulat in New York betreffend." (Lederer died at the end of December, 1842.)
June 15, 29, 1843. Three communications. Routine matters and current events.
July 12, 1843. Two communications. *Id.*
Sept. 12, 1843. One communication. *Id.*
Oct. 13, 1843. Two communications. "Bruits sur les relations entre les révolutionnaires italiens et des inhabitants des États Unis."
Oct. 23, 1843. Three communications. Routine matters.
Oct. 28, 1843. Two communications. "H. rend compte d'une conversation de Mr. Upshur, dans laquelle Mr. le Secrétaire d'État exprima le désir du gouvernement des États Unis, de faciliter les relations commerciales entre l'Autriche et ce pays-ci."
Nov. 4, 1843. "Das Vermögen von Emigranten betreffend."
Nov. 13, 1843. Routine matters.
Nov. 30, 1843. "Etwaige Beiträge zu den Wiener Jahrbüchern betreffend."
Dec. 6, 13, 26, 1843. Eight communications. Routine matters and current events.
Dec. 17, 1843. "H. transmet la constitution d'une société anti-catholique 'Christian Alliance'." (Printed constitution enclosed.)

1844.

Jan. 28, 29, 1844. Three communications. Routine and current events.
Feb. 22, 1844. Four communications, including: "Convention entre les États Unis et la Mexique sur des indemnités. L'Empereur d'Autriche désigné éventuellement comme arbitre. Le Mexique envoit un agent diplomatique à Vienne."
Feb. 27, 29, 1844. Two communications. Routine matters.
Mar. 4, 1844. "H. transmet une lettre du déporté G. Albinola."
Mar. 6, 1844. Four communications. Current events. (The first contains a number dated Mar. 2, 1844, of the *Deutsche Schnellpost,* a German semi-weekly published by Baron Eichthal and Bernhard.)
Mar. 28, 30, 1844. Three communications. Current events.
Apr. 14, 18, 28, 1844. Four communications. *Id.*
May 4, 13, 29, 30, 1844. Five communications. *Id.*
June 8, 1844. Three communications. "Concernant Texas; les inconvénients d'une organisation séparée des Irlandais, Allemands, etc.; Mr. Morse's télégraphe."
June 13, 1844. "Bruit de la prochaine nomination de Mr. Charles J. Ingersoll pour Vienne."

June 25, 1844. "La nomination de Mr. Charles J. Ingersoll n'a pas encore eu lieu."
June 26, 1844. Two communications. Current events.
July 24, 1844. Routine matters.
Aug. 13, 1844. Two communications. Routine and current events.
Sept. 24, 29, 1844. Two communications. *Id.*
Oct. 27, 1844. One communication. Current events.
Nov. 3, 9, 27, 1844. Three communications. *Id.*
Dec. 4, 13, 17, 23, 26, 1844. Six communications. Routine and current events.

Faszikel 5. 1845.

Jan. 13, 1845. " H. transmet une pétition de Giovanni Albinola."
Jan. 21, 1845. " H. transmet des extraits du *Democratic Review* concernant H—o H—g " (Harro Harring; see the biographical articles by Alexander H. Everett in the *Democratic Review,* Oct., Nov., Dec., 1844, XV. 337-347, 462-475, 561-579).
Jan. 22, 28, 30, 1845. Five communications. Routine and current events.
Feb. 4, 25, 28, 1845. Seven communications. *Id.*
Mar. 5, 10, 15, 16, 31, 1845. Eight communications. *Id.*
Apr. 14, 22, 28, 29, 1845. Five communications. *Id.*
May 9, 28, 1845. Three communications. *Id.*
June 11, 16, 28, 1845. Three communications. *Id.*
July 5, 1845. " H. übermacht eine Convention zwischen den Vereinigten Staaten und Hessen-Darmstadt zur Aufhebung des Abzugsrechts." (Droit d'aubaine, and taxes on emigration.)
July 6, 15, 1845. Current events.
July 30, 1845. *Id.* Texas.
Aug. 15, 1845. Two communications. Texas and Mexico.
Aug. 30, 1845. Two communications. Current events.
Sept. 14, 30, 1845. Two communications, including: " Expulsion de Mr. Albinola de la Toscane."
Oct. 1, 1845. Three communications, including: " H. transmet un rapport du sénateur Berrien sur des abus commis dans la naturalisation d'étrangers. Plusieurs gouverneurs allemands sont accusés par des dépositions jointes à ce rapport, d'encourager l'émigration des criminels aux Etats Unis."
Oct. 24, 29, 1845. Two communications, including: Question of war and peace.
Nov. 3, 25, 1845. Seven communications, including: " H. transmet la réponse faite par Mr. Buchanan à une réclamation de certains éditeurs de journaux allemands aux États Unis contre la défense de ces journaux par la Diète Germanique." (Referring to the prohibition by the German Diet of Frankfurt of all newspapers or periodicals in the German language.)
Dec. 4, 12, 24, 28, 1845. Four communications, including: Oregon question. Texas admitted.

1846.

Jan. 15, 1846. Current events.
Jan. 28, 1846. *Id.* " Quelle sera la position des Grandes Puissances continentales de l'Europe dans une guerre entre les États Unis et l'Angleterre? " H.'s solution, strict neutrality.

Feb. 8, 25, 26, 1846. Three communications. Routine matters and current events.
Mar. 29, 1846. Two communications. *Id.*
Apr. 6, 25, 1846. Two communications. *Id.*
May 4, 1846. Correspondence with Secretary Buchanan on a point in the President's message.
May 13, 19, 21, 22, 26, 1846. Five communications. Routine matters and current events, including War with Mexico.
June 16, 24, 1846. Three communications, including: Oregon treaty.
July 16, 30, 1846. Two communications, including: Mexico.
Aug. 14, 29, 1846. Five communications. Current events.
Aug. 31, 1846. " H. berichtet in Erledigung des hohen Rescriptes vom 3. Juli d. J., dass die nordamerikanische Regierung bereit ist, mit Sr. Kais. Majestät ein Uebereinkommen wegen wechselseitiger Auslieferung der Verbrecher abzuschliessen; sowie auch zur Regulirung sonstiger Schwierigkeiten durch additionelle Artikel."
Sept. 14, 1846. " Wegen Aufhebung von droit d'aubaine und Emigrantensteuern."
Sept. 15, 30, 1846. Two communications. Routine and current events.
Oct. 8, 14, 28, 1846. Two communications. Current events.
Nov. 24, 1846. One communication. *Id.*
Dec. 3, 12, 1846. Five communications. *Id.*

1847.

Jan. 27, 1847. One communication. Current events.
Feb. 1, 25, 1847. Two communications. Routine and current events.
Mar. 11, 29, 1847. Four communications. *Id.*
Apr. 2, 11, 28, 1847. Four communications. *Id.*
May 13, 1847. One communication. *Id.*
June 1, 1847. Observations on consequences of Mexican War. Sympathy for Mexico. European intervention? H. favors strict neutrality.
June 14, 1847. Current events.
June 25, 1847. " Observations sur l'Académie militaire de West Point."
May 8, 1847. Routine matters.
June 29, 1847. Two communications. Rumor of peace.
July 13, 26, 30, 31, 1847. Five communications. Routine and current events.
Aug. 14, 31, 1847. Two communications. *Id.*
Sept. 14, 23, 1847. Three communications. *Id.*
Sept. 24, 1847. " Observation de la question d'Italie. Entretien avec Mr. Buchanan sur les affaires d'Italie. Influence dangereuse de M. Hughes, Évêque de New-York, pour exciter la population irlandaise ", etc.
Sept. 30, 1847. Current events.
Oct. 6, 1847. " Occupation de la ville de Mexico."
Oct. 15, 28, 1847. " Nouvelles du Mexique."
Nov. 13, 1847. " Nouvelles du Mexique."
Nov. 16, 1847. " Projet d'une grande démonstration populaire à New York en faveur de la révolution italienne."
Dec. 13, 30, 1847. Four communications. Current events.

The diplomatic correspondence is not accessible after 1847. During the Hungarian revolution President Taylor sent an agent to Hungary (in 1849), for the purpose of obtaining information.[1] When the agent arrived, Russian intervention had already put down the Hungarian revolution. Hülsemann complained of the action of the United States government in sending a representative to investigate conditions in Hungary. Daniel Webster, secretary of state, replied in the " Hülsemann Letter ",[2] that the United States had the right to recognize any *de facto* revolutionary government, and to seek information in all proper ways in order to guide their action. The letter was meant as a sharp rebuke to the Austrian chargé, and was a very popular stroke, rousing national pride. Kossuth, who had sought refuge in Turkey, was brought from the Mediterranean to New York in a United States frigate in 1851. The general enthusiasm with which Kossuth was received everywhere was such a blow to Hülsemann that he left the country with indignation. *Cf.* Schurz, *Henry Clay*, II. 392; and Lodge, *Daniel Webster*, pp. 334-335.

WEISUNGEN.

F. 1. Convolut 1. Metternich an Bartholomäus Freiherrn von Stürmer. 1817-1819.

" Baron de Stürmer, commissaire de S. M. l'Empereur d'Autriche à Ste. Hélène nommés au poste de Consul Général aux États-Unis d'Amérique." Vienna, Nov. 26, 1817.

" Schreiben an den Staats Sekretär der Vereinigten Staaten von Amerika. Kreditiv für Freih. v. Stürmer als General Consul." Vienna, Nov. 26, 1817.

" Derselbe (Stürmer) wird von seiner Anstellung als K. K. Kommissär auf Helena enthoben, und erhält einstweilen 2000 Fl. Staatgeld jährlich, welches vom 16. Juli 1818, als dem Tage seiner Abreise von St. Helena flüssig gemacht worden ist." 2 documents, dated Vienna, Jan. 22, and Mar. 13, 1819.

F. 1. Convolut 2. Metternich an Alois Freiherrn von Lederer. 1821-1830.

Orders, rescripts, etc., largely concerning individuals to be traced, or whose property is to be looked after.

Note: " Weisungen in deutscher Sprache; amtlicher Briefwechsel in deutscher Sprache; die französische Sprache bleibt einzig für rein politische Berichte vorbehalten."

F. 1. Convolut 3. " Rescripte der Staats-Kanzley an den General Consul B. Lederer." 1830-1837.

F. 1. Convolut 4. Metternich an Mareschal. 1838-1841. " Historische Auseinandersetzung der von der kaiserlichen Regierung in Ausführung gebrachten Deportations-Massregel.—Grundsatz, der von der K. K. Gesandtschaft bei der Berührung mit den Deportirten fest im Auge zu halten ist."

" Liste der an Bord der Brigg *Ussaro* nach Nord Amerika deportirten, October 1836 zu New York gelandeten Verbrechern ": 1. Luigi Tinelli; 2. Giovanni Albinda; 3. Pietro Borsieri; 4. Cesare Benzoni; 5. Felice Argenti; 6. Alessandro Bargnani; 7. Felice Forresti; 8. Gaetano Castiglia. Federigo Confaloniere arrived at New York Feb. 22, 1837; he soon returned to Provence.

---

[1] The agent was A. Dudley Mann. His report, not published at the time, was printed in 1911 as 61 Cong., 1 and 2 sess., *Sen. Doc. No. 279.*

[2] See Moore, *Digest of International Law*, I. 223-234.

F. 1. Convolut 5. 1838. Weisungen, Staatskanzlei an General Consul und Minister.
F. 1. Convolut 6. 1839. Weisungen, an Baron v. Mareschal.
F. 1. Convolut 7. 1840. Weisungen, an Baron v. Mareschal.
F. 1. Convolut 8. 1841-1843. Weisungen, an den Gesandten Mareschal, den General Consul Lederer, den Geschäftsträger Hülsemann.
F. 1. Convolut 9. 1841-1847. Weisungen. Metternich an Hülsemann.

NOTEN.

F. 1. A. 1838-1844.
Letters to Metternich. Credentials of Henry Augustus Mühlenberg, U. S. minister. Letters concerning: Regulation of "Mauth-Tarif"; Jerome Bonaparte (Oct. 30, 1839); passport of Mühlenberg; estate of Mellen Chamberlain; notes on Daniel Jenifer, successor to Mühlenberg; etc.
Convolut 2. 1839-1846.
Routine matters. Mühlenberg and Jenifer. Notes of chargés d'affaires des États Unis: J. Randolph Clay and Wm. H. Stiles. Case of Bargnani (1846), etc.

VARIA.

F. 1. Pamphlets, containing printed reports of American state departments, associations, railroads, conventions, etc.
Newspaper clippings: American newspapers on contemporary events.
Letters, mostly translations into German of American originals, 1808, 1816, 1818. Copies of letters of Metternich, 1821.
V. Micarelli, Mémoire on advantages of commerce with United States. Trieste, May 1, 1827.
Letter concerning the estate of Mr. Shindle, of Lebanon, Pa.
Handelsvertrag zwischen Oesterreich u. d. Ver. Staaten, abgeschlossen d. 27. August, 1829. (Printed.)
Manuscripts and printed pamphlets on the "Leopoldinen Stiftung in Wien zur Unterstützung der katholischen Missionen in Nordamerika." 1829-1830.
Copy of letter of Buchanan to Stiles. (Mexican blockade.) May 14, 1846.
Letter of August Belmont to Freih. v. Kribeck, in Vienna, on Oregon question, Mexico, and financial situation. July 10, 1846.
Letter of August Belmont to Count Stadion, governor of Illyria and Trieste.

MANUSCRIPTS

in the K. K. Haus-, Hof- und Staatsarchiv relating to American history. A catalogue, descriptive of the entire manuscript collection, was published in 1873-1874: *Die Handschriften des kaiserlichen und königlichen Haus-, Hof- und Staatsarchivs,* beschrieben von Constantin Edlen von Böhm (Vienna, 1873; Supplement, Vienna, 1874).

33, 2. (B. 16.) Ansprüche Spaniens auf Amerika.
"Discorso delle Ragioni cha il Rè Catolico sopra il novo Hemispero et altri Regni d' Infideli secondo la scrittura con li Theologi, che di cio hanno scritto."
682. (B. 192.) "Relacion de las Indias de Fray Marcos de Nica. 1538."

683. (91.) Spanien Nr. 37. " Ueber die von der spanischen Regierung angewandten Mittel die Schätze Indiens nicht fremden Staaten zufliessen zu machen."

Fourteen manuscript pages in Spanish, in a collection of manuscripts entitled: " Promemoria eines Spaniers über die Nothwendigkeit den Krieg in Flandern auf irgend eine Weise zu beenden. 1623."

114. (62.) P. XVII Convolute Fol. und 4°. Collectanea historica. Franciscus Guillemann: " Diese durchgehends in lateinischer Sprache abgefasste Sammlung enthält Auszüge aus verschiedenen Schriftstellern und Chroniken, Notizen, etc., insbesondere zur Geschichte Oesterreichs und der deutschen Kaiser aus der Zeit vom 6. bis zum 17. Jahrhundert ; auch enthält sie Miscellanea de novo orbe."

ABTEILUNG: LÄNDER.

This section consists of a miscellaneous mass of material on foreign countries, material not otherwise classified. It has at present no adequate index, but it is proposed to provide an exhaustive guide to it at some time in the future. Meanwhile the following items from it have been listed for the present book by Dr. Hans Prankl, an assistant of the staff. A considerable number of the documents in this division, even among those described here by title, are understood to have been destroyed. On the other hand, the quantity of documents remaining is very large, since often ten pieces go with a single title such as is here given. Papers which are here listed, and which are still extant, can, it is understood, be found if needed, in spite of the absence of numbers, provided the rubric " Länder " and the year are given.

1768.

Holland. Der vielfältige Durchzug deutscher Emigranten nach Amerika durch Holland.

1774.

Spanien. Tätigkeiten zwischen Spaniern und Portugiesen am Fluss Rio Grande.

Irrungen zwischen Spanien und Portugal am Fluss Rio Grande bei Buenos Ayres, etc.

Prüfung verschiedener neuer Kanonen von Eisen aus Amerika.

Entdeckung der Stadt De los Cesares in Südamerika.

Holland. Irrungen mit dem dänischen Gouverneur der Inseln in Amerika wegen Sequestrierung der dem Amsterdamer Handels Haus Borck verhypothezierten Aktien.

Vorstellungen des dortigen englischen Botschafters gegen Zufuhr der Kriegsmunition nach den amerikanischen Kolonien auf holländischen Kauffahrteischiffen.

England. Die Händel mit den amerikanischen Kolonien und die diesfälligen Parlamentsverhandlungen.

Einführung einiger neuen Steuern in Canada und Quebec.

Reisen der Kapitäne Fourneau und Cook um die Welt mit den Fregatten *Aventure* und *Resolution*.

1775.

England. Die Zwistigkeiten zwischen England und den englischen Kolonien in Amerika.
Anmerkungen über die anwachsende Bevölkerung in den amerikanischen Kolonien.
Errichtung eines neuen Etablissement Cap Charles auf der Küste von Labrador.
Gerücht der Behandlung eines Subsidientraktates zwischen England, Preussen, etc., und Russland gegen Abschickung von 20,000 Russen nach Amerika.
Betrachtung über die kritische Lage der Irrungen mit den Amerikanern.
Die bourbonischen Höfe in Ansehung der engländischen Irrungen mit den Amerikanern.
Spanien. Die angebliche Entdeckung einer neuen Stadt in Südamerika.
Neue Entdeckungen in Nordamerika.
Ausrüstung einer kleinen Escadre nach Vera Cruz unter Commando des Dr. Ulloa.
Holland. Vorstellung des dortigen englischen Botschafters gegen die Zufuhr von Waffen und Munition auf holländischen Kauffahrteischiffen nach den amerikanischen englischen Kolonien.
Vorstellung der Generalstaaten gegen das Verbot der Aus- und Einfuhr der Esswaren in die englischen Kolonien von Nordamerika.
Anstände mit dem spanischen Hof wegen Debauchierung der Sklaven aus den holländischen Kolonien in Amerika.
Ansuchen des englischen Hofes bei den Generalstaaten um einstwillige Überlassung der in Diensten der Republik stehenden drei schottländischen Regimenter an England gegen die Kolonien in Amerika.

1776.

England. Nachricht des Erscheinens französischer Emissäre in den englisch-amerikanischen Kolonien.
Die Irrungen mit den amerikanischen Kolonien.
Kriegerische Vorfälle in Amerika: Verlust von Boston.
Eroberung von Neuyork. Diesfällige Karte.
Vermutung feindlicher Absichten von Seiten Englands auf die spanischen Besitzungen in Amerika.
Vergleichsunterhandlungen mit den englischen Kolonien in Amerika.
Frankreich. Beladung einiger amerikanischer Fahrzeuge mit Kriegsrüstungen im dortigen Hafen.
Dortige Massnahmen betreffend die Streitigkeiten zwischen England und den amerikanischen Kolonien gemeinschaftlich mit Spanien.
Dortige geheime Komerzialunterhandlungen mit den englischen Insurgenten in Amerika.
Holland. Drohungen und Memoires des dortigen englischen Botschafters wegen des holländischen Kriegsmunitionshandels nach Amerika mit Visitierung der Schiffe und Contrebanden.
Anstände mit Dänemark wegen Anhaltung zweier holländischer Schiffe auf dem Walfischfang an der grönländischen Küste.
Lissabon. Die Ausgleichung der Irrungen zwischen Portugal und Spanien bei Rio Janeiro.

Verordnung gegen das Erscheinen der Schiffe der englisch-amerikanischen Kolonien in den portugiesischen Häfen.
Neuerliche Feindseligkeiten der Portugiesen am Rio Grande gegen Spanien.

Neuyork. Karte von New-York.

Spanien. System des dortigen Hofes betreffs der Irrungen zwischen England und ihren amerikanischen Kolonien.
Projekt einer amerikanischen Leibgarde.
Neue Entdeckungen in Kalifornien.
Errichtung eines neuen Gouvernements in Amerika.
Ausrüstung einer Flotte zu Cadiz nach Neuspanien mit dem General Cevallos.
Freilassung eines amerikanischen Kapers aus dem Hafen zu Bilbao.
Abfahrt der Flotte von Vera-Cruz.

1777.

Amerika. Ansuchen des spanischen Hofes um Abschriften der in der k. k. Bibliothek oder in den k. k. österreich. Archiven etwa vorfindigen Briefschaften betreffend die Entdeckung von Amerika.

England. Verdankung der von dem französischen Grafen Bulkeley angebotenen Dienste gegen die Amerikaner.
Prisen der amerikanischen Kaper über die Engländer.
Gefechte mit den Kolonien in Amerika. Kriegsrüstungen gegen sie.
Die englischen Irrungen mit den amerikanischen Kolonien überhaupt.
Parlamentsverordnung wegen Verführung des Nutzholzes nach den westindischen Inseln.
Fliegende Schriften über die engländischen Streitigkeiten mit den Amerikanern.
Niederlagen der Rebellen in Amerika. Niederlagen der Engländer.
Die in dortiger Gefangenschaft befindlichen französischen Offiziere von der Partei der amerikanischen Insurgenten.
Bewegungen im Parlament wegen der Niederlagen der Engländer in Amerika. Massnahmen ungemeiner Kriegsrüstungen.
Gestattung der freien Getreideeinfuhr in England wegen des Krieges mit den Amerikanern.
Ansuchen des englischen Hofes bei dem k. k. österreichischen Hofe um die Befreiung der in den diesseitigen Häfen einlaufenden englischen Kriegsschiffe von der Visitation und um die Abweisung der etwa hier eintreffenden Emissäre der amerikanischen Kolonisten mit ihren Anträgen.
Verbot des Hofes des Verkaufes der von den Amerikanern den Engländern abgejagten Prisen.
Dortige Massnahmen in Ansehung der englischen Irrungen mit den amerikanischen Kolonien. Heimliche Begünstigung der letzteren.
Vorstellungen der allda befindlichen amerikanischen Insurgenten an den dortigen k. k. österreichischen Botschafter.

Frankreich. Heimliche Entweichung des Marquis de la Fayette zu den Insurgenten in Amerika.
Irrungen mit England wegen des freigelassenen amerikanischen Kapers Cunningham [Conyngham]. Französische Nachgiebigkeit.

Eintreffen französischer Schiffe mit Kriegsgerätschaften bei den Amerikanern in Boston.
Der Aufenthalt und die Bewegungen des bekannten Dr. Franklin aus Amerika und Insurgenten gegen England in Frankreich.
Holland. Dortiger Schleichhandel mit Waffen nach den englischen Kolonien in Amerika.
Englische Beschwerden über den Schleichhandel der Holländer zu S. Eustache mit den amerikanischen Rebellen.
Englisches Ansuchen um den freien Durchzug der nach Amerika bestimmten in Deutschland aufgebrachten Rekruten.
Verordnung der Generalstaaten wegen Aretierung der englisch-amerikanischen Kaper mit den gemachten Prisen.
Hinwegnahme eines amerikanischen Schiffes mit Reis durch ein englisches Kriegsschiff.
Vorstellungen der Handelsleute nach Westindien wegen der Notwendigkeit der Bedeckung ihrer Schiffe durch Kriegsschiffe.
Antrag der Errichtung einer Konvention mit Spanien wegen Zurückstellung der aus der holländischen Kolonie nach den spanischen Besitzungen in Amerika flüchtenden Sklaven.
Englische Insurgenten in Amerika. Antrag derselben einen Minister an den k. k. österreichischen Hof abzusenden, um das Commercium mit den österreichischen Untertanen zu pflegen.
Vorstellungsschreiben der englischen Insurgenten in Amerika an den k. k. österr. Botschafter zu Paris durch ihre dortigen Kommissäre.
Lissabon. Neuerliche Feindseligkeiten der Portugiesen am Rio Janeiro.
Vorteile der Spanier über die Portugiesen unter Commando des D. Cevallos in Südamerika. Eroberung der Insel St. Catharina.
Beschwerden des dortigen Hofes über den englischen Schiffskapitän wegen eigenmächtiger Anhaltung eines amerikanischen Schiffes im dortigen Hafen.
Die Entbindung der Prinzessin von Brasilien.
Tod der neugeborenen Infantin der Prinzessin von Brasilien.
Prisen der amerikanischen Kaper über die Portugiesen.
Verminderung der Abgaben auf das Gold aus Amerika.
Spanien. Nachrichten von der grossen spanischen Escadre unter Cevallos und Casatilly.
Abweisung eines Agenten der amerikanischen Insurgenten.
Verzeichnis der zu Mexiko ausgeprägten Gold- und Silbermünzen.
Entdeckung eines englischen Schleichhandels in Mexiko.
Anfrage des englischen Hofes beim spanischen Hofe wegen der Behandlung der Insurgenten in Amerika von Seite des Madrider Hofes. Antwort des letzeren Hofes.
Verlust des nach Acapulco bestimmten reich beladenen Schiffes durch einen Wetterstrahl zu Manilla.

1778.

Amerika. Die englischen Kolonien in Amerika. Französische Unterhandlungen mit denselben.
Die blühende Handlung der bourbonischen Häuser mit den amerikanisch-englischen Kolonien.

Anbringen der Deputierten der Kolonien zu Paris beim dortigen k. k. österr. Botschafter. Ankunft des William Lee[1] in Wien. Abfertigung desselben.
Schluss eines Freundschafts- und Kommerzientraktates zwischen Frankreich und den verbündeten Kolonien.
Gerücht von einer Alliance der Kolonien mit Preussen.
Aufnahme eines Darlehens in Amerika zur Bestreitung der Kriegskosten.
Französische und spanische Subsidien an die Kolonien.
Die Kommunizierung der in den k. k. österr. Erblanden vorfindigen Urkunden betreffend die Entdeckung von Amerika an den spanischen Hof.
Ankunft des Comte d'Estaing mit der französischen Flotte in Amerika.
Die Einleitung des Handels nach den amerikanisch-englischen Kolonien.
England. Erklärung des französischen Hofes an den englischen Hof von dem Abschluss eines Kommerzientraktates mit den amerikanisch-englischen Kolonien.
Eroberung der zwei Forts auf dem Delaware durch die Engländer.
Friedenspläne mit den Kolonien. Unterhandlungen.
Mündliche Versicherung des spanischen Hofes, dem französischen Traktat mit den amerikanischen Kolonien nicht beitreten zu wollen.
Der Krieg mit den Kolonien überhaupt.
Ernennen des Clinton zum Commando in Amerika an Stelle des Howe.
Rückkunft des Generals Howe aus Amerika.
Einfall der amerikanischen Kolonisten in West Florida.
Rückkunft der ost- und westindischen Flotte.
Spanien. Antrag auf Errichtung eines allgemeinen Schiffsbauwerfts in Amerika.
Verfall des Commercii in Amerika, Verwüstung der Städte Acapulco und Sonsonate durch ein Erdbeben.
Sammlung der Verordnungen, das amerikanische Commercium betreffend.
K. Verordnung, das freie Commercium in Amerika betreffend.
Erwartung der Silberflotte aus Vera Cruz. Ankunft.
Eroberung einer portugiesischen Festung, genannt Gataimai, in Paraguay durch die Spanier.
Plünderung einer spanischen Karawane unweit Buenos Ayres, durch die sogenannten Indios bravos.
Frankreich. Die französischen Unterhandlungen mit den amerikanischen Kolonien.
Absendung des Gerard zu den Amerikanern und Interimsanstellung des Hennin zum 1. Staats-Kommissär an die Stelle des ersteren.
Holland. Auslaufen des Convoi nach Holländisch-Westindien.
Die von den Spaniern angesprochene Insel Urica in Amerika betreffend.
Anhaltung eines amerikanischen Lagerschiffes zu S. Eustache.
Erbeutung eines holländischen nach Virginien bestimmten Schiffes durch einen englischen Kaper.
Ansuchen der holländischen Kolonie Demeray um einige Kriegsschiffe zur Bedeckung gegen die Engländer.

---

[1] *Cf.* Schlitter, *Beziehungen Oesterreichs zu Amerika*, pp. 5-6.

Antrag der englisch-amerikanischen Kolonien auf Errichtung eines Handlungs- und Freundschaftstraktates mit Holland.

1779.

Amerika. Der französische Traktat mit den dortigen engländischen Kolonien.
Ernennung des Franklin zum bevollmächtigten Minister des dortigen Kongresses in Paris. Dortiger Aufenthalt des Gerard von Seiten Frankreichs.
England. Der Krieg mit den englisch-amerikanischen Kolonien überhaupt. Spuren von einer russisch und preussischen Mediation zwischen England und Frankreich und den amerikanischen Kolonien.
Untersuchung des Betragens der englischen Generale in Amerika, desgleichen des Lord Sandwich.
Manifest, die Schiffahrt neutraler Mächte nach den Kolonien in Amerika betreffend.
Korrespondenz des General Howe aus Amerika mit dem amerikanischen Staats-Sekretär über den dortigen Krieg.
Gerücht von neuerlichen Friedensverhandlungen der Kolonien mit England.
Holland. Spanische Beschwerden über die Feindseligkeiten der Einwohner von Curaçao.
Frankreich. Audienzen verschiedener neuer Minister, darunter des Franklin von den vereinigten englischen Staaten in Amerika.
Antrag des k. k. österr. Konsuls zu Nantes auf Ausrüstung eines Schiffes mit k. k. Flaggen und Pässen zur Ueberbringung der Lebensmittel nach der französischen Insel St. Domingo.
Franklin. Ernennung des Franklin zum bevollmächtigten Minister des amerikanischen Kongresses in Paris.
Spanien. Neue Einrichtung des amerikanischen Commercii.

1780.

Amerika. Die englischen Friedensunterhandlungen mit den dortigen englischen Kolonien.
Druckschriften, die dortigen unierten englischen Kolonien betreffend.
Ankunft und Aufträge einiger amerikanischer Abgeordneten in Spanien.
Den erbländischen Handel nach den französischen und englischen Pflanzstädten in Amerika betreffend.
Der Handel mit den französischen Pflanzstädten.
England. Der Handel der k. k. österreichischen Untertanen nach den englischen Kolonien in Amerika.
Entdeckung einer dortigen geheimen Korrespondenz nach den amerikanischen Kolonien.
Zurückkunft der auf Entdeckungen im nördlichen Teile des Stillen Meeres zwischen Asien und Amerika ausgeschickten zwei Schiffe.
Aufgabe der Hoffnung, die Amerikaner unterwürfig zu machen.
Holland. Die Kommerzialunterhandlungen des Ratspensionaire von Amsterdam mit den englisch-amerikanischen Kolonien.
Die Viollierung des holländischen Territoriums zu St. Martin in Amerika durch die gewaltsame Kaperung der englisch-amerikanischen Schiffe von Seite der Engländer.

Frankreich. Der Antrag auf Verproviantierung der französischen Pflanzstädte im mexikanischen Meerbusen durch niederländische Schiffe.
Gedanken über die Einleitung des Commerciums aus den Niederlanden und den Häfen zu Triest und Fiume nach den französischen Kolonien.
Mexiko. Antrag des französischen Hofes auf Verproviantierung seiner Kolonien im mexikanischen Meerbusen durch k. k. österr. Untertanen.

1781.

Amerika. Erscheinen und Akzeptierung amerikanischer Wechsel in Spanien und Frankreich.
Absendung eines amerikanischen Emissärs nach Berlin und Kopenhagen zum Einkauf von Tuch und Gewehr.
Frankreich. Präsentierung des jungen Laurens als Deputierten der englisch-amerikanischen Stände beim französischen Hofe.
Gelddarlehen für die amerikanisch-englischen Kolonien.
Holland. Druckschriften der Unterhandlungen der Stadt Amsterdam mit den englischen Kolonien in Amerika; diesfälliger Untersuchungsprozess.
Bewegungen des Adams zur Erwirkung seiner Anerkennung als bevollmächtigten Minister des englisch-amerikanischen Kongresses allda.
Dänische und schwedische Geldnegotiationen allda, ebenso des englisch-amerikanischen Kongresses.
Geldnegotiationen für die englisch-amerikanischen Kolonien allda.
Die Angelegenheiten dortiger westindischer Kompanien.
Krieg. Eroberung der holländischen Inseln St. Eustache und St. Martin durch die Engländer, sowie mehrerer anderer solcher Besitzungen, sowie einiger Faktoreien.
Wiedereroberung der von den Engländern bei St. Eustache weggenommenen holländischen Kauffahrteiflotte durch die Franzosen.
Fehlgeschlagene englische Unternehmung auf St. Vincent, Neu-Orleans, La Mobile.
Spanische Wiedereroberung der Kolonie von St. Juan de Nicaraguas.
Fehlgeschlagene französische Unternehmung in der Bay von Chesapeake.
Krieg zwischen England und seinen Kolonien in Amerika, Vorteile der Engländer über die Kolonisten.
Abfall eines Teiles der Armee der Kolonisten an die Engländer.
Vorteile der Kolonisten über die Engländer.
Gefangennahme des Lord Cornwallis mit seiner Armee in Chesapeake.
Spanien. Der Aufruhr in Amerika.
Der allen Spaniern freigelassene Handel nach dem spanischen Westindien und die für die erbländischen Produkte hiebei zu erzielenden Vorteile.
Verfall des dortigen Handels.
Werbung. Die englischen Werbungen in den Reichslanden nach Amerika.
Heimliche Werbung der k. k. österr. Untertanen nach Amerika durch den Legationssekretär des hiesigen englischen Ministers Gerstenberg.

1782.

England. Debauchierung von k. k. österr. Untertanen nach Amerika durch den englischen Legationssekretär in Wien.
  Resignierung des amerikanischen Staatssekretärs Lord Germaine, dessen Nachfolger und übrige Veränderungen im Ministerium; gänzliche Abänderung desselben.
  Uebertragung des Generalkommandos in Amerika an General Carlton.
  Bewegungen im Parlament zur Beendigung des Krieges in Amerika mit den Kolonien.
Frieden. Abschluss der Friedenspräliminarien zwischen England und den amerikanischen Kolonien.
  Die englischen Friedensunterhandlungen mit den amerikanischen Kolonien.
Holland. Die Verrichtungen der Deputierten der englisch-amerikanischen Kolonien allda. Anerkennung ihres bevollmächtigten Ministers Mr. Adams.
  Projekt des holländischen Kommerzientraktates mit den nordamerikanischen Staaten, den englischen Kolonien.
  Dortige Behandlung eines Darlehens für die englisch-amerikanischen Kolonien.
Krieg. Eroberung der Insel St. Eustache durch die Franzosen.
  Nachrichten von einem förmlichen Angriff von Jamaica durch die Spanier und die Franzosen.
  Gefecht des englischen Admirals Hood über den französischen General De Grasse bei der Insel St. Christophe. Eroberung derselben durch die Franzosen.
  Verheerung der Hudsonsbay-Compagnie durch Paul Jones.
  Eroberung der Insel Roatan in der Bay von Honduras durch die Spanier.
  Eroberung der Insel Providence durch die Spanier.
  Eroberung von Essequibo und Demeray durch die Franzosen.
  Ankunft der Admirals Pigot in New-York mit 23 Linienschiffen. Erbeutung verschiedener spanischer und amerikanischer Kaper.
  Eroberung einiger englischer Besitzungen in der Hudsonsbay durch die Franzosen.
Spanien. Uebermachung der spanischen Schätze aus Amerika auf portugiesischen Schiffen.
Werbung. Heimliche Anwerbung von k. k. österr. Untertanen nach Amerika durch den Legationssekretär des hiesigen englischen Ministers.
  Die Werbungen des Fürsten von Anhalt-Zerbst für England nach Amerika.

1783.

Amerika. Die dortigen unabhängigen Staaten und vormaligen englischen Kolonien. Anfrage wegen Anerkennung ihrer auswärtigen Minister von Seite der k. k. Minister.
  Vorschlag eines Anonymi auf Einleitung eines erbländischen Handels mit den amerikanischen Kolonien.
  Die spanischen Kommerzial- und Grenzscheidungstraktate mit den amerikanischen Staaten.
  Der Antrag Englands zur Abschliessung einer geheimen Offensif- und Defensif-Alliance mit dasigen Staaten und Einladung des russischen Hofes zum Beitritte.

Die Errichtung eines diesseitigen Handels- und Freundschaftstraktates mit den amerikanischen Staaten und Dahinsendung eines diesseitigen Bevollmächtigten.
Vorhabende Handelsexpeditionen aus Triest nach den dortigen Staaten.
Die engländischen Kommerzialunterhandlungen mit den dortigen Staaten.
Der Handel nach Amerika überhaupt.
Die Geldnegotiationen für die dortigen vereinigten Staaten in Holland.
Antrag auf Behandlung eines Kommerzien-Traktates mit Portugal.
Das Misstrauen der dortigen Staaten gegen Frankreich und England.
Versuch des Dean [Francis Dana] in Petersburg um seine Anerkennung als Gesandter der neuen Staaten von Amerika.
Ernennung des Grafen Gansa zum dortigen spanischen Minister.
England. Ankunft eines amerikanischen Fahrzeuges.
Die englischen Handelstraktate mit den amerikanischen Staaten.
Eroberung der Bahamischen Inseln durch die Engländer.
Emigranten. Antrag auf Ansiedlung der aus Amerika zurückgekehrten deutschen Reichsuntertanen in den österr. Erblanden.
Frankreich. Errichtung eines monatlichen Paketbootes von Portlouis nach Amerika.
Holland. Ernennung des von Berkhel zum holländischen Gesandten bei den amerikanischen Staaten.
Auswechselung der Ratifikationen des holländischen Freundschafts- und Kommerzientraktates mit den vereinigten amerikanischen Staaten.
Spanien. Amnestie für die Rebellen in Mexiko und Behebung ihrer Beschwerden.
Empörungen im spanischen Amerika.
Ernennung des Carmichael zum amerikanischen Geschäftsträger alldort.

1784.

Amerika. Die Eröffnung des Commerciums mit der Reichsstadt Hamburg.
Die vereinigten amerikan. Staaten. Englische Verordnungen den Handel mit denselben betreffend.
Der Minister der dortigen Staaten in dem Haag verlangt die Gegenvisite vom dortigen k. k. österr. Minister.
Die Anhaltung eines Expressen des amerikanischen Ministers Adams in Brüssel.
Antrag der amerikanischen Staaten auf Abschluss eines Freundschafts- und Kommerzientraktates mit dem k. k. österr. Hofe.
Der Zustand der Handlung der Stadt Hamburg mit den dortigen Staaten.
Der toskanische Handel nach Amerika.
Kaperung eines amerikanischen Schiffes durch einen Marokkaner Korsar.
England. Emigrierung dortiger Fabrikanten, und aus Irland nach Amerika und Frankreich; diesfällige Verbote.
Häufige Emigrationen aus England nach Amerika.
Holland. Der amerikanische Minister allda verlangt Gegenvisite des k. k. österreichischen.
Spanien. Aufstand in Mexiko.
Irrungen mit England wegen der Grenzen von Florida.

1785.

Amerika. Die Errichtung eines diesseitigen Handelsvertrages mit den dortigen vereinigten Staaten.
Ernennung des John Temple zum dortigen englischen Generalkonsul und Verlängerung der Interimalhandlungsverordnung zwischen England und den vereinigten Staaten.
Die Beschwerden dortiger vereinigter Staaten über die Engländer wegen verzögerter Räumung der in dem Frieden abgetretenen Forts.
Plan einer Triester Handelskompagnie nach den dortigen vereinigten Staaten, bezw. die in Triest sich bildende österreichisch-amerikanische Handelsgesellschaft.
England. Die Kommerzialunterhandlungen mit den amerikanischen Staaten.
Parlamentsbewilligungen zur Entschädigung der amerikanischen Loyalisten.
Audienz des amerikanischen Ministers Adams.
Vorhabende Errichtung einer Handelskompagnie nach den Kuritischen [Kurilischen] Inseln.
Frankreich. Ankunft des neuen Ministers der amerikanischen Staaten Jefferson.
Spanien. Irrungen des dortigen Hofes mit England wegen der Grenzberichtigung von Florida und Fällung des Färbholzes.
Probe mit einem auf neue Art gebauten Linienschiff *S. Ildefons*.
Verzeichnis der 1784 aus Amerika nach Spanien und vice versa überbrachten Schätze und Waren.
Neuer Aufstand in Mexiko.
Königliche Gnade für den Vizekönig in Peru.
Abschaffung der Grabstätten auf St. Ildefons.

1786.

Amerika. Spanische Grenzirrungen mit den dortigen vereinigten Staaten und den Wilden.
Antrag auf Abschluss eines diesseitigen Handelsvertrages mit den vereinigten amerikanischen Staaten.
Handelspläne aus Nordamerika.
Gerücht von den englischen Unterhandlungen mit den unzufriedenen Provinzen wegen ihrer Wiedervereinigung mit England.
Irrungen des Kongresses mit den Staaten; diesfällige französische Intriguen.
Verfall des Handels aus Hamburg nach Amerika.
Preussischer Handelsvertrag mit den amerikanischen Staaten.
England. Die Forderungen der k. k. österr. Untertanen wegen ihrer in St. Eustache durch den Admiral Rodney eingezogenen Schiffe.
Konvention mit Spanien wegen Uebersetzung der im spanischen Amerika angesessenen Engländer.
Konvention mit Spanien wegen Beilegung der Irrungen betreffend Musquitos in Amerika.
Holland. Beschwerden der dortigen westindischen Kompagnie über die Engländer und Dänen auf der Küste von Guinea.
Beschwerden bei Frankreich wegen Debauchierung der Neger von Amerika und Essequibo.

Portugal. Begünstigung der Einfuhr der portugiesischen Weine nach den amerikanischen Staaten.
Ankunft der Silberflotte aus Brasilien.
Spanien. Tätigkeiten zwischen den Spaniern und Engländern in Amerika.
Verzeichnis der vorjährigen Warenladungen aus Spanien nach Amerika et vice versa.
Beilegung der Irrungen mit England wegen der Küste von Musquitos.
Gerücht von der Absendung eines spanischen Emissärs nach Ungarn zur Debauchierung dortiger Bergleute nach Amerika.

1787.

Amerika. Anfrage wegen Einsendung (Geschenk an den Kaiser) eines Gedichtes des Mr. Barlow auf die Freiheit der nordamerikanischen Staaten.
England. Debatten im Parlament gegen den mit Spanien geschlossenen Vertrag wegen Abtretung der Küste von Musquitos an Spanien.
Portugal. Vermutung eines französischen Anwurfs wegen Vermählung des Prinzen von Brasilien nach vorgängiger Scheidung mit der französischen Prinzessin Elisabeth.
Spanien. Spanische Irrungen mit England wegen Räumung der Küste von Musquitos.
Tod des Vizekönigs von Mexiko, Dn. Bern. de Galvez; dessen Nachfolger, Flore.
Werbung. Heimliche Werbungen im Reiche nach Amerika.

1788.

Louisiana. Der Einfall der Amerikaner in Louisiana.
England. Absendung von Truppen und Munition nach Ost- und Westindien.
Abberufung des dortigen Ministers der amerikanischen Staaten, Adams.
Seereise des Prinzen Wilhelm nach Amerika.
Holland. Abberufung des holländischen Ministers van Berckel von den nordamerikanischen Staaten.
Ernennung des van Berckel zum holländischen Residenten bei den amerikanischen Staaten.
Kriminalprozess gegen den van Berckel.
Absendung einiger Kommissäre nach Westindien zur Untersuchung dortiger Kolonien; Verordnungen, diesen Handel betreffend.
Portugal. Kommerzialunterhandlungen des dortigen Hofes mit den amerikanischen Staaten.
Blattern des Prinzen von Brasilien. Tod desselben. Eloge. Hoftrauer.
Gährungen im Ministerium nach dem Tode des Prinzen von Brasilien.
Dortige allgemeine Bestürzung über den Tod des Prinzen von Brasilien.
Beisorge wegen Erlöschen des Mannesstammes und der spanischen Sukzession in Portugal.
Charakter des nunmehrigen Prinzen von Brasilien und seiner Gemahlin.
Verwendung des Prinzen.
Wittum für die verwitwete Prinzessin von Brasilien.
Spanien. Entdeckung eines neuen Silberbergwerkes in Peru.
Verbot der Ausfuhr fremder Tücher aus Cadiz nach Amerika.
Schweiz. Auswanderungen aus der Schweiz nach Amerika.

1789.

Amerika. Behandlung eines Anlehens in Holland für die nordamerikanischen Staaten.
Ernennung des Carol zum dortigen katholischen Bischof.
England. Fortgang der Ansiedlungen der Delinquenten in Amerika.
Joseph II. Antrag der auf Vermählung Kaiser Josefs II. mit der verwitweten Prinzessin von Brasilien.
Portugal. Beträchtliche Einkünfte und Schmuck der verwitweten Prinzessin von Brasilien.
Antrag auf Vermählung der verwitweten Prinzessin von Brasilien mit dem spanischen Infanten Dn. Antonio.
Ausrüstung einer Escadre gegen die Algierer und nach Brasilien.
Aufstand in Pernambucos in Brasilien. Beilegung der Sache.
Krankheit des Prinzen von Brasilien. Genesung.
Fehlgeschlagener Versuch des Beichtvaters des Prinzen von Brasilien auf die Wiedereinräumung des Klosters zu Mafra an die Franziskaner.
Sonora. Eine angebliche goldreiche Provinz in Amerika.

1790.

Amerika. Die neuen russischen Kolonien in Nordamerika; diesfällige Unterhandlungen mit Spanien.
Der englische Pelzhandel in Nordamerika; diesfällige spanische Gegenvorkehrungen. Wegnahme einiger englischen Schiffe; englische Beschwerden hierüber.
Spanische Verordnung, die Freiheit der Negersklaven in Amerika betreffend.
Aufstand in französisch-amerikanischen Kolonien.
Frankreich. Gährungen in den französisch-amerikanischen Inseln.
Denunziation der Inwohner von St. Domingue gegen den Seeminister. Abdankung desselben.
Ernennung des Chr. Ternan zum französischen Minister bei den amerikanischen Staaten und des Grafen Du Moustier beim Berliner Hofe.
Spanien. Dortige Furcht vor Anzettelung eines Aufstandes in den spanisch-amerikanischen Besitzungen. Verteidigungsanstalten.
Gerücht von einer englischen Landung auf Pensacola in Florida.
Dortiger Aufenthalt und Unterhandlungen eines nordamerikanischen Emissärs.

1791.

Amerika. Die Reichsemigranten nach Amerika.
Angeblicher Antrag der dortigen vereinigten Staaten, das Pouvoir executiv einem englischen Prinzen zu überlassen.
England. Die Vorteile des vorigen Jahres zwischen England und Spanien geschlossenen Vergleichs für dortigen Hof in Bezug auf die Erweiterung des englischen Handels in Amerika.
Ernennung des Hammond zum englischen Minister bei den amerikanischen Staaten.

Frankreich. Bedenkliche Gährungen in St. Domingue und den übrigen französischen Inseln.
Untersuchung der französischen Nationalversammlung wegen der französischen Kolonien und des Negeraufstandes in St. Domingue.
Portugal. Portugiesische Beschwerden über die holländisch-westindische Kompagnie.
Akreditierung des Humphrey als dortigen Residenten der nordamerikanischen Staaten. Portugiesische Kommerzialunterhandlungen mit denselben.
Spanien. Die bedenklichen Folgen des vorjährigen Vergleichs zwischen Spanien und England in Bezug auf die spanisch-amerikanischen Besitzungen.
Dortige Massnahmen gegen die Verbreitung des Aufruhrs in St. Domingue.
Ankunft der Silberflotte aus Amerika.
Dortige Besorgnis wegen feindlicher englischer Absichten auf Louisiana und die Antillen.
Spuren neuer Feindseligkeiten zwischen Spanien und England in Amerika.
Spanische Irrungen mit den amerikanischen Staaten wegen der freien Schiffahrt auf dem Ohio und Mississippi im mexikanischen Meerbusen. Englische Intriguen.
Gibraltar. Antrag auf Ueberlassung dieser Festung an Spanien gegen Abtretung der spanisch-amerikanischen Besitzungen an England.

1792.

Amerika. Krieg der Indianer des Ohioflusses mit den vereinigten nordamerikanischen Staaten.
Uebermachung verschiedener Pflanzen aus Amerika für den botanischen Garten in Wien.
England. Gährungen in Jamaica.
Debatte wegen Aufhebung des Negerhandels.
St. Domingue. Französische Insel in Amerika. Aufruhr und Ravagen dortiger Sklaven.
Holland. Absendung einer kleinen holländischen Escadre nach Westindien gegen die Negersklaven.
Bewilligung einer Million zur Tilgung der Schulden der aufgehobenen westindischen Kompagnie.
Ankunft des Ministers der vereinigten amerikanischen Staaten, Short.
Portugal. Ansuchen des Prinzen von Brasilien um die päpstliche Dispens zur Beibehaltung des Malteser Grosspriorates.
Spanien. Spanien lässt eine Seekarte vom mitternächtlichen Amerika aufnehmen.
Vergleich mit England wegen der damnifizierten englischen Schiffe in dem Nootkasund.
Bedenkliche Forderungen der nordamerikanischen Staaten an Spanien wegen der freien Schiffahrt am Mississippi.
Anmerkungen über den spanischen Reichtum aus Amerika und den Handel.
Dortige Hoffnungen auf den Fall der Thronbesteigung des Prinzen von Brasilien in Portugal.

1793.

Amerika. Antrag dortiger französischer Inseln, sich unter englischen Schutz zu begeben.
Die Gesinnungen der vereinigten nordamerikanischen Staaten gegen Frankreich.
Häufige Getreide- und Munitionsausfuhr aus den nordamerikanischen Staaten nach Frankreich und feindliche Absichten derselben auf dortige holländische Kolonien.
England. Ausgleichung der Zwistigkeiten mit Spanien wegen der in dem Nootkasund angehaltenen englischen Schiffe.
Englische Eroberung der Insel Tabago.
Die fehlgeschlagene englische Landung auf Martinique.
Holland. Holländische Eroberung der Insel St. Martin.
Portugal. Schwangerschaft der Prinzessin von Brasilien. Entbindung von einer Prinzessin.
Wegnahme einer französischen Fregatte in Brasilien.
Nachrichten von einer Descente der Franzosen aus Cayenne in Brasilien.
Portugiesische Grenzirrungen mit Spanien in Amerika.
Neuerliche Schwangerschaft der Prinzessin von Brasilien.
Abreise des Beichtvaters der Prinzessin von Brasilien nach Spanien. Eloge desselben.
Promotionen und Gnadenverleihungen anlässlich der Entbindung der Prinzessin von Brasilien.
Spanien. Ankunft des nordamerikanischen Negotiateurs Short zur Ausgleichung der spanischen Irrungen mit dortigen Staaten wegen der Schiffahrt auf dem Ohio und Mississippi.
Unterhandlungen mit dem dortigen englischen Minister L. [Lord] St. Helens über die gemeinschaftlichen Kriegsoperationen gegen Frankreich; England dringt auf einen Landkrieg mit spanischen und portugiesischen Truppen gegen Garantierung der spanischen Besitzungen in Amerika.
Ankunft einer französischen Escadre mit französischen Emigranten aus Martinique in der spanischen Insel Trinidad.
Spanische Besorgnis wegen der zu befürchtenden Alleinherrschaft der Engländer zur See und der reichen spanisch-amerikanischen Besitzungen.
Ausrüstung einer Flotte nach Westindien.
Ankunft einer Silberflotte aus Amerika.
Errichtung eines Volontaires-Corps von Contrebandiers und Vermehrung des Gardes du Corps mit 200 Amerikanern.
Ernennung zweier Vicekönige nach Amerika.
Errichtung eines Paketbootes zwischen Corugna und Falmouth.
Quarantaine auf die nordamerikanischen Schiffe wegen des epidemischen Gelbfiebers in Amerika.

1794.

Amerika. Angebliche kriegerische Absichten Englands gegen die nordamerikanischen vereinigten Staaten.
England. Wiedereroberung der von den Franzosen gekaperten Kauffahrteischiffe aus Terre Neuve.

Holland. Dortige Besorgnis wegen eines Krieges zwischen England und
    den amerikanischen vereinigten Staaten.
Portugiesische Reklamierung eines nach St. Eustache entwichenen portugiesischen Korsaren.
Portugal. Ausrüstung einer Escadre gegen die Algierer Korsaren und nach
    Brasilien.
Abreise des dortigen Ministers der nordamerikanischen Staaten, Obristen
    Humphreys.
Spanien. Ankunft des nordamerikanischen Ministers Short.
Ankunft der Schätze aus Amerika.

1795.

Portugal. Schwangerschaft der Prinzessin von Brasilien. Taufpaten der
    Papst und die Königin von Spanien; Entbindung von einem
    Prinzen.
Erwartung der Schätze aus Brasilien. Ausrüstung einer Escadre zur
    Ueberbringung derselben; Auslaufen.
Spanien. Verzeichnis der im vorigen Jahr aus Amerika eingekommenen
    Schätze; Ankunft neuer Schätze.
Spuren der Behandlung eines Handelsvertrages zwischen Spanien und
    den nordamerikanischen Staaten. Schluss.
Ankunft der Schätze aus Amerika.
Einschiffung des im spanischen Sold stehenden Korps der französischen
    Émigrés in Cadiz nach St. Domingo.
Abschluss des spanischen Kommerzientraktates mit den nordamerikanischen Staaten.
Englische Vorstellung gegen die spanische Abtretung von St. Domingo
    an Frankreich.

1796.

Spanien. Unterhandlungen des dortigen englischen Botschafters wegen der
    Insel St. Domingo.
Abschlägige französische Antwort wegen Wiederabtretung von Domingo
    gegen ein Aequivalent. Diesfällige Unterhandlungen.
Verzeichnis der im vorigen Jahr aus Amerika überbrachten Geldschätze.
Ankunft neuer Schätze.
Negeraufstand im spanischen Domingo auf französisches Anstiften.
Schwäche der spanischen Truppen allda und im ganzen spanischen
    Amerika.
Absendung des französischen Kommissärs Rome auf einer spanischen
    Fregatte nach St. Domingo zur Uebernahme dieser Insel. Nachrichten aus St. Domingo.
Der zwischen dem dortigen Hof und den nordamerikanischen Staaten
    geschlossene Traktat.
Französische Forderung, dass der dortige Hof die Insel St. Domingo
    gegen einen feindlichen englischen Angriff verteidigen solle.
Gerüchte von einem Aufruhr in Mexiko.

1797.

Portugal. Auslaufen der portugiesischen Flotte von Brasilien.
Ankunft des nordamerikanischen Residenten Smith und des preussischen
    Abgesandten Freiherrn von Schladen.

Spanien. Gährungen in Mexiko; Ernennung des dortigen Erzbischofs zum Vizekönig an Stelle des Schwagers des Favoriten.
Ernennung des Humphreys zum dortigen bevollmächtigten Minister der nordamerikanischen vereinigten Staaten.
Besorgnis wegen eines Bruches der nordamerikanischen Staaten mit Frankreich und Spanien.

1798.

Spanien. Ankunft beladener Schiffe aus Mexiko.
Dortige grosse Besorgnis wegen der spanischen Besitzungen in Amerika bei Ausbruch des Krieges zwischen Frankreich und den nordamerikanischen Staaten.
Spanische eifrige Verwendung in Konstantinopel bei den nordamerikanischen Staaten und Barbaresquen zur Hintanhaltung eines Krieges gegen die Franzosen.
Französisches Anerbieten der Eroberung Portugals und der Einverleibung dieser Krone mit der spanischen gegen Abtretung von Brasilien und allen über den Ebro gegen die Pyrennäen gelegenen Provinzen.
Portugal. Auslauf der portugiesischen Flotte nach Brasilien.
Ankunft eines Teiles der Flotte aus Brasilien. Absendung eines englischen Konvois für den Rest.
Spuren heimlicher Anstalten zur Flucht des Hofes nach Brasilien auf den Fall der Annäherung französischer Truppen.
Ankunft der reichen Flotte aus Brasilien.
Entbindung der Prinzessin von Brasilien von einem Prinzen.

1799.

Portugal. Die Entbindung der Prinzessin von Brasilien von einem Infanten.
Entdeckung einer Revolutionsverschwörung in Brasilien.
Auslauf der grossen portugiesischen Konvoi nach Brasilien unter Bedeckung einiger Kriegsschiffe.
Amerika. Absendung zweier Gesandten der nordamerikanischen Staaten nach Paris zur Ausgleichung der Irrungen mit Frankreich.
Spanien. Nachrichten von bedenklichen Volksempörungen in den spanisch-amerikanischen Besitzungen.
Misshelligkeiten zwischen dem dortigen Hofe und den nordamerikanischen Staaten, wegen gekaperter amerikanischer Schiffe.

1800.

Portugal. Absegelung des grossen Konvoi nach Brasilien.
Entbindung der Prinzessin von Brasilien von einer Prinzessin.
Ankunft der portugiesischen Silberflotte aus Rio Janeiro und 7 spanischer reich beladener Gallionen; englische Beschwerde über die Freilassung der letzeren und Andringen auf den Beschlag; abschlägige Antwort des dortigen Hofes.
Spanien. Ernennung des Orosco zum spanischen Minister bei den nordamerikanischen Staaten und des D. Fruxo in gleicher Eigenschaft für die zisalpinische Republik.
Entbindung der Prinzessin von Brasilien.

1801.

Portugal. Zerstreuung der brasilianischen Flotte durch einen Sturm. Spuren heimlicher Unterhandlungen des dortigen Hofes mit dem englischen für den Fall eines feindlichen französischen Angriffes und des Antrages des Hofes nach Brasilien zu flüchten.
Entbindung der Prinzessin von Brasilien von einer Infantin.
Jesuiten. Abschaffung der Jesuiten aus Spanien und Amerika und Relegierung nach Italien.

1802.

Amerika. Ansuchen um neue k. k. Seeurkunden für das Schiff *Amerika*.
Ernennung des Lamson zum Konsul der nordamerikanischen Freistaaten in Triest.
Ankunft nordamerikanischer Handelsschiffe in Triest.
Antrag auf Einleitung des diesseitigen Handels mit nordamerikanischen Freistaaten.
Kriegserklärung der nordamerikanischen Staaten gegen Tripolis.
Ernennung des Wilhelm Riggin zum Konsul dortiger nordamerikanischer Freistaaten in Triest und den benachbarten Seehäfen.
Frankreich. Auslaufen der französisch-spanischen Flotte aus Brest, vermutlich nach Brasilien.
Portugal. Ankunft portugiesischer Schiffe aus Brasilien mit Gold.
Rückkunft des Vizegouverneurs aus Brasilien.
Besorgnis wegen eines Aufstandes in den portugiesischen Kolonien.
Spanien. Abschiedsaudienzen des dortigen Gesandten der nordamerikanischen Staaten Humphreys und Antrittsaudienzen seines Nachfolgers Pinckney.
Ankunft reich beladener Schiffe aus Amerika.
Ankunft der Schätze aus Amerika.
Angebliche Grenzirrungen zwischen Frankreich und Spanien hinsichtlich Louisiana.
Louisiana. Die beabsichtigte französische Expedition nach Louisiana.
Tripolis. Der König von Schweden und die nordamerikanischen Staaten erklären die Blockade des dortigen Hafens.

1803.

Amerika. Die Gestattung der Visitierung aller nordamerikanischen Konsulate in Italien durch den Gesandten dieser Staaten bei der italienischen Republik.
Holland. Englische Eroberung der batavischen Kolonien.
Louisiana. Die beabsichtigte französische Militärexpedition nach Louisiana; Einstellung.
Die Franzosen verkaufen Louisiana den nordamerikanischen Staaten.
Paolina. Reklamierung der von diesem österreichischen Schiffe durch einen Tunesischen Korsaren geraubten Effekten. Reklamierung des von einem amerikanischen Armateur unweit Malta weggenommenen österr. Schiffes, Kapitän Radich.
Portugal. Antwort des Kaisers und der Kaiserin an den dortigen Residenten wegen der Entbindung seiner Gemahlin, der Prinzessin von Brasilien, von einem Prinzen.
Gerücht von der Abtretung eines Teiles von Brasilien an Frankreich; England reklamiert das Kontingent von 6 Kriegsschiffen.

Riggin, William. Neuernannter amerikanischer Konsul in Triest, dessen Bitte um das Exequatur regium.
Spanien. Ankunft der Schätze aus Mexiko.
Irrungen des dortigen Hofes mit den amerikanischen Staaten wegen der Schiffahrt auf dem Mississippi.
Eine aus St. Domingue in Santander eingelaufene französische Kriegskorvette widersetzt sich der Quarantaine mit Gewalt.

1804.

Konsuln. Antrag, in Danzig und bei den nordamerikanischen Staaten einen k. k. österreichischen Konsul zu bestellen.
Frankreich. Eroberung von St. Domingo durch die Neger.
Batavische Republik. Wegnahme von Surinam durch die Engländer.
Louisiana. Eine von Frankreich an Nordamerika abgetretene Provinz. Verhandlungen zwischen Nordamerika und dem dagegen protestierenden Spanien.
Spanien. Irrungen zwischen dem dortigen Hofe und den nordamerikanischen Staaten. Abreise des amerikanischen Gesandten Pinkney.
Anfang der englischen Feindseligkeiten gegen Spanien wegen Wegnahme dreier reich beladener spanischer Schiffe aus Vera Cruz.
Embargo auf die spanischen Schiffe in England.
Ankunft der Silberflotte aus Vera Cruz.

1805.

Kolonisten. Aufstellung einer Kolonistenwerbung in Frankfurt für die nordamerikanischen Staaten. Abschaffung.
Spanien. Zerschlagen der Unterhandlungen mit den nordamerikanischen Staaten wegen der Grenzberichtigung von Louisiana.
Portugal. Der von der Prinzessin von Brasilien der Kaiserin Maria Theresia überschickte St. Elisabethorden.
Uebermachung eines Teiles der Schätze aus den spanischen Kolonien auf portugiesischen Schiffen.

1806.

Spanien. Die englische Eroberung von Buenos Ayres. Wiedereroberung.
Entdeckung einer Verschwörung in Buenos Ayres.
Spannung zwischen Spanien und den nordamerikanischen Staaten.

1807.

Spanien. Spanische Wiedereroberung von Buenos Ayres.

1808.

Amerika. Angebliches Dekret der französischen Regierung gegen die amerikanische Flagge. Die Sperrung aller französischen und Alliierten Häfen für sie.
Die Ausschliessung sämtlicher unter amerikanischer Flagge segelnder Schiffe aus den k. k. österreichischen Häfen.
England. Gerücht von dem Abschluss einer Alliance zwischen England und den amerikanischen Staaten.

1809.

Amerika. Die Einnahme der nordamerikanischen Schiffe in den k. k. österreichischen Häfen nach Wiederherstellung der freundschaftlichen Verhältnisse mit England.
Spanien. Vorteile der Spanier in St. Domingo über die Franzosen. Ankunft stärkerer Subsidiengelder aus England aus dem spanischen Amerika.

1811.

England. Gerüchte von dem Kriegsausbruche zwischen England und den amerikanischen Staaten.

1813.

Amerika. Absendung zweier Bevollmächtigter der nordamerikanischen Staaten, Gallatin und Bayard, ins preussische Hauptquartier wegen der von dem russischen Kaiser angebotenen Friedensvermittelung mit England.

1814.

Amerika. Englische Erklärung des Blockadezustandes der nordamerikanischen Küsten.
England. Englische Erklärung der Freiheit der Elbschiffahrt nach Abzug der Franzosen und der Blockade der Häfen, Flüsse, etc., an den Küsten der nordamerikanischen Staaten.
Spanien. Königliches Manifest für die amerikanischen Provinzen zur Rückkehr derselben in die spanische Oberherrschaft.

1815.

Amerika. Anzeige von den Feindseligkeiten amerikanischer Kriegsschiffe gegen die englischen Kauffahrteischiffe im Mittelländischen Meer.
Ansuchen dortiger Staaten um Gestattung der Aufnahme in den österreichischen Seehäfen der gegen die Barabaresquen-Korsaren kreuzenden amerikanischen Kriegsfahrzeuge.

1816.

Spanien. Ansuchen um ein Verbot der Waffenausfuhr aus den k. k. österr. Staaten für die spanischen Insurgenten in Amerika. Diesfällige Beschwerden.

1817.

Auswanderung. Die Auswanderungen aus dem Badischen und dem k. k. Oberamt Silbach, Breisgau, Ortenau, etc., nach Nordamerika.
Spanien. Erklärung der Küsten von Peru und Chili mit Ausnahme einiger Häfen in Blockadestand.
Ausrüstung spanischer Insurgenten-Korsarenschiffe in Buenos Ayres.
Korsaren. Das Auslaufen zahlreicher Korsaren mit Kaperbriefen der spanischen Insurgentenregierung in Buenos Ayres in Amerika zur Kreuzung in den europäischen Gewässern.

1818.

Allen, John. Amerikanischer Grosshändler, Anerbieten desselben, seine auf hiesigem Hauptmarkt liegenden 79 Fässer mit amerikanischen Häringen zur Verteilung an die Armee zu überlassen.

Amerika. Notizen über die von den nordamerikanischen Freistaaten auf alle englischen und spanischen Schiffe gelegte Embargo-Konfiszierung der auf selben befindlichen Güter.

Spanien. Königliche Proklamation zur Vermehrung der Population der weissen Menschen in der Insel Cuba.

Ansuchen des dortigen Hofes um ein Ausfuhrverbot aller Waffengattungen, des Pulvers aus den österreichischen Häfen nach Amerika, bis zur Dämpfung des Aufruhrs in den spanisch-amerikanischen Kolonien.

Edikt, die Bestrafung der mit Waffen in der Hand unter den Fahnen der Insurgenten in Amerika ergriffenen Fremden betreffend.

Anzeige des feindseligen Schrittes der Vereinigten Staaten von Nordamerika durch Verletzung des Gebietes von Florida gegen diesen Staat.

v. Stürmer, k. k. Generalkonsul bei den nordamerikanischen Staaten; die voreilige Kundmachung der Ernennung desselben zu diesem Posten in den Zeitungen betreffend.

Verleihung des preussischen roten Adlerordens an ihn.

Verständigung des englischen Hofes von seiner Ernennung zum k. k. österr. Generalkonsul in Philadelphia und Abberufung aus der Insel St. Helena. Antrag wegen seiner Reise nach Amerika.

1819.

Ansiedelung. Errichtung einer Gesellschaft in Stuttgart zur Erleichterung der Ansiedelung in Nordamerika. Statuten der Gesellschaft.

Amerika. Die Seeräubereien der südamerikanischen Freibeuter.

Nachrichten über den Handel in Nordamerika.

Die in England stattgehabte Subskription zu Gunsten der Amerikaner-Insurgenten.

Spanien. Spanische Verordnung der Todesstrafe auf alle Ausländer, die bei den amerikanischen Insurgenten in Amerika bewaffnet ergriffen werden, oder die ihnen Kriegslieferungen zuführen.

Uebermachung der späteren Verordnungen unter der Regierung der Cortes.

Ob den k. k. Schiffspatronen zu gestatten sei, ihre Schiffe zum Transport der spanischen Truppen nach Amerika gegen die Insurgenten auszumieten.

Ansuchen um ein Ausfuhrverbot wegen eines in Triest vorbereiteten für die Insel Thomas bestimmten Massentransports.

Schweiz. Die Auswanderungen aus der Schweiz nach Brasilien.

Antrag auf Errichtung schweizerischer Regimenter für den Hof von Brasilien.

Stürmer. Antrag auf ein Wartgeld von 2000 Fl. für ihn bis zum Antritt seiner neuen Anstellung.

1820.

Amerika. Die Verfassungspolitik der nordamerikanischen Staaten.
Die Behandlung fremder Handelsschiffe in holländischen Quarantainesachen.
Dortiger Aufenthalt des exilierten Franzosen Joseph Bonaparte.
Exequatur für den k. k. Generalkonsul allda, Freiherrn von Lederer.
Die Revolution in Spanisch-Amerika.
Spanien. Ansuchen der spanischen Botschaft um ein Verbot wegen der vorbereiteten Massenausfuhr von Triest nach Amerika.
Beschwerden des amerikanischen Gesandten bei dem dortigen Ministerium wegen seiner Effekten in Cadiz.
Stürmer. Dessen Ernennung zum k. k. Gesandten in Brasilien.
K. k. Gesandter in Brasilien. Die Liquidierung mehrerer Dienst- und Kurierrechnungen. Vergütung der Auslagen wegen Verzögerung der Ankunft des Schiffes *Carolina*.

1821.

Amerika. Antrag der nordamerikanischen Regierung wegen der Behandlung ihrer Nationalschiffe in den österreichischen Häfen.
Die Irrungen mit England wegen des Sklavenhandels und die spanische Abtretung von Florida an die dortige Regierung.
Die Gefechte mit den Insurgenten im spanischen und portugiesischen Amerika.
Spanien. Nachrichten von den Insurgenten in den spanischen Kolonien in Amerika.
Stürmer, k. k. Gesandter zu Rio Janeiro. Uebermachung eines Kreditbriefes für ihn, die Bezahlung eines neuen von 300 Pfund Sterling.
Nachrichten von der Reise desselben auf der *Carolina* nach Rio Janeiro.
Die Miete seines Gesandtschaftshauses.
Dessen Entfernung aus Brasilien.
Lederer, k. k. Generalkonsul in New-York. Anerkennung desselben von seite der nordamerikanischen Staaten.
Die Verfassung und Einrichtung seiner Berichte.
Dessen Bitte um Gestattung der Annahme des ihm verliehenen Toskanischen Generalkonsulates alldort.

K. u. K. KRIEGSARCHIV.

Location: Wien VII., Stiftgasse 2. The building was constructed in the eighteenth century, and was formerly the home of the "Technische Militärakademie". The archive is divided into: I. Die Direktion; II. Die Abteilung für Kriegsgeschichte; III. Das Schriftenarchiv (containing over 5,000,000 "Schriftstücke" since 1556, and 15,000 folio volumes of "Protokolle"); IV. Das Kartenarchiv; V. Die Kriegsbibliothek.

Hours: 10 a. m. to 2 p. m. daily, except Sundays and holidays.

Bibliography: Das K. K. Kriegs-Archiv: Geschichte und Monographie (Vienna, Verlag des K. K. Generalstabs, 1878).

J. Langer, *Das K. u. K. Kriegsarchiv von seiner Gründung bis zum Jahre 1900* (Vienna, second ed., 1900).

III. SCHRIFTENARCHIV.

The Schriftenarchiv contains no materials relating to American history prior to 1780. Indices to the " Protokolle " are very accessible for the period 1740-1848. The following entries appear, from 1780 on; some of the acta have been destroyed (cassiert), others preserved (asserviert).

1780.

G. 756. Nr. 1433. Rekruten werden von Reichs-Ständen an Engelland überlassen, u. nach Amerika abgeschickt. " Feldmarschall Lt. Prinz von Nassau-Usingen (Frankfurt den 23. Februar 1780) zeiget an, dass vermög. eingegangener Meldung des Obristlieutenants Otto auf der Margräflich Bayreutischen Berg-Vestung Blasenburg gegen 160 Rekruten meistens Ausländer und Deserteurs, worunter sich etliche 20 Kayserliche befinden sollen, verwahret, und zu Completirung deren vom Herrn Margrafen von Anspach an England nach Amerika abgegebenen Truppen bestimmt wären, und sollten selbe, der Sage nach, mit Anfang Märzens durch die Reichs Lande, und sodann weiters zu Wasser dahin transportiret werden." Frankfurt, Feb. 23, 1780.

Nr. 1434. " Major Grün und Hauptmann La Sollaye und den aus dem Reich gebürtigen Kaiserl. Soldaten Urlaub erteilt." (Inquiry added, whether it might be possible to get the deserters back.)

G. 1724. Nr. 3355. " Feldmarschall Lt. Prinz von Nassau-Usingen, den 31. May 1780, zeigt an, dass bei Höxter auf der Weser 1000 Recrouten nach Amerika vorbei passiret synd."

G. 2677. Nr. 5113. " Prinz zu Nassau-Usingen, Erfurt den 29. August 1780, zeiget an auf die Verordnung von—Juni Hindernisse, welche der Beförderung der diesseitigen Werbung im Reich im Weeg stehen, worunter besonders auch der in Mittel- und Nieder-Teutschland anhaltende Zulauf zu denen Werbungen der verschiedenen Reichsfürsten, so ihre Regimenter in Amerika zu ergänzen haben, vorzüglich aber die im ganzen Reich zerstreute Preussisch- und Dänische Werbungen begriffen sind, weil diese, und besonders die Preussische nun wiederum die vor dem letzten Krieg gehabten Hang und Zugang völlig, ja noch mehr hergestellet hat. [pag. 2678] Ohngeachtet dessen aber sey der Recruten Zuwachs in denen verflossenen Monaten dieses Jahres in seinem Verhältnis gegen die letzteren zwei Jahre nicht geringer. Indessen werde Berichtleger die untergebenen Werb Officiers die bessere Betreibung der Werbung einzubinden, auch wenn es diese Officiers besser kennen lernen, und darunter einige minder taugliche, oder unfleissige antreffen wird, deren Ablösung zu veranlassen nicht ermangeln."

Erledigung des Exhibiti, pag. 2677. " Soweit die Kayserl. Werbung in den Reichs Landen dadurch einen Abbruch zu erleiden hat, dass Reichs Unterthanen nacher America geschickt werden, muss der Reichswerbungs Directeur sich mit den betreffenden Ministres im Reich darüber einvernehmen, ob nicht etwa aus dem Grunde des Auswanderungs Edicts diesem Uebel Einhalt zu verschaffen thunlich seyn könnte, wohingegen, so viel die Anstalten betrifft, wodurch die Kayserlichen vor der Preussischen Werbung auf dem

Reichs Boden der Vorzug zuwege zu bringen seyn mag, in den pag. 2678 Reichswerbungs Directeur das Vertrauen gesetzet wird, es werde derselbe, je nachdem es hierzu schickliche Mittel und Wege vorkommen, sich solche zu Nutzen zu machen und derowegen ins besondere auch denen zur Werbung bestellten Offiziers die diensame Belehrung zu erteilen besorgt seyn."

B. 880. "Dass die Kayserl. Unterthanen mit ihren Schiffen von dem Französischen Droit de Frèt befreyet seyen." (An das Carlstädter General Commando.)

B. 944. Questions and inquiries.
"Einen proviantischen Handel aus diesseitigen Landen nach den französischen Besitzungen allda einzuleiten ist der Antrag, und wird dieserwegen das Nöthige veranlasset."

W. 1110. "Nur bis Toulon, Marseille u. dgl. wollen diesseitige Seefahrer die Körner liefern. Gefahr wegen der Barbaresquen. Zengger-Schiffe zur Fahrt nach America nicht erbaut."

B. 1187. Weitere Mitteilungen an das Carlstädter General Commando.

1781.

B. 247. "Mit Salz dahin handeln zu dürfen haben diesseitige Seefahrer gebethen, und ist das Nöthige darüber veranlasset worden."
"Susanni Marcus, Handelsmann von Zengg, bittet, eine Ladung Salzes von Trappani, welches das beste zu Einsalzung des Fleisches ist, mittelst seines Schiffes *La Madona del Carmine* genannt, nacher Zengg verführen lassen zu können, und sodann mit solchem weiter nacher Frankreich und America zu handeln." (Referred to Carlstädter General Commando, and granted.)

G. 1543. "Reichswerbungs Directeur Prinz Nassau zeiget an, dass den 5ten April 1500 Hessisch-Waldekische und Anspachische, dann den 18. dicti 800 Hannauische Recruten auf der Weser bei Höxter vorbeigeschifft seyen, um nach Engelland zu Verstärkung deren in America in englischem Sold dienenden Truppen abzufahren." May 10, 1781.

G. 1767. Acknowledgment of the above: "An verschiedenen Reichs Landen nach America abgegangene Truppen."

G. 2137. "Nassau-Usingen, Reichs Werbungs-Directeur zeiget an, dass nicht nur in der Reichsstadt Müllhausen und Nordhausen Chur-Hannöversche Werbungen eingenommen worden seyen, sondern auch dem Vernehmen nach diese Werbung sich in mehrere Reichsstädte vorbereiten solle, die ihre aufgebrachte Recruten zum Dienst der Crone Engellands nacher America fortschleppet, mit dem Beysatz, dass auch in Frankfurth einige Werbcommandirte eingerücket, und von diesen ein Officier mit einigen Commandirten nacher Wissbaden im Nassau-Usingschen aufgenommen worden seyn." July 14, 1781.

G. 2197. Erledigung des Exhibiti: "Das mit der Reichs Canzlei do. 1777 verabredete Hilfsmittel bestehe darin, dass bey den Chur- und Oberrheinischen Creisen, hauptsächlich bey Chur Pfalz, auch andern am Rheine liegenden Ständen erwürket werde, dass sie dem Volksauszuge Schranken setzen, den durchziehenden Transporten Unterthanen und Deserteurs abnehmen, allenfalls hierzu den Kayserl. Beystand aufrufen, zu welchem Ende diesseitige Werb Officiers ohne Aufsehen zu machen, auf alle Fälle, wo Reichs Unterthanen auswandern mögen, aufmerksam zu seyn, und davon im vertraulichen Wege, jene Stände, in deren Bezirke sie sich befinden, noch in Zeiten zu verständigen haben." Kriegshof Kanzlei, Aug. 2, 1781.

G. 2319. Acknowledgment of the above.

G. 2368. "Werbungen für die englischen Truppen in America werden im Reich aufgestellt, und wird wegen deren Abschaffung das Nöthige veranlasst."

"Werb Depot will in einigen Reichsstädten v. allda für die zum Dienst der englisch-ostindischen Compagnie allda v. in der Schweiz aufgebrachte Recruten errichtet werden, und wie diesfalls Abhülf zu treffen wird die Weisung gegeben."

G. 2664. "Englische Recruten Transports (aus dem oberen Theil Schwabens) sind von diesseitigen Militari angehalten worden." Erledigung: "Dürfen nur in so weit und so lange angehalten werden können, als nothwendig ist, die darunter befindliche diesseitige Landeskinder und Deserteure zu untersuchen und abzunehmen."

1782.

G. 974. "Recruten sind in Reichs Landen für fremde Mächte angeworben, und dahin transportirt worden, welches angezeigt, und das weitere darüber veranlasst worden."

Nr. 238: "Zu Anspach aufgebrachte Jäger über Hanau und Bremerleh für Cron Engelland nach America abgegangen."

1783.

G. 4, 164. "Werbungen sind für dortige Engelländische Truppen in Reichs Landen aufgestellet worden, und wird wegen deren Abschaffung, dann Verhinderung der Auswanderung der Reichs Unterthanen dahin die Vorsicht getroffen."

G. 1608. "Handlungsschiffe diesseitige sind auf der Rückreise von America zu Grund gegangen."

G. 2181, 2278. "Hessische Truppen in englischem Sold gestandene (und zurück erwartete) werden zu diesseitigen Diensten angebothen, und hierauf der Entschluss ertheilt."

B. 892. "Commerzienrath Kayserl. (Freyherr von Beelen) ist zur Beförderung der wechselseitigen Handlung zwischen dies- und jenseitigen Unterthanen dahin abgesendet und solches kundgemacht worden."

1784.

J. 1017, 1060. "Officiers dasige, bitten in K. K. Dienste angenommen zu werden, und folgt der Entschluss."

"Der Sohn des dortigen Hauptmanns von Brahm [*i. e.*, of Lieut.-Col. Ferdinand de Brahm, U. S. A.], welcher 10 Jahre als Ingenieurs Officier in Diensten des americanischen Congress gestanden auch wegen Wohlverhalten und ganz besonderen Kenntnissen zum

Obristlieut. ernannt, und mit dem Cincinnatus Orden beehrt worden ist, Gesundheits halber nach America zurückzukehren nicht mehr gesinnt, und da demselben andere Dienste in Europa angebothen worden, so wünschte gedachter K. Minister (Baron Duminique, Chur-Trier. Staatsminister), dass selber wegen seiner besonderen Fähigkeit vorzüglich in K. K. Dienste genommen werden möchte." Petition not granted, apparently in deference to monarchical principles.

1787.

A. 633. " Auswanderung nach America wird angesucht bewilliget oder abgeschlagen." (Passes granted to two women for Mexico.)

1789.

G. 221, 324, 472, 547, 1070, 1947, 2039. " Körner Lieferungen von America sind von Particularen (Beneke u. Pfister) angebothen, und das Nöthige veranlasset worden."

1791.

G. 8479. " Verordnungen den Zoll für Otterbälge betreffende, werden publicirt."

1794.

B. 80. " Pest Uebel soll alldort [Philadelphia] ausgebrochen seyn, und werden dagegen die nöthigen Vorkehrungen getroffen." (Quarantine of 14 days on ships from Philadelphia.)

G. 2692. " Ein Corps zu einer in Frankreichs Staaten auszuführenden Revolution aus französischen Deserteurs, Vertriebener, Emigrirten, und Kriegsgefangenen zusammenzusetzen wird vorgeschlagen, und das weitere verhandelt."

See also G. 2791, and acta fasc. 62, no. 574 ; also fasc. 9, no. 620.

1811.

G. 4–6/13, 25. " Kriegspässe dahin [America] Aufenthalt daselbst, ob solcher einigen Officiers ohne Compromittirung zu gestatten sey?"

G. 4–6/25. " Beurlaubung dahin, ob dagegen in politischer Hinsicht keine Umstände obwalten?"

1815.

M. 1–17/16. "Aufnahme, ob und welche den Nordamerikanischen Kriegsschiffen in diesseitigen Häfen zu gewähren sey?"

M. 1–1/9. " Fahrzeuge entbehrlicher, oder unbrauchbarer Veräusserung, oder Versteigerung, diesfällige Ausweise, Protokolle und Verhandlungen."

L. 4–13/211, 230. " Behandlung der unter der neapolitanischen Kriegsgefangenen befindlichen, jenseits der Meere gebürtigen Individuen, und ob entlassen werden dürfen."

1816.

N. 2–7/1. "Erbteil Erfolgmachungs Gesuche daher, und diesfällige Verfügung."
K. 11–1, K. 11–1/1. "Falschwerber ziehen herum—Massregeln gegen dieselben."
J. 1–13/98, 111, 132. "Massen Ausfuhr für die spanisch americanische Insurgenten zu verhindern."
M. 1–22/75. "Bestimmung einer Escadre zur Ueberschiffung der Gesandtschaft nach Brasilien."

1817.

M. 1–66/2-6. "Anschaffungen von Materialien für die nach Brasilien bestimmte Expedition sind nicht durch die bestimmte Gold Dotation, sondern durch den hierzu angewiesenen Vorschuss zu bewerkstelligen."
D. 9–3. "Einige allda sich aufhalten sollende Partheien."
N. 10–1. "Erbschaften auszufolgen wird angesucht und Entschluss."
"General Consuln werden für dortige Häfen angestellt."

1818.

[1] "Erbschaften auszufolgen wird angesucht, und Entschluss."

1819.

"Erbauung neuer Fregatten nach dem Modelle der Fregatten ersten Ranges in der dortigen [amerikanischer] Seemacht. Antrag und Entschluss."
"Unterstützungs Einwirkung in ministeriellem Weg von allda lebenden Verwandten, wird von Officiers Frauen angesucht, und Entschluss."
"Postportogebühren für Briefe nach America, oder den dortigen Colonien bestimmte."

1820.

"Anbau des californischen Waizens, Versuche und Resultate."
"Erbschaften auszufolgen."

1821.

"Nachrichten über die Fahrt, den Zustand und die sonstigen Ereignisse der Marine Expedition nach Brasilien und China."

1822.

"Marine Expedition nach China. Nachrichten über die Fahrt usw."
"Ausfuhrs Pässe für nach America auszuführende englische Feuergewehre abverlangte."
"Erbschaften auszufolgen, angesuchte und Entschluss."

[1] The very numerous references to volume and pages, in this and following years, may be found in the indices.

1823.

"Ausfuhrs Pässe für nach America auszuführende englische Feuergewehre."
Waffen Ausfuhrs Verbothe, Aufhebungsgesuche von Feuerwehr Fabrikanten.
Anbau ausländischer Getreide Arten, Versuche und Resultate.
Fürnüsz, neu erfundenen, oder den nordamerikanischen Feuerversicherungs Anstrich bei aerarial Gebäuden anzuwenden, Antrag."
"Erbschaften auszufolgen."

1824.

"Samengattungen ausländischer, Anbau, Versuch und Resultate."
"Confiscirtes Privat Eigentum während der Kriegs Ereignisse."
"Schiffbauhölzer, ob in Salzwasser zu legen, etc."
"Allerhöchste Zufriedenheit mit dem Kommandanten u. Equipagen der im Jahre 1817 gemachten Fahrt nach Brasilien."
"Grenzer und sonstige Partheien."
"Freypass Erfolglassungs Gesuche zur Pulverausfuhr dahin."
"Beschlagung der Marine Fahrzeuge unter der Wasserlinie mit Leder statt Kupfer und Zink."

1825.

"Samen Gattungen."
"Land- oder Seekarten der Marine."
"Privateigentum, confiscirtes, während der Kriegsjahre."
"Fregatten ersten Ranges."

1826.

"Erbauung neuer Fregatten vom Grunde aus nach dem Bauplan der nordamericanischen Fregatten ersten Ranges."
"Nordamericanische Erfindung: Telescop zur Durchforschung des Grundes der Ströme und Flüsse, etc., ob anwendbar?"
"Erbschaften auszufolgen."
"Waffen Ausfuhr Verbot."
"Zusammenstossen K. K. Kriegsfahrzeuge mit fremden."
"Rückkehr K. öster. Unterthanen in die K. K. Staaten."

1827.

"Land- und Seekarten." "Telescop."
"Urlaubs Anträge." "Reisepässe öster. Militairs."
"Unter dortiger Flagge escortirte Handelsschiffe."
"Erbschaften."

1828.

"Urlaubsbewilligung."
"Erbschaften."
"Kupferbeschlag der Fahrzeuge nach Art der Americaner."
"Schädlichkeit des Peches für den Kupferbeschlag."
"Hilfeleistungen einigen k. k. Kriegsfahrzeugen (bei unglücklichen Ereignissen) durch Mercantilfahrzeuge erwiesen."
"Differenzial Gebühren eingestellt."

1829.

" Erbschaften."
" Leopoldinenstiftung zur Unterstützung der americanischen katholischen Missionen."
" Einlaufen dortiger Fahrzeuge."
" Bericht des Secretairs für Kriegs- und Marine Angelegenheiten."
" Zerstörung der Schiffs Kupferbleche."
" Differenzial Gebühren eingestellt."
" Segel, baumwollene, statt der bisher üblichen hanfenen bei der nordamericanischen Marine."

1830.

" Marine Eisenbahnen."
" *Reise des Herzogs Bernhard von Sachsen Weimar nach Nordamerica.* Anschaffung und Uebermachung dieses Werkes."

1831.

" Verein zur Unterstützung der americanisch katholischen Mission, unter dem Namen Leopoldinen Errichtung, und Geldbeiträge Einsendung."
" Kupferbeschlag der Marinefahrzeuge nach americanischer Art."
" Handels- und Schiffahrts Traktat zwischen Oesterreich und den nordamericanischen Freistaaten."
" Merkantilfahrzeuge, dortige, in diesseitigen Häfen in Brand gerathene, ob und welche Hülfe denselben geleistet, dann deren Rettung oder Untergang."

1832.

" Verein zur Unterstützung der americanisch katholischen Mission- dann Geldbeiträge Einsendung."
" Paquetboots Fahrt Etablirung, zur Erhaltung eines regelmässigen überseeischen Dienstes Verbindung, im Wege der Aerarial Regie- oder einer zu patentierenden Privat-Entreprise, Anträge und Verfügungen."

1833.

" Dampfbootsmaschinen Verkaufs Offert an die k. k. Kriegsmarine und Entschluss."
" Dampfbootsmaschinen für die k. k. Kriegsmarine ob aus England oder aus Nordamerica vorzuziehen wäre?"
" Schiffszwieback nach America."
" Chronometer." " Blech Schüsseln für warme Getränke."
" Pharmaceutische Artikel." " Matrosen Mund-Razion."

1834.

" Sextanten englischer Construction von neuester Art."
" Sextanten alter Construction."
" New-Yorker Consulat."
" Zufriedenheit des Hofkriegsraths mit dem Stabe der Expedizion nach America."

" Original Constitute der nach Nordamerica überschifften russisch-polenschen Flüchtlinge, Deckstellung, nach Zurücklassung von deren Abschriften bei dem k. k. General Consulate in New York."

1835.

" Bücher, auf Dampfschiffbau und Dampfschiffahrt bezügliche, aus New York überbracht."
" Postporto für Amtspakete."
" Tabakpflanzen-Samen." " Thermometer Anschaffung."
" Dampfmaschinen Modelle. Anschaff und Bekostung."
" Fahrten der k. k. Kriegsfahrzeuge und Einlaufen derselben."
" Benehmen der russisch-polenschen Flüchtlinge bei ihrer Ueberschiffung auf k. k. Kriegsfahrzeugen nach Nordamerica."
" Kosten-Nachweisung. Vorbereitungen zur Expedizion einiger k. k. Kriegsfahrzeuge zur Reise nach Nordamerica."
" An Bordnahme italienischer Hochverrats Sträflinge und ihrer Familien auf k. k. Kriegsfahrzeugen, deren Behandlung, Verpflegung, Uebergabe und Uebernahme."
" Verbannung nach America der Hochverräter der Giovani Italia allergnädigst bewilligte, auch auf die Milt Sträflinge dieser Secte auszudehnen Ansuchen."

1836.

" Eigenschaften der grösseren Inbarkazion der verschiedenen Schiffsgattungen."
" Expedizion nach Nordamerica."
" An Bordnahme italienischer Hochverrats Sträflinge. Auslagen."
" Seekarten."
" Auslagen der Entsendung russisch-polnischer Flüchtlinge nach Nordamerica."
" Panatica höhere (bessere Verköstigung)."

1837.

" See Expedizion nach americanischen Häfen."
" Italienische Hochverraths Sträflinge."
" Medicamente etc." " Panatica höhere." " Speise- und Getränksartikel."
" Ueberführung russisch-polnischer Flüchtlinge."

1838.

" Gesandten Stelle Verleihung an Generals, ohne militärische Gebühren."
" Verpflegsauslagen."

1839.

" Mehrauslagen."
" Massregeln zum Verkehr fremder aus Gegenden, in welchen das gelbe Fieber herrscht, kommenden Schiffe."
" Pontons."
" Eigentum eines abgelebten Bürgers der Vereinigten Staaten ist ohne Einvernehmen des Consuls nicht zu veräussern."

1840.
"Mehrauslagen für Ueberschiffung russisch-polnischer Flüchtlinge."
"Marine Angelegenheiten." "Pontons."

1841.
Continuation of foregoing subjects.

1842.
Continuation as above.
"Einschiffungsbewilligung Ertheilung für Marine Officiers Söhne auf americanischen Schiffen."

1843.
"Umänderung im Leuchtfeuer System."
"Ankunft dortiger Kriegsfahrzeuge in österreichischen Häfen."
"Kriegsbrücken."

1844.
"Erbschaftsfälle, etc."
"Bekanntgebung der zwischen Oesterreich und den nordamericanischen Freystaaten Schiffahrts- und Handelstraktat."

1845.
Naval affairs and events.

1846.
"Mitgliedsdiploma des nordamericanischen National Instituts."
"Notizen über verstorbene ehemalige Officiers."

1847.
"Auswanderungsbewilligung."
Routine matters.

1848.
"Urlaubsbewilligung."
"Congressverhandlungen der Vereinigten Staaten."
"Russisch-polnische Flüchtlinge."

MEMOIREN.
Akten, Amerika betreffend.

Mem. 28/104. "Kapitulationen zwischen dem amerikanischen General Washington und dem französischen General Rochambeau, dann dem englischen General Lord Cornwallis [in York] und Gloucester." Two documents. 1781.

Mem. 28/606. "Ueber Amerika, dessen Unabhängigkeitskrieg, Sitten und Einrichtungen." Three note-books. 1824.

Mem. 22/55. "Statistik von Nordamerika, Columbia und Mexico." Quarto note-book. 1836.

Mem. 18/163. "Stand und Organisation der Armee und Seemacht Nordamerikas." Six documents. 1840.
Mem. 18/169. "Notizen über die Land- und Seemacht der nordamerikanischen Freistaaten." Bundle. 844.
Mem. 18/234. "Die spanische Armee in Amerika." One document, no date.

IV. KARTENARCHIV.

There is a card catalogue (Zettelkatalog) provided for this very large collection of maps. There are three divisions: (a) Politische, (b) Physikalische, (c) Fachwissenschaftliche Karten (including maps showing railroads, canals, postal-telegraph, military roads, etc.). The political maps include a section containing maps of Canada, the United States, Mexico, Central America, West Indies, etc. There are also maps of American cities. The war maps include the periods: "Engländer gegen die Spanier in Amerika"; "Nordamerikanischer Freiheitskrieg, 1775-1783"; "Krieg von 1861-1865."

A rare map is one in four volumes illustrating Santo Domingo. It is carefully executed by hand, and done in water-color. It is not complete, is without date, and bears the titles: "Plans des Lieux Principaux de St. Dominique.—Table des Plans relatifs au mémoire sur la defense Terrestre de St. Dominique." It was taken from Paris by the Allies in 1815.

ALLGEMEINES ARCHIV DES K. K. MINISTERIUMS DES INNERN.

Location: Wien I., Judenplatz 11. Building not modern.
Hours: Daily 9.30 a. m. to 3.30 p. m.
Bibliography: Inventar des Allgemeinen Archivs des Ministeriums des Innern, bearbeitet von den Beamten dieses Archivs (Vienna, 1909, pp. 95).

Recent works based on researches in this archive covering periods for which the documents are usually not accessible:

August Fournier, *Historische Studien und Skizzen,* 3 Teile (Vienna and Leipzig, 1912).
Heinrich Friedjung, *Oesterreich von 1848-1860,* two vols. (Stuttgart and Berlin, 1908).
L. Geiger, *Das junge Deutschland* (Berlin, 1907).
K. Glossy, *Literarische Geheimbericht aus dem Vormärz* (Vienna, 1913).
Herm. Gnau, *Die Zensur unter Joseph II.* (Strassburg and Leipzig, 1911).
Augusto Sandonà, *Contributo alla Storia dei Processi del Ventuno e dello Spielberg, 1821-1838* (Turin, 1910).

The only section of this archive which contains any materials relating to American history is the division "Polizeiakten", which reveals the inner workings of the Metternich spying system. The period not accessible, after 1848, probably contains more material on political refugees.

9. Neuere Polizeiakten 1793-1848, Fasz. 1-1902.

1804.

98. Auswanderungsversuche.
Amerikanische Werbkommissare.

1805.

317. Ansiedler, für Spanien und Nordamerika.

1812.

3131. " Vier Amerikaner, welche über Prag und Brünn in Presburg eingetroffen sind und ihre Reise über Pesth nach Constantinopel fortsetzen." Four names difficult to decipher: Miller, Rising, Wanhil[l] (?), Di[n]smore (?).

1813.

1311. Tyroler Ansiedlungsangelegenheiten.

1814.

4379. Auswanderung der Tyroler.

1815.

53. Auswanderung aus Südtyrol, etc., nach Spanien, etc.
486. Nordamerikaner wegen Tabakhandel.

1816.

119, 207, 2890. Auswanderung nach Nordamerika.

1817.

44. Auswanderung der Tyroler nach Spanien und Amerika.
283, 7072, 8611. Amerikanische Emisseure in Livorno.
5034, 5535. Nordamerikanische Regierung, welche geneigt sein soll die Schiffe im venezianischen Arsenal anzukaufen. Neger-Regierung.
5510. Nordamerikan. General Konsulat. Auskünfte über dessen Competenten.

1818.

11977/9. Americana, neue Sektenbenennung in Italien.

1819.

5541. Nordamerikanische Grundstücke. Verein in Deutschland zum Handel mit selben.

1820.

1043. Auswanderer nach Amerika, angeblich debauchiert durch den Kaufmann v. Meredyth.

1821.

2835. Amerikanische Gesellschaft in Bologna.
6317, 7786, 8797, 9667, etc. Americani Cacciatori.

1822.

3782. Auswanderung nach Brasilien.
606, 838, 2104, 2564, 5337, etc., etc. Americani Cacciatori, neue Sekte im Päpstlichen.
1817, 1959, 3973, 4202, etc. Natter, Joh. Jos., Commandeur und Pfarrer der Karlskirche allhier. Entweichung.

1823.

4526. Karl Postl gew. Sekretär der Kreuzherrn in Prag. Eleven acta concerning the fugitive monk Carl Postl, who fled from the Kreuzherrn monastery in Prague, travelled in the United States and Mexico, and wrote very popular novels descriptive of American life, under the pen-name Charles Sealsfield.
(a) Der Kreuzherr Commandeur Stöhr an den Bürger M. von Carlsbad. Eger, June 13, 1823.
(b) Dekret von der K. K. Polizei Ober Direkzion. Vienna, June 27, 1823.
(c) An den Hrn. Präs. der K. K. Polizeihofstelle. June 12, 1823.
(d) Jos. Köhler, Gen. Grossmeister an Hochw. Fürst-Erzbisch. Konsistorium. June 9, 1823.
(e) Zimmermann an d. Skriptor d. Universitätsbibliothek Hrn. Hanslik. Prag, May 29, 1823.
(f) Inquiries about Postl; unfavorable. " Es ist für den Orden besser, wenn zur Schonung des Ganzen der Einzelne nicht geschont wird." Vienna, June 6, 1823.
(g) Concerning Postl's movements. Karlsbad, June 2, 1823.
(h) Der Elbogener Dechant Pecher an d. Pater Joh. Fischer, Amtmeister d. Kreuzherrnordens in Prag. Elbogen, May 27, 1823.
(i) Der Bürger M. an d. Kreuzherrn Commandeur Stöhr in Eger. Karlsbad, June 2, 1823.
(j) Schraml an d. vormal. Sekretär d. Kreuzherrnordens Pater Karl Postl, nach Karlsbad. Wlaschin, May 24, 1823.
(k) Including a personal description of Postl. June 7, 1823.

1824.

7160. Auswanderung nach Brasilien.

1825.

3891. Auswanderung nach Brasilien.

1826.

1383, 2064. Flüchtlinge in der Schweiz.

1827.

1054, 1683, 3484. Neues Auswanderungs-patent.

1829.

828. Auswanderung nach Brasilien.

1830.

7080. Auswanderung nach Nordamerika.
3726, 7080. Religionsschwärmersekte des Bernhard Müller zu Offenbach (bundle of papers).
Religionsschwärmerische Gesellschaft, zu Frankfurt.
Maximilian Bernard Proli, zu Offenbach, angeblich Stifter einer politisch-religiösen Gesellschaft.[1]
6041. Nordamerikanische Gelehrte Gesellschaft u. Freymaurer.

1831.

7371. Nordamerikan. Schiffahrts- u. Handelsvertrag.
10838. Nordamerikanischer Freistaat, Bericht über den moralisch-politischen Zustand, durch die V. Magdalenengesellschaft.

1835.

6266, 6731. Amerikanische Auswanderung. Paul Szirmay (enthusiast for a plan of emigration) zu Giralth bei Eperjes.
5523. Paul Szirmay (Hermann), dessen Auswanderungsprojekt nach Amerika.
Reise nach Hüben, nach Amerika.
5523. Gottfried Duden in Bonn. Schreiben an ihn, des P. Szirmay.
8009. 11065. Deportation italienischer Hochverräter, Sträflinge.
8187. Flugschrift alldort gegen die katholische Religion und Oesterreich: *Foreign Conspiracy.*
11560. Amerikanische Gesellschaft zur Verbesserung des Zustandes und zur Bekehrung der Juden.
Colonien am Hudson, gegründet zur Besserung ihres (der Juden) Zustandes, von einer amerikanischen Gesellschaft.

1836.

5437. Auswanderungs-Patent v. 24. März, 1832. Bemerkungen hierüber des Mailänder Gen. Direktors.
31, 4413. Auswanderungsverfahren gegen lombardisch-venez. polit. Flüchtlinge.
7536, 8298. Auswanderungen aus Böhmen nach Amerika (Brasilien).
1610. Deportirte nach Amerika, in dem galizischen Hochverratsprozess verflochtene Individuen.
30. Deportirte, italienische, Hochverräter. Sträflinge nach Amerika. (Two pages of names.)

1837.

790, 4375. Auswanderungen, nach Amerika (Brasilien).
7087, 1470, 4472, 472. Schwierigkeiten bei Aufnahme der Emigranten in New York. (Lederer's report.)
455 (and numerous other references, see manuscript index). Deportirte, italienische Hochverräter in Amerika.

---

[1] *Cf.* J. Hanno Deiler, *Eine Vergessene Deutsche Colonie: eine Stimme zur Verteidigung des Grafen de Leon, alias Proli, alias Bernhard Müller* (New Orleans, 1900).

1838.
9289. Nordamerika, Auswanderungen dahin.
1490. Nordamerikanischer Konsul in Algier.
1444, etc., etc. Italienische Deportirte in Nordamerika. Hochverrats Sträflinge.

1840.
4490. Amerika, Passausstellungen dahin.
7352, 7963. Die katholisch-bischöfliche Administration in Nordamerika. Broschüre.
2622, 2668. Deportirte italienische Hochverräter. Behandlung.

1841.
10525. Friedrich Baraga, Priester aus Laibach, Missionär in Nordamerika. Manuskript: " Christliches Erbauungsbuch in der Sprache der amerikanischen Otawas-Indianer."
1993. Deportirte italienische Hochverräter.

1842.
2934, etc. Deportirte, italienische, nach Nordamerika.

1843.
7766, etc. Deportirte, italienische, nach Nordamerika.

1844.
4658, 7188. Amerikaner, reisende.

1846.
2098. Nordamerikanische Pässe, falsche.
2007, 2126, 613, 3358, etc., etc. Amerika, Auswanderungen dahin.
2997. Auswanderungen nach Texas.
3504. Kaufmann Leopold Förstl (Ferstl).

1847.
10139. Nordamerika, Auswanderung dahin. Friedrich Wilhelm Bornemann, Inhaber einer Agentur für Auswanderer nach Nordamerika zu Hannoverisch Münden.
8152. Nordamerika, Revolutionäre Teutschen-Vereine daselbst. Verein zur Beförderung revol. Umtriebe in Deutschland.
12606. Brünn, Press Confiszierung.
328, 1108, 1905, 2595, 5796, 6367, 6986, etc. Karl Heinzen. Dessen Pamphlet: *Der Teutsche Tribun.* Neue revol. Schrift v. K. Heinzen: *Die Teutsche Revolution.*

1848.
209, 210, 438, 1530. Karl Heinzen, Gewes. preuss. Landwehroffizier. Aus der Schweiz gewiesen; nach New York.

K. u. K. GEMEINSAMES FINANZ-ARCHIV (HOFKAMMER-ARCHIV).

Location: Wien I., Johannesgasse 6. Five-story building specially constructed for the purpose, in 1833.
Hours: 9 a. m. to 2 p. m., except Sundays and holidays.
Bibliography: Inventar des Archivs des K. K. Finanz-Ministeriums, hrg. v. d. Direktion dieses Archivs (Vienna, 1911, pp. 77).
Fellner-Kretschmayr, *Geschichte der Oesterreichischen Zentralverwaltung,* three vols. (Vienna, 1907).

Three divisions of the Hofkammerarchiv contain materials relating to American history, viz.: Commerz Litorale, containing material of the eighteenth century mainly; Commerz Kammer, from 1807 to 1830; Commerz Commission, from 1807 to 1830.

COMMERZ LITORALE.

Litorale 5401. Commerz. 1755-1798.

No. 122. Austria's declaration of neutrality, June 14, 1756, in war between France and England in America.
" Mémoire sur le commerce avec les Isles Françoises en Amérique." Fait en 1756.
Treaty of commerce with France, 1798 (use of French ships in American trade).

Litorale 5356. Commerz. 1763-1809.

No. 104. A bundle of reports on the East and West Indies. Mostly concerned with the beginnings of shipping and trade with the East Indies. A report on the ship *Città di Trieste,* designed in 1781 for the trade in both Indies, is followed by several others, mentioning trading vessels between 1783-1787.
No. 280. " Vorschläge des Filippo Fabrini, Chur-Pfälzischen Hofrathes, und Präsidenten zu Pisa, enthalten ein Verzeichnis aller Erzeugnisse der Natur und Kunst, so in dem Kayserl. Königl. Erblanden vorhanden, oder nicht vorhanden seyn mögen, mit welchen der Verschleusz [Verkauf] in alle Welt-Theile vornehmlich nach America getrieben werden sollte, und sehen einem Glücks-Haven ganz ähnlich, wo die fehlende, und treffende Numeri untereinander vermischet sind, jene aber diese unendlich übersteigen. Präsident des Hofkommerzienraths: Graf Andler-Witten." Nov. 6, 1763. (This is an elaborate report written in Italian.)
" Die Vorschläge des Filippo Fabrini, und sein Gesuch um das k. k. Consulat in Toscana betreffend." Nov. 6, 1763.
" Die Aeusserungen des hiesigen Handelsstandes über die Commercialvorschläge des Filippo Fabrini betreffend." Jan. 30, 1764.
Votum: " Da also die Sache nur auf Speculationen beruhet, und niemand sich darstellet, Hand an das Werk zu legen, um einige Waaren in die Canarischen Insulen, oder directa nach America zu versenden; so sieht man hier Orten auch noch nicht, was für ein Gebrauch von den Vorschlägen des Filippo Fabrini gemacht werden könne, und man muss sich lediglich auf den vorhinigen allerunterthänigsten Vortrag beziehen. Dass übrigens E. k. k. A. Maj. allerseits erkennet haben, dass einen Consul in Toscana anzustellen, der Zeit nicht diensam, noch anständig sey."

1776-1777.

Aug. 17, 1776. "America, Project ein Commerce dahin einzuleiten. Christoph Beller, Hauptmann des Fabrischen Regiments, machet den Vorschlag, ihn nach America zu schicken, um alldort bei denen zwischen den Engländern und Colonisten obwaltenden Zwistigkeiten das Commerce zum Vortheil der k. k. Erblande einzuleiten."

1780-1781.

July 29, 1780. "America, wegen Verproviantirung der dortigen französischen Besitzungen von Seite der diesseitigen Handelsleuten."

1782-1783.

Aug. 7, 1783. "Die Dahinsendung des Freiherrn von Beelen zur Beförderung des diesseitigen Handels."

1792-1793.

Oct. 11, 1792. "Auswanderung, eigenmächtige, wie sich hiebey zu benehmen."
Oct. 25, 1792. "Amerikanische Staaten, Gesuch des Joseph Mussi um das General Consulat in selben."

1796.

Mar. 4, 1796. "Die Einleitung eines Consulats allda." Franz von Silbernagel offers plan of consulate. Refused June 30, 1796.

1801-1803.

Jan., 1802. John Lamson appointed American consul, asks for exequatur regium.
Feb., 1802. His Majesty grants exequatur.
Oct., 1802. William Riggin appears, stating that he was appointed U. S. consul in Triest; request for exequatur.
Nov., 1802. Exequatur of John Lamson suspended until explanation can be obtained.
Same date. Reply to Riggin that the matter will have to be cleared up before exequatur can be given.
Jan., 1803. Same reply to Riggin's repeated request.
Mar., 1803. Action taken to request His Majesty to grant exequatur to William Riggin as successor to Lamson, consul at Triest.

COMMERZ KAMMER. 1807-1830.

1814.

Lit. 38. Amerika, dort entdeckte Quecksilber Minen.

1815.

f. 17. "Amerika, dortiges Consulat."
f. 9. "Amerikanische Handelsleute um Bewilligung ihrer Handelsbücher in englischer Sprache führen zu dürfen."

f. 16. " Steamböthe, deren Einführung vom Grosshändler Perry vorgeschlagen."
f. 5. " Amerika, dass die englische Regierung die Einfuhr der österreichischen Manufakte dorthin untersagt habe."

1816.

f. 17. " Amerika, dort zu besetzendes Consulat."
f. 5. " Amerika, Britisches Einfuhrsverboth der Oester. Fabrikate und Manufakte dorthin."

1824.

f. 22. " Amerikanische Provenienzen, ob die Contumatz Periode nicht abzukürzen wäre?"

1825.

f. 16. " Amerika, dortiger Leinwandhandel."

1826.

f. 16. " Abzuschliessender Handelstraktat."

1829.

f. 5. " Amerika. Abgeschlossener Handels- und Schiffahrtstraktat zwischen Preussen und den Hansa-Städten."
f. 5. " Id. Dortiger Handel mit Triest."
f. 5. " Id. Zolltarif und Handel mit England."
f. 5. " Id. Handel mit Oesterreich und Wirkung des dortigen Zolltarifs auf den Handel."
f. 17. " Id. Schwendler zum Consul in Frankfurt ernannt."
f. 22. " Amerikanische Provenienzen, Contumaz gegen dieselben, und Handelstraktat mit."
f. 5. " Amerikanische Congressakte, von dem österreichischen Consulate in N. Y. eingesendete."
f. 16. " Abzuschliessender Handelstraktat mit Amerika."
f. 5. " Ausfall der heuerlichen Getreideernte in Amerika."
f. 16. " Nordamerika. Versuch statt hanfenen Schiffssegeln baumwollene anzuwenden."
f. 17. " J. G. Schwarz, amerikanischer Consul in Wien bittet um das Exequatur regium."
f. 5. " Amerika, dortiger Handelszustand und Bericht des General Consuls in N. Y."

1830.

f. 16. " Amerika, dortige Versuche mit baumwollenen Schiffssegeln."
f. 5. " Amerika, Handelstraktat."
f. 17. " Amerikanischer Consul in Wien, J. G. Schwarz." Exequatur.
f. 16. " Amerikanische Staaten, deren Zustand."
f. 16. " Leuchtthurm bei der Mündung des Delaware aufzustellen."

f. 5. "Amerika, dortiger Beschluss allen Nationen gegen Reciprocität Schiffahrts- und Handelsbegünstigungen anzutragen."
f. 5. "Id. Bill wegen Handel mit den britischen Kolonien."
f. 5. "Id. Handelstraktat mit England und Dänemark."
f. 5. "Id. Dortige Handelsverordnungen."
f. 31. "Amerikanische Spinnmaschine zu verbessern. Privilegium des Franz Schulters."
f. 5. "Amerika, dortige Getreidepreise."
f. 16. "Schiffahrts- und Handelsreciprocität zwischen Amerika und England."

COMMERZ COMMISSION.

1816.

f. 22. "Amerikanische Provenienzen. Contumaz-Zeit für dieselben."

1821.

f. 5. "Amerika. Quecksilberverkehr dahin und Stand der dortigen Glas- und Wollwarenfabriken."

1824.

f. 22. "Amerika. Von da kommende Waren sind den Sanitätsanstalten zu unterziehen."
Commerzial Notizen aus New York. Feb. 18, 1824.

1827.

f. 16. "Nordamerika und Brasilien, abzuschliessender Handelstraktat und Handelsbeförderung dahin."
f. 16. "Amerika, dürfen spanische Schiffe unter fremder Flagge einstweilen Handel treiben?"

1828.

f. 22. "Amerikanische Provenienzen, Contumaz gegen dieselben und Handelstraktat mit."
f. 16. "Nordamerikanische und Preussische Flagge, deren Gleichstellung."
f. 33. "Amerikanisch-Swiftsche Tuchscheermaschine zu verbessern; diesfäll. Privilegium des Franz Ludwig."

IMPERIAL LIBRARY.

(HOFBIBLIOTHEK.)

Location: K. K. Hofburg, Wien I., Josefsplatz 1.
Hours: 9 a. m. to 4 p. m., except on Sundays and holidays.
The Imperial Library contains a good collection of printed books on America grouped as follows: A. Allgemeiner Teil; B. Nordamerika: 1. Literatur; 2. Geographie, Reisen, Einwanderung; 3. Religion, Politik, Geschichte; 4. Verwaltung, Justiz, Indianer; 5. Agrikultur, Handel, Gewerbe, Verkehr; 6. Sanität, Wissenschaften, Statistik; C. Central- und Südamerika, Westindien.

Codex in Imperial Library.

12613 (Suppl. 602) ch. XVIII. 77f. " Discours sur la grandeur et importance de la dernière révolution de l'Amérique septentrionale ; sur les causes principales qui l'ont déterminée et sur son influence vraisemblable sur l'état politique et sur le commerce des puissances européennes. Codex archetypus ab auctore exaratus multisque lituris, additamentis, etc., exornatus operis pro solvenda quaestione academiae condonati."

ARCHIV DER STADT WIEN.

Location: In the New Rathaus, fronting on the Franzensring. An imposing Gothic building, completed in 1882. The archive contains materials from the thirteenth century to the present time. Nothing relating to American history was found in the archive proper; the acta enumerated below are contained in the Stadt Haupt-Registratur, which is under the same directorship.

Hours: Daily except Sundays, 9 a. m. to 2 p. m. The privilege of working in the archive must be secured in advance.

AKTEN DER STADT HAUPT-REGISTRATUR.

Ad Arch. **Z 53**es 1913. Betr. Vereinigte Staaten von Nordamerika :

1783. Die nach dem vereinigten Amerika handelnden Vasallen können sich an den k. k. Kommerzialrath Baron von Beelen nach Philadelphia wenden. Hofdekret vom 7. August 1783 (*Josephinische Gesetzsammlung,* 3 Band, VI. Hauptabteilung, Kommerziensachen).

1850. Passwerber für Nordamerika sind auf die Schwierigkeiten der Reise, wenn selbe ohne hinlängliche Geldmittel und Vorbereitung unternommen wird, aufmerksam zu machen und dies sowie die Art, wie der Passwerber seine Subsistenz zu decken gedenkt, in der Passanweisung anzumerken. Normale 42 ex 1850.

1852. Vorschrift über Passwerbungen für Amerika. Normale 92 ex 1852.

1853. Wiedereinwanderung aus Amerika ; solche Gesuche sind in der Regel zurückzuweisen und es ist den Auswanderungsbewerbern mitzuteilen, dass sie durch diesen Schritt jedes Recht auf Wiedereinwanderung und Wiederverlangung der österreichischen Staatsbürgerschaft verlieren. Normale 21 ex 1853.

Reiseerlaubnis für Amerika ist nur ausnahmsweise zu erteilen. Normale 137 ex 1853.

1854. Auswanderungswerber nach Amerika haben Geldmittel auszuweisen. Den Auswanderungsagenten ist eifrig nachzuspüren. Normale 42 ex 1854.

1857. Das Normale 21 ex 1853 ist wieder aufgehoben und es sind die Gesuche um Wiederaufnahme in den österr. Staatsverband nach den allgemeinen gesetzlichen Bestimmungen zu behandeln. Normale 17 ex 1857.

1874. Bestallungs-Diplom des General-konsuls der Vereinigten Staaten in Wien P. Sidney-Post. F4—200606, 1874.

David M. M. Gregg wird Konsul der Vereinigten Staaten in Prag. F4—64182, 1874.

1875. Bekanntgabe jener Klassen von Fremden, welcher die Einwanderung nach den Vereinigten Staaten nicht gestattet ist. Normale 19 ex 1875.
1881. Verbot der Einfuhr von Schweinen, Schweinefleisch, Speck, und Würsten aus den Vereinigten Staaten. G8—99211, 1881.
1885. Otto Maas wird zum Vice-Generalkonsul ernannt. Normale 89 ex 1885.
Die Kenntnis des dortigen Auswanderungsgesetzes vom 3/8 1882, nach welchem Verbrechern, blöden, wahnsinnigen, und subsistenzlosen Personen die Landung in Amerika nicht gestattet wird, ist möglichst zu verbreiten, auch ist bei Passbewerbung die Nachweisung der Subsistenzmittel zu fordern. Normale 59 ex 1885.
1886. Auswanderungslustige sind auf die Wertlosigkeit der Fahrkarten des " Stettiner Lloyd " aufmerksam zu machen. Normale 69 ex 1886.

SALZBURG.
ARCHIV DER K. K. LANDESREGIERUNG.

Location: In the K. K. Landesregierungsgebäude. Entrance, Mozartplatz.

Hours: Week-days, in summer, 9 a. m. to 2 p. m.; in winter, 9 a. m. to 1 p. m., and 4 to 6 p. m. Permission to use the archive is granted by the director.

Bibliography: Inventar des Landesregierungsarchivs in Salzburg, bearbeitet von den Beamten dieses Archivs im Auftrage des K. K. Ministeriums des Innern, in *Inventare Oesterreichischer Landesarchive,* III. (Vienna, 1912, pp. 88).

A. Prinzinger (d. j.), " Die Ansiedlung der Salzburger im Staate Georgien in Nordamerika ", in *Mitteilungen der Gesellschaft für Salzburger Landeskunde,* XXII. Vereinsjahr, pp. 1-36 (Salzburg, 1882).

A collection of printed materials, described by Prinzinger (pp. 1-2), relating to the Salzburgers in America, is to be found in the Bibliothek des Städtischen Museums, and the Studienbibliothek zu Salzburg.

The archive at Salzburg consists of remnants left over after the larger part had been sent to Vienna, forming there the section of the K. u. K. Haus-, Hof- und Staatsarchiv called Das salzburgisch-erzbischöfliche und Domkapitelarchiv. The latter was searched for materials of American history, but nothing was found, nor does the archive in Salzburg contain anything bearing directly upon American history. For the study of the causes that led up to the large forced emigration of the Protestant Salzburgers in 1731, the Salzburg archive is, however, of very great value. Since there was an important colony of Salzburg emigrants who came to Georgia in 1734, the causes for their emigration also bear upon American colonial history. For this reason the principal sources in the archive have been enumerated below, and typical entries have been recorded.

AKTEN C. : UNTERBEHÖRDEN.
FACH XXX. PFLEG- UND LANDGERICHTE.

Pfleg Werfen. Fach 1, resp. 31-63. 1675-1775. (*Cf.* Ia., Repertorium über die Acten von 1675-1775; über alle Bücher, Acten, u. Schriften der Hochfürstlich. Salzburgischen Probstey, und Pfleg Werfen, und des Landgerichts Bischofshof v. J. 1675 in 1775.)

FACH XXXIII. DOMKAPITELSCHES ARCHIV.

Religions-Sachen, Commissions- u. Straf-Acten, 1675-1775. A few typical headings from among a very large number of acta are cited below, from the years 1729-1731.

1729.

Nr. 122. "Des Philipp Gumbers et Consorten 25 Reichsthaler Straf wegen Lesung verbothener Bücher, und Verachtung der Brüderschaften."
123. "Zur Aufsicht auf die hereinschleichend Lutherische Bücher werden zwei Personen bestimmt."
124. "Ein Act von Nr.— über jene Personen die mit Fleischkochen, und Bücherlesen u. d. g. verbrochen haben."
125. "Ein Act von Nr.— dass die im Glauben verdächtige zur Einschreibung in eine Brüderschaft angehalten werden oder emigriren sollen, wobei die Erklärungen."
126. "Hans Thaner wird wegen einem verdächtigen Buch constituirt."

1731.

131. "Getraud Häuszlin, Baurin zu Hinterholz, ihre zwei Söhne, Georg und Hanns, auch Magdalena Gwehnbergerin werden wegen Lutherischen Büchern constituirt."
134. "Bei Ruppert Eder zu———werden Lutherische Bücher gefunden."
135. "Hanns Hubers Lutherische Bücher."
140. "Ein Act den von Nürnberg anher gekommen und verdächtig gehaltenen Peter Schwer Bildschnitzers Lehrling betref."
147. "Georg Frommers emigrirter Bauers Sohn von Kraxenbiehl alda nunmehr Bürgers zu Regenspurg angehengte Klag wieder das tyrannische Verfahren des hiesigen Hr. Pflegers Roman von Motzl gegen die evangelische, und der hiesigen Emigranten angegebener Beschwerden, durch die Gesandtschaft in Regensburg."

FACH XXXVII. AUFRUHR- UND EMIGRATIONS SACHEN.

("Allda fangen die Acten erst vom Jahre 1731 an, weilen zu dieser Zeit sich eigentlich die wegen der Religion entstandene Salzburgische Emigration angesponnen hat, worauf eine sonderbare geheime Deputation gesetzt worden.")

Nr. 1. "Ein Schreiben von St. Johans nebst einem Constitut, dass nämlich die Gemeinde ihre in Glaubenssachen erlittene Bedrückungen den Protestantischen Gesandtschaften in Regenspurg vorgetragen, und ihr von dort Schutz sey versprochen worden."
2. "Die Unterthanen sollen, laut Hofrathsbefehl, ihre Beschwerden der ankommenden Commission schriftlich übergeben."
3. "Von Hr. Dechant bey der Pfarr anher communicirte Berichts Abschrift, samt einer Copie der Glaubens Bekenntnis der Lutherischen Bauern von St. Veit."
6. "Peter Holnsteiners sive Bernhofers Entweichung."
8. "Verzeichnis der Bauern, die vor der Commission sich für evangelisch angegeben haben."
9. "Schreibens Abschrift, dass Hr. Pfleger auch zur Verantwortung über die etwane Commissionaliter eingegebenen Beschwerden gelassen werde."
11. "Schreiben an die Commission wegen gehaltenen Zusammenkünften."

13. " Designation der sich in der Hofmarch Bischofshof für evangelisch erklärten Personen."
14. " Die überschickte Specification der Evangelischen Unterthanen."
15. " Commissions Befehl dass den Unterthanen eine Remedur ihrer Beschwerden erfolgen, sie aber sich friedlich und ohne Rottierung verhalten sollen."
16. " Bericht dass sich die Werfener Gemeinde friedlich aufzuführen erbiethe."
17. " Copie die Zusammenkünften in der Schwarzach, und dabei gemachten Schluss lutherische Brediger zu überkommen, und einig Deputirte nach Regenspurg zu schicken."
19. " Schreiben wegen verdächtig ins Land schleichenden Personen."
20. " Die von da abmarschierte Bauern Rothen [Rotten], und mitgenommenes vieles Gold."
21. " Schreiben die von den Bauern ausgesprengte Verhack- und Verlegung der Weg- und Strassen."
22. " Hofraths Befehl die Rothierungen, und offentliche Bredigten der Unterthanen sind Verbothen."
25. " Mathiasen Elmenthallers wider Se. Hochfürstlichen Gnaden ausgestossen vermessene Reden, die Zusammenkünfte der Bauern und Bredigten betreffent."
26. " Einige Radlführer werden allda um Mitternacht gefänglich eingezogen."
27. " Das Pfleggericht St. Johanns befürchtet einen Angriff."
28. " Die Evangelisch sich erklärte Unterthanen sollen specificirter nebst der Beyrückung der Profession eingesandt werden."
29. " An Hochlobl. Hofkammer die Berechnung der mit angefangen. Rebellionstroubeln erloffene [aufgelaufene] Unkosten, dann ein Verzeichnis der evangelisch sich erklärten Unterthanen nebst ihr Steuer sollen eingesendet werden."
30. " Alle Feuerschützen sollen beschrieben, und ihre Gewehr zu Gericht geliefert werden."
31. " Die Einrückung der Kaiserlichen Hilfsvölker, und ihre Verpflegung."
33. " Das General Mandat, und Emigrations Patent ist zu publiciren, und anzuschlagen."
34. " Endliche Erfahrung wegen des Hauptaufwiegler Peter Holnsteiner Entweichung nach Regenspurg, und von dem in der Festung Werfen der Schmiedin zu Hüttau an ihren eingekerkerten Mann geschriebenen Brief."
37. " Was diejenige zu thun, die sich anfangs evangelisch angeben, und wieder zum katholischen Glauben umschreiben lassen."
39. " Befehl, kraft dessen der Emigrations Termin der Unansessigen wird verlängert auf 8 Tage."
40. " Befehl, dass wegen den Emigranten solle vor ihrer Abfahrt Richtigkeit gepflogen werden."
41. " Befehl, wie die Passport sollen für die Emigranten eingerichtet werden."
42. " Der Emigrations Termin wird auf Hl. Georgy festgesetzt, und dass die Emigranten bis 1734 ihre Güter von Katholischen nach Belieben können verwalten lassen."

Archiv der K. K. Landesregierung

44. "Erläuterung über vorhin angesetzten Emigrationstermin und ob die Unterthanen damit zufrieden, sollen Erfahrungen eingesendet werden."
45. "Wegen den gefangenen Rädlführern sollen eidliche Erfahrungen eingesendet werden."
47. "Die aus Brandenburg angekommene und nun in Verhaft sitzende Elisabeth Kraftin betreffend."
51. "Die verdächtige Zusammenkunft wird bey Leib- und Lebensstraf verbothen, doch wird jedem unkatholischen Hausvater bewilliget in seinem Haus der Andacht abzuwarten."
52. "Denen zu Salzburg inliegenden Unterthanen solle zur Medizin und andern Nothdurften Geld hinausgeschickt werden."
53. "Den emigrirenden Unterthanen solle in Verkaufung ihrer Habschaften nichts in Weg gelegt werden."
54. "Das Pfleggericht St. Johanns notifizirt dass aldort die Lutherischen Handwerker abgeschafft werden."
55. "Landschaftsbefehl, das Abzugsgeld solle von den Emigranten eingelangt werden."
57. "Die unkatholischen Unterthanen mit Uebung ihres Glaubens abgewiesen, doch ihnen der freye Auszug gestattet werden."
62. "Jene, da sich zu keiner Religion erklären, sollen constituirt werden."
65. "Was bey den von den Emigranten verlangten Vermögens Beschreibungen zu beobachten."

1732.

68. "Des Mathias Elmanthallers Bestrafung wegen wider Sr. Hochfürstl. Gnaden ausgestossenen Lästerungen."
71. "Kammerbefehl. Von den zu Salzburg inhastirten Unterthanen werden Schuld Beschreibungen hieher gesendet, wovon den Weibern Abschrift solle hinaus gegeben werden."
72. "Kammerbefehl, dass den emigrirenden Unterthanen in Vieh- und Getreid Verkauf nichts in Weg zu legen sey."
73. "Ein Solcher, dass der Emigranten Güter mit Bestandleuten, und Käufern versehn und bebaut werden sollen."
78. "Den emigrirenden Unterthanen steht frey ihre Güter in Bestand zu lassen, wie sie wollen."
81. "Deputationsbefehl, wegen von den Emigranten hinterlassenen Büchern sollen die Häuser visitirt, und die neuen Besitzer davor gewarnt werden."
83. "Deputations-Befehl, dass man den Emigranten den Titel: Evangelisch nicht geben solle."
94. "Verbothener Verkauf aller gedruckten Bücher."
96. "Die PP. [Patres] Capucini sollen die hiesigen Pfarrkinder in Glaubenssachen unterweisen."
99. "Wegen gefährlicher Correspondenz sollen die Bothen alle Brief zu Gericht einliefern."
100. "General Befehl das wiederholte Verboth der Rottirungen enthaltend."
102. "Bei den rückgebliebenen Unterthanen sollen fremde Dienstboten angestellt werden."

103. " Die von den PP. Capucinis als verdächtig angegebenen Personen sollen constituirt werden."
106. " Zur Patrol wegen verdächtigen Personen werden vom Schloss täglich 3 Mann ausgesendet."
108. " Ein Band Correspondenzen den Abmarsch, sowohl der hiesigen als von andern Gerichten anher gebrachten Emigranten."

1733.

116. " Generale, wie in Klagsache wider die abwesende Emigranten zu verfahren sey."
117. " Revers der emigrirenden Unterthanen. Jährlicher Aufruhr Strafschilling."
118. " Verdächtigen Personen ist ohne Vorwissen der Deportation kein Heuraths Schein zu ertheilen."
119. " Das Einstandrecht bey den Emigrantengütern ist aufgehoben."

1734.

142. " Den Beamten ist bey Verlust des Dienstes verbothen die in Glaubenssachen verdächtige Personen zu verdeuthigen, Schenkungen anzunehmen, bei Verbstand [Verpacht] und Erkaufung der Emigrantengüter ungebührende Gelder einzutreiben."
143. " Peter Strobls zu Stroblhof in der Abtenau Landsverweisung wegen Lutherischen Büchern."
148. " General Patent vom 26. Aug. 1734 die Verkaufung der Emigranten Güter, Eintreibung der Activ. Schulden, dann die Vollmacht v. König v. Preussen ertheilt dem Erich Christoph Edeln vom Ploto für die ins Preussen emigrirte Salzburger betref. Nebst 2 gedruckten Verzeichnissen der Emigranten Güter."

1735.

185. " Bey Abhandlung der Emigranten Güter ist die Tax wie bey den Katholischen einzulegen."
186. " Die unbewussten Emigrantengelder sollen zu Gericht genommen, und zugewartet werden, bis ein rechtmässiger Ansprecher vorkommt."

1738.

227. " Mit Abfertigung des Preussischen Hr. Abgeordneten solle mit allem Ernst Richtigkeit gemacht werden."

11. Band zum XXXVII. Fach.

Nachstehende Nummern sind in folio gebunden und bestehen von Nr. 269 in 292.

269-273. " Zwei Bücher Vermögensbeschreibungen der Emigranten, welche angesessen waren, und im Jahre 1732 ausgezogen sind."
274-277. " Beschreibung der An- und Unangesessenen Personen, die zu emigriren gesonnen, und an der Zahl 4006 sind, diese verlangten im Jahre 1731 auszuziehen."

Archiv der K. K. Landesregierung 263

" Emigrations-Akten und Schriften " run on to Nr. 351, in the year 1764, which shows that it took over thirty years to settle property and other matters concerned with the expulsion of the Salzburgers.

RAURIS REPERTORIUM DES HOCHFURSTL. LAND- U. BERG-GERICHTS.

1 Band : Religions- und Emigrations-Sachen, 104.
    1730-1732. Acta Nr. 25-50.
    1733-1734.   " "   1-42.
    1735-1736.   " "   1-26.
    1737.   " "   1-33.
    1738-1739.   " "   1-27.
    1740-1742.   " "   1-19.
    1743-1745.   " "   1-22.
Continuous to 1785 with an occasional item on the Salzburgers.

K. K. HOFKOMMISSION.
1806-1807.

II. 259. Politicum. Regierung.
Auswanderung und Freyzügigkeit, sowohl überhaupt als in specie zwischen Oesterreich und Salzburg, dann Berchtesgaden. In specie :
Manumissionstaxe in Berchtesgaden.
Leibeigenschaftstaxe in Ytter.
Militärpflichtigkeits-Redimirungsgelder gegen Baiern.
Aus- und Einwanderer. Individuen.
II. 260. Politicum. Regierung. 1806-1807.
Aus- und Einwanderungstabellen.
III. 139. Camerale. Aus- and Einwanderungen, Abfahrtsgelder. 1806-1807.
Printed copies of *Verordnung* (1805), *Circularbefehl* (1796), *Publikandum* (1804), *Allgemeine Kundmachung* (1799), etc.
Auswanderungsverbot 30. März, 1774. No emigration permitted without consent, penalty loss of property left behind, punishment of those aiding emigrants.

KATENICH.
der Jahre 1729, 1730, 1731.

Contains among a large number of important printed documents, the famous edicts relating to the Salzburgers :
(1) *Emigrations Edikt vom 31. Oktober, 1731.* The edict of expulsion of the Protestant Salzburgers, with original signature of Archbishop Leopold, and H. Cristani (" Hof-Cantzler ").
All Protestants that have reached the age of 12 of both sexes compelled to emigrate, those without property within 8 days, those with property of the value of less than 150 fl. within one month, of 150-500 fl. within two months, of over 500 fl. within three months, under threat of loss of property and life.

ab anno 1734 et 1736 inclusive.

General-Patent, Salzburg den 26. August 1734.
Vollmacht vor den Legationsrath Edlen von Plotho, umb der in Preussen angesessenen emigrirten Saltzburgern in ihrem vormahligen Vater-Lande hinterlassene Vermögen einzufordern, und zu erheben. With:
Edikt des Königs von Preussen, Berlin den 22 Juni, 1734. (Making a claim on land owned by emigrant Salzburgers.)

FÜRST-ERZBISCHÖFLICHES CONSISTORIALARCHIV.

Location: Kapitelgasse 2. Salzburg.
Hours: By arrangement. Permission to use the archive must be obtained from the Consistorialrat.

Documents relating to religious trials; only ecclesiastical affairs concerning the consistory. Secular matters, partly in Vienna, partly in the Landesregierungsarchiv of Salzburg. Every deanery represented; for ecclesiastical affairs much more complete than what is in the Landesregierungsarchiv.

INNSBRUCK.

K. K. STAATSARCHIV.

Location: Central station, Statthalterei, Herrengasse.
Hours: Daily except Sundays and holidays, 8 a. m. to 1 p. m., and 3 to 5 p. m.
This is the oldest and second largest archive in Austria. In the economic history of Tyrol, America has been an important factor in so far as the monopoly in silver-mining held for a long time by this province was destroyed by the discovery of silver in America, principally in Mexico. It is conjectured, that Tyrolese miners (Knappen) were sent to Mexico in the earliest period, to work the mines. The history of the control acquired by the Fuggers over the Tyrolese silver mines can be studied in this archive. The following works on the subject were prepared with the aid of materials found in this archive:

Max Jansen, *Studien zur Fuggergeschichte.*
  I. Heft: *Die Anfänge der Fugger, bis 1494,* von Max Jansen (Leipzig, 1907).
  II. Heft: *Hans Fugger und die Kunst, 1531-1598,* von Geo. Lill (Leipzig, 1908).
  III. Heft: *Jakob Fugger der Reiche: sein Eintritt in die Kaufmannsschaft und seine ersten Unternehmungen,* von Max Jansen (Leipzig, 1910).

Cf. also, Konrad Haebler, *Die überseeischen Unternehmungen der Welser und ihrer Gesellschafter* (Leipzig, 1903).

BAIRISCHES ARCHIV.
IV. HAUPTABTEILUNG, KL. II.

Sekt. A. Aus- und Einwanderungen und Vermögens-Ex- und Importationen. II. Acta Specialia, No. 2.
Auswanderungs- und Vermögens- Exportations-Bewilligungen.
Alphabetisches Verzeichnis über die Auswanderungs- und Vermögens-Exportations-Bewilligungen.

DIALERSCHE NORMALIEN-SAMMLUNG.

Nos. 5233, 5332, 5416, 5436, 5656, 5775, 6445, 6446. (Auswanderung nach Amerika.)
Scattered acta mostly on consular business. 1850-1857.
Konsulats-Errichtung, 1851. Bundle of acta.

K. K. STATTHALTEREI-ARCHIV.

Aus- und Einwanderungstabellen in den Archiven der Tyrolischen Kreisämter, Imst, Schwatz, Bruneck, Bozen, Trient (ital. Tyrol), Rovereto, Bregenz (für Vorarlberg).

Annual statistics for 1815-1849 in fascicle " Publica ". (See Repertorium under the rubric " Auswanderung ".)[1]
The lists from 1850 on are contained in the " Registraturen der Bezirksämter ", and from 1868 (Sept. 1) in the " Bezirkshauptmannschaften ". There is a special rubric, " Auswanderung nach Amerika " (see Repertorien).

FERDINANDEUM.

Location: Museumstrasse.
Hours: Daily except Sunday, 9 a. m. to 5 p. m. Open also Sunday mornings.

The history of Tyrolese emigration to America since 1850 can best be studied in the library of the Tiroler Landes-Museum Ferdinandeum. An excellent subject-catalogue gives precisely every item on America in the numerous local or provincial newspapers, some of which have long ago ceased publication. Some few examples of titles of articles will illustrate; they are not exhaustive:

In the *Bothe für Tirol und Vorarlberg* (then a daily, now a weekly paper), there are over 40 articles on America (North and South) between the years 1850 and 1891. *E. g.:*

    1850, July 31, Aug. 2. " Korrespondenz eines jungen Innsbruckers aus Amerika an seine Eltern."

    1851, Dec. 24, 27, 29, 30, 31. " Brief eines Vorarlberger Missions Priesters aus Nord-Amerika." St. Anton bei Milwaukee, Wis., Aug. 15, 1851.

    1854, Jan. 30. " Auswanderer aus dem Oberinnthal nach Amerika."

    1866, Oct. 23. Monastery school founded by Tyrolese-American Franciscans, Louisville, Ky.

    1869, Jan. 21, 25, 28, Mar. 10, 24, Oct. 11. " Die neue Tyroler Ansiedelung in Virginien, Alpenburg, Henrico Co."

    1874, Oct. 14. " Tirolische Colonien in Amerika " (including one in Forestville, Mich., others in Brazil).

    Nov. 26, Dec. 2. " Tirol in der Fremde."

    1884, Dec. 23. " Südtirolische Auswanderer." An advertisement is mentioned of a Genoese immigration agency, exhibiting a woman with a barefooted child holding her hand. The woman's face beams at the sight of a beautiful transatlantic steamer. " Whither is the ship going, mother? " asks the poor little one. " To America, my child ", is the answer. Warning against such methods of advertising.

    1885, Feb. 9. " Die Odyssee einer Auswanderungs-Gesellschaft." Party of 29 from southern Tyrol embark for Buenos Aires. Cholera breaks out on board, what remained of the party is forced to return.

---

[1] Though the destination is given in the case of every emigrant, and the cause stated, there is a striking recurrence of the same destination and cause, viz.—Bavaria for the former, and " vortheilhafte Verehelichung " for the latter. The suspicion arises, that when young persons of either sex wished to emigrate, they found it most convenient and effective to give the neighboring country as their destination, and for the cause, bettering their condition by marriage. America very rarely appears as the destination named.

1886, May 11. "Florida, das amerikanische Eden." (Very unfavorable report.)
Dec. 2. Auswanderungsstatistik. Concerning emigration from Trent, 1870-1885. Out of population of 12,100, it is reported, 716 persons emigrated: 169 went to North, 547 to South America.
Tiroler Schützen-Zeitung: 1851, Dec. 26; 1852, June 1. (Increase of emigration.)
Volks- und Schützenzeitung: 1853, Nov. 23. (Plea to assist emigrants.)
1855, June 11, 13. (Texas.)
1862, Feb. 19, 21, 24. "Aus dem Tagebuch eines Tiroler-Freiwilligen bei der Armee von Nordamerika."
Oesterreichische Wochenschrift für Wissenschaft, Kunst u. öffentliches Leben (Vienna, 1863), pp. 296-304, article by G. A. Schimmer, giving statistics of emigration from 1820 to 1861. Government restrictions, and existence of fertile and uninhabited areas in interior of Austria-Hungary, are causes of slight emigration. Overpopulation only in Bohemia. After Bohemia, Tyrol has furnished largest contingent of emigrants (1820-1861).
Rechenschafts-Bericht des Tirolischen Landes-Ausschusses für das Jahr 1889 (Innsbruck, 1890), pp. 172-173. "Errichtung eines Auswanderer-Auskunftsbureaus."
Innsbrucker Zeitung: 1850, Oct. 8. Briefe. (Unfavorable.)
1852, Nov. 26. A group of gold-seekers, their misfortunes.
Tiroler Stimmen, für Gott, Kaiser, und Vaterland: 1866, Apr. 24. "Brief aus Nordamerika" (Cincinnati).
1868, Nov. 30. "Zum Aufruf d. Hrn. Ritters von Alpenburg (Virginien) betreff. Auswanderung."
1869, Feb. 3. "Aus u. über Amerika" (feuilleton), letter from Chicago.
Feb. 27. "Noch ein Wort über Auswanderung nach Virginien."
Mar. 9, 10. "Erlebnisse eines Auswanderers." Atchison, Kan.
Neue Tiroler Stimmen: 1897, Oct. 16. "Aus dem Goldlande. Briefe aus Alaska."
1898, May 12, Oct. 7. More letters concerning Alaska.

INDEX.

Aarau, aid to emigrants, 116; Registratur in, 140; state archive in, iv, 140
Aarburg, 45
Aargau, 2, 86, 140-143, 153, 154; aid to emigrants, 140-143; *Berichtliche und Statistische Notizen über Auswanderung vom Kanton,* 143; bills, 142; cantonal library, 140; citizenship. 142; commercial laws, 141; conference of 1846, 116; consul Wolff, complaint against, 69; death certificates, 141; emigration, 64, 75, 140-143, 153; emigration agents, 140; emigration bureau, 142; emigration proposals, 117; emigration regulations, 48, 61, 140, 141; emigration statistics, 64, 75, 142, 143; emigration tax, 140; emigration to Utah, 143; emigration via France, 141; insurance of wife's property, 141; loss of citizen and land rights, 140; *Rechenschaftsberichte des Kleinen Raths,* 143; Smaller Council, records of, 140-143; state archive vi, 140; warrants for criminals, 142
Abschieds-Bücher, *see* Fribourg
Abschreckende Relation von Philadelphia, Eine, see Rottenbühler
Acapulco, destroyed by earthquake, 220, 221
Ackermann, Anna and Franz, emigration of, 89
Acta Conventus Ecclesiastici, see Akten des Kirchenkonvents
Act of Mediation, 2. 9
Adams. Henry, *Life of Gallatin,* 180
Adams, John, minister to England, 226, 227; minister to the Netherlands, 223-225; transfer of University of Geneva, proposed by, 184
Adams, John Quincy. audience with, 190; eulogy of Lafayette, 198, 219; messages, 192, 194; pen-portrait of, 206; proposed for President, 190
Adet, Pierre Auguste. minister to U. S., 180
Adventure, frigate. 217
Aebnit, Peter Im, arrest, 47; attempt to escape, 5. 57; Bern refuses to surrender estate, 51; deportation, 47; emigrates to Carolina, 45, 56; emigration agent, 47; examination of, 55, 56; extradition of. 38, 39; imprisoned. 57; killed, 57; persecution of, 47, 56; return from Carolina, 47, 56; trial, 4; visit to English minister, 56
Africa, Swiss emigration to, 142
Agassiz, Louis, 149
Agricoltore Ticinese, L', article in, 148
Akten des Kirchenkonvents, Bern, 50-52, 58
Alabama, Swiss settlements in, 70
Alaska, letters from, 267
Albany, 196; deportation of Huber family, 22

Albinda, *see* Albinola
Albinola, Giovanni, deportation of, 208, 212, 213, 215
Alexander I., Russian emperor, ukase of, 190
Alexandria, Egypt, emigration from Bern to, 69
Alexandria, Va., Cazenova, consul in, 24; Swiss consulate in, 7, 64
Alfoltern, 23
Algeria, American consul in, 251; Swiss emigration to, 27, 96, 98, 116, 128
Algerian corsairs, Portuguese fleet against, 231
Allemann, 156
Allen, John, supply for U. S. army, 236
Allentown, Pa., 90
Allgemein Eidgenössische Bücher, 59
Almanaco del Popolo Ticinese, article in, 147
Alpena, W. Va., Swiss settlement, 71
Alpenburg, Va., Tyrolese settlement, 266, 267
Alpina, N. Y., colony of, 173; *Notice sur Alpina,* 173; Swiss settlers in, 161
Alpnacht, 86; letters from, 86; list of emigrants from, 87
Alsace, 13, 64
Alte und Neue Welt, article in, 85
Alter u. verbesserter Schreib-Kalender, 29
Altmann, Professor, 58
Altorf (Uri), cantonal archive in, 83
Altorf (Zurich), 20
America, discovery of, 221; emigration from Austria, 228, 235, 247; emigration from Switzerland, 6, 7, 25, 26, 48, 141; *Erdbeschreibung von ganz Amerika,* 188; learned societies, 195; newspapers, 190; papers concerning, 41, 51, 78, 84, 108, 117, 128, 141, 156; Russian colonies, 228; securities, 53; *Sichere Nachricht aus America.* 30; *Sur la Population de l'Amérique,* 51; Swiss colonies, 41; trials relating to, 19; Tyrolese colonies, 266; *Wunderbare Nachricht aus America,* 72
Americana, new sect in Italy, 248
American Historical Review, articles in, 7, 9, 55, 175. 186, 187
Americani Cacciatori, 248, 249
American Philosophical Society, 195
American Revolutionary War, 8, 218-224, 238, 240, 246, 256; Adams, minister to the Netherlands, 223, 224; alliance with Prussia, rumor of, 221; American drafts accepted in Spain and France, 223; American privateer Conyngham, 219; American ships with supplies leave French port, 218; capture of New York, 218; commercial relations with France, 220-222; commercial relations with the Netherlands. 222; commercial treaty with the Netherlands, 222,

269

224; complaint of insurgents to Austrian minister in France, 219; correspondence of Howe with Secretary of State, 222; debates in Parliament, 219, 224; desertion, 223; Discours sur la grandeur et importance de la révolution, 256; England complains of supplies on Dutch ships, 9, 217, 218, 220; England gives up hope of conquering the colonies, 222; England proposes to Austria to reject American emissaries, 219; English peace plans, 221, 222; English secret correspondence with colonies, 222; d'Estaing's arrival with French fleet, 221; evacuation of Boston, 218; evacuation of two Delaware forts, 221; France favors American cause, 219; Franklin appointed minister to France, 222; Franklin in France, 220; French capture English possession on Hudson Bay, 224; French opinion, 218; French law against sale of American prizes, 219; French officers taken prisoners, 219; French secret commercial relations with English insurgents, 218; French ships with supplies land in Boston, 220; French subsidies, 221; Lord G. Germain's resignation, 224; grievances with England, 218; increase in population, 218; invasion of West Florida, 221; Lafayette, 219; Laurens, deputy to France, 223; Lee arrives in Vienna, 221; Lisbon port closed to English-American ships, 219; loan in France, 221, 223; loan in the Netherlands, 223, 224; mission of emissary to Berlin and Copenhagen, 223; mission of Gerard to America, 221; peace debated in Parliament, 224; Pigott arrives with fleet in New York, 224; Portuguese prizes, 220; prizes of American privateers, 59, 219, 220, 224, 228, 232, 235; proposals to send minister to Austria, 220; Russian-Prussian mediation, rumor of, 222; Scottish troops against English colonies, 218; secret trading by way of St. Eustatius, 9, 217, 218, 220; seizure of American ship by English in Lisbon port, 220; Spain releases American privateers, 219; Spanish opinion, 219, 220; subsidies, 221; subsidy treaty between England, Prussia and Russia, 218; surrender of Cornwallis, 223, 246; treaty with France, 221, 222
Amerika, ship, 233
Amerika, Die Beziehungen Oesterreichs zu, see Schlitter, Dr. Hanns
Amerikanische Gesellschaft zur Verbesserung des Zustandes und zur Bekehrung der Juden, 250
Amerikanischer Wegweiser, see Ochs, Johann Rudolff
Amherst, Society of Natural History, 192
Amsterdam, 99; commerce with English-American colonies, 222; complaint of Swiss council, 157; complaint respecting Anabaptists, 37; East India Co., 37; emigration measures, 79, 157, 171; intervention of, 37; Jean Noblet, 178; letters from, 111, 179;

Swiss consul looks after emigrants, 61, 141; synod, 58; transportation rates, 128
Amtliche Sammlung der Bundesgesetze, 7, 69
Anabaptists, 3, 15, 23, 27, 36, 37, 38, 41, 50, 63, 72
Andelfingen, 22
Andermatt, Joseph, emigration of, 87
Andler-Witten, *Count*, 252
Anekli, Ferdinando Antonio, 205
Angliombi [Aglionby], English envoy, 37
Anhalt-Zerbst, *Prince* von, recruiting for England, 224
Annalen der Verbreitung des Glaubens, 84
Anne, *Queen*, letters to, 72
Anspach contingent, *see* Army, British
Anthracite coal, 199
Antilles, 179; Spain fears English aggression against, 229; *see also* West Indies, and names of islands
Antrag zur Aufnahme schweizerischer Colonisten in Texas, 80
Antwerp, free transportation of baggage to, 153; Swiss consulate, 92; Swiss emigration via, 135
Anzeiger für Schweizerische Geschichte, articles in, 13, 27, 33, 83, 89
Appenzell, 1, 2; emigration to Carolina, 18
Appenzell ausser Rhoden, 127; *Amtsblätter des Kantons*, 127; citizenship, 126; conference of 1846, 116; emigration, 62, 127; *Rechenschaftsberichte des Regierungsrats an den Kantonsrat*, 127
Appenzell inner Rhoden, 126; cantonal archive, iv, 126; citizenship, 126; emigration, 126
Archivalische Zeitschrift, article in, 101
Archives de l'Histoire de France, see Langlois, Ch. V.
Archiv für Schweizerische Geschichte, article in, 100
Arenenberg, archive of the castle, 144
Argentina, 128; Swiss emigration to, 69, 148, 156; Swiss consulate, 26; *see also* Buenos Aires; La Plata states
Argentini, Felice, deportation of, 207, 208, 211, 215
Arkansas, Catholic missions in, 85; Swiss settlement in, 70
Arlesheim, 78
Army, British, Anspach contingent, 9, 238, 239, 240; Austrian troops, 9, 223, 224, 240; Danish troops, 238; German troops, 220, 238; Hanau troops, 239, 240; Hanover troops, 239; Hesse-Waldeck troops, 239, 240; Prussian troops, 238; Scottish troops, 218; recruiting for, 52, 172, 224, 238, 239, 240
Arnay, A. M. d', emigrates to Santo Domingo, 72
Asheville, N. C., Swiss settlement, 71
Asia Minor, Swiss emigration to, 69
Atchison, Kan., 267
Aubert, H. V., article by, 184
Audience du Comte, *see* Neuchâtel
Audiences Générales, *see* Neuchâtel
Augusta, Ga., 204
Australia, Swiss emigration to, 69

Austria, American emissaries to, 219; American frigate used as model by, 11, 242, 243; American officers in Austrian service, 240; American vessels in port of, 241, 244; archives of, *see* Innsbruck, Salzburg, Tyrol, Vienna; *Austria as it Is*, 11; *Berichte des ersten Agenten Oesterreichs in den Vereinigten Staaten von Amerika*, 8, 186; *Beziehungen Oesterreichs zu den Vereinigten Staaten*, 8, 186, 221; Böcker, American consul general in. 25, 67, 84, 157; commercial relations with America, 188, 191, 222, 224, 233, 236, 254; commercial relations with France, 252; commercial treaty with U. S., 9, 10, 186, 187, 189, 192, 193, 209, 225, 244, 246, 250, 254; complaint to England over St. Eustatius affair, 226; convention between U. S. and, 196; deportation, 215; discrimination against American ships, 192, 194, 237; duty on Austrian wines, 195; emigration agents, 242, 247, 257; emigration laws, 9, 11, 25, 188, 236; emigration licenses, 249, 250; emigration to America, 8, 11, 188, 225, 228, 246-248, 250, 251, 263, 265; emigration to Brazil, 249, 250; emigration to Mexico, 241; emigration to Spain, 248; emigration to Texas, 251, 267; English ships in Austrian ports, 219; expeditions to America, 244, 245; extradition treaty with U. S., 11, 214; *Geschichte der Oesterreichischen Zentralverwaltung*, 252; military passes, 243; Mühlenberg, American minister to, 10, 199, 208, 209, 210, 216; neutrality of, 252; *Oesterreich von 1848-1860*, 247; *Oesterreichische Wochenschrift für Wissenschaft*, cited, 267; ports closed to American flag, 234; ports reopened, 235; position on slavery, 195; prevents Austrians from joining English troops, 9, 223, 224, 238, 239, 240; readmission of emigrants, 243, 256; recruiting for America, 227; steamship line to America, 244; steamship line to the Orient, 189; supplies for French possessions, 223, 239, 253; trade in salt, 239; warships, 243, 245; *see also* Beelen-Bertholff; Hülsemann; Innsbruck; Joseph II.; Lederer; Mareschal; Metternich; Salzburg; Stürmer; Tyrol; Vienna

Auswanderungs Zeitung, 68
Aventure, frigate, 217
Avisblatt, 45, 46

Bache, Alexander Dallas, 201
Bächthold, Martin (convict), and family, emigration of, 124
Baden (county), emigration laws, 58, 140
Baden (duchy), emigration decrees, 152; emigration from, 67, 116, 235
Baden (grandduchy), petition of Swiss in, 63
Baden (margraviate), list of Swiss emigrants to, 13
Bader, G., emigration of, 23
Baechli, Kaspar and family, petition of, 142
Bättiger, Benedikt. emigration of, 98
Bahama Islands, English occupation of, 225

Bahia. Swiss emigration to, 118
Baltimore, 120, 192, 208, 209
Bancroft, George, *History of the United States*, 72
Bandtli, 80
Bank, U. S., 196-198
Banking Act, N. Y., 202
Banking system and banks, 202, 203, 204, 206, 209, 211
Banks, Henry, letter from, 181
Baptists, 27; *see also* Anabaptists
Bär, return from Pennsylvania of, 22
Baraga, *Bishop* Friedrich, Indian missionary, 11, 251; letter from, 84
Barbe, T., emigration agency, 32, 118, 155
Bargnani, Alessandro, deportation of. 207, 208, 209, 211, 215, 216
Barlow, Joel, poem of, 227
Baron, Antoine, cantonal archivist, 159
Barrozo *vs.* Torlade, 195
Bartlome, Johannes, emigration of, 43
Barzizza, *Count* Philippo Ignazio, land claim of, 192, 193, 194
Basel-Landschaft, information concerning cantonal archive, vi, 121
Basel-Stadt, 1, 2, 50, 51, 171; aid to emigrants, 101, 107, 113, 116, 117, 118; American consulate in, 110, 153; Anabaptist New Testament printed at, 37; Armen-Seckel, 105; cantonal archive, vi, vii, 1, 4, 5, 101-120; circular letter, convicts to America, 118; conference of 1846, 116; Department of Commerce and Agriculture on emigration, 119; deportation of Hanhart, 23; Dreizehnerrat, 101; emigration, 3, 22, 63, 79, 101-120; emigration agencies, 92, 102, 105, 117 118, 119, 120, 123, 142; emigration laws, 101. 102, 104, 105, 106, 107, 108, 109, 111, 113, 114, 115, 116, 117, 118, 120; emigration of minors, 107, 115; emigration statistics, 103, 112, 114, 115, 119; emigration tax, 102, 103, 104, 105, 107, 109, 110, 112, 113, 114; emigration to Bahia, 118; emigration to Buenos Aires, 115; emigration to Carolina, 39, 101, 102, 103, 104, 106, 109, 110, 112; emigration to New Orleans, 116; emigration to Nova Scotia, 106; emigration to Pennsylvania, 103, 104, 106, 107, 110, 112; emigration to Spain, 107; emigration to Surinam, 111; emigration to Texas, 116; emigration to Uruguay, 118; emigration to Virginia, 107; emigration via France, 115; *Geschichte der Stadt und Landschaft Basel*, 113; *Handel und Industrie der Stadt Basel*, 131; Huber arrested, 46, 55, 56; Kennan's advertising scheme, 118; Kleiner Rat records concerning emigration, 101-108; land commission on emigration, 107; newspapers on emigration, 48; police department on emigration, 47, 118, 119; provisions for children of emigrants, 102, 105-106; release of emigrants from serfdom, 112, 113; *Repertorium des Staatsarchivs*, 101; Schweizerisches Wirtschaftsarchiv, 101
Basil, Ohio, Swiss settlement, 71
Basler, N. J., Swiss consul in Madison. Ind., 67

Batavian colonies, English occupation of, 233, 234
Baudin, *Adm.* Charles, negotiations with the Mexican government, 203; proclamation of, 202
Baumgardner, Pa., Swiss settlement at, 71
Baumgarten, emigration agency, 97, 118
Baumgartner, Andreas, *Ein Besuch in Neu Glarus*, 94
Bavaria, emigration from, 67; emigration to, 266
Bayard, James A., 235
Beacons, 246
Beck and Herzog, emigration bureau, 117, 118
Beda, *Abbot*, letter to, 129
Beelen-Bertholff, *Baron* de, Belgian agent, 8, 9, 240, 253, 236; reports of, 8, 187
Beerli, *Dr.* H., article by, 131n.
Belgiojoso, *Count* Barbiano de, plenipotentiary to Brussels, 187
Belgium, 196, 204; commerce with America, 187; emigration, 67; emigration law, 92; emigration via, 92, 154, 158; railroads, 10; *Railroads in Belgium*, 206; *see also* Netherlands
Bell County, Ky., Swiss emigration to, 129
Beller, Christoph, commercial scheme of, 9, 253
Bellinzona, cantonal archive of Canton Ticino, 147
Belmont, August, letter of, 216
Benedictines, 5, 84, 85, 87
Beneke and Pfister, 241
Benton, Thomas H., 206
Benziger, J. C., article by, 84
Benzinger, Pa., Swiss settlement at, 71
Benzoni, Cesare, deportation of, 215
Berchtesgaden, emigration from, 263; taxation in, 263
Bericht und Anleitung betr. die verschiedenen Reiserouten, 118
Berlin, 168; American commercial emissary to, 223
Bern, 1, 2, 25, 86, 93, 171; aid to returning emigrants, 22, 45, 54; American legation, archives of, vi, 6, 7, 33, 75-77; Amsterdam intervention rejected, 37; approval of colonial scheme, 3, 40; articles on Carolina forbidden, 43, 48; bibliography, 33; cantonal archive, vi, vii, 33-63; cantonal library, 81; census, first, 51; children not permitted to emigrate, 47; circular letter concerning Bolivar, 86; city library, 71-75; commission investigates emigration, 44, 51; complaint against confiscation of goods, 59; conference of 1846, 116; co-operation of Ratsherren with Ritter, 3; correspondence of the Quatre Ministraux, 73; deportation of paupers and criminals, 43, 61; Diplomatisches Departement, papers, 60-61; Direktion des Innern, papers, 61; Ehemaliges Fürstbisch. Baselsches Archiv, 63; emigration, a cantonal question, 62, 63; emigration agencies, 48, 68; emigration causes, 4, 60-62; emigration fever, 3, 43, 44, 46, 47, 55; emigration from, 3, 4, 5, 33-76; emigration laws, 33, 35-38, 41, 44-50, 55, 57, 59, 61, 62, 64-66, 68; emigration lists, 40, 53; emigration tax, 39, 40-48, 54, 61-63; emigràtion to California, 68; emigration to Carolina, 20, 34-36, 38, 39, 42-49, 54-57; emigration to Central America, 69; emigration to Danzig, 41; emigration to East Indies, 69; emigration to France, 69; emigration to French colonies, 69; emigration to Georgia, 45, 46; emigration to Hungary, 69; Evangelische und Drey-Oerthische Abscheiden, 58-60; Geheimes Missivenbuch, 48; government assists emigration, 41, 43; government declines Gasser's appeal, 50; government interested in lightning-rod, 52; Grosse Rat forbids emigration, 47; Grosse Rat rejects England's deportation scheme, 43; Grütli Verein, colonization scheme, 76; inheritance dispute with France, 59; inheritance dispute with Holland, 38; jurisdiction dispute, 38; Justiz Rath, Akten des, 61, 62; Kirchenkonvent, Akten des, 51, 52, 58; Kirchenkonvent favors aid to churches in Pennsylvania, 50; Klein Thurn-Buch der Stadt Bern, 56, 57; land rights imperilled by emigration, 33, 35, 40, 41, 47, 50, 61; Mandatenbuch, 33-36, 73; Manual der Recrouten Kammer der Stadt, 53; Manual der Täufer Kammer, 53, 54; Mississippi investments, failure of, 53; persecution of emigrants to Carolina, 39; persecution of recruiting agents, 52; plans to assist poor people, 55; police department on emigration, 23, 24, 46, 47; printed circulars against emigration to Carolina, 47; proposals concerning colony of Red River, 172; purchase of American securities, 52; purchase of land in America, 41; Raths-Manuale der Stadt, 3, 4, 40-54, 131; redemptioner system, 61, 62; religious books for emigrants, 40; religious permitted to emigrate, 41; reply to New York synod, 52; reports on Carolina, 43, 46; report on Prussian agents, 22; Responsa Prudentum, 55; Säckelschreiber Protocolle, 54, 55; sale of English securities, 53; synod in favor of Gasser's appeal, 50; Teutsche Missiven Buch der Stadt, 36-40; Thurn-Buch der Stadt, 4, 5, 55, 56, Vaud under authority of canton, 159; *see also* Vorort, Bern
Berne, Ind., Swiss settlement, 70
Berne, Mich., Swiss settlement, 70
Berne, N. Y., Swiss settlement, 71
Berne, Ohio, Swiss settlement, 71
Berne, Pa., Swiss settlement, 71
Berner Monatschrift, article in, 73
Bernese Oberland, *see* Oberland, Bernese
Bernhard, 212
Bernhard, *Duke*, of Saxe-Weimar, *Reise nach Nordamerika*, 11, 244
Bernhart, emigration of, 49
Bernhofer, 259
Bernstadt, colony in Kentucky, 69, 70
Berrien, John M., U. S. Senator, on abuse in naturalization, 213
Bersinger, of Weyach, complaint against, 19
Bersinger, Margaretta, death in Pennsylvania, 22

Index 273

Bertha, *Queen*, of Burgundy, grant to the abbey of Payerne, 161; will of, 150
Berthier, *Marshal* Alexandre, letter concerning Huguenin, 171; Prince of Neuchâtel, 166
Bertoni, Brenno, article by, 148
Beza, Theodore, 184
Beziehungen Oesterreichs zu den Vereinigten Staaten, *see* Schlitter, *Dr.* Hanns
Bible, Anabaptist New Testament, 37, 38; sent to Pennsylvania, 15
Bibliographie Nationale Suisse, 6
Biehl, Pa., Swiss settlement, 71
Bientz, Leonhard and Rudolf, examination of, 105
Bigamy, 77
Bilbao, 219
Billikon, emigration from, 20
Bills of lading, 119
Bischofshof, 258, 260
Bishops, Catholic, administration in America, 251
Biveleux, Antoine, president of the Central Committee, 179
Blasenberg, fortress, 238
Bleuler, Elisabeth, 22
Blockades, 200, 201, 202, 204, 216, 233, 235
Blonay, 161
Blumer, W., letter from, 90
Board of health, 255; *see also* Quarantine
Bodenstein, *Dr.* Gustav, vii
Böcker, J. G., American consul general, 25, 67, 84, 157
Böhm, Constantin Edler von, *Die Handschriften des K. u. K. Haus-, Hof-, und Staatsarchivs*, 186, 216
Boerlis, Barbara, 111
Böttstein, deportation of undesirables from, 118
Bohemia, 11; emigration, 11, 250; over-population, 267
Bohni, Eva, 103; *see also* Joggi Bohni
Bolivar, S. A., circular letter of Bern concerning, 86
Bolivar, *Gen.* Simón, 190
Bolivia, 201
Bologna, Amerikanische Gesellschaft in, 248
Bonaparte, Jerome, 216
Bonaparte, Joseph, 23, 190, 195, 208, 237
Bonaparte, Napoleon. 2; at St. Helena, 208
Bonn, 250
Bontà, Emilio, article by, 147
Boppelsen, 20
Borck, commercial house in Amsterdam, 217
Borgeaud, *Prof.* Charles, *Histoire de l'Université de Genève*, 184
Bornemann, Friedrich Wilhelm, emigration agent, 11, 251
Borsieri, Pietro, deportation of, 215
Boston, 197, 208, 220; charitable institution in, 27; evacuation of, 218
Bote der Urschweiz, 87
Bothe für Tirol und Vorarlberg, articles in, 266, 267
Boundary disputes, 190, 196, 201, 203, 224, 225, 226, 230, 233, 234
Bounties, 79
Bouquet, *Col.* Henry, 149, 162

Bourgogne, shipwreck of the, 81
Boutell, *Hon.* Henry S., iii
Boxborough, 59
Boycotting, 254
Boyd, John J., consular agent, 200
Bozen, 265
Bozzachi, J. Karl, 211
Braditsch, 205
Brahm, *Lieut.-Col.* Ferdinand de, in American army, 240
Brandenburg (Prussia), 216; Swiss emigration to, 40, 72
Bratteler, agent, persecution of, 49, 113
Brazil, 79, 82, 84, 128, 132, 156, 207; Austrian expedition, 242, 243; Conta-Gallo, 147; cession of part to France, 233; conference concerning Swiss colonists in, 86; declaration of independence, 157; emigration, Austrian, 249, 250; emigration, Swiss, 24, 27, 60, 69, 80, 86, 96, 124, 129, 132, 138, 144, 146, 152, 155, 157, 158, 236; fleet, Franco-Spanish, 233; fleet, Portuguese, 231, 232; fleet destroyed, 233; manuscript concerning, 82; Nouvelle-Fribourg, colony, 147; prince of, 227-229, 231, 232; princess of, 220, 228, 230-234; resolution, 189, 232; seizure of French frigate, 230; Stürmer, minister, 237; Swiss consulate, 26; Swiss troops for the court of, 236; treaty with Portugal, 157; treaty with U. S., 255; Tyrolese colonies, 266; vice-governor, return of, 233
Brechbühl, teacher, persecution of, 38
Bregenz, 265
Brei, Christ., and family, emigration to Tennessee, 134, 135
Breisgau, emigration from, 235
Breitenbach, 98
Breitenstein, Hans Heinrich, petition of, 101
Bremen, emigration bureau at, 96, 154; trip to N. Y. in nine days, 119
Bremen, Ind., Swiss settlement, 70
Bremerleh, 240
Brest, Franco-Spanish fleet leaves, 233
Bridel, Dean, *Le Conservateur Suisse*, 161
Britschgi, Alois, letter to, 86
Brodbecks, Pa., Swiss settlement, 71
Broglio, depopulated by emigration, 148
Brontallo, inscription in church in, 148
Brooklyn Naval Lyceum, 200
Brown and Co., emigration agency, 118, 123, 124
Brünigpass, emigration via, 46
Brünn, 248, 251; provincial archive, 8
Brugg, emigration from, 140
Brune, *see* Von Kapff and Brune
Bruneck, 265
Brunner, Anna, 36
Brunner, Hans, 35
Brunner, Johannes, petition of, 28
Brunnerville, Pa., Swiss settlement, 71
Brussels, Swiss consulate at, 92
Bruton Parish Church, 72
Bubendorf, 102
Buch, *see* Captalat de Buch
Buchanan, James, correspondence of, 214, 216; pen-portrait of, 206; reply to German Diet, 213

274   Index

Buchberg, emigration from, 124
Bucheckberg, 37, 38
Buchmann, Jacob, inheritance of, 23
Budapest, state archive of, 8
Büchele, Andreas, petition of, 137
Bücher, emigration of, 45
Büchi, Anna, deportation of, 142
Bühler, essay on the emigration to Brazil, 152
Bündner Tageblatt, 139
Bündner Zeitung, 139
Buenos Aires, 118, 217, 221; discovery of plot in, 234; emigration from Tyrol, 266; English occupation, 234; Spanish insurgents in, 235; Spanish reoccupation of, 234; Swiss emigration, 115; *see also* Argentina
Büren, emigration agents around, 48
Bürkli, Karl, *Das Evangelium der Armen*, 31
Büsserach, 98
Bugnon, *Rev.* Joseph, 174
Bulkeley, *Count*, offer of his services against Americans, 219
Bulle, 172
Bulletin Officiel, of Valais, 164
Bulletin Officiel des Lois, Fribourg, 151
Bundesarchiv, *see* Switzerland
Bundesblatt der Schweizerischen Eidgenossenschaft, 7, 69, 148
Bundesblatt, Sachregister zum, *see* Widmer, F.
Bundesrat, *see* Federal Council
Buochs, 89
Burkhardt, Wis., Swiss settlement, 71
Burnand, A., article by, 162
Burnett, Edmund C., article by, 186
Bustelli, *Signor*, vii

Cabinet, U. S., resignation of members, 196
Cadiz, 231, 237; exportation of clothing, 227; fleet for New Spain at, 219; steamship line to Spanish-American colonies, 188
Calhoun, John C., 206
California, Auswanderungsagenten der Kalifornischen Gesellschaft, 81; *Colonie Svizzere di*, 148; discoveries in, 219; Hardmeyer on the Ticinesi in, 148; *Novella Helvetia*, newspaper, 148; Swiss emigration to, 6, 87, 108, 138, 148, 154
Callava, *Col.* José, with Jackson at Pensacola, 190
Calvin, John, 183, 184
Calvinists, in Virginia, 13
Camenisch, Verena, petition of, 137
Canada, 201, 202, 204; *Auskunft für beabsichtigende Auswanderer*, 118; disturbances in, 200; Great Western, 200; Hülsemann's report on, 208; McLeod affair, 209; maps of, 247; pacification of, 200; Régiment de Meuron, 172; Swiss emigration, 97; taxation, 217
Canary Islands, trade relations, 252
Cantons, Swiss, 2
Cape Charles, Labrador, 218
Capital punishment, 23, 236
Captalat de Buch, Swiss emigration forbidden to, 36
Capuchins, 261, 262
Caribbee Islands, 179

Carleton, *Sir* Guy, 224
Carlsbad, 249
Carlstadt, General Commando, 239
Carmichael, William, arrival in Spain, 225
Carolina, v, 3; emigration literature on, 102; letters from, 4, 46, 50, 74, 111; Ludwig Michel's trip to, 72; printed articles and books concerning, 3, 4, 29, 30, 31, 45, 48, 118; " Rabies Carolina," 3, 55; Reformed Church in, 119; reports on, 44, 46, 111; Rodt in, 56; Swiss emigration laws, 32, 36; Swiss emigration to, 3, 14, 15, 17-22, 29-32, 34-36, 38, 39, 41-50, 54-57, 72-74, 101-104, 106, 109-112; Swiss Mennonites for, 3; travels in, 20; *see also* North Carolina; South Carolina
Caroline, ship, 203, 237
Carroll, Charles, 198
Carroll, *Bishop* John, 228
Casatilly, Spanish fleet under, 220
Castelli, Bernardino, petition of, 210
Castiglia, Gaetano, deportation of, 215
Castle Garden, 75
Catherine II., 173
Catholic Church in the United States, 85
Catholic Historical Review, article in, 208
Catholics, Roman, in Appenzell, 126; in U. S., 10, 85, 194, 208, 216, 244
Causes of the Present Crisis, 202
Cayenne, 230
Cazenova, Anthony Charles, Swiss consul in Alexandria, 24, 64
Cedar Mill, Ore., Swiss settlement, 71
Census, of Bern, 51; of U. S., 156, 190
Central America, 128, 206; consulate in, 26; maps of, 247; Swiss emigration to, 69
Cesares, Pueblo de los, South America, 217, 218
Cevallos, *Gen.*, Spanish fleet under, 219, 220
Ceylon, Régiment de Meuron at, 172
Chamberlain, Mellen, estate of, 216
Chambre des Bannerets, *see* Vaud
Chambre Économique, *see* Neuchâtel; Vaud
Chambrier, *Col.* A. de, 170, 171
Chaney, complaint against Maison Barbe by, 155
Charity institutions, 27, 64, 65, 84, 86, 90, 91, 92, 117, 118, 141, 142, 144, 145
Charleston, S. C., 120; Hülsemann's report on, 10, 204; immigration via, 135; letter from, 29; Swiss consulates in, 26, 110, 163
Charton, H. S., letter from, 181
Chateau d'Oex, 59
Châtelain, *Dr.*, article by, 172
Chatelanat, Henri, in charge of consulship at New Orleans, 65
Cheesland, Texas, Swiss settlement, 71
Chesapeake Bay, French failure on, 223; map of, 72
Chetlain, *Gen.* A. L., *The Red River Colony*, 172
Chicago, charitable institution at, 27; Exposition, 26, 110; Swiss consulate to, 129
Chicago Tribune, cited, 172
Chile, 128; blockade of the coast, 235; emigrants shipwrecked on way to, 79; Swiss consulate, 26; Swiss emigration, 97, 146, 157; treaty with U. S., 198

Chillon, notarial documents in the castle of, 160
China, Austrian expedition to, 242
Cholera, 116, 118, 197, 266
Christen, a widow, petition of, 45
Christen, A. M., emigration of, 89
Christen, Johannes, to collect inheritance, 51
Christen, *Father* Ulrich, journey to America, 85
Christholds Gedanken, 30
Christian Alliance, constitution of, 211
Cristofari, Peter, 191, 192
Chronometer, 244
Chur, cantonal archive in, vi, 132; city archive, 132; emigration to America, 138; emigration to Brazil, 138; Rathsprotokolls-Sbozzo, 133-136
Churer Wochenblatt, 139
Churer Zeitung, 139
Cincinnati, O., 120; charitable institution in, 27; letter from, 267; Swiss consulate in, 26, 110
Cincinnati Volksblatt, clippings from, 67
Citizenship, by marriage, 96, 142
Città di Trieste, ship, 252
Civil War, U. S., diary of Tyrolese volunteer, 267; military papers, 79; recruiting in Switzerland, 155
Claims, 81
Clarendon, *Earl* of (Edward Hyde), 180
Classis, *see* Neuchâtel
Clay, Henry, Austrian treaty, 10, 193; letter to Lederer, 192; limitation of power of, 194; pen-portrait of, 206; Schurz's *Henry Clay,* 215
Clay, J. Randolph, American chargé d'affaires, 216
Cleve (duchy), emigration via, 169
Clinton, *Sir* Henry, succeeds Howe, 221
Cliovitsch, 205
Clothing trade, 227
Cloth shears, 255
Clubs Insurgés, 179, 180
Cobenzl, *Count* Johann Philipp von, letter to, 187
Cochrane, *Vice-Adm.* Thomas, expedition against Peru, 190
Coinage, Swiss, value of, 104
Colladon and Hentsch, Gallatin gives power of attorney to, 181
Collection des Manuscrits Historiques, 176
Colombia, statistics of, 246; Swiss recognition of the republic, 79; Swiss troops for, 25; treaty with U. S., 192, 193
Colonie, Eine Vergessene Deutsche, see Deiler, J. Hanno
Columbia River, 203
Colville, letter to, 171
Comités d'Émigrations des Sociétés d'Utilité Publique, 7, 64
Commerce, *see* Trade
Commercial convention, Hülsemann's report on, 204
Commission Révolutionnaire, 180
Compagnie des Pasteurs et Professeurs, *see* Geneva
Company of Pastors, *see* Neuchâtel
Conception, abbey of, *see* New Engelberg

Conestoga, Pa., 54
Confaloniere, Federigo, deportation of, 215
Conference of 1818, concerning Swiss colonists in Brazil, 86, 155
Conference of 1846, concerning Swiss emigration, 116, 172
Confiscation, of Swiss goods, 59
Congress, U. S., 10, 11, 179, 180, 190, 197, 198, 199, 204, 206, 246; Canadian and Mexican affairs in, 202; reciprocity navigation bill, 192
Conner, *Father* Beda, *see* O'Connor
Conrad, *Father* Frowin, 87
Conseil Fédéral, *see* Federal Council
Conservateur Suisse, Le, see Bridel, Dean
Consistoire, archives of, *see* Geneva
Constantinople, 232, 248
Constitution, Swiss federal, 21
Consuls and consulates, *see* names of particular countries and places
Conta-Gallo, Swiss colony in Brazil, 147
Continental Congress, Franklin appointed minister to France, 222
Contraband, 9, 217, 218, 220
Convention, French, decree of, 78
Convention Internationale (1875), 156
Convention of 1818, *see* Conference of 1818
Convoys, 220, 221, 230, 232, 243
Conyngham, *Capt.* Gustavus, 219
Cook, *Capt.* James, voyage of, 217
Copenhagen, American emissary in, 223
Copia eines von einem Sohne N. N. Briefes, Philadelphia, Pastorius, 30
Coppeln, Mo., Swiss settlement, 70
Coppinger, *Col.* José, governor of East Florida, 190
Cornbury, *Lord* (Henry Hyde), crowned King of the Archers, 180; Swiss Council confers citizenship on, 180
Cornwallis, *Lord* (Charles), surrender of, 223, 246
Corpataux, Georges, 152
Cortes, government of the, 236
Coruña, ship line between Falmouth and, 230
Costa Rica, plan for colony in, 68, 155
Cotton duck, used in American sails, 11, 194, 244, 254
Cotton Hill, W. Va., Swiss settlement, 71
Cour d'Appellation Romande, *see* Vaud
Court, Antoine, papers of, 184
Couvet, 170
Covelle, Alfred L., *Le Livre des Bourgeois de Genève,* 175, 181, 182, 183
Cracow, provincial archive of, 8
Cramer, August, *Notes extraites des Registres du Consistoire de Genève,* 183-184
Créole, ship, 210
Cresson, Ellion, emigration of, 142
Crimea, emigration from Thurgau to the, 144
Cristani, H., Hof-Kanzler, 263
Crittenden, J. J., 206
Croft, Thomas, treatise on the potato disease, 67
Cross, Order of the, *see* Kreuzherren
Crousaz, Aymon, cantonal archivist, 159
Cuba, Lederer's report on, 191; white population in, 236

276 Index

Cuculli, Simon, 194, 195, 196
Cullman, Ala., Swiss settlement, 70
Cunningham, *Capt.* Gustavus, *see* Conyngham
Curaçao, Spanish complaints against hostilities in, 222
Curt, Hans, 48
Cushing, Caleb, 206; resolutions proposed in the House of Representatives, 202
Cuvelier, Joseph, article by, 186
Czech, *Prof.* Hermann, method of teaching deaf-mutes, 199

Dachelsen, 23
Dällikon, 22
Daily Advertiser, New York, 195
Dakota, Swiss settlement in, 70
Dampierre, 171
Dana, Francis, U. S. minister to Russia, 225
Danzig, Austrian consul in, 234; emigration from Bern to, 41
Décrets Romands, 161
Degerfelden, assembling of emigrants at, 142
De Grasse, François, *Comte, see* Grasse
Deiler, J. Hanno, *Eine Vergessene Deutsche Colonie*, 196, 250
Deisz, Johann M., 194
Delaware River, capture of forts on, 221; lighthouse at mouth of, 254
Delmonico Brothers, restaurant founded by, 147
Delplancq, letters to, 187
Demerara, appeal for convoys against English, 221; conquest by the French of, 224
Democratic convention (Baltimore, 1840), Hülsemann's report on the, 11, 209
Democratic Review, 213
Denmark, treaty between U. S. and, 193, 195, 255
Deschwanden, Theresia von, 86
Des Marez, G., article by, 186
Dessenzano, 205
Dettwyler, Joh., emigration of, 117
Deutsche Colonie, Eine Vergessene, see Deiler, Hanno
Deutsche Schnellpost, 212
Deutschland, Das junge, see Geiger, L.
Dialersche Normalien-Sammlung, *see* Innsbruck
Dielstorf, emigration list of, 13
Dierauer, *Prof. Dr.* Johannes, vii
Diet, German, 213; Swiss, *see* Swiss Confederation
Dietikon, emigration list of, 13
Dietsch, Andreas, emigration agency, 141
Dingley Bill, 131
Dinsmore, 248
Diplomatischen Departement, Bern, Manual des, 60
Domicile, *see* Freizügigkeitsvertrag
Dovere, Il, 147
Dreifuss, J., *Emigration*, 6
Duden, Gottfried, 250; travels in the Middle West, 11
Dür, Aloysia, birth certificate of, 203
Dürrenberger, Jacob, examination of, 111
Dürring, letters from, 108
Dürst, D., *Die Gründung der Kolonie Neu Glarus*, 94

Dufour, Jean-Jacques, founder of colony of Firstvineyard, 161
Dufour-Vernes, Louis, archivist, 175, 183; article by, 175, 177; Catalogue des Minutes de Notaires, 178; Index des Chambres, 177; Inventaire des Titres et Droits de la Seigneurie de Genève, 178, 183; Inventaire Général et Topographique des Archives de l'État, 178; Militaire, Justice et Police, 177
Duhamel, F., 178
Duminique, *Baron* de, minister of state in Trier, 241
Dunklen, Hans, emigration of, 123
Dunscomb, Andrew, letter from, 181
Dupaquier, emigration agent for Nova Scotia, 49
Du Ponceau, *see* Ponceau
Durham, *Earl* of (John George Lambton), departure of, 201; pacification of Canada, 200; remarks on, 201; resignation of, 200
Durrer, *Dr.* Robert, vii
Dutch West India Company, 179, 223, 229
Dye-wood, 226

Earthquake, 221
East India Company, recruiting Austrians for, 240; Swiss for, 52, 172; transportation of emigrants by, 37
East Indies, Austrian trade relations with, 252; return of fleet from, 221; Swiss emigration to, 69; travels in, 20; troops and munitions for, 227
Eben, C. T., translation by, 51
Eberle, *Oberstleutnant* Ludwig, vii
Eberle, Ill., Swiss settlement, 70
Eberly's Mill, Pa., Swiss settlement, 71
Echo des Alpes, 164
Ecuador, treaty with Switzerland, 96
Eder, Rupert, persecution of, 259
Educational Review, cited, 184
Eger, 249
Egger, Hans, emigration of, 45
Eglisau, emigrant from, 14, 19
Eichthal, *Count*, 212
Eidgenössische Abschiede, 1712-1743, 57
Eidgenössische Kanzlei, reports on emigration, 23
Eidgenössische Organisation der Auswanderung, conference of, 96; *see also* Federal Emigration Bureau
Eidgenössische Stände, Konferenz der, 86
Eidgenössische Vorort, *see* Vorort
Eidgenössiches Archiv, *see* Switzerland, Bundesarchiv
Eidgenössisches Auswanderungsamt, *see* Federal Emigration Bureau
Eidgenossenschaft, *see* Swiss Confederation
Einsiedeln, Benedictine monastery in, 5; Bezirksarchiv, 85; emigration from, 85; Stifts-Archiv, vi, 84, 85
Einsiedler Anzeiger, 85
Elbe, steamer, 119
Elbagen, 249
Elggau, 20
Ellikon, schoolmaster, 19
Elm, Gemeinderat, aid to emigrants, 92

Index

Elmenthaller, Mathias, persecution of, 260, 261
Elsau, letters of emigrants from, 19
Embrach, 25
Emigration, *see* names of countries and places
Emigration, see Dreifuss, J.
Emigration Suisse, see Karrer, L.
Engelberg, archive of, vi, 87, 88; Benedictine monastery in, 5. 87, 88
Engelberg, Ore., Swiss settlement, 71
Engelland Buch, 59
England, 205; ambassador received by Van Buren, 194; attitude towards U. S., 190; audience of the American minister, John Adams, 226; begins hostilities with Spain, 234; blockade of American coast, 235; boundary disputes with U. S., 190; commercial relations with America, 226, 228, 229, 236, 254; commercial treaties with America, 191, 193, 225; complaint of Dutch supply of arms, 9, 218, 220; convention with Spain, 226; Cushing's resolutions against, 202; deportation scheme of, 43; diplomatic exchanges with colonies, 218; disputes with colonies, 218; distrust by America of, 225; embargo on Spanish ships, 234; emigration from, 67, 225; Florida boundary dispute, 225, 226; free grain importation, 219; French emissaries in English colonies, 218; generals in America, 222; Graffenried's adventures in, 75; law against importation of Austrian goods, 254; McLeod affair, 209; manufacturers emigrate to America and France, 225; Mosquito Coast negotiations, 226, 227; navigation of neutral powers to the American colonies, 222; Nootka Sound negotiations, 229, 230; Parliament votes indemnities, 226; Parliamentary debate on slavery, 229, 237; Parliamentary debate on disputes with American colonies, 217; peace negotiations, 221, 222, 224; plantations, 51; proposals for offensive and defensive alliance 224; proposals to put French islands under English protection, 230; recapture of lost fleet, 230; rumor of alliance with U. S., 234; Scottish regiments in American colonies, 218; secret correspondence with colonies, 222; securities, 53; seizure of Spanish ships at Vera Cruz, 234; subscription in favor of American insurgents, 236; subsidies to Spain. 235; subsidy treaty between Prussia, Russia, and, 218; Van Buren's proposed trip to. 196; war with France, 252; war rumored with U. S., 235
England, ship, cholera on, 118
Englisch in Teutschland verschickte Erkläh-rung, Königlich, 30
Engwiller, report on supervision of agencies, 127
Enterprise, Kan., Swiss settlement, 70
Eperjes, 250
Erdbeschreibung von ganz Amerika, 188
Erguel, Anabaptists, 63; emigration to Pennsylvania, 36, 50
Erlach, 41, 42, 54
Ernst, emigration of, 20
Erschwil, 98

Escher, *Dr.* Hermann, vii
Escholzmatt, Gemeinderat, on emigration, 80
Esperanza, Argentina. Swiss settlers in, 161
Essequibo, conquest by the French of. 224; debauchery of negroes of, 226
Estaing, *Count* Charles d', arrival in America of, 221
Estates. *see* Inheritance
Études Économiques, article in, 104
Etzweiler-Merz. report on emigration agency of, 127
Evangelium der Armen, see Bürkli, Karl
Evarts, Wm. M., 77
Everett, Alexander H., 213
Exchange of official publications, 96, 155
Expositions, Chicago, 26; New York, 26; Philadelphia, 26, 142

Fabri regiment, 253
Fabrini, Filippo, scheme for world-wide trade, 9, 252
Falmouth, ship line between Coruña and, 230
Farnis, Hans, inheritance of, 38
Faust, A. B., article by, 162
Favarger, Charles Louis, manager of Alpina Co., 173; *Société en Commandite pour Alpina*, 173
Favin, *Madame*, 73
Fay, Theodore S., U. S. minister to Switzerland, 6. 75
Fechter, D. A., editor of *Eidgenössische Abschiede*, 57
Federal Chancery, on emigration via Havre. 170
Federal Council, 128; appropriation for aid to emigrants, 117; *Berichte des Schweizerischen Bundesrats*, 69; circular letters on emigration, 119, 127, 154, 155, 156; complaint against agencies, 118; emigration, a question for the, 153; emigration laws, 68, 76, 79; emigration list of Fribourg for the, 156, 157; emigration to Algeria, 27; emigration to Brazil, 27; emigration to New Orleans, 27; licensed agents and agencies, 119; Lincoln's assassination and. 78; proposals for emigration statistics, 119; Schweizerische Auswanderungsverein, petition to the, 68; warning concerning paupers and criminals, 93; *see also* Federal Emigration Bureau
Federal Directory, circular letters concerning emigration, 170, 172
Federal Emigration Bureau, vi, 5, 6. 33. 68-71. 97, 154
Fehre, Maria, petition of, 137
Fehre, Susanna, petition of, 137
Fellner-Kretschmayr, *Geschichte der Oesterreichischen Zentralverwaltung*, 252
Ferdinand I., arbitrator in indemnity dispute, 212
Ferdinandeum, *see* Innsbruck
Ferstl, 11; *see also* Foerstl
Fetscherin. Wilhelm. *Repertorium*, 62
Feuille Fédérale de la Confédération Suisse, see Bundesblatt
Feuille Officielle, 153

Fiess, brothers, 59
Filzbach, aid to emigration, 92
Financial situation in America, 170, 202, 206, 207, 216
Fire-engine, patent for, 141
Fire Islands, Swiss emigration to, 69
Firstvineyard, Ky., colony of, 161
Fischenthal, 25
Fischer, K., petition of, 116
Fischer, Ciprian, and family, emigration of, 134, 135
Fischer, *Father* Joh., 249
Fish, Nicholas, minister to Switzerland, 76, 77
Fitzgerald, *Bishop* Edward, 85
Fiume, trade relations with the French colonies, 223
Flag, U. S., 179, 180, 255
Flores, Manuel Antonio, viceroy, 227
Florida, 190, 199; article concerning, 267; boundary disputes, 225, 226; cession to U. S., 190. 237; free land in, 69; Swiss settlement in, 70; U. S. violation of, 236; *see also* West Florida
Fluebacher, Adam, estate of, 110
Flühli, 79
Förstl, Leopold, merchant, 11, 251
Fontes Rerum Austriacarum, 9, 186
Foreign Conspiracy, 198, 250
Forestville, Mich., Tyrolese colony in, 266
Forresti. Felice, deportation of, 207, 215
Forsyth, John, secretary of state, concerning minister to Austria, 199; conversation with Mühlenberg, 208; letter to Lederer, 199
Fort Douglas, 172
Fort York, 171, 172
Foster, Herbert D., article by, 175
Fourneau, *Capt.*, voyage of, 217
Fournier, August, *Historische Studien und Skizzen*, 247
Fox, Henry S., minister of Great Britain, 204
Fragmens Biographiques et Historiques de Genève, see Grenus-Saladin
France, 64, 171, 199, 205; ambassador received by Van Buren, 194; American drafts, 223; American vessels with supplies in ports of, 218; annexation of Geneva, 175; Austria recognizes new government, 195; boundary dispute with Spain, 233; commercial relations with American colonies. 220, 222, 223; commercial relations with English insurgents. 218; commercial treaty with U. S., 191, 193; complaint against Swiss paupers, 5; Conyngham affair, 219; correspondence of the Quatre Ministraux, 173; Cushing's resolutions against, 202; decrees regarding America, 78, 234; diplomatic negotiations with American colonies, 221; dispute with Switzerland, 60; distrust in America of, 225; droit de fret, 239; Elizabeth, princess, 227; emigration from, 67; émigrés in Spanish service. 231; emissaries in America, 218; d'Estaing arrives with fleet in America, 221; expedition against Louisiana, 233; fleet in America, 192; Franklin in Paris, 220, 222; French and Spanish subsidies for American colonies, 221; Gerard's mission to America, 221, 222; Graffenried's adventures, 75; indemnity treaty with U. S., 198; insurrection in French colonies, 228, 229; intrigues, 226; Jefferson, American minister, 226; Lafayette sails to America, 219; law against sale of American prizes, 219; loan for American colonies, 221, 223, 228; offer to conquer Portugal for Spain, 232; officers imprisoned in England, 219; opinion as to grievances between England and colonies, 218; ports closed to American flag, 234; refusal to exchange Santo Domingo, 231; reply to Swiss deportation scheme, 20, 116; revolutionary corps, 241; sale of Louisiana, 233, 234; secretly favors American cause, 219; steamship line from Port Louis to America, 225; subjugation of English possessions on Hudson Bay, 224; Swiss emigration to, 69, 116; Swiss emigration via, 14, 25, 62, 81, 95, 115. 116, 140, 141, 158, 170; Swiss troops for, 99; Ternant, minister to America, 228; treaty with English colonies, 221, 222; treaty with Mexico, 204; troubles in French-American colonies, 228, 229; supplies arrive in Boston, 220; war with England, 252; *see also* French
Franciscans, Tyrolese-American, 266
Franckendorf, 103
Frankfort (am Main), 171, 213; emigration from, 234; recruiting colonists for America in, 234; recruiting troops for England in, 250; religious fanaticism in, 250; Schwendler, American consul at, 254
Franklin, Benjamin, in France, 220; letter concerning Austrian treaty, 9, 187; letter to Count Mercy, 187; minister to France, 9, 187, 222
Frankreich Buch, Bern, 59
Frauenfeld, 20; cantonal archive in, 6, 144
Fredericksburg Gazette, article on Gallatin in, 181
Frederick William I., of Prussia, edict of 1734, 10, 264
Freemasons, 195, 250
Freiburger Geschichtsblätter, article in, 151
Freie Rätier, Der, 139
Freizügigkeitsvertrag, 7, 25. 68, 79, 81, 93, 95 110, 132, 152, 214
French cantons, emigration from, 149; order of, 149
French colonies, Swiss emigration to, 69
French convention, *see* Clubs Insurgés
Frey, Barbara, death of, 24; estate of, 25
Frey, Carl, death in Virginia, 24
Frey, *Col.* Emil, Swiss minister to U. S., 78
Frey, Friedrich, cantonal archivist, vii
Fribourg, 1, 2, 39, 149; archives of the bishopric, 152; archives of the commune, 151, 152; archives of the convents, 152; bishop of, 152: *Bulletin Officiel des Lois*, 151; Chancellerie, 150; circular letter on emigration, 154; Correspondance Extérieure, 150-151; deportation of criminals. 156; emigration agents, 157, 158; emigration from, 152-158; emigration laws, 154, 156, 157; emigration to Brazil. 152, 155, 157, 158; emigration to

Index 279

Chile, 157; emigration to Punta Arena, 156, 157; emigration under police supervision, 154; emigration via France, 158; emigration via the Netherlands, 157, 158; *état civil*, registers, 151; *Freiburger Geschichtsblätter*, 151; Grenette, 150; Hôtel de Ville, 150, 151, 152; Inventaire des Archives, 150; letter to Federal Council, 156; Livres de Bourgeoisie, 150, 151; Maison de Ville, 151; Mandaten-Bücher, 150; Manuaux du Conseil, 150, 151; Missiven-Bücher, 150; *Rapports du Conseil d'État*, 150; recruiting measures, 155; sale of railroad tickets, 154, 155; state archive, vi, 150-158; treasury accounts, 151; *Tableau des Notaires*, 151; viséing of passports, 154, 155, 158
Frick, emigration of, 14
Fridolin, *Count*, 205
Friedjung, Heinrich, *Oesterreich von 1848-1860*, 247
Friedrichsthal, *Ritter* von, 200, 201
Frigates, 11, 196, 217, 231, 242, 243
Froehlianists, 27
Frommer, Georg, complaint of, 259
Froschauer, New Testament, 38
Früh, Ulrich, a thief, emigration of, 145
Fruxo, D., Spanish minister, 232
Fürstenau, reformatory, 136
Für und Wider der Auswanderung nach Amerika, see Lanz, Johann
Fugger, Hans, und die Kunst, see Lill, Geo.
Fugger, Jacob, der Reiche, see Jansen, Max
Furrer, Jakob, petition of, 25
Fur-trade, 228

Gais, 127
Galena, Ill., Swiss colonists at, 172
Galicia, revolutionists deported to America, 11, 250
Gallati, Rud., petition of, 92
Gallatin, Albert, 149; Adam's *Life* of, 180; letter from P. S. du Ponceau, 181; report on emigrant transportation, 62; rumor of death of, 180-181; U. S. commissioner, 235
Gallatin family, nobility of, 180
Galveston, Tex., Swiss consulate at, 7, 65, 67
Galvez, Bernardo de, viceroy of Mexico, 227
Gambato, Alessandro, petition of, 210
Ganalh, Louis, 206
Gasc, Esaïe, syndic, 180
Gasser, minister, appeal of, 50; persecution of, 50
Gataimai, Paraguay, evacuation of, 221
Gautier, Jean-Antoine, *Histoire de Genève*, 179
Gazette d'Émigration, 156
Geering, T., *Handel und Industrie der Stadt Basel*, 131
Geheimbericht, Literarische, aus dem Vormärz, 247
Geiger, L., *Das junge Deutschland*, 247
Généalogique Suisse. Recueil, 183
Geneva, N. Y., Swiss settlers in, 161
Geneva, Ohio, Swiss settlement, 71
Geneva, Pa., Swiss settlement, 71
Geneva, Switzerland, 2, 149, 172; Allgemeine Gesellschaft gegenseitiger Unterstützung,

92; annexation of, 175; archives, inventories of, 177-178; *Archives de*, 175; *Archives de l'Église de*, 183; Archives d'État, 179-182; attempt to organize emigration, 80; Bibliothèque Publique et Universitaire, 184; Bourse Française, archives of, 177, 183; Calvin, Maison de, 176; Catalogue des Minutes des Notaires, 178; Catholic parish registers, 182, 183; Chancellerie, 175, 182, 183; Church of, 183; Collection des Manuscrits Historiques, 176; Communauté, registers of, 176, 182; Compagnie des Pasteurs et Professeurs, archives of, 183, 184; Conseil d'État, registers of, 175, 176, 179, 180, 183; Consistoire, archives of, 183, 184; Courts of Justice, archives, 177, 182; documents relating to refugees at, 182; ecclesiastical archives, 183-184; electors, registers of, 181; emigration, 64; emigration lists, 182; *état civil*, archives, 181-182, 183; État Général et Sommaire des Fonds, 177, 178; *Fragmens Biographiques et Historiques de*, 175; *Histoire de*, 179; Histoire de l'Université de, 184; Hôpital Général, archives of, 177, 178; Hôtel de Ville, 175, 176, 182; Index des Chambres, 177; inventories of archives, 177-178; *Journal de*, 77; letter of council to U. S. Congress, 180; Livre des Bourgeois de, 175, 181, 182, 183; member of Swiss Confederation, 175; *Notes extraites des Registres du Consistoire*, 184; *Notices Généalogiques sur les Familles Genevoises*, 183; part of the Département du Léman, 175; Portefeuilles des Pièces Historiques, 175, 176, 177, 178; records of baptisms and marriages, 181, 182, 183; records of parish churches, 181, 182, 183; *Regeste Genevois*, 183; Registres des Habitants, 183; St. Peter, documents of chapter of, 177, 178; St. Victor, priory of, 178; Société d'Histoire et d'Archéologie de, documents and publications of, 175, 176, 177, 179, 182, 184; Société d'Utilité Publique, Comité d'Émigration, 7, 64, 65, 66; Société des Catéchumènes, 177, 182; Société Économique, archives of, 178, 182; state archives, vi, 175-183; Tour Baudet, 176; University of, 184; Venerable Company, archives, 184; *see also* Léman, Département du
Genevoises, Notices Généalogiques sur les Familles, 183
George's Creek, Gallatin returns to, 181
Georgia, difficulties between federal and state government, 192; Hülsemann's report on, 204; preparing for secession, 192, 193; Swiss emigration to, 17, 29, 38, 45, 46, 70; Swiss settlements in, 70; *see also* Salzburger Protestants
Gerard, *Chevalier* Conrad Alexandre, mission to America of, 221, 222
Germain, *Lord* George, resignation of, 224
German American Annals, cited, 3, 73, 74, 162
Germanna, German colony in Virginia, 13
German Reformed Church in America, 119
Germantown, Pa., Pastorius, founder of, 13, 30

19

Index

Germany, 196; *Das junge Deutschland*, 247; *Der Teutsche Tribun*, 12, 251; *Die Teutsche Revolution*, 251; emigration, 62
Gerstenberg, secretary of legation at Vienna, secret recruiting for England, 9, 223, 224
Gerstner, Prof. François Antoine de, death of, 209; *Railroads in Belgium compared with those of the U. S.*, 206, 209
Gex, Pays de, civil registers of, 182, 183
Ghega, engineer, arrival in America of, 211
Gibraltar, proposal for exchange of, 229
Giegelmann, Hans, petition of, 102
Gilgen, emigration of, 45
Gilgiano, Christen, death of, 39
Gimpert, Rud., testimony of, 24
Gingins, 53
Giovane Italia, deportation of members of, 215, 245, 250, 251
Giralth, 250
Girard, Abbé François, *Histoire Abrégée des Officiers Suisses*, 100
Girard College, Philadelphia, 201
Glanzmann family, 79
Glarnischer Verein, see Glarus
Glarus, 1, 86; aid to emigrants, 90-92; bibliography, 94; conference of 1846, 116; deportation, 93; Dreifache Rath, 93; emigration agencies, 92, 93; emigration from, 62, 75, 90-93, 108, 116; emigration statistics, 92; Glarnischer Auswanderungs-Verein, 26, 90-93; *Handel und Industrie des Kantons Glarus*, 130; Kantonale Arbeiterbund, 93; *Neues Archiv des Kantons Glarus*, 6; police-commission, 91; property transfer, 90, 93; readmission of emigrants, 22; state archive, vi, 90-94; see also New Glarus
Glass factories in America, 255
Globe, Washington, 201
Glossy, K., *Literarische Geheimbericht aus dem Vormärz*, 247
Glücks-Hafen, oder Reicher Schatz-Kasten, 14, 59
Gloucester, Va., 246
Gnau, Herm., *Die Zensur unter Joseph II.*, 247
Goddard, F. W., accident of, 24
Göpfert, H., emigration of, 122, 123
Göttschi, Heinrich, 5; letter from, 18
Göttschi, Johann Moritz, 5, 18, 30; examination of, 14, 21; letter from, 14; petition of, 19, 20, 22
Goldbach, 24
Goldenberg, 24
Good, James I., *History of the Reformed Church*, 30
Good, Vinz., emigration of, 83
Goos, Dr. Roderick, vice-archivist, vii
Goundie, consul in Basel, concerning emigration, 95
Grabs, emigration from, 129
Graf, J. H., article by, 72
Graffenried, Anton, 75
Graffenried, Christoph von, 3, 60, 72-75; treaty with Tuscarora Indians, 74
Graffenried, Karl Emanuel, 60
Graffenried, Reese Calhoun de, member of U. S. Congress, 60
Graffenried family, 74; history of, 60
Graffenried manuscripts, vii, 4, 60, 73, 162
Grafstal, 18
Grain, crop in America, 254; prices in America, 255; trade, 9, 239, 241
Grant and Co. *vs.* Cornelius Specht, 205
Grasse, Comte François de, engagement with Hood, 224
Graubünden, 2, 86; aid to emigrants, 132-139; cantonal archive of, vi, 132; conference of 1846, 116; emigration, 132-139; emigration commission, 133-136; emigration of Catholics, 133; emigration proposals, 108, 172; emigration to Brazil, 132; Italian refugees, 132; Ratsprotokolle, Register of, 136; see also Tennessee Colonisationsgesellschaft
Graz, provincial archive of, 8
Great Western, ship, 204
Grebel, *Landvogt*, petition of, 20
Greece, commercial treaty with U. S., 202
Greenland, coast of, 218
Gregg, David M. M., American consul at Prague, 256
Grenaud, Abbé, manuscripts, 151
Grenaud Collection, Catalogue des MSS. de la, see Martin, Paul E.
Grenus-Saladin, *Fragmens Biographiques et Historiques de Genève*, 175
Greyffen See, 20
Grimm, teacher, persecution of, 38
Grindelwald, 47, 51, 56
Grisons, see Graubünden
Grivel, Ad. C., archivist, inventories by, 177, 178
Grob, Christian, death in Carolina, 22
Grob, Heinrich, power of attorney to, 22
Groszweibel, 49
Grün, *Maj.*, 238
Grünheim, Ky., Swiss settlement, 70
Grütli, Neb., Swiss settlement, 70
Grütli, Tenn., Swiss settlement, 71
Grütli Verein, colonization scheme of, 76
Gruner, Maria Rosalia, 198
Gruyères, emigration from, 153
Guatemala, 206
Gubler, D. Ursula, petition of, 138
Güggisberg, emigration from, 45
Guiana, Dutch, see Surinam
Guide to the German State Archives, see Learned, Marion Dexter
Guie, Friederich, 171
Guie, Jean Friederich, 171
Guie, Jeanne Marie, 171
Guienne, emigration to, 36
Guillemann, Franciscus, 217
Guinea, English and Danes on the coast of, 226
Gumbers, Philipp, persecution of, 259
Gustav, ship, 205
Guyenet, Jean Antoine, death in Philadelphia, 170
Guyot, Arnold, 149
Guyot, F. L., Swiss troops for Colombia, 25
Gwehnbergerin, Magdalena, persecution of, 259

Haebler, Konrad, *Die überseeischen Unternehmungen der Welser*, 265
Häfelfinger, inheritance, 110

Index 281

Hängi, *Denkschrift über die nordamerikanischen Verhältnisse*, 99
Hänszlin, Georg, Getraud, and Hanns, persecutions of, 259
Haga, Georg Friedrich, death in Philadelphia, 25
Hagemanns, of Pennsylvania, 21
Hague, American and Austrian ministers at the, 25
Haldimand, *Gen.* Frederick, 149, 162
Halifax, Nova Scotia, 203
Hallers Sammlung, 72
Hallwyl, Régiment de, 172
Hallwyl manuscripts, 140
Halter, H., report concerning transportation to America, 115
Hamburg, direct trade with America, 225, 226
Hammond, George, English minister to U. S., 228
Hanau, recruiting for England from, 239, 240
Handwörterbuch der Schweizerischen Volkswirtschaft, Reichesberg, 6
Hango, *Dr.* Hermann, vii
Hanhart, *Capt.*, deportation of, 23
Hannauer, article by, 104
Hanover, emigration from, 67; privileges to the Kingdom of, 193; troops in British service, 239
Hanover, Pa., Swiss near, 120
Hanse towns, treaty with Prussia, 254; treaty with U. S., 193, 194
Hanslik, 249
Hantz, pastor, letter of, 110
Harder, *Ober Vogt*, 122, 123
Harder Chronik, 124
Hardmeyer, Marie, 32
Hardmeyer, T., article by, 148
Harlan County, Ky., Swiss emigration to, 129
Harland, Richard, 198
Harmony, town in America, 23, 24
Harper, *Mrs.* Robert Goodloe, 198
Harring, Harro, 213
Harrisburg, Pa., disorder at the opening of the legislature at, 202
Hatz, Jeremias, blacksmith, petition of, 138
Hausen, 21
Hauser, expedition from Rotterdam to Fort York under, 171
Hauser, Kaspar, article by, 39
Havana, 206, 211
Havre, 117; cholera in, 116; complaint of Swiss consul, 153, 154; emigration port, 61, 75, 80, 81, 170; proposals of Swiss consul, 116; Werdenberg emigrants stranded at, 129
Hayti, 128
Hebron Church, 13
Hecht, Joseph, *Beschreibung der Meerfahrt ... nach Brasilien*, 82
Heimliche Emigranten, 5
Heinz, Johann Martin, surgeon, petition of, 136, 137
Heinzen, Karl, revolutionist, 11; deportation of, 251; *Der teutsche Tribun*, 12, 251; *Die Teutsche Revolution*, 251
Heisch, 24
Helffenstein, *Rev.* A., 59

Helvetia, Minn., Swiss settlement, 70
Helvetia, W. Va., Swiss settlement, 71
Helvetia, Wis., Swiss settlement, 71
Helvetia, ship, cholera on, 118
Helvetic Confederation, *see* Swiss Confederation
Helvetic Republic, 1, 159, 160, 163, 175
Helvetisches Archiv, Bern, 63
Hennin, successor to Gerard, 221
Herder, Ludwig, emigration agent, 21
Herisau, cantonal archive in, 127
Hermann, Pierre, 155
Hersche, Hans, 126
Hershey, Scott Funk, *History of the Hershey Family*, 126
Hershey family, in Lancaster Co., Pa., 126
Herziken, 21
Hesse-Darmstadt (grand-duchy), emigration from, 67
Hesse-Kassel (electorate), emigration from, 67
Hesserschweil, 23
Hessian troops, in British service, 239, 240
Heuser, *Dr.*, *Die Schweizer in St. Paolo*, 86; report on Brazil, 86
Heyer, Théophile, director of archives, 175
Highland, Ill., emigration from Luzern, 78; emigration from Sursee, 78; *Geschichte der Ansiedlung von*, 81; *Kurzer Reisebericht von Havre bis*, 81; Swiss consulate in, 26, 78, 110; Swiss settlers in, 70, 161
Highland, Ky., Swiss settlement, 70
Himmelrid, 98
Hinke, Wm. J., article by, 50; translator of Michel's journal, 72
Hinkender Bote, confiscated letters, 1752, 49
Hinderling, Ulr., emigration of, 23
Hinterholz, 259
Hirzel, 22
Hirzel, Johann Conrad, 14
Hirzel, L., article by, 31
Hisky, Joseph, 191
Historische Studien und Skizzen, 247
History of the Reformed Church, *see* Good, James I.
Höffern, *Frau* Antonia von, pension of, 206
Höxter, British recruits pass, 9, 238, 239
Hofmann, letters from, 108
Hohenberger, Carl Christ., consul in New Orleans, 200, 204
Holnsteiner, Peter, persecution of, 259, 260
Holzhofer, Michael, 194
Homburg, concerning emigration, 111
Hood, *Adm. Sir* Samuel, 224
Hôpital Général, Archives de l', 178
Horger, emigration of, 45
Horger, Barbara, petition of, 54
Hough, F. B., *History of Lewis County*, 173
Howard, Tilghman A., 206
Howe, *Sir* William, correspondence with Secretary of State, 222; return to England of, 221; superseded by Clinton, 221
Huber, a thief, receives aid to emigrate, 145
Huber, *Dr.* August, assistant archivist, vii
Huber, Hanns, 259
Huber, Heinrich, examination of, 22
Huber, Konrad, 146

Huber, Peter, agent, 39, 111; arrest of, 46, 47, 55, 111; attempt to smuggle letter, 4; deportation of, 46; emigrates to Carolina, 35, 38; escape of, 5; examination of. 55, 56, 57; extradition of, 22, 28; persecution of, 39, 46; return of, 46; trial of, 4
Huber, Ulrich, petition of, 21
Hudson Bay, 128
Hudson River, colony for Jews on, 250
Hudson's Bay Company, 171, 224
Hüber, emigration agent, 140
Hülsemann, *Chevalier* de, 10, 11, 210, 216; complaint to U. S. government, 215; departure of, 215; despatches to Metternich, 11, 211-215; on Canada, 208; on Catholic church in U. S., 208; on Charleston, 10, 204; on commercial convention, 204; on Democratic convention, 11, 209; on factories at Lowell, 10, 205; on Georgia, 204; on market for Austrian products, 204; on Norfolk. 10, 204; on North Carolina, 204; on products and commerce in Virginia, 204; on railroads. 10, 205; on Savannah, 10, 204; on South Carolina, 204; on trip to New England, 10, 205; on trip to Southern States, 10; on trip to the West, 208; on Whig convention. 11, 209; on white and black labor, 10, 204; on written constitution and the rights of neutrals on the sea, 10, 200; other reports, 207; pen-portraits of members of U. S. Congress, 11, 206
Hünigen, 20
Hüttau, 260
Hug, Alois, emigration of, 89
Hughes. *Bishop* John, influence over Irish population, 214
Huguenin, civil lieutenant, 171
Huguenot refugees, 177
Humphreys, *Col.* David, American minister to Portugal, 229, 231; minister to Spain, 232, 233
Hungary. miners to America from, 227; revolution in, 214, 215; Russian intervention, 215; Swiss emigration to, 69
Huser, Hieronymus, 54
Huttwyl. 80
Hyde, Edward, governor of North Carolina, 74

Illinois, 67; *Jahrbuch der Deutsch-Amerikanischen Historischen Gesellschaft von*, 74; Swiss settlements in, 6, 70
Imst, 265
Indemnities, 212, 226
India companies, deportation scheme of, 43; *see also* East India Company
Indiana, 67; Benedictine missions in, 84, 85; Swiss settlements in, 70
Indiana Magazine of History, 161
Indians, 181, 199, 208, 221, 251; hostilities with Spain, 226; treaty of Graffenried with Tuscarora Indians, 74; war with U. S., 229
India-rubber, 206
Ingersoll, Charles J., nomination of, 212
Inheritance cases, 22-25, 38, 39, 42, 50, 51, 54, 58-60, 63, 79, 86, 90, 93, 95, 105-107, 109, 110, 112-114, 116, 120, 124, 128, 141, 157, 188, 193, 194-197, 203, 206, 212, 242-246.
Innsbruck, archives of, v, vi, 8, 185; Bairisches Archiv, 265; Dialersche Normalien-Sammlung, 265; emigration records, 11, 265-267; Ferdinandeum, 266, 267; state archive, 265-266; Statthalterei-Archiv, 265, 266
Innsbrucker Zeitung, 267
Interlaken, Switzerland, emigrants from, 34, 39, 45, 46, 48, 50
Interlaken, Wis., Swiss settlement, 71
Inventare Schweizerischer Archive, 13, 27, 33, 89
Iowa, 67; Swiss settlements in, 70
Ireland, emigration from, 67
Iselin, Adrian Georg, founder of American branch, 120
Iselin, Heinrich, und sein Geschlecht, *see* Weiss-Frey, Fried.
Iselin brothers, transportation from Havre, 117
Iselin family, branches of, 120
Isenfluh, 50
Italia, Giovane, *see* Giovane Italia
Italiani negli Stati Uniti del Nord, Gl', 148
Italian-Swiss emigration, 147
Italy, Americana, new sect, 248; emigration from, 67; Italian refugees, 132; revolution, 214; Young, *see* Giovane Italia
Iten, Bländus, emigrates to Canada, 97
Iverten, 41

Jackson, Andrew, 206; and Col. Callava, 190; and Col. Coppinger, 190; attempted assassination of, 198; exequatur, 195; inaugural address, 194; messages, 194, 197, 198, 199; proclamation of, 194, 197; probable appointments of, 194; proposed for President, 191
Jägerlen, 19
Jäggi, letter of, 97
Jäggi-Gyger, *Auswanderungs-Zeitung*, 68
Jäggy, Valentin, emigration of, 140
Jahrbuch für Schweizerische Geschichte, 39, 53
Jamaica, disturbances in, 229; Spanish and French attack on, 224
Jameson. *Dr.* J. F., vi, 73, 149
Jansen, Max, *Jakob Fugger der Reiche*, 265; *Studien zur Fuggergeschichte*, 265
Jay, John, letters of Gallatin to, 180, 181
Jecklin, *Dr.* F. von, archivist, vii
Jefferson, Thomas, American minister to France, 226; letter to Tronchin. 181; University of Geneva and, 184; *Writings* of, 180
Jenifer, Daniel, envoy to Austria, 210; successor to Mühlenberg, 216
Jenny, Peter, plan for a charitable institution, 90, 91
Jenny-Trümpy, *Handel und Industrie des Kantons Glarus*, 130
Jesuits, 233
Jews, 95, 158, 250
Joggi Bohni, Eva, 103
Joggi Bohni, Hans, emigration and return of, 103
John, *Archduke*, 211

Index 283

Johnson, *Col.* R. M., 206
Joinville, *Prince* de, journey to U. S. of, 210
Joner, Jacob, agent, 49, 105, 106; deportation of, 49, 105, 106; examination of, 112; order to arrest, 48; return of, 48, 113; reward for arrest of, 106
Jones, John Paul, exploits of, 224
Joos, *Dr.* Wilhelm, colonial scheme of, 68, 155
Joseph II., emperor, 187, 228; *Die Zensur unter*, 247
Josephinische Gesetzsammlung, 256
Journal of the Presbyterian Historical Society, 50
Jovovich, Georgio, 194
Junt, and family, emigration of, 107
Jurisdiction, dispute over, 38

Kälin, Meinrad, article by, 85
Kahn, Dan., inheritance of, 59
Kaiser, *Dr.* Jakob. archivist, vii
Kalchrain, 117
Kallbruner, *Dr.* Josef, secretary, vii
Kambli, Heinrich. suspected as agent, 21
Kansas, Swiss settlements in, 70
Károlyi, *Hofrat* Árpad von, vi; *Katalog der Archivalien-Ausstellung*, 186
Karrer, L., *L'Émigration Suisse*, 6; *Das Schweizerische Auswanderungswesen*, 6
Karrer-Hallwyl regiment, *see* Merveilleux
Katholische Missionen im nordoestlichen Arkansas, 85
Katholische Studien, 84
Kaufmännisches Direktorium, Archive of, 130; *Berichte des*, 25, 131
Kaufmann, Isaac. deportation of, 37
Kaunitz, *Prince* Anton Wenzel von, report on treaty, 187
Keller, *Pastor*, recommendation of, 127
Keller, Gottfried, 29
Kendalia, W. Va., Swiss settlement, 71
Kennan, K. K., emigration agent, 118, 119
Kentucky, 67; Bernstadt colony in, 69, 70; Bureau of Geology and Immigration, 81; *Die materiellen Verhältnisse . . . für Einwanderer im Staate*, 81; Swiss settlements, 70, 161
Kerenzen, 92
Kilchberger, *Dean*, 58
Kilchenmann, I. E., article by, 100
Kissling, Daniel. letter from Carolina to, 46
Klagenfurth, provincial archive of, 8
Klein, Lisette. emigration of, 145
Kleinlützel, 98
Klenk, V., emigration agent, 117
Knonau, emigration from, 14, 20, 21, 22, 23
Knox, Julia L., article by, 161
Köhler, Jos., 249
Köpfli, Kaspar, *Licht und Schattenseite von New-Switzerland*, 81
Köpfli, Salomon. *Geschichte der Ansiedlung von Highland*, 81; *Neu Schweizerland*, 81; *Spiegel von Amerika*, 82
Köpfli family, 78; *Reisebericht der*, 81
Körner, J., petition of, 28
Kolbener, 126

Kossuth, Louis, *vs.* Hülsemann, 215
Koster, Gerard, defalcations of, 68; extradition of, 109, 141
Kraft, Elisabeth, persecution of, 261
Kraxenbiehl, 259
Kretschmayr, *Prof. Dr.* Heinrich, vii
Kretschmayr, *see also* Fellner-Kretschmayr
Kreuzherren, and Postl, 249
Kribeck, *Freiherr* von, 216
Kriens, 79
Kron, Andreas, and family, emigration of, 134, 135; petition for aid, 132
Kudlich, Hans, liberator of the Austrian peasantry, 12
Küntzi, Christian, emigration of, 43
Küntzlin, *see* Schmidt, Anna Barbara
Künzli, inheritance of, 59
Küssnacht, 24
Küttigen, 142
Kuhn, schoolmaster, petition of, 18
Kuhn, T. C., Swiss consul to Texas, 67
Kulm, 25
Kurile Islands, commercial relations with, 226
Kurz, G., assistant archivist, vii
Kyburg, 14, 20

Laborie, *Rev.* Jacques, letter of, 73
Labrador, 218
Lace, trade in, 7, 131
Lady, English ship, 59
Läufelfingen, 103
Lafayette, *Marquis* de, eulogy of, 198; goes to America, 219
Laibach, 251; provincial archive, 8
Lammer, Ed., 200
La Mothe Piquet, seizure of English ships by, 59
Lamson, John, American consul in Triest, 233, 253
Lancaster, Ohio, 120
Lancaster, Pa., 59
Lancaster Co., Pa., Hershey family in, 126; Swiss settlement, 63
Landau, commission receives letters from Carolina, 44
Landmann, article by, 53
Landry, John, article by, 162; *New Berne*, 73
Landsassen, an undesirable element of population, 3, 40
Lang, carpenter, emigration of, 124
Langer, J., *Das K. u. K. Kriegsarchiv*, 237
Langlois, Ch., and H. Stein, *Les Archives de l'Histoire de France*, 1n., 8, 186
Langnau, 42
Lanz, Johann, *Das Für und Wider der Auswanderung nach Amerika*, 80
La Planche, Jean-Lazare de, 180
La Plata states, Swiss emigration to, 93, 128
La Sollaye, *Capt.*, 238
Laurens, Henry, 223
Lausanne, 46; academy of, 160; Bishop of, 159; cantonal archives in, 159; city archives of, 161; Hôtel de Ville, 161; synod of the national church, archives, 161
Lawson, *New Voyage to Carolina*, 3

Learned, M. D., iii; *Guide to the German State Archives*, 149; *Life of Francis Daniel Pastorius*, 30
Lebanon, Pa., 113, 193, 216
Lechner, *Dr. A.*, Staatsschreiber, vii
Lederer, *Baron* Alois, Austrian consul general, 10, 189, 200, 210, 211, 237; application for post in Mexico, 205; audience with John Quincy Adams, 190; audience with President Monroe, 190; consular agents appointed by, 198; death of, 212; despatches to Metternich, 189-200; goes to Washington, 194, 199; instructions to, 215, 216; report on landing of immigrants, 250; report on Count Leon, 196; Tuscany consulate, 190, 237
Lee, William, mission to Vienna, 9, 221
Legacy, *see* Inheritance
Legaré, Hugh S., 206
Leghorn, American emissaries in, 248
Lehmann, Christoph, petition of, 116
Léman, Canton du, 159, 160, 161, 175
Léman, Département du, 159, 175, 177, 183
Lemberg, provincial archive of, 8
Leon, *Count, see* Müller, Bernhard
Leopold, *Archibishop*, 263
Leopoldina, Brazil, Swiss settlers in, 161
Leopoldina Institution, 208, 216, 244
Lerch, *Dr. E., Die Bernische Auswanderung nach Amerika*, 33, 50
Lerchenau, *Rittmeister* von, vii
Le Roy, Jean Jaques, commissary, 171
Leu, *Landvogt*, 20
Leutmerk, 146
Lewis County, N. Y., *History* of, 173
Leyder wahrhaffte Traurige Geschicht, Eine, 30
Liberale Alpenbote, der, 139
Liberté, La, article in, 151
Library of Congress, Washington, D. C., 190
Liebenau, *Dr. Theodor, Geschichte der Stadt Willisau*, 80
Liechstal, 103, 111
Liestal, archives, 121; emigration from, 114
Lighthouse, 254
Lightning-rod, 52
Lignières, 169
Lill, Geo., *Hans Fugger und die Kunst*, 265
Lincoln, Abraham, assassination of, 78; death of, 96; Lincoln album, 142
Lindau, 18
Linen, trade in, 131, 188, 254
Linherr, 126
Linnaean Society, New York, 192
Lisbon, 11, 210, 218, 220
Lithuania, 19
Little York, *see* York, Pa.
Livre des Bourgeois . . . de Genève, see Covelle, Alfred L.
Locarno, section near, depopulated by emigration, 148
Locle, 171
Lodge, H. C., *Daniel Webster*, 215
Lombard-Venetian conspirators of 1835, deportation of, 11, 250
Lombardy, history of, 185; political refugees from, 207

London, 14, 45, 46, 103; Austrian embassy in, 203
Longueville, house of, 166
Louisiana, American invasion, 227; boundary disputes, 233, 234; French expedition, 233; sale to U. S., 233; Spain fears English aggression against, 229; Spain protests against cession of, 234; *see also* Merveilleux, *Capt.*
Louisville, Ky., Franciscan monastery in, 266; Swiss consulate, 7, 26, 65, 67
Lowell, Hülsemann's report on factories at, 10, 205
Loyalists, indemnities to, 226
Luchsinger, John, *The Planting of the Swiss Colony at New Glarus*, 94; *The Swiss Colony of New Glarus*, 94
Ludwig, Franz, 255
Lusser, *Dr.* Karl, manuscript collection of, 83
Lutherans, in Virginia, 13
Luze, L. Ph. de, Swiss consul at New York, 64
Luzenberg, *Baron* Carl von, 206
Luzern, 1, 2, 25, 115; Bürgerbibliothek, 81, 82; city archives, 81, 82; emigrants in France, 116; emigration agencies, 81; emigration from, 79, 80; emigration laws, 78, 80, 81; emigration statistics, 81; emigration to Algeria, 116; emigration to Highland, Ill., 78; emigration via, 129; emigration via Prussian Rhine provinces, 115; emigration via the Netherlands, 62; in favor of Swiss consulates, 62; Jesuitenkollegium, 78; organized emigration, 81; state archive, vi, 78-81; *see also* Vorort, Luzern
Luzerne, Ia., Swiss settlement, 70
Luzerne, Mich., Swiss settlement, 70
Luzerne, Pa., Swiss settlement, 71

Maag, Hans Heinrich, emigration of, 18
Maas, Otto, Austrian vice-consul general to U. S., 257
McLaughlin, English territorial agent, 203
McLeod affair, 209, 210
Madison, Wis., letters from, 67; Swiss consulate in, 7, 65, 67, 110; Swiss emigration to, 67
Madonna del Carmine, La, ship, 239
Madrid, 220
Märk, emigration agent, 140
Märlis, Johann Jakob, 141
Märsteten, complaint against emigration from, 19
Mafra, Franciscan convent at, 228
Magdalenengesellschaft, 250
Magellan, Strait of, 69
Magny, Constantin de, dépositaire royal, 177
Mahler, Joseph, in U. S. army, 79
Maine, act on finance, 204; boundary dispute, 196, 203
Mainz, 92
Malacrida und Co., banking house, 53
Malta, priorships, 229
Mandatenbücher, Bern, 41, 73
Mangourit, M. A. B., consul at Charleston, 163
Manila, 220
Mann, A. Dudley, mission to Hungary, 215

Index

Maps, 72, 74, 218, 219, 229, 243, 245, 247
Marbach, 79
Marcos de Nizza, Fray, 216
Marcus, Susanni, trade in salt, 239
Mareschal, Wenzel Philipp *Freiherr* von, minister to U. S., 10, 200; despatches to Metternich, 10, 200-210; instructions to, 215, 216; receives post at Lisbon, 11, 210; trip to New England, 208; trip to the West and North, 205
Maria Stein, near Pocahontas, Ark., 85
Maria Theresia, empress, 185, 234
Marine railroads, 244
Maronielli, Pietro, 198, 199
Marret, Swiss consul in Mexico, assassinated, 95
Marriage, citizenship by, 96, 142
Martignier and Crousaz, *Dictionnaire Historique du Canton de Vaud*, 161
Marschner, Anton, inheritance of, 193, 195, 196, 197
Marseille, 239
Martin, *Father*, letter to, 84
Martin, *Lands-Venner*, letter to, 82
Martin, C., article by, 176
Martin, *Dr.* Franz, vii
Martin, Paul E., archivist, *Catalogue des MSS. de la Collection Grenaud*, 151; État Général et Sommaire de Fonds, 177, 178
Martinique, Dutch occupation of, 230
Maryland, 210
Maschwanden, 22
Masonic orders in U. S., movement against, 195
Massachusetts, railroad legislation in, 205
Mater, von, petition of, 24
Mather, Cotton, *Diary*, 184
Mathey, *Capt.*, letter to, 171
Mathisen, Heinrich, return of, 20
Maurer, Franz, claim of, 200
Maurer, Jakob, petition of, 29
Mauth-Tariff, regulation of, 216
Maximilian I., 185
May, Swiss commissioner to England, 45
May, Beath Ludwig, Säckelschreiber, 54
May, Emanuel, *Histoire Militaire de la Suisse*, 99
May, *Capt.* Emanuel, Red River colony, 61, 171, 172; *see also* Red River
May, *Capt.* Rudolph, Red River colony, 53, 61, 128, 171, 172; *Kurze und wahre Uebersicht*, 115; *see also* Red River
Mayence, *see* Mainz
Mayr, *Dr.* Michael, director, vii
Mead, Edwin D., article by, 184
Mediation, Russian and Prussian (1779), 222; Russian (1813), 235
Meiden, emigration of, 45
Meienthal, 83
Meier, J. P., petition of, 142
Memmingen, city council on emigration, 127
Mennonites, Dutch, 3; Swiss, 3
Menzingen, 97
Mediterranean, American warships in the, 235
Menzel, Joseph A., 210
Mercury, mines, 253; trade, 255
Mercy-Argenteau, *Count* Florimond von, criticism of treaty of commerce, 9, 187; letter of, 187
Meredyth, emigration agent, 248
Meriszhausen, emigration from, 122, 123, 124
Merle, John A., Swiss consul at New Orleans, 65
Merveilleux, *Capt.*, recruiting by, 3, 33, 34, 41, 42, 53, 54
Methodists, 27
Metmenstätten, 22
Mett, meeting at, 38
Metternich, *Prince* Clement Wenceslaus, 10, 11, 200; despatches to Hülsemann, 211-215; despatches of Lederer to, 189-200; despatches of Mareschal to, 200-210; despatches of Stürmer to, 189; instructions to Hülsemann, 216; instructions to Lederer, 215; instructions to Mareschal, 215; instructions to Stürmer, 215; letter to U. S. Secretary of State, 215; letters to, 199, 216; spying system of, 247
Meuron, Charles Daniel de, 172
Meuron, Th., articles by, 172; *Essai Historique sur le Régiment Suisse de Meuron*, 172
Meuron, Régiment de, 171, 172
Mexico, 10, 79, 84, 128, 202-205, 213, 216; amnesty for insurgents, 225; archbishop appointed viceroy, 232; Austrian emigration to, 241; blockade of coast, 200, 201, 204, 216; condition in, 195; convention between U. S. and, 212; diplomatic agent to Vienna, 212; emigration of Tyrolese miners to, 265; insurrections, 225, 226, 231, 232; list of gold and silver coins of, 220; maps of, 247; navigation treaty with U. S., 193; negotiations with Adm. Baudin, 203; occupation of city of Mexico, 214; Prince Paul von Württemberg in, 196; secret trading in, 220; statistics, 246; Swiss commercial treaty, 95; Swiss consul Marret assassinated, 95; Swiss consular reports on, 93; Swiss consulate in, 26; Swiss emigration to, 69; trade relations with, 25, 95; treaty with France, 204; treaty with Switzerland, 95; viceroy Don Bernardo de Galvez, death of, 227; war with Texas, 61; war with U. S., 214; *see also* New Spain
Mexico, Gulf of, Austrian supplies for French colonies on, 223
Meyer, Daniel, return of, 111
Meyer, Jacob, petition of, 24
Meyer, Joh., inheritance of, 23, 24
Meyer, Lucia, petition of, 137; petition refused, 138
Meyer von Knonau, G., *Der Kanton Zürich*, 28
Micarelli, V., commerce with U. S., mémoire on, 216
Michel, Franz Ludwig, article on, 72; contract with Ritter and Co., 74; letter of, 73; *Reisebeschreibung*, 72
Michigan, 67; Swiss settlements in, 70
Milan, 207, 250
Military pensions, *see* Pensions
Miller, 248
Milwaukee, consulate in, 26

Minder, Johann Baptist, 79
Minnesota, Swiss settlements in, 70
Mischler, emigration of, 45
Mississippi, 208; securities, 53; Swiss emigration to, 42, 54, 169; *see also* Merveilleux
Mississippi Company, 41
Mississippi River, free navigation of, 229, 230, 234
Missiven Buch, 54
Missouri, 87: Duden's book brings settlers to, 11; outline of the constitution of, 190; slave-trade, 190; Swiss settlements in, 6, 70
Mittelberger, Gottlieb, *Reise nach Pennsylvanien*, 20, 51
Mobile, English failure against, 223
Möhr, J., chief of the federal Auswanderungsamt, Bern, vii
Mölzel, Johann, death of, 206
Moering, *Ingenieur Captain* Carl, in U. S., 211, 212
Mohl, emigration of, 116
Mollis, 92
Moritz, colony in Brazil, 156
Monroe, James, messages, 190, 191; reception in Geneva of, 179, 180; *Writings*, 179, 180
Monticello, Fla., Swiss settlement, 70
Montjou, *Lieut.-Col.*, letter of, 171
Montreux, 161
Moore, J. B., *Digest of International Law*, 215n.
Morancour, articles on Carolina and Pennsylvania, 48
Morgenstern, 139
Morillo, *Gen.* Pablo, 190
Moritzi, F., petition for aid refused, 138
Mormons, Swiss, acta, 27; emigration, 7, 75, 77
Morris, Robert, letter from, 181
Morse, S. F. B., telegraph of, 212
Moser, Hans, return of, 50
Mosquito Coast, grievances between England and Spain concerning, 226, 227
Motta, E., archivist, 147, 148
Mottaz, E., *Dictionnaire Historique .... du Canton de Vaud*, 159, 160
Motzl, 259
Mount Angel College, Ore., architectural plans of, 88; *Die Benediktiner Kolonie*, 87; founding of, 87; newspaper articles on, 88
Moustier, *Count* de, French minister to Prussia, 228
Mudrich, *Dr.* Andreas, director, vii
Mühlenberg, Henry A., U. S. minister to Austria, 10, 208, 209, 210, 216
Mülinen, *Prof. Dr.* W. F. von, chief librarian, vii; *Christoph von Graffenried*, 74; library of, 74, 75
Müller, Bernhard, religionist, 11, 196, 250
Müller, Daniel, kidnapping of, 53
Müller, Jacob, petition of, 101
Müller, Maria, petition for aid refused, 145
Müller, Ulrich, 56
Müller und Co., banking house, 53
Müllhausen, recruiting for England in, 239
Münchenbuchsee, 43
Münden (Hanover), 251
Mumpf, 22
Murat, *Prince* Achille, 207, 208

Muri, Casimir, donation of Civil War papers, 79; pension for, 79
Musée Neuchâtelois, article in, 172
Mussi, Joseph, 253
Muttenz, emigration from, 48, 111
Myers, A. C., *Narratives of Early Pennsylvania*, 30
Nabholz, *Prof. Dr.* Hans, state archivist, vii
Nach dem fernen Westen, 87
Nachrichtsblättlein of Zürich, 18
Näf, Heinrich, agent, 21
Nägely, Jakob and Peter, petitions of, 35
Nantes, proposal for Austrian consul at, 222
Naples, treaty with U. S., 198
Napoleon I., *see* Bonaparte, Napoleon
Nassau-Saarbrücken, Swiss emigration to, 42
Nassau-Usingen, *Field Marshal Lieut. Prinz*, 238
Nater, Jakob, article by, 146
National Council, Bern, emigration laws discussed in, 76
National Gazette of Philadelphia, 190, 191, 195
National Institute, 246
National Intelligencer, 190, 191, 193, 208
Natter, *Rev.* John Jos., 249
Natural History, Society of, Amherst, 192
Naturalization, 213; *see also* Citizenship
Naval expeditions, 218, 219, 220, 221, 224, 228, 229, 230, 231, 232, 233, 242, 244, 245
Navy, U. S., Secretary of the, report of, 195
Nebraska, Swiss settlements in, 70
Netherlands, 67; Adams, American minister, 224, 225; commercial relations with America, 222, 224, 225; commercial relations with West Indies, 220, 227; complaint against Swiss emigrants, 5, 84, 115, 141, 144, 170; complaint against war supplies for the American colonies, 217, 218, 220; complaint of Dutch West India Co., 226; complaint over Anabaptists, 37; complaint to Denmark regarding whale fishery, 218; complaint to France and Spain regarding negroes, 218, 220, 226; convoys for ships to West Indies, 220, 221; debt of Dutch West India Co., 229; emigration from, 67; emigration laws, 23, 24, 25, 79, 115, 140, 141, 170, 171; emigration via, 25, 62, 84, 91, 140, 157, 158, 170, 171, 217; fear of war between England and U. S., 231; food supplies to English colonies, 218; foreign vessels in quarantine, 237; inheritance dispute with Bern, 38; list of Swiss emigrants to, 13; loan for American colonies, 224, 225, 228; Mennonites in, 3; Scottish regiments, 124; seizure of Dutch ships by English, 221; South Holland Synod, petition of, 106; Swiss emigrants, 13, 107, 115, 122; synod of the Reformed Church, 58; treaty with U. S., 205; Van Berckel, minister to U. S., 223, 227; *see also* Batavian; Belgium
Netzthal, emigration statistics from, 92
Neuchâtel, 38, 42, 49, 54, 57, 128, 149; Audience du Comte, 166; Audiences Générales, 166, 168; Chambre Économique, 168; Chancellerie, 166; church archives, 174; city ar-

Index   287

chives, 173; Classis, archives of, 166. 173-174; colonial scheme, 3; Commissaire Général, 166; communes. 168, 169; Company of Pastors, 166. 173-174; conference of 1846, 116; Corps Législatif, 166, 168; emigration from, 64, 169, 171; emigration laws, 38, 169, 170; emigration to Pennsylvania, 171; emigration to Russia, 173; *état civil*, registers, 168; Grand Council, 166, 168; independent principality, 2; insurrections, 166; *Le Véritable Messager Boiteux de*, 173; library of the city, 173; Manuaux du Conseil d'État, 167, 169; Missives, 168; *Musée Neuchâtelois*, cited, 172; notarial registers, 168; passport list since 1796, 171; Pièces Annexes, 167, 171; Prince of, 166; *Procès-Verbaux des Audiences Générales de*, 168; Protestants, 166; Quatre Ministraux, 173; reports on Carolina and Pennsylvania, 46; state archive, vi, 166-173; Tribunal des Trois États, 166; under King of Prussia, 2, 166, 168; uniform policy of emigration, 170; *see also* Pury, Jean Pierre
Neue Nachricht alter und neuer Merkwürdigkeiten, 31
Neuenburg, *see* Neuchâtel
Neu Engelberg, *see* New Engelberg
Neuengelberg, *see* Mount Angel
Neu-Gefundenes Eden, 29, 30
Neu Helvetia, Uruguay, Swiss at, 93, 146
Neujahrsblatt des Waisenhauses Zürich, 13
Neuländer, 109, 113
Neunkirch, 122, 123
Neutäufer, 27
Neutrality, 78, 252; violations of, 203, 222, 236
New Baden, Texas, Swiss settlement, 71
New Basel, Kan., Swiss settlement, 70
Newbern, Ala., Swiss settlement, 70
Newbern, Ind., Swiss settlement, 70
Newbern, Ia., Swiss settlement, 70
Newbern, Kan., Swiss settlement, 70
Newbern, Minn., Swiss settlement, 70
New Bern, N. C., article on, 73; description of, 3, 60, 73; map of. 74; Swiss settlement, 70
Newbern, Tenn., Swiss settlement, 71
Newbern, Va., Swiss settlement, 71
Newberne, Ill., Swiss settlement, 70
New Brunswick, boundary dispute, 203, 204
Newburgh, N. Y., 197
New Engelberg, Mo., Abbey of Conception, 88; petition to the Pope, 87; Swiss settlement, 70
New England, Hülsemann's trip to, 10, 205; Mareschal's trip to, 208
Newfoundland, 230
New Glarus, Wis., 6, 71. 92, 93; aid from canton Glarus, 9, 92; bibliography, 94; congratulatory message to, 93; founding of, 94; postoffice in. 92; report from, 91; report of the Glarner Verein on, 26
New Jersey, Swiss inhabitants in, 6
New Orleans, 65, 193, 195, 200. 204, 206; climatic conditions, 66; Die Deutsche Gesellschaft and its agency, 66; English failure against, 223; immigration statistics, 66; *Société de Bienfaisance de, Compte Rendu*, 65; Swiss charitable institution, 27, 65, 84, 117, 141; Swiss consulate in. 7, 26, 65, 66, 80. 110, 170, 172; Swiss immigration via, 65, 116, 135, 141; Swiss immigrants in, 27, 66, 141. 170, 172
New Oxford, Mass., 73
New St. Gallen, W. Va., Swiss settlement, 71
New Spain, 219; *see also* Mexico
New Subiaco Abbey. Ark., 84
New Switzerland, Ga., Swiss settlement. 70
New Switzerland, Ill., *see* Highland, Ill.
New York City, 52, 131, 154, 189, 192. 194, 195, 198, 199, 205, 207, 210, 250, 251, 255; Agricultural Society, 191; Austrian consulate in, 212. 245, 254; bureau of emigration, 96; capture of, 218; charitable institution in, 27; cholera, 197; commissioners of water works, report of, 201; Delmonico restaurant, 147; Exposition, 26; German Society offers aid to emigrants, 118; immigration statistics, 64; Italian newspaper in, 148; Italian revolution, demonstration in favor of, 214; Louis Kossuth in, 215; maps, 218, 219; Mareschal's arrival in, 200; *New Yorker Staatszeitung*, 191; riots in, 198; sequestration of silk in, 26; society for the benefit of Swiss immigrants, 64, 142; Swiss consulate, 7, 24, 26, 63, 64. 91, 110. 170; synod, 52; trip from Bremen to, 119; yellow fever in, 191
New York (state), 173; banking act, 202; immigration laws, 91; Swiss settlements in, 6, 71, 131;
Nicolaus, Simon, bishop of Basel, 63
Nicolet, Theodore, first consul at New Orleans, 65
Nidwalden, emigration from, 87; emigration list, 89; state archive, vi, 89; *see also* Unterwalden
Niederberg, *Dr.* Nikolaus, 193
Niles, Nathaniel, diplomatic mission to Austria, 199
Noblet, Jean. colonization scheme of, 178; letter of, 178; petition of, 179
Nootka Sound, 229, 230
Nordhausen, recruiting for England in. 239
Norfolk, Va., Hülsemann's report on, 10, 204
North Carolina, *Colonial Records* of, 73, 162; Hülsemann's report on, 204; letters from, 74; Swiss settlements in, 71; *see also* Carolina
Northeastern boundary question, 190, 196. 203, 204
North German Lloyd. 119
Northwest Company. 171
Nouvelle-Fribourg, Swiss colony in Brazil, 147
Nova Scotia, emigration to, 36, 48, 49. 106
Novella Helvetia, Italian newspaper. 148
Nüscheler, Solomon, emigration of, 21
Nuovo Secolo dell' Elvezia, article in, 148
Nuremberg, 259

Oberägeri, 97
Ob die Herrschaft Worb, 60
Oberdorf, 98

20

288 Index

Oberhasli, 38, 46, 55, 111; emigration from, 34, 39, 44, 45, 46
Oberhofen, emigration from, 34
Oberinnthal, emigration from, 266
Oberland, Bernese, 55; emigration from, 5, 39, 44, 46, 49
Oberried, 50
Ober-Simmenthal, Landschafts Commission, 60
Obwalden, emigration, 87; agencies, 87; statistics, 86, 87; state archive, vi, 86, 87; *see also* Unterwalden
Ochs, Johann Rudolff, 41; *Amerikanische Inseln*, 41; *Amerikanischer Wegweiser*, 3, 31; letter of, 73
Ochs, P., *Geschichte der Stadt und Landschaft Basel*, 113
O'Connor, *Father* Beda, journey to America, 84, 85
Odermatt, *Father* Adelhelm, founder of Mount Angel, 87
Oehrli, Christ., 50
Öri, cooper, returns from Carolina, 22
Öri, *Landvogt*, estate of, 21
Oesterreichische Wochenschrift für Wissenschaft, Kunst, u. öffentliches Leben, article in, 267
Oesterreich von 1848-1860, Friedjung, 247
Offenbach, religious fanaticism in, 250
Official publications, exchange of, 96, 155
Ohio, 67; Swiss settlements in, 6, 71
Ohio River, free navigation, 229, 230
Opfershofen, 122
Opfikon, 22
Orange, Anna Pavlovna, *Princess* of, 197
Ordinari Sambstagsblätlin, 44
Oregon, monastery in, 87; Swiss settlements, 71
Oregon question, 68, 203, 213, 214, 216
Orosco, appointment as Spanish minister, 232
Ortenau, emigration from, 235
Othmarsingen, 140
Ott, Swiss consul at Madison, 67
Ottawa Indians, 251
Otter-skins, tariff on, 241
Otto, *Col.*, 238
Ozark, Mo., Swiss settlement, 70

Pacific Ocean, 222
Pakenham, Richard, minister of England, 203
Palatinate, colonists from, 74; Swiss emigration to, 13
Palmerston, *Viscount*, correspondence over *Caroline*, 203
Panama, consulate in, 26
Paolina, ship, 233
Paquier, Joseph, letter of, 172
Paris, 171, 200, 221, 222
Parish, David, property of, 192, 193
Paraguay, 128
Passett, A., petition to emigrate, 138
Passports, American, 251; for Austrian officers during war, 241
Pastorius, Francis Daniel, founder of Germantown, 30; *Copia eines von einem Sohne, N. Y.*, 30; *Life* of, 30; *Sichere Nachricht*, 30

Patents, 141, 255
Patria e Progresso, 148
Payerne, abbey of, 161
Pecher, *Dean*, letter of, 249
Pecos River, 161
Pedro, *Dom.* accession of, 157
Pelizcaro, Pietro, 211
Pembina, 172
Pennsylvania, article on, 48; canal of, 206; *Das verlangte, nicht erlangte Canaan*, 31; description of, 14; German preachers for, 40; French colony in, 73; letters from, 4, 19, 49, 50; *Narratives of Early Pennsylvania*, 30; *Neu-Gefundenes Eden*, 29, 30; Reformed community of, 106, 130; *Reise nach Pennsylvanien*, 20, 51; Ritter plans colony in, 40; *Sichere Nachricht aus America*, 30; Swiss emigration to, v, 14, 15, 17-22, 29-31, 33, 36, 37, 39-43, 46, 48-51, 58, 63, 73, 101-107, 110-112, 123, 125, 171; Swiss Mennonites to, 3; Swiss settlements in, 71; travels in, 20; *Wahrhafte Erzehlung*, 19, 130
Pensacola, Jackson and Callava in, 190; rumor of English landing at, 228
Pensions, 7, 79, 124, 142, 156, 158, 206, 227
Percussion-locks, 195
Pernambuco, Brazil, 79; insurrection in, 228
Perry, merchant, recommends steamboats, 254
Peru, blockade of coast, 235; consulate in, 26; convention between U. S. and Peru-Bolivia confederation, 201; expedition of Vice-Admiral Cochrane, 190; silver-mines, 227; viceroy of, 226
Peter, estate of, 110
Péter, Jean Friederich, 171
Péter, Samuel, 171
Peterson, C. C., consular agent in New York, 192
Pewelef, Marguerite, 171
Pfäffikon, 22
Pfeiffer, Casper, agent, 129
Pfeiffer, Hans Jakob, 122, 123
Pfister, Balthazar, letter of, 19
Pfister, Joh. Jakob, power of attorney to, 59
Pfister (Beneke and Pfister), 241
Pharmaceutical articles, 244
Philadelphia, Jakob, 52
Philadelphia, 25, 30, 43, 120, 128, 170, 198, 200, 206, 211, 256; charitable institution in, 27; commissioners of water works, report, 201; Exposition, 26, 142; Handelskonsulat in, 66-67; letter from, 103; newspaper advertisements concerning Gallatin, 180; relation of, 51; Schlatter, Michael, 40, 49, 58; Stürmer, Austrian consul general in, 236; suspension of banks, 206; Swiss consul, complaint of, 97, 142; Swiss consulate in, 7, 26, 65, 66, 110; Swiss consulate's reply to Société d'Utilité, 66; synod report to Swiss Reformed Church, 52; yellow fever in, 241
Piaget, Arthur, archivist, 168
Pictet, Marc Antoine, correspondence of, 184
Pietists, 38
Pigot, *Adm.* Hugh, arrival in New York, 224
Pilots, Austrian signal for, 192
Pine Hill-Salzburg, Ky., Swiss settlement, 70

Pinckney, Charles, U. S. minister to Spain, 233, 234
Pirates, 34; Algerian, 231; of Barbary states, 235; of Morocco, 225; of South America, 236; of Tunis, 233; West India, 191
Pisa, 252
Pittsburgh, Pa., factories in, 206
Planta, consul general in Amsterdam, 115, 141, 157
Plattner, Verena, letter of, 110
Plitt, G., 205
Plöckli, Mathis and Peter, petitions for aid, 137
Plotho, Erich Christoph, *Edler vom*, property claims of the Salzburg Protestants, 262, 264
Plümacher, colonial scheme of, 69
Plüss, Jakob, estate of, 59
Pocahontas, Ark., Swiss settlement, 70
Point Breeze, 195
Poland, 19; Russian-Polish refugees, 245, 246; Swiss emigration to, 79, 96
Polignac, de, French ambassador, 59
Polk, James K., 206
Poll, arrested in Zürich, 36
Pomerania, Swiss emigration to, 3, 14, 18, 36
Ponceau, Peter S. du, letter of, 181
Population increase in American colonies, 218
Port Bretton, emigration to, 69
Portalès-Gorgier, *Count*, proposals on emigration, 168
Portefeuilles des Pièces Historiques, in Geneva archives, 175, 176, 177, 178
Porto Rico, 172, 194
Portugal, boundary disputes with Spain, 230; commercial relations with America, 227, 229; complaint against Dutch West India Co., 229; diplomatic agents of, 195; discord in ministry, 227; England claims warships, 233; English convoy for fleet, 232; exportation of wines, 227; fleet, 231, 232, 233, 234; fleet against Algiers, 228, 231; France proposes to conquer, 232; hostilities on Rio Grande between Spain and, 217, 218, 219, 220; Humphreys, American minister, 229, 231; insurrection in colonies, 233; invasion by France, rumor of, 232, 233; pensions, 227; ports closed to English-American vessels, 219; proposed commercial treaty with America, 232, 233; return of vice-governor to, 233; secret negotiations with England, 233; seizure of American ship at Lisbon, 220; seizure of French frigate, 230; silver fleet, 227, 231, 232; Spanish succession, 227; treaty of peace with Brazil, 157; Van Buren's proposed trip to, 196
Post, P. Sidney, American consul general in Vienna, 256
Postal relations, between Austria and America, 242, 245; Swiss, 7, 96, 97, 120
Poster, Hans, 56
Postl, Carl, 11, 249; *Austria as it Is*, 11
Potato disease, treatise on, 67
Potowmac, frigate, 196
Powder, exportation from Austria, 243
Powers, Swiss consul general to the U. S., 153, 158

Prague, 248, 249; archives, 8; Gregg, American consul at, 256
Prankl, *Dr.* Hans, vii, 217
Prattelen, 48
Presburg, 248
Presbyterian Historical Society, *Journal* of, 50n.
Preston, Wm. C., 206
Preziosi, G., *Gl'Italiani negli Stati Uniti del Nord*, 148
Prinzinger, A., jr., article by, 258
Prisoners, French officers in England, 219; Neapolitan, release of, 241
Prizes, American, 59, 219, 220, 224, 228, 233, 235; English, 220, 221, 222, 226, 234; French, 59, 230; Portuguese, 231; Spanish, 224, 229, 230, 232, 235
Proctor, John R., 81
Proli, *see* Müller, Bernhard
Proli, *Count* Balthasar de, diplomatic correspondence, 187
Property, private, confiscated, 243
Protestant cantons, emigration from, 5, 77
Protokollum Actorum Ecclesiasticorum, 18, 20
Providence Island, Spanish conquest of, 224
Prussia, 235; alliance with American colonies, 221; commercial treaty with Hanse towns, 254; commercial treaty with U. S., 226; complaint against Swiss paupers, 5; correspondence of the Quatre Ministraux with, 173; documents of the Neuchâtel administration, 168; emigration from, 67; emigration from Bern to, 38, 41; emigration from Schaffhausen to, 125; flag, 225; mediation, 9, 222; navigation treaty with U. S., 193; Prince of Neuchâtel, 166, 168, 169; reciprocity, 193; refuge of Mennonites in, 3; regulations, emigrant transports, 23, 79, 115, 140; subsidy treaty with England and Russia, 218; Wiedertäufer, 38; *see also* Frederick William I.; Neuchâtel; Salzburger Protestants
Prussia, East, Swiss emigration to, 42
Public Utility, Society of, *see* Société d' Utilité Publique
Punta Arena, emigration to, 156, 157
Purry, Jean Pierre, colonial scheme of, 3, 38, 42, 43, 54, 57, 169, 173
Purrysburgh, S. C., 3, 29, 174; article on, 169

Quarantine, 230, 234, 237, 241, 245
Quatre Ministraux, Neuchâtel, 173
Quebec, taxes, 217
Quinche, *Capt.*, emigration agent, 45, 54; persecution of, 45

"Rabies Carolina," 3, 55
Radich, *Capt.*, of the *Paolina*, 233
Raemy, Tobie de, state archivist, 151n., 152
Railroads, 10, 200, 204, 205, 206, 209, 211, 216, 244
Randolph, Edmund, mission to Vienna, 10, 195, 196
Ratgeber für die Schweizerischen Auswanderer, 6, 81
Ratsmanuale, *see* Bern. Zürich
Rauch, Bernhard, merchant, 191

Rauris Repertorium des Hochfürstl. Land- und Berg-Gerichts, 263
Reading, Pa., 59
Reciprocity, 190, 192, 193, 194, 197, 255
Recruiting, see Army, British
Recueil Généalogique Suisse, 183
Red River, colony on, 53, 61, 115, 128, 170, 171, 172
Reformed Church, History of, Good, 30
Regensberg, list of emigrants from, 13
Regensburg, Protestant Commission, 259
Regeste Genevois, 183
Register of German passengers, 62
Reiat, emigration from, 124
Reichenberg, English minister in, 56
Reichesberg, N., *Handwörterbuch der Schweizerischen Volkswirtschaft*, 6
Reily, James R., appeal for a theological seminary in U. S., 24
Rekruten-Kammer, Manual der (Bern), 52, 53-54
Repertorium der Abschiede der Eidgenössischen Tagsatzungen, 62
Repertorium des Staatsarchivs zu Basel, 101
Resolution, frigate, 217
Responsa Prudentum, 4, 55
Reutingen, 111
Reutlinger, deposition of, 24
Reuty, 91
Revolutionary Clubs, see Clubs Insurges
Revolutionary War, see American Revolutionary War
Revue de l'Université de Bruxelles, cited, 186
Revue des Bibliothèques et des Archives de Belgique, cited, 186
Revue Historique Vaudoise, cited, 73, 151, 162
Reybaz, minister of Geneva, 179, 180
Reymond, Maxime, article by, 159
Rham, H. C. de, Swiss consul in New York, 63
Rheinquellen, 139
Rheinthal, emigration law, 18
Rhodanique, République, 164
Richardton, N. D., abbey at, 84
Richmond, Va., 181
Ridgeway, N. C., Swiss settlement, 71
Rieden, Georg, 38
Rieger, and family, emigrate to Virginia, 107
Riehen, 117
Riemensperger, Hans, agent, 35, 38; persecution of, 46
Riggenbacher, H., letter from, 104
Riggenbagher, inheritance, 112
Riggin, William, appointment of, 233, 234, 253
Rights of domicile, see Freizügigkeitsvertrag
Ringholz, Dr. P. Odilo, vii; *Geschichte des Benediktinerstiftes Einsiedeln*, 85
Rio de Janeiro, 79, 218, 220, 232; Stürmer, Austrian minister to, 237
Rio de la Plata, blockade of the coast of, 204; see also La Plata states
Rio Grande River, Brazil, 217, 219
Rising, 248
Ritschard, Heinrich, return of, 50
Ritschard, Jacob, 56
Ritter, appeal of, 267

Ritter, Eugène, *Les Archives de l'Eglise de Genève*, 183, 184
Ritter, George, 72; colonial scheme of, 3, 37, 40, 41; contract of, 74; emigration of, 73
Ritter, Dr. Paul, iii
Rivaz, Charles Emmanuel de, journal of, 163; *Mémoires*, 163
Rivaz family, archives of, 163
Rives, Wm. C., 206
Roatan, see Ruatan
Roch, C., attaché of the Geneva archives of state, 183
Roch, Moïse, death in San Domingo, 59
Rochambeau, *Comte* de, in conference with Washington, 246
Rodney, *Adm.* Lord (George Brydges), capture of Austrian vessels, 226
Rodt, E., *Bern im XVIII. Jahrhundert*, 33
Rodt, Hans, 56
Röllin, Johannes, petition of, 97
Roenne, *Baron* L. von, minister of Prussia, 209
Röthlisberger, Ernest, article by, 6
Rohner, Joh., convict, petition for aid, 138, 139
Roman, complaint against, 259
Rome, French commissary on Spanish frigate, 231
Rommel and Co., emigration agency, 118, 120, 124
Rosati, Joseph, bishop of New Orleans and St. Louis, letter of, 208
Rosenfeld, 120
Rosenthal, Theodor A. T. von, 185
Rothschild, banking house in London, 203
Rottenbühler, Relation von Philadelphia, 51; *Theil von einem Schreiben eines Landsmanns aus Pennsylvanien*, 82
Rotterdam, 171; complaint over deportation of Anabaptists, 37
Rovereto, 265
Rovigo, 210
Royal Charter, ship, sinking of, 68
Ruatan, Spanish conquest of, 224
Rubi, *Lieut.*, letter to, 46
Ruckstuhl, J., thief, aid to emigrate, 145
Rübi, emigration of, 45
Rüdler, emigration of, 45
Rüdlingen, emigration from, 124
Rüger, Thebis, emigration of, 122, 123
Rüegger, Franz G., *Kurzer Reisebericht von Havre bis Highland*, 81
Rütschi, Rudolf, appeal of, 22
Rufenach, 141
Ruffener, Elise, pension for, 158
Rufli, Joseph, lawsuit against, 129
Russia, 205; claim to Northwest coast, 190; colonies in America, 228; concessions to colonists, 79; circulars concerning, 113; mediation, 9, 222, 235; secret alliance, 245; subsidy treaty between England, Prussia, and, 218; Russian-Polish refugees, 245, 246; Swiss emigrants to, 3, 22, 36, 69, 98, 115, 144, 173; treaty with U. S., 191, 198
Ryhinner, Charles, vice-consul of U. S., 152, 157
Ryken, 22

Index 291

Sachseln, 86
Sachsenspiegel, 127
Sackkalender, Zürich, 18
Säckelschreiber Protokolle, Bern, 54
Sails, *see* Cotton duck
St. Andreas, convent of, 87
St. Anton, Wis., letter from, 266
St. Christopher, captured by the French, 224; naval battle near, 224
St. Elizabeth, order of, 234
St. Eustatius, captured by the English, 223; captured by the French, 224; Dutch stop American vessel at, 221; Portuguese corsair in, 231; secret trading with Americans by way of, 9, 220; seizure of Austrian ships in, 226
St. Gallen, 2, 7, 29, 58, 106; archive of the township, 129, 130; cantonal library, 128; city archives, 130; emigration from, 128, 129; emigration statistics, 129, 130; emigration to Algeria, 128; emigration to Bell Co., Ky., 129; emigration to Brazil, 129; emigration to Chicago, 129; emigration to Harlan Co., Ky., 129; emigration to South America, 129; export to U. S., 131; *Industrie und Handel des Kantons*, 130; Kaufmännisches Direktorium, archive, vi, 7, 130-131; lace industry, 7, 131; May's colonial scheme rejected, 128; registers of preachers since the Reformation, 130; Stadtarchiv, 130; Stadtgemeinde, archive, 129-130; state archive, vi, 128-129; Stiftsarchiv, 129; *Tageblatt St. Gallen*, 129
St. Helena, recall of Stürmer from, 215, 236
St. Helens, *Lord* (Alleyne Fitzherbert), English minister to Spain, 230
St. John, 259, 260, 261
St. Louis, 81, 86, 172; charitable institution at, 27; letter from, 116: Swiss consulate, 26, 110
St. Martin, island, English conquest of, 223; neutrality, violation by the English of, 222; seizure of American ships by the English, 222
St. Mary's abbey, N. D., 84
St. Meinrad, Ind., abbey, 84, 85; Swiss settlement, 70
St. Peter, Geneva, 178
St. Thomas, troop ships from Triest to, 236, 237
St. Victor, priory of, 178
St. Vincent, English failure against, 223
St. Vincent's monastery, Pa., 84
Salt, trade in, 239
Salvador, commercial treaty with Switzerland, 96; extradition treaty with Switzerland, 83
Salzburg, 185; *Allgemeine Kundmachung*, 263; Bibliothek des Städtischen Museums, 258; *Circularbefehl*, 263: colony in Georgia, 258; Domkapitelsches Archiv, 258-259; emigration and emigration lists, 259-264; *Emigrations Edikt, Oct. 31, 1731*, 10, 263; Frederick William I., edict of, 10, 264; Fürst-Erzbischöfliches Consistorialarchiv, 264; *General-Patent, Aug. 26, 1734*, 264; Hofkommission, archive, 263; Katenich, 263-264; Landesregierung, archive, 258-264; *Landesregierungsarchivs, Inventar des*, 258; military service against Bavaria, 263; *Mitteilungen der Gesellschaft für Salzburger Landeskunde*, 258; Pfleg Werfen, 258; provincial archives, v, vi, 8, 10, 258-264; *Publikandum*, 263; Rauris Repertorium des Hochfürstl. Land- u. Berg-Gerichts, 263; Studienbibliothek, 258; *Verordnung*, 263
Salzburger Protestants, 10, 258, 264
Sancta Maria von Obernsee, *see* Sault St. Marie
Sandonà, Augusto, *Storia dei Processi del Ventuno e dello Spielberg*, 247
Sandwich, John, earl of, investigation of, 222
San Francisco, charitable institution, 27; Swiss consulate, 26, 110
San Ildefons, abolishing of cemetery at, 226
S. Ildefons, battleship, 226
San Juan, Nicaragua, Spanish reconquest of, 223
San Juan de Ulloa, French conquest of, 202
Santa Anna, *Gen.* Antonio López de, 199, 203
Santa Catharina, island, capitulation of, 220
Santander, French battleship at, 234
Santa Rosa, Llanos de, 206
Santee Forks, 50
Santiago de Cuba, 205
Santo Domingo, 228, 234; advantage of the Spaniards over French in, 235; cession to France, 231; complaint to France, 228; conquest by the negroes, 234; French troops in Spanish service for, 231; insurrections, 229, 231; maps, 247; Roch, death in, 59; supplies on Austrian ships for, 222; Swiss emigration to, 72
São Paulo, *Die Schweizer in*, 86; Swiss emigrants in, 132
Sardinia, King of, 177; treaty with U. S., 204
Sargans, emigration law, 18
Sarnen, convent of St. Andreas, 87; letters from, 86; state archive in, 86, 87
Sault St. Marie, *Bishop* of (Baraga), 84
Savannah, Ga., 203, 206, Hülsemann's report on, 10, 204
Savary, *Gen.* René, duc de Rovigo, letter of, 171
Savary de Valcoulon, letter of, 181
Savoy, 171
Savoyard communes, Geneva, civil registers of, 182
Schäublins, Martin, examination of, 106
Schaffhausen, 1, 19, 86; aid to emigrants, 122, 123, 124; *Akten der Gesetzgebungs- und Verwaltungsbehörden, Register*, 122; *Chronik der Stadt Schaffhausen*, 124; circular letter on emigration, 153; conference of 1846, 116; deportation, 124; emigration agencies, 123, 124; emigration from, 75, 123-125; emigration laws, 122-125; emigration literature, 122; emigration to Brazil, 86, 124; emigration to Prussia, 125; emigration to Venezuela, 124; *Offizielle Sammlung der Gesetze*, 124; Raths Protokolle, 122-123; refusal to readmit emigrants, 123; state archive, vi, 122-125; uniform emigration policy, 116

Schaffner, Martin, deportation of, 117
Schaub, Jacob, emigration of, 106
Schauenburg, Christ., petition to emigrate, 116
Scheitlin, J. M., president of the Verwaltungsrat, 129
Schenkel, Jakob, emigration of, 20
Scherz, Peter, 56
Scheuchzer, *Landvogt*, report of, 21
Schiess, *Dr.*, town archivist, vii
Schilling, Reinhard, convict, receives aid to emigrate, 144, 145, 146
Schimmer, G. A., article by, 267
Schinz, *Rev.*, 25
Schladen, Baron von, Prussian envoy to Portugal, 231
Schlatter, *Rev.* Michael, 5, 58, 130; petitions of, 19, 22, 39, 40, 40. 58, 106; *Wahrhafte Erzehlung*, 10, 130
Schlitter, *Dr.* Hanns, archivist, 5, 186; *Berichte des ersten Agenten Oesterreichs*, 8, 186; *Die Beziehungen Oesterreichs zu den Vereinigten Staaten*, 8, 186, 221
Schlötz, 79
Schmid, emigration agency, 118
Schmid, Franz Vincenz, article by, 83
Schmid, Simon and family, emigration of, 134, 135
Schmidt, Anna Barbara, inheritance of, 59
Schmidt, Michael, conveys power of attorney, 59
Schmidtmeyer, Peter, report of, 147
Schneebeli, emigration agency, 118
Schneebeli, E., death in America, 23
Schneebeli, Heinr., inheritance of, 23
Schneuwly, Joseph, state archivist, 151
Schnottwil, 98
Schöneck, Pa., letter from, 120
Schraml, letter of, 249
Schrantz, Hans, legacy of, 54
Schuler, Heinr., emigration of, 137
Schultz, Joh., petition for aid, 116
Schurz, Carl, *Henry Clay*, 215
Schwab, Johannes, examination of, 112
Schwaller, Benedikt, emigration of, 98
Schwanden, 90
Schwarz, brothers, emigration of, 42
Schwarz, J. G., American consul in Vienna, 198, 254
Schwarzach, 260
Schwarzenburg, emigration from, 40, 45
Schwatz, 265
Schweitzer, Jakob, letter from, 114
Schweizer, Heinrich, 22
Schweizer, Johannes, emigration of, 20, 21, 28
Schweizer, Paul, article by, 13
Schweizer Verein zum Wohlthun in New Orleans, letter from, 84
Schweizerische Auswanderer, Bern, Ratgeber für, 6
Schweizerische Auswanderungswesen, Das, Karrer, 6
Schweizerische Auswanderungs-Zeitung, 96, 97
Schweizerische Blätter für Handel und Industrie, 131
Schweizerische Hilfsgesellschaft, New York, 117

Schweizerischen Handels und Industrie Verein, Berichte des, 130
Schweizerischer Consular Agenten Berichte, 94
Schweizerisches Auswanderungsbureau, *see* Federal Emigration Bureau
Schweizerisches Wirtschaftsarchiv, Basel, 101
Schweizerische Unterstützungs- und Schutz-Gesellschaft für Auswanderer, 90
Schweizerische Wohltatigkeitsgesellschaft, complaint of, 86
Schwendler, American consul in Frankfort a. M., 254
Schwer, Peter, persecution of, 259
Schwyz, 1, 84, 85; cantonal archive, vi, 84; emigration from, 64, 84; *Mitteilungen des Historischen Vereins des Kantons*, 84
Scientific societies, 250
Scotland, emigration from, 67; regiments, 218
Sealsfield, Charles, *see* Postl, Carl
Seed varieties, 243
Seelisberg, Dak., Swiss settlement, 70
Seguin, Texas, Swiss settlement, 71
Seippel, Paul, *Die Schweiz im Neunzehnten Jahrhundert*, 6; *La Suisse au Dix-neuvième Siècle*, 6
Selkirk, Lord (Thomas Douglas), colonial scheme of, 53, 171, 172
Senate, U. S., 68; *see also* Congress
Separatists, 27
Servand, Martin, 177
Sextants, 244
Shindle, estate of, 216
Ships, 59, 68, 81, 96, 118, 119, 145, 196, 203, 205, 210, 212, 215, 217, 226, 233, 237, 239, 252; *see also* Frigates; Prizes; Steamships; names of particular ships
Shipwrecks, 30, 68, 79, 81, 96, 118, 145, 203, 204, 233
Short, William, American minister to the Netherlands, 229; mission to Spain, 230, 231
Shrok, J. M., extradition of, 109
Sieben, judgments of, 111, 112
Sierra Morena, Swiss emigration to, 36
Siggenthal, emigration from, 141
Signer, 126
Silbach, emigration from, 235
Silbernagel, Franz von, 253
Silk, trade in, 26, 131, 141
Simmlersche Sammlung, 4, 29
Singeisen, Mattis, emigration of, 111
Sion, bishopric archives destroyed by fire, 165; cantonal archive in, 163; Lycée-Collège, 163
Sissach, letter from, 114
Sizlen, 120, 140
Slavery, Austria's position on, 10, 105; question, 34, 190, 191, 195, 206, 218, 220, 226, 228, 229, 237
Smith, *Judge* H. A. M., article by, 169
Smith, Wm. L., arrival in Portugal of, 231
Smolinkary, letter of, 203
Société de Bienfaisance de la Nouvelle-Orléans, Compte Rendu, 65
Société d'Utilité Publique, Geneva and Vaud, 7, 64, 65, 66

Index 293

Société Économique, archives of, Geneva, 178, 182
Soleure, *see* Solothurn
Solothurn, 1, 149; archives entitled Frankreich, 99, 100; deportation of Anabaptists, 37; emigration from, 22, 75, 98, 99; emigration law, 98; emigration tax, 98, 99; French ambassadors resident in, 99; *Neues Solothurner Wochenblatt*, 100; state archive, vi, 98-100
Sonderbund, 2
Sonora, 228
Sonsonate, destroyed by earthquake, 221
Sordet, Louis, archivist, 175
South America, 79, 84, 188, 217, 218; articles on, 266, 267; corsairs, 236; emigration from Trent to, 267; insurgents in, 23, 190; report of Swiss consul in New Orleans on, 80; Swiss emigration to, 61, 69, 75, 93, 129; Swiss recognition of independence of states of, 190; Swiss troops in, 82
South Carolina, 50, 169; convention, 197; Hülsemann's report on, 10, 204; Swiss emigration to, 17; U. S. government and, 197; *see also* Carolina
South Carolina Historical Magazine, cited, 169
Southern States, Hülsemann's report on a trip to, 10
South Pittsburg, Tenn., Swiss settlement, 71
Spänhauwer, M., emigration agent, 48
Spain, 205, 216; advantages in Santo Domingo, 235; advantage under Cevallos, 220; American agent rejected by, 220; American emissary to, 228; American minister, complaint of, 237; American ships quarantined, 230; amnesty to the insurgents in Mexico, 225; anxious to prevent war with France, 232; appointment of two viceroys to America, 230; Austrian emigration to, 248; beginning of hostilities with England, 234; blockade of the coast of Peru and Chile, 235; boundary dispute with America and Indians, 226; boundary dispute with England concerning Florida, 190, 225, 226; boundary dispute with U. S. over Louisiana, 233, 234; capital punishment for aliens in the service of insurgents, 23, 236; capture of Gataimai, 221; capture of ships by England, 234; Carmichael, American envoy to, 225; cession of Florida to U. S., 190, 237; commercial and boundary treaties, 224, 226, 231; commercial relations with America, 221, 222, 226-229, 231, 233; commercial relations with Mexico, 232, 234; commercial relations with Spanish West Indies, 223; complaint against Austrian supplies to the insurgents, 235, 236, 242; complaint concerning hostilities in Curaçao, 222; complaint concerning troop ships from Triest to St. Thomas, 236, 237; complaint regarding relations at Rio Janeiro with Portugal, 218; complaint regarding relations of Mosquito Coast with England, 226, 227; concerning grievances between England and colonies, 18, 219; difficulties on Rio Grande with Portugal, 217, 219; discord between Spain and U. S., 234; embargo on ships, 234, 236; emigration from, 67; emigration from Swabia to Spanish colonies, 129; emigration from Tyrol to, 248; England objects to cession of Santo Domingo, 231; English conquest of Buenos Aires, 234; English designs upon Louisiana, 229; English landing at Pensacola, 228; English settlers in Spanish America, 226; escape of slaves from Dutch to Spanish colonies, 220; fear of English power at sea, 230; fear of rupture of America with France, 232; fleet for West Indies, 230; France proposes conquest of Portugal, 232; freedom for slaves, 228; free navigation of Ohio and Mississippi rivers, 229, 230, 234; French troops in Spanish service, 231; Gibraltar exchange proposition, 229; guns from America, 217; hostilities with Indians, 226; insurrections in Mexico, 225, 231, 232; insurrection in Santo Domingo, 229, 231; insurrections in Spanish America, 190, 225, 228, 232, 237; Jesuits driven out of, 233; negotiations with U. S. over captured ships, 232; nomination of archbishop as viceroy, 232; Nootka Sound affair, 229, 230; Orosco, Spanish minister to U. S., 232; Portuguese boundary dispute with, 230; position towards American insurgents, 220; proposed marriage of Princess of Brazil, 228; reconquest of Buenos Aires, 234; royal decree against American provinces, 235; royal decree concerning aid to South American insurgents, 23; royal decree concerning white population in Cuba, 236; ship-building yard in America, 221; silver fleet, 221, 229, 230, 234; Spanish America, serious effect of treaty of 1790 with England, 229; Spanish army in America, 247; Spanish colonies, 113, 128, 218; Spanish insurgent privateers in Buenos Aires, 235; Spanish position as to the treaty between France and colonies, 221; Spanish succession in Portugal, 227; Spanish troops on Austrian vessels, 236; steamship line to the Spanish-American colonies, 188; subsidies for the colonies, 221; subsidies from England and Spanish America to, 235; Swiss emigration to Spanish colonies, 3, 14, 22, 36, 58, 59, 98, 113, 129; transfer from Spanish to Portuguese ships, 224, 234; U. S. violation of Florida, 236; volunteer corps in, 230; war with France, English negotiations with Spain over, 230; yellow fever in Spanish colonies, 23
Specht, Cornelius, 205
Speiszegger, Hans Conrad, 122
Spiegel von Amerika, Köpfli, 82
Spielerville, Ark., 84
Spinning machinery, American, 255
Spotswood, Gov. Alexander, founder of Germanna, 13; letter of, 74
Spring, Franz, legacy of, 59
Spring, Hans, agent, 111
Spurzheim, *Dr.*, legacy of, 197

Index

Stadion, *Count*, governor of Illyria and Triest, 216
Stäbli, emigration of, 45
Stans, Stammbuchamt, 89; state archive in, 89
Stapfer, *Professor*, 51; on book *Sur la Population de l'Amérique*, 31, 32
Starhemberg, *Prince* Ludwig von, letter to Delplancq, 187
State, Department of, U. S., archives, 75
States General, *see* Netherlands
Stauffer, Pa., Swiss settlement, 71
Steamships, 244; lines, 188, 225, 230, 244; literature, 245
Steckborn, 50
Steffisburg, 38, 43
Steiger, R. von, article by, 100
Steinach, *Dr.* Adelrich, *Geschichte und Leben der Schweizer Kolonien*, 7
Steinauer, J. A., founder of Steinauer, Neb., 85
Steinauer, Neb., founding of, 85; Swiss settlement, 70
Steinimann, Andreas, petition to emigrate, 122
Stettiner Lloyd, 257
Stettler, 158
Stevenson, Andrew, American minister to England, 203
Stiger, writings of, 142, 155
Stiles, Wm. H., U. S. chargé d'affaires to Austria, 216
Stocker, *Landvogt*, report of, 20
Stöhr, *Kreuzherr Commandeur*, letter of, 249
Stössel and Co., emigration agency, complaint of, 69
Stoker, Peter, letters confiscated, 35
Stolz, *Dr.* Otto, vii
Stoll, C., convict, aid to emigrate, 32
Storker, Johannes, letter from, 49
Stovall, *Hon.* Pleasant A., iii
Straaszer, Peter, emigration of, 123
Streif, *Landvogt*, report of, 20
Striker, emigration agent, examination of, 43; expelled, 44; letter confiscated, 46
Strobl, Peter, persecution of, 262
Stroblhof, 262
Stuckey, Ga., Swiss settlement, 70
Studien und Mittheilungen aus dem Benediktiner- und Cistercienserorden, cited, 87
Studien zur Fuggergeschichte, Jansen, 265
Stürmer, *Freiherr* Bartholomaeus von, Austrian consul general, 10, 215, 236; despatches to Metternich from, 189; diplomatic post in Constantinople, 189; instructions from Metternich to, 215; minister to Brazil, 189, 237; order of the Red Eagle, 236; recall from Brazil, 237; recall from St. Helena, 189, 215, 236
Stuttgart, 31; emigration society, organization of, 236
Suchard, Philippe, 173
Süniken, 21
Suisse, Généalogique, Recueil, 183
Sulzer, goldsmith, emigration agent, 31
Sumiswald, 36, 98
Superior, Lake, 84
Suppiger, John [Joseph], emigration of, 78; justice of the peace, 78; *Reisebericht der Familie Köpfli und Suppiger*, 81;.vice-consul, 78
Surinam, Dutch colony, 104, 111; emigrants from, 112; English conquest of, 234
Sur la Population de l'Amérique, 31
Sursee, emigration from, 78
Suter, Andreas, convict, emigration of, 108
Svilovich, Joseph, inheritance of, 203
Svilovich, Peter, death in Savannah, 203
Svizzera Italiana, Bollettino Storico della, article in, 147
Swabia, 9; emigration to Spanish colonies from, 129; Swiss emigration to, 13
Sweden, blockade of port of Tripoli, 233; treaty with U. S., 193
Swift, patent of, 255
Swiss, Mo., Swiss settlement, 70
Swiss Alp. Tex., Swiss settlement, 71
Swiss Confederation, 2, 86, 149, 163, 164, 166, 175; correspondence of the Quatre Ministraux with the, 173; deportation scheme, 20; neutrality of, 78; registers of the diet, 161; *see also* Switzerland
Swissvale, Pa., Swiss settlement, 71
Switz City, Ind., Swiss settlement, 70
Switzer, Ohio, Swiss settlement, 71
Switzerland, American embassy, warning to emigrants, 117; American minister to, 6; American settlers liable to military duty, 120; archives, history and statistics, 1-7; Austrian refugees, 10, 249; *Bote der Urschweiz*, 87; *Bundesblatt*, 7, 9, 148; Bundesarchiv, iv, 1, 7, 33, 63-69, 97; charitable institution, 27; colony, 74; commercial laws, 25; commercial relations with Mexico, 25; commercial relations with U. S., 7, 25, 26, 64, 81, 83, 119, 128, 158; commercial treaty with Ecuador, 96; commercial treaty with Mexico, 95; commercial treaty with Salvador, 96; commercial treaty with U. S., 26, 95, 110, 128; conference of 1846, 116; *Le Conservateur Suisse*, 161; Department of Foreign Affairs, emigration, 119, 127; *Eidgenössischen Abschiede*, 57, 58; emigration agents, 4, 22, 24, 25; emigration in the 18th century, 3, 7, 227; emigration laws, 76, 157; emigration statistics, 3, 6, 68, 75, 93, 96; *Emigration Suisse*, 6; emigration tax, 5; emigration treaties, 81, 128; extradition treaty with Salvador, 83, 96; extradition treaty with U. S., 26, 68, 79, 95, 96, 109, 110, 128, 141, 153, 154; federal constitution, 2; *Geschichte und Leben der Schweizer Kolonien*, 7; *Handwörterbuch der Schweizerischen Volkswirtschaft*, 6; Helvetisches Archiv, 63; *Histoire Abrégée des Officiers Suisses*, 100; *Histoire Militaire de la Suisse*, 99; *Jahrbuch für Schweizerische Geschichte*, 39n., 53n.; military affairs, 120; ministers to U. S., 141; negotiations with Brazil, 152; *Neues Bundesarchiv*, 63; neutrality of, 72; population, 2; postal treaty with U. S., 96, 97; *Recueil Généalogique Suisse*, 183; reformers, letters of, 130; *Schweizerische Auswanderungswesen, Das*, 6; *Schweizerische Auswanderungszeitung*, 96.

97; *Schweizerische Blätter für Handel und Industrie,* 131n.; *Schweizerische Consular Agenten, Berichte,* 94; *Schweizerischer Handels- und Industrie Verein, Berichte,* 130; *Schweiz im Neunzehnten Jahrhundert,* 6; Tagsazungsarchiv, 63; troops in South America, 82; *Ueberseeische Auswanderung aus der Schweiz,* 70; see also Federal Council; Federal Directory: Federal Emigration Bureau; Freizügigkeitsvertrag; Helvetic Republic; Swiss Confederation
Switzerland, Ohio, Swiss settlement, 161
Synod, Dutch, appeal to Swiss Protestants, 50; of New York and Philadelphia, 52; *see also* Schlatter, Rev. Michael
Syz, Heinrich, inheritance of, 22
Syz, Jean, Swiss consul in Philadelphia, 66
Syz, Johann Georg, Swiss consul in Philadelphia, 66
Szirmay, P., emigration scheme of, 11, 250

Tacoma, Wash., Swiss settlers in, 87
Täufer-Jäger, *see* Anabaptists
Täufer-Kammer, Bern, Manual der, 53
Tagsatzungsarchiv, Bern, 63
Tallmadge, F. A., 206
Tampico, blockade of, 202
Tariff, 26, 81, 83, 131, 141, 191, 195, 197, 198, 216, 241, 254
Taylor, *Pres.* Zachary, agent sent to Hungary by, 214
Telegraph, 212
Telescope, 243
Tell, Pa., Swiss settlement, 71
Tell City, Ind., Swiss settlement, 70
Tell Cottage, Ohio, Swiss settlement, 71
Temple, *Sir* John, English consul general to America, 226
Tennessee, Plümacher's colonial scheme, 69; Swiss settlements in, 71
Tennessee Colonisationsgesellschaft, 133-136
Ternant, *Comte* Chr., French minister to U. S., 228
Terrasson, French consul, letter from, 181
Terzi, Franz Anton, legacy of, 193-197
Texas, 80, 199, 212, 213; admission of, 213; *Antrag zur Aufnahme Schweizerischer Colonisten in Texas,* 80; Austrian emigration to, 251; convention of 1838, 201; emigration from Tyrol, 267; free land in, 69; Kuhn, Swiss consul in, 67; Swiss consulate, 110; Swiss emigration to, 61, 116; Swiss settlements, 71; war with Mexico, 61
Thaner, Hans, persecution of, 259
Theological seminary, German Reformed, in U. S., 24
Thierachern, 43
Thorberg, convict, 61
Thun, 34
Thurgau, 2; aid to emigrants, 144-146; *Amtsblatt des Kantons Thurgau,* 146; cantonal archive, iv, 144-146; circular letter, emigration, 145; conference of 1846, 116; emigration from, 21; emigration laws, 18, 58; emigration statistics, 146; emigration to Brazil, 144, 146; emigration to Chile, 146; emigration to Russia, 144; emigration to the Crimea, 144; police department, 144; Schutzverein für entlassene Sträflinge, 144, 145; serfdom, 144; U. S. complaint against deportation from, 145; *Thurgauer Zeitung, Sonntagsblatt der,* 146
Thurn-Buch, Bern, 4, 5, 55, 56
Ticino, 2, 6; cantonal archive, vi, 147-148; conference of 1846, 116, 147; emigration from, 6, 147; emigration to Argentina, 148; emigration to California, 148; printed material in archive, 147-148; returning emigrants, 148
Tillier, Rudolph, petition of, 52
Timber, exportation of, 219
Tinelli, Anne, 208
Tinelli, Luigi, deportation of, 207, 208, 215; divorce case before Senate, 208; petition of, 207, 208
Tobacco, planters, convention of, 208; seed, 245; trade, 248
Tobago, English occupation of, 230
Tobler, Johann, *Alter u. verbesserter Schreib-Kalender,* article in, 29; *Eine ausführliche Relation aus Carolina,* 29
Todd, Vincent H., article by, 74
Toggenburg, 46; emigration from, 18, 35
Tonnage, tariff charge on, 191
Torlade, Barrozo *vs.*, 195
Torrenté, archives of the family of, 163
Toulon, 239
Tour Baudet, 176
Trachselwald, 36
Trachsler, Hans W., *Kurtz verfasste Reiss-Beschreibung,* 29
Trade, anthracite coal, 199; cannon, 217; clothing, 227; cotton, 131; dye-wood, 226; embroideries, 131; fur, 228; glassware, 255; grain, 9, 239, 241, 254, 255; india rubber, 206; lace, 7, 131; linen, 131, 188, 254; mercury, 255; milk, 7; otter skins, 241; pharmaceutical articles, 244; salt, 239; seed, 243; silk, 26, 131, 141; timber, 219; tobacco, 248; under neutral flag, 255; whale fishery, 218; wheat, 242; wine, 197, 205, 227; wool, 255; zwieback, 197; *see also* names of countries and places
Transportation, arrangements and terms, 61, 62, 68, 84, 115-118, 128, 132, 135, 153, 154, 155; reports on, 62, 115
Trappani, 239
Trautmannsdorf, *Count* Ferdinand von, correspondence of, 187
Travanet, 170
Travels, in America, 11; in the Middle West, 11
Treasury, U. S., Secretary of the, reports, 26, 197, 202, 206, 207
Trent, 265; Council of, 151; emigration to South America, 207
Tribunal des Trois États, Neuchâtel, 166
Triest, American merchant vessels in, 233; commercial expedition to U. S., 225; commercial relations with French colonies, 223; commercial relations with U. S., 192, 205, 234; Lamson, American consul, 233, 253; *Oesterreichische-Amerikanische Hand-*

lungsgesellschaft, 186, 188, 226; regulating ships visiting port of, 195; Riggin, American consul, 233, 234, 253; troop transports to St. Thomas, 236, 237; U. S. Treasury Department to the governor of, 204
Trinidad, French emigrants in, 230
Tripoli, blockade of port of, 233; U. S. at war with, 233
Trogen, cantonal archive, 127
Tronchin, letter from Jefferson to, 181
Troppau, provincial archive, 8
Tschan, Johann, emigration of, 98
Tschann, letter from, 62
Tschudi, mission of, 69
Tschudi, J. J., emigration agent, 49, 106, 112, 113
Tschudi, Martin and Nicolaus, 113
Türler, Dr. Heinrich, archivist, vii; *Uebersicht über den Inhalt des Staatsarchives des Kantons Bern*, 33
Tunis, corsair captures *Paolina*, 233
Turc, François, secretary, 179
Turin, treaty of 1816, 177
Turkey, relations with U. S., 195, 197
Turreau, Gen. Louis Marie, French minister to U. S., 163
Turrettini, F., *Les Archives de Genève*, 175
Tuscany, Austrian consulate in, 252; commercial relations with America, 225
Tuscarora Indians, treaty between Graffenried and, 74
Two Sicilies, 197
Tyler, Pres. John, letter to Mareschal, 210
Tyrol, article concerning emigrants from, 266; Auswanderer-Auskunftsbureau, 267; bibliography of emigration from, 266-267; *Bothe für Tirol und Vorarlberg*, cited, 266-267; colonies in Brazil, 266; colony in Forestville, Mich., 266; diary of a volunteer in U. S. army, 267; emigration from, 11, 248, 267; emigration to Buenos Aires, 266; emigration to Spain, 248; emigration to Virginia, 266, 267; emigration statistics, 265, 267; settlement in Alpenburg, Va., 266, 267; Tyrolese-American Franciscans, 266

Ueberseeische Auswanderung aus der Schweiz, Die, 70
Uelin, Verena, return of, 22
Ulloa, Dr. Antonio de, Spanish fleet under, 218
United States, alliance with England proposed, 224; army and navy, 244, 247; Austrian consuls, 10, 215, 234, 236; Austrian minister in, 10; Austro-Italian political refugees, 10; banking system, 203, 211; bankruptcy law, 209; banks, suspension of, 204, 206; Beelen-Bertholff, first agent to, 8; Benedictine monasteries in, 5, 84; blockade of port of Tripoli, 233; boundary dispute with Spain, 226; bounties, 79; census of, 156, 190; census of Swiss born in, 6, 110; chargé to Spain, 225; citizenship, 96; commercial conditions, 199; commercial laws, 255; commercial relations with Austria, 188, 191, 222, 224, 233, 236, 254; commercial relations with England, 228, 229, 236, 254; commercial relations with Portugal, 229; commercial relations with Spain, 228, 229, 231, 233; commercial relations with Switzerland, 7, 25, 26, 64, 81, 83, 119, 128, 131, 158; commercial relations with Triest, 192, 205, 225; commercial treaty with Brazil, 255; commercial treaty with Chile, 198; commercial treaty with Colombia, 192, 193; commercial treaty with Denmark, 193, 195, 255; commercial treaty with Greece, 202; commercial treaty with Hanse towns, 193, 194; commercial treaty with Mexico, 193; commercial treaty with Naples, 198; commercial treaty with Russia, 191, 198; commercial treaty with Sardinia, 204; commercial treaty with Sweden, 193; commercial treaty with Turkey, 195; consuls, 67, 233, 234, 237, 257; convention with Austria, 196; convention with Mexico, 212; deportation of undesirables, 6, 75, 76, 96, 117, 145, 156, 213; diplomatic correspondence concerning deportation, 75, 155; discrimination against ships of, 192, 194, 237; distrust of England and France in, 225; Dutch minister, 225; emigration from Austria to, 227; emigration from England to, 225; emigration literature, 60; English and Irish manufacturers for, 225; English blockade of coast of, 235; English consul in, 226; English delay in evacuating forts, 226; English law against importation of Austrian goods to, 254; English minister to, 228; exchange of official publications, 96, 156; feeling against France, 230; financial situation in, 170, 202, 206, 207, 216; flag, 179, 180, 255; freedom of religion in, 66; French intrigues in, 226; Gesellschaft in Stuttgart zur Erleichterung der Ansiedelung in, 236; government, 192, 237; high cost of living in, 201; hostilities against Indians, 229; immigration laws, 64, 67, 77, 257; inspection of consulates in Italy, 233; invasion of Louisiana, 227; loan negotiated in the Netherlands, 225, 228; McLeod affair, 210; maps, 247; marine inventions, 244; mercury mines, 253; ministers to Spain, 232, 233, 234; minister to the Netherlands, 229; mission to France, 226, 232; navigation of rivers of, 206, 229, 230, 234; neutrality, 78; payments of arrears to soldiers, 79, 96, 155; peace envoys, 235; pensions, 71, 124, 142, 156, 158; political conditions in, 190, 192, 196-200; ports closed to, 234; ports reopened to, 235; postal relations with Switzerland, 7, 96, 97, 120; purchase of Louisiana, 233, 234; railroads, 10, 200, 205, 206, 211, 244; relations with Austria, 158, 188, 196, 206, 233; relations with England, 195, 225, 226, 234, 235; relations with France, 199; relations with Hamburg, 225, 226; relations with Portugal, 227; relations with South America, 190; relations with Spain, 232; Russian mediation, 9, 222, 235; secession, 192; ships in Venice, 248; ships seized by pirates, 225; slavery differences with England, 237; Spanish ministers in,

Index 297

225, 232; statistics, 64, 96, 156, 199, 246; steamship line from Port Louis to, 225; Swiss consulates, 7, 24, 26, 79, 110, 153; Swiss settlements in, 70-71; Swiss soldiers in, 79, 110; treaty relations with Austria, 9, 10, 11, 186, 187, 189, 192, 193, 194, 209, 214, 216, 225, 226, 244, 246, 250, 254; treaty relations with England, 191, 193, 225, 255; treaty relations with France, 191, 193, 198; treaty relations with the Netherlands, 205, 225; treaty relations with Portugal, 225; treaty relations with Prussia, 193, 226; treaty relations with Spain, 224, 231; treaty relations with Switzerland, 26, 68, 79, 95, 96, 109, 110, 128, 141, 153, 154; value of Spanish money in, 25; war against Tripoli, 233; warships in Austrian ports, 237, 241, 246; warships in Mediterranean, 235; war with England, 235; war with Mexico, 214; war with Spain rumored, 192
Unteregeri, emigration from, 96
Unterehrendingen, 142
Unterhallau, emigration from, 125
Unter-Mettmenstetten, Huber family at, 22
Unterseen, emigration from, 34, 43
Unterwalden, 1, 2, 64, 86-89; *see also* Nidwalden; Obwalden
Upshur, Abel P., secretary of state, 212
Urech, Joh. Jakob, emigration of, 140
Uri, 1; circular letter, 83; emigration from, 64, 83; laws, 83; state archive, vi, 83
Urica, island, 221
Ussaro, brig, 215
Usteri, Theodor, article by, 27
Utah, 143
Utzendorf, 53
Uruguay, 128; Swiss emigration to, 69, 97, 118

Vadiana, 130
Valais, 2, 149, 163-165; administration of the archives of, 163, 164; *Bulletin Officiel*, 164; cantonal library, 163; *Conseil d'État, Rapport du*, 164; *état civil*, records of, 164; state archive, vi, 163
Valcoulon, *see* Savary de Valcoulon
Valangin, 38; emigration from, 169, 170, 171
Val-de-Travers, 169
Val Maggia, depopulated by emigration, 148
Val Verzasca, depopulated by emigration, 148
Van Berckel, P. J., Dutch minister to U. S., criminal process against, 227; recall of, 227
Van Buren, Martin, 197, 199, 206; appointed minister to England, 197; elected President, 199; Lederer invited to Washington by, 194; messages, 199-202, 207; proclamation of, 201; proposed trip to Portugal, 196; treaty with Austria, 10, 194
Van Houtte, Hubert, article by, 186
Vannaz, Friedrich, kidnapping of, 53
Vannoni, Giuseppe, political refugee, 208
Vaud, New Mexico, colony of, 161
Vaud, Switzerland, 1, 2, 149, 172, 175; Bernese administration, 159, 160; cantonal archives, vi, 159-161; Chambre des Bannerets, 160; Chambre Économique, 160; Commissariat, 160; communal archives, 161; conference

of 1846, 116; Conseil d'État, archives of, 161; Cour d'Appellation Romande, 160; *Dictionnaire Historique*, 159, 160, 161; emigration from, 161; *état civil*, registers of, 160; *Journal de la Société Vaudoise*, 159; national church, archives of, 161; part of the Canton du Léman, 159; part of the Département du Léman, 159; part of the French empire, 159; *Revue Historique Vaudoise*, 75, 151, 162; Société d'Utilité Publique, Comité d'Émigration, 7, 64, 65, 66
Venerable Company, *see* Geneva, Compagnie des Pasteurs
Venetia, documents relating to the history of, 185
Venezuela, Swiss emigration to, 69, 124
Ventuno e dello Spielberg, Storia dei processi del, Sandonà, 247
Vera Cruz, capitulation of, 202; declared open port, 202; renewal of hostilities at, 202; seizure of Spanish ships by the English at, 234; silver fleet from, 221, 234; Spanish fleet leaves, 219
Vergessene Deutsche Colonie, Eine, Deiler, 196, 250
Vergueiro and Co., agency, 132; lawsuit, 69, 158
Verlangte, nicht erlangte Canaan, Das, 31
Vermont, de, inquiry as to deportation, 20
Verrières, 171
Verzeichnis der Benediktinerinnen zur Hl. Gertrud., 87
Vespucci, Mlle. Ameriga dei, pretension of, 202, 203
Vevay, Ind., Swiss settlement, 66, 67, 70, 161
Vevey, Switzerland, 161
Vienna, American consulate, 248; American plants for botanical garden, 229; archives, distribution and survey of material, 7-12, 185; Belgische Archiv, 186; bibliography, 186, 237, 247, 252; Fürst-Erzbischöflisches Konsistorium, 249; Gemeinsames Finanzarchiv, 8, 185, 252-255; Haus-, Hof- und Staatsarchiv, vi, 8-10, 185-237, 258; Hofbibliothek, 8, 185, 255, 256; Hofkammerarchiv, vi, 8, 185, 252-255; Kartenarchiv, 247; Kriegsarchiv, vi, 8, 9, 185, 237-247; Ministerium des Innern, archive of, vi, 8, 11, 185, 247-251; Polizei Ober-Direction, decree of, 249; Porzellanfabrik, 198; Post, American consul general, 256; Royal Academy for the Deaf and Dumb, 199; Schwarz, American consul, 254; Schriftenarchiv, 238-247; Staatskanzlei, notes of, 186, 215, 216; Stadt Wien, archive of, 8, 185, 256, 257; *Wiener Jahrbücher*, 212
Virginia, 13, 24, 37, 60, 74, 181, 221; emigration from Tyrol, 266, 267; Hülsemann's report on, 10; Swiss emigration to, 13, 71, 107; Swiss settlements in, 71; travels in, 72; Tyrolese settlement in, 266; University of, 184; *Virginia Magazine of History*, 72
Virginia, ship, cholera on, 118
Voce del Popolo di S. Francisco, article in, 147
Vogel, Father Adalbert, *Die Benediktiner Kolonie in Neuengelberg*, 87

Vogel, Heinrich, aid to emigrate, 122
Vogel, William, letter of, 66
Vogt, letter of, 108
Vogt, Friedrich, aid for family to emigrate, 117
Vokinger, Adalbert, article by, 89
Volksfreund aus Schwaben, 118
Volks- und Schützenzeitung, cited, 267
Vollenweider, Emilie, aid to emigrate, 145
Vollmer, Joseph and family, emigration of, 134, 135
Von Kapff and Brune, Barzizza land claim, 192
Vorarlberg, 266; emigration statistics, 265
Vorort, Bern, circular letters, 109, 116, 128, 129; emigration, 63, 91, 116; seat of government, 2
Vorort, Luzern, circular letters, 115, 116, 128, 129
Vorort, Zürich, circular letters, 128, 129; commercial relations, 25, 26; Dutch emigration decree, 23, 24, 25; emigration, 26, 91, 116; emigration via France, 25; exportation, 25; extradition treaty, 26; inquiry as to Joh. Meyer, 24; passports, 25, 116; Prussian emigration decree, 23; Swiss commercial laws, 25; Swiss consuls to New York and Alexandria, 24
Vuagneux, Charles, notary in Porto Rico, 172
Vuagneux, Jacques, letter of, 172

Wackernagel, Dr. Rudolf, state archivist, vii, 108
Wäber, emigration of, 45
Wädenschweil, 22
Wänger, emigration of, 45
Wagner, Heini, estate of, 112
Wahrhafte Erzehlung, Schlatter, 19, 130
Waldenburg, emigration from, 111, 114, 115
Walder, Jacob, agent, 22
Waldstätter-Botc, 81
Waldvogel, Elisabeth, emigration of, 123
Wales, emigration from, 67
Wallbach, guarantee for emigrants, 140
Wallenstadt, 135
Wallimann, Franz, emigration of, 87
Walliszellen, 15
Waltenstein, 23
Walter, agent, 39
Walterswil, 99
Walzenhausen, 127
Wangen, 48
Wanhill, 248
Wanner, Swiss consul in Havre, complaint against, 69
War, Secretary of, U. S., report of, 195
Warburg, Tenn., Swiss settlement, 71
Wartmann, Dr. Hermann, vii, 7; *Industrie und Handel des Kantons St. Gallen*, 130
Washington, George, meeting with Rochambeau, 245; proposals concerning University of Geneva, 184
Washington, D. C., 11, 190, 191, 193, 194, 199-209; charitable institution, 27; Swiss consulate general, 26, 110; Swiss representation in, 96
Wasmer, emigration agent, 140

Wattenwil, 46
Wassen, 83
Watteville, Régiment de, 172
Weber, Hans, 122
Weber, J., vii
Weber, Ludwig, *Der Hinckende Bott von Carolina*, 30
Webster, Daniel, 206; Lodge's biography, 215; reply to Hülsemann on Hungarian question, 215
Wehrli, Marie, deportation of, 142
Weiach, 19, 22
Weidmann, Heinrich, emigration of, 21
Weinfeld, 146
Weiss-Frey, Fried., *Heinrich Iselin, und sein Geschlecht*, 120
Weisslingen, 24
Weisz, Johann M., 194
Welser, *Die überseeischen Unternehmungen der*, Haebler, 265
Werdenberg, emigration agent, 118
Werdenberg, emigration from, 129
Werdtman, Jacob, 194
Werfen, 258, 260
Werner, Dr. H., archivist, vii
West Florida, American invasion of, 221; see also Florida
West Indies, v, 30; appropriation to stop piracy in, 191; Austrian trade relations, 252; Dutch commercial relations, 227; Dutch fleet to, 229; English troops and war supplies to, 219; exportation of timber to, 219; fleet, return of, 221; maps, 247; Spanish fleet to, 230; Swiss emigration to, 37, 38; travels in, 20; see also Antilles and names of particular islands
West Point Military Academy, 206, 214
West Virginia, Swiss settlements in, 69, 71
Westphalia, treaty of, 1
Wetzstein, 19
Weyser, Konrad and family, emigration of, 106
Weysz, inquiry concerning, 106
Whale-fishery, Greenland, 218
Wheat, 242
Whig convention of 1839, 11, 209
White Lily, Ky., Swiss settlement, 70
Widerhold, Jean Herman, 180
Widmer, F., *Sachregister zum Bundesblatt*, 69
Wiedertäufer, see Anabaptists
Wiedlisbach, 49
Wiesbaden, recruiting for England in, 239
Wild, Philipp Friedrich, letter from, 47
William, *Prince*, of England, journey to America, 227
William and Mary, College of, 72
William Nelson, shipwreck of, 68, 81, 96, 118, 145
Williamsburg, Va., 192
Willisau, 80; *Geschichte der Stadt*, 80
Wimmis, 34
Winchester, Tenn., Swiss settlement, 71
Windisch, 142
Wine, trade in, 197, 205, 227
Winkel, 23, 24

Index 299

Winter, Gustav. *Die Gründung des K. K. Haus- Hof- und Staatsarchivs*, 186; *Das neue Gebäude des K. K. Haus- Hof- und Staatsarchivs*, 186; *Katalog der Archivalien-Ausstellung*, 186
Winterthur, city archive, 31, 32; emigration from, 5, 14, 32; inquiry concerning New Glarus, 91
Wisconsin, 67; commission of emigration bureau, literature, 119; Swiss settlements in, 71, 118, 119
Wlaschin, 249
Wolf, *Landvogt*, 20
Wolf, Gerson, *Geschichte der K. K. Archive in Wien*, 186
Wolf, Salomon, register of, 20
Wolfenbüttel, 116
Wolff, consul, complaint against, 69
Wool factories in America, 255
Worb, estate of the Graffenried family, 60; *Ob die Herrschaft*, 60
Wren, Christopher, 72
Wright, Silas, 206
Würenlingen, 142
Württemberg, emigration from, 67, 116; Prince Paul of, in Mexico, 196; Swiss emigration to, 13
Würths, Jacob, examination of, 113
Wüsten, examination of, 21
Wunderbare Nachricht aus America, 72
Wunderlich, H., see Merveilleux
Wysen, Peter, 30
Wyss, Hans, arrested, 50
Wysz, 60
Wysz, *Rev.*, 18
Wytenbach, theologian, 58

Yedy, brothers, emigration of, 25
Yellow fever, 23, 191, 230, 241, 245
York, Pa., death in, 24
Yorktown, Va., surrender of Cornwallis, 246
Ytter, taxation in, 263
Yverdon, 49; Graffenried's adventures in, 75; library of, 162

Zäuger, emigration of, 45
Zanini, *Baronne*, see Tinelli, Anne
Zeitschrift für Schweizerische Statistik, article in, 148
Zell, 18
Zengg, 239
Zensur unter Joseph II., Gnau, 247

Zimmermann, 249
Zimmermann, petition of, 28
Zimmermann, Jakob, protest against agency, 124
Zoller, *Landvogt*, reports on emigration, 20
Zoller, Hans Wilgert, 14
Zolliken, 22
Zollikofer, Jacob Christ., petition of, 13
Zschokke, Heinrich, *Ph. Suchard, Mein Besuch Amerikas*, 173; *Ph. Suchard, Un Voyage aux Etats Unis*, 173
Zuberbühler, Sebastian, 29
Zürich, Kan., Swiss settlement, 70
Zürich, Neb., Swiss settlement, 70
Zürich, N. Y., Swiss settlement, 71
Zürich, 1, 2, 36, 43, 46, 48, 86, 129, 172; aid to emigrants, 25, 28, 29; American consulate, 110; cantonal archive, Frauen Münster, 20; charity institution, 27; conference of 1846, 116; city archive, 27-29; city library, 29-31; criminal cases, 14; emigration agencies, 22, 27; emigration from, 3, 5, 14-29, 45, 57, 61, 101, 102, 113, 116, 137; emigration laws, 14-21, 23, 25, 27-29, 32, 44, 45, 57, 109, 113; emigration lists, 3, 13, 14, 21, 29; examination of emigrants, 14, 21, 22; *Kanton Zürich*, 28; land rights lost by emigration, 14-17; *Neue Züricher Zeitung*, 148; *Neujahrsblatt des Waisenhauses*, 13; Purry's books forbidden, 57; Rats Manuale, 15; seat of government, 2; Simmler'sche Sammlung, 4, 29; state archive, vi, vii, 13-27; Statthalteramt, circular letter, 29; *Züricher Verbot gegen Emigration nach Preussisch Pommern*, 113; see also Vorort, Zürich
Züricher, P. Franz, article by, 84
Zug, 1, 2, 149; cantonal archive, iv, 95-97; emigration agencies, 96; emigration from, 95, 96; emigration laws, 96; emigration statistics, 96; emigration via France, 95; milk industry, 7
Zurflüh, Hans, arrest of, 50
Zur-Lauben, *Baron, Histoire Militaire des Suisses au Service de la France*, 99
Zwahlen, emigration of, 45
Zweysimmen, 41
Zwiebach, American, 197
Zwilkchenbart, Andr., emigration agency, 27, 118, 120, 124, 155
Zwingle, Ia., Swiss settlement, 70
Zwingli, 130

Heritage Books by Don Heinrich Tolzmann:

Amana: William Rufus Perkins' and Barthinius L. Wick's History of the Amana Society, or Community of True Inspiration

Americana Germanica: Paul Ben Baginsky's Bibliography of German Works Relating to America, 1493–1800

Biography of Baron Von Steuben, the Army of the American Revolution and Its Organizer: Rudolf Cronau's Biography of Baron von Steuben

CD: German-American Biographical Index (Midwest Families)

CD: Germans, Volume 2

CD: The German Colonial Era (four volumes)

Cincinnati's German Heritage

Covington's German Heritage

Custer: Frederick Whittaker's Complete Life of General George A. Custer, Major General of Volunteers, Brevet Major General U.S. Army and Lieutenant-Colonel Seventh U.S. Cavalry

Dayton's German Heritage: Karl Karstaedt's Golden Jubilee History of the German Pioneer Society of Dayton, Ohio

Early German-American Newspapers: Daniel Miller's History

German Achievements in America: Rudolf Cronau's Survey History

German Americans in the Revolution

German Immigration to America: The First Wave

German Pioneer Life and Domestic Customs

German Pioneer Lifestyle

German Pioneers in Early California: Erwin G. Gudde's History

German-American Achievements: 400 Years of Contributions to America

German-Americana in Europe: Two Guides to Materials Relating to American History in the German, Austrian, and Swiss Archives

German-Americana: A Bibliography

Germany and America, 1450–1700

Kentucky's German Pioneers: H. A. Rattermann's History

Lives and Exploits of the Daring Frank and Jesse James: Thaddeus Thorndike's Graphic and Realistic Description of Their Many Deeds of Unparalleled Daring in the Robbing of Banks and Railroad Trains

Louisiana's German Heritage: Louis Voss' Introductory History

Maryland's German Heritage: Daniel Wunderlich Nead's History

Memories of the Battle of New Ulm: Personal Accounts of the Sioux Uprising. L. A. Fritsche's History of Brown County, Minnesota (1916)

*Michigan's German Heritage: John Andrew Russell's
History of the German Influence in the Making of Michigan*

Ohio's German Heritage

*Outbreak and Massacre by the Dakota Indians in Minnesota in 1862: Marion P. Satterlee's
Minute Account of the Outbreak, with Exact Locations, Names of All Victims, Prisoners
at Camp Release, Refugees at Fort Ridgely, etc. Complete List of Indians Killed in
Battle and Those Hung, and Those Pardoned at Rock Island, Iowa*

The German-American Soldier in the Wars of the U.S.: J. G. Rosengarten's History

The German Element in Virginia: Herrmann Schuricht's History

The German Immigrant in America

The Pennsylvania Germans: James Owen Knauss, Jr.'s Social History

The Pennsylvania Germans: Jesse Leonard Rosenberger's Sketch of Their History and Life

www.ingramcontent.com/pod-product-compliance
Lightning Source LLC
Chambersburg PA
CBHW071230300426
44116CB00008B/972